P9-DMY-052

DISCARD
REINHER
COLLEGE
LIBRARY

The Founders' Constitution

The Founders' Constitution

Edited by
Philip B. Kurland
and
Ralph Lerner

VOLUME FIVE
Amendments I–XII

The University of Chicago Press
Chicago and London

Philip B. Kurland is the William R. Kenan, Jr.,
Distinguished Service Professor in the College and
Professor in the Law School, University of Chicago.

Ralph Lerner is Professor in the Committee on Social
Thought and in the College, University of Chicago.

The University of Chicago Press, Chicago 60637
The University of Chicago Press, Ltd., London

© 1987 by The University of Chicago
All rights reserved. Published 1987
Printed in the United States of America
96 95 94 93 92 91 90 89 88 87 5 4 3 2

Library of Congress Cataloging-in-Publication Data

The Founders' Constitution.

    Includes bibliography and index.
    Contents: v. 1. Major themes.
      1. United States—Constitutional history—Sources.
I. Kurland, Philip B.   II. Lerner, Ralph.
KF4502.F68 1987   342.73′023   86-6958
ISBN 0-226-46387-7 (set)   347.30223
       0-226-46388-5 (v. 1)

All this is not the result of accident. It has a philosophical cause. Without the *Constitution* and the *Union*, we could not have attained the result; but even these, are not the primary cause of our great prosperity. There is something back of these, entwining itself more closely about the human heart. That something, is the principle of "Liberty to all"—the principle that clears the *path* for all—gives *hope* to all—and, by consequence, *enterprize,* and *industry* to all.

The *expression* of that principle, in our Declaration of Independence, was most happy, and fortunate. *Without* this, as well as *with* it, we could have declared our independence of Great Britain; but *without* it, we could not, I think, have secured our free government, and consequent prosperity. No oppressed, people will *fight,* and *endure,* as our fathers did, without the promise of something better, than a mere change of masters.

The assertion of that *principle,* at *that time,* was *the* word, *"fitly spoken"* which has proved an "apple of gold" to us. The *Union,* and the *Constitution,* are the *picture* of *silver,* subsequently framed around it. The picture was made, not to *conceal,* or *destroy* the apple; but to *adorn,* and *preserve* it. The *picture* was made *for* the apple—*not* the apple for the picture.

So let us act, that neither *picture,* or *apple* shall ever be blurred, or bruised or broken.

That we may so act, we must study, and understand the points of danger.

Abraham Lincoln, ca. January 1861

Contents

VOLUME FIVE: AMENDMENTS I–XII
(For detailed contents, see box at opening of each item or group of items listed below)

Note on References

References to documents follow a consistent pattern both in the cross-references (in the detailed tables of contents) and in the indexes. Where a document in volume 1 is being cited, reference is to chapter and document numbers: thus, for example, ch. 15, no. 23. Where the document is to be found in one of the subsequent volumes, which are organized by Constitutional article, section, and clause, or by amendment, reference is in this mode: 1.8.8, no. 12; or, Amend. I (religion), no. 66. Each document heading consists of its serial number in that particular chapter; an author and title (or letter writer and addressee, or speaker and forum); date of publication, writing, or speaking; and, where not given in the first part of the heading, an identification of the source of the text being reprinted. These sources are presented in short-title form, the author of the source volume being presumed (unless otherwise noted) to be the first proper name mentioned in the document heading. Thus, for example, in the case of a letter from Alexander Hamilton to Governor George Clinton, "Papers 1:425–28" would be understood to refer to the edition fully described under "Hamilton, Papers" in the list of short titles found at the back of each volume.

A somewhat different form has been followed in the case of the proceedings of the Constitutional Convention that met in Philadelphia from late May to mid-September of 1787. As might be expected, we have included many extracts from the various records kept by the participants while they were deliberating over the shape and character of a new charter of government. For any particular chapter or unit, those extracts have been grouped as a single document, titled "Records of the Federal Convention," and placed undated in that chapter's proper time slot. The bracketed note that precedes each segment within that selection of the "Records" lists the volume and opening page numbers in the printed source (Max Farrand's edition), the name of the participant whose notes are here being reproduced (overwhelmingly Madison, but also Mason, Yates, others, and the Convention's official Journal), and the month and day of 1787 when the reported transaction took place.

Bill of Rights

1

BILL OF RIGHTS
1 W. & M., 2d sess., c. 2,
16 Dec. 1689

An act for declaring the rights and liberties of the subject, and settling the succession of the crown.

Whereas the lords spiritual and temporal, and commons assembled at *Westminster,* lawfully, fully, and freely representing all the estates of the people of this realm, did upon the thirteenth day of *February,* in the year of our Lord one thousand six hundred eighty eight, present unto their Majesties, then called and known by the names and stile of *William* and *Mary,* prince and princess of *Orange,* being present in their proper persons, a certain declaration in writing, made by the said lords and commons, in the words following; *viz.*

Whereas the late King *James* the Second, by the assistance of divers evil counsellors, judges, and ministers employed by him, did endeavour to subvert and extirpate the protestant religion, and the laws and liberties of this kingdom.

1. By assuming and exercising a power of dispensing with and suspending of laws, and the execution of laws, without consent of parliament.

2. By committing and prosecuting divers worthy prelates, for humbly petitioning to be excused from concurring to the said assumed power.

3. By issuing and causing to be executed a commission under the great seal for erecting a court called, *The court of commissioners for ecclesiastical causes.*

4. By levying money for and to the use of the crown, by pretence of prerogative, for other time, and in other manner, than the same was granted by parliament.

5. By raising and keeping a standing army within this kingdom in time of peace, without consent of parliament, and quartering soldiers contrary to law.

6. By causing several good subjects, being protestants, to be disarmed, at the same time when papists were both armed and employed, contrary to law.

7. By violating the freedom of election of members to serve in parliament.

8. By prosecutions in the court of King's bench, for matters and causes cognizable only in parliament; and by divers other arbitrary and illegal courses.

9. And whereas of late years, partial, corrupt, and unqualified persons have been returned and served on juries in trials, and particularly divers jurors in trials for high treason, which were not freeholders.

10. And excessive bail hath been required of persons committed in criminal cases, to elude the benefit of the laws made for the liberty of the subjects.

11. And excessive fines have been imposed; and illegal and cruel punishments inflicted.

12. And several grants and promises made of fines and forfeitures, before any conviction or judgment against the persons, upon whom the same same were to be levied.

All which are utterly and directly contrary to the known laws and statutes, and freedom of this realm.

And whereas the said late King *James* the Second having abdicated the government, and the throne being thereby vacant, his highness the prince of *Orange* (whom it hath pleased Almighty God to make the glorious instrument of delivering this kingdom from popery and arbitrary power) did (by the advice of the lords spiritual and temporal, and divers principal persons of the commons) cause letters to be written to the lords spiritual and temporal, being protestants; and other letters to the several counties, cities, universities, boroughs, and cinque-ports, for the choosing of such persons to represent them, as were of right to be sent to parliament, to meet and sit at *Westminster* upon the two and twentieth day of *January,* in this year one thousand six hundred eighty and eight, in order to such an establishment, as that their religion, laws, and liberties might not again be in danger of being subverted: upon which letters, elections have been accordingly made,

And thereupon the said lords spiritual and temporal, and commons, pursuant to their respective letters and elections, being now assembled in a full and free representative of this nation, taking into their most serious consideration the best means for attaining the ends aforesaid; do in the first place (as their ancestors in like case have usually done) for the vindicating and asserting their ancient rights and liberties, declare;

1. That the pretended power of suspending of laws, or the execution of laws, by regal authority, without consent of parliament, is illegal.

2. That the pretended power of dispensing with laws, or the execution of laws, by regal authority, as it hath been assumed and exercised of late, is illegal.

3. That the commission for erecting the late court of commissioners for ecclesiastical causes, and other commissions and courts of like nature are illegal and pernicious.

4. That levying money for or to the use of the crown, by pretence of prerogative, without grant of parliament, for longer time, or in other manner than the same is or shall be granted, is illegal.

5. That it is the right of the subjects to petition the King, and all committments and prosecutions for such petitioning are illegal.

6. That the raising or keeping a standing army within the kingdom in time of peace, unless it be with consent of parliament, is against law.

7. That the subjects which are protestants, may have arms for their defence suitable to their conditions, and as allowed by law.

8. That election of members of parliament ought to be free.

9. That the freedom of speech, and debates or proceedings in parliament, ought not to be impeached or questioned in any court or place out of parliament.

10. That excessive bail ought not to be required, nor excessive fines imposed; nor cruel and unusual punishments inflicted.

11. That jurors ought to be duly impanelled and returned, and jurors which pass upon men in trials for high treason ought to be freeholders.

12. That all grants and promises of fines and forfeitures of particular persons before conviction, are illegal and void.

13. And that for redress of all grievances, and for the amending, strengthening, and preserving of the laws, parliaments ought to be held frequently.

And they do claim, demand, and insist upon all and singular the premises, as their undoubted rights and liberties; and that no declarations, judgments, doings or proceedings, to the prejudice of the people in any of the said premises, ought in any wise to be drawn hereafter into consequence or example.

To which demand of their rights they are particularly encouraged by the declaration of his highness the prince of *Orange*, as being the only means for obtaining a full redress and remedy therein.

Having therefore an entire confidence, That his said highness the prince of *Orange* will perfect the deliverance so far advanced by him, and will still preserve them from the violation of their rights, which they have here asserted, and from all other attempts upon their religion, rights, and liberties.

II. The said lords spiritual and temporal, and commons, assembled at *Westminster*, do resolve, that *William* and *Mary* prince and princess of *Orange* be, and be declared, King and Queen of *England, France* and *Ireland,* and the dominions thereunto belonging, to hold the crown and royal dignity of the said kingdoms and dominions to them the said prince and princess during their lives, and the life of the survivor of them; and that the sole and full exercise of the regal power be only in, and executed by the said prince of *Orange,* in the names of the said prince and princess, during their joint lives; and after their deceases, the said crown and royal dignity of the said kingdoms and dominions to be to the heirs of the body of the said princess; and for default of such issue to the princess *Anne* of *Denmark,* and the heirs of her body; and for default of such issue to the heirs of the body of the said prince of *Orange.* And the lords spiritual and temporal, and commons, do pray the said prince and princess to accept the same accordingly.

III. And that the oaths hereafter mentioned be taken by all persons of whom the oaths of allegiance and supremacy might be required by law, instead of them; and that the said oaths of allegiance and supremacy be abrogated.

I *A. B.* do sincerely promise and swear, That I will be faithful, and bear true allegiance, to their Majesties King *William* and Queen *Mary:*

So help me God.

I *A. B.* do swear, That I do from my heart abhor, detest, and abjure as impious and heretical, that damnable doctrine and position, *That princes excommunicated or deprived by the pope, or any authority of the see of* Rome, *may be deposed or murdered by their subjects, or any other whatsoever.* And I do declare, That no foreign prince, person, prelate, state, or potentate hath, or ought to have any jurisdiction, power, superiority, pre-eminence, or authority ecclesiastical or spiritual, within this realm:

So help me God.

IV. Upon which their said Majesties did accept the crown and royal dignity of the kingdoms of *England, France,* and *Ireland,* and the dominions thereunto belonging, according to the resolution and desire of the said lords and commons contained in the said declaration.

V. And thereupon their Majesties were pleased, That the said lords spiritual and temporal, and commons, being the two houses of parliament, should continue to sit, and with their Majesties royal concurrence make effectual provision for the settlement of the religion, laws and liberties of this kingdom, so that the same for the future might not be in danger again of being subverted; to which the said lords spiritual and temporal, and commons, did agree and proceed to act accordingly.

VI. *Now in pursuance of the premises, the said lords spiritual and temporal, and commons, in parliament assembled, for the ratifying, confirming and establishing the said declaration, and the articles, clauses, matters, and things therein contained, by the force of a law made in due form by authority of parliament, do pray that it may be declared and enacted, That all and singular the rights and liberties asserted and claimed in the said declaration, are the true, ancient, and indubitable rights and liberties of the people of this kingdom, and so shall be esteemed, allowed, adjudged, deemed, and taken to be, and that all and every the particulars aforesaid shall be firmly and strictly holden and observed, as they are expressed in the said declaration; and all officers and ministers whatsoever shall serve their Majesties and their successors according to the same in all times to come.*

2

Virginia Declaration of Rights
12 June 1776
Mason Papers 1:287–89

A DECLARATION OF RIGHTS made by the Representatives of the good people of VIRGINIA, assembled in full and free Convention; which rights do pertain to them and their posterity, as the basis and foundation of Government.

1. That all men are by nature equally free and independent, and have certain inherent rights, of which, when they enter into a state of society, they cannot, by any compact, deprive or divest their posterity; namely, the enjoyment of life and liberty, with the means of acquiring and possessing property, and pursuing and obtaining happiness and safety.

2. That all power is vested in, and consequently derived from, the People; that magistrates are their trustees and servants, and at all times amenable to them.

3. That Government is, or ought to be, instituted for the common benefit, protection, and security of the people, nation, or community;—of all the various modes and forms of Government that is best which is capable of producing the greatest degree of happiness and safety, and is most effectually secured against the danger of mal-administration;—and that, whenever any Government shall be found inadequate or contrary to these purposes, a majority of the community hath an indubitable, unalienable, and indefeasible right, to reform, alter, or abolish it, in such manner as shall be judged most conducive to the publick weal.

4. That no man, or set of men, are entitled to exclusive or separate emoluments and privileges from the community, but in consideration of publick services; which, not being descendible, neither ought the offices of Magistrate, Legislator, or Judge, to be hereditary.

5. That the Legislative and Executive powers of the State should be separate and distinct from the Judicative; and, that the members of the two first may be restrained from oppression, by feeling and participating the burdens of the people, they should, at fixed periods, be reduced to a private station, return into that body from which they were originally taken, and the vacancies be supplied by frequent, certain, and regular elections, in which all, or any part of the former members, to be again eligible, or ineligible, as the law shall direct.

6. That elections of members to serve as Representatives of the people, in Assembly, ought to be free; and that all men, having sufficient evidence of permanent common interest with, and attachment to, the community, have the right of suffrage, and cannot be taxed or deprived of their property for publick uses without their own consent or that of their Representative so elected, nor bound by any law to which they have not, in like manner, assented, for the publick good.

7. That all power of suspending laws, or the execution of laws, by any authority, without consent of the Representatives of the people, is injurious to their rights, and ought not to be exercised.

8. That in all capital or criminal prosecutions a man hath a right to demand the cause and nature of his accusation, to be confronted with the accusers and witnesses, to call for evidence in his favour, and to a speedy trial by an impartial jury of his vicinage, without whose unanimous consent he cannot be found guilty, nor can he be compelled to give evidence against himself; that no man be deprived of his liberty except by the law of the land, or the judgment of his peers.

9. That excessive bail ought not to be required, nor excessive fines imposed, nor cruel and unusual punishments inflicted.

10. That general warrants, whereby any officer or messenger may be commanded to search suspected places without evidence of a fact committed, or to seize any person or persons not named, or whose offence is not particularly described and supported by evidence, are grievous and oppressive, and ought not to be granted.

11. That in controversies respecting property, and in suits between man and man, the ancient trial by Jury is preferable to any other, and ought to be held sacred.

12. That the freedom of the Press is one of the greatest bulwarks of liberty, and can never be restrained but by despotick Governments.

13. That a well-regulated Militia, composed of the body of the people, trained to arms, is the proper, natural, and safe defence of a free State; that Standing Armies, in time of peace, should be avoided as dangerous to liberty; and that, in all cases, the military should be under strict subordination to, and governed by, the civil power.

14. That the people have a right to uniform Government; and, therefore, that no Government separate from, or independent of, the Government of *Virginia*, ought to be erected or established within the limits thereof.

15. That no free Government, or the blessing of liberty, can be preserved to any people but by a firm adherence to justice, moderation, temperance, frugality, and virtue, and by frequent recurrence to fundamental principles.

16. That Religion, or the duty which we owe to our *Creator*, and the manner of discharging it, can be directed only by reason and conviction, not by force or violence; and, therefore, all men are equally entitled to the free exercise of religion, according to the dictates of conscience;

and that it is the mutual duty of all to practise Christian forbearance, love, and charity, towards each other.

3

DECLARATION OF INDEPENDENCE
4 July 1776
Tansill 22–26

In Congress, July 4, 1776
The unanimous Declaration of the
thirteen united States of America

When in the Course of human events, it becomes necessary for one people to dissolve the political bands which have connected them with another, and to assume among the powers of the earth, the separate and equal station to which the Laws of Nature and of Nature's God entitle them, a decent respect to the opinions of mankind requires that they should declare the causes which impel them to the separation.—We hold these truths to be self-evident, that all men are created equal, that they are endowed by their Creator with certain unalienable Rights, that among these are Life, Liberty and the pursuit of Happiness.—That to secure these rights, Governments are instituted among Men, deriving their just powers from the consent of the governed,—That whenever any Form of Government becomes destructive of these ends, it is the Right of the People to alter or to abolish it, and to institute new Government, laying its foundation on such principles and organizing its powers in such form, as to them shall seem most likely to effect their Safety and Happiness. Prudence, indeed, will dictate that Governments long established should not be changed for light and transient causes; and accordingly all experience hath shown, that mankind are more disposed to suffer, while evils are sufferable, than to right themselves by abolishing the forms to which they are accustomed. But when a long train of abuses and usurpations, pursuing invariably the same Object evinces a design to reduce them under absolute Despotism, it is their right, it is their duty, to throw off such Government, and to provide new Guards for their future security.—Such has been the patient sufferance of these Colonies; and such is now the necessity which constrains them to alter their former Systems of Government. The history of the present King of Great Britain is a history of repeated injuries and usurpations, all having in direct object the establishment of an absolute Tyranny over these States. To prove this, let Facts be submitted to a candid world.—He has refused his Assent to Laws, the most wholesome and necessary for the public good.—He has forbidden his Governors to pass Laws of immediate and pressing importance, unless suspended in their operation till his Assent should be obtained; and when so suspended, he has utterly neglected to attend to them.—He has re-fused to pass other Laws for the accommodation of large districts of people, unless those people would relinquish the right of Representation in the Legislature, a right inestimable to them and formidable to tyrants only.—He has called together legislative bodies at places unusual, uncomfortable, and distant from the depository of their public Records, for the sole purpose of fatiguing them into compliance with his measures.—He has dissolved Representative Houses repeatedly, for opposing with manly firmness his invasions on the rights of the people.—He has refused for a long time, after such dissolutions, to cause others to be elected; whereby the Legislative powers, incapable of Annihilation, have returned to the People at large for their exercise; the State remaining in the mean time exposed to all the dangers of invasion from without, and convulsions within.—He has endeavoured to prevent the population of these States; for that purpose obstructing the Laws for Naturalization of Foreigners; refusing to pass others to encourage their migration hither, and raising the conditions of new Appropriations of Lands.—He has obstructed the Administration of Justice, by refusing his Assent to Laws for establishing Judiciary powers.—He has made Judges dependent on his Will alone, for the tenure of their offices, and the amount and payment of their salaries.—He has erected a multitude of New Offices, and sent hither swarms of Officers to harrass our people, and eat out their substance.—He has kept among us, in times of peace, Standing Armies, without the Consent of our legislatures.—He has affected to render the Military independent of and superior to the Civil power.—He has combined with others to subject us to a jurisdiction foreign to our constitution, and unacknowledged by our laws; giving his Assent to their Acts of pretended Legislation:—For quartering large bodies of armed troops among us:—For protecting them, by a mock Trial, from punishment for any Murders which they should commit on the Inhabitants of these States:—For cutting off our Trade with all parts of the world:—For imposing Taxes on us without our Consent:—For depriving us in many cases, of the benefits of Trial by Jury:—For transporting us beyond Seas to be tried for pretended offences:—For abolishing the free System of English Laws in a neighbouring Province, establishing therein an Arbitrary government, and enlarging its Boundaries so as to render it at once an example and fit instrument for introducing the same absolute rule into these Colonies:—For taking away our Charters, abolishing our most valuable Laws, and altering fundamentally the Forms of our Governments:—For suspending our own Legislatures, and declaring themselves invested with power to legislate for us in all cases whatsoever.—He has abdicated Government here, by declaring us out of his Protection and waging War against us.—He has plundered our seas, ravaged our Coasts, burnt our towns, and destroyed the lives of our people.—He is at this time transporting large Armies of foreign Mercenaries to compleat the works of death, desolation and tyranny, already begun with circumstances of Cruelty & perfidy scarcely paralleled in the most barbarous ages, and totally unworthy the Head of a civilized nation.—He has constrained our fellow Citizens taken Captive on the high Seas to bear Arms against their Country, to become the executioners of their friends and Brethren, or to fall themselves by their Hands.—He has excited domestic insurrections amongst us, and has endeavoured to bring on the inhabitants of our frontiers, the merciless Indian Savages, whose known rule of warfare, is an undistinguished destruction of all ages, sexes and conditions. In every stage of these Oppressions We have Petitioned for Redress in the most humble terms: Our repeated Petitions have been answered only by repeated injury. A Prince, whose character is thus marked by every act which may define a Tyrant, is unfit to be the ruler of a free people. Nor have We been wanting in attentions to our Brittish brethren. We have warned them from time to time of attempts by their legislature to extend an unwarrantable jurisdiction over us. We have reminded them of the circumstances of our emigration and settlement here. We have appealed to their native justice and magnanimity, and we have conjured them by the ties of our common kindred to disavow these usurpations, which, would inevitably interrupt our connections and correspondence. They too have been deaf to the voice of justice and of consanguinity. We must, therefore, acquiesce in the necessity, which denounces our Separation, and hold them, as we hold the rest of mankind, Enemies in War, in Peace Friends.—

WE, THEREFORE, the REPRESENTATIVES of the UNITED STATES OF AMERICA, in General Congress, Assembled, appealing to the Supreme Judge of the world for the rectitude of our intentions, do, in the Name, and by Authority of the good People of these Colonies, solemnly publish and declare, That these United Colonies are, and of Right ought to be FREE AND INDEPENDENT STATES; that they are Absolved from all Allegiance to the British Crown, and that all political connection between them and the State of Great Britain, is and ought to be totally dissolved; and that as Free and Independent States, they have full Power to levy War, conclude Peace, contract Alliances, establish Commerce, and to do all other Acts and Things which Independent States may of right do.—And for the support of this Declaration, with a firm reliance on the protection of Divine Providence, we mutually pledge to each other our Lives, our Fortunes and our sacred Honor.

John Hancock

[New Hampshire]
Josiah Bartlett
Wm. Whipple
Matthew Thornton

[Massachusetts Bay]
Saml. Adams
John Adams
Robt. Treat Paine
Elbridge Gerry

[Rhode Island]
Step. Hopkins
William Ellery

[Connecticut]
Roger Sherman
Sam'el Huntington
Wm. Williams
Oliver Wolcott

[New York]
Wm. Floyd
Phil. Livingston
Frans. Lewis
Lewis Morris

[New Jersey]
Richd. Stockton
Jno. Witherspoon
Fras. Hopkinson
John Hart
Abra. Clark

[Pennsylvania]
Robt. Morris
Benjamin Rush
Benja. Franklin
John Morton
Geo. Clymer
Jas. Smith
Geo. Taylor
James Wilson
Geo. Ross

[Delaware]
Caesar Rodney
Geo. Read
Tho. M'Kean

[Maryland]
Samuel Chase
Wm. Paca
Thos. Stone
Charles Carroll
of Carrollton

[Virginia]
George Wythe
Richard Henry Lee
Th. Jefferson
Benja. Harrison
Ths. Nelson, Jr.
Francis Lightfoot Lee
Carter Braxton

[North Carolina]
Wm. Hooper
Joseph Hewes
John Penn

[South Carolina]
Edward Rutledge
Thos. Heyward, Junr.
Thomas Lynch, Junr.
Arthur Middleton

[Georgia]
Button Gwinnett
Lyman Hall
Geo. Walton

4

DELAWARE DECLARATION OF RIGHTS
11 Sept. 1776
Sources 338–40

SECTION 1. That all government of right originates from the people, is founded in compact only, and instituted solely for the good of the whole.

SECT. 2. That all men have a natural and unalienable right to worship Almighty God according to the dictates of their own consciences and understandings; and that no man ought or of right can be compelled to attend any religious worship or maintain any ministry contrary to or against his own free will and consent, and that no authority can or ought to be vested in, or assumed by any power whatever that shall in any case interfere with, or in any manner controul the right of conscience in the free exercise of religious worship.

SECT. 3. That all persons professing the Christian religion ought forever to enjoy equal rights and privileges in this state, unless, under colour of religion, any man disturb the peace, the happiness or safety of society.

SECT. 4. That people of this state have the sole exclusive and inherent right of governing and regulating the internal police of the same.

SECT. 5. That persons intrusted with the Legislative and Executive Powers are the Trustees and Servants of the public, and as such accountable for their conduct; wherefore whenever the ends of government are perverted, and public liberty manifestly endangered by the Legislative singly, or a treacherous combination of both, the people may, and of right ought to establish a new, or reform the old government.

SECT. 6. That the right in the people to participate in the Legislature, is the foundation of liberty and of all free government, and for this end all elections ought to be free and frequent, and every freeman, having sufficient evidence of a permanent common interest with, and attachment to the community, hath a right of suffrage.

SECT. 7. That no power of suspending laws, or the execution of laws, ought to be exercised unless by the Legislature.

SECT. 8. That for redress of grievances, and for amending and strengthening of the laws, the Legislature ought to be frequently convened.

SECT. 9. That every man hath a right to petition the Legislature for the redress of grievances in a peaceable and orderly manner.

SECT. 10. That every member of society hath a right to be protected in the enjoyment of life, liberty and property, and therefore is bound to contribute his proportion towards the expense of that protection, and yield his personal service when necessary, or an equivalent thereto; but no part of a man's property can be justly taken from him or applied to public uses without his own consent or that of his legal Representatives: Nor can any man that is conscientiously scrupulous of bearing arms in any case be justly compelled thereto if he will pay such equivalent.

SECT. 11. That retrospective laws, punishing offences committed before the existence of such laws, are oppressive and unjust, and ought not to be made.

SECT. 12. That every freeman for every injury done him in his goods, lands or person, by any other person, ought to have remedy by the course of the law of the land, and ought to have justice and right for the injury done to him freely without sale, fully without any denial, and speedily without delay, according to the law of the land.

SECT. 13. That trial by jury of facts where they arise is one of the greatest securities of the lives, liberties and estates of the people.

SECT. 14. That in all prosecutions for criminal offences, every man hath a right to be informed of the accusation against him, to be allowed counsel, to be confronted with the accusers or witnesses, to examine evidence on oath in his favour, and to a speedy trial by an impartial jury, without whose unanimous consent he ought not to be found guilty.

SECT. 15. That no man in the Courts of Common Law ought to be compelled to give evidence against himself.

SECT. 16. That excessive bail ought not to be required, nor excessive fines imposed, nor cruel or unusual punishments inflicted.

SECT. 17. That all warrants without oath to search suspected places, or to seize any person or his property, are grievous and oppressive; and all general warrants to search suspected places, or to apprehend all persons suspected, without naming or describing the place or any person in special, are illegal and ought not to be granted.

SECT. 18. That a well regulated militia is the proper, natural and safe defence of a free government.

SECT. 19. That standing armies are dangerous to liberty, and ought not to be raised or kept up without the consent of the Legislature.

SECT. 20. That in all cases and at all times the military ought to be under strict subordination to and governed by the civil power.

SECT. 21. That no soldier ought to be quartered in any house in time of peace without the consent of the owner; and in time of war in such manner only as the Legislature shall direct.

SECT. 22. That the independency and uprightness of judges are essential to the impartial administration of justice, and a great security to the rights and liberties of the people.

SECT. 23. That the liberty of the press ought to be inviolably preserved.

5

PENNSYLVANIA CONSTITUTION OF 1776, DECLARATION OF RIGHTS

Thorpe 5:3082–84

I. That all men are born equally free and independent, and have certain natural, inherent and inalienable rights, amongst which are, the enjoying and defending life and liberty, acquiring, possessing and protecting property, and pursuing and obtaining happiness and safety.

II. That all men have a natural and unalienable right to worship Almighty God according to the dictates of their own consciences and understanding: And that no man ought or of right can be compelled to attend any religious worship, or erect or support any place of worship, or maintain any ministry, contrary to, or against, his own free will and consent: Nor can any man, who acknowledges the being of a God, be justly deprived or abridged of any civil right as a citizen, on account of his religious sentiments or peculiar mode of religious worship: And that no authority can or ought to be vested in, or assumed by any power whatever, that shall in any case interfere with, or in any manner controul, the right of conscience in the free exercise of religious worship.

III. That the people of this State have the sole, exclusive and inherent right of governing and regulating the internal police of the same.

IV. That all power being originally inherent in, and consequently derived from, the people; therefore all officers of government, whether legislative or executive, are their trustees and servants, and at all times accountable to them.

V. That government is, or ought to be, instituted for the common benefit, protection and security of the people, nation or community; and not for the particular emolument or advantage of any single man, family, or sett of men, who are a part only of that community; And that the community hath an indubitable, unalienable and indefeasible right to reform, alter, or abolish government in such manner as shall be by that community judged most conducive to the public weal.

VI. That those who are employed in the legislative and executive business of the State, may be restrained from oppression, the people have a right, at such periods as they may think proper, to reduce their public officers to a private station, and supply the vacancies by certain and regular elections.

VII. That all elections ought to be free; and that all free men having a sufficient evident common interest with, and attachment to the community, have a right to elect officers, or to be elected into office.

VIII. That every member of society hath a right to be protected in the enjoyment of life, liberty and property, and therefore is bound to contribute his proportion towards the expence of that protection, and yield his personal service when necessary, or an equivalent thereto: But no part of a man's property can be justly taken from him, or applied to public uses, without his own consent, or that of his legal representatives: Nor can any man who is conscientiously scrupulous of bearing arms, be justly compelled thereto, if he will pay such equivalent, nor are the people bound by any laws, but such as they have in like manner assented to, for their common good.

IX. That in all prosecutions for criminal offences, a man hath a right to be heard by himself and his council, to demand the cause and nature of his accusation, to be confronted with the witnesses, to call for evidence in his favour, and a speedy public trial, by an impartial jury of the country, without the unanimous consent of which jury he cannot be found guilty; nor can he be compelled to give evidence against himself; nor can any man be justly deprived of his liberty except by the laws of the land, or the judgment of his peers.

X. That the people have a right to hold themselves, their houses, papers, and possessions free from search and seizure, and therefore warrants without oaths or affirmations first made, affording a sufficient foundation for them, and whereby any officer or messenger may be commanded or required to search suspected places, or to seize any person or persons, his or their property, not particularly described, are contrary to that right, and ought not to be granted.

XI. That in controversies respecting property, and in suits between man and man, the parties have a right to trial by jury, which ought to be held sacred.

XII. That the people have a right to freedom of speech, and of writing, and publishing their sentiments; therefore the freedom of the press ought not to be restrained.

XIII. That the people have a right to bear arms for the defence of themselves and the state; and as standing armies in the time of peace are dangerous to liberty, they ought not to be kept up; And that the military should be kept under strict subordination to, and governed by, the civil power.

XIV. That a frequent recurrence to fundamental principles, and a firm adherence to justice, moderation, temperance, industry, and frugality are absolutely necessary to preserve the blessings of liberty, and keep a government free: The people ought therefore to pay particular attention to these points in the choice of officers and representatives, and have a right to exact a due and constant regard to them, from their legislatures and magistrates, in the making and executing such laws as are necessary for the good government of the state.

XV. That all men have a natural inherent right to emigrate from one state to another that will receive them, or to form a new state in vacant countries, or in such countries as they can purchase, whenever they think that thereby they may promote their own happiness.

XVI. That the people have a right to assemble together, to consult for their common good, to instruct their representatives, and to apply to the legislature for redress of grievances, by address, petition, or remonstrance.

6

MASSACHUSETTS CONSTITUTION OF 1780, PT. 1
Handlin 442–48

Part the First. A Declaration of the Rights of the Inhabitants of the Commonwealth of Massachusetts.

ART. I.—All men are born free and equal, and have certain natural, essential, and unalienable rights; among which may be reckoned the right of enjoying and defending their lives and liberties; that of acquiring, possessing, and protecting property; in fine, that of seeking and obtaining their safety and happiness.

II.—It is the right as well as the duty of all men in society, publicly, and at stated seasons, to worship the SUPREME BEING, the great creator and preserver of the universe. And no subject shall be hurt, molested, or restrained, in his person, liberty, or estate, for worshipping GOD in the manner and season most agreeable to the dictates of his own conscience; or for his religious profession or sentiments; provided he doth not disturb the public peace, or obstruct others in their religious worship.

III.—As the happiness of a people, and the good order and preservation of civil government, essentially depend upon piety, religion and morality; and as these cannot be generally diffused through a community, but by the institution of the public worship of GOD, and of public instructions in piety, religion and morality: Therefore, to promote their happiness and to secure the good order and preservation of their government, the people of this Commonwealth have a right to invest their legislature with power to authorize and require, and the legislature shall, from time to time, authorize and require, the several towns, parishes, precincts, and other bodies-politic, or religious societies, to make suitable provision, at their own expense, for the institution of the public worship of GOD, and for the support and maintenance of public protestant teachers of piety, religion and morality, in all cases where such provision shall not be made voluntarily.

And the people of this Commonwealth have also a right to, and do, invest their legislature with authority to enjoin upon all the subjects an attendance upon the instructions of the public teachers aforesaid, at stated times and seasons, if there be any on whose instructions they can conscientiously and conveniently attend.

Provided notwithstanding, that the several towns, parishes, precincts, and other bodies-politic, or religious societies, shall, at all times, have the exclusive right of electing their public teachers, and of contracting with them for their support and maintenance.

And all monies paid by the subject to the support of public worship, and of the public teachers aforesaid, shall, if he require it, be uniformly applied to the support of the public teacher or teachers of his own religious sect or denomination, provided there be any on whose instructions he attends: otherwise it may be paid towards the support of the teacher or teachers of the parish or precinct in which the said monies are raised.

And every denomination of christians, demeaning themselves peaceably, and as good subjects of the Commonwealth, shall be equally under the protection of the law: And no subordination of any one sect or denomination to another shall ever be established by law.

IV.—The people of this Commonwealth have the sole and exclusive right of governing themselves as a free, sovereign, and independent state; and do, and forever hereafter shall, exercise and enjoy every power, jurisdiction, and right, which is not, or may not hereafter, be by them expressly delegated to the United States of America, in Congress assembled.

V.—All power residing originally in the people, and being derived from them, the several magistrates and officers of government, vested with authority, whether legislative, executive, or judicial, are their substitutes and agents, and are at all times accountable to them.

VI.—No man, nor corporation, or association of men, have any other title to obtain advantages, or particular and exclusive privileges, distinct from those of the community, than what arises from the consideration of services rendered to the public; and this title being in nature neither hereditary, nor transmissible to children, or descendants, or relations by blood, the idea of a man born a magistrate, lawgiver, or judge, is absurd and unnatural.

VII.—Government is instituted for the common good; for the protection, safety, prosperity and happiness of the people; and not for the profit, honor, or private interest of any one man, family, or class of men; Therefore the people alone have an incontestible, unalienable, and indefeasible right to institute government; and to reform, alter, or totally change the same, when their protection, safety, prosperity and happiness require it.

VIII.—In order to prevent those, who are vested with authority, from becoming oppressors, the people have a right, at such periods and in such manner as they shall establish by their frame of government, to cause their public officers to return to private life; and to fill up vacant places by certain and regular elections and appointments.

IX.—All elections ought to be free; and all the inhabitants of this Commonwealth, having such qualifications as they shall establish by their frame of government, have an equal right to elect officers, and to be elected, for public employments.

X.—Each individual of the society has a right to be protected by it in the enjoyment of his life, liberty and property, according to standing laws. He is obliged, consequently, to contribute his share to the expense of this protection; to give his personal service, or an equivalent, when necessary: But no part of the property of any individual, can, with justice, be taken from him, or applied to public uses without his own consent, or that of the representative body of the people: In fine, the people of this Commonwealth are not controlable by any other laws, than those to which their constitutional representative body have given their consent. And whenever the public exigencies require, that the property of any individual should be appropriated to public uses, he shall receive a reasonable compensation therefor.

XI.—Every subject of the Commonwealth ought to find a certain remedy, by having recourse to the laws, for all injuries or wrongs which he may receive in his person, property, or character. He ought to obtain right and justice freely, and without being obliged to purchase it; completely, and without any denial; promptly, and without delay; conformably to the laws.

XII.—No subject shall be held to answer for any crime or offence, until the same is fully and plainly, substantially and formally, described to him; or be compelled to accuse, or furnish evidence against himself. And every subject shall have a right to produce all proofs, that may be favorable to him; to meet the witnesses against him face to face, and to be fully heard in his defence by himself, or his council, at his election. And no subject shall be arrested, imprisoned, despoiled, or deprived of his property, immunities, or privileges, put out of the protection of the law, exiled, or deprived of his life, liberty, or estate; but by the judgment of his peers, or the law of the land.

And the legislature shall not make any law, that shall subject any person to a capital or infamous punishment, excepting for the government of the army and navy, without trial by jury.

XIII.—In criminal prosecutions, the verification of facts in the vicinity where they happen, is one of the greatest securities of the life, liberty, and property of the citizen.

XIV.—Every subject has a right to be secure from all unreasonable searches, and seizures of his person, his houses, his papers, and all his possessions. All warrants, therefore, are contrary to this right, if the cause or foundation of them be not previously supported by oath or affirmation; and if the order in the warrant to a civil officer, to make search in suspected places, or to arrest one or more suspected persons, or to seize their property, be not accompanied with a special designation of the persons or objects of search, arrest, or seizure: and no warrant ought to be issued but in cases, and with the formalities, prescribed by the laws.

XV.—In all controversies concerning property, and in all suits between two or more persons, except in cases in which it has heretofore been otherways used and practised, the parties have a right to a trial by jury; and this method of procedure shall be held sacred, unless, in causes arising on the high-seas, and such as relate to mariners wages, the legislature shall hereafter find it necessary to alter it.

XVI.—The liberty of the press is essential to the security of freedom in a state: it ought not, therefore, to be restrained in this Commonwealth.

XVII.—The people have a right to keep and to bear arms for the common defence. And as in time of peace armies are dangerous to liberty, they ought not to be maintained without the consent of the legislature; and the military power shall always be held in an exact subordination to the civil authority, and be governed by it.

XVIII.—A frequent recurrence to the fundamental principles of the constitution, and a constant adherence to those of piety, justice, moderation, temperance, industry, and frugality, are absolutely necessary to preserve the advantages of liberty, and to maintain a free government: The people ought, consequently, to have a particular attention to all those principles, in the choice of their officers and representatives: And they have a right to require of their law-givers and magistrates, an exact and constant observance of them, in the formation and execution of the laws necessary for the good administration of the Commonwealth.

XIX.—The people have a right, in an orderly and peaceable manner, to assemble to consult upon the common good; give instructions to their representatives; and to request of the legislative body, by the way of addresses, petitions, or remonstrances, redress of the wrongs done them, and of the grievances they suffer.

XX.—The power of suspending the laws, or the execution of the laws, ought never to be exercised but by the legislature, or by authority derived from it, to be exercised in such particular cases only as the legislature shall expressly provide for.

XXI.—The freedom of deliberation, speech and debate, in either house of the legislature, is so essential to the rights of the people, that it cannot be the foundation of any accusation or prosecution, action or complaint, in any other court or place whatsoever.

XXII.—The legislature ought frequently to assemble for the redress of grievances, for correcting, strengthening, and confirming the laws, and for making new laws, as the common good may require.

XXIII.—No subsidy, charge, tax, impost, or duties, ought to be established, fixed, laid, or levied, under any pretext whatsoever, without the consent of the people, or their representatives in the legislature.

XXIV.—Laws made to punish for actions done before the existence of such laws, and which have not been declared crimes by preceding laws, are unjust, oppressive, and inconsistent with the fundamental principles of a free government.

XXV.—No subject ought, in any case, or in any time, to be declared guilty of treason or felony by the legislature.

XXVI.—No magistrate or court of law shall demand excessive bail or sureties, impose excessive fines, or inflict cruel or unusual punishments.

XXVII.—In time of peace no soldier ought to be quartered in any house without the consent of the owner; and in time of war such quarters ought not to be made but by the civil magistrate, in a manner ordained by the legislature.

XXVIII.—No person can in any case be subjected to law-martial, or to any penalties or pains, by virtue of that law, except those employed in the army or navy, and except the militia in actual service, but by authority of the legislature.

XXIX.—It is essential to the preservation of the rights of every individual, his life, liberty, property and character, that there be an impartial interpretation of the laws, and administration of justice. It is the right of every citizen to be tried by judges as free, impartial and independent as the lot of humanity will admit. It is therefore not only the best policy, but for the security of the rights of the people, and of every citizen, that the judges of the supreme judicial court should hold their offices as long as they behave themselves well; and that they should have honorable salaries ascertained and established by standing laws.

XXX.—In the government of this Commonwealth, the legislative department shall never exercise the executive and judicial powers, or either of them: The executive shall never exercise the legislative and judicial powers, or either of them: The judicial shall never exercise the legislative and executive powers, or either of them: to the end it may be a government of laws and not of men.

7

Alexander Hamilton, Federalist, no. 84, 575–81
28 May 1788

The most considerable of these remaining objections is, that the plan of the convention contains no bill of rights. Among other answers given to this, it has been upon different occasions remarked, that the constitutions of several of the states are in a similar predicament. I add, that New-

York is of this number. And yet the opposers of the new system in this state, who profess an unlimited admiration for its constitution, are among the most intemperate partizans of a bill of rights. To justify their zeal in this matter, they alledge two things; one is, that though the constitution of New-York has no bill of rights prefixed to it, yet it contains in the body of it various provisions in favour of particular privileges and rights, which in substance amount to the same thing; the other is, that the constitution adopts in their full extent the common and statute law of Great-Britain, by which many other rights not expressed in it are equally secured.

To the first I answer, that the constitution proposed by the convention contains, as well as the constitution of this state, a number of such provisions.

Independent of those, which relate to the structure of the government, we find the following: Article I. section 3. clause 7. "Judgment in cases of impeachment shall not extend further than to removal from office, and disqualification to hold and enjoy any office of honour, trust or profit under the United States; but the party convicted shall nevertheless be liable and subject to indictment, trial, judgment and punishment, according to law." Section 9. of the same article, clause 2. "The privilege of the writ of *habeas corpus* shall not be suspended, unless when in cases of rebellion or invasion the public safety may require it." Clause 3. "No bill of attainder or *ex post facto* law shall be passed." Clause [8]. "No title of nobility shall be granted by the United States: And no person holding any office of profit or trust under them, shall, without the consent of the congress, accept of any present, emolument, office or title, of any kind whatever, from any king, prince or foreign state." Article III. section 2. clause 3. "The trial of all crimes, except in cases of impeachment, shall be by jury; and such trial shall be held in the state where the said crimes shall have been committed; but when not committed within any state, the trial shall be at such place or places as the congress may by law have directed." Section 3, of the same article, "Treason against the United States shall consist only in levying war against them, or in adhering to their enemies, giving them aid and comfort. No person shall be convicted of treason unless on the testimony of two witnesses to the same overt act, or on confession in open court." And clause [2], of the same section. "The congress shall have power to declare the punishment of treason, but no attainder of treason shall work corruption of blood, or forfeiture, except during the life of the person attainted."

It may well be a question whether these are not upon the whole, of equal importance with any which are to be found in the constitution of this state. The establishment of the writ of *habeas corpus,* the prohibition of *ex post facto* laws, and of TITLES OF NOBILITY, *to which we have no corresponding provisions in our constitution,* are perhaps greater securities to liberty and republicanism than any it contains. The creation of crimes after the commission of the fact, or in other words, the subjecting of men to punishment for things which, when they were done, were breaches of no law, and the practice of arbitrary imprisonments have been in all ages the favourite and most formidable instruments of tyranny. The observations of the judicious Blackstone in reference to the latter, are well worthy of recital. "To bereave a man of life (says he) or by violence to confiscate his estate, without accusation or trial, would be so gross and notorious an act of despotism, as must at once convey the alarm of tyranny throughout the whole nation; but confinement of the person by secretly hurrying him to goal, where his sufferings are unknown or forgotten, is a less public, a less striking, and therefore *a more dangerous engine* of arbitrary government." And as a remedy for this fatal evil, he is every where peculiarly emphatical in his encomiums on the *habeas corpus* act, which in one place he calls "the BULWARK of the British constitution."

Nothing need be said to illustrate the importance of the prohibition of titles of nobility. This may truly be denominated the corner stone of republican government; for so long as they are excluded, there can never be serious danger that the government will be any other than that of the people.

To the second, that is, to the pretended establishment of the common and statute law by the constitution, I answer, that they are expressly made subject "to such alterations and provisions as the legislature shall from time to time make concerning the same." They are therefore at any moment liable to repeal by the ordinary legislative power, and of course have no constitutional sanction. The only use of the declaration was to recognize the ancient law, and to remove doubts which might have been occasioned by the revolution. This consequently can be considered as no part of a declaration of rights, which under our constitutions must be intended as limitations of the power of the government itself.

It has been several times truly remarked, that bills of rights are in their origin, stipulations between kings and their subjects, abridgments of prerogative in favor of privilege, reservations of rights not surrendered to the prince. Such was MAGNA CHARTA, obtained by the Barons, sword in hand, from king John. Such were the subsequent confirmations of that charter by subsequent princes. Such was the *petition of right* assented to by Charles the First, in the beginning of his reign. Such also was the declaration of right presented by the lords and commons to the prince of Orange in 1688, and afterwards thrown into the form of an act of parliament, called the bill of rights. It is evident, therefore, that according to their primitive signification, they have no application to constitutions professedly founded upon the power of the people, and executed by their immediate representatives and servants. Here, in strictness, the people surrender nothing, and as they retain every thing, they have no need of particular reservations. "WE THE PEOPLE of the United States, to secure the blessings of liberty to ourselves and our posterity, do *ordain* and *establish* this constitution for the United States of America." Here is a better recognition of popular rights than volumes of those aphorisms which make the principal figure in several of our state bills of rights, and which would sound much better in a treatise of ethics than in a constitution of government.

But a minute detail of particular rights is certainly far less applicable to a constitution like that under consideration, which is merely intended to regulate the general political interests of the nation, than to a constitution which has the regulation of every species of personal and private concerns. If therefore the loud clamours against the plan of the convention on this score, are well founded, no epithets of reprobation will be too strong for the constitution of this state. But the truth is, that both of them contain all, which in relation to their objects, is reasonably to be desired.

I go further, and affirm that bills of rights, in the sense and in the extent in which they are contended for, are not only unnecessary in the proposed constitution, but would even be dangerous. They would contain various exceptions to powers which are not granted; and on this very account, would afford a colourable pretext to claim more than were granted. For why declare that things shall not be done which there is no power to do? Why for instance, should it be said, that the liberty of the press shall not be restrained, when no power is given by which restrictions may be imposed? I will not contend that such a provision would confer a regulating power; but it is evident that it would furnish, to men disposed to usurp, a plausible pretence for claiming that power. They might urge with a semblance of reason, that the constitution ought not to be charged with the absurdity of providing against the abuse of an authority, which was not given, and that the provision against restraining the liberty of the press afforded a clear implication, that a power to prescribe proper regulations concerning it, was intended to be vested in the national government. This may serve as a specimen of the numerous handles which would be given to the doctrine of constructive powers, by the indulgence of an injudicious zeal for bills of rights.

On the subject of the liberty of the press, as much has been said, I cannot forbear adding a remark or two: In the first place, I observe that there is not a syllable concerning it in the constitution of this state, and in the next, I contend that whatever has been said about it in that of any other state, amounts to nothing. What signifies a declaration that "the liberty of the press shall be inviolably preserved?" What is the liberty of the press? Who can give it any definition which would not leave the utmost latitude for evasion? I hold it to be impracticable; and from this, I infer, that its security, whatever fine declarations may be inserted in any constitution respecting it, must altogether depend on public opinion, and on the general spirit of the people and of the government.* And here, after all, as intimated upon another occasion, must we seek for the only solid basis of all our rights.

*To show that there is a power in the constitution by which the liberty of the press may be affected, recourse has been had to the power of taxation. It is said that duties may be laid upon publications so high as to amount to a prohibition. I know not by what logic it could be maintained that the declarations in the state constitutions, in favour of the freedom of the press, would be a constitutional impediment to the imposition of duties upon publications by the state legislatures. It cannot certainly be pretended that any degree of duties, however low, would be an abrigement of the liberty of the press. We know that newspapers are taxed in Great-Britain, and yet it is notorious that the press no where enjoys greater liberty than in that country. And if duties of any kind may be laid without a violation of that liberty, it is evident that the extent must depend on legislative discretion, regulated by public opinion; so that after all, general declarations respecting the liberty of the press will give it no greater security than it will have without them. The same invasions of it may be effected under the state constitutions which contain those declarations through the means of taxation, as under the proposed constitution which has nothing of the kind. It would be quite as significant to declare that government ought to be free, that taxes ought not to be excessive, &c., as that the liberty of the press ought not to be restrained.

There remains but one other view of this matter to conclude the point. The truth is, after all the declamation we have heard, that the constitution is itself in every rational sense, and to every useful purpose, A BILL OF RIGHTS. The several bills of rights, in Great-Britain, form its constitution, and conversely the constitution of each state is its bill of rights. And the proposed constitution, if adopted, will be the bill of rights of the union. Is it one object of a bill of rights to declare and specify the political privileges of the citizens in the structure and administration of the government? This is done in the most ample and precise manner in the plan of the convention, comprehending various precautions for the public security, which are not to be found in any of the state constitutions. Is another object of a bill of rights to define certain immunities and modes of proceeding, which are relative to personal and private concerns? This we have seen has also been attended to, in a variety of cases, in the same plan. Adverting therefore to the substantial meaning of a bill of rights, it is absurd to allege that it is not to be found in the work of the convention. It may be said that it does not go far enough, though it will not be easy to make this appear; but it can with no propriety be contended that there is no such thing. It certainly must be immaterial what mode is observed as to the order of declaring the rights of the citizens, if they are to be found in any part of the instrument which establishes the government. And hence it must be apparent that much of what has been said on this subject rests merely on verbal and nominal distinctions, which are entirely foreign from the substance of the thing.

8

NEW YORK RATIFICATION OF CONSTITUTION
26 July 1788
Elliot 1:327–31

We, the delegates of the people of the state of New York, duly elected and met in Convention, having maturely considered the Constitution for the United States of America, agreed to on the 17th day of September, in the year 1787, by the Convention then assembled at Philadelphia, in the commonwealth of Pennsylvania, (a copy whereof precedes these presents,) and having also seriously and deliberately concurrence of two thirds of the senators and representatives present in each house.

That the privilege of the *habeas corpus* shall not, by any law, be suspended for a longer term than six months, or until twenty days after the meeting of the Congress next following the passing the act for such suspension.

That the right of Congress to exercise exclusive legislation over such district, not exceeding ten miles square, as may, by cession of a particular state, and the acceptance of Congress, become the seat of government of the United States, shall not be so exercised as to exempt the inhabitants of such district from paying the like taxes, imposts, duties, and excises, as shall be imposed on the other inhabitants of the state in which such district may be; and that no person shall be privileged within the said district from arrest for crimes committed, or debts contracted, out of the said district.

That the right of exclusive legislation, with respect to such places as may be purchased for the erection of forts, magazines, arsenals, dock-yards, and other needful buildings, shall not authorize the Congress to make any law to prevent the laws of the states, respectively, in which they may be, from extending to such places in all civil and criminal matters, except as to such persons as shall be in the service of the United States; nor to them with respect to crimes committed without such places.

That the compensation for the senators and representatives be ascertained by standing laws; and that no alteration of the existing rate of compensation shall operate for the benefit of the representatives until after a subsequent election shall have been had.

That the Journals of the Congress shall be published at least once a year, with the exception of such parts, relating to treaties or military operations, as, in the judgment of either house, shall require secrecy; and that both houses of Congress shall always keep their doors open during their sessions, unless the business may, in their opinion, require secrecy. That the yeas and nays shall be entered on the Journals whenever two members in either house may require it.

That no capitation tax shall ever be laid by Congress.

That no person be eligible as a senator for more than six years in any term of twelve years; and that the legislatures of the respective states may recall their senators, or either of them, and elect others in their stead, to serve the remainder of the time for which the senators so recalled were appointed.

That no senator or representative shall, during the time for which he was elected, be appointed to any office under the authority of the United States.

That the authority given to the executives of the states to fill up the vacancies of senators be abolished, and that such vacancies be filled by the respective legislatures.

That the power of Congress to pass uniform laws concerning bankruptcy shall only extend to merchants and other traders; and the states, respectively, may pass laws for the relief of other insolvent debtors.

That no person shall be eligible to the office of President of the United States a third time.

That the executive shall not grant pardons for treason, unless with the consent of the Congress; but may, at his discretion, grant reprieves to persons convicted of treason, until their cases can be laid before the Congress.

That the President, or person exercising his powers for the time being, shall not command an army in the field in person, without the previous desire of the Congress.

That all letters patent, commissions, pardons, writs, and processes of the United States, shall run in the name of *the people of the United States*, and be tested in the name of the President of the United States, or the person exercising his powers for the time being, or the first judge of the court out of which the same shall issue, as the case may be.

That the Congress shall not constitute, ordain, or establish, any tribunals of inferior courts, with any other than appellate jurisdiction, except such as may be necessary for the trial of cases of admiralty and maritime jurisdiction, and for the trial of piracies and felonies committed on the high seas; and in all other cases to which the judicial power of the United States extends, and in which the Supreme Court of the United States has not original jurisdiction, the causes shall be heard, tried, and determined, in some one of the state courts, with the right of appeal to the Supreme Court of the United States, or other proper tribunal, to be established for that purpose by the Congress, with such exceptions, and under such regulations, as the Congress shall make.

That the court for the trial of impeachments shall consist of the Senate, the judges of the Supreme Court of the United States, and the first or senior judge, for the time being, of the highest court of general and ordinary common-law jurisdiction in each state; that the Congress shall, by standing laws, designate the courts in the respective states answering this description, and, in states having no courts exactly answering this description, shall designate some other court, preferring such, if any there be, whose judge or judges may hold their places during good behavior; provided, that no more than one judge, other than judges of the Supreme Court of the United States, shall come from one state.

That the Congress be authorized to pass laws for compensating the judges for such services, and for compelling their attendance; and that a majority, at least, of the said judges shall be requisite to constitute the said court. That no person impeached shall sit as a member thereof; that each member shall, previous to the entering upon any trial, take an oath or affirmation honestly and impartially to hear and determine the cause; and that a majority of the members present shall be necessary to a conviction.

That persons aggrieved by any judgment, sentence, or decree, of the Supreme Court of the United States, in any cause in which that court has original jurisdiction, with such exceptions, and under such regulations, as the Congress shall make concerning the same, shall, upon application, have a commission, to be issued by the President of the United States to such men learned in the law as he shall nominate, and by and with the advice and consent of the Senate appoint, not less than seven, authorizing such commissioners, or any seven or more of them, to correct

tion, which is merely intended to regulate the general political interests of the nation, than to a constitution which has the regulation of every species of personal and private concerns. If therefore the loud clamours against the plan of the convention on this score, are well founded, no epithets of reprobation will be too strong for the constitution of this state. But the truth is, that both of them contain all, which in relation to their objects, is reasonably to be desired.

I go further, and affirm that bills of rights, in the sense and in the extent in which they are contended for, are not only unnecessary in the proposed constitution, but would even be dangerous. They would contain various exceptions to powers which are not granted; and on this very account, would afford a colourable pretext to claim more than were granted. For why declare that things shall not be done which there is no power to do? Why for instance, should it be said, that the liberty of the press shall not be restrained, when no power is given by which restrictions may be imposed? I will not contend that such a provision would confer a regulating power; but it is evident that it would furnish, to men disposed to usurp, a plausible pretence for claiming that power. They might urge with a semblance of reason, that the constitution ought not to be charged with the absurdity of providing against the abuse of an authority, which was not given, and that the provision against restraining the liberty of the press afforded a clear implication, that a power to prescribe proper regulations concerning it, was intended to be vested in the national government. This may serve as a specimen of the numerous handles which would be given to the doctrine of constructive powers, by the indulgence of an injudicious zeal for bills of rights.

On the subject of the liberty of the press, as much has been said, I cannot forbear adding a remark or two: In the first place, I observe that there is not a syllable concerning it in the constitution of this state, and in the next, I contend that whatever has been said about it in that of any other state, amounts to nothing. What signifies a declaration that "the liberty of the press shall be inviolably preserved?" What is the liberty of the press? Who can give it any definition which would not leave the utmost latitude for evasion? I hold it to be impracticable; and from this, I infer, that its security, whatever fine declarations may be inserted in any constitution respecting it, must altogether depend on public opinion, and on the general spirit of the people and of the government.* And here, after all, as intimated upon another occasion, must we seek for the only solid basis of all our rights.

There remains but one other view of this matter to conclude the point. The truth is, after all the declamation we have heard, that the constitution is itself in every rational sense, and to every useful purpose, A BILL OF RIGHTS. The several bills of rights, in Great-Britain, form its constitution, and conversely the constitution of each state is its bill of rights. And the proposed constitution, if adopted, will be the bill of rights of the union. Is it one object of a bill of rights to declare and specify the political privileges of the citizens in the structure and administration of the government? This is done in the most ample and precise manner in the plan of the convention, comprehending various precautions for the public security, which are not to be found in any of the state constitutions. Is another object of a bill of rights to define certain immunities and modes of proceeding, which are relative to personal and private concerns? This we have seen has also been attended to, in a variety of cases, in the same plan. Adverting therefore to the substantial meaning of a bill of rights, it is absurd to allege that it is not to be found in the work of the convention. It may be said that it does not go far enough, though it will not be easy to make this appear; but it can with no propriety be contended that there is no such thing. It certainly must be immaterial what mode is observed as to the order of declaring the rights of the citizens, if they are to be found in any part of the instrument which establishes the government. And hence it must be apparent that much of what has been said on this subject rests merely on verbal and nominal distinctions, which are entirely foreign from the substance of the thing.

8

NEW YORK RATIFICATION OF CONSTITUTION
26 July 1788
Elliot 1:327–31

We, the delegates of the people of the state of New York, duly elected and met in Convention, having maturely considered the Constitution for the United States of America, agreed to on the 17th day of September, in the year 1787, by the Convention then assembled at Philadelphia, in the commonwealth of Pennsylvania, (a copy whereof precedes these presents,) and having also seriously and deliberately

---

*To show that there is a power in the constitution by which the liberty of the press may be affected, recourse has been had to the power of taxation. It is said that duties may be laid upon publications so high as to amount to a prohibition. I know not by what logic it could be maintained that the declarations in the state constitutions, in favour of the freedom of the press, would be a constitutional impediment to the imposition of duties upon publications by the state legislatures. It cannot certainly be pretended that any degree of duties, however low, would be an abridgement of the liberty of the press. We know that newspapers are taxed in Great-Britain, and yet it is notorious that the press no where enjoys greater liberty than in that country. And if duties of any kind

may be laid without a violation of that liberty, it is evident that the extent must depend on legislative discretion, regulated by public opinion; so that after all, general declarations respecting the liberty of the press will give it no greater security than it will have without them. The same invasions of it may be effected under the state constitutions which contain those declarations through the means of taxation, as under the proposed constitution which has nothing of the kind. It would be quite as significant to declare that government ought to be free, that taxes ought not to be excessive, &c., as that the liberty of the press ought not to be restrained.

considered the present situation of the United States,—Do declare and make known,—

That all power is originally vested in, and consequently derived from, the people, and that government is instituted by them for their common interest, protection, and security.

That the enjoyment of life, liberty, and the pursuit of happiness, are essential rights, which every government ought to respect and preserve.

That the powers of government may be reassumed by the people whensoever it shall become necessary to their happiness; that every power, jurisdiction, and right, which is not by the said Constitution clearly delegated to the Congress of the United States, or the departments of the government thereof, remains to the people of the several states, or to their respective state governments, to whom they may have granted the same; and that those clauses in the said Constitution, which declare that Congress shall not have or exercise certain powers, do not imply that Congress is entitled to any powers not given by the said Constitution; but such clauses are to be construed either as exceptions to certain specified powers, or as inserted merely for greater caution.

That the people have an equal, natural, and unalienable right freely and peaceably to exercise their religion, according to the dictates of conscience; and that no religious sect or society ought to be favored or established by law in preference to others.

That the people have a right to keep and bear arms; that a well-regulated militia, including the body of the people *capable of bearing arms*, is the proper, natural, and safe defence of a free state.

That the militia should not be subject to martial law, except in time of war, rebellion, or insurrection.

That standing armies, in time of peace, are dangerous to liberty, and ought not to be kept up, except in cases of necessity; and that at all times the military should be under strict subordination to the civil power.

That, in time of peace, no soldier ought to be quartered in any house without the consent of the owner, and in time of war only by the civil magistrate, in such manner as the laws may direct.

That no person ought to be taken, imprisoned, or disseized of his freehold, or be exiled, or deprived of his privileges, franchises, life, liberty, or property, but by due process of law.

That no person ought to be put twice in jeopardy of life or limb, for one and the same offence; nor, unless in case of impeachment, be punished more than once for the same offence.

That every person restrained of his liberty is entitled to an inquiry into the lawfulness of such restraint, and to a removal thereof if unlawful; and that such inquiry or removal ought not to be denied or delayed, except when, on account of public danger, the Congress shall suspend the privilege of the writ of *habeas corpus*.

That excessive bail ought not to be required, nor excessive fines imposed, nor cruel or unusual punishments inflicted.

That (except in the government of the land and naval forces, and of the militia when in actual service, and in cases of impeachment) a presentment or indictment by a grand jury ought to be observed as a necessary preliminary to the trial of all crimes cognizable by the judiciary of the United States; and such trial should be speedy, public, and by an impartial jury of the county where the crime was committed; and that no person can be found guilty without the unanimous consent of such jury. But in cases of crimes not committed within any county of any of the United States, and in cases of crimes committed within any county in which a general insurrection may prevail, or which may be in the possession of a foreign enemy, the inquiry and trial may be in such county as the Congress shall by law direct; which county, in the two cases last mentioned, should be as near as conveniently may be to that county in which the crime may have been committed;— and that, in all criminal prosecutions, the accused ought to be informed of the cause and nature of his accusation, to be confronted with his accusers and the witnesses against him, to have the means of producing his witnesses, and the assistance of counsel for his defence; and should not be compelled to give evidence against himself.

That the trial by jury, in the extent that it obtains by the common law of England, is one of the greatest securities to the rights of a free people, and ought to remain inviolate.

That every freeman has a right to be secure from all unreasonable searches and seizures of his person, his papers, or his property; and therefore, that all warrants to search suspected places, or seize any freeman, his papers, or property, without information, upon oath or affirmation, of sufficient cause, are grievous and oppressive; and that all general warrants (or such in which the place or person suspected are not particularly designated) are dangerous, and ought not to be granted.

That the people have a right peaceably to assemble together to consult for their common good, or to instruct their representatives, and that every person has a right to petition or apply to the legislature for redress of grievances.

That the freedom of the press ought not to be violated or restrained.

That there should be, once in four years, an election of the President and Vice-President, so that no officer, who may be appointed by the Congress to act as President, in case of the removal, death, resignation, or inability, of the President and Vice-President, can in any case continue to act beyond the termination of the period for which the last President and Vice-President were elected.

That nothing contained in the said Constitution is to be construed to prevent the legislature of any state from passing laws at its discretion, from time to time, to divide such state into convenient districts, and to apportion its representatives to and amongst such districts.

That the prohibition contained in the said Constitution, against *ex post facto* laws, extends only to laws concerning crimes.

That all appeals in causes determinable according to the course of the common law, ought to be by writ of error, and not otherwise.

That the judicial power of the United States, in cases in which a state may be a party, does not extend to criminal prosecutions, or to authorize any suit by any person against a state.

That the judicial power of the United States, as to controversies between citizens of the same state, claiming lands under grants from different states, is not to be construed to extend to any other controversies between them, except those which relate to such lands, so claimed, under grants of different states.

That the jurisdiction of the Supreme Court of the United States, or of any other court to be instituted by the Congress, is not in any case to be increased, enlarged, or extended, by any faction, collusion, or mere suggestion; and that no treaty is to be construed so to operate as to alter the Constitution of any state.

Under these impressions, and declaring that the rights aforesaid cannot be abridged or violated, and that the explanations aforesaid are consistent with the said Constitution, and in confidence that the amendments which shall have been proposed to the said Constitution will receive an early and mature consideration,—We, the said delegates, in the name and in the behalf of the people of the state of New York, do, by these presents, assent to and ratify the said Constitution. In full confidence, nevertheless, that, until a convention shall be called and convened for proposing amendments to the said Constitution, the militia of this state will not be continued in service out of this state for a longer term than six weeks, without the consent of the legislature thereof; that the Congress will not make or alter any regulation in this state, respecting the times, places, and manner, of holding elections for senators or representatives, unless the legislature of this state shall neglect or refuse to make laws or regulations for the purpose, or from any circumstance be incapable of making the same, and that, in those cases, such power will only be exercised until the legislature of this state shall make provision in the premises; that no excise will be imposed on any article of the growth, production, or manufacture of the United States, or any of them, within this state, ardent spirits excepted; and the Congress will not lay direct taxes within this state, but when the moneys arising from the impost and excise shall be insufficient for the public exigencies, nor then, until Congress shall first have made a requisition upon this state to assess, levy, and pay, the amount of such requisition, made agreeably to the census fixed in the said Constitution, in such way and manner as the legislature of this state shall judge best; but that in such case, if the state shall neglect or refuse to pay its proportion, pursuant to such requisition, then the Congress may assess and levy this state's proportion, together with interest, at the rate of six per centum per annum, from the time at which the same was required to be paid.

Done in Convention, at Poughkeepsie, in the county of Duchess, in the state of New York, the 26th day of July, in the year of our Lord 1788.

By order of the Convention.   GEO. CLINTON,
                                                                    President.

Attested. JOHN M'KESSON, A. B. BANKER, *Secretaries.*

And the Convention do, in the name and behalf of the people of the state of New York, enjoin it upon their representatives in Congress to exert all their influence, and use all reasonable means, to obtain a ratification of the following amendments to the said Constitution, in the manner prescribed therein; and in all laws to be passed by the Congress, in the mean time, to conform to the spirit of the said amendments, as far as the Constitution will admit.

That there shall be one representative for every thirty thousand inhabitants, according to the enumeration or census mentioned in the Constitution, until the whole number of representatives amounts to two hundred, after which that number shall be continued or increased, but not diminished, as the Congress shall direct, and according to such ratio as the Congress shall fix, in conformity to the rule prescribed for the apportionment of representatives and direct taxes.

That the Congress do not impose any excise on any article (ardent spirits excepted) of the growth, production, or manufacture of the United States, or any of them.

That Congress do not lay direct taxes but when the moneys arising from the impost and excise shall be insufficient for the public exigencies, nor then, until Congress shall first have made a requisition upon the states to assess, levy, and pay, their respective proportions of such requisition, agreeably to the census fixed in the said Constitution, in such way and manner as the legislatures of the respective states shall judge best; and in such case, if any state shall neglect or refuse to pay its proportion, pursuant to such requisition, then Congress may assess and levy such state's proportion, together with interest at the rate of six per centum per annum, from the time of payment prescribed in such requisition.

That the Congress shall not make or alter any regulation, in any state, respecting the times, places, and manner, of holding elections for senators and representatives, unless the legislature of such state shall neglect or refuse to make laws or regulations for the purpose, or from any circumstance be incapable of making the same, and then only until the legislature of such state shall make provision in the premises; provided, that Congress may prescribe the time for the election of representatives.

That no persons, except natural-born citizens, or such as were citizens on or before the 4th day of July, 1776, or such as held commissions under the United States during the war, and have at any time since the 4th day of July, 1776, become citizens of one or other of the United States, and who shall be freeholders, shall be eligible to the places of President, Vice-President, or members of either house of the Congress of the United States.

That the Congress do not grant monopolies, or erect any company with exclusive advantages of commerce.

That no standing army or regular troops shall be raised, or kept up, in time of peace, without the consent of two thirds of the senators and representatives present in each house.

That no money be borrowed on the credit of the United States without the assent of two thirds of the senators and representatives present in each house.

That the Congress shall not declare war without the

concurrence of two thirds of the senators and representatives present in each house.

That the privilege of the *habeas corpus* shall not, by any law, be suspended for a longer term than six months, or until twenty days after the meeting of the Congress next following the passing the act for such suspension.

That the right of Congress to exercise exclusive legislation over such district, not exceeding ten miles square, as may, by cession of a particular state, and the acceptance of Congress, become the seat of government of the United States, shall not be so exercised as to exempt the inhabitants of such district from paying the like taxes, imposts, duties, and excises, as shall be imposed on the other inhabitants of the state in which such district may be; and that no person shall be privileged within the said district from arrest for crimes committed, or debts contracted, out of the said district.

That the right of exclusive legislation, with respect to such places as may be purchased for the erection of forts, magazines, arsenals, dock-yards, and other needful buildings, shall not authorize the Congress to make any law to prevent the laws of the states, respectively, in which they may be, from extending to such places in all civil and criminal matters, except as to such persons as shall be in the service of the United States; nor to them with respect to crimes committed without such places.

That the compensation for the senators and representatives be ascertained by standing laws; and that no alteration of the existing rate of compensation shall operate for the benefit of the representatives until after a subsequent election shall have been had.

That the Journals of the Congress shall be published at least once a year, with the exception of such parts, relating to treaties or military operations, as, in the judgment of either house, shall require secrecy; and that both houses of Congress shall always keep their doors open during their sessions, unless the business may, in their opinion, require secrecy. That the yeas and nays shall be entered on the Journals whenever two members in either house may require it.

That no capitation tax shall ever be laid by Congress.

That no person be eligible as a senator for more than six years in any term of twelve years; and that the legislatures of the respective states may recall their senators, or either of them, and elect others in their stead, to serve the remainder of the time for which the senators so recalled were appointed.

That no senator or representative shall, during the time for which he was elected, be appointed to any office under the authority of the United States.

That the authority given to the executives of the states to fill up the vacancies of senators be abolished, and that such vacancies be filled by the respective legislatures.

That the power of Congress to pass uniform laws concerning bankruptcy shall only extend to merchants and other traders; and the states, respectively, may pass laws for the relief of other insolvent debtors.

That no person shall be eligible to the office of President of the United States a third time.

That the executive shall not grant pardons for treason, unless with the consent of the Congress; but may, at his discretion, grant reprieves to persons convicted of treason, until their cases can be laid before the Congress.

That the President, or person exercising his powers for the time being, shall not command an army in the field in person, without the previous desire of the Congress.

That all letters patent, commissions, pardons, writs, and processes of the United States, shall run in the name of *the people of the United States*, and be tested in the name of the President of the United States, or the person exercising his powers for the time being, or the first judge of the court out of which the same shall issue, as the case may be.

That the Congress shall not constitute, ordain, or establish, any tribunals of inferior courts, with any other than appellate jurisdiction, except such as may be necessary for the trial of cases of admiralty and maritime jurisdiction, and for the trial of piracies and felonies committed on the high seas; and in all other cases to which the judicial power of the United States extends, and in which the Supreme Court of the United States has not original jurisdiction, the causes shall be heard, tried, and determined, in some one of the state courts, with the right of appeal to the Supreme Court of the United States, or other proper tribunal, to be established for that purpose by the Congress, with such exceptions, and under such regulations, as the Congress shall make.

That the court for the trial of impeachments shall consist of the Senate, the judges of the Supreme Court of the United States, and the first or senior judge, for the time being, of the highest court of general and ordinary common-law jurisdiction in each state; that the Congress shall, by standing laws, designate the courts in the respective states answering this description, and, in states having no courts exactly answering this description, shall designate some other court, preferring such, if any there be, whose judge or judges may hold their places during good behavior; provided, that no more than one judge, other than judges of the Supreme Court of the United States, shall come from one state.

That the Congress be authorized to pass laws for compensating the judges for such services, and for compelling their attendance; and that a majority, at least, of the said judges shall be requisite to constitute the said court. That no person impeached shall sit as a member thereof; that each member shall, previous to the entering upon any trial, take an oath or affirmation honestly and impartially to hear and determine the cause; and that a majority of the members present shall be necessary to a conviction.

That persons aggrieved by any judgment, sentence, or decree, of the Supreme Court of the United States, in any cause in which that court has original jurisdiction, with such exceptions, and under such regulations, as the Congress shall make concerning the same, shall, upon application, have a commission, to be issued by the President of the United States to such men learned in the law as he shall nominate, and by and with the advice and consent of the Senate appoint, not less than seven, authorizing such commissioners, or any seven or more of them, to correct the errors in such judgment, or to review such sentence and decree, as the case may be, and to do justice to the parties in the premises.

That no judge of the Supreme Court of the United States shall hold any other office under the United States, or any of them.

That the judicial power of the United States shall extend to no controversies respecting land, unless it relate to claims of territory or jurisdiction between states, and individuals under the grants of different states.

That the militia of any state shall not be compelled to serve without the limits of the state, for a longer term than six weeks, without the consent of the legislature thereof.

That the words *without the consent of the Congress*, in the seventh clause of the ninth section of the first article of the Constitution, be expunged.

That the senators and representatives, and all executive and judicial officers of the United States, shall be bound by oath or affirmation not to infringe or violate the constitutions or rights of the respective states.

That the legislatures of the respective states may make provision, by law, that the electors of the election districts, to be by them appointed, shall choose a citizen of the United States, who shall have been an inhabitant of such district for the term of one year immediately preceding the time of his election, for one of the representatives of such state

9

VIRGINIA RATIFYING CONVENTION, PROPOSED
AMENDMENTS TO THE CONSTITUTION
27 June 1788
Elliot 3:657–61

Mr. WYTHE reported, from the committee appointed, such *amendments* to the proposed Constitution of government for the United States as were by them deemed necessary to be recommended to the consideration of the Congress which shall first assemble under the said Constitution, to be acted upon according to the mode prescribed in the 5th article thereof; and he read the same in his place, and afterwards delivered them in at the clerk's table, where the same were again read, and are as follows:—

"That there be a declaration or bill of rights asserting, and securing from encroachment, the essential and unalienable rights of the people, in some such manner as the following:—

"1st. That there are certain natural rights, of which men, when they form a social compact, cannot deprive or divest their posterity; among which are the enjoyment of life and liberty, with the means of acquiring, possessing, and protecting property, and pursuing and obtaining happiness and safety.

"2d. That all power is naturally invested in, and consequently derived from, the people; that magistrates therefore are their *trustees* and *agents,* at all times amenable to them.

"3d. That government ought to be instituted for the common benefit, protection, and security of the people; and that the doctrine of non-resistance against arbitrary power and oppression is absurd, slavish, and destructive to the good and happiness of mankind.

"4th. That no man or set of men are entitled to separate or exclusive public emoluments or privileges from the community, but in consideration of public services, which not being descendible, neither ought the offices of magistrate, legislator, or judge, or any other public office, to be hereditary.

"5th. That the legislative, executive, and judicial powers of government should be separate and distinct; and, that the members of the two first may be restrained from oppression by feeling and participating the public burdens, they should, at fixed periods, be reduced to a private station, return into the mass of the people, and the vacancies be supplied by certain and regular elections, in which all or any part of the former members to be eligible or ineligible, as the rules of the Constitution of government, and the laws, shall direct.

"6th. That the elections of representatives in the legislature ought to be free and frequent, and all men having sufficient evidence of permanent common interest with, and attachment to, the community, ought to have the right of suffrage; and no aid, charge, tax, or fee, can be set, rated, or levied, upon the people without their own consent, or that of their representatives, so elected; nor can they be bound by any law to which they have not, in like manner, assented, for the public good.

"7th. That all power of suspending laws, or the execution of laws, by any authority, without the consent of the representatives of the people in the legislature, is injurious to their rights, and ought not to be exercised.

"8th. That, in all criminal and capital prosecutions, a man hath a right to demand the cause and nature of his accusation, to be confronted with the accusers and witnesses, to call for evidence, and be allowed counsel in his favor, and to a fair and speedy trial by an impartial jury of his vicinage, without whose unanimous consent he cannot be found guilty, (except in the government of the land and naval forces;) nor can he be compelled to give evidence against himself.

"9th. That no freeman ought to be taken, imprisoned, or disseized of his freehold, liberties, privileges, or franchises, or outlawed, or exiled, or in any manner destroyed, or deprived of his life, liberty, or property, but by the law of the land.

"10th. That every freeman restrained of his liberty is entitled to a remedy, to inquire into the lawfulness thereof, and to remove the same, if unlawful, and that such remedy ought not to be denied nor delayed.

"11th. That, in controversies respecting property, and in suits between man and man, the ancient trial by jury is one of the greatest securities to the rights of the people, and to remain sacred and inviolable.

"12th. That every freeman ought to find a certain remedy, by recourse to the laws, for all injuries and wrongs he may receive in his person, property, or character. He ought to obtain right and justice freely, without sale, completely and without denial, promptly and without delay; and that all establishments or regulations contravening these rights are oppressive and unjust.

"13th. That excessive bail ought not to be required, nor excessive fines imposed, nor cruel and unusual punishments inflicted.

"14th. That every freeman has a right to be secure from all unreasonable searches and seizures of his person, his papers, and property; all warrants, therefore, to search suspected places, or seize any freeman, his papers, or property, without information on oath (or affirmation of a person religiously scrupulous of taking an oath) of legal and sufficient cause, are grievous and oppressive; and all general warrants to search suspected places, or to apprehend any suspected person, without specially naming or describing the place or person, are dangerous, and ought not to be granted.

"15th. That the people have a right peaceably to assemble together to consult for the common good, or to instruct their representatives; and that every freeman has a right to petition or apply to the legislature for redress of grievances.

"16th. That the people have a right to freedom of speech, and of writing and publishing their sentiments; that the freedom of the press is one of the greatest bulwarks of liberty, and ought not to be violated.

"17th. That the people have a right to keep and bear arms; that a well-regulated militia, composed of the body of the people trained to arms, is the proper, natural, and safe defence of a free state; that standing armies, in time of peace, are dangerous to liberty, and therefore ought to be avoided, as far as the circumstances and protection of the community will admit; and that, in all cases, the military should be under strict subordination to, and governed by, the civil power.

"18th. That no soldier in time of peace ought to be quartered in any house without the consent of the owner, and in time of war in such manner only as the law directs.

"19th. That any person religiously scrupulous of bearing arms ought to be exempted, upon payment of an equivalent to employ another to bear arms in his stead.

"20th. That religion, or the duty which we owe to our Creator, and the manner of discharging it, can be directed only by reason and conviction, not by force or violence; and therefore all men have an equal, natural, and unalienable right to the free exercise of religion, according to the dictates of conscience, and that no particular religious sect or society ought to be favored or established, by law, in preference to others."

Amendments to the Constitution.

"1st. That each state in the Union shall respectively retain every power, jurisdiction, and right, which is not by this Constitution delegated to the Congress of the United States, or to the departments of the federal government.

"2d. That there shall be one representative for every thirty thousand, according to the enumeration or census mentioned in the Constitution, until the whole number of representatives amounts to two hundred; after which, that number shall be continued or increased, as Congress shall direct, upon the principles fixed in the Constitution, by apportioning the representatives of each state to some greater number of people, from time to time, as population increases.

"3d. When the Congress shall lay direct taxes or excises, they shall immediately inform the executive power of each state, of the quota of such state, according to the census herein directed, which is proposed to be thereby raised; and if the legislature of any state shall pass a law which shall be effectual for raising such quota at the time required by Congress, the taxes and excises laid by Congress shall not be collected in such state.

"4th. That the members of the Senate and House of Representatives shall be ineligible to, and incapable of holding, any civil office under the authority of the United States, during the time for which they shall respectively be elected.

"5th. That the journals of the proceedings of the Senate and House of Representatives shall be published at least once in every year. except such parts thereof, relating to treaties, alliances, or military operations, as, in their judgment, require secrecy.

"6th. That a regular statement and account of the receipts and expenditures of public money shall be published at least once a year.

"7th. That no commercial treaty shall be ratified without the concurrence of two thirds of the whole number of the members of the Senate; and no treaty ceding, contracting, restraining, or suspending, the territorial rights or claims of the United States, or any of them, or their, or any of their rights or claims to fishing in the American seas, or navigating the American rivers, shall be made, but in cases of the most urgent and extreme necessity; nor shall any such treaty be ratified without the concurrence of three fourths of the whole number of the members of both houses respectively.

"8th. That no navigation law, or law regulating commerce, shall be passed without the consent of two thirds of the members present, in both houses.

"9th. That no standing army, or regular troops, shall be raised, or kept up, in time of peace, without the consent of two thirds of the members present, in both houses.

"10th. That no soldier shall be enlisted for any longer term than four years, except in time of war, and then for no longer term than the continuance of the war.

"11th. That each state respectively shall have the power to provide for organizing, arming, and disciplining its own militia, whensoever Congress shall omit or neglect to provide for the same. That the militia shall not be subject to martial law, except when in actual service, in time of war, invasion, or rebellion; and when not in the actual service of the United States, shall be subject only to such fines, penalties, and punishments, as shall be directed or inflicted by the laws of its own state.

"12th. That the exclusive power of legislation given to Congress over the federal town and its adjacent district, and other places, purchased or to be purchased by Congress of any of the states, shall extend only to such regulations as respect the police and good government thereof.

"13th. That no person shall be capable of being President of the United States for more than eight years in any term of sixteen years.

"14th. That the judicial power of the United States shall be vested in one Supreme Court, and in such courts of admiralty as Congress may from time to time ordain and establish in any of the different states. The judicial power shall extend to all cases in law and equity arising under treaties made, or which shall be made, under the authority of the United States; to all cases affecting ambassadors, other foreign ministers, and consuls; to all cases of admiralty and maritime jurisdiction; to controversies to which the United States shall be a party; to controversies between two or more states, and between parties claiming lands under the grants of different states. In all cases affecting ambassadors, other foreign ministers, and consuls, and those in which a state shall be a party, the Supreme Court shall have original jurisdiction; in all other cases before mentioned, the Supreme Court shall have appellate jurisdiction, as to matters of law only, except in cases of equity, and of admiralty, and maritime jurisdiction, in which the Supreme Court shall have appellate jurisdiction both as to law and fact, with such exceptions and under such regulations as the Congress shall make: but the judicial power of the United States shall extend to no case where the cause of action shall have originated before the ratification of the Constitution, except in disputes between states about their territory, disputes between persons claiming lands under the grants of different states, and suits for debts due to the United States.

"15th. That, in criminal prosecutions, no man shall be restrained in the exercise of the usual and accustomed right of challenging or excepting to the jury.

"16th. That Congress shall not alter, modify, or interfere in the times, places, or manner of holding elections for senators and representatives, or either of them, except when the legislature of any state shall neglect, refuse, or be disabled, by invasion or rebellion, to prescribe the same.

"17th. That those clauses which declare that Congress shall not exercise certain powers, be not interpreted, in any manner whatsoever, to extend the powers of Congress; but that they be construed either as making exceptions to the specified powers where this shall be the case, or otherwise, as inserted merely for greater caution.

"18th. That the laws ascertaining the compensation of senators and representatives for their services, be postponed, in their operation, until after the election of representatives immediately succeeding the passing thereof; that excepted which shall first be passed on the subject.

"19th. That some tribunal other than the Senate be provided for trying impeachments of senators.

"20th. That the salary of a judge shall not be increased or diminished during his continuance in office, otherwise than by general regulations of salary, which may take place on a revision of the subject at stated periods of not less than seven years, to commence from the time such salaries shall be first ascertained by Congress."

10

NORTH CAROLINA RATIFYING CONVENTION, DECLARATION OF RIGHTS AND OTHER AMENDMENTS
1 Aug. 1788
Elliot 4:242–46, 248–49

The resolution was accordingly read and entered, as follows, viz.:—

Resolved, That a declaration of rights, asserting and securing from encroachment the great principles of civil and religious liberty, and the unalienable rights of the people, together with amendments to the most ambiguous and exceptionable parts of the said Constitution of government, ought to be laid before Congress, and the convention of the states that shall or may be called for the purpose of amending the said Constitution, for their consideration, previous to the ratification of the Constitution aforesaid on the part of the state of North Carolina.

Declaration of Rights.

1. That there are certain natural rights, of which men, when they form a social compact, cannot deprive or divest their posterity, among which are the enjoyment of life and liberty, with the means of acquiring, possessing, and protecting property, and pursuing and obtaining happiness and safety.

2. That all power is naturally vested in, and consequently derived from, the people; that magistrates, therefore, are their trustees and agents, and at all times amenable to them.

3. That government ought to be instituted for the common benefit, protection, and security, of the people; and that the doctrine of non-resistance against arbitrary power and oppression is absurd, slavish, and destructive to the good and happiness of mankind.

4. That no man or set of men are entitled to exclusive or separate public emoluments or privileges from the community, but in consideration of public services, which not being descendible, neither ought the offices of magistrate, legislator, or judge, or any other public office, to be hereditary.

5. That the legislative, executive, and judiciary powers of government should be separate and distinct, and that the members of the two first may be restrained from oppression by feeling and participating the public burdens: they should, at fixed periods, be reduced to a private station, return into the mass of the people, and the vacancies be supplied by certain and regular elections, in which all or any part of the former members to be eligible or ineligible, as the rules of the constitution of government and the laws shall direct.

6. That elections of representatives in the legislature ought to be free and frequent, and all men having sufficient evidence of permanent common interest with, and attachment to, the community, ought to have the right of

suffrage; and no aid, charge, tax, or fee, can be set, rated, or levied, upon the people without their own consent, or that of their representatives so elected; nor can they be bound by any law to which they have not in like manner assented for the public good.

7. That all power of suspending laws, or the execution of laws, by any authority, without the consent of the representatives of the people in the legislature, is injurious to their rights, and ought not to be exercised.

8. That, in all capital and criminal prosecutions, a man hath a right to demand the cause and nature of his accusation, to be confronted with the accusers and witnesses, to call for evidence, and be allowed counsel in his favor, and a fair and speedy trial by an impartial jury of his vicinage, without whose unanimous consent he cannot be found guilty, (except in the government of the land and naval forces;) nor can he be compelled to give evidence against himself.

9. That no freeman ought to be taken, imprisoned, or disseized of his freehold, liberties, privileges, or franchises, or outlawed or exiled, or in any manner destroyed, or deprived of his life, liberty, or property, but by the law of the land.

10. That every freeman, restrained of his liberty, is entitled to a remedy to inquire into the lawfulness thereof, and to remove the same if unlawful; and that such remedy ought not to be denied nor delayed.

11. That, in controversies respecting property, and in suits between man and man, the ancient trial by jury is one of the greatest securities to the rights of the people, and ought to remain sacred and inviolable.

12. That every freeman ought to find a certain remedy, by recourse to the laws, for all injuries and wrongs he may receive in his person, property, or character; he ought to obtain right and justice freely without sale, completely and without denial, promptly and without delay; and that all establishments or regulations contravening these rights are oppressive and unjust.

13. That excessive bail ought not to be required, nor excessive fines imposed, nor cruel and unusual punishments inflicted.

14. That every freeman has a right to be secure from all unreasonable searches and seizures of his person, his papers and property; all warrants, therefore, to search suspected places, or to apprehend any suspected person, without specially naming or describing the place or person, are dangerous, and ought not to be granted.

15. That the people have a right peaceably to assemble together, to consult for the common good, or to instruct their representatives; and that every freeman has a right to petition or apply to the legislature for redress of grievances.

16. That the people have a right to freedom of speech, and of writing and publishing their sentiments; that freedom of the press is one of the greatest bulwarks of liberty, and ought not to be violated.

17. That the people have a right to keep and bear arms; that a well regulated militia, composed of the body of the people, trained to arms, is the proper, natural, and safe defence of a free state; that standing armies, in time of peace, are dangerous to liberty, and therefore ought to be avoided, as far as the circumstances and protection of the community will admit; and that, in all cases, the military should be under strict subordination to, and governed by, the civil power.

18. That no soldier, in time of peace, ought to be quartered in any house without the consent of the owner, and in time of war, in such manner only as the laws direct.

19. That any person religiously scrupulous of bearing arms ought to be exempted, upon payment of an equivalent to employ another to bear arms in his stead.

20. That religion, or the duty which we owe to our Creator, and the manner of discharging it, can be directed only by reason and conviction, not by force or violence; and therefore all men have an equal, natural, and unalienable right to the free exercise of religion, according to the dictates of conscience; and that no particular religious sect or society ought to be favored or established by law in preference to others.

Amendments to the Constitution.

1. That each state in the Union shall respectively retain every power, jurisdiction, and right, which is not by this Constitution delegated to the Congress of the United States, or to the departments of the federal government.

2. That there shall be one representative for every thirty thousand, according to the enumeration or census mentioned in the Constitution, until the whole number of representatives amounts to two hundred; after which that number shall be continued or increased as Congress shall direct, upon the principles fixed in the Constitution, by apportioning the representatives of each state to some greater number of the people, from time to time, as the population increases.

3. When Congress shall lay direct taxes or excises, they shall immediately inform the executive power of each state of the quota of such state, according to the census herein directed, which is proposed to be thereby raised; and if the legislature of any state shall pass any law which shall be effectual for raising such quota at the time required by Congress, the taxes and excises laid by Congress shall not be collected in such state.

4. That the members of the Senate and House of Representatives shall be ineligible to, and incapable of holding, any civil office under the authority of the United States, during the time for which they shall respectively be elected.

5. That the Journals of the proceedings of the Senate and House of Representatives shall be published at least once in every year, except such parts thereof relating to treaties, alliances, or military operations, as in their judgment require secrecy.

6. That a regular statement and account of receipts and expenditures of all public moneys shall be published at least once in every year.

7. That no commercial treaty shall be ratified without the concurrence of two thirds of the whole number of the members of the Senate. And no treaty, ceding, contracting, restraining, or suspending, the territorial rights or claims of the United States, or any of them, or their, or

any of their, rights or claims of fishing in the American seas, or navigating the American rivers, shall be made, but in cases of the most urgent and extreme necessity; nor shall any such treaty be ratified without the concurrence of three fourths of the whole number of the members of both houses respectively.

8. That no navigation law, or law regulating commerce, shall be passed without the consent of two thirds of the members present in both houses.

9. That no standing army or regular troops shall be raised or kept up in time of peace, without the consent of two thirds of the members present in both houses.

10. That no soldier shall be enlisted for any longer term than four years, except in time of war, and then for no longer term than the continuance of the war.

11. That each state respectively shall have the power to provide for organizing, arming, and disciplining its own militia, whensoever Congress shall omit or neglect to provide for the same; that the militia shall not be subject to martial law, except when in actual service in time of war, invasion, or rebellion; and when not in the actual service of the United States, shall be subject only to such fines, penalties, and punishments, as shall be directed or inflicted by the laws of its own state.

12. That Congress shall not declare any state to be in rebellion, without the consent of at least two thirds of all the members present in both houses.

13. That the exclusive power of legislation given to Congress over the federal town and its adjacent district, and other places purchased or to be purchased by Congress of any of the states, shall extend only to such regulations as respect the police and good government thereof.

14. That no person shall be capable of being President of the United States for more than eight years in any term of fifteen years.

15. That the judicial power of the United States shall be vested in one Supreme Court, and in such courts of admiralty as Congress may from time to time ordain and establish in any of the different states. The judicial power shall extend to all cases in law and equity arising under treaties made, or which shall be made, under the authority of the United States; to all cases affecting ambassadors, other foreign ministers, and consuls; to all cases of admiralty and maritime jurisdiction; to controversies to which the United States shall be a party; to controversies between two or more states, and between parties claiming lands under the grants of different states. In all cases affecting ambassadors, other foreign ministers, and consuls, and those in which a state shall be a party, the Supreme Court shall have original jurisdiction. In all other cases before mentioned, the Supreme Court shall have appellate jurisdiction as to matters of law only, except in cases of equity, and of admiralty and maritime jurisdiction, in which the Supreme Court shall have appellate jurisdiction both as to law and fact, with such exceptions, and under such regulations, as the Congress shall make: but the judicial power of the United States shall extend to no case where the cause of action shall have originated before the ratification of this Constitution, except in disputes between states about their territory, disputes between persons claiming lands under the grants of different states, and suits for debts due to the United States.

16. That, in criminal prosecutions, no man shall be restrained in the exercise of the usual and accustomed right of challenging or excepting to the jury.

17. That Congress shall not alter, modify, or interfere in, the times, places, or manner, of holding elections for senators and representatives, or either of them, except when the legislature of any state shall neglect, refuse, or be disabled, by invasion or rebellion, to prescribe the same.

18. That those clauses which declare that Congress shall not exercise certain powers be not interpreted in any manner whatsoever to extend the power of Congress; but that they be construed either as making exceptions to the specified powers, where this shall be the case, or otherwise as inserted merely for greater caution.

19. That the laws ascertaining the compensation of senators and representatives for their services, be postponed in their operation until after the election of representatives immediately succeeding the passing thereof, that excepted which shall first be passed on the subject.

20. That some tribunal other than the Senate be provided for trying impeachments of senators.

21. That the salary of a judge shall not be increased or diminished during his continuance in office, otherwise than by general regulations of salary, which may take place on a revision of the subject at stated periods of not less than seven years, to commence from the time such salaries shall be first ascertained by Congress.

22. That Congress erect no company of merchants with exclusive advantages of commerce.

23. That no treaties which shall be directly opposed to the existing laws of the United States in Congress assembled shall be valid until such laws shall be repealed, or made conformable to such treaty; nor shall any treaty be valid which is contradictory to the Constitution of the United States.

24. That the latter part of the 5th paragraph of the 9th section of the 1st article be altered to read thus: 'Nor shall vessels bound to a particular state be obliged to enter or pay duties in any other; nor, when bound from any one of the states, be obliged to clear in another.'

25. That Congress shall not, directly or indirectly, either by themselves or through the judiciary, interfere with any one of the states in the redemption of paper money already emitted and now in circulation, or in liquidating and discharging the public securities of any one of the states, but each and every state shall have the exclusive right of making such laws and regulations, for the above purposes, as they shall think proper.

26. That Congress shall not introduce foreign troops into the United States without the consent of two thirds of the members present of both houses.

. . . . .

Mr. IREDELL then moved as follows, viz.:—

That the report of the committee be amended, by striking out all the words of the said report except the two first, viz.: "Resolved, That," and that the following words be inserted in their room, viz.:—"this Convention, having fully deliberated on the Constitution proposed for the future government of the United States of America by the Federal Convention lately held, at Philadelphia, on the 17th day of September last, and having taken into their serious and solemn consideration the present critical situation of America, which induces them to be of opinion that, though certain amendments to the said Constitution may be wished for, yet that those amendments should be proposed subsequent to the ratification on the part of this state, and not previous to it:—they do, therefore, on behalf of the state of North Carolina, and the good people thereof, and by virtue of the authority to them delegated, ratify the said Constitution on the part of this state; and they do at the same time recommend that, as early as possible, the following amendments to the said Constitution may be proposed for the consideration and adoption of the several states in the Union, in one of the modes prescribed by the 5th article thereof:"—

"Amendments.

"1. Each state in the Union shall respectively retain every power, jurisdiction, and right, which is not by this Constitution delegated to the Congress of the United States, or to the departments of the general government; nor shall the said Congress, nor any department of the said government, exercise any act of authority over any individual in any of the said states, but such as can be justified under some power particularly given in this Constitution; but the said Constitution shall be considered at all times a solemn instrument, defining the extent of their authority, and the limits of which they cannot rightfully in any instance exceed.

"2. There shall be one representative for every thirty thousand, according to the enumeration or census mentioned in the Constitution, until the whole number of representatives amounts to two hundred; after which, that number shall be continued or increased, as Congress shall direct, upon the principles fixed in the Constitution, by apportioning the representatives of each state to some greater number of people, from time to time, as the population increases.

"3. Each state respectively shall have the power to provide for organizing, arming, and disciplining, its own militia, whensoever Congress shall omit or neglect to provide for the same. The militia shall not be subject to martial law, except when in actual service in time of war, invasion, or rebellion; and when they are not in the actual service of the United States, they shall be subject only to such fines, penalties, and punishments, as shall be directed or inflicted by the laws of its own state.

"4. The Congress shall not alter, modify, or interfere in the times, places, or manner, of holding elections for senators and representatives, or either of them, except when the legislature of any state shall neglect, refuse, or be disabled by invasion or rebellion, to prescribe the same.

"5. The laws ascertaining the compensation of senators and representatives, for their services, shall be postponed in their operation until after the election of representatives immediately succeeding the passing thereof; that excepted which shall first be passed on the subject.

"6. Instead of the following words in the 9th section of the 1st article, viz., 'Nor shall vessels bound to or from one state be obliged to enter, clear, or pay duties, in another,' [the meaning of which is by many deemed not sufficiently explicit,] it is proposed that the following shall be substituted: 'No vessel bound to one state shall be obliged to enter or pay duties, to which such vessel may be liable at any port of entry, in any other state than that to which such vessel is bound; nor shall any vessel bound from one state be obliged to clear, or pay duties to which such vessel shall be liable at any port of clearance, in any other state than that from which such vessel is bound.' "

11

House of Representatives, Amendments to the Constitution
8 June, 21 July, 13, 18–19 Aug. 1789
Annals 1:424–50, 661–65, 707–17, 757–59, 766

[*8 June*]

Mr. MADISON rose, and reminded the House that this was the day that he had heretofore named for bringing forward amendments to the Constitution, as contemplated in the fifth article of the Constitution, addressing the Speaker as follows: This day, Mr. Speaker, is the day assigned for taking into consideration the subject of amendments to the Constitution. As I considered myself bound in honor and in duty to do what I have done on this subject, I shall proceed to bring the amendments before you as soon as possible, and advocate them until they shall be finally adopted or rejected by a Constitutional majority of this House. With a view of drawing your attention to this important object, I shall move that this House do now resolve itself into a Committee of the Whole on the state of the Union; by which an opportunity will be given, to bring forward some propositions, which I have strong hopes will meet with the unanimous approbation of this House, after the fullest discussion and most serious regard. I therefore move you, that the House now go into a committee on this business.

Mr. SMITH was not inclined to interrupt the measures which the public were so anxiously expecting, by going into a Committee of the Whole at this time. He observed there were two modes of introducing this business to the House. One by appointing a select committee to take into consideration the several amendments proposed by the State Conventions; this he thought the most likely way to shorten the business. The other was, that the gentleman should lay his propositions on the table, for the consideration of the members; that they should be printed, and taken up for discussion at a future day. Either of these modes would enable the House to enter upon business better prepared than could be the case by a sudden transition from other important concerns to which their minds were strongly bent. He therefore hoped that the honorable gentleman would consent to bring the subject forward in one of those ways, in preference to going into a Committee of the Whole. For, said he, it must appear extremely impolitic to go into the consideration of amending the Government, before it is organized, before it has begun to operate. Certainly, upon reflection, it must appear to be premature. I wish, therefore, gentlemen would consent to the delay: for the business which lies in an unfinished state—I mean particularly the collection bill—is necessary to be passed; else all we have hitherto done is of no effect. If we go into the discussion of this subject, it will take us three weeks or a month; and during all this time, every other business must be suspended, because we cannot proceed with either accuracy or despatch when the mind is perpetually shifted from one subject to another.

Mr. JACKSON.—I am of opinion we ought not to be in a hurry with respect to altering the Constitution. For my part, I have no idea of speculating in this serious manner on theory. If I agree to alterations in the mode of administering this Government, I shall like to stand on the sure ground of experience, and not be treading air. What experience have we had of the good or bad qualities of this Constitution? Can any gentleman affirm to me one proposition that is a certain and absolute amendment? I deny that he can. Our Constitution, sir, is like a vessel just launched, and lying at the wharf; she is untried, you can hardly discover any one of her properties. It is not known how she will answer her helm, or lay her course; whether she will bear with safety the precious freight to be deposited in her hold. But, in this state, will the prudent merchant attempt alterations? Will he employ workmen to tear off the planking and take asunder the frame? He certainly will not. Let us, gentlemen, fit out our vessel, set up her masts, and expand her sails, and be guided by the experiment in our alterations. If she sails upon an uneven keel, let us right her by adding weight where it is wanting. In this way, we may remedy her defects to the satisfaction of all concerned; but if we proceed now to make alterations, we may deface a beauty, or deform a well proportioned piece of workmanship. In short, Mr. Speaker, I am not for amendments at this time; but if gentlemen should think it a subject deserving of attention, they will surely not neglect the more important business which is now unfinished before them. Without we pass the collection bill we can get no revenue, and without revenue the wheels of Government cannot move. I am against taking up the subject at present, and shall therefore be totally against the amendments, if the Government is not organized, that I may see whether it is grievous or not.

When the propriety of making amendments shall be obvious from experience, I trust there will be virtue enough in my country to make them. Much has been said by the opponents to this Constitution, respecting the insecurity of jury trials, that great bulwark of personal safety. All their objections may be done away, by proper regulations on this point, and I do not fear but such regulations will take place. The bill is now before the Senate, and a proper attention is shown to this business. Indeed, I cannot conceive how it could be opposed; I think an almost omnipotent Emperor would not be hardy enough to set himself against it. Then why should we fear a power which cannot be improperly exercised?

We have proceeded to make some regulations under the Constitution; but have met with no inaccuracy, unless it may be said that the clause respecting vessels bound to or from one State be obliged to enter, clear, or pay duties in another, is somewhat obscure; yet that is not sufficient, I trust, in any gentleman's opinion to induce an amendment. But let me ask what will be the consequence of taking up this subject? Are we going to finish it in an hour? I believe not; it will take us more than a day, a week, a month—it will take a year to complete it! And will it be doing our duty to our country, to neglect or delay putting the Government in motion, when every thing depends upon its being speedily done?

Let the Constitution have a fair trial; let it be examined by experience, discover by that test what its errors are, and then talk of amending; but to attempt it now is doing it at a risk, which is certainly imprudent. I have the honor of coming from a State that ratified the Constitution by the unanimous vote of a numerous convention: the people of Georgia have manifested their attachment to it, by adopting a State Constitution framed upon the same plan as this. But although they are thus satisfied, I shall not be against such amendments as will gratify the inhabitants of other States, provided they are judged of by experience and not merely on theory. For this reason, I wish the consideration of the subject postponed until the 1st of March, 1790.

Mr. GOODHUE.—I believe it would be perfectly right in the gentleman who spoke last, to move a postponement to the time he has mentioned; because he is opposed to the consideration of amendments altogether. But I believe it will be proper to attend to the subject earlier; because it is the wish of many of our constituents, that something should be added to the Constitution, to secure in a stronger manner their liberties from the inroads of power. Yet I think the present time premature; inasmuch as we have other business before us, which is incomplete, but essential to the public interest. When that is finished, I shall concur in taking up the subject of amendments.

Mr. BURKE thought amendments to the Constitution necessary, but this was not the proper time to bring them forward. He wished the Government completely organized before they entered upon this ground. The law for collecting the revenue is immediately necessary; the Treasury Department must be established; till this, and other important subjects are determined, he was against taking this up. He said it might interrupt the harmony of the House, which was necessary to be preserved in order to despatch the great objects of legislation. He hoped it would be postponed for the present, and pledged himself to bring it forward hereafter, if nobody else would.

Mr. MADISON.—The gentleman from Georgia (Mr. JACKSON) is certainly right in his opposition to my motion for going into a Committee of the Whole, because he is unfriendly to the object I have in contemplation; but I cannot see that the gentlemen who wish for amendments to be proposed at the present session, stand on good ground when they object to the House going into committee on this business.

When I first hinted to the House my intention of calling their deliberations to this object, I mentioned the pressure of other important subjects, and submitted the propriety of postponing this till the more urgent business was despatched; but finding that business not despatched, when the order of the day for considering amendments arrived, I thought it a good reason for a farther delay; I moved the postponement accordingly. I am sorry the same reason still exists in some degree, but operates with less force, when it is considered that it is not now proposed to enter into a full and minute discussion of every part of the subject, but merely to bring it before the House, that our constituents may see we pay a proper attention to a subject they have much at heart; and if it does not give that full gratification which is to be wished, they will discover that it proceeds from the urgency of business of a very important nature. But if we continue to postpone from time to time, and refuse to let the subject come into view, it may occasion suspicions, which, though not well founded, may tend to inflame or prejudice the public mind against our decisions. They may think we are not sincere in our desire to incorporate such amendments in the Constitution as will secure those rights, which they consider as not sufficiently guarded. The applications for amendments come from a very respectable number of our constituents, and it is certainly proper for Congress to consider the subject, in order to quiet that anxiety which prevails in the public mind. Indeed, I think it would have been of advantage to the Government, if it had been practicable to have made some propositions for amendments the first business we entered upon; it would have stifled the voice of complaint, and made friends of many who doubted the merits of the Constitution. Our future measures would then have been more generally agreeably supported; but the justifiable anxiety to put the Government into operation prevented that; it therefore remains for us to take it up as soon as possible. I wish then to commence the consideration at the present moment; I hold it to be my duty to unfold my ideas, and explain myself to the House in some form or other without delay. I only wish to introduce the great work, and, as I said before, I do not expect it will be decided immediately; but if some step is taken in the business, it will give reason to believe that we may come to a final result. This will inspire a reasonable hope in the advocates for amendments, that full justice will be done to the important subject; and I have reason to believe their expectation will not be defeated. I hope the House will not decline my motion for going into a committee.

Mr. SHERMAN.—I am willing that this matter should be brought before the House at a proper time. I suppose a number of gentlemen think it their duty to bring it forward; so that there is no apprehension it will be passed over in silence. Other gentlemen may be disposed to let the subject rest until the more important objects of Government are attended to; and I should conclude, from the

nature of the case, that the people expect the latter from us in preference to altering the Constitution; because they have ratified that instrument, in order that the Government may begin to operate. If this was not their wish, they might as well have rejected the Constitution, as North Carolina has done, until the amendments took place. The State I have the honor to come from adopted this system by a very great majority, because they wished for the Government; but they desired no amendments. I suppose this was the case in other States; it will therefore be imprudent to neglect much more important concerns for this. The executive part of the Government wants organization; the business of the revenue is incomplete, to say nothing of the judiciary business. Now, will gentlemen give up these points to go into a discussion of amendments, when no advantage can arise from them? For my part, I question if any alteration which can be now proposed would be an amendment, in the true sense of the word; but nevertheless, I am willing to let the subject be introduced. If the gentleman only desires to go into committee for the purpose of receiving his propositions, I shall consent; but I have strong objections to being interrupted in completing the more important business; because I am well satisfied it will alarm the fears of twenty of our constituents where it will please one.

Mr. WHITE.—I hope the House will not spend much time on this subject, till the more pressing business is despatched; but, at the same time, I hope we shall not dismiss it altogether, because I think a majority of the people who have ratified the Constitution, did it under the expectation that Congress would, at some convenient time, examine its texture and point out where it was defective, in order that it might be judiciously amended. Whether, while we are without experience, amendments can be digested in such a manner as to give satisfaction to a Constitutional majority of this House, I will not pretend to say; but I hope the subject may be considered with all convenient speed. I think it would tend to tranquillize the public mind; therefore, I shall vote in favor of going into a Committee of the Whole, and, after receiving the subject, shall be content to refer it to a special committee to arrange and report. I fear, if we refuse to take up the subject, it will irritate many of our constituents, which I do not wish to do. If we cannot, after mature consideration, gratify their wishes, the cause of complaint will be lessened, if not removed. But a doubt on this head will not be a good reason why we should refuse to inquire. I do not say this as it affects my immediate constituents, because I believe a majority of the district which elected me do not require alterations; but I know there are people in other parts who will not be satisfied unless some amendments are proposed.

Mr. SMITH, of South Carolina, thought the gentleman who brought forward the subject had done his duty: he had supported his motion with ability and candor, and if he did not succeed, he was not to blame. On considering what had been urged for going into a committee, he was induced to join the gentleman; but it would be merely to receive his propositions, after which he would move something to that effect: That, however desirous this House may be to go into the consideration of amendments to the Constitution, in order to establish the liberties of the people of America on the securest foundation, yet the important and pressing business of the Government prevents their entering upon that subject at present.

Mr. PAGE.—My colleague tells you he is ready to submit to the Committee of the Whole his ideas on this subject. If no objection had been made to his motion, the whole business might have been finished before this. He has done me the honor of showing me certain propositions which he has drawn up; they are very important, and I sincerely wish the House may receive them. After they are published, I think the people will wait with patience till we are at leisure to resume them. But it must be very disagreeable to them to have it postponed from time to time, in the manner it has been for six weeks past; they will be tired out by a fruitless expectation. Putting myself into the place of those who favor amendments, I should suspect Congress did not mean seriously to enter upon the subject; that it was vain to expect redress from them. I should begin to turn my attention to the alternative contained in the fifth article, and think of joining the Legislatures of those States which have applied for calling a new convention. How dangerous such an expedient would be I need not mention; but I venture to affirm, that unless you take early notice of this subject, you will not have power to deliberate. The people will clamor for a new convention, they will not trust the House any longer. Those, therefore, who dread the assembling of a convention, will do well to acquiesce in the present motion, and lay the foundation of a most important work. I do not think we need consume more than half an hour in the Committee of the Whole; this is not so much time but we may conveniently spare it, considering the nature of the business. I do not wish to divert the attention of Congress from the organization of the Government, nor do I think it need be done, if we comply with the present motion.

Mr. VINING.—I hope the House will not go into a Committee of the Whole. It strikes me that the great amendment which the Government wants is expedition in the despatch of business. The wheels of the national machine cannot turn, until the impost and collection bill are perfected; these are the desiderata which the public mind is anxiously expecting. It is well known, that all we have hitherto done amounts to nothing, if we leave the business in its present state. True; but, say gentlemen, let us go into committee; it will take up but a short time; yet may it not take a considerable proportion of our time? May it not be procrastinated into days, weeks, nay, months? It is not the most facile subject that can come before the Legislature of the Union. Gentlemen's opinions do not run in a parallel on this topic; it may take up more time to unite or concentre them than is now imagined. And what object is to be attained by going into a committee? If information is what we seek after, cannot that be obtained by the gentleman's laying his propositions on the table; they can be read, or they can be printed. But I have two other reasons for opposing this motion; the first is, the uncertainty with which we must decide on questions of amendment,

founded merely on speculative theory; the second is a previous question, how far it is proper to take the subject of amendments into consideration, without the consent of two-thirds of both Houses? I will submit it to gentlemen, whether the words of the Constitution, "the Congress, whenever two-thirds of both Houses shall deem it necessary, shall propose amendments," do not bear my construction, that it is as requisite for two-thirds to sanction the expediency of going into the measure at present, as it will be to determine the necessity of amending at all. I take it that the fifth article admits of this construction, and think that two-thirds of the Senate and House of Representatives must concur in the expediency, as to the time and manner of amendments, before we can proceed to the consideration of the amendments themselves. For my part, I do not see the expediency of proposing amendments. I think, sir, the most likely way to quiet the perturbation of the public mind, will be to pass salutary laws; to give permanency and stability to Constitutional regulations, founded on principles of equity and adjusted by wisdom. Although hitherto we have done nothing to tranquillize that agitation which the adoption of the Constitution threw some people into, yet the storm has abated and a calm succeeds. The people are not afraid of leaving the question of amendments to the discussion of their representatives; but is this the juncture for discussing it? What have Congress done towards completing the business of their appointment? They have passed a law regulating certain oaths; they have passed the impost bill; but are not vessels daily arriving, and the revenue slipping through our fingers? Is it not very strange that we neglect the completion of the revenue system? Is the system of jurisprudence unnecessary? And here let me ask gentlemen how they propose to amend that part of the Constitution which embraces the judicial branch of Government, when they do not know the regulations proposed by the Senate, who are forming a bill on this subject?

If the honorable mover of the question before the House does not think he discharges his duty without bringing his propositions forward, let him take the mode I have mentioned, by which there will be little loss of time. He knows, as well as any gentleman, the importance of completing the business on your table, and that it is best to finish one subject before the introduction of another. He will not, therefore, persist in a motion which tends to distract our minds, and incapacitates us from making a proper decision on any subject. Suppose every gentleman who desires alterations to be made in the Constitution were to submit his propositions to a Committee of the Whole; what would be the consequence? We should have strings of them contradictory to each other, and be necessarily engaged in a discussion that would consume too much of our precious time.

Though the State I represent had the honor of taking the lead in the adoption of this Constitution, and did it by a unanimous vote; and although I have the strongest predilection for the present form of Government, yet I am open to information, and willing to be convinced of its imperfections. If this be done, I shall cheerfully assist in correcting them. But I cannot think this a proper time to enter upon the subject, because more important business is suspended; and, for want of experience, we are as likely to do injury by our prescriptions as good. I wish to see every proposition which comes from that worthy gentleman on the science of Government; but I think it can be presented better by staying where we are, than by going into committee, and therefore shall vote against his motion.

Mr. MADISON.—I am sorry to be accessary to the loss of a single moment of time by the House. If I had been indulged in my motion, and we had gone into a Committee of the Whole, I think we might have rose and resumed the consideration of other business before this time; that is, so far as it depended upon what I proposed to bring forward. As that mode seems not to give satisfaction, I will withdraw the motion, and move you, sir, that a select committee be appointed to consider and report such amendments as are proper for Congress to propose to the Legislatures of the several States, conformably to the fifth article of the Constitution.

I will state my reasons why I think it proper to propose amendments, and state the amendments themselves, so far as I think they ought to be proposed. If I thought I could fulfil the duty which I owe to myself and my constituents, to let the subject pass over in silence, I most certainly should not trespass upon the indulgence of this House. But I cannot do this, and am therefore compelled to beg a patient hearing to what I have to lay before you. And I do most sincerely believe, that if Congress will devote but one day to this subject, so far as to satisfy the public that we do not disregard their wishes, it will have a salutary influence on the public councils, and prepare the way for a favorable reception of our future measures. It appears to me that this House is bound by every motive of prudence, not to let the first session pass over without proposing to the State Legislatures some things to be incorporated into the Constitution, that will render it as acceptable to the whole people of the United States, as it has been found acceptable to a majority of them. I wish, among other reasons why something should be done, that those who have been friendly to the adoption of this Constitution may have the opportunity of proving to those who were opposed to it that they were as sincerely devoted to liberty and a Republican Government, as those who charged them with wishing the adoption of this Constitution in order to lay the foundation of an aristocracy or despotism. It will be a desirable thing to extinguish from the bosom of every member of the community, any apprehensions that there are those among his countrymen who wish to deprive them of the liberty for which they valiantly fought and honorably bled. And if there are amendments desired of such a nature as will not injure the Constitution, and they can be ingrafted so as to give satisfaction to the doubting part of our fellow-citizens, the friends of the Federal Government will evince that spirit of deference and concession for which they have hitherto been distinguished.

It cannot be a secret to the gentlemen in this House, that, notwithstanding the ratification of this system of Gov-

ernment by eleven of the thirteen United States, in some cases unanimously, in others by large majorities; yet still there is a great number of our constituents who are dissatisfied with it; among whom are many respectable for their talents and patriotism, and respectable for the jealousy they have for their liberty, which, though mistaken in its object, is laudable in its motive. There is a great body of the people falling under this description, who at present feel much inclined to join their support to the cause of Federalism, if they were satisfied on this one point. We ought not to disregard their inclination, but, on principles of amity and moderation, conform to their wishes, and expressly declare the great rights of mankind secured under this constitution. The acquiescence which our fellow-citizens show under the Government, calls upon us for a like return of moderation. But perhaps there is a stronger motive than this for our going into a consideration of the subject. It is to provide those securities for liberty which are required by a part of the community; I allude in a particular manner to those two States that have not thought fit to throw themselves into the bosom of the Confederacy. It is a desirable thing, on our part as well as theirs, that a reunion should take place as soon as possible. I have no doubt, if we proceed to take those steps which would be prudent and requisite at this juncture, that in a short time we should see that disposition prevailing in those States which have not come in, that we have seen prevailing in those States which have embraced the Constitution.

But I will candidly acknowledge, that, over and above all these considerations, I do conceive that the Constitution may be amended; that is to say, if all power is subject to abuse, that then it is possible the abuse of the powers of the General Government may be guarded against in a more secure manner than is now done, while no one advantage arising from the exercise of that power shall be damaged or endangered by it. We have in this way something to gain, and, if we proceed with caution, nothing to lose. And in this case it is necessary to proceed with caution; for while we feel all these inducements to go into a revisal of the Constitution, we must feel for the Constitution itself, and make that revisal a moderate one. I should be unwilling to see a door opened for a reconsideration of the whole structure of the Government—for a re-consideration of the principles and the substance of the powers given; because I doubt, if such a door were opened, we should be very likely to stop at that point which would be safe to the Government itself. But I do wish to see a door opened to consider, so far as to incorporate those provisions for the security of rights, against which I believe no serious objection has been made by any class of our constituents: such as would be likely to meet with the concurrence of two-thirds of both Houses, and the approbation of three-fourths of the State Legislatures. I will not propose a single alteration which I do not wish to see take place, as intrinsically proper in itself, or proper because it is wished for by a respectable number of my fellow-citizens; and therefore I shall not propose a single alteration but is likely to meet the concurrence required by the Constitution. There have been objections of various kinds made against the Constitution. Some were levelled against its structure because the President was without a council; because the Senate, which is a legislative body, had judicial powers in trials on impeachments; and because the powers of that body were compounded in other respects, in a manner that did not correspond with a particular theory; because it grants more power than is supposed to be necessary for every good purpose, and controls the ordinary powers of the State Governments. I know some respectable characters who opposed this Government on these grounds; but I believe that the great mass of the people who opposed it, disliked it because it did not contain effectual provisions against encroachments on particular rights, and those safeguards which they have been long accustomed to have interposed between them and the magistrate who exercises the sovereign power; nor ought we to consider them safe, while a great number of our fellow-citizens think these securities necessary.

It is a fortunate thing that the objection to the Government has been made on the ground I stated; because it will be practicable, on that ground, to obviate the objection, so far as to satisfy the public mind that their liberties will be perpetual, and this without endangering any part of the Constitution, which is considered as essential to the existence of the Government by those who promoted its adoption.

The amendments which have occurred to me, proper to be recommended by Congress to the State Legislatures, are these.

First, That there be prefixed to the Constitution a declaration, that all power is originally vested in, and consequently derived from, the people.

That Government is instituted and ought to be exercised for the benefit of the people; which consists in the enjoyment of life and liberty, with the right of acquiring and using property, and generally of pursuing and obtaining happiness and safety.

That the people have an indubitable, unalienable, and indefeasible right to reform or change their Government, whenever it be found adverse or inadequate to the purposes of its institution.

Secondly. That in article 1st, section 2, clause 3, these words be struck out, to wit: "The number of Representatives shall not exceed one for every thirty thousand, but each State shall have at least one Representative, and until such enumeration shall be made;" and that in place thereof be inserted these words, to wit: "After the first actual enumeration, there shall be one Representative for every thirty thousand, until the number amounts to ———, after which the proportion shall be so regulated by Congress, that the number shall never be less than ———, nor more than ———, but each State shall, after the first enumeration, have at least two Representatives; and prior thereto."

Thirdly. That in article 1st, section 6, clause 1, there be added to the end of the first sentence, these words, to wit: "But no law varying the compensation last ascertained shall operate before the next ensuing election of Representatives."

Fourthly. That in article 1st, section 9, between clauses 3 and 4, be inserted these clauses, to wit: The civil rights of none shall be abridged on account of religious belief or worship, nor shall any national religion be established, nor shall the full and equal rights of conscience be in any manner, or on any pretext, infringed.

The people shall not be deprived or abridged of their right to speak, to write, or to publish their sentiments; and the freedom of the press, as one of the great bulwarks of liberty, shall be inviolable.

The people shall not be restrained from peaceably assembling and consulting for their common good; nor from applying to the Legislature by petitions, or remonstrances, for redress of their grievances.

The right of the people to keep and bear arms shall not be infringed; a well armed and well regulated militia being the best security of a free country: but no person religiously scrupulous of bearing arms shall be compelled to render military service in person.

No soldier shall in time of peace be quartered in any house without the consent of the owner; nor at any time, but in a manner warranted by law.

No person shall be subject, except in cases of impeachment, to more than one punishment or one trial for the same offence; nor shall be compelled to be a witness against himself; nor be deprived of life, liberty, or property, without due process of law; nor be obliged to relinquish his property, where it may be necessary for public use, without a just compensation.

Excessive bail shall not be required, nor excessive fines imposed, nor cruel and unusual punishments inflicted.

The rights of the people to be secured in their persons; their houses, their papers, and their other property, from all unreasonable searches and seizures, shall not be violated by warrants issued without probable cause, supported by oath or affirmation, or not particularly describing the places to be searched, or the persons or things to be seized.

In all criminal prosecutions, the accused shall enjoy the right to a speedy and public trial, to be informed of the cause and nature of the accusation, to be confronted with his accusers, and the witnesses against him; to have a compulsory process for obtaining witnesses in his favor; and to have the assistance of counsel for his defence.

The exceptions here or elsewhere in the Constitution, made in favor of particular rights, shall not be so construed as to diminish the just importance of other rights retained by the people, or as to enlarge the powers delegated by the Constitution; but either as actual limitations of such powers, or as inserted merely for greater caution.

Fifthly. That in article 1st, section 10, between clauses 1 and 2, be inserted this clause, to wit:

No State shall violate the equal rights of conscience, or the freedom of the press, or the trial by jury in criminal cases.

Sixthly. That, in article 3d, section 2, be annexed to the end of clause 2d, these words, to wit:

But no appeal to such court shall be allowed where the value in controversy shall not amount to ——— dollars: nor shall any fact triable by jury, according to the course of common law, be otherwise re-examinable than may consist with the principles of common law.

Seventhly. That in article 3d, section 2, the third clause be struck out, and in its place be inserted the clauses following, to wit:

The trial of all crimes (except in cases of impeachments, and cases arising in the land or naval forces, or the militia when on actual service, in time of war or public danger) shall be by an impartial jury of freeholders of the vicinage, with the requisite of unanimity for conviction, of the right of challenge, and other accustomed requisites; and in all crimes punishable with loss of life or member, presentment or indictment by a grand jury shall be an essential preliminary, provided that in cases of crimes committed within any county which may be in possession of an enemy, or in which a general insurrection may prevail, the trial may by law be authorized in some other county of the same State, as near as may be to the seat of the offence.

In cases of crimes committed not within any county, the trial may by law be in such county as the laws shall have prescribed. In suits at common law, between man and man, the trial by jury, as one of the best securities to the rights of the people, ought to remain inviolate.

Eighthly. That immediately after article 6th, be inserted, as article 7th, the clauses following, to wit:

The powers delegated by this Constitution are appropriated to the departments to which they are respectively distributed: so that the Legislative Department shall never exercise the powers vested in the Executive or Judicial nor the Executive exercise the powers vested in the Legislative or Judicial, nor the Judicial exercise the powers vested in the Legislative or Executive Departments.

The powers not delegated by this Constitution, nor prohibited by it to the States, are reserved to the States respectively.

Ninthly. That article 7th be numbered as article 8th.

The first of these amendments relates to what may be called a bill of rights. I will own that I never considered this provision so essential to the Federal Constitution, as to make it improper to ratify it, until such an amendment was added; at the same time, I always conceived, that in a certain form, and to a certain extent, such a provision was neither improper nor altogether useless. I am aware, that a great number of the most respectable friends to the Government, and champions for republican liberty, have thought such a provision, not only unnecessary, but even improper; nay, I believe some have gone so far as to think it even dangerous. Some policy has been made use of, perhaps, by gentlemen on both sides of the question: I acknowledge the ingenuity of those arguments which were drawn against the Constitution, by a comparison with the policy of Great Britain, in establishing a declaration of rights; but there is too great a difference in the case to warrant the comparison: therefore, the arguments drawn from that source were in a great measure inapplicable. In the declaration of rights which that country has established, the truth is, they have gone no farther than to raise a barrier against the power of the Crown; the power of the Legislature is left altogether indefinite. Although I know whenever the great rights, the trial by jury, freedom of the press, or liberty of conscience, come in question in

that body, the invasion of them is resisted by able advocates, yet their Magna Charta does not contain any one provision for the security of those rights, respecting which the people of America are most alarmed. The freedom of the press and rights of conscience, those choicest privileges of the people, are unguarded in the British Constitution.

But although the case may be widely different, and it may not be thought necessary to provide limits for the legislative power in that country, yet a different opinion prevails in the United States. The people of many States have thought it necessary to raise barriers against power in all forms and departments of Government, and I am inclined to believe, if once bills of rights are established in all the States as well as the Federal Constitution, we shall find that although some of them are rather unimportant, yet, upon the whole, they will have a salutary tendency.

It may be said, in some instances, they do no more than state the perfect equality of mankind. This, to be sure, is an absolute truth, yet it is not absolutely necessary to be inserted at the head of a Constitution.

In some instances they assert those rights which are exercised by the people in forming and establishing a plan of Government. In other instances, they specify those rights which are retained when particular powers are given up to be exercised by the Legislature. In other instances, they specify positive rights, which may seem to result from the nature of the compact. Trial by jury cannot be considered as a natural right, but a right resulting from a social compact which regulates the action of the community, but is as essential to secure the liberty of the people as any one of the pre-existent rights of nature. In other instances, they lay down dogmatic maxims with respect to the construction of the Government; declaring that the Legislative, Executive, and Judicial branches shall be kept separate and distinct. Perhaps the best way of securing this in practice is, to provide such checks as will prevent the encroachment of the one upon the other.

But whatever may be the form which the several States have adopted in making declarations in favor of particular rights, the great object in view is to limit and qualify the powers of Government, by excepting out of the grant of power those cases in which the Government ought not to act, or to act only in a particular mode. They point these exceptions sometimes against the abuse of the Executive power, sometimes against the Legislative, and, in some cases, against the community itself; or, in other words, against the majority in favor of the minority.

In our Government it is, perhaps, less necessary to guard against the abuse in the Executive Department than any other; because it is not the stronger branch of the system, but the weaker: It therefore must be levelled against the Legislative, for it is the most powerful, and most likely to be abused, because it is under the least control. Hence, so far as a declaration of rights can tend to prevent the exercise of undue power, it cannot be doubted but such declaration is proper. But I confess that I do conceive, that in a Government modified like this of the United States, the great danger lies rather in the abuse of the community than in the Legislative body. The prescriptions in favor of liberty ought to be levelled against that quarter where the greatest danger lies, namely, that which possesses the highest prerogative of power. But this is not found in either the Executive or Legislative departments of Government, but in the body of the people, operating by the majority against the minority.

It may be thought that all paper barriers against the power of the community are too weak to be worthy of attention. I am sensible they are not so strong as to satisfy gentlemen of every description who have seen and examined thoroughly the texture of such a defence; yet, as they have a tendency to impress some degree of respect for them, to establish the public opinion in their favor, and rouse the attention of the whole community, it may be one means to control the majority from those acts to which they might be otherwise inclined.

It has been said, by way of objection to a bill of rights, by many respectable gentlemen out of doors, and I find opposition on the same principles likely to be made by gentlemen on this floor, that they are unnecessary articles of a Republican Government, upon the presumption that the people have those rights in their own hands, and that is the proper place for them to rest. It would be a sufficient answer to say, that this objection lies against such provisions under the State Governments, as well as under the General Government; and there are, I believe, but few gentlemen who are inclined to push their theory so far as to say that a declaration of rights in those cases is either ineffectual or improper. It has been said, that in the Federal Government they are unnecessary, because the powers are enumerated, and it follows, that all that are not granted by the Constitution are retained; that the Constitution is a bill of powers, the great residuum being the rights of the people; and, therefore, a bill of rights cannot be so necessary as if the residuum was thrown into the hands of the Government. I admit that these arguments are not entirely without foundation; but they are not conclusive to the extent which has been supposed. It is true, the powers of the General Government are circumscribed, they are directed to particular objects; but even if Government keeps within those limits, it has certain discretionary powers with respect to the means, which may admit of abuse to a certain extent, in the same manner as the powers of the State Governments under their constitutions may to an indefinite extent; because in the Constitution of the United States, there is a clause granting to Congress the power to make all laws which shall be necessary and proper for carrying into execution all the powers vested in the Government of the United States, or in any department or officer thereof; this enables them to fulfil every purpose for which the Government was established. Now, may not laws be considered necessary and proper by Congress, for it is for them to judge of the necessity and propriety to accomplish those special purposes which they may have in contemplation, which laws in themselves are neither necessary nor proper; as well as improper laws could be enacted by the State Legislatures, for fulfilling the more extended objects of those Governments. I will state an instance, which I think in point, and proves that this might be the case. The General Government has a right to pass all laws which shall be necessary to collect its revenue; the means for enforcing the collection are within the direction of the Legislature: may not general warrants be considered necessary for this purpose, as well as for some purposes which it was supposed at the framing of their constitutions the State Governments had in view? If there was reason for restraining the State Governments from exercising this power, there is like reason for restraining the Federal Government.

It may be said, indeed it has been said, that a bill of rights is not necessary, because the establishment of this Government has not repealed those declarations of rights which are added to the several State constitutions; that those rights of the people, which had been established by the most solemn act, could not be annihilated by a subsequent act of that people, who meant, and declared at the head of the instrument, that they ordained and established a new system, for the express purpose of securing to themselves and posterity the liberties they had gained by an arduous conflict.

I admit the force of this observation, but I do not look upon it to be conclusive. In the first place, it is too uncertain ground to leave this provision upon, if a provision is at all necessary to secure rights so important as many of those I have mentioned are conceived to be, by the public in general, as well as those in particular who opposed the adoption of this Constitution. Besides, some States have no bills of rights, there are others provided with very defective ones, and there are others whose bills of rights are not only defective, but absolutely improper; instead of securing some in the full extent which republican principles would require, they limit them too much to agree with the common ideas of liberty.

It has been objected also against a bill of rights, that, by enumerating particular exceptions to the grant of power, it would disparage those rights which were not placed in that enumeration; and it might follow, by implication, that those rights which were not singled out, were intended to be assigned into the hands of the General Government, and were consequently insecure. This is one of the most plausible arguments I have ever heard urged against the admission of a bill of rights into this system; but, I conceive, that it may be guarded against. I have attempted it, as gentlemen may see by turning to the last clause of the fourth resolution.

It has been said, that it is unnecessary to load the Constitution with this provision, because it was not found effectual in the constitution of the particular States. It is true, there are a few particular States in which some of the most valuable articles have not, at one time or other, been violated; but it does not follow but they may have, to a certain degree, a salutary effect against the abuse of power. If they are incorporated into the Constitution, independent tribunals of justice will consider themselves in a peculiar manner the guardians of those rights; they will be an impenetrable bulwark against every assumption of power in the Legislative or Executive; they will be naturally led to resist every encroachment upon rights expressly stipulated for in the Constitution by the declaration of rights. Besides this security, there is a great probability that such a declaration in the federal system would be enforced; because the State Legislatures will jealously and closely watch the operations of this Government, and be able to resist with more effect every assumption of power, than any other power on earth can do; and the greatest opponents to a Federal Government admit the State Legislatures to be sure guardians of the people's liberty. I conclude, from this view of the subject, that it will be proper in itself, and highly politic, for the tranquillity of the public mind, and the stability of the Government, that we should offer something, in the form I have proposed, to be incorporated in the system of Government, as a declaration of the rights of the people.

In the next place, I wish to see that part of the Constitution revised which declares that the number of Representatives shall not exceed the proportion of one for every thirty thousand persons, and allows one Representative to every State which rates below that proportion. If we attend to the discussion of this subject, which has taken place in the State conventions, and even in the opinion of the friends to the Constitution, an alteration here is proper. It is the sense of the people of America, that the number of Representatives ought to be increased, but particularly that it should not be left in the discretion of the Government to diminish them, below that proportion which certainly is in the power of the Legislature as the Constitution now stands; and they may, as the population of the country increases, increase the House of Representatives to a very unwieldy degree. I confess I always thought this part of the Constitution defective, though not dangerous; and that it ought to be particularly attended to whenever Congress should go into the consideration of amendments.

There are several minor cases enumerated in my proposition, in which I wish also to see some alteration take place. That article which leaves it in the power of the Legislature to ascertain its own emolument, is one to which I allude. I do not believe this is a power which, in the ordinary course of Government, is likely to be abused. Perhaps of all the powers granted, it is least likely to abuse; but there is a seeming impropriety in leaving any set of men without control to put their hand into the public coffers, to take out money to put in their pockets; there is a seeming indecorum in such power, which leads me to propose a change. We have a guide to this alteration in several of the amendments which the different conventions have proposed. I have gone, therefore, so far as to fix it, that no law, varying the compensation, shall operate until there is a change in the Legislature; in which case it cannot be for the particular benefit of those who are concerned in determining the value of the service.

I wish also, in revising the Constitution, we may throw into that section, which interdicts the abuse of certain powers in the State Legislatures, some other provisions of equal, if not greater importance than those already made. The words, "No State shall pass any bill of attainder, *ex post facto* law," &c. were wise and proper restrictions in the Constitution. I think there is more danger of those powers being abused by the State Governments than by the Government of the United States. The same may be said of other powers which they possess, if not controlled by the general principle, that laws are unconstitutional which infringe the rights of the community. I should therefore wish to extend this interdiction, and add, as I have stated in the 5th resolution, that no State shall violate the equal right of conscience, freedom of the press, or trial by jury in criminal cases; because it is proper that every Government should be disarmed of powers which trench upon those particular rights. I know, in some of the State constitutions, the power of the Government is controlled by such a declaration; but others are not. I cannot see any reason against obtaining even a double security on those points; and nothing can give a more sincere proof of the attachment of those who opposed this Constitution to these great and important rights, than to see them join in obtaining the security I have now proposed; because it must be admitted, on all hands, that the State Governments are as liable to attack these invaluable privileges as the General Government is, and therefore ought to be as cautiously guarded against.

I think it will be proper, with respect to the judiciary powers, to satisfy the public mind on those points which I have mentioned. Great inconvenience has been apprehended to suitors from the distance they would be dragged to obtain justice in the Supreme Court of the United States, upon an appeal on an action for a small debt. To remedy this, declare that no appeal shall be made unless the matter in controversy amounts to a particular sum; this, with the regulations respecting jury trials in criminal cases, and suits at common law, it is to be hoped, will quiet and reconcile the minds of the people to that part of the Constitution.

I find, from looking into the amendments proposed by the State conventions, that several are particularly anxious that it should be declared in the Constitution, that the powers not therein delegated should be reserved to the several States. Perhaps words which may define this more precisely than the whole of the instrument now does, may be considered as superfluous. I admit they may be deemed unnecessary: but there can be no harm in making such a declaration, if gentlemen will allow that the fact is as stated. I am sure I understand it so, and do therefore propose it.

These are the points on which I wish to see a revision of the Constitution take place. How far they will accord with the sense of this body, I cannot take upon me absolutely to determine; but I believe every gentleman will readily admit that nothing is in contemplation, so far as I have mentioned, that can endanger the beauty of the Government in any one important feature, even in the eyes of its most sanguine admirers. I have proposed nothing that does not appear to me as proper in itself, or eligible as patronized by a respectable number of our fellow-citizens; and if we can make the Constitution better in the opinion of those who are opposed to it, without weakening its frame, or abridging its usefulness, in the judgment of those who are attached to it, we act the part of wise and liberal men to make such alterations as shall produce that effect.

Having done what I conceived was my duty, in bringing before this House the subject of amendments, and also stated such as I wish for and approve, and offered the reasons which occurred to me in their support, I shall content myself, for the present, with moving "that a committee be appointed to consider of and report such amendments as ought to be proposed by Congress to the Legislatures of the States, to become, if ratified by three-fourths thereof, part of the Constitution of the United States." By agreeing to this motion, the subject may be going on in the committee, while other important business is proceeding to a conclusion in the House. I should advocate greater despatch in the business of amendments, if I were not convinced of the absolute necessity there is of pursuing the organization of the Government; because I think we should obtain the confidence of our fellow-citizens, in proportion as we fortify the rights of the people against the encroachments of the Government.

Mr. JACKSON.—The more I consider the subject of amendments, the more I am convinced it is improper. I revere the rights of my constituents as much as any gentleman in Congress, yet I am against inserting a declaration of rights in the Constitution, and that for some of the reasons referred to by the gentleman last up. If such an addition is not dangerous or improper, it is at least unnecessary: that is a sufficient reason for not entering into the subject at a time when there are urgent calls for our attention to important business. Let me ask gentlemen, what reason there is for the suspicions which are to be removed by this measure? Who are Congress, that such apprehensions should be entertained of them? Do we not belong to the mass of the people? Is there a single right that, if infringed, will not affect us and our connexions as much as any other person? Do we not return at the expiration of two years into private life? and is not this a security against encroachments? Are we not sent here to guard those rights which might be endangered, if the Government was an aristocracy or a despotism? View for a moment the situation of Rhode Island, and say whether the people's rights are more safe under State Legislatures than under a Government of limited powers? Their liberty is changed to licentiousness. But do gentlemen suppose bills of rights necessary to secure liberty? If they do, let them look at New York, New Jersey, Virginia, South Carolina, and Georgia. Those States have no bills of rights, and is the liberty of the citizens less safe in those States, than in the other of the United States? I believe it is not.

There is a maxim in law, and it will apply to bills of rights, that when you enumerate exceptions, the exceptions operate to the exclusion of all circumstances that are omitted; consequently, unless you except every right from the grant of power, those omitted are inferred to be resigned to the discretion of the Government.

The gentleman endeavors to secure the liberty of the press; pray how is this in danger? There is no power given to Congress to regulate this subject as they can commerce, or peace, or war. Has any transaction taken place to make us suppose such an amendment necessary? An honorable gentleman, a member of this House, has been attacked in the public newspapers on account of sentiments delivered on this floor. Have Congress taken any notice of it? Have they ordered the writer before them, even for a breach of privilege, although the Constitution provides that a member shall not be questioned in any place for any speech or debate in the House? No, these things are offered to the public view, and held up to the inspection of the world. These are principles which will always prevail. I am not afraid, nor are other members I believe, our conduct should meet the severest scrutiny. Where, then, is the necessity of taking measures to secure what neither is nor can be in danger?

I hold, Mr. Speaker, that the present is not a proper time for considering of amendments. The States of Rhode Island and North Carolina are not in the Union. As to the latter, we have every presumption that she will come in. But in Rhode Island I think the anti-federal interest yet prevails. I am sorry for it, particularly on account of the firm friends of the Union, who are kept without the embrace of the Confederacy by their countrymen. These persons are worthy of our patronage; and I wish they would apply to us for protection; they should have my consent to be taken into the Union upon such application. I understand there are some important mercantile and manufacturing towns in that State, who ardently wish to live under the laws of the General Government; if they were to come forward and request us to take measures for this purpose, I would give my sanction to any which would be likely to bring about such an event.

But to return to my argument. It being the case that those States are not yet come into the Union, when they join us, we shall have another list of amendments to consider, and another bill of rights to frame. Now, in my judgment, it is better to make but one work of it whenever we set about the business.

But in what a situation shall we be with respect to those foreign Powers with whom we desire to be in treaty? They look upon us as a nation emerging into figure and importance. But what will be their opinion, if they see us unable to retain the national advantages we have just gained? They will smile at our infantine efforts to obtain consequence, and treat us with the contempt we have hitherto borne by reason of the imbecility of our Government. Can we expect to enter into a commercial competition with any of them, while our system is incomplete? And how long it will remain in such a situation, if we enter upon amendments, God only knows. Our instability will make us objects of scorn. We are not content with two revolutions in less than fourteen years; we must enter upon a third, without necessity or propriety. Our faith will be like the *punica fides* of Carthage; and we shall have none that will repose confidence in us. Why will gentlemen press us to propose amendments, while we are without experience? Can they assure themselves that the amendments, as they call them, will not want amendments, as soon as they are adopted? I will not tax gentlemen with a desire of amusing the people; I believe they venerate their country too much for this; but what more can amendments lead to? That part of the Constitution which is proposed to be altered, may be the most valuable part of the whole; and perhaps those who now clamor for alterations may, ere long, discover that they have marred a good Government, and rendered their own liberties insecure. I again repeat it, this is not the time for bringing forward amendments; and, notwithstanding the honorable gentleman's ingenious arguments on that point, I am now more strongly persuaded it is wrong.

If we actually find the Constitution bad upon experience, or the rights and privileges of the people in danger, I here pledge myself to step forward among the first friends of liberty to prevent the evil; and if nothing else will avail, I will draw my sword in the defence of freedom, and cheerfully immolate at that shrine my property and my life. But how are we now proceeding? Why, on nothing more than the theoretical speculation pursuing a mere *ignis fatuus*, which may lead us into serious embarrassments. The imperfections of the Government are now unknown; let it have a fair trial, and I will be bound they show themselves; then we can tell where to apply the remedy, so as to secure the great object we are aiming at.

There are, Mr. Speaker, a number of important bills on the table, which require despatch; but I am afraid, if we enter on this business, we shall not be able to attend to them for a long time. Look, sir, over the long list of amendments proposed by some of the adopting States, and say, when the House could get through the discussion; and I believe, sir, every one of those amendments will come before us. Gentlemen may feel themselves called by duty or inclination to oppose them. How are we then to extricate ourselves from this labyrinth of business? Certainly we shall lose much of our valuable time, without any advantage whatsoever. I hope, therefore, the gentleman will press us no further; he has done his duty, and acquitted himself of the obligation under which he lay. He may now accede to what I take to be the sense of the House, and let the business of amendments lie over until next Spring; that will be soon enough to take it up to any good purpose.

Mr. GERRY.—I do not rise to go into the merits or demerits of the subject of amendments; nor shall I make any other observations on the motion for going into a Committee of the Whole on the state of the Union, which is now withdrawn, than merely to say, that, referring the subject to that committee, is treating it with the dignity its importance requires. But I consider it improper to take up this business, when our attention is occupied by other important objects. We should despatch the subjects now on the table, and let this lie over until a period of more leisure for discussion and attention. The gentleman from Virginia says it is necessary to go into a consideration of this subject, in order to satisfy the people. For my part, I cannot be of his opinion. The people know we are employed in the organization of the Government, and cannot expect that we should forego this business for any other. But I would not have it understood, that I am against entering

upon amendments when the proper time arrives. I shall be glad to set about it as soon as possible, but I would not stay the operations of the Government on this account. I think with the gentleman from Delaware, (Mr. VINING,) that the great wheels of the political machine should first be set in motion; and with the gentleman from Georgia, (Mr. JACKSON,) that the vessel ought to be got under way, lest she lie by the wharf till she beat off her rudder, and run herself a wreck on shore.

I say I wish as early a day as possible may be assigned for taking up this business, in order to prevent the necessity which the States may think themselves under of calling a new convention. For I am not, sir, one of those blind admirers of this system, who think it all perfection; nor am I so blind as not to see its beauties. The truth is, it partakes of humanity; in it is blended virtue and vice, errors and excellence. But I think, if it is referred to a new convention, we run the risk of losing some of its best properties; this is a case I never wish to see. Whatever might have been my sentiments of the ratification of the Constitution without amendments, my sense now is, that the salvation of America depends upon the establishment of this Government, whether amended or not. If the Constitution which is now ratified should not be supported, I despair of ever having a Government of these United States.

I wish the subject to be considered early for another reason. There are two States not in the Union; it would be a very desirable circumstance to gain them. I should therefore be in favor of such amendments as might tend to invite them and gain their confidence; good policy will dictate to us to expedite that event. Gentlemen say, that we shall not obtain the consent of two-thirds of both Houses to amendments. Are gentlemen willing then to throw Rhode Island and North Carolina into the situation of foreign nations? They have told you that they cannot accede to the Union, unless certain amendments are made to the Constitution; if you deny a compliance with their request in that particular, you refuse an accommodation to bring about that desirable event, and leave them detached from the Union.

I have another reason for going early into this business. It is necessary to establish an energetic Government. My idea of such a Government is, that due deliberation be had in making laws, and efficiency in the execution. I hope, in this country, the latter may obtain without the dread of despotism. I would wish to see the execution of good laws irresistible. But from the view which we have already had of the disposition of the Government, we seem really to be afraid to administer the powers with which we are invested, lest we give offence. We appear afraid to exercise the Constitutional powers of the Government, which the welfare of the State requires, lest a jealousy of our powers be the consequence. What is the reason of this timidity? Why, because we see a great body of our constituents opposed to the Constitution as it now stands, who are apprehensive of the enormous powers of Government. But if this business is taken up, and it is thought proper to make amendments, it will remove this difficulty. Let us deal fairly and candidly with our constituents, and give the subject a full discussion; after that, I have no doubt but the decision will be such as, upon examination, we shall discover to be right. If it shall then appear proper and wise to reject the amendments, I dare to say the reasons for so doing will bring conviction to the people out of doors, as well as it will to the members of this House; and they will acquiesce in the decision, though they may regret the disappointment of their fondest hopes for the security of the liberties of themselves and their posterity. Thus, and thus only, the Government will have its due energy, and accomplish the end for which it was instituted.

I am against referring the subject to a select committee, because I conceive it would be disrespectful to those States which have proposed amendments. The conventions of the States consisted of the most wise and virtuous men of the community; they have ratified this Constitution, in full confidence that their objections would at least be considered; and shall we, sir, preclude them by the appointment of a special committee, to consider of a few propositions brought forward by an individual gentleman? Is it in contemplation that the committee should have the subject at large before them, or that they should report upon the particular amendments just mentioned, as they think proper? And are we to be precluded from the consideration of any other amendments but those the committee may report? A select committee must be considered improper, because it is putting their judgments against that of the conventions which have proposed amendments, but if the committee are to consider the matter at large, they will be liable to this objection, that their report will only be waste of time. For if they do not bring forward the whole of the amendments recommended, individual members will consider themselves bound to bring them forward for the decision of the House. I would therefore submit, if gentlemen are determined to proceed in the business at this time, whether it is not better that it should go, in the first instance, to a Committee of the Whole, as first proposed by the gentleman from Virginia?

Some gentlemen consider it necessary to do this to satisfy our constituents. I think referring the business to a special committee will be attempting to amuse them with trifles. Our fellow-citizens are possessed of too much discernment not to be able to discover the intention of Congress by such procedure. It will be the duty of their representatives to tell them, if they were not able to discover it of themselves, they require the subject to be fairly considered; and if it be found to be improper to comply with their reasonable expectations, to tell them so. I hope there is no analogy between federal and punic faith; but unless Congress shall candidly consider the amendments which have been proposed in confidence by the State conventions, federal faith will not be considered very different from the *punica fides* of Carthage. The ratification of the Constitution in several States would never have taken place, had they not been assured that the objections would have been duly attended to by Congress. And I believe many members of these conventions would never have voted for it, if they had not been persuaded that Congress would notice them with that candor and attention which their importance requires. I will say nothing respecting the amendments themselves; they ought to stand or fall on their own merits. If any of them are eligible, they will be adopted; if not, they will be rejected.

Mr. LIVERMORE was against this motion; not that he was against amendments at a proper time. It is enjoined on him to act a rational part in procuring certain amendments, and he meant to do so; but he could not say what amendments were requisite, until the Government was organized. He supposed the judiciary law would contain certain regulations that would remove the anxiety of the people respecting such amendments as related thereto; because he thought much of the minutiae respecting suits between citizens of different States, &c. might be provided for by law. He could not agree to make jury trials necessary on every occasion; they were not practised even at this time, and there were some cases in which a cause could be better decided without a jury than with one.

In addition to the judiciary business, there is that which relates to the revenue. Gentlemen had let an opportunity go through their hands of getting a considerable supply from the impost on the Spring importations. He reminded them of this; and would tell them now was the time to finish that business; for if they did not sow in seed-time, they would be beggars in harvest. He was well satisfied in his own mind, that the people of America did not look for amendments at present; they never could imagine it to be the first work of Congress.

He wished the concurrence of the Senate upon entering on this business, because if they opposed the measure, all the House did would be mere waste of time; and there was some little difficulty on this point, because it required the consent of two-thirds of both Houses to agree to what was proper on this occasion. He said, moreover, it would be better to refer the subject generally, if referred to them at all, than to take up the propositions of individual members.

Mr. SHERMAN.—I do not suppose the Constitution to be perfect, nor do I imagine if Congress and all the Legislatures on the continent were to revise it, that their united labors would make it perfect. I do not expect any perfection on this side the grave in the works of man; but my opinion is, that we are not at present in circumstances to make it better. It is a wonder that there has been such unanimity in adopting it, considering the ordeal it had to undergo; and the unanimity which prevailed at its formation is equally astonishing; amidst all the members from the twelve States present at the Federal Convention, there were only three who did not sign the instrument to attest their opinion of its goodness. Of the eleven States who have received it, the majority have ratified it without proposing a single amendment. This circumstance leads me to suppose that we shall not be able to propose any alterations that are likely to be adopted by nine States; and gentlemen know, before the alterations take effect, they must be agreed to by the Legislatures of three-fourths of the States in the Union. Those States which have not recommended alterations, will hardly adopt them, unless it is clear that they tend to make the Constitution better. Now how this can be made out to their satisfaction I am yet to learn; they know of no defect from experience. It seems to be the opinion of gentlemen generally, that this is not the time for entering upon the discussion of amendments: our only question therefore is, how to get rid of the subject. Now, for my own part, I would prefer to have it referred to a Committee of the Whole, rather than a special committee, and therefore shall not agree to the motion now before the House.

Mr. GERRY moved, that the business lie over until the 1st day of July next, and that it be the order for that day.

Mr. SUMTER.—I consider the subject of amendments of such great importance to the Union, that I shall be glad to see it undertaken in any manner. I am not, Mr. Speaker, disposed to sacrifice substance to form; therefore, whether the business shall originate in a Committee of the Whole, or in the House, is a matter of indifference to me, so that it be put in train. Although I am seriously inclined to give this subject a full discussion, yet I do not wish it to be fully entered into at present, but am willing it should be postponed to a future day, when we shall have more leisure. With respect to referring to a select committee, I am rather against it; because I consider it as treating the applications of the State conventions rather slightly; and I presume it is the intention of the House to take those applications into consideration as well as any other. If it is not, I think it will give fresh cause for jealousy; it will rouse the alarm which is now suspended, and the people will become clamorous for amendments. They will decline any further application to Congress, and resort to the other alternative pointed out in the Constitution. I hope, therefore, this House, when they do go into the business, will receive those propositions generally. This I apprehend will tend to tranquillize the public mind, and promote that harmony which ought to be kept up between those in the exercise of the powers of Government, and those who have clothed them with the authority, or, in other words, between Congress and the people. Without a harmony and confidence subsist between them, the measures of Government will prove abortive, and we shall have still to lament that imbecility and weakness which have long marked our public councils.

Mr. VINING found himself in a delicate situation respecting the subject of amendments. He came from a small State, and therefore his sentiments would not be considered of so much weight as the sentiments of those gentlemen who spoke the sense of much larger States. Besides, his constituents had prejudged the question, by a unanimous adoption of the Constitution, without suggesting any amendments thereto. His sense accorded with the declared sense of the State of Delaware, and he was doubly bound to object to amendments which were either improper or unnecessary. But he had good reasons for opposing the consideration of even proper alterations at this time. He would ask the gentleman who pressed them, whether he would be responsible for the risk the Government would run of being injured by an *interregnum?* Proposing amendments at this time, is suspending the operations of Government, and may be productive of its ruin.

He would not follow the gentleman in his arguments, though he supposed them all answerable, because he would not take up the time of the House; he contented himself with saying, that a bill of rights was unnecessary in a Government deriving all its powers from the people; and the Constitution enforced the principle in the strongest manner by the practical declaration prefixed to that instrument; he alluded to the words, "We the people do ordain and establish."

There were many things mentioned by some of the State Conventions which he would never agree to, on any conditions whatever; they changed the principles of the Government, and were therefore obnoxious to its friends. The honorable gentleman from Virginia had not touched upon any of them; he was glad of it, because he could by no means bear the idea of an alteration respecting them; he referred to the mode of obtaining direct taxes, judging of elections, &c.

He found he was not speaking to the question; he would therefore return to it, and declare he was against committing the subject to a select committee; if it was to be committed at all, he preferred a Committee of the Whole, but hoped the subject would be postponed.

Mr. MADISON found himself unfortunate in not satisfying gentlemen with respect to the mode of introducing the business; he thought, from the dignity and peculiarity of the subject, that it ought to be referred to a Committee of the Whole. He accordingly made that motion first, but finding himself not likely to succeed in that way, he had changed his ground. Fearing again to be discomfited, he would change his mode, and move the propositions he had stated before, and the House might do what they thought proper with them. He accordingly moved the propositions by way of resolutions to be adopted by the House.

Mr. LIVERMORE objected to these propositions, because they did not take up the amendments of the several States.

Mr. PAGE was much obliged to his colleague for bringing the subject forward in the manner he had done. He conceived it to be just and fair. What was to be done when the House would not refer it to a committee of any sort, but bring the question at once before them? He hoped it would be the means of bringing about a decision.

Mr. LAWRENCE moved to refer Mr. MADISON's motion to the Committee of the Whole on the state of the Union.

Mr. LEE thought it ought to be taken up in that committee; and hoped his colleague would bring the propositions before the committee, when on the state of the Union, as he had originally intended.

Mr. BOUDINOT wished the appointment of a select committee, but afterwards withdrew his motion.

At length Mr. LAWRENCE's motion was agreed to, and Mr. MADISON's propositions were ordered to be referred to a Committee of the Whole. Adjourned.

[21 July]

Mr. SHERMAN.—The provision for amendments made in the fifth article of the Constitution, was intended to facilitate the adoption of those which experience should point out to be necessary. This Constitution has been adopted by eleven States, a majority of those eleven have received it without expressing a wish for amendments; now, is it probable that three-fourths of the eleven States will agree to amendments offered on mere speculative points, when the Constitution has had no kind of trial whatever? It is hardly to be expected that they will. Consequently we shall lose our labor, and had better decline having any thing further to do with it for the present.

But if the House are to go into a consideration, it had better be done in such a way as not to interfere much with the organization of the Government.

Mr. PAGE hoped the business would proceed as heretofore directed. He thought it would be very agreeable to the majority of the Union, he knew it would be to his constituents, to find that the Government meant to give every security to the rights and liberties of the people, and to examine carefully into the grounds of the apprehensions expressed by several of the State conventions; he thought they would be satisfied with the amendments brought forward by his colleague, when the subject was last before the House.

. . . . .

Mr. JACKSON was sorry to see the House was to be troubled any further on the subject; he looked upon it as a mere waste of time; but as he always chose the least of two evils, he acquiesced in the motion for referring it to a special committee.

Mr. GERRY asked, whether the House had cognizance of the amendments proposed by the State conventions? If they had not, he would make a motion to bring them forward.

Mr. PAGE replied, that such motion would be out of order, until the present question was determined.

A desultory conversation ensued, and it was questioned whether the subject generally was to be before the Committee of the Whole, or those specific propositions only which had already been introduced.

Mr. GERRY said, that it was a matter of indifference how this question was understood, because no gentleman could pretend to deny another the privilege of bringing forward propositions conformably to his sentiments. If gentlemen, then, might bring forward resolutions to be added, or motions of amendment, there would be no time saved by referring the subject to a special committee. But such procedure might tend to prejudice the House against an amendment neglected by the committee, and thereby induce them not to show that attention to the State which proposed it that would be delicate and proper.

He wished gentlemen to consider the situation of the States; seven out of thirteen had thought the Constitution very defective, yet five of them have adopted it with a perfect reliance on Congress for its improvement. Now, what will these States feel if the subject is discussed in a select committee, and their recommendations totally neglected? The indelicacy of treating the application of five States in a manner different from other important subjects, will give no small occasion for disgust, which is a circumstance that this Government ought carefully to avoid. If, then, the House could gain nothing by this manner of proceeding, he hoped they would not hesitate to adhere to their former vote for going into a Committee of the Whole. That they would gain nothing was pretty certain, for gentlemen must necessarily come forward with their amendments to the report when it was brought in. The members from Massachusetts were particularly instructed to press

the amendments recommended by the convention of that State at all times, until they had been maturely considered by Congress; the same duties were made incumbent on the members from some other States; consequently, any attempt to smother the business, or prevent a full investigation, must be nugatory, while the House paid a proper deference to their own rules and orders. He did not contend for going into a Committee of the whole at the present moment; he would prefer a time of greater leisure than the present, from the business of organizing the Government.

Mr. AMES declared to the House, that he was no enemy to the consideration of amendments; but he had moved to rescind their former vote, in order to save time, which he was confident would be the consequence of referring it to a select committee.

He was sorry to hear an intention avowed by his colleague, of considering every part of the frame of this Constitution. It was the same as forming themselves into a convention of the United States. He did not stand for words, the thing would be the same in fact. He could not but express a degree of anxiety at seeing the system of Government encounter another ordeal, when it ought to be extending itself to furnish security to others. He apprehended, if the zeal of some gentlemen broke out on this occasion, that there would be no limits to the time necessary to discuss the subject; he was certain the session would not be long enough; perhaps they might be bounded by the period of their appointment, but he questioned it.

When gentlemen suppose themselves called upon to vent their ardor in some favorite pursuit, in securing to themselves and their posterity the inestimable rights and liberties they have just snatched from the hand of despotism, they are apt to carry their exertions to an extreme; but he hoped the subject itself would be limited; not that he objected to the consideration of the amendments proposed, indeed he should move himself for the consideration, by the committee, of those recommended by Massachusetts, if his colleagues omitted to do it; but he hoped gentlemen would not think of bringing in new amendments, such as were not recommended, but went to tear the frame of Government into pieces.

He had considered a select committee much better calculated to consider and arrange a complex business, than a Committee of the Whole; he thought they were like the senses to the soul, and on an occasion like the present, could be made equally useful.

If he recollected rightly the decision made by the House on the 8th of June, it was that certain specific amendments be referred to the Committee of the Whole; not that the subject generally be referred, and that amendments be made in the committee that were not contemplated, before. This public discussion would be like a dissection of the Constitution, it would be defacing its symmetry, laying bare its sinews and tendons, ripping up the whole form, and tearing out its vitals; but is it presumable that such conduct would be attended with success? Two thirds of both Houses must agree in all these operations, before they can have effect. His opposition to going into a Committee of the Whole, did not arise from any fear that the Constitution would suffer by a fair discussion in this, or any other House; but while such business was going on, the Government was laid prostrate, and every artery ceased to beat. The unfair advantages that might be taken in such a situation, were easier apprehended than resisted. Wherefore, he wished to avoid the danger, by a more prudent line of conduct.

Mr. TUCKER would not say whether the discussion alluded to by the gentleman last up would do good or harm, but he was certain it ought to take place no where but in a Committee of the Whole; the subject is of too much importance for a select committee. Now, suppose such a committee to be appointed, and that the amendments proposed by the several States, together with those brought forward by the gentleman from Virginia, are referred to them: after some consideration they report, but not one of the amendments proposed by either State; what is the inference? They have considered them, and as they were better capable than the House of considering them, the House ought to reject every proposition coming from the State conventions. Will this give satisfaction to the States who have required amendments? Very far from it. They will expect that their propositions would be fully brought before the House, and regularly and fully considered; if indeed then they are rejected, it may be some satisfaction to them, to know that their applications have been treated with respect.

What I have said with respect to the propositions of the several States, may apply in some degree to the propositions brought forward by the gentleman (Mr. MADISON) from Virginia; the select committee may single out one or two, and reject the remainder, notwithstanding the vote of the House for considering them. The gentleman would have a right to complain, and every State would be justly disgusted.

Will it tend to reconcile the Government to that great body of the people who are dissatisfied, who think themselves and all they hold most dear, unsafe under it, without certain amendments are made? Will it answer any one good purpose to slur over this business, and reject the propositions without giving them a fair chance of a full discussion? I think not, Mr. Speaker. Both the Senate and this House ought to treat the present subject with delicacy and impartiality.

The select committee will have it in their power so to keep this business back, that it may never again come before the House; this is an imprudent step for us to take; not that I would insinuate it is an event likely to take place, or which any gentleman has in contemplation. I give every gentleman credit for his declaration, and believe the honorable mover means to save time by this arrangement; but do not let us differ on this point. I would rather the business should lie over for a month, nay, for a whole session, than have it put into other hands, and passed over without investigation.

Mr. GERRY inquired of his colleague, how it was possible that the House could be a federal convention without the Senate, and when two-thirds of both Houses are to agree to the amendments? He would also be glad to find out how

a committee was the same to the House as the senses to the soul? What, said he, can we neither see, hear, smell, or feel, without we employ a committee for the purpose? My colleague further tells us, that if we proceed in this way, we shall lay bare the sinews and tendons of the constitution; that we shall butcher it, and put it to death. Now, what does this argument tend to prove? Why, sir, to my mind, nothing more nor less than this, that we ought to adopt the report of the committee, whatever the report may be; for we are to judge by the knowledge derived through our senses, and not to proceed on to commit murder. If these are the arguments to induce the House to refer the subject to a select committee, they are arguments to engage to go further, and give into the hands of select committees the whole legislative power. But what was said respecting a public discussion? Are gentlemen afraid to meet the public ear on this topic? Do they wish to shut the gallery doors? Perhaps nothing would be attended with more dangerous consequences. No, sir, let us not be afraid of full and public investigation. Let our means, like our conclusions, be justified; let our constituents see, hear, and judge for themselves.

The question on discharging the Committee of the Whole on the state of the Union from proceeding on the subject of amendments, as referred to them, was put, and carried in the affirmative—the House divided, 34 for it, and 15 against it.

It was then ordered that Mr. MADISON's motion, stating certain specific amendments, proper to be proposed by Congress to the Legislatures of the States, to become, if ratified by three-fourths thereof, part of the Constitution of the United States, together with the amendments to the said Constitution, as proposed by the several States, be referred to a committee, to consist of a member from each State, with instruction to take the subject of amendments to the Constitution of the United States generally into their consideration, and to report thereupon to the House.

[13 August]

The House then resolved itself into a Committee of the Whole, Mr. BOUDINOT in the chair, and took the amendments under consideration. The first article ran thus: "In the introductory paragraph of the Constitution, before the words 'We the people,' add 'Government being intended for the benefit of the people, and the rightful establishment thereof being derived from their authority alone.'"

Mr. SHERMAN.—I believe, Mr. Chairman, this is not the proper mode of amending the Constitution. We ought not to interweave our propositions into the work itself, because it will be destructive of the whole fabric. We might as well endeavor to mix brass, iron, and clay, as to incorporate such heterogeneous articles; the one contradictory to the other. Its absurdity will be discovered by comparing it with a law. Would any Legislature endeavor to introduce into a former act a subsequent amendment, and let them stand so connected? When an alteration is made in an act, it is done by way of supplement; the latter act always repealing the former in every specified case of difference.

Besides this, sir, it is questionable whether we have the right to propose amendments in this way. The Constitution is the act of the people, and ought to remain entire. But the amendments will be the act of the State Governments. Again, all the authority we possess is derived from that instrument; if we mean to destroy the whole, and establish a new Constitution, we remove the basis on which we mean to build. For these reasons, I will move to strike out that paragraph and substitute another.

The paragraph proposed was to the following effect:

Resolved by the Senate and House of Representatives of the United States in Congress assembled, That the following articles be proposed as amendments to the Constitution, and when ratified by three-fourths of the State Legislatures shall become valid to all intents and purposes, as part of the same.

Under this title, the amendments might come in nearly as stated in the report, only varying the phraseology so as to accommodate them to a supplementary form.

Mr. MADISON.—Form, sir, is always of less importance than the substance; but on this occasion, I admit that form is of some consequence, and it will be well for the House to pursue that which, upon reflection, shall appear to be the most eligible. Now it apears to me, that there is a neatness and propriety in incorporating the amendments into the Constitution itself; in that case the system will remain uniform and entire; it will certainly be more simple, when the amendments are interwoven into those parts to which they naturally belong, than it will if they consist of separate and distinct parts. We shall then be able to determine its meaning without references or comparison; whereas, if they are supplementary, its meaning can only be ascertained by a comparison of the two instruments, which will be a very considerable embarrassment. It will be difficult to ascertain to what parts of the instrument the amendments particularly refer; they will create unfavorable comparisons; whereas, if they are placed upon the footing here proposed, they will stand upon as good foundation as the original work.

Nor is it so uncommon a thing as gentlemen suppose; systematic men frequently take up the whole law, and, with its amendments and alterations, reduce it into one act. I am not, however, very solicitous about the form, provided the business is but well completed.

Mr. SMITH did not think the amendment proposed by the honorable gentlemen from Connecticut was compatible with the Constitution, which declared, that the amendments recommended by Congress, and ratified by the Legislatures of three-fourths of the several States, should be part of this Constitution; in which case it would form one complete system; but according to the idea of the amendment, the instrument is to have five or six suits of improvements. Such a mode seems more calculated to embarrass the people than any thing else, while nothing in his opinion was a juster cause of complaint than the difficulties of knowing the law, arising from Legislative obscurities that might easily be avoided. He said, that it had certainly been the custom in several of the State Governments, to amend their laws by way of supplement. But South Carolina had been an instance of the contrary prac-

tice, in revising the old code; instead of making acts in addition to acts, which is always attended with perplexity, she has incorporated them, and brought them forward as a complete system, repealing the old. This is what he understood was intended to be done by the committee; the present copy of the Constitution was to be done away, and a new one substituted in its stead.

Mr. TUCKER wished to know whether the deliberations of the committee were intended to be confined to the propositions on the table. If they were not, he should beg leave to bring before them the amendments proposed by South Carolina. He considered himself as instructed to bring them forward, and he meant to perform his duty by an early and prompt obedience. He wished to have the sense of the House on this point, whether he was in order to bring them forward.

Mr. LIVERMORE was clearly of opinion, that whatever amendments were made to the constitution, they ought to stand separate from the original instrument. We have no right, said he, to alter a clause, any otherwise than by a new proposition. We have well-established precedents for such a mode of procedure in the practice of the British Parliament and the State Legislatures throughout America. I do not mean, however, to assert that there has been no instance of a repeal of the whole law on enacting another; but this has generally taken place on account of the complexity of the original, with its supplements. Were we a mere Legislative body, no doubt it might be warrantable in us to pursue a similar method; but it is questionable whether it is possible for us, consistent with the oath we have taken, to attempt a repeal of the Constitution of the United States, by making a new one to substitute in its place; the reason of this is grounded on a very simple consideration. It is by virtue of the present Constitution, I presume, that we attempt to make another; now, if we proceed to the repeal of this, I cannot see upon what authority we shall erect another; if we destroy the base, the superstructure falls of course. At some future day it may be asked upon what authority we proceeded to raise and appropriate public moneys. We suppose we do it in virtue of the present Constitution; but it may be doubted whether we have a right to exercise any of its authorities while it is suspended, as it will certainly be from the time that two-thirds of both Houses have agreed to submit it to the State Legislatures; so that, unless we mean to destroy the whole Constitution, we ought to be careful how we attempt to amend it in the way proposed by the committee. From hence, I presume it will be more prudent to adopt the mode proposed by the gentleman from Connecticut, than it will be to risk the destruction of the whole by proposing amendments in the manner recommended by the committee.

Mr. VINING disliked a supplementary form, and said it was a bad reason to urge the practice of former ages, when there was a more convenient method of doing the business at hand. He had seen an act entitled an act to amend a supplement to an act entitled an act for altering part of an act entitled an act for certain purposes therein mentioned. If gentlemen were disposed to run into such jargon in amending and altering the Constitution, he could not help it; but he trusted they would adopt a plainness and simplicity of style on this and every other occasion, which should be easily understood. If the mode proposed by the gentleman from Connecticut was adopted, the system would be distorted, and, like a careless written letter, have more attached to it in a postscript than was contained in the original composition.

The Constitution being a great and important work, ought all to be brought into one view, and made as intelligible as possible.

Mr. CLYMER was of opinion with the gentleman from Connecticut, that the amendments ought not to be incorporated in the body of the work, which he hoped would remain a monument to justify those who made it; by a comparison, the world would discover the perfection of the original, and the superfluity of the amendments. He made this distinction, because he did not conceive any of the amendments essential, but as they were solicited by his fellow-citizens, and for that reason they were acquiesced in by others; he therefore wished the motion for throwing them into a supplementary form might be carried.

Mr. STONE.—It is not a matter of much consequence, with respect to the preservation of the original instrument, whether the amendments are incorporated or made distinct; because the records will always show the original form in which it stood. But in my opinion, we ought to mark its progress with truth in every step we take. If the amendments are incorporated in the body of the work, it will appear, unless we refer to the archives of Congress, that GEORGE WASHINGTON, and the other worthy characters who composed the convention, signed an instrument which they never had in contemplation. The one to which he affixed his signature purports to be adopted by the unanimous consent of the delegates from every State there assembled. Now if we incorporate these amendments, we must undoubtedly go further, and say that the Constitution so formed was defective, and had need of alteration; we therefore purpose to repeal the old and substitute a new one in its place. From this consideration alone, I think we ought not to pursue the line of conduct drawn for us by the committee. This perhaps is not the last amendment the Constitution may receive; we ought therefore to be careful how we set a precedent which, in dangerous and turbulent times, may unhinge the whole.

With respect to the observations of the gentleman from South Carolina, I shall just remark, that we have no authority to repeal the whole Constitution. The words referred to in that instrument only authorize us to propose amendments to it, which, when properly ratified, are to become valid as a part of the same; but these can never be construed to empower us to make a new Constitution.

For these reasons, I would wish our expressions might be so guarded, as to purport nothing but what we really have in view.

Mr. LIVERMORE.—The mode adopted by the committee might be very proper, provided Congress had the forming of a Constitution in contemplation; then they, or an individual member, might propose to strike out a clause and insert another, as is done with respect to article 3, section 2. But certainly no gentleman acquainted with legislative business would pretend to alter and amend, in this manner, a law already passed. He was convinced it could not be done properly in any other way than by the one proposed by the gentleman from Connecticut.

Mr. GERRY asked, if the mode could make any possible difference, provided the sanction was the same; or whether it would operate differently in any one instance? If it will not, we are disputing about form, and the question will turn on the expediency. Now one gentleman tells you, that he is so attached to this instrument, that he is unwilling to lose any part of it; therefore, to gratify him, we may throw it into a supplementary form. But let me ask, will not this as effectually destroy some parts, as if the correction had been made by way of incorporation? or will posterity have a more favorable opinion of the original, because it has been amended by distinct acts? For my part, I cannot see what advantage can accrue from adopting the motion of the honorable gentleman from Connecticut, unless it be to give every one the trouble of erasing out of his copy of the Constitution certain words and sentences, and inserting others. But, perhaps, in our great veneration for the original composition, we may go further, and pass an act to prohibit these interpolations, as it may injure the text.

All this, sir, I take to be trifling about matters of little consequence. The Constitution has undoubtedly provided that the amendments shall be incorporated if I understand the import of the words, "and shall be valid to all intents and purposes, as part of the Constitution." If it had said that the present form should be preserved, then it would be proper to propose the alterations by way of a supplement. One gentleman has said we shall lose the names that are now annexed to the instrument. They are names, sir, I admit, of high respect; but I would ask that gentleman, if they would give validity to the Constitution if it were not ratified by the several States? or if their names were struck out, whether it would be of less force than it is at present? If he answers these questions in the negative, I shall consider it of no consequence whether the names are appended to it or not. But it will be time enough to discuss this point, when a motion is made for striking them out.

If we proceed in the way proposed by the honorable gentleman from Connecticut, I presume the title of our first amendment will be, a supplement to the Constitution of the United States; the next a supplement to the supplement, and so on, until we have supplements annexed five times in five years, wrapping up the Constitution in a maze of perplexity; and as great an adept as that honorable gentleman is at finding out the truth, it will take him, I apprehend, a week or a fortnight's study to ascertain the true meaning of the Constitution.

It is said, if the amendments are incorporated, it will be a virtual repeal of the Constitution. I say the effect will be the same in a supplementary way; consequently the objection goes for nothing, or it goes against making any amendments whatever.

It is said that the present form of the amendments is contrary to the 5th article. I will not undertake to define the extent of the word amendment, as it stands in the fifth article; but I suppose if we proposed to change the division of the powers given to the three branches of the Government, and that proposition is accepted and ratified by three-fourths of the State Legislatures, it will become as valid, to all intents and purposes, as any part of the Constitution; but if it is the opinion of gentlemen that the original is to be kept sacred, amendments will be of no use, and had better be omitted; whereas, on the other hand, if they are to be received as equal in authority, we shall have five or six constitutions, perhaps differing in material points from each other, but all equally valid; so that they may require a man of science to determine what is or is not the Constitution. This will certainly be attended with great inconvenience, as the several States are bound not to make laws contradictory thereto, and all officers are sworn to support it, without knowing precisely what it is.

Mr. STONE asked the gentleman last up, how he meant to have the amendments incorporated? Was it intended to have the Constitution republished, and the alterations inserted in their proper places? He did not see how it was practicable to propose amendments, without making out a new Constitution, in the manner brought forward by the committee.

Mr. LAWRENCE could not conceive how gentlemen meant to engraft the amendments into the Constitution. The original one, executed by the convention at Philadelphia, was lodged in the archives of the late Congress, it was impossible for this House to take, and correct, and interpolate that without making it speak a different language: this would be supposing several things which never were contemplated. But what would become of the acts of Congress? They will certainly be vitiated, unless they are provided for by an additional clause in the Constitution.

What shall we say with respect to the ratifications of the several States? They adopted the original Constitution, but they have not thereby enabled us to change the one form of Government for another. It is true, amendments were proposed by some of them; but it does not follow, of necessity, that we should alter the form of the original which they have ratified. Amendments in this way are only proper in legislative business, while the bill is on its passage, as was justly observed before.

Mr. BENSON said, that this question had been agitated in the select committee, and determined in favor of the form in which it was reported; he believed this decision was founded in a great degree upon the recommendation of the State conventions, which had proposed amendments in this very form. This pointed out the mode most agreeable to the people of America, and therefore the one most eligible for Congress to pursue; it will likewise be the most convenient way. Suppose the amendments ratified by the several States; Congress may order a number of copies to be printed, into which the alterations will be inserted, and the work stand perfect and entire.

I believe it never was contemplated by any gentleman to alter the original constitution deposited in the archives of the Union, that will remain there with the names of those who formed it, while the Government has a being. But certainly there is convenience and propriety in completing the work in a way provided for in itself. The records of Congress and the several States will mark the progress of the business, and nothing will appear to be done but what is actually performed.

Mr. MADISON.—The gentleman last up has left me but one remark to add, and that is, if we adopt the amendment, we shall so far unhinge the business, as to occasion alterations in every article and clause of the report.

Mr. HARTLEY hoped the committee would not agree to the alteration, because it would perplex the business. He wished the propositions to be simple and entire, that the State Legislatures might decide without hesitation, and every man know what was the ground on which he rested his political welfare. Besides, the consequent changes which the motion would induce, were such as, he feared, would take up some days, if not weeks; and the time of the House was too precious to be squandered away in discussing mere matter of form.

Mr. PAGE was sorry to find the gentlemen stop at the preamble; he hoped they would proceed as soon as the obstruction was removed, and that would be when the motion was negatived.

He thought the best way to view this subject, was to look at the Constitution as a bill on its passage through the House, and to consider and amend its defects, article by article; for which reason he was for entering at once upon the main business. After that was gone through, it would be time enough to arrange the materials with which the House intended to form the preamble.

Mr. LIVERMORE insisted, that neither this Legislature, nor all the Legislatures in America, were authorized to repeal a Constitution; and that must be an inevitable consequence of an attempt to amend it in a way proposed by the committee. He then submitted to gentlemen the propriety of the alteration.

As to the difficulty which had been supposed in understanding supplemental laws, he thought but little of it; he imagined there were things in the Constitution more difficult to comprehend than any thing he had yet seen in the amendments.

Mr. JACKSON.—I do not like to differ with gentlemen about form; but as so much has been said, I wish to give my opinion; it is this: that the original Constitution ought to remain inviolate, and not be patched up, from time to time, with various stuffs resembling Joseph's coat of many colors.

Some gentlemen talk of repealing the present Constitution, and adopting an improved one. If we have this power, we may go on from year to year, making new ones; and in this way, we shall render the basis of the superstructure the most fluctuating thing imaginable, and the people will never know what the Constitution is. As for the alteration proposed by the committee to prefix before "We the people," certain dogmas, I cannot agree to it; the words, as they now stand, speak as much as it is possible to speak; it is a practical recognition of the right of the people to ordain and establish Governments, and is more expressive than any other mere paper declaration.

But why will gentlemen contend for incorporating amendments into the Constitution? They say, that it is necessary for the people to have the whole before them in one view. Have they precedent for this assertion? Look at the

Constitution of Great Britain; is that all contained in one instrument? It is well known, that *magna charta* was extorted by the barons from King John some centuries ago. Has that been altered since by the incorporation of amendments? Or does it speak the same language now, as it did at the time it was obtained? Sir, it is not altered a tittle from its original form. Yet there have been many amendments and improvements in the Constitution of Great Britain since that period. In the subsequent reign of his son, the great charters were confirmed with some supplemental acts. Is the *habeas corpus* act, or the statute *De Tollagio non concedendo* incorporated in *magna charta?* And yet there is not an Englishman but would spill the last drop of his blood in their defence; it is these, with some other acts of Parliament and *magna charta*, that form the basis of English liberty. We have seen amendments to their Constitution during the present reign, by establishing the independence of the judges, who are hereafter to be appointed during good behavior; formerly they were at the pleasure of the Crown. But was this done by striking out and inserting other words in the great charter? No, sir, the Constitution is composed of many distinct acts; but an Englishman would be ashamed to own that, on this account, he could not ascertain his own privileges or the authority of the Government.

The Constitution of the Union has been ratified and established by the people; let their act remain inviolable; if any thing we can do has a tendency to improve it, let it be done, but without mutilating and defacing the original.

Mr. SHERMAN.—If I had looked upon this question as mere matter of form, I should not have brought it forward or troubled the committee with such a lengthy discussion. But, sir, I contend that amendments made in the way proposed by the committee are void. No gentleman ever knew an addition and alteration introduced into an existing law, and that any part of such law was left in force; but if it was improved or altered by a supplemental act, the original retained all its validity and importance, in every case where the two were not incompatible. But if these observations alone should be thought insufficient to support my motion, I would desire gentlemen to consider the authorities upon which the two Constitutions are to stand. The original was established by the people at large, by conventions chosen by them for the express purpose. The preamble to the Constitution declares the act: but will it be a truth in ratifying the next Constitution, which is to be done perhaps by the State Legislatures, and not conventions chosen for the purpose? Will gentlemen say it is "We the people" in this case? Certainly they cannot; for, by the present Constitution, we, nor all the Legislatures in the Union together, do not possess the power of repealing it. All that is granted us by the 5th article is, that whenever we shall think it necessary, we may propose amendments to the Constitution; not that we may propose to repeal the old, and substitute a new one.

Gentlemen say, it would be convenient to have it in one instrument, that people might see the whole at once; for my part, I view no difficulty on this point. The amendments reported are a declaration of rights; the people are secure in them, whether we declare them or not; the last amendment but one provides that the three branches of Government shall each exercise its own rights. This is well secured already; and, in short, I do not see that they lessen the force of any article in the Constitution; if so, there can be little more difficulty in comprehending them whether they are combined in these or stand distinct instruments.

Mr. SMITH read extracts from the amendments proposed by several of the State conventions at the time they ratified the Constitution, from which, he said, it appeared that they were generally of opinion that the phraseology of the Constitution ought to be altered; nor would this mode of proceeding repeal any part of the Constitution but such as it touched, the remainder will be in force during the time of considering it and ever after.

As to the observations made by the honorable gentleman from Georgia, respecting the amendments made to the Constitution of Great Britain, they did not apply; the cases were nothing like similar, and consequently, could not be drawn into precedent. The Constitution of Britain is neither the *magna charta* of John, nor the *habeas corpus* act, nor all the charters put together; it is what the Parliament wills. It is true, there are rights granted to the subject that cannot be resumed; but the Constitution, or form of Government, may be altered by the authority of Parliament, whose power is absolute without control.

Mr. SENEY was afraid the House would consume more time than was at first apprehended in discussing the subject of amendments, if he was to infer any thing from what had now taken place. He hoped the question would soon be put and decided.

Mr. VINING was an enemy to unnecessary debate, but he conceived the question to be an important one, and was not displeased with the discussion that had taken place; he should, however, vote in favor of the most simple mode.

Mr. GERRY.—The honorable gentleman from Connecticut, if I understand him right, says that the words "We the people" cannot be retained, if Congress should propose amendments, and they be ratified by the State Legislatures. Now, if this is a fact, we ought most undoubtedly to adopt his motion; because if we do not, we cannot obtain any amendment whatever. But upon what ground does the gentleman's opinion stand? The Constitution of the United States was proposed by a convention met at Philadelphia; but, with all its importance, it did not possess as high authority as the President, Senate, and House of Representatives of the Union. For that convention was not convened in consequence of any express will of the people, but an implied one, through their members in the State Legislatures. The Constitution derived no authority from the first convention; it was concurred in by conventions of the people, and that concurrence armed it with power and invested it with dignity. Now the Congress of the United States are expressly authorized by the sovereign and uncontrollable voice of the people, to propose amendments whenever two-thirds of both Houses shall think fit. Now, if this is the fact, the propositions of amendment will be found to originate with a higher authority than the original system. The conventions of the States, respectively, have agreed for the people, that the State Legislatures shall be authorized to decide upon these amendments in the manner of a convention. If these acts of the State Legislatures are not good, because they are not specifically instructed by their constituents, neither were the acts calling the first and subsequent conventions.

Does he mean to put amendments on this ground, that after they have been ratified by the State Legislatures, they are not to have the same authority as the original instrument? If this is his meaning, let him avow it; and if it is well founded, we may save ourselves the trouble of proceeding in the business. But, for my part, I have no doubt but a ratification of the amendments, in any form, would be as valid as any part of the Constitution. The Legislatures are elected by the people. I know no difference between them and conventions, unless it be that the former will generally be composed of men of higher characters than may be expected in conventions; and in this case, the ratification by the Legislatures would have the preference.

Now, if it is clear that the effect will be the same in either mode, will gentlemen hesitate to approve the most simple and clear? It will undoubtedly be more agreeable to have it all brought into one instrument, than have to refer to five or six different acts.

Mr. SHERMAN.—The gentlemen who oppose the motion say we contend for matter of form; they think it nothing more. Now we say we contend for substance, and therefore cannot agree to amendments in this way. If they are so desirous of having the business completed, they had better sacrifice what they consider but a matter of indifference to gentlemen, to go more unanimously along with them in altering the Constitution.

The question on Mr. SHERMAN's motion was now put and lost.

Mr. LIVERMORE wished to know whether it was necessary, in order to carry a motion in committee, that two-thirds should agree.

Mr. HARTLEY mentioned, that in Pennsylvania, they had a council of censors who were authorized to call a convention to amend the Constitution when it was thought necessary, but two-thirds were required for that purpose. He had been a member of that body, when they had examined the business in a committee of council; the majority made a report, which was lost for want of two-thirds to carry it through the council.

Some desultory conversation took place on this subject, when it was decided by the chairman of the committee that a majority of the committee were sufficient to form a report.

An appeal being made from the opinion of the Chair, it was, after some observations, confirmed by the committee. After which the committee rose and reported progress.

Adjourned.

[18 Aug.]

Mr. GERRY moved,

"That such of the amendments to the Constitution proposed by the several States, as are not in substance comprised in the report of the select committee appointed to consider amendments, be referred to a Committee of the whole House; and that all amendments which shall be agreed to by the committee last mentioned be included in one report."

Mr. TUCKER remarked, that many citizens expected that the amendments proposed by the conventions would be attended to by the House, and that several members conceived it to be their duty to bring them forward. If the House should decline taking them into consideration, it might tend to destroy that harmony which had hitherto existed, and which did great honor to their proceedings; it might affect all their future measures, and promote such feuds as might embarrass the Government exceedingly. The States who had proposed these amendments would feel some degree of chagrin at having misplaced their confidence in the General Government. Five important States have pretty plainly expressed their apprehensions of the danger to which the rights of their citizens are exposed. Finding these cannot be secured in the mode they had wished, they will naturally recur to the alternative, and endeavor to obtain a Federal Convention; the consequence of this may be disagreeable to the Union; party spirit may be revived, and animosities rekindled destructive of tranquillity. States that exert themselves to obtain a federal convention, and those that oppose the measure, may feel so strongly the spirit of discord, as to sever the Union asunder.

If in this conflict the advocates for a federal convention should prove successful, the consequences may be alarming; we may lose many of the valuable principles now established in the present Constitution. If, on the other hand, a convention should not be obtained, the consequences resulting are equally to be dreaded; it would render the administration of this system of government weak, if not impracticable; for no Government can be administered with energy, however energetic its system, unless it obtains the confidence and support of the people. Which of the two evils is the greatest would be difficult to ascertain.

It is essential to our deliberations that the harmony of the House be preserved; by it alone we shall be enabled to perfect the organization of the Government—a Government but in embryo, or at best but in its infancy.

My idea relative to this Constitution, whilst it was dependent upon the assent of the several States, was, that it required amendment, and that the proper time for amendment was previous to the ratification. My reasons were, that I conceived it difficult, if not impossible, to obtain essential amendments by the way pointed out in the Constitution; nor have I been mistaken in this suspicion. It will be found, I fear, still more difficult than I apprehended; for perhaps these amendments, should they be agreed to by two-thirds of both Houses of Congress, will be submitted for ratification to the Legislatures of the several States, instead of State conventions, in which case the chance is still worse. The Legislatures of almost all the States consist of two independent, distinct bodies; the amendments must be adopted by three-fourths of such Legislatures; that is to say, they must meet the approbation of the majority of each of eighteen deliberative assemblies. But, notwithstanding all these objections to obtaining amendments after the ratification of the Constitution, it will tend to give a great degree of satisfaction to those who are desirous of them, if this House shall take them up, and consider them with that degree of candor and attention they have hitherto displayed on the subjects that have come before them; consider the amendments separately, and, after fair deliberation, either approve or disapprove of them. By such conduct, we answer in some degree the expectations of those citizens in the several States who have shown so great a tenacity to the preservation of those rights and liberties they secured to themselves by an arduous, persevering, and successful conflict.

I have hopes that the States will be reconciled to this disappointment, in consequence of such procedure.

A great variety of arguments might be urged in favor of the motion; but I shall rest it here, and not trespass any further upon the patience of the House.

Mr. MADISON was just going to move to refer these amendments, in order that they might be considered in the fullest manner; but it would be very inconvenient to have them made up into one report, or all of them discussed at the present time.

Mr. VINING had no objection to the bringing them forward in the fullest point of view; but his objection arose from the informality attending the introduction of the business.

The order of the House was to refer the report of the Committee of Eleven to a Committee of the Whole, and therefore it was improper to propose any thing additional.

A desultory conversation arose on this motion, when Mr. VINING moved the previous question, in which, being supported by five members, it was put, and the question was, Shall the main question, to agree to the motion, be now put? The yeas and nays being demanded by one-fifth of the members present, on this last motion, they were taken as follows:

YEAS.—Messrs. Burke, Coles, Floyd, Gerry, Griffin, Grout, Hathorn, Livermore, Page, Parker, Van Rensselaer, Sherman, Stone, Sturgis, Sumter, and Tucker.—16.

NAYS.—Messrs. Ames, Baldwin, Benson, Boudinot, Brown, Cadwalader, Carroll, Clymer, Fitzsimons, Foster, Gilman, Goodhue, Hartley, Heister, Huntington, Lawrence, Lee, Madison, Moore, Muhlenburg, Partridge, Schureman, Scott, Sedgwick, Seney, Sylvester, Sinnickson, Smith, of Maryland, Smith, of South Carolina, Thatcher, Trumbull, Vining, Wadsworth, and Wynkoop.—34.

[19 Aug.]

The House then took into consideration the amendments to the Constitution, as reported by the Committee of the Whole.

Mr. SHERMAN renewed his motion for adding the amendments to the Constitution by way of supplement.

Hereupon ensued a debate similar to what took place in the Committee of the Whole. . . ; but, on the question, Mr. SHERMAN's motion was carried by two-thirds of the House; in consequence it was agreed to.

12

PROPOSED AMENDMENTS AND RATIFICATION
1789

Elliot 1:338–40

CONGRESS OF THE UNITED STATES;

Begun and held at the City of New York, on Wednesday, the 4th of March, 1789.

The conventions of a number of the states having, at the time of their adopting the Constitution, expressed a desire, in order to prevent misconstruction or abuse of its powers, that further declaratory and restrictive clauses should be added; and as extending the ground of public confidence in the government will best insure the beneficent ends of its institution;—

Resolved, by the Senate and House of Representatives of the United States of America, in Congress assembled, two thirds of both houses concurring, that the following articles be proposed to the legislatures of the several states, as amendments to the Constitution of the United States, all or any of which articles, when ratified by three fourths of the said legislatures, to be valid, to all intents and purposes, as part of the said Constitution, namely,—

Articles in Addition to, and Amendment of, the Constitution of the United States of America, proposed by Congress, and ratified by the Legislatures of the several States, pursuant to the Fifth Article of the original Constitution.

ART. I. After the first enumeration required by the first article of the Constitution, there shall be one representative for every thirty thousand, until the number shall amount to one hundred, after which the proportion shall be so regulated by Congress, that there shall not be less than one hundred representatives, nor less than one representative for every forty thousand persons, until the number of representatives shall amount to two hundred, after which the proportion shall be so regulated by Congress, that there shall not be less than two hundred representatives, nor more than one representative for every fifty thousand.

ART. II. No law varying the compensation for services of the senators and representatives shall take effect, until an election of representatives shall have intervened.

ART. III. Congress shall make no law respecting an establishment of religion, or prohibiting the free exercise thereof, or abridging the freedom of speech, or of the press, or the right of the people peaceably to assemble, and to petition the government for a redress of grievances.

ART. IV. A well-regulated militia being necessary to the security of a free state, the right of the people to keep and bear arms shall not be infringed.

ART. V. No soldier shall, in time of peace, be quartered in any house without the consent of the owner, nor in time of war, but in a manner prescribed by law.

Art. VI. The right of the people to be secure in their persons, houses, papers, effects, against unreasonable searches and seizures, shall not be violated; and no warrants shall issue, but upon principal cause, supported by oath or affirmation, and particularly describing the place to be searched, and the persons or things to be seized.

Art. VII. No person shall be held to answer for a capital or otherwise infamous crime, unless on a presentment or indictment of a grand jury, except in cases arising in the land or naval forces, or in the militia when in actual service, in time of war or public danger; nor shall any person be subject, for the same offence, to be twice put in jeopardy of life or limb; nor shall be compelled, in any criminal case, to be a witness against himself; nor be deprived of life, liberty, or property, without due process of law; nor shall private property be taken for public use without just compensation.

Art. VIII. In all criminal prosecutions, the accused shall enjoy the right of a speedy and public trial, by an impartial jury of the state and district wherein the crime shall have been committed, which district shall have been previously ascertained by law; and to be informed of the nature and cause of the accusation; to be confronted with the witnesses against him; to have compulsory process for obtaining witnesses in his favor; and to have the assistance of counsel for his defence.

Art. IX. In suits at common law, where the value in controversy shall exceed twenty dollars, the right of trial by jury shall be preserved, and no fact tried by a jury shall be otherwise reëxamined, in any court of the United States, than according to the rules in common law.

Art. X. Excessive bail shall not be required, nor excessive fines imposed, nor cruel and unusual punishments inflicted.

Art. XI. The enumeration, in the Constitution, of certain rights, shall not be construed to deny or disparage others retained by the people.

Art. XII. The powers not delegated to the United States by the Constitution, nor prohibited by it to the states, are reserved to the states, respectively, or to the people.

FREDERICK AUGUSTUS MUHLENBERG,
Speaker of the House of Representatives.
JOHN ADAMS, *Vice-President of the United States,*
and President of the Senate.

Attest. JOHN BECKLEY,
Clerk of the House of Representatives.
SAMUEL A. OTIS, *Secretary of the Senate.*

Which, being transmitted to the several state legislatures, were decided upon by them, according to the following returns:—

By the State of New Hampshire.—Agreed to the whole of the said amendments, except the 2d article.

By the State of New York.—Agreed to the whole of the said amendments, except the 2d article.

By the State of Pennsylvania.—Agreed to the 3d, 4th, 5th, 6th, 7th, 8th, 9th, 10th, 11th, and 12th articles of the said amendments.

By the State of Delaware.—Agreed to the whole of the said amendments, except the 1st article.

By the State of Maryland.—Agreed to the whole of the said twelve amendments.

By the State of South Carolina.—Agreed to the whole said twelve amendments.

By the State of North Carolina.—Agreed to the whole of the said twelve amendments.

By the State of Rhode Island and Providence Plantations.—Agreed to the whole of the said twelve articles.

By the State of New Jersey.—Agreed to the whole of the said amendments, except the second article.

By the State of Virginia.—Agreed to the whole of the said twelve articles.

No returns were made by the states of Massachusetts, Connecticut, Georgia, and Kentucky.

The amendments thus proposed became a part of the Constitution, the first and second of them excepted, which were not ratified by a sufficient number of the state legislatures.

13

AMENDMENTS TO THE CONSTITUTION
1791–1804
Tansill 1066–69

Article I

Congress shall make no law respecting an establishment of religion, or prohibiting the free exercise thereof; or abridging the freedom of speech, or of the press; or the right of the people peaceably to assemble, and to petition the Government for a redress of grievances.

Article II

A well regulated Militia, being necessary to the security of a free State, the right of the people to keep and bear Arms, shall not be infringed.

Article III

No Soldier shall, in time of peace be quartered in any house, without the consent of the Owner, nor in time of war, but in a manner to be prescribed by law.

Article IV

The right of the people to be secure in their persons, houses, papers, and effects, against unreasonable searches and seizures, shall not be violated, and no Warrants shall issue, but upon probable cause, supported by Oath or affirmation, and particularly describing the place to be searched, and the persons or things to be seized.

Article V

No person shall be held to answer for a capital, or otherwise infamous crime, unless on a presentment or indictment of a Grand Jury, except in cases arising in the land or naval forces, or in the Militia, when in actual service in time of War or public danger; nor shall any person be subject for the same offence to be twice put in jeopardy of life or limb; nor shall be compelled in any criminal case to be a witness against himself, nor be deprived of life, liberty, or property, without due process of law; nor shall private property be taken for public use, without just compensation.

Article VI

In all criminal prosecutions, the accused shall enjoy the right to a speedy and public trial, by an impartial jury of the State and district wherein the crime shall have been committed, which district shall have been previously ascertained by law, and to be informed of the nature and cause of the accusation; to be confronted with the witnesses against him; to have compulsory process for obtaining witnesses in his favor, and to have the Assistance of Counsel for his defence.

Article VII

In Suits at common law, where the value in controversy shall exceed twenty dollars, the right of trial by jury shall be preserved, and no fact tried by a jury, shall be otherwise re-examined in any Court of the United States, than according to the rules of the common law.

Article VIII

Excessive bail shall not be required, nor excessive fines imposed, nor cruel and unusual punishments inflicted.

Article IX

The enumeration in the Constitution, of certain rights, shall not be construed to deny or disparage others retained by the people.

Article X

The powers not delegated to the United States by the Constitution, nor prohibited by it to the States, are reserved to the States respectively, or to the people.

Article XI

The Judicial power of the United States shall not be construed to extend to any suit in law or equity, commenced or prosecuted against one of the United States by Citizens of another State, or by Citizens or Subjects of any Foreign State.

Article XII

The Electors shall meet in their respective states, and vote by ballot for President and Vice-President, one of whom, at least, shall not be an inhabitant of the same state with themselves; they shall name in their ballots the person voted for as President, and in distinct ballots the person voted for as Vice-President, and they shall make distinct lists of all persons voted for as President, and of all persons voted for as Vice-President, and of the number of votes for each, which lists they shall sign and certify, and transmit sealed to the seat of the government of the United States, directed to the President of the Senate;—The President of the Senate shall, in the presence of the Senate and House of Representatives, open all the certificates and the votes shall then be counted;—The person having the greatest number of votes for President, shall be the President, if such number be a majority of the whole number of Electors appointed; and if no person have such majority, then from the persons having the highest numbers not exceeding three on the list of those voted for as President, the House of Representatives shall choose immediately, by ballot, the President. But in choosing the President, the votes shall be taken by states, the representation from each state having one vote; a quorum for this purpose shall consist of a member or members from two-thirds of the states, and a majority of all the states shall be necessary to a choice. And if the House of Representatives shall not choose a President whenever the right of choice shall devolve upon them, before the fourth day of March next following, then the Vice-President shall act as President, as in the case of the death or other constitutional disability of the President. The person having the greatest number of votes as Vice-President, shall be the Vice-President, if such number be a majority of the whole number of Electors appointed, and if no person have a majority, then from the two highest numbers on the list, the Senate shall choose the Vice-President; a quorum for the purpose shall consist of two-thirds of the whole number of Senators, and a majority of the whole number shall be necessary to a choice. But no person constitutionally ineligible to the office of President shall be eligible to that of Vice-President of the United States.

SEE ALSO:

Generally 5; Amends. I–X.

Charter of Libertyes and Priviledges, 30 Oct. 1683, The Colonial Laws of New York from the Year 1664 to the Revolution (1894), 1:111–16

Act Declareing What Are the Rights and Priviledges of Their Majesties Subjects Inhabiting within Their Province of New York, 13 May 1691, The Colonial Laws of New York from the Year 1664 to the Revolution (1894), 1:244–48

Samuel Adams, The Rights of the Colonists and a List of Infringements and Violations of Rights, 1772, Writings 2:350–69

Maryland Declaration of Rights, 1776, Thorpe 3:1686–91

North Carolina Constitution of 1776, Thorpe 5:2787–88

Vermont Constitution of 1777, Thorpe 6:3739–42

New Hampshire Constitution of 1784, Thorpe 4:2453–57

Vermont Constitution of 1786, Thorpe 6:3751–54

North Carolina Delegates to Governor Caswell, 7 Aug. 1787, Farrand 3:68

Debate in Pennsylvania Ratifying Convention, 28 Oct.–11 Dec. 1787, Elliot 2:434–38, 529–42

James Iredell, Marcus, Answers to Mr. Mason's Objections to the Constitution, 1788, Pamphlets 335–36

Debate in Massachusetts Ratifying Convention, 1, 4–6 Feb. 1788, Elliot 2:130–33, 134–37, 148–78

Amendment I

Congress shall make no law respecting an establishment of religion, or prohibiting the free exercise thereof; or abridging the freedom of speech, or of the press; or the right of the people peaceably to assemble, and to petition the Government for a redress of grievances.

RELIGION

31. Adam Smith, Wealth of Nations, bk. 5, ch. 1, pt. 3, art. 3 (1776)
32. Thomas Jefferson, Draft of Bill Exempting Dissenters from Contributing to the Support of the Church, 30 Nov. 1776
33. George Mason, Amendment to the Bill Exempting Dissenters from Contributions to the Established Church, 5 Dec. 1776
34. New York Constitution of 1777, arts. 38, 39
35. Vermont Constitution of 1777, ch. 1, sec. 3; ch. 2, sec. 41
36. South Carolina Constitution of 1778, arts. 21, 38
37. Thomas Jefferson, A Bill for Establishing Religious Freedom, 12 June 1779
38. Massachusetts Constitution of 1780, pt. 1, arts. 2, 3
39. Benjamin Rush to John Armstrong, 19 Mar. 1783
40. Thomas Jefferson, Notes on the State of Virginia, Query 17 (1784)
41. John Blair to James Madison, 21 June 1784
42. New Hampshire Constitution of 1784, pt. 1, arts. 4, 5, 6, 13
43. James Madison, Memorial and Remonstrance against Religious Assessments, 20 June 1785
44. Virginia, Act for Establishing Religious Freedom, 31 Oct. 1785
45. Thomas Jefferson, Autobiography, 1821
46. Vermont Constitution of 1786, ch. 1, art. 3
47. An Old Whig, no. 5, Fall 1787
48. A [Maryland] Farmer, no. 7, 11 Apr. 1788
49. James Madison, Virginia Ratifying Convention, 12 June 1788
50. Patrick Henry, Virginia Ratifying Convention, 12 June 1788
51. Virginia Ratifying Convention, Proposed Amendments, 27 June 1788
52. Debate in North Carolina Ratifying Convention, 30 July 1788
53. House of Representatives, Amendments to the Constitution, 15, 17, 20 Aug. 1789
54. George Washington, Proclamation: A National Thanksgiving, 3 Oct. 1789
55. Tench Coxe, Notes concerning the United States of America, 1790
56. Alexander Hamilton, Report on Manufactures, 5 Dec. 1791
57. Thomas Paine, Rights of Man, pt. 1, 1791
58. Thomas Jefferson to Danbury Baptist Association, 1 Jan. 1802
59. St. George Tucker, Blackstone's Commentaries (1803)
60. Thomas Jefferson to Rev. Samuel Miller, 23 Jan. 1808
61. House of Representatives, Returned Bill, 21, 23 Feb. 1811
62. *People* v. *Ruggles*, 8 Johns. R. 290 (N.Y. 1811)
63. James Madison, Proclamation, 16 Nov. 1814
64. James Madison, Detached Memoranda, ca. 1817
65. Thomas Jefferson to Albert Gallatin, 16 June 1817
66. James Madison to Edward Livingston, 10 July 1822
67. William Rawle, A View of the Constitution of the United States (2d ed. 1829)
68. James Madison to Rev. Adams, 1832
69. Joseph Story, Commentaries on the Constitution (1833)

1

JOHN CALVIN, INSTITUTES OF THE
CHRISTIAN RELIGION
1536
Stokes 1:110

III. The opinion entertained by some persons, that . . . all civil magistrates were strangers to the profession of Christianity, is a mistake, for want of considering the great distinction, and the nature of the difference, between the ecclesiastical and civil power. For the Church has no power of the sword to punish or to coerce, no authority to compel, no prisons, fines, or other punishments, like those inflicted by the civil magistrate. Besides, the object of this power is, not that he who has transgressed may be punished against his will, but that he may profess his repentance by a voluntary submission to chastisement. The difference therefore is very great; because the Church does not assume to itself what belongs to the magistrate, nor can the magistrate execute that which is executed by the Church. . . .

Nor let any one think it strange that I now refer to human polity the charge of the due maintenance of religion, which I may appear to have placed beyond the jurisdiction of men. For I do not allow men to make laws respecting religion and the worship of God now, any more than I did before: though I approve of civil government, which provides that the true religion which is contained in the law of God, be not violated, and polluted by public blasphemies, with impunity.

. . . . .

XXII. The first duty of subjects towards their magistrates is to entertain the most honourable sentiments of their function, which they know to be a jurisdiction delegated to them from God, and on that account to esteem and reverence them as God's ministers and vicegerents. . . .

XXIII. Hence follows another duty, that, with minds disposed to honour and reverence magistrates, subjects approve their obedience to them, in submitting to their edicts, in paying taxes, in discharging public duties and bearing burdens which relate to the common defence, and in fulfilling all their other commands.

. . . . .

XXXII. But in the obedience which we have shewn to be due to the authority of governors, it is always necessary to make one exception, and that is entitled to our first attention, that it do not seduce us from obedience to him, to whose will the desires of all kings ought to be subject, to whose decrees all their commands ought to yield, to whose majesty all their sceptres ought to submit.

2

THE FUNDAMENTAL AGREEMENT OR ORIGINAL
CONSTITUTION OF THE COLONY
OF NEW-HAVEN
4 June 1639
Old South Leaflets, no. 8, 6–10

The 4th day of the 4th month, called June, 1639, all the free planters assembled together in a general meeting, to consult about settling civil government, according to GOD, and the nomination of persons that might be found, by consent of all, fittest in all respects for the foundation work of a church, which was intended to be gathered in Quinipiack. After solemn invocation in the name of GOD, in prayer for the presence and help of his spirit and grace, in those weighty businesses, they were reminded of the business whereabout they met, (viz.) for the establishment of such civil order as might be most pleasing unto GOD, and for the choosing the fittest men for the foundation work of a church to be gathered. For the better enabling them to discern the mind of GOD, and to agree accordingly concerning the establishment of civil order, Mr. John Davenport propounded divers queries to them publicly, praying them to consider seriously in the presence and fear of GOD, the weight of the business they met about, and not to be rash or slight in giving their votes to things they understood not; but to digest fully and thoroughly what should be propounded to them, and without respect to men, as they should be satisfied and persuaded in their own minds, to give their answers in such sort as they would be willing should stand upon record for posterity.

This being earnestly pressed by Mr. Davenport, Mr. Robert Newman was intreated to write, in characters, and to read distinctly and audibly in the hearing of all the people, what was propounded and accorded on, that it might appear, that all consented to matters propounded, according to words written by him.

Query I. Whether the scriptures do hold forth a perfect rule for the direction and government of all men in all duties which they are to perform to GOD and men, as well in families and commonwealth, as in matters of the church? This was assented unto by all, no man dissenting, as was expressed by holding up of hands. Afterwards it was read over to them that they might see in what words

their vote was expressed. They again expressed their consent by holding up their hands, no man dissenting.

Query II. Whereas there was a covenant solemnly made by the whole assembly of free planters of this plantation, the first day of extraordinary humiliation, which we had after we came together, that as in matters that concern the gathering and ordering of a church, so likewise in all public officers which concern civil order, as choice of magistrates and officers, making and repealing laws, dividing allotments of inheritance, and all things of like nature, we would all of us be ordered by those rules which the scripture holds forth to us; this covenant was called a plantation covenant, to distinguish it from a church covenant, which could not at that time be made, a church not being then gathered, but was deferred till a church might be gathered, according to GOD: It was demanded whether all the free planters do hold themselves bound by that covenant, in all businesses of that nature which are expressed in the covenant, to submit themselves to be ordered by the rules held forth in the scripture?

This also was assented unto by all, and no man gainsayed it; and they did testify the same by holding up their hands, both when it was first propounded, and confirmed the same by holding up their hands when it was read unto them in public John Clark being absent, when the covenant was made, doth now manifest his consent to it. Also Richard Beach, Andrew Law, Goodman Banister, Arthur Halbridge, John Potter, Robert Hill, John Brocket, and John Johnson, these persons, being not admitted planters when the covenant was made, do now express their consent to it.

Query III. Those who have desired to be received as free planters, and are settled in the plantation, with a purpose, resolution and desire, that they may be admitted into church fellowship, according to CHRIST, as soon as GOD shall fit them thereunto, were desired to express it by holding up hands. According all did express this to be their desire and purpose by holding up their hands twice (viz.) at the proposal of it, and after when these written words were read unto them.

Query IV. All the free planters were called upon to express, whether they held themselves bound to establish such civil order as might best conduce to the securing of the purity and peace of the ordinance to themselves and their posterity according to GOD? In answer hereunto they expressed by holding up their hands twice as before, that they held themselves bound to establish such civil order as might best conduce to the ends aforesaid.

Then Mr. Davenport declared unto them, by the scripture, what kind of persons might best be trusted with matters of government; and by sundry arguments from scripture proved that such men as were described in Exod. xviii. 2, Deut. i. 13, with Deut. xvii. 15, and 1 Cor. vi. 1, 6, 7. ought to be intrusted by them, seeing they were free to cast themselves into that mould and form of commonwealth which appeared best for them in reference to the securing the peace and peaceable improvement of all CHRIST his ordinances in the church according to GOD, whereunto they have bound themselves, as hath been acknowledged.

Having thus said he sat down praying the company freely to consider, whether they would have it voted at this time or not. After some space of silence, Mr. Theophilus Eaton answered, it might be voted, and some others also spake to the same purpose, none at all opposing it. Then it was propounded to vote.

Query V. Whether free burgesses shall be chosen out of the church members, they that are in the foundation work of the church being actually free burgesses, and to choose to themselves out of the like estate of church fellowship, and the power of choosing magistrates and officers from among themselves, and the power of making and repealing laws, according to the word, and the dividing of inheritances, and deciding of differences that may arise, and all the businesses of like nature are to be transacted by those free burgesses? This was put to vote and agreed unto by lifting up of hands twice, as in the former it was done. Then one man stood up and expressed his dissenting from the rest in part; yet granting, 1. That magistrates should be men fearing GOD. 2. That the church is the company where, ordinarily, such men may be expected. 3. That they that choose them ought to be men fearing GOD; only at this he stuck, that free planters ought not to give this power out of their hands. Another stood up and answered, that nothing was done, but with their consent. The former answered, that all the free planters ought to resume this power into their own hands again, if things were not orderly carried. Mr. Theophilus Eaton answered, that in all places they choose committees in like manner. The companies in London choose the liveries by whom the public magistrates are chosen. In this the rest are not wronged, because they expect, in time, to be of the livery themselves, and to have the same power. Some others intreated the former to give his arguments and reasons whereupon he dissented. He refused to do it, and said, they might not rationally demand it, seeing he let the vote pass on freely and did not speak till after it was past, because he would not hinder what they agreed upon. Then Mr. Davenport, after a short relation of some former passages between them two about this question, prayed the company that nothing might be concluded by them on this weighty question, but what themselves were persuaded to be agreeing with the mind of GOD, and they had heard what had been said since the voting; he intreated them again to consider of it, and put it again to vote as before. Again all of them, by holding up their hands, did show their consent as before. And some of them confessed that, whereas they did waver before they came to the assembly, they were now fully convinced, that it is the mind of GOD. One of them said that in the morning before he came reading Deut. xvii. 15, he was convinced at home. Another said, that he came doubting to the assembly, but he blessed GOD, by what had been said, he was now fully satisfied, that the choice of burgesses out of church members, and to intrust those with the power before spoken of is according to the mind of GOD revealed in the scriptures. All having spoken their apprehensions it was agreed upon, and Mr. Robert Newman was desired to write it as an order whereunto every one, that hereafter should be admitted here as planters, should submit, and testify the same by subscribing their names to the order: Namely, that church members only shall be free burgesses, and that they only shall choose magistrates and officers among themselves, to have power of transacting all the public civil affairs of this plantation; of making and repealing laws, dividing of inheritances, deciding of differences that may arise, and doing all things and businesses of like nature.

This being thus settled, as a fundamental agreement concerning civil government, Mr. Davenport proceeded to propound something to consideration about the gathering of a church, and to prevent the blemishing of the first beginnings of the church work, Mr. Davenport advised, that the names of such as were to be admitted might be publicly propounded, to the end that they who were most approved might be chosen; for the town being cast into several private meetings, wherein they that lived nearest together gave their accounts one to another of GOD's gracious work upon them, and prayed together and conferred to their mutual edification, sundry of them had knowledge one of another; and in every meeting some one was more approved of all than any other; for this reason and to prevent scandals, the whole company was intreated to consider whom they found fittest to nominate for this work.

3

THE BODY OF LIBERTIES OF THE MASSACHUSETS COLLONIE IN NEW ENGLAND
1641

MHS Collections (3d ser.), 8:216, 226, 231, 232, 234–36

The free fruition of such liberties Immunities and priveledges as humanitie, Civilitie, and Christianitie call for as due to every man in his place and proportion without impeachment and Infringement hath ever bene and ever will be the tranquillitie and Stabilitie of Churches and Commonwealths. And the deniall or deprivall thereof, the disturbance if not the ruine of both.

We hould it therefore our dutie and safetie whilst we are about the further establishing of this Government to collect and expresse all such freedomes as for present we foresee may concerne us, and our posteritie after us, And to ratify them with our sollemne consent.

Wee doe therefore this day religiously and unanimously decree and confirme these following Rites, liberties and priveledges concerneing our Churches, and Civill State to be respectively impartiallie and inviolably enjoyed and observed throughout our Jurisdiction for ever.

1. No mans life shall be taken away, no mans honour or good name shall be stayned, no mans person shall be arrested, restrayned, banished, dismembred, nor any wayes punished, no man shall be deprived of his wife or children, no mans goods or estaite shall be taken away from him, nor any way indammaged under colour of law or

Countenance of Authoritie, unlesse it be by vertue or equitie of some expresse law of the Country waranting the same, established by a generall Court and sufficiently published, or in case of the defect of a law in any parteculer case by the word of God.

. . . . .

Liberties more peculiarlie concerning the free men.

58. Civill Authoritie hath power and libertie to see the peace, ordinances and Rules of Christ observed in every church according to his word. so it be done in a Civill and not in an Ecclesiasticall way.

59. Civil Authoritie hath power and libertie to deale with any Church member in a way of Civill Justice, notwithstanding any Church relation, office or interest.

60. No church censure shall degrade or depose any man from any Civill dignitie, office, or Authoritie he shall have in the Commonwealth.

. . . . .

Liberties of Forreiners and Strangers.

89. If any people of other Nations professing the true Christian Religion shall flee to us from the Tiranny or oppression of their perscecutors, or from famyne, warres, or the like necessary and compulsarie cause, They shall be entertayned and succoured amongst us, according to that power and prudence, god shall give us.

. . . . .

91. There shall never be any bond slaverie, villinage or Captivitie amongst us unles it be lawfull Captives taken in just warres, and such strangers as willingly selle themselves or are sold to us. And these shall have all the liberties and Christian usages which the law of god established in Israell concerning such persons doeth morally require. This exempts none from servitude who shall be Judged thereto by Authoritie.

. . . . .

94. *Capitall Laws.*

1.

Deut. 13. 6, 10.
Deut. 17. 2, 6.
Ex. 22. 20.

If any man after legall conviction shall have or worship any other god, but the lord god, he shall be put to death.

2.

Ex. 22. 18.
Lev. 20. 27.
Dut. 18. 10.

If any man or woeman be a witch, (that is hath or consulteth with a familiar spirit,) They shall be put to death.

3.

If any person shall Blaspheme the name of god, the father, Sonne or Holie Ghost, with direct, expresse, presumptuous or high handed blasphemie, or shall curse god in the like manner, he shall be put to death.

Lev. 24. 15, 16.

. . . . .

95. *A Declaration of the Liberties the Lord Jesus hath given to the Churches.*

1.

All the people of god within this Jurisdiction who are not in a church way, and be orthodox in Judgement, and not scandalous in life, shall have full libertie to gather themselves into a Church Estaite. Provided they doe it in a Christian way, with due observation of the rules of Christ revealed in his word.

2.

Every Church hath full libertie to exercise all the ordinances of god, according to the rules of scripture.

3.

Every Church hath free libertie of Election and ordination of all their officers from time to time, provided they be able, pious and orthodox.

4.

Every Church hath free libertie of Admission, Recommendation, Dismission, and Expulsion, or deposall of their officers, and members, upon due cause, with free exercise of the Discipline and Censures of Christ according to the rules of his word.

5.

No Injunctions are to be put upon any Church, Church officers or member in point of Doctrine, worship or Discipline, whether for substance or cercumstance besides the Institutions of the lord.

6.

Every Church of Christ hath freedome to celebrate days of fasting and prayer, and of thanksgiveing according to the word of god.

7.

The Elders of Churches have free libertie to meete monthly, Quarterly, or otherwise, in convenient numbers and places, for conferences, and consultations about Christian and Church questions and occasions.

8.

All Churches have libertie to deale with any of their members in a church way that are in the hand of Justice. So it be not to retard or hinder the course thereof.

9.

Every Church hath libertie to deale with any magestrate, Deputie of Court or other officer what soe ever that is a member in a church way in case of apparent and just offence given in their places, so it be done with due observance and respect.

10.

Wee allowe private meetings for edification in religion amongst Christians of all sortes of people. So it be without just offence for number, time, place, and other cercumstances.

11.

For the preventing and removeing of errour and offence that may grow and spread in any of the Churches in this Jurisdiction, And for the preserveing of trueith and peace in the severall churches within themselves, and for the maintenance and exercise of brotherly communion, amongst all the churches in the Countrie, It is allowed and ratified, by the Authoritie of this Generall Court as a lawfull libertie of the Churches of Christ. That once in every month of the yeare (when the season will beare it) It shall be lawfull for the minesters and Elders, of the Churches neere adjoyneing together, with any other of the breetheren with the consent of the churches to assemble by course in each severall Church one after an other. To the intent after the preaching of the word by such a minister as shall be requested thereto by the Elders of the church where the Assembly is held, The rest of the day may be spent in publique Christian Conference about the discussing and resolveing of any such doubts and cases of conscience concerning matter of doctrine or worship or government of the church as shall be propounded by any of the Breetheren of that church, with leave also to any other Brother to propound his objections or answeres for further satisfaction according to the word of god. Provided that the whole action be guided and moderated by the Elders of the Church where the Assemblie is helde, or by such others as they shall appoint. And that no thing be concluded and imposed by way of Authoritie from one or more churches upon an other, but onely by way of Brotherly conference and consultations. That the trueth may be searched out to the satisfying of every mans conscience in the sight of god according his worde. And because such an Assembly and the worke thereof can not be duely attended to if other lectures be held in the same weeke. It is therefore agreed with the consent of the Churches. That in that weeke when such an Assembly is held, All the lectures in all the neighbouring Churches for the weeke shall be forborne. That so the publique service of Christ in this more solemne Assembly may be transacted with greater deligence and attention.

96. Howsoever these above specified rites, freedomes Immunities, Authorites and priveledges, both Civill and Ecclesiastical are expressed onely under the name and title of Liberties, and not in the exact forme of Laws or Statutes, yet we do with one consent fullie Authorise, and earnestly intreate all that are and shall be in Authoritie to consider them as laws, and not to faile to inflict condigne and proportionable punishments upon every man impartiallie, that shall infringe or violate any of them.

4

ROGER WILLIAMS, THE BLOODY TENENT, OF PERSECUTION FOR CAUSE OF CONSCIENCE 1644
Stokes 1:196–97, 198, 199

All civil states with their officers of justice, in their respective constitutions and administrations, are . . . essentially civil, and therefore not judges, governors, or defenders of the Spiritual, or Christian, State and worship. . . . It is the will and command of God that, since the coming of His Son, the Lord Jesus, a permission of the most Paganish, Jewish, Turkish or anti-Christian consciences and worship be granted to all men, in all nations and countries; and they are only to be fought against with that sword which is only, in Soul matters able to conquer, to wit; the sword of the Spirit—the Word of God. . . . God requireth not an uniformity of religion to be enacted and enforced in any civil state; which enforced uniformity, sooner or later, is the greatest occasion of civil war, ravishing consciences, persecution of Christ Jesus in His servants, and of the hypocrisy and destruction of millions of souls. . . . An enforced uniformity of religion throughout a nation or civil state confounds the civil and religious, denies the principles of Christianity and civility, and that Jesus Christ is come in the flesh.

. . . . .

The *Church* or company of *worshippers* (whether true or false) is like unto a . . . *Corporation, Society* or *Company* . . . in *London;* which Companies may hold their *Courts,* keep their *Records,* hold *disputations;* and in matters concerning their *Societie,* may dissent, divide, break into Schisms and Factions, sue and implead each other at the *Law,* yea wholly break up and dissolve into pieces and nothing, and yet the *peace* of the *Citie* not be in the least measure impaired or disturbed; because the *essence* or being of the *Citie,* and so the *well-being* and *peace* thereof is essentially distinct from those particular *Societies;* the *Citie-Courts, Citie-Lawes, Citie-punishments* distinct from theirs. The *Citie* was before them, and stands absolute and intire, when such a *Corporation* or *Societie* is taken down.

. . . . .

Summary

First, That the blood of so many hundred thousand soules of *Protestants* and *Papists,* split in the *Wars* of *present* and *former Ages,* for their respective *Consciences,* is not *required* nor *accepted* by *Jesus Christ* the *Prince* of *Peace.*

Secondly, Pregnant *Scriptures* and *Arguments* are throughout the Worke proposed against the *Doctrine* of *persecution* for the *cause* of *Conscience.*

Thirdly, *Satisfactorie* Answers are given to *Scriptures,* and objections produced by Mr. *Calvin, Beza,* Mr. *Cotton,* and the Ministers of the New English Churches and others former and later, tending to prove the *Doctrine* of *persecution* for cause of *Conscience*.

Fourthly, The *Doctrine of persecution* for cause of *Conscience*, is proved guilty of all the *blood* of the *Soules* crying for *vengeance* under the Altar.

Fifthly, All *Civill States* with their *Officers of justice* in their respective *constitutions* and *administrations* are proved *essentially Civill*, and therefore not *Judges, Governours* or *Defendours* of the Spirituall or Christian State and Worship.

Sixthly, It is the will and command of *God*, that (since the comming of his Sonne the *Lord Jesus*) a *permission* of the most *Paganish, Jewish*, Turkish, or Antichristian consciences and worships, bee granted to all men in all *Nations* and *Countries:* and they are onely to bee *fought* against with that *Sword* which is only (in *Soule* matters) able to *conquer*, to wit, the *Sword of Gods Spirit*, the *Word of God*.

Seventhly, The *State* of the Land of *Israel*, the *Kings* and *people* thereof in *Peace & War*, is proved *figurative* and *ceremoniall*, and no *patterne* nor *president* for any *Kingdome* or *civill State* in the *world* to follow.

Eighthly, *God* requireth not an *uniformity* of *Religion* to be *inacted* and *inforced* in any *civill State;* which inforced *uniformity* (sooner or later) is the greatest occasion of *civill Warre*, ravishing of *conscience*, persecution of *Christ Jesus* in his servants, and of the *hypocrisie* and *destruction* of *millions* of *souls*.

Ninthly, In holding an inforced *uniformity of Religion* in a *civill state*, wee must necessarily *disclaime* our desires and hopes of the *Jewes conversion* to *Christ*.

Tenthly, An inforced *uniformity* of *Religion* throughout a *Nation* or *civill State*, confounds the *Civill* and *Religious*, denies the principles of Christianity and civility, and that *Jesus Christ* is come in the *Flesh*.

Eleventhly, The *permission* of other *consciences* and *worships* then a state *professeth*, only can (according to God) procure a firme and lasting *peace*, (good *assurance* being taken according to the *wisedome* of the *civill State* for *uniformity* of *civill obedience* from all sorts.)

Twelfthly, lastly, true *civility* and *Christianity* may both flourish in a *state* or *Kingdome*, notwithstanding the *permission* of divers and contrary *consciences*, either of *Jew* or *Gentile*.

5

MARYLAND ACT CONCERNING RELIGION 1649

Maryland Archives 1:244–47

An Act concerning Religion

Forasmuch as in a well governed and Xpian Comon Weath matters concerning Religion and the honor of God ought in the first place to bee taken, into serious consideracōn and endeavoured to bee settled. Be it therefore ordered and enacted by the Right Hoble Cecilius Lord Baron of Baltemore absolute Lord and Proprietary of this Province with the advise and consent of this Generall Assembly. That whatsoever pson or psons within this Province and the Islands thereunto belonging shall from henceforth blaspheme God, that is Curse him, or deny our Saviour Jesus Christ to bee the sonne of God, or shall deny the holy Trinity the ffather sonne and holy Ghost, or the Godhead of any of the said Three psons of the Trinity or the Vnity of the Godhead, or shall use or utter any reproachfull Speeches, words or language concerning the said Holy Trinity, or any of the said three psons thereof, shalbe punished with death and confiscatōn or forfeiture of all his or her lands and goods to the Lord Proprietary and his heires, And bee it also Enacted by the Authority and with the advise and assent aforesaid. That whatsoever pson or psons shall from henceforth use or utter any reproachfull words or Speeches concerning the blessed Virgin Mary the Mother of our Saviour or the holy Apostles or Evangelists or any of them shall in such case for the first offence forfeit to the said Lord Proprietary and his heirs Lords and Proprietaries of this Province the sume of ffive pound Sterling or the value thereof to be Levyed on the goods and chattells of every such pson soe offending, but in case such Offender or Offenders, shall not then have goods and chattells sufficient for the satisfyeing of such forfeiture, or that the same bee not otherwise speedily satisfyed that then such Offender or Offenders shalbe publiquely whipt and bee ymprisoned during the pleasure of the Lord Proprietary or the Leivet. or cheife Governor of this Province for the time being. And that every such Offender or Offenders for every second offence shall forfeit tenne pound sterling or the value thereof to bee levyed as aforesaid, or in case such offender or Offenders shall not then haue goods and chattells within this Province sufficient for that purpose then to bee publiquely and severely whipt and imprisoned as before is expressed. And that every pson or psons before mentioned offending herein the third time, shall for such third Offence forfeit all his lands and Goods and bee for ever banished and expelled out of this Province. And be it also further Enacted by the same authority advise and assent that whatsoever pson or psons shall from henceforth vppon any occasion of Offence or otherwise in a reproachful manner or Way declare call or denominate any pson or psons whatsoever inhabiting residing traffiqueing trading or comerceing within this Province or within any the Ports, Harbors, Creeks or Havens to the same belonging an heritick, Scismatick, Idolator, puritan, Independant, Prespiterian popish prest, Jesuite, Jesuited papist, Lutheran, Calvenist, Anabaptist, Brownist, Antinomian, Barrowist, Roundhead, Sepatist, or any other name or terme in a reproachfull manner relating to matter of Religion shall for every such Offence forfeit and loose the some or tenne shillings sterling or the value thereof to bee levyed on the goods and chattells of every such Offender and Offenders, the one half thereof to be forfeited and paid unto the person and persons of whom such reproachfull words are or shalbe spoken or vttered, and the other half thereof to the Lord Proprietary and his heires Lords and Proprietaries of this

Province, But if such pson or psons who shall at any time vtter or speake any such reproachfull words or Language shall not have Goods or Chattells sufficient and overt within this Province to bee taken to satisfie the penalty aforesaid or that the same bee not otherwise speedily satisfyed, that then the pson or persons soe offending shalbe publickly whipt, and shall suffer imprisonmt. without baile or maineprise vntill hee shee or they respectively shall satisfy the party soe offended or greived by such reproachfull Language by asking him or her respectively forgivenes publiquely for such his Offence before the Magistrate or cheife Officer or Officers of the Towne or place where such Offence shalbe given. And be it further likewise Enacted by the Authority and consent aforesaid That every person and persons within this Province that shall at any time hereafter p̄phane the Sabbath or Lords day called Sunday by frequent swearing, drunkennes or by any uncivill or disorderly recreacōn, or by working on that day when absolute necessity doth not require it shall for every such first offence forfeit 2s 6d sterling or the value thereof, and for the second offence 5s sterling or the value thereof, and for the third offence and soe for every time he shall offend in like manner afterwards 10s sterling or the value thereof. And in case such offender and offenders shall not have sufficient goods or chattells within this Province to satisfy any of the said Penalties respectively hereby imposed for prophaning the Sabbath or Lords day called Sunday as aforesaid, That in Every such case the p̄tie soe offending shall for the first and second offence in that kinde be imprisoned till hee or shee shall publickly in open Court before the cheife Commander Judge or Magistrate, of that County Towne or precinct where such offence shalbe committed acknowledg the Scandall and offence he hath in that respect given against God and the good and civill Governemt. of this Province And for the third offence and for every time after shall also bee publickly whipt. And whereas the inforceing of the conscience in matters of Religion hath frequently fallen out to be of dangerous Consequence in those commonwealthes where it hath been practised, And for the more quiett and peaceable governemt. of this Province, and the better to p̄serve mutuall Love and amity amongst the Inhabitants thereof. Be it Therefore also by the Lo: Proprietary with the advise and consent of this Assembly Ordeyned & enacted (except as in this p̄sent Act is before Declared and sett forth) that noe person or psons whatsoever within this Province, or the Islands, Ports, Harbors, Creekes, or havens thereunto belonging professing to beleive in Jesus Christ, shall from henceforth bee any waies troubled, Molested or discountenanced for or in respect of his or her religion nor in the free exercise thereof within this Province or the Islands thereunto belonging nor any way compelled to the beleife or exercise of any other Religion against his or her consent, soe as they be not unfaithfull to the Lord Proprietary, or molest or conspire against the civill Governemt. established or to bee established in this Province vnder him or his heires. And that all & every pson and psons that shall presume Contrary to this Act and the true intent and meaning thereof directly or indirectly either in person or estate willfully to wrong disturbe trouble or molest any

person whatsoever within this Province professing to beleive in Jesus Christ for or in respect of his or her religion or the free exercise thereof within this Province other than is provided for in this Act that such pson or psons soe offending, shalbe compelled to pay trebble damages to the party soe wronged or molested, and for every such offence shall also forfeit 20s sterling in money or the value thereof, half thereof for the vse of the Lo: Proprietary, and his heires Lords and Proprietaries of this Province, and the other half for the vse of the party soe wronged or molested as aforesaid, Or if the ptie soe offending as aforesaid shall refuse or bee vnable to recompense the party soe wronged, or to satisfy such ffyne or forfeiture, then such Offender shalbe severely punished by publick whipping & imprisonmt. during the pleasure of the Lord Proprietary, or his Leivetenāt or cheife Governor of this Province for the tyme being without baile or maineprise And bee it further alsoe Enacted by the authority and consent aforesaid That the Sheriff or other Officer or Officers from time to time to bee appointed & authorized for that purpose, of the County Towne or precinct where every particular offence in this p̄sent Act conteyned shall happen at any time to bee comĩtted and wherevppon there is hereby a fforfeiture ffyne or penalty imposed shall from time to time distraine and seise the goods and estate of every such pson soe offending as aforesaid against this p̄sent Act or any p̄t thereof, and sell the same or any part thereof for the full satisfaccōn of such forfeiture, ffine, or penalty as aforesaid, Restoring vnto the p̄tie soe offending the Remainder or overplus of the said goods or estate after such satisfaccōn soe made as aforesaid

---

6

ROGER WILLIAMS TO THE TOWN OF PROVIDENCE
Jan. 1655
Stokes 1:197–98

That ever I should speak or write a tittle, that tends to such an infinite liberty of conscience, is a mistake, and which I have ever disclaimed and abhorred. To prevent such mistakes, I shall at present only propose this case: There goes many a ship to sea, with many hundred souls in one ship, whose weal and woe is common, and is a true picture of a commonwealth, or a human combination or society. It hath fallen out sometimes, that both papists and protestants, Jews and Turks, may be embarked in one ship; upon which supposal I affirm, that all the liberty of conscience, that ever I pleaded for, turns upon these two hinges—that none of the papists, protestants, Jews, or Turks, be forced to come to the ship's prayers of worship, nor compelled from their own particular prayers or worship, if they practice any. I further add, that I never denied, that notwithstanding this liberty, the commander of this ship ought to command the ship's course, yea, and also command that justice, peace and sobriety, be kept and practiced, both among the seamen and all the passengers. If any of the seamen refuse to perform their services, or passengers to pay their freight; if any refuse to help, in person or purse, towards the common charges or defence; if any refuse to obey the common laws and orders of the ship, concerning their common peace or preservation; if any shall mutiny and rise up against their commanders and officers; if any should preach or write that there ought to be no commanders or officers, because all are equal in Christ, therefore no masters nor officers, no laws nor orders, nor corrections nor punishments;—I say, I never denied, but in such cases, whatever is pretended, the commander or commanders may judge, resist, compel and punish such transgressors, according to their deserts and merits. This if seriously and honestly minded, may, if it so please the Father of lights, let in some light to such as willingly shut not their eyes.

I remain studious of your common peace and liberty.

7

Carolina Fundamental Constitutions of 1669

Thorpe 5:2783–84

Ninety-five. No man shall be permitted to be a freeman of Carolina, or to have any estate or habitation within it, that doth not acknowledge a God; and that God is publicly and solemnly to be worshipped.

Ninety-six. [As the country comes to be sufficiently planted and distributed into fit divisions, it shall belong to the parliament to take care for the building of churches, and the public maintenance of divines, to be employed in the exercise of religion, according to the Church of England; which being the only true and orthodox, and the national religion of all the King's dominions, is so also of Carolina; and, therefore, it alone shall be allowed to receive public maintenance, by grant of parliament.]

Ninety-seven. But since the natives of that place, who will be concerned in our plantation, are utterly strangers to Christianity, whose idolatry, ignorance, or mistake gives us no right to expel or use them ill; and those who remove from other parts to plant there will unavoidably be of different opinions concerning matters of religion, the liberty whereof they will expect to have allowed them, and it will not be reasonable for us, on this account, to keep them out, that civil peace may be maintained amidst diversity of opinions, and our agreement and compact with all men may be duly and faithfully observed; the violation whereof, upon what pretence soever, cannot be without great offence to Almighty God, and great scandal to the true religion which we profess; and also that Jews, heathens, and other dissenters from the purity of Christian religion may not be scared and kept at a distance from it, but, by having an opportunity of acquainting themselves with the truth and reasonableness of its doctrines, and the peaceableness and inoffensiveness of its professors, may, by

good usage and persuasion, and all those convincing methods of gentleness and meekness, suitable to the rules and design of the gospel, be won ever to embrace and unfeignedly receive the truth; therefore, any seven or more persons agreeing in any religion, shall constitute a church or profession, to which they shall give some name, to distinguish it from others.

Ninety-eight. The terms of admittance and communion with any church or profession shall be written in a book, and therein be subscribed by all the members of the said church or profession; which book shall be kept by the public register of the precinct wherein they reside.

Ninety-nine. The time of every one's subscription and admittance shall be dated in the said book or religious record.

One hundred. In the terms of communion of every church or profession, these following shall be three; without which no agreement or assembly of men, upon pretence of religion, shall be accounted a church or profession within these rules:

1st. "That there is a God."

II. "That God is publicly to be worshipped."

III. "That it is lawful and the duty of every man, being thereunto called by those that govern, to bear witness to truth; and that every church or profession shall, in their terms of communion, set down the external way whereby they witness a truth as in the presence of God, whether it be by laying hands on or kissing the bible, as in the Church of England, or by holding up the hand, or any other sensible way."

One hundred and one. No person above seventeen years of age shall have any benefit or protection of the law, or be capable of any place of profit or honor, who is not a member of some church or profession, having his name recorded in some one, and but one religious record at once.

One hundred and two. No person of any other church or profession shall disturb or molest any religious assembly.

One hundred and three. No person whatsoever shall speak anything in their religious assembly irreverently or seditiously of the government or governors, or of state matters.

One hundred and four. Any person subscribing the terms of communion, in the record of the said church or profession, before the precinct register, and any five members of the said church or profession, shall be thereby made a member of the said church or profession.

One hundred and five. Any person striking out his own name out of any religious record, or his name being struck out by any officer thereunto authorized by each church or profession respectively, shall cease to be a member of that church or profession.

One hundred and six. No man shall use any reproachful, reviling, or abusive language against any religion of any church or profession; that being the certain way of disturbing the peace, and of hindering the conversion of any to the truth, by engaging them in quarrels and animosities, to the hatred of the professors and that profession which otherwise they might be brought to assent to.

One hundred and seven. Since charity obliges us to wish well to the souls of all men, and religion ought to alter nothing in any man's civil estate or right, it shall be lawful for slaves, as well as others, to enter themselves, and be of what church or profession any of them shall think best, and, therefore, be as fully members as any freeman. But yet no slave shall hereby be exempted from that civil dominion his master hath over him, but be in all things in the same state and condition he was in before.

One hundred and eight. Assemblies, upon what pretence soever of religion, not observing and performing the above said rules, shall not be esteemed as churches, but unlawful meetings, and be punished as other riots.

One hundred and nine. No person whatsoever shall disturb, molest, or persecute another for his speculative opinions in religion, or his way of worship.

8

KING JAMES II, INSTRUCTIONS TO GOVERNOR THOMAS DONGAN
1682

Stokes 1:166

You shall permit all persons of what Religion soever quietly to inhabit within your Government without giving them any disturbance or disquiet whatsoever for or by reason of their differing Opinions in matters of Religion, Provided they give no disturbance to ye public peace, nor do molest or disquiet others in ye free Exercise of their Religion.

9

PENNSYLVANIA CHARTER OF LIBERTY, LAWS AGREED UPON IN ENGLAND, ETC.
1682

Thorpe 5:3062–63

XXXIV. That all Treasurers, Judges, Masters of the Rolls, Sheriffs, Justices of the Peace, and other officers and persons whatsoever, relating to courts, or trials of causes, or any other service in the government; and all Members elected to serve in provincial Council and General Assembly, and all that have right to elect such Members, shall be such as possess faith in Jesus Christ, and that are not convicted of ill fame, or unsober and dishonest conversation, and that are of twenty-one years of age, at least; and that all such so qualified, shall be capable of the said several employments and privileges, as aforesaid.

XXXV. That all persons living in this province, who confess and acknowledge the one Almighty and eternal God, to be the Creator, Upholder and Ruler of the world;

and that hold themselves obliged in conscience to live peaceably and justly in civil society, shall, in no ways, be molested or prejudiced for their religious persuasion, or practice, in matters of faith and worship, nor shall they be compelled, at any time, to frequent or maintain any religious worship, place or ministry whatever.

XXXVI. That, according to the good example of the primitive Christians, and the ease of the creation, every first day of the week, called the Lord's day, people shall abstain from their common daily labour, that they may the better dispose themselves to worship God according to their understandings.

XXXVII. That as a careless and corrupt administration of justice draws the wrath of God upon magistrates, so the wildness and looseness of the people provoke the indignation of God against a country: therefore, that all such offences against God, as swearing, cursing, lying, prophane talking, drunkenness, drinking of healths, obscene words, incest, sodomy, rapes, whoredom, fornication, and other uncleanness (not to be repeated) all treasons, misprisions, murders, duels, felony, seditions, maims, forcible entries, and other violences, to the persons and estates of the inhabitants within this province; all prizes, stage-players, cards, dice, May-games, gamesters, masques, revels, bull-baitings, cock-fightings, bear-baitings, and the like, which excite the people to rudeness, cruelty, looseness, and irreligion, shall be respectively discouraged, and severely punished, according to the appointment of the Governor and freemen in provincial Council and General Assembly; as also all proceedings contrary to these laws, that are not here made expressly penal.

10

JOHN LOCKE, A LETTER CONCERNING TOLERATION
1689

Montuori 17–25, 31–33, 45, 55, 65–69, 89, 91, 93

Now that the whole jurisdiction of the magistrate reaches only to these civil concernments, and that all civil power, right, and dominion, is bounded and confined to the only care of promoting these things; and that it neither can nor ought in any manner to be extended to the salvation of souls, these following considerations seem unto me abundantly to demonstrate.

First. Because the care of souls is not committed to the civil magistrate, any more than to other men. It is not committed unto him, I say, by God; because it appears not that God has ever given any such authority to one man over another, as to compel any one to his religion. Nor can any such power be vested in the magistrate by the *consent of the people,* because no man can so far abandon the care of his own salvation as blindly to leave to the choice of any other, whether prince or subject, to prescribe to him what faith or worship he shall embrace. For no man can, if he would, conform his faith to the dictates of another. All the life and power of true religion consist in the inward and full persuasion of the mind; and faith is not faith without believing. Whatever profession we make, to whatever outward worship we conform, if we are not fully satisfied in our own mind that the one is true, and the other well pleasing unto God, such profession and such practice, far from being any furtherance, are indeed great obstacles to our salvation. For in this manner, instead of expiating other sins by the exercise of religion, I say, in offering thus unto God Almighty such a worship as we esteem to be displeasing unto him, we add unto the number of our other sins those also of hypocrisy, and contempt of his Divine Majesty.

In the second place. The care of souls cannot belong to the civil magistrate, because his power consists only in outward force; but true and saving religion consists in the inward persuasion of the mind, without which nothing can be acceptable to God. And such is the nature of the understanding, that it cannot be compelled to the belief of anything by outward force. Confiscation of estate, imprisonment, torments, nothing of that nature can have any such efficacy as to make men change the inward judgment that they have framed of things.

It may indeed be alleged that the magistrate may make use of arguments, and thereby draw the heterodox into the way of truth, and procure their salvation. I grant it; but this is common to him with other men. In teaching, instructing, and redressing the erroneous by reason, he may certainly do what becomes any good man to do. Magistracy does not oblige him to put off either humanity or Christianity; but it is one thing to persuade, another to command; one thing to press with arguments, another with penalties. This the civil power alone has a right to do; to the other good-will is authority enough. Every man has commission to admonish, exhort, convince another of error, and, by reasoning, to draw him into truth; but to give laws, receive obedience, and compel with the sword, belongs to none but the magistrate. And upon this ground, I affirm that the magistrate's power extends not to the establishing of any articles of faith, or forms of worship, by the force of his laws. For laws are of no force at all without penalties, and penalties in this case are absolutely impertinent, because they are not proper to convince the mind. Neither the profession of any articles of faith, nor the conformity to any outward form of worship (as has been already said), can be available to the salvation of souls, unless the truth of the one, and the acceptableness of the other unto God, be thoroughly believed by those that so profess and practise. But penalties are no way capable to produce such belief. It is only light and evidence that can work a change in men's opinions; and that light can in no manner proceed from corporal sufferings, or any other outward penalties.

In the third place. The care of the salvation of men's souls cannot belong to the magistrate; because, though the rigour of laws and the force of penalties were capable to convince and change men's minds, yet would not that help at all to the salvation of their souls. For there being but one truth, one way to heaven, what hope is there that more men would be led into it if they had no other rule to follow but the religion of the court, and were put under the necessity to quit the light of their own reason, to oppose the dictates of their own consciences, and blindly to resign themselves up to the will of their governors, and to the religion which either ignorance, ambition, or superstition had chanced to establish in the countries where they were born? In the variety and contradiction of opinions in religion, wherein the princes of the world are as much divided as in their secular interests, the narrow way would be much straitened; one country alone would be in the right, and all the rest of the world put under an obligation of following their princes in the ways that lead to destruction; and that which heightens the absurdity, and very ill suits the notion of a Deity, men would owe their eternal happiness or misery to the places of their nativity.

These considerations, to omit many others that might have been urged to the same purpose, seem unto me sufficient to conclude that all the power of civil government relates only to men's civil interests, is confined to the care of the things of this world, and hath nothing to do with the world to come.

Let us now consider what a church is. A church, then, I take to be a voluntary society of men, joining themselves together of their own accord in order to the public worshipping of God in such manner as they judge acceptable to him, and effectual to the salvation of their souls.

I say it is a free and voluntary society. Nobody is born a member of any church; otherwise the religion of parents would descend unto children by the same right of inheritance as their temporal estates, and every one would hold his faith by the same tenure he does his lands, than which nothing can be imagined more absurd. Thus, therefore, that matter stands. No man by nature is bound unto any particular church or sect, but every one joins himself voluntarily to that society in which he believes he has found that profession and worship which is truly acceptable to God. The hope of salvation, as it was the only cause of his entrance into that communion, so it can be the only reason of his stay there. For if afterwards he discover anything either erroneous in the doctrine or incongruous in the worship of that society to which he has joined himself, why should it not be as free for him to go out as it was to enter? No member of a religious society can be tied with any other bonds but what proceed from the certain expectation of eternal life. A church, then, is a society of members voluntarily uniting to this end.

It follows now that we consider what is the power of this church, and unto what laws it is subject.

Forasmuch as no society, how free soever, or upon whatsoever slight occasion instituted, whether of philosophers for learning, of merchants for commerce, or of men of leisure for mutual conversation and discourse, no church or company, I say, can in the least subsist and hold together, but will presently dissolve and break to pieces, unless it be regulated by some laws, and the members all consent to observe some order. Place and time of meeting must be agreed on; rules for admitting and excluding members must be established; distinction of officers, and putting things into a regular course, and such-like, cannot be omitted. But since the joining together of several members into this church-society, as has already been demonstrated, is absolutely free and spontaneous, it necessarily follows that the right of making its laws can belong to none but the society itself; or, at least (which is the same thing), to those whom the society by common consent has authorized thereunto.

. . . . .

These things being thus determined, let us inquire, in the next place, how far the duty of toleration extends, and what is required from every one by it.

And, first, I hold that no church is bound, by the duty of toleration, to retain any such person in her bosom as, after admonition, continues obstinately to offend against the laws of the society. . . .

Secondly, no private person has any right in any manner to prejudice another person in his civil enjoyments because he is of another church or religion. All the rights and franchises that belong to him as a man, or as a denizen, are inviolably to be preserved to him. These are not the business of religion. No violence nor injury is to be offered him, whether he be Christian or Pagan. Nay, we must not content ourselves with the narrow measures of bare justice; charity, bounty, and liberality must be added to it. This the Gospel enjoins, this reason directs, and this that natural fellowship we are born into requires of us. If any man err from the right way, it is his own misfortune, no injury to thee; nor therefore art thou to punish him in the things of this life because thou supposest he will be miserable in that which is to come.

What I say concerning the mutual toleration of private persons differing from one another in religion, I understand also of particular churches which stand, as it were, in the same relation to each other as private persons among themselves: nor has any one of them any manner of jurisdiction over any other; no, not even when the civil magistrate (as it sometimes happens) comes to be of this or the other communion. For the civil government can give no new right to the church, nor the church to the civil government. So that whether the magistrate join himself to any church, or separate from it, the church remains always as it was before, a free and voluntary society. It neither requires the power of the sword by the magistrate's coming to it, nor does it lose the right of instruction and excommunication by his going from it. This is the fundamental and immutable right of a spontaneous society; that it has power to remove any of its members who transgress the rules of its institution; but it cannot, by the accession of any new members, acquire any right of jurisdiction over those that are not joined with it. And therefore peace, equity, and friendship are always mutually to be observed by particular churches, in the same manner as by private persons, without any pretence of superiority or jurisdiction over one another.

. . . . .

In the last place. Let us now consider *what is the magistrate's duty* in the business of toleration, which certainly is very considerable.

We have already proved that the care of souls does not belong to the magistrate. Not a magisterial care, I mean (if I may so call it), which consists in prescribing by laws and compelling by punishments. But a charitable care, which consists in teaching, admonishing, and persuading, cannot be denied unto any man. The care, therefore, of every man's soul belongs unto himself, and is to be left unto himself. But what if he neglect the care of his soul? I answer: What if he neglect the care of his health or of his estate, which things are nearlier related to the government of the magistrate than the other? Will the magistrate provide by an express law that such a one shall not become poor or sick? Laws provide, as much as is possible, that the goods and health of subjects be not injured by the fraud and violence of others; they do not guard them from the negligence or ill-husbandry of the possessors themselves. No man can be forced to be rich or healthful whether he will or no.

. . . . .

But, after all, the *principal consideration,* and which absolutely determines this controversy, is this: Although the magistrate's opinion in religion be sound, and the way that he appoints be truly evangelical, yet, if I be not thoroughly persuaded thereof in my own mind, there will be no safety for me in following it. No way whatsoever that I shall walk in against the dictates of my conscience will ever bring me to the mansions of the blessed. I may grow rich by an art that I take not delight in, I may be cured of some disease by remedies that I have not faith in; but I cannot be saved by a religion that I distrust, and by a worship that I abhor. It is in vain for an unbeliever to take up the outward show of another man's profession. Faith only, and inward sincerity, are the things that procure acceptance with God. The most likely and most approved remedy can have no effect upon the patient if his stomach reject it as soon as taken; and you will in vain cram a medicine down a sick man's throat, which his particular constitution will be sure to turn into poison. In a word, whatsoever may be doubtful in religion, yet this at least is certain, that no religion which I believe not to be true can be either true or profitable unto me. In vain, therefore, do princes compel their subjects to come into their church communion, under pretence of saving their souls. If they believe, they will come of their own accord; if they believe not, their coming will nothing avail them. How great soever, in fine, may be the pretence of good-will and charity, and concern for the salvation of men's souls, men cannot be forced to be saved whether they will or no. And therefore, when all is done, they must be left to their own consciences.

. . . . .

In the next place: As the magistrate has no power to *impose* by his laws the use of any rites and ceremonies in any church, so neither has he any power to *forbid* the use of such rites and ceremonies as are already received, approved, and practised by any church; because, if he did so, he would destroy the church itself: the end of whose institution is only to worship God with freedom after its own manner.

You will say, by this rule, if some congregations should have a mind to *sacrifice infants,* or (as the primitive Christians were falsely accused) *lustfully pollute themselves in promiscuous uncleanness,* or practise any other such heinous enormities, is the magistrate obliged to tolerate them, because they are committed in a religious assembly? I answer: No. These things are not lawful in the ordinary course of life, nor in any private house; and therefore neither are they so in the worship of God, or in any religious meeting. But, indeed, if any people congregated upon account of religion should be desirous to sacrifice a calf, I deny that that ought to be prohibited by a law. *Melibaeus*, whose calf it is, may lawfully kill his calf at home, and burn any part of it that he thinks fit. For no injury is thereby done to any one, no prejudice to another man's goods. And for the same reason he may kill his calf also in a religious meeting. Whether the doing so be well-pleasing to God or no, it is their part to consider that do it. The part of the magistrate is only to take care that the commonwealth receive no prejudice, and that there be no injury done to any man, either in life or estate. And thus what may be spent on a feast may be spent on a sacrifice. But if peradventure such were the state of things that the interest of the commonwealth required all slaughter of beasts should be forborne for some while, in order to the increasing of the stock of cattle that had been destroyed by some extraordinary murrain, who sees not that the magistrate, in such a case, may forbid all his subjects to kill any calves for any use whatsoever? Only it is to be observed that, in this case, the law is not made about a religious, but a political matter; nor is the sacrifice, but the slaughter of calves, thereby prohibited.

By this we see what difference there is between the church and the commonwealth. Whatsoever is lawful in the commonwealth cannot be prohibited by the magistrate in the church. Whatsoever is permitted unto any of his subjects for their ordinary use, neither can nor ought to be forbidden by him to any sect of people for their religious uses. If any man may lawfully take bread or wine, either sitting or kneeling in his own house, the law ought not to abridge him of the same liberty in his religious worship; though in the church the use of bread and wine be very different, and be there applied to the mysteries of faith and rites of divine worship. But those things that are prejudicial to the commonweal of a people in their ordinary use, and are therefore forbidden by laws, those things ought not to be permitted to churches in their sacred rites. Only the magistrate ought always to be very careful that he do not misuse his authority to the oppression of any church, under pretence of public good.

It may be said: *what if a church be idolatrous, is that also to be tolerated by the magistrate?* In answer, I ask: What power can be given to the magistrate for the suppression of an idolatrous church, which may not in time and place be made use of to the ruin of an orthodox one? For it must be remembered that the civil power is the same everywhere, and the religion of every prince is orthodox to himself. If, therefore, such a power be granted unto the civil magistrate in spirituals, as that at *Geneva* (for example) he may extirpate, by violence and blood, the religion which is there reputed idolatrous, by the same rule another magistrate, in some neighbouring country, may oppress the reformed religion, and, in *India,* the Christian. The civil power can either change everything in religion, according to the prince's pleasure, or it can change noth-

ing. If it be once permitted to introduce anything into religion, by the means of laws and penalties, there can be no bounds put to it; but it will in the same manner be lawful to alter everything, according to that rule of truth which the magistrate has framed unto himself. No man whatsoever ought therefore to be deprived of his terrestrial enjoyments upon account of his religion. Not even *Americans,* subjected unto a Christian prince, are to be punished either in body or goods for not embracing our faith and worship. If they are persuaded that they please God in observing the rites of their own country, and that they shall obtain happiness by that means, they are to be left unto God and themselves.

. . . . .

But to come to particulars. I say, *first,* no opinions contrary to human society, or to those moral rules which are necessary to the preservation of civil society, are to be tolerated by the magistrate.

. . . . .

Again: That church can have no right to be tolerated by the magistrate which is constituted upon such a bottom that all those who enter into it do thereby *ipso facto* deliver themselves up to the protection and service of another prince. For by this means the magistrate would give way to the settling of a foreign jurisdiction in his own country, and suffer his own people to be listed, as it were, for soldiers against his own government.

. . . . .

Lastly, those are not at all to be tolerated who *deny the being of a God.* Promises, covenants, and oaths, which are the bonds of human society, can have no hold upon an atheist. The taking away of God, though but even in thought, dissolves all; besides also, those that by their atheism undermine and destroy all religion, can have no pretence of religion whereupon to challenge the privilege of a toleration. As for other practical opinions, though not absolutely free from all error, yet if they do not tend to establish domination over others, or civil impunity to the church in which they are taught, there can be no reason why they should not be tolerated.

11

DELAWARE CHARTER OF 1701, ARTS. 1, 8
Thorpe 1:558, 560–61

I.

Because no People can be truly happy, though under the greatest Enjoyment of Civil Liberties, if abridged of the Freedom of their Consciences, as to their Religious Profession and Worship: And Almighty God being the only Lord of Conscience, Father of Lights and Spirits; and the Author as well as Object of all divine Knowledge, Faith and Worship, who only doth enlighten the Minds, and persuade and convince the Understandings of People, I do hereby grant and declare, That no Person or Persons, inhabiting in this Province or Territories, who shall confess and acknowledge *One* almighty God, the Creator, Upholder and Ruler of the World; and professes him or themselves obliged to live quietly under the Civil Government, shall be in any Case molested or prejudiced, in his or their Person or Estate, because of his or their consciencious Persuasion or Practice, nor be compelled to frequent or maintain any religious Worship, Place or Ministry, contrary to his or their Mind, or to do or suffer any other Act or Thing, contrary to their religious Persuasion.

And that all Persons who also profess to believe in *Jesus Christ,* the Saviour of the World, shall be capable (notwithstanding their other Persuasions and Practices in Point of Conscience and Religion) to serve this Government in any Capacity, both legislatively and executively, he or they solemnly promising, when lawfully required, Allegiance to the King as Sovereign, and Fidelity to the Proprietary and Governor, and taking the Attests as now established by the Law made at *Newcastle,* in the Year *One Thousand and Seven Hundred,* entitled, *An Act directing the Attests of several Officers and Ministers,* as now amended and confirmed this present Assembly.

VIII.

But, because the Happiness of Mankind depends so much upon the Enjoying of Liberty of their Consciences, as aforesaid, I do hereby solemnly declare, promise and grant, for me, my Heirs and Assigns, That the *First* Article of this Charter relating to Liberty of Conscience, and every Part and Clause therein, according to the true Intent and Meaning thereof, shall be kept and remain, without any Alteration, inviolably for ever.

12

MONTESQUIEU, SPIRIT OF LAWS, BK. 12, CHS. 4, 5;
BK. 24, CHS. 7, 8; BK. 25, CHS. 9, 10, 12
1748

[Book 12]

4.—*That Liberty is favored by the Nature and Proportion of Punishments*

Liberty is in perfection when criminal laws derive each punishment from the particular nature of the crime. There are then no arbitrary decisions; the punishment does not flow from the capriciousness of the legislator, but from the very nature of the thing; and man uses no violence to man.

There are four sorts of crimes. Those of the first species are prejudicial to religion, the second to morals, the third to the public tranquillity, and the fourth to the security of the subject. The punishments inflicted for these crimes ought to proceed from the nature of each of these species.

In the class of crimes that concern religion, I rank only those which attack it directly, such as all simple sacrileges. For as to crimes that disturb the exercise of it, they are of the nature of those which prejudice the tranquillity or security of the subject, and ought to be referred to those classes.

In order to derive the punishment of simple sacrileges from the nature of the thing, it should consist in depriving people of the advantages conferred by religion in expelling them out of the temples, in a temporary or perpetual exclusion from the society of the faithful, in shunning their presence, in execrations, comminations, and conjurations.

In things that prejudice the tranquillity or security of the state, secret actions are subject to human jurisdiction. But in those which offend the Deity, where there is no public act, there can be no criminal matter, the whole passes between man and God, who knows the measure and time of His vengeance. Now if magistrates confounding things should inquire also into hidden sacrileges, this inquisition would be directed to a kind of action that does not at all require it: the liberty of the subject would be subverted by arming the zeal of timorous as well as of presumptuous consciences against him.

The mischief arises from a notion which some people have entertained of revenging the cause of the Deity. But we must honor the Deity and leave him to avenge his own cause. And, indeed, were we to be directed by such a notion, where would be the end of punishments? If human laws are to avenge the cause of an infinite Being, they will be directed by his infinity, and not by the weakness, ignorance, and caprice of man.

An historian of Provence relates a fact which furnishes us with an excellent description of the consequences that may arise in weak capacities from the notion of avenging the Deity's cause. A Jew was accused of having blasphemed against the Virgin Mary; and upon conviction was condemned to be flayed alive. A strange spectacle was then exhibited: gentlemen masked, with knives in their hands, mounted the scaffold, and drove away the executioner, in order to be the avengers themselves of the honor of the blessed Virgin. I do not here choose to anticipate the reflections of the reader.

. . . . .

5.—*Of certain Accusations that require particular Moderation and Prudence*

It is an important maxim, that we ought to be very circumspect in the prosecution of witchcraft and heresy. The accusation of these two crimes may be vastly injurious to liberty, and productive of infinite oppression, if the legislator knows not how to set bounds to it. For as it does not directly point at a person's actions, but at his character, it grows dangerous in proportion to the ignorance of the people; and then a man is sure to be always in danger, because the most exceptional conduct, the purest morals, and the constant practice of every duty in life are not a sufficient security against the suspicion of his being guilty of the like crimes.

Under Manuel Comnenus, the Protestator was accused

of having conspired against the emperor, and of having employed for that purpose some secrets that render men invisible. It is mentioned in the life of this emperor that Aaron was detected, as he was poring over a book of Solomon's, the reading of which was sufficient to conjure up whole legions of devils. Now by supposing a power in witchcraft to rouse the infernal spirits to arms, people look upon a man whom they call a sorcerer as the person in the world most likely to disturb and subvert society; and, of course, they are disposed to punish him with the utmost severity.

But their indignation increases when witchcraft is supposed to have the power of subverting religion. The history of Constantinople informs us that in consequence of a revelation made to a bishop of a miracle having ceased because of the magic practices of a certain person, both that person and his son were put to death. On how many surprising things did not this single crime depend? That revelations should not be uncommon, that the bishop should be favored with one, that it was real, that there had been a miracle in the case, that this miracle had ceased, that there was an art magic, that magic could subvert religion, that this particular person was a magician, and, in fine, that he had committed that magic act.

The Emperor Theodorus Lascarus attributed his illness to witchcraft. Those who were accused of this crime had no other resource left than to handle a red-hot iron without being hurt. Thus among the Greeks a person ought to have been a sorcerer to be able to clear himself of the imputation of witchcraft. Such was the excess of their stupidity that to the most dubious crime in the world they joined the most dubious proofs of innocence.

Under the reign of Philip the Long, the Jews were expelled from France, being accused of having poisoned the springs with their lepers. So absurd an accusation ought to make us doubt all those that are founded on public hatred.

I have not here asserted that heresy ought not to be punished; I said only that we ought to be extremely circumspect in punishing it.

[Book 24]

7.—Of the Laws of Perfection in Religion

Human laws, made to direct the will, ought to give precepts, and not counsels; religion, made to influence the heart, should give many counsels, and few precepts.

When, for instance, it gives rules, not for what is good, but for what is better; not to direct to what is right, but to what is perfect; it is expedient that these should be counsels, and not laws: for perfection can have no relation to the universality of men or things. Besides, if these were laws, there would be a necessity for an infinite number of others, to make people observe the first. Celibacy was advised by Christianity; when they made it a law in respect to a certain order of men, it became necessary to make new ones every day, in order to oblige those men to observe it. The legislator wearied himself, and he wearied society, to make men execute by precept what those who love perfection would have executed as counsel.

8.—Of the Connection between the moral Laws and those of Religion

In a country so unfortunate as to have a religion that God has not revealed, it is necessary for it to be agreeable to morality; because even a false religion is the best security we can have of the probity of men.

The principal points of religion of the inhabitants of Pegu are, not to commit murder, not to steal, to avoid uncleanliness, not to give the least uneasiness to their neighbor, but to do him, on the contrary, all the good in their power. With these rules they think they should be saved in any religion whatsoever. Hence it proceeds that those people, though poor and proud, behave with gentleness and compassion to the unhappy.

[Book 25]

9.—Of Toleration in point of Religion

We are here politicians, and not divines; but the divines themselves must allow that there is a great difference between tolerating and approving a religion.

When the legislator has believed it a duty to permit the exercise of many religions, it is necessary that he should enforce also a toleration among these religions themselves. It is a principle that every religion which is persecuted becomes itself persecuting; for as soon as by some accidental turn it arises from persecution, it attacks the religion which persecuted it; not as religion, but as tyranny.

It is necessary, then, that the laws require from the several religions, not only that they shall not embroil the state, but that they shall not raise disturbances among themselves. A citizen does not fulfil the laws by not disturbing the government; it is requisite that he should not trouble any citizen whomsoever.

10.—The same Subject continued

As there are scarcely any but persecuting religions that have an extraordinary zeal for being established in other places (because a religion that can tolerate others seldom thinks of its own propagation), it must, therefore, be a very good civil law, when the state is already satisfied with the established religion, not to suffer the establishment of another.

This is then a fundamental principle of the political laws in regard to religion; that when the state is at liberty to receive or to reject a new religion it ought to be rejected; when it is received it ought to be tolerated.

. . . . .

12.—Of penal Laws

Penal laws ought to be avoided in respect to religion: they imprint fear, it is true; but as religion has also penal laws which inspire the same passion, the one is effaced by the other, and between these two different kinds of fear the mind becomes hardened.

The threatenings of religion are so terrible, and its promises so great, that when they actuate the mind, whatever efforts the magistrate may use to oblige us to re-nounce it, he seems to leave us nothing when he deprives us of the exercise of our religion, and to bereave us of nothing when we are allowed to profess it.

It is not, therefore, by filling the soul with the idea of this great object, by hastening her approach to that critical moment in which it ought to be of the highest importance, that religion can be most successfully attacked: a more certain way is, to tempt her by favors, by the conveniences of life, by hopes of fortune; not by that which revives, but by that which extinguishes the sense of her duty; not by that which shocks her, but by that which throws her into indifference at the time when other passions actuate the mind, and those which religion inspires are hushed into silence. As a general rule in changing a religion the invitations should be much stronger than the penalties.

The temper of the human mind has appeared even in the nature of punishments. If we take a survey of the persecutions in Japan, we shall find that they were more shocked at cruel torments than at long sufferings, which rather weary than affright, which are the more difficult to surmount, from their appearing less difficult.

In a word, history sufficiently informs us that penal laws have never had any other effect than to destroy.

13

PATRICK HENRY, RELIGIOUS TOLERANCE
1766

Stokes 1:311–12

Much learning hath been displayed to show the necessity of establishing one church in England in the present form. But these reasonings do not reach the case of this colony. . . .

. . . A general toleration of Religion appears to me the best means of peopling our country, and enabling our people to procure those necessarys among themselves, the purchase of which from abroad has so nearly ruined a colony, enjoying, from nature and time, the means of becoming the most prosperous on the continent. . . .

. . . When I say that the article of religion is deemed a trifle by our people in the general, I assert a known truth. But when we suppose that the poorer sort of European emigrants set as light by it, we are greatly mistaken. The free exercise of religion hath stocked the Northern part of the continent with inhabitants; and altho' Europe hath in great measure adopted a more moderate policy, yet the profession of Protestantism is extremely inconvenient in many places there. A Calvinist, a Lutheran, or Quaker, who hath felt these inconveniences in Europe, sails not to Virginia, where they are felt perhaps in a (greater degree).

14

BENJAMIN FRANKLIN, LETTER TO THE
LONDON PACKET
3 June 1772

Papers 19:163–68

I Understand from the public papers, that in the debates on the bill for relieving the Dissenters in the point of subscription to the Church Articles, sundry reflections were thrown out against that people, importing, "that they themselves are of a persecuting intolerant spirit, for that when they had here the superiority they persecuted the church, and still persecute it in America, where they compel its members to pay taxes for maintaining the Presbyterian or independent worship, and at the same time refuse them a toleration in the full exercise of their religion by the administrations of a bishop."

If we look back into history for the character of present sects in Christianity, we shall find few that have not in their turns been persecutors, and complainers of persecution. The primitive Christians thought persecution extremely wrong in the Pagans, but practised it on one another. The first Protestants of the Church of England, blamed persecution in the Roman church, but practised it against the Puritans: these found it wrong in the Bishops, but fell into the same practice themselves both here and in New England. To account for this we should remember, that the doctrine of *toleration* was not then known, or had not prevailed in the world. Persecution was therefore not so much the fault of the sect as of the times. It was not in those days deemed wrong *in itself*. The general opinion was only, that those *who are in error* ought not to persecute *the truth*: But the *possessors of truth* were in the right to persecute *error*, in order to destroy it. Thus every sect believing itself possessed of *all truth*, and that every tenet differing from theirs was *error*, conceived that when the power was in their hands, persecution was a duty required of them by that God whom they supposed to be offended with heresy. By degrees more moderate *and more modest* sentiments have taken place in the Christian world; and among Protestants particularly all disclaim persecution, none vindicate it, and few practise it. We should then cease to reproach each other with what was done by our ancestors, but judge of the present character of sects or churches by their *present conduct* only.

Now to determine on the justice of this charge against the present dissenters, particularly those in America, let us consider the following facts. They went from England to establish a new country for themselves, *at their own expence*, where they might enjoy the free exercise of religion in their own way. When they had purchased the territory of the natives, they granted the lands out in townships, requiring for it neither purchase-money nor quit-rent, but this condition only to be complied with, that the freeholders should for ever support a gospel minister (meaning probably one of the then governing sects) and a free-school within the township. Thus, what is commonly called Presbyterianism became the *established religion* of that country. All went on well in this way while the same religious opinions were general, the support of minister and school being raised by a proportionate tax on the lands. But in process of time, some becoming Quakers, some Baptists, and, of late years some returning to the Church of England (through the laudable endeavours and a *proper application* of their funds by the society for propagating the gospel) objections were made to the payment of a tax appropriated to the support of a church they disapproved and had forsaken. The civil magistrates, however, continued for a time to collect and apply the tax according to the original laws which remained in force; and they did it the more freely, as thinking it just and equitable that the holders of lands should pay what was contracted to be paid when they were granted, as the only consideration for the grant, and what had been considered by all subsequent purchasers as a perpetual incumbrance on the estate, bought therefore at a proportionably cheaper rate; a payment which it was thought no honest man ought to avoid under the pretence of his having changed his religious persuasion. And this I suppose is one of the best grounds of demanding tythes of dissenters now in England. But the practice being clamoured against by the episcopalians as persecution, the legislature of the Province of the Massachusets-Bay, near thirty years since, passed an act for their relief, requiring indeed the tax to be paid as usual, but directing that the several sums levied from members of the Church of England, should be paid over to the Minister of that Church, with whom such members usually attended divine worship, which Minister had power given him to receive and on occasion *to recover the same by law.*

It seems that legislature considered the *end* of the tax was, to secure and improve the morals of the people, and promote their happiness, by supporting among them the public worship of God and the preaching of the gospel; that where particular people fancied a particular mode, that mode might probably therefore be of most use to those people; and that if the good was done, it was not so material in what mode or by whom it was done. The consideration that their brethren the dissenters in England were still compelled to pay tythes to the clergy of the Church, had not weight enough with the legislature to prevent this moderate act, which still continues in full force, and I hope no uncharitable conduct of the church toward the dissenters will ever provoke them to repeal it.

With regard to a bishop, I know not upon what ground the dissenters, either here or in America, are charged with refusing the benefit of such an officer to the church in that country. *Here* they seem to have naturally no concern in the affair. *There* they have no power to prevent it, if government should think fit to send one. They would probably *dislike,* indeed, to see an order of men established among them, from whose persecutions their fathers fled into that wilderness, and whose future domination they may possibly fear, *not knowing that their natures are changed.* But the non-appointment of bishops for America seems to arise from another quarter. The same wisdom of government, probably, that prevents the sitting of convocations, and forbids, by *noli prosequi's,* the persecution of Dissenters for non-subscription, avoids establishing bishops where the minds of people are not yet prepared to receive them cordially, lest the public peace should be endangered.

And now let us see how this *persecution-account* stands between the parties.

In New-England, where the legislative bodies are almost to a man Dissenters from the Church of England,

1. There is no test to prevent Churchmen holding offices.

2. The sons of Churchmen have the full benefit of the Universities.

3. The taxes for support of public worship, when paid by Churchmen, are given to the Episcopal minister.

In Old England,

1. Dissenters are excluded from all offices of profit and honour.

2. The benefits of education in the Universities are appropriated to the sons of Churchmen.

3. The clergy of the Dissenters receive none of the tythes paid by their people, who must be at the additional charge of maintaining their own separate worship.

But it is said, the Dissenters of America *oppose* the introduction of a Bishop.

In fact, it is not alone the Dissenters there that give the opposition (if *not encouraging* must be termed *opposing*) but the laity in general dislike the project, and some even of the clergy. The inhabitants of Virginia are almost all Episcopalians. The Church is fully established there, and the Council and General Assembly are perhaps to a man its members, yet when lately at a meeting of the clergy, a resolution was taken to apply for a Bishop, against which several however protested; the assembly of the province at their next meeting, expressed their disapprobation of the thing in the strongest manner, by unanimously ordering the thanks of the house to the protesters: for many of the American laity of the church think it some advantage, whether their own young men come to England for ordination, and improve themselves at the same time by conversation with the learned here, or the congregations are supplied by Englishmen, who have had the benefit of education in English universities, and are ordained before they come abroad. They do not therefore see the necessity of a Bishop merely for ordination, and confirmation is among them deemed a ceremony of no very great importance, since few seek it in England where Bishops are in plenty. These sentiments prevail with many churchmen there, not to promote a design, which they think must sooner or later saddle them with great expences to support it. As to the Dissenters, their minds might probably be more conciliated to the measure, if the Bishops here should, in their wisdom and goodness, think fit to set their sacred character in a more friendly light, by dropping their opposition to the Dissenters application for relief in subscription, and declaring their willingness that Dissenters should be capable of offices, enjoy the benefit of education in the universities, and the privilege of appropriating their tythes to the support of their own clergy. In all these points of toleration, they appear far behind the present Dissenters of New-England, and it may seem to some a step below the dignity of Bishops, to follow the example of such inferiors. I do not, however, despair of their doing it some time or other, since nothing of the kind is too hard for *true christian humility.* I am, Sir, your's, &c.

A NEW-ENGLAND-MAN.

15

SAMUEL ADAMS, THE RIGHTS OF THE COLONISTS
20 Nov. 1772

Writings 2:352–53

As neither reason requires, nor religeon permits the contrary, every Man living in or out of a state of civil society, has a right peaceably and quietly to worship God according to the dictates of his conscience.—

"Just and true liberty, equal and impartial liberty" in matters spiritual and temporal, is a thing that all Men are clearly entitled to, by the eternal and immutable laws Of God and nature, as well as by the law of Nations, & all well grounded municipal laws, which must have their foundation in the former.—

In regard to Religeon, mutual tolleration in the different professions thereof, is what all good and candid minds in all ages have ever practiced; and both by precept and example inculcated on mankind: And it is now generally agreed among christians that this spirit of toleration in the fullest extent consistent with the being of civil society "is the chief characteristical mark of the true church"* & In so much that Mr. Lock has asserted, and proved beyond the possibility of contradiction on any solid ground, that such toleration ought to be extended to all whose doctrines are not subversive of society. The only Sects which he thinks ought to be, and which by all wise laws are excluded from such toleration, are those who teach Doctrines subversive of the Civil Government under which they live. The Roman Catholicks or Papists are excluded by reason of such Doctrines as these "that Princes excommunicated may be deposed, and those they call *Hereticks* may be destroyed without mercy; besides their recognizing the Pope in so absolute a manner, in subversion of Government, by introducing as far as possible into the states, under whose protection they enjoy life, liberty and property, that solecism in politicks, Imperium in imperio† leading directly to the worst anarchy and confusion, civil discord, war and blood shed—

The natural liberty of Men by entring into society is abridg'd or restrained so far only as is necessary for the Great end of Society the best good of the whole—

*See Locks Letters on Toleration.
†A Government within a Government—

16

JAMES MADISON TO WILLIAM BRADFORD
24 Jan. 1774

Papers 1:106

I want again to breathe your free Air. I expect it will mend my Constitution & confirm my principles. I have indeed as good an Atmosphere at home as the Climate will allow: but have nothing to brag of as to the State and Liberty of my Country. Poverty and Luxury prevail among all sorts: Pride ignorance and Knavery among the Priesthood and Vice and Wickedness among the Laity. This is bad enough But It is not the worst I have to tell you. That diabolical Hell conceived principle of persecution rages among some and to their eternal Infamy the Clergy can furnish their Quota of Imps for such business. This vexes me the most of any thing whatever. There are at this [time?] in the adjacent County not less than 5 or 6 well meaning men in close [Gaol] for publishing their religious Sentiments which in the main are very orthodox. I have neither patience to hear talk or think of any thing relative to this matter, for I have squabbled and scolded abused and ridiculed so long about it, [to so lit]tle purpose that I am without common patience. So I [leave you] to pity me and pray for Liberty of Conscience [to revive among us.]

17

WILLIAM BRADFORD TO JAMES MADISON
4 Mar. 1774

Madison Papers 1:109

I am sorry to hear that Persecution has got so much footing among you. The discription you give of your Country makes me more in love with mine. Indeed I have ever looked on America as the land of freedom when compared with the rest of the world, but compared with the rest of america Tis Pennsylvania that is so. Persecution is a weed that grows not in our happy soil: and I do no[t] remember that any Person was ever imprisoned here for his religious sentiments however heritical or unepiscopal they might be. Liberty (As Caspipina says in his Letters) [is] the Genius of Pennsylvania; and it[s] inhabitants think speak and act with a freedom unknow[n]—I do indeed pity you; & long to see you according to your own expression, "breathing our purer air." The Synod will meet here about the middle of may. You will then have an opportunity of seeing most of your Nassovian friends, and higthing the felicity that friends long seperated enjoy when they meet.

18

JAMES MADISON TO WILLIAM BRADFORD
1 Apr. 1774
Papers 1:112–13

Our Assembly is to meet the first of May When It is expected something will be done in behalf of the Dissenters: Petitions I hear are already forming among the Persecuted Baptists and I fancy it is in the thoughts of the Presbyterians also to intercede for greater liberty in matters of Religion. For my part I can not help being very doubtful of their succeeding in the Attempt. The Affair was on the Carpet during the last Session; but such incredible and extravagant stories were told in the House of the monstrous effects of the Enthusiasm prevalent among the Sectaries and so greedily swallowed by their Enemies that I believe they lost footing by it and the bad name they still have with those who pretend too much contempt to examine into their principles and Conduct and are too much devoted to the ecclesiastical establishment to hear of the Toleration of Dissentients, I am apprehensive, will be again made a pretext for rejecting their requests. The Sentiments of our people of Fortune & fashion on this subject are vastly different from what you have been used to. That liberal catholic and equitable way of thinking as to the rights of Conscience, which is one of the Characteristics of a free people and so strongly marks the People of your province is but little known among the Zealous adherents to our Hierarchy. We have it is true some persons in the Legislature of generous Principles both in Religion & Politicks but number, not merit, you know, is necessary to carry points there. Besides[,] the Clergy are a numerous and powerful body[,] have great influence at home by reason of their connection with & dependence on the Bishops and Crown and will naturally employ all their art & Interest to depress their rising Adversaries; for such they must consider dissenters who rob them of the good will of the people and may in time endanger their livings & security.

You are happy in dwelling in a Land where those inestimable privileges are fully enjoyed and public has long felt the good effects of their religious as well as Civil Liberty. Foreigners have been encouraged to settle amg. you. Industry and Virtue have been promoted by mutual emulation and mutual Inspection, Commerce and the Arts have flourished and I can not help attributing those continual exertions of Gen[i]us which appear among you to the inspiration of Liberty and that love of Fame and Knowledge which always accompany it. Religious bondage shackles and debilitates the mind and unfits it for every noble enterprize every expanded prospect. How far this is the Case with Virginia will more clearly appear when the ensuing Trial is made.

19

CONTINENTAL CONGRESS TO THE PEOPLE OF
GREAT BRITAIN
21 Oct. 1774
Journals 1:83, 87–88

That we think the Legislature of Great-Britain is not authorized by the constitution to establish a religion, fraught with sanguinary and impious tenets, or, to erect an arbitrary form of government, in any quarter of the globe. These rights, we, as well as you, deem sacred. And yet sacred as they are, they have, with many others been repeatedly and flagrantly violated.

. . . . .

And by another Act the dominion of Canada is to be so extended, modelled, and governed, as that by being disunited from us, detached from our interests, by civil as well as religious prejudices, that by their numbers daily swelling with Catholic emigrants from Europe, and by their devotion to Administration, so friendly to their religion, they might become formidable to us, and on occasion, be fit instruments in the hands of power, to reduce the ancient free Protestant Colonies to the same state of slavery with themselves.

This was evidently the object of the Act:—And in this view, being extremely dangerous to our liberty and quiet, we cannot forebear complaining of it, as hostile to British America.—Superadded to these considerations, we cannot help deploring the unhappy condition to which it has reduced the many English settlers, who, encouraged by the Royal Proclamation, promising the enjoyment of all their rights, have purchased estates in that country.—They are now the subjects of an arbitrary government, deprived of trial by jury, and when imprisoned cannot claim the benefit of the habeas corpus Act, that great bulwark and palladium of English liberty:—Nor can we suppress our astonishment, that a British Parliament should ever consent to establish in that country a religion that has deluged your island in blood, and dispersed bigotry, persecution, murder and rebellion through every part of the world.

20

CONTINENTAL CONGRESS TO THE INHABITANTS OF
THE PROVINCE OF QUEBEC
26 Oct. 1774
Journals 1:105–13

Friends and fellow-subjects,
We, the Delegates of the Colonies of New-Hampshire, Massachusetts-Bay, Rhode-Island and Providence Planta-

tions, Connecticut, New-York, New-Jersey, Pennsylvania, the Counties of Newcastle Kent and Sussex on Delaware, Maryland, Virginia, North-Carolina and South-Carolina, deputed by the inhabitants of the said Colonies, to represent them in a General Congress at Philadelphia, in the province of Pennsylvania, to consult together concerning the best methods to obtain redress of our afflicting grievances, having accordingly assembled, and taken into our most serious consideration the state of public affairs on this continent, have thought proper to address your province, as a member therein deeply interested.

When the fortune of war, after a gallant and glorious resistance, had incorporated you with the body of English subjects, we rejoiced in the truly valuable addition, both on our own and your account; expecting, as courage and generosity are naturally united, our brave enemies would become our hearty friends, and that the Divine Being would bless to you the dispensations of his over-ruling providence, by securing to you and your latest posterity the inestimable advantages of a free English constitution of government, which it is the privilege of all English subjects to enjoy.

These hopes were confirmed by the King's proclamation, issued in the year 1763, plighting the public faith for your full enjoyment of those advantages.

Little did we imagine that any succeeding Ministers would so audaciously and cruelly abuse the royal authority, as to with-hold from you the fruition of the irrevocable rights, to which you were thus justly entitled.

But since we have lived to see the unexpected time, when Ministers of this flagitious temper, have dared to violate the most sacred compacts and obligations, and as you, educated under another form of government, have artfully been kept from discovering the unspeakable worth of *that* form you are now undoubtedly entitled to, we esteem it our duty, for the weighty reasons herein after mentioned, to explain to you some of its most important branches.

"In every human society," says the celebrated Marquis *Beccaria*, "there is an *effort, continually tending* to confer on one part the heighth of power and happiness, and to reduce the other to the extreme of weakness and misery. The intent of good laws is to *oppose this effort,* and to diffuse their influence *universally* and *equally*."

Rulers stimulated by this pernicious "effort," and subjects animated by the just "intent of opposing good laws against it," have occasioned that vast variety of events, that fill the histories of so many nations. All these histories demonstrate the truth of this simple position, that to live by the will of one man, or sett of men, is the production of misery to all men.

On the solid foundation of this principle, Englishmen reared up the fabrick of their constitution with such a strength, as for ages to defy time, tyranny, treachery, internal and foreign wars: And, as an illustrious author of your nation, hereafter mentioned, observes,—"They gave the people of their Colonies, the form of their own government, and this government carrying prosperity along with it, they have grown great nations in the forests they were sent to inhabit."

In this form, the first grand right, is that of the people having a share in their own government by their representatives chosen by themselves, and, in consequence, of being ruled by *laws*, which they themselves approve, not by *edicts* of *men* over whom they have no controul. This is a bulwark surrounding and defending their property, which by their honest cares and labours they have acquired, so that no portions of it can legally be taken from them, but with their own full and free consent, when they in their judgment deem it just and necessary to give them for public service, and precisely direct the easiest, cheapest, and most equal methods, in which they shall be collected.

The influence of this right extends still farther. If money is wanted by Rulers, who have in any manner oppressed the people, they may retain it, until their grievances are redressed; and thus peaceably procure relief, without trusting to despised petitions, or disturbing the public tranquillity.

The next great right is that of trial by jury. This provides, that neither life, liberty nor property, can be taken from the possessor, until twelve of his unexceptionable countrymen and peers of his vicinage, who from that neighbourhood may reasonably be supposed to be acquainted with his character, and the characters of the witnesses, upon a fair trial, and full enquiry, face to face, in open Court, before as many of the people as chuse to attend, shall pass their sentence upon oath against him; a sentence that cannot injure him, without injuring their own reputation, and probably their interest also; as the question may turn on points, that, in some degree, concern the general welfare; and if it does not, their verdict may form a precedent, that, on a similar trial of their own, may militate against themselves.

Another right relates merely to the liberty of the person. If a subject is seized and imprisoned, tho' by order of Government, he may, by virtue of this right, immediately obtain a writ, termed a Habeas Corpus, from a Judge, whose sworn duty it is to grant it, and thereupon procure any illegal restraint to be quickly enquired into and redressed.

A fourth right, is that of holding lands by the tenure of easy rents, and not by rigorous and oppressive services, frequently forcing the possessors from their families and their business, to perform what ought to be done, in all well regulated states, by men hired for the purpose.

The last right we shall mention, regards the freedom of the press. The importance of this consists, besides the advancement of truth, science, morality, and arts in general, in its diffusion of liberal sentiments on the administration of Government, its ready communication of thoughts between subjects, and its consequential promotion of union among them, whereby oppressive officers are shamed or intimidated, into more honourable and just modes of conducting affairs.

These are the invaluable rights, that form a considerable part of our mild system of government; that, sending its equitable energy through all ranks and classes of men, defends the poor from the rich, the weak from the powerful, the industrious from the rapacious, the peaceable from the violent, the tenants from the lords, and all from their superiors.

These are the rights, without which a people cannot be free and happy, and under the protecting and encouraging influence of which, these colonies have hitherto so amazingly flourished and increased. These are the rights, a profligate Ministry are now striving, by force of arms, to ravish from us, and which we are, with one mind, resolved never to resign but with our lives.

These are the rights *you* are entitled to and ought at this moment in perfection, to exercise. And what is offered to you by the late Act of Parliament in their place? Liberty of conscience in your religion? No. God gave it to you; and the temporal powers with which you have been and are connected, firmly stipulated for your enjoyment of it. If laws, divine and human, could secure it against the despotic caprices of wicked men, it was secured before. Are the French laws in *civil* cases restored? *It seems so.* But observe the cautious kindness of the Ministers, who pretend to be your benefactors. The words of the statute are—that those "laws shall be the rule, until they shall be *varied* or *altered* by any ordinances of the Governor and Council." Is the "certainty and lenity of the *criminal* law of England, and its benefits and advantages," commended in the said statute, and said to "have been sensibly felt by you," secured to you and your descendants? No. They too are subjected to arbitrary "*alterations*" by the Governor and Council; and a power is expressly reserved of appointing "such courts of *criminal, civil,* and *ecclesiastical* jurisdiction, as shall be thought proper." Such is the precarious tenure of mere *will,* by which you hold your lives and religion. The Crown and its Ministers are impowered, as far as they could be by Parliament, to establish even the *Inquisition* itself among you. Have you an Assembly composed of worthy men, elected by yourselves, and in whom you can confide, to make laws for you, to watch over your welfare, and to direct in what quantity, and in what manner, your money shall be taken from you? No. The power of making laws for you is lodged in the governor and council, all of them dependent upon, and removeable at, the *pleasure* of a Minister. Besides, another late statute, made without your consent, has subjected you to the impositions of *Excise,* the horror of all free states; thus wresting your property from you by the most odious of taxes, and laying open to insolent tax-gatherers, houses, the scenes of domestic peace and comfort, and called the castles of English subjects in the books of their law. And in the very act for altering your government, and intended to flatter you, you are not authorized to "assess, levy, or apply any *rates* and *taxes,* but for the inferior purposes of *making roads,* and erecting and repairing *public buildings,* or for other *local* conveniences, within your respective towns and districts." Why this degrading distinction? Ought not the property, honestly acquired by *Canadians,* to be held as sacred as that of *Englishmen?* Have not Canadians sense enough to attend to any other public affairs, than gathering stones from one place, and piling them up in another? Unhappy people! who are not only injured, but insulted. Nay more!—With such a superlative contempt of your understanding and spirit, has an insolent Ministry presumed to think of you, our respectable fellow-subjects, according to the information we have received, as firmly to perswade themselves that your gratitude, for the injuries and insults they have recently offered to you, will engage you to take up arms, and render yourselves the ridicule and detestation of the world, by becoming tools, in their hands, to assist them in taking that freedom from *us,* which they have treacherously denied to *you;* the unavoidable consequence of which attempt, if successful, would be the extinction of all hopes of you or your posterity being ever restored to freedom: For idiocy itself cannot believe, that, when their drudgery is performed, they will treat you with less cruelty than they have us, who are of the same blood with themselves.

What would your countryman, the immortal *Montesquieu,* have said to such a plan of domination, as has been framed for you? Hear his words, with an intenseness of thought suited to the importance of the subject.—"In a free state, every man, who is supposed a free agent, *ought to be concerned in his own government:* Therefore the *legislative* should reside in the whole body of the *people,* or their representatives."—"The political liberty of the subject is *a tranquillity of mind,* arising from the opinion each person has of his *safety.* In order to have this liberty, it is requisite the government be so constituted, as that one man need not be *afraid* of another. When the power of *making* laws, and the power of *executing* them, are *united* in the same person, or in the same body of Magistrates, *there can be no liberty;* because apprehensions may arise, lest the same *Monarch* or *Senate,* should *enact* tyrannical laws, to *execute* them in a tyrannical manner."

"The power of *judging* should be exercised by persons taken from the *body of the people,* at certain times of the year, and pursuant to a form and manner prescribed by law. *There is no liberty,* if the power of *judging* be not *separated* from the *legislative* and *executive* powers."

"Military men belong to a profession, which *may be* useful, but *is often* dangerous."—"The enjoyment of liberty, and even its support and preservation, consists in every man's being allowed to speak his thoughts, and lay open his sentiments."

Apply these decisive maxims, sanctified by the authority of a name which all Europe reveres, to your own state. You have a Governor, it may be urged, vested with the *executive* powers, or the powers of *administration:* In him, and in your Council, is lodged the power of *making laws.* You have *Judges,* who are to *decide* every cause affecting your lives, liberty or property. Here is, indeed, an appearance of the several powers being *separated* and *distributed* into *different* hands, for checks one upon another, the only effectual mode ever invented by the wit of men, to promote their freedom and prosperity. But scorning to be illuded by a tinsel'd outside, and exerting the natural sagacity of Frenchmen, *examine* the specious device, and you will find it, to use an expression of holy writ, "a whited sepulchre," for burying your lives, liberty and property.

Your *Judges,* and your *Legislative Council,* as it is called, are *dependant* on your *Governor,* and *he* is *dependant* on the servant of the Crown, in Great-Britain. The *legislative, executive* and *judging* powers are *all* moved by the nods of a

Minister. Privileges and immunities last no longer than his smiles. When he frowns, their feeble forms dissolve. Such a treacherous ingenuity has been exerted in drawing up the code lately offered you, that every sentence, beginning with a benevolent pretension, concludes with a destructive power; and the substance of the whole, divested of its smooth words, is—that the Crown and its Ministers shall be as absolute throughout your extended province, as the despots of Asia or Africa. What can protect your property from taxing edicts, and the rapacity of necessitous and cruel masters? your persons from Letters de Cachet, gaols, dungeons, and oppressive services? your lives and general liberty from arbitrary and unfeeling rulers? We defy you, casting your view upon every side, to discover a single circumstance, promising from any quarter the faintest hope of liberty to you or your posterity, but from an entire adoption into the union of these Colonies.

What advice would the truly great man before-mentioned, that advocate of freedom and humanity, give you, was he now living, and knew that we, your numerous and powerful neighbours, animated by a just love of our invaded rights, and united by the indissoluble bands of affection and interest, called upon you, by every obligation of regard for yourselves and your children, as we now do, to join us in our righteous contest, to make common cause with us therein, and take a noble chance for emerging from a humiliating subjection under Governors, Intendants, and Military Tyrants, into the firm rank and condition of English freemen, whose custom it is, derived from their ancestors, to make those tremble, who dare to think of making them miserable?

Would not this be the purport of his address? "Seize the opportunity presented to you by Providence itself. You have been conquered into liberty, if you act as you ought. This work is not of man. You are a small people, compared to those who with open arms invite you into a fellowship. A moment's reflection should convince you which will be most for your interest and happiness, to have all the rest of North-America your unalterable friends, or your inveterate enemies. The injuries of Boston have roused and associated every colony, from Nova-Scotia to Georgia. Your province is the only link wanting, to compleat the bright and strong chain of union. Nature has joined your country to theirs. Do you join your political interests. For their own sakes, they never will desert or betray you. Be assured, that the happiness of a people inevitably depends on their liberty, and their spirit to assert it. The value and extent of the advantages tendered to you are immense. Heaven grant you may not discover them to be blessings after they have bid you an eternal adieu."

We are too well acquainted with the liberality of sentiment distinguishing your nation, to imagine, that difference of religion will prejudice you against a hearty amity with us. You know, that the transcendant nature of freedom elevates those, who unite in her cause, above all such low-minded infirmities. The Swiss Cantons furnish a memorable proof of this truth. Their union is composed of Roman Catholic and Protestant States, living in the utmost concord and peace with one another, and thereby enabled, ever since they bravely vindicated their freedom, to defy and defeat every tyrant that has invaded them.

Should there be any among you, as there generally are in all societies, who prefer the favours of Ministers, and their own private interests, to the welfare of their country, the temper of such selfish persons will render them incredibly active in opposing all public-spirited measures, from an expectation of being well rewarded for their sordid industry, by their superiors; but we doubt not you will be upon your guard against such men, and not sacrifice the liberty and happiness of the whole Canadian people and their posterity, to gratify the avarice and ambition of individuals.

We do not ask you, by this address, to commence acts of hostility against the government of our common Sovereign. We only invite you to consult your own glory and welfare, and not to suffer yourselves to be inveigled or intimidated by infamous ministers so far, as to become the instruments of their cruelty and despotism, but to unite with us in one social compact, formed on the generous principles of equal liberty, and cemented by such an exchange of beneficial and endearing offices as to render it perpetual. In order to complete this highly desirable union, we submit it to your consideration, whether it may not be expedient for you to meet together in your several towns and districts, and elect Deputies, who afterwards meeting in a provincial Congress, may chuse Delegates, to represent your province in the continental Congress to be held at Philadelphia on the tenth day of May, 1775.

In this present Congress, beginning on the fifth of the last month, and continued to this day, it has been, with universal pleasure and an unanimous vote, resolved, That we should consider the violation of your rights, by the act for altering the government of your province, as a violation of our own, and that you should be invited to accede to our confederation, which has no other objects than the perfect security of the natural and civil rights of all the constituent members, according to their respective circumstances, and the preservation of a happy and lasting connection with Great-Britain, on the salutary and constitutional principles herein before mentioned. For effecting these purposes, we have addressed an humble and loyal petition to his Majesty, praying relief of our and your grievances; and have associated to stop all importations from Great-Britain and Ireland, after the first day of December, and all exportations to those Kingdoms and the West-Indies, after the tenth day of next September, unless the said grievances are redressed.

That Almighty God may incline your minds to approve our equitable and necessary measures, to add yourselves to us, to put your fate, whenever you suffer injuries which you are determined to oppose, not on the small influence of your single province, but on the consolidated powers of North-America, and may grant to our joint exertions an event as happy as our cause is just, is the fervent prayer of us, your sincere and affectionate friends and fellow-subjects.

21

ISAAC BACKUS, A HISTORY OF NEW ENGLAND
1774–75
Stokes 1:307–9

To the Honorable Delegates of the several colonies in North America, met in a general Congress in Philadelphia:

Honorable Gentlemen: As the Antipaedobaptist churches in New England are most heartily concerned for the preservation and defense of the rights and privileges of this country, and are deeply affected by the encroachments upon the same, which have lately been made by the British parliament, and are willing to unite with our dear countrymen, vigorously to pursue every prudent measure for relief, so we would beg leave to say that, as a distinct denomination of Protestants, we conceive that we have an equal claim to charter-rights with the rest of our fellow-subjects; and yet have long been denied the free and full enjoyment of those rights, as to the support of religious worship. Therefor we, the elders and brethren of twenty Baptist churches met in Association at Medfield, twenty miles from Boston, September 14, 1774, have unanimously chosen and sent unto you the reverend and beloved Mr. Isaac Backus as our agent, to lay our case, in these respects, before you, or otherwise to use all the prudent means he can for our relief. . . .

It may now be asked, *What is the liberty desired?* The answer is: As the kingdom of Christ is not of this world, and religion is a concern between God and the soul, with which no human authority can intermeddle, consistently with the principles of Christianity, and according to the dictates of Protestantism, we claim and expect the liberty of worshipping God according to our consciences, not being obliged to support a ministry we cannot attend, whilst we demean ourselves as faithful subjects. These we have an undoubted right to, as men, as Christians, and by charter as inhabitants of Massachusetts Bay. . . .

John Adams made a long speech and Samuel Adams another; both of whom said, "There is, indeed, an ecclesiastical establishment in our province; but a very slender one, hardly to be called an establishment." When they would permit, we brought up facts, which they tried to explain away, but could not. Then they shifted their plea, and asserted that our General Court was clear of blame, and had always been ready to hear our complaints, and to grant all reasonable help, whatever might have been done by executive officers; and S. Adams and R. T. Paine spent near an hour more on this plea. When they stopped, I told them I was very sorry to have any accusations to bring against the government which I belonged to, and which I would gladly serve to the utmost of my power, but I must say that facts proved the contrary to their plea; and gave a short account of our Legislature's treatment of Ashfield, which was very puzzling to them. In their plea, S. Adams tried to represent that *regular* Baptists were quite easy among us; and more than once insinuated that these complaints came from enthusiasts who made it a merit to suffer persecution; and also that enemies had a hand therein. Paine said, there was nothing of conscience in the matter; it was only a contending about paying a little money; and also that we would not be neighborly and let them know who we were, which was all they wanted, and they would readily exempt us.

In answer, I told them they might call it enthusiasm or what they pleased; but I freely own, before all these gentlemen, that it is absolutely a point of conscience with me; for I cannot give in the certificates they require without implicitly acknowledging that power in man which I believe belongs only to God. This shocked them; and Cushing said: "*It quite altered the case;* for if it were a point of conscience, he had nothing to say to that." And the conference of about four hours continuance, closed with their promising to do what they could for our relief; though to deter us from thinking of their coming upon equal footing with us as to religion, John Adams at one time said, we might as well expect a change in the solar system, as to expect they would give up their establishment.

1775 Resolution to the Massachusetts Assembly:

Our real grievances are, that we, as well as our fathers, have, from time to time, been taxed on religious accounts where we were not represented; and when we have sued for our rights, our causes have been tried by interested judges. That the Representatives in former Assemblies, as well as the present, were elected by virtue only of civil and worldly qualifications, is a truth so evident, that we presume it need not be proved to this Assembly; and for a civil Legislature to impose religious taxes, is, we conceive, a power which their constituents never had to give; and is therefore going entirely out of their jurisdiction. . . . Under the legal dispensation, where God himself prescribed the exact proportion of what the people were to give, yet none but persons of the worst characters ever attempted to *take it by force.* I Sam. ii. 12, 16; Mic. iii. 5–9. How daring then, must it be for any to do it for Christ's ministers, who says, *My kingdom is not of this world!* . . . We beseech this honorable Assembly to take these matters into their wise and serious consideration, before him who has said, With what measure ye mete it shall be measured to you again. Is not all America now appealing to heaven against the injustice of being taxed where we are not represented, and against being judged by men who are interested in getting away our money? And will heaven approve of your *doing the same thing* to your fellow servants? No, surely. . . . We have no desire of representing this government as the worst of any who have imposed religious taxes; we fully believe the contrary. Yet, as we are persuaded that an entire freedom from being taxed by civil rulers to religious worship, is not a mere favor, from any man or men in the world, but a right and property granted us by God, who commands us to stand fast in it, we have not only the same reason to refuse an acknowledgement of such a taxing power here, as America has the above-said power, but also, according to our present light, we should wrong our consciences in allowing that power to men, which we believe belongs only to God.

22

John Adams, Novanglus, no. 4
13 Feb. 1775
Papers 2:265–67

It is true that the people of this country in general, and of this province in special, have an hereditary apprehension of and aversion to lordships temporal and spiritual. Their ancestors fled to this wilderness to avoid them—they suffer'd sufficiently under them in England. And there are few of the present generation who have not been warned of the danger of them by their fathers or grandfathers, and injoined to oppose them. And neither Bernard nor Oliver ever dared to avow before them, the designs which they had certainly formed to introduce them. Nor does Massachusettensis dare to avow his opinion in their favour. I don't mean that such avowal would expose their persons to danger, but their characters and writings to universal contempt.

When you were told that the people of England were depraved, the parliament venal, and the ministry corrupt, were you not told most melancholly truths? Will Massachusettensis deny any of them? Does not every man who comes from England, whig or tory, tell you the same thing? Do they make any secret of it, or use any delicacy about it? Do they not most of them avow that corruption is so established there, as to be incurable, and a necessary instrument of government? Is not the British constitution arrived nearly to that point, where the Roman republic was when Jugurtha left it, and pronounc'd it a venal city ripe for destruction, if it can only find a purchaser? If Massachusettensis can prove that it is not, he will remove from my mind, one of the heaviest loads which lies upon it.

Who has censured the tories for remissness, I know not. Whoever it was, he did them great injustice. Every one that I know of that character, has been thro' the whole tempestuous period, as indefatigable as human nature will admit, going about seeking whom he might devour, making use of art, flattery, terror, temptation and alurement, in every shape in which human wit could dress it up, in public and private. But all to no purpose. The people have grown more and more weary of them every day, untill now the land mourns under them.

Massachusettensis is then seized with a violent fit of anger at the clergy. It is curious to observe the conduct of the Tories towards this sacred body. If a clergyman preaches against the principles of the revolution, and tells the people that upon pain of damnation they must submit to an established government of whatever character, the Tories cry him up as an excellent man, and a wonderful preacher, invite him to their tables, procure him missions from the society, and chaplainships to the navy, and flatter him with the hopes of lawn sleeves. But if a clergyman preaches Christianity, and tells the magistrates that they were not distinguished from their brethren for their pri-

vate emolument, but for the good of the people, that the people are bound in conscience to obey a good government, but are not bound to submit to one that aims at destroying all the ends of government—Oh Sedition! Treason!

The clergy in all ages and countries, and in this in particular, are disposed enough to be on the side of government, as long as it is tolerable: If they have not been generally in the late administrations on that side, it is demonstration that the late administration has been universally odious.

The clergy of this province are a virtuous, sensible and learned set of men, and they don't take their sermons from news-papers but the bible, unless it be a few who preach passive obedience. These are not generally curious enough to read Hobbs.

It is the duty of the clergy to accommodate their discourses to the times, to preach against such sins as are most prevalent, and recommend such virtues as are most wanted. For example, if exorbitant ambition, and venality are predominant, ought they not to warn their hearers against these vices? If public spirit is much wanted, should they not inculcate this great virtue? If the rights and duties of christian magistrates and subjects are disputed, should they not explain them, shew their nature, ends, limitations and restrictions, how much soever it may move the gall of Massachusettensis?

Let me put a supposition. Justice is a great christian as well as moral duty and virtue, which the clergy ought to inculcate and explain. Suppose a great man of a parish should for seven years together receive 600 sterling a year, for discharging the duties of an important office; but during the whole time, should never do one act or take one step about it. Would not this be great injustice to the public? And ought not the parson of the parish to cry aloud and spare not, and shew such a bold transgressor his sin? Shew that justice was due to the public as well as to an individual, and that cheating the public of four thousand two hundred pounds sterling, is at least as great a sin as taking a chicken from a private hen roost, or perhaps a watch from a fob!

Then we are told that news-papers and preachers have excited outrages disgraceful to humanity. Upon this subject I will venture to say, that there have been outrages in this province which I neither justify, excuse or extenuate; but these were not excited, that I know of, by news-papers or sermons. That however, if we run through the last ten years, and consider all the tumults and outrages that have happened, and at the same time recollect the insults, provocations, and oppressions which this people have endured; we shall find the two characteristicks of this people, religion and humanity, strongly marked on all their proceedings, not a life, nor that I have ever heard, a single limb has been lost thro' the whole. I will take upon me to say, there is not another province on this continent, nor in his majesty's dominions, where the people, under the same indignities, would not have gone greater lengths. Consider the tumults in the three kingdoms, consider the tumults in ancient Rome, in the most virtuous of her periods, and compare them with ours. It is a saying of Machiavel, which no wise man ever contradicted, which has been literally verified in this province that "while the mass of the people is not corrupted, tumults do no hurt." By which he means, that they leave no lasting ill effects behind.

23

Edmund Burke, Speech on Conciliation
with the Colonies
22 Mar. 1775
Works 1:464–71

In this character of the Americans, a love of freedom is the predominating feature which marks and distinguishes the whole: and as an ardent is always a jealous affection, your colonies become suspicious, restive, and untractable, whenever they see the least attempt to wrest from them by force, or shuffle from them by chicane, what they think the only advantage worth living for. This fierce spirit of liberty is stronger in the English colonies probably than in any other people of the earth; and this from a great variety of powerful causes; which, to understand the true temper of their minds, and the direction which this spirit takes, it will not be amiss to lay open somewhat more largely.

First, the people of the colonies are descendants of Englishmen. England, Sir, is a nation, which still I hope respects, and formerly adored, her freedom. The colonists emigrated from you when this part of your character was most predominant; and they took this bias and direction the moment they parted from your hands. They are therefore not only devoted to liberty, but to liberty according to English ideas, and on English principles. Abstract liberty, like other mere abstractions, is not to be found. Liberty inheres in some sensible object; and every nation has formed to itself some favourite point, which by way of eminence becomes the criterion of their happiness. It happened, you know, Sir, that the great contests for freedom in this country were from the earliest times chiefly upon the question of taxing. Most of the contests in the ancient commonwealths turned primarily on the right of election of magistrates; or on the balance among the several orders of the state. The question of money was not with them so immediate. But in England it was otherwise. On this point of taxes the ablest pens, and most eloquent tongues, have been exercised; the greatest spirits have acted and suffered. In order to give the fullest satisfaction concerning the importance of this point, it was not only necessary for those who in argument defended the excellence of the English constitution, to insist on this privilege of granting money as a dry point of fact, and to prove, that the right had been acknowledged in ancient parchments, and blind usages, to reside in a certain body called a House of Commons. They went much farther; they attempted to prove, and they succeeded, that in theory it ought to be so, from the particular nature of a House of Commons, as an immediate representative of the people; whether the old records had delivered this oracle or not. They took infinite pains to inculcate, as a fundamental principle, that in all monarchies the people must in effect themselves, mediately or immediately, possess the power of granting their own money, or no shadow of liberty could subsist. The colonies draw from you, as with their life-blood, these ideas and principles. Their love of liberty, as with you, fixed and attached on this specific point of taxing. Liberty might be safe, or might be endangered, in twenty other particulars, without their being much pleased or alarmed. Here they felt its pulse; and as they found that beat, they thought themselves sick or sound. I do not say whether they were right or wrong in applying your general arguments to their own case. It is not easy indeed to make a monopoly of theorems and corollaries. The fact is, that they did thus apply those general arguments; and your mode of governing them, whether through lenity or indolence, through wisdom or mistake, confirmed them in the imagination, that they, as well as you, had an interest in these common principles.

They were further confirmed in this pleasing error by the form of their provincial legislative assemblies. Their governments are popular in a high degree; some are merely popular; in all, the popular representative is the most weighty; and this share of the people in their ordinary government never fails to inspire them with lofty sentiments, and with a strong aversion from whatever tends to deprive them of their chief importance.

If anything were wanting to this necessary operation of the form of government, religion would have given it a complete effect. Religion, always a principle of energy, in this new people is no way worn out or impaired; and their mode of professing it is also one main cause of this free spirit. The people are Protestants; and of that kind which is the most adverse to all implicit submission of mind and opinion. This is a persuasion not only favourable to liberty, but built upon it. I do not think, Sir, that the reason of this averseness in the dissenting churches, from all that looks like absolute government, is so much to be sought in their religious tenets, as in their history. Every one knows that the Roman Catholic religion is at least coeval with most of the governments where it prevails; that it has generally gone hand in hand with them, and received great favour and every kind of support from authority. The Church of England too was formed from her cradle under the nursing care of regular government. But the dissenting interests have sprung up in direct opposition to all the ordinary powers of the world; and could justify that opposition only on a strong claim to natural liberty. Their very existence depended on the powerful and unremitted assertion of that claim. All Protestantism, even the most cold and passive, is a sort of dissent. But the religion most prevalent in our northern colonies is a refinement on the principle of resistance; it is the dissidence of dissent, and the Protestantism of the Protestant religion. This religion, under a variety of denominations agreeing in nothing but in the communion of the spirit of liberty, is predominant in most of the northern provinces; where the Church of England, notwithstanding its legal rights, is in reality no more than a sort of private sect, not composing most probably the tenth of the people. The colonists left England when this spirit was high, and in the emigrants was the highest of all; and even that stream of foreigners, which has been constantly flowing into these colonies, has, for the greatest part, been composed of dissenters from the establishments of their several countries, and have brought with them a temper and character far from alien to that of the people with whom they mixed.

Sir, I can perceive by their manner, that some gentlemen object to the latitude of this description; because in the southern colonies the Church of England forms a large body, and has a regular establishment. It is certainly true. There is, however, a circumstance attending these colonies, which, in my opinion, fully counterbalances this difference, and makes the spirit of liberty still more high and haughty than in those to the northward. It is, that in Virginia and the Carolinas they have a vast multitude of slaves. Where this is the case in any part of the world, those who are free, are by far the most proud and jealous of their freedom. Freedom is to them not only an enjoyment, but a kind of rank and privilege. Not seeing there, that freedom, as in countries where it is a common blessing, and as broad and general as the air, may be united with much abject toil, with great misery, with all the exterior of servitude, liberty looks, amongst them, like something that is more noble and liberal. I do not mean, Sir, to commend the superior morality of this sentiment, which has at least as much pride as virtue in it; but I cannot alter the nature of man. The fact is so; and these people of the southern colonies are much more strongly, and with a higher and more stubborn spirit, attached to liberty, than those to the northward. Such were all the ancient commonwealths; such were our Gothic ancestors; such in our days were the Poles; and such will be all masters of slaves, who are not slaves themselves. In such a people, the haughtiness of domination combines with the spirit of freedom, fortifies it, and renders it invincible.

Permit me, Sir, to add another circumstance in our colonies, which contributes no mean part towards the growth and effect of this untractable spirit. I mean their education. In no country perhaps in the world is the law so general a study. The profession itself is numerous and powerful; and in most provinces it takes the lead. The greater number of the deputies sent to the congress were lawyers. But all who read, and most do read, endeavour to obtain some smattering in that science. I have been told by an eminent bookseller, that in no branch of his business, after tracts of popular devotion, were so many books as those on the law exported to the plantations. The colonists have now fallen into the way of printing them for their own use. I hear that they have sold nearly as many of Blackstone's Commentaries in America as in England. General Gage marks out this disposition very particularly in a letter on your table. He states, that all the people in his government are lawyers, or smatterers in law; and that in Boston they have been enabled, by successful chicane, wholly to evade many parts of one of your capital penal constitutions. The smartness of debate will say, that this knowledge ought to teach them more clearly the rights of legislature, their obligations to obedience, and the penalties of rebellion. All

this is mighty well. But my honourable and learned friend on the floor, who condescends to mark what I say for animadversion, will disdain that ground. He has heard, as well as I, that when great honours and great emoluments do not win over this knowledge to the service of the state, it is a formidable adversary to government. If the spirit be not tamed and broken by these happy methods, it is stubborn and litigious. *Abeunt studia in mores.* This study renders men acute, inquisitive, dexterous, prompt in attack, ready in defence, full of resources. In other countries, the people, more simple, and of a less mercurial cast, judge of an ill principle in government only by an actual grievance; here they anticipate the evil, and judge of the pressure of the grievance by the badness of the principle. They augur misgovernment at a distance; and snuff the approach of tyranny in every tainted breeze.

The last cause of this disobedient spirit in the colonies is hardly less powerful than the rest, as it is not merely moral, but laid deep in the natural constitution of things. Three thousand miles of ocean lie between you and them. No contrivance can prevent the effect of this distance in weakening government. Seas roll, and months pass, between the order and the execution; and the want of a speedy explanation of a single point is enough to defeat a whole system. You have, indeed, winged ministers of vengeance, who carry your bolts in their pounces to the remotest verge of the sea. But there a power steps in, that limits the arrogance of raging passions and furious elements, and says, "So far shalt thou go, and no farther." Who are you, that should fret and rage, and bite the chains of nature?—Nothing worse happens to you than does to all nations who have extensive empire; and it happens in all the forms into which empire can be thrown. In large bodies, the circulation of power must be less vigorous at the extremities. Nature has said it. The Turk cannot govern Egypt, and Arabia, and Curdistan, as he governs Thrace; nor has he the same dominion in Crimea and Algiers, which he has at Brusa and Smyrna. Despotism itself is obliged to truck and huckster. The Sultan gets such obedience as he can. He governs with a loose rein, that he may govern at all; and the whole of the force and vigour of his authority in his centre is derived from a prudent relaxation in all his borders. Spain, in her provinces, is, perhaps, not so well obeyed as you are in yours. She complies too; she submits; she watches times. This is the immutable condition, the eternal law, of extensive and detached empire.

Then, Sir, from these six capital sources; of descent; of form of government; of religion in the northern provinces; of manners in the southern; of education; of the remoteness of situation from the first mover of government; from all these causes a fierce spirit of liberty has grown up. It has grown with the growth of the people in your colonies, and increased with the increase of their wealth; a spirit, that unhappily meeting with an exercise of power in England, which, however lawful, is not reconcilable to any ideas of liberty, much less with theirs, has kindled this flame that is ready to consume us.

I do not mean to commend either the spirit in this excess, or the moral causes which produce it. Perhaps a more smooth and accommodating spirit of freedom in them would be more acceptable to us. Perhaps ideas of liberty might be desired, more reconcilable with an arbitrary and boundless authority. Perhaps we might wish the colonists to be persuaded, that their liberty is more secure when held in trust for them by us (as their guardians during a perpetual minority) than with any part of it in their own hands. The question is, not whether their spirit deserves praise or blame, but—what, in the name of God, shall we do with it? You have before you the object, such as it is, with all its glories, with all its imperfections on its head. You see the magnitude; the importance; the temper; the habits; the disorders. By all these considerations we are strongly urged to determine something concerning it. We are called upon to fix some rule and line for our future conduct, which may give a little stability to our politics, and prevent the return of such unhappy deliberations as the present. Every such return will bring the matter before us in a still more untractable form. For, what astonishing and incredible things have we not seen already! What monsters have not been generated from this unnatural contention! Whilst every principle of authority and resistance has been pushed, upon both sides, as far as it would go, there is nothing so solid and certain, either in reasoning or in practice, that has not been shaken. Until very lately, all authority in America seemed to be nothing but an emanation from yours. Even the popular part of the colony constitution derived all its activity, and its first vital movement, from the pleasure of the crown. We thought, Sir, that the utmost which the discontented colonists could do, was to disturb authority; we never dreamt they could of themselves supply it; knowing in general what an operose business it is to establish a government absolutely new. But having, for our purposes in this contention, resolved, that none but an obedient assembly should sit; the humours of the people there, finding all passage through the legal channel stopped, with great violence broke out another way. Some provinces have tried their experiment, as we have tried ours; and theirs has succeeded. They have formed a government sufficient for its purposes, without the bustle of a revolution, or the troublesome formality of an election. Evident necessity, and tacit consent, have done the business in an instant. So well they have done it, that Lord Dunmore (the account is among the fragments on your table) tells you, that the new institution is infinitely better obeyed than the ancient government ever was in its most fortunate periods. Obedience is what makes government, and not the names by which it is called; not the name of governor, as formerly, or committee, as at present. This new government has originated directly from the people; and was not transmitted through any of the ordinary artificial media of a positive constitution. It was not a manufacture ready formed, and transmitted to them in that condition from England. The evil arising from hence is this; that the colonists having once found the possibility of enjoying the advantages of order in the midst of a struggle for liberty, such struggles will not henceforward seem so terrible to the settled and sober part of mankind as they had appeared before the trial.

Pursuing the same plan of punishing by the denial of the exercise of government to still greater lengths, we wholly abrogated the ancient government of Massachusetts. We were confident that the first feeling, if not the very prospect of anarchy, would instantly enforce a complete submission. The experiment was tried. A new, strange, unexpected face of things appeared. Anarchy is found tolerable. A vast province has now subsisted, and subsisted in a considerable degree of health and vigour, for near a twelvemonth, without governor, without public council, without judges, without executive magistrates. How long it will continue in this state, or what may arise out of this unheard-of situation, how can the wisest of us conjecture? Our late experience has taught us that many of those fundamental principles, formerly believed infallible, are either not of the importance they were imagined to be; or that we have not at all adverted to some other far more important and far more powerful principles, which entirely overrule those we had considered as omnipotent. I am much against any further experiments, which tend to put to the proof any more of these allowed opinions, which contribute so much to the public tranquillity. In effect, we suffer as much at home by this loosening of all ties, and this concussion of all established opinions, as we do abroad. For, in order to prove that the Americans have no right to their liberties, we are every day endeavouring to subvert the maxims which preserve the whole spirit of our own. To prove that the Americans ought not to be free, we are obliged to depreciate the value of freedom itself; and we never seem to gain a paltry advantage over them in debate, without attacking some of those principles, or deriding some of those feelings, for which our ancestors have shed their blood.

24

THOMAS PAINE, COMMON SENSE
10 Jan. 1776
Life 2:162–63

As to religion, I hold it to be the indispensible duty of every government, to protect all conscientious professors thereof, and I know of no other business which government hath to do therewith. Let a man throw aside that narrowness of soul, that selfishness of principle, which the niggards of all professions are so unwilling to part with; and he will be at once delivered of his fears on that head. Suspicion is the companion of mean souls, and the bane of all good society. For myself, I fully and conscientiously believe, that it is the will of the Almighty, that there should be a diversity of religious opinions among us: it affords a larger field for our Christian kindness. Were we all of one way of thinking, our religious dispositions would want matter for probation; and on this liberal principle, I look on the various denominations among us, to be like children of the same family, differing only, in what is called, their Christian names.

25

VIRGINIA DECLARATION OF RIGHTS, SEC. 16
12 June 1776

16. That religion, or the duty which we owe to our CRE-ATOR, and the manner of discharging it, can be directed only by reason and conviction, not by force or violence; and therefore all men are equally entitled to the free exercise of religion, according to the dictates of conscience; and that it is the mutual duty of all to practice Christian forbearance, love, and charity, towards each other.

26

DELAWARE DECLARATION OF RIGHTS AND FUNDAMENTAL RULES
11 Sept. 1776
Sources 338

2. That all Men have a natural and unalienable Right to worship Almighty God according to the Dictates of their own Consciences and Understandings; that no Man ought or of Right can be compelled to attend any religious Worship or maintain any Ministry contrary to or against his own free Will and Consent, and that no Authority can or ought to be vested in, or assumed by any Power whatever that shall in any Case interfere with, or in any Manner controul the Right of Conscience in the Free Exercise of Religious Worship.

3. That all Persons professing the Christian Religion ought forever to enjoy equal Rights and Privileges in this State, unless, under Colour of Religion, any Man disturb the Peace, the Happiness or Safety of Society.

27

MARYLAND CONSTITUTION OF 1776, DECLARATION OF RIGHTS, NOS. 33–36
Thorpe 3:1689–90

XXXIII. That, as it is the duty of every man to worship God in such manner as he thinks most acceptable to him; all persons, professing the Christian religion, are equally entitled to protection in their religious liberty; wherefore no person ought by any law to be molested in his person or estate on account of his religious persuasion or profession, or for his religious practice; unless, under colour of religion, any man shall disturb the good order, peace or safety of the State, or shall infringe the laws of morality, or injure others, in their natural, civil, or religious rights; nor ought any person to be compelled to frequent or maintain, or contribute, unless on contract, to maintain any particular place of worship, or any particular ministry; yet the Legislature may, in their discretion, lay a general and equal tax, for the support of the Christian religion; leaving to each individual the power of appointing the payment over of the money, collected from him, to the support of any particular place of worship or minister, or for the benefit of the poor of his own denomination, or the poor in general of any particular county: but the churches, chapels, glebes, and all other property now belonging to the church of England, ought to remain to the church of England forever. And all acts of Assembly, lately passed, for collecting monies for building or repairing particular churches or chapels of ease, shall continue in force, and be executed, unless the Legislature shall, by act, supersede or repeal the same: but no county court shall assess any quantity of tobacco, or sum of money, hereafter, on the application of any vestry-men or church-wardens; and every encumbent of the church of England, who hath remained in his parish, and performed his duty, shall be entitled to receive the provision and support established by the act, entitled "An act for the support of the clergy of the church of England, in this Province," till the November court of this present year, to be held for the county in which his parish shall lie, or partly lie, or for such time as he hath remained in his parish, and performed his duty.

XXXIV. That every gift, sale, or devise of lands, to any minister, public teacher, or preacher of the gospel, as such, or to any religious sect, order or denomination, or to or for the support, use or benefit of, or in trust for, any minister, public teacher, or preacher of the gospel, as such, or any religious sect order or denomination—and every gift or sale of goods, or chattels, to go in succession, or to take place after the death of the seller or donor, or to or for such support, use or benefit—and also every devise of goods or chattels to or for the support, use or benefit of any minister, public teacher, or preacher of the gospel, as such, or any religious sect, order, or denomination, without the leave of the Legislature, shall be void; except always any sale, gift, lease or devise of any quantity of land, not exceeding two acres, for a church, meeting, or other house of worship, and for a burying-ground, which shall be improved, enjoyed or used only for such purpose—or such sale, gift, lease, or devise, shall be void.

XXXV. That no other test or qualification ought to be required, on admission to any office of trust or profit, than such oath of support and fidelity to this State, and such oath of office, as shall be directed by this Convention, or the Legislature of this State, and a declaration of a belief in the Christian religion.

XXXVI. That the manner of administering an oath to any person, ought to be such, as those of the religious persuasion, profession, or denomination, of which such person is one, generally esteem the most effectual confirmation, by the attestation of the Divine Being. And that the people called Quakers, those called Dunkers, and those called Menonists, holding it unlawful to take an oath on any occasion, ought to be allowed to make their solemn affirmation, in the manner that Quakers have been here-tofore allowed to affirm; and to be of the same avail as an oath, in all such cases, as the affirmation of Quakers hath been allowed and accepted within this State, instead of an oath. And further, on such affirmation, warrants to search for stolen goods, or for the apprehension or commitment of offenders, ought to be granted, or security for the peace awarded, and Quakers, Dunkers or Menonists ought also, on their solemn affirmation as aforesaid, to be admit-ted as witnesses, in all criminal cases not capital.

28

NEW JERSEY CONSTITUTION OF 1776, ARTS. 18, 19

Thorpe 5:2597–98

XVIII. That no person shall ever, within this Colony, be deprived of the inestimable privilege of worshipping Al-mighty God in a manner agreeable to the dictates of his own conscience; nor, under any pretence whatever, be compelled to attend any place of worship, contrary to his own faith and judgment; nor shall any person, within this Colony, ever be obliged to pay tithes, taxes, or any other rates, for the purpose of building or repairing any other church or churches, place or places of worship, or for the maintenance of any minister or ministry, contrary to what he believes to be right, or has deliberately or voluntarily engaged himself to perform.

XIX. That there shall be no establishment of any one religious sect in this Province, in preference to another; and that no Protestant inhabitant of this Colony shall be denied the enjoyment of any civil right, merely on account of his religious principles; but that all persons, professing a belief in the faith of any Protestant sect, who shall de-mean themselves peaceably under the government, as hereby established, shall be capable of being elected into any office of profit or trust, or being a member of either branch of the Legislature, and shall fully and freely enjoy every privilege and immunity, enjoyed by others their fel-low subjects.

29

NORTH CAROLINA CONSTITUTION OF 1776, ARTS. 19, 31–32, 34

Thorpe 5:2788, 2793

[Declaration of Rights]

XIX. That all men have a natural and unalienable right to worship Almighty God according to the dictates of their own consciences.

[Constitution]

XXXI. That no clergyman, or preacher of the gospel, of any denomination, shall be capable of being a member of either the Senate, House of Commons, or Council of State, while he continues in the exercise of the pastoral function.

XXXII. That no person, who shall deny the being of God or the truth of the Protestant religion, or the divine authority either of the Old or New Testaments, or who shall hold religious principles incompatible with the free-dom and safety of the State, shall be capable of holding any office or place of trust or profit in the civil department within this State. . . .

XXXIV. That there shall be no establishment of any one religious church or denomination in this State, in preference to any other; neither shall any person, on any pretence whatsoever, be compelled to attend any place of worship contrary to his own faith or judgment, nor be obliged to pay, for the purchase of any glebe, or the build-ing of any house of worship, or for the maintenance of any minister or ministry, contrary to what he believes right, or has voluntarily and personally engaged to per-form; but all persons shall be at liberty to exercise their own mode of worship:—*Provided,* That nothing herein contained shall be construed to exempt preachers of trea-sonable or seditious discourses, from legal trial and pun-ishment.

30

PENNSYLVANIA CONSTITUTION OF 1776, DECLARATION OF RIGHTS

Thorpe 5:3082, 3083

II. That all men have a natural and unalienable right to worship Almighty God according to the dictates of their own consciences and understanding: And that no man ought or of right can be compelled to attend any religious worship, or erect or support any place of worship, or maintain any ministry, contrary to, or against, his own free will and consent: Nor can any man, who acknowledges the being of a God, be justly deprived or abridged of any civil right as a citizen, on account of his religious sentiments or peculiar mode of religious worship: And that no authority can or ought to be vested in, or assumed by any power whatever, that shall in any case interfere with, or in any manner controul, the right of conscience in the free exer-cise of religious worship.

. . . . .

VIII. That every member of society hath a right to be protected in the enjoyment of life, liberty and property, and therefore is bound to contribute his proportion to-wards the expence of that protection, and yield his per-sonal service when necessary, or an equivalent thereto: But no part of a man's property can be justly taken from him, or applied to public uses, without his own consent, or that of his legal representatives: Nor can any man who is conscientiously scrupulous of bearing arms, be justly compelled thereto, if he will pay such equivalent, nor are the people bound by any laws, but such as they have in like manner assented to, for their common good.

31

ADAM SMITH, WEALTH OF NATIONS,
BK. 5, CH. 1, PT. 3, ART. 3
1776

Of the Expence of the Institutions for the Instruction of People of all Ages

The institutions for the instruction of people of all ages are chiefly those for religious instruction. This is a species of instruction of which the object is not so much to render the people good citizens in this world, as to prepare them for another and a better world in a life to come. The teachers of the doctrine which contains this instruction, in the same manner as other teachers, may either depend altogether for their subsistence upon the voluntary contributions of their hearers; or they may derive it from some other fund to which the law of their country may entitle them; such as a landed estate, a tythe or land tax, an established salary or stipend. Their exertion, their zeal and industry, are likely to be much greater in the former situation than in the latter. In this respect the teachers of new religions have always had a considerable advantage in attacking those ancient and established systems of which the clergy, reposing themselves upon their benefices, had neglected to keep up the fervour of faith and devotion in the great body of the people; and having given themselves up to indolence, were become altogether incapable of making any vigorous exertion in defence even of their own establishment. The clergy of an established and well-endowed religion frequently become men of learning and elegance, who possess all the virtues of gentlemen, or which can recommend them to the esteem of gentlemen; but they are apt gradually to lose the qualities, both good and bad, which gave them authority and influence with the inferior ranks of people, and which had perhaps been the original causes of the success and establishment of their religion. Such a clergy, when attacked by a set of popular and bold, though perhaps stupid and ignorant enthusiasts, feel themselves as perfectly defenceless as the indolent, effeminate, and full-fed nations of the southern parts of Asia, when they were invaded by the active, hardy, and hungry Tartars of the North. Such a clergy, upon such an emergency, have commonly no other resource than to call upon the civil magistrate to persecute, destroy, or drive out their adversaries, as disturbers of the public peace. It was thus that the Roman catholic clergy called upon the civil magistrate to persecute the protestants; and the church of England, to persecute the dissenters; and that in general every religious sect, when it has once enjoyed for a century or

two the security of a legal establishment, has found itself incapable of making any vigorous defence against any new sect which chose to attack its doctrine or discipline. Upon such occasions the advantage in point of learning and good writing may sometimes be on the side of the established church. But the arts of popularity, all the arts of gaining proselytes, are constantly on the side of its adversaries. In England those arts have been long neglected by the well-endowed clergy of the established church, and are at present chiefly cultivated by the dissenters and by the methodists. The independent provisions, however, which in many places have been made for dissenting teachers, by means of voluntary subscriptions, of trust rights, and other evasions of the law, seem very much to have abated the zeal and activity of those teachers. They have many of them become very learned, ingenious, and respectable men; but they have in general ceased to be very popular preachers. The methodists, without half the learning of the dissenters, are much more in vogue.

In the church of Rome, the industry and zeal of the inferior clergy are kept more alive by the powerful motive of self-interest, than perhaps in any established protestant church. The parochial clergy derive, many of them, a very considerable part of their subsistence from the voluntary oblations of the people; a source of revenue which confession gives them many opportunities of improving. The mendicant orders derive their whole subsistence from such oblations. It is with them, as with the hussars and light infantry of some armies; no plunder, no pay. The parochial clergy are like those teachers whose reward depends partly upon their salary, and partly upon the fee or honoraries which they get from their pupils; and these must always depend more or less upon their industry and reputation. The mendicant orders are like those teachers whose subsistence depends altogether upon their industry. They are obliged, therefore, to use every art which can animate the devotion of the common people. The establishment of the two great mendicant orders of St. Dominic and St. Francis, it is observed by Machiavel, revived, in the thirteenth and fourteenth centuries, the languishing faith and devotion of the catholic church. In Roman catholic countries the spirit of devotion is supported altogether by the monks and by the poorer parochial clergy. The great dignitaries of the church, with all the accomplishments of gentlemen and men of the world, and sometimes with those of men of learning, are careful enough to maintain the necessary discipline over their inferiors, but seldom give themselves any trouble about the instruction of the people.

"Most of the arts and professions in a state," says by far the most illustrious philosopher and historian of the present age, "are of such a nature, that, while they promote the interests of the society, they are also useful or agreeable to some individuals; and in that case, the constant rule of the magistrate, except, perhaps, on the first introduction of any art, is, to leave the profession to itself, and trust its encouragement to the individuals who reap the benefit of it. The artizans, finding their profits to rise by the favour of their customers, increase, as much as possible, their skill and industry; and as matters are not disturbed by any injudicious tampering, the commodity is always sure to be at all times nearly proportioned to the demand.

"But there are also some callings, which, though useful and even necessary in a state, bring no advantage or pleasure to any individual, and the supreme power is obliged to alter its conduct with regard to the retainers of those professions. It must give them public encouragement in order to their subsistence; and it must provide against that negligence to which they will naturally be subject, either by annexing particular honours to the profession, by establishing a long subordination of ranks and a strict dependence, or by some other expedient. The persons employed in the finances, fleets, and magistracy, are instances of this order of men.

"It may naturally be thought, at first sight, that the ecclesiastics belong to the first class, and that their encouragement, as well as that of lawyers and physicians, may safely be entrusted to the liberality of individuals, who are attached to their doctrines, and who find benefit or consolation from their spiritual ministry and assistance. Their industry and vigilance will, no doubt, be whetted by such an additional motive; and their skill in the profession, as well as their address in governing the minds of the people, must receive daily increase, from their increasing practice, study, and attention.

"But if we consider the matter more closely, we shall find, that this interested diligence of the clergy is what every wise legislator will study to prevent, because, in every religion except the true, it is highly pernicious, and it has even a natural tendency to pervert the true, by infusing into it a strong mixture of superstition, folly, and delusion. Each ghostly practitioner, in order to render himself more precious and sacred in the eyes of his retainers, will inspire them with the most violent abhorrence of all other sects, and continually endeavour, by some novelty, to excite the languid devotion of his audience. No regard will be paid to truth, morals, or decency in the doctrines inculcated. Every tenet will be adopted that best suits the disorderly affections of the human frame. Customers will be drawn to each conventicle by new industry and address in practising on the passions and credulity of the populace. And in the end, the civil magistrate will find, that he has dearly paid for his pretended frugality, in saving a fixed establishment for the priests; and that in reality the most decent and advantageous composition, which he can make with the spiritual guides, is to bribe their indolence, by assigning stated salaries to their profession, and rendering it superfluous for them to be farther active, than merely to prevent their flock from straying in quest of new pastures. And in this manner ecclesiastical establishments, though commonly they arose at first from religious views, prove in the end advantageous to the political interests of society." [David Hume, *History of England*, ch. 29.]

But whatever may have been the good or bad effects of the independent provision of the clergy; it has, perhaps, been very seldom bestowed upon them from any view to those effects. Times of violent religious controversy have generally been times of equally violent political faction. Upon such occasions, each political party has either found

it, or imagined it, for its interest, to league itself with some one or other of the contending religious sects. But this could be done only by adopting, or at least by favouring, the tenets of that particular sect. The sect which had the good fortune to be leagued with the conquering party, necessarily shared in the victory of its ally, by whose favour and protection it was soon enabled in some degree to silence and subdue all its adversaries. Those adversaries had generally leagued themselves with the enemies of the conquering party, and were therefore the enemies of that party. The clergy of this particular sect having thus become complete masters of the field, and their influence and authority with the great body of the people being in its highest vigour, they were powerful enough to over-awe the chiefs and leaders of their own party, and to oblige the civil magistrate to respect their opinions and inclinations. Their first demand was generally, that he should silence and subdue all their adversaries; and their second, that he should bestow an independent provision on themselves. As they had generally contributed a good deal to the victory, it seemed not unreasonable that they should have some share in the spoil. They were weary, besides, of humouring the people, and of depending upon their caprice for a subsistence. In making this demand therefore they consulted their own ease and comfort, without troubling themselves about the effect which it might have in future times upon the influence and authority of their order. The civil magistrate, who could comply with this demand only by giving them something which he would have chosen much rather to take, or to keep to himself, was seldom very forward to grant it. Necessity, however, always forced him to submit at last, though frequently not till after many delays, evasions, and affected excuses.

But if politics had never called in the aid of religion, had the conquering party never adopted the tenets of one sect more than those of another, when it had gained the victory, it would probably have dealt equally and impartially with all the different sects, and have allowed every man to chuse his own priest and his own religion as he thought proper. There would in this case, no doubt, have been a great multitude of religious sects. Almost every different congregation might probably have made a little sect by itself, or have entertained some peculiar tenets of its own. Each teacher would no doubt have felt himself under the necessity of making the utmost exertion, and of using every art both to preserve and to increase the number of his disciples. But as every other teacher would have felt himself under the same necessity, the success of no one teacher, or sect of teachers, could have been very great. The interested and active zeal of religious teachers can be dangerous and troublesome only where there is, either but one sect tolerated in the society, or where the whole of a large society is divided into two or three great sects; the teachers of each acting by concert, and under a regular discipline and subordination. But that zeal must be altogether innocent where the society is divided into two or three hundred, or perhaps into as many thousand small sects, of which no one could be considerable enough to disturb the public tranquillity. The teachers of each sect, seeing themselves surrounded on all sides with more adversaries than friends, would be obliged to learn that candour and moderation which is so seldom to be found among the teachers of those great sects, whose tenets, being supported by the civil magistrate, are held in veneration by almost all the inhabitants of extensive kingdoms and empires, and who therefore see nothing round them but followers, disciples, and humble admirers. The teachers of each little sect, finding themselves almost alone, would be obliged to respect those of almost every other sect, and the concessions which they would mutually find it both convenient and agreeable to make to one another, might in time probably reduce the doctrine of the greater part of them to that pure and rational religion, free from every mixture of absurdity, imposture, and fanaticism, such as wise men have in all ages of the world wished to see established; but such as positive law has perhaps never yet established, and probably never will establish in any country: because, with regard to religion, positive law always has been, and probably always will be, more or less influenced by popular superstition and enthusiasm. This plan of ecclesiastical government, or more properly of no ecclesiastical government, was what the sect called Independents, a sect no doubt of very wild enthusiasts, proposed to establish in England towards the end of the civil war. If it had been established, though of a very unphilosophical origin, it would probably by this time have been productive of the most philosophical good temper and moderation with regard to every sort of religious principle. It has been established in Pennsylvania, where, though the Quakers happen to be the most numerous, the law in reality favours no one sect more than another, and it is there said to have been productive of this philosophical good temper and moderation.

But though this equality of treatment should not be productive of this good temper and moderation in all, or even in the greater part of the religious sects of a particular country; yet provided those sects were sufficiently numerous, and each of them consequently too small to disturb the public tranquillity, the excessive zeal of each for its particular tenets could not well be productive of any very hurtful effects, but, on the contrary, of several good ones: and if the government was perfectly decided both to let them all alone, and to oblige them all to let alone one another, there is little danger that they would not of their own accord subdivide themselves fast enough, so as soon to become sufficiently numerous.

<hr/>

32

THOMAS JEFFERSON, DRAFT OF BILL EXEMPTING
DISSENTERS FROM CONTRIBUTING TO THE
SUPPORT OF THE CHURCH
30 Nov. 1776
Papers 1:532–33

<hr/>

Whereas it is represented by many of the Inhabitants of this Country who dissent from the Church of England as by Law established that they consider the Assessments and Contributions which they have been hitherto obliged to make towards the support and Maintenance of the said Church and its Ministry as grievous and oppressive, and an Infringement of their religious Freedom. For Remedy whereof and that equal Liberty as well religious as civil may be universally extended to all the good People of this Common Wealth, Be it Enacted by the General Assembly of the Common Wealth of Virginia and it is hereby Enacted by the Authority of the same that all Dissenters of whatever Denomination from the said Church shall from and after the passing this Act be totally free and exempt from all Levies Taxes and Impositions whatever towards supporting and maintaining the said Church as it now is or may hereafter be established and its Ministers. Provided nevertheless and it is hereby farther Enacted by the Authority aforesaid that the Vestries of the several Parishes where the same hath not been already done shall and may and they are hereby authorized and required at such times as they shall appoint to levy and assess on all Tithables within their respective Parishes as well Dissenters as others all such Salaries and Arrears of Salaries as are or may be due to the Ministers or Incumbents of their Parishes for past Services; moreover to make such Assessments on all Tithables as will enable the said Vestries to comply with their legal parochial Engagements already entered into and lastly to continue such future Provision for the poor in their respective Parishes as they have hitherto by Law been accustomed to make. And be it farther Enacted by the Authority aforesaid that there shall in all time coming be saved and reserved to the Use of the Church by Law established the several Tracts of Glebe Land already purchased; the Churches and Chapels already built for the use of the Parishes; all Books Plate & ornaments belonging or appropriated to the use of the said Church and all arrears of Money or Tobacco arising from former Assessments or otherwise and that there shall moreover be saved and reserved to the use of such Parishes as may have received private Donations for the better support of the said Church and its Ministers the perpetual Benefit and enjoyment of all such Donations.

And whereas great Varieties of Opinions have arisen touching the Propriety of a general Assessment or whether every religious society should be left to voluntary Contributions for the support and maintenance of the several Ministers and Teachers of the Gospel who are of different Persuasions and Denominations, and this Difference of Sentiments cannot now be well accommodated, so that it is thought most prudent to defer this matter to the Discussion and final Determination of a future assembly when the Opinions of the Country in General may be better known. To the End therefore that so important a Subject may in no Sort be prejudged, Be it Enacted by the Authority aforesaid that nothing in this Act contained shall be construed to affect or influence the said Question of a general Assessment or voluntary Contribution in any respect whatever.

Provided always that in the mean time the Members of the Established Church shall not in any Parish be subject to the payment of a greater tax for the support of the said

Church & its Minister than they would have been, had the Dissenters not been exempted from paying their accustomed proportion, any Law to the contrary notwithstanding.

And whereas it is represented that in some Counties Lists of Tithables have been omitted to be taken, For remedy whereof be it further enacted, that the Courts of the several Counties, where it may be necessary, shall have Power & they are hereby required so soon as may be convenient to appoint some of their own Members to take the Lists of Tithables throughout their respective Counties.

33

George Mason, Amendment to the Bill Exempting Dissenters from Contributions to the Established Church
5 Dec. 1776
Papers 1:318

[To stand before the preamble.]

Whereas several oppressive Acts of Parliament respecting Religion have been formerly enacted, and Doubts have arisen and may hereafter arise whether the same are in Force within this Common-Wealth or not, for Prevention whereof Be it enacted by the General Assembly of the Common-Wealth of Virginia, and it is hereby enacted by the Authority of the same, That all and every Act or Statute either of the Parliament of England, or of Great Britain, by whatsoever Title known or distinguished, which renders criminal the maintaining of any Opinions in Matters of Religion, forbearing to repair to Church, or the exercising any Mode of worship whatsoever, or which prescribes punishments for the same, shall henceforth be of no Validity or Force within this Common-Wealth.

[agreed]

34

New York Constitution of 1777, arts. 38, 39
Thorpe 5:2636–37

XXXVIII. And whereas we are required, by the benevolent principles of rational liberty, not only to expel civil tyranny, but also to guard against that spiritual oppression and intolerance wherewith the bigotry and ambition of weak and wicked priests and princes have scourged mankind, this convention doth further, in the name and by the authority of the good people of this State, ordain, determine, and declare, that the free exercise and enjoyment of religious profession and worship, without discrimination or preference, shall forever hereafter be allowed, within this State, to all mankind: *Provided,* That the liberty of conscience, hereby granted, shall not be so construed as to excuse acts of licentiousness, or justify practices inconsistent with the peace or safety of this State.

XXXIX. And whereas the ministers of the gospel are, by their profession, dedicated to the service of God and the care of souls, and ought not to be diverted from the great duties of their function; therefore, no minister of the gospel, or priest of any denomination whatsoever, shall, at any time hereafter, under any pretence or description whatever, be eligible to, or capable of holding, any civil or military office or place within this State.

35

Vermont Constitution of 1777, ch. 1, sec. 3; ch. 2, sec. 41
Thorpe 6:3740, 3748

[Chapter 1]

III. That all men have a natural and unalienable right to worship Almighty God, according to the dictates of their own consciences and understanding, regulated by the word of God; and that no man ought, or of right can be compelled to attend any religious worship, or erect, or support any place of worship, or maintain any minister, contrary to the dictates of his conscience; nor can any man who professes the protestant religion, be justly deprived or abridged of any civil right, as a citizen, on account of his religious sentiment, or peculiar mode of religious worship, and that no authority can, or ought to be vested in, or assumed by, any power whatsoever, that shall, in any case, interfere with, or in any manner controul, the rights of conscience, in the free exercise of religious worship: nevertheless, every sect or denomination of people ought to observe the Sabbath, or the Lord's day, and keep up, and support, some sort of religious worship, which to them shall seem most agreeable to the revealed will of God.

[Chapter 2]

Section XLI. Laws for the encouragement of virtue and prevention of vice and immorality, shall be made and constantly kept in force; and provision shall be made for their due execution; and all religious societies or bodies of men, that have or may be hereafter united and incorporated, for the advancement of religion and learning, or for other pious and charitable purposes, shall be encouraged and protected in the enjoyment of the privileges, immunities and estates which they, in justice, ought to enjoy, under such regulations, as the General Assembly of this State shall direct.

36

SOUTH CAROLINA CONSTITUTION OF 1778, ARTS. 21, 38

Thorpe 6:3253, 3255–56

XXI. And whereas the ministers of the gospel are by their profession dedicated to the service of God and the cure of souls, and ought not to be diverted from the great duties of their function, therefore no minister of the gospel or public preacher of any religious persuasion, while he continues in the exercise of his pastoral function, and for two years after, shall be eligible either as governor, lieutenant-governor, a member of the senate, house of representatives, or privy council in this State.

. . . . .

XXXVIII. That all persons and religious societies who acknowledge that there is one God, and a future state of rewards and punishments, and that God is publicly to be worshipped, shall be freely tolerated. The Christian Protestant religion shall be deemed, and is hereby constituted and declared to be, the established religion of this State. That all denominations of Christian Protestants in this State, demeaning themselves peaceably and faithfully, shall enjoy equal religious and civil privileges. To accomplish this desirable purpose without injury to the religious property of those societies of Christians which are by law already incorporated for the purpose of religious worship, and to put it fully into the power of every other society of Christian Protestants, either already formed or hereafter to be formed, to obtain the like incorporation, it is hereby constituted, appointed, and declared that the respective societies of the Church of England that are already formed in this State for the purpose of religious worship shall still continue incorporate and hold the religious property now in their possession. And that whenever fifteen or more male persons, not under twenty-one years of age, professing the Christian Protestant religion, and agreeing to unite themselves in a society for the purposes of religious worship, they shall, (on complying with the terms hereinafter mentioned,) be, and be constituted a church, and be esteemed and regarded in law as of the established religion of the State, and on a petition to the legislature shall be entitled to be incorporated and to enjoy equal privileges. That every society of Christians so formed shall give themselves a name or denomination by which they shall be called and known in law, and all that associate with them for the purposes of worship shall be esteemed as belonging to the society so called. But that previous to the establishment and incorporation of the respective societies of every denomination as aforesaid, and in order to entitle them thereto, each society so petitioning shall have agreed to and subscribed in a book the following five articles, without which no agreement or union of men upon pretence of religion shall entitle them to be incorporated and esteemed as a church of the established religion of this State:

1st. That there is one eternal God, and a future state of rewards and punishments.

2d. That God is publicly to be worshipped.

3d. That the Christian religion is the true religion.

4th. That the holy scriptures of the Old and New Testaments are of divine inspiration, and are the rule of faith and practice.

5th. That it is lawful and the duty of every man being thereunto called by those that govern, to bear witness to the truth.

And that every inhabitant of this State, when called to make an appeal to God as a witness to truth, shall be permitted to do it in that way which is most agreeable to the dictates of his own conscience. And that the people of this State may forever enjoy the right of electing their own pastors or clergy, and at the same time that the State may have sufficient security for the due discharge of the pastoral office, by those who shall be admitted to be clergymen, no person shall officiate as minister of any established church who shall not have been chosen by a majority of the society to which he shall minister, or by persons appointed by the said majority, to choose and procure a minister for them; nor until the minister so chosen and appointed shall have made and subscribed to the following declaration, over and above the aforesaid five articles, viz: "That he is determined by God's grace out of the holy scriptures, to instruct the people committed to his charge, and to teach nothing as required of necessity to eternal salvation but that which he shall be persuaded may be concluded and proved from the scripture; that he will use both public and private admonitions, as well to the sick as to the whole within his cure, as need shall require and occasion shall be given, and that he will be diligent in prayers, and in reading of the same; that he will be diligent to frame and fashion his own self and his family according to the doctrine of Christ, and to make both himself and them, as much as in him lieth, wholesome examples and patterns to the flock of Christ; that he will maintain and set forwards, as much as he can, quietness, peace, and love among all people, and especially among those that are or shall be committed to his charge. No person shall disturb or molest any religious assembly; nor shall use any reproachful, reviling, or abusive language against any church, that being the certain way of disturbing the peace, and of hindering the conversion of any to the truth, by engaging them in quarrels and animosities, to the hatred of the professors, and that profession which otherwise they might be brought to assent to. No person whatsoever shall speak anything in their religious assembly irreverently or seditiously of the government of this State. No person shall, by law, be obliged to pay towards the maintenance and support of a religious worship that he does not freely join in, or has not voluntarily engaged to support. But the churches, chapels, parsonages, glebes, and all other property now belonging to any societies of the Church of England, or any other religious societies, shall remain and be secured to them forever. The poor shall be supported, and elections managed in the accustomed manner, until laws shall be provided to adjust those matters in the most equitable way.

37

THOMAS JEFFERSON, A BILL FOR ESTABLISHING
RELIGIOUS FREEDOM
12 June 1779
Papers 2: facing 305

Well aware that the opinions and belief of men depend not on their own will, but follow involuntarily the evidence proposed to their minds, that Almighty God hath created the mind free, and manifested his Supreme will that free it shall remain, by making it altogether insusceptible of restraint: That all attempts to influence it by temporal punishments or burthens, or by civil incapacitations, tend only to beget habits of hypocrisy and meanness, and are a departure from the plan of the holy author of our religion, who being Lord both of body and mind, yet chose not to propagate it by coercions on either, as was in his Almighty power to do, but to extend it by its influence on reason alone: That the impious presumption of legislators and rulers, civil as well as ecclesiastical, who, being themselves but fallible and uninspired men, have assumed dominion over the faith of others, setting up their own opinions and modes of thinking, as the only true and infallible, and as such, endeavouring to impose them on others, hath established and maintained false religions over the greatest part of the world, and through all time: That to compel a man to furnish contributions of money for the propagation of opinions which he disbelieves and abhors, is sinful and tyrannical: That even the forcing him to support this or that teacher of his own religious persuasion, is depriving him of the comfortable liberty of giving his contributions to the particular pastor whose morals he would make his pattern, and whose powers he feels most persuasive to righteousness, and is withdrawing from the Ministry those temporal rewards which, proceeding from an approbation of their personal conduct, are an additional incitement to earnest and unremitting labour for the instruction of mankind: That our civil rights have no dependance on our religious opinions, any more than on our opinions in physicks or geometry: That therefore the proscribing any citizen as unworthy the publick confidence, by laying upon him an incapacity of being called to offices of trust and emolument, unless he profess or renounce this or that religious opinion, is depriving him injuriously of those privileges and advantages to which, in common with his fellow citizens he has a natural right: That it tends also to corrupt the principles of that very religion it is meant to encourage, by bribing with a monopoly of worldly honours and emoluments, those who will externally profess and conform to it: That though indeed these are criminal who do not withstand such temptation, yet neither are those innocent who lay the bait in their way : That the opinions of men are not the object of civil government, nor under its jurisdiction: That to suffer the civil Magistrate to intrude his powers into the field of opinion, and to restrain the profession or propagation of principles on supposition of their ill tendency, is a dangerous fallacy, which at once destroys all religious liberty; because he being of course Judge of that tendency will make his own opinions the rule of judgment, and approve or condemn the sentiments of others only as they shall square with, or differ from his own: That it is time enough for the rightful purposes of civil government for its officers to interfere when principles break out into overt acts against peace and good order: And finally, that truth is great and will prevail if left to herself; that she is the proper and sufficient antagonist to errour, and has nothing to fear from the conflict, unless by human interposition, disarmed of her natural weapons, free argument and debate; errours ceasing to be dangerous when it is permitted freely to contract them.

We the General Assembly of *Virginia* do enact, that no man shall be compelled to frequent or support any relig[i]ous Worship place or Ministry whatsoever, nor shall be enforced, restrained, molested, or burthened in his body or goods, nor shall otherwise suffer on account of his religious opinions or belief, but that all men shall be free to profess, and by argument to maintain their opinions in matters of religion, and that the same shall in no wise diminish, enlarge, or affect their civil capacities.

And though we know that this Assembly, elected by the people for the ordinary purposes of legislation only, have no power to restrain the acts of succeeding Assemblies, constituted with powers equal to our own, and that therefore to declare this act irrevocable would be of no effect in law; yet we are free to declare, and do declare, that the rights hereby asserted are of the natural rights of mankind, and that if any act shall be hereafter passed to repeal the present, or to narrow its operation, such act will be an infringement of natural right.

38

MASSACHUSETTS CONSTITUTION OF 1780, PT. 1,
ARTS. 2, 3
Thorpe 3:1189–90

[*Declaration of Rights*]

Art. II. It is the right as well as the duty of all men in society, publicly and at stated seasons, to worship the Supreme Being, the great Creator and Preserver of the universe. And no subject shall be hurt, molested, or restrained, in his person, liberty, or estate, for worshipping God in the manner and season most agreeable to the dictates of his own conscience, or for his religious profession or sentiments, provided he doth not disturb the public peace or obstruct others in their religious worship.

Art. III. As the happiness of a people and the good order and preservation of civil government essentially depend upon piety, religion, and morality, and as these cannot be generally diffused through a community but by the institution of the public worship of God and of public instructions in piety, religion, and morality: Therefore, To promote their happiness and to secure the good order and preservation of their government, the people of this commonwealth have a right to invest their legislature with power to authorize and require, and the legislature shall, from time to time, authorize and require, the several towns, parishes, precincts, and other bodies-politic or religious societies to make suitable provision, at their own expense, for the institution of the public worship of God and for the support and maintenance of public Protestant teachers of piety, religion, and morality in all cases where such provision shall not be made voluntarily.

And the people of this commonwealth have also a right to, and do, invest their legislature with authority to enjoin upon all the subjects an attendance upon the instructions of the public teachers aforesaid, at stated times and seasons, if there be any on whose instructions they can conscientiously and conveniently attend.

Provided, notwithstanding, That the several towns, parishes, precincts, and other bodies-politic, or religious societies, shall at all times have the exclusive right of electing their public teachers and of contracting with them for their support and maintenance.

And all moneys paid by the subject to the support of public worship and of the public teachers aforesaid shall, if he require it, be uniformly applied to the support of the public teacher or teachers of his own religious sect or denomination, provided there be any on whose instructions he attends; otherwise it may be paid toward the support of the teacher or teachers of the parish or precinct in which the said moneys are raised.

And every denomination of Christians, demeaning themselves peaceably and as good subjects of the commonwealth, shall be equally under the protection of the law; and no subordination of any one sect or denomination to another shall ever be established by law.

39

BENJAMIN RUSH TO JOHN ARMSTRONG
19 Mar. 1783
Letters 1:294–95

The early respect I was taught to entertain for your character, and the agreeable connection we once had together, are the only apologies I shall offer for opening a correspondence with you upon the subject of a college at Carlisle.

I am no stranger to the opposition that has been excited against the scheme in your county by some gentlemen in this city, nor am I unacquainted with the very illiberal reflections that have been thrown upon me for favoring the design by two of those gentlemen. I have nothing to say against them by way of retaliation. The only design of this letter is to explain more fully to you the advantages to be derived to the state at large and the Presbyterian society in particular from a nursery of religion and learning on the west side of the river Susquehannah.

The manner in which the Presbyterians seized their present share of power in the University of Philadelphia has given such general offense that there is little doubt of an attempt being made in the course of a few years to restore it to its original owners. The old trustees say that the present charter is contrary to the Constitution of the state and to every principle of justice, and I find a great many of the most respectable members of the Assembly are of the same opinion, among whom is the Reverend Mr. Joseph Montgomery.

But supposing the present trustees held the University by the most equitable and constitutional tenure, it cannot be viewed as a nursery for the Presbyterian Church. Only 11 out of 24 of the present trustees are Presbyterians. Dr. Ewing was elected by a majority of a single vote. He will probably be the last Presbyterian clergyman that ever will be placed at the head of that institution, should it even continue upon its present footing. From its extreme catholicism, I am sorry to say that, as no one religion prevails, so no religious principles are inculcated in it. The fault here is only in the charter, for all the teachers I believe are friends to Christianity and men of pious and moral characters.

Religion is best supported under the patronage of particular societies. Instead of encouraging bigotry, I believe it prevents it by removing young men from those opportunities of controversy which a variety of sects mixed together are apt to create and which are the certain fuel of bigotry. Religion is necessary to correct the effects of learning. Without religion I believe learning does real mischief to the morals and principles of mankind; a mode of worship is necessary to support religion; and education is the surest way of producing a preference and constant attachment to a mode of worship. Religion could not long be maintained in the world without forms and the distinctions of sects. The weaknesses of human nature require them. The distinction of sects is as necessary in the Christian Church towards the perfection and government of the whole as regiments and brigades are in an army. Some people talk loudly of the increase of liberality of sentiment upon religious subjects since the war, but I suspect that this boasted catholicism arises chiefly from an indifference acquired since the war to religion itself. We only change the names of our vices and follies in different periods of time. Religious bigotry has yielded to political intolerance. The man who used to hate his neighbor for being a Churchman or a Quaker now hates him with equal cordiality for being a tory. Colleges are the best schools for [divinity. But divinity] cannot be taught without a system, and this system must partake of the doctrines of some one sect of Christians—hence the necessity of the College being in the hands of some one religious society. The universities of England, Scotland, and Ireland, and I believe of every other kingdom in Europe are in the hands of particular societies, and it is from this circumstance they have become the bulwarks of the Christian religion throughout the world.

The expense of an education in Philadelphia alone, exclusive of the influence of a large city upon the morals of youth, is sufficient to deter the farmers from sending their sons to the University of Philadelphia. The distance of the College of New Jersey from the western counties of this state makes the difference of *one fifth* of the expense in the education of a young man in traveling twice a year backwards and forwards to and from his father's house.

It has long been a subject of complaint among us that the principal part of the emigrants from Pennsylvania into new countries were Presbyterians. This has greatly reduced our numbers and influence in government. It is I believe pretty certain that we do not now compose more than one fourth or fifth part of the inhabitants of the state. A college at Carlisle, by diffusing the light of science and religion more generally through our society, may check this spirit of emigration among them. It may teach them to prefer civil, social, and religious advantages, with a small farm and old land, to the loss of them all with extensive tracts of woods and a more fertile soil.

40

THOMAS JEFFERSON, NOTES ON THE STATE OF VIRGINIA, QUERY 17, 157–61
1784

The first settlers in this country were emigrants from England, of the English church, just at a point of time when it was flushed with complete victory over the religious of all other persuasions. Possessed, as they became, of the powers of making, administering, and executing the laws, they shewed equal intolerance in this country with their Presbyterian brethren, who had emigrated to the northern government. The poor Quakers were flying from persecution in England. They cast their eyes on these new countries as asylums of civil and religious freedom; but they found them free only for the reigning sect. Several acts of the Virginia assembly of 1659, 1662, and 1693, had made it penal in parents to refuse to have their children baptized; had prohibited the unlawful assembling of Quakers; had made it penal for any master of a vessel to bring a Quaker into the state; had ordered those already here, and such as should come thereafter, to be imprisoned till they should abjure the country; provided a milder punishment for their first and second return, but death for their third; had inhibited all persons from suffering their meetings in or near their houses, entertaining them individually, or disposing of books which supported their tenets. If no capital execution took place here, as did in New-England, it was not owing to the moderation of the church, or spirit of the legislature, as may be inferred from the law itself; but to historical circumstances which have not been handed down to us. The Anglicans retained full possession of the country about a century. Other opinions began then to creep in, and the great care of the government to support their own church, having begotten an equal degree of indolence in its clergy, two-thirds of the people had become dissenters at the commencement of the present revolution. The laws indeed were still oppressive on them, but

the spirit of the one party had subsided into moderation, and of the other had risen to a degree of determination which commanded respect.

The present state of our laws on the subject of religion is this. The convention of May 1776, in their declaration of rights, declared it to be a truth, and a natural right, that the exercise of religion should be free; but when they proceeded to form on that declaration the ordinance of government, instead of taking up every principle declared in the bill of rights, and guarding it by legislative sanction, they passed over that which asserted our religious rights, leaving them as they found them. The same convention, however, when they met as a member of the general assembly in October 1776, repealed all *acts of parliament* which had rendered criminal the maintaining any opinions in matters of religion, the forbearing to repair to church, and the exercising any mode of worship; and suspended the laws giving salaries to the clergy, which suspension was made perpetual in October 1779. Statutory oppressions in religion being thus wiped away, we remain at present under those only imposed by the common law, or by our own acts of assembly. At the common law, *heresy* was a capital offence, punishable by burning. Its definition was left to the ecclesiastical judges, before whom the conviction was, till the statute of the 1 El. c. 1. circumscribed it, by declaring, that nothing should be deemed heresy, but what had been so determined by authority of the canonical scriptures, or by one of the four first general councils, or by some other council having for the grounds of their declaration the express and plain words of the scriptures. Heresy, thus circumscribed, being an offence at the common law, our act of assembly of October 1777, c. 17. gives cognizance of it to the general court, by declaring, that the jurisdiction of that court shall be general in all matters at the common law. The execution is by the writ *De haeretico comburendo*. By our own act of assembly of 1705, c. 30, if a person brought up in the Christian religion denies the being of a God, or the Trinity, or asserts there are more Gods than one, or denies the Christian religion to be true, or the scriptures to be of divine authority, he is punishable on the first offence by incapacity to hold any office or employment ecclesiastical, civil, or military; on the second by disability to sue, to take any gift or legacy, to be guardian, executor, or administrator, and by three years imprisonment, without bail. A father's right to the custody of his own children being founded in law on his right of guardianship, this being taken away, they may of course be severed from him, and put, by the authority of a court, into more orthodox hands. This is a summary view of that religious slavery, under which a people have been willing to remain, who have lavished their lives and fortunes for the establishment of their civil freedom.

The error seems not sufficiently eradicated, that the operations of the mind, as well as the acts of the body, are subject to the coercion of the laws. But our rulers can have authority over such natural rights only as we have submitted to them. The rights of conscience we never submitted, we could not submit. We are answerable for them to our God. The legitimate powers of government extend to such acts only as are injurious to others. But it does me no injury for my neighbour to say there are twenty gods, or no god. It neither picks my pocket nor breaks my leg. If it be said, his testimony in a court of justice cannot be relied on, reject it then, and be the stigma on him. Constraint may make him worse by making him a hypocrite, but it will never make him a truer man. It may fix him obstinately in his errors, but will not cure them. Reason and free enquiry are the only effectual agents against error. Give a loose to them, they will support the true religion, by bringing every false one to their tribunal, to the test of their investigation. They are the natural enemies of error, and of error only. Had not the Roman government permitted free enquiry, Christianity could never have been introduced. Had not free enquiry been indulged, at the aera of the reformation, the corruptions of Christianity could not have been purged away. If it be restrained now, the present corruptions will be protected, and new ones encouraged. Was the government to prescribe to us our medicine and diet, our bodies would be in such keeping as our souls are now. Thus in France the emetic was once forbidden as a medicine, and the potatoe as an article of food. Government is just as infallible too when it fixes systems in physics. Galileo was sent to the inquisition for affirming that the earth was a sphere: the government had declared it to be as flat as a trencher, and Galileo was obliged to abjure his error. This error however at length prevailed, the earth became a globe, and Descartes declared it was whirled round its axis by a vortex. The government in which he lived was wise enough to see that this was no question of civil jurisdiction, or we should all have been involved by authority in vortices. In fact, the vortices have been exploded, and the Newtonian principle of gravitation is now more firmly established, on the basis of reason, than it would be were the government to step in, and to make it an article of necessary faith. Reason and experiment have been indulged, and error has fled before them. It is error alone which needs the support of government. Truth can stand by itself. Subject opinion to coercion: whom will you make your inquisitors? Fallible men; men governed by bad passions, by private as well as public reasons. And why subject it to coercion? To produce uniformity. But is uniformity of opinion desireable? No more than of face and stature. Introduce the bed of Procrustes then, and as there is danger that the large men may beat the small, make us all of a size, by lopping the former and stretching the latter. Difference of opinion is advantageous in religion. The several sects perform the office of a Censor morum over each other. Is uniformity attainable? Millions of innocent men, women, and children, since the introduction of Christianity, have been burnt, tortured, fined, imprisoned; yet we have not advanced one inch towards uniformity. What has been the effect of coercion? To make one half the world fools, and the other half hypocrites. To support roguery and error all over the earth. Let us reflect that it is inhabited by a thousand millions of people. That these profess probably a thousand different systems of religion. That ours is but one of that thousand. That if there be but one right, and ours that one, we should wish to see the 999 wandering sects gathered into the fold of truth. But against such a majority we cannot effect this by force. Rea-

son and persuasion are the only practicable instruments. To make way for these, free enquiry must be indulged; and how can we wish others to indulge it while we refuse it ourselves. But every state, says an inquisitor, has established some religion. No two, say I, have established the same. Is this a proof of the infallibility of establishments? Our sister states of Pennsylvania and New York, however, have long subsisted without any establishment at all. The experiment was new and doubtful when they made it. It has answered beyond conception. They flourish infinitely. Religion is well supported; of various kinds, indeed, but all good enough; all sufficient to preserve peace and order: or if a sect arises, whose tenets would subvert morals, good sense has fair play, and reasons and laughs it out of doors, without suffering the state to be troubled with it. They do not hang more malefactors than we do. They are not more disturbed with religious dissensions. On the contrary, their harmony is unparalleled, and can be ascribed to nothing but their unbounded tolerance, because there is no other circumstance in which they differ from every nation on earth. They have made the happy discovery, that the way to silence religious disputes, is to take no notice of them. Let us too give this experiment fair play, and get rid, while we may, of those tyrannical laws. It is true, we are as yet secured against them by the spirit of the times. I doubt whether the people of this country would suffer an execution for heresy, or a three years imprisonment for not comprehending the mysteries of the Trinity. But is the spirit of the people an infallible, a permanent reliance? Is it government? Is this the kind of protection we receive in return for the rights we give up? Besides, the spirit of the times may alter, will alter. Our rulers will become corrupt, our people careless. A single zealot may commence persecutor, and better men be his victims. It can never be too often repeated, that the time for fixing every essential right on a legal basis is while our rulers are honest, and ourselves united. From the conclusion of this war we shall be going down hill. It will not then be necessary to resort every moment to the people for support. They will be forgotten, therefore, and their rights disregarded. They will forget themselves, but in the sole faculty of making money, and will never think of uniting to effect a due respect for their rights. The shackles, therefore, which shall not be knocked off at the conclusion of this war, will remain on us long, will be made heavier and heavier, till our rights shall revive or expire in a convulsion.

41

JOHN BLAIR TO JAMES MADISON
21 June 1784
Madison Papers 8:81–82

Since my arrival at home, I have seen a part of your Journals, & by them have learned the objects of the Petition from the Episcopal Clergy, which in one or two instances, appear to me very exceptionable. The first part of their prayer is necessary & proper; & the whole of it might pass without much animadversion to its disadvantage, 'till you hear them requesting that "they, the Clergy, may be incorporated by law;" & then an attentive mind must revolt against it as very unjustifiable, & very insulting to the members of their communion in general. Had they requested that an incorporating act should pass, in favour of that Church as a party of Christians, whereby the *people* might have had a share in the direction of ecclesiastical regulations, & the appointment of Church officers for that purpose, it would have been extremely proper. But as the matter now stands, the Clergy seem desirous to exclud[e] *them* from any share in such a privilege & willing to oblige the members of their Churches to sit down patiently, under such regulations as an incorporated body of Clergymen, who wish to be peculiarly considered as ministers in the view of the law, shall chuse to make, without a legal right to interfere in any manner, but such as these spiritual leaders may think fit to allow. I should expect that such an Idea of spiritual domination, would be resented & opposed by every adherent to that Society. I should suppose that every one of them who felt the spirit of his station would regard the attempt as an indefensible remain of Star-chamber tyranny, & resist it accordingly. However, if the Gentlemen, of the communion are so used to Dictators, that they either have not observed the Jure divino pretension to domineer over them, or have not inclination of Spirit to oppose it, perhaps it may be thought proper for one so little interested in the matter as myself to be Silent. I confess that I have less reason to interfere than many others: but as a Citizen of a free State I am interested in the Spirit which my Countrymen discover, & am sorry that there is room to suppose them too insensible of their own importance in any instance whatever.

But that part of the petition, which concerns me most, as well as every Non-Episcopalian in the state, is, where these Clergymen pray for an act of the Assembly to *Enable,* them to regulate all the spiritual concerns of that Church &c. This is an express attempt to draw the State into an illicit connexion & commerce with them, which is already the ground of that uneasiness which at present prevails thro' a great part of the State. According to the spirit of that prayer, the Legislature is to consider itself as the head of that Party, & consequently they as Members are to be fostered with particular care. This is unreasonable & highly improper, as well as dangerous. It ought therefore to [be] treated by the assembly as an ill-digested Scheme of policy in the present State of affairs. I am sorry that Christian Ministers should virtually declare their Church a mere political machine, which the State may regulate at pleasure; but I shall be surprized if the Assembly shall assume the improper office. The interference of the Legislature is always dangerous, where it is unnecessary. And I am sure it is plainly so in this case. It would be to decide upon a matter which a Superior power, I mean the Convention in the Bill of Rights, has already determined. It would be to give leave to do what every class of Citizens has a natural, unalienable right to do without any such

leave; for surely every religious society in the State possesses full power to regulate their internal police; without depending upon the Assembly for leave to do so. Surely we are not again to be irritated & harassed with the heavy weight of a State-Church, that is to sit as sovereign over the rest, by depending in a more particular manner for direction in Spirituals, upon that antiquated fountain head of influences, the secular power.

I have here hastily throw[n] together the very first thoughts which occurred to me upon reading the Journals; & as you certainly have taken notice of the same improprieties in the petition which I have now done, I hope you will use your extensive influence to prevent the consequences intended to flow from it.

42

NEW HAMPSHIRE CONSTITUTION OF 1784, PT. 1, ARTS. 4, 5, 6, 13

Thorpe 4:2454–55

IV. Among the natural rights, some are in their very nature unalienable, because no equivalent can be given or received for them. Of this kind are the RIGHTS OF CONSCIENCE.

V. Every individual has a natural and unalienable right to worship GOD according to the dictates of his own conscience, and reason; and no subject shall be hurt, molested, or restrained in his person, liberty or estate for worshipping GOD, in the manner and season most agreeable to the dictates of his own conscience, or for his religious profession, sentiments or persuasion; provided he doth not disturb the public peace, or disturb others, in their religious worship.

VI. As morality and piety, rightly grounded on evangelical principles, will give the best and greatest security to government, and will lay in the hearts of men the strongest obligations to due subjection; and as the knowledge of these, is most likely to be propagated through a society by the institution of the public worship of the DEITY, and of public instruction in morality and religion; therefore, to promote those important purposes, the people of this state have a right to impower, and do hereby fully impower the legislature to authorize from time to time, the several towns, parishes, bodies-corporate, or religious societies within this state, to make adequate provision at their own expence, for the support and maintenance of public protestant teachers of piety, religion and morality:

Provided notwithstanding, That the several towns, parishes, bodies-corporate, or religious societies, shall at all times have the exclusive right of electing their own public teachers, and of contracting with them for their support and maintenance. And no person of any one particular religious sect or denomination, shall ever be compelled to pay towards the support of the teacher or teachers of another persuasion, sect or denomination.

And every denomination of christians demeaning themselves quietly, and as good subjects of the state, shall be equally under the protection of the law: and no subordination of any one sect or denomination to another, shall ever be established by law.

And nothing herein shall be understood to affect any former contracts made for the support of the ministry; but all such contracts shall remain, and be in the same state as if this constitution had not been made.

· · · · ·

XIII. No person who is conscientiously scrupulous about the lawfulness of bearing arms, shall be compelled thereto, provided he will pay an equivalent.

43

JAMES MADISON, MEMORIAL AND REMONSTRANCE AGAINST RELIGIOUS ASSESSMENTS
20 June 1785
Papers 8:298–304

*To the Honorable the General Assembly
of the Commonwealth of Virginia
A Memorial and Remonstrance*

We the subscribers, citizens of the said Commonwealth, having taken into serious consideration, a Bill printed by order of the last Session of General Assembly, entitled "A Bill establishing a provision for Teachers of the Christian Religion," and conceiving that the same if finally armed with the sanctions of a law, will be a dangerous abuse of power, are bound as faithful members of a free State to remonstrate against it, and to declare the reasons by which we are determined. We remonstrate against the said Bill,

1. Because we hold it for a fundamental and undeniable truth, "that Religion or the duty which we owe to our Creator and the manner of discharging it, can be directed only by reason and conviction, not by force or violence." [Virginia Declaration of Rights, art. 16] The Religion then of every man must be left to the conviction and conscience of every man; and it is the right of every man to exercise it as these may dictate. This right is in its nature an unalienable right. It is unalienable, because the opinions of men, depending only on the evidence contemplated by their own minds cannot follow the dictates of other men: It is unalienable also, because what is here a right towards men, is a duty towards the Creator. It is the duty of every man to render to the Creator such homage and such only as he believes to be acceptable to him. This duty is precedent, both in order of time and in degree of obligation, to the claims of Civil Society. Before any man can be considered as a member of Civil Society, he must be considered as a subject of the Governour of the Universe: And if a member of Civil Society, who enters into any subordinate Association, must always do it with a reservation of his duty to the General Authority; much more must every man who becomes a member of any particular Civil Society, do it with a saving of his allegiance to the Universal Sovereign. We maintain therefore that in matters of Religion, no mans right is abridged by the institution of Civil Society and that Religion is wholly exempt from its cognizance. True it is, that no other rule exists, by which any question which may divide a Society, can be ultimately determined, but the will of the majority; but it is also true that the majority may trespass on the rights of the minority.

2. Because if Religion be exempt from the authority of the Society at large, still less can it be subject to that of the Legislative Body. The latter are but the creatures and vicegerents of the former. Their jurisdiction is both derivative and limited: it is limited with regard to the co-ordinate departments, more necessarily is it limited with regard to the constituents. The preservation of a free Government requires not merely, that the metes and bounds which separate each department of power be invariably maintained; but more especially that neither of them be suffered to overleap the great Barrier which defends the rights of the people. The Rulers who are guilty of such an encroachment, exceed the commission from which they derive their authority, and are Tyrants. The People who submit to it are governed by laws made neither by themselves nor by an authority derived from them, and are slaves.

3. Because it is proper to take alarm at the first experiment on our liberties. We hold this prudent jealousy to be the first duty of Citizens, and one of the noblest characteristics of the late Revolution. The free men of America did not wait till usurped power had strengthened itself by exercise, and entangled the question in precedents. They saw all the consequences in the principle, and they avoided the consequences by denying the principle. We revere this lesson too much soon to forget it. Who does not see that the same authority which can establish Christianity, in exclusion of all other Religions, may establish with the same ease any particular sect of Christians, in exclusion of all other Sects? that the same authority which can force a citizen to contribute three pence only of his property for the support of any one establishment, may force him to conform to any other establishment in all cases whatsoever?

4. Because the Bill violates that equality which ought to be the basis of every law, and which is more indispensible, in proportion as the validity or expediency of any law is more liable to be impeached. If "all men are by nature equally free and independent," [Virginia Declaration of Rights, art. 1] all men are to be considered as entering into Society on equal conditions; as relinquishing no more, and therefore retaining no less, one than another, of their natural rights. Above all are they to be considered as retaining an *"equal* title to the free exercise of Religion according to the dictates of Conscience." [Virginia Declaration of Rights, art. 16] Whilst we assert for ourselves a freedom to embrace, to profess and to observe the Religion which we believe to be of divine origin, we cannot deny an equal freedom to those whose minds have not yet yielded to the evidence which has convinced us. If this freedom be abused, it is an offence against God, not against man: To God, therefore, not to man, must an account of it be rendered. As the Bill violates equality by subjecting some to

peculiar burdens, so it violates the same principle, by granting to others peculiar exemptions. Are the Quakers and Menonists the only sects who think a compulsive support of their Religions unnecessary and unwarrantable? Can their piety alone be entrusted with the care of public worship? Ought their Religions to be endowed above all others with extraordinary privileges by which proselytes may be enticed from all others? We think too favorably of the justice and good sense of these denominations to believe that they either covet pre-eminences over their fellow citizens or that they will be seduced by them from the common opposition to the measure.

5. Because the Bill implies either that the Civil Magistrate is a competent Judge of Religious Truth; or that he may employ Religion as an engine of Civil policy. The first is an arrogant pretension falsified by the contradictory opinions of Rulers in all ages, and throughout the world: the second an unhallowed perversion of the means of salvation.

6. Because the establishment proposed by the Bill is not requisite for the support of the Christian Religion. To say that it is, is a contradiction to the Christian Religion itself, for every page of it disavows a dependence on the powers of this world: it is a contradiction to fact; for it is known that this Religion both existed and flourished, not only without the support of human laws, but in spite of every opposition from them, and not only during the period of miraculous aid, but long after it had been left to its own evidence and the ordinary care of Providence. Nay, it is a contradiction in terms; for a Religion not invented by human policy, must have pre-existed and been supported, before it was established by human policy. It is moreover to weaken in those who profess this Religion a pious confidence in its innate excellence and the patronage of its Author; and to foster in those who still reject it, a suspicion that its friends are too conscious of its fallacies to trust it to its own merits.

7. Because experience witnesseth that ecclesiastical establishments, instead of maintaining the purity and efficacy of Religion, have had a contrary operation. During almost fifteen centuries has the legal establishment of Christianity been on trial. What have been its fruits? More or less in all places, pride and indolence in the Clergy, ignorance and servility in the laity, in both, superstition, bigotry and persecution. Enquire of the Teachers of Christianity for the ages in which it appeared in its greatest lustre; those of every sect, point to the ages prior to its incorporation with Civil policy. Propose a restoration of this primitive State in which its Teachers depended on the voluntary rewards of their flocks, many of them predict its downfall. On which Side ought their testimony to have greatest weight, when for or when against their interest?

8. Because the establishment in question is not necessary for the support of Civil Government. If it be urged as necessary for the support of Civil Government only as it is a means of supporting Religion, and it be not necessary for the latter purpose, it cannot be necessary for the former. If Religion be not within the cognizance of Civil Government how can its legal establishment be neccessary to Civil Government? What influence in fact have ecclesiastical establishments had on Civil Society? In some instances they have been seen to erect a spiritual tyranny on the ruins of the Civil authority; in many instances they have been seen upholding the thrones of political tyranny: in no instance have they been seen the guardians of the liberties of the people. Rulers who wished to subvert the public liberty, may have found an established Clergy convenient auxiliaries. A just Government instituted to secure & perpetuate it needs them not. Such a Government will be best supported by protecting every Citizen in the enjoyment of his Religion with the same equal hand which protects his person and his property; by neither invading the equal rights of any Sect, nor suffering any Sect to invade those of another.

9. Because the proposed establishment is a departure from that generous policy, which, offering an Asylum to the persecuted and oppressed of every Nation and Religion, promised a lustre to our country, and an accession to the number of its citizens. What a melancholy mark is the Bill of sudden degeneracy? Instead of holding forth an Asylum to the persecuted, it is itself a signal of persecution. It degrades from the equal rank of Citizens all those whose opinions in Religion do not bend to those of the Legislative authority. Distant as it may be in its present form from the Inquisition, it differs from it only in degree. The one is the first step, the other the last in the career of intolerance. The magnanimous sufferer under this cruel scourge in foreign Regions, must view the Bill as a Beacon on our Coast, warning him to seek some other haven, where liberty and philanthrophy in their due extent, may offer a more certain repose from his Troubles.

10. Because it will have a like tendency to banish our Citizens. The allurements presented by other situations are every day thinning their number. To superadd a fresh motive to emigration by revoking the liberty which they now enjoy, would be the same species of folly which has dishonoured and depopulated flourishing kingdoms.

11. Because it will destroy that moderation and harmony which the forbearance of our laws to intermeddle with Religion has produced among its several sects. Torrents of blood have been spilt in the old world, by vain attempts of the secular arm, to extinguish Religious discord, by proscribing all difference in Religious opinion. Time has at length revealed the true remedy. Every relaxation of narrow and rigorous policy, wherever it has been tried, has been found to assuage the disease. The American Theatre has exhibited proofs that equal and compleat liberty, if it does not wholly eradicate it, sufficiently destroys its malignant influence on the health and prosperity of the State. If with the salutary effects of this system under our own eyes, we begin to contract the bounds of Religious freedom, we know no name that will too severely reproach our folly. At least let warning be taken at the first fruits of the threatened innovation. The very appearance of the Bill has transformed "that Christian forbearance, love and charity," [Virginia Declaration of Rights, art. 16] which of late mutually prevailed, into animosities and jealousies, which may not soon be appeased. What mischiefs may not be dreaded, should this enemy to the public quiet be armed with the force of a law?

12. Because the policy of the Bill is adverse to the diffusion of the light of Christianity. The first wish of those who enjoy this precious gift ought to be that it may be imparted to the whole race of mankind. Compare the number of those who have as yet received it with the number still remaining under the dominion of false Religions; and how small is the former! Does the policy of the Bill tend to lessen the disproportion? No; it at once discourages those who are strangers to the light of revelation from coming into the Region of it; and countenances by example the nations who continue in darkness, in shutting out those who might convey it to them. Instead of Levelling as far as possible, every obstacle to the victorious progress of Truth, the Bill with an ignoble and unchristian timidity would circumscribe it with a wall of defence against the encroachments of error.

13. Because attempts to enforce by legal sanctions, acts obnoxious to so great a proportion of Citizens, tend to enervate the laws in general, and to slacken the bands of Society. If it be difficult to execute any law which is not generally deemed necessary or salutary, what must be the case, where it is deemed invalid and dangerous? And what may be the effect of so striking an example of impotency in the Government, on its general authority?

14. Because a measure of such singular magnitude and delicacy ought not to be imposed, without the clearest evidence that it is called for by a majority of citizens, and no satisfactory method is yet proposed by which the voice of the majority in this case may be determined, or its influence secured. "The people of the respective counties are indeed requested to signify their opinion respecting the adoption of the Bill to the next Session of Assembly." But the representation must be made equal, before the voice either of the Representatives or of the Counties will be that of the people. Our hope is that neither of the former will, after due consideration, espouse the dangerous principle of the Bill. Should the event disappoint us, it will still leave us in full confidence, that a fair appeal to the latter will reverse the sentence against our liberties.

15. Because finally, "the equal right of every citizen to the free exercise of his Religion according to the dictates of conscience" is held by the same tenure with all our other rights. If we recur to its origin, it is equally the gift of nature; if we weigh its importance, it cannot be less dear to us; if we consult the "Declaration of those rights which pertain to the good people of Virginia, as the basis and foundation of Government," it is enumerated with equal solemnity, or rather studied emphasis. Either then, we must say, that the Will of the Legislature is the only measure of their authority; and that in the plenitude of this authority, they may sweep away all our fundamental rights; or, that they are bound to leave this particular right untouched and sacred: Either we must say, that they may controul the freedom of the press, may abolish the Trial by Jury, may swallow up the Executive and Judiciary Powers of the State; nay that they may despoil us of our very right of suffrage, and erect themselves into an independent and hereditary Assembly or, we must say, that they have no authority to enact into law the Bill under consideration. We the Subscribers say, that the General Assembly

of this Commonwealth have no such authority: And that no effort may be omitted on our part against so dangerous an usurpation, we oppose to it, this remonstrance; earnestly praying, as we are in duty bound, that the Supreme Lawgiver of the Universe, by illuminating those to whom it is addressed, may on the one hand, turn their Councils from every act which would affront his holy prerogative, or violate the trust committed to them: and on the other, guide them into every measure which may be worthy of his blessing,.may redound to their own praise, and may establish more firmly the liberties, the prosperity and the happiness of the Commonwealth.

44

VIRGINIA, ACT FOR ESTABLISHING RELIGIOUS FREEDOM
31 Oct. 1785
Madison Papers 8:399–401

I. Whereas Almighty God hath created the mind free; that all attempts to influence it by temporal punishments or burthens, or by civil incapacitations, tend only to beget habits of hypocrisy and meanness, and are a departure from the plan of the Holy author of our religion, who being Lord both of body and mind, yet chose not to propagate it by coercions on either, as was in his Almighty power to do; that the impious presumption of legislators and rulers, civil as well as ecclesiastical, who being themselves but fallible and uninspired men, have assumed dominion over the faith of others, setting up their own opinions and modes of thinking as the only true and infallible, and as such endeavouring to impose them on others, hath established and maintained false religions over the greatest part of the world, and through all time; that to compel a man to furnish contributions of money for the propagation of opinions which he disbelieves, is sinful and tyrannical; that even the forcing him to support this or that teacher of his own religious persuasion, is depriving him of the comfortable liberty of giving his contributions to the particular pastor, whose morals he would make his pattern, and whose powers he feels most persuasive to righteousness, and is withdrawing from the ministry those temporary rewards, which proceeding from an approbation of their personal conduct, are an additional incitement to earnest and unremitting labours for the instruction of mankind; that our civil rights have no dependence on our religious opinions, any more than our opinions in physics or geometry; that therefore the proscribing any citizen as unworthy the public confidence by laying upon him an incapacity of being called to offices of trust and emolument, unless he profess or renounce this or that religious opinion, is depriving him injuriously of those privileges and advantages to which in common with his fellow-citizens he has a natural right; that it tends only to corrupt the principles of that religion it is meant to encourage, by bribing with a monopoly of wor[l]dly honours and emoluments, those who will externally profess and conform to it; that though indeed these are criminal who do not withstand such temptation, yet neither are those innocent who lay the bait in their way; that to suffer the civil magistrate to intrude his powers into the field of opinion, and to restrain the profession or propagation of principles on supposition of their ill tendency, is a dangerous fallacy, which at once destroys all religious liberty, because he being of course judge of that tendency will make his opinions the rule of judgement; and approve or condemn the sentiments of others only as they shall square with or differ from his own; that it is time enough for the rightful purposes of civil government, for its officers to interfere when principles break out into overt acts against peace and good order; and finally, that truth is great and will prevail if left to herself, that she is the proper and sufficient antagonist to error, and has nothing to fear from the conflict, unless by human interposition disarmed of her natural weapons, free argument and debate, errors ceasing to be dangerous when it is permitted freely to contradict them:

II. *Be it enacted by the General Assembly,* That no man shall be compelled to frequent or support any religious worship, place, or ministry whatsoever, nor shall be enforced restrained, molested, or burthened in his body or goods, nor shall otherwise suffer on account of his religious opinions or belief; but that all men shall be free to profess, and by argument to maintain, their opinion in matters of religion, and that the same shall in no wise diminish, enlarge, or affect their civil capacities.

III. And though we well know that this assembly elected by the people for the ordinary purposes of legislation only, have no power to restrain the acts of succeeding assemblies, constituted with powers equal to our own, and that therefore to declare this act to be irrevocable would be of no effect in law; yet we are free to declare, and do declare, that the rights hereby asserted are of the natural rights of mankind, and that if any act shall be hereafter passed to repeal the present, or to narrow its operation such act will be an infringement of natural right.

45

THOMAS JEFFERSON, AUTOBIOGRAPHY
1821
Works 1:71

The bill for establishing religious freedom, the principles of which had, to a certain degree, been enacted before, I had drawn in all the latitude of reason and right. It still met with opposition; but, with some mutilations in the preamble, it was finally passed; and a singular proposition proved that its protection of opinion was meant to be universal. Where the preamble declares, that coercion is a departure from the plan of the holy author of our religion, an amendment was proposed, by inserting the word "Jesus

Christ," so that it should read, "a departure from the plan of Jesus Christ, the holy author of our religion;" the insertion was rejected by a great majority, in proof that they meant to comprehend, within the mantle of its protection, the Jew and the Gentile, the Christian and Mahometan, the Hindoo, and Infidel of every denomination.

46

VERMONT CONSTITUTION OF 1786,
CH. 1, ART. 3
Thorpe 6:3752

III. That all men have a natural and unalienable right to worship Almighty God according to the dictates of their own consciences and understandings, as in their opinion shall be regulated by the word of God; and that no man ought, or of right can be compelled to attend any religious worship, or erect or support any place of worship, or maintain any minister, contrary to the dictates of his conscience; nor can any man be justly deprived or abridged of any civil right as a citizen, on account of his religious sentiments, or peculiar mode of religious worship; and that no authority can, or ought to be vested in, or assumed by any power whatsoever, that shall in any case interfere with, or in any manner control the rights of conscience, in the free exercise of religious worship: Nevertheless, every sect or denomination of Christians ought to observe the Sabbath or Lord's day, and keep up some sort of religious worship, which to them shall seem most agreeable to the revealed will of God.

47

AN OLD WHIG, NO. 5
Fall 1787
Storing 3.3.25–29

In order that people may be sufficiently impressed, with the necessity of establishing a BILL OF RIGHTS in the forming of a new constitution, it is very proper to take a short view of some of those liberties, which it is of the greatest importance for Freemen to retain to themselves, when they surrender up a part of their natural rights for the good of society.

The first of these, which it is of the utmost importance for the people to retain to themselves, which indeed they have not even the right to surrender, and which at the same time it is of no kind of advantage to government to strip them of, is the LIBERTY OF CONSCIENCE. I know that a ready answer is at hand, to any objections upon this head. We shall be told that in this enlightened age, the rights of conscience are perfectly secure: There is no necessity of guarding them; for no man has the remotest thoughts of invading them. If this be the case, I beg leave to reply that now is the very time to secure them.—Wise and prudent men always take care to guard against danger beforehand, and to make themselves safe whilst it is yet in their power to do it without inconvenience or risk.—[W]ho shall answer for the ebbings and flowings of opinion, or be able to say what will be the fashionable frenzy of the next generation? It would have been treated as a very ridiculous supposition, a year ago, that the charge of witchcraft would cost a person her life in the city of Philadelphia; yet the fate of the unhappy old woman called *Corbmaker,* who was beaten—repeatedly wounded with knives—mangled and at last killed in our streets, in obedience to the commandment which requires "that we shall not suffer a witch to live," without a possibility of punishing or even of detecting the authors of this inhuman folly, should be an example to warn us how little we ought to trust to the unrestrained discretion of human nature.

Uniformity of opinion in science, morality, politics or religion, is undoubtedly a very great happiness to mankind; and there have not been wanting zealous champions in every age, to promote the means of securing so invaluable a blessing. If in America we have not lighted up fires to consume Heretics in religion, if we have not persecuted unbelievers to promote the unity of the faith, in matters which pertain to our final salvation in a future world, I think we have all of us been witness to something very like the same spirit, in matters which are supposed to regard our political salvation in this world. In Boston it seems at this very moment, that no man is permitted to publish a doubt of the infalibility of the late convention, without giving up his name to the people, that he may be delivered over to speedy destruction; and it is but a short time since the case was little better in this city. Now this is a portion of the very same spirit, which has so often kindled the fires of the inquisition: and the same Zealot who would hunt a man down for a difference of opinion upon a political question which is the subject of public enquiry, if he should happen to be fired with zeal for a particular species of religion, would be equally intolerant. The fact is, that human nature is still the same that ever it was: the fashion indeed changes; but the seeds of superstition, bigotry and enthusiasm, are too deeply implanted in our minds, ever to be eradicated; and fifty years hence, the French may renew the persecution of the Huguenots, whilst the Spaniards in their turn may become indifferent to their forms of religion. They are idiots who trust their future security to the whim of the present hour. One extreme is always apt to produce the contrary, and those countries, which are now the most lax in their religious notions, may in a few years become the most rigid, just as the people of this country from not being able to bear any continental government at all, are now flying into the opposite extreme of surrendering up all the powers of the different states, to one continental government.

The more I reflect upon the history of mankind, the more I am disposed to think that it is our duty to secure the essential rights of the people, by every precaution; for not an avenue has been left unguarded, through which

oppression could possibly enter in any government[,] without some enemy of the public peace and happiness improving the opportunity to break in upon the liberties of the people; and none have been more frequently successful in the attempt, than those who have covered their ambitious designs under the garb of a fiery zeal for religious orthodoxy. What has happened in other countries and in other ages, may very possibly happen again in our own country, and for aught we know, before the present generation quits the stage of life. We ought therefore in a *bill of rights* to secure, in the first place, by the most express stipulations, the sacred rights of conscience. Has this been done in the constitution, which is now proposed for the consideration of the people of this country?—Not a word on this subject has been mentioned in any part of it; but we are left in this important article, as well as many others, entirely to the mercy of our future rulers.

But supposing our future rulers to be wicked enough to attempt to invade the rights of conscience; I may be asked how will they be able to effect so horrible a design? I will tell you my friends—*The unlimited power of taxation* will give them the command of all the treasures of the continent; *a standing army* will be wholly at their devotion, and the authority which is given them over the *militia,* by virtue of which they may, if they please, change all the officers of the militia on the continent in one day, and put in new officers whom they can better trust; by which they can subject all the militia to strict military laws, and punish the disobedient with death, or otherwise, as they shall think right: by which they can march the militia back and forward from one end of the continent to the other, at their discretion; these powers, if they should ever fall into bad hands, may be abused to the worst of purposes. Let us instance one thing arising from this right of organizing and governing the militia. Suppose a man alledges that he is conscientiously scrupulous of bearing Arms.—By the bill of rights of Pennsylvania he is bound only to pay an equivalent for his personal service.—What is there in the new proposed constitution to prevent his being dragged like a Prussian soldier to the camp and there compelled to bear arms?—This will depend wholly upon the wisdom and discretion of the future legislature of the continent in the framing their militia laws; and I have lived long enough to hear the practice *of commuting personal service for a paltry fine* in time of war and foreign invasion most severely reprobated by some persons who ought to have judged more rightly on the subject—Such flagrant oppressions as these I dare say will not happen at the beginning of the new government; probably not till the powers of government shall be firmly fixed; but it is a duty we owe to ourselves and our posterity if possible to prevent their ever happening. I hope and trust that there are few persons at present hardy enough to entertain thoughts of creating any religious establishment for this country; although I have lately read a piece in the newspaper, which speaks of *religious* as well as civil and military *offices,* as being hereafter to be disposed of by the new government; but if a majority of the continental legislature should at any time think fit to establish a form of religion, for the good people of this continent, with all the pains and penalties which in other countries are annexed to the establishment of a national church, what is there in the proposed constitution to hinder their doing so? Nothing; for we have no bill of rights, and every thing therefore is in their power and at their discretion. And at whose discretion? We know not any more than we know the fates of those generations which are yet unborn.

48

A [MARYLAND] FARMER, NO. 7
11 Apr. 1788
Storing 5.1.105–7

Thus it is that barbarity—cruelty and blood which stain the history of religion, spring from the corruption of civil government, and from that never-dying hope and fondness for a state of equality, which constitutes an essential part of the soul of man:—A chaos of darkness obscures the downfal of empire, intermixed with gleams of light, which serve only to disclose scenes of desolation and horror—From the last confusion springs order:—The bold spirits who pull down the ancient fabric—erect a new one, founded on the natural liberties of mankind, and *where civil government is preserved free, there can be no religious tyranny*—the sparks of bigotry and enthusiasm may and will crackle, but can never light into a blaze.—

The truth of these remarks appear from the histories of those two great revolutions of European government, which seem to have convulsed this earth to the centre of its orb, and of which we have compleat record—The Roman and the Gothic, or as it is more commonly called the feudal constitution:—In the infancy of the Roman republic, when enterprizing and free, their conquests were rapid, because beneficial to the conquered (who were admitted to a participation of their liberty) their religion, although devoid, was not only unstained by persecution, but censurably liberal—they received without discrimination the Gods of the countries they subdued, into the list of their deities, until Olympus was covered with an army of demigods as numerous as the legions of Popish Saints; and we find the Grecian divinities adored with more sincere piety at Rome, than at Athens.—Rome was then in the zenith of her glory—in the days of her wretched decline—in the miserable reigns of Caracalla, Eliagabalus and Commodus.—Ammianus and others, inform us that the Christians were butchered like sheep, for reviving the old exploded doctrine of a future state, in which Emperors and Senators were to be placed on a level with the poorest and most abject of mankind:—And in the succeeding despotisms when christianity became the established religion, it grew immediately as corrupt in its infancy, as ever it has proved at any period since—the most subtle disquisitions of a metaphysical nature became the universal rage—the more incomprehensible—the more obstinately were they maintained, and in fine, the canonized Austin or Ambrose,

(I forget which) closed his laborious enquiries, with this holy position—*that he believed, because it was impossible.* At length the great question, whether the three persons of the divinity, were three or one, became publickly agitated, and threw all mankind into a flame—Councils after councils, composed of all the wisdom of the divines, were assembled, and at length the doctrine that three were one prevailed, and such would have been the determination had it been proposed that three were sixteen—because misery is the foundation, upon which error erects her tyranny over the vulgar mind.—After this determination the arm of the Magistrate was called in, and those poor misled Arians who were still so wicked as to imagine that three must be three, were not only declared guilty of a most abominable and damnable heresy, but were thenceforth exterminated by fire and sword.

In the first age of the *Gothic* government, those free and hardy adventurers, deserted their Idols and embraced the doctrines of Christianity with ardent sincerity:—The King and a large majority of a nation, would be converted and baptized with as much celerity as the ceremony could be performed—but still liberty in the temporal, secured freedom in the spiritual administration: Christians and Pagan citizens lived together in the utmost harmony—Those bold and hardy conquerors would never listen to Bishops who advised persecution, and held in sovereign contempt all those metaphysical distinctions with which a pure religion has been disgraced, in order to cloak villainous designs and support artful usurpations of civil powers in feeble and turbulent governments. The Gothic institutions were however much sooner corrupted from internal vices than the Roman, and the undeniable reason was, that in the former, government by representation was admitted almost coeval with their first inundations;—whereas with the Romans, the democratic branch of power, exercised by the people personally, rendered them invinsible both in war and peace—the virtue of this internal institution could only be subdued by the greatness of its external acquisition—extensive empire ruined this mighty fabric—a superstructure, which overshadowed the then known world, was too mighty for the foundation confined within the walls of a city—the wealth imported by the Scipios from Spain and Afric, and by Flaminius, Lucullus, Sylla and Pompey, from the East, enabled the *few* to corrupt the *many*—a case that can never exist but where the legislative power resides exclusively in the citizens of the town—The Roman republic then became diseased at the heart, but as it was ages in forming, so it required ages of corruption to destroy a robust constitution where every atom was a nerve: It was not so with the Gothic constitution, mortal disease soon made its appearance there—Civil liberty was early destroyed by the insolence and oppressions of the great—The temporal power availed itself of that spiritual influence which nature has given religion over the hearts of men—A religion, the divinity of which is demonstrable by reason alone, unassisted by revelation became the corrupt instrument of usurpation.—Those who were the authors of the disorders which disgraced civil government, cut the reins of ecclesiastical persecution: And an universal and tyrannic confusion was mingled with absurdities that excite both ridicule and horror. We see a Duke of Gandia (who was betrayed and assassinated by that monster of perfidy Caesar Borgia, the bastard of the infamous Pope Alexander the VIth) in the last moments of his existence, begging the cut throat son, that he would intercede with his father, the Pope, in favour of his poor soul, that it might not be kept long in purgatory, but dispatched as soon as possible to Heaven, to dispute the infallibility of those vice-gerents of God, who generally patterned after the devil, was considered as an heresy more damnable than blaspheming the most high. Religious tyranny continued in this state, during those convulsions which broke the aristocracies of Europe, and settled their governments into mixed monarchies: A ray of light then beamed—but only for a moment—the turbulent state and quick corruption of mixed monarchy, opened a new scene of religious horror—Pardons for all crimes committed and to be committed, were regulated by ecclesiastical law, with a mercantile exactitude, and a Christian knew what he must pay for murdering another better than he now does the price of a pair of boots: At length some bold spirits began to doubt whether wheat flour, made into paste, could be actually human flesh, or whether the wine made in the last vintage could be the real blood of Christ, who had been crucified upwards of 1400 years— Such was the origin of the Protestant reformation—at the bare mention of such heretical and dangerous doctrine, striking (as they said) at the root of all religion, the sword of power leaped from its scabbard, the smoke that arose from the flames, to which the most virtuous of mankind, were without mercy committed, darkened all Europe for ages; tribunals, armed with frightful tortures, were every where erected, to make men confess opinions, and then they were solemnly burned for confessing, whilst priest and people sang hymns around them; and the fires of persecution are scarcely yet extinguished. *Civil and religious liberty are inseparably interwoven—whilst government is pure and equal—religion will be uncontaminated:—The moment government becomes disordered, bigotry and fanaticism take root and grow—they are soon converted to serve the purpose of usurpation, and finally, religious persecution reciprocally supports and is supported by the tyranny of the temporal powers.*

49

JAMES MADISON, VIRGINIA RATIFYING CONVENTION
12 June 1788
Papers 11:130–31

The honorable member has introduced the subject of religion. Religion is not guarded—there is no bill of rights declaring that religion should be secure. Is a bill of rights a security for religion? Would the bill of rights, in this state, exempt the people from paying for the support of one particular sect, if such sect were exclusively established

by law? If there were a majority of one sect, a bill of rights would be a poor protection for liberty. Happily for the states, they enjoy the utmost freedom of religion. This freedom arises from that multiplicity of sects, which pervades America, and which is the best and only security for religious liberty in any society. For where there is such a variety of sects, there cannot be a majority of any one sect to oppress and persecute the rest. Fortunately for this commonwealth, a majority of the people are decidedly against any exclusive establishment—I believe it to be so in the other states. There is not a shadow of right in the general government to intermeddle with religion. Its least interference with it, would be a most flagrant usurpation. I can appeal to my uniform conduct on this subject, that I have warmly supported religious freedom. It is better that this security should be depended upon from the general legislature, than from one particular state. A particular state might concur in one religious project. But the United States abound in such a variety of sects, that it is a strong security against religious persecution, and it is sufficient to authorise a conclusion, that no one sect will ever be able to outnumber or depress the rest.

50

PATRICK HENRY, VIRGINIA RATIFYING CONVENTION
12 June 1788
Elliot 3:317–18

Wherefore is religious liberty not secured? One honorable gentlemen, who favors adoption, said that he had had his fears on the subject. If I can well recollect, he informed us that he was perfectly satisfied, by the powers of reasoning, (with which he is so happily endowed,) that those fears were not well grounded. There is many a religious man who knows nothing of argumentative reasoning; there are many of our most worthy citizens who cannot go through all the labyrinths of syllogistic, argumentative deductions, when they think that the rights of conscience are invaded. This sacred right ought not to depend on constructive, logical reasoning.

. . . That sacred and lovely thing, religion, ought not to rest on the ingenuity of logical deduction. Holy religion, sir, will be prostituted to the lowest purposes of human policy. What has been more productive of mischief among mankind than religious disputes? Then here, sir, is a foundation for such disputes, when it requires learning and logical deduction to perceive that religious liberty is secure.

51

VIRGINIA RATIFYING CONVENTION,
PROPOSED AMENDMENTS
27 June 1788
Dumbauld 185

Nineteenth, That any person religiously scrupulous of bearing arms ought to be exempted upon payment of an equivalent to employ another to bear arms in his stead.

Twentieth, That religion or the duty which we owe to our Creator, and the manner of discharging it can be directed only by reason and conviction, not by force or violence, and therefore all men have an equal, natural and unalienable right to the free exercise of religion according to the dictates of conscience, and that no particular religious sect or society ought to be favored or established by Law in preference to others.

52

DEBATE IN NORTH CAROLINA RATIFYING
CONVENTION
30 July 1788
Elliot 4:191–200, 208–9

Mr. HENRY ABBOT, after a short exordium, which was not distinctly heard, proceeded thus: Some are afraid, Mr. Chairman, that, should the Constitution be received, they would be deprived of the privilege of worshipping God according to their consciences, which would be taking from them a benefit they enjoy under the present constitution. They wish to know if their religious and civil liberties be secured under this system, or whether the general government may not make laws infringing their religious liberties. The worthy member from Edenton mentioned sundry political reasons why treaties should be the supreme law of the land. It is feared, by some people, that, by the power of making treaties, they might make a treaty engaging with foreign powers to adopt the Roman Catholic religion in the United States, which would prevent the people from worshipping God according to their own consciences. The worthy member from Halifax has in some measure satisfied my mind on this subject. But others may be dissatisfied. Many wish to know what *religion* shall be established. I believe a majority of the community are Presbyterians. I am, for my part, against any exclusive establishment; but if there were any, I would prefer the Episcopal. The exclusion of religious tests is by many thought dangerous and impolitic. They suppose that if there be no religious test required, pagans, deists, and Mahometans might obtain offices among us, and that the senators and representatives might all be pagans. Every person employed by the general and state governments is to take an oath to support the former. Some are desirous to know how and by whom they are to swear, since no religious tests are required—whether they are to swear by Jupiter, Juno, Minerva, Proserpine, or Pluto. We ought to be suspicious of our liberties. We have felt the effects of oppressive measures, and know the happy consequences of being jealous of our rights. I would be glad some gentleman would endeavor to obviate these objections, in order to satisfy the religious part of the society. Could I be convinced that the objections were well founded, I would then declare my opinion against the Constitution. [Mr. Abbot added several other observations, but spoke too low to be heard.]

Mr. IREDELL. Mr. Chairman, nothing is more desirable than to remove the scruples of any gentleman on this interesting subject. Those concerning religion are entitled to particular respect. I did not expect any objection to this particular regulation, which, in my opinion, is calculated to prevent evils of the most pernicious consequences to society. Every person in the least conversant in the history of mankind, knows what dreadful mischiefs have been committed by religious persecutions. Under the color of religious tests, the utmost cruelties have been exercised. Those in power have generally considered all wisdom centred in themselves; that they alone had a right to dictate to the rest of mankind; and that all opposition to their tenets was profane and impious. The consequence of this intolerant spirit had been, that each church has in turn set itself up against every other; and persecutions and wars of the most implacable and bloody nature have taken place in every part of the world. America has set an example to mankind to think more modestly and reasonably—that a man may be of different religious sentiments from our own, without being a bad member of society. The principles of toleration, to the honor of this age, are doing away those errors and prejudices which have so long prevailed, even in the most intolerant countries. In the Roman Catholic countries, principles of moderation are adopted which would have been spurned at a century or two ago. I should be sorry to find, when examples of toleration are set even by arbitrary governments, that this country, so impressed with the highest sense of liberty, should adopt principles on this subject that were narrow and illiberal.

I consider the clause under consideration as one of the strongest proofs that could be adduced, that it was the intention of those who formed this system to establish a general religious liberty in America. Were we to judge from the examples of religious tests in other countries, we should be persuaded that they do not answer the purpose for which they are intended. What is the consequence of such in England? In that country no man can be a member in the House of Commons, or hold any office under the crown, without taking the sacrament according to the rites of the Church. This, in the first instance, must degrade and profane a rite which never ought to be taken but from a sincere principle of devotion. To a man of base principles, it is made a mere instrument of civil policy. The intention was, to exclude all persons from offices but the members of the Church of England. Yet it is notorious that dissenters qualify themselves for offices in this manner, though they never conform to the Church on any other occasion; and men of no religion at all have no scruple to make use of this qualification. It never was known that a man who had no principles of religion hesitated to perform any rite when it was convenient for his private interest. No test can bind such a one. I am therefore clearly of opinion that such a discrimination would neither be effectual for its own purposes, nor, if it could, ought it by any means to be made. Upon the principles I have stated, I confess the restriction on the power of Congress, in this particular, has my hearty approbation. They certainly have no authority to interfere in the establishment of any religion whatsoever; and I am astonished that any gentleman should conceive they have. Is there any power given to Congress in matters of religion? Can they pass a single act to impair our religious liberties? If they could, it would be a just cause of alarm. If they could, sir, no man would have more horror against it than myself. Happily, no sect here is superior to another. As long as this is the case, we shall be free from those persecutions and distractions with which other countries have been torn. If any future Congress should pass an act concerning the religion of the country, it would be an act which they are not authorized to pass, by the Constitution, and which the people would not obey. Every one would ask, "Who authorized the government to pass such an act? It is not warranted by the Constitution, and is barefaced usurpation." The power to make treaties can never be supposed to include a right to establish a foreign religion among ourselves, though it might authorize a toleration of others.

But it is objected that the people of America may, perhaps, choose representatives who have no religion at all, and that pagans and Mahometans may be admitted into offices. But how is it possible to exclude any set of men, without taking away that principle of religious freedom which we ourselves so warmly contend for? This is the foundation on which persecution has been raised in every part of the world. The people in power were always right, and every body else wrong. If you admit the least difference, the door to persecution is opened. Nor would it answer the purpose, for the worst part of the excluded sects would comply with the test, and the best men only be kept out of our counsels. But it is never to be supposed that the people of America will trust their dearest rights to persons who have no religion at all, or a religion materially different from their own. It would be happy for mankind if religion was permitted to take its own course, and maintain itself by the excellence of its own doctrines. The divine Author of our religion never wished for its support by worldly authority. Has he not said that the gates of hell shall not prevail against it? It made much greater progress for itself, than when supported by the greatest authority upon earth.

It has been asked by that respectable gentleman (Mr. Abbot) what is the meaning of that part, where it is said that the United States shall *guaranty* to every state in the Union a republican form of government, and why a *guaranty* of religious freedom was not included. The meaning of the guaranty provided was this: There being thirteen

governments confederated upon a republican principle, it was essential to the existence and harmony of the confederacy that each should be a republican government, and that no state should have a right to establish an aristocracy or monarchy. That clause was therefore inserted to prevent any state from establishing any government but a republican one. Every one must be convinced of the mischief that would ensue, if any state had a right to change its government to a monarchy. If a monarchy was established in any one state, it would endeavor to subvert the freedom of the others, and would, probably, by degrees succeed in it. This must strike the mind of every person here, who recollects the history of Greece, when she had confederated governments. The king of Macedon, by his arts and intrigues, got himself admitted a member of the Amphictyonic council, which was the superintending government of the Grecian republics; and in a short time he became master of them all. It is, then, necessary that the members of a confederacy should have similar governments. But consistently with this restriction, the states may make what change in their own governments they think proper. Had Congress undertaken to guaranty religious freedom, or any particular species of it, they would then have had a pretence to interfere in a subject they have nothing to do with. Each state, so far as the clause in question does not interfere, must be left to the operation of its own principles.

There is a degree of jealousy which it is impossible to satisfy. Jealousy in a free government ought to be respected; but it may be carried to too great an extent. It is impracticable to guard against all possible danger of people's choosing their officers indiscreetly. If they have a right to choose, they may make a bad choice.

I met, by accident, with a pamphlet, this morning, in which the author states, as a very serious danger, that the pope of Rome might be elected President. I confess this never struck me before; and if the author had read all the qualifications of a President, perhaps his fears might have been quieted. No man but a native, or who has resided fourteen years in America, can be chosen President. I know not all the qualifications for pope, but I believe he must be taken from the college of cardinals; and probably there are many previous steps necessary before he arrives at this dignity. A native of America must have very singular good fortune, who, after residing fourteen years in his own country, should go to Europe, enter into Romish orders, obtain the promotion of cardinal, afterwards that of pope, and at length be so much in the confidence of his own country as to be elected President. It would be still more extraordinary if he should give up his popedom for our presidency. Sir, it is impossible to treat such idle fears with any degree of gravity. Why is it not objected, that there is no provision in the Constitution against electing one of the kings of Europe President? It would be a clause equally rational and judicious.

I hope that I have in some degree satisfied the doubts of the gentleman. This article is calculated to secure universal religious liberty, by putting all sects on a level—the only way to prevent persecution. I thought nobody would have objected to this clause, which deserves, in my opinion, the highest approbation. This country has already had the honor of setting an example of civil freedom, and I trust it will likewise have the honor of teaching the rest of the world the way to religious freedom also. God grant both may be perpetuated to the end of time!

Mr. ABBOT, after expressing his obligations for the explanation which had been given, observed that no answer had been given to the question he put concerning the form of an *oath*.

Mr. IREDELL. Mr. Chairman, I beg pardon for having omitted to take notice of that part which the worthy gentleman has mentioned. It was by no means from design, but from its having escaped my memory, as I have not the conveniency of taking notes. I shall now satisfy him in that particular in the best manner in my power.

According to the modern definition of an oath, it is considered a "solemn appeal to the Supreme Being, for the truth of what is said, by a person who believes in the existence of a Supreme Being and in a future state of rewards and punishments, according to that form which will bind his conscience most." It was long held that no oath could be administered but upon the New Testament, except to a Jew, who was allowed to swear upon the Old. According to this notion, none but Jews and Christians could take an oath; and heathens were altogether excluded. At length, by the operation of principles of toleration, these narrow notions were done away. Men at length considered that there were many virtuous men in the world who had not had an opportunity of being instructed either in the Old or New Testament, who yet very sincerely believed in a Supreme Being, and in a future state of rewards and punishments. It is well known that many nations entertain this belief who do not believe either in the Jewish or Christian religion. Indeed, there are few people so grossly ignorant or barbarous as to have no religion at all. And if none but Christians or Jews could be examined upon oath, many innocent persons might suffer for want of the testimony of others. In regard to the form of an oath, that ought to be governed by the religion of the person taking it. I remember to have read an instance which happened in England, I believe in the time of Charles II. A man who was a material witness in a cause, refused to swear upon the book, and was admitted to swear with his uplifted hand. The jury had a difficulty in crediting him; but the chief justice told them, he had, in his opinion, taken as strong an oath as any of the other witnesses, though, had he been to swear himself, he should have kissed the book. A very remarkable instance also happened in England, about forty years ago, of a person who was admitted to take an oath according to the rites of his own country, though he was a heathen. He was an East Indian, who had a great suit in chancery, and his answer upon oath to a bill filed against him was absolutely necessary. Not believing either in the Old or New Testament, he could not be sworn in the accustomed manner, but was sworn according to the form of the Gentoo religion, which he professed, by touching the foot of a priest. It appeared that, according to the tenets of this religion, its members believed in a Supreme Being, and in a future state of rewards and punishments. It was accordingly held by the judges, upon great

consideration, that the oath ought to be received; they considering that it was probable those of that religion were equally bound in conscience by an oath according to their form of swearing, as they themselves were by one of theirs; and that it would be a reproach to the justice of the country, if a man, merely because he was of a different religion from their own, should be denied redress of an injury he had sustained. Ever since this great case, it has been universally considered that, in administering an oath, it is only necessary to inquire if the person who is to take it, believes in a Supreme Being, and in a future state of rewards and punishments. If he does, the oath is to be administered according to that form which it is supposed will bind his conscience most. It is, however, necessary that such a belief should be entertained, because otherwise there would be nothing to bind his conscience that could be relied on; since there are many cases where the terror of punishment in this world for perjury could not be dreaded. I have endeavored to satisfy the committee. We may, I think, very safely leave religion to itself; and as to the form of the oath, I think this may well be trusted to the general government, to be applied on the principles I have mentioned.

Gov. JOHNSTON expressed great astonishment that the people were alarmed on the subject of religion. This, he said, must have arisen from the great pains which had been taken to prejudice men's minds against the Constitution. He begged leave to add the following few observations to what had been so ably said by the gentleman last up.

I read the Constitution over and over, but could not see one cause of apprehension or jealousy on this subject. When I heard there were apprehensions that the pope of Rome could be the President of the United States, I was greatly astonished. It might as well be said that the king of England or France, or the Grand Turk, could be chosen to that office. It would have been as good an argument. It appears to me that it would have been dangerous, if Congress could intermeddle with the subject of religion. True religion is derived from a much higher source than human laws. When any attempt is made, by any government, to restrain men's consciences, no good consequence can possibly follow. It is apprehended that Jews, Mahometans, pagans, &c., may be elected to high offices under the government of the United States. Those who are Mahometans, or any others who are not professors of the Christian religion, can never be elected to the office of President, or other high office, but in one of two cases. First, if the people of America lay aside the Christian religion altogether, it may happen. Should this unfortunately take place, the people will choose such men as think as they do themselves. Another case is, if any persons of such descriptions should, notwithstanding their religion, acquire the confidence and esteem of the people of America by their good conduct and practice of virtue, they may be chosen. I leave it to gentlemen's candor to judge what probability there is of the people's choosing men of different sentiments from themselves.

But great apprehensions have been raised as to the influence of the Eastern States. When you attend to circumstances, this will have no weight. I know but two or three states where there is the least chance of establishing any particular religion. The people of Massachusetts and Connecticut are mostly Presbyterians. In every other state, the people are divided into a great number of sects. In Rhode Island, the tenets of the Baptists, I believe, prevail. In New York, they are divided very much: the most numerous are the Episcopalians and the Baptists. In New Jersey, they are as much divided as we are. In Pennsylvania, if any sect prevails more than others, it is that of the Quakers. In Maryland, the Episcopalians are most numerous, though there are other sects. In Virginia, there are many sects; you all know what their religious sentiments are. So in all the Southern States they differ; as also in New Hampshire. I hope, therefore, that gentlemen will see there is no cause of fear that any one religion shall be exclusively established.

Mr. CALDWELL thought that some danger might arise. He imagined it might be objected to in a political as well as in a religious view. In the first place, he said, there was an invitation for Jews and pagans of every kind to come among us. At some future period, said he, this might endanger the character of the United States. Moreover, even those who do not regard religion, acknowledge that the Christian religion is best calculated, of all religions, to make good members of society, on account of its morality. I think, then, added he, that, in a political view, those gentlemen who formed this Constitution should not have given this invitation to Jews and heathens. All those who have any religion are against the emigration of those people from the eastern hemisphere.

Mr. SPENCER was an advocate for securing every unalienable right, and that of worshipping God according to the dictates of conscience in particular. He therefore thought that no one particular religion should be established. Religious tests, said he, have been the foundation of persecutions in all countries. Persons who are conscientious will not take the oath required by religious tests, and will therefore be excluded from offices, though equally capable of discharging them as any member of the society. It is feared, continued he, that persons of bad principles, deists, atheists, &c., may come into this country; and there is nothing to restrain them from being eligible to offices. He asked if it was reasonable to suppose that the people would choose men without regarding their characters. Mr. Spencer then continued thus: Gentlemen urge that the want of a test admits the most vicious characters to offices. I desire to know what test could bind them. If they were of such principles, it would not keep them from enjoying those offices. On the other hand, it would exclude from offices conscientious and truly religious people, though equally capable as others. Conscientious persons would not take such an oath, and would be therefore excluded. This would be a great cause of objection to a religious test. But in this case, as there is not a religious test required, it leaves religion on the solid foundation of its own inherent validity, without any connection with temporal authority; and no kind of oppression can take place. I confess it strikes me so. I am sorry to differ from the worthy gentlemen. I cannot object to this part of the Constitution. I wish every other part was as good and proper.

Gov. JOHNSTON approved of the worthy member's candor. He admitted a possibility of Jews, pagans, &c., emigrating to the United States; yet, he said, they could not be in proportion to the emigration of Christians who should come from other countries; that, in all probability, the children even of such people would be Christians; and that this, with the rapid population of the United States, their zeal for religion, and love of liberty, would, he trusted, add to the progress of the Christian religion among us.

. . . . .

Mr. SPAIGHT. As to the subject of religion, I thought what had been said would fully satisfy that gentleman and every other. No power is given to the general government to interfere with it at all. Any act of Congress on this subject would be a usurpation.

No sect is preferred to another. Every man has a right to worship the Supreme Being in the manner he thinks proper. No test is required. All men of equal capacity and integrity, are equally eligible to offices. Temporal violence might make mankind wicked, but never religious. A test would enable the prevailing sect to persecute the rest. I do not suppose an infidel, or any such person, will ever be chosen to any office, unless the people themselves be of the same opinion. He says that Congress may establish ecclesiastical courts. I do not know what part of the Constitution warrants that assertion. It is impossible. No such power is given them. The gentleman advises such amendments as would satisfy him, and proposes a mode of amending before ratifying. If we do not adopt first, we are no more a part of the Union than any foreign power. It will be also throwing away the influence of our state to propose amendments as the condition of our ratification. If we adopt first, our representatives will have a proportionable weight in bringing about amendments, which will not be the case if we do not adopt. It is adopted by ten states already. The question, then, is, not whether the Constitution be good, but whether we will or will not confederate with the other states. The gentleman supposes that the liberty of the press is not secured. The Constitution does not take it away. It says nothing of it, and can do nothing to injure it. But it is secured by the constitution of every state in the Union in the most ample manner.

53

HOUSE OF REPRESENTATIVES, AMENDMENTS
TO THE CONSTITUTION
15, 17, 20 Aug. 1789
Annals 1:729–31, 755, 766

[*15 Aug.*]

The House again went into a Committee of the Whole on the proposed amendments to the constitution, Mr. BOUDINOT in the Chair.

The fourth proposition being under consideration, as follows:

Article 1. Section 9. Between paragraphs two and three insert "no religion shall be established by law, nor shall the equal rights of conscience be infringed."

Mr. SYLVESTER had some doubts of the propriety of the mode of expression used in this paragraph. He apprehended that it was liable to a construction different from what had been made by the committee. He feared it might be thought to have a tendency to abolish religion altogether.

Mr. VINING suggested the propriety of transposing the two members of the sentence.

Mr. GERRY said it would read better if it was, that no religious doctrine shall be established by law.

Mr. SHERMAN thought the amendment altogether unnecessary, inasmuch as Congress had no authority whatever delegated to them by the Constitution to make religious establishments; he would, therefore, move to have it struck out.

Mr. [Daniel] CARROLL.—As the rights of conscience are, in their nature, of peculiar delicacy, and will little bear the gentlest touch of governmental hand; and as many sects have concurred in opinion that they are not well secured under the present constitution, he said he was much in favor of adopting the words. He thought it would tend more towards conciliating the minds of the people to the Government than almost any other amendment he had heard proposed. He would not contend with gentlemen about the phraseology, his object was to secure the substance in such a manner as to satisfy the wishes of the honest part of the community.

Mr. MADISON said, he apprehended the meaning of the words to be, that Congress should not establish a religion, and enforce the legal observation of it by law, nor compel men to worship God in any manner contrary to their conscience. Whether the words are necessary or not, he did not mean to say, but they had been required by some of the State Conventions, who seemed to entertain an opinion that under the clause of the Constitution, which gave power to Congress to make all laws necessary and proper to carry into execution the Constitution, and the laws made under it, enabled them to make laws of such a nature as might infringe the rights of conscience and establish a national religion; to prevent these effects he presumed the amendment was intended, and he thought it as well expressed as the nature of the language would admit.

Mr. HUNTINGTON said that he feared, with the gentleman first up on this subject, that the words might be taken in such latitude as to be extremely hurtful to the cause of religion. He understood the amendment to mean what had been expressed by the gentleman from Virginia; but others might find it convenient to put another construction upon it. The ministers of their congregations to the Eastward were maintained by the contributions of those who belonged to their society; the expense of building meetinghouses was contributed in the same manner. These things were regulated by by-laws. If an action was brought before a Federal Court on any of these cases, the person who had neglected to perform his engagements could not be compelled to do it; for a support of ministers, or building of places of worship might be construed into a religious establishment.

By the charter of Rhode Island, no religion could be established by law; he could give a history of the effects of such a regulation; indeed the people were now enjoying the blessed fruits of it. He hoped, therefore, the amendment would be made in such a way as to secure the rights of conscience, and a free exercise of the rights of religion, but not to patronize those who professed no religion at all.

Mr. MADISON thought, if the word national was inserted before religion, it would satisfy the minds of honorable gentlemen. He believed that the people feared one sect might obtain a pre-eminence, or two combine together, and establish a religion to which they would compel others to conform. He thought if the word national was introduced, it would point the amendment directly to the object it was intended to prevent.

Mr. LIVERMORE was not satisfied with that amendment; but he did not wish them to dwell long on the subject. He thought it would be better if it was altered, and made to read in this manner, that Congress shall make no laws touching religion, or infringing the rights of conscience.

Mr. GERRY did not like the term national, proposed by the gentleman from Virginia, and he hoped it would not be adopted by the House. It brought to his mind some observations that had taken place in the conventions at the time they were considering the present Constitution. It had been insisted upon by those who were called antifederalists, that this form of Government consolidated the Union; the honorable gentleman's motion shows that he considers it in the same light. Those who were called antifederalists at that time complained that they had injustice done them by the title, because they were in favor of a Federal Government, and the others were in favor of a national one; the federalists were for ratifying the constitution as it stood, and the others not until amendments were made. Their names then ought not to have been distinguished by federalists and antifederalists, but rats and antirats.

Mr. MADISON withdrew his motion, but observed that the words "no national religion shall be established by law," did not imply that the Government was a national one; the question was then taken on Livermore's motion, and passed in the affirmative, thirty-one for, and twenty against it.

[17 Aug.]

The committee then proceeded to the fifth proposition:

Article 1, section 10, between the first and second paragraph, insert "no State shall infringe the equal rights of conscience, nor the freedom of speech or of the press, nor of the right of trial by jury in criminal cases."

Mr. TUCKER.—This is offered, I presume, as an amendment to the Constitution of the United States, but it goes only to the alteration of the constitutions of particular States. It will be much better, I apprehend, to leave the State Governments to themselves, and not to interfere with them more than we already do; and that is thought by many to be rather too much. I therefore move, sir, to strike out these words.

Mr. MADISON conceived this to be the most valuable amendment in the whole list. If there was any reason to restrain the Government of the United States from infringing upon these essential rights, it was equally necessary that they should be secured against the State Governments. He thought that if they provided against the one, it was as necessary to provide against the other, and was satisfied that it would be equally grateful to the people.

Mr. LIVERMORE had no great objection to the sentiment, but he thought it not well expressed. He wished to make it an affirmative proposition; "the equal rights of conscience, the freedom of speech or of the press, and the right of trial by jury in criminal cases, shall not be infringed by any State."

This transposition being agreed to, and Mr. TUCKER's motion being rejected, the clause was adopted.

[20 Aug.]

On motion of Mr. AMES, the fourth amendment was altered so as to read "Congress shall make no law establishing religion, or to prevent the free exercise thereof, or to infringe the rights of conscience." This being adopted. . . .

which we have since enjoyed; for the peaceable and rational manner in which we have been enabled to establish constitutions of government for our safety and happiness, and particularly the national one now lately instituted; for the civil and religious liberty with which we are blessed, and the means we have of acquiring and diffusing useful knowledge; and, in general, for all the great and various favors which He has been pleased to confer upon us.

And also that we may then unite in most humbly offering our prayers and supplications to the great Lord and Ruler of Nations, and beseech Him to pardon our national and other trangressions; to enable us all, whether in public or private stations, to perform our several and relative duties properly and punctually; to render our National Government a blessing to all the people by constantly being a Government of wise, just, and constitutional laws, discreetly and faithfully executed and obeyed; to protect and guide all sovereigns and nations (especially such as have shown kindness to us), and to bless them with good governments, peace, and concord; to promote the knowledge and practice of true religion and virtue, and the increase of science among them and us; and, generally, to grant unto all mankind such a degree of temporal prosperity as He alone knows to be best.

54

GEORGE WASHINGTON, PROCLAMATION: A NATIONAL THANKSGIVING
3 Oct. 1789

1 Richardson 64

Whereas it is the duty of all nations to acknowledge the providence of Almighty God, to obey His will, to be grateful for His benefits, and humbly to implore His protection and favor; and

Whereas both Houses of Congress have, by their joint committee, requested me "to recommend to the people of the United States a day of public thanksgiving and prayer, to be observed by acknowledging with grateful hearts the many and signal favors of Almighty God, especially by affording them an opportunity peaceably to establish a form of government for their safety and happiness:"

Now, therefore, I do recommend and assign Thursday, the 26th day of November next, to be devoted by the people of these States to the service of that great and glorious Being who is the beneficent author of all the good that was, that is, or that will be; that we may then all unite in rendering unto Him our sincere and humble thanks for His kind care and protection of the people of this country previous to their becoming a nation; for the signal and manifold mercies and the favorable interpositions of His providence in the course and conclusion of the late war; for the great degree of tranquillity, union, and plenty

55

TENCH COXE, NOTES CONCERNING THE UNITED STATES OF AMERICA
1790

Stokes 1:275

The situation of religious rights in the American states, though also well known, is too important, too precious a circumstance to be omitted. Almost every sect and form of Christianity is known here—as also the Hebrew church. None are tolerated. All are admitted, aided by mutual charity and concord, and supported and cherished by the laws. In this land of promise for the good men of all denominations, are actually to be found, the independent or congregational church from England, the protestant episcopal church (separated by our revolution from the church of England) the quaker church, the English, Scotch, Irish and Dutch presbyterian or calvinist churches, the Roman catholic church, the German Lutheran church, the German reformed church, the baptist and anabaptist churches, the hugonot or French protestant church, the Moravian church, the Swedish episcopal church, the seceders from the Scotch church, the menonist church, with other christian sects, and the Hebrew church. Mere toleration is a doctrine exploded by our general condition; instead of which have been substituted an unqualified admission, and assertion, "that their own modes of worship and of faith equally belong to all the worshippers of God, of whatever church, sect, or denomination."

56

ALEXANDER HAMILTON, REPORT ON MANUFACTURES
5 Dec. 1791

Papers 10:253–54

IV As to the promoting of emigration from foreign countries.

Men reluctantly quit one course of occupation and livelihood for another, unless invited to it by very apparent and proximate advantages. Many, who would go from one country to another, if they had a prospect of continuing, with more benefit, the callings to which they have been educated, will often not be tempted to change their situation by the hope of doing better in some other way. Manufacturers, who (listening to the powerful invitations of a better price for their fabrics, or their labour, of greater cheapness of provisions and raw materials, of an exemption from the chief part of the taxes, burdens and restraints, which they endure in the old world, of greater personal independence and consequence, under the operation of a more equal government, and of, what is far more precious than mere religious toleration, a perfect equality of religious privileges) would probably flock from Europe to the united states to pursue their own trades or professions, if they were once made sensible of the advantages they would enjoy, and were inspired with an assurance of encouragement and employment. . . .

57

THOMAS PAINE, RIGHTS OF MAN, PT. 1
1791

Life 6:101–6

The French Constitution hath abolished or renounced *toleration*, and *intolerance* also, and hath established UNIVERSAL RIGHT OF CONSCIENCE.

Toleration is not the *opposite* of intoleration, but is the *counterfeit* of it. Both are despotisms. The one assumes to itself the right of withholding liberty of conscience, and the other of granting it. The one is the Pope, armed with fire and faggot, and the other is the Pope selling or granting indulgences. The former is church and state, and the latter is church and traffic.

But toleration may be viewed in a much stronger light. Man worships not himself, but his Maker: and the liberty of conscience which he claims, is not for the service of himself, but of his God. In this case, therefore, we must necessarily have the associated idea of two beings; the *mortal* who renders the worship, and the *immortal being* who is worshipped.

Toleration therefore, places itself not between man and man, nor between church and church, nor between one denomination of religion and another, but between God and man; between the being who worships, and the *being* who is worshipped; and by the same act of assumed authority by which it tolerates man to pay his worship, it presumptuously and blasphemously sets up itself to tolerate the Almighty to receive it.

Were a bill brought into Parliament, entitled, "An *act* to tolerate or grant liberty to the Almighty to receive the worship of a Jew or a Turk," or "to prohibit the Almighty from receiving it," all men would startle, and call it blasphemy. There would be an uproar. The presumption of toleration in religious matters would then, present itself unmasked; but the presumption is not the less because the name of "Man" only appears to those laws, for the associated idea of the *worshipper* and the *worshipped* cannot be separated.

Who, then, art thou, vain dust and ashes! by whatever name thou art called, whether a king, a bishop, a church or a state, a parliament or any thing else, that obtrudest thine insignificance between the soul of man and his Maker? Mind thine own concerns. If he believes not as thou believest, it is a proof that thou believest not as he believeth, and there is no earthly power can determine between you.

With respect to what are called denominations of religion, if every one is left to judge of his own religion, there is no such thing as a religion that is wrong; but if they are to judge of each other's religion, there is no such thing as a religion that is right; and therefore all the world is right, or all the world is wrong.

But with respect to religion itself, without regard to names, and as directing itself from the universal family of mankind to the divine object of all adoration, *it is man bringing to his Maker the fruits of his heart;* and though these fruits may differ from each other like the fruits of the earth, the grateful tribute of every one is accepted.

A bishop of Durham, or a bishop of Winchester, or the archbishop who heads the dukes, will not refuse a tithe-sheaf of wheat, because it is not a cock of hay; nor a cock of hay, because it is not a sheaf of wheat; nor a pig, because it is neither the one nor the other: but these same persons, under the figure of an established church, will not permit their Maker to receive the various tithes of man's devotion.

One of the continual choruses of Mr. Burke's book, is "church and state." He does not mean some one particular church, or some one particular state, but any church and state; and he uses the term as a general figure to hold forth the political doctrine of always uniting the church with the state in every country, and he censures the National Assembly for not having done this in France. Let us bestow a few thoughts on this subject.

All religions are in their nature mild and benign, and united with principles of morality. They could not have made proselytes at first, by professing anything that was vicious, cruel, persecuting or immoral. Like every thing else, they had their beginning; and they proceeded by persuasion, exhortation, and example. How then is it that they lose their native mildness, and become morose and intolerant?

It proceeds from the connection which Mr. Burke recommends. By engendering the church with the state, a sort of mule-animal, capable only of destroying, and not of breeding up, is produced, called, *The Church established by Law*. It is a stranger, even from its birth to any parent mother on which it is begotten, and whom in time it kicks out and destroys.

The Inquisition in Spain does not proceed from the religion originally professed, but from this mule-animal, engendered between the church and the state. The burnings in Smithfield proceeded from the same heterogeneous production; and it was the regeneration of this strange animal in England afterwards, that renewed rancor and irreligion among the inhabitants, and that drove the people called Quakers and Dissenters to America.

Persecution is not an original feature in *any* religion; but it is always the strongly marked feature of all law-religions, or religions established by law. Take away the law-establishment, and every religion reassumes its original benignity. In America, a Catholic priest is a good citizen, a good character, and a good neighbor; an Episcopal minister is of the same description: and this proceeds, independently of the men, from there being no law-establishment in America.

If also we view this matter in a temporal sense, we shall see the ill effects it has had on the prosperity of nations. The union of church and state has impoverished Spain. The revoking the edict of Nantes drove the silk manufacture from France into England; and church and state are now driving the cotton manufacture from England to America and France.

Let then Mr. Burke continue to preach his anti-political doctrine of Church and State. It will do some good. The National Assembly will not follow his advice, but will benefit by his folly. It was by observing the ill effects of it in England, that America has been warned against it; and it is by experiencing them in France, that the National Assembly have abolished it, and, like America, have established UNIVERSAL RIGHT OF CONSCIENCE, AND UNIVERSAL RIGHT OF CITIZENSHIP.

58

THOMAS JEFFERSON TO DANBURY BAPTIST ASSOCIATION
1 Jan. 1802
Writings 16:281

Believing with you that religion is a matter which lies solely between man and his God, that he owes account to none other for his faith or his worship, that the legislative powers of government reach actions only, and not opinions, I contemplate with sovereign reverence that act of the whole American people which declared that their legislature should "make no law respecting an establishment of religion, or prohibiting the free exercise thereof," thus building a wall of separation between Church and State. Adhering to this expression of the supreme will of the nation in behalf of the rights of conscience, I shall see with sincere satisfaction the progress of those sentiments which tend to restore to man all his natural rights, convinced he has no natural right in opposition to his social duties.

59

ST. GEORGE TUCKER,
BLACKSTONE'S COMMENTARIES,
1:App. 296–97, 2:App. 3–11
1803

On the first of these subjects, our state bill of rights contains, what, if prejudice were not incapable of perceiving truth, might be deemed an axiom, concerning the human mind. That "religion, or the duty we owe to our Creator, and the manner of discharging it, can be dictated only by reason and conviction, not by force or violence." In vain, therefore, may the civil magistrate interpose the authority of human laws, to prescribe that belief, or produce that conviction, which human reason rejects: in vain may the secular arm be extended, the rack stretched, and the flames kindled, to realize the tortures denounced against unbelievers by all the various sects of the various denominations of fanatics and enthusiasts throughout the globe. The martyr at the stake, glories in his tortures, and proves that human laws may punish, but cannot convince. The pretext of religion, and the pretences of sanctity and humility, have been employed throughout the world, as the most direct means of gaining influence and power. Hence the numberless martyrdoms and massacres which have drenched the whole earth with blood, from the first moment that civil and religious institutions were blended together. To separate them by mounds which can never be overleaped, is the only means by which our duty to God, the peace of mankind, and the genuine fruits of charity and fraternal love, can be preserved or properly discharged. This prohibition, therefore, may be regarded as the most powerful cement of the federal government, or rather, the violation of it will prove the most powerful engine of separation. Those who prize the union of the states will never think of touching this article with unhallowed hands. The ministry of the unsanctified sons of Aaron scarcely produced a flame more sudden, more violent, or more destructive, than such an attempt would inevitably excite. . . . I forbear to say more, in this place, upon this subject, having treated of it somewhat at large in a succeeding note.

. . . . .

The right of personal opinion is one of those absolute rights which man hath received from the immediate gift of his Creator, but which the policy of all governments, from the first institution of society to the foundation of the

American republics, hath endeavoured to restrain, in some mode or other. The mind being created free by the author of our nature, in vain have the arts of man endeavoured to shackle it: it may indeed be imprisoned a while by ignorance, or restrained from a due exertion of it's powers by tyranny and oppression; but let the rays of science, or the dawn of freedom, penetrate the dungeon, its faculties are instantly rarified and burst their prison. This right of personal opinion, comprehends first, liberty of conscience in all matters relative to religion; and, secondly, liberty of speech and of discussion in all speculative matters, whether religious, philosophical, or political.

1. Liberty of conscience in matters of religion consists in the absolute and unrestrained exercise of our religious opinions, and duties, in that mode which our own reason and conviction dictate, without the control or intervention of any human power or authority whatsoever. This liberty though made a part of our constitution, and interwoven in the nature of man by his Creator; so far as the arts of fraud and terrors of violence have been capable of abridging it, hath been the subject of coercion by human laws in all ages and in all countries as far as the annals of mankind extend. The infallibility of the rulers of nations, in matters of religion, hath been a doctrine practically enforced from the earliest periods of history to the present moment among jews, pagans, mahometans, and christians, alike. The altars of Moloch and of Jehovah have been equally stained with the blood of victims, whose conscience did not receive conviction from the polluted doctrines of blood thirsty priests and tyrants. Even in countries where the crucifix, the rack, and the flames have ceased to be the engines of proselitism, civil incapacities have been invariably attached to a dissent from the national religion: the ceasing to persecute by more violent means, has in such nations obtained the name of toleration*. In liberty of conscience says the elegant Dr. Price, I include much more than toleration. Jesus Christ has established a perfect equality among his followers. His command is, that they shall assume no jurisdiction over one another, and acknowledge no master besides himself. It is, therefore, presumption in any of them to claim a right to any superiority or pre-eminence over their bretheren. Such a claim is implied, whenever any of them pretend to tolerate the rest. Not only all christians, but all men of all religions, ought to be considered by a state as equally entitled to it's protection, as far as they demean themselves honestly and peaceably. Toleration can take place only where there is a civil establishment of a particular mode of religion; that is, where a predominant sect enjoys exclusive advantages, and makes the encouragement of it's own mode of faith and worship a part of the constitution of the state; but at the same time thinks fit to suffer the exercise of other modes of faith and worship. Thanks be to God, the new American states are at present strangers to such establishments. In this respect, as well as many others, they have shewn in framing their constitutions, a degree of wisdom and liberality which is above all praise.

*[EDITORS' NOTE.—Tucker here reproduces a passage from Paine's *Rights of Man*, to be found at no. 57 *supra*.]

Civil establishments of formularies of faith and worship, are inconsistent with the rights of private judgement. They engender strife . . . they turn religion into a trade . . . they shore up error . . . they produce hypocrisy and prevarication . . . they lay an undue bias on the human mind in its inquiries, and obstruct the progress of truth . . . genuine religion is a concern that lies entirely between God and our own souls. It is incapable of receiving any aid from human laws. It is contaminated as soon as worldly motives and sanctions mix their influence with it. Statesmen should countenance it only by exhibiting, in their own example, a conscientious regard to it in those forms which are most agreeable to their own judgments, and by encouraging their fellow citizens in doing the same. They cannot, as public men, give it any other assistance. All, besides, that has been called a public leading in religion, has done it an essential injury, and produced some of the worst consequences.

The church establishment in England is one of the mildest sort. But even there what a snare has it been to integrity? And what a check to free inquiry? What dispositions favourable to despotism has it fostered? What a turn to pride and narrowness and domination has it given the clerical character? What struggles has it produced in its members to accommodate their opinions to the subscriptions and tests which it imposes? What a perversion of learning has it occasioned to defend obsolete creeds and absurdities? What a burthen is it on the consciences of some of its best clergy, who, in consequence of being bound down to a system they do not approve, and having no support except that which they derive from conforming to it, find themselves under the hard necessity of either prevaricating or starving? No one doubts but that the English clergy in general could with more truth declare that they do not, than that they do give their unfeigned assent to all and every thing contained in the thirty-nine articles, and the book of common prayer: and, yet, with a solemn declaration to this purpose, are they obliged to enter upon an office which above all offices requires those who exercise it to be examples of simplicity and sincerity . . . Who can help execrating the cause of such an evil?

But what I wish most to urge is the tendency of religious establishments to impede the improvement of the world. They are boundaries prescribed by human folly to human investigation; and enclosures, which intercept the light, and confine the exertions of reason. Let any one imagine to himself what effects similar establishments would have in philosophy, navigation, metaphisics, medicine, or mathematics. Something like this, took place in logic and philosophy, while the *ipse dixit* of Aristotle, and the nonsense of the schools, maintained, an authority like that of the creeds of churchmen; and the effect was a longer continuance of the world in the ignorance and barbarity of the dark ages. But civil establishments of religion are more pernicious. So apt are mankind to misrepresent the character of the Deity, and to connect his favour with particular modes of faith, that it must be expected that a religion so settled will be what it has hitherto been . . . a gloomy and cruel superstition, bearing the name of religion.

It has been long a subject of dispute, which is worse in

it's effects on society, such a religion or speculative atheism. For my own part, I could almost give the preference to the latter . . . Atheism is so repugnant to every principle of common sense, that it is not possible it should ever gain much ground, or become very prevalent. On the contrary, there is a particular proneness in the human mind to superstition, and nothing is more likely to become prevalent . . . Atheism leaves us to the full influence of most of our natural feelings and social principles; and these are so strong in their operation, that, in general, they are a sufficient guard to the order of society. But superstition counteracts these principles, by holding forth men to one another as objects of divine hatred; and by putting them on harrassing, silenceing, imprissoning and burning one another, in order to do God service . . . Atheism is a sanctuary for vice, by taking away the motives to virtue arising from the will of God, and the fear of future judgment. But superstition is more a sanctuary for vice, by teaching men ways of pleasing God, without moral virtue; and by leading them even to compound for wickedness, by ritual services, by bodily penances and mortifications; by adoring shrines, going pilgrimages, saying many prayers, receiving absolution from the priests, exterminating heretics, &c. . . . Atheism destroys the sacredness and obligation of an oath. But is there not also a religion (so called) which does this, by teaching, that there is power which can dispense with the obligation of oaths; that *pious* frauds are right, and that faith is not to be kept with heretics.

It is indeed only a rational and liberal religion; a religion founded on just notions of the Deity, as a Being who regards equally every sincere worshipper, and by whom all are alike favoured as far as they act up to the light they enjoy: a religion which consists in the imitation of the moral perfections of an Almighty but Benevolent Governor of Nature, who directs for the best, all events, in confidence in the care of his providence, in resignation to his will, and in the faithful discharge of every duty of piety and morality from a regard to his authority, and the apprehension of a future righteous retribution. It is only this religion (the inspiring principle of every thing fair and worthy, and joyful, and which, in truth is nothing but the love of God to man, and virtue warming the heart and directing the conduct). It is only this kind of religion that can bless the world, or be an advantage to society. This is the religion that every enlightened friend to mankind will be zealous to support. But it is a religion that the powers of the world know little of, and which will always be best promoted by being left free and open. The following passage from the same author, deserves too much attention to be pretermitted: "Let no such monster be known there, [in the United States] as human authority in matters of religion. Let every honest and peaceable man, whatever is his faith, be protected there; and find an effectual defence against the attacks of bigotry and intolerance. In the United States may religion flourish! They cannot be very great and happy if it does not. But let it be a better religion than most of those which have been hitherto professed in the world. Let it be a religion which enforces moral obligations; not a religion which relaxes and evades them . . . A tolerant and catholic religion; not a rage for proselytism . . . A religion of peace and charity; not a religion that persecutes curses and damns. In a word, let it be the genuine gospel of peace, lifting above the world, warming the heart with the love of God and his creatures, and sustaining the fortitude of good men, by the assured hope of a future deliverance from death, and an infinite reward in the everlasting kingdom of our Lord and Saviour."

This inestimable and imprescriptible right is guaranteed to the citizens of the United States, as such, by the constitution of the United States, which declares, that no religious test shall ever be required as a qualification to any office or public trust under the United States; and by that amendment to the constitution of the United States, which prohibits congress from making any law respecting the establishment of religion, or prohibiting the free exercise thereof; and to the citizens of Virginia by the bill of rights, which declares, "that religion, or the duty which we owe to our Creator, and the manner of discharging it, can be directed only by reason and conviction, not by force or violence, and therefore all men are equally entitled to the free exercise of religion, according to the dictates of conscience: and that it is the mutual duty of all to practice christian forbearance, love, and charity, towards each other." And further, by the act for establishing religious freedom, by which it is also declared, "that no man shall be compelled to frequent or support any religious worship, place, or ministry, whatsoever, nor shall be enforced, restrained, molested or burthened in his body or goods, nor shall otherwise suffer on account of his religious opinions or belief; but that all men shall be free to profess, and by argument maintain their opinions in matters of religion, and that the same shall in no wise diminish, enlarge, or affect their civil capacities."

60

THOMAS JEFFERSON TO REV. SAMUEL MILLER
23 Jan. 1808
Works 11:7–9

I have duly received your favor of the 18th and am thankful to you for having written it, because it is more agreeable to prevent than to refuse what I do not think myself authorized to comply with. I consider the government of the US. as interdicted by the Constitution from intermeddling with religious institutions, their doctrines, discipline, or exercises. This results not only from the provision that no law shall be made respecting the establishment, or free exercise, of religion, but from that also which reserves to the states the powers not delegated to the U. S. Certainly no power to prescribe any religious exercise, or to assume authority in religious discipline, has been delegated to the general government. It must then rest with the states, as far as it can be in any human authority. But it is only proposed that I should *recommend*, not prescribe a day of fasting & prayer. That is, that I should *indirectly* assume to the U. S. an authority over religious exercises which the Constitution has directly precluded them from. It must be meant too that this recommendation is to carry some authority, and to be sanctioned by some penalty on those who disregard it; not indeed of fine and imprisonment, but of some degree of proscription perhaps in public opinion. And does the change in the nature of the penalty make the recommendation the less *a law* of conduct for those to whom it is directed? I do not believe it is for the interest of religion to invite the civil magistrate to direct it's exercises, it's discipline, or it's doctrines; nor of the religious societies that the general government should be invested with the power of effecting any uniformity of time or matter among them. Fasting & prayer are religious exercises. The enjoining them an act of discipline. Every religious society has a right to determine for itself the times for these exercises, & the objects proper for them, according to their own particular tenets; and this right can never be safer than in their own hands, where the constitution has deposited it.

I am aware that the practice of my predecessors may be quoted. But I have ever believed that the example of state executives led to the assumption of that authority by the general government, without due examination, which would have discovered that what might be a right in a state government, was a violation of that right when assumed by another. Be this as it may, every one must act according to the dictates of his own reason, & mine tells me that civil powers alone have been given to the President of the US. and no authority to direct the religious exercises of his constituents.

I again express my satisfaction that you have been so good as to give me an opportunity of explaining myself in a private letter, in which I could give my reasons more in detail than might have been done in a public answer: and I pray you to accept the assurances of my high esteem & respect.

61

HOUSE OF REPRESENTATIVES, RETURNED BILL
21, 23 Feb. 1811
Annals 22:982–85, 995, 997

[*21 Feb.*]

A Message was received from the President of the United States, by Mr. Edward Coles, his Secretary, who, by command of the President, returned to the House the bill passed by the two Houses entitled "An act incorporating the Protestant Episcopal Church in the town of Alexandria, in the District of Columbia," and presented to the President for his approbation and signature, on Thursday the fourteenth instant, to which bill the President having made objections, the same were also delivered in by the said Secretary, who then withdrew.

The objections were read, and ordered to be entered at large on the Journal, as follows:

To the House of Representatives of the United States:

Having examined and considered the bill, entitled "An act incorporating the Protestant Episcopal Church in the town of Alexandria, in the District of Columbia," I now return the bill to the House of Representatives," in which it originated, with the following objections:

Because the bill exceeds the rightful authority to which Governments are limited, by the essential distinction between civil and religious functions, and violates, in particular, the article of the Constitution of the United States, which declares, that "Congress shall make no law respecting a religious establishment." The bill enacts into, and establishes by law, sundry rules and proceedings relative purely to the organization and polity of the church incorporated, and comprehending even the election and removal of the Minister of the same; so that no change could be made therein by the particular society, or by the general church of which it is a member, and whose authority it recognises. This particular church, therefore, would so far be a religious establishment by law; a legal force and sanction being given to certain articles in its constitution and administration. Nor can it be considered, that the articles thus established are to be taken as the descriptive criteria only of the corporate identity of the society, inasmuch as this identity must depend on other characteristics; as the regulations established are generally unessential, and alterable according to the principles and canons, by which churches of that denomination govern themselves; and as the injunctions and prohibitions contained in the regulations, would be enforced by the penal consequences applicable to a violation of them according to the local law:

Because the bill vests in the said incorporated church an authority to provide for the support of the poor, and the education of poor children of the same; an authority which being altogether superfluous, if the provision is to be the result of pious charity, would be a precedent for giving to religious societies, as such, a legal agency in carrying into effect a public and civil duty.

JAMES MADISON

February 21, 1811.

Mr. BASSETT suggested the reference of the Message to a select committee.

The SPEAKER conceived that the article on the Constitution on this subject required that the House should proceed to a reconsideration of the bill.

On motion of Mr. PITKIN, the House proceeded to reconsider the bill.

The Message was again read, as also was the following clause of the Constitution:

"Every bill which shall have passed the House of Representatives and the Senate, shall, before it becomes a law, be presented to the President of the United States; if he approve, he shall sign it;

but if not, he shall return it, with his objections, to that House in which it shall have originated, who shall enter the objections at large on their Journal, and proceed to reconsider it. If, after such reconsideration, two-thirds of that House shall agree to pass the bill, it shall be sent, together with the objections, to the other House, by which it shall likewise be reconsidered, and, if approved by two-thirds of that House, it shall become a law."

Mr. RANDOLPH asked whether a motion for indefinite postponement would, in the opinion of the Speaker, lie in this case?

The SPEAKER believed not.

The following article of the Constitution was then read by request:

"Congress shall make no law respecting an establishment of religion, or prohibiting the free exercise thereof; or abridging the freedom of speech, or of the press; or the right of the people peaceably to assemble, and to petition the Government for a redress of grievances."

Mr. BASSETT said, though the Constitution had prescribed a reconsideration of the bill when returned, the mode of reconsideration was not prescribed; and it might as well be by reference to a select committee as in any other mode. The bill might, perhaps, be amended. Of their power to amend it in its present stage, however, he was not certain.

Mr. SMILIE conceived the Constitution peremptorily to require an immediate decision.

Mr. PITKIN said, that this question was new to him. He had no idea that the Constitution precluded Congress from passing laws to incorporate religious societies for the purpose of enabling them to hold property, &c. He had always held the Constitution to intend to prevent the establishment of a National Church, such as the Church of England—a refusal to subscribe to the tenets of which was to exclude a citizen from office, &c. Desiring time for reflection, he therefore wished the bill to lie on the table for further consideration.

Mr. PICKMAN said, it appeared to him that the bill was not an important one, a refusal to pass which would be productive of any serious injury; and yet, that a full discussion of the principles it involved would occupy the whole of the remainder of the session. If two-thirds of the House were to refuse to proceed to a reconsideration, the bill would be *ipso facto* at an end; and this he thought would be the best course, &c., considering all the circumstances.

Mr. WHEATON said he differed widely from his colleague (Mr. PICKMAN) as to the importance of the bill now under consideration. He did not imagine that they were to assume the objections of the President to be valid, and of course to dismiss the bill. They had a duty to perform as well as the President. He had performed his duty in the case presented for consideration. And would gentlemen assume it as a correct position because the bill was objected to by the President that the House ought not to act understandingly? This was not a correct principle. In his view the objections made by the President to this bill were altogether futile. Mr. W. said he did not consider this bill any infringement of the Constitution. If it was, both branches of the Legislature, since the commencement of the Government, had been guilty of such infringement. It could not be said, indeed, that they had been guilty of doing much about religion; but they had at every session appointed Chaplains, to be of different denominations, to interchange weekly between the two Houses. Now, if a bill for regulating the funds of a religious society could be an infringement of the Constitution, the two Houses had so far infringed it by electing, paying or contracting with their Chaplains; for so far it established two different denominations of religion. Mr. W. deemed this question of very great consequence. Were the people of this District never to have any religion? Was it to be entirely excluded from these ten miles square? He should be afraid to come if that were to be the case. The want of time was no sufficient reason against giving this subject a mature consideration. What was done ought to be well done. For these reasons he was in favor of the bill lying on the table.

Mr. MACON quoted a precedent of the proceedings in a case similar to this in GENERAL WASHINGTON's Administration; in which the House, after a consideration of the Message, had come to the following resolution:

"*Resolved,* That to-morrow be assigned for the reconsideration of said bill, according to the Constitution of the United States."

He moved that the same resolution be now adopted.

Messrs. LYON and BOYD were in favor of an immediate decision.

Mr. SOUTHARD wished a postponement to give him time to examine the bill. He was convinced that a bill might be passed for regulating the temporal concerns of a religious society, which would not violate the Constitution; but did not say, till he could examine whether this was such a bill or not.

Mr. QUINCY quoted cases of laws which had passed the signature of the late President, which, in every material respect, appeared to him to contain the same provisions as this bill.

The motion of Mr. MACON was adopted without a division.

[*23 Feb.*]

The House resumed the reconsideration of the bill passed by the two Houses, entitled "An act incorporating the Protestant Episcopal Church, in the town of Alexandria, in the District of Columbia," which was presented for approbation on Thursday, the 14th instant, and returned by the President on the 21st instant, with objections.

The said bill was read at the Clerk's table.

· · · · ·

The President's objections were also again read; and, after debate, the question "That the House on reconsideration, do agree to pass the bill," was taken in the mode prescribed by the Constitution of the United States, and determined in the negative—yeas 29, nays 74.

62

PEOPLE V. RUGGLES

8 Johns. R. 290 (N.Y. 1811)

Kent, Ch. J. delivered the opinion of the Court. The offence charged is, that the defendant below did "wickedly, maliciously, and blasphemously utter, in the presence and hearing of divers good and christian people, these false, feigned, scandalous, malicious, wicked and blasphemous words, to wit, *"Jesus Christ* was a bastard, and his mother must be a whore;" and the single question is, whether this be a public offence by the law of the land. After conviction, we must intend that these words were uttered in a wanton manner, and, as they evidently import, with a wicked and malicious disposition, and not in a serious discussion upon any controverted point in religion. The language was blasphemous not only in a popular, but in a legal sense; for blasphemy, according to the most precise definitions, consists in maliciously reviling God, or religion, and this was reviling christianity through its author. (*Emlyn's Preface to the State Trials,* p. 8. See, also, *Whitlock's Speech, State Trials,* vol. 2, 273.) The jury have passed upon the intent or *quo animo,* and if those words spoken, in any case, will amount to a misdemeanor, the indictment is good.

Such words, uttered with such a disposition, were an offence at common law. In *Taylor's case,* (1 *Vent.* 293. 3 *Keb.* 607. *Tremaine's Pleas of the Crown,* 226. S. C.) the defendant was convicted upon information of speaking similar words, and the court of *K. B.* said, that christianity was parcel of the law, and to cast contumelious reproaches upon it, tended to weaken the foundation of moral obligation, and the efficacy of oaths. And in the case of *Rex* v. *Woolston,* (*Str.* 834. *Fitzg.* 64.) on a like conviction, the court said they would not suffer it to be debated whether defaming christianity in general was not an offence at common law, for that whatever strikes at the root of christianity, tends manifestly to the dissolution of civil government. But the court were careful to say, that they did not intend to include disputes between learned men upon particular controverted points. The same doctrine was laid down in the late case of *The King* v. *Williams,* for the publication of *Paine's "Age of Reason,"* which was tried before Lord *Kenyon,* in *July,* 1797. The authorities show that blasphemy against God, and contumelious reproaches and profane ridicule of Christ or the Holy Scriptures, (which are equally treated as blasphemy,) are offences punishable at common law, whether uttered by words or writings. (*Taylor's case,* 1 *Vent.* 293. 4 *Blacks. Com.* 59. 1 *Hawk.* b. 1. c. 5. 1 *East's P. C.* 3. *Tremaine's Entries,* 225. *Rex* v. *Doyley.*) The consequences may be less extensively pernicious in the one case than in the other, but in both instances, the

reviling is still an offence, because it tends to corrupt the morals of the people, and to destroy good order. Such offences have always been considered independent of any religious establishment or the rights of the church. They are treated as affecting the essential interests of civil society.

And why should not the language contained in the indictment be still an offence with us? There is nothing in our manners or institutions which has prevented the application or the necessity of this part of the common law. We stand equally in need, now as formerly, of all the moral discipline, and of those principles of virtue, which help to bind society together. The people of this state, in common with the people of this country, profess the general doctrines of christianity, as the rule of their faith and practice; and to scandalize the author of these doctrines is not only, in a religious point of view, extremely impious, but, even in respect to the obligations due to society, is a gross violation of decency and good order. Nothing could be more offensive to the virtuous part of the community, or more injurious to the tender morals of the young, than to declare such profanity lawful. It would go to confound all distinction between things sacred and profane; for, to use the words of one of the greatest oracles of human wisdom, "profane scoffing doth by little and little deface the reverence for religion;" and who adds, in another place, "two principal causes have I ever known of atheism—curious controversies and profane scoffing." (Lord *Bacon's Works,* vol. 2. 291. 503.) Things which corrupt moral sentiment, as obscene actions, prints and writings, and even gross instances of seduction, have, upon the same principle, been held indictable; and shall we form an exception in these particulars to the rest of the civilized world? No government among any of the polished nations of antiquity, and none of the institutions of modern *Europe,* (a single and monitory case excepted,) ever hazarded such a bold experiment upon the solidity of the public morals, as to permit with impunity, and under the sanction of their tribunals, the general religion of the community to be openly insulted and defamed. The very idea of jurisprudence with the ancient lawgivers and philosophers, embraced the religion of the country. *Jurisprudentia est divinarum atque humanarum rerum notitia.* (*Dig.* b. 1. 10. 2. *Cic. De Legibus,* b. 2. *passim.*)

The free, equal, and undisturbed, enjoyment of religious opinion, whatever it may be, and free and decent discussions on any religious subject, is granted and secured; but to revile, with malicious and blasphemous contempt, the religion professed by almost the whole community, is an abuse of that right. Nor are we bound, by any expressions in the constitution, as some have strangely supposed, either not to punish at all, or to punish indiscriminately the like attacks upon the religion of *Mahomet* or of the grand *Lama;* and for this plain reason, that the case assumes that we are a christian people, and the morality of the country is deeply ingrafted upon christianity, and not upon the doctrines or worship of those impostors. Besides, the offence is *crimen malitiae,* and the imputation of malice could not be inferred from any invectives upon superstitions equally false and unknown. We are not to be

101

restrained from animadversion upon offences against public decency, like those committed by Sir *Charles Sedley,* (1 *Sid.* 168,) or by one *Rollo,* (*Sayer,* 158,) merely because there may be savage tribes, and perhaps semibarbarous nations, whose sense of shame would not be affected by what we should consider the most audacious outrages upon decorum. It is sufficient that the common law checks upon words and actions, dangerous to the public welfare, apply to our case, and are suited to the condition of this and every other people whose manners are refined, and whose morals have been elevated and inspired with a more enlarged benevolence, by means of the christian religion.

Though the constitution has discarded religious establishments, it does not forbid judicial cognisance of those offences against religion and morality which have no reference to any such establishment, or to any particular form of government, but are punishable because they strike at the root of moral obligation, and weaken the security of the social ties. The object of the 38th article of the constitution, was, to "guard against spiritual oppression and intolerance," by declaring that "the free exercise and enjoyment of religious profession and worship, without discrimination or preference, should for ever thereafter be allowed within this state, to all mankind." This declaration, (noble and magnanimous as it is, when duly understood,) never meant to withdraw religion in general, and with it the best sanctions of moral and social obligation from all consideration and notice of the law. It will be fully satisfied by a free and universal toleration, without any of the tests, disabilities, or discriminations, incident to a religious establishment. To construe it as breaking down the common law barriers against licentious, wanton, and impious attacks upon christianity itself, would be an enormous perversion of its meaning. The *proviso* guards the article from such dangerous latitude of construction, when it declares, the "*the liberty of conscience hereby granted,* shall not be so construed as to excuse acts of licentiousness, or justify practices inconsistent with the peace and safety of this state." The preamble and this *proviso* are a species of commentary upon the meaning of the article, and they sufficiently show that the framers of the constitution intended only to banish test oaths, disabilities and the burdens, and sometimes the oppressions, of church establishments; and to secure to the people of this state, freedom from coercion, and an equality of right, on the subject of religion. This was no doubt the consummation of their wishes. It was all that reasonable minds could require, and it had long been a favorite object, on both sides of the *Atlantic,* with some of the most enlightened friends to the rights of mankind, whose indignation had been roused by infringements of the liberty of conscience, and whose zeal was inflamed in the pursuit of its enjoyment. That this was the meaning of the constitution is further confirmed by a paragraph in a preceding article, which specially provides that "such parts of the common law as might be construed to establish or maintain any particular denomination of christians, or their ministers," were thereby abrogated.

The legislative exposition of the constitution is conformable to this view of it. Christianity, in its enlarged sense, as a religion revealed and taught in the Bible, is not unknown to our law. The *statute for preventing immorality* (*Laws,* vol. 1. 224. *R. S.* 675, s. 69, *et seq.*) consecrates the first day of the week, as holy time, and considers the violation of it as immoral. This was only the continuation, in substance, of a law of the colony which declared, that the profanation of the Lord's day was "the great scandal of the christian faith." The act *concerning oaths,* (*Laws,* vol. 1. p. 405. [2 *R. S.* 407, s. 82,]) recognises the common law mode of administering an oath, "by laying the hand on and kissing the gospels." Surely, then, we are bound to conclude, that wicked and malicious words, writings and actions which go to vilify those gospels, continue, as at common law, to be an offence against the public peace and safety. They are inconsistent with the reverence due to the administration of an oath, and among their other evil consequences, they tend to lessen, in the public mind, its religious sanction.

63

JAMES MADISON, PROCLAMATION
16 Nov. 1814
Richardson 1:558

The two Houses of the National Legislature having by a joint resolution expressed their desire that in the present time of public calamity and war a day may be recommended to be observed by the people of the United States as a day of public humiliation and fasting and of prayer to Almighty God for the safety and welfare of these States, His blessing on their arms, and a speedy restoration of peace, I have deemed it proper by this proclamation to recommend that Thursday, the 12th of January next, be set apart as a day on which all may have an opportunity of voluntarily offering at the same time in their respective religious assemblies their humble adoration to the Great Sovereign of the Universe, of confessing their sins and transgressions, and of strengthening their vows of repentance and amendment. They will be invited by the same solemn occasion to call to mind the distinguished favors conferred on the American people in the general health which has been enjoyed, in the abundant fruits of the season, in the progress of the arts instrumental to their comfort, their prosperity, and their security, and in the victories which have so powerfully contributed to the defense and protection of our country, a devout thankfulness for all which ought to be mingled with their supplications to the Beneficent Parent of the Human Race that He would be graciously pleased to pardon all their offenses against Him; to support and animate them in the discharge of their respective duties; to continue to them the precious advantages flowing from political institutions so auspicious to their safety against dangers from abroad, to their tranquillity at home, and to their liberties, civil and religious; and that He would in a special manner preside over the nation in its public councils and constituted authorities, giving wisdom to its measures and success to its arms in maintaining its rights and in overcoming all hostile designs and attempts against it; and, finally, that by inspiring the enemy with dispositions favorable to a just and reasonable peace its blessings may be speedily and happily restored.

64

JAMES MADISON, DETACHED MEMORANDA
ca. 1817

W. & M. Q., 3d ser., 3:554–60 (1946)

The danger of silent accumulations & encroachments by Ecclesiastical Bodies have not sufficiently engaged attention in the U. S. They have the noble merit of first unshackling the conscience from persecuting laws, and of establishing among religious Sects a legal equality. If some of the States have not embraced this just and this truly Xn principle in its proper latitude, all of them present examples by which the most enlightened States of the old world may be instructed; and there is one State at least, Virginia, where religious liberty is placed on its true foundation and is defined in its full latitude. The general principle is contained in her declaration of rights, prefixed to her Constitution: but it is unfolded and defined, in its precise extent, in the act of the Legislature, usually named the Religious Bill, which passed into a law in the year 1786. Here the separation between the authority of human laws, and the natural rights of Man excepted from the grant on which all political authority is founded, is traced as distinctly as words can admit, and the limits to this authority established with as much solemnity as the forms of legislation can express. The law has the further advantage of having been the result of a formal appeal to the sense of the Community and a deliberate sanction of a vast majority, comprizing every sect of Christians in the State. This act is a true standard of Religious liberty: its principle the great barrier agst usurpations on the rights of conscience. As long as it is respected & no longer, these will be safe. Every provision for them short of this principle, will be found to leave crevices at least thro' which bigotry may introduce persecution; a monster, that feeding & thriving on its own venom, gradually swells to a size and strength overwhelming all laws divine & human.

Ye States of America, which retain in your Constitutions or Codes, any aberration from the sacred principle of religious liberty, by giving to Caesar what belongs to God, or joining together what God has put asunder, hasten to revise & purify your systems, and make the example of your Country as pure & compleat, in what relates to the freedom of the mind and its allegiance to its maker, as in what belongs to the legitimate objects of political & civil institutions.

Strongly guarded as is the separation between Religion & Govt in the Constitution of the United States the danger of encroachment by Ecclesiastical Bodies, may be illustrated by precedents already furnished in their short history. (See the cases in which negatives were put by J. M. on two bills passd by Congs and his signature withheld from another. See also attempt in Kentucky for example, where it was proposed to exempt Houses of Worship from taxes.

The most notable attempt was that in Virga to establish a Genl assessment for the support of all Xn sects. This was proposed in the year   by P. H. and supported by all his eloquence, aided by the remaining prejudices of the Sect which before the Revolution had been established by law. The progress of the measure was arrested by urging that the respect due to the people required in so extraordinary a case an appeal to their deliberate will. The bill was accordingly printed & published with that view. At the instance of Col: George Nicholas, Col: George Mason & others, the memorial & remonstrance agst it was drawn up, (which see) and printed Copies of it circulated thro' the State, to be signed by the people at large. It met with the approbation of the Baptists, the Presbyterians, the Quakers, and the few Roman Catholics, universally; of the Methodists in part; and even of not a few of the Sect formerly established by law. When the Legislature assembled, the number of Copies & signatures prescribed displayed such an overwhelming opposition of the people, that the proposed plan of a genl assessmt was crushed under it; and advantage taken of the crisis to carry thro' the Legisl: the Bill above referred to, establishing religious liberty. In the course of the opposition to the bill in the House of Delegates, which was warm & strenuous from some of the minority, an experiment was made on the reverence entertained for the name & sactity of the Saviour, by proposing to insert the words "Jesus Christ" after the words "our lord" in the preamble, the object of which, would have been, to imply a restriction of the liberty defined in the Bill, to those professing his religion only. The amendment was discussed, and rejected by a vote of   agst (See letter of J. M. to Mr Jefferson dated   ) The opponents of the amendment having turned the feeling as well as judgment of the House agst it, by successfully contending that the better proof of reverence for that holy name wd be not to profane it by making it a topic of legisl. discussion, & particularly by making his religion the means of abridging the natural and equal rights of all men, in defiance of his own declaration that his Kingdom was not of this world. This view of the subject was much enforced by the circumstance that it was espoused by some members who were particularly distinguished by their reputed piety and Christian zeal.

But besides the danger of a direct mixture of Religion & civil Government, there is an evil which ought to be guarded agst in the indefinite accumulation of property from the capacity of holding it in perpetuity by ecclesiastical corporations. The power of all corporations, ought to be limited in this respect. The growing wealth acquired by them never fails to be a source of abuses. A warning on this subject is emphatically given in the example of the various Charitable establishments in G. B. the management of which has been lately scrutinized. The excessive wealth of ecclesiastical Corporations and the misuse of it in many Countries of Europe has long been a topic of complaint. In some of them the Church has amassed half perhaps the property of the nation. When the reformation took place, an event promoted if not caused, by that disordered state of things, how enormous were the treasures of religious societies, and how gross the corruptions engendered by them; so enormous & so gross as to produce in the Cabinets & Councils of the Protestant states a disregard, of all the pleas of the interested party drawn from the sanctions of the law, and the sacredness of property held in religious trust. The history of England during the period of the reformation offers a sufficient illustration for the present purpose.

Are the U. S. duly awake to the tendency of the precedents they are establishing, in the multiplied incorporations of Religious Congregations with the faculty of acquiring & holding property real as well as personal? Do not many of these acts give this faculty, without limit either as to time or as to amount? And must not bodies, perpetual in their existence, and which may be always gaining without ever losing, speedily gain more than is useful, and in time more than is safe? Are there not already examples in the U. S. of ecclesiastical wealth equally beyond its object and the foresight of those who laid the foundation of it? In the U. S. there is a double motive for fixing limits in this case, because wealth may increase not only from additional gifts, but from exorbitant advances in the value of the primitive one. In grants of vacant lands, and of lands in the vicinity of growing towns & Cities the increase of value is often such as if foreseen, would essentially controul the liberality confirming them. The people of the U. S. owe their Independence & their liberty, to the wisdom of descrying in the minute tax of 3 pence on tea, the magnitude of the evil comprized in the precedent. Let them exert the same wisdom, in watching agst every evil lurking under plausible disguises, and growing up from small beginnings. Obsta principiis.

> see the Treatise of Father Paul on beneficiary matters.

Is the appointment of Chaplains to the two Houses of Congress consistent with the Constitution, and with the pure principle of religious freedom?

In strictness the answer on both points must be in the negative. The Constitution of the U. S. forbids everything like an establishment of a national religion. The law appointing Chaplains establishes a religious worship for the national representatives, to be performed by Ministers of religion, elected by a majority of them; and these are to be paid out of the national taxes. Does not this involve the principle of a national establishment, applicable to a provision for a religious worship for the Constituent as well as of the representative Body, approved by the majority, and conducted by Ministers of religion paid by the entire nation.

The establishment of the chaplainship to Congs is a palpable violation of equal rights, as well as of Constitutional principles: The tenets of the chaplains elected [by the majority] shut the door of worship agst the members whose creeds & consciences forbid a participation in that of the majority. To say nothing of other sects, this is the case with that of Roman Catholics & Quakers who have always had members in one or both of the Legislative branches. Could a Catholic clergyman ever hope to be appointed a Chaplain? To say that his religious principles are obnoxious or that his sect is small, is to lift the evil at once and exhibit in its naked deformity the doctrine that religious truth is to be tested by numbers. or that the major sects have a right to govern the minor.

If Religion consist in voluntary acts of individuals, singly, or voluntarily associated, and it be proper that public functionaries, as well as their Constituents shd discharge their religious duties, let them like their Constituents, do so at their own expence. How small a contribution from each member of Congs wd suffice for the purpose? How just wd it be in its principle? How noble in its exemplary sacrifice to the genius of the Constitution; and the divine right of conscience? Why should the expence of a religious worship be allowed for the Legislature, be paid by the public, more than that for the Ex. or Judiciary branch of the Govt

Were the establishment to be tried by its fruits, are not the daily devotions conducted by these legal Ecclesiastics, already degenerating into a scanty attendance, and a tiresome formality?

Rather than let this step beyond the landmarks of power have the effect of a legitimate precedent, it will be better to apply to it the legal aphorism de minimis non curat lex: or to class it cum "maculis quas aut incuria fudit, aut humana parum cavit natura."

Better also to disarm in the same way, the precedent of Chaplainships for the army and navy, than erect them into a political authority in matters of religion. The object of this establishment is seducing; the motive to it is laudable. But is it not safer to adhere to a right pinciple, and trust to its consequences, than confide in the reasoning however specious in favor of a wrong one. Look thro' the armies & navies of the world, and say whether in the appointment of their ministers of religion, the spiritual interest of the flocks or the temporal interest of the Shepherds, be most in view: whether here, as elsewhere the political care of religion is not a nominal more than a real aid. If the spirit of armies be devout, the spirit out of the armies will never be less so; and a failure of religious instruction & exhortation from a voluntary source within or without, will rarely happen: and if such be not the spirit of armies, the official services of their Teachers are not likely to produce it. It is more likely to flow from the labours of a spontaneous zeal. The armies of the Puritans had their appointed Chaplains; but without these there would have been no lack of public devotion in that devout age.

The case of navies with insulated crews may be less within the scope of these reflections. But it is not entirely so. The chance of a devout officer, might be of as much worth to religion, as the service of an ordinary chaplain. [were it admitted that religion has a real interest in the latter.] But we are always to keep in mind that it is safer to trust the consequences of a right principle, than reasonings in support of a bad one.

Religious proclamations by the Executive recommending thanksgivings & fasts are shoots from the same root with the legislative acts reviewed.

Altho' recommendations only, they imply a religious agency, making no part of the trust delegated to political rulers.

The objections to them are 1. that Govts ought not to interpose in relation to those subject to their authority but in cases where they can do it with effect. An *advisory* Govt is a contradiction in terms. 2. The members of a Govt as such can in no sense, be regarded as possessing an advisory trust from their Constituents in their religious capacities. They cannot form an ecclesiastical Assembly, Convocation, Council, or Synod, and as such issue decrees or injunctions addressed to the faith or the Consciences of the people. In their individual capacities, as distinct from their official station, they might unite in recommendations of any sort whatever, in the same manner as any other individuals might do. But then their recommendations ought to express the true character from which they emanate. 3. They seem to imply and certainly nourish the erronious idea of a *national* religion. The idea just as it related to the Jewish nation under a theocracy, having been improperly adopted by so many nations which have embraced Xnity, is too apt to lurk in the bosoms even of Americans, who in general are aware of the distinction between religious & political societies. The idea also of a union of all to form one nation under one Govt in acts of devotion to the God of all is an imposing idea.

65

THOMAS JEFFERSON TO ALBERT GALLATIN
16 June 1817
Works 12:73

Three of our papers have presented us the copy of an act of the legislature of New York, which, if it has really passed, will carry us back to the times of the darkest bigotry and barbarism, to find a parallel. Its purport is, that all those who shall *hereafter* join in communion with the religious sect of Shaking Quakers, shall be deemed civilly dead, their marriages dissolved, and all their children and property taken out of their hands. This act being published nakedly in the papers, without the usual signatures, or any history of the circumstances of its passage, I am not without a hope it may have been a mere abortive attempt. It contrasts singularly with a cotemporary vote of the Pennsylvania legislature, who, on a proposition to make the belief in God a necessary qualification for office, rejected it by a great majority, although assuredly there was not a single atheist in their body. And you remember to have heard, that when the act for religious freedom was before the Virginia Assembly, a motion to insert the name of Jesus Christ before the phrase, "the author of our holy religion," which stood in the bill, was rejected, although that was the creed of a great majority of them.

66

JAMES MADISON TO EDWARD LIVINGSTON
10 July 1822
Writings 9:100–103

I observe with particular pleasure the view you have taken of the immunity of Religion from civil jurisdiction, in every case where it does not trespass on private rights or the public peace. This has always been a favorite principle with me; and it was not with my approbation, that the deviation from it took place in Congs., when they appointed Chaplains, to be paid from the Natl. Treasury. It would have been a much better proof to their Constituents of their pious feeling if the members had contributed for the purpose, a pittance from their own pockets. As the precedent is not likely to be rescinded, the best that can now be done, may be to apply to the Constn. the maxim of the law, de minimis non curat.

There has been another deviation from the strict principle in the Executive Proclamations of fasts & festivals, so far, at least, as they have spoken the language of *injunction,* or have lost sight of the equality of *all* religious sects in the eye of the Constitution. Whilst I was honored with the Executive Trust I found it necessary on more than one occasion to follow the example of predecessors. But I was always careful to make the Proclamations absolutely indiscriminate, and merely recommendatory; or rather mere *designations* of a day, on which all who thought proper might *unite* in consecrating it to religious purposes, according to their own faith & forms. In this sense, I presume you reserve to the Govt. a right to *appoint* particular days for religious worship throughout the State, without any penal sanction *enforcing* the worship. I know not what may be the way of thinking on this subject in Louisiana. I should suppose the Catholic portion of the people, at least, as a small & even unpopular sect in the U. S., would rally, as they did in Virga. when religious liberty was a Legislative topic, to its broadest principle. Notwithstanding the general progress made within the two last centuries in favour of this branch of liberty, & the full establishment of it, in some parts of our Country, there remains in others a strong bias towards the old error, that without some sort of alliance or coalition between Govt. & Religion neither can be duly supported. Such indeed is the tendency to such a coalition, and such its corrupting influence on both the parties, that the danger cannot be too carefully guarded agst. And in a Govt. of opinion, like ours, the only effectual guard must be found in the soundness and stability of the general opinion on the subject. Every new & successful example therefore of a perfect separation between ecclesiastical and civil matters, is of importance. And

I have no doubt that every new example, will succeed, as every past one has done, in shewing that religion & Govt. will both exist in greater purity, the less they are mixed together. It was the belief of all sects at one time that the establishment of Religion by law, was right & necessary; that the true religion ought to be established in exclusion of every other; And that the only question to be decided was which was the true religion. The example of Holland proved that a toleration of sects, dissenting from the established sect, was safe & even useful. The example of the Colonies, now States, which rejected religious establishments altogether, proved that all Sects might be safely & advantageously put on a footing of equal & entire freedom; and a continuance of their example since the declaration of Independence, has shewn that its success in Colonies was not to be ascribed to their connection with the parent Country. If a further confirmation of the truth could be wanted, it is to be found in the examples furnished by the States, which have abolished their religious establishments. I cannot speak particularly of any of the cases excepting that of Virga. where it is impossible to deny that Religion prevails with more zeal, and a more exemplary priesthood than it ever did when established and patronised by Public authority. We are teaching the world the great truth that Govts. do better without Kings & Nobles than with them. The merit will be doubled by the other lesson that Religion flourishes in greater purity, without than with the aid of Govt.

67

WILLIAM RAWLE, A VIEW OF THE CONSTITUTION OF THE UNITED STATES 121–23
1829 (2d ed.)

The first amendment prohibits congress from passing *any law respecting an establishment of religion, or preventing the free exercise of it.* It would be difficult to conceive on what possible construction of the Constitution such a power could ever be claimed by congress. The time has long passed by when enlightened men in this country entertained the opinion that the *general welfare of a nation* could be promoted by religious intolerance, and under no other clause could a pretence for it be found. Individual states whose legislatures are not restrained by their own constitutions, have been occasionally found to make some distinctions; but when we advert to those parts of the Constitution of the United States, which so strongly enforce the equality of all our citizens, we may reasonably doubt whether the denial of the smallest civic right under this pretence can be reconciled to it. In most of the governments of Europe, some one religious system enjoys a preference, enforced with more or less severity, according to circumstances. Opinions and modes of worship differing from those which form the established religion, are sometimes expressly forbidden, sometimes punished, and in the mildest

cases, only tolerated without patronage or encouragement. Thus a human government interposes between the Creator and his creature, intercepts the devotion of the latter, or condescends to permit it only under political regulations. From injustice so gross, and impiety so manifest, multitudes sought an asylum in America, and hence she ought to be the hospitable and benign receiver of every variety of religious opinion. It is true, that in her early provincial stage, the equality of those rights does not seem to have been universally admitted. Those who claimed religious freedom for themselves, did not immediately perceive that others were also entitled to it; but the history of the stern exclusion or reluctant admission of other sects in several of the provinces, would be an improper digression in this work. In tracing the annals of some of the provinces, it is pleasing to observe that in the very outset, their enlightened founders publicly recognised the perfect freedom of conscience. There was indeed sometimes an inconsistency, perhaps not adverted to in the occlusion of public offices to all but Christians, which was the case in Pennsylvania, but it was then of little practical importance. In the constitution adopted by that state in 1776, the same inconsistency, though expressed in language somewhat different, was retained, but in her present constitution, nothing abridges, nothing qualifies, nothing defeats, the full effect of the original declaration. Both the elector and the elected are entitled, whatever their religious tenets may be, to the fullest enjoyment of political rights, provided in the latter description, the party publicly declares his belief in the being of a God, and a future state of rewards and punishments. This qualification is not expressly required of an elector, and perhaps was introduced in respect to those elected, chiefly for the purpose of more particularly explaining the sense of a preceding section. It is indeed to such a degree doubtful whether any can be found so weak and depraved as to disbelieve these cardinal points of all religions, that it can scarcely be supposed to have been introduced for any other purpose.*

Just and liberal principles on this subject, throw a lustre round the Constitution in which they are found, and while they dignify the nation, promote its internal peace and harmony. No predominant religion overpowers another, the votaries of which are few and humble; no lordly hierarchy excites odium or terror; legal persecution is unknown, and freedom of discussion, while it tends to promote the knowledge, contributes to increase the fervour of piety.

---

*There are now but two states in the Union whose constitutions contain exclusive provisions in regard to religious opinions. In Maryland, no one who does not believe in the Christian religion can be admitted to an office of trust or profit. In North Carolina, the same exclusion is extended to all who deny the truth of the protestant religion. But in every other respect than the capacity to hold such offices, all stand on the same footing in both states.

68

JAMES MADISON TO REV. ADAMS
1832
Writings 9:484–87

I recd in due time the printed copy of your Convention sermon on the relation of Xnity to Civil Govt with a manuscript request of my opinion on the subject.

There appears to be in the nature of man what insures his belief in an invisible cause of his present existence, and anticipation of his future existence. Hence the propensities & susceptibilities in that case of religion which with a few doubtful or individual exceptions have prevailed throughout the world.

Waiving the rights of Conscience, not included in the surrender implied by the social State, and more or less invaded by all religious Establishments, the simple question to be decided is whether a support of the best & purest religion, the Xn religion itself ought not so far at least as pecuniary means are involved, to be provided for by the Govt. rather than be left to the voluntary provisions of those who profess it. And on this question experience will be an admitted Umpire, the more adequate as the connection between Govts. & Religion have existed in such various degrees & forms, and now can be compared with examples where connection has been entirely dissolved.

In the Papal System, Government and Religion are in a manner consolidated, & that is found to be the worst of Govts.

In most of the Govts. of the old world, the legal establishment of a particular religion and without or with very little toleration of others makes a part of the Political and Civil organization and there are few of the most enlightened judges who will maintain that the system has been favorable either to Religion or to Govt.

Until Holland ventured on the experiment of combining a liberal toleration with the establishment of a particular creed, it was taken for granted, that an exclusive & intolerant establishment was essential, and notwithstanding the light thrown on the subject by the experiment, the prevailing opinion in Europe, England not excepted, has been that Religion could not be preserved without the support of Govt. nor Govt. be supported witht. an established religion that there must be at least an alliance of some sort between them.

It remained for North America to bring the great & interesting subject to a fair, and finally to a decisive test.

In the Colonial State of the Country, there were four examples, R. I. N. J. Penna. and Delaware, & the greater part of N. Y. where there were no religious Establishments; the support of Religion being left to the voluntary associations & contributions of individuals; and certainly the religious condition of those Colonies, will well bear a comparison with that where establishments existed.

As it may be suggested that experiments made in Colonies more or less under the Controul of a foreign Government, had not the full scope necessary to display their tendency, it is fortunate that the appeal can now be made to their effects under a compleat exemption from any such controul.

It is true that the New England States have not discontinued establishments of Religion formed under very peculiar circumstances; but they have by successive relaxations advanced towards the prevailing example; and without any evidence of disadvantage either to Religion or good Government.

And if we turn to the Southern States where there was, previous to the Declaration of independence, a legal provision for the support of Religion; and since that event a surrender of it to a spontaneous support by the people, it may be said that the difference amounts nearly to the contrast in the greater purity & industry of the Pastors and in the greater devotion of their flocks, in the latter period than in the former. In Virginia the contrast is particularly striking, to those whose memories can make the comparison. It will not be denied that causes other than the abolition of the legal establishment of Religion are to be taken into view in accountg for the change in the Religious character of the community. But the existing character, distinguished as it is by its religious features, and the lapse of time now more than 50 years since the legal support of Religion was withdrawn sufficiently prove that it does not need the support of Govt. and it will scarcely be contended that Government has suffered by the exemption of Religion from its cognizance, or its pecuniary aid.

The apprehension of some seems to be that Religion left entirely to itself may run into extravagances injurious both to Religion and to social order; but besides the question whether the interference of Govt. *in any form* wd. not be more likely to increase than controul the tendency, it is a safe calculation that in this as in other cases of excessive excitement, Reason will gradually regain its ascendancey. Great excitements are less apt to be permanent than to vibrate to the opposite extreme.

Under another aspect of the subject there may be less danger that Religion, if left to itself, will suffer from a failure of the pecuniary support applicable to it than that an omission of the public authorities to limit the duration of their Charters to Religious Corporations, and the amount of property acquirable by them, may lead to an injurious accumulation of wealth from the lavish donations and bequests prompted by a pious zeal or by an atoning remorse. Some monitory examples have already appeared.

Whilst I thus frankly express my view of the subject presented in your sermon, I must do you the justice to observe that you very ably maintained yours. I must admit moreover that it may not be easy, in every possible case, to trace the line of separation between the rights of religion and the Civil authority with such distinctness as to avoid collisions & doubts on unessential points. The tendency to a usurpation on one side or the other, or to a corrupting coalition or alliance between them, will be best guarded agst. by an entire abstinance of the Govt. from interference in any way whatever, beyond the necessity of preserving public order, & protecting each sect agst. trespasses on its legal rights by others.

I owe you Sir an apology for the delay in complying with the request of my opinion on the subject discussed in your sermon; if not also for the brevity & it may be thought crudeness of the opinion itself. I must rest the apology on my great age now in its 83d. year, with more than the ordinary infirmities. . . .

69

JOSEPH STORY, COMMENTARIES ON THE CONSTITUTION 3:§§ 1865–73
1833

§ 1865. How far any government has a right to interfere in matters touching religion, has been a subject much discussed by writers upon public and political law. The right and the duty of the interference of government, in matters of religion, have been maintained by many distinguished authors, as well those, who were the warmest advocates of free government, as those, who were attached to governments of a more arbitrary character. Indeed, the right of a society or government to interfere in matters of religion will hardly be contested by any persons, who believe that piety, religion, and morality are intimately connected with the well being of the state, and indispensable to the administration of civil justice. The promulgation of the great doctrines of religion, the being, and attributes, and providence of one Almighty God; the responsibility to him for all our actions, founded upon moral freedom and accountability; a future state of rewards and punishments; the cultivation of all the personal, social, and benevolent virtues;—these never can be a matter of indifference in any well ordered community. It is, indeed, difficult to conceive, how any civilized society can well exist without them. And at all events, it is impossible for those, who believe in the truth of Christianity, as a divine revelation, to doubt, that it is the especial duty of government to foster, and encourage it among all the citizens and subjects. This is a point wholly distinct from that of the right of private judgment in matters of religion, and of the freedom of public worship according to the dictates of one's conscience.

§ 1866. The real difficulty lies in ascertaining the limits, to which government may rightfully go in fostering and encouraging religion. Three cases may easily be supposed. One, where a government affords aid to a particular religion, leaving all persons free to adopt any other; another, where it creates an ecclesiastical establishment for the propagation of the doctrines of a particular sect of that religion, leaving a like freedom to all others; and a third, where it creates such an establishment, and excludes all persons, not belonging to it, either wholly, or in part, from any participation in the public honours, trusts, emoluments, privileges, and immunities of the state. For instance, a government may simply declare, that the Chris-

tian religion shall be the religion of the state, and shall be aided, and encouraged in all the varieties of sects belonging to it; or it may declare, that the Catholic or Protestant religion shall be the religion of the state, leaving every man to the free enjoyment of his own religious opinions; or it may establish the doctrines of a particular sect, as of Episcopalians, as the religion of the state, with a like freedom; or it may establish the doctrines of a particular sect, as exclusively the religion of the state, tolerating others to a limited extent, or excluding all, not belonging to it, from all public honours, trusts, emoluments, privileges, and immunities.

§ 1867. Now, there will probably be found few persons in this, or any other Christian country, who would deliberately contend, that it was unreasonable, or unjust to foster and encourage the Christian religion generally, as a matter of sound policy, as well as of revealed truth. In fact, every American colony, from its foundation down to the revolution, with the exception of Rhode Island, (if, indeed, that state be an exception,) did openly, by the whole course of its laws and institutions, support and sustain, in some form, the Christian religion; and almost invariably gave a peculiar sanction to some of its fundamental doctrines. And this has continued to be the case in some of the states down to the present period, without the slightest suspicion, that it was against the principles of public law, or republican liberty. Indeed, in a republic, there would seem to be a peculiar propriety in viewing the Christian religion, as the great basis, on which it must rest for its support and permanence, if it be, what it has ever been deemed by its truest friends to be, the religion of liberty. Montesquieu has remarked, that the Christian religion is a stranger to mere despotic power. The mildness so frequently recommended in the gospel is incompatible with the despotic rage, with which a prince punishes his subjects, and exercises himself in cruelty. He has gone even further, and affirmed, that the Protestant religion is far more congenial with the spirit of political freedom, than the Catholic. "When," says he, "the Christian religion, two centuries ago, became unhappily, divided into Catholic and Protestant, the people of the north embraced the Protestant, and those of the south still adhered to the Catholic. The reason is plain. The people of the north have, and will ever have, a spirit of liberty and independence, which the people of the south have not. And, therefore, a religion, which has no visible head, is more agreeable to the independency of climate, than that, which has one." Without stopping to inquire, whether this remark be well founded, it is certainly true, that the parent country has acted upon it with a severe and vigilant zeal; and in most of the colonies the same rigid jealousy has been maintained almost down to our own times. Massachusetts, while she has promulgated in her BILL OF RIGHTS the importance and necessity of the public support of religion, and the worship of God, has authorized the legislature to require it only for Protestantism. The language of that bill of rights is remarkable for its pointed affirmation of the duty of government to support Christianity, and the reasons for it. "As," says the third article, "the happiness of a people, and the good order and preservation of civil government, essentially depend upon piety, religion, and morality; and as these cannot be generally diffused through the community, but by the institution of the public worship of God, and of public instructions in piety, religion, and morality; therefore, to promote their happiness and to secure the good order and preservation of their government, the people of this Commonwealth have a right to invest their legislature with power to authorize, and require, and the legislature shall from time to time authorize and require, the several towns, parishes, &c. &c. to make suitable provision at their own expense for the institution of the public worship of God, and for the support and maintenance of public *protestant* teachers of piety, religion, and morality, in all cases where such provision shall not be made voluntarily." Afterwards there follow provisions, prohibiting any superiority of one sect over another, and securing to all citizens the free exercise of religion.

§ 1868. Probably at the time of the adoption of the constitution, and of the amendment to it, now under consideration, the general, if not the universal, sentiment in America was, that Christianity ought to receive encouragement from the state, so far as was not incompatible with the private rights of conscience, and the freedom of religious worship. An attempt to level all religions, and to make it a matter of state policy to hold all in utter indifference, would have created universal disapprobation, if not universal indignation.

§ 1869. It yet remains a problem to be solved in human affairs, whether any free government can be permanent, where the public worship of God, and the support of religion, constitute no part of the policy or duty of the state in any assignable shape. The future experience of Christendom, and chiefly of the American states, must settle this problem, as yet new in the history of the world, abundant, as it has been, in experiments in the theory of government.

§ 1870. But the duty of supporting religion, and especially the Christian religion, is very different from the right to force the consciences of other men, or to punish them for worshipping God in the manner, which, they believe, their accountability to him requires. It has been truly said, that "religion, or the duty we owe to our Creator, and the manner of discharging it, can be dictated only by reason and conviction, not by force or violence." Mr. Locke himself, who did not doubt the right of government to interfere in matters of religion, and especially to encourage Christianity, at the same time has expressed his opinion of the right of private judgment, and liberty of conscience, in a manner becoming his character, as a sincere friend of civil and religious liberty. "No man, or society of men," says he, "have any authority to impose their opinions or interpretations on any other, the meanest Christian; since, in matters of religion, every man must know, and believe, and give an account for himself." The rights of conscience are, indeed, beyond the just reach of any human power. They are given by God, and cannot be encroached upon by human authority, without a criminal disobedience of the precepts of natural, as well as of revealed religion.

§ 1871. The real object of the amendment was, not to countenance, much less to advance Mahometanism, or Judaism, or infidelity, by prostrating Christianity; but to exclude all rivalry among Christian sects, and to prevent any national ecclesiastical establishment, which should give to an hierarchy the exclusive patronage of the national government. It thus cut off the means of religious persecution, (the vice and pest of former ages,) and of the subversion of the rights of conscience in matters of religion, which had been trampled upon almost from the days of the Apostles to the present age. The history of the parent country had afforded the most solemn warnings and melancholy instructions on this head; and even New England, the land of the persecuted puritans, as well as other colonies, where the Church of England had maintained its superiority, would furnish out a chapter, as full of the darkest bigotry and intolerance, as any, which could be found to disgrace the pages of foreign annals. Apostacy, heresy, and nonconformity had been standard crimes for public appeals, to kindle the flames of persecution, and apologize for the most atrocious triumphs over innocence and virtue.

§ 1872. Mr. Justice Blackstone, after having spoken with a manly freedom of the abuses in the Romish church respecting heresy; and, that Christianity had been deformed by the demon of persecution upon the continent, and that the island of Great Britain had not been *entirely* free from the scourge, defends the final enactments against nonconformity in England, in the following set phrases, to which, without any material change, might be justly applied his own sarcastic remarks upon the conduct of the Roman ecclesiastics in punishing heresy. "For nonconformity to the worship of the church," (says he,) "there is much more to be pleaded than for the former, (that is, reviling the ordinances of the church,) being a matter of private conscience, to the scruples of which our *present* laws have shown a very just, and Christian indulgence. For undoubtedly all persecution and oppression of weak consciences, on the score of religious persuasions, are highly unjustifiable upon every principle of natural reason, civil liberty, or sound religion. But care must be taken not to carry this indulgence into such extremes, as may endanger the national church. There is always a difference to be made between toleration and establishment." Let it be remembered, that at the very moment, when the learned commentator was penning these cold remarks, the laws of England merely tolerated protestant dissenters in their public worship upon certain conditions, at once irritating and degrading; that the test and corporation acts excluded them from public and corporate offices, both of trust and profit; that the learned commentator avows, that the object of the test and corporation acts to exclude them from office, in common with Turks, Jews, heretics, papists, and other sectaries; that to deny the Trinity, however conscientiously disbelieved, was a public offence, punishable by fine and imprisonment; and that, in the rear of all these disabilities and grievances, came the long list of acts against papists, by which they were reduced to a state of political and religious slavery, and cut off from some of the dearest privileges of mankind.

§ 1873. It was under a solemn consciousness of the

dangers from ecclesiastical ambition, the bigotry of spiritual pride, and the intolerance of sects, thus exemplified in our domestic, as well as in foreign annals, that it was deemed advisable to exclude from the national government all power to act upon the subject. The situation, too, of the different states equally proclaimed the policy, as well as the necessity of such an exclusion. In some of the states, episcopalians constituted the predominant sect; in others, presbyterians; in others, congregationalists; in others, quakers; and in others again, there was a close numerical rivalry among contending sects. It was impossible, that there should not arise perpetual strife and perpetual jealousy on the subject of ecclesiastical ascendancy, if the national government were left free to create a religious establishment. The only security was in extirpating the power. But this alone would have been an imperfect security, if it had not been followed up by a declaration of the right of the free exercise of religion, and a prohibition (as we have seen) of all religious tests. Thus, the whole power over the subject of religion is left exclusively to the state governments, to be acted upon according to their own sense of justice, and the state constitutions; and the Catholic and the Protestant, the Calvinist and the Arminian, the Jew and the Infidel, may sit down at the common table of the national councils, without any inquisition into their faith, or mode of worship.

SEE ALSO:

Generally 6.3; Bill of Rights
Leonard Busher, Petition to James I, 1614, Stokes 1:113
Plan of Government for New Haven Colony, 1643, Thorpe 1:526–27
Oliver Cromwell, 1644, Stokes 1:121
Congregationalist Churches of England, Savoy Declaration, 1658, Stokes 1:117
John Milton, A Treatise of Civil Power in Ecclesiastical Causes (1659)
Quaker Statement of Belief, 1675, Stokes 1:114
Pennsylvania Charter of Privileges, 1701, Thorpe 5:3077–78
The Constitution of Free-Masons, 1734, Stokes 1:246
Plantation Act of 1740, 13 Geo. 2, c. 7
William Blackstone, Commentaries 1:269 (1765)
Letter of the General Association of Congregational Pastors, 1768, Stokes 1:235–36
Massachusetts House of Representatives to Dennis deBert, 12 Jan. 1768, Stokes 1:235
Letter of "Society of Dissenters," 28 Feb. 1769, Stokes 1:236–38
Samuel Adams, The Rights of the Colonists as Christians, 20 Nov. 1772, Writings 2:355–56
John Adams to Abigail Adams, 16 Sept. 1774, Butterfield 74–76
Alexander Hamilton, Remarks on the Quebec Bill, pt. 2, 22 June 1775, Papers 1:169–75
Resolution to the Massachusetts Assembly, 1775, Stokes 1:308–9
Journal of the Virginia Convention of 1776, 20 June 1776, Stokes 1:370
Memorial of the Hanover Presbytery to the Virginia Assembly, 24 Oct. 1776, Stokes 1:376–77
Thomas Paine, Epistle to Quakers, 1776, Life 2:183–84, 191–92
George Washington, General Orders, 9 July 1776, 2 May 1778, Writings 5:244–45, 11:342–43
Maryland Constitution of 1776, Amendments, arts. 3, 5, 13, Thorpe 3:1702, 1705
Thomas Jefferson, Notes on Locke and Shaftesbury, ca. 1776, Papers 1:544–50
Petition of Dissenters in Albemarle and Amherst Counties, 1776, Jefferson Papers 1:586
Declaration of the Virginia Association of Baptists, 25 Dec. 1776, Jefferson Papers 1:660–61
John Jay, New York Constitutional Convention, 20–21 Mar. 1777, Unpublished Papers 1:392
Georgia Constitution of 1777, arts. 56, 62, Thorpe 2:784, 785
John Jay, Charge to Grand Jury of Ulster County, 9 Sept. 1777, Correspondence 1:162–63
Governor William Livingston, Remarks on Liberty of Conscience, 1778, Niles 199
Rev. John Todd to Thomas Jefferson, 16 Aug. 1779, Jefferson Papers 3:68–69
Baptist Petition to the Virginia Assembly, 8 Nov. 1780, Stokes 1:371–72
Returns of the Towns on the Massachusetts Constitution of 1780, Handlin 557–58, 633–34, 640–41, 645–48, 660–61, 763–64
John Wilson Campbell, History of Virginia to 1781 (1813), Stokes 1:238–39
Petition from Rockingham Assembly, 18 Nov. 1784, Stokes 1:362–63
Richard Henry Lee to James Madison, 26 Nov. 1784, Madison Papers 8:149–50
James Madison, Notes for Debate on General Assessment Bill, 23–24 Dec. 1784, Papers 8:197–99
Incorporation of Protestant Episcopal Church in Virginia, 1784, Stokes 1:385–86
Treaty with Prussia, art. 11, 1785
James Madison to James Monroe, 21 June 1785, Papers 8:306
Copy of Protestant Episcopal Church Petition to General Assembly of Virginia, July 1785, Madison Papers 8:312–13
John Dickinson to George Read, 28 Apr. 1786, Read Life 412
Memorial of the Convention of Baptists of New England to the Constitutional Convention of 1787, Stokes 1:307
Records of the Federal Convention, Farrand 1:450–52
Proposed Amendments by Pennsylvania Ratifying Convention Minority, 12 Dec. 1787, Dumbauld 173
Thomas Jefferson to John Rutledge, Jr., 2 Feb. 1788, Papers 12:557
Proposed Amendments by Minority of Maryland Convention Committee, 29 Apr. 1788, Dumbauld 179
Edmund Randolph, Virginia Ratifying Convention, 10 June 1788, Elliot 3:204–5
New Hampshire Ratifying Convention, Proposed Amendment, 21 June 1788, Dumbauld 182
New York Ratifying Convention, Proposed Amendment, 26 July 1788, Dumbauld 189
North Carolina Ratifying Convention, Proposed Amendments, 1 Aug. 1788, Dumbauld 201
George Washington to the General Committee of the United Baptist Churches of Virginia, May 1789, Stokes 1:495
Georgia Constitution of 1789, art. 4, Thorpe 2:789
Noah Webster, Miscellaneous Remarks, Feb. 1790, Collection, 345–47, 362–64
Pennsylvania Constitution of 1790, art. 9, secs. 3, 4, Thorpe 5:3100
South Carolina Constitution of 1790, art. 8, secs. 1, 2, Thorpe 6:3264
George Washington to the Hebrew Congregation of Newport, R.I., Fall 1790, Stokes 1:861–62
William Livingston, Observations on the Support of the Clergy, Dec. 1790, Stokes 1:278
Delaware Constitution of 1792, Preamble and art. 1, Thorpe 1:568

Kentucky Constitution of 1792, art. 1, sec. 24, art. 12, sec. 4, Thorpe 3:1267, 1274

Vermont Constitution of 1793, ch. 1, art. 3, Thorpe 6:3762

Tennessee Constitution of 1796, art. 7, sec. 7, art. 8, secs. 1, 2, Thorpe 6:3420

Treaty between United States and Tripoli, art. 4, sec. 10, art. 11, 10 Feb. 1797

Kentucky Constitution of 1799, art. 2, sec. 26, art. 3, sec. 6, art. 10, secs. 3, 4, Thorpe 3:1280, 1281, 1289

Thomas Jefferson to Jeremiah Moor, 14 Aug. 1800, Works 9:143

Benjamin Rush to Thomas Jefferson, 6 Oct. 1800, Letter 2:824–25

Ohio Constitution of 1802, art. 8, sec. 3, Thorpe 5:2910

Samuel Adams to Thomas Paine, 30 Nov. 1802, Writings 4:412–13

Washburn v. *Springfield,* 1 Mass. 32 (1804)

Elbridge Gerry, 1811, Life 335–37

Louisiana Constitution of 1812, art. 2, sec. 22, Thorpe 3:1384

John Adams to Thomas Jefferson, 25 June 1813, Cappon 2:334

John Adams to Thomas Jefferson, 28 June 1813, Cappon 2:338–40

John Adams to Thomas Jefferson, 14 Sept. 1813, Cappon 2:373–74

Terrett v. *Taylor,* 9 Cranch 43 (1815)

Indiana Constitution of 1816, art. 1, sec. 3, Thorpe 2:1058

John Adams to Thomas Jefferson, 6 May 1816, Cappon 2:474

Thomas Jefferson to John Adams, 1 Aug. 1816, Cappon 2:484

Mississippi Constitution of 1817, art. 1, secs. 3, 4, Thorpe 4:2033

John Adams to Thomas Jefferson, 18 May 1817, Cappon 2:515, 516

Adams v. *Howe,* 14 Mass. 340 (1817)

Connecticut Constitution of 1818, art. 1, sec. 3, 4, art. 7, secs. 1, 2, Thorpe 1:537, 544–45

Illinois Constitution of 1818, art. 13, secs. 3, 4, Thorpe 2:1007

Alabama Constitution of 1819, art. 1, secs. 3–7, Thorpe 1:97

Constitution of Maine of 1819, art. 1, sec. 3, Thorpe 3:1647

Missouri Constitution of 1820, art. 13, secs. 4, 5, 18, Thorpe 4:2163, 2164

Baker v. *Fales,* 16 Mass. 488 (1820)

New York Constitution of 1821, art. 7, secs. 3, 4, Thorpe 5:2648

Thomas Jefferson, Report of the Rector to the Board of Visitors of the University of Virginia, 7 Oct. 1822, Writings 19:413–16

Bishop John England, The Substance of a Discourse Preached in the Hall of the House of Representatives, 8 Jan. 1826, Stokes 1:503–4

John Marshall to William B. Sprague, 22 July 1828, in R. Faulkner, The Jurisprudence of John Marshall 140, n. 22 (1965)

Virginia Constitution of 1830, art. 3, sec. 11, Thorpe 7:3824–25

Delaware Constitution of 1831, art. 1, secs. 1, 2, Thorpe 1:582

James Madison to Edward Everett, 1832, Stokes 1:348

Mississippi Constitution of 1832, art. 1, secs. 3, 4, Thorpe 4:2049

Gallego's ex'ors v. *Attorney General,* 3 Leigh 450, 477–81 (Va. 1832)

Magill v. *Brown,* 16 Fed. Cas. 408, no. 8,952 (C.C.E.D.Pa. 1833)

Michigan Constitution of 1835, art. 1, secs. 4–6, Thorpe 1:1931

Commonwealth v. *Kneeland,* 20 Pick. 206 (Mass. 1838)

SPEECH AND PRESS

1. An Act for Preventing the Frequent Abuses in Printing Seditious Treasonable and Unlicensed Books and Pamphlets and for Regulating Printing and Printing Presses, 14 Chas. 2, c. 33 (1662)

2. David Hume, Of the Liberty of the Press (1742)

3. Montesquieu, Spirit of Laws, bk. 12, chs. 12–13 (1748)

4. William Blackstone, Commentaries (1769)

5. James Burgh, Political Disquisitions (1775)

6. Virginia Declaration of Rights, sec. 12, 12 June 1776

7. Albemarle County Instructions concerning the Virginia Constitution, Fall 1776

8. Thomas Jefferson to Edward Carrington, 16 Jan. 1787

9. Cincinnatus, no. 2, to James Wilson, 8 Nov. 1787

10. James Wilson, Pennsylvania Ratifying Convention, 1 Dec. 1787

11. Federal Farmer, no. 16, 20 Jan. 1788

12. A Plebeian, An Address to the People of the State of New-York, Spring 1788

13. *Respublica* v. *Oswald,* 1 Dall. 319 (Pa. 1788)

14. Congress, Amendments to the Constitution, June–Sept. 1789

15. Thomas Jefferson to James Madison, 28 Aug. 1789

16. Benjamin Franklin, An Account of the Supremest Court of Judicature in Pennsylvania, viz., The Court of the Press, 12 Sept. 1789

17. John Marshall to a Freeholder, 20 Sept. 1798

18. Kentucky Resolutions, 10 Nov. 1798, 14 Nov. 1799

19. James Madison, Virginia Resolutions, 21 Dec. 1798

20. John Marshall, Report of the Minority on the Virginia Resolutions, 22 Jan. 1799

21. James Madison, Address of the General Assembly to the People of the Commonwealth of Virginia, 23 Jan. 1799

22. James Iredell, Charge to the Grand Jury, in *Case of Fries,* 9 Fed. Cas. 829, no. 5,126 (C.C.D.Pa. 1799)

23. Kentucky Constitution of 1799, art. 10, sec. 7

24. James Madison, Report on the Virginia Resolutions, Jan. 1800

25. *United States* v. *Cooper,* 25 Fed. Cas. 631, no. 14,865 (C.C.D.Pa. 1800)

26. Thomas Jefferson, First Inaugural Address, 4 Mar. 1801

27. St. George Tucker, Blackstone's Commentaries (1803)

28. *People* v. *Croswell,* 3 Johns. Cas. 337 (N.Y. 1804)

29. Thomas Jefferson to John Norvell, 14 June 1807

30. *Updegraph* v. *Commonwealth,* 11 Serg. & Rawle 394 (Pa. 1824)

31. *Commonwealth* v. *Blanding,* 3 Pick. 304 (Mass. 1825)

32. James Kent, Commentaries (1826)

33. Joseph Story, Commentaries on the Constitution (1833)

1

AN ACT FOR PREVENTING THE FREQUENT ABUSES
IN PRINTING SEDITIOUS TREASONABLE AND
UNLICENSED BOOKS AND PAMPHLETS AND
FOR REGULATING PRINTING AND
PRINTING PRESSES
14 Chas. 2, c. 33, 1662

Whereas the well-government and regulating of Printers and Printing Presses is matter of Publique care and of great concernment especially considering that by the general licentiousnes of the late times many evil disposed persons have been encouraged to print and sell heretical schismatical blasphemous seditious and treasonable Bookes Pamphlets and Papers and still doe continue such theire unlawfull and exorbitant practice to the high dishonour of Almighty God the endangering the peace of these Kingdomes and raising a disaffection to His most Excellent Majesty and His Government For prevention whereof no surer meanes can be advised then by reducing and limiting the number of Printing Presses and by ordering and setling the said Art or Mystery of Printing by Act of Parliament in manner as herein after is expressed. The Kings most Excellent Majesty by and with the Consent and Advise of the Lords Spiritual and Temporal & Commons in this present Parliament assembled doth therefore ordaine and enact And be it ordained and enacted by the Authority aforesaid That no person or persons whatsoever shall presume to print or cause to be printed either within this Realm of England or any other His Majesties Dominions or in the parts beyond the Seas any heretical seditious schismatical or offensive Bookes or Pamphlets wherein any Doctrine or Opinion shall be asserted or maintained which is contrary to Christian Faith or the Doctrine or Discipline of the Church of England or which shall or may tend or be to the scandall of Religion or the Church or the Government or Governors of the Church State or Common wealth or of any Corporation or particular person or persons whatsoever nor shall import publish sell or dispose any such Booke or Books or Pamphlets nor shall cause or procure any such to be published or put to sale or to be bound stitched or sowed togeather.

And be it further ordained and enacted by the Authority aforesaid That no private person or persons whatsoever shall att any time hereafter print or cause to be printed any Booke or Pamphlet whatsoever unlesse the same Booke and Pamphlet togeather with all and every the Titles Epistles Prefaces Proems Preambles Introductions Tables Dedications and other matters and things thereunto annexed be first entred in the Booke of the Register of the Company of Stationers of London except Acts of Parliament Proclamations and such other Books and Papers as shall be appointed to be printed by vertue of any Warrant under the Kings Majesties Sign Manual or under the Hand of one or both of His Majesties Principal Secretaries of State and unlesse the same Booke and Pamphlet

and also all and every the said Titles Epistles Prefaces Proems Preambles Introductions Tables Dedications and other matters and things whatsoever thereunto annexed or therewith to be imprinted shall be first lawfully licensed and authorized to be printed by such person and persons only as shall be constituted and appointed to license the same according to the direction and true meaning of this present Act herein after expressed and by no other (that is to say) That all Books concerning the Common Lawes of this Realm shall be printed by the special allowance of the Lord Chancellor or Lord Keeper of the Great Seal of England for the time being the Lords Cheife Justices and Lord Cheife Baron for the time being or one or more of them or by theire or one or more of theire appointments And that all Books of History concerning the State of this Realm or other Books concerning any affaires of State shall be licensed by the Principal Secretaries of State for the time being or one of them or by theire or one of theire appointments And that all Bookes to bee imprinted concerning Heraldry Titles of Honour and Armes or otherwise concerning the Office of Earle Marshal shall be licensed by the Earl Marshal for the time being or by his appointment or in case there shall not then be an Earl Marshal shall be licensed by the Three Kings of Armes Garter. Clarenceux and Norroy or any two of them whereof Garter Principal King of Armes to be one And that all other Bookes to bee imprinted or reprinted whether of Divinity Phisick Philosophy or whatsoever other Science or Art shall be first licensed and allowed by the Lord Arch Bishop of Canterbury and the Lord Bishop of London for the time being or one of them or by theire or one of theire appointments or by either one of the Chancellors or Vice-Chancellors of either of the Universities of this Realme for the time being Provided alwaies that the said Chancellors or Vice Chancellors of either of the said Universities shall only license such Bookes as are to be imprinted or reprinted within the limits of the said Universities respectively but not in London or else where not medling either with Bookes of the Common Lawes or matters of State or Government nor any Booke or Bookes the right of printing whereof doth solely and properly belong to any particular person or persons without his or theire Consent first obtained in that behalfe

And be it enacted by the Authority aforesaid That every person and persons who by vertue of this present Act are or shall be appointed or authorized to license the imprinting of Bookes or reprinting thereof with any Additions or Amendments as aforesaid shall have one written Copy of the same Booke or Bookes which shall be soe licensed to be imprinted or reprinted with the Titles Epistles Prefaces Tables Dedications and all other things whatsoever thereunto annexed which said Copy shall be delivered by such Licenser or Licensers to the Printer or Owner for the imprinting thereof and shall be safely and intirely returned by such Printer or owner after the imprinting thereof unto such Licenser or Licensers to be kept in the publick Registrys of the said Lord Archbishop or Lord Bishop of London respectively or in the Office of the Chancellor or Vice Chancellor of either the said Universities or with the said Lord Chancellor or Lord Keeper of the Great Seal for the time being or Lord Cheife Justices or Cheif Baron or one of them or the said Principal Secretaries of State or with the Earle Marshall or the said Kings of Armes or one of them of all such Books as shall be licensed by them respectively and if such Booke so to be licensed shall be an English Booke or of the English Tongue there shall be twoe Written Copies thereof delivered to the Licenser or Licensers (if he or they shall so require) one Copy whereof so licensed shall be delivered back to the said Printer or Owner and the other Copy shall be reserved and kept as is aforesaid to the end such Licenser or Licensers may be secured that the Copy so licensed shall not be altered without his or theire privity And upon the said Copy licensed to be imprinted he or they who shall so license the same shall testifie under his or their hand or hands That there is not any thing in the same contained that is contrary to Christian Faith or the Doctrine or Discipline of the Church of England or against the State or Government of this Realm or contrary to good life or good manners or otherwise as the nature and subject of the Worke shall require which License or Approbation shall be printed in the begining of the same Booke with the Name or Names of him or them that shall authorize or license the same for a Testimony of the allowance thereof

And be it further enacted by the Authority aforesaid That every Merchant of Bookes and person and persons whatsoever who doth or hereafter shall import or bring any Booke or Books into this Realm from any parts beyond the Seas shall import the same in the Port of London only and not elsewhere without the special License of the Archbishop of Canterbury and Bishop of London for the time being or one of them who are hereby authorized to grant Licenses for that purpose and shall before such time as the same Booke or Books or any of them be delivered forth or out of his or theire hand or hands or exposed to sale give and present a true Note or Catalogue in writing of all and every such Booke or Bookes unto the Lord Archbishop of Canterbury and Lord Bishop of London for the time being or to one of them And no Merchant or other person or persons whatsoever which shall import or bring any Booke or Books into the Port of London aforesaid from any parts beyond the Seas shall presume to open any Dry Fats Bales Packs Maunds or other Fardels of Bookes or wherein Bookes are nor shall any Searcher Waiter or other Officer belonging to the Custom house upon pain of losing his or their place or places suffer the same to passe or to be delivered out of his or theire hands or Custody before such time as the Lord Archbishop of Canterbury and the Lord Bishop of London for the time being or one of them shall have appointed some Scholar or learned man with one or more of the said Company of Stationers and such others they shall call to theire assistance to be present at the opening thereof and to view the same And if there shall happen to be found any Heretical Seditious Scandalous Schismatical or other dangerous or offensive Booke or Books or any part of such Booke or Bookes printed in English they shall forthwith be brought to the said Lord Archbishop of Canterbury and Lord Bishop of London for the time being or to one of them or to some publick place to be assigned and chosen by the

said Lord Archbishop and Lord Bishop for the time being to the end the person and persons which importeth or causeth the said Offensive Books to bee imported may be proceeded against as an offender against this present Act And alsoe that such further course may be taken concerning the same offensive Booke or Books as by the said Lord Archbishop and Bishop for the time being shall be thought fitting for the suppressing thereof

And be it further enacted by the Authority aforesaid That no person or persons shall within this Kingdome or else where imprint or cause to bee imprinted nor shall import or bring in or cause to be imported or brought into this Kingdome from or out of any other His Majesties Dominions nor from any other parts beyond the Seas any Copy or Copies Booke or Bookes or part of any Book or Bookes or Forms of blank Bills or Indentures for any His Majesties Islands printed beyond the Seas or else where which any person or persons by force or vertue of any Letters Patents granted or assigned or which shall hereafter be granted or assigned to him or them or (where the same are not granted by any Letters Patents) by force or vertue of any Entry or Entries thereof duly made or to be made in the Register Booke of the said Company of Stationers or in the Register Booke of either of the Universities respectively have or shall have the Right Priviledge Authority or Allowance solely to print without the consent of the Owner or Owners of such Booke or Bookes Copy or Copies Form or Forms of such blank Bills nor shall binde stitch or put to Sale any such Booke or Books or part of any such Booke or Books Form or Forms without the like consent upon pain of losse and forfeiture of the same and of being proceeded against as an Offender against this present Act and upon the further penalty and forfeiture of Six shillings eight pence for every such Booke or Books or part of such Booke or Bookes Copy or Copies or Form or Forms of any such blank Bills or Indentures so imprinted or imported bound stitched or put to sale The Moyetie of which said Forfeiture & Forfeitures shall be to the use of our Soveraigne Lord the King His Heirs and Successors and the other Moyety to the use of the Owner or Owners Proprietor or Proprietors of such Copy or Copies Booke or Bookes or Form of such blank Bills or Indentures if he or they shall sue for the same within Six moneths next after such imprinting importing binding stitching or putting to Sale And in default of such Suit by the Owner or Owners Proprietor or Proprietors commenced within the said Six moneths Then the same Moyety shall be to the use and behoofe of such other person or persons as within the space of one yeare next after the said Offence committed shall sue for the same to be recovered by Action of Debt Bill Plaint or Information in any of his Majesties Courts of Record held att Westminster called the Kings Bench Common Pleas or Exchequer wherein no Essoign Wager of Law or Protection shall be allowed to the Defendant or Defendants

And be it further enacted and declared That every person and persons that shall hereafter print or cause to be printed any Booke Ballad Chart Pourtracture or any other thing or things whatsoever shall thereunto or thereon print and set his or theire owne Name or Names and alsoe shall declare the Name of the Author thereof if he be thereunto required by the Licenser under whose Approbation the licensing of the said Booke Ballad Chart or Pourtraiture shall be authorized and by and for whom any such Booke or other thing is or shall be printed upon paine of Forfeiture of all such Books Ballads Charts Pourtraitures and other thing or things printed contrary to the Tenor hereof And the Presses Letters and other Instruments for printing wherewith such Book Ballad Pourtraiture or other thing or things shall be so imprinted or sett or prepared for the printing thereof to be defaced and made unserviceable And that no person or persons shall hereafter print or cause to bee imprinted nor shall forge put or counterfeit in or upon any Booke or Pamphlet the Name Title Marke or Vinnet of any other person or persons which hath or shall have lawfull Priviledge Authority or Allowance of sole printing the same without the free consent of the person and persons so priviledged first had and obtained upon pain that every person and persons so offending shall forfeit and lose all such Books and Pamphlets upon which such counterfeit Name or Marke shall be imprinted and shall further be proceeded against as an Offender against this present Act.

And be it further enacted by the Authority aforesaid That no Haberdasher of Small Wares Ironmonger Chandler Shopkeeper or other person or persons whatsoever not being licensed in that behalfe by the Lord Bishop of the Diocese wherein such Booke or Bookes shall be having been Seven yeares Apprentice to the Trade of Booke seller Printer or Bookbinder nor being a Freeman of the City of London by Patrimonial Right as Son of a Booke seller Printer or Booke binder nor being a Member of the said Company of Stationers shall within the City or Suburbs of London or any other Market Towne or elsewhere receive take or buy or barter sell againe change or doe away any Bibles Testaments Psalm books Common Prayer books Primers Abcees Licensed Almanacks Grammar School books or other Book or Books whatsoever upon pain of forfeiture of the same

And for that printing is and for many yeares hath been an Art & Manufacture of this Kingdom Therefore for the better encouraging thereof and the prevention of divers Libels Pamphlets and Seditious Books printed beyond the Seas in English and thence transported into this Realm Be it further enacted and ordained by the Authority aforesaid That no Merchant Bookseller or other person or persons whatsoever shall imprint or cause to be imprinted beyond the Seas nor shall import or bring nor knowingly assist or consent to the importation or bringing from beyond the Seas into this Realm any English Booke or Books or part of any Booke which is or shall bee or the greater part thereof is or shall be English or of the English Tongue whether the same Booke Books or part of such Book have been here formerly printed or not upon pain of forfeiture of all such English Books so imprinted or imported contrary to the tenour hereof And that no Alien or Forreiner whatsoever shall hereafter bring in or be suffered to vend here within this Realm any Book or Books printed beyond the Seas in any Language whatsoever either by himselfe or his Factor or Factors except such only as bee

Free Printers or Stationers of London or such as have been brought up in that Profession without the special License of the Archbishop of Canterbury and Bishop of London for the time being or one of them who are hereby authorized to grant Licenses for that purpose upon like pain of forfeiture of all such Books as shall be soe imprinted or vended contrary to the purport and true intent hereof

And be it further enacted by the Authority aforesaid That no person or persons within the City of London or the Liberties thereof or elsewhere shall erect or cause to be erected any Presse or Printing House nor shall knowingly demise or let or willingly suffer to be held or used any House Vault Cellar or other Room whatsoever to or by any person or persons for a Printing House or Place to print in unlesse he or they who erect such Presse or shall so knowingly demise or let such House Cellar Vault or room or willingly suffer the same to be used shall first give notice to the Master or Wardens of the said Company of Stationers for the time being of the erecting of such Presse or of such demise or suffering to worke or print in such House Vault Cellar or Room And that no Joyner Carpenter or other person shall make any Printing Presse no Smith shall forge any Iron worke for a Printing Presse no Founder shall cast any Letters which may be used for printing for any person or persons whatsoever neither shall any person or persons bring or cause to be brought in from any parts beyond the Seas any Letters founded or cast nor shall buy any such Letters for printing Printing Presses or other Materials belonging unto printing unlesse he or they respectively shall first acquaint the said Master and Wardens of the said Company of Stationers for the time being or some or one of them for whom the same Presses Iron Worke or Letters are to be made forged cast brought or imported upon pain that every person who shall erect any such Printing Press or shall demise or let any House or Room or suffer the same to be held or used and every person who shall make any Printing Press or any Iron worke for a Printing Presse or shall make import or buy any Letters for printing without giving notice as aforesaid shall forfeit for every such offence the sum of Five pounds the one Moyety whereof shall be to the use of our Soveraign Lord the King His Heires and Successors and the other Moyety to the use of such person or persons as shall sue for the same

And be it further enacted by the Authority aforesaid That for the time to come no man shall be admitted to be a Master Printer untill they who are now actually Master Printers shall be by death or otherwise reduced to the number of Twenty and from thence forth the number of Twenty Master Printers shall be continued and no more besides the Kings Printers and the Printers allowed for the Universities to have the use and exercise of printing of Books at one time and but four Master Founders of Letters for printing The which said Master Printers and four Master Founders of Letters for printing shall be nominated appointed and allowed by the Lord Archbishop of Canterbury and Lord Bishop of London for the time being And in case of death of any one of the said four Master Founders of Letters or of the said Master Printers or of Forfeiture or avoidance of any of their Places and Priviledges to print by vertue of this Act for any Offence contrary to the same or otherwise that then the Lord Archbishop of Canterbury and Lord Bishop of London for the time being or one of them shall nominate and appoint such other fit person or persons to succeed and supply the place of such Master Printer or Founder of Letters as shall be void by Death Forfeiture or otherwise as aforesaid And every person and persons which shall hereafter be allowed or permitted to have the use of a Printing Presse or Printing House upon or before such his allowance obtained shall become bound with Sureties to His Majesty in the Court of Kings Bench or before some one or more of the Justices of Assize or the Justices of the Peace at theire several Quarter Sessions in the sum of three hundred pounds not to print or suffer to be printed in his house or presse any Booke or Bookes whatsoever but such as shall from time to time be lawfully licensed.

And be it further enacted by the Authority aforesaid That none of the said Master Printers to be allowed from time to time as aforesaid shall keep above Two Printing Presses at once unlesse he hath been Master or Upper Warden of the Company who are hereby allowed to keepe Three Presses and no more unlesse for some great and special occasion for the Publique he or they have for a time leave of the said Lord Archishop of Canterbury or Lord Bishop of London for the time being to have or use one or more above the aforesaid Number as their Lordships or either of them shall thinke fit

And be it alsoe enacted by the Authority aforesaid That no Printer or Printers (except the Kings Printers) nor Founder or Founders of Letters for printing shall take or retain any more or greater number of Apprentices then is herein after limited and appointed (that is to say) every Master Printer and Master Founder of Letters for printing that is or hath been Master or Upper Warden of his Company may have three Apprentices at one time and no more And every Master Printer and Master Founder of Letters for printing that is of the Livery of his Company may have two Apprentices at one time and no more And every Master Printer and Master Founder of Letters for printing of the Yeomanry of his Company may have one Apprentice at one time and no more neither by Copartnership binding at the Scriveners nor any other way whatsoever neither shall it be lawfull for any Master Printer or Master Founder of Letters when any Apprentice or Apprentices shall run or be put away to take another Apprentice or other Apprentices in his or theire place or places unlesse the name or names of him or them so gone away be rased out of the Hall Booke and never admitted againe

And because a great part of the secret Printing in corners hath been caused for want of orderly imployment for Journey men Printers The said several Master Printers and Master Founders of Letters for Printing so to be allowed as aforesaid are hereby required to take special Care that all Journey men Printers and Journey men Founders of Letters for printing who are lawfully Free of the said respective Mysteries be set to worke and imployed in theire respective Trades And if any such Journey man Printer or Journey man Founder of Letters being of honest and good behaviour and able in his Trade do want Imployment he shall repair to any of the said Master Printer or Master Founders of Letters respectively for the time being who thereupon shall receive him or them into work If such Master Printer or Master Founder of Letters have not a Journeyman already although such M̄r Printer or M̄r Founder of Letters respectively with his Apprentice or Apprentices be able without the helpe of the said Journey man to discharge his owne Work upon pain that every Master Printer and Master Founder of Letters respectively refuseing to receive such Journey man repairing to him as aforesaid shall forfeit five pounds to be recovered by Bill Plaint or Information in any Court of Record wherein no Essoign Wager at Law Priviledge or Protection shall be admitted the Moyety of which forfeiture shall go to the Kings Majesty his Heires and Successors and the other Moyety to the Informer who shall sue for the same within six monthes next after the said offence committed And if any Journey man or Journey men Printers or Founders of Letters for Printing shall refuse imployment being offered to him or them by any Master Printer or Master Founder of Letters respectively or neglect it when he or they have undertaken it he or they so refuseing or neglecting shall suffer three months Imprisonment at the least without Bail or Mainprize upon conviction of such his said refusal or neglect by two Witnesses before any one or more Justice or Justices of the Peace who are hereby impowered to heare and examine the said offence and to commit the said Offender and Offenders to the Common Gaol of the County where he or they shall be apprehended And no Master Printer or Master Founder of Letters for Printing shall from henceforth imploy either to worke at the Case or Press or otherwise about his Printing any other person or persons than such only as are Englishmen and Freemen or the Sons of Free men or Apprentices to the said Trades or Mysteries of Printing or Founding of Letters for Printing respectively

And for the better discovering of printing in Corners without License Be it further enacted by the Authority aforesaid That one or more of the Messengers of his Majesties Chamber by Warrant under His Majesties Sign Manual or under the Hand of one or both of His Majesties principal Secretares of State or the Master and Wardens of the said Company of Stationers or any one of them shall have power and authority with a constable to take unto them such assistance as they shall thinke needfull and att what time they shall thinke fitt to search all Houses and Shops where they shall knowe or upon some probable reason suspect any Books or Papers to be printed bound or stitched especially Printing Houses Booksellers Shops and Warehouses and Bookbinders Houses and Shops and to view there what is imprinting binding or stitching and to examine whether the same be licensed and to demand a sight of the said License and if the said Booke soe imprinting binding or stitching shall not be licensed then to seize upon so much thereof as shall be found imprinted togeather with the several Offenders and to bring them before one or more Justices of the Peace whoe are hereby authorized and required to commit such Offenders to Prison there to remaine untill they shall be tried and acquitted or convicted and punished for the said Offences And in case the said Searchers shall upon theire said Search find any Booke or Bookes or part of Bookes unlicensed which they shall suspect to contain matters therein contrary to the Doctrine or Discipline of the Church of England or against the State and Government Then upon such suspition to seise upon such Book or Books or part of Book or Books and to bring the same unto the said Lord Archbishop of Canterbury and Lord Bishop of London for the time being or one of them or to the Secretaries of State or one of them respectively who shall take such further course for the suppressing thereof as to them or any of them shall seeme fit.

And be it ordained and enacted by the Authority aforesaid That all and every Printer and Printers of Books Founder and Founders of Letters for Printing and all and every other person and persons working in or for the said Trades who from and after the Tenth day of June in the Yeare One thousand six hundred sixty and two shall offend against this present Act or any Article Clause or Thing herein contained and shall be thereof convicted by verdict confession or otherwise shall for the first offence be disenabled from exercising his respective Trade for the space of three yeares and for the second offence shall for ever thence after be disabled to use or exercise the Art or Mystery of Printing or of Founding Letters for Printing and shall alsoe have and receive such further punishment by Fine Imprisonment or other Corporal Punishment not extending to Life or Limb as by the Justices of the Court of Kings Bench or Justices of Oyer and Terminer or Justices of Assize in theire several Circuits or Justices of the Peace in theire several Quarter Sessions shall be thought fitt to be inflicted The which said Justices of the Peace in theire several Quarter Sessions shall have full power and authority to heare and determine all and every offence and offences that shall be committed against this Act or against any branch thereof upon indictment or information by any person or persons to be taken before them in theire Sessions of Peace respectively and shall yearely certifie into the Court of Exchequer as in other like Cases they are bound to doe the Fines by them imposed for any the offences aforesaid and shall and may alsoe by vertue hereof award process and execution for the taking or punishing such Offenders as in any other Case they lawfully may do by any the Lawes and Statutes of this Realm

And be it further enacted by the Authority aforesaid That every Printer shall reserve three printed Copies of the best and largest Paper of every Book new printed or reprinted by him with Additions and shall before any publick venting of the said Book bring them to the Master of the Company of Stationers and deliver them to him one whereof shall be delivered to the Keeper of his Majesties Library and the other two to be sent to the Vice-Chancellors of the two Universities respectively for the use of the Publique Libraries of the said Universities

Provided alwaies That nothing in this Act contained shall be construed to extend to the p[re]judice or infringing of any the just Rights and Priviledges of either of the two Universities of this Realm touching and concerning the licensing or printing of Books in either of the said Universities

Provided alwaies That no search shall be att any time made in the House or Houses of any the Peers of this Realm or of any other person or persons not being free of or using any of the Trades in this Act before mentioned but by special Warrant from the Kings Majestie under His Sign Manual or under the Hand of one or both of His Majesties principal Secretaries of State or for any other Books then such as are in printing or shall be printed after the Tenth of June One thousand six hundred sixty two Any thing in this Act to the contrary thereof in any wise notwithstanding

Provided alsoe and be it further enacted by the Authority aforesaid That neither this Act nor any thing therein contained shall be construed to prohibit any person or persons to sell Books or Papers who have sold Books or Papers within Westminster Hall the Palace of Westminster or in any Shopp or Shopps within twenty yards of the great Gate of Westminster Hall aforesaid before the Twentieth day of November One thousand six hundred sixty and one but they and every of them may sell Books and Papers as they have or did before the said Twentieth Day of November One thousand six hundred sixty one within the said Hall Pallace and twenty yards aforesaid but not else where Any thing in this Act to the contrary in any wise notwithstanding

Provided alsoe That neither this Act nor any thing therein contained shall extend to p[re]judice the just Rights or Priviledges granted by His Majesty or any of his Royall Predecessors to any person or persons under His Majesties Great Seale or otherwise but that such person or persons may exercise and use such Rights and Priviledges as aforesaid according to theire respective Grants Any thing in this Act to the contrary notwithstanding

Provided alsoe That neither this Act nor any therein contained shall extend to prohibit John Streater Stationer from printing Bookes and Papers but that he may still follow the Art and Mistery of Printing as if this Act had never beene made Any thing therein to the contrary notwithstanding

Provided alsoe That neither this Act nor any thing therein contained shall extend to restrain the keeping and using of a Printing Presse in the City of Yorke so as all Bookes of Divinity there printed be first licensed by the Archbishop of Yorke for the time being or such person or persons whom he shall appoint and all other Bookes whatsoever there printed be first licensed by such persons respectively to whom the licensing thereof doth or shall appertain by the rules herein before mentioned and so as no Bibles be there printed nor any other Booke whereof the Original Copy is or shall be belonging to the Company of Stationers in London or any Member thereof and so as the Archbishop or Lord Mayor of Yorke for the time being do execute within the said City (which they are hereby impowered to do) all the Powers and Rules in this Act concerning Searchers for unlicensed Bookes and impose and levy the said penalties in the like cases Any thing in this Act to the contrary notwithstanding

Provided That this Act shall continue and be in force for two yeares to commence from the Tenth of June One thousand six hundred sixty and two and no longer.

2

DAVID HUME, OF THE LIBERTY OF THE PRESS 1742

Nothing is more apt to surprise a foreigner than the extreme liberty which we enjoy in this country of communicating whatever we please to the public and of openly censuring every measure entered into by the king or his ministers. If the administration resolve upon war, it is affirmed that, either willfully or ignorantly, they mistake the interests of the nation; and that peace, in the present situation of affairs, is infinitely preferable. If the passion of the ministers lie toward peace, our political writers breathe nothing but war and devastation, and represent the specific conduct of the government as mean and pusillanimous. As this liberty is not indulged in any other government, either republican or monarchical—in Holland and Venice more than in France or Spain—it may very naturally give occasion to the question: *How it happens that Great Britain alone enjoys this peculiar privilege?* And whether the unlimited exercise of this liberty be advantageous or prejudicial to the public.

The reason why the laws indulge us in such a liberty seems to be derived from our mixed form of government, which is neither wholly monarchical nor wholly republican. It will be found, if I mistake not, a true observation in politics that the two extremes in government, liberty and slavery, commonly approach nearest to each other; and that, as you depart from the extremes and mix a little of monarchy with liberty, the government becomes always the more free, and on the other hand, when you mix a little of liberty with monarchy, the yoke becomes always the more grievous and intolerable. In a government, such as that of France, which is absolute and where law, custom, and religion concur, all of them, to make the people fully satisfied with their condition, the monarch cannot entertain any *jealousy* against his subjects and therefore is apt to indulge them in great *liberties*, both of speech and action. In a government altogether republican, such as that of Holland, where there is no magistrate so eminent as to give *jealousy* to the state, there is no danger in entrusting the magistrates with large discretionary powers; and though many advantages result from such powers, in preserving peace and order, yet they lay a considerable restraint on men's actions and make every private citizen pay a great respect to the government. Thus it seems evident that the two extremes of absolute monarchy and of a republic approach near to each other in some material circumstances. In the *first* the magistrate has no jealousy of the people, in the *second* the people have none of the magistrate; which want of jealousy begets a mutual confidence and trust in both cases and produces a species of liberty in monarchies and of arbitrary power in republics. . . .

[A]s the republican part of the government prevails in England, though with a great mixture of monarchy, it is obliged, for its own preservation, to maintain a watchful *jealousy* over the magistrates, to remove all discretionary powers, and to secure everyone's life and fortune by general and inflexible laws. No action must be deemed a crime but what the law has plainly determined to be such; no crime must be imputed to a man but from a legal proof before his judges, and even these judges must be his fellow subjects, who are obliged by their own interest to have a watchful eye over the encroachments and violence of the ministers. From these causes it proceeds that there is as much liberty, and even perhaps licentiousness, in Great Britain as there were formerly slavery and tyranny in Rome.

These principles account for the great liberty of the press in these kingdoms beyond what is indulged in any other government. It is apprehended that arbitrary power would steal in upon us were we not careful to prevent its progress and were there not an easy method of conveying the alarm from one end of the kingdom to the other. The spirit of the people must frequently be roused in order to curb the ambition of the court, and the dread of rousing this spirit must be employed to prevent that ambition. Nothing so effectual to this purpose as the liberty of the press, by which all the learning, wit, and genius of the nation may be employed on the side of freedom and everyone be animated to its defense. As long, therefore, as the republican part of our government can maintain itself against the monarchical, it will naturally be careful to keep the press open, as of importance to its own preservation.

Since, therefore, the liberty of the press is so essential to the support of our mixed government, this sufficiently decides the second question: *Whether this liberty be advantageous or prejudicial*, there being nothing of greater importance in every state than the preservation of the ancient government, especially if it be a free one. But I would fain go a step further and assert that such a liberty is attended with so few inconveniences that it may be claimed as the common right of mankind and ought to be indulged them almost in every government except the ecclesiastical, to which, indeed, it would be fatal. We need not dread from this liberty any such ill consequences as followed from the harangues of the popular demagogues of Athens and tribunes of Rome. A man reads a book or pamphlet alone and coolly. There is none present from whom he can catch the passion by contagion. He is not hurried away by the force and energy of action. And should he be wrought up to never so seditious a humor, there is no violent resolution presented to him by which he can immediately vent his passion. The liberty of the press, therefore, however abused, can scarce ever excite popular tumults or rebellion. And as to those murmurs or secret discontents it may occasion, it is better they should get vent in words, that they may come to the knowledge of the magistrate before it be too late, in order to his providing a remedy against them. Mankind, it is true, have always a greater propension to believe what is said to the disadvantage of their governors than the contrary; but this inclination is inseparable from them whether they have liberty or not. A whisper may fly as quick and be as pernicious as a pamphlet. Nay, it will be more pernicious where men are not accustomed to think freely or distinguish betwixt truth and falsehood. . . .

It is a very comfortable reflection to the lovers of liberty that this peculiar privilege of *Britain* is of a kind that cannot easily be wrested from us and must last as long as our government remains in any degree free and independent. It is seldom that liberty of any kind is lost all at once. Slavery has so frightful an aspect to men accustomed to freedom that it must steal in upon them by degrees and must disguise itself in a thousand shapes in order to be received. But if the liberty of the press ever be lost, it must be lost at once. The general laws against sedition and libeling are at present as strong as they possibly can be made. Nothing can impose a further restraint but either the clapping an imprimatur upon the press or the giving very large discretionary powers to the court to punish whatever displeases them. But these concessions would be such a barefaced violation of liberty that they will probably be the last efforts of a despotic government. We may conclude that the liberty of *Britain* is gone forever when these attempts shall succeed.

It must however be allowed that the unbounded liberty of the press, though it be difficult—perhaps impossible—to propose a suitable remedy for it, is one of the evils attending those mixed forms of government.

3

MONTESQUIEU, SPIRIT OF LAWS, BK. 12, CHS. 12–13
1748

12.—Of indiscreet Speeches

Nothing renders the crime of high treason more arbitrary than declaring people guilty of it for indiscreet speeches. Speech is so subject to interpretation; there is so great a difference between indiscretion and malice; and frequently so little is there of the latter in the freedom of expression, that the law can hardly subject people to a capital punishment for words unless it expressly declares what words they are.

Words do not constitute an overt act; they remain only in idea. When considered by themselves, they have generally no determinate signification; for this depends on the tone in which they are uttered. It often happens that in repeating the same words they have not the same meaning; this depends on their connection with other things, and sometimes more is signified by silence than by any expression whatever. Since there can be nothing so equivocal and ambiguous as all this, how is it possible to convert it into a crime of high treason? Wherever this law is estab-

lished, there is an end not only of liberty, but even of its very shadow.

In the manifesto of the late Czarina against the family of the D'Olgoruckys, one of those princes is condemned to death for having uttered some indecent words concerning her person: another, for having maliciously interpreted her imperial laws, and for having offended her sacred person by disrespectful expressions.

Not that I pretend to diminish the just indignation of the public against those who presume to stain the glory of their sovereign; what I mean is, that if despotic princes are willing to moderate their power, a milder chastisement would be more proper on those occasions than the charge of high treason—a thing always terrible even to innocence itself.

Overt acts do not happen every day; they are exposed to the eye of the public; and a false charge with regard to matters of fact may be easily detected. Words carried into action assume the nature of that action. Thus a man who goes into a public market-place to incite the subject to revolt incurs the guilt of high treason, because the words are joined to the action, and partake of its nature. It is not the words that are punished, but an action in which words are employed. They do not become criminal, but when they are annexed to a criminal action: everything is confounded if words are construed into a capital crime, instead of considering them only as a mark of that crime.

The Emperors Theodosius, Arcadius, and Honorius wrote thus to Rufinus, who was *praefectus praetorio:* "Though a man should happen to speak amiss of our person or government, we do not intend to punish him: if he has spoken through levity, we must despise him; if through folly, we must pity him; and if he wrongs us, we must forgive him. Therefore, leaving things as they are, you are to inform us accordingly, that we may be able to judge of words by persons, and that we may duly consider whether we ought to punish or overlook them."

13.—Of Writings

In writings there is something more permanent than in words, but when they are in no way preparative to high treason they cannot amount to that charge.

And yet Augustus and Tiberius subjected satirical writers to the same punishment as for having violated the law of majesty. Augustus, because of some libels that had been written against persons of the first quality; Tiberius, because of those which he suspected to have been written against himself. Nothing was more fatal to Roman liberty. Cremutius Cordus was accused of having called Cassius in his annals the last of the Romans.

Satirical writings are hardly known in despotic governments, where dejection of mind on the one hand, and ignorance on the other, afford neither abilities nor will to write. In democracies they are not hindered, for the very same reason which causes them to be prohibited in monarchies; being generally levelled against men of power and authority, they flatter the malignancy of the people, who are the governing party. In monarchies they are forbidden, but rather as a subject of civil animadversion than as a capital crime. They may amuse the general malevolence, please the malcontents, diminish the envy against public employments, give the people patience to suffer, and make them laugh at their sufferings.

But no government is so averse to satirical writings as the aristocratic. There the magistrates are petty sovereigns, but not great enough to despise affronts. If in a monarchy a satirical stroke is designed against the prince, he is placed on such an eminence that it does not reach him; but an aristocratic lord is pierced to the very heart. Hence the decemvirs, who formed an aristocracy, punished satirical writings with death.

4

WILLIAM BLACKSTONE, Commentaries 4:150–53
1769

---

13. Of a nature very similar to challenges are *libels, libelli famosi*, which, taken in their largest and most extensive sense, signify any writings, pictures, or the like, of an immoral or illegal tendency; but, in the sense under which we are now to consider them, are malicious defamations of any person, and especially a magistrate, made public by either printing, writing, signs, or pictures, in order to provoke him to wrath, or expose him to public hatred, contempt, and ridicule. The direct tendency of these libels is the breach of the public peace, by stirring up the objects of them to revenge, and perhaps to bloodshed. The communication of a libel to any one person is a publication in the eye of the law: and therefore the sending an abusive private letter to a man is as much a libel as if it were openly printed, for it equally tends to a breach of the peace. For the same reason it is immaterial with respect to the essence of a libel, whether the matter of it be true or false; since the provocation, and not the falsity, is the thing to be punished criminally: though, doubtless, the falsehood of it may aggravate it's guilt, and enhance it's punishment. In a civil action, we may remember, a libel must appear to be false, as well as scandalous; for, if the charge be true, the plaintiff has received no private injury, and has no ground to demand a compensation for himself, whatever offence it may be against the public peace: and therefore, upon a civil action, the truth of the accusation may be pleaded in bar of the suit. But, in a criminal prosecution, the tendency which all libels have to create animosities, and to disturb the public peace, is the sole consideration of the law. And therefore, in such prosecutions, the only facts to be considered are, first, the making or publishing of the book or writing; and secondly, whether the matter be criminal: and, if both these points are against the defendant, the offence against the public is complete. The punishment of such libellers, for either making, repeating, printing, or publishing the libel, is fine, and such corporal punishment as the court in their discretion shall inflict; regarding the quantity of the offence, and the quality of the offender. By the law of the twelve tables at Rome, libels, which affected the reputation of another, were made a capital offence: but, before the reign of Augustus, the punishment became corporal only. Under the emperor Valentinian it was again made capital, not only to write, but to publish, or even to omit destroying them. Our law, in this and many other respects, corresponds rather with the middle age of Roman jurisprudence, when liberty, learning, and humanity, were in their full vigour, than with the cruel edicts that were established in the dark and tyrannical ages of the antient *decemviri*, or the later emperors.

In this, and the other instances which we have lately considered, where blasphemous, immoral, treasonable, schismatical, seditious, or scandalous libels are punished by the English law, some with a greater, others with a less degree of severity; the *liberty of the press*, properly understood, is by no means infringed or violated. The liberty of the press is indeed essential to the nature of a free state: but this consists in laying no *previous* restraints upon publications, and not in freedom from censure for criminal matter when published. Every freeman has an undoubted right to lay what sentiments he pleases before the public: to forbid this, is to destroy the freedom of the press: but if he publishes what is improper, mischievous, or illegal, he must take the consequence of his own temerity. To subject the press to the restrictive power of a licenser, as was formerly done, both before and since the revolution, is to subject all freedom of sentiment to the prejudices of one man, and make him the arbitrary and infallible judge of all controverted points in learning, religion, and government. But to punish (as the law does at present) any dangerous or offensive writings, which, when published, shall on a fair and impartial trial be adjudged of a pernicious tendency, is necessary for the preservation of peace and good order, of government and religion, the only solid foundations of civil liberty. Thus the will of individuals is still left free; the abuse only of that free will is the object of legal punishment. Neither is any restraint hereby laid upon freedom of thought or enquiry: liberty of private sentiment is still left; the disseminating, or making public, of bad sentiments, destructive of the ends of society, is the crime which society corrects. A man (says a fine writer on this subject) may be allowed to keep poisons in his closet, but not publicly to vend them as cordials. And to this we may add, that the only plausible argument heretofore used for restraining the just freedom of the press, "that it was necessary to prevent the daily abuse of it," will entirely lose it's force, when it is shewn (by a seasonable exertion of the laws) that the press cannot be abused to any bad purpose, without incurring a suitable punishment: whereas it never can be used to any good one, when under the control of an inspector. So true will it be found, that to censure the licentiousness, is to maintain the liberty, of the press.

5

JAMES BURGH, POLITICAL DISQUISITIONS 3:246–52
1775

Of the Liberty of Speech and Writing in Political Subjects

In an inquiry into public abuses no one will wonder to find punishment inflicted by government upon complainers, reckoned as an abuse; for it certainly is one of the most atrocious abuses, that a free subject should be restrained in his inquiries into the conduct of those who undertake to manage his affairs; I mean the administrators of government: for all such are undertakers, and are answerable for what they undertake: but if it be dangerous and penal to inquire into their conduct, the state may be ruined by their blunders, or by their villanies, beyond the possibility of redress.

There seems to be somewhat unnatural in attempting to lay a restraint on those who would criticise the conduct of men who undertake to do other people's business. It is an offense, if we remark on the decision of a court of law, on the proceedings of either house of parliament, or of the administration; all whose proceedings we are immediately concerned in. At the same time, if a man builds a house for himself, marries a wife for himself, or writes a book, by which the public gets more than the author, it is no offence to make very severe and unjust remarks.

Are Judges, Juries, Counsellors, Members of the House of Commons, Peers, Secretaries of State, or Kings, infallible? Or are they short-sighted, and perhaps interested, mortals?

In a petition to parliament, a bill in chancery, and proceedings at law, libellous words are not punishable; because freedom of speech and writing are indispensably necessary to the carrying on of business. But it may be said, there is no necessity for a private writer to be indulged the liberty of attacking the conduct of those who take upon themselves to govern the state. The answer is easy, viz. That all history shews the necessity, in order to the preservation of liberty, of every subject's having a watchful eye on the conduct of Kings, Ministers, and Parliament, and of every subject's being not only secured, but encouraged in alarming his fellow-subjects on occasion of every attempt upon public liberty, and that private, independent subjects *only* are likely to give fair warning of such attempts; their betters (as to rank and fortune) being more likely to conceal, than detect the abuses committed by those in power. If, therefore, private writers are to be intimidated in shewing their fidelity to their country, the principal security of liberty is taken away.

Punishing libels public or private is foolish, because it does not answer the end, and because the end is a bad one, if it could be answered.

The Attorney General *De Grey* confessed in the House of Commons, A.D. 1770, "that his power of filing informations *ex officio* is an odious power, and that it does not answer the purpose intended; for that he had not been able to bring any libeller to justice." Mr. *Pownal* shewed that power to be illegal and unconstitutional; for that, according to law, no *Englishman* is to be brought upon his trial, but by presentment of his country; a few particular cases excepted.

When the lawyers say a libel is criminal, though true, they mean, because it is, according to them, a breach of the peace, and tends to excite revenge. They allow, that the *falsehood* of the charge is an aggravation, and that, therefore, the person libelled has no right to damages, if the charges laid against him be *true*. But by this rule it should seem, that the *truth* of the libel should take away all its criminality. For if I have no right to damages, I have no pretence to seek revenge. Therefore to libel me for what I cannot affirm myself to be innocent of, is no breach of the peace, as it does not naturally tend to excite revenge, but rather ingenuous shame and reformation.

Let us hear on this subject the excellent Lord *Chesterfield*, on the bill for licensing the stage, A.D. 1737.

"In public, as well as private life, the only way to prevent being ridiculed or censured, is to avoid all ridiculous or wicked measures, and to pursue such only as are virtuous and worthy. The people never endeavor to ridicule those they love and esteem, nor will they suffer them to be ridiculed. If any one attempts it, their ridicule returns upon the author; he makes himself only the object of public hatred and contempt. The actions or behaviour of a private man may pass unobserved, and consequently unapplauded and uncensured; but the actions of these in high stations, can neither pass without notice nor without censure or applause; and therefore an administration without esteem, without authority, among the people, let their power be ever so great or ever so arbitrary, will be ridiculed: the severest edicts, the most terrible punishments cannot prevent it. If any man, therefore, thinks he has been censured, if any man thinks he has been ridiculed, upon any of our public theatres, let him examine his actions he will find the cause, let him alter his conduct he will find a remedy. As no man is perfect, as no man is infallible, the greatest may err, the most circumspect may be guilty of some piece of ridiculous behavior. It is not licentiousness, it is an useful liberty always indulged the stage in a free country, that some great men may there meet with a just reproof, which none of their friends will be free enough, or rather faithful enough to give them. Of this we have a famous influence in the *Roman* history. The great *Pompey*, after the many victories he had obtained, and the great conquests he had made, had certainly a good title to the esteem of the people of *Rome*. Yet that great man by some error in his conduct, became an object of general dislike; and therefore in the representation of an old play, when *Diphilus* the actor came to repeat these words, *Nostrâ miseriâ tu es magnus*, the audience immediately applied them to *Pompey*, who at that time was as well known by the name of *Magnus* as by the name *Pompey*, and were so highly pleased with the satire, that, as *Cicero* tells us, they made the actor repeat the words one hundred times over. An account of this was immediately sent to *Pompey,* who, instead of resenting it as an injury, was so wise as to take it for a just reproof. He examined his conduct, he altered his measures, he regained by degrees the esteem of the people, and then he neither feared the wit, nor felt the satire of the stage. This is an example which ought to be followed by great men in all countries."

Even the cruel *Tiberius,* when in good humour, could say, In a free state, the mind and the tongue "ought to be free." *Titus* defied any one to scandalize him. *Trajan* published absolute liberty of speech and writing. *Constantine,* when he was told that some ill-disposed persons had battered his head and face, meaning those of his statue, felt himself all about those parts, and told his courtiers, he found nothing amiss; desiring that they would take no trouble about finding out the violators of the statue.

Mr. *Gordon* allows the maxim, that a libel is not the less a libel for being true. But this holds, he says, only in respect of *private* characters; and it is quite otherwise, when the crimes of men affect the *public.* We are to take care of the public safety at all adventures. And the loss of an individual's, or a whole ministry's *political* characters, ought to be despised, when put in competition with the fate of a kingdom. Therefore no free subject ought to be under the least restraint in respect to accusing the greatest, so long as his accusation strikes only at the *political* conduct of the accused: his private we have no right to meddle with, but in so far as a known vicious private character indicates an unfitness for public power or truth. But it may be said, this is a grievous hardship on those who undertake the administration of a nation; that they are to run the hazard of being thus publicly accused of corruption, embezzlement, and other political crimes, without having it in their power to punish their slanderers. To this I answer, It is no hardship at all, but the unavoidable inconvenience attendant upon a high station, which he who dislikes must avoid, and keep himself private. *Cato* was forty times tried. But we do not think the worse of *Cato* for this. If a statesman is liable to be falsely accused, let him comfort himself by recollecting, that he is well paid. An ensign is liable to be killed in war; and he has but 3 *s.* 6 *d.* a day. If a statesman has designedly behaved amiss, he ought to be punished with the utmost severity; because the injury he has done, is unboundedly extensive. If he has injured the public through weakness, and without wicked intention, he is still punishable; because he ought not to have thrust himself into a station for which he was unfit. But, indeed, these cases are so rare (want of *honesty* being the general cause of maladministration), that it is scarce worth while to touch upon them. If a statesman is falsely accused, he has only to clear his character, and he appears in a fairer light than before. He must not insist on punishing his accuser: for the public security requires, that there be no danger in accusing those who undertake the administration of national affairs. The punishment of political satyrists gains credit to their writings, nor do unjust govenments reap any fruit from such severities, but insults to themselves, and honour to those whom they prosecute.

A libel is in fact (criminally speaking) a *non entity, i.e.* there is no such offence as scandal. For if the punishment was taken away, the whole of the evil would be taken away, because nobody would regard scandal; but people would believe every person's character to be what they knew it.

6

VIRGINIA DECLARATION OF RIGHTS, SEC. 12
12 June 1776

---

12. That the freedom of the press is one of the great bulwarks of liberty, and can never be restrained but by despotick governments.

7

ALBEMARLE COUNTY INSTRUCTIONS CONCERNING THE VIRGINIA CONSTITUTION
Fall 1776
Jefferson Papers 6:288

In regard to the freedom of the press, which certainly is, as mentioned in the Bill of Rights, one of the great bulwarks of Liberty, we think that the Printers should never be liable for any thing they print, provided they may give up authors, who are responsible, but on the contrary that they should print nothing without. Many good people have been lately mislead by the artifices of ingenious, but malicious, interested and corrupt writers. Had their names been published, their Characters would have been the antidote to their own poison. We are convinced, that by such a regulation many inconveniencies may be avoided, and whether the objections to it are of greater weight we submit to the consideration of our Representatives.

8

THOMAS JEFFERSON TO EDWARD CARRINGTON
16 Jan. 1787
Papers 11:48–49

The tumults in America I expected would have produced in Europe an unfavorable opinion of our political state. But it has not. On the contrary, the small effect of those tumults seems to have given more confidence in the firmness of our governments. The interposition of the people themselves on the side of government has had a great effect on the opinion here. I am persuaded myself that the good sense of the people will always be found to be the best army. They may be led astray for a moment, but will soon correct themselves. The people are the only censors of their governors: and even their errors will tend to keep these to the true principles of their institution. To punish these errors too severely would be to suppress the only safeguard of the public liberty. The way to prevent these irregular interpositions of the people is to give them full information of their affairs thro' the channel of the public papers, and to contrive that those papers should penetrate the whole mass of the people. The basis of our governments being the opinion of the people, the very first object should be to keep that right; and were it left to me to decide whether we should have a government without newspapers, or newspapers without a government, I should not hesitate a moment to prefer the latter. But I should mean that every man should receive those papers and be capable of reading them. I am convinced that those societies (as the Indians) which live without government enjoy in their general mass an infinitely greater degree of happiness than those who live under European governments. Among the former, public opinion is in the place of law, and restrains morals as powerfully as laws ever did any where. Among the latter, under pretence of governing they have divided their nations into two classes, wolves and sheep. I do not exaggerate. This is a true picture of Europe. Cherish therefore the spirit of our people, and keep alive their attention. Do not be too severe upon their errors, but reclaim them by enlightening them. If once they become inattentive to the public affairs, you and I, and Congress, and Assemblies, judges and governors shall all become wolves. It seems to be the law of our general nature, in spite of individual exceptions; and experience declares that man is the only animal which devours his own kind, for I can apply no milder term to the governments of Europe, and to the general prey of the rich on the poor.

9

CINCINNATUS, NO. 2, TO JAMES WILSON
8 Nov. 1787
Storing 6.1.11–12

I have proved, sir, that not only some power is given in the constitution to restrain, and even to subject the press, but that it is a power totally unlimited; and may certainly annihilate the freedom of the press, and convert it from being the palladium of liberty to become an engine of imposition and tyranny. It is an easy step from restraining the press to making it place the worst actions of government in so favorable a light, that we may groan under tyranny and oppression without knowing from whence it comes.

But you comfort us, by saying,—"there is no reason to suspect so popular a privilege will be neglected." The wolf, in the fable, said as much to the sheep, when he was persuading them to trust him as their protector, and to dismiss their guardian dogs. Do you indeed suppose, Mr.

Wilson, that if the people give up their privileges to these new rulers they will render them back again to the people? Indeed, sir, you should not trifle upon a question so serious—You would not have us to suspect any ill. If we throw away suspicion—to be sure, the thing will go smoothly enough, and we shall deserve to continue a free, respectable, and happy people. Suspicion shackles rulers and prevents good government. All great and honest politicians, *like yourself*, have reprobated it. Lord Mansfield is a great authority against it, and has often treated it as the worst of libels. But such men as Milton, Sidney, Locke, Montesquieu, and Trenchard, have thought it essential to the preservation of liberty against the artful and persevering encroachments of those with whom power is trusted. You will pardon me, sir, if I pay some respect to these opinions, and wish that the freedom of the press may be *previously* secured as a *constitutional* and *unalienable right*, and not left to the precarious care of popular privileges which may or may not influence our new rulers.

10

JAMES WILSON, PENNSYLVANIA
RATIFYING CONVENTION
1 Dec. 1787
Elliot 2:448–50

In answer to the gentleman from Fayette, (Mr. Smilie,) on the subject of the press, I beg leave to make an observation. It is very true, sir, that this Constitution says nothing with regard to that subject, nor was it necessary; because it will be found that there is given to the general government no power whatsoever concerning it; and no law, in pursuance of the Constitution, can possibly be enacted to destroy that liberty.

I heard the honorable gentleman make this general assertion, that the Congress was certainly vested with power to make such a law; but I would be glad to know by what part of this Constitution such a power is given? Until that is done, I shall not enter into a minute investigation of the matter, but shall at present satisfy myself with giving an answer to a question that has been put. It has been asked, If a law should be made to punish libels, and the judges should proceed under that law, what chance would the printer have of an acquittal? And it has been said he would drop into a den of devouring monsters!

I presume it was not in the view of the honorable gentleman to say there is no such thing as a libel, or that the writers of such ought not to be punished. The idea of the liberty of the press is not carried so far as this in any country. What is meant by the liberty of the press is, that there should be no antecedent restraint upon it; but that every author is responsible when he attacks the security or welfare of the government, or the safety, character, and property of the individual.

With regard to attacks upon the public, the mode of

proceeding is by a prosecution. Now, if a libel is written, it must be within some one of the United States, or the district of Congress. With regard to that district, I hope it will take care to preserve this as well as the other rights of freemen; for, whatever district Congress may choose, the cession of it cannot be completed without the consent of its inhabitants. Now, sir, if this *libel* is to be tried, it must be tried where the offence was committed; for, under this Constitution, as declared in the 2d section of the 3d article, the trial must be held in the state; therefore, on this occasion, it must be tried where it was published, if the indictment is for publishing; and it must be tried likewise by a jury of that state. Now, I would ask, is the person prosecuted in a worse situation under the general government, even if it had the power to make laws on this subject, than he is at present under the state government? It is true, there is no particular regulation made, to have the jury come from the body of the county in which the offence was committed; but there are some states in which this mode of collecting juries is contrary to their established custom, and gentlemen ought to consider that this Constitution was not meant merely for Pennsylvania. In some states, the juries are not taken from a single county. In Virginia, the sheriff, I believe, is not confined even to the inhabitants of the state, but is at liberty to take any man he pleases, and put him on the jury. In Maryland, I think, a set of jurors serve for the whole western shore, and another for the eastern shore.

11

FEDERAL FARMER, NO. 16
20 Jan. 1788
Storing 2.8.203

All parties apparently agree, that the freedom of the press is a fundamental right, and ought not to be restrained by any taxes, duties, or in any manner whatever. Why should not the people, in adopting a federal constitution, declare this, even if there are only doubts about it. But, say the advocates, all powers not given are reserved:—true; but the great question is, are not powers given, in the exercise of which this right may be destroyed? The people's or the printers claim to a free press, is founded on the fundamental laws, that is, compacts, and state constitutions, made by the people. The people, who can annihilate or alter those constitutions, can annihilate or limit this right. This may be done by giving general powers, as well as by using particular words. No right claimed under a state constitution, will avail against a law of the union, made in pursuance of the federal constitution: therefore the question is, what laws will congress have a right to make by the constitution of the union, and particularly touching the press? By art. 1. sect. 8. congress will have power to lay and collect taxes, duties, imposts and excise. By this congress will clearly have power to lay and collect all kind of

taxes whatever—taxes on houses, lands, polls, industry, merchandize, &c.—taxes on deeds, bonds, and all written instruments—on writs, pleas, and all judicial proceedings, on licences, naval officers papers, &c. on newspapers, advertisements, &c. and to require bonds of the naval officers, clerks, printers, &c. to account for the taxes that may become due on papers that go through their hands. Printing, like all other business, must cease when taxed beyond its profits; and it appears to me, that a power to tax the press at discretion, is a power to destroy or restrain the freedom of it. There may be other powers given, in the exercise of which this freedom may be effected; and certainly it is of too much importance to be left thus liable to be taxed, and constantly to constructions and inferences. A free press is the channel of communication as to mercantile and public affairs; by means of it the people in large countries ascertain each others sentiments; are enabled to unite, and become formidable to those rulers who adopt improper measures. Newspapers may sometimes be the vehicles of abuse, and of many things not true; but these are but small inconveniences, in my mind, among many advantages. A celebrated writer, I have several times quoted, speaking in high terms of the English liberties, says, "lastly the key stone was put to the arch, by the final establishment of the freedom of the press."

12

A PLEBEIAN, AN ADDRESS TO THE PEOPLE OF
THE STATE OF NEW-YORK
Spring 1788
Storing 6.11.31–33

"We are told, (says he [John Jay]) among other strange things, that the liberty of the press is left insecure by the proposed constitution, and yet that constitution says neither more nor less about it, than the constitution of the state of New-York does. We are told it deprives us of trial by jury, whereas the fact is, that it expressly secures it in certain cases, and takes it away in none, &c. It is absurd to construe the silence of this, or of our own constitution relative to a great number of our rights into a total extinction of them; silence and a blank paper neither grant nor take away anything."

It may be a strange thing to this author to hear the people of America anxious for the preservation of their rights, but those who understand the true principles of liberty, are no strangers to their importance. The man who supposes the constitution, in any part of it, is like a blank piece of paper, has very erroneous ideas of it. He may be assured every clause has a meaning, and many of them such extensive meaning, as would take a volume to unfold. The suggestion, that the liberty of the press is secure, because it is not in express words spoken of in the constitution, and that the trial by jury is not taken away, because it is not said in so many words and letters it is so, is puerile and unworthy of a man who pretends to reason. We contend, that by the indefinite powers granted to the general government, the liberty of the press may be restricted by duties, &c. and therefore the constitution ought to have stipulated for its freedom. The trial by jury, in all civil cases is left at the discretion of the general government, except in the supreme court on the appellate jurisdiction, and in this I affirm it is taken away, not by express words, but by fair and legitimate construction and inference; for the supreme court have expressly given them an appellate jurisdiction, in every case to which their powers extend (with two or three exceptions) both as to *law and fact.* The court are the judges; every man in the country, who has served as a juror, knows, that there is a distinction between the court and the jury, and that the lawyers in their pleading, make the distinction. If the court, upon appeals, are to determine both the law and the fact, there is no room for a jury, and the right of trial in this mode is taken away.

The author manifests equal levity in referring to the constitution of this state, to shew that it was useless to stipulate for the liberty of the press, or to insert a bill of rights in the constitution. With regard to the first, it is perhaps an imperfection in our consitution that the liberty of the press is not expressly reserved; but still there was not equal necessity of making this reservation in our State as in the general Constitution, for the commmon and statute law of England, and the laws of the colony are established, in which this privilege is fully defined and secured. It is true, a bill of rights is not prefixed to our constitution, as it is in that of some of the states; but still this author knows, that many essential rights are reserved in the body of it; and I will promise, that every opposer of this system will be satisfied, if the stipulations that they contend for are agreed to, whether they are prefixed, affixed, or inserted in the body of the constitution, and that they will not contend which way this is done, if it be but done.

13

RESPUBLICA V. OSWALD
1 Dall. 319 (Pa. 1788)

On the 12th of July, *Lewis* moved for a rule to show cause why an attachment should not issue against Eleazer Oswald, the printer and publisher of the Independent Gazetteer.

The case was this: Oswald having inserted in his newspapers several anonymous pieces against the character of Andrew Browne, the master of a female academy, in the city of Philadelphia, Browne applied to him to give up the authors of those pieces: but being refused that satisfaction, he brought an action for the libel against Oswald, returnable into the supreme court, on the 2d day of July; and therein demanded bail for 1000*l.* Previously to the return-day of the writ, the question of bail being brought by citation before Mr. Justice BRYAN, at his chambers, the judge, on a full hearing of the cause of action, in the presence of both the parties, ordered the defendant to be discharged on common bail; and the plaintiff appealed from this order to the court. Afterwards, on the first of July, Oswald published, under his own signature, an address to the public, which contained a narrative of these proceedings, and the following passages, which, I conceive, to have been the material grounds of the present motion.

"When violent attacks are made upon a person, under pretext of justice, and legal steps are taken on the occasion, not perhaps to redress the supposed injury, but to feed and gratify partisaning and temporising resentments, it is not unwarrantable in such person to represent the real statement of his case, and appeal to the world for their sentiments and countenance.

"Upon these considerations, principally, I am now emboldened to trespass on the public patience, and must solicit the indulgence of my friends and customers, while I present to their notice, an account of the steps lately exercised with me; from which it will appear that my situation as *a printer, and the rights of the press and of freemen,* are fundamentally struck at; and an earnest endeavor is on the carpet to involve me in difficulties to please the malicious dispositions of old and permanent enemies.

"But until the news had arrrived last Thursday, that the ninth state had acceded to the new federal government, I was not called upon; and Mr. Page, in the afternoon of that day, visited me, in due form of law, with a writ. Had Mr. Browne pursued me in this line, 'without loss of time,' agreeably to his lawyer's letter, I should not have supposed it extraordinary—but to arrest me the moment the federal intelligence came to hand, indicated that the commencement of this suit was not so much the child of his own fancy, as it has probably been dictated to and urged on him by others, whose sentiments upon the new constitution have not in every respect coincided with mine. In fact, it was my idea, in the first progress of the business, that Mr. Browne was merely the hand-maid of some of my enemies among the federalists: and in this class, I must rank his great patron, Doctor Rush (whose brother is a judge of the supreme court): I think, Mr. Browne's conduct has since confirmed the idea beyond a doubt.

"Enemies I have had in the legal profession, and it may perhaps add to the hopes of malignity, that this action is instituted in the supreme court of Pennsylvania. However, if former prejudices should be found to operate against me on the bench, it is with a jury of my country, properly elected and impannelled, a jury of freemen and independent citizens, I must rest the suit. I have escaped the jaws of persecution through this channel, on certain memorable occasions, and hope I shall never be a sufferer, let the blast of faction blow with all its furies!

"The doctrine of libels being a doctrine incompatible with law and liberty, and at once destructive of the privileges of free country, in the communication of our thoughts, has not hitherto gained any footing in Pennsylvania: and the vile measures formerly taken to lay me by the heels, on this subject, only brought down obloquy upon the conductors themselves. I may well suppose, the same love of liberty yet pervades my fellow-citizens, and that they will not allow the freedom of the press to be violated, upon any refined pretence, which oppressive ingenuity or courtly study can invent.

"Upon trial of the cause, the public will decide for themselves, whether Mr. Browne's motives have been laudable and dignified; whether his conduct, in declining an acquittal of his character in the paper, and suing me in the manner he did, was decent and consistent; and in a word, whether he is not actuated by some of my inveterate foes and opponents, to lend his name in their service, for the purpose of harassing and injuring me."

A transcript from the records was read, to show that the action between *Browne* and *Oswald* was depending in the court; James Martin proved that the paper containing Oswald's address was bought at his printing-office, fresh and damp from the press; and a deposition, made by Browne, was read, to prove the preceding facts relative to the cause of action, the hearing before Mr. Justice BRYAN, and the appeal from his order.

Lewis, then adverted to the various pieces, which were charged as libellous in the depending action; and argued, that, though the liberty of the press was invaluable in its nature, and ought not to be infringed; yet, that its value did not consist in a boundless licentiousness of slander and defamation. He contended, that the profession of Browne, to whom the education of more than a hundred children was sometimes intrusted, exposed him, in a peculiar manner, to be injured by wanton aspersions of his character; and he inferred the necessity of the action, which had been instituted, from this consideration, that if Browne were really the monster which the papers in question described him to be, he ought to be hunted from society; but, that if he had been falsely accused, if he had been maliciously traduced, it was a duty that he owed to himself and to the public to vindicate his reputation, and to call upon the justice of the laws, to punish so gross a violation of truth and decency. For this purpose, he continued, a writ had been issued, and bail was required. The defendant, if not before, was certainly, on the hearing at the judge's chambers, apprised of the cause of action; the order of Mr. Justice BRYAN on that occasion, and the appeal to the court, were circumstances perfectly within his knowledge; and yet, while the whole merits of the cause were thus in suspense, he thought proper to address the public in language evidently calculated to excite the popular resentment against Browne; to create doubts and suspicions of the integrity and impartiality of the judges, who must preside upon the trial; and to promote an unmerited compassion in his own favor. He has described himself as the object of former persecutions upon similar principles; he has asserted that, in this instance, an individual is made the instrument of a party to destroy him; and he artfully calls upon his fellow-citizens to interest themselves to preserve the freedom of the press, which he considers as attacked in his person. . . .

Lewis then added, that the address to the public manifestly tended to interrupt the course of justice; it was an attempt to prejudice the minds of the people in a cause then depending, and, by that means, to defeat the plaintiff's claim to justice, and to stigmatize the judges, whose duty it was to administer the laws. There could be no doubt, therefore, that it amounted to a contempt of the court; and it only remained, in support of his motion, to show that an attachment was the legal mode of proceeding against the offender. For this he cited 4 Black. Com. 280; 2 Atk. 469. . . .

. . . whatever the law might be in England, *Sergeant* insisted, that it could not avail in Pennsylvania. Even in England, indeed, though it is said to be a contempt, to report the decisions of the courts, unless under the *imprimatur* of the judges; yet, we find Burrow, and all the subsequent reporters, proceeding without that sanction. But the constitution of Pennsylvania authorizes many things to be done, which in England are prohibited. Here, the press is laid open to the inspection of every citizen, who wishes to examine the proceedings of the government; of which the judicial authority is certainly to be considered as a branch. Const. Penn. § 35.

McKEAN, C. J.—Could not this be done in England? Certainly it could: for, in short, there is nothing in the constitution of this state, respecting the liberty of the press, that has not been authorised by the constitution of that Kingdom for near a century past.

Sergeant.—The 9th section of the bill of rights, however, puts this supposed offence into such a form, as must entitle the defendant to a trial by jury; and precludes every attempt to compel him to give evidence against himself. It declares, "that, in all prosecutions for criminal offences, a man has a right to be heard by himself and his counsel, to demand the cause and nature of his accusation, to be confronted with the witnesses, to call for evidence in his favor, and a speedy public trial, by an impartial jury of the country, without the unanimous consent of which jury, he cannot be found guilty; nor can he be compelled to give evidence against himself; nor can any man be justly deprived of his liberty, except by the laws of the land, or the judgment of his peers." Now, the present proceeding against the defendant, is for a criminal offence; and, yet, if the attachment issues, the essential parts of this section must be defeated: for, in that case, the defendant cannot be tried by a jury; and, according to the practice upon attachments, he will be compelled to answer interrogatories, in doing which, he must either be guilty of perjury, or give evidence against himself. The proceeding by attachment is, indeed, a novelty in this country, except for the purpose of enforcing the attendance of witnesses. Those contempts which are committed in the face of a court, stand upon a very different ground. Even the court of admiralty (which is not a court of record) possesses a power to punish them; and the reason arises from the necessity that every jurisdiction should be competent to protect itself from immediate violence and interruption. But contempts which are alleged to have been committed out of doors, are not within this reason; they come properly within the class of criminal offences; and, as such, by the 9th sect. of the bill of rights, they can only be tried by a jury.

McKEAN, C. J.—Do you then apprehend that the 9th sect. of the bill of rights introduced something new on the subject of trials? I have always understood it to be the law, independent of this section, that the twelve jurors must be unanimous in their verdict, and yet this section makes this express provision. . . .

Heatly and *Lewis*, in support of the motion, contended, that under the circumstances of the case, Oswald's publication, whether true or false, amounted to a contempt of the court, as it respected a cause then depending in judgment, and reflected upon one of the judges in his official capacity; that the argument of the adverse counsel went so far as to assert, there could be no such offence as a contempt, even in England, since the very words inserted in the constitution of Pennsylvania, were used in the *Magna Charta* of that kingdom; that, in truth, neither the bill of rights nor the constitution extended to the case of contempts, for they mean only to secure to every citizen the right of expressing his sentiments with a manly freedom, but not to authorize wanton attacks upon private reputation, or to deprive the court of a power essential to its own existence, and to the due administration of justice; that the court were as competent to judge of the fact and the law, upon the inspection of the publication in question, as the chancellor was, in the authority cited from Atkins; and that although the prosecutor could, perhaps, proceed either by indictment or information, yet that the abuses of the Star Chamber had rendered the process by information odious, and an attachment, which was sanctified by immemorial usage, was the most expeditious, and therefore, the most proper remedy for the evil complaint of.

The Chief Justice delivered the opinion of the court to the following effect—Judge BRYAN having shortly before taken his seat.

MCKEAN, C. J.—This is a motion for an attachment against Eleazer Oswald, the printer and publisher of the Independent Gazetteer, of the 1st of July last, No. 796. As a ground for granting the attachment, it is proved, that an action for a libel had been instituted in this court, in which Andrew Browne is the plaintiff, and Eleazer Oswald the defendant; that a question with respect to bail in that action, had been agitated before one of the judges, from whose order, discharging the defendant on common bail, the plaintiff had appealed to the court; and that Mr. Oswald's address to the public, which is the immediate subject of complaint, relates to the action thus depending before us.

The counsel in support of their motion, have argued, that this address was intended to prejudice the public mind upon the merits of the cause, by propagating an opinion that Browne was the instrument of a party to persecute and destroy the defendant; that he acted under the particular influence of Dr. Rush, whose brother is a judge of this court; and, in short, that from the ancient prejudices of all the judges, the defendant did not stand a chance of a fair trial.

Assertions and imputations of this kind are certainly calculated to defeat and discredit the administration of justice. Let us, therefore, inquire, first, whether they ought to be considered as a contempt of the court; and, secondly, whether, if so, the offender is punishable by attachment.

And here, I must be allowed to observe, that libelling is a great crime, whatever sentiments may be entertained by those who live by it. With respect to the heart of the libeller, it is more dark and base than that of the assassin, or than his who commits a midnight arson. It is true, that I may never discover the wretch who has burned my house, or set fire to my barn; but these losses are easily repaired, and bring with them no portion of ignominy or reproach. But the attacks of the libeller admit not of this consolation: the injuries which are done to character and reputation seldom can be cured, and the most innocent man may, in a moment, be deprived of his good name, upon which, perhaps, he depends for all the prosperity, and all the happiness of his life. To what tribunal can he then resort? how shall he be tried, and by whom shall he be acquitted? It is in vain to object, those who know him will disregard the slander, since the wide circulation of public prints must render it impracticable to apply the antidote so far as the poison has been extended. Nor can it be fairly said, that the same opportunity is given to vindicate, which has been employed to defame him: for, many will read the charge, who may never see the answer; and while the object of accusation is publicly pointed at, the malicious and malignant author rests in the dishonorable security of an anonymous signature. Where much has been said, something will be believed; and it is one of the many artifices of the libeller, to give to his charges an aspect of general support, by changing and multiplying the style and name of his performances. But shall such things be transacted with impunity in a free country and among an enlightened people? Let every honest man make this appeal to his heart and understanding, and the answer must be—no!

What then is the meaning of the bill of rights, and constitution of Pennsylvania, when they declare, "That the freedom of the press shall not be restrained," and "that the printing presses shall be free to every person who undertakes to examine the proceedings of the legislature, or any part of the government?" However ingenuity may torture the expressions there can be little doubt of the just sense of these sections; they give to every citizen a right of investigating the conduct of those who are intrusted with the public business; and they effectually preclude any attempt to fetter the press by the institution of a licenser. The same principles were settled in England, so far back as the reign of *William III.*, and since that time, we all know, there has been the freest animadversion upon the conduct of the ministers of that nation. But is there anything in the language of the constitution (much less in its spirit and intention) which authorizes one man to impute crimes to another, for which the law has provided the mode of trial, and the degree of punishment? Can it be presumed, that the slanderous words, which, when spoken to a few individuals, would expose the speaker to punishment, become sacred, by the authority of the constitution, when delivered to the public through the more permanent and diffusive medium of the press? Or, will it be said, that the constitutional right to examine the proceedings of government, extends to warrant an anticipation of the acts of the legislature, or the judgments of the court? and not only to authorize a candid commentary upon what has been done, but to permit every endeavor to bias and intimidate with respect to matters still in suspense? The futility of any attempt to establish a construction of this sort, must be obvious to every intelligent mind. The true liberty of the press is amply secured by permitting every man to publish his opinion; but it is due to the peace and dignity of society, to inquire into the motives of such publications, and to distinguish between those which are meant for use and reformation, and with an eye solely to the public good, and those which are intended merely to delude and defame. To the latter description, it is impossible that any good government should afford protection and impunity.

If, then, the liberty of the press is regulated by any just principle, there can be little doubt, that he who attempts to raise a prejudice against his antagonist, in the minds of those that must ultimately determine the dispute between them; who, for that purpose, represents himself as a persecuted man, and asserts that his judges are influenced by passion and prejudice—wilfully seeks to corrupt the source, and to dishonor the administration of justice.

Such is evidently the object and tendency of Mr. Oswald's address to the public. Nor can that artifice prevail, which insinuates that the decision of this court will be the effect of personal resentment; for, if it could, every man could evade the punishment due to his offences, by first pouring a torrent of abuse upon his judges, and then asserting that they act from passion, because their treatment has been such as would naturally excite resentment in the human disposition. But it must be remembered, that judges discharge their functions under the solemn obligations of an oath; and, if their virtue entitles them to their station, they can neither be corrupted by favor to swerve from, nor influenced by fear to desert their duty. That judge, indeed, who courts popularity by unworthy means, while he weakens his pretensions, diminishes, likewise, the chance of attaining his object; and he will eventually find that he has sacrificed the substantial blessing of a good conscience, in an idle and visionary pursuit.

Upon the whole, we consider the publication in question, as having the tendency which has been ascribed to it, that of prejudicing the public (a part of whom must hereafter be summoned as jurors), with respect to the merits of a cause depending in this court, and of corrupting the administration of justice; we are, therefore, unanimously of opinion on the first point, that it amounts to a contempt.

It only remains then to consider, whether the offense is punishable in the way that the present motion has proposed.

It is certain, that the proceeding by attachment is as old as the law itself, and no act of the legislature, or section of the constitution, has interposed to alter or suspend it. Besides the sections which have been already read from the constitution, there is another section which declares, that "trials by jury shall be as heretofore;" and surely it cannot be contended, that the offence, with which the defendant is now charged, was heretofore tried by that tribunal.[a] If a

man commits an outrage in the face of the court, what is there to be tried?—what further evidence can be necessary to convict him of the offence, than the actual view of the judges? A man has been compelled to enter into security for his good behavior, for giving the lie in the presence of the judges in Westminster Hall.

On the present occasion, is not the proof, from the inspection of the paper, as full and satisfactory as any that can be offered? And whether the publication amounts to a contempt, or not, is a point of law, which, after all, it is the province of the judges, and not of the jury, to determine. Being a contempt, if it is not punished immediately, how shall the mischief be corrected? Leave it to the customary forms of a trial by jury, and the cause may be continued long in suspense, while the party perseveres in his misconduct. The injurious consequences might then be justly imputed to the court, for refusing to exercise their legal power in preventing them.

For these reasons, we have no doubt of the competency of our jurisdiction; and, we think, that justice and propriety call upon us to proceed by attachment.

The Chief Justice pronounced the judgment of the court in the following words:—

McKEAN, Chief Justice.—Eleazer Oswald: Having yesterday considered the charge against you, we were unanimously of opinion, that it amounted to a contempt of the court. Some doubts were suggested, whether, even a contempt of the court was punishable by attachment: but, not only my brethren and myself, but, likewise, all the judges of England, think, that without this power, no court could possibly exist—nay, that no contempt could, indeed, be committed against us, we should be so truly contemptible. The law upon the subject is of immemorial antiquity; and there is not any period when it can be said to have ceased or discontinued. On this point, therefore, we entertain no doubt.[b]

But some difficulty has arisen with respect to our sentence; for, on the one hand, we have been informed of your circumstances, and on the other, we have seen your conduct; your circumstances are small, but your offence is great and persisted in. Since, however, the question seems to resolve itself into this, whether you shall bend to the law, or the law shall bend to you, it is our duty to determine that the former shall be the case.

---

[a]In Hollingsworth v. Duane (Wall. C. C. 77, 106), the circuit court of the United States held that a similar provision in the constitution of the United States did not deprive the courts of the right to punish contempts in a summary mode.

[b]In Respublica v. Passmore, 3 Yeates 438, it was held, that a publication, attempting to prejudice the public mind on the merits of a suit pending at court, was punishable by attachment; and the defendant in that case was sentenced to fine and imprisonment. The power of the courts to punish in a summary way, for what are called constructive contempts, has since been taken away by the act of 19th April 1809 (5 Sm. I. 55), which restricts their power of summary punishment, to cases of "official misconduct of the officers of the courts, to the negligence or disobedience of officers, parties, jurors or witnesses, against the lawful process of the court, and to the misbehavior of any person in the presence of the court, obstructing the administration of justice." The act, however, declares that publications tending to bias the public mind respecting any question depending in court, may be punished by indictment, or by a civil action.

Upon the whole, therefore, the COURT pronounce this sentence:—That you pay a fine of 10*l.* to the commonwealth; that you be imprisoned for the space of one month, that is, from the 15th day of July to the 15th day of August next; and afterwards, until the fine and costs are paid.

14

CONGRESS, AMENDMENTS TO THE CONSTITUTION
June–Sept. 1789

[*House Debate, 8 June; Annals 1:434–36, 440–43*]

[Mr. MADISON] The people shall not be deprived or abridged of their right to speak, to write, or to publish their sentiments; and the freedom of the press, as one of the great bulwarks of liberty, shall be inviolable.

. . . . .

No State shall violate the equal rights of conscience, or the freedom of the press, or the trial by jury in criminal cases.

. . . . .

The first of these amendments relates to what may be called a bill of rights. I will own that I never considered this provision so essential to the federal constitution, as to make it improper to ratify it, until such an amendment was added; at the same time, I always conceived, that in a certain form, and to a certain extent, such a provision was neither improper nor altogether useless. I am aware, that a great number of the most respectable friends to the Government, and champions for republican liberty, have thought such a provision, not only unnecessary, but even improper; nay, I believe some have gone so far as to think it even dangerous. Some policy has been made use of, perhaps, by gentlemen on both sides of the question: I acknowledge the ingenuity of those arguments which were drawn against the constitution, by a comparison with the policy of Great Britain, in establishing a declaration of rights; but there is too great a difference in the case to warrant the comparison: therefore, the arguments drawn from that source were in a great measure inapplicable. In the declaration of rights which that country has established, the truth is, they have gone no farther than to raise a barrier against the power of the Crown; the power of the Legislature is left altogether indefinite. Although I know whenever the great rights, the trial by jury, freedom of the press, or liberty of conscience, come in question in that body, the invasion of them is resisted by able advocates, yet their Magna Charta does not contain any one provision for the security of those rights, respecting which the people of America are most alarmed. The freedom of the press and rights of conscience, those choicest privileges of the people, are unguarded in the British constitution.

. . . . .

I wish also, in revising the constitution, we may throw into that section, which interdict the abuse of certain powers in the State Legislatures, some other provisions of equal, if not greater importance than those already made. The words, "No State shall pass any bill of attainder, ex post facto law," &c. were wise and proper restrictions in the constitution. I think there is more danger of those powers being abused by the State Governments than by the Government of the United States. The same may be said of other powers which they possess, if not controlled by the general principle, that laws are unconstitutional which infringe the rights of the community. I should therefore wish to extend this interdiction, and add, as I have stated in the 5th resolution, that no State shall violate the equal right of conscience, freedom of the press, or trial by jury in criminal cases; because it is proper that every Government should be disarmed of powers which trench upon those particular rights. I know, in some of the State constitutions, the power of the Government is controlled by such a declaration; but others are not. I cannot see any reason against obtaining even a double security on those points; and nothing can give a more sincere proof of the attachment of those who opposed this constitution to these great and important rights, than to see them join in obtaining the security I have now proposed; because it must be admitted, on all hands, that the State Governments are as liable to attack the invaluable privileges as the General Government is, and therefore ought to be as cautiously guarded against.

. . . . .

[Mr. JACKSON] The gentleman endeavors to secure the liberty of the press; pray how is this in danger? There is no power given to Congress to regulate this subject as they can commerce, or peace, or war. Has any transaction taken place to make us suppose such an amendment necessary? An honorable gentleman, a member of this House, has been attacked in the public newspapers on account of sentiments delivered on this floor. Have Congress taken any notice of it? Have they ordered the writer before them, even for a breach of privilege, although the constitution provides that a member shall not be questioned in any place for any speech or debate in the House? No, these things are offered to the public view, and held up to the inspection of the world. These are principles which will always prevail. I am not afraid, nor are other members I believe, our conduct should meet the severest scrutiny. Where, then, is the necessity of taking measures to secure what neither is nor can be in danger?

[*House Debate, 15 Aug.; Annals 1:731, 738*]

The next clause of the fourth proposition was taken into consideration, and was as follows: "The freedom of speech and of the press, and the right of the people peaceably to assemble and consult for their common good, and to apply to the Government for redress of grievances, shall not be infringed.

Mr. SEDGWICK submitted to those gentlemen who had contemplated the subject, what effect such an amendment as this would have; he feared it would tend to make them appear trifling in the eyes of their constituents; what, said he, shall we secure the freedom of speech, and think it necessary, at the same time, to allow the right of assembling? If people freely converse together, they must assemble for that purpose; it is a self-evident, unalienable right which the people possess; it is certainly a thing that never would be called in question; it is derogatory to the dignity of the House to descend to such minutiae; he therefore moved to strike out "assemble and."

. . . . .

[Mr. MADISON] The right of freedom of speech is secured; the liberty of the press is expressly declared to be beyond the reach of this Government; the people may therefore publicly address their representatives, may privately advise them, or declare their sentiment by petition to the whole body; in all these ways they may communicate their will. If gentlemen mean to go further, and to say that the people have a right to instruct their representatives in such a sense as that the delegates are obliged to conform to those instructions, the declaration is not true.

[*House Debate, 17 Aug.; Annals 1:755*]

The committee then proceeded to the fifth proposition:

Article 1, section 10. between the first and second paragraph, insert "no State shall infringe the equal rights of conscience, nor the freedom of speech or of the press, nor of the right of trial by jury in criminal cases."

Mr. TUCKER: This is offered, I presume, as an amendment to the constitution of the United States, but it goes only to the alteration of the constitutions of particular States. It will be much better, I apprehend, to leave the State Governments to themselves, and not to interfere with them more than we already do; and that is thought by many to be rather too much. I therefore move, sir, to strike out these words.

Mr. MADISON conceived this to be the most valuable amendment in the whole list. If there was any reason to restrain the Government of the United States from infringing upon these essential rights, it was equally necessary that they should be secured against the State Governments. He thought that if they provided against the one, it was necessary to provide against the other, and was satisfied that it would be equally grateful to the people.

Mr. LIVERMORE had no great objection to the sentiment, but he thought it not well expressed. He wished to make it an affirmative proposition; "the equal rights of conscience, the freedom of speech or of the press, and the right of trial by jury in criminal cases, shall not be infringed by any State."

[*Senate Journal, 3–4 Sept.; History of Congress 161–62*]

The fourth article was then taken up, namely: "The freedom of speech and of the press, and the right of the people peaceably to assemble and consult for their common good, and to apply to the government for redress of grievances, shall not be infringed." It was moved to insert, after the words "common good," these words: "to instruct their representatives." On this question, the yeas and nays being required, it was decided as follows:—

Yeas—Messrs. Grayson and Lee.—2.

Nays—Messrs. Bassett, Carroll, Dalton, Ellsworth, Elmer, Gunn, Henry, Johnson, Izard, King, Morris, Paterson, Read, Wingate.—14.

A motion was then made to insert after the word "press," these words: "in as ample a manner as hath at any time been secured by the common law;" but this motion was unsuccessful; as also was a subsequent motion to strike out the words, "and consult for their common good, and." The further consideration of this article was then postponed until the next day, (the 4th,) when it was adopted in the following form:— "That Congress shall make no law abridging the freedom of speech, or of the press, or the right of the people peaceably to assemble and consult for their common good, and to petition the government for a redress of grievances."

[*Senate Journal, 9 Sept.; History of Congress 167*]

On the 9th of September, the subject was resumed. The third article was then amended to read as follows: "Congress shall make no law establishing articles of faith, or a mode of worship, or prohibiting the free exercise of religion, or abridging the freedom of speech, or the press, or the right of the people peaceably to assemble, and petition to the government for the redress of grievances."

[*Senate Journal, 24 Sept.; History of Congress 169–70*]

On the 23d, Mr. Madison made a report to the House of Representatives on the subject, which was taken up for consideration on the 24th; whereupon,

"*Resolved*—That this house doth recede from their disagreement to the first, third, fifth, sixth, seventh, ninth, tenth, eleventh, fourteenth, fifteenth, seventeenth, twentieth, twenty-first, twenty-second, twenty-third, and twenty-fourth amendments, insisted on by the Senate: *Provided,* That the two articles which by the amendments of the Senate are now proposed to be inserted as the third and eighth articles, shall be amended to read as followeth:—

"*Article the third.* Congress shall make no law respecting an establishment of religion, or prohibiting the free exercise thereof; or abridging the freedom of speech, or of the press; or the right of the people peaceably to assemble, and to petition the government for a redress of grievances.

15

THOMAS JEFFERSON TO JAMES MADISON
28 Aug. 1789
Papers 15:367

. . . the following alterations and additions would have pleased me. Art 4. "The people shall not be deprived or abridged of their right to speak to write or *otherwise* to publish any thing but false facts affecting injuriously the life, property, or reputation of others or affecting the peace of the confederacy with foreign nations."

16

BENJAMIN FRANKLIN, AN ACCOUNT OF THE
SUPREMEST COURT OF JUDICATURE IN
PENNSYLVANIA, VIZ., THE COURT OF THE PRESS
12 Sept. 1789
Writings 10:36–40

Power of this Court.

It may receive and promulgate accusations of all kinds, against all persons and characters among the citizens of the State, and even against all inferior courts; and may judge, sentence, and condemn to infamy, not only private individuals, but public bodies, &c., with or without inquiry or hearing, *at the court's discretion.*

In whose Favour and for whose Emolument this Court is established.

In favour of about one citizen in five hundred, who, by education or practice in scribbling, has acquired a tolerable style as to grammar and construction, so as to bear printing; or who is possessed of a press and a few types. This five hundredth part of the citizens have the privilege of accusing and abusing the other four hundred and ninety-nine parts at their pleasure; or they may hire out their pens and press to others for that purpose.

Practice of the Court.

It is not governed by any of the rules of common courts of law. The accused is allowed no grand jury to judge of the truth of the accusation before it is publicly made, nor is the Name of the Accuser made known to him, nor has he an Opportunity of confronting the Witnesses against him; for they are kept in the dark, as in the Spanish Court of Inquisition. Nor is there any petty Jury of his Peers, sworn to try the Truth of the Charges. The Proceedings are also sometimes so rapid, that an honest, good Citizen may find himself suddenly and unexpectedly accus'd, and in the same Morning judg'd and condemn'd, and sentence pronounc'd against him, that he is a *Rogue* and a *Villain.* Yet, if an officer of this court receives the slightest check for misconduct in this his office, he claims immediately the rights of a free citizen by the constitution, and demands to know his accuser, to confront the witnesses, and to have a fair trial by a jury of his peers.

The Foundation of its Authority.

It is said to be founded on an Article of the Constitution of the State, which establishes *the Liberty of the Press;* a Lib-

erty which every Pennsylvanian would fight and die for; tho' few of us, I believe, have distinct Ideas of its Nature and Extent. It seems indeed somewhat like the *Liberty of the Press* that Felons have, by the Common Law of England, before Conviction, that is, to be *press'd* to death or hanged. If by the *Liberty of the Press* were understood merely the Liberty of discussing the Propriety of Public Measures and political opinions, let us have as much of it as you please: But if it means the Liberty of affronting, calumniating, and defaming one another, I, for my part, own myself willing to part with my Share of it when our Legislators shall please so to alter the Law, and shall cheerfully consent to exchange my *Liberty* of Abusing others for the *Privilege* of not being abus'd myself.

By Whom this Court is commissioned or constituted.

It is not by any Commission from the Supreme Executive Council, who might previously judge of the Abilities, Integrity, Knowledge, &c. of the Persons to be appointed to this great Trust, of deciding upon the Characters and good Fame of the Citizens; for this Court is above that Council, and may *accuse, judge,* and *condemn* it, at pleasure. Nor is it hereditary, as in the Court of *dernier Resort,* in the Peerage of England. But any Man who can procure Pen, Ink, and Paper, with a Press, and a huge pair of BLACKING Balls, may commissionate himself; and his court is immediately established in the plenary Possession and exercise of its rights. For, if you make the least complaint of the *judge's* conduct, he daubs his blacking balls in your face wherever he meets you; and, besides tearing your private character to flitters, marks you out for the odium of the public, as an *enemy to the liberty of the press.*

Of the natural Support of these Courts.

Their support is founded in the depravity of such minds, as have not been mended by religion, nor improved by good education;

> "There is a Lust in Man no Charm can tame,
> Of loudly publishing his Neighbour's Shame."

Hence;

> "On Eagle's Wings immortal Scandals fly,
> While virtuous Actions are but born and die."
>   DRYDEN.

Whoever feels pain in hearing a good character of his neighbour, will feel a pleasure in the reverse. And of those who, despairing to rise into distinction by their virtues, are happy if others can be depressed to a level with themselves, there are a number sufficient in every great town to maintain one of these courts by their subscriptions. A shrewd observer once said, that, in walking the streets in a slippery morning, one might see where the good-natured people lived by the ashes thrown on the ice before their doors; probably he would have formed a different conjecture of the temper of those whom he might find engaged in such a subscription.

*Of the Checks proper to be established against the
Abuse of Power in these Courts.*

Hitherto there are none. But since so much has been written and published on the federal Constitution, and the necessity of checks in all other parts of good government has been so clearly and learnedly explained, I find myself so far enlightened as to suspect some check may be proper in this part also; but I have been at a loss to imagine any that may not be construed an infringement of the sacred *liberty of the press.* At length, however, I think I have found one that, instead of diminishing general liberty, shall augment it; which is, by restoring to the people a species of liberty, of which they have been deprived by our laws, I mean the *liberty of the cudgel.* In the rude state of society prior to the existence of laws, if one man gave another ill language, the affronted person would return it by a box on the ear, and, if repeated, by a good drubbing; and this without offending against any law. But now the right of making such returns is denied, and they are punished as breaches of the peace; while the right of abusing seems to remain in full force, the laws made against it being rendered ineffectual by the *liberty of the press.*

My proposal then is, to leave the liberty of the press untouched, to be exercised in its full extent, force, and vigor; but to permit the *liberty of the cudgel* to go with it *pari passu.* Thus, my fellow-citizens, if an impudent writer attacks your reputation, dearer to you perhaps than your life, and puts his name to the charge, you may go to him as openly and break his head. If he conceals himself behind the printer, and you can nevertheless discover who he is, you may in like manner way-lay him in the night, attack him behind, and give him a good drubbing. Thus far goes my project as to *private* resentment and retribution. But if the public should ever happen to be affronted, *as it ought to be,* with the conduct of such writers, I would not advise proceeding immediately to these extremities; but that we should in moderation content ourselves with tarring and feathering, and tossing them in a blanket.

If, however, it should be thought that this proposal of mine may disturb the public peace, I would then humbly recommend to our legislators to take up the consideration of both liberties, that of the *press,* and that of the *cudgel,* and by an explicit law mark their extent and limits; and, at the same time that they secure the person of a citizen from *assaults,* they would likewise provide for the security of his *reputation.*

17

JOHN MARSHALL TO A FREEHOLDER
20 Sept. 1798
Life 2:577

5th. I am not an advocate for the alien and sedition bills; had I been in Congress when they passed, I should, unless my judgment could have been changed, certainly have opposed them. Yet, I do not think them fraught with all those mischiefs which many gentlemen ascribe to them. I should have opposed them because I think them useless; and because they are calculated to create unnecessary discontents and jealousies at a time when our very existence, as a nation, may depend on our union—

I believe that these laws, had they been opposed on these principles by a man, not suspected of intending to destroy the government, or being hostile to it, would never have been enacted. With respect to their repeal, the effort will be made before I can become a member of Congress.

If it succeeds there will be an end of the busines—if it fails, I shall on the question of renewing the effort, should I be chosen to represent the district, obey the voice of my constituents. My own private opinion is, that it will be unwise to renew it for this reason: the laws will expire of themselves, if I recollect rightly the time for which they are enacted, during the term of the ensuing Congress. I shall indisputably oppose their revival; and I believe that opposition will be more successful, if men's minds are not too much irritated by the struggle about a repeal of laws which will, at the time, be expiring of themselves.

18

KENTUCKY RESOLUTIONS
10 Nov. 1798, 14 Nov. 1799
Elliot 4:540–45

[*10 Nov. 1798*]

1. *Resolved,* That the several states composing the United States of America are not united on the principle of unlimited submission to their general government; but that, by compact, under the style and title of a Constitution for the United States, and of amendments thereto, they constituted a general government for special purposes, delegated to that government certain definite powers, reserving, each state to itself, the residuary mass of right to their own self-government; and that whensoever the general government assumes undelegated powers, its acts are unauthoritative, void, and of no force; that to this compact each state acceded as a state, and is an integral party; that this government, created by this compact, was not made the exclusive or final judge of the extent of the powers delegated to itself, since that would have made its discretion, and not the Constitution, the measure of its powers; but that, as in all other cases of compact among parties having no common judge, *each party has an equal right to judge for itself, as well of infractions as of the mode and measure of redress.*

2. *Resolved,* That the Constitution of the United States having delegated to Congress a power to punish treason, counterfeiting the securities and current coin of the United States, piracies and felonies committed on the high seas, and offences against the laws of nations, and no other crimes whatever; and it being true, as a general principle,

and one of the amendments to the Constitution having also declared "that the powers not delegated to the United States by the Constitution, nor prohibited by it to the states, are reserved to the states respectively, or to the people,"—therefore, also, the same act of Congress, passed on the 14th day of July, 1798, and entitled "An Act in Addition to the Act entitled 'An Act for the Punishment of certain Crimes against the United States;'" as also the act passed by them on the 27th day of June, 1798, entitled "An Act to punish Frauds committed on the Bank of the United States," (and all other their acts which assume to create, define, or punish crimes other than those enumerated in the Constitution,) are altogether void, and of no force; and that the power to create, define, and punish, such other crimes is reserved, and of right appertains, solely and exclusively, to the respective states, each within its own territory.

3. *Resolved*, That it is true, as a general principle, and is also expressly declared by one of the amendments to the Constitution, that "the powers not delegated to the United States by the Constitution, nor prohibited by it to the states, are reserved to the states respectively, or to the people;" and that, no power over the freedom of religion, freedom of speech, or freedom of the press, being delegated to the United States by the Constitution, nor prohibited by it to the states, all lawful powers respecting the same did of right remain, and were reserved to the states, or to the people; that thus was manifested their determination to retain to themselves the right of judging how far the licentiousness of speech, and of the press, may be abridged without lessening their useful freedom, and how far those abuses which cannot be separated from their use, should be tolerated rather than the use be destroyed; and thus also they guarded against all abridgment, by the United States, of the freedom of religious principles and exercises, and retained to themselves the right of protecting the same, as this, stated by a law passed on the general demand of its citizens, had already protected them from all human restraint or interference; and that, in addition to this general principle and express declaration, another and more special provision has been made by one of the amendments to the Constitution, which expressly declares, that "Congress shall make no laws respecting an establishment of religion, or prohibiting the free exercise thereof, or abridging the freedom of speech, or of the press," thereby guarding, in the same sentence, and under the same words, the freedom of religion, of speech, and of the press, insomuch that whatever violates either throws down the sanctuary which covers the others,—and that libels, falsehood, and defamation, equally with heresy and false religion, are withheld from the cognizance of federal tribunals. That therefore the act of the Congress of the United States, passed on the 14th of July, 1798, entitled "An Act in Addition to the Act entitled 'An Act for the Punishment of certain Crimes against the United States,'" which does abridge the freedom of the press, is not law, but is altogether void, and of no force.

4. *Resolved*, That alien friends are under the jurisdiction and protection of the laws of the state wherein they are; that no power over them has been delegated to the United States, nor prohibited to the individual states, distinct from their power over citizens; and it being true, as a general principle, and one of the amendments to the Constitution having also declared, that "the powers not delegated to the United States by the Constitution, nor prohibited to the states, are reserved to the states, respectively, or to the people," the act of the Congress of the United States, passed the 22d day of June, 1798, entitled "An Act concerning Aliens," which assumes power over alien friends not delegated by the Constitution, is not law, but is altogether void and of no force.

5. *Resolved*, That, in addition to the general principle, as well as the express declaration, that powers not delegated are reserved, another and more special provision inserted in the Constitution from abundant caution, has declared, "that the migration or importation of such persons as any of the states now existing shall think proper to admit, shall not be prohibited by the Congress prior to the year 1808." That this commonwealth does admit the migration of alien friends described as the subject of the said act concerning aliens; that a provision against prohibiting their migration is a provision against all acts equivalent thereto, or it would be nugatory; that to remove them, when migrated, is equivalent to a prohibition of their migration, and is, therefore, contrary to the said provision of the Constitution, and *void*.

6. *Resolved*, That the imprisonment of a person under the protection of the laws of this commonwealth, on his failure to obey the simple order of the President to depart out of the United States, as is undertaken by the said act, entitled, "An Act concerning Aliens," is contrary to the Constitution, one amendment in which has provided, that "no person shall be deprived of liberty without due process of law;" and that another having provided, "that, in all criminal prosecutions, the accused shall enjoy the right of a public trial by an impartial jury, to be informed as to the nature and cause of the accusation, to be confronted with the witnesses against him, to have compulsory process for obtaining witnesses in his favor, and to have assistance of counsel for his defence," the same act undertaking to authorize the President to remove a person out of the United States who is under the protection of the law, on his own suspicion, without jury, without public trial, without confrontation of the witnesses against him, without having witnesses in his favor, without defence, without counsel—contrary to these provisions also of the Constitution—is therefore not law, but utterly void, and of no force.

That transferring the power of judging any person who is under the protection of the laws, from the courts to the President of the United States, as is undertaken by the same act concerning aliens, is against the article of the Constitution which provides, that "the judicial power of the United States shall be vested in the courts, the judges of which shall hold their office during good behavior," and that the said act is void for that reason also; and it is further to be noted that this transfer of judiciary power is to that magistrate of the general government who already possesses all the executive, and a qualified negative in all the legislative powers.

7. *Resolved*, That the construction applied by the general government (as is evident by sundry of their proceedings) to those parts of the Constitution of the United States which delegate to Congress power to lay and collect taxes, duties, imposts, excises; to pay the debts, and provide for the common defence and general welfare, of the United States, and to make all laws which shall be necessary and proper for carrying into execution the powers vested by the Constitution in the government of the United States, or any department thereof, goes to the destruction of all the limits prescribed to their power by the Constitution; that words meant by that instrument to be subsidiary only to the execution of the limited powers, ought not to be so construed as themselves to give unlimited powers, nor a part so to be taken as to destroy the whole residue of the instrument; that the proceedings of the general government, under color of those articles, will be a fit and necessary subject for revisal and correction at a time of greater tranquillity, while those specified in the preceding resolutions call for immediate redress.

8. *Resolved*, That the preceding resolutions be transmitted to the senators and representatives in Congress from this commonwealth, who are enjoined to present the same to their respective houses, and to use their best endeavors to procure, at the next session of Congress, a repeal of the aforesaid unconstitutional and obnoxious acts.

9. *Resolved*, lastly, That the governor of this commonwealth be, and is, authorized and requested to communicate the preceding resolutions to the legislatures of the several states, to assure them that this commonwealth considers union for special national purposes, and particularly for those specified in their late federal compact, to be friendly to the peace, happiness, and prosperity, of all the states; that, faithful to that compact, according to the plain intent and meaning in which it was understood and acceded to by the several parties, it is sincerely anxious for its preservation; that it does also believe, that, to take from the states all the powers of self-government, and transfer them to a general and consolidated government, without regard to the special government, and reservations solemnly agreed to in that compact, is not for the peace, happiness, or prosperity of these states; and that, therefore, this commonwealth is determined, as it doubts not its co-states are, to submit to undelegated and consequently unlimited powers in no man, or body of men, on earth; that, if the acts before specified should stand, these conclusions would flow from them—that the general government may place any act they think proper on the list of crimes, and punish it themselves, whether enumerated or not enumerated by the Constitution as cognizable by them; that they may transfer its cognizance to the President, or any other person, who may himself be the accuser, counsel, judge, and jury, whose suspicions may be the evidence, his order the sentence, his officer the executioner, and his breast the sole record of the transaction; that a very numerous and valuable description of the inhabitants of these states, being, by this precedent, reduced, as outlaws, to absolute dominion of one man, and the barriers of the Constitution thus swept from us all, no rampart now remains against the passions and the power of a majority of

Congress, to protect from a like exportation, or other grievous punishment, the minority of the same body, the legislatures, judges, governors, and counsellors of the states, nor their other peaceable inhabitants, who may venture to reclaim the constitutional rights and liberties of the states and people, or who, for other causes, good or bad, may be obnoxious to the view, or marked by the suspicions, of the President, or be thought dangerous to his or their elections, or other interests, public or personal; that the friendless alien has been selected as the safest subject of a first experiment; but the citizen will soon follow, or rather has already followed; for already has a Sedition Act marked him as a prey: That these and successive acts of the same character, unless arrested on the threshold, may tend to drive these states into revolution and blood, and will furnish new calumnies against republican governments, and new pretexts for those who wish it to be believed that man cannot be governed but by a rod of iron; that it would be a dangerous delusion were a confidence in the men of our choice to silence our fears for the safety of our rights; that confidence is every where the parent of despotism; free government is founded in jealousy, and not in confidence; it is jealousy, and not confidence, which prescribes limited constitutions to bind down those whom we are obliged to trust with power; that our Constitution has accordingly fixed the limits to which, and no farther, our confidence may go; and let the honest advocate of confidence read the Alien and Sedition Acts, and say if the Constitution has not been wise in fixing limits to the government it created, and whether we should be wise in destroying those limits; let him say what the government is, if it be not a tyranny, which the men of our choice have conferred on the President, and the President of our choice has assented to and accepted, over the friendly strangers, to whom the mild spirit of our country and its laws had pledged hospitality and protection; that the men of our choice have more respected the bare suspicions of the President than the solid rights of innocence, the claims of justification, the sacred force of truth, and the forms and substance of law and justice.

In questions of power, then, let no more be said of confidence in man, but bind him down from mischief by the chains of the Constitution. That this commonwealth does therefore call on its co-states for an expression of their sentiments on the acts concerning aliens, and for the punishment of certain crimes herein before specified, plainly declaring whether these acts are or are not authorized by the federal compact. And it doubts not that their sense will be so announced as to prove their attachment to limited government, whether general or particular, and that the rights and liberties of their co-states will be exposed to no dangers by remaining embarked on a common bottom with their own; but they will concur with this commonwealth in considering the said acts as so palpably against the Constitution as to amount to an undisguised declaration, that the compact is not meant to be the measure of the powers of the general government, but that it will proceed in the exercise over these states of all powers whatsoever. That they will view this as seizing the rights of the states, and consolidating them in the hands of the general government, with a power assumed to bind the states, not merely in cases made federal, but in all cases whatsoever, by laws made, not with their consent, but by others against their consent; that this would be to surrender the form of government we have chosen, and live under one deriving its powers from its own will, and not from our authority; and that the co-states, recurring to their natural rights not made federal, will concur in declaring these void and of no force, and will each unite with this commonwealth in requesting their repeal at the next session of Congress.*

[*14 Nov. 1799*]

The house, according to the standing order of the day, resolved itself into a committee of the whole house, on the state of the commonwealth, (Mr. Desha in the chair,) and, after some time spent therein, the speaker resumed the

*[EDITORS' NOTE.—Thomas Jefferson's original draft of Resolutions 8 and 9, which he supplied to the Kentucky legislature, ran as follows (*Writings* 17:385–91):

"8th. *Resolved,* That a committee of conference and correspondence be appointed, who shall have in charge to communicate the preceding resolutions to the legislatures of the several States; to assure them that this commonwealth continues in the same esteem of their friendship and union which it has manifested from that moment at which a common danger first suggested a common union: that it considers union, for specified national purposes, and particularly to those specified in their late federal compact, to be friendly to the peace, happiness and prosperity of all the States: that faithful to that compact, according to the plain intent and meaning in which it was understood and acceded to by the several parties, it is sincerely anxious for its preservation: that it does also believe, that to take from the States all the powers of self-government and transfer them to a general and consolidated government, without regard to the special delegations and reservations solemnly agreed to in that compact, is not for the peace, happiness or prosperity of these States; and that therefore this commonwealth is determined, as it doubts not its co-States are, to submit to undelegated, and consequently unlimited powers in no man, or body of men on earth: that in cases of an abuse of the delegated powers, the members of the General Government, being chosen by the people, a change by the people would be the constitutional remedy; but, where powers are assumed which have not been delegated, a nullification of the act is the rightful remedy: that every State has a natural right in cases not within the compact, (casus non foederis,) to nullify of their own authority all assumptions of power by others within their limits: that without this right, they would be under the dominion, absolute and unlimited, of whosoever might exercise this right of judgment for them: that nevertheless, this commonwealth, from motives of regard and respect for its co-States, has wished to communicate with them on the subject: that with them alone it is proper to communicate, they alone being parties to the compact, and solely authorized to judge in the last resort of the powers exercised under it, Congress being not a party, but merely the creature of the compact, and subject as to its assumptions of power to the final judgment of those by whom, and for whose use itself and its powers were all created and modified: that if the acts before specified should stand, these conclusions would flow from them; that the General Government may place any act they think proper on the list of crimes, and punish it themselves whether enumerated or not enumerated by the Constitution as cognizable by them: that they may transfer its cognizance to the President, or any other person, who may himself be the accuser, counsel, judge and jury, whose *suspicions* may be the evidence, his *order* the sentence, his *officer* the executioner, and his breast the sole record of the transaction: that a very numerous and valuable description of the inhabitants of these States being, by this precedent, reduced, as outlaws, to the absolute dominion of one man, and the barrier of the

Constitution thus swept away from us all, no rampart now remains against the passions and the powers of a majority in Congress to protect from a like exportation, or other more grievous punishment, the minority of the same body, the legislatures, judges, governors, and counsellors of the States, nor their other peaceable inhabitants, who may venture to reclaim the constitutional rights and liberties of the States and people, or who for other causes, good or bad, may be obnoxious to the views, or marked by the suspicions of the President, or be thought dangerous to his or their election, or other interests, public or personal: that the friendless alien has indeed been selected as the safest subject of a first experiment; but the citizen will soon follow, or rather, has already followed, for already has a sedition act marked him as its prey: that these and successive acts of the same character, unless arrested at the threshold, necessarily drive these States into revolution and blood, and will furnish new calumnies against republican government, and new pretexts for those who wish it to be believed that man cannot be governed but by a rod of iron: that it would be a dangerous delusion were a confidence in the men of our choice to silence our fears for the safety of our rights: that confidence is everywhere the parent of despotism—free government is founded in jealousy, and not in confidence; it is jealousy and not confidence which prescribes limited constitutions, to bind down those whom we are obliged to trust with power: that our Constitution has accordingly fixed the limits to which, and no further, our confidence may go; and let the honest advocate of confidence read the alien and sedition acts, and say if the Constitution has not been wise in fixing limits to the government it created, and whether we should be wise in destroying those limits. Let him say what the government is, if it be not a tyranny, which the men of our choice have conferred on our President, and the President of our choice has assented to, and accepted over the friendly strangers to whom the mild spirit of our country and its laws have pledged hospitality and protection: that the men of our choice have more respected the bare *suspicions* of the President, than the solid right of innocence, the claims of justification, the sacred force of truth, and the forms and substance of law and justice. In questions of power, then, let no more be heard of confidence in man, but bind him down from mischief by the chains of the Constitution. That this commonwealth does therefore call on its co-States for an expression of their sentiments on the acts concerning aliens, and for the punishment of certain crimes herein before specified, plainly declaring whether these acts are or are not authorized by the federal compact. And it doubts not that their sense will be so announced as to prove their attachment unaltered to limited government, whether general or particular. And that the rights and liberties of their co-States will be exposed to no dangers by remaining embarked in a common bottom with their own. That they will concur with this commonwealth in considering the said acts as so palpably against the Constitution as to amount to an undisguised declaration that that compact is not meant to be the measure of the powers of the General Government, but that it will proceed in the exercise over these States, of all powers whatsoever: that they will view this as seizing the rights of the States, and consolidating them in the hands of the General Government, with a power assumed to bind the States, (not merely as the cases made federal, (casus foederis,) but) in all cases whatsoever, by laws made, not with their consent, but by others against their consent: that this would be to surrender the form of government we have chosen, and live under one deriving its powers from its own will, and not from our authority; and that the co-States, recurring to their natural right in cases not made federal, will concur in declaring these acts void, and of no force, and will each take measures of its own for providing that neither these acts, nor any others of the General Government not plainly and intentionally authorized by the Constitution, shall be exercised within their respective territories.

"9th. *Resolved,* That the said committee be authorized to communicate by writing or personal conferences, at any times or places whatever, with any person or persons who may be appointed by any one or more co-States to correspond or confer with them; and that they lay their proceedings before the next session of Assembly."]

chair, and Mr. Desha reported, that the committee had taken under consideration sundry resolutions passed by several state legislatures, on the subject of the Alien and Sedition Laws, and had come to a resolution thereupon, which he delivered in at the clerk's table, where it was read and *unanimously* agreed to by the house, as follows:—

The representatives of the good people of this commonwealth, in General Assembly convened, having maturely considered the answers of sundry states in the Union to their resolutions, passed the last session, respecting certain unconstitutional laws of Congress, commonly called the Alien and Sedition Laws, would be faithless, indeed, to themselves, and to those they represent, were they silently to acquiesce in the principles and doctrines attempted to be maintained in all those answers, that of Virginia only excepted. To again enter the field of argument, and attempt more fully or forcibly to expose the unconstitutionality of those obnoxious laws, would, it is apprehended, be as unnecessary as unavailing. We cannot, however, but lament that, in the discussion of those interesting subjects by sundry of the legislatures of our sister states, unfounded suggestions and uncandid insinuations, derogatory to the true character and principles of this commonwealth, have been substituted in place of fair reasoning and sound argument. Our opinions of these alarming measures of the general government, together with our reasons for those opinions, were detailed with decency and with temper, and submitted to the discussion and judgment of our fellow-citizens throughout the Union. Whether the like decency and temper have been observed in the answers of most of those states who have denied, or attempted to obviate, the great truths contained in those resolutions, we have now only to submit to a candid world. Faithful to the true principles of the federal Union, unconscious of any designs to disturb the harmony of that Union, and anxious only to escape the fangs of despotism, the good people of this commonwealth are regardless of censure or calumniation. Lest, however, the silence of this commonwealth should be construed into an acquiescence in the doctrines and principles advanced, and attempted to be maintained, by the said answers; or at least those of our fellow-citizens, throughout the Union, who so widely differ from us on those important subjcts, should be deluded by the expectation that we shall be deterred from what we conceive our duty, or shrink from the principles contained in those resolutions,—therefore,

Resolved, That this commonwealth considers the federal Union, upon the terms and for the purposes specified in the late compact, conducive to the liberty and happiness of the several states: That it does now unequivocally declare its attachment to the Union, and to that compact, agreeably to its obvious and real intention, and will be among the last to seek its dissolution: That, if those who administer the general government be permitted to transgress the limits fixed by that compact, by a total disregard to the special delegations of power therein contained, an annihilation of the state governments, and the creation, upon their ruins, of a general consolidated government, will be the inevitable consequence: That the principle and construction, contended for by sundry of the state legislatures, that the general government is the exclusive judge of the extent of the powers delegated to it, stop not short of *despotism*—since the discretion of those who administer the government, and not the *Constitution,* would be the measure of their powers: That the several states who formed that instrument, being sovereign and independent, have the unquestionable right to judge of the infraction; and, *That a nullification, by those sovereignties, of all unauthorized acts done under color of that instrument, is the rightful remedy:* That this commonwealth does, under the most deliberate reconsideration, declare, that the said Alien and Sedition Laws are, in their opinion, palpable violations of the said Constitution; and, however cheerfully it may be disposed to surrender its opinion to a majority of its sister states, in matters of ordinary or doubtful policy, yet, in momentous regulations like the present, which so vitally wound the best rights of the citizen, it would consider a silent acquiescence as highly criminal: That, although this commonwealth, as a party to the federal compact, will bow to the laws of the Union, yet it does, at the same time, declare, that it will not now, or ever hereafter, cease to oppose, in a constitutional manner, every attempt, at what quarter soever offered, to violate that compact: And finally, in order that no pretext or arguments may be drawn from a supposed acquiescence, on the part of this commonwealth, in the constitutionality of those laws, and be thereby used as precedents for similar future violations of the federal compact, this commonwealth does now enter against them its solemn PROTEST.

19

JAMES MADISON, VIRGINIA RESOLUTIONS
21 Dec. 1798
Elliot 4:528–29

Resolved, That the General Assembly of Virginia doth unequivocally express a firm resolution to maintain and defend the Constitution of the United States, and the Constitution of this state, against every aggression, either foreign or domestic; and that they will support the government of the United States in all measures warranted by the former.

That this Assembly most solemnly declares a warm attachment to the union of the states, to maintain which it pledges its powers; and that, for this end, it is their duty to watch over and oppose every infraction of those principles which constitute the only basis of that union, because a faithful observance of them can alone secure its existence and the public happiness.

That this Assembly doth explicitly and peremptorily declare, that it views the powers of the federal government as resulting from the compact to which the states are parties, as limited by the plain sense and intention of the instrument constituting that compact, as no further valid than they are authorized by the grants enumerated in that compact; and that, in case of a deliberate, palpable, and dangerous exercise of other powers, not granted by the said compact, the states, who are parties thereto, have the right, and are in duty bound, to interpose, for arresting the progress of the evil, and for maintaining, within their respective limits, the authorities, rights and liberties, appertaining to them.

That the General Assembly doth also express its deep regret, that a spirit has, in sundry instances, been manifested by the federal government to enlarge it powers by forced constructions of the constitutional charter which defines them; and that indications have appeared of a design to expound certain general phrases (which, having been copied from the very limited grant of powers in the former Articles of Confederation, were the less liable to be misconstrued) so as to desroy the meaning and effect of the particular enumeration which necessarily explains and limits the general phrases, and so as to consolidate the states, by degrees, into one sovereignty, the obvious tendency and inevitable result of which would be, to transform the present republican system of the United States into an absolute, or, at best, a mixed monarchy.

That the General Assembly doth particularly PROTEST against the palpable and alarming infractions of the Constitution, in the two late cases of the "Alien and Sedition Acts," passed at the last session of Congress; the first of which exercises a power nowhere delegated to the federal govenment, and which, by uniting legislative and judicial powers to those of executive, subverts the general principles of free government, as well as the particular organization and positive provisions of the Federal Constitution; and the other of which acts exercises, in like manner, a power not delegated by the Constitution, but, on the contrary, expressly and positively forbidden by one of the amendments thereto,—a power which, more than any other, ought to produce universal alarm, because it is levelled against the right of freely examining public characters and measures, and of free communication among the people thereon, which has ever been justly deemed the only effectual guardian of every other right.

That this state having, by its Convention, which ratified the Federal Constitution, expressly declared that, among other essential rights, "the liberty of conscience and the press cannot be cancelled, abridged, restrained, or modified, by any authority of the United States," and from its extreme anxiety to guard these rights from every possible attack of sophistry and ambition, having, with other states, recommended an amendment for that purpose, which amendment was, in due time, annexed to the Constitution,—it would mark a reproachful inconsistency, and criminal degeneracy, if an indifference were now shown to the most palpable violation of one of the rights thus declared and secured, and to the establishment of a precedent which may be fatal to the other.

That the good people of this commonwealth, having ever felt, and continuing to feel, the most sincere affection for their brethren of the other states; the truest anxiety for establishing and perpetuating the union of all; and the most scrupulous fidelity to that Constitution, which is the pledge of mutual friendship, and the instrument of mutual happiness,—the General Assembly doth solemnly appeal to the like dispositions in the other states, in confi-

dence that they will concur with this commonwealth in declaring, as it does hereby declare, that the acts aforesaid are unconstitutional; and that the necessary and proper measures will be taken *by each* for coöperating with this state, in maintaining unimpaired the authorities, rights, and liberties, reserved to the states respectively, or to the people.

That the governor be desired to transmit a copy of the foregoing resolutions to the executive authority of each of the other states, with a request that the same may be communicated to the legislature thereof, and that a copy be furnished to each of the senators and representatives representing this state in the Congress of the United States.

20

JOHN MARSHALL, REPORT OF THE MINORITY ON THE VIRGINIA RESOLUTIONS
22 Jan. 1799

J. House of Delegates (Va.) 6:93–95 (1798–99)

The act intitled "An act in addition to the act instituted as an act for the punishment of certain crimes against the United States," and which is commonly called the sedition law, subjects to a fine not exceeding two thousand dollars, and to imprisonment not exceeding two years, any person who shall write, print, utter, or publish, or cause or procure to be written, printed, uttered or published, any false, scandalous, malicious writing or writings against the government of the United States, with intent to defame the said government of the United States, or either house of Congress of the United States, or the President of the United States, with intent to defame the said government, or either house of Congress, or the said President, or to bring them, or either of them, into contempt or disrepute, or to excite against them, or either or any of them, the hatred of the good people of the United States, or to stir up any sedition within the United States, or to excite any unlawful combination therein for opposing or resisting any law of the United States, or any act of the President of the United States, done in pursuance of such law, or of the powers in him vested by the constitution of the United States, or to resist, oppress, or defeat any such law or act, or to aid, encourage, or abet hostile designs of any foreign nation, against the United States, their people, or government; the person accused is to be tried by jury, and may give in evidence the truth of the matter contained in the libel.

To constitute the crime, the writing must be false, scandalous, and malicious, and the intent must be to effect some of the ill purposes described in the act.

To contend that there does not exist a power to punish writings coming within the description of this law, would be to assert the inability of our nation to preserve its own peace, and to protect themselves from the attempts of wicked citizens, who, incapable of quiet themselves, are incessantly employed in devising means to disturb the public repose.

Government is instituted and preserved for the general happiness and safety—the people therefore are interested in its preservation, and have a right to adopt measures for its security, as well against secret plots as open hostility. But government cannot be thus secured, if by falsehood and malicious slander, it is to be deprived of the confidence and affection of the people. It is vain to urge that truth will prevail, and that slander, when detected, recoils on the calumniator. The experience of the world, and our own experience, prove that a continued course of defamation will at length sully the fairest reputation, and will throw suspicion on the purest conduct. Although the calumnies of the factious and discontented may not poison the minds of the majority of the citizens, yet they will infect a very considerable number, and prompt them to deeds destructive of the public peace and dangerous to the general safety.

This, the people have a right to prevent: and therefore, in all the nations of the earth, where presses are known, some corrective of their licentiousness has been deemed indispensable. But it is contended that though this may be theoretically true, such is the peculiar structure of our government, that this power has either never been confided to, or has been withdrawn from the legislature of this union.—We will examine these positions. The power of making all laws which shall be necessary and proper for carrying into execution all powers vested by the constitution in the government of the United States, or in any department or officer thereof, is by the concluding clause of the eighth section of the first article, expressly delegated to congress. This clause is admitted to authorize congress to pass any act for the punishment of those who would resist the execution of the laws, because such an act would be incontestably necessary and proper for carrying into execution the powers vested in the government. If it authorizes the punishment of actual resistance, does it not also authorize the punishment of those acts, which are criminal in themselves, and which obviously lead to and prepare resistance? Would it not be strange, if, for the purpose of executing the legitimate powers of the government, a clause like that which has been cited should be so construed as to permit the passage of laws punishing open resistance, and yet to forbid the passage of laws punishing acts which constitute the germ from which resistance springs? That the government must look on, and see preparations for resistance which it shall be unable to control, until they shall break out in open force? This would be an unreasonable and improvident construction of the article under consideration. That continued calumnies against the government have this tendency, is demonstrated by uninterrupted experience. They will, if unrestrained, produce in any society convulsions, which if not totally destructive of, will yet be very injurious to, its prosperity and welfare. It is not to be believed that the people of the western parts of Pennsylvania could have been deluded into that unprovoked and wanton insurrection, which called forth the militia of the neighbouring states, if they had not been at the same time irritated and seduced by calumnies

with which certain presses incessantly teemed into the opinion that the people of America, instead of supporting their government and their laws, would join in their subversion. Those calumnies then, tended to prevent the execution of the laws of the union, and such seems to be their obvious and necessary tendency.

To punish all malicious calumnies against an individual with an intent to defame him, is a wrong on the part of the calumniator, and an injury to the individual, for which the laws afford redress. To write or print these calumnies is such an aggravation of the crime, as to constitute an offence against the government, and the author of the libel is subject to the additional punishment which may be inflicted under an indictment. To publish malicious calumnies against government itself, is a wrong on the part of the calumniator, and an injury to all those who have an interest in the government. Those who have this interest and have sustained the injury, have the natural right to an adequate remedy. The people of the United States have a common interest in their government, and sustain in common the injury which affects that government. The people of the United States therefore have a right to the remedy for that injury, and are substantially the party seeking redress. By the 2d section of the 3d article of the constitution, the judicial power of the United States is extended to controversies to which the United States shall be a party; and by the same article it is extended to all cases in law and equity arising under the constitution, the laws of the United States, and treaties made or which shall be made under their authority. What are cases arising under the constitution, as contradistinguished from those which arise under the laws made in pursuance thereof? They must be cases triable by a rule which exists independent of any act of the legislature of the union. That rule is the common or unwritten law which pervades all America, and which declaring libels against government to be a punishable offence, applies itself to and protects any government which the will of the people may establish. The judicial power of the United States, then, being extended to the punishment of libels against the government, as a common law offence, arising under the constitution which create the government, the general clause gives to the legislature of the union the right to make such laws as shall give that power effect.

That such was the contemporaneous construction of the constitution, is obvious from one of the amendments which have been made to it. The 3d amendment which declares, that Congress shall make no law abridging the liberty of the press, is a general construction made by all America on the original instrument admitting its application to the subject. It would have been certainly unnecessary thus to have modified the legislative powers of Congress concerning the press, if the power itself does not exist.

But altho' the original constitution may be supposed to have enabled the government to defend itself against false and malicious libels, endangering the peace, and threatening the tranquility of the American people, yet it is contended that the 3d amendment to that instrument, has deprived it of this power.

The amendment is in these words,—"Congress shall make no law respecting an establishment of religion, or prohibiting the free exercise thereof, or ABRIDGING the freedom of speech or of the press."

In a solemn instrument, as is a constitution, words are well weighed and considered before they are adopted. A remarkable diversity of expression is not used, unless it be designed to manifest a difference of intention. Congress is prohibited from making any law RESPECTING a religious establishment, but not from making any law RESPECTING the press. When the power of Congress relative to the press is to be limited, the word RESPECTING is dropt, and Congress is only restrained from the passing any law ABRIDGING its liberty. This difference of expression with respect to religion and the press, manifests a difference of intention with respect to the power of the national legislature over those subjects, both in the person who drew, and in those who adopted this amendment.

All ABRIDGMENT of the freedom of the press is forbidden, but it is only an ABRIDGEMENT of that freedom which is forbidden. It becomes then necessary in order to determine whether the act in question be unconstitutional or not, to inquire whether it does in fact ABRIDGE the freedom of the press.

The act is believed not to have that operation, for two reasons.

1st. A punishment of the licentiousness is not considered as a restriction of the freedom of the press,

2d. The act complained of does not punish any writing not before punishable, nor does it inflict a more severe penalty than that to which the same writing was before liable.

1st. If by freedom of the press is meant a perfect exemption from all punishment for whatever may be published, that freedom never has, and most probably never will exist. It is known to all, that the person who writes or publishes a libel, may be both sued and indicted, and must bear the penalty which the judgment of his country inflicts upon him. It is also known to all that the person who shall libel the government of the state, is for that offence, punishable in the like manner. Yet this liability to punishment for slanderous and malicious publications has never been considered as detracting from the liberty of the press. In fact the liberty of the press is a term which has a definite and appropriate signification, completely understood. It signifies a liberty to publish, free from previous restraint, any thing and every thing at the discretion of the printer only, but not the liberty of spreading with impunity false and scandalous slanders which may destroy the peace and mangle the reputation of an individual or of a community.

If this definition of the term be correct, and it is presumed that its correctness is not to be questioned, then a law punishing the authors and publishers of false, malicious and scandalous libels can be no attack on the liberty of the press.

But the act complained of is no abridgment of the liberty of the press, for another reason.

2d. It does not punish any writing not before punishable, nor does it inflict a heavier penalty than the same writing was before liable to.

No man will deny, that at common law, the author and publisher of a false, scandalous and malicious libel against the government or an individual, were subject to fine and imprisonment, at the discretion of the judge. Nor will it be denied, that previous to our revolution, the common law was the law of the land throughout the now United States.

We believe it to be a principle incontestibly true, that a change of government does not dissolve obligations previously created, does not annihilate existing laws, and dissolve the bonds of society; but that a People passing from one form of government to another, retain in full force all their municipal institutions not necessarily changed by the change of government. If this be true, then the common law continued to be the law of the land after the revolution, and was of complete obligation even before the act of our Assembly for its adoption. Whether similar acts have been passed by the legislature of other states or not, it is certain that in every state the common law is admitted to be in full force, except as it may have been altered by the statute law. The only question is, whether the doctrines of the common law are applicable to libels against the government of the United States, as well as to libels against the governments of particular states. For such a distinction there seems to be no sufficient reason. It is not to a magistrate of this or that description that the rules of the common law apply. That he is a magistrate, that he is cloathed with the authority of the laws, that he is invested with power by the people, is a sufficient title to the protection of the common law. The government of the United States is for certain purposes as entirely the government of each state, chosen by the people thereof, and cloathed with their authority, as the government of each particular state is the government of every subdivision of that state; and no satisfactory reason has been heretofore assigned why a general rule common to all, and punishing generally the malicious calumniators of magistrates, should not be as applicable to magistrates chosen for the whole, as to those chosen for its different parts.

If then it were even true that the punishment of the printer of malicious falsehoods affected the liberty of the press, yet the act does not abridge that liberty, since it does not substitute a harsher or severer rule of punishment than that which before existed.

On points so extremely interesting, a difference of opinion will be entertained. On such occasions all parties must be expected to maintain their real opinions, but to maintain them with moderation and with decency. The will of the majority must prevail, or the republican principle is abandoned and the nation is destroyed. If upon every constitutional question which presents itself, or on every question we choose to term constitutional, the construction of the majority shall be forcibly opposed, and hostility to the government excited throughout the nation, there is an end of our domestic peace, and we may ever bid adieu to our representative government.

The legislature of Virginia has itself passed more than one unconstitutional law, but they have not been passed with an intention to violate the constitution. On being decided to be unconstitutional by the legitimate authority, they have been permitted to fall. Had the judges deemed them constitutional, they should have been maintained. The same check, nor is it a less efficient one, exists in the government of the union. The judges of the United States are as independent as the judges of the state of Virginia, nor is there any reason to believe them less wise and less virtuous. It is their province, and their duty to construe the constitution and the laws, and it cannot be doubted, but that they will perform this duty faithfully and truly. They will perform it unwarmed by political debate, uninfluenced by party zeal. Let us in the mean time seek a repeal of any acts we may disapprove, by means authorized by our happy constitution, but let us not endeavor to disseminate among our fellow citizens the most deadly hate against the government of their own creation, against the government, on the preservation of which we firmly believe the peace and liberty of America to depend, because in some respects its judgment has differed from our own.

21

JAMES MADISON, ADDRESS OF THE GENERAL
ASSEMBLY TO THE PEOPLE OF THE
COMMONWEALTH OF VIRGINIA
23 Jan. 1799
Writings 6:333–36

The sedition act presents a scene which was never expected by the early friends of the Constitution. It was then admitted that the State sovereignties were only diminished by powers specifically enumerated, or necessary to carry the specified powers into effect. Now, Federal authority is deduced from implication; and from the existence of State law, it is inferred that Congress possess a similar power of legislation; whence Congress will be endowed with a power of legislation in all cases whatsoever, and the States will be stripped of every right reserved, by the concurrent claims of a paramount Legislature.

The sedition act is the offspring of these tremendous pretensions, which inflict a death-wound on the sovereignty of the States.

For the honor of American understanding, we will not believe that the people have been allured into the adoption of the Constitution by an affectation of defining powers, whilst the *preamble* would admit a construction which would erect the will of Congress into a power paramount in all cases, and therefore limited in none. On the contrary, it is evident that the objects for which the Constitution was formed were deemed attainable only by a particular enumeration and specification of each power granted to the Federal Government; reserving all others to the people, or to the States. And yet it is in vain we search for any specified power embracing the right of legislation against the freedom of the press.

Had the States been despoiled of their sovereignty by the generality of the preamble, and had the Federal Government been endowed with whatever they should judge to be instrumental towards union, justice, tranquillity, common defence, general welfare, and the preservation of liberty, nothing could have been more frivolous than an enumeration of powers.

It is vicious in the extreme to calumniate meritorious public servants; but it is both artful and vicious to arouse the public indignation against calumny in order to conceal usurpation. Calumny is forbidden by the laws, usurpation by the Constitution. Calumny injures individuals, usurpation, States. Calumny may be redressed by the common judicatures; usurpation can only be controlled by the act of society. Ought *usurpation*, which is most mischievous, to be rendered less hateful by *calumny*, which, though injurious, is in a degree less pernicious? But the laws for the correction of calumny were not defective. Every libellous writing or expression might receive its punishment in the State courts, from juries summoned by an officer, who does not receive his appointment from the President, and is under no influence to court the pleasure of Government, whether it injured public officers or private citizens. Nor is there any distinction in the Constitution empowering Congress exclusively to punish calumny directed against an officer of the General Government; so that a construction assuming the power of protecting the reputation of a citizen officer will extend to the case of any other citizen, and open to Congress a right of legislation in every conceivable case which can arise between individuals.

In answer to this, it is urged that every Government possesses an inherent power of self-preservation, entitling it to do whatever it shall judge necessary for that purpose.

This is a repetition of the doctrine of implication and expediency in different language, and admits of a similar and decisive answer, namely, that as the powers of Congress are defined, powers inherent, implied, or expedient, are obviously the creatures of ambition; because the care expended in defining powers would otherwise have been superfluous. Powers extracted from such sources will be indefinitely multiplied by the aid of armies and patronage, which, with the impossibility of controlling them by any demarcation, would presently terminate reasoning, and ultimately swallow up the State sovereignties.

So insatiable is a love of power that it has resorted to a distinction between the freedom and licentiousness of the press for the purpose of converting the third amendment of the Constitution, which was dictated by the most lively anxiety to preserve that freedom, into an instrument for abridging it. Thus usurpation even justifies itself by a precaution against usurpation; and thus an amendment universally designed to quiet every fear is adduced as the source of an act which has produced general terror and alarm.

The distinction between liberty and licentiousness is still a repetition of the Protean doctrine of implication, which is ever ready to work its ends by varying its shape. By its help, the judge as to what is licentious may escape through any constitutional restriction. Under it men of a particular religious opinion might be excluded from office, because such exclusion would not amount to an establishment of religion, and because it might be said that their opinions are licentious. And under it Congress might denominate a religion to be heretical and licentious, and proceed to its suppression. Remember that precedents once established are so much positive power; and that the nation which reposes on the pillow of political confidence, will sooner or later end its political existence in a deadly lethargy. Remember, also, that it is to the press mankind are indebted for having dispelled the clouds which long encompassed religion, for disclosing her genuine lustre, and disseminating her salutary doctrines.

The sophistry of a distinction between the liberty and the licentiousness of the press is so forcibly exposed in a late memorial from our late envoys to the Minister of the French Republic, that we here present it to you in their own words:

"The genius of the Constitution, and the opinion of the people of the United States, cannot be overruled by those who administer the Government. Among those principles deemed sacred in America, among those sacred rights considered as forming the bulwark of their liberty, which the Government contemplates with awful reverence and would approach only with the most cautious circumspection, there is no one of which the importance is more deeply impressed on the public mind than the liberty of the press. That this *liberty* is often carried to excess; that it has sometimes degenerated into *licentiousness*, is seen and lamented, *but the remedy has not yet been discovered. Perhaps it is an evil inseparable from the good with which it is allied; perhaps it is a shoot which cannot be stripped from the stalk without wounding vitally the plant from which it is torn. However desirable those measures might be which might correct without enslaving the press, they have never yet been devised in America.* No regulations exist which enable the Government to suppress whatever calumnies or invectives any individual may choose to offer to the public eye, or to punish such calumnies and invectives otherwise than by a legal prosecution in courts which are alike open to all who consider themselves as injured."

'As if we were bound to look for security from the personal probity of Congress amidst the frailties of man, and not from the barriers of the Constitution, it has been urged that the accused under the sedition act is allowed to prove the truth of the charge. This argument will not for a moment disguise the unconstitutionality of the act, if it be recollected that opinions as well as facts are made punishable, and that the truth of an opinion is not susceptible of proof. By subjecting the truth of opinion to the regulation, fine, and imprisonment, to be inflicted by those who are of a different opinion, the free range of the human mind is injuriously restrained. The sacred obligations of religion flow from the due exercise of opinion, in the solemn discharge of which man is accountable to his God alone; yet, under this precedent the truth of religion itself may be ascertained, and its pretended licentiousness punished by a jury of a different creed from that held by the person accused. This law, then, commits the double sacrilege of arresting reason in her progress towards perfection, and of placing in a state of danger the free exercise of religious opinions. But where does the Constitution allow Congress to create crimes and inflict punishment, pro-

vided they allow the accused to exhibit evidence in his defense? This doctrine, united with the assertion, that sedition is a common law offence, and therefore within the correcting power of Congress, opens at once the hideous volumes of penal law, and turns loose upon us the utmost invention of insatiable malice and ambition, which, in all ages, have debauched morals, depressed liberty, shackled religion, supported despotism, and deluged the scaffold with blood.

22

JAMES IREDELL, CHARGE TO THE GRAND JURY, IN CASE OF FRIES

9 Fed. Cas. 829, no. 5,126 (C.C.D.Pa. 1799)

---

4. That objection is, that the act is in violation of this amendment of the constitution. 3 Swift's Ed. p. 455, art. 3 [1 Stat. 21]. "Congress shall make no law respecting an establishment of religion, or prohibiting the free exercise thereof; or abridging the freedom of speech, or of the press, or the right of the people peaceably to assemble, and to petition the government for a redress of grievances."

The question then is, whether this law has abridged the freedom of the press? Here is a remarkable difference in expressions as to the different objects in the same clause. They are to make no law respecting an establishment of religion, or prohibiting the free exercise thereof, or abridging the freedom of speech, or of the press. When, as to one object, they entirely prohibit any act whatever, and, as to another object, only limit the exercise of the power, they must, in reason, be supposed to mean different things. I presume, therefore, that congress may make a law respecting the press, provided the law be such as not to abridge its freedom. What might be deemed the freedom of the press, if it had been a new subject, and never before in discussion, might indeed admit of some controversy. But, so far as precedent, habit, laws, and practices are concerned, there can scarcely be a more definite meaning than that which all these have affixed to the term in question. We derive our principles of law originally from England. There, the press, I believe, is as free as in any country of the world, and so it has been for near a century. The definition of it is, in my opinion, no where more happily or justly expressed than by the great author of the commentaries on the laws of England, which book deserves more particular regard on this occasion, because for near thirty years it has been the manual of almost every student of law in the United States, and its uncommon excellence has also introduced it into the libraries, and often to the favourite reading of private gentlemen; so that his views of the subject could scarcely be unknown to those who framed the amendments to the constitution: and if they were not, unless his explanation had been satisfactory, I presume the amendment would have been more particularly worded, to guard against any possible mistake. His explanation is as follows: "The liberty of the press is indeed essential to the nature of a free state. And this consists in laying no previous restraints upon publications, and not in freedom from censure for criminal matter when published. Every freeman has an undoubted right to lay what sentiments he pleases before the public; to forbid this, is to destroy the freedom of the press: but if he publishes what is improper, mischievous, or illegal, he must take the consequence of his own temerity. To subject the press to the restrictive power of a licenser, as was formerly done, both before and since the Revolution, is to subject all freedom of sentiment to the prejudices of one man, and make him the arbitrary and infallible judge of all controversial points in learning, religion, and government. But to punish (as the law does at present) any dangerous or offensive writings, which, when published, shall, on a fair and impartial trial, be adjudged of a pernicious tendency, is necessary for the preservation of peace and good order, of government and religion, the only solid foundations of civil liberty. Thus the will of individuals is still left free; the abuse only of that free will is the object of legal punishment. Neither is any restraint hereby laid upon freedom of thought or inquiry: liberty of private sentiment is still left; the disseminating, or making public, of bad sentiments, destructive of the ends of society, is the crime which society corrects. A man (says a fine writer on this subject) may be allowed to keep poisons in his closet, but not publicly to vend them as cordials. And to this we may add, that the only plausible argument heretofore used for the restraining the just freedom of the press, 'that it was necessary to prevent the daily abuse of it,' will entirely lose its force when it is shown (by a reasonable exercise of the laws) that the press cannot be abused to any bad purpose, without incurring a suitable punishment: whereas, it never can be used to any good one when under the control of an inspector. So true will it be found, that to censure the licentiousness is to maintain the liberty of the press." 4 Bl. Comm. 151.

It is believed that, in every state in the Union, the common law principles concerning libels apply; and in some of the states words similar to the words of the amendment are used in the constitution itself or a contemporary bill of rights, of equal authority, without ever being supposed to exclude any law being passed on the subject. So that there is the strongest proof that can be of a universal concurrence in America on this point, that the freedom of the press does not require that libellers shall be protected from punishment. But, in some respects the act of congress is much more restrictive than the principles of the common law, or than, perhaps, the principles of any state in the Union. For, under the law of the United States, the truth of the matter may be given in evidence, which at common law, in criminal prosecutions, was held not to be admissible; and the punishment of fine and imprisonment, which at common law was discretionary, is limited in point of severity, though not of lenity. It is to be observed, too, that by the express words of the act, both malice and falsehood must combine in the publication, with the seditious intent particularly described. So that if the writing be false, yet not malicious, or malicious and not false, no conviction can take place. This, therefore, fully provides for any publication arising from inadvertency, mistake, false confidence, or anything short of a wilful and atrocious falsehood. And none surely will contend, that the publication of such a falsehood is among the indefeasible rights of men, for that would be to make the freedom of liars greater than that of men of truth and integrity.

23

KENTUCKY CONSTITUTION OF 1799, ART. 10, SEC. 7
Thorpe 3:1289

SEC. 7. That printing-presses shall be free to every person who undertakes to examine the proceedings of the legislature or any branch of government, and no law shall ever be made to restrain the right thereof. The free communication of thoughts and opinions is one of the invaluable rights of man, and every citizen may freely speak, write, and print on any subject, being responsible for the abuse of that liberty.

SEC. 8. In prosecutions for the publication of papers investigating the official conduct of officers or men in a public capacity, or where the matter published is proper for public information, the truth thereof may be given in evidence. And in all indictments for libels, the jury shall have a right to determine the law and the facts, under the direction of the court, as in other cases.

24

JAMES MADISON, REPORT ON THE VIRGINIA
RESOLUTIONS
Jan. 1800
Writings 6:385–401

2. The next point which the resolution requires to be proved is, that the power over the press exercised by the Sedition Act is positively forbidden by one of the amendments to the Constitution.

The amendment stands in these words: "Congress shall make no law respecting an establishment of religion, or prohibiting the free exercise thereof, *or abridging the freedom of speech or of the press; or the right of the people peaceably to assemble and to petition the Government for a redress of grievances."

In the attempts to vindicate the Sedition Act it has been contended—1. That the "freedom of the press" is to be determined by the meaning of these terms in the common law. 2. That the article supposes the power over the press to be in Congress, and prohibits them only from *abridging* the freedom allowed to it by the common law.

Although it will be shown, on examining the second of these positions, that the amendment is a denial to Congress of all power over the press, it may not be useless to make the following observations on the first of them:

It is deemed to be a sound opinion, that the Sedition Act, in its definition of some of the crimes created, is an abridgment of the freedom of publication, recognised by principles of the common law in England.

The freedom of the press under the common law is, in the defences of the Sedition Act, made to consist in an exemption from all *previous* restraint on printed publications by persons authorized to inspect and prohibit them. It appears to the committee that this idea of the freedom of the press can never be admitted to be the American idea of it; since a law inflicting penalties on printed publications would have a similar effect with a law authorizing a previous restraint on them. It would seem a mockery to say that no laws should be passed preventing publications from being made, but that laws might be passed for punishing them in case they should be made.

The essential difference between the British Government and the American Constitutions will place this subject in the clearest light.

In the British Government the danger of encroachments on the rights of the people is understood to be confined to the executive magistrate. The representatives of the people in the Legislature are not only exempt themselves from distrust, but are considered as sufficient guardians of the rights of their constituents against the danger from the Executive. Hence it is a principle, that the Parliament is unlimited in its power; or, in their own language, is omnipotent. Hence, too, all the ramparts for protecting the rights of the people—such as their Magna Charta, their Bill of Rights, &c.—are not reared against the Parliament, but against the royal prerogative. They are merely legislative precautions against executive usurpations. Under such a government as this, an exemption of the press from previous restraint, by licensers appointed by the King, is all the freedom that can be secured to it.

In the United States the case is altogether different. The People, not the Government, possess the absolute sovereignty. The Legislature, no less than the Executive, is under limitations of power. Encroachments are regarded as possible from the one as well as from the other. Hence, in the United States the great and essential rights of the people are secured against legislative as well as against executive ambition. They are secured, not by laws paramount to prerogative, but by constitutions paramount to laws. This security of the freedom of the press requires that it should be exempt not only from previous restraint by the Executive, as in Great Britain, but from legislative restraint also; and this exemption, to be effectual, must be an exemption not only from the previous inspection of licensers, but from the subsequent penalty of laws.

The state of the press, therefore, under the common law, cannot, in this point of view, be the standard of its freedom in the United States.

But there is another view under which it may be necessary to consider this subject. It may be alleged that although the security for the freedom of the press be different in Great Britain and in this country, being a legal security only in the former, and a constitutional security in the latter; and although there may be a further difference, in an extension of the freedom of the press, here, beyond an exemption from previous restraint, to an exemption from subsequent penalties also; yet that the actual legal freedom of the press, under the common law, must determine the degree of freedom which is meant by the terms, and which is constitutionally secured against both previous and subsequent restraints.

The committee are not unaware of the difficulty of all general questions which may turn on the proper boundary between the liberty and licentiousness of the press. They will leave it, therefore, for consideration only how far the difference between the nature of the British Government and the nature of the American Governments, and the practice under the latter may show the degree of rigor in the former to be inapplicable to and not obligatory in the latter.

The nature of governments elective, limited, and responsible, in all their branches, may well be supposed to require a greater freedom of animadversion than might be tolerated by the genius of such a government as that of Great Britain. In the latter it is a maxim that the King, an hereditary, not a responsible magistrate, can do no wrong, and that the Legislature, which in two-thirds of its composition is also hereditary, not responsible, can do what it pleases. In the United States the executive magistrates are not held to be infallible, nor the Legislatures to be omnipotent; and both being elective, are both responsible. Is it not natural and necessary, under such different circumstances, that a different degree of freedom in the use of the press should be contemplated?

Is not such an inference favoured by what is observable in Great Britain itself? Notwithstanding the general doctrine of the common law on the subject of the press, and the occasional punishment of those who use it with a freedom offensive to the Government, it is well known that with respect to the responsible members of the Government, where the reasons operating here become applicable there, the freedom exercised by the press and protected by public opinion far exceeds the limits prescribed by the ordinary rules of law. The ministry, who are responsible to impeachment, are at all times animadverted on by the press with peculiar freedom, and during the elections for the House of Commons, the other responsible part of the Government, the press is employed with as little reserve towards the candidates.

The practice in America must be entitled to much more respect. In every State, probably, in the Union, the press has exerted a freedom in canvassing the merits and measures of public men of every description which has not been confined to the strict limits of the common law. On this footing the freedom of the press has stood; on this footing it yet stands. And it will not be a breach either of truth or of candour to say, that no persons or presses are in the habit of more unrestrained animadversions on the proceedings and functionaries of the State governments than the persons and presses most zealous in vindicating the act of Congress for punishing similar animadversions on the Government of the United States.

The last remark will not be understood as claiming for the State governments an immunity greater than they have heretofore enjoyed. Some degree of abuse is inseparable from the proper use of every thing, and in no instance is this more true than in that of the press. It has accordingly been decided by the practice of the States, that it is better to leave a few of its noxious branches to their luxuriant growth, than, by pruning them away, to injure the vigour of those yielding the proper fruits. And can the wisdom of this policy be doubted by any who reflect that to the press alone, chequered as it is with abuses, the world is indebted for all the triumphs which have been gained by reason and humanity over error and oppression; who reflect that to the same beneficent source the United States owe much of the lights which conducted them to the ranks of a free and independent nation, and which have improved their political system into a shape so auspicious to their happiness? Had "Sedition Acts," forbidding every publication that might bring the constituted agents into contempt or disrepute, or that might excite the hatred of the people against the authors of unjust or pernicious measures, been uniformly enforced against the press, might not the United States have been languishing at this day under the infirmities of a sickly Confederation? Might they not, possibly, be miserable colonies, groaning under a foreign yoke?

To these observations one fact will be added, which demonstrates that the common law cannot be admitted as the *universal* expositor of American terms, which may be the same with those contained in that law. The freedom of conscience and of religion are found in the same instruments which assert the freedom of the press. It will never be admitted that the meaning of the former, in the common law of England, is to limit their meaning in the United States.

Whatever weight may be allowed to these considerations, the committee do not, however, by any means intend to rest the question on them. They contend that the article of amendment, instead of supposing in Congress a power that might be exercised over the press, provided its freedom was not abridged, was meant as a positive denial to Congress of any power whatever on the subject.

To demonstrate that this was the true object of the article, it will be sufficient to recall the circumstances which led to it, and to refer to the explanation accompanying the article.

When the Constitution was under the discussions which preceded its ratification, it is well known that great apprehensions were expressed by many, lest the omission of some positive exception, from the powers delegated, of certain rights, and of the freedom of the press particularly, might expose them to the danger of being drawn, by construction, within some of the powers vested in Congress, more especially of the power to make all laws necessary and proper for carrying their other powers into execution. In reply to this objection, it was invariably urged to be a fundamental and characteristic principle of the Constitution, that all powers not given by it were reserved; that no powers were given beyond those enumerated in the Constitution, and such as were fairly incident to them: that the power over the rights in question, and particularly over the press, was neither among the enumerated powers, nor incident to any of them; and consequently that an exercise of any such power would be manifest usurpation. It is painful to remark how much the arguments now employed in behalf of the Sedition Act are at variance with the reasoning which then justified the Constitution, and invited its ratification.

From this posture of the subject resulted the interesting question, in so many of the Conventions, whether the doubts and dangers ascribed to the Constitution should be removed by any amendments previous to the ratification, or be postponed in confidence that, as far as they might be proper, they would be introduced in the form provided by the Constitution. The latter course was adopted; and in most of the States, ratifications were followed by propositions and instructions for rendering the Constitution more explicit, and more safe to the rights not meant to be delegated by it. Among those rights, the freedom of the press, in most instances, is particularly and emphatically mentioned. The firm and very pointed manner in which it is asserted in the proceedings of the Convention of this State will be hereafter seen.

In pursuance of the wishes thus expressed, the first Congress that assembled under the Constitution proposed certain amendments, which have since, by the necessary ratifications, been made a part of it; among which amendments is the article containing, among other prohibitions on the Congress, an express declaration that they should make no law abridging the freedom of the press.

Without tracing farther the evidence on this subject, it would seem scarcely possible to doubt that no power whatever over the press was supposed to be delegated by the Constitution, as it originally stood, and that the amendment was intended as a positive and absolute reservation of it.

But the evidence is still stronger. The proposition of amendments made by Congress is introduced in the following terms:

"The Conventions of a number of the States having, at the time of their adopting the Constitution, expressed a desire, in order to prevent misconstructions or abuse of its powers, that further declaratory and restrictive clauses should be added; and as extending the ground of public confidence in the Government will best insure the beneficent ends of its institutions."

Here is the most satisfactory and authentic proof that the several amendments proposed were to be considered as either declaratory or restrictive, and, whether the one or the other as corresponding with the desire expressed by a number of the States, and as extending the ground of public confidence in the Government.

Under any other construction of the amendment relating to the press, than that it declared the press to be wholly exempt from the power of Congress, the amendment could neither be said to correspond with the desire expressed by a number of the States, nor be calculated to extend the ground of public confidence in the Government.

Nay, more; the construction employed to justify the Sedition Act would exhibit a phenomenon without a parallel in the political world. It would exhibit a number of respectable States, as denying, first, that any power over the press was delegated by the Constitution; as proposing, next, that an amendment to it should explicitly declare that no such power was delegated; and, finally, as concurring in an amendment actually recognising or delegating such a power.

Is, then, the Federal Government, it will be asked, destitute of every authority for restraining the licentiousness of the press, and for shielding itself against the libellous attacks which may be made on those who administer it?

The Constitution alone can answer this question. If no such power be expressly delegated, and if it be not both necessary and proper to carry into execution an express power—above all, if it be expressly forbidden, by a declaratory amendment to the Constitution—the answer must be, that the Federal Government is destitute of all such authority.

And might it not be asked, in turn, whether it is not more probable, under all the circumstances which have been reviewed, that the authority should be withheld by the Constitution, than that it should be left to a vague and violent construction, whilst so much pains were bestowed in enumerating other powers, and so many less important powers are included in the enumeration?

Might it not be likewise asked, whether the anxious circumspection which dictated so many peculiar limitations on the general authority would be unlikely to exempt the press altogether from that authority? The peculiar magnitude of some of the powers necessarily committed to the Federal Government; the peculiar duration required for the functions of some of its departments; the peculiar distance of the seat of its proceedings from the great body of its constituents; and the peculiar difficulty of circulating an adequate knowledge of them through any other channel; will not these considerations, some or other of which produced other exceptions from the powers of ordinary governments, all together, account for the policy of binding the hand of the Federal Government from touching the channel which alone can give efficacy to its responsibility to its constituents, and of leaving those who administer it to a remedy, for their injured reputations, under the same laws, and in the same tribunals, which protect their lives, their liberties, and their properties?

But the question does not turn either on the wisdom of the Constitution or on the policy which gave rise to its particular organization. It turns on the actual meaning of the instrument, by which it has appeared that a power over the press is clearly excluded from the number of powers delegated to the Federal Government.

3. And, in the opinion of the committee, well may it be said, as the resolution concludes with saying, that the unconstitutional power exercised over the press by the Sedition Act ought, "more than any other, to produce univer-sal alarm; because it is levelled against that right of freely examining public characters and measures, and of free communication among the people thereon, which has ever been justly deemed the only effectual guardian of every other right."

Without scrutinizing minutely into all the provisions of the Sedition Act, it will be sufficient to cite so much of section 2d as follows: "And be it further enacted, that if any person shall write, print, utter, or publish, or shall cause or procure to be written, printed, uttered, or published, or shall knowingly and willingly assist or aid in writing, printing, uttering, or publishing, any false, scandalous, and malicious writing or writings against the Government of the United States, or either house of the Congress of the United States, or the President of the United States, with an intent to defame the said Government or either house of the said Congress, or the President, or to bring them or either of them into contempt or disrepute, or to excite against them, or either or any of them, the hatred of the good people of the United States, &c.—then such person, being thereof convicted before any court of the United States having jurisdiction thereof, shall be punished by a fine not exceeding two thousand dollars, and by imprisonment not exceeding two years."

On this part of the act, the following observations present themselves:

1. The Constitution supposes that the President, the Congress, and each of its Houses, may not discharge their trusts, either from defect of judgment or other causes. Hence they are all made responsible to their constituents, at the returning periods of election; and the President, who is singly intrusted with very great powers, is, as a further guard, subjected to an intermediate impeachment.

2. Should it happen, as the Constitution supposes it may happen, that either of these branches of the Government may not have duly discharged its trust; it is natural and proper, that, according to the cause and degree of their faults, they should be brought into contempt or disrepute, and incur the hatred of the people.

3. Whether it has, in any case, happened that the proceedings of either or all of those branches evince such a violation of duty as to justify a contempt, a disrepute, or hatred among the people, can only be determined by a free examination thereof, and a free communication among the people thereon.

4. Whenever it may have actually happened that proceedings of this sort are chargeable on all or either of the branches of the Government, it is the duty, as well as right, of intelligent and faithful citizens to discuss and promulge them freely, as well to control them by the censorship of the public opinion, as to promote a remedy according to the rules of the Constitution. And it cannot be avoided that those who are to apply the remedy must feel, in some degree, a contempt or hatred against the transgressing party.

5. As the act was passed on July 14, 1798, and is to be in force until March 3, 1801, it was of course that, during its continuance, two elections of the entire House of Representatives, an election of a part of the Senate, and an election of a President, were to take place.

6. That consequently, during all these elections, intended by the Constitution to preserve the purity or to purge the faults of the Administration, the great remedial rights of the people were to be exercised, and the responsibility of their public agents to be screened, under the penalties of this act.

May it not be asked of every intelligent friend to the liberties of his country, whether the power exercised in such an act as this ought not to produce great and universal alarm? Whether a rigid execution of such an act, in time past, would not have repressed that information and communication among the people which is indispensable to the just exercise of their electoral rights? And whether such an act, if made perpetual, and enforced with rigor, would not, in time to come, either destroy our free system of government, or prepare a convulsion that might prove equally fatal to it?

In answer to such questions, it has been pleaded that the writings and publications forbidden by the act are those only which are false and malicious, and intended to defame; and merit is claimed for the privilege allowed to authors to justify, by proving the truth of their publications, and for the limitations to which the sentence of fine and imprisonment is subjected.

To those who concurred in the act, under the extraordinary belief that the option lay between the passing of such an act and leaving in force the common law of libels, which punishes truth equally with falsehood, and submits the fine and imprisonment to the indefinite discretion of the court, the merit of good intentions ought surely not to be refused. A like merit may perhaps be due for the discontinuance of the corporal punishment, which the common law also leaves to the discretion of the court. This merit of intention, however, would have been greater, if the several mitigations had not been limited to so short a period; and the apparent inconsistency would have been avoided, between justifying the act, at one time, by contrasting it with the rigors of the common law otherwise in force; and at another time, by appealing to the nature of the crisis, as requiring the temporary rigor exerted by the act.

But, whatever may have been the meritorious intentions of all or any who contributed to the Sedition Act, a very few reflections will prove that its baleful tendency is little diminished by the privilege of giving in evidence the truth of the matter contained in political writings.

In the first place, where simple and naked facts alone are in question, there is sufficient difficulty in some cases, and sufficient trouble and vexation in all, of meeting a prosecution from the Government with the full and formal proof necessary in a court of law.

But in the next place, it must be obvious to the plainest minds, that opinions and inferences, and conjectural observations, are not only in many cases inseparable from the facts, but may often be more the objects of the prosecution than the facts themselves; or may even be altogether abstracted from particular facts; and that opinions, and inferences, and conjectural observations, cannot be subjects of that kind of proof which appertains to facts, before a court of law.

Again: it is no less obvious that the intent to defame, or bring into contempt, or disrepute, or hatred—which is made a condition of the offence created by the act—cannot prevent its pernicious influence on the freedom of the press. For, omitting the inquiry, how far the malice of the intent is an inference of the law from the mere publication, it is manifestly impossible to punish the intent to bring those who administer the Government into disrepute or contempt, without striking at the right of freely discussing public characters and measures; because those who engage in such discussions must expect and intend to excite these unfavorable sentiments, so far as they may be thought to be deserved. To prohibit, therefore, the intent to excite those unfavorable sentiments against those who administer the Government, is equivalent to a prohibition of the actual excitement of them; and to prohibit the actual excitement of them is equivalent to a prohibition of discussions having that tendency and effect; which, again, is equivalent to a protection of those who administer the Government, if they should at any time deserve the contempt or hatred of the people, against being exposed to it by free animadversions on their characters and conduct. Nor can there be a doubt, if those in public trust be shielded by penal laws from such strictures of the press as may expose them to contempt, or disrepute, or hatred, where they may deserve it, that, in exact proportion as they may deserve to be exposed, will be the certainty and criminality of the intent to expose them, and the vigilance of prosecuting and punishing it; nor a doubt that a government thus intrenched in penal statutes against the just and natural effects of a culpable administration will easily evade the responsibility which is essential to a faithful discharge of its duty.

Let it be recollected, lastly, that the right of electing the members of the Government constitutes more particularly the essence of a free and responsible government. The value and efficacy of this right depends on the knowledge of the comparative merits and demerits of the candidates for public trust, and on the equal freedom, consequently, of examining and discussing these merits and demerits of the candidates respectively. It has been seen that a number of important elections will take place while the act is in force, although it should not be continued beyond the term to which it is limited. Should there happen, then, as is extremely probable in relation to some or other of the branches of the Government, to be competitions between those who are and those who are not members of the Government, what will be the situations of the competitors? Not equal; because the characters of the former will be covered by the Sedition Act from animadversions exposing them to disrepute among the people, whilst the latter may be exposed to the contempt and hatred of the people without a violation of the act. What will be the situation of the people? Not free; because they will be compelled to make their election between competitors whose pretensions they are not permitted by the act equally to examine, to discuss, and to ascertain. And from both these situations will not those in power derive an undue advantage for continuing themselves in it, which, by impairing the right of election, endangers the blessings of the Government founded on it?

It is with justice, therefore, that the General Assembly have affirmed, in the resolution, as well that the right of freely examining public characters and measures, and of free communication thereon, is the only effectual guardian of every other right, as that this particular right is levelled at by the power exercised in the Sedition Act.

The Resolution next in order is as follows:

"That this State having, by its Convention, which ratified the Federal Constitution, expressly declared that, among other essential rights, 'the liberty of conscience and of the press cannot be cancelled, abridged, restrained, or modified, by any authority of the United States;' and, from its extreme anxiety to guard these rights from every possible attack of sophistry and ambition, having, with other States, recommended an amendment for that purpose, which amendment was in due time annexed to the Constitution, it would mark a reproachful inconsistency, and criminal degeneracy, if an indifference were now shown to the most palpable violation of one of the rights thus declared and secured, and to the establishment of a precedent which may be fatal to the other."

To place this Resolution in its just light, it will be necessary to recur to the act of ratification by Virginia, which stands in the ensuing form:

"We, the delegates of the people of Virginia, duly elected in pursuance of a recommendation from the General Assembly and now met in Convention, having fully and freely investigated and discussed the proceedings of the Federal Convention, and being prepared, as well as the most mature deliberation hath enabled us, to decide thereon—DO, in the name and in behalf of the people of Virginia declare and make known that the powers granted under the Constitution, being derived from the people of the United States, may be resumed by them whensoever the same shall be perverted to their injury or oppression; and that every power not granted thereby remains with them, and at their will. That, therefore, no right of any denomination can be cancelled, abridged, restrained, or modified, by the Congress, by the Senate or House of Representatives, acting in any capacity, by the President, or any department or officer of the United States, except in those instances in which power is given by the Constitution for those purposes; and that, among other essential rights, the liberty of conscience and of the press cannot be cancelled, abridged, restrained, or modified, by any authority of the United States."

Here is an express and solemn declaration by the Convention of the State, that they ratified the Constitution in the sense that no right of any denomination can be cancelled, abridged, restrained, or modified, by the Government of the United States, or any part of it, except in those instances in which power is given by the Constitution; and in the sense, particularly, "that among other essential rights, the liberty of conscience and freedom of the press cannot be cancelled, abridged, restrained, or modified, by any authority of the United States."

Words could not well express in a fuller or more forcible manner the understanding of the Convention, that the liberty of conscience and the freedom of the press were *equally* and *completely* exempted from all authority whatever of the United States.

Under an anxiety to guard more effectually these rights against every possible danger, the Convention, after ratifying the Constitution, proceeded to prefix to certain amendments proposed by them a declaration of rights, in which are two articles providing, the one for the liberty of conscience, the other for the freedom of speech and of the press.

Similar recommendations having proceeded from a number of other States, and Congress, as has been seen, having, in consequence thereof, and with a view to extend the ground of public confidence, proposed, among other declaratory and restrictive clauses, a clause expressly securing the liberty of conscience and of the press, and Virginia having concurred in the ratifications which made them a part of the Constitution, it will remain with a candid public to decide whether it would not mark an inconsistency and degeneracy, if an indifference were now shown to a palpable violation of one of those rights—the freedom of the press; and to a precedent, therein, which may be fatal to the other—the free exercise of religion.

That the precedent established by the violation of the former of these rights may, as is affirmed by the resolution, be fatal to the latter, appears to be demonstrable by a comparison of the grounds on which they respectively rest, and from the scope of reasoning by which the power over the former has been vindicated.

First. Both of these rights, the liberty of conscience and of the press, rest equally on the original ground of not being delegated by the Constitution, and, consequently, withheld from the Government. Any construction, therefore, that would attack this original security for the one must have the like effect on the other.

Secondly. They are both equally secured by the supplement to the Constitution, being both included in the same amendment, made at the same time, and by the same authority. Any construction or argument, then, which would turn the amendment into a grant or acknowledgment of power with respect to the press, might be equally applied to the freedom of religion.

Thirdly. If it be admitted that the extent of the freedom of the press secured by the amendment is to be measured by the common law on this subject, the same authority may be resorted to for the standard which is to fix the extent of the "free exercise of religion." It cannot be necessary to say what this standard would be; whether the common law be taken solely as the unwritten, or as varied by the written law of England.

Fourthly. If the words and phrases in the amendment are to be considered as chosen with a studied discrimination, which yields an argument for a power over the press under the limitation that its freedom be not abridged, the same argument results from the same consideration for a power over the exercise of religion, under the limitation that its freedom be not prohibited.

For if Congress may regulate the freedom of the press, provided they do not abridge it, because it is said only "they shall not abridge it," and is not said, "they shall make no law respecting it," the analogy of reasoning is conclusive that Congress may *regulate* and even *abridge* the free exercise of religion, provided they do not *prohibit* it; because it is said only "they shall not prohibit it," and is *not* said, "they shall make no law *respecting*, or no law *abridging* it."

The General Assembly were governed by the clearest reason, then, in considering the Sedition Act, which legislates on the freedom of the press, as establishing a precedent that may be fatal to the liberty of conscience; and it will be the duty of all, in proportion as they value the security of the latter, to take the alarm at every encroachment on the former.

25

UNITED STATES V. COOPER
25 Fed. Cas. 631, no. 14,865 (C.C.D.Pa. 1800)

CHASE, Circuit Justice (charging jury). Gentlemen of the jury: When men are found rash enough to commit an offence such as the traverser is charged with, it becomes the duty of the government to take care that they should not pass with impunity. It is my duty to state to you the law on which this indictment is preferred, and the substance of the accusation and defence. Thomas Cooper, the traverser, stands charged with having published a false, scandalous and malicious libel against the president of the United States, in his official character as president. There is no civilized country that I know of, that does not punish such offences; and it is necessary to the peace and welfare of this country, that these offences should meet with their proper punishment, since ours is a government founded on the opinions and confidence of the people. The representatives and the president are chosen by the people. It is a government made by themselves; and their officers are chosen by themselves; and, therefore, if any improper law is enacted, the people have it in their power to obtain the repeal of such law, or even of the constitution itself, if found defective, since provision is made for its amendment. Our government, therefore, is really republican; the people are truly represented, since all power is derived from them. It is a government of representation and responsibility. All officers of the government are liable to be displaced or removed, or their duration in office limited by elections at fixed periods. There is one department only, the judiciary, which is not subject to such removal; their offices being held "during good behaviour," and therefore they can only be removed for misbehaviour. All governments which I have ever read or heard of punish libels against themselves. If a man attempts to destroy the confidence of the people in their officers, their supreme magistrate, and their legislature, he effectually saps the foundation of the government. A republican government can only be destroyed in two ways: the introduction of lux-

ury, or the licentiousness of the press. This latter is the more slow, but most sure and certain, means of bringing about the destruction of the government. The legislature of this country, knowing this maxim, has thought proper to pass a law to check this licentiousness of the press: by a clause in that law it is enacted. (Judge CHASE here read the second section of the sedition law.) It must, therefore, be observed, gentlemen of the jury, that the intent must be plainly manifest. It is an important word in the law; for if there is no such intent to defame, &c., there is no offence created by that law. Thomas Cooper, then, stands indicted for having published a false, scandalous and malicious libel upon the president of the United States, with intent to defame the president, to bring him into contempt and disrepute, and to excite against him the hatred of the good people of the United States. This is the charge. The traverser has pleaded not guilty, and that he has not published, &c., with these views. He has also pleaded in justification (which the law provides for), that the matters asserted by him are true, and that he will give the same in evidence.

It is incumbent on the part of the prosecution to prove two facts: (1) That the traverser did publish the matters contained in the indictment. (2) That he did publish with intent to defame, &c. For the intent is as much a fact as the other, and must be proved in the same manner as other facts; and must be proved as stated in the law of congress—the mere publication is no offence; and in making up your verdict, though you consider them separately, you must take the whole tenor and import of the publication, since the offence is committed by the two coupled together.

First, then, as to the publication. The fact of writing and publishing is clearly proved; nay, in fact, it is not denied. It is proved to have taken place at Sunbury, a considerable distance from the seat of government. It appears from the evidence that the traverser went to the house of a justice of the peace with this paper, whom, of all others, he ought to have avoided; for he must know that it was the duty of the justice of the peace to deliver it immediately to those who administer the government. He did so. It was indecent to deliver such a paper to a justice of the peace, and the manner in which it was delivered was yet more outrageous—if it was done in joke, as the traverser would wish to imply, it was still very improper—but there was the same solemnity in his expression, "This is my name, and I am the author of this handbill," as if the traverser was going to part with an estate. This conduct showed that he intended to dare and defy the government, and to provoke them, and his subsequent conduct satisfies my mind that such was his disposition. For he justifies the publication in all its parts, and declares it to be founded in truth. It is proved most clearly to be his publication. It is your business to consider the intent as coupled with that, and view the whole together. You must take that publication, and compare it with the indictment. If there are doubts as to the motives of the traverser, he has removed them; for, though he states in his defence that he does not arraign the motives of the president, yet he has boldly avowed that his own motives in this publication were to censure the conduct of the president, which his conduct, as he thought, deserved. Now, gentlemen, the motives of the president, in his official capacity, are not a subject of inquiry with you. Shall we say to the president, you are not fit for the government of this country? It is no apology for a man to say, that he believes the president to be honest, but that he has done acts which prove him unworthy the confidence of the people, incapable of executing the duties of his high station, and unfit for the important office to which the people have elected him: the motives and intent of the traverser, not of the president, are the subject to be inquired into by you.

Now we will consider this libel as published by the defendant, and observe what were his motives. You will find the traverser speaking of the president in the following words: "Even those who doubted his capacity, thought well of his intentions." This the traverser might suppose would be considered as a compliment as to the intentions of the president; but I have no doubt that it was meant to carry a sting with it which should be felt; for it was in substance saying of the president, "You may have good intentions, but I doubt your capacity." He then goes on to say: "Nor were we yet saddled with the expense of a permanent navy, nor threatened, under his (the president's) auspices, with the existence of a standing army. Our credit was not yet reduced so low as to borrow money at eight per cent. in time of peace." Now, gentlemen, if these things were true, can any one doubt what effect they would have on the public mind? If the people believed those things, what would be the consequence? What! the president of the United States saddle us with a permanent navy, encourage a standing army, and borrow money at a large premium? And are we told, too, that this is in time of peace? If you believe this to be true, what opinion can you, gentlemen, form of the president? One observation must strike you, viz.: That these charges are made not only against the president, but against yourselves who elect the house of representatives, for these acts cannot be done without first having been approved of by congress. Can a navy be built, can an army be raised, or money borrowed, without the consent of congress? The president is further charged for that "the unnecessary violence of his official expressions might justly have provoked a war." This is a very serious charge indeed. What, the president, by unnecessary violence, plunge this country into a war! and that a just war? It cannot be—I say, gentlemen, again, if you believe this, what opinion can you form of the president? Certainly the worst you can form: you would certainly consider him totally unfit for the high station which he has so honorably filled, and with such benefit to his country. The traverser states that, under the auspices of the president, "our credit is so low that we are obliged to borrow money at eight per cent. in time of peace." I cannot suppress my feelings at this gross attack upon the president. Can this be true? Can you believe it? Are we now in time of peace? Is there no war? No hostilities with France? Has she not captured our vessels and plundered us of our property to the amount of millions? Has not the intercourse been prohibited with her? Have we not armed our vessels to defend ourselves,

and have we not captured several of her vessels of war? Although no formal declaration of war has been made, is it not notorious that actual hostilities have taken place? And is this, then, a time of peace? The very expense incurred, which rendered a loan necessary, was in consequence of the conduct of France. The traverser, therefore, has published an untruth, knowing it to be an untruth.

The other part of the publication is much more offensive. I do not allude to his assertions relating to the embassies to Prussia, Russia, and the Sublime Porte. They are matters of little consequence, and, therefore, I shall pass over them. The part to which I allude is that where the traverser charges the president with having influenced the judiciary department. I know of no charge which can be more injurious to the president than that of an attempt to influence a court of judicature; the judicature of the country is of the greatest consequence to the liberties and existence of a nation. If your constitution was destroyed, so long as the judiciary department remained free and uncontrolled, the liberties of the people would not be endangered. Suffer your courts of judicature to be destroyed; there is an end to your liberties. The traverser says that this interference was a stretch of authority that the monarch of Great Britain would have shrunk from; an interference without precedent, against law and against mercy. Is not this an attack, and a most serious attack on the character of the president? The traverser goes on thus: "This melancholy case of Jonathan Robbins, a native of America, forcibly impressed by the British, and delivered, with the advice of Mr. Adams, to the mock trial of a British court-martial, had not yet astonished the republican citizens of this free country,—a case too little known, but of which the people ought to be fully apprised before the election, and they shall be." Now, gentlemen, there are circumstances in this publication which greatly aggravate the offence. The traverser does not only tell you that the president interfered to influence a court of justice without precedent, against law and against mercy; but that he so interfered in order to deliver up a native American citizen to be executed by a British court-martial under a mock trial, against law and against mercy. Another circumstance is adduced to complete the picture. He tells you that this Robbins was not only an American, but a native American, forcibly impressed by the British; and yet that the president of the United States, without precedent, against law and against mercy, interfered with a court of justice, and ordered this native American to be delivered up to a mock trial by a British court-martial. I can scarcely conceive a charge can be made against the president of so much consequence, or of a more heinous nature. But, says Mr. Cooper, he has done it. I will show you the case in which he has done it. It is the case of Jonathan Robbins. It appears then that this is a charge on the president, not only false and scandalous, but evidently made with intent to injure his character, and the manner in which it is made is well calculated to operate on the passions of Americans, and I fear such has been the effect. If this charge were true, there is not a man amongst you but would hate the president. I am sure I should hate him myself if I had thought he had done this. Upon the purity and independence of the judges depend the existence of your government and the preservation of your liberties. They should be under no influence—they are only accountable to God and their own consciences—your present judges are in that situation.

There is a little circumstance which the attorney-general, in his observations to you, omitted to state, but which I think it right to recall to your recollection, as it appears with what design the traverser made this publication. In this allusion to Jonathan Robbins he expressly tells you this is "a case too little known, but of which the people ought to be fully apprised before the election, and they shall be." Here, then, the evident design of the traverser was, to arouse the people against the president so as to influence their minds against him on the next election. I think it right to explain this to you, because it proves, that the traverser was actuated by improper motives to make this charge against the president. It is a very heavy charge, and made with intent to bring the president into contempt and disrepute, and excite against him the hatred of the people of the United States. The traverser has read in evidence a report made by the president to the house of representatives, and a letter written by the secretary of state, to show that the president had advised and directed this Robbins to be given up; but subsequent facts could not excuse the traverser for what he had written before. Now, gentlemen, with regard to this delivery of Jonathan Robbins, I am clearly of opinion that the president could not refuse to deliver him up. This same Jonathan Robbins, whose real name appears to have been Nash, was charged with murder committed on board the Hermione, British ship of war. This Nash being discovered in America, the British minister made a requisition to the president that he should be delivered up. Then we must inquire whether the president was obliged to give him up? By the twenty-seventh article of the treaty with Great Britain, it is stipulated, "that either of the contracting parties will deliver up to justice all persons who, being charged with murder or forgery committed within the jurisdiction of either, shall seek an asylum within any of the countries of the other, provided this shall be done only on such evidence of criminality as, according to the laws of the place where the fugitive or person so charged shall be found, would justify his apprehension and commitment for trial, if the offence had been there committed." If the president, therefore, by this treaty, was bound to give this Nash up to justice, he was so bound by law; for the treaty is the law of the land: if so, the charge of interference to influence the decisions of a court of justice, is without foundation. The reason why this article was inserted in the treaty, is evident. Murder is a crime against the laws of God and man, and ought never to be committed with impunity. Forgery is an offence affecting all commercial countries, and should never go unpunished; and therefore every government, especially a commercial one, acts wisely in delivering fugitives guilty of such crimes to justice. Nash was charged with having committed murder on board a British ship of war. Now a dispute has arisen whether murder committed on board such a ship of war, was committed within the jurisdiction of Great Britain. I have no doubt as to the point.

All vessels, whether public or private, are part of the territory and within the jurisdiction of the nation to which they belong. This is according to the law of nations. All nations have this jurisdiction, and the reason is obvious, for every country carrying on commerce, is answerable to other nations for the conduct of their subjects on the ocean. Were it not so, crimes committed on board vessels of war would go unpunished; for no other country can claim jurisdiction. This person, then, was charged with murder committed on board a British ship of war. I say it was committed within the jurisdiction of Great Britain. By the constitution, (since the treaty is the law of the land,) America was bound to give him up: but who is the person to deliver up a fugitive according to that article in the treaty? The president was the only person to take the proper steps, and to take cognizance of the business. He represents the United States in their concerns with foreign powers. This affair could not be tried before a court of law. No court of justice here has jurisdiction over the crime of murder committed on board a British ship of war. Now, as the requisition was made to the president on the part of the British government to deliver this man up, it became necessary to know whether there was sufficient evidence of his criminality pursuant to the treaty. The judge of the court of Carolina was therefore called upon to inquire into the evidence of his criminality. He was the instrument made use of by the president to ascertain that fact. His delivery was the necessary act of the president, which he was by the treaty and the law of the land, bound to perform: and had he not done so, we should have heard louder complaints from that party who are incessantly opposing and calumniating the government, that the president had grossly neglected his duty by not carrying a solemn treaty into effect. Was this, then, an interference on the part of the president with the judiciary without precedent, against law and against mercy; for doing an act which he was bound by the law of the land to carry into effect, and over which a court of justice had no jurisdiction? Surely not; neither has it merited to be treated in the manner in which the traverser has done in his publication. A defence of greater novelty I never heard before.

Take this publication in all its parts, and it is the boldest attempt I have known to poison the minds of the people. He asserts that Mr. Adams has countenanced a navy, that he has brought forward measures for raising a standing army in the country. The traverser is certainly a scholar, and has shown himself a man of learning, and has read much on the subject of armies. But to assert, as he has done, that we have a standing army in this country, betrays the most egregious ignorance, or the most wilful intentions to deceive the public. We have two descriptions of armies in this country—we have an army which is generally called the Western army, enlisted for five years only—can this be a standing army? Who raises them? Congress. Who pays them? The people. We have also another army, called the provisional army, which is enlisted during the existence of the war with France—neither of these can, with any propriety, be called a standing army. In fact, we cannot have a standing army in this country, the constitution having expressly declared that no appropriation shall be made for the support of an army longer than two years. Therefore, as congress may appropriate money for the support of the army annually, and are obliged to do it only for two years, there can be no standing army in this country until the constitution is first destroyed. There is no subject on which the people of America feel more alarm, than the establishment of a standing army. Once persuade them that the government is attempting to promote such a measure, and you destroy their confidence in the government. Therefore, to say, that under the auspices of the president, we were saddled with a standing army, was directly calculated to bring him into contempt with the people, and excite their hatred against him.

It is too much to press this point on the traverser. But he deserves it. This publication is evidently intended to mislead the ignorant, and inflame their minds against the president, and to influence their votes on the next election. The traverser says, he has proved that the president has advocated a standing army—how has he proved it? There is no standing army; I have before stated, the army is only raised for five years, and during the existing differences— he tells you, Mr. Adams is a friend to the establishment of a navy; I wonder who is not a friend to a navy which is to protect the commerce and power of this country. The traverser has, to prove these points, read to you many extracts from the addresses and answers to the president. He has selected a number of passages, which, he asserts, prove the approbation of the president to the creation of a navy, and forming a standing army. But we are to recollect gentlemen, that when in consequence of the unjust proceedings of France, the great mass of the people thought proper to address the president, expressing in those addresses, sentiments of attachment and confidence in the president, and their determination to resist the oppression of the French government, the president replied to them, in answers which generally were the echo of their sentiments, and in fact, his expressions were as general as the nature of the addresses would permit—therefore, the traverser ought to have blamed the addresses, and not the president. The Marine Society of Boston, as old seamen, address the president in favour of a navy. The president in reply, thinks a navy is the proper defence of the country.

I believe, gentlemen, in the first part of my charge, I made remarks on the assertions of the traverser, that the president had borrowed money at eight per cent. in time of peace. Therefore, it will not be necessary to enlarge on that point. You will please to notice, gentlemen, that the traverser in his defence must prove every charge he has made to be true; he must prove it to the marrow. If he asserts three things, and proves but one, he fails; if he proves but two, he fails in his defence, for he must prove the whole of his assertions to be true. If he were to prove, that the president had done everything charged against him in the first paragraph of the publication—though he should prove to your satisfaction, that the president had interfered to influence the decisions of a court of justice, that he had delivered up Jonathan Robbins without precedent, against law and against mercy, this would not be sufficient, unless he proved at the same time, that Jona-

than Robbins was a native American, and had been forcibly impressed, and compelled to serve on board a British ship of war. If he fails, therefore, gentlemen, in this proof, you must then consider whether his intention in making these charges against the president were malicious or not. It is not necessary for me to go more minutely into an investigation of the defence. You must judge for yourselves—you must find the publication, and judge of the intent with which that publication was made, whether it was malice or not? If you believe that he has published it without malice, or an intent to defame the president of the United States, you must acquit him. If he has proved the truth of the facts asserted by him, you must find him not guilty.

After the jury had returned with a verdict of guilty:

CHASE, Circuit Justice. Mr. Cooper, as the jury have found you guilty, we wish to hear any circumstances you have to offer in point of the mitigation of the fine the court may think proper to impose on you, and also in extenuation of your punishment. We should therefore wish to know your situation in life, in regard to your circumstances. It will be proper for you to consider of this. As you are under recognizance, you will attend the court some time the latter end of the week. (The court appointed Wednesday.)

Proceedings on Wednesday, April 30, 1800.

CHASE, Circuit Justice. Mr. Cooper, have you anything to offer to the court previous to passing sentence?

Mr. Cooper. The court have desired me to offer anything relating to my circumstances in mitigation of the fine, or any observation that occurs to me in extenuation of the offence. I have thought it my duty (not for the purpose of deprecating any punishment which the court may deem it proper to inflict, but) to prevent any accidental or apparent harshness of punishment on part of the court, for want of that information which it is in my power to give. For this reason, therefore, and that the court may not be misled, I think it right to say, that my property in this country is moderate. That some resources I had in England, commercial failures there have lately cut off: that I depend principally on my practice: that practice, imprisonment will annihilate. Be it so. I have been accustomed to make sacrifices to opinion, and I can make this. As to circumstances in extenuation, not being conscious that I have set down aught in malice, I have nothing to extenuate.

CHASE, Circuit Justice. I have heard what you have to say. I am sorry you did not think proper to make an affidavit in regard to your circumstances; you are a perfect stranger to the court, to me at least. I do not know you personally—I know nothing of you, more than having lately heard your name mentioned in some publication. Every person knows the political disputes which have existed amongst us. It is notorious that there are two parties in the country; you have stated this yourself. You have taken one side—we do not pretend to say, that you have not a right to express your sentiments, only taking care not to injure the characters of those to whom you are opposed.

Your circumstances ought to have been disclosed, on affidavit, that the court might have judged as to the amount of the offence; nor did we want to hurt you, by this open disclosure.

Mr. Cooper. I have nothing to disclose that I am ashamed of.

CHASE, Circuit Justice. If we were to indulge our own ideas, there is room to suspect that in cases of this kind, where one party is against the government, gentlemen who write for that party would be indemnified against any pecuniary loss; and that the party would pay any fine which might be imposed on the person convicted. You must know, I suppose, before you made any publication of this kind, whether you were to be supported by a party or not, and whether you would not be indemnified against any pecuniary loss. If the fine were only to fall on yourself, I would consider your circumstances; but, if I could believe you were supported by a party inimical to the government, and that they were to pay the fine, not you, I would go to the utmost extent of the power of the court. I understand you have a family, but you have not thought proper to state that to the court. From what I can gather from you, it appears that you depend on your profession for support; we do not wish to impose so rigorous a fine as to be beyond a person's abilities to support, but the government must be secured against these malicious attacks. You say that you are not conscious of having acted from malicious motives. It may be so; saying so, we must believe you; but, the jury have found otherwise. You are a gentleman of the profession, of such capacity and knowledge, as to have it more in your power to mislead the ignorant. I do not want to oppress, but I will restrain, as far as I can, all such licentious attacks on the government of the country.

Mr. Cooper. I have been asked by the court whether, in case of a fine being imposed upon me, I shall be supported by a party. Sir, I solemnly aver, that throughout my life, here and elsewhere, among all the political questions in which I have been concerned, I have never so far demeaned myself as to be a party writer. I never was in the pay or under the support of any party; there is no party in this, or any other country, that can offer me a temptation to prostitute my pen. If there are any persons here who are acquainted with what I have published, they must feel and be satisfied that I have had higher and better motives, than a party could suggest. I have written, to the best of my ability, what I seriously thought would conduce to the general good of mankind. The exertions of my talents, such as they are, have been unbought, and so they shall continue; they have indeed been paid for, but they have been paid for by myself, and by myself only, and sometimes dearly. The public is my debtor, and what I have paid or suffered for them, if my duty should again call upon me to write or to act, I shall again most readily submit to. I do not pretend to have no party opinions, to have no predilection for particular descriptions of men or of measures; but I do not act upon minor considerations; I belong here, as in my former country, to the great party of mankind. With regard to any offers which may have been made to me, to enable me to discharge the fine which

may be imposed, I will state candidly to the court what has passed, for I wish not to conceal the truth; I have had no previous communication or promise whatever. I have since had no specific promises of money or anything else. I wrote from my own suggestions. But, many of my friends have, in the expectation of a verdict against me, come forward with general offers of pecuniary assistance; these offers I have, hitherto, neither accepted nor rejected. If the court should impose a fine beyond my ability to pay, I shall accept them without hesitation; but if the fine be within my circumstances to discharge, I shall pay it myself. But the insinuations of the court are ill founded, and if you, sir, from misapprehension or misinformation have been tempted to make them, your mistake should be corrected.

PETERS, District Judge. I think we have nothing to do with parties; we are only to consider the subject before us. I wish you had thought proper to make an affidavit of your property. I have nothing to do, sitting here, to inquire whether a party in whose favour you may be, or you, are to pay the fine. I shall only consider your circumstances, and impose a fine which I think adequate; we ought to avoid any oppression. It appears that you depend chiefly upon your profession for support. Imprisonment for any time would tend to increase the fine, as your family would be deprived of your professional abilities to maintain them.

CHASE, Circuit Justice. We will take time to consider this. Mr. Cooper, you may attend here again.

Thursday, Mr. Cooper attended, and the court sentenced him to pay a fine of four hundred dollars; to be imprisoned for six months, and, at the end of that period, to find surety for his good behaviour, himself in a thousand, and two sureties in five hundred dollars each.

26

THOMAS JEFFERSON, FIRST INAUGURAL ADDRESS
4 Mar. 1801
Richardson 1:322–23

During the contest of opinion through which we have passed the animation of discussions and of exertions has sometimes worn an aspect which might impose on strangers unused to think freely and to speak and to write what they think; but this being now decided by the voice of the nation, announced according to the rules of the Constitution, all will, of course, arrange themselves under the will of the law, and unite in common efforts for the common good. All, too, will bear in mind this sacred principle, that though the will of the majority is in all cases to prevail, that will to be rightful must be reasonable; that the minority possess their equal rights, which equal law must protect, and to violate would be oppression. Let us, then, fellow-citizens, unite with one heart and one mind. Let us restore to social intercourse that harmony and affection without which liberty and even life itself are but dreary things. And let us reflect that, having banished from our land that religious intolerance under which mankind so long bled and suffered, we have yet gained little if we countenance a political intolerance as despotic, as wicked, and capable of as bitter and bloody persecutions. During the throes and convulsions of the ancient world, during the agonizing spasms of infuriated man, seeking through blood and slaughter his long-lost liberty, it was not wonderful that the agitation of the billows should reach even this distant and peaceful shore; that this should be more felt and feared by some and less by others, and should divide opinions as to measures of safety. But every difference of opinion is not a difference of principle. We have called by different names brethren of the same principle. We are all Republicans, we are all Federalists. If there be any among us who would wish to dissolve this Union or to change its republican form, let them stand undisturbed as monuments of the safety with which error of opinion may be tolerated where reason is left free to combat it. I know, indeed, that some honest men fear that a republican government can not be strong, that this Government is not strong enough; but would the honest patriot, in the full tide of successful experiment, abandon a government which has so far kept us free and firm on the theoretic and visionary fear that this Government, the world's best hope, may by possibility want energy to preserve itself? I trust not. I believe this, on the contrary, the strongest Government on earth. I believe it the only one where every man, at the call of the law, would fly to the standard of the law, and would meet invasions of the public order as his own personal concern. Sometimes it is said that man can not be trusted with the government of himself. Can he, then, be trusted with the government of others? Or have we found angels in the forms of kings to govern him? Let history answer this question.

Let us, then, with courage and confidence pursue our own Federal and Republican principles, our attachment to union and representative government.

27

St. George Tucker,
Blackstone's Commentaries, 1:App. 298–99,
2:App. 12–25, 27–30
1803

Our state bill of rights declares, that the freedom of the press is one of the great bulwarks of liberty, and can never be restrained but by despotic governments. The constitutions of most of the other states in the union contain articles to the same effect. When the constitution of the United States was adopted by the convention of Virginia, they inserted the following declaration in the instrument of ratification: "that among other essential rights, the liberty of conscience, and of the press, cannot be cancelled, abridged, restrained, or modified by any authority of the United States."

An ingenious foreigner seems to have been a good deal puzzled to discover the law which establishes the freedom of the press in England: after many vain researches, he concludes, (very rightly, as it relates to that government,) that the liberty of the press there, is grounded on its not being prohibited*. But with us, there is a visible solid foundation to be met with in the constitutional declarations which we have noticed. The English doctrine, therefore, that the liberty of the press consists only in this, that there shall be no previous restraint laid upon the publication of any thing which any person may think proper, as was formerly the case in that country, is not applicable to the nature of our government, and still less to the express tenor of the constitution. That this necessary and invaluable liberty has been sometimes abused, and "carried to excess; that it has sometimes degenerated into licentiousness, is seen and lamented; but the remedy has not been discovered. Perhaps it is an evil inseparable from the good to which it is allied; perhaps it is a shoot which cannot be stripped from the stalk, without wounding vitally the plant from which it is torn. However desirable those measures might be which correct without enslaving the press, they have never yet been devised in America†."

It may be asked; is there no protection for any man in America from the wanton, malicious, and unfounded attacks of envenomed calumny? Is there no security for his good name? Is there no value put upon reputation? No reparation for an injury done to it?

To this we may answer with confidence, that the judicial courts of the respective states are open to all persons alike, for the redress of injuries of this nature; there, no distinction is made between one individual and another; the farmer, and the man in authority, stand upon the same ground: both are equally entitled to redress for any false aspersion on their respective characters, nor is there any thing in our laws or constitution which abridges this right. But the genius of our government will not permit the federal legislature to interfere with the subject; and the federal courts are, I presume, equally restrained by the principles of the constitution, and the amendments which have since been adopted.

Such, I contend, is the true interpretation of the constitution of the United States: it has received a very different interpretation both in congress and in the federal courts.

. . . . .

In England during the existence of the court of star chamber, and after it's abolition, from the time of the long parliament to the year 1694, the liberty of the press, and the right of vending books, was restrained to very narrow limits, by various ordinances and acts of parliament; all books printed were previously licensed by some of the great offices of state, or the two universities, and all foreign books were exposed to a similar scrutiny before they

---

*De Lolme on the English constitution. 317. Phila. printed.

†Letter from the American envoys to the French minister of foreign affairs. This nervous passage bespeaks its author [John Marshall]; a gentleman who now fills the highest judicial office under the federal government.

were vended. No shopkeeper could buy a book to sell again, or sell any book, unless he were a licensed bookseller. By these and other restrictions the communication of knowledge was utterly subjected to the control of those, whose interest led them rather to promote ignorance than the knowledge of truth. In 1694, the parliament refused to continue these prohibitions any longer, and thereby, according to De Lolme, established the freedom of the press in England. But although this negative establishment may satisfy the subjects of England, the people of America have not thought proper to suffer the freedom of speech, and of the press to rest upon such an uncertain foundation, as the will and pleasure of the government. Accordingly, when it was discovered that the constitution of the United States had not provided any barrier against the possible encroachments of the government thereby to be established, great complaints were made of the omission, and most of the states instructed their representatives to obtain an amendment in that respect; and so sensible was the first congress of the general prevalence of this sentiment throughout America, that in their first session they proposed an amendment since adopted by all the states and made a part of the constitution; "that congress shall make no law abridging the freedom of speech, or of the press." And our state bill of rights declares, "that the freedom of the press is one of the great bulwarks of liberty, and cannot be restrained, but by despotic governments." And so tenacious of this right, was the convention of Virginia, by which the constitution of the United States was ratified, that they further declared, as an article of the bill of rights then agreed to, "that the people have a right to the freedom of speech, and of writing and publishing their sentiments; that the freedom of the press is one of the greatest bulwarks of liberty, and ought not to be violated[*]." Nay, so reasonably jealous were they of the possibility of this declaration being disregarded, as not forming a part of the constitution, at that time, that the following declaration is inserted in, and forms a part of, the instrument of ratification, viz. "That the powers granted under the constitution, being derived from the people of the United States, may be resumed by them, whensoever the same shall be perverted to their injury or oppression; and that, every power not granted thereby, remains with them, and at their will: that, therefore no right; of any denomination, can be cancelled, abridged, restrained, or modified by the congress, by the senate, or house of representatives, acting in any capacity; by the president, or any department, or officer of the United States, except in those instances where power is given by the constitution for those purposes: that among other essential rights, the liberty of conscience, and of the press, cannot be cancelled, abridged, restrained, or modified, by any authority of the United States[†]."

As this latter declaration forms a part of the instrument by which the constitution of the United States became obligatory upon the state, and citizens of Virginia; and as

the act of ratification has been accepted in that form; no principle is more clear, than that the state of Virginia is no otherwise bound thereby, than according to the very tenor of the instrument, by which she has bound herself. For as no free state can be bound to another, or to a number of others, but by it's own voluntary consent and act, so not only the evidence of that consent, but the nature and terms of it, can be ascertained only by recurrence to the very instrument, by which it was first given. And as the foregoing declaration not only constitutes a part of that instrument, but contains a preliminary protest against any extension of the enumerated powers thereby granted to the federal government, it could scarcely have been imagined, that any violation of a principle so strenuously asserted, and made, as it were, the sole ground of the pragmatic sanction, would ever have been attempted by the federal government.

But however reasonable such an expectation might have been, a very few years evinced a determination on the part of those who then ruled the public councils of the United States, to set at nought all such restraints. An act accordingly was passed by the congress, on the fourteenth of July 1798, whereby it was enacted, that "if any person shall write, print, utter or publish any false and malicious writing against the government of the United States, or either house of congress, or the president, with intent to defame them, or either of them, or to bring them or either of them into contempt, or disrepute; or to excite against them or either of them, the hatred of the good people of the United States, then such person, being thereof convicted before any court of the United States having jurisdiction thereof shall be punished by a fine not exceeding two thousand dollars, and by imprisonment not exceeding two years." The act was limited in it's duration to the third day of March, 1801, the very day on which the period for which the then president was elected, was to expire; and, previous to which the event of the next presidential election must be known.

The consequences of this act, as might have been foreseen, were a general astonishment, and dissatisfaction, among all those who considered the government of the United States, as a limited system of government; in it's nature altogether federal, and essentially different from all others which might lay claim to unlimited powers; or even to national, instead of federal authority. The constitutionality of the act was accordingly very generally denied, or questioned, by them. They alleged, that it is to the freedom of the press, and of speech, that the American nation is indebted for its liberty, it's happiness, it's enlightened state, nay more, for it's existence. That in these states the people are the only sovereign: that the government established by themselves, is for their benefit; that those who administer the government, whether it be that of the state, or of the federal union, are the agents and servants of the people, not their rulers or tyrants. . . . That these agents must be, and are, from the nature and principles of our governments, responsible to the people, for their conduct. That to enforce this responsibility, it is indispensibly necessary that the people should inquire into the conduct of their agents; that in this inquiry, they must,

[*]Bill of Rights agreed to by the convention of Virginia, by which the C. U. S. was adopted Art. 16.

[†]C. U. S. as ratified by the convention of Virginia.

or ought to scrutinize their motives, sift their intentions, and penetrate their designs; and that it was therefore, an unimpeachable right in them to censure as well as to applaud; to condemn or to acquit; and to reject, or to employ them again, as the most severe scrutiny might advise. That as no man can be forced into the service of the people against his own will and consent; so if any man employed by them in any office, should find the tenure of it too severe, because responsibility is inseparably annexed to it, he might retire: if he can not bear scrutiny, he might resign: if his motives, or designs, will not bear sifting; or if censure be too galling to his feelings, he might avoid it in the shades of domestic privacy. That if flattery be the only music to his ear, or the only balm to his heart; if he sickened when it is withheld, or turned pale when denied him; or if power, like the dagger of Macbeth, should invite his willing imagination to grasp it, the indignation of the people ought immediately to mark him, and hurl him from their councils, and their confidence forever. That if this absolute freedom of inquiry may be, in any manner, abridged, or impaired by those who administer the government, the nature of it will be instantly changed from a federal union of representative democracies, in which the people of the several states are the sovereign, and the administrators of the government their agents, to a consolidated oligarchy, aristocracy, or monarchy, according to the prevailing caprice of the constituted authorities, or of those who may usurp them. That where absolute freedom of discussion is prohibited, or restrained, responsibility vanishes. That any attempt to prohibit, or restrain that freedom, may well be construed to proceed from conscious guilt. That the people of America have always manifested a most jealous sensibility, on the subject of this inestimable right, and have ever regarded it as a fundamental principle in their government, and carefully engrafted in the constitution. That this sentiment was generated in the American mind, by an abhorrence of the maxims and principles of that government which they had shaken off, and a detestation of the abominable persecutions, and extrajudicial dogmas, of the still odious court of star-chamber; whose tyrannical proceedings and persecutions, among other motives of the like nature, prompted and impelled our ancestors to fly from the pestilential government of their native country, to seek an asylum here; where they might enjoy, and their posterity establish, and transmit to all future generations, freedom, unshackled, unlimited, undefined. That in our time we have vindicated, fought for, and established that freedom by our arms, and made it the solid, and immovable basis and foundation both of the state, and federal government. That nothing could more clearly evince the inestimable value that the American people have set upon the liberty of the press, than their uniting it in the same sentence, and even in the same member of a sentence, with the rights of conscience, and the freedom of speech. And since congress are equally prohibited from making any law abridging the freedom of speech, or of the press, they boldly challenged their adversaries to point out the constitutional distinction, between those two modes of discussion, or inquiry. If the unrestrained freedom of the press, said they,

be not guaranteed, by the constitution, neither is that of speech. If on the contrary the unrestrained freedom of speech is guaranteed, so also, is that of the press. If then the genius of our federal constitution has vested the people of the United States, not only with a censorial power, but even with the sovereignty itself; if magistrates are, indeed, their agents: if they are responsible for their acts of agency; if the people may not only censure whom they disapprove, but reject whom they may find unworthy; if approbation or censure, election or rejection, ought to be the result of inquiry, scrutiny, and mature deliberation; why, said they, is the exercise of this censorial power, this sovereign right, this necessary inquiry, and scrutiny to be confined to the freedom of speech? Is it because this mode of discussion better answers the purposes of the censorial power? Surely not. The best speech can not be heard, by any great number of persons. The best speech may be misunderstood, misrepresented, and imperfectly remembered by those who are present. To all the rest of mankind, it is, as if it had never been. The best speech must also be short for the investigation of any subject of an intricate nature, or even a plain one, if it be of more than ordinary length. The best speech then must be altogether inadequate to the due exercise of the censorial power, by the people. The only adequate supplementary aid for these defects, is the absolute freedom of the press. A freedom unlimited as the human mind; viewing all things, penetrating the recesses of the human heart, unfolding the motives of human actions, and estimating all things by one invaluable standard, truth; applauding those who deserve well; censuring the undeserving; and condemning the unworthy, according to the measure of their demerits.

In vindication of the act, the promoters and supporters of it, said, that a law to punish false, scandalous, and malicious writings against the government, with intent to stir up sedition, is a law necessary for carrying into effect the power vested by the constitution in the government of the United States, and consequently such a law as congress may pass. To which it was answered, that even were the premises true, it would not authorize congress to pass an act to punish writings calculated to bring congress, or the president into contempt or disrepute. Inasmuch as such contempt or disrepute may be entertained for them, or either of them, without incurring the guilt of sedition, against the government, and without the most remote design of opposing, or resisting any law, or any act of the president done in pursuance of any law: one or the other of which would seem necessary to constitute the offence, which this argument defends the right of congress to punish, or prevent.

It was further urged in vindication of the act, that the liberty of the press consists not in a licence for every man to publish what he pleases, without being liable to punishment for any abuse of that licence; but in a permission to publish without previous restraint; and, therefore, that a law to restrain the licentiousness of the press, cannot be considered as an abridgment of its liberty.

To which it was answered that this exposition of the liberty of the press, was only to be found in the theoretical writings of the commentators on the *English* government, where the liberty of the press rests upon no other ground, than that there is now no law which imposes any actual previous restraint upon the press, as was formerly the case: which is very different from the footing upon which it stands in the United States, where it is made a fundamental article of the constitutions, both of the federal and state governments, that no such restraint shall be imposed by the authority of either. . . . That if the sense of the state governments be wanting on the occasion, nothing can be more explicit than the meaning and intention of the state of Virginia, at the moment of adopting the constitution of the United States; by which it will clearly appear that it never was the intention of that state (and probably of no other in the union) to permit congress to distinguish between the liberty and licentiousness of the press; or, in any manner to "cancel, abridge, restrain, or modify" that inestimable right.

Thirdly it was alleged, that the act could not be unconstitutional because it made nothing penal, which was not penal before, being merely declaratory of the common law, viz. of England.

To this it was, among other arguments, answered. That the United States as a federal government have no common law. That although the common law of England, is, under different modifications, admitted to be the common law of the states respectively, yet the whole of the common law of England has been no where introduced: that there is a great and essential difference, in this respect, in the several states, not only in the subjects to which it is applied, but in the extent of its application. That the common law of one state, therefore, is not the common law of another. That the constitution of the United States has neither created it, nor conferred it upon the federal government. And, therefore, that government has no power or authority to assume the right of punishing any action, merely because it is punishable in England, or may be punishable in any, or all the states, by the common law.

The essential difference between the British government and the American constitutions was moreover insisted on, as placing this subject in the clearest light. In the former, the danger of encroachments on the rights of the people, was understood to be confined to the executive magistrate. The representatives of the people in the legislature are not only exempt themselves, from distrust, but are considered as sufficient guardians of the rights of their constituents against the danger from the executive. Hence it is a principle, that the parliament is unlimited in it's power, or, in their own language, is omnipotent. Hence too, all the ramparts for protecting the rights of the people, such as their *magna charta*, their bill of rights, &c. are not reared against the parliament, but against the royal prerogative. They are mere legislative precautions against executive usurpations. Under such a government as that, an exemption of the press from previous restraints, by licencers from the king, is all the freedom that can be secured to it, there: but, that in the United States the case is altogether different. The people, not the government, possess the absolute sovereignty. The legislature, no less than the executive, is under limitations of power. Encroachments are regarded as possible from the one, as well

as from the other. Hence in the United States, the great and essential rights of the people, are secured against legislative, as well as against executive ambition. They are secured, not by laws paramount to prerogative; but by constitutions paramount to laws. This security of the freedom of the press requires, that it should be exempt, not only from previous restraint by the executive, as in Great-Britain; but from legislative restraint also; and this exemption, to be effectual, must be an exemption, not only from the previous inspection of licencers, but from the subsequent penalty of laws. . . . A further difference between the two governments was also insisted on. In Great-Britain, it is a maxim, that the king, an hereditary, not a responsible magistrate, can do no wrong; and that the legislature, which in two thirds of it's composition, is also hereditary, not responsible, can do what it pleases. In the United States, the executive magistrates are not held to be infallible, nor the legislatures to be omnipotent; and both being elective, are both responsible. That the latter may well be supposed to require a greater degree of freedom of animadversion than might be tolerated by the genius of the former. That even in England, notwithstanding the general doctrine of the common law, the ministry, who are responsible to impeachment, are at all times animadverted on, by the press, with peculiar freedom. That the practice in America must be entitled to much more respect: being in most instances founded upon the express declarations contained in the respective constitutions, or bill of rights of the confederated states*. That even in those states where no such guarantee could be found, the press had always exerted a freedom in canvassing the merits, and measures of public men of every description, not confined to the limits of the common law. That on this footing the press has stood even in those states, at least, from the period of the revolution.

The advocates and supporters of the act alleged, fourthly; That had the constitution intended to prohibit congress from legislating at all, on the subject of the press, it would have used the same expressions as in that part of the clause, which relates to religion, and religious tests; whereas, said they, there is a manifest difference; it being evident that the constitution intended to prohibit congress from legislating at all, on the subject of religious establishments, and the prohibition is made in the most express terms. Had the same intention prevailed respecting the press, the same expression would have been used, viz. "Congress shall make no law respecting the press." They are not, however, prohibited, added they, from legislating at all, on the subject, but merely from abridging the liberty of the press. It is evident, therefore, said they, that congress may legislate respecting the press: may pass laws for it's regulation, and to punish those who pervert it into an

*See the Virginia bill of rights, Art. 12. Massachusetts, Art. 16. Pennsylvania, Art. 12. Delaware, Art. 23. Maryland, Art. 38. North-Carolina, Art. 15. South-Carolina, Art. 43. Georgia, Art. 61. The constitution of Pennsylvania, Art. 35, declares, "That the printing presses shall be free to every person who undertakes to examine the proceedings of the legislature or any part of the government. And, the bill of rights of Vermont, Art. 15, is to the same effect.

engine of mischief, provided those laws do not abridge it's liberty. A law to impose previous restraints upon the press, and not one to inflict punishment on wicked and malicious publications, would be a law to abridge the liberty of the press*.

To this it was answered, that laws to regulate, must, according to the true interpretation of that word, impose rules, or regulations, not before imposed; that to impose rules is to restrain; that to restrain must necessarily imply an abridgment of some former existing rights, or power: consequently, when the constitution prohibits congress from making any law abridging the freedom of speech, or of the press, it forbids them to make any law respecting either of these subjects. That this conclusion was an inevitable consequence of the injunction contained in the amendment, unless it could be shown, that the existing restraints upon the freedom of the press in the United States, were such as to require a remedy, by a law regulating (but not abridging) the manner in which it might be exercised with greater freedom and security. A supposition, which it was believed no person would maintain. That the necessary consequence of these things is, that the amendment was meant as a positive denial to congress, of any power whatever, on the subject.

As an evidence on this subject, which must be deemed absolutely conclusive, it was observed, That the proposition of amendments made by congress, is introduced in the following terms: "The conventions of a number of states, having, at the time of their adopting the constitution, expressed a desire, in order to prevent misconstruction, or abuse of its powers, that further declaratory and restrictive clauses should be added; and, as extending the ground of public confidence in the government, will best ensure the beneficent ends of it's institution:" which affords the most satisfactory and authentic proof, that the several amendments proposed, were to be considered as either declaratory, or restrictive; and whether the one or the other, as corresponding with the desire expressed by a number of states, and as extending the ground of public confidence in the government. That under any other construction of the amendment relating to the press, than that it declared the press to be wholly exempt from the power of congress . . . the amendment could neither be said to correspond with the desire expressed by a number of the states, nor be calculated to extend the ground of public confidence in the government. Nay more; that the construction employed to justify the "Sedition Act," would exhibit a phaenomenon without a parallel in the political world. It would exhibit a number of respectable states, as denying first that any power over the press was delegated by the constitution; as proposing next, that an amendment to it should explicitly declare, that no such power was delegated; and finally as concurring in an amendment actually recognizing, or delegating such a power.

But, the part of the constitution which seems to have been most recurred to, and even relied on, in defence of the act of congress, is the last clause of the eighth section of the first article, empowering congress "to make all laws which shall be necessary and proper for carrying into execution the foregoing powers, and all other powers vested by the constitution in the government of the United States, or in any department or officer thereof†."

To this it was answered, that the plain import of that clause is, that congress shall have all the incidental, or instrumental powers, necessary and proper for carrying into execution all the express powers; whether they be vested in the government of the United States, more collectively, or in the several departments, or officers thereof. That it is not a grant of new powers to congress, but merely a declaration, for the removal of all uncertainty, that the means of carrying into execution, those otherwise granted, are included in the grant. Whenever, therefore, a question arises concerning the constitutionality of a particular power, the first question is, whether the power be expressed in the constitution. If it be, the question is decided. If it be not expressed, the next inquiry must be, whether it is properly incidental to an express power, and necessary to its execution. If it be, it may be exercised by congress. If it be not, congress cannot exercise it. . . . That, if the sedition law be brought to this kind of test, it is not even pretended by the framers of that act, that the power over the press, which is exercised thereby, can be found among the powers expressly vested in congress. That if it be asked, whether there is any express power, for executing which, that act is a necessary and a proper power: the answer is, that the express power which has been selected, as least remote from that exercised by the act, is the power of "suppressing insurrections;" which is said to imply a power to prevent insurrections, by punishing whatever may lead, or tend to them. But it surely cannot, with the least plausibility, be said, that a regulation of the press, and the punishment of libels, are exercises of a power to suppress insurrections. That if it be asked, whether the federal government has no power to prevent, as well as punish, resistance to the laws; the proper answer is, that they have the power, which the constitution deemed most proper in their hands for the purpose. That congress has power, before it happens, to pass laws for punishing such resistance; and the executive and judiciary have a power to enforce those laws, whenever it does actually happen. That it must be recollected by many, and could be shewn to the satisfaction of all, that this construction of the terms "necessary and proper," is precisely the construction which prevailed during the discussions and ratifications of the constitution; and that it is a construction absolutely necessary to maintain their consistency with the peculiar character of the government, as possessed of particular and defined powers only; not of the general and indefinite powers vested in ordinary governments. That if this construction be rejected, it must be wholly immaterial, whether unlimited powers be exercised under the name of

---

*See the report of a committee of congress, to whom were referred several petitions for the repeal of the alien and sedition laws. February 25, 1799.

†See the report of a committee of congress, Feb. 25, 1799; and the answer of the senate and house of representatives of Massachusetts, (Feb. 9th and 13th, 1799), to the communications from the state of Virginia, on the subject of the alien and sedition laws.

unlimited powers, or be exercised under the name of un-limited means of carrying into execution limited powers.

To those who asked, if the federal government be des-titute of every authority for restraining the licentiousness of the press, and for shielding itself against the libellous attacks which may be made on those who administer it; the reply given was, that the constitution alone can answer the question: that no such power being expressly given; and such a power not being both necessary and proper to carry into execution any express power; but, above all, such a power being expressly forbidden by a declaratory amend-ment to the constitution, the answer must be, that the fed-eral government is destitute of all such authority*.

This very imperfect sketch may be sufficient to afford the student some idea of the magnitude and importance of a question, which agitated every part of the United States, almost to a degree of convulsion: the controversy not being confined to the closets of speculative politicians, or to the ordinary channels of discussion through the me-dium of the press; but engrossing the attention, and call-ing forth the talents and exertions of the legislatures of several of the states in the union, on the one hand, and of the federal government, and all its branches, legislative, executive, and judiciary, on the other. For no sooner had the act passed, than prosecutions were commenced against individuals in several of the states: they were conducted, in some cases, with a rigour, which seemed to betray a de-termination to convert into a scourge that, which it had been pretended was meant only to serve as a shield.

The state of Kentucky was the first which took the act under consideration, and by a resolution passed with two dissenting voices only, declared the act of congress not law, but altogether void, and of no force. The state of Virginia, though posterior to her younger sister in point of time, was not behind her in energy.

. . . . .

Answers were received from the legislatures of seven states, disapproving of the resolutions of Virginia and Kentucky, which had also been transmitted with a similar proposition. The general assembly of Massachusetts, alone, condescended to reason with her sister states; the others scarcely paid them the common respect that is held to be due from individuals, to each other. The assembly of Virginia at their next session, entered into a critical review and examination of their former resolutions, and sup-ported them by a train of arguments, and of powerful, convincing, and unsophistic reasoning, to which, probably, the equal cannot be produced in any public document, in any country†. They concluded this examination and re-view (which occupied more than eighty pages) with resolv-ing, "That having carefully and respectfully attended to

*In the preceding sketch of the arguments used to demonstrate the unconstitutionality of the act of congress, I have extracted a few of those contained in the report of the committee of the house of delegates of Virginia, agreed to by the house, Jan. 11, 1800, and afterwards concurred in by the senate. This most valu-able document is very long, and is incapable of being abridged, without manifest injury.

†See the report of the committee, on this subject, agreed to in the house of delegates, Jan. 11, 1800.

the proceedings of a number of the states, in answer to their former resolutions, and having accurately and fully re-examined and re-considered the latter, they found it to be their indispensible duty to adhere to the same, as founded in truth, as consonant with the constitution, and as conducive to its preservation; and more especially to be their duty, to renew, as they do hereby renew their protest against the alien and sedition acts, as palpable and alarm-ing infractions of the constitution."

Mean time, petitions had been presented to congress for the repeal of those obnoxious acts: on the 25th of Febru-ary 1799, congress agreed to the report of a committee advising them, that it would be inexpedient to repeal them. A majority of four members, only, prevailed on this occasion. During the session which succeeded, strenuous exertions were made for the continuance of the act com-monly called the sedition act, (the other concerning aliens, having expired:) After a severe struggle, the attempt failed, and the act was permitted to expire, at the same moment that put a period to the political importance of those, for whose benefit, alone, it seems to have been in-tended. . . . .

It may be asked, perhaps: is there no remedy in the United States for injuries done to the good fame and rep-utation of a man; injuries, which to a man of sensibility, and of conscious integrity, are the most grievous that can be inflicted; injuries, which when offered through the me-dium of the press, may be diffused throughout the globe, and transmitted to latest posterity; may render him odious, and detestable in the eyes of the world, his coun-try, his neighbours, his friends, and even his own family; may seclude him from society as a monster of depravity, and iniquity; and even may deprive him of sustenance, by destroying all confidence in him, and discouraging that commerce, or intercourse with him, which may be neces-sary to obtain the means?

Heaven forbid, that in a country which boasts of rational freedom, and of affording perfect security to the citizen for the complete enjoyment of all his rights, the most valu-able of all should be exposed without remedy, or redress, to the vile arts of detraction and slander! Every individual, certainly, has a right to speak, or publish, his sentiments on the measures of government: to do this without re-straint, control, or fear of punishment for so doing, is that which constitutes the genuine freedom of the press. The danger justly apprehended by those states which insisted that the federal government should possess no power, di-rectly or indirectly, over the subject, was, that those who were entrusted with the administration might be forward in considering every thing as a crime against the govern-ment, which might operate to their own personal disad-vantage; it was therefore made a fundamental article of the federal compact, that no such power should be exer-cised, or claimed by the federal government; leaving it to the state governments to exercise such jurisdiction and control over the subject, as their several constitutions and laws permit. In contending therefore for the absolute free-dom of the press, and its total exemption from all re-straint, control, or jurisdiction of the federal government, the writer of these sheets most explicitly disavows the most distant approbation of its licentiousness. A free press, conducted with ability, firmness, decorum, and impartiality, may be regarded as the chaste nurse of genuine liberty; but a press stained with falsehood, imposture, detraction, and personal slander, resembles a contaminated prostitute, whose touch is pollution, and whose offspring bears the foul marks of the parent's ignominy.

Whoever makes use of the press as the vehicle of his sentiments on any subject, ought to do it in such language as to shew he has a deference for the sentiments of others; that while he asserts the right of expressing and vindicating his own judgment, he acknowledges the obligation to submit to the judgment of those whose authority he cannot legally, or constitutionally dispute. In his statement of facts he is bound to adhere strictly to the truth; for any deviation from the truth is both an imposition upon the public, and an injury to the individual whom it may respect. In his restrictures on the conduct of men, in public stations, he is bound to do justice to their characters, and not to criminate them without substantial reason. The right of character is a sacred and invaluable right, and is not forfeited by accepting a public employment. Whoever knowingly departs from any of these maxims is guilty of a crime against the community, as well as against the person injured; and though both the letter and the spirit of our federal constitution wisely prohibit the congress of the United States from making any law, by which the freedom of speech, or of the press, may be exposed to restraint or persecution under the authority of the federal government, yet for injuries done the reputation of any person, as *an individual*, the state-courts are always open, and may afford ample, and competent redress, as the records of the courts of this commonwealth abundantly testify.

28

PEOPLE V. CROSWELL
3 Johns. Cas. 337 (N.Y. 1804)

An indictment was found against the defendant on a *libel*, at the general sessions of the peace in Columbia county, which was removed, by *certiorari*, into this court, in January term, 1803, and the issue of traverse thereon was tried, at the Columbia circuit, in July, 1803, before Mr. Chief Justice Lewis.

The indictment was as follows, to wit: "At a court of general sessions of the peace, holden, &c. It is represented that Harry Croswell, late of the city of Hudson, in the county of Columbia aforesaid, printer, being a malicious and seditious man, of a depraved mind and wicked and diabolical disposition, and also deceitfully, wickedly, and maliciously devising, contriving and intending, Thomas Jefferson, Esq., President of the United States of America, to detract from, scandalize, traduce, vilify, and to represent him, the said Thomas Jefferson, as unworthy the confidence, respect, and attachment of the people of the said

United States, and to alienate and withdraw from the said Thomas Jefferson, Esq., President as aforesaid, the obedience, fidelity, and allegiance of the citizens of the state of New York, and also of the said United States; and wickedly and seditiously to disturb the peace and tranquility, as well of the people of the state of New York, as of the United States; and also to bring the said Thomas Jefferson, Esq., (as much as in him the said Harry Croswell lay) into great hatred, contempt, and disgrace, not only with the people of the state of New York, and the said people of the United States, but also with the citizens and subjects of other nations; and for that purpose the said Harry Croswell did, on the ninth day of September, in the year of our Lord one thousand eight hundred and two, with force and arms, at the said city of Hudson, in the said county of Columbia, wickedly, maliciously, and seditiously, print and publish, and cause and procure to be printed and published, a certain scandalous, malicious, and seditious libel, in a certain paper or publication, entitled 'The Wasp;' containing therein, among other things, certain scandalous, malicious, inflammatory, and seditious matters, of and concerning the said Thomas Jefferson, Esq., then and yet being President of the United States of America, that is to say, in one part thereof, according to the tenor and effect following, that is to say: Jefferson (the said Thomas Jefferson, Esq., meaning,) paid Callender (meaning one James Thompson Callender) for calling Washington (meaning George Washington, Esq., deceased, late President of the said United States,) a traitor, a robber, and a perjurer; for calling Adams (meaning John Adams, Esq., late President of the said United States,) a hoary-headed incendiary, and for most grossly slandering the private characters of men who he (meaning the said Thomas Jefferson) well knew to be virtuous; to the great scandal and infamy of the said Thomas Jefferson, Esq., President of the said United States, in contempt of the people of the said state of New York, in open violation of the laws of the said state, to the evil example of all others in like case offending, and against the peace of the people of the state of New York, and their dignity."

The defendant applied to the judge, at the circuit, to put off the trial of the cause, on affidavit, which stated that James Thompson Callender, of the state of Virginia, was a material witness for the defendant, without the benefit of whose testimony the defendant could not, as he was advised, safely proceed to the trial of the cause; that the defendant expected to be able to prove, by the said witness, the *truth of the charge* set forth in the indictment, so far forth as this; that the said James Thompson Callender was the writer of a certain pamphlet called "The Prospect before us," and that he caused the same to be printed, which pamphlet contains the charges against Washington and Adams, as in the publication set forth in the indictment, &c., &c., and that Mr. Jefferson, well knowing the contents of the said publication, paid, or caused to be paid, to the said J. T. Callender, two several sums of 50 dollars each, one of which was prior to the publication of the said pamphlet, and the other subsequent to the publication thereof, as a reward, thereby showing his approbation thereof, &c., &c. That it had been wholly out of the power of the defendant to procure the voluntary attendance of the said Callender, at that court, though he had, at the last general sessions of the peace, and since, until a few days past, good reason to believe, that he would attend, as a witness, at the then court; and that the defendant expected to be able to procure the voluntary attendance of the said Callender at the next circuit court, to be held in the said county, &c., unless the court would grant a commission to examine the said Callender, upon the application of the defendant, which he intended to make, at the next term of the court, for that purpose.

The Chief Justice refused to put off the trial, on this affidavit. It was proved, on the part of the public prosecutor, that the defendant was editor of a newspaper entitled "The Wasp," a series of which were printed and published in the city of Hudson. In one of them (number 7,) was contained a piece, from which was extracted the matter charged in the indictment, as the libel, the whole of which piece was read by the prosecutor, in the following words: "Holt says, the burden of the federal song is, that Mr. Jefferson paid Callender for writing against the late administration. This is wholly false. The charge is explicitly this: Jefferson paid Callender for calling Washington a traitor, a robber and a perjurer; for calling Adams a hoary-headed incendiary, and for most grossly slandering the private characters of men whom he well knew were virtuous. These charges, not a democratic editor has yet dared, or ever will dare, to meet in an open and manly discussion." It was further proved, on the part of the prosecutor, that a file of The Wasp, from number 1 to number 12, inclusive, was purchased at the office where they had been printed; from number 1 to number 5 had been sold by the defendant, and the residue by one of the journeymen in his office. The prosecutor then called a witness, to prove the truth of the *innuendoes*; to this the counsel for the defendant objected; but the Chief Justice overruled the objection. The witness was examined and testified, that he understood the epithets Jefferson, Washington and Adams, mentioned in the alleged libel, to be as stated in the *innuendoes* in the indictment, and that he had seen similar charges, in other papers, previous to the publication in The Wasp; which was one of the reasons which induced his opinion, that the *innuendoes* were correct.

The prosecutor having rested on this evidence, the defendant offered to prove, that he had no agency in devising, writing, or inditing the publication in question, and that the same was handed to be printed to a person in his employ, and in his absence, without his knowledge. To the introduction of this testimony, the prosecutor objected, and the Chief Justice refused to receive the same, unless the defendant meant also to prove, that he was not privy to the printing and publication of the alleged libel. This the defendant's counsel did not offer to prove. The defendant's counsel proceeded to sum up the evidence, and read a paragraph in The Bee, a newspaper printed in Hudson by Holt, the person in the alleged libellous piece mentioned, to show that he declared the burden of the federal song to be such, as mentioned in the libel. Though this had not been previously proved or read in evidence, it was not objected to. In the course of the summing up,

on the part of the prosecution, the Attorney-General offered to read certain passages, from number 7 of "The Wasp," and the prospectus contained in the first number, which had not before been shown, or pointed out to the defendant's counsel, or read in evidence. To this, objections were made, but the Chief Justice decided that the prosecutor had a right to read such passages, from such numbers of The Wasp, as he thought fit. The Attorney-General accordingly read, in order to show the intent of the defendant in publishing the alleged libel to be such as charged in the indictment, from number 1 of The Wasp, the prospectus, and another piece from number 7, in neither of which passages was there anything alleged against Thomas Jefferson, in his private or official capacity. The Attorney-General further stated, that from an examination of every number of The Wasp, it would be manifest, that the intent of the defendant was malicious.

The judge charged the jury, among other things, that the rule of law which confined jurors to the consideration of facts alone, was strictly applicable to the case of libels, where the question of libel or no libel was an inference of law from the fact; and that it was, perhaps, the only case in which courts invariably regarded a general as a special verdict; and where they would, *ex mero motu*, arrest the judgment, if the law was with the defendant.

His honor then read to the jury the opinion of Lord Mansfield, in the case of The Dean of St. Asaph, (as reported in a note in 3 Term Rep. 428,) and charged them, that the law therein laid down was the law of this state; that it was no part of the province of a jury to inquire or decide on the intent of the defendant, or whether the publication in question was true, or false, or malicious; that the only questions for their consideration and decision were, first, whether the defendant was the publisher of the piece charged in the indictment; and, second, as to the truth of the *innuendoes*; that if they were satisfied as to these two points, it was their duty to find him guilty; that the intent of the publisher, and whether the publication in question was libellous or not, was, upon the return of the *postea*, to be decided *exclusively* by the court, and, therefore, it was not his duty to give any opinion to them, on these points; and accordingly no opinion was given.

A motion was made, in behalf of the defendant, for a new trial, on the following grounds:

1. Because the trial ought to have been put off, in order to give an opportunity to the defendant to procure the testimony in the affidavit mentioned.

2. That the piece alleged to be libellous, and which was read in evidence, from number 7 of The Wasp, is materially and substantially different from that charged in the indictment, and the piece so read is not libellous.

3. For the misdirection of the judge, in his charge to the jury, that in cases of libel, they were not the judges of law and fact; that in case of libel only, could a court set aside a general verdict of guilty; that the law laid down in the case of The Dean of St. Asaph, is the law of this state; that the intent was simply a question of law, and, therefore, not to be left to the jury, but to be decided exclusively by the court on the return of the *postea*; and that whether the piece in question was libellous or not, was not to be de-

cided by the jury; and because the judge did not, as he ought to have done, give his opinion to the jury, on the point last mentioned.

. . . . .

The following is a brief summary of the argument of [Alexander] Hamilton, in reply.

He said, that the two great questions that arose in the cause were: 1. Can the truth be given in evidence? 2. Are the jury to judge of the intent and the law? The first point might be more embarrassing, but the second was clear.

The liberty of the press consisted in publishing with impunity, truth with good motives, and for justifiable ends, whether it related to men or to measures. To discuss measures without reference to men, was impracticable. Why examine measures, but to prove them bad, and to point out their pernicious authors, so that the people might correct the evil by removing the men? There was no other way to preserve liberty, and bring down a tyrannical faction. If this right was not permitted to exist in vigor and in exercise, good men would become silent; corruption and tyranny would go on, step by step, in usurpation, until at last, nothing that was worth speaking, or writing, or acting for, would be left in our country.

But he did not mean to be understood as being the advocate of a press wholly without control. He reprobated the novel, the visionary, the pestilential doctrine of an unchecked press, and ill fated would be our country, if this doctrine was to prevail. It would encourage vice, compel the virtuous to retire, destroy confidence, and confound the innocent with the guilty. Single drops of water constantly falling may wear out adamant. The best character of our country, he to whom it was most indebted, and who is now removed beyond the reach of calumny, felt its corrosive effects. No, he did not contend for this terrible liberty of the press, but he contended for the right of publishing truth, with good motives, although the censure might light upon the government, magistrates, or individuals.

The check upon the press ought to be deposited, not in a permanent body of magistrates, as the court, but in an occasional and fluctuating body, the jury, who are to be selected by lot. Judges might be tempted to enter into the views of government, and to extend, by arbitrary constructions, the law of libels. In the theory of our government, the executive and legislative departments are operated upon by one influence, and act in one course, by means of popular election. How, then, are our judges to be independent? How can they withstand the combined force and spirit of the other departments? The judicial is less independent here than in England, and, of course, we have more reason, and stronger necessity, to cling to the trial by jury, as our greatest safety.

Men are not to be implicitly trusted, in elevated stations. The experience of mankind teaches us, that persons have often arrived at power by means of flattery and hypocrisy; but instead of continuing humble lovers of the people, have changed into their most deadly persecutors.

Lord Camden said, that he had not been able to find a satisfactory definition of a libel. He would venture, however, but with much diffidence, after the embarrassment which that great man had discovered, to submit to the court the following definition. *A libel is a censorious or ridiculing writing, picture or sign, made with a mischievous and malicious intent towards government, magistrates or individuals.* According to Blackstone, it is a malicious defamation made public, with intent to provoke or expose to public hatred and ridicule. The malice and intent enter into the essence of the crime, and must be proved, and are, accordingly, to be left to the jury, as parcel of the fact. The definition of Lord Coke does not oppose this result. He speaks of a libel, as having a tendency to break the peace. This, also, is a fact to be proved to the jury, for the tendency depends upon time, manner, circumstance, and must of necessity be a question of fact.

Texts taken from the holy scriptures and scattered among the people, may, in certain times, and under certain circumstances, become libellous, nay, treasonable. These texts are, then, innocent, libellous, or treasonable, according to the time and intent; and surely the time, manner, and intent are matters of fact for a jury. It is the intent that constitutes the crime. This is a fundamental principle of jurisprudence. . . . Whether crime or not, will always depend upon intent, tendency, quality, manner, &c., and these must be matters of fact for the jury. The law cannot adjudge a paper to be a libel, until a jury have found the circumstances connected with the publication.

But it is not only the province of the jury, in all criminal cases, to judge of the intent with which the act was done, as being parcel of the fact; they are also authorized to judge of the law as connected with the fact. In civil cases, the court are the exclusive judges of the law, and this arose from the nature of pleadings in civil suits; for anciently, matters of law arising in the defence, were required to be spread upon the record, by a special plea, and the jury were liable to an *attaint* for finding a verdict contrary to law. But in criminal cases, the law and fact are necessarily blended by the general issue, and a general verdict was always final and conclusive, both upon the law and the fact. Nor were the jury ever exposed to an *attaint* for a verdict in a criminal case; and this is decisive to prove that they had a concurrent jurisdiction with the court on questions of law; for where the law allows an act to be valid or definitive, it presupposes a legal and rightful authority to do it. This is a sure and infallible test of a legal power.

In England trial by jury has always been cherished, as the great security of the subject against the oppression of government; but it never could have been a solid refuge and security, unless the jury had the right to judge of the intent, and the law.

The jury ought undoubtedly to pay every respectful regard to the opinion of the court; but suppose a trial in a capital case, and the jury are satisfied from the arguments of counsel, the law authorities that are read, and their own judgment, upon the application of the law to the facts, (for the criminal law consists in general of plain principles,) that the law arising in the case is different from that which the court advances, are they not bound by their oaths, by their duty to their creator and themselves, to pronounce according to their own convictions? To oblige them, in such a case, to follow implicitly the direction of the court, is to make them commit perjury, and homicide, under the forms of law.

The case of the Seven Bishops, and Fuller's and Tuchin's Cases, are a series of precedents in favor of the right of the jury. The opposite precedents begin with Lord Raymond, but they have not been uniform nor undisputed. It has been constantly a floating and litigious question in Westminster Hall. A series of precedents only can form law. There can be no embarrassment in the court; they are at liberty to examine the question upon principles. The English declaratory act recites that doubts had existed, and being declaratory, it is evidence of the sense of the nation. The Marquis of Lansdowne observed, in the house of lords, that the same declaratory bill had been brought in twenty years before, and was then deemed unnecessary.

The question how far the truth is to be given in evidence, depends much on the question of intent; for if the intent be a subject of inquiry for the jury, the giving the truth in evidence is requisite as a means to determine the intent. Truth is a material ingredient in the evidence of intent. In the whole system of law there is no other case in which the truth cannot be shown; and this is sufficient to prove the proposition, which denies it in the present case, to be a paradox.

The Roman law permitted the truth to justify a libel. The ancient English statutes prove also, that in the root and origin of our law, falsity was an ingredient in the crime, and those statutes were declaratory of the common law. The ancient records and precedents prove the same thing, and they are the most authoritative evidence of the ancient law. In the celebrated case of the Seven Bishops, the court permitted the defendants to prove the truth of the facts stated in the petition. That case is also very important, in various views. It establishes the necessity of inquiring into the circumstances and intent of the act. It was an instance of a firm and successful effort to recall the principles of the common law, and was an important link in the chain of events that led on to the glorious aera of their revolution.

In *Fuller's Case*, Lord Holt allowed the defendant to go into proof of the truth of the charge. But while, he said, he advocated the admission of the truth, he subscribed to the doctrine of *Want's Case*, in Moore, that the truth ought only to be given in evidence, to determine *quo animo* the act was done. It ought not to be a justification in every case, for it may be published maliciously. It may be abused, to the gratification of the worst of passions, as in the promulgation of a man's personal defects or deformity.

The court of Star Chamber was the polluted source from whence the prosecutor's doctrine was derived. That is not the court from which we are to expect principles and precedents friendly to freedom. It was a most arbitrary, tyrannical and hated tribunal, under the control of a permanent body of magistrates, without the wholesome restraints of a jury. The Whigs in England, after the revolution, in order to prop up their power, adopted, as in *Franklin's Case*, the arbitrary maxims of that court which had been reprobated at the revolution; and this ought to serve as a monitory lesson to rulers at the present day, for such is the nature, progress and effect of the human passions.

The right of giving the truth in evidence, in cases of libels, is all-important to the liberties of the people. Truth is an ingredient in the eternal order of things, in judging of the quality of acts. He hoped to see the axiom, that truth was admissible, recognized by our legislative and judicial bodies. He always had a profound reverence for this doctrine, and he felt a proud elevation of sentiment in reflecting, that the act of congress, which had been the object of so much unmerited abuse, and had been most grossly misrepresented by designing men, established this great vital principle. It was an honorable, a worthy and glorious effort in favor of public liberty. He reflected also, with much pleasure, on the fact, that so illustrious a patriot as Mr. Jay had laid down, correctly and broadly, the power of the jury. These acts were monuments, were consoling vestiges of the wisdom and virtue of the administration and character that produced them.

He maintained that the common law applied to the United States. That the common law was principally the application of natural law to the state and condition of society.

That the constitution of the United States used terms and ideas which had a reference to the common law, and were inexplicable without its aid. That the definition of treason, of the writ of *habeas corpus*, of crimes and misdemeanors, &c., were all to be expounded by the rules of the common law. That the constitution would be frittered away or borne down by factions, (the evil *genu*, the pest of republics,) if the common law was not applicable. That without this guide, any political tenet or indiscretion might be made a crime or pretext to impeach, convict and remove from office the judges of the federal courts. That if we departed from common law principles, we would degenerate into anarchy, and become the sport of the fury of conflicting passions. The transition from anarchy was to despotism, to an armed master.

The real danger to our liberties was not from a few provisional troops. The road to tyranny will be opened by making dependent judges, by packing juries, by stifling the press, by silencing leaders and patriots. His apprehensions were not from single acts of open violence. Murder rouses to vengeance; it awakens sympathy, and spreads alarm. But the most dangerous, the most sure, the most fatal of tyrannies, was by selecting and sacrificing single individuals, under the mask and forms of law, by dependent and partial tribunals. Against such measures we ought to keep a vigilant eye, and take a manly stand. Whenever they arise, we ought to resist, and resist, till we have hurled the demagogues and tyrants from their imagined thrones. He concurred most readily with the learned counsel opposed to him, in the opinion that the English were a free, a gloriously free people. That country is free where the people have a representation in the government, so that no law can pass without their consent; and where they are secured in the administration of justice, by the trial by jury. We have gone further in this country into the popular principle, and he cordially united his prayers with the opposite counsel, that the experiment with us might be successful.

The question on the present libel ought to be again tried. It concerns the reputation of Mr. Jefferson. It concerned deeply the honor of our country. It concerned the fame of that bright and excellent character General Washington, in which he had left a national legacy of inestimable value.

He concluded, by recapitulating the substance of the doctrine for which he contended, in the following words:

"1. The liberty of the press consists in the right to publish, with impunity, truth, with good motives, for justifiable ends, though reflecting on government, magistracy, or individuals.

"2. That the allowance of this right is essential to the preservation of a free government; the disallowance of it fatal.

"3. That its abuse is to be guarded against by subjecting the exercise of it to the animadversion and control of the tribunals of justice; but that this control cannot safely be intrusted to a permanent body of magistracy, and requires the effectual co-operation of court and jury.

"4. That to confine the jury to the mere question of publication, and the application of terms, without the right of inquiry into the intent or tendency, reserving to the court the exclusive right of pronouncing upon the construction, tendency, and intent of the alleged libel, is calculated to render nugatory the function of the jury; enabling the court to make a libel of any writing whatsoever, the most innocent or commendable.

"5. That it is the general rule of criminal law, that the intent constitutes the crime; and that it is equally a general rule, that the intent, mind, or *quo animo*, is an inference of fact to be drawn by the jury.

"6. That if there are exceptions to this rule, they are confined to cases in which not only the principal fact, but its circumstances, can be, and are, specifically defined by statute or judicial precedent.

"7. That, in respect to libel, there is no such specific and precise definition of facts and circumstances to be found; that, consequently, it is difficult, if not impossible, to pronounce that any writing is *per se*, and exclusive of all circumstances, libellous; that its libellous character must depend on intent and tendency; the one and the other being matter of fact.

"8. That the definitions or descriptions of libels to be met with in the books, founded them upon some malicious or mischievous intent or tendency, to expose individuals to hatred or contempt, or to occasion a disturbance or a breach of the peace.

"9. That in determining the character of a libel, the truth or falsehood is, in the nature of things, a material ingredient, though the truth may not always be decisive; but being abused may still admit of a malicious and mischievous intent, which may constitute a libel.

"10. That, in the Roman law, one source of the doctrine of a libel, the truth, in cases interesting to the public, was given in evidence; that the ancient statutes, probably declaratory of the common law, make the falsehood an ingredient of the crime; that the ancient precedents in the courts of justice correspond, and that the precedents to this day charge a malicious intent.

"11. That the doctrine of excluding the truth, as immaterial, originated in a tyrannical and polluted source, in the court of Star Chamber; and though it prevailed a considerable length of time, yet there are leading precedents down to the revolution, and ever since, in which a contrary practice prevailed.

"12. That the doctrine being against reason and natural justice, and contrary to the original principles of the common law, enforced by statutory provisions, the precedents which support it deserve to be considered in no better light than as a *malus usus*, which ought to be abolished.

"13. That, in the general distribution of power, in any system of jurisprudence, the cognizance of law belongs to the court, of fact to the jury; that as often as they are not blended, the power of the court is absolute and exclusive. That, in civil cases, it is always so, and may rightfully be so exerted. That, in criminal cases, the law and fact being always blended, the jury, for reasons of a political and peculiar nature, for the security of life and liberty, are intrusted with the power of deciding both law and fact."

. . . . .

The following are the opinions of KENT, J., and LEWIS, Ch. J., as prepared, and intended to have been delivered by them.

KENT, J. The defendant was convicted, at the last circuit court in Columbia county, of printing and publishing a scandalous, malicious and seditious libel upon Thomas Jefferson, the President of the United States. . . .

1 The criminality of the charge in the indictment consisted in a malicious and seditious *intention*. (Hawk. tit. Libel, s. 1. 2 Wils. 403. 1 Esp. Cas. 228.) There can be no crime without an evil mind. . . . The simple act of publication, which was all that was left to the jury, in the present case, was not, in itself, criminal. It is the applications to times, persons and circumstances; it is the *particular* intent and tendency that constitutes the libel. Opinions and acts may be innocent under one set of circumstances, and criminal under another. This application to circumstances, and this particular intent, are as much *matters of fact*, as the printing and publishing. (Winne's Eunomus, dial. 3, s. 53.) Where an act, innocent in itself, becomes criminal, when done with a particular intent, that intent is the material *fact* to constitute the crime. (Lord Mansfield, 3 Term Rep. 429, in the note.) And I think there cannot be a doubt, that the mere publication of a paper is not, *per se*, criminal; for otherwise, the copying of the indictment by the clerk, or writing a friendly and admonitory letter to a father, on the vices of his son, would be criminal. The intention of the publisher, and every circumstance attending the act, must therefore be cognizable by the jury, as questions of fact. And if they are satisfied that the publication is innocent; that it has no mischievous or evil tendency; that the mind of the writer was not in fault; that the publication was inadvertent, or from any other cause was no libel, how can they conscientiously pronounce the defendant guilty, from the mere fact of publication? A verdict of *guilty*, embraces the whole charge upon the record, and are the jury not

permitted to take into consideration the only thing that constitutes the crime, which is the malicious intent? According to the doctrine laid down at the trial, all that results from a verdict of guilty is, that the defendant has published a certain paper, and that it applies to certain persons, according to the *innuendoes;* but whether the paper be lawful or unlawful; whether it be criminal, or innocent, or meritorious; whether the intent was wicked or virtuous, are matters of law which do not belong to the jury, but are reserved for the determination of the court. . . .

To deny to the jury the right of judging of the intent and tendency of the act, is to take away the substance, and with it the value and security of this mode of trial. It is to transfer the exclusive cognizance of crimes from the jury to the court, and to give the judges the absolute control of the press. There is nothing peculiar in the law of libels, to withdraw it from the jurisdiction of the jury. The twelve judges, in their opinion to the house of lords, (April, 1792,) admitted that the general criminal law of England was the law of libel. And by the general criminal law of England, the office of the jury is judicial. "They only are the judges," as Lord Somers observes, (Essay on the Power and Duty of Grand Juries, p. 7,) "from whose sentence the indicted are to expect life or death. Upon their integrity and understanding, the lives of all that are brought into judgment do ultimately depend. From their verdict there lies no appeal. They resolve both law and fact, and this has always been their custom and practice."

If the criminal intent be in this case an inference of law, the right of the jury is still the same. In every criminal case, upon the plea of not guilty, the jury may, and indeed they *must*, unless they choose to find a special verdict, take upon themselves the decision of the law, as well as the fact, and bring in a verdict as comprehensive as the issue; because, in every such case, they are charged with the deliverance of the defendant from the crime of which he is accused. The indictment not only sets forth the particular fact committed, but it specifies the nature of the crime. Treasons are laid to be done traitorously, felonies feloniously, and public libels to be published seditiously. . . . So in the case of a public libeller, the jury are to try, not only whether he published such a writing, but whether he published it *seditiously*. In all these cases, from the nature of the issue, the jury are to try not only the *fact*, but the *crime*, and in doing so they must judge of the *intent*, in order to determine whether the charge be true, as set forth in the indictment. (Dagge on Criminal Law, b. 1, c. 11, s. 2.) The law and fact are so involved, that the jury are under an indispensable necessity to decide both, unless they separate them by a special verdict.

This right in the jury to determine the law as well as the fact has received the sanction of some of the highest authorities in the law. . . .

To meet and resist directly this stream of authority, is impossible. But while the *power* of the jury is admitted, it is denied that they can *rightfully* or *lawfully* exercise it, without compromitting their consciences, and that they are bound implicitly, in all cases, to receive the law from the court. The law must, however, have intended, in granting

this power to a jury, to grant them a lawful and rightful power, or it would have provided a remedy against the undue exercise of it. The true criterion of a legal power is its capacity to produce a definitive effect liable neither to censure nor review. And the verdict of not guilty, in a criminal case, is, in every respect, absolutely final. . . .

The first case I have met with, in which the question arose between the jurisdiction of the court and jury, was upon the trial of Lilburne for high treason, in 1549. (2 St. Tr. 69, 81, 82.) He insisted, in coarse but intelligible language, that the jury were judges of law and fact, but the court, in language equally rude, denied it. He insisted upon the privilege of reading law to the jury, but the court refused it. The jury, however, acquitted him, and they declared that they took themselves to be judges of the law as well as of the fact, notwithstanding the court had said otherwise. *Bushell's Case* followed soon after, and it is in every view important. (Vaughan, 132. Sir T. Jones, 13.) He was one of the jurors, on the trial of an indictment for a misdemeanor, before the court of *oyer and terminer* in London, and was fined and committed, because he and the other jurors acquitted the defendant against full proof, *and against the direction of the court, in matter of law.* He was brought into the court of C. B. upon *habeas corpus* and discharged; and Lord Ch. J. Vaughan delivered, upon that occasion, in behalf of the court, a learned and profound argument in favor of the rights of the jury. He admitted that where the law and fact were distinct, the provinces of the court and jury were exclusive of each other, so that if it be demanded what is a fact, the judge cannot answer it, and if what is the law, the jury cannot answer it. But that upon all general issues, where the jury find a general verdict, they resolve both law and fact completely, and not the fact by itself.

Upon the trial of Algernon Sidney, (3 St. Tr. 817,) the question did not distinctly arise, but Lord Ch. J. Jeffries, in his charge to the jury, told them it was the duty of the court to declare the law to the jury, and *the jury were bound to receive their declaration of the law.* They did, in that case, unfortunately, receive the law from the court, and convicted the prisoner, but his *attainder* was afterwards reversed by parliament; and the law, as laid down on that trial, was denied and reprobated, and the violence of the judge, and the severity of the jury, held up to the reproach and detestation of posterity. The case of the Seven Bishops (4 St. Tr.) is a precedent of a more consoling kind; it was an auspicious and memorable instance of the exercise of the right of the jury to determine both the law and the fact. I shall have occasion to notice this case hereafter, and shall only observe for the present, that the counsel on the trial went at large into the consideration of the law, the intent and the fact; and although the judges differed in opinion, as to what constituted a libel, they all gave their opinions in the style of advice, not of direction, and expressly referred the law and the fact to the jury. Mr. J. Holloway, in particular, observed, that whether libel or not, depended upon the *ill intent*, and concluded by telling the jury, *it was left to them* to determine.

In the case of *Tuchin*, (5 St. Tr. 542,) who was tried for a libel before Ch. J. Holt, in 1704, the judge, in his charge to the jury, expressly submitted to them the whole question on the libel. After reasoning on the libellous nature of the publication, he observes that *now they are to consider whether the words he had read to them, did not tend to beget an ill opinion of the administration of the government.*

The weight of the decisions thus far, was clearly in favor of the right of the jury to decide generally upon the law and the fact. But, since the time of Lord Holt, the question before us has been an unsettled and litigious one in Westminster Hall. Lord Mansfield was of opinion (3 Term Rep. 429) that the formal direction of every judge, since the revolution, had been agreeable to that given in the case of the Dean of St. Asaph; but the earliest case he mentions is that of Franklin, before Lord Raymond, in 1751; (9 St. Tr. 255,) and that has been considered as the formal introduction of the doctrine now under review. The charge of Sir John Holt, in *Tuchin's Case*, appears to me to be decidedly to the contrary; and in another case before Holt, (11 Mod. 86, *Queen v. Brown*,) the attorney-general admitted that the jury were the judges *quo animo* the libel was made. The new doctrine, as laid down in the present case, may, therefore, be referred to the case of Franklin. But in *Oneby's Case*, (2 Ld. Raym. 1485; 2 Str. 766,) who was tried a few years before, for murder, Lord Raymond and the court of K. B. advanced a general doctrine, which may perhaps be supposed to curtail the power of the jury as much as the decision in the case before us. He said, that all the judges agreed in the proposition, that the court were the judges of the malice, and not the jury; that upon the trial the judge directs the jury, as to the law arising upon the facts, and the jury may, if they think proper, give a general verdict; or if they find a special verdict, the court is to form their judgment from the facts found, whether there was malice or not; because, in special verdicts, the jury never find, in express terms, the malice, but it is left to be drawn by the court.

The case to which this opinion applied, was that of a special verdict, and taking it together, I see nothing in it inconsistent with my view of the subject. . . .

. . . .To say that the jury cannot rightfully judge of the *malus animus* of the prisoner, in which his crime consists, is, in my opinion, a monstrous proposition, destructive of the essence and excellence of trial by jury, and inconsistent with the genius of the English judiciary, as drawn from its history and constitutional policy.

To return to the case of Franklin; the counsel for the defendant, who were very able lawyers, contended that the jury had a right to judge of the intent and tendency of the publication; but Lord Raymond, in his direction to the jury, went the whole length of the charge in the present case. He told the jury that there were two things only for their consideration; 1st. Whether the defendant was guilty of publishing; and, 2d. Whether the *innuendoes* were justly stated and applied, and that the third question, whether the publication was libellous, belonged exclusively to the court as matter of law. The same doctrine was laid down by Ch. J. Lee, in the case of Owen; (10 St. Tr. Appendix, 196,) by Sir Dudley Ryder, in the case of Nutt; and by Lord Mansfield, in the cases of Shebbeare, Woodfall and others. (5 Burr. 2661. 3 Term Rep. 430.) It is to be ob-

served, however, that in none of these cases did the counsel for the defendants renounce what they conceived to be the privilege of the defendants, and the right of the jury. Lord Camden was counsel for the defendants, in the cases of Owen and Shebbeare, and he claimed and exercised the right of addressing the jury, on the whole matter of the libel. (Parliamentary Senator, vol. 5, p. 822.) In the case of Woodfall, the defendant's counsel likewise pressed the jury to acquit him, on the ground that the intent was innocent, and the paper not libellous; and the counsel for the crown, on the other hand, urged to the jury the criminal intent and pernicious tendency of the paper. The same steps were followed by counsel, in the case of the Dean of St. Asaph. (3 Term Rep. 428.) This *uniform* practice of counsel of the first rank at the bar, is pretty strong evidence that the rule laid down in *Franklin's Case* was never acquiesced in, nor regarded as the settled law. But it was not the counsel only who dissented from this doctrine. Lord Camden and Lord Loughborough did, as judges, uniformly resist it, and one of them declared, that it had always been his practice, in cases of libel, to state the law as it bore on the facts, and to refer the combined consideration to the jury. (Senator, vol. 3, pp. 647, 650, 651; vol. 5, pp. 686, 822.) So Lord Mansfield departed from Lord Raymond's rule, upon the trial of John Horne. (11 St. Tr. 283.) He told the jury there were two points for them to satisfy themselves in, in order to form their verdict. 1st. Did the defendant compose and publish? 2d. Was the sense of the paper libellous, as charged? He concluded by telling them, that *they would judge of the meaning of it; that it was a matter for their judgment.* His lordship admits to us, in another place, (3 Term Rep. 418,) that the counsel for the crown and the judges have sometimes expatiated to the jury on the enormity of the libel, with the view to remove prejudices, and obviate captivating harangues; and this confession shows the difficulty and danger of attempting to separate the law and the fact, the publication and the intent, when the issue, the arguments of counsel, and the verdict, comprehended both.

The constant struggle of counsel and of the jury, against the rule, so emphatically laid down by Lord Raymond, the disagreement among the judges, and the dangerous tendency of the doctrine, as it affected two very conspicuous and proud monuments of English liberty, trial by jury, and the freedom of the press, at length attracted and roused the attention of the nation. The question was brought before the parliament, and debated in two successive sessions. (In 1791 and 1792, see Debates in the Senator, vols. 3, 4, 5.) There was combined, in the discussion of this dry law question, an assemblage of talents, of constitutional knowledge, of practical wisdom, and of professional erudition, rarely if ever before surpassed. It underwent a patient investigation and severe scrutiny, upon principle and precedent, and a bill *declaratory* of the right of the jury to give a general verdict upon the whole matter put in issue, without being required or directed to find the defendant guilty merely on the proof of publication and the truth of the *innuendoes*, was at length agreed to and passed with uncommon unanimity. It is entitled "An act to remove doubts respecting the functions of juries in cases of libel;"

and, although I admit, that a declaratory statute is not to be received as conclusive evidence of the common law, yet it must be considered as a very respectable authority in the case; and especially, as the circumstances attending the passage of this bill, reflect the highest honor on the moderation, the good sense, and the free and independent spirit of the British parliament.

It was, no doubt, under similar impressions of the subject, that the act of congress, for punishing certain libels against the United States, (Laws U. S. vol. 4, p. 204,) enacted and *declared* that the jury who should try the cause, should have a right to determine the law and fact, under the direction of the court, as in other cases; and before the passing of that statute, the same doctrine was laid down in full latitude, and in explicit terms, by the supreme court of the United States. (3 Dallas, 4.)

The result, from this view, is, to my mind, a firm conviction that this court is not bound by the decisions of Lord Raymond, and his successors. By withdrawing from the jury the consideration of the essence of the charge, they render their function nugatory and contemptible. Those opinions are repugnant to the more ancient authorities which had given to the jury the power, and with it the right, to judge of the law and fact, when they were blended by the issue, and which rendered their decisions, in criminal cases, final and conclusive. The English bar steadily resisted those decisions, as usurpations on the rights of the jury. Some of the judges treated the doctrine as erroneous, and the parliament, at last, declared it an innovation, by restoring the trial by jury, in cases of libel, to that ancient vigor and independence, by which it had grown so precious to the nation as the guardian of liberty and life, against the power of the court, the vindictive persecution of the prosecutor, and the oppression of the government.

I am aware of the objection to the fitness and competency of a jury to decide upon questions of law, and especially, with a power to overrule the directions of the judge. In the first place, however, it is not likely often to happen, that the jury will resist the opinion of the court on the matter of law. That opinion will generally receive its due weight and effect; and in civil cases it can, and always ought to be, ultimately enforced by the power of setting aside the verdict. But in human institutions, the question is not, whether every evil contingency can be avoided, but what arrangement will be productive of the least inconvenience. And it appears to be most consistent with the permanent security of the subject, that in criminal cases the jury should, after receiving the advice and assistance of the judge, as to the law, take into their consideration all the circumstances of the case, and the intention with which the act was done, and to determine upon the whole, whether the act done, be, or be not, within the meaning of the law. This distribution of power, by which the court and jury mutually assist, and mutually check each other, seems to be the safest, and, consequently, the wisest, arrangement, in respect to the trial of crimes. The constructions of judges on the intention of the party may often be (with the most upright motives) too speculative and refined, and not altogether just in their application to every case. Their

rules may have too technical a cast, and become, in their operation, severe and oppressive. To judge accurately of motives and intentions, does not require a master's skill in the science of law. It depends more on a knowledge of the passions, and of the springs of human action, and may be the lot of ordinary experience and sagacity.

My conclusion on this first point then, is, that upon every indictment or information for a libel, where the defendant puts himself upon the country, by a plea of not guilty, the jury have a right to judge, not only of the fact of the publication, and the truth of the *innuendoes*, but of the intent and tendency of the paper, and whether it be a libel or not; and, in short, of "the whole matter put in issue upon such indictment or information." (Stat. 32 Geo. III.) That in this, as in other criminal cases, it is the duty of the court, "according to their discretion, to give their opinion and direction to the jury on the matter in issue;" and it is the duty of the jury to receive the same with respectful deference and attention, and, unless they choose to find a special verdict, they are then to exercise their own judgments on the matter in issue, with discretion and integrity.

2. The second point in the case, although a question of evidence merely, is equally important, and still more difficult. It was made a very prominent point upon the argument, and the decision of it is essential for the direction of the judge who is to preside at the new trial that may be awarded.

As a libel is a defamatory publication, made with a malicious intent, the truth or falsehood of the charge may, in many cases, be a very material and pertinent consideration with the jury, in order to ascertain that intent. There can be no doubt that it is competent for the defendant to rebut the presumption of malice, drawn from the fact of publication; and it is consonant to the general theory of evidence, and the dictates of justice, that the defendant should be allowed to avail himself of every fact and circumstance that may serve to repel that presumption. And what can be a more important circumstance than the truth of the charge, to determine the goodness of the motive in making it, if it be a charge against the competency or purity of a character in public trust, or of a candidate for public favor, or a charge of actions in which the community have an interest, and are deeply concerned? To shut out wholly the inquiry into the truth of the accusation, is to abridge essentially the means of defence. It is to weaken the arm of the defendant, and to convict him, by means of a presumption, which he might easily destroy by proof that the charge was true, and that, considering the nature of the accusation, the circumstances and time under which it was made, and the situation of the person implicated, his motive could have been no other than a pure and disinterested regard for the public welfare. At the same time, this doctrine will not go to tolerate libels upon private character or the circulation of charges for seditious and wicked ends, or to justify exposing to the public eye one's personal defects or misfortunes. The public have no concern with, nor are they injured by such information, and the truth of the charge would rather aggravate than lessen the baseness and evil tendency of the publication. It will, therefore, still remain, in every case, a question for the jury, what was the intent and tendency of the paper, and how far the truth, in the given case, has been used for commendable, or abused for malicious purposes.

This principle in the law of libels is considered as rational and sound, in an ethical point of view; (Paley's Moral Philosophy, p. 188,) and to this extent, the writers on the civil law have allowed the truth to excuse a defamatory accusation. . . .

That falsehood is a material ingredient in a public libel, is a doctrine not without precedent in former times; it has always been asserted, and occasionally admitted, by the English courts. In this country it has taken firmer root, and in regard to the measures of government, and the character and qualifications of candidates for public trust, it is considered as the vital support of the liberty of the press.

The English decisions on the subject of libels have not been consistent in principle. The reason assigned for the punishment of libels, whether true or false, is because they tend to a breach of the peace, by inciting the libelled party to revenge, or the people to sedition. It is not the matter, but the manner, say the books, which is punishable. (1 Hawk. tit. Libel, s. 3, 6, 7. Hudson on the Star Chamber, p. 102.) This reason, however, according to some late decisions, is made to yield to stronger reasons of a public nature, although the instances given come equally within the rule, as they equally tend to defame and provoke. It is no libel to publish a true account of proceedings in parliament or courts of justice, notwithstanding the paper may be very injurious to the character of individuals or of magistrates; because those proceedings are open to all the world, and it is of vast importance to the public, that they should be generally known. (8 Term Rep. 297, 298; 1 Bos. & Pull. 226.) It was held no libel to treat with asperity the character of the officers of Greenwich hospital, where the publication was distributed only among the governors of the hospital, because they are the persons who, from their situation, are called upon to redress the grievance, and have the power to do it. (*Rex* v. *Baillie*, Mich. 20 Geo. III, by Lord Mansfield. Esp. Dig. 506.) It might be easily perceived, that according to the same doctrine, it ought not to be a libel to publish generally a true account of the character and conduct of public rulers, because it is of vast importance that their character and actions should be accurately understood, and especially by the public, to whom alone they are responsible. This rule of decision, in the different cases, varies, but the principle applies equally to each.

The doctrine that the truth of the matter charged was no defence to a public prosecution for a libel, came from the court of Star Chamber. William Hudson, who was an eminent practiser in that court, in the reign of James I., compiled, early under his successor, a very copious and learned treatise on its jurisdiction and practice. (See 2 Collectanea Juridica.) He says, that libels had in all ages been severely punished there, but especially when they began to grow frequent, about the reign of Elizabeth. This fact would lead to interesting reflection. The era here referred to, was the very time when the use of printing had grown familiar, when learning was disseminated, when civil and political rights became objects of inquiry, and, to use the words of Mr. Hume, when "symptoms had appeared of a more free and independent genius in the nation." Hudson cites upwards of twenty adjudged cases, in the Star Chamber, upon libels, and says that there were two gross errors, which had crept into the world concerning libels, one of which was, that it was not a libel, if true, but this, he adds, had been long since expelled out of that court; and he mentions the case of *Breverton*, (Mich. 2 Jac. I.) in which that species of defence was attempted to a charge of bribery and extortion in a public trust, and was overruled. This treatise of Hudson establishes two very important facts; the one that the court of Star Chamber established the doctrine in question, and the other, that it was still the public sentiment, which he calls "a gross error in the world," that the truth might be a defence to a libel; and this defence was attempted in that court as late as the reign of James. Mr. Barrington (Observations on the Statutes, 68,) has given us a part of a curious letter, written at that time by the Dean of St. Paul's, from which we may infer his alarm and disgust at the new libel doctrines of the Star Chamber. "There be many cases," he observes, "where a man may do his country good service, by libelling; for where a man is either too great, or his vices too general to be brought under a judiciary accusation, there is no way but this extraordinary method of accusation. *Sealed letters in the Star Chamber have nowadays been judged libels.*" Lord Coke has reported some of those Star Chamber decisions, on this very subject, and in one of which we find the same point resolved, that had been ruled the year before in the case of *Breverton*, (Pasch. 3 Jac. I.; 5 Co. 125.) He was, in his time, says Hudson, as well exercised in the case of libels, as all the attorneys that ever were before him; and yet it appears he was not so well disciplined in the new doctrine, but that in the case of *Lake* v. *Hutton*, (Hob. 252,) which afterwards arose in the Star Chamber, he insisted, that if the libel was true, the defendant might justify it. These cases and facts are sufficient to show that the doctrine in question was not considered then as the settled law; that it was regarded as an innovation, for it gave dissatisfaction, and met with opposition.

The proceedings in the star chamber were according to the course of those courts which follow the civil law. They proceeded by bill, without a jury, and compelled the party accused to answer upon oath. The decisions of that court upon libels, were probably borrowed, in a great degree, from Justinian's code. The very definition of a libel, and the title of one of Coke's cases, was taken from thence, and *Halliwood's Case*, in the 43 and 44 Eliz. (5 Co. 125, 126, a.) was grounded entirely upon the severe edict of Valentinian and Valens. (Code lib. 9, tit. 36.) And yet there is good reason to believe, that in the best ages of the Roman law, it spoke a milder and more rational language; for Paulus, in the Digest, (lib. 47, tit. 10, c. 18,) holds it to be against good conscience, to condemn a man for publishing the truth; and the civilians are generally of opinion, that the truth will excuse defamation, if the charge relate to matter proper for public information. (Vinnius, ubi supra, Perezii Praelec. vol. 2, 208.)

Mr. Barrington, who is so well known to the profession

as a legal antiquarian, admits (Observations on the Statutes, 68,) that the rule of refusing evidence of the truth of a libel, was adopted by the more modern determination of the common law courts, from the star chamber decisions. And if we recur back to the more ancient English statutes and records, which are the highest evidence of the common law, we shall find that the falsity of the charge was always made a material ingredient in the libel. . . .

Sir E. Coke, in his Commentary on the statute of Westm. 1, (2 Inst. 226,) uniformly describes the offence, by the epithets *false* and *feigned*; and he says, that no punishment was inflicted by this statute, upon the devisor or inventor himself of such false scandal, but he was left to the common law to be punished according to the offence which was aggravated, inasmuch as it was prohibited by statute. This passage shows conclusively, that in the opinion of Coke, this statute was in affirmance of the common law, and this was the opinion of *Atkins*, J., in the case of *Townsend* v. *Hughes*, (2 Mod. 151, 152.) This statute is, therefore, a very sure index of the meaning of defamation at common law; and as a further evidence on the subject, I refer to Fleta, (lib. 2, c. 1, s. 10,) which was written under Edw. I., and was a treatise upon the whole law, as it then stood. It is there stated that there are certain atrocious injuries which are punished by imprisonment, such as the inventors of evil rumors, (*sicut de inventoribus malorum rumorum*,) by whom the public peace is destroyed.

The form of the record of a conviction of one John Northampton in the K. B., for a libellous letter upon the court, is given by Coke, in his 3d Institute (p. 174.) The defendant confessed a libel, and was imprisoned and bound to his good behavior, and the record stated that the libel was false: *quae litera continet in se nullam veritatem.* The records of the courts have always been esteemed as the most authentic memorials of the law; and it is an important fact, which may now be noticed, that the indictments for libels have always charged the libel to be *false*, as well as malicious; and it was not until very lately that this epithet has been omitted. (7 Term Rep. 4.) I am aware that it has been said, (9 St. Tr. 302,) that the falsehood of the libel was not the ground of the judgment in this case of Northampton; but I see no reason for that assertion, for the words could have no other use or meaning upon the record; and it is absurd to suppose they were inserted by the judges, in order to acquit themselves to the king.

It appears clear, from this historical survey, that the doctrine now under review, originated in the court of Star Chamber, and was introduced and settled there about the beginning of the reign of James I. . . .

After the abolition of the Star Chamber under Charles I. we hear very little of the doctrine of libels, till we have followed the judicial precedents down to the era of the revolution. During the reign of the Stuarts, the press was stifled by the *imprimaturs* of government, which were first introduced by the acts of uniformity and borrowed from the inquisition. (1 Bl. Rep. 114, 115. 4 Bl. Comm. 152, note.) After the Star Chamber had ceased, the parliament subjected all publications to the arbitrary control of a license. Whoever has the curiosity to examine the licensing act of 13 and 14 Car. II. c. 33, will at once perceive that

there was no longer any need, either of the jurisdiction or doctrines of the Star Chamber, to control seditious and libellous publications. The case of the seven bishops (4 St. Tr.) is the first instance in which the new doctrine of libel was brought into the court of K. B. and submitted to the test of a jury; and here we consult once more the genuine oracles of the common law, and although their responses may not be altogether consistent or unequivocal, we listen to them with delight and instruction. On this trial, the Attorney-General contended that it was not to be made a question, whether the libel was true or false, and he grounded himself entirely upon the decisions in the Star Chamber, as he cited no other. But the counsel for the defendants, under the permission of the court, went at large into argument and proof, to show the dispensing power of the crown illegal, and that the allegation in the petition was true. And when the judges came to charge the jury, which they did separately, two of them were of opinion that the petition was a libel, and that whether true or false, was immaterial. The third judge placed the question altogether upon the *quo animo* of the defendants, but the fourth judge (Mr. Justice Powell) told the jury, that to make a libel, it must be *false*, it must be malicious, and it must tend to sedition; and that if there was no dispensing power in the king, which he believed, then it was no libel to say that the king's declaration was illegal. The jury were of his opinion, and acquitted the defendants.

The next case that meets our attention is that of Fuller, (5 St. Tr. 442, 444; 8 St. Tr. 78,) who was tried before Lord Ch. J. Holt, on an information for a libel upon the government; and when the defendant came to his defence, being without counsel, the Chief Justice asked him, in these words: "Can you make it appear that these books are true? If you take it on you to write such things as you are charged with, it lies upon you to prove them, at your peril. These persons are scandalized, if you produce no proof of what you charge them with. If you can offer any matter to prove what you have written, let us hear it. If you have any witnesses, produce them." Nothing can be plainer or more decisive than this language of the Ch. J. To do away the force of this case, it has been urged (9 St. Tr. 303,) that Fuller was prosecuted as a cheat and impostor. But the information says no such thing. The charge is expressly laid to consist in publishing two *false, scandalous and defamatory libels*. The judge calls them libels, and charges the jury to convict him of publishing the scandalous books. . . .

After this we meet only with two *dicta*, the one of Holt himself, and the other of Ch. J. Pratt, (11 Mod. 99, Str. 498,) declaring generally, that the truth was no justification on an indictment for a libel, until we come to Franklin's Case, in 1731. (9 St. Tr. 269.) There the defendant's counsel (Mr. Bootle and Sir J. Strange) offered evidence to prove the libel true, but Lord Ch. J. Raymond overruled the evidence, and observed, that it was not material whether the facts charged in the libel were true or false. "Then I submit," replies Mr. Bootle, "whether this will not tend to the utter suppression of the liberty of the press, which has been so beneficial to the nation. As the Star Chamber is now abolished, I don't know how far that doctrine may be adhered to. I should be glad to have one instance or authority of this, where a publisher of news is not allowed to say this piece of news is true. Is there no distinction to be made between false news and true news, and cannot we now animadvert or take notice of public affairs as well as formerly?" The attorney-general, although thus pressed for his authorities, produced no case to the point, but the case *de libellis famosis*, in 5 Coke; and he laid down a doctrine totally incompatible with any freedom of the press, which was, that a printer may lawfully print what belongs to his own trade, but he is not to publish anything reflecting on the character and reputation and administration of his majesty or his ministers.

It is a little remarkable, that the prohibition to the jury to judge of the criminality of the libel, and the prohibition to the defendant to give the truth in evidence, received together their first authoritative sanction in a court of common law, by this *nisi prius* decision of Lord Raymond. It seems, however, to have been acquiesced in, and to have been, from that time, generally taken as a law, without further inquiry or examination. And yet upon the trial of John Horne, (11 St. Tr. 283), before Lord Mansfield, upon an information, for a libel, in charging the king's troops with murdering the Americans, at Lexington, the defendant was permitted to call witnesses to prove the truth of the libel; and the Attorney-General, (Thurlow,) in his reply, observed, that the defendant was to prove the charge, and that it was the first hour that it ever entered his imagination, that that species of proof could be allowed. Lord Mansfield, in charging the jury, observed that, if it was a criminal arraignment of the king's troops, they would find their verdict one way; but that if they were of opinion that the contest was to reduce innocent subjects to slavery, and that they were all murdered, why then they might form a different conclusion with regard to the meaning and application of the paper.

This case, and the others I have mentioned, show that the admission of the truth in evidence, and that the jury are to judge of the intent, have been considered as very much connected together, and have shared the same fate. In this case of Horne, Lord Mansfield placed the question undoubtedly on its true ground, which is, that if the libel be false, the jury are to conclude one way, but if true, they may then form a different conclusion as to the meaning and application of the libel.

In addition to this case, there are decisive proofs that the opinions even of the highest professional characters were unsettled and at variance, so late as the year 1792, on this interesting and litigious question. It was one of the questions proposed, in that year, by the house of lords to the judges; and Lord Kenyon, (Senator, vol. 5, p. 684,) after vindicating the practice of the courts as to the control of the jury, said, that the only doubt in practice was, whether the truth should be taken as part of the defence, and that he thought a clause to determine that point would be necessary to the bill. Lord Camden (Senator, vol. 3, p. 649,) went further and made a vigorous and eloquent defence of the freedom of the press. "A paper," he observed, "that tended to excite sedition, was libellous; but a paper that reflected upon the conduct of the ministry, that

pointed out their base and mischievous proceedings, that went to open the eyes of the world, ought not to be considered as libellous. The jury must judge of the seditious tendency of the libel. Some would have every censure on the measures of government a libel. If this were the case, the voice of truth would cease to be heard amidst the notes of adulation. *It ought to be left to a jury to decide, whether what was called calumny, was well or ill founded.*"

I have thus shown, that the rule denying permission to give the truth in evidence, was not an original rule of the common law. The ancient statutes and precedents, which are the only memorials to which we can resort, all place the crime on its falsity. The court of Star Chamber originated the doctrine, and it was considered an innovation. When it was brought into a court of common law, it was resisted and denied; the court dared not practice upon it, and the jury gave it their negative. Lord Holt totally disregarded the rule, in the case of Fuller; and it did not become an express decision of a court of common law till Franklin's case, in 1731; and there the counsel made a zealous struggle against it, as new, dangerous and arbitrary. In the trial of Horne, Lord Mansfield laid the rule aside, and the counsel for the crown rejoiced at an opportunity to meet the defendant upon the merits of the accusation. In 1792, it was made a questionable point, in the house of lords, and one of the highest law characters in the house seems to have borne his testimony against it. I feel myself, therefore, at full liberty to examine this question upon principle, and to lay the doctrine aside, if it shall appear unjust in itself or incompatible with public liberty, and the rights of the press.

But, whatever may be our opinion on the English law, there is another and a very important view of the subject to be taken, and that is with respect to the true standard of the freedom of the American press. In England they have never taken notice of the press in any parliamentary recognition of the principles of the government, or of the rights of the subject, whereas the people of this country have always classed the freedom of the press among their fundamental rights. This I can easily illustrate by a few examples.

The first American congress, in 1774, in one of their public addresses, (Journals, vol. 1, p. 57,) enumerated five invaluable rights, without which a people cannot be free and happy, and under the protecting and encouraging influence of which these colonies had hitherto so amazingly flourished and increased. One of these rights was the *freedom of the press*, and the importance of this right consisted, as they observed, "besides the advancement of truth, science, morality, and arts in general, in its diffusion of liberal sentiments on the administration of government, its ready communication of thoughts between subjects, and its consequential promotion of union among them, whereby oppressive officers are shamed or intimidated into more honorable and just modes of conducting affairs." The next high authority I shall mention, is the Convention of the people of this state, which met in 1788. They declared unanimously, (Journals, pp. 44, 51, 52, 73, 74,) that the freedom of the press was a right which could not be abridged or violated. The same opinion is contained in the amendment to the constitution of the United States, and to which this state was a party. It is also made an article in most of the state constitutions, that the liberty of the press was essential to the security of freedom, and ought to be inviolably preserved; and in two of those constitutions, (Pennsylvania and Ohio,) this freedom of the press is specifically defined, by saying that in prosecutions for any publications, respecting the official conduct of men in a public capacity, or where the matter is proper for public information, the truth may always be given in evidence. I shall mention, lastly, the act of congress, of the 14th July, 1798, which prescribed penalties for certain specified libels upon the government of the United States, and allowed the truth to be given in evidence, on every prosecution under that act; and it is worthy of notice that the part of the act allowing the truth to be given in evidence, was *declaratory*, and thereby conveyed the sense of congress that such was the already existing law.

These multiplied acts and declarations are the highest, the most solemn, and commanding authorities, that the state or the nation can produce. They are generally the acts of the people themselves, when they came forward in their original character, to change the constitution of the country, and to assert their indubitable rights. And it seems impossible that they could have spoken with so much explicitness and energy, if they had intended nothing more than that restricted and slavish press, which may not publish anything, true or false, that reflects on the character and administration of public men. Such is the English doctrine of the liberty of the press, as asserted in Franklin's Case. (See also, Hawk. tit. Libels, 7.) A treatise on hereditary right has been held a libel, although it contained no reflections on any part of the subsisting government. (*Queen* v. *Bedford*, Str. 189; Gilbert's Rep. K. B. 297.) And if the theory of the prevailing doctrine in England, (for even there it is now scarcely anything more than theory,) had been strictly put in practice with us, where would have been all those enlightened and manly discussions which prepared and matured the great events of our revolution, or which, in a more recent period, pointed out the weakness and folly of the confederation, and roused the nation to throw it aside, and to erect a better government upon its ruins? They were, no doubt, libels upon the existing establishments, because they tended to defame them, and to expose them to the contempt and hatred of the people. They were, however, libels founded in truth, and dictated by worthy motives.

I am far from intending that these authorities mean, by the freedom of the press, a press wholly beyond the reach of the law, for that would be emphatically *Pandora's box, the source of every evil*. And yet the house of delegates in Virginia, by their resolution of the 7th January, 1800, and which appears to have been intended for the benefit and instruction of the union, came forward as the advocates of a press totally unshackled, and declare, in so many words, that "the baneful tendency of the *sedition act* was but little diminished by the privilege of giving in evidence the truth of the matter contained in political writings." They seem also to consider it as the exercise of a pernicious influence, and as striking at the root of free discussion, to punish,

even for a *false and malicious* writing, published *with intent* to defame those who administer the government. If this doctrine was to prevail, the press would become a pest, and destroy the public morals. Against such a commentary upon the freedom of the American press, I beg leave to enter my protest. The founders of our governments were too wise and too just, ever to have intended, by the freedom of the press, a right to circulate falsehood as well as truth, or that the press should be the lawful vehicle of malicious defamation, or an engine for evil and designing men, to cherish, for mischievous purposes, sedition, irreligion, and impurity. Such an abuse of the press would be incompatible with the existence and good order of civil society. The true rule of law is, that the intent and tendency of the publication is, in every instance, to be the substantial inquiry on the trial, and that the truth is admissible in evidence, to explain that intent, and not in every instance to justify it. I adopt, in this case, as perfectly correct, the comprehensive and accurate definition of one of the counsel at the bar, (Gen. Hamilton,) *that the liberty of the press consists in the right to publish, with impunity, truth, with good motives, and for justifiable ends, whether it respects government, magistracy, or individuals.*

THOMPSON, J., concurred in the opinion of Kent. LEWIS, Ch. J., reviewing the same English authorities came to the conclusion that the law required the affirmance of the conviction.

29

THOMAS JEFFERSON TO JOHN NORVELL
14 June 1807
Works 10:417–18

To your request of my opinion of the manner in which a newspaper should be conducted, so as to be most useful, I should answer, "by restraining it to true facts & sound principles only." Yet I fear such a paper would find few subscribers. It is a melancholy truth, that a suppression of the press could not more compleatly deprive the nation of it's benefits, than is done by it's abandoned prostitution to falsehood. Nothing can now be believed which is seen in a newspaper. Truth itself becomes suspicious by being put into that polluted vehicle. The real extent of this state of misinformation is known only to those who are in situations to confront facts within their knolege with the lies of the day. I really look with commiseration over the great body of my fellow citizens, who, reading newspapers, live & die in the belief, that they have known something of what has been passing in the world in their time; whereas the accounts they have read in newspapers are just as true a history of any other period of the world as of the present, except that the real names of the day are affixed to their fables. General facts may indeed be collected from them, such as that Europe is now at war, that Bonaparte has been a successful warrior, that he has subjected a great portion of Europe to his will, &c., &c.; but no details can be relied on. I will add, that the man who never looks into a newspaper is better informed than he who reads them; inasmuch as he who knows nothing is nearer to truth than he whose mind is filled with falsehoods & errors. He who reads nothing will still learn the great facts, and the details are all false.

Perhaps an editor might begin a reformation in some such way as this. Divide his paper into 4 chapters, heading the 1st, Truths. 2d, Probabilities. 3d, Possibilities. 4th, Lies. The first chapter would be very short, as it would contain little more than authentic papers, and information from such sources as the editor would be willing to risk his own reputation for their truth. The 2d would contain what, from a mature consideration of all circumstances, his judgment should conclude to be probably true. This, however, should rather contain too little than too much. The 3d & 4th should be professedly for those readers who would rather have lies for their money than the blank paper they would occupy.

30

UPDEGRAPH V. COMMONWEALTH
11 Serg. & Rawle 394 (Pa. 1824)

DUNCAN, J. This was an indictment for blasphemy, founded on an act of assembly, passed in 1700, which enacts, that whosoever shall wilfully, premeditatedly, and despitefully blaspheme, and speak loosely and *profanely* of Almighty God, Christ Jesus, the Holy Spirit, or the Scriptures of Truth, and is legally convicted thereof, shall forfeit and pay the sum of *ten pounds.*

It charges the defendant with contriving and intending to scandalize and bring into disrepute, and vilify the Christian Religion, and the Scriptures of Truth; and that he, in the presence and hearing of several persons, unlawfully, wickedly, and premeditatedly, despitefully and blasphemously, did say, among other things, in substance as follows: "That the Holy Scriptures were a mere fable, that they were a contradiction, and that although they contained a number of good things, yet they contained a great many lies," and the indictment concludes, to the great dishonour of Almighty God, to the great scandal of the profession of the Christian Religion, to the evil example of all others in like case offending, and against the form of the act of assembly in such case made and provided.

The jury have found that the defendant did speak words of that substance, in the temper and with the intent stated. This verdict excludes every thing like innocence of intention; it finds a malicious intention in the speaker to vilify the Christian Religion, and the Scriptures, and this court cannot look beyond the record, nor take any notice of the allegation, that the words were uttered by the defendant, a member of a debating association, which convened weekly for discussion and mutual information, and

that the expressions were used in the course of argument on a religious question. That there is an association in which so serious a subject is treated with so much levity, indecency, and scurrility, existing in this city, I am sorry to hear, for it would prove a nursery of vice, a school of preparation to qualify young men for the gallows, and young women for the brothel, and there is not a skeptic of decent manners and good morals, who would not consider such debating clubs as a common nuisance and disgrace to the city. From the tenor of the words, it is impossible that they could be spoken seriously and conscientiously, in the discussion of a religious or theological topic; there is nothing of argument in the language; it was the out-pouring of an invective so vulgarly shocking and insulting, that the lowest grade of civil authority ought not to be subject to it, but when spoken in a Christian land, and to a Christian audience, the highest offence *contra bonos mores*; and even if Christianity was not part of the law of the land, it is the popular religion of the country, an insult on which would be indictable, as directly tending to disturb the public peace. The bold ground is taken, though it has often been exploded, and nothing but what is trite can be said upon it—it is a barren soil, upon which no flower ever blossomed;—the assertion is once more made, that Christianity never was received as part of the common law of this Christian land; and it is added, that if it was, it was virtually repealed by the constitution of the *United States*, and of this state, as inconsistent with the liberty of the people, the freedom of religious worship, and hostile to the genius and spirit of our government, and, with it, the act against blasphemy; and if the argument is worth any thing, all the laws which have Christianity for their object—all would be carried away at one fell swoop—the act against cursing and swearing, and breach of the Lord's day; the act forbidding incestuous marriages, perjury by taking a false oath upon the book, fornication and adultery, *et peccatum illud horribile non nominandum inter christianos*—for all these are founded on Christianity—for all these are restraints upon civil liberty, according to the argument—edicts of religious and civic tyranny, "when enlightened notions of the rights of man were not so universally diffused as at the present day."

Another *exception* is taken. However technical it may be, and however heinous the offence, still, if it is not charged as the law requires, the plaintiff in error is entitled to the full benefit of the exception. The objection is, that the words are not laid to have been spoken profanely.

We will first dispose of what is considered the grand objection—*the constitutionality of Christianity*—for in effect that is *the question.*

Christianity, general Christianity, is, and always has been, a part of the common law of *Pennsylvania*; Christianity, without the spiritual artillery of *European* countries; for this Christianity was one of the considerations of the royal charter, and the very basis of its great founder, *William Penn*; not Christianity founded on any particular religious tenets; not Christianity with an established church, and tithes, and spiritual courts; but Christianity with liberty of conscience to all men. *William Penn* and Lord *Baltimore* were the first legislators who passed laws in favour of liberty of conscience; for before that period the principle of liberty of conscience appeared in the laws of no people, the axiom of no government, the institutes of no society, and scarcely in the temper of any man. Even the reformers were as furious against contumacious errors, as they were loud in asserting the liberty of conscience. And to the wilds of America, peopled by a stock cut off by persecution from a Christian society, does Christianity owe true freedom of religious opinion and religious worship. There is, in this very act of 1700, a precision of definition, and a discrimination so perfect between prosecutions for opinions seriously, temperately, and argumentatively expressed, and despiteful railings, as to command our admiration and reverence for the enlightened framers. From the time of *Bracton*, Christianity has been received as part of the common law of *England*. I will not go back to remote periods, but state a series of prominent decisions, in which the doctrine is to be found. *The King* v. *Taylor, Ventr.* 93. 3 *Keb.* 507, the defendant was convicted on an information for saying, that *Christ Jesus* was a bastard, a whoremaster, and religion a cheat. Lord Chief Baron HALE, the great and the good Lord HALE, (no stickler for church establishments) observed, "that such kind of wicked and blasphemous words were not only an offence against God and religion, but against the laws of the state and government, and therefore punishable; that to say, religion is a cheat, is to dissolve all those obligations by which civil societies are preserved; and that Christianity is part of the law of *England*, and therefore to reproach the Christian religion is to speak in subversion of the laws." In the case of *The King* v. *Woolaston*, 2 *Stra.* 884. *Fitzg.* 64. *Raymond*, 162, the defendant had been convicted of publishing five libels, ridiculing the miracles of *Jesus Christ*, his life and conversation; and was moved in arrest of judgment, that this offence was not punishable in the temporal courts, but the court said, they would not suffer it to be debated, "whether to write against Christianity generally was not an offence of temporal cognizance." It was further contended, that it was merely to show that those miracles were not to be taken in a literal but allegorical sense; and, therefore, the book could not be aimed at Christianity in general, but merely attacking one proof of the divine mission. But the court said, the main design of the book, though professing to establish Christianity upon a true bottom, considers the narrations of scripture as explanative and prophetical, yet that these professions could not be credited, and the rule is *allegatio contra factum non est admittendum*. In that case the court laid great stress on the term *general*, and did not intend to include disputes between learned men on particular and controverted points, and Lord Chief Justice RAYMOND, *Fitzg.* 66, said "I would have it taken notice of, that we do not meddle with the difference of opinion, and that we interfere only where the root of Christianity is struck at." The information filed against the celebrated *Wilkes* was for publishing an obscene and infamous libel, tending to vitiate and corrupt the minds of the subjects, and to introduce a total contempt of religion, morality, and virtue, to blaspheme Almighty God, to ridicule our Saviour, and the Christian religion. In the justly admired speech of Lord MANSFIELD, in a case which made

much noise at the time—*Evens* v. *Chamberlain of London. Furneaux's Letters to Sir W. Blackstone. Appx. to Black. Com.* and 2 *Burns' Eccles. Law, p.* 95. Conscience, he observed, is not controllable by human laws, nor amenable to human tribunals; persecution, or attempts to force conscience, will never produce conviction, and were only calculated to make hypocrites or martyrs. There never was a single instance from the *Saxon* times down to our own, in which a man was punished for erroneous opinions. For atheism, blasphemy, and reviling the Christian religion, there have been instances of prosecution at the common law; but bare non-conformity is no sin by the common law, and all pains and penalties for non-conformity to the established rites and modes are repealed by the acts of toleration, and dissenters exempted from ecclesiastical censures. What bloodshed and confusion have been occasioned, from the reign of *Henry* IV., when the first penal statutes were enacted, down to the revolution, by laws made to force conscience. There is certainly nothing more unreasonable, nor inconsistent with the rights of human nature, more contrary to the spirit and precepts of the Christian religion, more iniquitous and unjust, more impolitic, than persecution against natural religion, revealed religion and sound policy. The great, and wise, and learned judge observes, "The true principles of natural religion are part of the common law; the essential principles of revealed religion are part of the common law; so that a person vilifying, subverting or ridiculing them may be prosecuted at common law; but temporal punishments ought not to be inflicted for mere opinions." Long before this, much suffering, and a mind of a strong and liberal cast, had taught this sound doctrine and this Christian precept to *William Penn*. The charter of *Charles* II. recites, that "Whereas our trusty and beloved *William Penn*, out of a commendable desire to enlarge our *English* empire, as also to reduce the savages, by gentle and just measures, to the love of civil society, and the Christian religion, hath humbly besought our leave to translate a colony," &c. The first legislative act in the colony was the recognition of the Christian religion, and establishment of liberty of conscience. Before this, in 1646, Lord *Baltimore* passed a law in *Maryland* in favour of religious freedom, and it is a memorable fact, that of the first legislators, who established religious freedom, one was a Roman Catholic and the other a Friend. It is called the great law, of the body of laws, in the province of *Pennsylvania*, passed at an assembly at *Chester*, the 7th of the 12th month, *December*. After the following preamble and declaration, viz.: "Whereas ye glory of Almighty God, and ye good of mankind, is ye reason and end of government, and therefore government in itself is a venerable ordinance of God; and forasmuch as it is principally desired and intended by ye proprietary and governor, and ye freemen of ye province of *Pennsylvania*, and territorys thereunto belonging, to make and establish such laws as shall best preserve true Christians, and civil liberty, in opposition to all unchristian, licentious, and unjust practices, whereby God may have his due, *Caesar* his due, and ye people their due, from tiranny and oppression on ye one side, and insolency and licentiousness on ye other, so that ye best and firmest foundation may be laid for ye present and future happiness both of ye governor and people of this province and territorys aforesaid, and their posterity:—Be it therefore enacted by *William Penn*, proprietary and governor, by and with ye advice and consent of the deputys of ye freemen of this province and counties aforesaid in assembly mett, and by ye authority of ye same, that these following chapters and paragraphs shall be the laws of *Pennsylvania*, and the territorys thereof.

"Almighty God, being only Lord of conscience, Father of lyghts and spirits, and ye author as well as object of all divine knowledge, faith, and worship, who only can enlighten ye minds, and persuade and convince ye understandings of people in due reverence to his sovereignty over the souls of mankind: It is enacted by the authority aforesaid, yt no person at any time hereafter living in this province, who shall confess and acknowledge one Almighty God to be ye creator, upholder, and ruler of ye world, and that professeth him or herself obliged in conscience to live peaceably and justly under ye civil government, shall in any wise be molested or prejudiced for his or her conscientious persuasion or practice, nor shall he or she at any time be compelled to frequent or maintain any religious worship, plan or ministry, whatever, contrary to his or her mind, but shall freely and fully enjoy his or her Christian liberty in yt respect, without any interruption or reflection; and if any person shall abuse or deride any other for his or her different persuasion and practice in a matter of religion, such shall be lookt upon as a disturber of ye peace, and be punished accordingly." And to the end that looseness, irreligion, and atheism may not creep in under the pretence of conscience, it provides for the observance of the Lord's day, punishes profane cursing and swearing, and further enacts, for the better preventing corrupt communication, "that whoever shall speak loosely and profanely of Almighty God, Christ Jesus, the Holy Spirit, or Scriptures of Truth, and is thereof legally convicted, shall forfeit and pay 5 pounds, and be imprisoned for five days in the house of correction." Thus this wise legislature framed this great body of laws for a Christian country and Christian people. Infidelity was then rare, and no infidels were among the first colonists. They fled from religious intolerance, to a country where all were allowed to worship according to their own understanding, and as was justly observed by the learned Chancellor of the associated members of the Bar of *Philadelphia*, in the city of *Philadelphia*, in his address to that body, 22d of *June*, 1822, the number of *Jews* was too inconsiderable to excite alarm, and the believers in *Mahomet* were not likely to intrude. Every one had the right of adopting for himself whatever opinion appeared to be the most rational, concerning all matters of religious belief; thus, securing by law this inestimable freedom of conscience, one of the highest privileges, and greatest interests of the human race. This is the Christianity of the common law, incorporated into the great law of *Pennsylvania*, and thus, it is irrefragably proved, that the laws and institutions of this state are built on the foundation of reverence for Christianity. Here was complete liberty of conscience, with the exception of disqualification for office of all who did not profess faith in Jesus Christ. This disqualification was not contained in the constitution of 1776; the door was open to any believer in a God, and so it continued under our present constitution, with the necessary addition of a belief in a future state of rewards and punishments. On this the constitution of the *United States* has made no alteration, nor in the great body of the laws which was an incorporation of the common law doctrine of Christianity, as suited to the condition of the colony, and without which no free government can long exist. Under the constitution, penalties against cursing and swearing have been exacted. If Christianity was abolished, all false oaths, all tests by oath in the common form by the book, would cease to be indictable as perjury. The indictment must state the oath to be on the holy Evangelists of Almighty God. The accused on his trial might argue that the book by which he was sworn, so far from being holy writ, was a pack of lies, containing as little truth as *Robinson Crusoe*. And is every jury in the box to decide as a fact whether the Scriptures are of divine origin?

Let us now see what have been the opinions of our judges and courts. The late Judge *Wilson*, of the Supreme Court of the *United States*, Professor of Law in the College in *Philadelphia*, was appointed in 1791, unanimously by the House of Representatives of this state to "revise and digest the laws of this commonwealth, to ascertain and determine how far any *British* statutes extended to it, and to prepare bills containing such alterations and additions as the code of laws, and the principles and forms of the constitution, then lately adopted, might require." He had just risen from his seat in the convention which formed the constitution of the *United States*, and of this state; and it is well known, that for our present form of government we are greatly indebted to his exertions and influence. With his fresh recollection of both constitutions, in his course of Lectures, 3d vol. of his works, 112, he states, that profaneness and blasphemy are offences punishable by fine and imprisonment, and that Christianity is part of the common law. It is in vain to object that the law is obsolete; this is not so; it has seldom been called into operation, because this, like some other offences, has been rare. It has been retained in our recollection of laws now in force, made by the direction of the legislature, and it has not been a dead letter.

In the Mayor's Court of the city of *Philadelphia*, in 1818, one *Murray* was convicted of a most scandalous blasphemy. He attempted by advertisement to call a meeting of the enemies of persecution; but this ended in mere vapour; the good sense of the people frowned upon it, and he was most justly sentenced. An account of the proceedings will be found in the *Franklin Gazette*, of the 21st of *November*, 1818. If the doctrine advanced in the written argument delivered to the court was just, (and it is but justice to the counsel for the plaintiff in error for the court to acknowledge the propriety of his conduct in preferring this course to a declamation in open court,) impiety and profanity must reach their acme with impunity, and every debating club might dedicate the club room to the worship of the Goddess of Reason, and adore the deity in the person of a naked prostitute. The people would not tolerate these flagitious acts, and would themselves punish; and it is for this, among other reasons, that the law interposes to prevent the disturbance of the public peace. It is sometimes asked with a sneer, Why not leave it to Almighty God to revenge his own cause? Temporal courts do so leave it. "Bold and presumptuous would be the man who would attempt to arrest the thunder of heaven from the hand of God, and direct the bolts of vengeance where to fall." It is not on this principle courts act, but on the dangerous temporal consequences likely to proceed from the removal of religious and moral restraints; this is the ground of punishment for blasphemous and criminal publications; and without any view to spiritual correction of the offender. 4 *Bla. C.* 59. *Fitz.* 67. *Stark. on Libels*, 487.

"Shall each blasphemer quite escape the rod,
And plead the insult's not to man but God?"

It is not an *auto da fe*, displaying vengeance; but a law, punishing with great mildness, a gross offence against public decency and public order, tending directly to disturb the peace of the commonwealth. Chief Justice SWIFT, in his system of Laws, 2 vol. 825, has some very just reasoning on the subject. He observes, "To prohibit the open, public, and explicit denial of the popular religion of a country, is a necessary measure to preserve the tranquillity of a government. Of this, no person in a Christian country can complain; for, admitting him to be an infidel, he must acknowledge that no benefit can be derived from the subversion of a religion which enforces the purest morality." In the Supreme Court of *New York* it was solemnly determined, that Christianity was part of the law of the land, and that to revile the Holy Scriptures was an indictable offence. The case assumes, says Chief Justice KENT, that we are a Christian people, and the morality of the country is deeply engrafted on Christianity. Nor are we bound by any expression in the constitution, as some have strangely supposed, not to punish at all, or to punish indiscriminately the like attack upon *Mahomet* or the *Grand Luma*. *The People* v. *Ruggles*, 8 *Johnston*, 290. This decision was much canvassed in the *New York* convention, 1821. Debates 463. An article was proposed in the new constitution, declaring that the judiciary should not declare any particular religion the law of the land. This was lost by a vote of 74 to 41. It is a mistake to suppose that this decision was founded on any special provision in the constitution. It has long been firmly settled, that blasphemy against the Deity generally, or an attack on the Christian religion indirectly, for the purpose of exposing its doctrines to ridicule and contempt, is indictable and punishable as a temporal offence. The principles and actual decisions are, that the publication, whether written or oral, must be malicious, and designed for that end and purpose; both the language of indictments, and the guarded expressions of judges show, that it never was a crime at the common law, seriously and conscientiously to discuss theological and religious topics, though in the course of such discussions doubts may have been created and expressed, on doctrinal points, and the force of a particular proof of Scripture evidence casually weakened, or the authority of particular important texts disputed; and persons of a different religion, as *Jews*, though they must necessarily deny the au-

thenticity of other religions, have never been punished as blasphemers or libellers at common law, for so doing. All men, of conscientious religious feeling, ought to concede outward respect to every mode of religious worship. Upon the whole, it may not be going too far to infer, from the decisions, that no author or printer, who fairly and conscientiously promulgates the opinions with whose truths he is impressed, for the benefit of others, is answerable as a criminal; that a malicious and mischievous intention is, in such a case, the broad boundary between right and wrong, and that is to be collected from the offensive levity, scurrilous and opprobrious language, and other circumstances, whether the act of the party was malicious; and since the law has no means of distinguishing between different degrees of evil tendency, if the matter published contains any such evil tendency, it is a public wrong. An offence against the public peace may consist either of an actual breach of the peace, or doing that which tends to provoke and excite others to do it. Within the latter description fall all acts and all attempts to produce disorder, by written, printed, or oral communications, for the purpose of generally weakening those religious and moral restraints, without the aid of which mere legislative provisions would prove ineffectual. No society can tolerate a wilful and despiteful attempt to subvert its religion, no more than it would break down its laws—a general, malicious, and deliberate intent to overthrow Christianity, general Christianity. This is the line of indication, where crime commences, and the offence becomes the subject of penal visitation. The species of offence may be classed under the following heads—1. Denying the Being and Providence of God. 2. Contumelious reproaches of Jesus Christ; profane and malevolent scoffing at the Scriptures, or exposing any part of them to contempt and ridicule. 3. Certain immoralities tending to subvert all religion and morality, which are the foundations of all governments. Without these restraints no free government could long exist. It is liberty run mad, to declaim against the punishment of these offences, or to assert that the punishment is hostile to the spirit and genius of our government. They are far from being true friends to liberty who support this doctrine, and the promulgation of such opinions, and general receipt of them among the people, would be the sure forerunners of anarchy, and finally of despotism. Amidst the concurrent testimony of political and philosophical writers among the Pagans, in the most absolute state of democratic freedom, the sentiments of *Plutarch*, on this subject, are too remarkable to be omitted. After reciting that the first and greatest care of the legislators of *Rome*, *Athens*, *Lacedaemon*, and *Greece* in general, was by instituting solemn supplications and forms of oaths, to inspire them with a sense of the favour or displeasure of Heaven, that learned historian declares, that we have met with towns unfortified, illiterate, and without the conveniences of habitations; but a people wholly without religion, no traveller hath yet seen; and a city might as well be erected in the air, as a state be made to unite, where no divine worship is attended. Religion he terms the cement of civil union, and the essential support of legislation. No free government now exists in the world, unless where Christianity is acknowledged, and is the religion of the country. So far from Christianity, as the counsel contends, being part of the machinery necessary to despotism, the reverse is the fact. Christianity is part of the common law of this state. It is not proclaimed by the commanding voice of any human superior, but expressed in the calm and mild accents of customary law. Its foundations are broad, and strong, and deep: they are laid in the authority, the interest, the affections of the people. Waiving all questions of hereafter, it is the purest system of morality, the firmest auxiliary, and only stable support of all human laws. It is impossible to administer the laws without taking the religion which the defendant in error has scoffed at, that Scripture which he has reviled, as their basis; to lay aside these is at least to weaken the confidence in human veracity, so essential to the purposes of society, and without which no question of property could be decided, and no criminal brought to justice; an oath in the common form, on a discredited book, would be a most idle ceremony. This act was not passed, as the counsel supposed, when religious and civil tyranny were at their height; but on the breaking forth of the sun of religious liberty, by those who had suffered much for conscience' sake, and fled from ecclesiastical oppression. The counsel is greatly mistaken in attributing to the common law the punishment at the stake, and by the faggot. No man ever suffered at common law for any heresy. The writ *de haeretico comburendo*, and all the sufferings which he has stated in such lively colours, and which give such a frightful, though not exaggerated picture, were the enactments of positive laws, equally barbarous and impolitic. There is no reason for the counsel's exclamation, are these things to be revived in this country, where Christianity does not form part of the law of the land!—it does form, as we have seen, a necessary part of our common law; it inflicts no punishment for a non-belief in its truths; it is a stranger to fire and to faggots, and this abused statute merely inflicts a mild sentence on him who bids defiance to all public order, disregards all decency, by contumelious reproaches, scoffing at and reviling that which is certainly the religion of the country; and when the counsel compared this act against blasphemy to the act against witchcraft, and declared this was equally absurd, I do not impute to him that which I know his heart abhors, a scoffing at religion, but to the triteness of the topics. It is but a barren field, and must contain a repetition of that which has been so often advanced and so often refuted. It is not argument. He has likewise fallen into error with respect to the report of the Judges of the Supreme Court on the *British* statute *de religiosis*, and of *mortmain*, parts of which are not incorporated, as being inapplicable to the state of the country; these statutes were made to resist the encroachments of religious bodies, in engrossing great landed estates, and holding them in *mortmain*, but these are adopted so far as relates to the avoidance of conveyances to the use of bodies corporate, unless sanctioned by the charter declaring void all conveyances to superstitious uses. The present statute is called the statute *de religiosis*, from the initiatory words of the act. It clipped the wings of ecclesiastical monopoly, and avoided conveyances to su-

perstitious uses, but had no more relation to the doctrines of Christ than of *Mahomet;* the counsel has confounded the name *de religiosis* with the doctrines of Christianity, and drawn a false conclusion; because the statute *de religiosis* was not applicable to the country, therefore religion itself was not, and because they incorporated only part of the statutes avoiding conveyances to superstitious uses, therefore Christianity was superstition, and is abolished. This argument is founded on misconception, and is a nullity. The plaintiff in error has totally failed to support his grand objection to this indictment, for Christianity is part of the common law. The act against blasphemy is neither obsolete nor virtually repealed, nor is Christianity inconsistent with our free governments or the genius of the people.

As I understand this writ of error was taken out with a view to decide the question, whether Christianity was part of the law of the land, and whether it was consistent with our civil institutions, I have considered it a duty to be thus explicit. No preference is given by law to any particular religious persuasion. Protection is given to all by our laws. It is only the malicious reviler of Christianity who is punished. By general Christianity is not intended the doctrine of worship of any particular church or sect; the law leaves these disputes to theologians; it is not known as a standard by which to decide political dogmas. The worship of the Jews is under the protection of the law, and all prosecutions against Unitarians have been discontinued in *England.* The statute of *William III. Ch. 3,* with its penalties against Anti-Trinitarians, is repealed, and it never was punishable at common law; and no partial mode of belief or unbelief were the objects of coercion by the civil magistrate. Whatever doctrines were heretical, were left to the ecclesiastical judges, who had a most arbitrary latitude allowed to them. Freedom from the demon of persecution, and the scourge of established churches, was not on the *European,* but on our side of the Atlantic. I do not by this allude to any particular church, for the Puritans in turn became persecutors, when they got the upper hand. By an ordinance of 23d of *August,* 1645, which continued until the restoration, to preach, write or print any thing in derogation, or disapproving of the directory to the established puritanical form of worship, subjected the offender, when convicted, to a discretionary fine, not exceeding 50 pounds. *Scofill,* 98. While our own free constitution secures liberty of conscience and freedom of religious worship to all, it is not necessary to maintain that any man should have the right publicly to vilify the religion of his neighbours and of the country. These two privileges are directly opposed. It is open, public vilification of the religion of the country that is punished, not to force conscience by punishment, but to preserve the peace of the country by an outward respect to the religion of the country, and not as a restraint upon the liberty of conscience; but licentiousness endangering the public peace, when tending to corrupt society, is considered as a breach of the peace, and punishable by indictment. Every immoral act is not indictable, but when it is destructive of morality generally, it is because it weakens the bonds by which society is held together, and government is nothing more than public order. This was the opinion of the court in the case of *Commonwealth* v. *Sharpless*, 2 *Serg. & Rawle*, 101. It is not now, for the first time, determined in this court, that Christianity is part of the common law of *Pennsylvania*. In the case of the *Guardians of the Poor* v. *Green*, 5 *Binn.* 55. Judge BRACKENBRIDGE observed, the church establishment of *England* has become a part of the common law, but was the common law in this particular, or any part of it, carried with us in our emigration and planting a colony in *Pennsylvania*? Not a particle of it. On the contrary, the getting quit of the ecclesiastical establishment and tyranny, was a great cause of the emigration. All things were reduced to a primitive Christianity, and we went into a new state. And Chief Justice TILGHMAN observes, that every country has its own common law; ours is composed partly of our own usages. When our ancestors emigrated from *England*, they took with them such of the English principles as were convenient for the situation in which they were about to be placed. It required time and experience to ascertain how much of the *English* law would be suitable to this country. The minds of *William Penn* and his followers, would have revolted at the idea of an established church. Liberty to all, preference to none; equal privilege is extended to the mitred Bishop and the unadorned Friend.

This is the Christianity which is the law of our land, and I do not think it will be an invasion of any man's right of private judgment, or of the most extended privilege of propagating his sentiments with regard to religion, in the manner which he thinks most conclusive. If from a regard to decency and the good order of society, profane swearing, breach of the Sabbath, and blasphemy, are punishable by civil magistrates, these are not punished as sins or offences against God, but crimes injurious to, and having a malignant influence on society; for it is certain, that by these practices, no one pretends to prove any supposed truths, detect any supposed error, or advance any sentiment whatever.

The reasoning of the counsel of the plaintiff in error is quite conclusive on the subaltern objection to the form of the indictment. The word *profanely* used in the act, should have been inserted in the indictment. It is a description of the offence, and though the words blasphemously and despitefully, may be synonymous with profanely, and tantamount in common understanding, yet as the legislature has adopted this word as a description or definition of the crime, the omission is fatal. As for blasphemy at the common law, the indictment cannot be sustained, for the sentence is founded on the act of assembly, and distribution of the fine to the poor, is not a part of a common law punishment. The general rule is, that all indictments on statutes, must state all the circumstances which constitute the definition of the offence, so as to bring the defendant precisely within it; and not even the fullest description of the offence, even the terms of a legal definition, would be sufficient, without keeping to the expressions of the act. A case directly in point is the indictment for perjury, on the statute; the word wilfully must be inserted, because it is

part of the description the act gives of the crime; though in indictments for some offences at common law, that precise term is not essential, but may be supplied by others conveying the same idea; and in indictments on the black act, the term wilfully is essential, as being used by the legislature, and maliciously, will not suffice. 1 *Chitty's Crim. Law*, where the various authorities are referred to. The judgment is for this reason reversed. I very much incline to think the indictment is defective on another ground. It should have stated the very words: here it is laid, that among other things, he said in substance as follows. In all indictments for words, the words themselves ought to be set out. In an accusation of this nature, particularly, the words ought to be set out, for it is from the mode and manner the words were spoken, that the malicious intention must appear. One individual attending a long sermon, with particular dogmas of his own always uppermost in his head, and with strong prejudice against the speaker and his sect, whose opinions he might hold to be heretical, and who, from that very prejudice, would put the worst construction on all he said, might conclude from an argument in which no vituperative language was used, that in substance, the speaker said the Scriptures were fabulous, and contained many lies. He might conscientiously suppose, because some favourite opinion of his own was touched, it in substance, amounted to a declaration that the Scriptures were a fable and a lie. When a man undertakes to give an account of the substance of what he has heard or read, he by no means undertakes for the accuracy of expressions; he avoids that; he only states what was his own conclusion from the whole discourse of writing; the speaker in substance intended it; it would be dangerous either to speaker or preacher, if this latitude were allowed. The thing itself, must be stated explicitly and directly, in such an open and palpable form, that any one who heard the words, shall know the law to be infringed. A very serious, conscientious discourse, on a subject or text of Scripture, on which the different sects thought differently, might make the preacher the victim of ignorance, prejudice, fanaticism, or ill will, by taking up a sentence and disjoining it from the whole discourse and scope of reasoning of the speaker. Even in a declaration in slander in *England*, it is not sufficient to state, that the defendant among other things said in substance as follows; the words must be set out, though it would be sufficient to prove the substance. But it has been determined in this court, that in an action of slander the words may be so laid, but it never has been carried so far as to say this would do in indictments. In an indictment for a libel, *Commonwealth* v. *Sweney*, 10 *Serg. & Rawle*, 173, it was decided, that this mode of laying written slander would not be sufficient.

I am not required to give an opinion on this point, and only throw out this hint to gentlemen who may have occasion to draw bills of this nature.

Judgment reversed.

31

COMMONWEALTH v. BLANDING
3 Pick. 304 (Mass. 1825)

This was an indictment charging the defendant with making, framing and causing to be published in a newspaper, called the Providence Gazette, at Rehoboth, in the county of Bristol, on the 20th of February, 1822, a false, scandalous and libellous paragraph concerning one Enoch Fowler, he then being an innholder in that county, and a good and peaceable citizen, &c.

On the trial, before *Wilde* J., it was proved that the defendant delivered the writing set forth in the indictment to the printer of the Providence Gazette, at Providence in the State of Rhode Island, and that it was published in the paper at the request of the defendant, who acknowledged that he was the author of it; and it was proved that that paper circulates in Rehoboth, and had so circulated previously to such publication; and that the number containing this writing was received and circulated in that town.

The defendant offered to give in evidence a coroner's inquest alluded to in the libel, to prove that the allegations contained therein were true; and he also offered to prove the truth of all the allegations in the writing. But this evidence was not admitted.

The defendant contended that there was no evidence that the writing was composed or published in the county of Bristol; but the jury were instructed, that the causing of it to be published in the Providence Gazette, the defendant knowing that that newspaper was taken and circulated in Rehoboth, was a sufficient publication within the county.

The jury were also instructed, that the malicious intent charged in the indictment was an inference of law, it not being competent for the defendant to prove the truth of the facts alleged, and there being no such proof in the case; and that although the jury were, with the advice of the Court, the judges of the law and the fact, yet they were bound to decide according to the law as actually established, whatever might be their opinion of its policy; and that unless they knew the law to be otherwise, they ought to receive it from the judge, whose instructions, if incorrect, would be subject to revision and correction by the whole Court.

A verdict was returned against the defendant; but if these instructions were wrong, or if the evidence offered by the defendant should have been admitted, the verdict was to be set aside and a new trial granted, or the defendant was to be discharged, according as the whole Court might direct. . . .

PARKER C. J. delivered the opinion of the Court. As to the first question, which relates to the publication of the supposed libel, we think the admitted facts, that it was at the request of the defendant inserted in a public newspaper printed in Providence, which, though in another State, borders on the county of Bristol, and that that paper usually circulates in the town of Rehoboth in that county, and that the number containing the libel was actually received and did circulate in that town, were competent and conclusive evidence of a publication in the county of Bristol. In this respect the case is like that of *Rex* v. *Burdett*, 4 Barn. & Ald. 95.

As to that part of the instructions of the judge, which states that the malicious intent charged in the indictment (there being no evidence admitted to prove the truth of the facts alleged) was an inference of law,—this is certainly the common law doctrine, and it never has been repealed by any statute of this commonwealth, nor overruled by any decision of this Court; and if the doctrine be true, that the gist or essence of the offence of libel is, that it tends to provoke a breach of the peace, and this certainly is maintained in all the books, then it must follow, that when the publication complained of is of a libellous nature, it must be taken to be of a malicious character, unless the defendant shall within some of the known provisions of law be admitted to prove, and shall in fact prove, that the allegations made are true, and that he had some warrantable purpose, inconsistent with a malicious intent, in causing the publication.

There are certain cases in which the defendant in a prosecution for a libel may acquit himself by showing an honest purpose and proving the truth of his allegations. The general principles upon which such a right depends, are stated in the case of *Commonwealth* v. *Clap*, 4 Mass. R. 168, though without doubt there are cases, other than those mentioned in the opinion of the Court in that case as illustrations of the general doctrine, in which the same principles will apply.

The law as laid down in the case above cited, has stood before the public nearly twenty years, and successive legislatures must be presumed to have acquiesced in its wisdom and policy, or it would have been altered by statute.

The general principle decided is, that it is immaterial to the character of a libel *as a public offence*, whether the matter of it be true or false; not, as some have affirmed, because the law makes no distinction between truth and falsehood, but because the interest of the public requires, that men not invested with authority by the laws, shall not usurp the power of public accusation, and arraign before the public, with malicious motives, their neighbours and fellow citizens, exposing them to partial trials in forms not warranted by the constitution or laws, and condemning them to a species of ignomy which is often a heavier punishment than the law would inflict for the offences or misconduct of which they are thus officiously accused. And surely so long as preventive justice shall be deemed more salutary than vindictive, all wise governments will hold it necessary to curb the disposition, always too prevalent, to excite ill temper and ill blood by exposing the offences, faults or foibles of men, who, if guilty of any violation of law, are amenable to punishment in the ordinary way, and if liable to censure for private vices, irregularities of temper or unaccommodating manners, should be left, as the law leaves them, to the corrections of conscience and those silent but powerful punishments which their misconduct itself will supply.

No state of society would be more deplorable than that which would admit an indiscriminate right in every citizen to arraign the conduct of every other, before the public, in newspapers, handbills or other modes of publication, not only for crimes, but for faults, foibles, deformities of mind or person, even admitting all such allegations to be true. When the accusation is made by public bodies or officers whose duty it is by law to detect and prosecute offences, the charge and the investigation are submitted to, and no spirit of revenge is produced, but if private intermeddlers, assuming the character of reformers, should have the right to become public accusers, and when called to account, to defend themselves by breaking into the circle of friends, families, children and domestics, to prove the existence of errors or faults which may have been overlooked or forgiven where they were most injurious, the man who is thus accused without lawful process might be expected to avenge himself by unlawful means, and duels or assassinations would be the common occurrences of the times. Instances are recollected where violence, and even death, has ensued from such proceedings. It was with a wise regard to these evils, that the common law has put a check upon the *licentiousness* of the press, and the expression of opinion by writing, painting, &c. when the effect and object is to blacken the character of any one, or to disturb his comfort, the public good not being the end and purpose of such publication, or if that is professed, the public peace requiring a different mode of accusation.

Nor does our constitution or declaration of rights abrogate the common law in this respect, as some have insisted. The 16th article declares, that "the liberty of the press is essential to the security of freedom in a state; it ought not, therefore, to be restrained in this commonwealth." The *liberty* of the press, not its *licentiousness;* this is the construction which a just regard to the other parts of that instrument, and to the wisdom of those who formed it, requires. In the 11th article it is declared, that every "subject of the commonwealth ought to find a certain remedy, by having recourse to the laws, for all injuries or wrongs which he may receive in his person, property or *character.*" And thus the general declaration in the 16th article is qualified. Besides, it is well understood, and received as a commentary on this provision for the liberty of the press, that it was intended to prevent all such *previous restraints* upon publications as had been practised by other governments, and in early times here, to stifle the efforts of patriots towards enlightening their fellow subjects upon their rights and the duties of rulers. The liberty of the press was to be unrestrained, but he who used it was to be responsible in case of its abuse; like the right to keep fire arms, which does not protect him who uses them for annoyance or destruction.

The common law therefore is left unimpaired by the constitution, except as will hereafter be stated, and by that law, unquestionably, the propagator of written or printed tales to the essential prejudice of any one in his estate or reputation, is a public offender, and is not allowed to ex-

cuse himself by the additional wrong of proving in a court of justice, in a collateral way, the facts which he has unwarrantably promulgated.

And yet there are some exceptions to this general rule, recognised by the common law; and others, which are rendered necessary by the principles of our government.

These exceptions are all founded in regard to certain public interests, which are of more importance than the character or tranquillity of any individual. All proceedings in legislative assemblies, whether by speech, written documents or otherwise, are protected from scrutiny elsewhere than in those bodies themselves, because it is essential to the maintenance of public liberty, that in such assemblies the tongue and the press should be wholly unshackled. So proceedings in courts of justice, in which the reputation of individuals may be involved, are to be free from future animadversions, because the investigation of right demands the utmost latitude of inquiry, and men ought not to be deterred from prosecuting or defending there by fear of punishment or damages. Yet in *these* instances, if this necessary indulgence is abused for malicious purposes, a pretence only being made of the forms of legislative or judicial process, the party so conducting himself is amenable to the law. The right also of complaining to any public constituted body, of the malversation or oppressive conduct of any of its officers or agents, with a view to redress for actual wrong, or the removal of an unfaithful officer, may be justified, because the case will show that the proceeding does not arise from malicious motives, or if it does, because the common interest requires that such representations should be free. And there are cases of mere private import, such as an honest though mistaken character of a servant, which, when requested by any one having an interest, the law considers innocent. These cases are all provided for by the common law, and they go far to render harmless that much decried rule, that the truth is no defence in a prosecution for libel. *Rex* v. *Wright,* 8 T. R. 293; *Rex* v. *Creevey,* 1 Maule & Selw. 273; *Lake* v. *King,* 1 Saund. 131; *Astley* v. *Younge,* 2 Burr. 807; *Rogers* v. *Clifton,* 3 Bos. & Pul. 587; Esp. Dig. (3d ed.) 505; *Thorn* v. *Blanchard,* 5 Johns. R. 508; *Rex* v. *Fisher,* 2 Campb. 563; Starkie on Slander, c. 11.

That by the common law always, so far as it can be traced back, the doctrine as now mentioned in regard to excluding the truth of the matters alleged, as a defence in a public presecution for libel, with the exceptions stated, has been recognised and enforced, will be denied by no lawyer who has thoroughly examined the subject. *De Libellis Famosis,* 5 Co. 125; 4 Bl. Com. 150. Indeed it has always been objected as one of the imperfections of that system, by those who have chosen to question its title to veneration. But like most other principles of the common law, it is founded in common sense and common justice, and is not peculiar to that system, for it prevails in the civil law, and indeed the code of no civilized country would repudiate it. It may be altered, or, as may be thought, mitigated by legislative enactments in some States, but this very legislative interference is grounded upon the existence of the principle at common law. If any reformation therefore is wanted, which under the judicial expositions in this commonwealth may well be doubted, none but the legislature is competent to make it.*

For a very sensible, learned and manly discussion of this subject, I refer to the opinion of the Court of Appeals in South Carolina, delivered by *Waties* J. in the case of *The State* v. *Lehre*, published in 4 Hall's Law Journ. 48. The doctrine so laid down had the sanction of the intelligent bar of the State.

The truth is, that the rule, with the exceptions stated, has never been complained of, except when applied to prosecutions for libel of political bearing and character. In such prosecutions the passions of men are always much inflamed, and there is a desire on one side or the other to break through those wholesome restraints which the law has devised for the protection of private character and the preservation of the public peace. An attack upon public men, even in regard to their private characters, has been viewed as a right growing out of our free institutions and essential to the support of them. And so far forth as this notion is correct and salutary, it has been incorporated into our law, and serves to form an exception to the general rule, not distinctly admitted by the common law, though not at all inconsistent with its general character. The case of *Commonwealth* v. *Clap* was the first, since the adoption of the constitution, which called for a discussion of these principles, and in that case it is very clearly and distinctly settled, that if the *truth only* is told of public elective officers, or of acknowledged candidates for offices, in a decent manner and with a view properly to influence an election, it is justifiable. For the reasons upon which that doctrine is founded, we refer to the case above cited. The force of them will not be disputed.

But there are certain other cases not yet distinctly adjudicated upon, where the truth of charges is a legitimate ground of defence, by clear inference from principles recognised by the common law and our own tribunals.

In *Commonwealth* v. *Clap*, it is stated, "that a man may apply by complaint to the legislature to remove an unworthy officer; and if the complaint be true, and made with the honest intention of giving useful information, and not maliciously, or with intent to defame, the complaint will not be a libel."

This is put for illustration of the principle, not to exhibit the only instance in which it is to be applied. A complaint to the *executive* against an officer holding his place at its pleasure,—to a court against an officer whom they have the power to dismiss,—to any body of men having power over its officers,—the subject of the complaint being of a public nature, or the person complaining having a particular interest in it,—falls within the same principle.

Thus if a minister of the gospel should be guilty of gross immoralities, and one of his parish should complain to the church in order that an inquiry might be instituted; or if a *candidate* for the ministry should from vicious habits be unfit for the station he seeks; since all are interested in the purity of the ministerial character, information to those whose duty it is to determine his qualifications, would not be libellous, if communicated in a spirit of truth and candor. Various other cases might be put, in which if it appeared that the purpose was sincere and upright, and wholly free from malice, the truth of the facts stated would be a good defence. But in all such cases, the information is to be given to those who have a right to act upon it, and whose interest and duty are concerned in it; for a promiscuous promulgation of the same facts would of itself be the strongest evidence of malice, and in such cases the court must judge whether the occasion is a fit and proper one for the admission of such defence, and the jury must determine the motives and the end.

With this exposition of the law of libel in this commonwealth, in which we are warranted by the common law, by the constitution, and by judicial decisions, there seems to be no reason for complaint against that general rule, which is so often the theme of popular declamation. A further relaxation can scarcely take place without involving the community, families and individuals, in those contentions and acrimonious conflicts which will render the social state little, if at all, better than the savage.

The principal difference between the common law, as admitted here, and the statute provisions of the State of New York is, that *there* the jury are to judge of the occasion, as well as the motives and ends of the publication; whereas, with us, it must appear first to the court that the case is a proper one for the admission of the truth in evidence. The difficulty with the New York system is, that in every prosecution for a libel, whether of a public or a private nature, the whole matter must be made the subject of open investigation; so that a man's whole domestic relations may be brought before the public, in order to ascertain whether the motives of the alleged libeller were good and his end justifiable; whereas our system proceeds on the ground that private individuals have nothing to do with the conduct of their neighbours, as it may affect the public, unless they proceed in due course of legal process against them in some tribunal, where, instead of being crushed by public opinion factitiously made up on newspaper paragraphs, they will have full opportunity to vindicate their innocence, or if guilty, meet only the punishment which the law has awarded for their offence. If the public sentiment in this commonwealth is in favor of a more relaxed system, the power is in the hands of the legislature, which can mould the law at its pleasure.

Having thus attempted to vindicate the law of libel, as established in this commonwealth, from the aspersions which are frequently cast upon it, we will consider its application to the case before us, in order to determine

---

*Immediately after this decision the legislature enacted, that in every prosecution for writing or for publishing a libel, the defendant may give in evidence in his defence, upon the trial, the truth of the matter contained in the publication charged as libellous, provided that such evidence shall not be deemed a sufficient justification, unless it shall be further made to appear, on the trial, that the matter charged to be libellous was published with good motives and for justifiable ends. *St.* 1826, *c.* 107, § 1; [Revised Stat. *c.* 133, § 6.] . . .

So in Connecticut, New York and some other of the States, the truth of the supposed libellous matter may be given in evidence in public prosecutions, by virtue of the constitutions of some, and the statutes of others, made for that purpose, subject to different degrees of limitation.

whether, upon either of the grounds assumed, a new trial ought to be granted.

The first ground, to wit, the want of legal proof that the libel was published, as alleged, within the county of Bristol, has been considered and overruled; as has also the objection to the charge to the jury.

The other objection, which opens the general question, is that the judge refused to admit in evidence the inquisition which is alluded to in the publication, and with a view to prove the truth of the facts therein stated. Had the inquisition been published without any defamatory comment, it certainly would not have furnished ground for this prosecution; for it does not of itself contain any libellous matter, and it is in the nature of a judicial inquiry, the publication of which would not be criminal, unaccompanied by direct proof of malice. The inquisition merely states that a deceased stranger, who was found dead in a tavern kept by Fowler, came to his death by intoxication. Now this may be true, without any implication against Fowler, for every innholder is liable to have drunken people come to his house, and if they die there, he may be entirely innocent of the cause of their death. But the remarks made by the defendant charge Fowler with having administered the *liquid poison*, and thus being the cause of the death of the stranger; and the public are warned against resorting to the house where such practice is allowed, and the municipal authorities are invoked to exert their power by taking away or withholding the license of Fowler to keep a public house. The matter of this publication is certainly libellous, as it insinuates gross misconduct against Fowler, and directly charges him with a violation of his duty, and exposes him to the loss of his livelihood, so far as that depends upon the reputation of his inn for regularity and order. Admitting the account of the inquisition to be correct as published, yet the addition of comments and insinuations tending to asperse Fowler's character renders it libellous. *Thomas* v. *Croswell*, 7 Johns. R. 264.

But it is said, that this is a matter of public concern, and that the defendant was impelled by a sense of public duty to warn travellers and others from a house which was thus deservedly stigmatized. The answer is, that the defendant did not select a proper vehicle for the communication. The natural effect of a publication of this sort in a newspaper, is, to procure a condemnation in the public mind of the party accused, and his punishment, by bringing his house into disrepute, without any opportunity of defence on his part; so that the accuser becomes judge and executioner at one stroke, and his purpose, if a malicious one, is answered, without any means of relief; for the mischief to the person libelled would be quite as great if he were innocent as if he were guilty. If it should be said in answer, that all this is right if the allegation be true, and if not true, he may recover his damages in an action of slander, it may justly be replied, that this remedy is uncertain and incomplete; for in many cases the slanderer will be unable to respond in damages, and the suffering party will be subjected to the additional injury of a troublesome and expensive lawsuit with little or no hope of recompense.

There may be cases where (there being no other mode by which great mischief can be warded off from the public) a newspaper communication, made with the sole view of preserving the citizens from injury to their life or health, would be justifiable. Such might be the case of an apothecary selling and distributing poison in the form of medicine, stated by a distinguished member of the late convention for revising the constitution. This is an extreme case, where to delay information until the forms of law should be pursued might endanger the lives of hundreds, and such a case would be a law to itself; the public safety being the supreme law, and it being every citizen's duty to give warning in such cases. There may be cases of gross swindling, where nothing but immediate notice would secure the public against depredation, which would be governed by the same principle.

But in the case before us there was no such urgent necessity. The statute regulating licensed houses provides the restrictions and the punishment which the legislature has thought adequate to the offences of the nature contained in this libel. . . . There was then no necessity for this newspaper publication, and the defendant, by resorting to it, has taken the law into his own hands unwarrantably, instead of resorting to those tribunals which the laws have constituted for the correction of these offences. This then is a case in which the defendant cannot be allowed to excuse himself by showing the truth of the accusation which he has unjustifiably made. He had no right to arraign the prosecutor before the public in the form which he adopted, and thus destroy the reputation of his house, without leaving him any means of showing his innocence of the charges made against him. The occasion was not a proper one for a newspaper denunciation.

32

JAMES KENT, COMMENTARIES 2:12–22
1826

As a part of the right of personal security, the preservation of every person's good name from the vile arts of detraction is justly included. The laws of the ancients, no less than those of modern nations, made private reputation one of the objects of their protection. The Roman law took a just distinction between slander spoken and written; and the same distinction prevails in our law, which considers the slander of a private person by words, in no other light than a civil injury, for which a pecuniary compensation may be obtained. The injury consists in falsely and maliciously charging another with the commission of some public offence, or the breach of some public trust, or with any matter in relation to his particular trade or vocation, and which, if true, would render him unworthy of employment; or, lastly, with any other matter or thing, by which special injury is sustained. But if the slander be communicated by pictures, or signs, or writing, or printing, it is calculated to have a wider circulation, to make a deeper impression, and to become proportionably more injurious. Expressions which tend to render a man ridiculous, or lower him in the esteem and opinion of the world, would be libellous if printed, though they would not be actionable if spoken. A libel, as applicable to individuals, has been well defined to be a malicious publication, expressed either in printing or writing, or by signs or pictures, tending either to blacken the memory of one dead, or the reputation of one alive, and expose him to public hatred, contempt, or ridicule. A malicious intent towards government, magistrates, or individuals, and an injurious or offensive tendency, must concur to constitute the libel. It then becomes a grievance, and the law has accordingly considered it in the light of a public as well as a private injury, and has rendered the party not only liable to a private suit at the instance of the party libelled, but answerable to the state by indictment, as guilty of an offence tending directly to a breach of the public peace.

But though the law be solicitous to protect every man in his fair fame and character, it is equally careful that the liberty of speech, and of the press, should be duly preserved. The liberal communication of sentiment, and entire freedom of discussion, in respect to the character and conduct of public men, and of candidates for public favour, is deemed essential to the judicious exercise of the right of suffrage, and of that control over their rulers, which resides in the free people of these United States. It has, accordingly, become a constitutional principle in this country, that "every citizen may freely speak, write, and publish his sentiments, on all subjects, being responsible for the abuse of that right, and that no law can rightfully be passed to restrain or abridge the freedom of speech, or of the press."

The law of England, even under the Anglo-Saxon line of princes, took severe and exemplary notice of defamation, as an offence against the public peace, and in the time of Henry III., Bracton adopted the language of the Institutes of Justinian, and held slander and libellous writings to be actionable injuries. But the first private suit for slanderous words to be met with in the English law, was in the reign of Edward III., and for the high offence of charging another with a crime which endangered his life. The mischiefs of licensed abuse were felt to be so extensive, and so incompatible with the preservation of peace, that several acts of parliament, known as the statutes *de scandalis magnatum*, were passed to suppress and punish the propagation of false and malicious slander. They are said to have been declaratory of the common law, and actions of slander were slowly, but gradually multiplied, between the time of Edward III., and the reign of Elizabeth, when they had become frequent. The remedy was applied to a variety of cases; and in a private action of slander for damages, and even in the action of *scandalum magnatum*, the defendant was allowed to justify, by showing the truth of the fact charged, for if the words were true, it was then a case of *damnum absque injuria*, according to the just opinion of Paulus, in the civil law. But in the case of a public prosecution for a libel, it became the established principle of the English law, as declared in the Court of Star Chamber, about the beginning of the reign of James I. that the truth of the libel could not be shown by way of justification, because, whether true or false, it was equally dangerous to the public peace. The same doctrine remains in England to this day unshaken; and in the case of *The King* v. *Burdett*, it was held, that where a libel imputes to others the commission of a triable crime, the evidence of the truth of it was inadmissible, and that the intention was to be collected from the paper itself, unless explained by the mode of publication, or other circumstances, and that if the contents were likely to produce mischief, the defendant must be presumed to intend *that* which his act was likely to produce. "The liberty of the press," as one of the judges in that case observed, "cannot impute criminal conduct to others without violating the right of character, and that right can only be attacked in a court of justice, where the party attacked has a fair opportunity of defending himself. Where vituperation begins, the liberty of the press ends." Whether the rule of the English law was founded on a just basis, and whether it was applicable to the free press and free institutions in this country, has been a question extensively and laboriously discussed in several cases which have been brought before our American tribunals.

In the case of *The People* v. *Croswell*, which came before the Supreme Court of this state in 1804, and was argued at the bar with very great ability, the court were equally divided in opinion on the point, whether, on an indictment for a libel, the defendant was entitled to give in evidence to the jury the truth of the charges contained in the libel. In the Court of Appeals in South Carolina, in 1811, the court unanimously decided, in the case of *The State* v. *Lehre*, that by the English common law it was settled, on sound principles of policy derived from the civil law, that the defendant had no right to justify the libel by giving the truth of it in evidence. The court, in the learned and able opinion which was delivered in that case, considered that the law, as then declared, was not only the law of England, but probably the law of all Europe, and of most of the free states of America. The same question has been frequently discussed in Massachusetts. In the case of *The Commonwealth* v. *Chase*, in 1808, it was decided, that the publication of a libel maliciously, and with intent to defame, was clearly a public offence, whether the libel be true or not; and the rule was held to be founded on sound principles, indispensable to restrain all tendencies to breaches of the peace, and to private animosity and revenge. The essence of the offence consisted in the malicious intent to defame the reputation of another; and a man may maliciously publish the truth against another with the intent to defame his character, and if the publication be true, the tendency of the publication to inflame the passions, and to excite revenge, is not diminished. But though a defendant, on an indictment for a libel, cannot justify himself for publishing the libel, merely by proving the truth of it, yet he may repel the criminal charge by proving that the publication was for a justifiable purpose, and not malicious; and if the purpose be justifiable, the defendant may give in evidence the truth of the words, when such evidence will tend to negative the malicious intent to defame. The same question was again agitated and discussed before the same court in 1825, in the case of *The Commonwealth* v. *Blanding*, and the court strongly enforced the doctrine of the former case, that, as a general rule, the truth of the libel was not admissible in evidence upon the trial of the indictment; and this principle of the common law was declared to be founded in common sense and common justice, and prevailed in the codes of every civilized country. It was further held, that whether in any particular case such evidence be admissible, was to be determined by the court; and, if admissible, then the jury were to determine whether the publication was made with good motives, and for justifiable ends. The same rule, that the truth cannot be admitted in evidence on indictment for a libel, though it may in a civil suit for damages, has been adjudged in Louisiana; and the weight of judicial authority undoubtedly is, that the English common law doctrine of libel is the common law doctrine in this country, in all cases in which it has not been expressly controlled by constitutional or legislative provisions. The decisions in Massachusetts and Louisiana were made notwithstanding the constitution of the one state had declared, that "the liberty of the press ought not to be restrained," and that the other had said, that "every citizen might freely speak, write, and print, on any subject, being responsible for the abuse of that liberty." Those decisions went only to control the malicious abuse or licentiousness of the press, and that is the most effectual way to preserve its freedom in the genuine sense of the constitutional declarations on the subject. Without such a check, the press, in the hands of evil and designing men, would become a most formidable engine, and as mighty for mischief as for good. Since the decision in 1825, the legislature of Massachusetts have interposed, and by an act passed in March, 1827, have allowed the truth to be given in evidence in all prosecutions for libels, but with a proviso that such evidence should not be a justification, unless it should be made satisfactorily to appear upon the trial, that the matter charged as libellous was published with good motives, and for justifiable ends.

The constitutions of several of the United States have made special provision in favour of giving the truth in evidence in public prosecutions for libels. In the constitutions of Pennsylvania, Delaware, Tennessee, Kentucky, Ohio, Indiana, and Illinois, it is declared, that in prosecutions for libels on men in respect to their public official conduct, the truth may be given in evidence, when the matter published was proper for public information. In the constitutions of Mississippi and Missouri, the extension of the right to give the truth in evidence is more at large, and applies to all prosecutions or indictments for libels, without any qualifications annexed in restraint of the privilege; and an act of the legislature of New-Jersey, in 1799, allowed the same unrestricted privilege. The legislature of Pennsylvania, in 1809, went far beyond their own constitution, and declared by statute, that no person should be indictable for a publication on the official conduct of men in public trust; and that in all actions or criminal prosecutions for a libel, the defendant might plead the truth in justification, or give it in evidence. The decision of the Court of Errors of this state, in *Thorn* v. *Blanchard*, carried the toleration of a libellous publication to as great an extent as the Pennsylvania law; for it appeared to be the doctrine of a majority of the court, that where a person petitioned the council of

appointment to remove a public officer for corruption in office, public policy would not permit the officer libelled to have any redress by private action, whether the charge was true or false, or the motives of the petitioner innocent or malicious. The English law on the point seems to be founded in a juster policy. Petitions to the king, or to parliament, or to the secretary at war, for the redress of any grievance, are privileged communications, and not actionable libels, provided the privilege be not abused; but if it appear that the communication was made maliciously, and without probable cause, the pretence under which it is made aggravates the case, and an action lies. The constitution of this state, as amended in 1821, is a little varied in its language from those provisions which have been mentioned, and is not quite so latitudinary in its indulgence as some of them. It declares, that "in all prosecutions or indictments for libels, the truth may be given in evidence to the jury; and if it shall appear to the jury, that the matter charged as libellous, is true, and was published with good motives, and for justifiable ends, the party shall be acquitted." These provisions in favour of giving the truth in evidence, are to be found only in those constitutions which have been promulgated long since our revolution; and the current of opinion seems to have been setting strongly, not only in favour of erecting barriers against any previous restraints upon publications, (and which was all that the earlier sages of the revolution had in view,) but in favour of the policy that would diminish or destroy altogether every obstacle or responsibility in the way of the publication of the truth. The subject is not without its difficulties, and it has been found embarrassing to preserve equally, and in just harmony and proportion, the protection which is due to character, and the protection which ought to be afforded to liberty of speech, and of the press. These rights are frequently brought into dangerous collision, and the tendency of measures in this country has been to relax too far the vigilance with which the common law surrounded and guarded character, while we are animated with a generous anxiety to maintain freedom of discussion. The constitution of this state makes the facts in every possible case a necessary subject of open investigation; and however improper or unfit those facts may be for public information, and however painful or injurious to the individuals concerned, yet it would seem, that they may, in the first instance, be laid bare before the jury. The facts are to go to them, at all events; for the jury are to determine, *as it shall appear to them,* whether the motives of the libeller were good, and his end justifiable.

The act of Congress of the 14th of July, 1798, made it an indictable offence to libel the government, or Congress, or the President of the United States; and it made it lawful for the defendant, upon the trial, to give in evidence in his defence, the truth of the matter contained in the publication charged as a libel. This act was, by the terms of it, *declaratory,* and it was intended to convey the sense of Congress, that in prosecutions of that kind it was the common right of the defendant to give the truth in evidence. So, the case of *The People* v. *Croswell,* in this state, was followed by an act of the legislature on the 6th of April, 1805, enacting and *declaring,* that in every prosecution, for a libel, (and which included public and private prosecutions) it should be lawful for the defendant to give in evidence in his defence the truth of the matter charged; but such evidence was not to be a justification, unless, on the trial, it should be made satisfactorily to appear, that the matter charged as libellous was published with good motives, and for justifiable ends; and this was the whole extent of the doctrine which had been claimed in favour of the press in the case of *The People* v. *Croswell.*

There appears to have been some contrariety of opinion in the English books on the point, whether a defendant in a private action upon a libel, could be permitted to justify the charge, by pleading the truth. But the prevailing, and the better opinion is, that the truth may, in all cases, be pleaded by way of justification, in a private action for damages, arising from written or printed defamation, as well as in an action for slanderous words. The ground of the private action, is the injury which the party has sustained, and his consequent right to damages as a recompense for that injury; but if the charge, in its substance and measure, be true in point of fact, the law considers the plaintiff as coming into court without any equitable title to relief. And yet it is easy to be perceived, that in the case of libels upon private character, greater strictness as to allowing the truth in evidence, by way of justification, ought to be observed, than in the case of public prosecutions; for the public have no interest in the detail of private vices and defects, when the individual charged is not a candidate for any public trust; and publications of that kind, are apt to be infected with malice, and to be very injurious to the peace and happiness of families. If the libel was made, in order to expose to the public eye personal defects, or misfortunes, or vices, the proof of the truth of the charge would rather aggravate than lessen the baseness and evil tendency of the publication; and there is much justice and sound policy in the opinion, that in private, as well as public prosecutions for libels, the inquiry should be pointed to the innocence or malice of the publisher's intentions. The truth ought to be admissible in evidence to explain that intent, and not in every instance to justify it. The guilt and the essential ground of action for defamation, consist in the malicious intention; and when the mind is not in fault, no prosecution can be sustained. On the other hand, the truth may be printed and published maliciously, and with an evil intent, and for no good purpose, and when it would be productive only of private misery, and public scandal and disgrace.

33

JOSEPH STORY, COMMENTARIES ON THE
CONSTITUTION 3:§§ 1874, 1876–83, 1885–86
1833

---

§ 1874. . . . "Congress shall make no law abridging the freedom of speech, or of the press." That this amendment was intended to secure to every citizen an absolute right to speak, or write, or print, whatever he might please, without any responsibility, public or private, therefor, is a supposition too wild to be indulged by any rational man. This would be to allow to every citizen a right to destroy, at his pleasure, the reputation, the peace, the property, and even the personal safety of every other citizen. A man might, out of mere malice and revenge, accuse another of the most infamous crimes; might excite against him the indignation of all his fellow citizens by the most atrocious calumnies; might disturb, nay, overturn all his domestic peace, and embitter his parental affections; might inflict the most distressing punishments upon the weak, the timid, and the innocent; might prejudice all a man's civil, and political, and private rights; and might stir up sedition, rebellion, and treason even against the government itself, in the wantonness of his passions, or the corruption of his heart. Civil society could not go on under such circumstances. Men would then be obliged to resort to private vengeance, to make up for the deficiencies of the law; and assassinations, and savage cruelties, would be perpetrated with all the frequency belonging to barbarous and brutal communities. It is plain, then, that the language of this amendment imports no more, than that every man shall have a right to speak, write, and print his opinions upon any subject whatsoever, without any prior restraint, so always, that he does not injure any other person in his rights, person, property, or reputation; and so always, that he does not thereby disturb the public peace, or attempt to subvert the government. It is neither more nor less, than an expansion of the great doctrine, recently brought into operation in the law of libel, that every man shall be at liberty to publish what is true, with good motives and for justifiable ends. And with this reasonable limitation it is not only right in itself, but it is an inestimable privilege in a free government. Without such a limitation, it might become the scourge of the republic, first denouncing the principles of liberty, and then, by rendering the most virtuous patriots odious through the terrors of the press, introducing despotism in its worst form.

. . . . .

§ 1876. . . . The art of printing, soon after its introduction, (we are told,) was looked upon, as well in England, as in other countries, as merely a matter of state, and subject to the coercion of the crown. It was therefore regulated in England by the king's proclamations, prohibitions, charters of privilege, and licenses, and finally by the decrees of the court of Star Chamber; which limited the number of printers, and of presses, which each should employ, and prohibited new publications, unless previously approved by proper licensers. On the demolition of this odious jurisdiction, in 1641, the long parliament of Charles the First, after their rupture with that prince, assumed the same powers, which the Star Chamber exercised, with respect to licensing books; and during the commonwealth, (such is human frailty, and the love of power, even in republics!) they issued their ordinances for that purpose, founded principally upon a Star Chamber decree, in 1637. After the restoration of Charles the Second, a statute on the same subject was passed, copied, with some few alterations, from the parliamentary ordinances.

The act expired in 1679, and was revived and continued for a few years after the revolution of 1688. Many attempts were made by the government to keep it in force; but it was so strongly resisted by parliament, that it expired in 1694, and has never since been revived. To this very hour the liberty of the press in England stands upon this negative foundation. The power to restrain it is dormant, not dead. It has never constituted an article of any of her numerous bills of rights; and that of the revolution of 1688, after securing other civil and political privileges, left this without notice, as unworthy of care, or fit for restraint.

§ 1877. This short review exhibits, in a striking light, the gradual progress of opinion in favour of the liberty of publishing and printing opinions in England, and the frail and uncertain tenure, by which it has been held. Down to this very day it is a contempt of parliament, and a high breach of privilege, to publish the speech of any member of either house, without its consent. It is true, that it is now silently established by the course of popular opinion to be innocent in practice, though not in law. But it is notorious, that within the last fifty years the publication was connived at, rather than allowed; and that for a considerable time the reports were given in a stealthy manner, covered up under the garb of speeches in a fictitious assembly.

§ 1878. There is a good deal of loose reasoning on the subject of the liberty of the press, as if its inviolability were constitutionally such, that, like the king of England, it could do no wrong, and was free from every inquiry, and afforded a perfect sanctuary for every abuse, that, in short, it implied a despotic sovereignty to do every sort of wrong, without the slightest accountability to private or public justice. Such a notion is too extravagant to be held by any sound constitutional lawyer, with regard to the rights and duties belonging to governments generally, or to the state governments in particular. If it were admitted to be correct, it might be justly affirmed, that the liberty of the press was incompatible with the permanent existence of any free government. Mr. Justice Blackstone has remarked, that the liberty of the press, properly understood, is essential to the nature of a free state; but that this consists in laying no *previous* restraints upon publications, and not in freedom from censure for criminal matter, when published. Every freeman has an undoubted right to lay what sentiments he pleases before the public; to forbid this is to destroy the freedom of the press. But, if he publishes what is improper, mischievous, or illegal, he must take the consequences of his own temerity. To subject the press to the restrictive power of a licenser, as was formerly done before, and since the revolution (of 1688), is to subject all freedom of sentiment to the prejudices of one man, and make him the arbitrary and infallible judge of all controverted points in learning, religion, and government. But to punish any dangerous or offensive writings, which, when published, shall, on a fair and impartial trial, be adjudged of a pernicious tendency, is necessary for the preservation of peace and good order, of government and religion, the only solid foundations of civil liberty. Thus, the will of individuals is still left free; the abuse only of that

free will is the object of legal punishment. Neither is any restraint hereby laid upon freedom of thought or inquiry; liberty of private sentiment is still left; the disseminating, or making public of bad sentiments, destructive of the ends of society, is the crime, which society corrects. A man may be allowed to keep poisons in his closet; but not publicly to vend them as cordials. And after some additional reflections, he concludes with this memorable sentence: "So true will it be found, that to censure the licentiousness, is to maintain the liberty of the press."[1]

§ 1879. De Lolme states the same view of the subject; and, indeed, the liberty of the press, as understood by all England, is the right to publish without any previous restraint, or license; so, that neither the courts of justice, nor other persons, are authorized to take notice of writings intended for the press; but are confined to those, which are printed. And, in such cases, if their character is questioned, whether they are lawful, or libellous, is to be tried by a jury, according to due proceedings at law. The noblest patriots of England, and the most distinguished friends of liberty, both in parliament, and at the bar, have never contended for a total exemption from responsibility, but have asked only, that the guilt or innocence of the publication should be ascertained by a trial by jury.[2]

§ 1880. It would seem, that a very different view of the subject was taken by a learned American commentator, though it is not, perhaps, very easy to ascertain the exact extent of his opinions. In one part of his disquisitions, he [St. George Tucker] seems broadly to contend, that the security of the freedom of the press requires, that it

[1] 1 Black. Comm. 152, 153; *Rex v. Burdett*, 4 Barn. & Ald. R. 95.—Mr. Justice Best in *Rex v. Burdett*, (4 Barn. & Ald. R. 95, 132,) said "my opinion of the liberty of the press is, that every man ought to be permitted to instruct his fellow subjects; that every man may fearlessly advance any new doctrines, provided he does so with proper respect to the religion and government of the country; that he may point out errors in the measures of public men; but, he must not impute criminal conduct to them. The liberty of the press cannot be carried to this extent, without violating another equally sacred right, the right of character. This right can only be attacked in a court of justice, where the party attacked has a fair opportunity of defending himself. Where vituperation begins, the liberty of the press ends."

[2] See also *Rex v. Burdett*, 4 Barn. & Ald. 95.—The celebrated act of parliament of Mr. Fox, giving the right to the jury, in trials for libels, to judge of the whole matter of the charge, and to return a general verdict, did not affect to go farther. The celebrated defence of Mr. Erskine, on the trial of the Dean of St. Asaph, took the same ground. Even Junius, with his severe and bitter assaults upon established authority and doctrines, stopped here. "The liberty of the press," (said he,) "is the palladium of all the civil, political, and religious rights of an Englishman, and the right of juries to return a general verdict in all cases whatsoever, is an essential part of our constitution." "The laws of England, provide as effectually, as any human laws can do, for the protection of the subject in his reputation, as well as in his person and property. If the characters of private men are insulted, or injured, a double remedy is open to them, by action and by indictment."—"With regard to strictures upon the characters of men in office, and the measures of government, the case is a *little* different. A *considerable* latitude must be allowed in the discussion of public affairs, or the liberty of the press will be of no benefit to society." But he no where contends for the right to publish seditious libels; and, on the contrary, through his whole reasoning he admits the duty to punish those, which are really so.

should be exempt, not only from previous restraint by the executive, as in Great Britain; but, from legislative restraint also; and that this exemption, to be effectual, must be an exemption, not only from the previous inspection of licensers, but from the subsequent penalty of laws. In other places, he seems as explicitly to admit, that the liberty of the press does not include the right to do injury to the reputation of another, or to take from him the enjoyment of his rights or property, or to justify slander and calumny upon him, as a private or public man. And yet it is added, that every individual certainly has a right to speak, or publish his sentiments on the measures of government. To do this without restraint, control, or *fear of punishment for so doing,* is that which constitutes the genuine freedom of the press. Perhaps the apparent contrariety of these opinions may arise from mixing up, in the same disquisitions, a discussion of the right of the state governments, with that of the national government, to interfere in cases of this sort, which may stand upon very different foundations. Or, perhaps, it is meant to be contended, that the liberty of the press, in all cases, excludes public punishment for public wrongs; but not civil redress for private wrongs, by calumny and libels.

§ 1881. The true mode of considering the subject is, to examine the case with reference to a state government, whose constitution, like that, for instance, of Massachusetts, declares, that "the liberty of the press is essential to the security of freedom in a state; it ought not, therefore, to be restrained in this commonwealth." What is the true interpretation of this clause? Does it prohibit the legislature from passing any laws, which shall control the licentiousness of the press, or afford adequate protection to individuals, whose private comfort, or good reputations are assailed, and violated by the press? Does it stop the legislature from passing any laws to punish libels and inflammatory publications, the object of which is to excite sedition against the government, to stir up resistance to its laws, to urge on conspiracies to destroy it, to create odium and indignation against virtuous citizens, to compel them to yield up their rights, or to make them the objects of popular vengeance? Would such a declaration in Virginia (for she has, on more than one occasion, boldly proclaimed, that the liberty of the press ought not to be restrained,) prohibit the legislature from passing laws to punish a man, who should publish, and circulate writings, the design of which avowedly is to excite the slaves to general insurrection against their masters, or to inculcate upon them the policy of secretly poisoning, or murdering them? In short, is it contended, that the liberty of the press is so much more valuable, than all other rights in society, that the public safety, nay the existence of the government itself is to yield to it? Is private redress for libels and calumny more important, or more valuable, than the maintenance of the good order, peace, and safety of society? It would be difficult to answer these questions in favour of the liberty of the press, without at the same time declaring, that such a licentiousness belonged, and could belong only to a despotism; and was utterly incompatible with the principles of a free government.

§ 1882. Besides:—What is meant by restraint of the press, or an abridgment of its liberty? If to publish without control, or responsibility be its genuine meaning; is not that equally violated by allowing a private compensation for damages, as by a public fine? Is not a man as much restrained from doing a thing by the fear of heavy damages, as by public punishment? Is he not often as severely punished by one, as by the other? Surely, it can make no difference in the case, what is the nature or extent of the restraint, if all restraint is prohibited. The legislative power is just as much prohibited from one mode, as from another. And it may be asked, where is the ground for distinguishing between public and private amesnability for the wrong? The prohibition itself states no distinction. It is general; it is universal. Why, then, is the distinction attempted to be made? Plainly, because of the monstrous consequences flowing from such a doctrine. It would prostrate all personal liberty, all private peace, all enjoyment of property, and good reputation. These are the great objects, for which government is instituted; and, if the licentiousness of the press must endanger, not only these, but all public rights and public liberties, is it not as plain, that the right of government to punish the violators of them (the only mode of redress, which it can pursue) flows from the primary duty of self-preservation? No one can doubt the importance, in a free government, of a right to canvass the acts of public men, and the tendency of public measures, to censure boldly the conduct of rulers, and to scrutinize closely the policy, and plans of the government. This is the great security of a free government. If we would preserve it, public opinion must be enlightened; political vigilance must be inculcated; free, but not licentious, discussion must be encouraged. But the exercise of a right is essentially different from an abuse of it. The one is no legitimate inference from the other. Common sense here promulgates the broad doctrine, *sic utere tuo, ut non alienum laedas;* so exercise your own freedom, as not to infringe the rights of others, or the public peace and safety.

§ 1883. The doctrine laid down by Mr. Justice Blackstone, respecting the liberty of the press, has not been repudiated (as far as is known) by any solemn decision of any of the state courts, in respect to their own municipal jurisprudence. On the contrary, it has been repeatedly affirmed in several of the states, notwithstanding their constitutions, or laws recognize, that "the liberty of the press ought not to be restrained," or more emphatically, that "the liberty of the press shall be inviolably maintained." This is especially true in regard to Massachusetts, South-Carolina, and Louisiana. Nay; it has farther been held, that the truth of the facts is not alone sufficient to justify the publication, unless it is done from good motives, and for justifiable purposes, or, in other words, on an occasion, (as upon the canvass of candidates for public office,) when public duty, or private right requires it. And the very circumstance, that, in the constitutions of several other states, provision is made for giving the truth in evidence, in prosecutions for libels for official conduct, when the matter published is proper for public information, is exceedingly strong to show, how the general law is understood. The exception establishes in all other cases the propriety of the doctrine. And Mr. Chancellor Kent, upon a large survey of the whole subject, has not scrupled to declare, that "it has become a constitutional principle in this country, that every citizen may freely speak, write, and publish his sentiments on all subjects, *being responsible for the abuse of that right;* and, that no law can rightfully be passed, to restrain, or abridge the freedom of the press."

. . . . .

§ 1885. Whether the national government possesses a power to pass any law, not restraining the liberty of the press, but punishing the licentiousness of the press, is a question of a very different nature, upon which the commentator abstains from expressing any opinion. In 1798, Congress, believing that they possessed a constitutional authority for that purpose, passed an act, punishing all unlawful combinations, and conspiracies, to oppose the measures of the government, or to impede the operation of the laws, or to intimidate and prevent any officer of the United States from undertaking, or executing his duty. The same act further provided, for a public presentation, and punishment by fine, and imprisonment, of all persons, who should write, print, utter, or publish any false, scandalous, and malicious writing, or writings against the government of the United States, or of either house of congress, or of the president, with an intent to defame them, or bring them into contempt, or disrepute, or to excite against them the hatred of the good people of the United States; or to excite them to oppose any law, or act of the president, in pursuance of law of his constitutional powers; or to resist, or oppose, or defeat any law; or to aid, encourage, or abet any hostile designs of any foreign nation against the United States. And the same act authorized the truth to be given in evidence on any such prosecution; and the jury, upon the trial, to determine the law and the fact, as in other cases.

§ 1886. This act was immediately assailed, as unconstitutional, both in the state legislatures, and the courts of law, where prosecutions were pending. Its constitutionality was deliberately affirmed by the courts of law; and in a report made by a committee of congress. It was denied by a considerable number of the states; but affirmed by a majority. It became one of the most prominent points of attack upon the existing administration; and the appeal thus made was, probably, more successful with the people, and more consonant with the feelings of the time, than any other made upon that occasion. The act, being limited to a short period, expired by its own limitation, in March, 1801; and has never been renewed. It has continued, down to this very day, to be a theme of reproach with many of those, who have since succeeded to power.

SEE ALSO:

Generally Bill of Rights
Stroud's Case, 3 How. St. Tr. 235 (1629)
John Milton, Areopagitica, A Speech for Liberty of Unlicensed Printing to the Parliament of England (1644)
Thomas Gordon, Cato's Letters, no. 15, 4 Feb. 1720, Jacobson 38–44
Thomas Gordon, Cato's Letters, no. 32, 10 June 1721, Jacobson 73–80
John Trenchard, Cato's Letters, nos. 100–101, 27 Oct.–3 Nov. 1722, Jacobson 230–42
James Alexander, A Brief Narrative of the Case and Trial of John Peter Zenger, 1735 (S. Katz ed., 1963)
King v. *Almon*, 97 Eng. Rep. 94 (K.B. 1765)
Continental Congress to the Inhabitants of Quebec, 26 Oct. 1774, Journals 1:105–13
John Adams, Novanglus, no. 3, 6 Feb. 1775, Papers 2:243–47
Delaware Declaration of Rights and Fundamental Rules, 11 Sept. 1776, Sources 340
Maryland Constitution of 1776, Declaration of Rights, art. 38, Thorpe 3:1690
North Carolina Constitution of 1776, Declaration of Rights, art. 15, Thorpe 5:2788
Pennsylvania Constitution of 1776, Declaration of Rights, art. 12, Thorpe 5:3083
Vermont Constitution of 1777, ch. 1, art. 14, Thorpe 6:3741
South Carolina Constitution of 1778, art. 43, Thorpe 6:3257
Massachusetts Declaration of Rights, 1780, pt. 1, art. 16, Handlin 446
New Hampshire Constitution of 1784, pt. 1, art. 22, Thorpe 4:2456
Vermont Constitution of 1786, ch. 1, art. 15, Thorpe 6:3753
Federal Farmer, no. 4, 12 Oct. 1787, Storing 2.8.56
James Wilson, An Address to a Meeting of the Citizens of Philadelphia, 1787, Pamphlets 155–57
A Democratic Federalist, 17 Oct. 1787, Storing 3.5.3–4
James Wilson, Pennsylvania Ratifying Convention, 1 Dec. 1787, Elliot 2:448–49, 449–50
Noah Webster, Address to the Dissenting Members of the Late Convention of Pennsylvania, Dec. 1787, Collection 144–46
Pennsylvania Ratifying Convention Minority, Proposed Amendment, 12 Dec. 1787, Dumbauld 174
Alexander Contee Hanson, Aristides, Remarks, 1788, Pamphlets 256
James Iredell, Marcus, Answers to Mr. Mason's Objections to the New Constitution, 1788, Pamphlets 356, 360–61
Hugh Williamson, Remarks on the New Plan of Government, 1788, Essays 395–406
James Monroe, Observations on the Proposed Plan of Government, 1788, Writings 1:394–95
Elbridge Gerry, Observations on the New Constitution and the Federal and State Conventions, 1788, Pamphlets 9
John Jay, Address to the People of New York on the Constitution, 1788, Correspondence 3:305
Debate in South Carolina Ratifying Convention, 18 Jan. 1788, Elliot 4:314, 315–16
Luther Martin, Letter no. 4, 21 Mar. 1788, Essays 365
Proposed Amendment, Maryland Ratifying Convention Committee, 29 Apr. 1788, Dumbauld 178
Debate in Virginia Ratifying Convention, 10, 16–17 June 1788, Elliot 3:246–47, 449, 469
Proposed Amendment, Virginia Ratifying Convention, 27 June 1788, Dumbauld 185
North Carolina Ratifying Convention, Proposed Amendment, 1 Aug. 1788, Dumbauld 201
House of Representatives, Debates of the House, 26 Sept. 1789, Annals 1:917–20
Georgia Constitution of 1789, art. 4, sec. 3, Thorpe 2:1789
Pennsylvania Constitution of 1790, art. 9, sec. 7, Thorpe 5:3100
House of Representatives, Government Support of Newspapers, 14 Apr., 9 Dec. 1790, Annals 2:1528–29, 1789–90
James Wilson, Lectures on Law, 1791, Works 2:647–52
Delaware Constitution of 1792, art. 1, sec. 5, Thorpe 1:569
Kentucky Constitution of 1792, art. 12, secs. 7, 8, Thorpe 3:1274
Vermont Constitution of 1793, ch. 1, art. 13, Thorpe 6:3763

William Bradford, Libellous Publications, 17 Sept. 1794, 1 Ops. Atty. Gen. 52

Tennessee Constitution of 1796, art. 1, sec. 19, Thorpe 6:3428

Charles Lee, Libellous Publications, 27 July 1797, 1 Ops. Atty. Gen. 71, 74

Georgia Constitution of 1798, art. 4, sec. 5, Thorpe 2:800

House of Representatives, Seditious Practices, 16 June 1798, Annals 8:1954–71

House of Representatives, Punishment of Crime, 5, 6, 10 July 1798, Annals 8:2093–2113, 2115–16, 2139–71

Charge of Chief Justice Thomas McKean of Pennsylvania to the Grand Jury, Sept. 1798, Addison R. 270–89

Trial of Matthew Lyon, 7 Oct. 1798, State Trials 333

The Sedition Act, 1 Stat. 596–97 (1798)

Responses of Delaware, Rhode Island, Massachusetts, New York, Connecticut, New Hampshire and Vermont Legislatures to Virginia Resolutions of 1798, Elliot 4:532–37

House of Representatives, Alien and Sedition Laws, 25 Feb. 1799, Annals 9:2985–3014, 3016

William Pitt, House of Commons, Hansard (1st ser.) 34:987 (1799)

James Iredell, Charge to the Grand Jury, 9 Fed. Cas. 826, no. 5,126 (C.C.D.Pa. 1799)

Kentucky Constitution of 1799, art. 10, sec. 7, Thorpe 3:1289

An Act for the Punishment of Certain Crimes, 1 Stat. 613 (1799)

Trial of David Frothingham, 1799, State Trials 649

Trial of Anthony Haswell, 1800, State Trials 684

Trial of James Thompson Callender, 1800, State Trials 688

Tunis Wortman, A Treatise concerning Political Enquiry (1800)

House of Representatives, The Sedition Law, 23 Jan. 1800, 21–23 Jan. 1801, Annals 10:404–19, 420–23, 424–25, 916–40, 946–58, 960–75

United States v. *Duane,* 25 Fed. Cas. 920, no. 14,997 (C.C.D.Pa. 1801)

Hollingsworth v. *Duane,* 12 Fed. Cas. 359, no. 6,619 (C.C.D.Pa. 1801)

Thomas Jefferson to Levi Lincoln, 24 Mar. 1802, Works 9:357–58

Ohio Constitution of 1802, art. 8, sec. 6, Thorpe 5:2910

Thomas Jefferson to Thomas McKean, 19 Feb. 1803, Works 9:451–52

Thomas Jefferson to John Tyler, 28 June 1804, Writings 11:32–34

Thomas Jefferson to Abigail Adams, 22 July 1804, Writings 11:43–44

Thomas Jefferson to Abigail Adams, 11 Sept. 1804, Writings 11:51–52

Thomas Jefferson, Second Inaugural Address, 4 Mar. 1805, Richardson 1:381

Thomas Jefferson to Thomas Seymour, 11 Feb. 1807, Works 10:367–69

Commonwealth v. *Clap,* 4 Mass. 163 (1808)

Thorn v. *Blanchard,* 5 Johns. R. 508 (N.Y. 1809)

Commonwealth v. *Duane,* 1 Binney 601 (Pa. 1809)

Thomas v. *Croswell,* 7 Johns. R. 264 (N.Y. 1810)

Louisiana Constitution of 1812, art. 6, sec. 21, Thorpe 3:1390

Thomas Jefferson to Walter Jones, 2 Jan. 1814, Writings 14:46

Gray v. *Pentland,* 2 Serg. & Rawle 23 (Pa. 1815)

Indiana Constitution of 1816, art. 1, secs. 9, 10, Thorpe 2:1058

Mississippi Constitution of 1817, art. 1, secs. 6–8, Thorpe 2:2033

Connecticut Constitution of 1818, art. 1, sec. 5, Thorpe 1:537

Illinois Constitution of 1818, secs. 22, 23, Thorpe 2:983

Alabama Constitution of 1819, art. 1, sec. 8, art. 6, sec. 14, Thorpe 1:97, 109

Maine Constitution of 1819, art. 1, sec. 4, Thorpe 3:1647

Missouri Constitution of 1820, art. 13, sec. 16, Thorpe 4:2164

New York Constitution of 1821, art. 7, sec. 8, Thorpe 5:2648

Thomas Jefferson to A. Coray, 31 Oct. 1823, Writings 15:489

William Rawle, A View of the Constitution of the United States 123–24 (2d ed. 1829)

Mississippi Constitution of 1832, art. 1, secs. 6–8, Thorpe 4:2049

A. J. Stansbury, Report of the Trial of James H. Peck 49–52, 85–92, 102–4, 298–99, 447–49, 475, 479–80, 573 (1833)

Arnold v. *Clifford,* 1 Fed. Cas. 1177, no. 555 (C.C.D.R.I. 1835)

Michigan Constitution of 1835, art. 1, sec. 7, Thorpe 4:1931

Senate, Debate on Incendiary Publications Bill, and Senate Report Thereon, 4, 9 Feb., 11, 12 Apr., 8 June 1836, Debates 12:1126, 1128–32, 1146–48, 1721–22, 1731–32; 12:App. 72–74

PETITION AND ASSEMBLY

1

MAGNA CARTA, c. 61
1215
Sources 21

. . . if we or our justiciar, or our bailiffs, or any of our servants shall have done wrong in any way toward any one, or shall have transgressed any of the articles of peace or security; and the wrong shall have been shown to four barons of the aforesaid twenty-five barons, let those four barons come to us or to our justiciar, if we are out of the kingdom, laying before us the transgression, and let them ask that we cause that transgression to be corrected without delay.

2

WILLIAM LAMBARDE, EIRENARCHA 175–76
1614 cd.

An unlawfull Assembly, is the companie of three or moe persons, disorderly comming together, forcibly to commit an unlawful act: as, to beate a man, or to enter upon his possession, or such like. . . .

A Route is a disordered assembly of three or moe persons, moving forwarde to commit by force an unlawfull acte. For it is a Route, whether they put their purpose in ful execution, or no, if so be that they doe goe, ride, or move forward after their first meeting. . . .

A Riot, is thought to bee, where three or moe persons, be disorderly assembled to commit with force any such unlawfull acte, and do accordingly execute the same. . . .

And thus (upon the whole reckoning) an unlawfull assembly is the first degree, or beginning: a Route, the next step, or proceeding: and a Riot the ful effect and consummation, of such a disordered and forbidden action.

3

PETITION OF RIGHT
3 Chas. 1, c. 1, 7 June 1628

To the King's most excellent majesty.

HUMBLY *shew unto our sovereign lord the King, the lords spiritual and temporal, and commons in parliament assembled,*

That whereas it is declared and enacted by a statute made in the time of the reign of King Edward *the First commonly called* Statutum de tallagio non concedendo, *That no tallage or aid shall be laid or levied by the King or his heirs in this realm, without the good will and assent of the archbishops, bishops, earls, barons, knights, burgesses, and other the freemen of the commonalty of this realm;* (2) *and by authority of parliament holden in the five and twentieth year of the reign of King* Edward *the Third, it is declared and enacted, That from thenceforth no person should be compelled to make any loans to the King against his will, because such loans were against reason and the franchise of the land;* (3) *and by other laws of this realm it is provided, That none should be charged by any charge or imposition called a benevolence, nor by such like charge:* (4) *by which the statutes before mentioned, and other the good laws and statutes of this realm, your subjects have inherited this freedom, That they should not be compelled to contribute to any tax, tallage, aid or other like charge not set by common consent in parliament.*

II. *Yet nevertheless, of late divers commissions directed to sundry commissioners in several counties, with instructions, have issued; by means whereof your people have been in divers places assembled, and required to lend certain sums of money unto your Majesty, and many of them, upon their refusal so to do, have had an oath administred unto them not warrantable by the laws of statutes of this realm, and have been constrained to become bound to make appearance and give attendance before your privy council and in other places, and others of them have been therefore imprisoned, confined, and sundry other ways molested and disquieted;* (2) *and divers other charges have been laid and levied upon your people in several counties by lord lieutenants, deputy lieutenants, commissioners for musters, justices of peace and others, by command or direction from your Majesty, or your privy council, against the laws and free customs of the realm.*

III. *And where also by the statute called* The great charter of the liberties of England, *it is declared and enacted, That no freeman may be taken or imprisoned, or be disseised of his freehold or liberties, or his free customs, or be outlawed or exiled, or in manner destroyed, but by the lawful judgment of his peers, or by the law of the land.*

IV. *And in the eight and twentieth year of the reign of King* Edward *the Third, it was declared and enacted by authority of parliament, That no man of what estate or condition that he be, should be put out of his land or tenements, nor taken, nor imprisoned, nor disherited, nor put to death without being brought to answer by due process of law:*

V. *Nevertheless against the tenor of the said statutes, and other the good laws and statutes of your realm to that end provided, divers of your subjects have of late been imprisoned without any cause shewed;* (2) *and when for their deliverance they were brought before your justices by your Majesty's writs of habeas corpus, there to undergo and receive as the court should order, and their keepers commanded to certify the causes of their detainer, no cause was certified, but that they were detained by your Majesty's special command, signified by the lords of your privy council, and yet were returned back to several prisons, without being charged with any thing to which they might make answer according to the law:*

VI. *And whereas of late great companies of soldiers and mariners have been dispersed into divers counties of the realm, and the inhabitants against their wills have been compelled to receive them into their houses, and there to suffer them to sojourn, against the laws and customs of this realm, and to the great grievance and vexation of the people:*

VII. *And whereas also by authority of parliament, in the five and twentieth year of the reign of King* Edward *the Third, it is declared and enacted, That no man should be forejudged of life or limb against the form of the* great charter *and the law of the land; (2) and by the said* great charter *and other the laws and statutes of this your realm, no man ought to be adjudged to death but by the laws established in this your realm, either by the customs of the same realm, or by acts of parliament: (3) and whereas no offender of what kind soever is exempted from the proceedings to be used, and punishments to be inflicted by the laws and statutes of this your realm: nevertheless of late time divers commissions under your Majesty's great seal have issued forth, by which certain persons have been assigned and appointed commissioners with power and authority to proceed within the land, according to the justice of martial law, against such soldiers or mariners, or other dissolute persons joining with them, as should commit any murder, robbery, felony, mutiny or other outrage or misdemeanor whatsoever, and by such summary course and order as is agreeable to martial law, and as is used in armies in time of war, to proceed to the trial and condemnation of such offenders, and them to cause to be executed and put to death according to the law martial:*

VIII. *By pretext whereof some of your Majesty's subjects have been by some of the said commissioners put to death, when and where, if by the laws and statutes of the land they had deserved death, by the same laws and statutes also they might, and by no other ought to have been judged and executed:*

IX. *And also sundry grievous offenders, by colour thereof claiming an exemption, have escaped the punishments due to them by the laws and statutes of this your realm, by reason that divers of your officers and ministers of justice have unjustly refused or forborn to proceed against such offenders according to the same laws and statutes, upon pretence that the said offenders were punishable only by martial law, and by authority of such commissions as aforesaid: (2) which commissions, and all other of like nature, are wholly and directly contrary to the said laws and statutes of this your realm:*

X. They do therefore humbly pray your most excellent Majesty, That no man hereafter be compelled to make or yield any gift, loan, benevolence, tax, or such-like charge, without common consent by act of parliament; (2) and that none be called to make answer, or take such oath, or to give attendance, or be confined, or otherwise molested or disquieted concerning the same, or for refusal thereof; (3) and that no freeman, in any such manner as is beforementioned, be imprisoned or detained; (4) and that your Majesty would be pleased to remove the said soldiers and mariners, and that your people may not be so burthened in time to come; (5) and that the aforesaid commissions, for proceeding by martial law, may be revoked and annulled; and that hereafter no commissions of like nature may issue forth to any person or persons whatsoever to be executed as aforesaid, lest by colour of them any of your Majesty's subjects to destroyed, or put to death contrary to the laws and franchise of the land.

XI. All which they most humbly pray of your most excellent Majesty as their rights and liberties, according to the laws and statutes of this realm; and that your Majesty would also vouchsafe to declare, That the awards, doings and proceedings, to the prejudice of your people in any of the premisses, shall not be drawn hereafter into consequence or example; (2) and that your Majesty would be also graciously pleased, for the further comfort and safety of your people, to declare your royal will and pleasure, That in the things aforesaid all your officers and ministers shall serve you according to the laws and statutes of this realm, as they tender the honour of your Majesty, and the prosperity of this kingdom. *Qua quidem petitione lecta & plenius intellecta per dictum dominum regem taliter est responsum in pleno parliamento, viz. Soit droit fait come est desire.*

4

THE TUMULTUOUS PETITION ACT
13 Chas. 2, st. 1, c. 5 (1661)

. . . no person or persons whatsoever shall repaire to his Majesty or both or either of the Houses of Parliament upon p[re]tence of presenting or delivering any peticion complaint remonstrance or declaracion or other addresses accompanied with excessive number of people nor att any one time with above the number of ten persons upon pain of incurring a penalty not exceeding the sum of one hundred pounds in money and three months imprisonment . . . for every offence which offence to be prosecuted at the Court of Kings Bench or att the assizes or generall quarter sessions within six monthes after the offence committed and proved by two or more credible witnesses.

2. PROVIDED alwaies that this Act or any thing therein contained shall not be construed to extend to debar or hinder any person or persons not exceeding the number of ten aforesaid to present any publique or private greivance or complaint to any member or members of Parliament after his election and during the continuance of the Parliament or to the Kings Majesty for any remedy to bee thereupon had nor to extend to any address whatsoever to his Majesty by all or any the members of both or either Houses of Parliament during the sitting of Parliament but that they may enjoye theire freedome of accesse to his Majesty as heretofore hath beene used.

5

RESOLUTION OF THE HOUSE OF COMMONS
1669
Robertson 27

(1) That it is an inherent right of every commoner in England to prepare and present Petitions to the House of

Commons in case of grievances, and the House of Commons to receive the same.

(2) That it is an undoubted right and privilege of the Commons to judge and determine concerning the nature and matter of such petitions, how far they are fit or unfit to be received.

6

TRIAL OF THE SEVEN BISHOPS FOR PUBLISHING A LIBEL

12 How. St. Tr. 183, 415 (1688)

[*Sol. Gen.*] Now, my lord, I come to that which is very plain from the case of De Libellis Famosis, in lord Coke's Reports: if any person have slandered the government in writing, you are to examine the truth of that fact in such writing, but the slander which it imports to the king or government; and be it never so true, yet if slanderous to the king or the government, it is a libel, and to be punished: in that case, the right or wrong is not to be examined, or if what was done by the government be legal or no; but whether the party have done such an act. If the king have a power (for still I keep to that) to issue forth proclamations to his subjects, and to make orders and constitutions in matters ecclesiastical, if he do issue forth his proclamation, and make an order upon the matters within his power and prerogative; and if any one would come and bring that power in question otherwise than in parliament, that the matter of that proclamation be not legal, I say that is sedition, and you are not to examine the legality or illegality of the order or proclamation, but the slander and reflexion upon the government, and that, I think, is very plain upon that case, in the fifth Report De Libellis Famosis; for it says, If a person do a thing that is libellous, you shall not examine the fact, but the consequence of it; whether it tended to stir up sedition against the public, or to stir up strife between man and man, in the case of private persons: as if a man should say of a judge, he has taken a bribe, and I will prove it; this is not to be sent in a letter, but they must take a regular way to prosecute it according to law.

If it be so in the case of an inferior magistrate, what must it be in the case of a king? To come to the king's face, and tell him, as they do here, that he has acted illegally, doth certainly sufficiently prove the matter to be libellous. What do they say to the king? They say and admit, that they have an averseness for the declaration, and they tell him from whence that averseness doth proceed: and yet they insinuate that they had an inclination to gratify the king, and embrace the dissenters, that were as averse to them as could be, with due tenderness, when it should be settled by parliament and convocation. Pray what hath their convocation to do in this matter?

L. C. J. Mr. Solicitor-General, I will not interrupt you; but, pray come to the business before us. Shew us that this is in diminution of the king's prerogative, or that the king ever had such a prerogative.

Sol. Gen. I will, my lord, I am observing what it is they say in this petition—They tell the king it is inconsistent with their honour, prudence and conscience, to do what he would have them to do: And if these things be not reflective upon the king and government, I know not what is. This is not in a way of judicature: possibly it might have been allowable to petition the king to put it into a course of justice, whereby it may be tried; but alas! there is no such thing in this matter.

It is not their desire to put it into any method for trial, and so it comes in the case de Libellis Famosis; for by this way they make themselves judges, which no man by law is permitted to do. My lords the bishops have gone out of the way, and all that they have offered does not come home to justify them; and therefore I take it, under favour, that we have made it a good case for the king: We have proved what they have done, and whether this be warrantable or not, is the question, gentlemen, that you are to try. The whole case appears upon record; the declaration and petition are set forth, and the order of the king and council. When the verdict is brought in, they may move any thing what they please in arrest of judgment. They have had a great deal of latitude, and taken a great deal of liberty; but truly, I apprehend, not so very pertinently. But I hope we have made a very good case of it for the king, and that you, gentlemen, will give us a verdict.

Just. *Holloway.* Mr. Solicitor, there is one thing I would fain be satisfied in: You say the bishops have no power to petition the king.

Sol. Gen. Not out of parliament, Sir.

Just. *Holloway.* Pray give me leave, Sir: Then the king having made such a declaration of a general toleration and liberty of conscience, and afterwards he comes and requires the bishops to disperse this declaration; this, they say, out of a tenderness of conscience, they cannot do, because they apprehend it is contrary to law, and contrary to their function: What can they do, if they may not petition?

Sol. Gen. I'll tell you what they should have done, Sir. If they were commanded to do any thing against their consciences, they should have acquiesced till the meeting of the parliament. [At which some people in the court hissed.]

Att. Gen. This is very fine indeed! I hope the court and the jury will take notice of this carriage.

Sol. Gen. My Lord, it is one thing for a man to submit to his prince, if the king lay a command upon him that he cannot obey, and another thing to affront him. If the king will impose upon a man what he cannot do, he must acquiesce; but shall he come and fly in the face of his prince? Shall he say it is illegal? and the prince acts against prudence, honour or conscience, and throw dirt in the king's face? Sure that is not permitted; that is libelling with a witness.

L. C. J. Truly, Mr. Solicitor, I am of opinion that the bishops might petition the king; but this is not the right way of bringing it in. I am not of that mind that they cannot petition the king out of parliament; but if they may

189

petition, yet they ought to have done it after another manner: for if they may in this reflective way petition the king, I am sure it will make the government very precarious.

Just. *Powell.* Mr. Solicitor, it would have been too late to stay for a parliament; for it was to have been distributed by such a time.

Sol. Gen. They might have lain under it and submitted.

Just. *Powell.* No, they would have run into contempt of the king's command, without petitioning the king not to insist upon it; and if they had petitioned, and not have shewn the reason why they could not obey, it would have been looked upon as a piece of sullenness, and that they would have been blamed for as much on the other side.

Serj. *Baldock.* After so long a debate, I shall not trouble you long; most things that are to be said have been said; but I shall only say this in short: I cannot deny, nor shall not, but that the subject has a right to petition; but I shall affirm it also, he has a duty to obey; and that in this case, the power of the king to dispense with penal laws in matters ecclesiastical, is not a thing that is now in question, nor need we here have had these long debates on both sides. It may be perceived plainly, by the proofs that have been read, that the kings and princes have thought themselves that they had such a power, though it may be the parliament thought they had not; and therefore the declarations of the one or the other I shall not meddle with in this case. That power itself which the king has, as king of this realm, in matters rather ecclesiastical and criminal, than matters of property, may somewhat appear by what has been read before your lordship. But all this will be nothing in our case, neither has his majesty now depended so much upon this thing. The declaration has been read to you, and what's there said? The king there says, That for those reasons he was ready to suspend those laws; and be they suspended. Yet, my lord, with this too, that he refers it to, and hopes to make it secure by a parliament. So that there being this, it has not gone, I think, very far; and it not having been touched here, it is not a point of duty in my lords the bishops, as bishops, that's here inquired into. Whether they should have meddled with this or no, in this manner, is the question. That the king is supreme over all of us, and has a particular supremacy over them, as supreme ordinary and governor, and moderator of the church, is very plain; and, my lord, it is as plain, that in such things as concern the church, he has a particular power to command them. This is not unknown, but very frequent and common in matters ecclesiastical, and matters of state. It is not here a question now, whether these declarations which they were commanded to take care of getting read, were legal or not legal? What prudence there was, what honour there was, what conscience there was, for their not reading it, is not the question neither: But the point was, the king as supreme ordinary of his kingdom, to whom the bishops are subject, does in council order; and what is it he orders? Their sending out and distributing his declaration. They were concerned in no more than that, and it had been a very pretty [petty?] thing, a small thing, to send out the king's declaration to be read by the clergy. All the clergy were ordered to read it, but my lords the bishops were only commanded to distribute

it. This he might do by virtue of his power ecclesiastical. And if this be not an evil in itself, and if it be not against the word of God, certainly obedience was due from my lords the bishops; active obedience was due from them to do so much as this. It was no consent of theirs, it was no approbation of theirs of what they read, that was required. So that if they had read it, or another had read it by the king's order, especially if that order be legal, they are bound to do it by virtue of their obedience, and not to examine more.

And, my lord, in this petition, here they come to relieve, not only themselves that were present, (for I speak to the preamble, as others before me have spoke to the conclusion) but they do involve the rest of the bishops that were absent; for it is in behalf of themselves, and their brethren, and all the clergy of that province. Now that all these should join in the petition, is a thing very uncertain. How does it construe here, whether they were all together and consented to it, or how all their minds could be so fully known, that they would be all involved in the disobedience to this order of the king? Then, my lord, what is the thing they are greatly averse to? There are two things required in the order: the bishops required to distribute the declaration to the inferior clergy, and the inferior clergy are required to read it. Then their averseness must be to distribute it, and the others to read it, and so they will be involved; none of whom did ever appear to have joined in it. And then they give reasons for their averseness; and it is true, reasons might have been given, and good reasons should be given, why they should not do this in duty to his majesty; more gentle reasons, and other kind of reasons than those that they have given.

L. C. J. Pray, brother, will you come to the matter before us?

Serj. *Baldock.* I have almost done, my lord.

Just. *Powell.* The information is not for disobedience, brother, but for a libel.

Serj. *Baldock.* No, Sir, it is not for disobedience, but it is for giving reasons for the disobedience in a libellous petition, and I am going on to that. The declaration is said in the petition to be illegal; which is a charge upon the king, that he has done an illegal act. They say, they cannot in honour, conscience, or prudence, do it; which is a reflection upon the prudence, justice, and honour of the king in commanding them to do such a thing: and this appearing to have been delivered to the king by my lords the bishops, persons to whom certainly we all owe a deference, as our spiritual masters, to believe what things they say as most likely to be true; and therefore it having an universal influence upon all the people, I shall leave it here to your lordship and the jury, whether they ought not to answer for it.

Recorder. Will your lordship please to spare me one word?

L. C. J. I hope we shall have done by and bye.

Recorder. If your lordship don't think fit, I can sit down.

L. C. J. No, no, go on, sir Bartholomew Shower, you'll say I have spoiled a good speech.

Recorder. I have no good one to make, my lord, I have but a very few words to say.

L. C. J. Well, go on, Sir.

Recorder. That which I would urge, my lord, is only this: I think, my lord, we have proved our information, and that they have made no answer to it; for the answer they have made is but argumentative, and taken either from the persons of the defendants, as peers, or from the form of its being a petition. As peers, it is said they have a right to petition to, and advise the king; but that is no excuse at all; for if it contains matter reproachful or scandalous, it is a libel in them as well as in any other subject; and they have no more right to libel the king than his majesty's other subjects have; nor will the privilege of their peerage exempt them from being punished. And for the form of this paper, as being a petition, there is no more excuse in that neither: for every man has as much right to publish a book, or pamphlet, as they had to present their petition. And as it would be punishable in that man to write a scandalous book, so it would be punishable in them to make a scandalous, and a libellous petition. And the author of Julian the Apostate, because he was a clergyman, and a learned man too, had as much right to publish his book, as my lords the bishops had to deliver this libel to the king. And if the city of London were so severely punished as to lose their charter, for petitioning for the sitting of a parliament, in which there were reflecting words, but more soft—

Just. Holloway. Pray, good Mr. Recorder, don't compare the writing of a book to the making of a petition; for it is the birthright of the subject to petition.

Recorder. My lord, it was as lawful for the city of London to petition for the sitting of a parliament, as it was for my lords the bishops to give reasons for their disobedience to the king's command: and if the matter of the city of London's petition was reckoned to be libellous, in saying that what the king had done in dissolving the parliament, was an obstruction of justice, what other construction can be made of my lords the bishops saying that the king's declaration is illegal? And if the matter of this petition be of the same nature with that of the city of London, your lordship can make no other judgment of it, but that it ought to have the same condemnation.

Just. Powell. Mr. Recorder, you will as soon bring the two poles together, as make this petition to agree with Johnson's book. They are no more alike than the most different things you can name.

Serj. *Trinder.* My lord, I have but one word.

L. C. J. How unreasonable is this now, that we must have so many speeches at this time of day! But we must hear it; go on, brother.

Serj. *Trinder.* My lord, if your lordship pleases, that which they seem most to insist upon on the other side, and which has not been much spoken to on our side, is, that this power which his majesty has exerted, in setting forth his declaration, was illegal, and their arguments were hypothetical. If it were illegal, they had not offended; and they offered at some arguments to prove it illegal; but as to that, my lord, we need not go much further than a case which is very well known here, which I crave leave to mention, only because the jury, perhaps, have not heard of it, and that was the case of sir Edward Hales; where, after a long debate, it was resolved, That the king had a power to dispense with penal laws.

But, my lord, if I should go higher into our books of law, that which they seem to make so strange of, might easily be made appear to have been made a frequent and constant practice.—

L. C. J. That is quite out of the case, brother.

Serj. *Trinder.* I beg your lordship's favour for a word or two. If your lordship please to consider the power the king has, as supreme ordinary, we say, he has a power to dispense with these statutes as he is king, and to give ease to his subjects, as supreme ordinary of the whole kingdom, and as having supreme ecclesiastical authority throughout the kingdom. There might be abundance of cases cited for this, if there were need: the statute of *primo* Eliz. doubtless is in force at this time, and a great many of the statutes that have been made since that time, have express savings of the king's supremacy: so that the king's power is unquestionable. And if they have come and questioned this power in this manner, by referring themselves to the declarations in parliament, they have done that which of late days has been always looked upon as an ill thing; as if the king's authority was under the suffrages of a parliament. But when they come to make out their parliament declarations, there was never a one, unless it be first in Richard the second's time, that can properly be called a parliament declaration, so that of the several parliaments is a matter perfectly mistaken; and if they have mistaken it, it is in the nature of false news, which is a crime for which the law will punish them. More things might be added, but I consider your lordship has had a great deal of patience already, and much time has been spent, and therefore I shall conclude, begging your lordship's pardon for what I have said.

L. C. J. I do assure you, if it had not been a case of great concern, I would not have heard you so long. It is a case of very great concern to the king and the government on the one side, and to my lords the bishops on the other; and I have taken all the care I can to observe what has been said on both sides. It is not to be expected that I should repeat all the speeches, or the particular facts, but I will put the jury in mind of the most material things, as well as my memory will give me leave; but I have been interrupted by so many long and learned speeches, and by the length of the evidence which has been brought in, in a very broken, unmethodical way, that I shall not be able to do so well as I would.

Gentlemen, thus stands the case: it is an information against my lords the bishops, his grace my lord of Canterbury, and the other six noble lords; and it is for preferring, composing, making, and publishing, and causing to be published, a seditious libel: the way that the information goes is special, and it sets forth, that the king was graciously pleased, by his royal power and prerogative, to set forth a declaration of indulgence for liberty of conscience, in the third year of his reign; and afterwards upon the 27th of April, in the fourth year, he comes and makes another declaration; and afterwards in May, orders in council that this declaration should be published by my lords the bishops in their several dioceses; and after this was done, my lords the bishops come and present a petition to the king, in which were contained the words which you have seen.

Now, gentlemen, the proofs that have been upon this, you will see what they are. The two declarations are proved by the clerks of the council, and they are brought here under the great seal. A question did arise, whether the prints were the same with the original declarations, and that is proved by Hills, or his man, that they were examined, and are the same. Then the order of the council was produced by sir John Nicholas, and has likewise been read to you. Then they come to prove the fact against the bishops, and first they fall to proving their hands. They begun indeed a great way off, and did not come so close to it as they afterwards did; for some of their hands they could hardly prove, but my lord archbishop's hand was only proved, and some others; but there might have been some question about that proof. But afterwards it came to be proved, that my lords the bishops owned their hands; which if they had produced at first, would have made the cause something shorter than it was.

The next question that did arise, was about the publishing of it, whether my lords the bishops had published it? And it was insisted upon, that no body could prove the delivery of it to the king. It was proved, the king gave it to the council, and my lords the bishops were called in, and there they acknowledged their hands; but nobody could prove how it came to the king's hands. Upon which we were all of opinion, that it was not such a publishing as was within the information; and I was going to have directed you to find my lords the bishops not guilty: but it happened, that being interrupted in my directions, by an honest, worthy, learned gentleman, the king's counsel took the advantage, and informing the court that they had further evidence for the king, we staid till my lord president came, who told us how the bishops came to him to his office at Whitehall, and after they had told him their design, that they had a mind to petition the king, they asked him the method they were to take for it, and desired him to help them to the speech of the king: and he tells them he will acquaint the king with their desire, which he does; and the king giving leave, he comes down and tells the bishops, that they might go and speak with the king when they would; and, says he, I have given direction that the door shall be opened for you as soon as you come. With that the two bishops went away, and said, they would go and fetch their other brethren, and they did bring the other four, but my lord archbishop was not there; and immediately when they came back, they went up into the chamber, and there a petition was delivered to the king. He cannot speak to that particular petition, because he did not read it, and that is all that he knew of the matter; only it was all done the same day, and that was before my lords the bishops appeared at the council.

Gentlemen, after this was proved, then the defendants came to their part; and these gentlemen that were of counsel for my lords, let themselves into their defence, by notable learned speeches, by telling you that my lords the bishops are guardians to the church, and great peers of

the realm, and were bound in conscience to take care of the church. They have read you a clause of a statute made in queen Elizabeth's time, by which they say, my lords the bishops were under a curse, if they did not take care of that law: then they shew you some records; one in Richard the second's time, which they could make little of, by reason their witness could not read it; but it was, in short, a liberty given to the king, to dispense with the statute of provisors. Then they shew you some journals of parliament; first in the year 1662, where the king had granted an indulgence, and the house of commons declared it was not fit to be done, unless it were by act of parliament: and they read the king's speech, wherein he says, he wished he had such a power; and so likewise that in 1672, which is all nothing but addresses and votes, or orders of the house, or discourses; either the king's speech, or the subjects addresses; but these are not declarations in parliament. That is insisted upon by the counsel for the king, that what is a declaration in parliament is a law, and that must be by the king, lords, and commons; the other is but common discourse, but a vote of the house, or a signification of their opinion, and cannot be said to be a declaration in parliament. Then they come to that in 1685, where the commons take notice of something about the soldiers in the army that had not taken the test, and make an address to the king about it: but in all these things (as far as I can observe) nothing can be gathered out of them one way or the other; it is nothing but discourses. Sometimes this dispensing power has been allowed, as in Richard the 2nd's time, and sometimes it has been denied, and the king did once wave it: Mr. Solicitor tells you the reason, there was a lump of money in the case; but I wonder indeed to hear it come from him.

Sol. Gen. My lord, I never gave my vote for money, I assure you.

L. C. J. But those concessions which the king sometimes makes for the good of the people, and sometimes for the profit of the prince himself (but I would not be thought to distinguish between the profit of the prince and the good of the people, for they are both one; and what is the profit of the prince is always for the good of the people), but I say, those concessions must not be made law, for that is reserved in the king's breast, to do what he pleases in it at any time.

The truth of it is, the dispensing power is out of the case, it is only a word used in the petition; but truly, I will not take upon me to give my opinion in the question, to determine that now, for it is not before me: the only question before me is, and so it is before you, gentlemen, it being a question of fact, whether here be a certain proof of a publication? And then the next question is a question of law indeed, whether if there be a publication proved, it be a libel?

Gentlemen, upon the point of the publication, I have summed up all the evidence to you; and if you believe that the petition which these lords presented to the king was this petition, truly, I think, that is a publication sufficient: if you do not believe it was this petition, then my lords the bishops are not guilty of what is laid to their charge in this information, and consequently there needs no inquiry whether they are guilty of a libel? but if you do believe that this was the petition they presented to the king, then we must come to inquire whether this be a libel.

Now, gentlemen, any thing that shall disturb the government, or make mischief and a stir among the people, is certainly within the case of "Libellis Famosis;" and I must in short give you my opinion, I do take it to be a libel. Now this being a point of law, if my brothers have any thing to say to it, I suppose they will deliver their opinions.

Just. *Holloway.* Look you, gentlemen, it is not usual for any person to say any thing after the Chief Justice has summed up the evidence; it is not according to the course of the court: but this is a case of an extraordinary nature, and there being a point of law in it, it is very fit every body should deliver their own opinion. The question is, Whether this petition of my lords the bishops be a libel or no. Gentlemen, the end and intention of every action is to be considered; and likewise, in this case, we are to consider the nature of the offence that these noble persons are charged with; it is for delivering a petition, which, according as they have made their defence, was with all the humility and decency that could be: so that if there was no ill intent, and they were not (as it is not, nor can be pretended they were) men of evil lives, or the like, to deliver a petition cannot be a fault, it being the right of every subject to petition. If you are satisfied there was an ill intention of sedition, or the like, you ought to find them guilty: but if there be nothing in the case that you find, but only that they did deliver a petition to save themselves harmless, and to free themselves from blame, by shewing the reason of their disobedience to the king's command, which they apprehended to be a grievance to them, and which they could not in conscience give obedience to, I cannot think it is a libel: it is left to you, gentlemen, but that is my opinion.

L. C. J. Look you, by the way, brother, I did not ask you to sum up the evidence (for that is not usual) but only to deliver your opinion, whether it be a libel or no.

Just. *Powell.* Truly I cannot see, for my part, any thing of sedition, or any other crime, fixed upon these reverend fathers, my lords the bishops.

For, gentlemen, to make it a libel, it must be false, it must be malicious, and it must tend to sedition. As to the falshood, I see nothing that is offered by the king's counsel, nor any thing as to the malice: it was presented with all the humility and decency that became the king's subjects to approach their prince with.

Now, gentlemen, the matter of it is before you; you are to consider of it, and it is worth your consideration. They tell his majesty, it is not out of averseness to pay all due obedience to the king, nor out of a want of tenderness to their dissenting fellow subjects, that made them not perform the command imposed upon them; but they say, that because they do conceive that the thing that was commanded them was against the law of the land, therefore they do desire his majesty, that he would be pleased to forbear to insist upon it, that they should perform that command which they take to be illegal.

Gentlemen, we must consider what they say is illegal in it. They say, they apprehend the declaration is illegal, because it is founded upon a dispensing power, which the king claims, to dispense with the laws concerning ecclesiastical affairs.

Gentlemen, I do not remember, in any case in all our law (and I have taken some pains upon this occasion to look into it), that there is any such power in the king, and the case must turn upon that. In short, if there be no such dispensing power in the king, then that can be no libel which they presented to the king, which says, that the declaration, being founded upon such a pretended power, is illegal.

Now, gentlemen, this is a dispensation with a witness; it amounts to an abrogation and utter repeal of all the laws; for I can see no difference, nor know of none in law, between the king's power to dispense with laws ecclesiastical, and his power to dispense with any other laws whatsoever. If this be once allowed of, there will need no parliament; all the legislature will be in the king, which is a thing worth considering, and I leave the issue to God and your consciences.

Just. *Allybone.* The single question that falls to my share is, to give my sense of this petition, whether it shall be in construction of law a libel in itself, or a thing of great innocence. I shall endeavour to express myself in as plain terms as I can, and as much as I can, by way of proposition.

And I think, in the first place, that no man can take upon him to write against the actual exercise of the government, unless he have leave from the government, but he makes a libel, be what he writes true or false; for if once we come to impeach the government by way of argument, it is the argument that makes it the government or not the government. So that I lay down that, in the first place, the government ought not to be impeached by argument, nor the exercise of the government shaken by argument; because I can manage a proposition in itself doubtful, with a better pen than another man: this, say I, is a libel.

Then I lay down this for my next position, that no private man can take upon him to write concerning the government at all; for what has any private man to do with the government, if his interest be not stirred or shaken? It is the business of the government to manage matters relating to the government; it is the business of subjects to mind only their own properties and interests. If my interest is not shaken, what have I to do with matters of government? They are not within my sphere. If the government does come to shake my particular interest, the law is open for me, and I may redress myself by law: and when I intrude myself into other men's business that does not concern my particular interest, I am a libeller.

These I have laid down for plain propositions; now then let us consider further, whether, if I will take upon me to contradict the government, any specious pretence that I shall put upon it shall dress it up in another form, and give it a better denomination? And truly I think it is the worse, because it comes in a better dress; for by that rule, every man that can put on a good vizard, may be as mischievous as he will to the government at the bottom: so that whether it be in the form of a supplication, or an address, or a petition, if it be what it ought not to be, let us call it by its true name, and give it its right denomination—it is a libel.

Then, gentlemen, consider what this petition is: this is a petition relating to something that was done and ordered by the government. Whether the reasons of the petition be true or false, I will not examine that now, nor will I examine the prerogative of the crown, but only take notice that this relates to the act of the government. The government here has published such a declaration as this that has been read, relating to matters of government; and shall, or ought any body to come and impeach that as illegal, which the government has done? Truly, in my opinion, I do not think he should, or ought; for by this rule may every act of the government be shaken, when there is not a parliament *de facto* sitting.

I do agree, that every man may petition the government, or the king, in a matter that relates to his own private interest, but to meddle with a matter that relates to the government, I do not think my lords the bishops had any power to do more than any others. When the house of lords and commons are in being, it is a proper way of applying to the king: there is all the openness in the world for those that are members of parliament, to make what addresses they please to the government, for the rectifying, altering, regulating, and making of what law they please; but if every private man shall come and interpose his advice, I think there can never be an end of advising the government. I think there was an instance of this in king James's time, when by a solemn resolution it was declared to be a high misdemeanor, and next to treason, the king to put the penal laws in execution.

Just. *Powell.* Brother, I think you do mistake a little.

Just. *Allybone.* Brother I dare rely upon it that I am right: it was so declared by all the judges.

Sol. Gen. The Puritans presented a petition to that purpose, and in it they said, if it would not be granted, they would come with a great number.

Just. *Powell.* Aye, there it is.

Just. *Allybone.* I tell you, Mr. Solicitor, the resolution of the judges is, That such a petition is next door to treason, a very great misdemeanor.

Just. *Powell.* They accompanying it with threats of the people's being discontented.

Just. *Allybone.* As I remember, it is in the second part of the folio 35, or 37, where the resolution of the judges is, That to frame a petition to the king, to put the penal laws in execution, is next to treason; for, say they, no man ought to intermeddle with matters of government without leave of the government.

Serj. *Pemberton.* That was a petition against the penal laws.

Just. *Allybone.* Then I am quite mistaken indeed, in case it be so.

Serj. *Trinder.* That is not material at all which it was.

Mr. *Pollexfen.* They there threatened, unless their request were granted, several thousands of the king's subjects would be discontented.

Just. *Powell.* That is the reason of that judgment, I affirm it.

Just. *Allybone.* But then I'll tell you, brother, again, what is said in that case that you hinted at, and put Mr. Solicitor in mind of: for any man to raise a report that the king will or will not permit a toleration, if either of these be disagreeable to the people, whether he may or may not, it is against law; for we are not to measure things from any truth they have in themselves, but from that aspect they have upon the government; for there may be every tittle of a libel true, and yet it may be a libel still: so that I put no great stress upon that objection, that the matter of it is not false; and for sedition, it is that which every libel carries in itself; and as every trespass implies *vi & armis*, so every libel against the government carries in it sedition, and all the other epithets that are in the information. This is my opinion as to law in general. I will not debate the prerogatives of the king, nor the privileges of the subject; but as this fact is, I think these venerable bishops did meddle with that which did not belong to them: they took upon them, in a petitionary, to contradict the actual exercise of the government, which I think no particular persons, or singular body, may do.

L. C. J. Gentlemen of the jury, have you a mind to drink before you go?

Jury. Yes, my lord, if you please. [Wine was sent for for the jury.]

Juryman. My lord, we humbly pray that your lordship will be pleased to let us have the papers that have been given in evidence.

L. C. J. What is that you would have, Sir?

Sol. Gen. He desires this, my lord, that you would be pleased to direct that the jury may have the use of such writings and statute-books as may be necessary for them to make use of.

L. C. J. The statute-book they shall have.

Sol. Gen. But they can have no papers but what are under seal.

Serj. *Levinz.* They may have them by consent, and they may have a copy of the information.

L. C. J. They shall have a copy of the information, and the declarations under seal.

Mr. *Pollexfen.* If they have those, and the libel, as they call it, they will not need a copy of the information.

Att. Gen. My lord, we pray that your lordship would be pleased to ascertain what it is they shall have.

L. C. J. They shall have a copy of the information, the libel, and the declarations under the great seal.

Sol. Gen. But not the Votes of the House of Commons, nor the Journals, for they are not evidence.

L. C. J. No, I don't intend they shall.

Sir *R. Sawyer.* My lord, we pray they may have the whole petition.

Just. *Holloway.* That is, with the direction and prayer, you mean.

Att. Gen. Yes, with all our hearts.

[Then the court arose, and the jury went together, to consider of their verdict, and stayed together all night, without fire or candle.]

On Saturday the 30th day of June, 1688, about ten o'clock in the morning, the archbishop, and the rest of the bishops, came again into the court, and immediately after the jury were brought to the bar.

Sir *S. Astry.* Crier, take the appearance of the jury. Sir Roger Langley.

Sir *Roger Langley.* Here.

Crier. Vous avez, &c. And so all the rest were called, and answered. Then proclamation for silence was made.

Sir *S. Astry.* Gentlemen, are you agreed on your verdict?

Jury. Yes.

Sir *S. Astry.* Who shall say for you?

Jury. Foreman.

Sir *S. Astry.* Do you find the defendants, or any of them, guilty of the misdemeanor whereof they are impeached, or not guilty?

Foreman. Not guilty.

Sir *S. Astry.* Then hearken to your verdict, as the court hath recorded it.—You say, the defendants, and every of them, are not guilty of the misdemeanor whereof they are impeached; and so you say all?—*Jury.* Yes.

[At which there were several great shouts in court, and throughout the hall.]

Mr. Solicitor General taking notice of some persons in court that shouted, moved very earnestly that they might be committed: whereupon a gentleman of Gray's-Inn was laid hold of, but was soon after discharged. And after the shouting was over, the Lord Chief Justice reproving the gentleman, said;

L. C. J. I am as glad as you can be that my lords the bishops are acquitted; but your manner of rejoicing here in court is indecent, you might rejoice in your chamber, or elsewhere, and not here. [Then speaking to Mr. Attorney, he said:]

Have you any thing more to say to my lords the bishops, Mr. Attorney?

Att. Gen. No, my lord. [Then the Court arose, and the bishops went away.]

After the revolution, complaint was made against the proceedings in this case, as in others.

I find in the Lords' Journal, that on May 1st, 1689, "The earl of Huntingdon made report from the committee of privileges, 'That the duke of Grafton, the lord Lovelace, the archbishop of Canterbury, the bishops of St. Asaph, Bristol, Peterborough, Ely, Bath and Wells, and Chichester, having been desired by the lords of the committee to cause to be brought this day before their lordships, a relation in writing of the proceedings against their lordships, in the court of King's Bench, in prejudice to the privileges of the peers in general, as well as to their persons in particular; which having not been done by any of the said lords, that it is the opinion of the committee, that the House be moved to take some effectual order therein.'

"Upon report from the lords committees for privileges, it is ordered, by the lords spiritual and temporal in parliament assembled, That Mr. Ince do attend their lordships, with an account, in writing, of the proceedings that were had, in the court of King's Bench, against the archbishop of Canterbury, the bishop of Bath and Wells, the bishop of St. Asaph, the bishop of Bristol, bishop of Ely, bishop of Chichester, and bishop of Peterborough, in Trinity term last."

But I have not discovered that any farther proceedings were had on the matter.

All the historians of this period relate the expressions of joy which this acquittal of the bishops called forth. Kennett writes as follows:

"There were immediately very loud acclamations through Westminster-hall, and the words 'Not guilty,' 'Not guilty,' went round with such shouts and huzzas, that the king's Solicitor moved very earnestly that such as had shouted in the court might be committed. But the shouts were carried on through the cities of Westminster and London, and flew presently to Hounslow-heath, where the soldiers in the camp echoed them so loud that it startled the king, who was that day entertained in the earl of Feversham's tent: insomuch that his majesty sent him out to know what was the matter. The earl came back and told the king, 'It was nothing but the soldiers shouting upon the news of the bishops being acquitted.' The king replied, 'And do you call that nothing? but so much the worse for them.' What his majesty meant by the last words he had not much time to interpret: he could only shew some indignation, that the bishops had escaped a legal penalty, and he threatened to deliver them up to the ecclesiastical commissioners. And for the two judges, Holloway and Powell, he immediately turned them out, and would have meditated some farther severity, if his following reign would have allowed it.

"This acquitment of the bishops encouraged the clergy in their honest resolutions of not reading the Declaration; but the ecclesiastical commissioners were instructed to call them to an account for it, for which purpose, on July 12, they met in the council-chamber and made an order, 'That whereas they had received information that divers rectors, vicars and curates, had omitted or neglected to read the said Declaration, to the manifest contempt of his majesty's authority-royal, they do hereby command and require all chancellors, archdeacons, commissaries and officials, to inquire strictly within their respective jurisdictions, in what churches and chapels his majesty's said Declaration was read, and in what churches and chapels the same was omitted, and to transmit an account thereof upon the 16th of August next.' The commissioners met again on that day, and finding that little or no inquiry had been made, they were much divided what to do in the matter. After a long consultation they were content to give longer time, and therefore published another order, 'Commanding all chancellors, archdeacons, commissaries, officials, and others having ecclesiastical jurisdiction, strictly to inquire of the church-wardens, as one of their articles of inquiry, at their respective visitations, (which visitations they were required to hold and keep before the 15th day of November next) in what churches and chapels his majesty's said Declaration was read, and in what the same was omitted, and to transmit an account thereof to them on the 6th day of December next.' But Providence prevented a return to this inquiry. The bishop of Rochester finding by this time the drift of the ecclesiastical commission, thought it inconsistent with his profession and character to act any longer in it, and therefore he wrote a letter to his colleagues, desiring to be excused from sitting amongst them."

It appears, that the "Declaration" was not read in more than seven churches in London, and two hundred throughout England. See Kennett, Rapin, Burnet, and Hume.

May 20th, 1688, being the day appointed for reading the King's Declaration in London, it was only read in some few places, as at Westminster-abbey," [Sprat being Dean. See the Introduction to the Trials for the Rye-House Plot, vol. 9, p. 362], "at Serjeants'-Inn, in Fleet-street," [a chapel, I apprehend, belonging to the Judges and other Serjeants at Law], "Mr. Hall's in Wood-street, Mr. Elliott's at Duke's-place," and some few others.

"The bishops that were for reading the King's Declaration, and dispersed it into their bishoprics, were the bishops of Durham," [Crew: he absconded for some time, but returned and took the oaths to King William.* He was excepted out of the "Bill of Indemnity and Free Pardon," passed in 1690, but made his peace and retained his bishopric many years]. "Lincoln," [Barlow. He took the oaths to King William]. "Hereford," [Croft. He wrote "The Naked Truth." He was deprived for not taking the oaths to King William]. "Rochester," [Sprat, who was one of King James's privy councillors. See some account of him as above. He took the oaths to King William]. "Chester," [Cartwright. See some account of him, p. 27, of this Volume], and "St. David's," [Watson. He took the oaths to King William; but, in 1699, was deprived for simony. See his Case in this Collection]. Narcissus Luttrell's MS. "Brief Historical Relation," &c.

"It generally happened wherever it was read, that the congregation immediately left the church. One minister, before he began to read it, told his flock, 'that he could not refuse the order sent him to read the Declaration, but that he knew no order which obliged them to hear it.' " Rapin.

After the acquittal of the bishops on the prosecution for their petition, it appears that James entertained the design of proceeding before the ecclesiastical commissioners against them for not causing his "Declaration" to be read. No such proceedings, however, were instituted; but the ecclesiastical commissioners endeavoured to enforce the reading of the Declaration by the compelled instrumentality of the archdeacons and chancellors, of whom some undisguisedly resisted the attempt, and some less resolutely excused their non-compliance. Narcissus Luttrell relates, that on October the 5th, the king declared in council that the ecclesiastical commission was dissolved.

---

*"The bishop of Durham, who had been at the House but twice before, came to day to give his vote against the king, who had raised him." Clarendon's Diary, Feb. 6, 1689.

7

JOHN LOCKE, A LETTER CONCERNING TOLERATION
1689
Montuori 93–101

Lastly, those are not at all to be tolerated who *deny the being of a God.* Promises, covenants, and oaths, which are the bonds of human society, can have no hold upon an atheist. The taking away of God, though but even in thought, dissolves all; besides also, those that by their atheism undermine and destroy all religion, can have no pretence of religion whereupon to challenge the privilege of a toleration. As for other practical opinions, though not absolutely free from all error, yet if they do not tend to establish domination over others, or civil impunity to the church in which they are taught, there can be no reason why they should not be tolerated.

It remains that I say something concerning those assemblies which being vulgarly called, and perhaps having sometimes been *conventicles* and nurseries of factions and seditions, are thought to afford the strongest matter of objection against this doctrine of toleration. But this has not happened by anything peculiar unto the genius of such assemblies, but by the unhappy circumstances of an oppressed or ill-settled liberty. These accusations would soon cease if the law of toleration were once so settled that all churches were obliged to lay down toleration as the foundation of their own liberty, and teach that liberty of conscience is every man's natural right, equally belonging to dissenters as to themselves; and that nobody ought to be compelled in matters of religion either by law or force. The establishment of this one thing would take away all ground of complaints and tumults upon account of conscience; and these causes of discontents and animosities being once removed, there would remain nothing in these assemblies that were not more peaceable and less apt to produce disturbance of state than in any other meetings whatsoever. But let us examine particularly the heads of these accusations.

You will say that *assemblies and meetings endanger the public peace, and threaten the commonwealth.* I answer: If this be so, why are there daily such numerous meetings in markets and courts of judicature? Why are crowds upon the exchange, and a concourse of people in cities suffered? You will reply: These are civil assemblies, but those we object against are ecclesiastical. I answer: It is a likely thing indeed, that such assemblies as are altogether remote from civil affairs should be most apt to embroil them. Oh, but civil assemblies are composed of men that differ from one another in matters of religion, but these ecclesiastical meetings are of persons that are all of one opinion. As if an agreement in matters of religion were in effect a conspiracy against the commonwealth; or as if men would not be so much the more warmly unanimous in religion the less liberty they had of assembling. But it will be urged still, that civil assemblies are open and free for any one to enter into, whereas religious conventicles are more private, and thereby give opportunity to clandestine machinations. I answer, that this is not strictly true, for many civil assemblies are not open to every one. And if some religious meetings be private, who are they (I beseech you) that are to be blamed for it? Those that desire, or those that forbid their being public? Again, you will say that religious communion does exceedingly unite men's minds and affections to one another, and is therefore the more dangerous. But if this be so, why is not the magistrate afraid of his own church; and why does he not forbid their assemblies as things dangerous to his government? You will say because he himself is a part, and even the head of them. As if he were not also a part of the commonwealth, and the head of the whole people.

Let us therefore deal plainly. The magistrate is afraid of other churches, but not of his own; because he is kind and favourable to the one, but severe and cruel to the other. These he treats like children, and indulges them even to wantonness. Those he uses as slaves, and how blamelessly soever they demean themselves, recompenses them no otherwise th[a]n by galleys, prisons, confiscations, and death. These he cherishes and defends; those he continually scourges and oppresses. Let him turn the tables. Or let those dissenters enjoy but the same privileges in civils as his other subjects, and he will quickly find that these religious meetings will be no longer dangerous. For if men enter into seditious conspiracies, it is not religion inspires them to it in their meetings, but their sufferings and oppressions that make them willing to ease themselves. Just and moderate governments are everywhere quiet, everywhere safe; but oppression raises ferments and makes men struggle to cast off an uneasy and tyrannical yoke. I know that seditions are very frequently raised upon pretence of religion, but it is as true that for religion subjects are frequently ill treated, and live miserably. Believe me, the stirs that are made proceed not from any peculiar temper of this or that church or religious society, but from the common disposition of all mankind, who when they groan under any heavy burthen endeavour naturally to shake off the yoke that galls their necks. Suppose this business of religion were let alone, and that there were some other distinction made between men and men upon account of their different complexions, shapes, and features, so that those who have black hair (for example) or grey eyes should not enjoy the same privileges as other citizens; that they should not be permitted either to buy or sell, or live by their callings; that parents should not have the government and education of their own children; that they should either be excluded from the benefit of the laws, or meet with partial judges; can it be doubted but these persons, thus distinguished from others by the colour of their hair and eyes, and united together by one common persecution, would be as dangerous to the magistrate as any others that had associated themselves merely upon the account of religion? Some enter into company for trade and profit, others for want of business have their clubs for claret. Neighbourhood joins some, and religion others. But there is only one thing which gathers people into seditious commotions, and that is oppression.

You will say: What, will you have people to meet at divine service *against the magistrate's will*? I answer: Why, I pray, against his will? Is it not both lawful and necessary that they should meet? Against his will, do you say? That is what I complain of; that is the very root of all the mischief. Why are assemblies less sufferable in a church than in a theatre or market? Those that meet there are not either more vicious or more turbulent than those that meet elsewhere. The business in that is that they are ill used, and therefore they are not to be suffered. Take away the partiality that is used towards them in matters of common right; change the laws, take away the penalties unto which they are subjected, and all things will immediately become safe and peaceable; nay, those that are averse to the religion of the magistrate will think themselves so much the more bound to maintain the peace of the commonwealth as their condition is better in that place than elsewhere; and all the several separate congregations, like so many guardians of the public peace, will watch one another, that nothing may be innovated or changed in the form of the government, because they can hope for nothing better than what they already enjoy; that is, an equal condition with their fellow-subjects under a just and moderate government. Now if that church which agrees in religion with the prince be esteemed the chief support of any civil government, and that for no other reason (as has already been shewn) than because the prince is kind and the laws are favourable to it, how much greater will be the security of government where all good subjects, of whatsoever church they be, without any distinction upon account of religion, enjoying the same favour of the prince and the same benefit of the laws, shall become the common support and guard of it, and where none will have any occasion to fear the severity of the laws but those that do injuries to their neighbours and offend against the civil peace?

8

BILL OF RIGHTS, SECS. 5, 13
1 W. & M., 2d sess., c. 2, 16 Dec. 1689

---

5. That it is the right of the subjects to petition the King, and all committments [*sic*] and prosecutions for such petitioning are illegal.

. . . . .

13. And that for redress of all grievances, and for the amending, strengthening, and preserving of the laws, parliaments ought to be held frequently.

9

STAMP ACT CONGRESS, DECLARATION OF RIGHTS, SEC. 13
19 Oct. 1765
Sources 271

13th. That it is the right of the British subjects in these colonies, to petition the king or either house of parliament.

10

WILLIAM BLACKSTONE, COMMENTARIES 1:138–39
1765

---

4. If there should happen any uncommon injury, or infringement of the rights beforementioned, which the ordinary course of law is too defective to reach, there still remains a fourth subordinate right appertaining to every individual, namely, the right of petitioning the king, or either house of parliament, for the redress of grievances. In Russia we are told that the czar Peter established a law, that no subject might petition the throne, till he had first petitioned two different ministers of state. In case he obtained justice from neither, he might then present a third petition to the prince; but upon pain of death, if found to be in the wrong. The consequence of which was, that no one dared to offer such third petition; and grievances seldom falling under the notice of the sovereign, he had little opportunity to redress them. The restrictions, for some there are, which are laid upon petitioning in England, are of a nature extremely different; and while they promote the spirit of peace, they are no check upon that of liberty. Care only must be taken, lest, under the pretence of petitioning, the subject be guilty of any riot or tumult; as happened in the opening of the memorable parliament in 1640: and, to prevent this, it is provided by the statute 13 Car. II. st. 1. c. 5. that no petition to the king, or either house of parliament, for any alterations in church or state, shall be signed by above twenty persons, unless the matter thereof be approved by three justices of the peace or the major part of the grand jury, in the country; and in London by the lord mayor, aldermen, and common council; nor shall any petition be presented by more than two persons at a time. But under these regulations, it is declared by the statute 1 W. & M. st. 2. c. 2. that the subject hath a right to petition; and that all commitments and prosecutions for such petitioning are illegal.

11

WILLIAM BLACKSTONE, COMMENTARIES 4:146–47
1769

---

6. *Riots, routs,* and *unlawful assemblies* must have *three* persons at least to constitute them. An *unlawful assembly* is when three, or more, do assemble themselves together to do an unlawful act, as to pull down inclosures, to destroy a warren or the game therein; and part without doing it, or making any motion towards it. A *rout* is where three or more meet to do an unlawful act upon a common quarrel, as forcibly breaking down fences upon a right claimed of common, or of way; and make some advances towards it. A *riot* is where three or more actually do an unlawful act of violence, either with or without a common cause or quarrel: as if they beat a man; or hunt and kill game in another's park, chase, warren, or liberty; or do any other unlawful act with force and violence; or even do a lawful act, as removing a nuisance, in a violent and tumultuous manner. The punishment of unlawful assemblies, if to the number of twelve, we have just now seen may be capital, according to the circumstances that attend it; but, from the number of three to eleven, is by fine and imprisonment only. The same is the case in riots and routs by the common law; to which the pillory in very enormous cases has been sometimes superadded. And by the statute 13 Hen. IV. c. 7. any two justices, together with the sheriff or under-sheriff of the county, may come with the *posse comitatus,* if need be, and suppress any such riot, assembly, or rout, arrest the rioters, and record upon the spot the nature and circumstances of the whole transaction; which record alone shall be a sufficient conviction of the offenders. In the interpretation of which statute it hath been holden, that all persons, noblemen and others, except women, clergymen, persons decrepit, and infants under fifteen, are bound to attend the justices in suppressing a riot, upon pain of fine and imprisonment; and that any battery, wounding, or killing the rioters, that may happen in suppressing the riot, is justifiable. So that our antient law, previous to the modern riot act, seems pretty well to have guarded against any violent breach of the public peace; especially as any riotous assembly on a public or general account, as to redress grievances or pull down all inclosures, and also resisting the king's forces if sent to keep the peace, may amount to overt acts of high treason, by levying war against the king.

7. Nearly related to this head of riots is the offence of *tumultuous petitioning;* which was carried to an enormous height in the times preceding the grand rebellion. Wherefore by statute 13 Car. II. st. 1. c. 5. it is enacted, that not more than twenty names shall be signed to any petition to the king or either house of parliament, for any alteration of matters established by law in church or state; unless the contents thereof be previously approved, in the country, by three justices, or the majority of the grand jury at the

assises or quarter sessions; and, in London, by the lord mayor, aldermen, and common council: and that no petition shall be delivered by a company of more than ten persons: on pain in either case of incurring a penalty not exceeding 100 *l*, and three months imprisonment.

12

THOMAS JEFFERSON, INSTRUCTIONS IN THE VIRGINIA CONVENTION TO THE DELEGATES TO CONGRESS
Aug. 1774
Papers 1:142–43

The Proclamation issued by General Gage, in the Government of the Province of the Massachusetts Bay, declaring it Treason for the Inhabitants of that Province to assemble themselves to consider of their Grievances and form Associations for their common Conduct on the Occasion, and requiring the Civil Magistrates and Officers to apprehend all such Persons to be tried for their supposed Offences, is the most alarming Process that ever appeared in a British Government; that the said General Gage hath thereby assumed and taken upon himself Powers denied by the Constitution to our legal Sovereign; that he, not having condescended to disclose by what Authority he exercises such extensive and unheard of Powers, we are at a Loss to determine whether he intends to justify himself as the Representative of the King or as the Commander in Chief of his Majesty's Forces in America. If he considers himself as acting in the Character of his Majesty's Representative, we would remind him that the Statute 25th Edward III. has expressed and defined all treasonable Offences, and that the Legislature of Great Britain hath declared that no Offence shall be construed to be Treason but such as is pointed out by that Statute, and that this was done to take out of the Hands of tyrannical Kings, and of weak and wicked Ministers, that deadly Weapon which constructive Treason had furnished them with, and which had drawn the Blood of the best and honestest Men in the Kingdom; and that the King of Great Britain hath no Right by his Proclamation to subject his People to Imprisonment, Pains, and Penalties.

That if the said General Gage conceives he is empowered to act in this Manner, as the Commander in Chief of his Majesty's Forces in America, this odious and illegal Proclamation must be considered as a plain and full Declaration that this despotick Viceroy will be bound by no Law, nor regard the constitutional Rights of his Majesty's Subjects, whenever they interfere with the Plan he has formed for oppressing the good People of the Massachusetts Bay; and therefore, that the executing, or attempting to execute, such Proclamation, will justify Resistance and Reprisal.

13

CONTINENTAL CONGRESS, DECLARATION AND RESOLVES
14 Oct. 1774
Tansill 3

Resolved, N. C. D. 8. That they have a right peaceably to assemble, consider of their grievances, and petition the king; and that all prosecutions, prohibitory proclamations, and commitments for the same, are illegal.

14

DECLARATION OF INDEPENDENCE
4 July 1776
Tansill 24–25

In every stage of these Oppressions We have Petitioned for Redress in the most humble terms: Our repeated Petitions have been answered only by repeated injury. A Prince, whose character is thus marked by every act which may define a Tyrant, is unfit to be the ruler of a free people. Nor have We been wanting in attentions to our Brittish brethren. We have warned them from time to time of attempts by their legislature to extend an unwarrantable jurisdiction over us. We have reminded them of the circumstances of our emigration and settlement here. We have appealed to their native justice and magnanimity, and we have conjured them by the ties of our common kindred to disavow these usurpations, which, would inevitably interrupt our connections and correspondence. They too have been deaf to the voice of justice and of consanguinity. We must, therefore, acquiesce in the necessity, which denounces our Separation, and hold them, as we hold the rest of mankind. Enemies in War, in Peace Friends.—

15

MASSACHUSETTS CONSTITUTION OF 1780, PT. 1, ART. 19
Thorpe 3:1892

ART. XIX. The people have a right, in an orderly and peaceable manner, to assemble to consult upon the common good; give instructions to their representatives, and to request of the legislative body, by the way of addresses, petitions, or remonstrances, redress of the wrongs done them, and of the grievances they suffer.

16

MARYLAND RATIFYING CONVENTION, PROPOSED AMENDMENT
29 Apr. 1788
Dumbauld 179

14. That every man hath a right to petition the legislature for the redress of grievances, in a peaceable and orderly manner.

17

HOUSE OF REPRESENTATIVES, AMENDMENTS TO THE CONSTITUTION
15 Aug. 1789
Annals 1:731–45

The next clause of the fourth proposition was taken into consideration, and was as follows: "The freedom of speech and of the press, and the right of the people peaceably to assemble and consult for their common good, and to apply to the Government for redress of grievances, shall not be infringed.

Mr. SEDGWICK submitted to those gentlemen who had contemplated the subject, what effect such an amendment as this would have; he feared it would tend to make them appear trifling in the eyes of their constituents; what, said he, shall we secure the freedom of speech, and think it necessary, at the same time, to allow the right of assembling? If people freely converse together, they must assemble for that purpose; it is a self-evident, unalienable right which the people possess; it is certainly a thing that never would be called in question; it is derogatory to the dignity of the House to descend to such minutiae; he therefore moved to strike out "assemble and."

Mr. BENSON.—The committee who framed this report proceeded on the principle that these rights belonged to the people; they conceived them to be inherent; and all that they meant to provide against was their being infringed by the Government.

Mr. SEDGWICK replied, that if the committee were governed by that general principle, they might have gone into a very lengthy enumeration of rights; they might have declared that a man should have a right to wear his hat if he pleased; that he might get up when he pleased, and go to bed when he thought proper; but he would ask the gentleman whether he thought it necessary to enter these trifles in a declaration of rights, in a Government where none of them were intended to be infringed.

Mr. TUCKER hoped the words would not be struck out, for he considered them of importance; besides, they were recommended by the States of Virginia and North Carolina, though he noticed that the most material part proposed by those States was omitted, which was, a declaration that the people should have a right to instruct their representatives. He would move to have those words inserted as soon as the motion for striking out was decided.

Mr. GERRY was also against the words being struck out, because he conceived it to be an essential right; it was inserted in the constitutions of several States; and though it had been abused in the year 1786 in Massachusetts, yet that abuse ought not to operate as an argument against the use of it. The people ought to be secure in the peaceable enjoyment of this privilege, and that can only be done by making a declaration to that effect in the constitution.

Mr. PAGE.—The gentleman from Massachusetts, (Mr. SEDGWICK,) who made this motion, objects to the clause, because the right is of so trivial a nature. He supposes it no more essential than whether a man has a right to wear his hat or not; but let me observe to him that such rights have been opposed, and a man has been obliged to pull off his hat when he appeared before the face of authority; people have also been prevented from assembling together on their lawful occasions, therefore it is well to guard against such stretches of authority, by inserting the privilege in the declaration of rights. If the people could be deprived of the power of assembling under any pretext whatsoever, they might be deprived of every other privilege contained in the clause.

Mr. VINING said, if the thing was harmless, and it would tend to gratify the States that had proposed amendments, he should agree to it.

Mr. HARTLEY observed, that it had been asserted in the convention of Pennsylvania, by the friends of the constitution, that all the rights and powers that were not given to the Government were retained by the States and the people thereof. This was also his own opinion; but as four or five States had required to be secured in those rights by an express declaration in the constitution, he was disposed to gratify them; he thought every thing that was not incompatible with the general good ought to be granted, if it would tend to obtain the confidence of the people in the Government; and, upon the whole, he thought these words were as necessary to be inserted in the declaration of rights as most in the clause.

Mr. GERRY said, that his colleague contended for nothing, if he supposed that the people had a right to consult for the common good, because they could not consult unless they met for the purpose.

Mr. SEDGWICK replied that if they were understood or implied in the word consult, they were utterly unnecessary, and upon that ground he moved to have them struck out.

The question was now put upon Mr. SEDGWICK's motion, and lost by a considerable majority.

Mr. TUCKER then moved to insert these words, "to instruct their Representatives."

Mr. HARTLEY wished the motion had not been made, for gentlemen acquainted with the circumstances of this country, and the history of the country from which we separated, differed exceedingly on this point. The members of the House of Representatives, said he, are chosen for two years, the members of the Senate for six.

According to the principles laid down in the Constitution, it is presumable that the persons elected know the interests and the circumstances of their constituents, and being checked in their determinations by a division of the Legislative power into two branches, there is little danger of error. At least it ought to be supposed that they have the confidence of the people during the period for which they are elected; and if, by misconduct, they forfeit it, their constituents have the power of leaving them out at the expiration of that time—thus they are answerable for the part they have taken in measures that may be contrary to the general wish.

Representation is the principle of our Government; the people ought to have confidence in the honor and integrity of those they send forward to transact their business; their right to instruct them is a problematical subject. We have seen it attended with bad consequences, both in England and America. When the passions of the people are excited, instructions have been resorted to and obtained, to answer party purposes; and although the public opinion is generally respectable, yet at such moments it has been known to be often wrong; and happy is that Government composed of men of firmness and wisdom to discover, and resist popular error.

If, in a small community, where the interests, habits, and manners are neither so numerous or diversified, instructions bind not, what shall we say of instructions to this body? Can it be supposed that the inhabitants of a single district in a State, are better informed with respect to the general interests of the Union, than a select body assembled from every part? Can it be supposed that a part will be more desirous of promoting the good of the whole than the whole will of the part? I apprehend, sir, that Congress will be the best judges of proper measures, and that instructions will never be resorted to but for party purposes, when they will generally contain the prejudices and acrimony of the party, rather than the dictates of honest reason and sound policy.

In England, this question has been considerably agitated. The representatives of some towns in Parliament have acknowledged, and submitted to the binding force of instructions, while the majority have thrown off the shackles with disdain. I would not have this precedent influence our decision; but let the doctrine be tried upon its own merits, and stand or fall as it shall be found to deserve.

It appears to my mind, that the principle of representation is distinct from an agency, which may require written instructions. The great end of meeting is to consult for the common good; but can the common good be discerned without the object is reflected and shown in every light. A local or partial view does not necessarily enable any man to comprehend it clearly; this can only result from an inspection into the aggregate. Instructions viewed in this light will be found to embarrass the best and wisest men. And were all the members to take their seats in order to obey instructions, and those instructions were as various as it is probable they would be, what possibility would there exist of so accommodating each to the other as to produce any act whatever? Perhaps a majority of the whole might not be instructed to agree to any one point, and is it thus the people of the United States propose to form a more perfect union, provide for the common defence, and promote the general welfare?

Sir, I have known within my own time so many inconveniences and real evils arise from adopting the popular opinions on the moment, that although I respect them as much as any man, I hope this Government will particularly guard against them, at least that they will not bind themselves by a constitutional act, and by oath, to submit to their influence; if they do, the great object which this Government has been established to attain, will inevitably elude our grasp on the uncertain and veering winds of popular commotion.

Mr. PAGE.—The gentleman from Pennsylvania tells you, that in England this principle is doubted; how far this is consonant with the nature of the Government I will not pretend to say; but I am not astonished to find that the administrators of a monarchical Government are unassailable by the weak voice of the people; but under a democracy, whose great end is to form a code of laws congenial with the public sentiment, the popular opinion ought to be collected and attended to. Our present object is, I presume, to secure to our constituents and to posterity these inestimable rights. Our Government is derived from the people, of consequence the people have a right to consult for the common good; but to what end will this be done, if they have not the power of instructing their representatives? Instruction and representation in a republic appear to me to be inseparably connected; but were I the subject of a monarch, I should doubt whether the public good did not depend more upon the prince's will than the will of the people. I should dread a popular assembly consulting for the public good, because, under its influence, commotions and tumults might arise that would shake the foundation of the monarch's throne, and make the empire tremble in expectation. The people of England have submitted the crown to the Hanover family, and have rejected the Stuarts. If instructions upon such a revolution were considered binding, it is difficult to know what would have been the effects. It might be well, therefore, to have the doctrine exploded from that kingdom; but it will not be advanced as a substantial reason in favor of our treading in the same steps.

The honorable gentleman has said, that when once the people have chosen a representative, they must rely on his integrity and judgment during the period for which he is elected. I think, sir, to doubt the authority of the people to instruct their representatives, will give them just cause to be alarmed for their fate. I look upon it as a dangerous doctrine, subversive of the great end for which the United States have confederated. Every friend of mankind, every well-wisher of his country, will be desirous of obtaining the sense of the people on every occasion of magnitude; but how can this be so well expressed as in instructions to their representatives? I hope, therefore, that gentlemen will not oppose the insertion of it in this part of the report.

Mr. CLYMER.—I hope the amendment will not be

adopted; but if our constituents choose to instruct us, that they may be left at liberty to do so. Do gentlemen foresee the extent of these words? If they have a constitutional right to instruct us, it infers that we are bound by those instructions; and as we ought not to decide constitutional questions by implication, I presume we shall be called upon to go further, and expressly declare the members of the Legislature bound by the instruction of their constituents. This is a most dangerous principle, utterly destructive of all ideas of an independent and deliberative body, which are essential requisites in the Legislatures of free Governments; they prevent men of abilities and experience from rendering those services to the community that are in their power, destroying the object contemplated by establishing an efficient General Government, and rendering Congress a mere passive machine.

Mr. SHERMAN.—It appears to me, that the words are calculated to mislead the people, by conveying an idea that they have a right to control the debates of the Legislature. This cannot be admitted to be just, because it would destroy the object of their meeting. I think, when the people have chosen a representative, it is his duty to meet others from the different parts of the Union, and consult, and agree with them to such acts as are for the general benefit of the whole community. If they were to be guided by instructions, there would be no use in deliberation; all that a man would have to do, would be to produce his instructions, and lay them on the table, and let them speak for him. From hence I think it may be fairly inferred, that the right of the people to consult for the common good can go no further than to petition the Legislature, or apply for a redress of grievances. It is the duty of a good representative to inquire what measures are most likely to promote the general welfare, and, after he has discovered them, to give them his support. Should his instructions, therefore, coincide with his ideas on any measure, they would be unnecessary; if they were contrary to the conviction of his own mind, he must be bound by every principle of justice to disregard them.

Mr. JACKSON was in favor of the right of the people to assemble and consult for the common good; it had been used in this country as one of the best checks on the British Legislature in their unjustifiable attempts to tax the colonies without their consent. America had no representatives in the British Parliament, therefore they could instruct none, yet they exercised the power of consultation to a good effect. He begged gentlemen to consider the dangerous tendency of establishing such a doctrine; it would necessarily drive the house into a number of factions. There might be different instructions from every State, and the representation from each State would be a faction to support its own measures.

If we establish this as a right, we shall be bound by those instructions; now, I am willing to leave both the people and representatives to their own discretion on this subject. Let the people consult and give their opinion; let the representative judge of it; and if it is just, let him govern himself by it as a good member ought to do; but if it is otherwise, let him have it in his power to reject their advice.

What may be the consequence of binding a man to vote in all cases according to the will of others? He is to decide upon a constitutional point, and on this question his conscience is bound by the obligation of a solemn oath; you now involve him in a serious dilemma. If he votes according to his conscience, he decides against his instructions; but in deciding against his instructions, he commits a breach of the constitution, by infringing the prerogative of the people, secured to them by this declaration. In short, it will give rise to such a variety of absurdities and inconsistencies, as no prudent Legislature would wish to involve themselves in.

Mr. GERRY.—By the checks provided in the constitution, we have good grounds to believe that the very framers of it conceived that the Government would be liable to maladministration, and I presume that the gentlemen of this House do not mean to arrogate to themselves more perfection than human nature has as yet been found to be capable of; if they do not, they will admit an additional check against abuses which this, like every other Government, is subject to. Instruction from the people will furnish this in a considerable degree.

It has been said that the amendment proposed by the honorable gentleman from South Carolina (Mr. TUCKER) determines this point, "that the people can bind their representatives to follow their instructions." I do not conceive that this necessarily follows. I think the representative, notwithstanding the insertion of these words, would be at liberty to act as he pleased; if he declined to pursue such measures as he was directed to attain, the people would have a right to refuse him their suffrages at a future election.

Now, though I do not believe the amendment would bind the representatives to obey the instructions, yet I think the people have a right both to instruct and bind them. Do gentlemen conceive that on any occasion instructions would be so general as to proceed from all our constituents? If they do, it is the sovereign will; for gentlemen will not contend that the sovereign will resides in the Legislature. The friends and patrons of this constitution have always declared that the sovereignty resides in the people, and that they do not part with it on any occasion; to say the sovereignty vests in the people, and that they have not a right to instruct and control their representatives, is absurd to the last degree. They must either give up their principle, or grant that the people have a right to exercise their sovereignty to control the whole Government, as well as this branch of it. But the amendment does not carry the principle to such an extent, it only declares the right of the people to send instructions; the representative will, if he thinks proper, communicate his instructions to the House, but how far they shall operate on his conduct, he will judge for himself.

The honorable gentleman from Georgia (Mr. JACKSON) supposes that instructions will tend to generate factions in this House; but he did not see how it could have that effect, any more than the freedom of debate had. If the representative entertains the same opinion with his constituents, he will decide with them in favor of the measure; if other gentlemen, who are not instructed on this point, are convinced by argument that the measure is proper, they will also vote with them; consequently, the influence of debate and of instruction is the same.

The gentleman says further, that the people have the right of instructing their representatives; if so, why not declare it? Does he mean that it shall lie dormant and never be exercised? If so, it will be a right of no utility. But much good may result from a declaration in the constitution that they possess this privilege; the people will be encouraged to come forward with their instructions, which will form a fund of useful information for the Legislature. We cannot, I apprehend, be too well informed of the true state, condition, and sentiment of our constituents, and perhaps this is the best mode in our power of obtaining information. I hope we shall never shut our ears against that information which is to be derived from the petitions and instructions of our constituents. I hope we shall never presume to think that all the wisdom of this country is concentred within the walls of this House. Men, unambitious of distinctions from their fellow-citizens, remain within their own domestic walk, unheard of and unseen, possessing all the advantages resulting from a watchful observance of public men and public measures, whose voice, if we would descend to listen to it, would give us knowledge superior to what could be acquired amidst the cares and bustles of a public life; let us then adopt the amendment, and encourage the diffident to enrich our stock of knowledge with the treasure of their remarks and observations.

Mr. MADISON.—I think the committee acted prudently in omitting to insert these words in the report they have brought forward; if, unfortunately, the attempt of proposing amendments should prove abortive, it will not arise from the want of a disposition in the friends of the constitution to do what is right with respect to securing the rights and privileges of the people of America, but from the difficulties arising from discussing and proposing abstract propositions, of which the judgment may not be convinced. I venture to say, that if we confine ourselves to an enumeration of simple, acknowledged principles, the ratification will meet with but little difficulty. Amendments of a doubtful nature will have a tendency to prejudice the whole system; the proposition now suggested partakes highly of this nature. It is doubted by many gentlemen here; it has been objected to in intelligent publications throughout the Union; it is doubted by many members of the State Legislatures. In one sense this declaration is true, in many others it is certainly not true; in the sense in which it is true, we have asserted the right sufficiently in what we have done; if we mean nothing more than this, that the people have a right to express and communicate their sentiments and wishes, we have provided for it already. The right of freedom of speech is secured; the liberty of the press is expressly declared to be beyond the reach of this Government; the people may therefore publicly address their representatives, may privately advise them, or declare their sentiments by petition to the whole body; in all these ways they may communicate their will. If gentlemen mean to go further, and to say that the people have a right to instruct their representatives in such a sense as that the delegates are obliged to conform to those instructions, the declaration is not true. Suppose they instruct a representative, by his vote, to violate the constitution; is he at liberty to obey such instructions? Suppose he is instructed to patronize certain measures, and from circumstances known to him, but not to his constituents, he is convinced that they will endanger the public good; is he obliged to sacrifice his own judgment to them? Is he absolutely bound to perform what he is instructed to do? Suppose he refuses, will his vote be the less valid, or the community be disengaged from that obedience which is due to the laws of the Union? If his vote must inevitably have the same effect, what sort of a right is this in the constitution, to instruct a representative who has a right to disregard the order, if he pleases? In this sense the right does not exist, in the other sense it does exist, and is provided largely for.

The honorable gentleman from Massachusetts asks if the sovereignty is not with the people at large. Does he infer that the people can, in detached bodies, contravene an act established by the whole people? My idea of the sovereignty of the people is, that the people can change the constitution if they please; but while the constitution exists, they must conform themselves to its dictates. But I do not believe that the inhabitants of any district can speak the voice of the people; so far from it, their ideas may contradict the sense of the whole people; hence the consequence that instructions are binding on the representative is of a doubtful, if not of a dangerous nature. I do not conceive, therefore, that it is necessary to agree to the proposition now made; so far as any real good is to arise from it, so far that real good is provided for; so far as it is of a doubtful nature, so far it obliges us to run the risk of losing the whole system.

Mr. SMITH, of South Carolina.—I am opposed to this motion, because I conceive it will operate as a partial inconvenience to the more distant States. If every member is to be bound by instructions how to vote, what are gentlemen from the extremities of the continent to do? Members from the neighboring States can obtain their instructions earlier than those from the Southern ones, and I presume that particular instructions will be necessary for particular measures; of consequence, we vote perhaps against instructions on their way to us, or we must decline voting at all. But what is the necessity of having a numerous representation? One member from a State can receive the instructions, and by his vote answer all the purposes of many, provided his vote is allowed to count for the proportion the State ought to send; in this way the business might be done at a less expense than having one or two hundred members in the House, which had been strongly contended for yesterday.

Mr. STONE.—I think the clause would change the Government entirely; instead of being a Government founded upon representation, it would be a democracy of singular properties.

I differ from the gentleman from Virginia, (Mr. MADISON,) if he thinks this clause would not bind the representative; in my opinion, it would bind him effectually, and I venture to assert, without diffidence, that any law passed by the Legislature would be of no force, if a majority of the members of this House were instructed to the contrary, provided the amendment became part of the constitution. What would follow from this? Instead of looking in the code of laws passed by Congress, your Judiciary would have to collect and examine the instructions from the various parts of the Union. It follows very clearly from hence, that the Government would be altered from a representative one to a democracy, wherein all laws are made immediately by the voice of the people.

This is a power not to be found in any part of the earth except among the Swiss cantons; there the body of the people vote upon the laws, and give instructions to their delegates. But here we have a different form of Government; the people at large are not authorized under it to vote upon the law, nor did I ever hear that any man required it. Why, then, are we called upon to propose amendments subversive of the principles of the constitution, which were never desired?

Several members now called for the question, and the Chairman being about to put the same:

Mr. GERRY.—Gentlemen seem in a great hurry to get this business through. I think, Mr. Chairman, it requires a further discussion; for my part, I had rather do less business and do it well, than precipitate measures before they are fully understood.

The honorable gentleman from Virginia (Mr. MADISON) stated, that if the proposed amendments are defeated, it will be by the delay attending the discussion of doubtful propositions; and he declares this to partake of that quality. It is natural, sir, for us to be fond of our own work. We do not like to see it disfigured by other hands. That honorable gentleman brought forward a string of propositions; among them was the clause now proposed to be amended: he is no doubt ready for the question, and determined not to admit what we think an improvement. The gentlemen who were on the committee, and brought in the report, have considered the subject, and are also ripe for a decision. But other gentlemen may crave a like indulgence. Is not the report before us for deliberation and discussion, and to obtain the sense of the House upon it; and will not gentlemen allow us a day or two for these purposes, after they have forced us to proceed upon them at this time? I appeal to their candor and good sense on the occasion, and am sure not to be refused; and I must inform them now, that they may not be surprised hereafter, that I wish all the amendments proposed by the respective States to be considered. Gentlemen say it is necessary to finish the subject, in order to reconcile a number of our fellow-citizens to the Government. If this is their principle, they ought to consider the wishes and intentions which the convention has expressed for them; if they do this, they will find that they expect and wish for the declaration proposed by the honorable gentleman over the way, (Mr. TUCKER,) and, of consequence, they ought to agree to it; and why it, with others recommended in the same way, were not reported, I cannot pretend to say; the committee know this best themselves.

The honorable gentleman near me (Mr. STONE) says, that the laws passed contrary to instruction will be nugatory. And other gentlemen ask, if their constituents instruct them to violate the constitution, whether they must do it, Sir, does not the constitution declare that all laws passed by Congress are paramount to the laws and constitutions of the several States; if our decrees are of such force as to set aside the State laws and constitutions, certainly they may be repugnant to any instructions whatever, without being injured thereby. But can we conceive that our constituents would be so absurd as to instruct us to violate our oath, and act directly contrary to the principles of a Government ordained by themselves? We must look upon them to be absolutely abandoned and false to their own interests, to suppose them capable of giving such instructions.

If this amendment is introduced into the constitution, I do not think we shall be much troubled with instructions; a knowledge of the right will operate to check a spirit that would render instruction necessary.

The honorable gentleman from Virginia asked, will not the affirmative of a member who votes repugnant to his instructions bind the community as much as the votes of those who conform? There is no doubt, sir, but it will; but does this tend to show that the constituent has no right to instruct? Surely not. I admit, sir, that instructions contrary to the constitution ought not to bind, though the sovereignty resides in the people. The honorable gentleman acknowledges that the sovereignty vests there; if so, it may exercise its will in any case not inconsistent with a previous contract. The same gentleman asks if we are to give the power to the people in detached bodies to contravene the Government while it exists. Certainly not; nor does the proposed proposition extend to that point; it is only intended to open for them a convenient mode in which they may convey their sense to their agents. The gentleman therefore takes for granted what is inadmissible, that Congress will always be doing illegal things, and make it necessary for the sovereign to declare its pleasure.

He says the people have a right to alter the constitution, but they have no right to oppose the Government. If, while the Government exists, they have no right to control it, it appears they have divested themselves of the sovereignty over the constitution. Therefore, our language, with our principles, must change, and we ought to say that the sovereignty existed in the people previous to the establishment of this Government. This will be ground for alarm indeed, if it is true; but I trust, sir, too much to the good sense of my fellow-citizens ever to believe that the doctrine will generally obtain in this country of freedom.

Mr. VINING.—If, Mr. Chairman, there appears on one side too great an urgency to despatch this business, there appears on the other an unnecessary delay and procrastination equally improper and unpardonable. I think this business has been already well considered by the House, and every gentleman in it; however, I am not for an unseemly expedition.

The gentleman last up has insinuated a reflection upon the committee for not reporting all the amendments proposed by some of the State conventions. I can assign a reason for this. The committee conceived some of them superfluous or dangerous, and found many of them so contradictory that it was impossible to make any thing of them; and this is a circumstance the gentleman cannot pretend ignorance of.

Is it not inconsistent in that honorable member to complain of hurry, when he comes day after day reiterating the same train of arguments, and demanding the attention of this body by rising six or seven times on a question? I wish, sir, this subject discussed coolly and dispassionately, but hope we shall have no more reiterations or tedious discussions; let gentlemen try to expedite public business, and their arguments will be conducted in a laconic and consistent manner. As to the business of instruction, I look upon it inconsistent with the general good. Suppose our constituents were to instruct us to make paper money; no gentleman pretends to say it would be unconstitutional, yet every honest mind must shudder at the thought. How can we then assert that instructions ought to bind us in all cases not contrary to the constitution?

Mr. LIVERMORE was not very anxious whether the words were inserted or not, but he had a great deal of doubt on the meaning of this whole amendment; it provides that the people may meet and consult for the common good. Does this mean a part of the people in a township or district, or does it mean the representatives in the State Legislatures? If it means the latter, there is no occasion for a provision that the Legislature may instruct the members of this body.

In some States the representatives are chosen by districts. In such case, perhaps, the instructions may be considered as coming from the district; but in other States, each representative is chosen by the whole people. In New Hampshire it is the case; the instructions of any particular place would have but little weight, but a legislative instruction would have considerable influence upon each representative. If, therefore, the words mean that the Legislature may instruct, he presumed it would have considerable effect, though he did not believe it binding. Indeed, he was inclined to pay a deference to any information he might receive from any number of gentlemen, even by a private letter; but as for full binding force, no instructions contained that quality. They could not, nor ought not to have it, because different parties pursue different measures; and it might be expedient, nay, absolutely necessary, to sacrifice them in mutual concessions.

The doctrine of instructions would hold better in England than here, because the boroughs and corporations might have an interest to pursue totally immaterial to the rest of the kingdom: in that case, it would be prudent to instruct their members in Parliament.

Mr. GERRY wished the constitution amended without his having any hand in it; but if he must interfere, he would do his duty. The honorable gentleman from Delaware had given him an example of moderation and laconic and consistent debate that he meant to follow; and would just observe to the worthy gentleman last up, that several States had proposed the amendment, and among the rest New Hampshire.

There was one remark which escaped him, when he was up before. The gentleman from Maryland (Mr. STONE) had said that the amendment would change the nature of the Government, and make it a democracy. Now he had always heard that it was a democracy; but perhaps he was misled, and the honorable gentleman was right in distinguishing it by some other appellation; perhaps an aristocracy was a term better adapted to it.

Mr. SEDGWICK opposed the idea of the gentleman from New Hampshire, that the State Legislature had the power of instructing the members of this House; he looked upon it as a subornation of the rights of the people to admit such an authority. We stand not here, said he, the representatives of the State Legislatures, as under the former Congress, but as the representatives of the great body of the people. The sovereignty, the independence, and the rights of the States are intended to be guarded by the Senate; if we are to be viewed in any other light, the greatest security the people have for their rights and privileges is destroyed.

But with respect to instructions, it is well worthy of consideration how they are to be procured. It is not the opinion of an individual that is to control my conduct; I consider myself as the representative of the whole Union. An individual may give me information, but his sentiments may be in opposition to the sense of the majority of the people. If instructions are to be of any efficacy, they must speak the sense of the majority of the people, at least of a State. In a State so large as Massachusetts it will behoove gentlemen to consider how the sense of the majority of the freemen is to be obtained and communicated. Let us take care to avoid the insertion of crude and indigested propositions, more likely to produce acrimony than that spirit of harmony which we ought to cultivate.

Mr. LIVERMORE said that he did not understand the honorable gentleman, or was not understood by him; he did not presume peremptorily to say what degree of influence the legislative instructions would have on a representative. He knew it was not the thing in contemplation here; and what he had said respected only the influence it would have on his private judgment.

Mr. AMES said there would be a very great inconvenience attending the establishment of the doctrine contended for by his colleague. Those States which had selected their members by districts would have no right to give them instructions, consequently the members ought to withdraw; in which case the House might be reduced below a majority, and not be able, according to the constitution, to do any business at all.

According to the doctrine of the gentleman from New Hampshire, one part of the Government would be annihilated; for of what avail is it that the people have the appointment of a representative, if he is to pay obedience to the dictates of another body?

Several members now rose, and called for the question.

Mr. PAGE was sorry to see gentlemen so impatient; the more so, as he saw there was very little attention paid to any thing that was said; but he would express his sentiments if he was only heard by the Chair. He discovered clearly, notwithstanding what had been observed by the most ingenious supporters of the opposition, that there was an absolute necessity for adopting the amendment. It was strictly compatible with the spirit and the nature of the Government; all power vests in the people of the United States; it is, therefore, a Government of the people, a democracy. If it were consistent with the peace and tranquillity of the inhabitants, every freeman would have a right to come and give his vote upon the law; but, inasmuch as this cannot be done, by reason of the extent of territory, and some other causes, the people have agreed that their representatives shall exercise a part of their authority. To pretend to refuse them the power of instructing their agents, appears to me to deny them a right. One gentleman asks how the instructions are to be collected. Many parts of this country have been in the practice of instructing their representatives; they found no difficulty in communicating their sense. Another gentleman asks if they were to instruct us to make paper money, what we would do. I would tell them, said he, it was unconstitutional; alter that, and we will consider on the point. Unless laws are made satisfactory to the people, they will lose their support, they will be abused or done away; this tends to destroy the efficiency of the Government.

It is the sense of several of the conventions that this amendment should take place; I think it my duty to support it, and fear it will spread an alarm among our constituents if we decline to do it.

Mr. WADSWORTH.—Instructions have frequently been given to the representatives of the United States; but the people did not claim as a right that they should have any obligation upon the representatives; it is not right that they should. In troublesome times, designing men have drawn the people to instruct the representatives to their harm; the representatives have, on such occasions, refused to comply with their instructions. I have known, myself, that they have been disobeyed, and yet the representative was not brought to account for it; on the contrary, he was caressed and reelected, while those who have obeyed them, contrary to their private sentiments, have ever after been despised for it. Now, if people considered it an inherent right in them to instruct their representatives, they would have undoubtedly punished the violation of them. I have no idea of instructions, unless they are obeyed; a discretional power is incompatible with them.

The honorable gentleman who was up last says, if he were instructed to make paper money, he would tell his constituents it was unconstitutional. I believe that is not the case, for this body would have a right to make paper money; but if my constituents were to instruct me to vote for such a measure, I would disobey them, let the consequence be what it would.

Mr. SUMTER.—The honorable gentlemen who are opposed to the motion of my colleague, do not treat it fairly. They suppose that it is meant to bind the representative to conform to his instructions. The mover of this question, I presume to say, has no such thing in idea. That they shall notice them and obey them, as far as is consistent and proper, may be very just; perhaps they ought to produce them to the House, and let them have as much influence as they deserve; nothing further, I believe, is contended for.

18

PENNSYLVANIA V. MORRISON
1 Addison 274 (Pa. 1795)

These men were indicted for having, on 18th *August,* 1794, unlawfully, riotously, and routously assembled together, to disturb the peace, and, in *Market Street* in *Pittsburgh,* raised a pole or standard, called a *liberty-pole,* in defiance of the laws of the state of *Pennsylvania,* and of the *United States,* and as an indignity and insult to the honourable *James Ross, Jasper Yeates,* and *William Bradford,* Esquires, commissioners on behalf of the *United States* of *America,* and the honourable *Thomas McKean* and *William Irwin,* Esquires, commissioners on behalf of the state of *Pennsylvania,* to confer with the citizens of the counties west of the *Allegheny* mountains; to the great disturbance of the peace, and to the ill example of others.

Woods, for the defendants. These men acted under force, as those had done, who went from *Pittsburgh* to the meeting at *Braddock's-Field.* They had no view to oppose the government. Many did not sign the terms of amnesty, because they supposed themselves innocent. It was not the intention of the defendants to oppose the laws, but to save the town from violence.

PRESIDENT. *Thomas White* must be acquitted: there is no evidence against him. *John McWilliams* has signed the amnesty.

You have no evidence of any constraint from a mob from the country, but in the declarations of the defendants themselves. This is not like the case of *Braddock's Field,* where five or six thousand men were assembled, and threatened the town. There must be first some evidence, that violence was threatened, and danger existed, to the town, before they can found any excuse for their conduct, on this ground.

Pole-raising was a notorious symptom of dissatisfaction, and the exhibition of this, in the only part of this country, where government was supposed to have strength, must have made an impression very unfavourable to the whole country, promoted violence in the people here, and induced force on the part of government.

All the evidence of their acting under duress, is their saying so. It is, at least, as probable, that this was a cover for their real motives, an opposition to the civil authority. Why did not these men sign the amnesty, when almost every man besides in the town signed it? They surely refrained not from a consciousness of innocence. It is somewhat singular, if danger then existed, that the only men in this town anxious for its safety, were men of little or no property in it; and that then all the men of property were against this measure. When there was real danger, all the town went to *Braddock's-Field.*

The act of raising a pole in the street is itself unlawful, independent of any other ill intention. The probability is, that the intention was an unlawful opposition to the government, and that the excuse was feigned, to cover their real designs.

Verdict guilty, except as to *White* and *McWilliams*.

19

ST. GEORGE TUCKER,
BLACKSTONE'S COMMENTARIES 1:APP. 299–300
1803

The same article secures to the people the right of assembling peaceably; and of petitioning the government for the redress of grievances. The convention of Virginia proposed an article expressed in terms more consonant with the nature of our representative democracy, declaring, that the people have a right, peaceably to assemble together to consult for their common good, or to instruct their representatives: that every freeman has a right to petition, or apply to the legislature, for the redress of grievances. This is the language of a free people asserting their rights: the other savours of that stile of condescension, in which favours are supposed to be granted. In England, no petition to the king, or either house of parliament for any alteration in church or state, shall be signed by above twenty persons, unless the matter thereof be approved by three justices of the peace, or a major part of the grand-jury in the county; nor be presented by more than ten persons. In America, there is no such restraint.

20

WILLIAM RAWLE, A VIEW OF THE CONSTITUTION
OF THE UNITED STATES 124
1829 (2d ed.)

The right of the people peaceably to assemble and petition government for a redress of grievances concludes the article.

Of this right in the abstract there cannot be a doubt. To withhold from the injured, the privilege of complaint, and to debar the rulers from the benefit of information that may apprize them of their errors, is mutually unjust. It may, however, be urged, that history shows how those meetings and petitions have been abused, and we may be turned to an English statute, which, though ill observed, is said to be still in force, and which is understood to have been founded on the mischiefs and disorders experienced from large and tumultuous assemblies, presenting petitions for the redress of grievances in the reign of Charles I. But besides the well known irrelevancy of the argument from the abuse of any thing against its use, we must remember that by requiring the assembly to be peaceable, the usual remedies of the law are retained, if the right is illegally exercised.

21

JOSEPH STORY, COMMENTARIES ON THE
CONSTITUTION 3:§§ 1887–88
1833

§ 1887. This would seem unnecessary to be expressly provided for in a republican government, since it results from the very nature of its structure and institutions. It is impossible, that it could be practically denied, until the spirit of liberty had wholly disappeared, and the people had become so servile and debased, as to be unfit to exercise any of the privileges of freemen.

§ 1888. The provision was probably borrowed from the declaration of rights in England, on the revolution of 1688, in which the right to petition the king for a redress of grievances was insisted on; and the right to petition parliament in the like manner has been provided for, and guarded by statutes passed before, as well as since that period. Mr. Tucker has indulged himself in a disparaging criticism upon the phraseology of this clause, as savouring too much of that style of condescension, in which favours are supposed to be granted. But this seems to be quite overstrained; since it speaks the voice of the people in the language of prohibition, and not in that of affirmance of a right, supposed to be unquestionable, and inherent.

22

SENATE, RECEPTION OF ABOLITION PETITIONS
1836
Elliot 4:597–98

Mr. BUCHANAN. Although the Constitution, as it came from the hands of its framers, gave to Congress no power to touch the right of petition, yet some of the states to whom it was submitted for ratification, apprehending that the time might arrive when Congress would be disposed to act like the British Parliament, (in Charles II.'s time,) expressly withdrew the subject from our control. Not satisfied with the fact, that no power over it had been granted by the Constitution, they determined to prohibit us, in express terms, from ever exercising such a power.

The proposition [the right of petition] is almost too plain for argument, that, if the people have a constitutional right to petition, a corresponding duty is imposed upon us to receive their petitions. From the very nature of things, rights and duties are reciprocal. The human mind cannot conceive of the one without the other. They are relative terms. If the people have a right to command, it is the duty of their servants to obey. If I have a right to a sum of money, it is the duty of my debtor to pay it to me.

If the people have a right to petition their representatives, it is our duty to receive their petition.

This question was solemnly determined by the Senate more than thirty years ago. Neither before nor since that time, so far as I can learn, has the general right of petition ever been called in question; until the motion now under consideration was made by the senator from South Carolina.

Mr. KING, (of Georgia.) Congress, under this article, [the first amendment] can pass no law to "abridge" the right of the people to petition the government. A modern commentator on the Constitution, of some note and much ability, in noticing this part of the article, dismissed it with the remark, that it was totally unnecessary. This is obvious to every one who will consider for a moment the relation between a free people and the government of their own choice. The privilege belonged (Mr. K. said) to the form of government—was united with it, and inseparable from it. It as clearly belonged to the people, on the formation of the government, as did the right to use the English language without any constitutional provision for that purpose; and, said Mr. K., if gentlemen will only look at the Constitution, and not evade it, they will see that the right was not ACQUIRED by the Constitution, but only SECURED by it. The right, as a preëxisting one, was expressly recognized by the language of the Constitution itself. What was the language applicable to the question before the Senate? It prevented Congress from passing any law "abridging the right of the people to petition," &c.

The right belonged to the people as inseparably incident to their form of government; was acknowledged to exist by the language of the Constitution; and was guardedly secured by the provisions of that instrument.

Mr. CALHOUN. The first amended article of the Constitution, which provides that Congress shall pass no law to prevent the people from peaceably assembling and petitioning for a redress of grievances, was clearly intended to prescribe the limits within which the right might be exercised. It is not pretended that to refuse to receive petitions, touches, in the slightest degree, on these limits. To suppose that the framers of the Constitution—no, not the framers, but those jealous patriots who were not satisfied with that instrument as it came from the hands of the framers, and who proposed this very provision to guard what they considered a sacred right—performed their task so bunglingly as to omit any essential guard, would be to do great injustice to the memory of those stern and sagacious men.

If the Constitution makes it our duty to receive, we should have no discretion left to reject, as the motion presupposes. Our rules of proceeding must accord with the Constitution. Thus, in the case of revenue bills, which, by the Constitution, must originate in the other house, it would be out of order to introduce them here; and it has accordingly been so decided. For like reasons, if we are bound to receive petitions, the present motion would be out of order; and, if such should be your opinion, it is your duty, as the presiding officer, to call me to order, and to arrest all further discussion on the question of reception.

SEE ALSO:

Generally Bill of Rights

The Riot Act, 1 Geo. 1, c. 5 (1714–16)

Delaware Declaration of Rights and Fundamental Rules, 11 Sept. 1776, Sources 339

North Carolina Constitution of 1776, Declaration of Rights, art. 18, Thorpe 5:2788

Pennsylvania Constitution of 1776, Declaration of Rights, art. 16, Thorpe 5:1508

Vermont Constitution of 1777, ch. 1, sec. 18, ch. 2, sec. 12, Thorpe 6:3741–42, 3744

Closing Arguments of Thomas Erskine for Defendant, Solicitor General James Mansfield for Prosecution, and Summation of Lord Mansfield, Proceedings against Lord George Gordon for Treason, 21 How. St. Tr. 587–647 (1781)

New Hampshire Constitution of 1784, arts. 31–32, Thorpe 4:2457

Vermont Constitution of 1786, ch. 1, sec. 4, Thorpe 6:3752

Virginia Ratifying Convention, Proposed Amendment, 27 June 1788, Dumbauld 184–85

New York Ratifying Convention, Proposed Amendment, 26 July 1788, Dumbauld 191

North Carolina Ratifying Convention, Proposed Amendment, 1 Aug. 1788, Dumbauld 201

Kentucky Constitution of 1792, art. 12, sec. 22, Thorpe 3:1275

House of Representatives, President's Speech, 24–27 Nov. 1794, Annals 4:899–945

House of Representatives, Yazoo Land Claims, 4 Jan. 1808, Annals 17:1283–85, 1294

Illinois Constitution of 1818, art. 8, sec. 19, Thorpe 2:983

Amendment II

A well regulated Militia, being necessary to the security of a free State,
the right of the people to keep and bear Arms, shall not be infringed.

---

1. Statute of Northampton, 2 Edw. 3, c. 3 (1328)
2. *Sir John Knight's Case*, 87 Eng. Rep. 75 (K.B. 1686)
3. Bill of Rights, sec. 7, 1 W. & M., 2d sess., c. 2, 16 Dec. 1689
4. William Blackstone, Commentaries (1765)
5. Pennsylvania Constitution of 1776, Declaration of Rights, art. 13
6. House of Representatives, Amendments to the Constitution, 17, 20 Aug. 1789
7. St. George Tucker, Blackstone's Commentaries (1803)
8. *Bliss* v. *Commonwealth*, 12 Littell 90 (Ky. 1822)
9. William Rawle, A View of the Constitution of the United States (2d ed. 1829)
10. Joseph Story, Commentaries on the Constitution (1833)
11. *State* v. *Mitchell*, 3 Ind. 229 (1833)

1

STATUTE OF NORTHAMPTON
2 Edw. 3, c. 3 (1328)

Item, it is enacted, that no man great nor small, of what condition soever he be, except the king's servants in his presence, and his ministers in executing of the king's precepts, or of their office, and such as be in their company assisting them, and also [upon a cry made for arms to keep the peace, and the same in such places where such acts happen,] be so hardy to come before the King's justices, or other of the King's ministers doing their office, with force and arms, nor bring no force in affray of the peace, nor to go nor ride armed by night nor by day, in fairs, markets, nor in the presence of the justices or other ministers, nor in no part elsewhere, upon pain to forfeit their armour to the King, and their bodies to prison at the King's pleasure. And that the King's justices in their presence, sheriffs, and other ministers in their bailiwicks, lords of franchises, and their bailiffs in the same, and mayors and bailiffs of cities and boroughs, within the same cities and boroughs, and borough-holders, constables, and wardens of the peace within their wards, shall have power to execute this act. And that the justices assigned, at their coming down into the country, shall have power to enquire how such officers and lords have exercised their offices in this case, and to punish them whom they find that have not done that which pertained to their office.

2

SIR JOHN KNIGHT'S CASE
87 Eng. Rep. 75 (K.B. 1686)

An information was exhibited against him by the Attorney General, upon the statute of 2 Edw. 3, c. 3, which prohibits "all persons from coming with force and arms before the King's Justices, &c., and from going or riding armed in affray of peace, on pain to forfeit his armour, and suffer imprisonment at the King's pleasure." This statute is confirmed by that of 20 Rich. 2, c. 1, with an addition of a further punishment, which is to make a fine to the King.

The information sets forth, that the defendant did walk about the streets armed with guns, and that he went into the church of St. Michael, in Bristol, in the time of divine service, with a gun, to terrify the King's subjects, *contra formam statuti*.

This case was tried at the Bar, and the defendant was acquitted.

The Chief Justice said, that the meaning of the statute of 2 Edw. 3, c. 3, was to punish people who go armed to terrify the King's subjects. It is likewise a great offence at the *common law*, as if the King were not able or willing to protect his subjects; and therefore this Act is but an affirmance of that law; and it having appointed a penalty, this Court can inflict no other punishment than what is therein directed.

3

BILL OF RIGHTS, SEC. 7
1 W. & M., 2d sess., c. 2, 16 Dec. 1689

7. That the subjects which are protestants, may have arms for their defence suitable to their conditions, and as allowed by law.

4

WILLIAM BLACKSTONE, COMMENTARIES 1:139
1765

5. The fifth and last auxiliary right of the subject, that I shall at present mention, is that of having arms for their defence, suitable to their condition and degree, and such as are allowed by law. Which is also declared by the same statute I W. & M. st. 2. c. 2. and is indeed a public allowance, under due restrictions, of the natural right of resistance and self-preservation, when the sanctions of society and laws are found insufficient to restrain the violence of oppression.

5

PENNSYLVANIA CONSTITUTION OF 1776,
DECLARATION OF RIGHTS, ART. 13
Thorpe 5:3083

XIII. That the people have a right to bear arms for the defence of themselves and the state; and as standing armies in the time of peace are dangerous to liberty, they ought not to be kept up; And that the military should be kept under strict subordination to, and governed by, the civil power.

6

HOUSE OF REPRESENTATIVES, AMENDMENTS TO
THE CONSTITUTION
17, 20 Aug. 1789
Annals 1:749–52, 766–67

[*17 Aug.*]
The House again resolved itself into a committee, Mr. BOUDINOT in the chair, on the proposed amendments to the constitution. The third clause of the fourth proposition in the report was taken into consideration, being as follows: "A well regulated militia, composed of the body of the people, being the best security of a free state, the right of the people to keep and bear arms shall not be infringed; but no person religiously scrupulous shall be compelled to bear arms."

MR. GERRY.—This declaration of rights, I take it, is intended to secure the people against the mal-administration of the Government; if we could suppose that, in all cases, the rights of the people would be attended to, the occasion for guards of this kind would be removed. Now, I am apprehensive, sir, that this clause would give an opportunity to the people in power to destroy the constitution itself. They can declare who are those religiously scrupulous, and prevent them from bearing arms.

What, sir, is the use of a militia? It is to prevent the establishment of a standing army, the bane of liberty. Now, it must be evident, that, under this provision, together with their other powers, Congress could take such measures with respect to a militia, as to make a standing army necessary. Whenever Governments mean to invade the rights and liberties of the people, they always attempt to destroy the militia, in order to raise an army upon their ruins. This was actually done by Great Britain at the commencement of the late revolution. They used every means in their power to prevent the establishment of an effective militia to the eastward. The Assembly of Massachusetts, seeing the rapid progress that administration were making to divest them of their inherent privileges, endeavored to counteract them by the organization of the militia; but they were always defeated by the influence of the Crown.

Mr. SENEY wished to know what question there was before the committee, in order to ascertain the point upon which the gentleman was speaking.

Mr. GERRY replied that he meant to make a motion, as he disapproved of the words as they read. He then proceeded. No attempts that they made were successful, until they engaged in the struggle which emancipated them at once from their thraldom. Now, if we give a discretionary power to exclude those from militia duty who have religious scruples, we may as well make no provision on this head. For this reason, he wished the words to be altered so as to be confined to persons belonging to a religious sect scrupulous of bearing arms.

Mr. JACKSON did not expect that all the people of the United States would turn Quakers or Moravians; consequently, one part would have to defend the other in case of invasion. Now this, in his opinion, was unjust, unless the constitution secured an equivalent: for this reason he moved to amend the clause, by inserting at the end of it, "upon paying an equivalent, to be established by law."

Mr. SMITH, of South Carolina, inquired what were the words used by the conventions respecting this amendment. If the gentleman would conform to what was proposed by Virginia and Carolina, he would second him. He thought they were to be excused provided they found a substitute.

Mr. JACKSON was willing to accommodate. He thought the expression was, "No one, religiously scrupulous of bearing arms, shall be compelled to render military service, in person, upon paying an equivalent."

Mr. SHERMAN conceived it difficult to modify the clause and make it better. It is well known that those who are religiously scrupulous of bearing arms, are equally scrupulous of getting substitutes or paying an equivalent. Many of them would rather die than do either one or the other; but he did not see an absolute necessity for a clause of this kind. We do not live under an arbitrary Government, said he, and the States, respectively, will have the government of the militia, unless when called into actual service; besides, it would not do to alter it so as to exclude the whole of any sect, because there are men amongst the Quakers who will turn out, notwithstanding the religious principles of the society, and defend the cause of their country. Certainly it will be improper to prevent the exercise of such favorable dispositions, at least whilst it is the practice of nations to determine their contests by the slaughter of their citizens and subjects.

Mr. VINING hoped the clause would be suffered to remain as it stood, because he saw no use in it if it was amended so as to compel a man to find a substitute, which, with respect to the Government, was the same as if the person himself turned out to fight.

Mr. STONE inquired what the words "religiously scrupulous" had reference to: was it of bearing arms? If it was, it ought so to be expressed.

Mr. BENSON moved to have the words "but no person religiously scrupulous shall be compelled to bear arms," struck out. He would always leave it to the benevolence of the Legislature, for, modify it as you please, it will be impossible to express it in such a manner as to clear it from ambiguity. No man can claim this indulgence of right. It may be a religious persuasion, but it is no natural right, and therefore ought to be left to the discretion of the Government. If this stands part of the constitution, it will be a question before the Judiciary on every regulation you make with respect to the organization of the militia, whether it comports with this declaration or not. It is extremely injudicious to intermix matters of doubt with fundamentals.

I have no reason to believe but the Legislature will always possess humanity enough to indulge this class of citizens in a matter they are so desirous of; but they ought to be left to their discretion.

The motion for striking out the whole clause being seconded, was put, and decided in the negative—22 members voting for it, and 24 against it.

Mr. GERRY objected to the first part of the clause, on account of the uncertainty with which it is expressed. A well regulated militia being the best security of a free State, admitted an idea that a standing army was a secondary one. It ought to read, "a well regulated militia, trained to arms;" in which case it would become the duty of the Government to provide this security, and furnish a greater certainty of its being done.

Mr. GERRY's motion not being seconded, the question was put on the clause as reported; which being adopted,

Mr. BURKE proposed to add to the clause just agreed to, an amendment to the following effect: "A standing army of regular troops in time of peace is dangerous to public liberty, and such shall not be raised or kept up in time of peace but from necessity, and for the security of the people, nor then without the consent of two-thirds of the members present of both Houses; and in all cases the military shall be subordinate to the civil authority." This being seconded.

Mr. VINING asked whether this was to be considered as an addition to the last clause, or an amendment by itself. If the former, he would remind the gentleman the clause was decided; if the latter, it was improper to introduce new matter, as the House had referred the report specially to the Committee of the whole.

Mr. BURKE feared that, what with being trammelled in rules, and the apparent disposition of the committee, he should not be able to get them to consider any amendment; he submitted to such proceeding because he could not help himself.

Mr. HARTLEY thought the amendment in order, and was ready to give his opinion on it. He hoped the people of America would always be satisfied with having a majority to govern. He never wished to see two-thirds or three-fourths required, because it might put it in the power of a small minority to govern the whole Union.

[20 Aug.]

Mr. SCOTT objected to the clause in the sixth amendment, "No person religiously scrupulous shall be compelled to bear arms." He observed that if this becomes part of the constitution, such persons can neither be called upon for their services, nor can an equivalent be demanded; it is also attended with still further difficulties, for a militia can never be depended upon. This would lead to the violation of another article in the constitution, which secures to the people the right of keeping arms, and in this case recourse must be had to a standing army. I conceive it, said he, to be a legislative right altogether. There are many sects I know, who are religiously scrupulous in this respect; I do not mean to deprive them of any indulgence the law affords; my design is to guard against those who are of no religion. It has been urged that religion is on the decline; if so, the argument is more strong in my favor, for when the time comes that religion shall be discarded, the generality of persons will have recourse to these pretexts to get excused from bearing arms.

Mr. BOUDINOT thought the provision in the clause, or something similar to it, was necessary. Can any dependence, said he, be placed in men who are conscientious in this respect? or what justice can there be in compelling them to bear arms, when, according to their religious principles, they would rather die than use them? He adverted to several instances of oppression on this point, that occurred during the war. In forming a militia, an effectual defence ought to be calculated, and no characters of this religious description ought to be compelled to take up arms. I hope that in establishing this Government, we may show the world that proper care is taken that the Government may not interfere with the religious sentiments of any person. Now, by striking out the clause, people may be led to believe that there is an intention in the General Government to compel all its citizens to bear arms.

7

St. George Tucker,
Blackstone's Commentaries 1:App. 300
1803

This may be considered as the true palladium of liberty. . . . The right of self defence is the first law of nature: in most governments it has been the study of rulers to confine this right within the narrowest limits possible. Wherever standing armies are kept up, and the right of the people to keep and bear arms is, under any colour or pretext whatsoever, prohibited, liberty, if not already annihilated, is on the brink of destruction. In England, the people have been disarmed, generally, under the specious pretext of preserving the game: a never failing lure to bring over the landed aristocracy to support any measure, under that mask, though calculated for very different purposes. True it is, their bill of rights seems at first view to counteract this policy: but the right of bearing arms is confined to protestants, and the words suitable to their condition and degree, have been interpreted to authorise the prohibition of keeping a gun or other engine for the destruction of game, to any farmer, or inferior tradesman, or other person not qualified to kill game. So that not one man in five hundred can keep a gun in his house without being subject to a penalty.

8

Bliss v. Commonwealth
12 Littell 90 (Ky. 1822)

This was an indictment founded on the act of the legislature of this state, "to prevent persons in this commonwealth from wearing concealed arms."

The act provides, that any person in this commonwealth, who shall hereafter wear a pocket pistol, dirk, large knife, or sword in a cane, concealed as a weapon, unless when travelling on a journey, shall be fined in any sum not less than one hundred dollars; which may be recovered in any court having jurisdiction of like sums, by action of debt, or on presentment of a grand jury.

The indictment, in the words of the act, charges Bliss with having *worn concealed as a weapon, a sword in a cane.*

Bliss was found guilty of the charge, and a fine of one hundred dollars assessed by the jury, and judgment was thereon rendered by the court. To reverse that judgment, Bliss appealed to this court.

2. In argument the judgment was assailed by the counsel of Bliss, exclusively on the ground of the act, on which the indictment is founded, being in conflict with the twenty third section of the tenth article of the constitution of this state.

That section provides, "that the right of the citizens to bear arms in defence of themselves and the state, shall not be questioned."

The provision contained in this section, perhaps, is as well calculated to secure to the citizens the right to bear arms in defence of themselves and the state, as any that could have been adopted by the makers of the constitution. If the right be assailed, immaterial through what medium, whether by an act of the legislature or in any other form, it is equally opposed to the comprehensive import of the section. The legislature is no where expressly mentioned in the section; but the language employed is general, without containing any expression restricting its import to any particular department of government; and in the twenty eighth section of the same article of the constitution, it is expressly declared, "that every thing in that article is excepted out of the general powers of government, and shall forever remain inviolate; and that all laws contrary thereto, or contrary to the constitution, shall be *void.*"

It was not, however, contended by the attorney for the commonwealth, that it would be competent for the legislature, by the enactment of any law, to prevent the citizens from bearing arms either in defence of themselves or the state; but a distinction was taken between a law prohibiting the exercise of the right, and a law merely regulating the manner of exercising that right; and whilst the former was admitted to be incompatible with the constitution, it was insisted, that the latter is not so, and under that distinction, and by assigning the act in question a place in the latter description of laws, its consistency with the constitution was attempted to be maintained.

3. That the provisions of the act in question do not import an entire destruction of the right of the citizens to bear arms in defence of themselves and the state, will not be controverted by the court; for though the citizens are forbid wearing weapons concealed in the manner described in the act, they may, nevertheless, bear arms in any other admissible form. But to be in conflict with the constitution, it is not essential that the act should contain a prohibition against bearing arms in every possible form— it is the *right* to bear arms in defence of the citizens and the state, that is secured by the constitution, and whatever restrains the full and complete exercise of that right, though not an entire destruction of it, is forbidden by the explicit language of the constitution.

If, therefore, the act in question imposes any restraint on the right, immaterial what appellation may be given to the act, whether it be an act regulating the manner of bearing arms or any other, the consequence, in reference to the constitution, is precisely the same, and its collision with that instrument equally obvious.

And can there be entertained a reasonable doubt but the provisions of the act import a restraint on the right of the citizens to bear arms? The court apprehends not. The right existed at the adoption of the constitution; it had then no limits short of the moral power of the citizens to exercise it, and it in fact consisted in nothing else but in the liberty of the citizens to bear arms. Diminish that liberty, therefore, and you necessarily restrain the right; and such is the diminution and restraint, which the act in question most indisputably imports, by prohibiting the citizens wearing weapons in a manner which was lawful to wear them when the constitution was adopted. In truth, the right of the citizens to bear arms, has been as directly assailed by the provisions of the act, as though they were forbid carrying guns on their shoulders, swords in scabbards, or when in conflict with an enemy, were not allowed the use of bayonets; and if the act be consistent with the constitution, it cannot be incompatible with that instrument for the legislature, by successive enactments, to entirely cut off the exercise of the right of the citizens to bear arms. For, in principle, there is no difference between a law prohibiting the wearing concealed arms, and a law forbidding the wearing such as are exposed; and if the former be unconstitutional, the latter must be so likewise.

We may possibly be told, that though a law of either description, may be enacted consistently with the constitution, it would be incompatible with that instrument to enact laws of both descriptions. But if either, when alone, be consistent with the constitution, which, it may be asked, would be incompatible with that instrument, if both were enacted?

The law first enacted would not be; for, as the argument supposes either may be enacted consistent with the constitution, that which is first enacted must, at the time of enactment, be consistent with the constitution; and if then consistent, it cannot become otherwise, by any subsequent act of the legislature. It must, therefore, be the latter act, which the argument infers would be incompatible with the constitution.

But suppose the order of enactment were reversed, and instead of being the first, that which was first, had been the last; the argument, to be consistent, should, nevertheless, insist on the last enactment being in conflict with the constitution. So, that the absurd consequence would thence follow, of making the same act of the legislature, either consistent with the constitution, or not so, according as it may precede or follow some other enactment of a different import. Besides, by insisting on the previous act producing any effect on the latter, the argument implies that the previous one operates as a partial restraint on the right of the citizens to bear arms, and proceeds on the notion, that by prohibiting the exercise of the residue of right, not affected by the first act, the latter act comes in collision with the constitution. But it should not be forgotten, that it is not only a part of the right that is secured by the constitution; it is the right entire and complete, as it existed at the adoption of the constitution; and if any portion of that right be impaired, immaterial how small the part may be, and immaterial the order of time at which it be done, it is equally forbidden by the constitution.

4. Hence, we infer, that the act upon which the indictment against Bliss is founded, is in conflict with the constitution; and if so, the result is obvious—the result is what the constitution has declared it shall be, that the act is *void*.

And if to be incompatible with the constitution makes void the act, we must have been correct, throughout the examination of this case, in treating the question of compatibility, as one proper to be decided by the court. For it is emphatically the duty of the court to decide what the law is; and how is the law to be decided, unless it be known? and how can it be known without ascertaining, from a comparison with the constitution, whether there exist such an incompatibility between the acts of the legislature and the constitution, as to make void the acts?

A blind enforcement of every act of the legislature, might relieve the court from the trouble and responsibility of deciding on the consistency of the legislative acts with the constitution; but the court would not be thereby released from its obligations to obey the mandates of the constitution, and maintain the paramount authority of that instrument; and those obligations must cease to be acknowledged, or the court become insensible to the impressions of moral sentiment, before the provisions of any act of the legislature, which in the opinion of the court, conflict with the constitution, can be enforced.

Whether or not an act of the legislature conflicts with the constitution, is, at all times, a question of great delicacy, and deserves the most mature and deliberate consideration of the court. But though a question of delicacy, yet as it is a judicial one, the court would be unworthy its station, were it to shrink from deciding it, whenever in the course of judicial examination, a decision becomes material to the right in contest. The court should never, on slight implication or vague conjecture, pronounce the legislature to have transcended its authority in the enactment of law; but when a clear and strong conviction is entertained, that an act of the legislature is incompatible with the constitution, there is no alternative for the court to pursue, but to declare that conviction, and pronounce the act inoperative and *void*. And such is the conviction entertained by a majority of the court, (Judge MILLS dissenting,) in relation to the act in question.

9

WILLIAM RAWLE, A VIEW OF THE CONSTITUTION
OF THE UNITED STATES 125–26
1829 (2d ed.)

In the second article, it is declared, that a *well regulated militia is necessary to the security of a free state;* a proposition from which few will dissent. Although in actual war, the services of regular troops are confessedly more valuable; yet, while peace prevails, and in the commencement of a war before a regular force can be raised, the militia form the palladium of the country. They are ready to repel invasion, to suppress insurrection, and preserve the good order and peace of government. That they should be well regulated, is judiciously added. A disorderly militia is disgraceful to itself, and dangerous not to the enemy, but to its own country. The duty of the state government is, to adopt such regulations as will tend to make good soldiers with the least interruptions of the ordinary and useful occupations of civil life. In this all the Union has a strong and visible interest.

The corollary, from the first position, is, that *the right of the people to keep and bear arms shall not be infringed.*

The prohibition is general. No clause in the Constitution could by any rule of construction be conceived to give to congress a power to disarm the people. Such a flagitious attempt could only be made under some general pretence by a state legislature. But if in any blind pursuit of inordinate power, either should attempt it, this amendment may be appealed to as a restraint on both.

In most of the countries of Europe, this right does not seem to be denied, although it is allowed more or less sparingly, according to circumstances. In England, a country which boasts so much of its freedom, the right was secured to protestant subjects only, on the revolution of 1688; and it is cautiously described to be that of bearing arms for their defence, "suitable to their conditions, and as allowed by law." An arbitrary code for the preservation of game in that country has long disgraced them. A very small proportion of the people being permitted to kill it, though for their own subsistence; a gun or other instrument, used for that purpose by an unqualified person, may be seized and forfeited. Blackstone, in whom we regret that we cannot always trace the expanded principles of rational liberty, observes however, on this subject, that the prevention of popular insurrections and resistance to government by disarming the people, is oftener meant than avowed, by the makers of forest and game laws.

This right ought not, however, in any government, to be abused to the disturbance of the public peace.

An assemblage of persons with arms, for an unlawful purpose, is an indictable offence, and even the carrying of arms abroad by a single individual, attended with circumstances giving just reason to fear that he purposes to make an unlawful use of them, would be sufficient cause to require him to give surety of the peace. If he refused he would be liable to imprisonment.

10

JOSEPH STORY, COMMENTARIES ON THE
CONSTITUTION 3:§§ 1890–91
1833

---

§ 1890. The importance of this article will scarcely be doubted by any persons, who have duly reflected upon the subject. The militia is the natural defence of a free country against sudden foreign invasions, domestic insurrections, and domestic usurpations of power by rulers. It is against sound policy for a free people to keep up large military establishments and standing armies in time of peace, both from the enormous expenses, with which they are attended, and the facile means, which they afford to ambitious and unprincipled rulers, to subvert the government, or trample upon the rights of the people. The right of the citizens to keep and bear arms has justly been considered, as the palladium of the liberties of a republic; since it offers a strong moral check against the usurpation and arbitrary power of rulers; and will generally, even if these are successful in the first instance, enable the people to resist and triumph over them. And yet, though this truth would seem so clear, and the importance of a well regulated militia would seem so undeniable, it cannot be disguised, that among the American people there is a growing indifference to any system of militia discipline, and a strong disposition, from a sense of its burthens, to be rid of all regulations. How it is practicable to keep the people duly armed without some organization, it is difficult to see. There is certainly no small danger, that indifference may lead to disgust, and disgust to contempt; and thus gradually undermine all the protection intended by this clause of our national bill of rights.

§ 1891. A similar provision in favour of protestants (for to them it is confined) is to be found in the bill of rights of 1688, it being declared, "that the subjects, which are protestants, may have arms for their defence suitable to their condition, and as allowed by law." But under various pretences the effect of this provision has been greatly narrowed; and it is at present in England more nominal than real, as a defensive privilege.

11

STATE V. MITCHELL
3 Ind. 229 (1833)

It was *held* in this case, that the statute of 1831, prohibiting all persons, except travelers, from wearing or carrying concealed weapons, is not unconstitutional.

SEE ALSO:

Generally Bill of Rights
Vermont Constitution of 1777, ch. 1, art. 15, Thorpe 6:3741
Kentucky Constitution of 1792, art. 12, cl. 23, Thorpe 3:1275
State v. Reid, 1 Ala. (n.s.) 612 (1840)
State v. Buzzard, 4 Ark. 18 (1842)
Nunn v. Georgia, 1 Ga. 243 (1846)

Amendment III

No Soldier shall, in time of peace be quartered in any house, without the consent of the Owner, nor in time of war, but in a manner to be prescribed by law.

1

BENJAMIN FRANKLIN, THE GAZETEER AND NEW DAILY ADVERTISER
2 May 1765
Papers 12:119–20

The North-American agents beg you will insert the following card, in answer to Mr. C. D——'s letter in your Saturday's paper.

The agents of North-America present their most grateful compliments to Mr. C. D. (who they conceive to be the S—— at ——'s first clerk) and are extremely obliged to him for the alternative, which his right honourable master has allowed him to offer. Conceiving themselves the *only representatives* of America, they most chearfully acquiesce in his last proposition, and hereby declare their *choice* to defend themselves without any *military aid.* They dread no enemy but the mother country, and wish to preserve America as an asylum for the wrecks of liberty. Mr. C. D. must pardon the agents if they think his knowledge is inferior to his zeal. There are no want of barracks in Quebec, or any part of America; but if an increase of them is necessary, at whose expence should that be? What is the practice in England? All that the agents contend for is, that the same protection of property and domestic security which prevails in England, should be preserved in America. Let Mr. C. D. or his master, first try the effects of quartering soldiers on butchers, bakers, or other private houses here, and then transport the measure to America. Parental example may produce filial obedience. But no —— at ——, or his clerk, can ever conceive, that the people of America, or those in England, (whose interest depend on a commercial connexion and strictest amity with them) will tamely submit to encroachments on so dear a part of their liberties, which they call on the bill of rights to defend. The people of England and America are the same; one King, and one law; and those who endeavour to promote a distinction, are truly enemies to both.

2

SAMUEL ADAMS, BOSTON GAZETTE
17 Oct. 1768
Writings 1:251–53

"Where Law ends, (says Mr. Locke) TYRANNY begins, if the Law be *transgress'd* to *anothers harm*": No one I believe will deny the truth of the observation, and therefore I again appeal to *common sense,* whether the act which provides for the quartering and billeting the King's troops, was not TRANSGRESS'D, when the barracks at the Castle WHICH ARE SUFFICIENT TO CONTAIN MORE than the whole number of soldiers now in this town, were ABSOLUTELY REFUS'D: This I presume cannot be contested. Should any one say that the law is not transgres'd *"to anothers harm,"* the assertion I dare say would contradict the feelings of every sober householder in the town. No man can pretend to say that the *peace* and *good order* of the community is so secure with soldiers quartered in *the body of a city* as without them. Besides, where *military power* is introduced, *military maxims* are propagated and adopted, which are inconsistent with and must soon eradicate every idea of *civil government*. Do we not already find some persons weak enough to believe, that an officer is *oblig'd* to obey the orders of his superior, tho' it be even AGAINST the law! And let any one consider whether this doctrine does not directly lead even to the setting up that superior officer, whoever he may be, as a tyrant. It is morever to be observ'd that military government and civil, are so different from each other, if not opposite, that they cannot long subsist together. Soldiers are not govern'd properly by the laws of their country, but by a law made *for them only:* This may in time make them look upon themselves as a body of men *different* from the rest of the people; and as they and they only have *the sword* in their hands, they may sooner or later begin to look upon themselves as the LORDS and not the SERVANTS of the people: Instead of enforcing the execution of law, which by the way is far from being the original intent of soldiers, they may *refuse to obey* it themselves: Nay, they may even *make laws for themselves,* and enforce them by the *power of the sword!* Such instances are not uncommon in history, and they always will happen when troops are put under the direction of an *ambitious* or a *covetous* governor! And if there is any reason for fear that this may be the consequence of a transgression of the act of parliament, it is a transgression not *"to the harm"* of individuals only, but of THE PUBLICK. It behoves *the publick* then to be aware of the danger, and like sober men *to avail themselves of the remedy of the law*, while it is *in their power*. It is always *safe* to AD-HERE TO THE LAW, and to keep every man of every denomination and character WITHIN ITS BOUNDS—Not to do this would be in the highest degree IMPRUDENT: Whenever it becomes a question in *prudence*, whether we shall make use of *legal* and *constitutional* methods to prevent the *incroachments* of ANY KIND OF POWER, what will it be but to depart from the *straight line*, to give up the LAW and the CONSTITUTION, which is fixed and stable, and is the *collected* and *long digested* sentiment OF THE WHOLE, and to substitute in its room the *opinion* of *individuals*, than which *nothing can be more uncertain:* The sentiments of men in such a case would in all likelihood be as *various* as their sentiments in religion or anything else; and as there would then be no *settled rule* for the publick to advert to, the safety of the people would probably be at an end.

3

CONTINENTAL CONGRESS, DECLARATION AND RESOLVES
14 Oct. 1774
Tansill 4, 5

Resolved, N. C. D. 9. That the keeping a standing army in these colonies, in times of peace, without the consent of the legislature of that colony, in which such army is kept, is against law.

. . . . .

Also the act passed in the same session, for the better providing suitable quarters for officers and soldiers in his majesty's service, in North-America.

4

JOSEPH HAWLEY TO ELBRIDGE GERRY
18 Feb. 1776
Gerry Life 1:162–63

Secondly, I hope, sir, you will by no means forget to endeavour that there be the most peremptory and absolute order and injunction on all the generals and officers of the American army, that quarters for the army or any part of them, shall in no case be impressed, but by the intervention of a civil magistrate, or direction of the legislature of the colony. They have again (I suppose through the resentment and pique of Park, the assistant quarter-master) quartered a company on Major Thompson, against his will. Our assembly is so much on the wing, and the active members so generally gone, that it is impossible to make any proper remonstrance thereof to the general.

It is not easy to imagine what a handle such conduct as this gives to the tories, and how much they rejoice to be able to take such exceptions; besides, it is downright and intolerably wrong. It is much more necessary that congress should make some express order and regulation for their forces in every part, touching their behaviour in this particular; because, you know that the colonies in general, and this in particular, are in the hands and power of the army, by reason of the militia being in a great degree stripped of their arms and ammunition for the sake of furnishing the army.

5

DECLARATION OF INDEPENDENCE
4 July 1776
Tansill 23–24

—He has kept among us, in times of peace, Standing Armies, without the Consent of our legislatures.—He has affected to render the Military independent of and superior to the Civil power. . . . —For quartering large bodies of armed troops among us:—For protecting them, by a mock Trial, from punishment for any Murders which they should commit on the Inhabitants of these States:

6

Delaware Declaration of Rights and Fundamental Rules
11 Sept. 1776
Sources 339

21. That no Soldier ought to be quartered in any House in Time of Peace without the Consent of the Owner; and in Time of War in such Manner only as the Legislature shall direct.

7

Federal Farmer, no. 16
20 Jan. 1788
Storing 2.8.202

The constitution will give congress general powers to raise and support armies. General powers carry with them incidental ones, and the means necessary to the end. In the exercise of these powers, is there any provision in the constitution to prevent the quartering of soldiers on the inhabitants? you will answer, there is not. This may sometimes be deemed a necessary measure in the support of armies; on what principle can the people claim the right to be exempt from this burden? they will urge, perhaps, the practice of the country, and the provisions made in some of the state constitutions—they will be answered, that their claim thus to be exempt is not founded in nature, but only in custom and opinion, or at best, in stipulations in some of the state constitutions, which are local, and inferior in their operation, and can have no controul over the general government—that they had adopted a federal constitution—had noticed several rights, but had been totally silent about this exemption—that they had given general powers relative to the subject, which, in their operation, regularly destroyed the claim. Though it is not to be presumed, that we are in any immediate danger from this quarter, yet it is fit and proper to establish, beyond dispute, those rights which are particularly valuable to individuals, and essential to the permanency and duration of free government. An excellent writer observes, that the English, always in possession of their freedom, are frequently unmindful of the value of it: we, at this period, do not seem to be so well off, having, in some instances abused ours; many of us are quite disposed to barter it away for what we call energy, coercion, and some other terms we use as vaguely as that of liberty—There is often as great a rage for change and novelty in politics, as in amusements and fashions.

8

Debate in Virginia Ratifying Convention
16 June 1788
Elliot 3:411, 413

[Mr. Henry:] . . . One of our first complaints, under the former government, was the quartering of troops upon us. This was one of the principal reasons for dissolving the connection with Great Britain. Here we may have troops in time of peace. They may be billeted in any manner—to tyrannize, oppress, and crush us.

. . . . .

[Mr. Madison:] . . . He says that one ground of complaint, at the beginning of the revolution, was, that a standing army was quartered upon us. This was not the whole complaint. We complained because it was done without the local authority of this country—without the consent of the people of America. As to the exclusion of standing armies in the bill of rights of the states, we shall find that though, in one or two of them, there is something like a prohibition, yet, in most of them, it is only provided that no armies shall be kept without the legislative authority; that is, without the consent of the community itself. Where is the impropriety of saying that we shall have an army, if necessary? Does not the notoriety of this constitute security? If inimical nations were to fall upon us when defenceless, what would be the consequence? Would it be wise to say, that we should have no defence? Give me leave to say, that the only possible way to provide against standing armies is to make them unnecessary.

9

House of Representatives, Amendments to the Constitution
17 Aug. 1789
Annals 1:752

The fourth clause of the fourth proposition was taken up as follows: "No soldier shall, in time of peace, be quartered in any house, without the consent of the owner, nor in time of war, but in a manner to be prescribed by law."

Mr. Sumter hoped soldiers would never be quartered on the inhabitants, either in time of peace or war, without the consent of the owner. It was a burthen, and very oppressive, even in cases where the owner gave his consent; but where this was wanting, it would be a hardship indeed! Their property would lie at the mercy of men irritated by a refusal, and well disposed to destroy the peace of the family.

He moved to strike out all the words from the clause but "no soldier shall be quartered in any house without the consent of the owner."

Mr. Sherman observed that it was absolutely necessary that marching troops should have quarters, whether in time of peace or war, and that it ought not to be put in the power of an individual to obstruct the public service; if quarters were not to be obtained in public barracks, they must be procured elsewhere. In England, where they paid considerable attention to private rights, they billeted the troops upon the keepers of public houses, and upon private houses also, with the consent of the magistracy.

Mr. Sumter's motion being put, was lost by a majority of sixteen.

Mr. Gerry moved to insert between "but" and, "in a manner" the words "by a civil magistrate," observing that there was no part of the Union but where they could have access to such authority.

Mr. Hartley said those things ought to be entrusted to the Legislature; that cases might arise where the public safety would be endangered by putting it in the power of one person to keep a division of troops standing in the inclemency of the weather for many hours; therefore he was against inserting the words.

10

St. George Tucker,
Blackstone's Commentaries
1:App. 300–301
1803

Our state bill of rights, conforming to the experience of all nations, declares, that standing armies in time of peace, should be avoided as dangerous to liberty; this article of the constitution, seems by a kind of side wind, to countenance, or at least, not to prohibit them. The billeting of soldiers upon the citizens of a state, has been generally found burthensome to the people, and so far as this article may prevent that evil it may be deemed valuable; but it certainly adds nothing to the national security.

11

William Rawle, A View of the Constitution
of the United States 126–27
1829 (2d ed.)

No soldier shall in time of peace be quartered in any house without the consent of the owner, (here the restriction is general,) *nor in time of war, but in a manner to be prescribed by law; and*

this must be construed a law of the United States when the war is general, or of the state when in the authorized exercise of the right of self-defence on the sudden emergencies adverted to in the Constitution, immediate state operations have become necessary. In the former case, the sole conduct of the war is given to the general government, and it ought not to be dependent on, or controlled by the state governments in its modes of proceeding. In the latter, the state, relying on its own energies, is entitled to the benefit of the same principle. The practice would be needlessly burthensome to the people in time of peace, and by a government having improper views, it might be rendered an indirect and odious mean of compelling submission to improper measures. During a war, when it becomes necessary to garrison a town, or station a body of troops for a time in a particular place, the common interest will naturally supersede minor objections.

By the general term soldier, we are to understand as well the militia in actual service as regular troops.

12

Joseph Story, Commentaries on the
Constitution 3:§ 1893
1833

§ 1893. This provision speaks for itself. Its plain object is to secure the perfect enjoyment of that great right of the common law, that a man's house shall be his own castle, privileged against all civil and military intrusion. The billeting of soldiers in time of peace upon the people has been a common resort of arbitrary princes, and is full of inconvenience and peril. In the petition of right (3 Charles I.), it was declared by parliament to be a great grievance.

SEE ALSO:

Generally Bill of Rights
Petition of Right, 3 Chas. 1, c. 1, 7 June 1628
Kentucky Constitution of 1792, art. 12, sec. 25, Thorpe 3:1275–76

Amendment IV

The right of the people to be secure in their persons, houses, papers, and effects, against unreasonable searches and seizures, shall not be violated, and no Warrants shall issue, but upon probable cause, supported by Oath or affirmation, and particularly describing the place to be searched, and the persons or things to be seized.

1. *The King* v. *Dr. Purnell,* 96 Eng. Rep. 20 (K.B. 1748)
2. Writs of Assistance, 1761–72, Quincy's Rep. (Mass.)
3. *Huckle* v. *Money,* 95 Eng. Rep. 768 (C.P. 1763)
4. *Wilkes* v. *Wood,* 98 Eng. Rep. 489, 498–99 (C.P. 1763)
5. *Rex* v. *Wilkes,* 95 Eng. Rep. 737 (C.P. 1763)
6. *Entick* v. *Carrington,* 95 Eng. Rep. 807 (K.B. 1765)
7. *Money* v. *Leach,* 97 Eng. Rep. 1075, 1088 (K.B. 1765)
8. William Blackstone, Commentaries (1768, 1769)
9. Virginia Declaration of Rights, sec. 10, 12 June 1776
10. Maryland Constitution of 1776, Declaration of Rights, art. 23
11. Massachusetts Constitution of 1780, pt. 1, art. 14
12. *Frisbie* v. *Butler,* Kirby 213 (Conn. 1787)
13. House of Representatives, Amendments to the Constitution, 17 Aug. 1789
14. St. George Tucker, Blackstone's Commentaries (1803)
15. *Ex parte Burford,* 3 Cranch 448 (1806)
16. *Conner* v. *Commonwealth,* 3 Binney 38 (Pa. 1810)
17. *Bell* v. *Clapp,* 10 Johns. R. 263 (N.Y. 1813)
18. *Grumon* v. *Raymond,* 1 Conn. 40 (1814)
19. *Treasurer* v. *Moore,* 3 Brev. 550 (S.C. 1815)
20. *The Antelope,* 10 Wheat. 66 (1825)

1

THE KING v. DR. PURNELL
96 Eng. Rep. 20 (K.B. 1748)

The defendant was vice chancellor of Oxford; and the Attorney-General had ex officio exhibited against him an information, for not taking the deposition of Blacow the evidence, and for neglect of his duty both as vice chancellor and justice of the peace, in not punishing Whitmore and Dawes, who had spoken treasonable words in the streets of Oxford. The defendant appeared to the first information, upon which a noli prosequi was entered, and a second filed, to which also the defendant appeared and pleaded; and a trial at Bar was appointed November 21, but it was countermanded, and a new day, viz. February 6th was afterwards appointed. And now, the last day of the term, the attorney, without any affidavit, moved for a rule directed to the proper officers of the university to permit their books, records and archives to be inspected, in order to furnish evidence against the vice chancellor. This was moved as a motion of course for a peremptory rule, on a suggestion that the King, being visitor of the university, had a right to inspect their books whenever he thought proper. Notice of motion was however given the night before at nine o'clock, and it was opposed by Henley and Evans. And the Court, being of opinion it was not a peremptory motion, only granted a rule to shew cause.

In the next term, Mr. Wilbraham, standing counsel for the university, shewed cause. That the rule was made on no affidavit: that it was drawn in very general terms, (to inspect books, records, and archives).—Records, if any, may be seen elsewhere. Archives cannot be inspected but by a figure, continens pro contenta. But this is a case of too much concern, to stand upon form. The principal case is, whether on a prosecution of a public officer for a supposed misdemesnor, the Court ought to grant inspection of the public books of a corporation. The rule is on Dr. Purnell himself. Nemo tenetur seipsum accusare. The law will not tempt a man to make shipwreck of his conscience, in order to disculpate himself. In Chancery, a man may demur, if on the face of the bill it appears, that the matter to be discovered will affect the defendant in a criminal way. It will be said, the Court usually grants rules to inspect public books. True, but then it is usually when franchises are contested, and the like; when inspection of those books are the only evidence, and the corporation are considered only as trustees, just as lords of manors are, of the public evidences belonging to the manor. But in no case has the Court ever interposed in a criminal prosecution to grant such a rule, and force such inspection. Many indeed have been granted to inspect poor's rates; but those are public evidences which every body has a right to. Was there never any prosecution carried on with the same spirit as this? Why then are no examples produced? By the same reason every person indicted might be obliged to shew, whether he had any evidence against himself. In *Bradshaw qui tam* v. *Philips*, A. D. 1735, in an action for bribery, motion was, to inspect the books of a corporation, to prove the defendant a freeman. Hardwicke, C.J., denied the rule, because the plaintiff was a stranger. This case is much stronger. It is a precedent of the first impression. There seems to be a general want of evidence; but it is to be hoped, there is no other view than for evidence in this particular case. A hundred cases may be shewn where such rules have been granted in quo warranto's &c. but none in criminal cases. [The Attorney "mentioned *K. and Burkins*, 7 Geo. 1, which was an indictment at a borough sessions, removed into B. R. by certiorari. Court said, the defendant might have a rule on the clerk of the peace, to have a copy of the names on the back of the indictment."] This is by no means a case. The indictment is a public record; he might have had it without a rule.

Mr. Henley on the same side.—This is a rule of the greatest importance to the most respectable body in the nation. It gives authority to the lowest agent of the Crown to rummage the MSS. of the university. One rule, in applications of this kind, is, that the person applying has an interest in the books and papers, so that in justice he is at all times entitled to have recourse to them. Another, that the person in possession is a trustee for the person applying (as a lord of a manor, &c.), and then the trust must be the subject in dispute; the suit must be about land in the manor, and averred by affidavit so to be. So corporations are the trustees and repository of the common franchises, and there is no instance of such a rule against a corporation, but where the franchise has been disputed, as on mandamus or quo warranto. The present rule is on an information against a vice chancellor and justice of peace. The Crown commences a prosecution against an individual of the university, and therefore desires to inspect the records of the university. By parity of reason, on an indictment against a citizen of London, they might inspect the records of the city. But it is suggested, that the King is visitor, and therefore entitled to a rule. I question the fact. The Court will require to be well satisfied of that. But, if so, 'tis a strong reason against granting the rule, for then the Crown may enforce its demands in a visitatorial way. Suppose the Crown has a general interest in the books of a corporation; that will not entitle them to an inspection, except the books are the subject of the dispute. *Crew qui tam and Blackburn*, H. 8 G. 2, an action for interfering in elections of members of Parliament, being a clerk of the post-office: the Court would not grant a rule to inspect the post-office books (though public books), because the cause did not concern them. *Benson and Cole*, M. 22 G. 2; motion to inspect Custom-House books, to prove the plaintiff in an insurance cause had no interest: urged that they were public books: refused, because they were not the subject of dispute. These were civil actions; the present otherwise. The avowed design of this motion being to furnish evidence, some precedent will be necessary; especially as a very bad use may be made of such a rule, when the university is much out of favour with some people.

Mr. Ford, on the same side.—*The College of Physicians* v. *Dr. West*, H. 2 G. 1; action for practising sans licence; motion to inspect the public books of the college; denied, because the defendant is a stranger to the college. *Cox and Copping*, 5 Mod. 395; dispute about the glebe: Court would not grant rule to inspect the churchwardens' books; because it was a private dispute. There is no reason to grant this inspection, because the vice-chancellor is a justice. Is it because he is vice-chancellor? Why? Not on account of his supposed visitatorial power; for in *Dr. Walker's case*, the Court quashed a rule because they would not take upon themselves to act the part of visitors. The Court will not assist visitors, but only in support of their visitatorial authority. The visitatorial authority is not now in quesiton; the vice-chancellor is prosecuted for a supposed offence at common law. If a witness has a question put to him that may affect himself, the Court will not oblige him to answer it. *Qu. and Mead*, 2 Lord Raym. 927; defendant was an attorney, and with others incorporated by Act of Parliament as surveyors of highways, &c. Action against him, for not taking the oaths to qualify. Motion to inspect the corporation books; but denied, because they would not force a man to produce evidence against himself. *K. and Lee*, M. 17 G. 2; information against defendant as overseer, for making rate without churchwardens. Rule obtained by surprise, to inspect papers: not obeyed. Motion against Lee for an attachment. Lee C.J., cited *Bradshaw and Philips;* Court refused to grant attachment, enlarged the rule, and it was dropped. The *K. and Burkins* only shews the tenderness which the Court always shews for persons under prosecution, and was to let him know his accusers. If the present defendant has evidence in his custody, and refuses to obey the rule, an attachment must issue; which would be as strange, as to grant one against a man, for not confessing his crime.

Mr. Evans on the same side.—Had this been an information for exercising the office of vice-chancellor, motion might have been regular. In ecclesiastical jurisdictions, they used to compel a man to furnish evidence against himself: but by Stat. Car. 2, oaths ex officio are taken away. On indictment for coining, the attorney might as well move, to have a prisoner discover all his correspondence. 'Tis true, the crimes are less, and the punishment less; but the barrier of liberty is the same. If this rule be granted, the Court of K. B. would be no longer a Court of Justice, but an aid to an inquisition of State. This is an information ex officio, and all legal stops should be put to such informations. This Court sits to hear, not to furnish evidence.

Mr. Morton, on the same side would not repeat.

Ryder, Attorney General, in support of the rule. This prosecution is out of favour to the university; to keep up a spirit of religion and loyalty there. Hard, that the university should interest themselves, to vindicate a member of their body that is under prosecution. If the prosecution be just, or unjust, it cannot hurt the university. Motion relates only to the public records, not to MSS. letters, &c.

therefore cannot be so prejudicial as is represented. The intent is to see the statutes of the university, to which the motion shall be confined. The information is for not taking depositions against an enormous crime, as vice-chancellor and as justice of the peace: and these statutes direct the conduct of the vice-chancellor. The Court grants motions of course to inspect public books. It is as reasonable that public records should be produced for public justice, as private papers for private justice. It is not desired that the vice-chancellor but the public officer should produce them: should he prove to be the public officer, that is no reason against the motion; for it does not respect him as defendant, but as public officer. The public is interested in the university statutes. We do not apply on behalf of the King as visitor, but as guardian of the public peace. In *K. and Burkins*, there was a rule of this kind made in a penal prosecution; a rule on a public officer, keeping a public record, for an inspection in a criminal prosecution. Informations in nature of quo warranto are public and criminal suits. There, rules of this sort are frequent. The case of *Bradshaw and Philips* was not of a public nature. *K. and Blackburn;* post-office books are not public, but the King's private books. *Benson and Cole;* same answer. As to the case of *College of Physicians,* that was the case of plaintiffs, and the Court will not compel the plaintiff to produce evidence against himself. In *The Qu. and Mead,* the books were of a private nature, and it appeared that the defendant was the person who kept the books. In *The K. and Lee,* it was plain, that the defendant was himself the person against whom the motion was made. Not so here; the vice-chancellor is not the person on whom the rule is to be made.

[Hereupon Mr. Henley suggested, that the vice-chancellor had the custody of the original statutes.]

Sir John Strange for the Crown.—Affidavits are not usual in such cases. In the case of *The Skinners' Company,* the clerk refused to grant inspection, and an attachment was granted; but it was argued, whether the papers required were proper to be seen, and the Court held that they were. So here, if any thing improper be demanded, the inspection may be refused. Strange, that the university should conceal their statutes; since they are of so public a nature, that all the youth there entered, take oaths to observe them, and yet they are secreted from them. The Crown is the founder and lawgiver of the university, and as such has a right to inspect those laws.

[Lee, C.J.—I apprehend this case is argued to differ from all others (as qui tam actions, &c.) because in those the party applying is a stranger; but that in the present case the King is no stranger, because he is the founder. But how does that appear? Another question; is there any instance of an information against an officer of a corporation for breach of by-laws, and a rule granted to inspect those by-laws?]

Murray, Solicitor-General for the Crown.—Four necessary requisites for inspections of this kind. First, that they be public books. Second, that the party applying has an interest in them. Third, that they be material in a suit in this Court. Fourth, that the person in possession be forced to discover nothing to charge himself criminally.—First,

these are of a public nature, given by the King, and open to all members of the university. The very youngest have a copy given them at their matriculation. Second, the King has an interest; he gave them, and has an interest in seeing them obeyed; and may enforce that obedience two ways; as visitor, and as King, where an offence at common law is mixed with the breach of them. Third, there is a suit in this Court, and the statutes may be material; and, if it is suggested that they will be so, the Court will grant the rule. Fourth, the objection is, that in criminal suits no one is bound to furnish evidence against himself. Agreed, but a distinction may be made. When a man is a magistrate, and as such has books in his custody; his having the office shall not secrete those books, which another vice-chancellor must have produced. Besides, the statutes are not in the vice-chancellor's custody only, but also in the hands of the custos archivorum.

Sir R. Lloyd, on the same side.—The university is not accused; the university may therefore very safely produce their books. The King is as much related to the Corporation of the University of Oxford, as to that of the City of York, and no more a stranger to one than the other. It is to be hoped, that the King is no stranger to either university. If a man were to be indicted for burning the records of a corporation; no doubt but such a rule would then be granted, and why not now? Per Lee, C.J.—This is quite a new case. There is no precedent to warrant it, I therefore chuse to consider of it.

Afterwards, Lee C.J., delivered the opinion of the Court. This rule has been much narrowed, since it was first moved by Mr. Attorney. But still we are all of opinion, that we cannot, consistently with the rules of this Court, make such a rule. We ground ourselves on what has been done in similar cases, though none so strong as this. No case has been cited to support this application, but *The K. and Burkin,* which is not apposite. The clerk of the peace ought ex officio to have given a copy of the indictment, and the Court would have granted a rule on him to do it. The cases which we apprehend to be close to this are, 1st. *Qu. and Mead,* 2 Ann. Ld. Raym. 927. The reasons for denying the motion were, because, 1. The books were of a private nature. 2. Granting such rule would be to make a man produce evidence against himself, in a criminal prosecution. The second case is *The K. and Cornelius and Others, Justices of Ipswich,* T. 17 & 18 Geo. 2, an information for exacting money from persons for licensing ale-houses: a motion to inspect the corporation books; cause was shewn against it by Sir J. Strange and Sir R. Lloyd. The Court on consideration were of opinion, that the rule could not be granted; as it was in a criminal proceeding, and it tended to make the defendants furnish evidence against themselves. These cases are very similar, only the present is rather stronger; because the information here is for a breach of and crime against the laws of the land, and this is an application to search books, which relate to the defendant's behaviour, as a member of a particular corporation. This case differs much from informations in nature of quo warranto; because these concern franchises, whereof the corporation books are the proper and only evidence, and they concern the Crown and the defendants equally. We know no instance, wherein this Court has granted a rule to inspect books in a criminal prosecution nakedly considered.

The rule was discharged per totam Curiam.

2

WRITS OF ASSISTANCE
1761–72

Quincy's Rep. (Mass.), App. 1:395–99, 401–5, 452–54, 457–60, 461, 495–98, 512–40

A. What are Writs of Assistance?

This term has been applied in the books of the law to many different processes, which may conveniently be classed under three heads.

I. Writs of assistance, more usually called "writs of aid," issuing from the Court of Exchequer, addressed to the sheriff, and commanding him to be in aid—"*quod sit in auxilium*"—of the King's tenants by knight service, or the King's collectors, debtors, or accountants, to enforce payment of their own dues, in order to enable them to pay their dues to the King. These writs are very ancient. A like writ, issued in 20 James I., to levy debts due to the Prince of Wales, is entitled on the record "*breve de assistendo.*"

Under this head may conveniently be mentioned the writs issued by King Edward I. to the Barons of the Exchequer, commanding them to aid a particular creditor to obtain a preference over other creditors of the same debtor, out of a surplus of his goods remaining in the Exchequer, after paying a debt due to the King, or to some other creditor who had sued there.

2. Writs to the sheriff, to assist a receiver, sequestrator, or other party to a suit in chancery, to get possession, under a decree of the Court, of lands withheld from him by another party to the suit. These writs, which issue from the equity side of the Court of Exchequer, or from any other Court of Chancery, are at least as old as the reign of James I., and are still in common use in England, Ireland, and some of the United States. But, whether from the odium attached to the name here, or from the practice in this Commonwealth to conform processes in equity to those at law, no instance is known of such a writ having been issued in Massachusetts.

3. Writs of assistance to seize uncustomed goods were introduced by a statute of Charles II., and were perhaps copied from the sheriff's patent of assistance. The book of precedents, quoted at the first argument here in 1761, is so rare, and the form therein given is so curious a justification of Otis's suggestion that it was framed "by some ignorant clerk of the Exchequer," that it is exactly reprinted in the margin. The same form, with very little change, is still followed in England, as appears by comparing the old writ with one issued in the first year of the present reign,

for a copy of which the writer is indebted to Henry T. Parker, Esq., of London.

. . . . .

B. Writs of Assistance granted in Massachusetts Bay in the Reign of George II.

Hutchinson says, that under the administration of Governor *Shirley,* (which ended in 1756,) "he, as the civil magistrate, gave out his warrants to the officers of the customs to enter;" and "these warrants were in use some years," until a dispute of their legality caused the Governor "to direct the officers to apply for warrants from the Superior Court; and, from that time, writs issued, not exactly in the form, but of the nature of writs of assistance issued from the Court of Exchequer in England." The accuracy of this last statement is fully corroborated by the contemporaneous records. The foremost to apply to the Court was *Charles Paxton.*

"Province of the Massachusetts Bay } To the Honourable his Majestys Justices of his Superiour Court for said Province to be held at York in and for the County of York on the third Tuesday of June 1755.

"HUMBLY SHEWS Charles Paxton Esqr: That he is lawfully authorized to Execute the Office of Surveyor of all Rates Duties and Impositions arising and growing due to his Majesty at Boston in this Province & cannot fully Exercise said Office in such Manner as his Majestys Service and the Laws in such Cases Require Unless Your Honours who are vested with the Power of a Court of Exchequer for this Province will please to Grant him a Writ of Assistants, he therefore prays he & his Deputys may be Aided in the Execution of said office within his District by a Writ of Assistants under the Seal of this Superiour Court in Legal form & according to Usage in his Majestys Court of Exchequer & in Great Britain, & your Petitioner &Ca:

"CHAS PAXTON"

This case first appears on the records of the Court at the ensuing August term in Suffolk, (which the docket shows to have been held by *Sewall,* C. J., *Lynde, Cushing & Russell,* JJ., and which was finally adjourned on the 30th of August,) in this form:

"UPON READING the petition of Charles Paxton Esquire wherein he shewed that he is lawfully authorized to execute the office of Surveyor of all Rates Duties and Impositions arising & growing due to his Majesty at Boston in this Province, and could not fully exercise said office in such manner as his Majestys Service and the Laws in such cases require, unless said Court who are vested with the power of a Court of Exchequer for this province would grant him a writ of Assistants, he therefore prayed that he and his Deputies might be aided in the Execution of said office with his District by a writ of Assistants under the Seal of said Court in Legal form and according to Usuage in his Majestys Court of Exchequer & in Great Britain. ALLOWED, AND TIS ORDERED BY SAID COURT that a writ be issued as prayed for."

The writ was afterwards issued in the following form:

"Province of the Massachusetts Bay. } GEORGE the Second by the Grace of God of Great Britain, France and Ireland King, Defender of the Faith &c—

"To all and singular Justices of the Peace, Sheriffs and Constables, and to all other our officers and Subjects within said Prov. & to each of you Greeting—

"WHEREAS the Commissioners of our Customs have by their Deputation dated the 8th day of Jany 1752, assignd Charles Paxton Esqr Surveyor of all Rates, Duties, and Impositions arising and growing due within the Port of Boston in said Province as by said Deputation at large appears, WE THEREFORE command you and each of you that you permit ye said C. P. and his Deputies and Servants from Time to time at his or their Will as well in the day as in the Night to enter and go on board any Ship, Boat or other Vessel riding lying or being within or coming to the said Port or any Places or Creeks appertaining to said Port, such Ship, Boat or Vessell then & there found to View & Search & strictly to examine in the same, touching the Customs and Subsidies to us due, And also in the day Time together with a Constable or other public officer inhabiting near unto the Place to enter and go into any Vaults, Cellars, Warehouses, Shops or other Places to search and see whether any Goods, Wares or Merchandises, in ye same Ships, Boats or Vessells, Vaults, Cellars, Warehouses, Shops or other Places are or shall be there hid or concealed, having been imported, ship't or laden in order to be exported from or out of the said Port or any Creeks or Places appertain'g to the same Port; and to open any Trunks, Chests, Boxes, fardells or Packs made up or in Bulk, whatever in wh any Goods, Wares, or Merchandises are suspected to be packed or concealed and further to do all Things which of Rt and according to Law and the Statutes in such Cases provided, is in this Part to be done: And We strictly command you and every of you that you, from Time to Time be aiding and assisting to the said C. P. his Deputies and Servants and every of them in the Execution of the Premises in all Things as becometh: Fail not at your Peril: WITNESS Stephen Sewall Esqr &c—"

· · · · ·

Case.

Opinion of Attorney General De Grey upon Writs of Assistance.

"7th Geo. 3d, Ch. 46. } By this Act of Parliament, after reciting 'That by an Act of Parliament made in the 14th CHA. 2d, intitled an Act for preventing Frauds and regulating Abuses in His Majesty's Customs, and several other Acts now in Force, it is lawful for any Officer of His Majesty's Customs, authorized by Writ of Assistants under the Seal of His Majesty's Court of Exchequer, to take a Constable, Headborough, or any other public Officer inhabiting near unto the Place, and in the Day Time, to enter and go into any House, Shop, Cellar, Warehouse or Room, or other Place, and in Case of Resistance to break open Doors, Chests, Trunks and other Package, there to seize, and from thence to bring any kinds of Goods or Merchandize whatsoever, prohibited or uncustomed; and to put and secure the same in His Majesty's Storehouse, next to the Place where the Seizure shall be made. And further reciting, That by an Act made in the 7th and 8th of WILLIAM the 3d, intitled an Act for preventing Frauds and regulating Abuses in the Plantation Trade, it was amongst other Things enacted, That the Officers for collecting and managing His Majesty's Revenue, and inspecting the Plantation Trade in *America*, should have the same Powers and Authorities to enter Houses or Warehouses, to search for and seize Goods prohibited to be imported or exported into, or out of, any of the said Plantations, or for which any Duties were payable, or ought to have been paid, and that the like Assistance should be given to the said Officers in the Execution of their Office, as by the said recited Act of the 14th CHA. 2d, is provided for the Officers in *England*, but no Authority being expressly given by the said Act of 7th and 8th of WILLIAM 3d, to any particular Court to grant such Writs of Assistants for the Officers of the Customs in the said Plantations, it was doubted whether such Officers could legally enter Houses and other Places on Land to search for and seize Goods in the Manner directed by the said Acts; to obviate which Doubts for the future, and in order to carry the intention of the said Acts into effectual Execution.

"*It is enacted,* 'That after the 20th of *November,* 1767, such Writs of Assistants to authorize and empower the Officers of His Majesty's Customs to enter and go into any House, Warehouse, Shop, Cellar or other Place, in the *British* Colonies or Plantations in *America*, to search for and seize prohibited or uncustomed Goods in the Manner directed by the said recited Acts, shall and may be granted by the Superior or Supreme Court of Justice having Jurisdiction within such Colony or Plantation respectively.'

"IN PURSUANCE of this Act of Parliament, the Officers of the Customs in *America*, have applied to the Judges of the Superior Courts of Judicature in the respective Provinces, for Writs of Assistants, but most of them have refused to grant such Writs, seemingly for this Reason, that no informations had been made to them of any special Occasion for such Writ, and that it will be unconstitutional to lodge such Writ in the Hands of the Officer, as it will give him a discretionary Power to act under it in such Manner as he shall think necessary.

"But it must be observed, that if such a General Writ of Assistants is not granted to the Officer, the true Intent of the Act may in almost every Case be evaded, for if he is obliged, every Time he knows, or has received information of prohibited or uncustomed Goods being concealed, to apply to the Supreme Court of Judicature for a Writ of Assistants, such concealed Goods may be conveyed away before the Writ can be obtained. Inquiry has been made into the Manner of granting Writs of Assistants in *England,* and it appears that such Writs are issued out of the Court of Exchequer whenever the Commissioners of the Customs apply for them. Every Officer of the Customs here, is armed with such a Writ, and whenever a new Officer is appointed, the Commissioners direct their Sollicitor to procure a Writ of Assistants, which is issued as a matter of Course by the Clerks of the Exchequer without any Application to the Court. This Writ is directed to all Officers and Ministers who have any Office, Power or Authority from or under the Jurisdiction of the Lord High Admiral of *England,* to all and every Vice Admirals, Justices of the Peace, Mayors, Sheriffs, Constables, Bailiffs, Headboroughs, and all other the King's Officers, Ministers and Subjects, commanding them to be aiding, assisting and helping the Commissioners of the Customs and their Deputies, Ministers, Servants, and other Officers in the Execution of their Duty.

"Quest. *Whether the Superior Courts of Justice in the* British *Colonies or Plantations in* America, *ought not upon Application, to issue Writs of Assistants in the same Manner as is practised in the Court of Exchequer in* England, *and what steps should be taken by Government in Order to Enforce the Issuing of these Writs for the Protection of the Officers of the Customs abroad?*

"There can be no doubt, but that the Superior Courts of Justice in *America* are bound by the 7th GEO. 3d. to issue such Writs of Assistants, as the Court of Exchequer in *England* issues in similar Cases, to the Officers of the Customs.

"As this Process was probably new to many of the Judges there, and they seem to have had no Opportunity of informing themselves about it, it is perhaps in some measure excusable, that they wished to have time to consider of it, and to inquire into the Practice of the Court of Exchequer and of other Colonies; and I think it can only be because the Subject was entirely misunderstood, and the Practice in *England* unknown, that the Chief Justice of *Pennsylvania,* who is generally well spoken of, could imagine, that 'He was not Warranted by Law' to issue a Writ commanded by the Legislature; which Writ was founded upon the Common Law, enforced by Acts of Parliament and in daily use in *England,* and which from the general import of the 7th WILL. 3d. ought to have been set on foot from that time in *America,* and which Statute the late Act only meant to Explain. And it appears accordingly that in *Boston* where a very able Judge presides and some Experience had been had upon the Subject, no Difficulty was made in granting it.

"I think therefore it is advisable that the Form of the Writ issued by the Court of Exchequer in *England,* should be sent over to the several Colonies in *America,* together with the Manner of applying for it and of granting it, by which they will see, that the power of the Custom House Officers is given by Act of Parliament and not by this Writ, which does nothing more than facilitate the Execution of his Power by making the Disobedience of the Writ a Contempt of the Court: The Writ only requiring all Subjects to permit the exercise of it and to Aid it. The Writ is a

Notification of the Character of the Bearer to the Constable and others to whom he applies, and a Security to the Subject against others who might pretend to such Authority. No Body has it but a Custom House Officer armed with such a Writ. The Writ is not granted upon a previous Information, nor to any particular Person, nor on a special Occasion. The inconvenience of that was experienced upon the Act of 12th CHA. 2d, C. 19. and the present Method of proceeding adopted in lieu of what that Statute had prescribed.

"*Wm DeGrey.*

"*20th August,* 1768."

. . . . .

Jonathan Sewal vs. John Hancock.

Advocate General *v.* Hancock. Information.

"Prov. &c. Before the Honl. Robert Auchmuty Esqr

"Be it remembered, that on the 29 day of October in the Ninth Year of the Reign of his Majesty George the Third, Jonathan Sewall Esqr Advocate General for the said Lord the King, in his proper Person comes and as well on behalf of the said Lord the King, as of the Governor of this Province, gives the said Court to understand and be informed, that on the ninth day of May last, a certain Sloop called the Liberty, arrived at the Port of Boston in said Province, from the Islands of Madeira, having on Board, one hundred and twenty seven Pipes of Wine of the Growth of the Madeira's; of which said Sloop, one Nathaniel Barnard was then Master, and that in the Night Time of the same day the said Nathaniel Barnard with Intent to defraud the said Lord the King of his lawfull Customs, did unlawfully and clandestinely unship and land on Shore in Boston aforesaid one hundred of the aforesaid Pipes of Wine of the Value of Thirty Pounds Sterling Money of Great Britain, each Pipe, the Duties thereon not having been first paid, or secured to be paid, agreeable to Law. And that John Hancock of Boston aforesaid Esqr was then and there *willfully and unlawfully aiding and assisting in unshiping & landing* the same one hundred Pipes of Wine, he the said John Hancock, at the same time *well knowing, that the Duties thereon were not paid or secured* and that the unshipping and landing the same, as aforesaid, was with Intent to defraud the said Lord the King as aforesaid, and contrary to Law; against the Peace of the said Lord the King and the Form of the Statute in such Case made and provided, whereby and by Force of the same Statute, the said John has forfeited Treble the Value of the said Goods, so unshipped and landed as aforesaid, amounting in the whole to the Sum of Nine Thousand Pounds Sterling Money of Great Britain, to be divided, paid and applied in manner following, that is to say, after deducting the Charges of Prosecution, one Third Part thereof to be paid into the Hands of the Collector of his Majesty's Customs for the said Port of Boston, for the Use of his Majesty, his Heirs and Successors, one Third Part to the Governor of said Province, and the other Third Part to him that informs for the same.

Whereupon as this is a matter properly within the Jurisdiction of this Honl. Court, the said Advocate General prays the Advisement of the said Court in the Premises, and that the said John Hancock may be attached and held to answer to this Information, and may by a Decree of this honourable Court be adjudged to pay the aforesaid sum of Nine Thousand Pounds to be applied to the Uses aforesaid.

"JON SEWALL Advo. for the King."

"Octr. 29, 1768. Filed and allowed and ordered that the Register of this Court or his Deputy issue out a Warrant for the Marshall of this Court or his Deputy to arrest the Body of the said John Hancock and him keep in safe Custody so that he have him at a Court of Vice Admiralty to be holden at Boston on the seventh day of November next at Nine of Clock before noon and that he take Bail for Three Thousand Pounds Sterling Money of Great Britain.

"ROBERT AUCHMUTY Judge &c."

Hancock was arrested on the night of November 2d, and gave the required bail. "Journal of the Times" of November 3, 1768, in Boston Evening Post of January 9, 1769. The Court adjourned from time to time until January 2d, when "a number of witnesses were examined by the court in a most extraordinary and curious manner; Mr. *Hancock's* nearest relations, and even his tradesmen, were summoned as evidences;" and the Court afterwards sat repeatedly and examined other witnesses. "Journal of the Times" of December 5 & 14, 1768, January 2, 5, 7, 23, 28, 30, February 11, 18, 21, 1769, in Boston Evening Post of January 30, February 6, 20, 27, March 13, 20, 27, April 10, 17, 1769. Observations published by the Merchants of Boston in 1769, 19, note. The grounds of defence, as stated in the notes of *John Adams,* were as follows:

1st. That even if Captain *Marshall* had landed the wines before the duties were paid, (of which there was evidence,) Mr. *Hancock,* if he "neither consented to this Frolick, nor knew of it," could not be held to be "assisting or otherwise concerned in the unshipping or landing inwards," within St. 4 G. 3, c. 15, § 87, which *Adams* compared with St. 8 Anne, c. 7, § 17.

2d. That the St. of 4 G. 3 was to be construed with the utmost strictness; because it was "the most poenal of almost any Law in the whole British Pandect," forfeiting the whole ship and cargo for withholding a small amount of duties.

"But among the Groupe of Hardships which attend this Statute, the first that ought always to be mentioned, and that ought never to be forgotten is

"That it was made without our Consent. My Clyent Mr Hancock never consented to it. He never voted for it himself, and he never voted for any Man to make such a Law for him. In this Respect therefore the greatest Consolation of an Englishman, suffering under any Law, is torn from him, I mean the Reflection, that it is a Law of his own Making, a Law that he sees the Necessity of for the Public. Indeed the Consent of the subject to all Laws, is so clearly necessary that no Man has yet been found hardy enough to deny it. The Patrons of these Acts allow that Consent is necessary, they only contend for a Consent by Construc-

tion, by Interpretation, a virtual Consent. But this is only deluding Men with Shadows instead of Substances. Construction, has made Treason where the law has made none. Constructions, in short and arbitrary Distinctions, made in short only, for so many by Words, so many Cries to deceive a Mob have always been the Instruments of arbitrary Power, the means of lulling and ensnaring Men into their own Servitude, for whenever we leave Principles and clear positive Laws, and wander after Constructions, one Construction or Consequence is piled up upon another untill we get at an immense distance from Fact and Truth and Nature, lost in the wild Regions of Imagination and Possibility, where arbitrary Power sitts upon her brazen Throne and governs with an iron Scepter. It is an Hardship therefore, scarcely to be endured that such a penal Statute, should be made to govern a Man and his Property, without his actual Consent and only upon such a wild Chimaera as a virtual and constructive Consent.

"But there are greater Proofs of the Severity of this Statute, yet behind. The Legislative Authority by which it was made is not only grievous, but the Executive Courts by which it is to be carried into Effect, is another. In the 41st. § of this Act 4 G. 3, c. 15, we find that all the forfeitures and penalties inflicted by this or any other Act of Parliament, relating to the Trade and Revenues of the said British Colonies or Plantations in America, which shall be incurred there, shall and may be prosecuted, sued for, and recovered, in any Court of Record, or *in any Court of Admiralty,*" &c. "Thus, these extraordinary Penalties and Forfeitures are to be heard and try'd,—how? Not by a Jury, not by the Law of the Land, but by the civil Law and a Single Judge. Unlike the ancient Barons who *una Voce responderunt, Nolumus Leges Angliae mutari*—The Barons of modern Times, have answered, that they are willing, that the Laws of England should be changed, at least with Regard to all America, in the most tender Point, the most fundamental Principle. And this Hardship is the more severe as we see in the same Page of the Statute and the very preceeding Section, § 40, That all Penalties and Forfeitures, herein before mentioned, which shall be incurred in Great Britain, shall be prosecuted, sued for and recovered in any of his Majesty's Courts of Record in Westminster or in the Court of Exchequer in Scotland respectively. Here is the Contrast that stares us in the Face! The Parliament in one Clause guarding the People of the Realm, and securing to them the benefit of a Tryal by the Law of the Land, and by the next Clause, depriving all Americans of that Priviledge. What shall we say to this Distinction? Is there not in this Clause, a Brand of Infamy, of Degradation, and Disgrace, fixed upon every American? Is he not degraded below the Rank of an Englishman? Is it not directly, a Repeal of Magna Charta, as far as America is concerned. It is not att all surprising that the Tryals of Forfeitures & Penalties are confined to the Courts of Record at Westminster, in England—The Wonder only is that they are not confined to Courts of common Law here." He then refers to the attachment of Englishmen to c. 29 of Magna Charta; and to Lord *Coke's* commentary thereon in 2 Inst. 51, as "concluding with a Reflection, which if properly attended to might be sufficient even to make a Parliament tremble."

. . . . .

3d. Adams also said: "We are here to be tryed by a Court of civil not of common Law, we are therefore to be tryed by the Rules of Evidence that we find in the civil Law, not by those that we find in the common Law.—We are to be tryed, both Fact and Law is to be tryed by a single Judge, not by a Jury.—We therefore claim it as a Right that Witnesses not Presumptions nor Circumstances are to be the Evidence." And he argued that by the rules of the civil law, in order to convict a person of any crime, there must be two witnesses, free from all exception; that "if there were two or ten such Witnesses as *Mezle*, they would not amount to Proof sufficient for condemnation;" that the respondents had "a right to examine the Witnesses whole past life, and his Character at large;" and to prove by other witnesses that (as it is stated in the "Journal of the Times") "he was a *fugitive* from his native country to *avoid the punishment* due to a very *heinous crime;*" for which he cited the following authorities: "New Inst. Civil Law, 315, 316. Dig. Lib. 22, Tit. 5, §§ 3, 12. Codicis, Lib. 4, Tit. 19, § 25; Tit. 20, s. 9, § 1, & note 32. Deut. 19, 15. Calv. Lex Testis. Fortescue de Laudibus Legum, c. 21, p. 38. Wood Inst. 310. Domat, V. 1, p. 13, Preliminary Book, Tit. 1, § 2, IV. 15."

"On the contrary," *Adams* argued, "if we are to be governed by the Rules of the common Law we ought to adopt it as a whole and summon a Jury and be tryed by Magna Charta—Every Examination of Witnesses ought to be in open Court, in Presence of the Parties, Face to Face—and there ought to be regular Adjournments from one Time to another. What other Hypothesis shall we assume? Shall we say that we are to be governed by some Rules of the common Law and some Rules of the civil Law, that the Judge at his Discretion shall choose out of each System such Rules as please him, and discard the rest, if so, *Misera servitus est.* Examinations of Witnesses upon Interrogatories, are only by the Civil Law. Interrogatories are unknown at common Law, and Englishmen & common Lawyers have an aversion to them if not an abhorrence of them. Shall we suffer under the odious Rules of the civil Law, and receive no advantage from the beneficial Rules of it? This, instead of favouring the Accused, would be favouring the Accuser, which is against the Maxims of both Laws."

. . . . .

G. Subsequent Action of the General Court.

At the next session of the General Court, on the 22d of February 1762, the following bill was introduced and passed to be engrossed in the Council:

"An Act for the better enabling the Officers of his Majesty's Customs to carry the Acts of Trade into Execution.

"Whereas it is the Desire of this Court, that the Officers of his Majesty's Customs in this Province may be assisted in the due Execution of their Office, for the securing his Majesty's Dues, and for the preventing of Fraud:

"Be it enacted by the Governour, Council and House of Representatives, That upon Application of any of the Officers of his Majesty's Customs in this Province, impowred by Commission to seise upon Oath made to the Superiour Court of Judicature, Court of Assize, and General Goal Delivery, or to the Court of General Sessions of the Peace, or to the Inferiour Court of Common Pleas, or to either of the Justices of said Courts, or to any one of his Majesty's Justices of the Peace of the County, that he has had information of the Breach of any of the Acts of Trade; and that he verily believes or knows such Information to be true; it shall be lawful in every such Case, for such Court or Justice, to whom Application may be made as aforesaid, upon reducing such Oath to Writing, with the Name of the Person [Informing and the place] informed against, and not otherwise, to issue a Writ or Warrant of Assistance, which Writ or Warrant of Assistance shall be in the Form following and no other, Vizt.

"   ss. To the Sheriff and Coroner of the County of   and to their respective deputies; and to the respective Constables of the Town of   in said County —Greetings

"Whereas A. B.   of his Majesty's Customs, hath this Day made Complaint on Oath, That (setting forth the Complaint and Oath with the name of the Person complained of) You and every of You in his Majesty's Name, upon Sight thereof, are strictly Commanded to be aiding and assisting to the said A. B. in the due Execution of his Office relating to the Information aforesaid. Hereof fail Not at your Peril, and make Return of this Warrant and of your Doings thereon unto myself in seven Days from the Date hereof. Dated at B. the   Day of   In the   Year of his Majesty's Reign: Anno Domini

"And be it further enacted, That it shall be lawful for any Person or Persons authorized by Writ or Warrant of Assistance, in matter and Form as aforesaid, and not otherwise, in the Daytime to enter and go into any House, Shop, Cellar, Warehouse, or other Place; and in Case of Resistance, to break open Doors, Chests, Trunks and other Packages, them to seize and from thence to bring any Kind of Goods or Merchandize whatsoever prohibited and unaccustomed there found and them secure. And all his Majesty's good Subjects are required to be aiding and assisting in the due Execution of said Writ or Warrant of Assistance, and all such shall hereby be defended and saved harmless."

The bill was also passed through all its stages by the House, with the amendment inclosed in brackets in the third paragraph, and was returned to the Council on the 6th of March, and there passed on the same day. After the bill had been sent up from the House, the Governor sent a message to the House that he had signed certain bills, of which this was not one; and the House thereupon sent a message to the Council by *James Otis* to inquire if they had passed on this bill, and the Council returned a message to acquaint the House that the Council had passed it to be enacted.

At a Council held on the 6th of March 1762, "His Excellency informed the Council that he had a Bill laid before him for his consent intituled an Act for the better enabling the Officers of his Majesty's Customs to carry the Acts of Trade into Execution which appeared to him to be repugnant and contrary to the Laws of the Realm and particularly to the Act of Parliament of the 7th: and 8th: of William the Third Chap: 22, in pursuance of which Act the Judges of the Superior Court heretofore granted Writs of Assistance to the Officers of the Custom House, Wherefore he thought proper in Council to take the opinion of the Judges upon this Question,

"Whether if this Bill should be enacted, The Superior Court as a Court of Exchequer could (consistently with such Act) grant a Writ of Assistance in pursuance of the Act of Parliament of the 7th: and 8th: of William the Third in the same manner as if such Bill was not enacted.

"The Judges having the Question in Writing given to them retired into the Lobby, and soon after returning, unanimously declared their opinion,

"That if this Bill should pass into a Law the Superiour Court would be restrained from granting a Writ of Assistance in the manner they have heretofore done and in the manner such Writs of Assistance are granted by the Court of Exchequer in England."

On the 6th of March the Governor prorogued the General Court, after making a speech to the two Houses, in which he gave these reasons for refusing to sign this bill:

"I have had a Bill laid before me, which I have not Power to pass to be enacted, I mean the Bill Intituled 'An Act for the better enabling the Officers of his Majesty's Customs, to carry the Acts of Trade into Execution;' which is so plainly repugnant and contrary to the laws of England, and particularly to the Act of Parliament of the seventh and eighth of King William the Third, Chapter twenty-second, that if I could overlook, it is impossible it should escape the Penetration of the Lords of Trade: In such Case, if I was to transmit this Bill as passed here, it would have no other Effect than to give a Proof of my Ignorance of my Business, and your Inattention to the Conditions upon which we are intrusted with the Power of Legislation."

. . . . .

I. Were the Writs of Assistance legal?

A report of the controversy upon the Writs of Assistance would be incomplete without an examination of the legal correctness of the decision of *Hutchinson* and his associates. Such an examination naturally resolves itself into four questions.

1st. Did Acts of the Parliament of Great Britain bind the Colonies?

2d. Were those Acts of Parliament, which provided for Writs of Assistance, void for unconstitutionality?

3d. Did those Acts, properly construed, authorize the issuing of general Writs of Assistance?

4th. Had the Superior Court of Judicature of the Province the powers of the English Court of Exchequer in this respect?

I. The inseparableness of taxation and representation, and the distinction between external and internal taxes, were familiar to the law of England before the discovery of America.

In the reign of Edward 3 Irish nobles were sometimes summoned to the English Parliament— "an excellent president to be followed," says Lord *Coke,* "whenever any Act of Parliament shall be made in England concerning the state of Ireland." In 1441 Chief Justice *Fortescue* held, that an act of the Irish Parliament, forfeiting offices in Ireland held by absentees, vacated an office previously expressly granted by the King to one or his deputy; and said that an English statute granting a tax would not bind the Irish, unless approved by their Parliament. For this last position the counsel for the losing party suggested the reason, that they were not represented in Parliament. In 1486 the same doctrine and the same reason were laid down by all the Judges of England, limited however to internal as opposed to external legislation.

Lord *Coke* declared in the House of Commons in 1627 that "the lord may tax his villein high or low, but it is against the franchises of the land, for freemen to be taxed, but by their consent in Parliament." Lord *Hale* is said to have been of opinion that "no acts here can bind the Irish in point of subsidies." Even Sir *William Blackstone,* in the debate on the repeal of the Stamp Act, is reported to have "declared, Tory as he was, that Parliament had no right to impose internal taxes." And Lord *Camden,* in his first speech in the House of Lords, said that the Act of 1766, declaring the right of the British Parliament to make laws to bind the American Colonies in all cases whatsoever was "illegal, absolutely illegal, contrary to the fundamental laws of nature, contrary to the fundamental laws of this Constitution;" and, nine years later, speaking "not only as a statesman, politician and philosopher, but as a common lawyer," told the house, "You have no right to tax America."

Yet *Coke* agreed with the uniform current of English authority, in holding that an Act of Parliament bound Ireland or the Colonies, if expressly named or necessarily included therein. And *Camden,* in the winter of 1767–8, said in the House of Lords that "though he had been clearly of opinion that Parliament had no such right, yet since it had been declared by Parliament, he did not think himself, or any man else, at liberty to call it in question." The reason of this is to be found in that principle of the English law, which attributes to Parliament the supreme legislative authority and the ultimate power of deciding what accords with the Constitution. In England, as has been truly said by Lord *Brougham,* though it sounds to American ears like a paradox, "things may be legal and yet unconstitutional."

Under the Colony Charter, Massachusetts constantly asserted her right of exemption from Parliamentary taxation, upon the ground of not being represented in Parliament. And upon this theory several acts were passed by the General Court to carry into effect the Acts of Trade and Navigation.

Under the Province Charter the subjection to the authority of Parliament seems to have been less disputed on grounds of legal right. The first statute of the Province was "an act setting forth general priveledges," one of which was that no tax should be imposed or levied on persons or estates, "on any colour or pretence whatsoever, but by the act and consent of the Governour, Council and Representatives of the People, assembled in General Court." But this act was disallowed by the King, under the power reserved to him in the new Charter. Three years later Parliament expressly extended the Acts of Trade to the American Colonies, and declared all laws, by-laws, usages or customs, repugnant to those or any future acts which should relate to and mention the Colonies, to be illegal and void. And the lawful authority of all Acts of Parliament, which concerned the Colonies and in terms applied to them, was acknowledged in the Provincial Courts of law, and expressly admitted in the addresses of the General Court of Massachusetts Bay to the Governor in 1757 and 1761; and in matters of external commerce, at least, was not seriously disputed until after the passage of the Stamp Act.

The opposite position, if taken in the argument upon the Writs of Assistance, would have been too striking to have been omitted in the contemporary reports. Yet none of them contain anything which could bear that construction, except a single expression in *Quincy's* Report. And the elaborate argument printed in the Boston Gazette immediately after the decision, as well as the later published writings of *Otis* and *Thacher*, assert in the most explicit terms the rightful authority of Parliament to legislate for the Colonies.

II. But *Otis*, while he recognized the jurisdiction of Parliament over the Colonies, denied that it was the final arbiter of the justice and constitutionality of its own acts; and relying upon words of the greatest English lawyers, and putting out of sight the circumstances under which they were uttered, contended that the validity of statutes must be judged by the Courts of Justice; and thus foreshadowed the principle of American Constitutional Law, that it is the duty of the judiciary to declare unconstitutional statutes void.

His main reliance was the well known statement of Lord *Coke* in *Dr. Bonham's case*—"It appeareth in our books, that in many cases the common law will control Acts of Parliament and adjudge them to be utterly void; for where an Act of Parliament is against common right and reason or repugnant or impossible to be performed, the common law will control it and adjudge it to be void." *Otis* seems also to have had in mind the equally familiar *dictum* of Lord *Hobart*—"Even an Act of Parliament made against natural equity, as to make a man judge in his own case, is void in itself: for *jura naturae sunt immutabilia*, and they are *leges legum*." Lord *Holt* is reported to have said, "What my Lord *Coke* says in *Dr. Bonham's case* in his 8 Rep. is far from any extravagancy, for it is a very reasonable and true saying, That if an Act of Parliament should ordain that the same person should be party and judge, or what is the same thing, judge in his own cause, it would be a void Act of Parliament."

The law was laid down in the same way, on the authority of the above cases, in Bacon's Abridgment, first published in 1735; in Viner's Abridgment, published 1741–51, from which *Otis* quoted it; and in Comyn's Digest, published 1762–7, but written more than twenty years before. And there are older authorities to the same effect. So that at the time of *Otis's* agreement his position appeared to be supported by some of the highest authorities in the English law.

The same doctrine was repeatedly asserted by *Otis*, and was a favorite in the Colonies before the Revolution. There are later *dicta* of many eminent judges to the effect that a statute may be void as exceeding the just limits of legislative power; but it is believed there is no instance, except one case in South Carolina, in which an act of the legislature has been set aside by the courts, except for conflict with some written constitutional provision.

The reduction of the fundamental principles of government in the American States to the form of written constitutions, established by the people themselves, and beyond the control of their representatives, necessarily obliged the judicial department, in case of a conflict between a constitutional provision and a legislative act, to obey the Constitution as the fundamental law and disregard the statute. This duty was recognized, and unconstitutional acts set aside, by courts of justice, even before the adoption of the Constitution of the United States. Since the ratification of that Constitution the power of the courts to declare unconstitutional statutes void has become too well settled to require an accumulation of authorities. But as the office of the judiciary is to decide particular cases, and not to issue general edicts, only so much of a statute is to be declared void as is repugnant to the Constitution and covers the case before the court, unless the constitutional and unconstitutional provisions are so interwoven as to convince the court that the legislature would not have passed the one without the other.

III. The St. of 13 & 14 Car. 2, c. II, § 5, declared that it should be lawful for any person "authorized by writ of assistance under the seal of his Majesty's Court of Exchequer" to take an officer and go into any house or shop and seize and bring out uncustomed goods. This statute, in which the name first appeared as applied to this process, did not define what it was, but assumed it to be already known. The only process, mentioned in any earlier statute or law book, to which the name could be referred, would seem to be the warrant mentioned in St. 12 Car. 2, c. 19, (confirmed by St. 13 Car. 2, St. 1, c. 7, and subsequent statutes,) which could only issue upon information on oath, and authorized the entry of a house for one month only after the offence, and by which, "if the information upon which any house is searched should prove to be false," the informer was made liable in full costs and damages to the party injured.

As general warrants were not authorized by the common law, *Otis* argued that the writ of assistance mentioned in St. 13 & 14 Car. 2, must be special, according to St. 12 Car. 2. This seems to have been considered at the time of the argument and afterwards the most important point; and upon the ordinary rules of interpreting statutes *in pari materia* together, and according to the rule and reason of the common law, the conclusion of *Otis* seems inevitable.

If the writ of assistance contemplated by the Sts. of Charles 2 was general to search all houses and issued without oath, it is a little remarkable that Lord *Hale*, neither in discussing general warrants, nor in speaking of these very statutes, gives any hint of such a departure from the principles of the common law.

It must be admitted that in practice general writs of assistance were commonly used in England. But they do not seem to have been the subject of judicial remark there before the argument in Massachusetts, after which Lord *Mansfield* took every opportunity to assert that general writs of assistance were expressly authorized by statute, which was certainly not the fact. And the practice was no more uniform nor better established than that which was allowed no force, either by Lord *Camden*, or by Lord *Mansfield* and his associates, in the matter of general warrants. But Lord *Camden*, who led the way in that matter, had not yet been raised to the Bench.

It is hard to imagine that the same House of Commons which condemned general warrants in 1766 intended to authorize general writs of assistance in 1767. Even after the passage of the St. of 7 G. 3, some of the American courts refused to issue anything but special writs of assistance; and attempts were made to limit them by statute. But in England the practice of issuing general writs of assistance continued until 1817, when a limit was imposed upon their use by an order of the Board of Customs, providing that no writ of assistance should in future be delivered to any officer of the customs, unless he should previously make oath before a magistrate of his belief and grounds of belief that smuggled goods were lodged in a certain house. And thus the reasonableness of the position of the Colonies was finally vindicated in the mother country.

In Massachusetts, the General Court recognized and applied the principles of the common law on the subject of general warrants, even in time of war, not allowing general warrants to issue even for the arrest of deserters in the Old French War, or to search for the arms of disaffected persons at the beginning of the War of the Revolution. Those principles were confirmed in 1780 by the Declaration of Rights, prefixed to the Constitution of Massachusetts, as follows: "Every subject has a right to be secure from all unreasonable searches and seizures of his person, his houses, his papers and all his possessions. All warrants therefore are contrary to this right, if the cause or foundation of them be not previously supported by oath or affirmation; and if the order in the warrant to a civil officer to make search in suspected places, or to arrest one or more suspected persons, or to seize their property, be not accompanied with a special designation of the persons or objects of search, arrest, or seizure; and no warrant ought to be issued but in cases, and with the formalities, prescribed by the laws." And the substance of this article was incorporated into one of the earliest amendments of the Constitution of the United States.

IV. The only question remaining is, whether the Superior Court of Judicature of the Province had in this matter the powers of the Court of Exchequer in England.

Upon this point *Gridley's* argument seems hard to meet.

The Act of Parliament of 13 & 14 Car. 2, c. 11, § 5, one of the Acts of Trade, empowered "any person authorized by writ of assistance under the seal of his Majesty's Court of Exchequer," to enter with a peace officer houses, &c. The General Court of the Colony afterwards provided for the strict observation of those acts. And the English St. of 7 & 8 W. 3, c. 22, § 6, provided "that the like assistance shall be given" to officers of the customs in the American Colonies, "as by the said" Act of Car. 2 "is provided for the officers in England." By the Province Charter "the great and general court of assembly" was vested with power "to erect and constitute judicatories or courts of record, or other courts," to try all crimes and civil actions; reserving the probate jurisdiction to the Governor and Council, and the jurisdiction in admiralty to Judges to be commissioned by the King. And under the power thus conferred, the General Court of the Province, by the first Judiciary Act which obtained the King's approval, established a Superior Court of Judicature, and bestowed upon it all the jurisdiction which "the Courts of King's Bench, Common Bench and Exchequer within his Majesty's Kingdom of England have or ought to have."

In support of the argument that the Superior Court had not the powers of the Court of Exchequer, much reliance was placed upon their refusal to entertain jurisdiction of a bill in equity. But no Court of the Province could well have assumed, on any pretence, a general equity jurisdiction, in the face of the opinions repeatedly expressed by the English Government upon that subject.

Whether the authority of the Court of Exchequer in matters of revenue was a part of its jurisdiction in equity does not appear to have been determined when the case of the Writs of Assistance came up. But the opinion seems to have since prevailed in England, that the revenue jurisdiction of that Court was strictly a common law jurisdiction, although some of its incidental proceedings might take the form of processes in equity. And the writs of assistance to officers of the customs certainly seem to bear a closer analogy to the common law writs of aid, which always issued from the Exchequer, than to the writs of assistance out of Chancery to take possession of lands.

Yet it is evident that the exercise of the jurisdiction of the Exchequer by the Superior Court was considered by both parties to be very doubtful. No instance was shown in which this Court had exercised any of the powers of the Exchequer, which might not have been exercised by the King's Bench or Common Bench; and it certainly did not possess all the powers of that Court even in matters of revenue. And this objection seems to have been thought the only one worthy of notice in England.

A careful examination of the subject compels the conclusion that the decision of *Hutchinson* and his associates has been too strongly condemned as illegal: and that there was at least reasonable ground for holding, as matter of mere law, that the British Parliament had power to bind the Colonies; that even a statute contrary to the Constitution could not be declared void by the judicial Courts; that by the English statutes, as practically construed by the Courts in England, Writs of Assistance might be general in form; that the Superior Court of Judicature of the

Province had the power of the English Court of Exchequer; and that the Writs of Assistance prayed for, though contrary to the spirit of the English Constitution, could hardly be refused by a Provincial Court, before general warrants had been condemned in England, and before the Revolution had actually begun in America. The remedy adopted by the Colonies was to throw off the yoke of Parliament; to confer on the judiciary the power to declare unconstitutional statutes void; to declare general warrants unconstitutional in express terms; and thus to put an end here to general Writs of Assistance.

3

HUCKLE V. MONEY
95 Eng. Rep. 768 (C.P. 1763)

Lord Chief Justice.—In all motions for new trials, it is as absolutely necessary for the Court to enter into the nature of the cause, the evidence, facts, and circumstances of the case, as for a jury; the law has not laid down what shall be the measure of damages in actions of tort; the measure is vague and uncertain, depending upon a vast variety of causes, facts, and circumstances; torts or injuries which may be done by one man to another are infinite; in cases of criminal conversation, battery, imprisonment, slander, malicious prosecutions, &c. the state, degree, quality, trade or profession of the party injured, as well as of the person who did the injury, must be, and generally are, considered by a jury in giving damages. The few cases to be found in the books of new trials for torts, shews that Courts of Justice have most commonly set their faces against them; and the Courts interfering in these cases would be laying aside juries. Before the time of granting new trials, there is no instance that the Judges ever intermeddled with the damages.

I shall now state the nature of this case, as it appeared upon the evidence at the trial: a warrant was granted by Lord Halifax, Secretary of State, directed to four messengers, to apprehend and seize the printers and publishers of a paper called the *North Briton*, Number 45, without any information or charge laid before the Secretary of State, previous to the granting thereof, and without naming any person whatsoever in the warrant; Carrington, the first of the messengers to whom the warrant was directed, from some private intelligence he had got that Leech was the printer of the *North Briton*, Number 45, directed the defendant to execute the warrant upon the plaintiff, (one of Leech's journeymen,) and took him into custody for about six hours, and during that time treated him well; the personal injury done to him was very small, so that if the jury had been confined by their oath to consider the mere personal injury only, perhaps 20 *l.* damages would have been thought damages sufficient; but the small injury done to the plaintiff, or the inconsiderableness of his sta-

tion and rank in life did not appear to the jury in that striking light in which the great point of law touching the liberty of the subject appeared to them at the trial; they saw a magistrate over all the King's subjects, exercising arbitrary power, violating Magna Charta, and attempting to destroy the liberty of the kingdom, by insisting upon the legality of this general warrant before them; they heard the King's Counsel, and saw the solicitor of the Treasury endeavouring to support and maintain the legality of the warrant in a tyrannical and severe manner. These are the ideas which struck the jury on the trial; and I think they have done right in giving exemplary damages. To enter a man's house by virtue of a nameless warrant, in order to procure evidence, is worse than the Spanish Inquisition; a law under which no Englishman would wish to live an hour; it was a most daring public attack made upon the liberty of the subject. I thought that the 29th chapter of Magna Charta, Nullus liber homo capiatur vel imprisonetur, &c. nec super eum ibimus, &c. nisi per legale judicium parium suorum vel per legem terrae, &c. which is pointed against arbitrary power, was violated. I cannot say what damages I should have given if I had been upon the jury; but I directed and told them they were not bound to any certain damages against the Solicitor-General's argument. Upon the whole, I am of opinion the damages are not excessive; and that it is very dangerous for the Judges to intermeddle in damages for torts; it must be a glaring case indeed of outrageous damages in a tort, and which all mankind at first blush must think so, to induce a Court to grant a new trial for excessive damages.

Bathurst J.—I am of my Lord's opinion, and particularly in the matter of damages, wherein he directed the jury that they were not bound to certain damages. This is a motion to set aside 15 verdicts in effect; for all the other persons who have brought actions against these messengers have had verdicts for 200 *l.* in each cause by consent, after two of the actions were fully heard and tried. Clive J. absent.

Per Curiam.—New trial refused.

4

WILKES V. WOOD
98 Eng. Rep. 489, 498–99 (C.P. 1763)

The Lord Chief Justice then summoned up the evidence of the whole, and observed it was an action of trespass, to which the defendant had pleaded first not guilty, and then a special justification. He then went through the particulars relating to the justification, the King's speech, the libel No. 45.

Information given, that such a libel was published,

Lord Hallifax granting a warrant; messengers entering Mr. Wilkes's house; Mr. Wood directed to go thither only with a message, and remaining altogether inactive in the affair.

If the jury should be of opinion, that every step was properly taken as represented in the justification, and should esteem it fully proved, they must find a verdict for the defendant. But if on the other hand they should view Mr. Wood as a party in the affair, they must find a verdict for the plaintiff, with damages. This was a general direction his Lordship gave the jury, and he then went into the particulars of the evidence. The chief part of the justification, he observed, consisted in proving Mr. Wilkes the author, and the evidence given, together with the letters to Kearsley plainly shew, that Mr. Wilkes was generally so. Then as to No. 45, the evidence was of two sorts, first a letter to fix it upon him, and the other general: as to the proof of the republication of *The North Britons* given by Currie, supposing it of itself sufficient, of which there was a doubt, it did not extend to the present case, to justify a warrant issued several weeks previous to that period. As to the letter, the gentlemen must take that out with them, together with *The North Briton,* No. 45, and allow all the weight to the circumstance they think it will admit of.

If upon the whole they should esteem Mr. Wilkes to be the author and publisher, the justification would be fully proved. But that, to do this, it was essentially necessary to have the enclosed paper in the letter to Balff, as, without that, all the rest was but inference, and not the proof positive which the law required. As to Mr. Wood, he was described on one side as very active in the affair, and on the other side as quite inoffensive. Aiders and abetters are always esteemed parties: but if a person present remains only a spectator, he cannot be affected. The evidence on the one side had been positive, and on the other side only negative. Mr. Wood might have said and done as represented on the one side, when the evidences on the other side were not present: if upon the whole they should be of opinion, that Mr. Wood was active in the affair, they must find a verdict for the plaintiff with damages. His Lordship then went upon the warrant, which he declared was a point of the greatest consequence he had ever met with in his whole practice. The defendants claimed a right, under precedents, to force persons houses, break open escrutores, seize their papers, &c. upon a general warrant, where no inventory is made of the things thus taken away, and where no offenders names are specified in the warrant, and therefore a discretionary power given to messengers to search wherever their suspicions may chance to fall. If such a power is truly invested in a Secretary of State, and he can delegate this power, it certainly may affect the person and property of every man in this kingdom, and is totally subversive of the liberty of the subject.

And as for the precedents, will that be esteemed law in a Secretary of State which is not law in any other magistrate of this kingdom? If they should be found to be legal, they are certainly of the most dangerous consequences; if not legal, must aggravate damages. Notwithstanding what Mr. Solicitor-General has said, I have formerly delivered it as my opinion on another occasion, and I still continue of the same mind, that a jury have it in their power to give damages for more than the injury received. Damages are designed not only as a satisfaction to the injured person, but likewise as a punishment to the guilty, to deter from any such proceeding for the future, and as a proof of the detestation of the jury to the action itself.

As to the proof of what papers were taken away, the plaintiff could have no account of them; and those who were able to have given an account (which might have been an extenuation of their guilt) have produced none. It lays upon the jury to allow what weight they think proper to that part of the evidence. It is my opinion the office precedents, which had been produced since the Revolution, are no justification of a practice in itself illegal, and contrary to the fundamental principles of the constitution; though its having been the constant practice of the office, might fairly be pleaded in mitigation of damages.

He then told the jury they had a very material affair to determine upon, and recommended it to them to be particularly cautious in bringing in their verdict. Observed, that if the jury found Mr. Wilkes the author or publisher of No. 45, it will be filed, and stand upon record in the Court of Common Pleas, and of course be produced as proof, upon the criminal cause depending, in barr of any future more ample discussion of that matter on both sides; that on the other side they should be equally careful to do justice, according to the evidence; he therefore left it to their consideration.

The jury, after withdrawing for near half an hour, returned, and found a general verdict upon both issues for the plaintiff, with a thousand pounds damages.

After the verdict was recorded, the Solicitor-General offered to prefer a bill of exceptions, which the Lord Chief Justice refused to accept, saying it was out of time.

The Court sat at nine o'clock in the morning, and the verdict was brought in at twenty minutes past eleven o'clock at night.

5

REX v. WILKES
95 Eng. Rep. 737 (C.P. 1763)

Lord Chief Justice Pratt, after stating the warrant of commitment, said, there are two objections taken to the legality of this warrant, and a third matter insisted on for the defendant, is privilege of Parliament.

The first objection is, that it does not appear to the Court that Mr. Wilkes was charged by any evidence before the Secretaries of State, that he was the author or publisher of the *North Briton,* Number XLV. In answer to this, we are all of opinion, that it is not necessary to state in the warrant that Mr. Wilkes was charged by any evidence before the Secretaries of State, and that this objection has no weight. Whether a justice of peace can, ex officio, without any evidence or information, issue a warrant for apprehending for a crime, is a different question: if a crime be done in his sight, he may commit the criminal upon the spot; but where he is not present, he ought not to commit upon discretion. Suppose a magistrate hath notice, or a particular knowledge that a person has been guilty of an offence, yet I do not think it is a sufficient ground for him to commit the criminal; but in that case he is rather a witness than a magistrate, and ought to make oath of the fact before some other magistrate, who should thereupon act the official part, by granting a warrant to apprehend the offender, it being more fit that the accuser should appear as a witness than act as a magistrate. But that is not the question upon this warrant; the question here is, whether it is an essential part of the warrant that the information, evidence, or grounds of the charge before the Secretaries of State, should be set forth in the warrant? And we think it is not. *Thomas Rudyard's case,* 2 Vent. 22, cannot be applied to this case, for in the case of a conviction it is otherwise. It was said that a charge by witness was the ground of a warrant; but we think it not requisite to set out more than the offence, and the particular species of it. It may be objected, if this be good every man's liberty will be in the power of a justice of peace. But Hale, Coke, and Hawkins take no notice that a charge is necessary to be set out in the warrant. In the case of *The Seven Bishops* their counsel did not take this objection, which no doubt but they would have done if they had thought there had been any weight in it. I do not rely upon the determination of the Judges who then presided in the King's Bench. I have been attended with many precedents of warrants returned into the King's Bench; they are almost universally like this; and in *Sir William Wyndham's case,* 1 Stra. 2, 3, this very point before us is determined. And Hawkins, in his 2 Pl. Coron. 120, sect. 17, says, "It is safe to set forth that the party is charged upon oath; but this is not necessary; for it hath been resolved that a commitment for treason, or for suspicion of it, without setting forth any particular accusation, or ground of suspicion, is good;" and cites *Sir William Wyndham's case,* Trin. 2 Geo. Dalt. cap. 125. Cromp. 233 b.

The second objection is, that the libel ought to be set forth in the warrant in haec verba, or at least so much thereof as the Secretaries of State deemed infamous, seditious, &c. that the Court may judge whether any such paper ever existed, or if it does exist, whether it be an infamous and seditious libel or not. But we are all of a contrary opinion: a warrant of commitment for felony must contain the species of felony briefly, "as for felony for the death of J. S., or for burglary in breaking the house of J. S. &c.; and the reason is, because it may appear to the Judges upon the return of an habeas corpus, whether it be felony or not." The magistrate forms his judgment upon the writing, whether it be an infamous and seditious libel or not, at his peril, and perhaps the paper itself may not contain the whole of the libel; inuendoes may be necessary to make the whole out: there is no other word in the law but libel whereby to express the true idea of an infamous writing; we understand the nature of a libel as well as a species of felony; it is said the libel ought to be stated, because the Court cannot judge whether it is a libel or not without it; but that is a matter for the Judge and jury to determine at the trial. If the paper was here, I should be afraid to read it. We might perhaps be able to

determine that it was a libel, but we could not judge that it was not a libel, because of inuendoes, &c. It may be said, that without seeing the libel we are not able to fix the quantum of the bail; but in answer to this, the nature of the offence is known by us; it is said to be an infamous and seditious libel, &c.: it is such a misdemeanor as we should require good bail for, (moderation to be observed,) and such as the party may be able to procure.

The third matter insisted upon for Mr. Wilkes is, that he is a member of Parliament, (which has been admitted by the King's Serjeants,) and entitled to privilege to be free from arrests in all cases except treason, felony, and actual breach of the peace, and therefore ought to be discharged from imprisonment without bail; and we are all of opinion that he is entitled to that privilege, and must be discharged without bail. In the case of *The Seven Bishops* the Court took notice of the privilege of Parliament, and thought the bishops would have been entitled to it if they had not judged them to have been guilty of a breach of the peace; for three of them, Wright, Holloway, and Allybone, deemed a seditious libel to be an actual breach of the peace, and therefore they were ousted of their privilege most unjustly. If Mr. Wilkes had been described as a member of Parliament in the return, we must have taken notice of the law of privilege of Parliament, otherwise the members would be without remedy where they are wrongfully arrested against the law of Parliament; we are bound to take notice of their privileges, as being part of the law of the land. 4 Inst. 25 says, the privilege of Parliament holds unless it be in three cases, viz. treason, felony, and the peace; these are the words of Coke. In the trial of *The Seven Bishops* the word peace, in this case of privilege, is explained to mean where surety of the peace is required. Privilege of Parliament holds in informations for the King, unless in the cases before excepted; the case of an information against Lord Tankerville for bribery, 4 Annae, was within the privilege of Parliament. See the resolution of the Lords and Commons, anno 1675. We are all of opinion that a libel is not a breach of the peace: it tends to the breach of the peace, and that is the utmost. 1 Lev. 139. But that which only tends to the breach of the peace cannot be a breach of it. Suppose a libel be a breach of the peace, yet I think it cannot exclude privilege, because I cannot find that a libeller is bound to find surety of the peace, in any book whatever, nor ever was, in any case, except one, viz. the case of *The Seven Bishops,* where three Judges said, that surety of the peace was required in the case of a libel: Judge Powell, the only honest man of the four Judges, dissented, and I am bold to be of his opinion, and to say that case is not law; but it shews the miserable condition of the State at that time. Upon the whole, it is absurd to require surety of the peace or bail in the case of a libeller, and therefore Mr. Wilkes must be discharged from his imprisonment: whereupon there was a loud huzza in Westminster-Hall. He was discharged accordingly.

6

ENTICK V. CARRINGTON
95 Eng. Rep. 807 (K.B. 1765)

Lord Chief Justice.—I shall not give any opinion at present, because this case, which is of the utmost consequence to the public, is to be argued again; I shall only just mention a matter which has slipped the sagacity of the counsel on both sides, that it may be taken notice of upon the next argument. Suppose a warrant which is against law be granted, such as no justice of peace, or other magistrate high or low whomsoever, has power to issue, whether that magistrate or justice who grants such warrant, or the officer who executes it, are within the stat. 24 Geo. 2, c. 44? To put one case (among an hundred that might happen); suppose a justice of peace issues a warrant to search a house for stolen goods, and directs it to four of his servants, who search and find no stolen goods, but seize all the books and papers of the owners of the house, whether in such a case would the justice of peace, his officers or servants, be within the Stat. 24 Geo. 2? I desire that every point of this case may be argued to the bottom; for I shall think myself bound, when I come to give judgment, to give my opinion upon every point in the case.

. . . . .

Curia.—The defendants make two defences; first, that they are within the stat. 24 Geo. 2, c. 44; 2dly, that such warrants have frequently been granted by Secretaries of State ever since the Revolution, and have never been controverted, and that they are legal; upon both which defences the defendants rely.

A Secretary of State, who is a Privy Counsellor, if he be a conservator of the peace, whatever power he has to commit is by the common law: if he be considered only as a Privy Counsellor, he is the only one at the board who has exercised this authority of late years; if as a conservator, he never binds to the peace; no other conservator ever did that we can find: he has no power to administer an oath, or take bail; but yet it must be admitted that he is in the full exercise of this power to commit, for treason and seditious libels against the Government, whatever was the original source of that power; as appears from the cases of *The Queen and Derby, The King and Earbury,* and *Kendale and Roe's case.*

We must know what a Secretary of State is, before we can tell whether he is within the stat. 24 Geo. 2, c. 44. He is the keeper of the King's signet wherewith the King's private letters are signed. 2 Inst. 556. Coke upon Articuli Super Chartas, 28 Ed. 1. Lord Coke's silence is a strong presumption that no such power as he now exercises was in him at that time; formerly he was not a Privy Counsellor, or considered as a magistrate; he began to be significant about the time of the Revolution, and grew great when the princes of Europe sent ambassadors hither; it seems inconsistent that a Secretary of State should have power to commit, and no power to administer an oath, or take bail; who can commit and not have power to examine? the House of Commons indeed commit without oath, but that is nothing to the present case; there is no account in our law-books of Secretaries of State, except in the few cases mentioned; he is not to be found among the old conservators; in Lambert, Crompton, Fitzherbert, &c. &c. nor is a Privy Counsellor to be found among our old books till *Kendall and Roe's case,* and 1 Leon. 70, 71, 29 Eliz. is the first case that takes notice of a commitment by a Secretary of State; but in 2 Leon. 175 the Judges knew no such committing magistrate as the Secretary of State. It appears by the Petitition of Right, that the King and Council claimed a power to commit; if the Secretary of State had claimed any such power, then certainly the Petition of Right would have taken notice of it; but from its silence on that head we may fairly conclude he neither claimed nor had any such power; the Stat. 16 Car. 1, for Regulating the Privy Council, and taking away the Court of Star-Chamber, binds the King not to commit, and in such case gives a habeas corpus; it is strange that House of Commons should take no notice of the Secretary of State, if he then had claimed power to commit. This power of a Secretary of State to commit was derivative from the commitment per mandatum Regis: Ephemeris Parliamentaria. Coke says in his speech to the House, "If I do my duty to the King, I must commit without shewing the cause;" 1 Leon. 70, 71, shews that a commitment by a single Privy Counsellor was not warranted. By the Licensing Statute of 13 & 14 Car. 2, cap. 33, sec. 15, licence is given to a messenger under a warrant of the Secretary of State to search for books unlicensed, and if they find any against the religion of the Church of England, to bring them before the Secretary of State; the warrant in that case expressed that it was by the King's command. See Stamford's comment on the mandate of the King, and Lambert, cap. Bailment. All the Judges temp. Eliz. held that in a warrant or commitment by one Privy Counsellor he must shew it was by the mandate of the King in Council. See And. 297, the opinion of all the Judges; they remonstrated to the King that no subject ought to be committed by a Privy Counsellor against the law of the realm. Before the 3 Car. 1 all the Privy Counsellors exercised this power to commit; from that aera they disused this power, but then they prescribed still to commit per mandatum Regis. Journal of the House of Commons 195. 16 Car. 1. Coke, Selden, &c. argued that the King's power to commit, meant that he had such power by his Courts of Justice. In the case of *The Seven Bishops* all the Court and King's Council admit, that supposing the warrant had been signed out of the Council, that it would have been bad, but the Court presumed it to be signed at the board; Pollexfen in his argument says, we do not deny but the Council board have power to commit, but not out of Council; this is a very strong authority; the whole body of the law seem not to know that Privy Counsellors out of Council had any power to commit, if there had been any such power they could not have been ignorant of it; and this power was only in cases of high treason, they never claimed it in any other case. It was argued that if a Secretary of State hath power to commit in high treason, he hath it in cases of lessor crimes: but this we deny, for if it appears that he hath power to commit in one case only, how can we then without authority say he has that power in other cases? he is not a conservator of the peace; Justice Rokeby only says he is in the nature of a conservator of the peace: we are now bound by the cases of *The Queen and Derby,* and *The King and Earbury.*

The Secretary of State is no conservator nor a justice of the peace, quasi secretary, within the words or equity of the Stat. 24 Geo. 2, admitting him (for arguments sake) to be a conservator, the preamble of the statute shews why it was made, and for what purpose; the only grantor of a warrant therein mentioned, is a justice of the peace; justice of peace and conservator are not convertible terms; the cases of construction upon old statutes, in regard to the warden of the Fleet, the Bishop of Norwich, &c. are not to be applied to cases upon modern statutes. The best way to construe modern statutes is to follow the words thereof; let us compare a justice of peace and a conservator; the justice is liable to actions, as the statute takes notice, it is applicable to him who acts by warrant directed to constables; a conservator is not intrusted with the execution of laws, which by this Act is meant statutes, which gives justices jurisdiction; a conservator is not liable to actions; he never acts: he is almost forgotten; there never was an action against a conservator of the peace as such; he is antiquated, and could never be thought of when this Act was made; and ad ea quae frequenter accidunt jura adaptantur. There is no act of a constable or tithingman as conservator taken notice of in the statute; will the Secretary of State be ranked with the highest or lowest of these conservators? the Statute of Jac. 1, for officers acting by authority to plead the general issue, and give the special matter in evidence, when considered with this Statute of 24 Geo. 2, the latter seems to be a second part of the Act of Jac. 1, and we are all clearly of opinion that neither the Secretary of State, nor the messengers, are within the Stat. 24 Geo. 2, but if the messengers had been within it, as they did not take a constable with them according to the warrant, that alone would have been fatal to them, nor did they pursue the warrant in the execution thereof, when they carried the plaintiff and his books, &c. before Lovel Stanhope, and not before Lord Halifax; that was wrong, because a Secretary of State cannot delegate his power, but ought to act in this part of his office personally.

The defendants having failed in their defence under the Statute 24 Geo. 2; we shall now consider the special justification, whether it can be supported in law, and this depends upon the jurisdiction of the Secretary of State; for if he has no jurisdiction to grant a warrant to break open doors, locks, boxes, and to seize a man and all his books, &c. in the first instance upon an information of his being guilty of publishing a libel, the warrant will not justify the defendants: it was resolved by B. R. in the case of *Shergold* v. *Holloway,* that a justice's warrant expressly to arrest the party will not justify the officer, there being no jurisdiction. 2 Stran. 1002. The warrant in our case was an execution in the first instance, without any previous summons, examination, hearing the plaintiff, or proof that he was

the author of the supposed libels; a power claimed by no other magistrate whatever (Scroggs C.J. always excepted); it was left to the discretion of these defendants to execute the warrant in the absence or presence of the plaintiff, when he might have no witness present to see what they did; for they were to seize all papers, bank bills, or any other valuable papers they might take away if they were so disposed; there might be nobody to detect them. If this be lawful, both Houses of Parliament are involved in it, for they have both ruled, that privilege doth not extend to this case. In the case of *Wilkes,* a member of the Commons House, all his books and papers were seized and taken away; we were told by one of these messengers that he was obliged by his oath to sweep away all papers whatsoever; if this is law it would be found in our books, but no such law ever existed in this country; our law holds the property of every man so sacred, that no man can set his foot upon his neighbour's close without his leave; if he does he is a trespasser, though he does no damage at all; if he will tread upon his neighbour's ground, he must justify it by law. The defendants have no right to avail themselves of the usage of these warrants since the Revolution, and if that would have justified them they have not averred it in their plea, so it could not be put, nor was in issue at the trial; we can safely say there is no law in this country to justify the defendants in what they have done; if there was, it would destroy all the comforts of society; for papers are often the dearest property a man can have. This case was compared to that of stolen goods; Lord Coke denied the lawfulness of granting warrants to search for stolen goods, 4 Inst. 176, 177, though now it prevails to be law; but in that case the justice and the informer must proceed with great caution; there must be an oath that the party has had his goods stolen, and his strong reason to believe they are concealed in such a place; but if the goods are not found there, he is a trespasser; the officer in that case is a witness; there are none in this case, no inventory taken; if it had been legal many guards of property would have attended it. We shall now consider the usage of these warrants since the Revolution; if it began then, it is too modern to be law; the common law did not begin with the Revolution; the ancient constitution which had been almost overthrown and destroyed, was then repaired and revived; the Revolution added a new buttress to the ancient venerable edifice: the K. B. lately said that no objection had ever been taken to general warrants, they have passed sub silentio: this is the first instance of an attempt to prove a modern practice of a private office to make and execute warrants to enter a man's house, search for and take away all his books and papers in the first instance, to be law, which is not to be found in our books. It must have been the guilt or poverty of those upon whom such warrants have been executed, that deterred or hindered them from contending against the power of a Secretary of State and the Solicitor of the Treasury, or such warrants could never have passed for lawful till this time. We are inclined to think the present warrant took its first rise from the Licensing Act, 13 & 14 Car. 2, c. 33, and are all of opinion that it cannot be justified by law, notwithstanding the resolution of the Judges in the time of Cha. 2, and Jac. 2, that such search warrants are lawful. State Trials, vol. 3, 58, the trial of Carr for a libel. There is no authority but of the Judges of that time that a house may be searched for a libel, but the twelve Judges cannot make law; and if a man is punishable for having a libel in his private custody, as many cases say he is, half the kingdom would be guilty in the case of a favourable libel, if libels may be searched for and seized by whomsoever and wheresoever the Secretary of State thinks fit. It is said it is better for the Government and the public to seize the libel before it is published; if the Legislature be of that opinion they will make it lawful. Sir Samuel Astry was committed to the Tower, for asserting there was a law of State distinct from the common law. The law never forces evidence from the party in whose power it is; when an adversary has got your deeds, there is no lawful way of getting them again but by an action. 2 Stran. 1210, *The King and Cornelius. The King and Dr. Purnell*, Hil. 22 Geo. B. R. Our law is wise and merciful, and supposes every man accused to be innocent before he is tried by his peers: upon the whole, we are all of opinion that this warrant is wholly illegal and void. One word more for ourselves; we are no advocates for libels, all Governments must set their faces against them, and whenever they come before us and a jury we shall set our faces against them; and if juries do not prevent them they may prove fatal to liberty, destroy Government and introduce anarchy; but tyranny is better than anarchy, and the worst Government better than none at all.

Judgment for the plaintiff.

7

MONEY V. LEACH
97 Eng. Rep. 1075, 1088 (K. B. 1765)

[LORD MANSFIELD]. . . . The last point is, "whether this general warrant be good."—

One part of it may be laid out of the case: for, as to what relates to the seizing his papers, that part of it was never executed; and therefore it is out of the case.

It is not material to determine, "whether the warrant be good or bad;" except in the event of the case being within 7 J. 1, but not within 24 G. 2.

At present—As to the validity of the warrant, upon the single objection of the incertainty of the person, being neither named nor described—The common law, in many cases, gives authority to arrest without warrant; more especially, where taken in the very act: and there are many cases where particular Acts of Parliament have given authority to apprehend, under general warrants; as in the case of writs of assistance, or warrants to take up loose, idle and disorderly people. But here it is not contended, that the common law gave the officer authority to apprehend; nor that there is any Act of Parliament which warrants this case.

Therefore it must stand upon principles of common law.

It is not fit, that the receiving or judging of the information should be left to the discretion of the officer. The magistrate ought to judge; and should give certain directions to the officer. This is so, upon reason and convenience.

Then as to authorities—Hale and all others hold such an uncertain warrant void: and there is no case or book to the contrary.

It is said, "that the usage has been so; and that many such have been issued, since the Revolution, down to this time."

But a usage, to grow into law, ought to be a general usage, communiter usitata et approbata; and which, after a long continuance, it would be mischievous to overturn.

This is only the usage of a particular office, and contrary to the usage of all other justices and conservators of the peace.

There is the less reason for regarding this usage; because the form of the warrant probably took its rise from a positive statute; and the former precedents were inadvertently followed, after that law was expired.

Mr. Justice Wilmot declared, that he had no doubt, nor ever had, upon these warrants: he thought them illegal and void.

Neither had the two other Judges, Mr. Justice Yates, and Mr. Justice Aston, any doubt (upon this first argument) of the illegality of them: for, no degree of antiquity can give sanction to a usage bad in itself. And they esteemed this usage to be so. They were clear and unanimous in opinion "that this warrant was illegal and bad."

8

WILLIAM BLACKSTONE, COMMENTARIES
3:288, 4:286–90
1768, 1769

An *arrest* must be by corporal seising or touching the defendant's body; after which the bailiff may justify breaking open the house in which he is, to take him: otherwise he has no such power; but must watch his opportunity to arrest him. For every man's house is looked upon by the law to be his castle of defence and asylum, wherein he should suffer no violence. Which principle is carried so far in the civil law, that for the most part not so much as a common citation or summons, much less an arrest, can be executed upon a man within his own walls.

. . . . .

First then, of an *arrest:* which is the apprehending or restraining of one's person, in order to be forthcoming to answer an alleged or suspected crime. To this arrest all persons whatsoever are, without distinction, equally liable to all criminal cases: but no man is to be arrested, unless charged with such a crime, as will at least justify holding him to bail, when taken. And, in general, an arrest may be made four ways: 1. By warrant: 2. By an officer without warrant: 3. By a private person also without warrant: 4. By an hue and cry.

1. A warrant may be granted in extraordinary cases by the privy council, or secretaries of state; but ordinarily by justices of the peace. This they may do in any cases where they have a jurisdiction over the offence; in order to compel the person accused to appear before them: for it would be absurd to give them power to examine an offender, unless they had also a power to compel him to attend, and submit to such examination. And this extends undoubtedly to all treasons, felonies, and breaches of the peace; and also to all such offences as they have power to punish by statute. Sir Edward Coke indeed hath laid it down, that a justice of the peace cannot issue a warrant to apprehend a felon upon bare suspicion; no, not even till an indictment be actually found: and the contrary practice is by others held to be grounded rather upon connivance, than the express rule of law; though now by long custom established. A doctrine, which would in most cases give a loose to felons to escape without punishment; and therefore sir Matthew Hale hath combated it with invincible authority, and strength of reason: maintaining, 1. That a justice of peace hath power to issue a warrant to apprehend a person *accused* of felony, though not yet *indicted;* and 2. That he may also issue a warrant to apprehend a person *suspected* of felony, though the original suspicion be not in himself, but in the party that prays his warrant; because he is a competent judge of the probability offered to him of such suspicion. But in both cases it is fitting to examine upon oath the party requiring a warrant, as well to ascertain that there *is* a felony or other crime actually committed, without which no warrant should be granted; as also to *prove* the cause and probability of suspecting the party, against whom the warrant is prayed. This warrant ought to be under the hand and seal of the justice, should set forth the time and place of making, and the cause for which it is made, and should be directed to the constable, or other peace officer, requiring him to bring the party either generally before *any* justice of the peace for the county, or only before the justice who granted it; the warrant in the latter case being called a *special* warrant. A *general* warrant to apprehend all persons suspected, without naming or particularly describing any person in special, is illegal and void for it's uncertainty; for it is the duty of the magistrate, and ought not to be left to the officer, to judge of the ground of suspicion. And a warrant to apprehend all persons guilty of a crime therein specified, is no legal warrant: for the point, upon which it's authority rests, is a fact to be decided on a subsequent trial; namely, whether the person apprehended thereupon be really guilty or not. It is therefore in fact no warrant at all: for it will not justify the officer who acts under it; whereas a lawful warrant will at all events indemnify the officer, who executes the same ministerially. When a warrant is received by the officer, he is bound to execute it, so far as the jurisdiction of the magistrate and himself extends. A warrant from the chief, or other, justice of the court of king's bench extends all over the kingdom: and is *teste*'d, or dated, *England;* not Oxfordshire, Berks, or other particular county. But the warrant

of a justice of the peace in one county, as Yorkshire, must be backed, that is, signed by a justice of the peace in another, as Middlesex, before it can be executed there. Formerly, regularly speaking, there ought to have been a fresh warrant in every fresh county; but the practice of backing warrants had long prevailed without law, and was at last authorized by statutes 23 Geo. II. c. 26. and 24 Geo. II. c. 55.

2. Arrests by *officers, without warrant,* may be executed, 1. By a justice of the peace; who may himself apprehend, or cause to be apprehended, by word only, any person committing a felony or breach of the peace in his presence. 2. The sheriff, and 3. The coroner, may apprehend any felon within the county without warrant. 4. The constable, of whose office we formerly spoke, hath great original and inherent authority with regard to arrests. He may, without warrant, arrest any one for a breach of the peace, and carry him before a justice of the peace. And, in case of felony actually committed, or a dangerous wounding whereby felony is like to ensue, he may upon probable suspicion arrest the felon; and for that purpose is authorized (as upon a justice's warrant) to break open doors, and even to kill the felon if he cannot otherwise be taken; and, if he or his assistants be killed in attempting such arrest, it is murder in all concerned. 5. Watchmen, either those appointed by the statute of Winchester, 13 Edw. I. c. 4. to keep watch and ward in all towns from sunsetting to sunrising, or such as are mere assistants to the constable, may *virtute officii* arrest all offenders, and particularly nightwalkers, and commit them to custody till the morning.

3. Any private person (and *a fortiori* a peace officer) that is present when any felony is committed, is bound by the law to arrest the felon; on pain of fine and imprisonment, if he escapes through the negligence of the standers by. And they may justify breaking open doors upon following such felon: and if *they kill him,* provided he cannot be otherwise taken, it is justifiable; though if *they are killed* in endeavouring to make such arrest, it is murder. Upon probable suspicion also a private person may arrest the felon, or other person so suspected, but he cannot justify breaking open doors to do it; and if either party kill the other in the attempt, it is manslaughter, and no more. It is no more, because there is no malicious design to kill: but it amounts to so much, because it would be of most pernicious consequence, if, under pretence of suspecting felony, any private person might break open a house, or kill another; and also because such arrest upon suspicion is barely *permitted* by the law, and not *enjoined,* as in the case of those who are present when a felony is committed.

4. There is yet another species of arrest, wherein both officers and private men are concerned, and that is upon an *hue* and *cry* raised upon a felony committed. An hue (from *huer,* to shout) and cry, *hutesium et clamor,* is the old common law process of pursuing, with horn and with voice, all felons, and such as have dangerously wounded another.

9

VIRGINIA DECLARATION OF RIGHTS, SEC. 10
12 June 1776

10. That general warrants, whereby any officer or messenger may be commanded to search suspected places without evidence of a fact committed, or to seize any person or persons not named, or whose offence is not particularly described and supported by evidence, are grievous and oppressive, and ought not to be granted.

10

MARYLAND CONSTITUTION OF 1776, DECLARATION OF RIGHTS, ART. 23
Thorpe 3:1688

That all warrants, without oath or affirmation, to search suspected places, or to seize any person or property, are grievous and oppressive; and all general warrants—to search suspected places, or to apprehend suspected persons, without naming or describing the place, or the person in special—are illegal, and ought not to be granted.

11

MASSACHUSETTS CONSTITUTION OF 1780, PT. 1, ART. 14
Thorpe 3:1891

XIV. Every subject has a right to be secure from all unreasonable searches, and seizures of his person, his houses, his papers, and all his possessions. All warrants, therefore, are contrary to this right, if the cause or foundation of them be not previously supported by oath or affirmation; and if the order in the warrant to a civil officer, to make search in suspected places, or to arrest one or more suspected persons, or to seize their property, be not accompanied with a special designation of the persons or objects of search, arrest, or seizure: and no warrant ought to be issued but in cases, and with the formalities, prescribed by the laws.

12

FRISBIE V. BUTLER
Kirby 213 (Conn. 1787)

With regard to the warrant—Although it is the duty of a justice of the peace granting a search warrant (in doing which he acts judicially) to limit the search to such particular place or places, as he, from the circumstances, shall judge there is reason to suspect; and the arrest to such person or persons as the goods shall be found with: And the warrant in the present case, being general, to search all places, and arrest all persons, the complainant should suspect, is clearly illegal; yet, how far this vitiates the proceedings upon the arraignment, may be a question, which is not necessary now to determine; as also the sufficiency of several of the other matters assigned in error.

13

HOUSE OF REPRESENTATIVES, AMENDMENTS TO THE CONSTITUTION
17 Aug. 1789
Annals 1:754

The committee went on to the consideration of the seventh clause of the fourth proposition, being as follows: "The right of the people to be secured in their persons, houses, papers, and effects, shall not be violated by warrants issuing without probable cause, supported by oath or affirmation, and not particularly describing the place to be searched, and the persons or things to be seized."

Mr. GERRY said he presumed there was a mistake in the wording of this clause; it ought to be "the right of the people to be secure in their persons, houses, papers, and effects, against unreasonable seizures and searches," and therefore moved that amendment.

Mr. BENSON objected to the words "by warrants issuing." This declaratory provision was good as far as it went, but he thought it was not sufficient; he therefore proposed to alter it so as to read "and no warrant shall issue."

The question was put on this motion and lost by a considerable majority.

Mr. LIVERMORE objected to the words "and not" between "affirmation" and "particularly." He moved to strike them out, in order to make it an affirmative proposition.

But the motion passed in the negative.

The clause as amended being now agreed to.

14

St. George Tucker,
Blackstone's Commentaries
1:App. 301–4
1803

The case of general warrants, under which term all warrants not comprehended within the description of the preceding article may be included, was warmly contested in England about thirty or thirty-five years ago, and after much altercation they were finally pronounced to be illegal by the common law. The constitutional sanction here given to the same doctrine, and the test which it affords for trying the legality of any warrant by which a man may be deprived of his liberty, or disturbed in the enjoyment of his property, can not be too highly valued by a free people.

But, notwithstanding this constitutional sanction, and the security which it promises to all persons, an act passed during the second session of the fifth congress, entitled an act concerning aliens, which was supposed to violate this article of the constitution, in the most flagrant and unjustifiable degree: by authorising the president of the United States to order all such aliens as he should judge dangerous to the peace and safety of the United States, or have reasonable grounds to suspect of any treasonable or secret machinations against the government thereof, to depart out of the territory of the United States within a limited time; and in case of disobedience, every alien so ordered was liable on conviction to be imprisoned for any term not exceeding three years. And any alien so ordered to depart, and remaining in the United States without a licence from the president might be arrested, and sent out of them, by his order: and, in case of his voluntary return, might be imprisoned so long, as in the opinion of the president, the public safety might require. Alien friends, only, were the objects of this act, another act being passed at the same session, respecting alien enemies. . . . The general assembly of Virginia at their session in 1798, "protested against the palpable, and alarming infractions of the constitution in this act; which exercises a power no where delegated to the federal government; and which, by uniting legislative and judicial powers to those of executive, subverts the general principles of a free government, as well as the particular organization, and positive provisions of the federal constitution." Kentucky had before adopted a similar conduct.

Among the arguments used by the general assembly of Virginia in their strictures upon this act, the following seem to be more peculiarly apposite to the subject of this article.

In the administration of preventive justice, the following principles have been held sacred; that some probable ground of suspicion be exhibited before some judicial authority; that it be supported by oath or affirmation; that the party may avoid being thrown into confinement, by finding pledges or securities for his legal conduct, sufficient in the judgment of some judicial authority; that he may have the benefit of a writ of *habeas corpus,* and thus obtain his release, if wrongfully confined; and that he may at any time be discharged from his recognizance, or his confinement, and restored to his former liberty and rights, on the order of the proper judicial authority; if it shall see sufficient cause.

Let the student diligently compare these principles of the only preventive justice known to American jurisprudence, and he will probably find that they are all violated by the alien act. The ground of suspicion is to be judged of, not by any judicial authority, but by the executive magistrate, alone; no oath, or affirmation is required; if the suspicion be held reasonable by the president, (whatever be the grounds of it) he may order the suspected alien to depart, without the opportunity of avoiding the sentence by finding pledges for his future good conduct, as the president may limit the time of departure as he pleases, the benefit of the writ of *habeas corpus* may be suspended with respect to the party, although the constitution ordains, that it shall not be suspended, unless when the public safety may require it, in case of rebellion, or invasion, neither of which existed at the passage of that act: and the party being, under the sentence of the president, either removed from the United States, or punished by imprisonment, or disqualification ever to become a citizen on conviction of his not obeying the order of removal, or on returning without the leave of the president, he can not be discharged from the proceedings against him, and restored to the benefits of his former situation, although the highest judicial authority should see the most sufficient cause for it.

Among the reasons alledged by a committee of congress, in support of the constitutionality of the alien law, one was; "that the constitution was made for citizens, not for aliens, who of consequence have no rights under it, but remain in the country, and enjoy the benefit of the laws, not as matter of right, but merely as matter of favour and permission; which may be withdrawn whenever the government may judge their further continuance dangerous."

To this it was answered; that, "although aliens are not parties to the constitution, it does not follow that the constitution has vested in Congress an absolute right over them; or that whilst they actually conform to it, they have no right to it's protection. That if they had no rights under it, they might not only be banished, but even capitally punished, without a jury, or other incidents to a fair trial." A doctrine so far from being sound, that a jury, one half of which shall be aliens, is allowed, it is believed, by the laws of every state, except in cases of treason. To which we may add that the word *"persons"* in this, and the subsequent articles of the amendments to the constitution, most clearly designate, that aliens, as *persons,* must be entitled to the benefits therein secured to all *persons* alike.

15

EX PARTE BURFORD
3 Cranch 448 (1806)

The Judges of this Court were unanimously of opinion, that the warrant of commitment was illegal, for want of stating some good cause certain, supported by oath. If the circuit court had proceeded *de novo,* perhaps, it might have made a difference. But this court is of opinion, that that court has gone only upon the proceedings before the justices. It has gone so far as to correct two of the errors committed, but the rest remain. If the prisoner is really a person of ill fame, and ought to find sureties for his good behavior, the justices may proceed *de novo,* and take care that their proceedings are regular.

16

CONNER V. COMMONWEALTH
3 Binney 38 (Pa. 1810)

TILGHMAN C. J. The plaintiff in error was indicted in the Court of Oyer and Terminer of Northumberland county, for refusing to execute a warrant issued by Thomas Cooper, esq., president of the Court of Common Pleas of the said county, for the arrest of a certain Jacob Langs, of the said county. The warrant was set forth at large in the indictment, and it appeared on the face of it, that it was issued without any previous oath or affirmation, on the following ground—"that it appeared to the judge from *common report,* that there was strong reason to suspect the said Langs of having knowingly uttered as true and genuine, certain false and forged notes, purporting to be notes of the Farmers and Mechanics' Bank of Philadelphia, and that the said Langs was likely to depart from, and quit the county of Northumberland, and retreat to parts unknown, before the witnesses to said uttering could be duly summoned and appear before the said judge, to enable him to issue a warrant on their testimony on oath."

Judge Cooper acted with great candor and propriety in stating on the face of the warrant, that it was issued without oath, and there is no doubt but he was actuated solely by the desire of preventing the escape of a criminal. The question is, whether this warrant does not appear to be illegal, from matter contained in the body of it? Of such matter the constable had a right to judge; and if it was illegal, he was not bound to execute it.

It is declared by the 8th section of the 9th article of the constitution of Pennsylvania, that no warrant shall be issued to seize any person, without probable cause supported by oath or affirmation. These expressions are very plain and very comprehensive. But it has been contended that the public safety requires that they should be subject to some exceptions; that in cases of necessity the oath may be dispensed with; and that the magistrate who issues the warrant must be the judge of that necessity. It appears to me, that if this be the true construction, the provision in the constitution is a dead letter; because in every instance, the magistrate who issued the warrant, would say that he thought it a case of necessity. It is true, that by insisting on an oath, felons may sometimes escape. This must have been very well known to the framers of our constitution; but they thought it better that the guilty should sometimes escape, than that every individual should be subject to vexation and oppression. It is unnecessary to consider whether there is no possible case, in which a warrant may be issued without oath, a case for instance, in which a crime is committed under the eye of a magistrate; or whether in cases of great and imminent public danger, the *salus populi* will not form an exception to the general rule. When such cases arise it will be time enough to decide them. It is dangerous for a court to lay down general propositions, from which unforeseen consequences may be drawn. I shall therefore confine my opinion to the warrant set forth in the indictment. It was commonly reported that Langs was guilty of uttering counterfeit notes; this common report came to the ears of the judge, and on that he issued his warrant. The constitution says a warrant shall not be issued without oath, which is more than common report. If the constitution did not mean, that a man charged with or suspected of a particular offence, should not be arrested, unless some person swore either that he believed him to be guilty, or to some facts from which it might be reasonably inferred that he was guilty, then I confess I can see no meaning in it. As for the necessity set forth in the warrant, that is to say the probability that the criminal might escape, I cannot think that it is of that nature, which can form an exception to the constitution; even supposing (which I do not affirm) that any necessity can form an exception. I am therefore of opinion, that the warrant was illegal, on the face of it, and the defendant not bound to execute it; consequently when he refused to execute it, he was guilty of no offence. But the refusal to execute the warrant is the only matter charged against the defendant in the indictment. Therefore, although the jury have convicted him of the matter charged, it does not appear on the record that he has been convicted of any crime. It follows, that the judgment of the Court of Oyer and Terminer was erroneous and must be reversed.

17

BELL V. CLAPP
10 Johns. R. 263 (N.Y. 1813)

Per Curiam. The matter set forth in the plea is a justification of the trespass. The search warrant was founded on oath, and the information stated that one hundred barrels of flour had been stolen from the wharf, in the first ward, by *Richard and Isaac Jaques,* and that the same, or a part thereof, was concealed in a cellar of *Gideon Jaques.* The plea then states that the warrant, being under the hand and seal of the magistrate, (who was one of the special justices of the city of *New-York,* an officer created by a public statute,) and being directed to the constables and marshals, authorized and required them to enter the said cellar, in the day-time, and search for the flour, and to bring it, together with the said *Gideon,* or the person in whose custody it might be found, before the justice; that in pursuance of the warrant, the defendants, the one being a constable and the other a marshal, did go to the cellar, which was part and parcel of the dwelling-house of the plaintiff, and, after being refused entrance, did open the door by force, and seize the flour in as peaceable a manner as possible. This, then, was a valid warrant duly executed by these officers. The warrant had all the essential qualities of a legal warrant. It was founded on oath, and was specific as to place and object, and the stolen goods were taken, and taken in as peaceable a manner as the nature of the case admitted.

In *Entick* v. *Carrington,* (*2 Wils.* 275. 11 *St. Tr.* 313–316,) Lord *Camden* admitted a search warrant, so well guarded, to be a lawful authority. The warrant did not state in whom the property of the flour resided, nor was this essential to its validity: a person may even be indicted and convicted of stealing the goods of a person unknown. Nor did it affect the legality of the warrant that it directed the officer to bring *Jaques,* to whom the cellar belonged, *or the person in whose custody the flour might be found.* It was impossible for any warrant to be more explicit and particular; and it would, probably, have been the duty of the officer to have arrested any person in possession of the stolen goods at the place designated, without any directions in the warrant, and to have carried him before the justice for examination.

Sir Mathew Hale, in one part of his treatise, (*H. P. C.* v. 2. 114. 116, 117,) denies to the officer the right of breaking open the door, on a warrant to search for stolen goods. but he, afterwards, (*Ibid.* 151,) admits this power in the officer, if the door be shut, and if upon demand it is refused to be opened. This past opinion is founded on the better reason, for search warrants are often indispensable to the detection of crimes; and they would be of little or no efficacy without this power attached to them. All the checks which the *English* law, and which even the constitution of the *United States,* have imposed upon the operation of these search warrants, and with the manifestation of a strong jealousy of the abuses incident to them, would scarcely have been thought of, or have been deemed necessary, if the warrant did not communicate the power of opening the outer door of a house. In the case of *Entick* v. *Carrington,* it was asserted by the counsel for the defendant, that on a search warrant to search for stolen goods, the officer might break open doors, &c., and this power was not questioned by the other side, nor by Lord *Camden* in the able and elaborate view which he took of the legality and effect of these warrants.

The defendants are, accordingly, entitled to judgment upon the demurrers.   Judgment for the defendants.

18

GRUMON v. RAYMOND
1 Conn. 40 (1814)

REEVE, Ch. J. That this warrant was such as no justice ought to have issued will be admitted; for it is not only a warrant to search for stolen goods supposed to be concealed in a particular place, but it is a warrant to search all suspected places, stores, shops and barns in *Wilton.* Where those suspected places were in *Wilton* is not pointed out, or by whom suspected: so that all the dwelling-houses and out-houses within the town of *Wilton* were by this warrant made liable to search. The officer also was directed to search suspected persons, and arrest them. By whom they were suspected, whether by the justice, the officer, or complainant, is not mentioned; so that every citizen of the *United States* within the jurisdiction of the justice to try for theft, was liable to be arrested and carried before the justice for trial. The warrant was this: Search every house, store or barn within the town of *Wilton,* that is suspected of having certain bags concealed in it, said to be stolen, and all persons who are suspected of having stolen them. This is a general search-warrant, which has always been determined to be illegal, not only in cases of searching for stolen goods, but in all other cases.

In all the history of legal proceedings there is no such warrant to be found as to arrest all suspected persons; for in those general warrants issued by Lord *Halifax,* as secretary of state, in search of libels, the persons to be arrested were pointed out in every warrant; but is was to ransack a man's house, and to bring all his books, papers, &c. before Lord *Halifax.* A number of suits were brought against those employed by Lord *Halifax* for having executed these warrants; and in every instance, the plaintiff prevailed, and recovered exemplary damages, by verdicts of the jury; which verdicts were approbated by the court; for in all the applications for new trials, they refused them.

It cannot be said, that those cases differed from the present one; that in this case the justice had jurisdiction over theft, and might issue a proper warrant in the case; and having issued an improper one, it is only an error in judgment respecting a subject over which he has jurisdiction, and therefore he cannot be accountable; but that Lord *Halifax,* as secretary of state, had no jurisdiction over the subject matter. This is not the case. A secretary of state has power to commit for treason and seditious libels upon a proper warrant. *Rex* v. *Kendall* and *Row, Skinn.* 596. S. C. 1 *Salk* 347. S. C. 1 *Ld. Raym.* 65. *Rex* v. *Wyndham,* 1 *Stra.* 2. *Searche's* case, 1 *Leon.* 70. *pl.* 93. *Yaxley's* case, *Carth.* 291. *Hellyard's* case, 2 *Leon.* 175. *pl.* 213. 2 *Hawk. P. C. c.* 16. *s.* 4. And this doctrine was held to be correct by the court who tried the cases. 2 *Wils.* 288. The ground on which the defendants were held liable was not that the secretary had no jurisdiction in case of libels against the government, but that he had no jurisdiction to issue such a process; for there must be not only a jurisdiction of the subject matter, but also a jurisdiction of the process. This point was expressly determined in the case of *Martin* v. *Marshall* and *Key, Hob.* 63. In a case tried by the mayor of *York*, the action brought was trespass *vi et armis*. The mayor of *York* was judge of a court of limited jurisdiction, and issued a process which was illegal. Though he had full jurisdiction over the subject matter tried, yet the court held him liable; for, say the court, the judge had a limited jurisdiction of the subject matter, but had no jurisdiction of such process as was issued. This doctrine was recognized as correct in *Perkin* v. *Proctor & al.* 2 *Wils.* 386. where the court say, there must be jurisdiction of the *process* as well as of the person and cause.

In the principal case, the law knows of no such process as one to arrest all suspected persons, and bring them before a court for trial. It is an idea not to be endured for a moment. It would open a door for the gratification of the most malignant passions, if such process issued by a magistrate should skreen him from damages.

As there is no such process known to the law as the record presents, no person could be arrested under it. The case, then, stands on no better ground than it would if there had been no process, and a verbal direction had been given to arrest all suspected persons, and bring them before the justice. But the magistrate who issued a verbal process to arrest was held liable in trespass; and this is recognized as good law in 2 *Wils.* 386.

Should it be asked, if a justice issues a warrant which has some defect in it, so that the person arrested cannot be held by it, is the justice liable? I answer, he is not, if he aims at issuing a process which the law recognizes, and fails though some oversight or mistake. If he should attempt to issue an attachment against the goods, estate or person of a debtor, and direct the officer for want of property to take the debtor, and him have before the court &c., and it should be so defective as to abate, the justice would not be liable; for he had jurisdiction over that kind of process which he issued. But if he should direct the officer, for want of property, to take the body of the debtor, and put him in irons, and confine him in *Newgate*, he would be liable; for the law knows of no such process.

Where there is a want of jurisdiction over the persons, as in the *Marshalsea* case, 10 *Co.* 70.; or over the cause, as if a justice should try a man for murder; or over the process, as in the case cited from *Hobart*; it is the same as though there was no court. It is *coram non judice*.

From the case of *Entick* v. *Carrington*, 2 *Wils.* 275. we have the opinion of the Chief Justice, that if a warrant which is against law be granted, such as no justice of the peace or other magistrate, high or low, has power to issue, the justice who issues and the officer who executes it are liable in an action of trespass. And no man can hesitate to say, that the law knows of no such warrant as one to arrest suspected persons without naming them, without any complaint, against any person, leaving it to the officer to suspect whom he pleases, or to arrest every person that any other person suspects.

But there is another point of light in which this subject may be viewed. The justice never had any jurisdiction of the subject matter. This purports to be a search-warrant

for stolen goods; and the law requires, that before any justice can have power to issue a warrant in such case, certain requisites be complied with.

It is comparatively of modern date that such a warrant could, under any circumstances, issue. In the time of Lord *Coke* it could not be done. 4 *Inst.* 176, 7. But it is now allowed of under certain circumstances. There must be an oath by the applicant that he has had his goods stolen, and strongly suspects that they are concealed in such a place; and the warrant cannot give a direction to search any other place than the particular place pointed out.

By the complaint on record in writing, it does not appear, that any oath was made, that the bags were stolen; nor that any place was pointed out where they were concealed; both of which were necessary, and without them no warrant could issue.

But it is said, that from the warrant under the hand of the justice it appears, that there was an oath that the bags were stolen; and that they were concealed at *Aaron Hyatt's,* or some other place. It is true, the justice so says; but it will be remarked, that he says, "as will appear by the complaint;" and upon examination of that, there is no oath ever made that there was any felony, or any place pointed out where the stolen bags were supposed to be; so that the justice had no jurisdiction over the case so as to issue a search-warrant.

But admitting that the warrant under the hand of the justice presents to us correctly the facts, it will not help the defendants; for there is no place pointed out, only at *Aaron Hyatt's or somewhere else*, which is equivalent to saying, that they were somewhere concealed. This would not be sufficient to warrant the issuing of a search-warrant.

If it should be contended, that it would authorize the issuing of a warrant to search *Aaron Hyatt's*, yet it laid no foundation to search any other place, for no other place is mentioned; and notwithstanding this, the warrant directs all suspected places in *Wilton* to be searched, whether houses, barns or stores; and under a warrant so issued the plaintiff was arrested.

It is no uncommon thing where there is a court of limited jurisdiction, that their jurisdiction depends upon the existence of certain things, and for want of these the court has no jurisdiction; and every thing done by the court, where these are wanting, is *coram non judice;* and the judge and officer are, in such case, liable in trespass to any person who may be arrested by a warrant issuing from the court.

There is a notable case in 2 *Stra.* 993. which fully establishes this doctrine. It is the case of *Smith* v. *Bouchier* and others, *viz.* the vice-chancellor of the university of *Oxford*, the judge, gaoler and party. The question arose upon a custom, that a plaintiff making oath that he has a personal action against any person within the precincts of the university, and that he believes the defendant will not appear, but run away, the judge may award a warrant to arrest him, and detain him until security is given for answering the complaint. On the 7th of *August* 1731, the defendant *Bouchier*, having the privilege of the university, made a complaint to the defendant *Shippen*, the vice-chancellor, of a personal action against the plaintiff *Smith*, to his damage

1000*l.*, according to his estimation, and that he suspected that the plaintiff *Smith* would run away. He took his oath of and upon the truth of the premises; upon which a warrant was granted to the other defendants, who arrested *Smith*, and kept him in prison eight days for want of sureties.

Here, it will be observed, the requisite was, that the plaintiff should swear to his *belief* that the defendant would run away, whereas the oath was, that he *suspected*. The court held, that it was necessary, to give jurisdiction to the court, that he should swear to his belief; and because he did not, all that was done was *coram non judice*, and void. The vice-chancellor, judge, officer and party were, therefore, all held to be liable in an action of trespass and false imprisonment.

As in that case there was no jurisdiction without an oath that the plaintiff believed; so in this case there is no jurisdiction without an oath that the bags were concealed in some specific place. As there was no such oath, the justice had no jurisdiction. This case is precisely in point.

When this case is viewed in either point of light, the case is with the plaintiff; for although the justice had jurisdiction of the subject matter of theft, yet he had no jurisdiction over such a process. It was unknown in law and illegal, and could not be issued by any magistrate high or low, as is expressed by Lord *Camden*, without making that magistrate liable, provided any person was arrested under it.

As to the warrant to search for stolen goods; this could in no case be issued, unless certain requisites had been observed, which were not observed in this case, and of course the justice had no jurisdiction in the case.

The justice, therefore, was liable to this action, and the officer also who executed it; for although an officer is not always liable when he executes an improper warrant; yet this is in a case where it does not appear on the face of the warrant that it is illegal. It may, for any thing that the officer can discover, be legal; and in such case, it is his duty to obey, and to presume that it is lawful. But an officer is bound to know the law; and when the warrant, on the face of it, appears to be illegal, and he executes it, he is liable to the person arrested. Such was the present case.

19

TREASURER V. MOORE
3 Brev. 550 (S.C. 1815)

COLCOCK, J. I am in favor of the motion. I think the witness should have made a return as to the *duces tecum*, or that part of the subpoena which required him to bring the books. I also think that a sheriff's books are public property, and that whoever may be in possession of them, is bound to produce them, when called for by legal authority, even though as evidence against himself; nor can I conceive that there can be a doubt, but that when a sale has taken place, a sheriff, or his representatives, are bound to account for the proceeds.

20

THE ANTELOPE
10 Wheat. 66 (1825)

Mr. Chief Justice MARSHALL delivered the opinion of the court, and after stating the case, proceeded as follows:

In prosecuting this appeal, the United States assert no property in themselves. They appear in the character of guardians, or next friends, of these Africans, who are brought, without any act of their own, into the bosom of our country, insist on their right to freedom, and submit their claim to the laws of the land, and to the tribunals of the nation.

The consuls of Spain and Portugal, respectively, demand these Africans as slaves, who have, in the regular course of legitimate commerce, been acquired as property by the subjects of their respective sovereigns, and claim their restitution under the laws of the United States.

In examining claims of this momentous importance; claims in which the sacred rights of liberty and of property come in conflict with each other; which have drawn from the bar a degree of talent and of eloquence worthy of the questions that have been discussed; this court must not yield to feelings which might seduce it from the path of duty, and must obey the mandate of the law.

That the course of opinion on the slave trade should be unsettled, ought to excite no surprise. The Christian and civilized nations of the world, with whom we have most intercourse, have all been engaged in it. However abhorrent this traffic may be to a mind whose original feelings are not blunted by familiarity with the practice, it has been sanctioned in modern times by the laws of all nations who possess distant colonies, each of whom has engaged in it as a common commercial business which no other could rightfully interrupt. It has claimed all the sanction which could be derived from long usage, and general acquiescence. That trade could not be considered as contrary to the law of nations which was authorized and protected by the laws of all commercial nations; the right to carry on which was claimed by each, and allowed by each.

The course of unexamined opinion, which was founded on this inveterate usage, received its first check in America; and, as soon as these states acquired the right of self-government, the traffic was forbidden by most of them. In the beginning of this century, several humane and enlightened individuals of Great Britain devoted themselves to the cause of the Africans; and, by frequent appeals to the nation, in which the enormity of this commerce was unveiled and exposed to the public eye, the general sentiment was at length roused against it, and the feelings of justice and humanity, regaining their long lost ascendency, prevailed so far in the British Parliament as to obtain an act for its abolition. The utmost efforts of the British government, as well as of that of the United States, have since been assiduously employed in its suppression. It has been denounced by both in terms of great severity, and those concerned in it are subjected to the heaviest penalties which law can inflict. In addition to these measures operating on their own people, they have used all their influence to bring other nations into the same system, and to interdict this trade by the consent of all.

Public sentiment has, in both countries, kept pace with the measures of government; and the opinion is extensively, if not universally entertained, that this unnatural traffic ought to be suppressed. While its illegality is asserted by some governments, but not admitted by all; while the detestation in which it is held is growing daily, and even those nations who tolerate it in fact, almost disavow their own conduct, and rather connive at, than legalize, the acts of their subjects; it is not wonderful that public feeling should march somewhat in advance of strict law, and that opposite opinions should be entertained on the precise cases in which our own laws may control and limit the practice of others. Indeed, we ought not to be surprised, if, on this novel series of cases, even courts of justice should, in some instances, have carried the principle of suppression farther than a more deliberate consideration of the subject would justify.

The Amedie (1 Acton's Rep., 240), which was an American vessel employed in the African trade, was captured by a British cruiser, and condemned in the Vice-Admiralty Court of Tortola. An appeal was prayed; and Sir William Grant, in delivering the opinion of the court, said, that the trade being then declared unjust and unlawful by Great Britain, "a claimant could have no right, upon principles of universal law, to claim restitution in a prize court, of human beings carried as his slaves. He must show some right that has been violated by the capture, some property of which he has been dispossessed, and to which he ought to be restored. In this case, the laws of the claimant's country allow of no right of property such as he claims. There can, therefore, be no right of restitution. The consequence is, that the judgment must be affirmed."

The Fortuna (1 Dodson's Rep., 81), was condemned on the authority of *The Amedie,* and the same principle was again affirmed.

The Diana (1 Dodson's Rep., 95), was a Swedish vessel, captured with a cargo of slaves, by a British cruiser, and condemned in the Court of Vice-Admiralty at Sierra Leone. This sentence was reversed on appeal, and Sir William Scott, in pronouncing the sentence of reversal, said, "the condemnation also took place on a principle which this court cannot in any manner recognize, inasmuch as the sentence affirms, 'that the slave trade, from motives of humanity, hath been abolished by most civilized nations, and is not, at the present time, legally authorized by any.' This appears to me to be an assertion by no means sustainable." The ship and cargo were restored, on the principle that the trade was allowed by the laws of Sweden.

The principle common to these cases is, that the legality of the capture of a vessel engaged in the slave trade, depends on the law of the country to which the vessel belongs. If that law gives its sanction to the trade, restitution will be decreed; if that law prohibits it, the vessel and cargo will be condemned as good prize.

This whole subject came on afterwards to be considered in *The Louis* (2 Dodson's Rep., 238). The opinion of Sir William Scott, in that case, demonstrates the attention he had bestowed upon it, and gives full assurance that it may be considered as settling the law in the British courts of admiralty as far as it goes.

The Louis was a French vessel, captured on a slaving voyage, before she had purchased any slaves, brought into Sierra Leone, and condemned by the Vice-Admiralty Court at that place. On an appeal to the Court of Admiralty in England, the sentence was reversed.

In the very full and elaborate opinion given on this case, Sir William Scott, in explicit terms, lays down the broad principle that the right of search is confined to a state of war. It is a right strictly belligerent in its character, which can never be exercised by a nation at peace, except against professed pirates, who are the enemies of the human race. The act of trading in slaves, however detestable, was not, he said, "the act of freebooters, enemies of the human race, renouncing every country, and ravaging every country, in its coasts and vessels, indiscriminately." It was not piracy.

He also said that this trade could not be pronounced contrary to the law of nations. "A court, in the administration of law, cannot attribute criminality to an act where the law imputes none. It must look to the legal standard of morality; and, upon a question of this nature, that standard must be found in the law of nations, as fixed and evidenced by general, and ancient, and admitted practice, by treaties, and by the general tenor of the laws and ordinances, and the formal transactions of civilized states; and, looking to those authorities, he found a difficulty in maintaining that the transaction was legally criminal."

The right of visitation and search being strictly a belligerent right, and the slave trade being neither piratical nor contrary to the law of nations, the principle is asserted and maintained with great strength of reasoning, that it cannot be exercised on the vessels of a foreign power, unless permitted by treaty. France had refused to assent to the insertion of such an article in her treaty with Great Britain, and, consequently, the right could not be exercised on the high seas by a British cruiser on a French vessel.

"It is pressed as a a difficulty," says the judge, "what is to be done, if a French ship, laden with slaves, is brought in? I answer, without hesitation, restore the possession which has been unlawfully devested; rescind the illegal act done by your own subject, and leave the foreigner to the justice of his own country."

This reasoning goes far in support of the proposition that, in the British courts of admiralty, the vessel even of a nation which had forbidden the slave trade, but had not conceded the right of search, must, if wrongfully brought in, be restored to the original owner. But the judge goes farther, and shows that no evidence existed to prove that France had, by law, forbidden that trade. Consequently, for this reason, as well as for that previously assigned, the sentence of condemnation was reversed, and restitution awarded.

In the United States, different opinions have been entertained in the different circuits and districts; and the subject is now, for the first time, before this court.

The question whether the slave trade is prohibited by the law of nations has been seriously propounded, and both the affirmative and negative of the proposition have been maintained with equal earnestness.

That it is contrary to the law of nature will scarcely be denied. That every man has a natural right to the fruits of his own labor, is generally admitted; and that no other person can rightfully deprive him of those fruits, and appropriate them against his will, seems to be the necessary result of this admission. But from the earliest times war has existed, and war confers rights in which all have acquiesced. Among the most enlightened nations of antiquity, one of these was, that the victor might enslave the vanquished. This, which was the usage of all, could not be pronounced repugnant to the law of nations, which is certainly to be tried by the test of general usage. That which has received the assent of all, must be the law of all.

Slavery, then, has its origin in force; but as the world has agreed that it is a legitimate result of force, the state of things which is thus produced by general consent, cannot be pronounced unlawful.

Throughout Christendom, this harsh rule has been exploded, and war is no longer considered as giving a right to enslave captives. But this triumph of humanity has not been universal. The parties to the modern law of nations do not propagate their principles by force; and Africa has not yet adopted them. Throughout the whole extent of that immense continent, so far as we know its history, it is still the law of nations that prisoners are slaves. Can those who have themselves renounced this law, be permitted to participate in its effects by purchasing the beings who are its victims?

Whatever might be the answer of a moralist to this question, a jurist must search for its legal solution in those principles of action which are sanctioned by the usages, the national acts, and the general assent of that portion of the world of which he considers himself as a part, and to whose law the appeal is made. If we resort to this standard as the test of international law, the question, as has already been observed, is decided in favor of the legality of the trade. Both Europe and America embarked in it; and for nearly two centuries it was carried on without opposition, and without censure. A jurist could not say that a practice thus supported was illegal, and that those engaged in it might be punished, either personally, or by deprivation of property.

In this commerce, thus sanctioned by universal assent, every nation had an equal right to engage. How is this right to be lost? Each may renounce it for its own people; but can this renunciation affect others?

No principle of general law is more universally acknowledged than the perfect equality of nations. Russia and Geneva have equal rights. It results from this equality, that no one can rightfully impose a rule on another. Each legislates for itself, but its legislation can operate on itself alone. A right, then, which is vested in all by the consent of all, can be devested only by consent; and this trade, in which all have participated, must remain lawful to those who cannot be induced to relinquish it. As no nation can prescribe a rule for others, none can make a law of nations; and this traffic remains lawful to those whose governments have not forbidden it.

If it is consistent with the law of nations, it cannot in itself be piracy. It can be made so only by statute; and the obligation of the statute cannot transcend the legislative power of the state which may enact it.

If it be neither repugnant to the law of nations, nor piracy, it is almost superfluous to say in this court that the right of bringing in for adjudication in time of peace, even where the vessel belongs to a nation which has prohibited the trade, cannot exist. The courts of no country execute the penal laws of another; and the course of the American government on the subject of visitation and search, would decide any case in which that right had been exercised by an American cruiser, on the vessel of a foreign nation, not violating our municipal laws, against the captors.

It follows, that a foreign vessel engaged in the African slave trade, captured on the high seas in time of peace, by an American cruiser, and brought in for adjudication, would be restored.

SEE ALSO:

Generally Bill of Rights
An Act to Prevent Frauds and Concealments of His Majesty's Customs and Subsidies, 12 Chas. 2, c. 19 (1660)
Regina v. *Mead*, 92 Eng. Rep. 119 (Q.B. 1703)
Delaware Declaration of Rights and Fundamental Rules, 11 Sept. 1776, Sources 339
Vermont Constitution of 1777, ch. 1, arts. 11, 12, Thorpe 6:3741
Customs Act, 1 Stat. 29 (1789)
An Act Repealing Duties, 1 Stat. 199 (1790)
Kentucky Constitution of 1792, art. 12, sec. 9, Thorpe 3:1274
Camfranque v. *Burnell*, 4 Fed. Cas. 1130, no. 2,342 (C.C.D.Pa. 1806)
Sailly v. *Smith*, 11 Johns. R. 500 (N.Y. 1814)
An Act Further to Provide for the Collection of Duties, 3 Stat. 231 (1815)
William Wirt, The Power to Cause an Arrest, 8 Sept. 1818, 1 Ops. Atty. Gen. 229
Illinois Constitution of 1818, art. 8, sec. 7, Thorpe 2:981
Ex parte Pool, 2 Va. Cas. 276 (1821)
Read v. *Case*, 4 Conn. 166 (1822)
John Macpherson Berrien, Proof Necessary to an Arrest, 10 Sept. 1829, 2 Ops. Atty. Gen. 266
William Rawle, A View of the Constitution of the United States 127 (2d ed. 1829)
Joseph Story, Commentaries on the Constitution 3:§ 1895 (1833)
Roger B. Taney, Criminal Jurisdiction of Circuit and District Judges, 14 May 1833, 2 Ops. Atty. Gen. 564

Amendments V and VI
(Criminal Process)

V

No person shall be held to answer for a capital, or otherwise infamous crime, unless on a presentment or indictment of a Grand Jury, except in cases arising in the land or naval forces, or in the Militia, when in actual service in time of War or public danger; nor shall any person be subject for the same offence to be twice put in jeopardy of life or limb; nor shall be compelled in any criminal case to be a witness against himself, nor be deprived of life, liberty, or property, without due process of law; nor shall private property be taken for public use, without just compensation.

VI

In all criminal prosecutions, the accused shall enjoy the right to a speedy and public trial, by an impartial jury of the State and district wherein the crime shall have been committed, which district shall have been previously ascertained by law, and to be informed of the nature and cause of the accusation; to be confronted with the witnesses against him; to have compulsory process for obtaining witnesses in his favor, and to have the Assistance of Counsel for his defence.

1. Assize of Clarendon, 1166
2. The Body of Liberties of the Massachusets Collonie in New England, 1641
3. *Earl of Shaftesbury's Trial,* 8 How. St. Tr. 759, 771–74 (1681)
4. Bill of Rights, sec. 11, 1 W. & M., 2d sess., c. 2, 16 Dec. 1689
5. *Fenwick's Trial,* 13 How. St. Tr. 537, 591–92, 638 (1696)
6. Delaware Charter of 1701, arts. 5, 6
7. Sir Matthew Hale, History of the Common Law (1713 [posthumous])
8. William Hawkins, Pleas of the Crown (1721 ed.)
9. Sir Matthew Hale, History of the Pleas of the Crown (1736 [posthumous])
10. Montesquieu, Spirit of Laws, bk. 6, ch. 2 (1748)
11. *Brownsword* v. *Edwards,* 28 Eng. Rep. 157 (Ch. 1751)
12. John Adams, Instructions of the Town of Braintree on the Stamp Act, 10 Oct. 1765
13. Stamp Act Congress, Declaration of Rights, 19 Oct. 1765
14. William Blackstone, Commentaries (1769)
15. Continental Congress, Declaration and Resolves, 14 Oct. 1774
16. John Adams, Novanglus, no. 5, 20 Feb. 1775
17. Connecticut Constitutional Ordinance of 1776
18. Virginia Declaration of Rights, sec. 8, 12 June 1776
19. Delaware Declaration of Rights and Fundamental Rules, 11 Sept. 1776
20. Georgia Constitution of 1777, arts. 39, 58
21. Vermont Constitution of 1777, ch. 1, arts. 10, 19
22. Debate in Massachusetts Ratifying Convention, 30 Jan. 1788
23. *Respublica* v. *Shaffer,* 1 Dall. 236 (Pa. 1788)
24. House of Representatives, Amendments to the Constitution, 17–18 Aug. 1789
25. *Holmes* v. *Comegys,* 1 Dall. 439 (Pa. 1789)
26. *Commonwealth* v. *Dillon,* 4 Dall. 116 (Pa. 1792)
27. *United States* v. *Insurgents,* 26 Fed. Cas. 499, no. 15,443 (C.C.D.Pa. 1795)
28. *State* v. *Garrigues,* 1 Hayw. 241 (N.C. 1795)
29. Zephaniah Swift, A System of Laws of the State of Connecticut (1796)
30. *State* v. *Squires,* 1 Tyler 147 (Vt. 1801)
31. *Respublica* v. *Gibbs,* 3 Yeates 429 (Pa. 1802)
32. *People* v. *Barrett,* 1 Johns. R. 66 (N.Y. 1806)
33. *United States* v. *Burr,* 25 Fed. Cas. 25, no. 14,692b (C.C.D.Va. 1807)
34. *United States* v. *Burr,* 25 Fed. Cas. 38, no. 14,692e (C.C.D.Va. 1807)
35. *United States* v. *Burr,* 25 Fed. Cas. 49, no. 14,692g (C.C.D.Va. 1807)

36. *United States* v. *Charles*, 25 Fed. Cas. 409, no. 14,786 (C.C.D.C. 1813)

37. *Meade* v. *Deputy Marshal*, 1 Marshall's C.C. 324 (C.C.D.Va. 1815)

38. *People* v. *Casborus*, 13 Johns. R. 351 (N.Y. 1816)

39. *State* v. *Edwards*, 2 Nott. & McC. 376 (S.C. 1819)

40. *People* v. *Goodwin*, 18 Johns. R. 187 (N.Y. 1820)

41. *United States* v. *Miller*, 26 Fed. Cas. 1254, no. 15,772 (C.C.D.C. 1821)

42. *Commonwealth* v. *Cook*, 6 Serg. & Rawle 577 (Pa. 1822)

43. *United States* v. *Perez*, 9 Wheat. 579 (1824)

44. *Crenshaw* v. *Tennessee*, 1 Mart. & Y. 134 (Tenn. 1827)

45. *United States* v. *Gooding*, 12 Wheat. 460 (1827)

46. *United States* v. *Marchant*, 12 Wheat. 480 (1827)

47. *United States* v. *Saline Bank*, 1 Pet. 100 (1828)

48. *In the matter of Spier*, 1 Dev. 491 (N.C. 1828)

49. *Sanderson's Case*, 21 Fed. Cas. 326, no. 12,297 (C.C.D.C. 1829)

50. *Bull* v. *Loveland*, 10 Pick. 9 (Mass. 1830)

51. *United States* v. *Shive*, 27 Fed. Cas. 1065, no. 16,278 (C.C.E.D.Pa. 1832)

52. Joseph Story, Commentaries on the Constitution (1833)

53. *United States* v. *Gibert*, 25 Fed. Cas. 1287, no. 15,204 (C.C.D.Mass. 1834)

1

ASSIZE OF CLARENDON
1166

*Plucknett, Concise History of the
Common Law 108 (1936)*

---

4. And when a robber or murderer or thief or receiver of them has been arrested through the aforesaid oath, if the justices are not about to come speedily enough into the country where they have been taken, let the sheriffs send word to the nearest justice by some well-informed person that they have arrested such men, and the justices shall send back word to the sheriffs informing them where they desire the men to be brought before them; and let the sheriffs bring them before the justices.

2

THE BODY OF LIBERTIES OF THE MASSACHUSETS
COLLONIE IN NEW ENGLAND
1641

Sources 151, 153, 155

Every man that findeth himselfe unfit to plead his owne cause in any Court shall have Libertie to imploy any man against whom the Court doth not except, to helpe him, Provided he give him noe fee or reward for his paines.

. . . . .

No man shall be twise sentenced by Civill Justice for one and the same Crime, offence, or Trespasse.

. . . . .

Everie Action betweene partie and partie, and proceedings against delinquents in Criminall causes shall be briefly

and destinctly entered on the Rolles of every Court by the Recorder thereof. That such actions be not afterwards brought againe to the vexation of any man.

3

EARL OF SHAFTESBURY'S TRIAL
8 How. St. Tr. 759, 771–74 (1681)

(Sir F. Withins moved, after the charge to the grand jury, that the evidence be heard in court; and Pemberton, L.C.J., declared that he would grant the motion; the jury then desired to have a copy of their oath, which was given them, and they withdrew; after returning shortly, the following colloquy ensued):

Foreman. My Lord Chief Justice, it is the opinion of the jury, that they ought to examine the witnesses in private, and it hath been the constant practice of our ancestors and predecessors to do it; and they insist upon it as their right to examine in private, because they are bound to keep the king's secrets, which they cannot do, if it be done in court.

[PEMBERTON, L.C.J.] Look ye, gentlemen of the jury, it may very probably be, that some late usage has brought you into this error, that it is your right, but it is not your right in truth. . . . What you say concerning keeping your counsels, that is quite of another nature, that is, your debates, and those things, there you shall be in private, for to consider of what you hear publicly. But certainly it is the best way, both for the king, and for you, that there should, in a case of this nature, be an open and plain examination of the witnesses, that all the world may see what they say.

Foreman. My lord, if your lordship pleases, I must beg your lordship's pardon, if I mistake in anything, it is contrary to the sense of what the jury apprehend. First, they apprehend that the very words of the oath doth bind them, it says, "That they shall keep the counsel's, and their own secrets:" Now, my lord, there can be no secret in public; the very intimation of that doth imply, that the examination should be secret; besides, my lord, I beg your lordship's pardon if we mistake, we do not understand anything of law.

Mr. *Papillon* [a juror]. . . . [I]f it be the ancient custom of the kingdom to examine in private, then there is something may be very prejudicial to the king in this public examination; for sometimes in examining witnesses in private, there come to be discovered some persons guilty of treason, and misprision of treason, that were not known, nor thought on before. Then the jury sends down to the court, and gives them intimation, and these men are presently secured; whereas, my lord, in case they be examined in open court publicly, then presently there is intimation given and these men are gone away. Another thing that may be prejudicial to the king, is, that all the evidences here, will be foreknown before they come to the main trial upon issue by the petty jury; then if there be not a very great deal of care, these witnesses may be confronted by raising up witnesses to prejudice them, as in some cases it has been: Then besides, the jury do apprehend, that in private they are more free to examine things in particular, for the satisfying their own consciences, and that without favour or affection; and we hope we shall do our duty.

[PEMBERTON, L.C.J.] . . . [T]he king's counsel have examined whether he hath cause to accuse these persons, or not; and, gentlemen, they understand very well, that it will be no prejudice to the king to have the evidence heard openly in court; or else the king would never desire it.

Foreman. My lord, the gentlemen of the jury desire that it may be recorded, that we insisted upon it as our right; but if the court over-rule, we must submit to it.

4

BILL OF RIGHTS, SEC. 11
1 W. & M., 2d sess., c. 2, 16 Dec. 1689

---

11. That jurors ought to be duly impanelled and returned, and jurors which pass upon men in trials for high treason ought to be freeholders.

5

FENWICK'S TRIAL
13 How. St. Tr. 537, 591–92, 638 (1696)

Sergt. *Lovel* (for the prosecution): "We have Mr. Goodman's examination under the hand of Mr. Vernon; we pray it may be read." Sir. B. *Shower* (for the accused): "Mr. Speaker, . . . I humbly oppose the reading of this examination, as not agreeable to the rules of practice and evi-

dence, and that which is wholly new. . . . No deposition of a person can be read, though beyond sea, unless in cases where the party it is to be read against was privy to the examination and might have cross-examined him or examined to his credit, if he thought fit. . . . Our law requires persons to appear and give their testimony 'viva voce'; and we see that their testimony appears credible or not by their very countenances and the manner of their delivery; and their falsity may sometimes be discovered by questions that the party may ask them, and by examining them to particular circumstances which may lay open the falsity of a well-laid scheme, which otherwise, as he himself had put it together, might have looked well at first; and this we are deprived of, if this examination should be admitted to be read. . . . We oppose it at present for that we were not present nor privy nor could have cross-examined him." Sir T. *Powis*, arguing: "How contrary this is to a fundamental rule in our law, that no evidence shall be given against a man, when he is on trial for his life, but in the presence of the prisoner, because he may cross-examine him who gives such evidence; and that is due to every man in justice."

6

DELAWARE CHARTER OF 1701, ARTS. 5, 6
Thorpe 1:560

V.

That all Criminals shall have the same Privileges of Witnesses and Council as their Prosecutors.

VI.

That no Person or Persons shall or may, at any Time hereafter, be obliged to answer any Complaint, Matter or Thing whatsoever, relating to Property, before the Governor and Council, or in any other Place, but in ordinary Course of Justice, unless Appeals thereunto shall be hereafter by Law appointed.

7

SIR MATTHEW HALE, HISTORY OF THE COMMON LAW
1713 (posthumous)
Gray 26-27, 163–64

But touching the Business of Martial Law, these Things are to be observed, *viz.*

First, That in Truth and Reality it is not a Law, but something indulged rather than allowed as a Law; the Necessity of Government, Order and Discipline in an Army, is that only which can give those Laws a Countenance, *Quod enim Necessitas cogit desendi.*

Secondly, This indulged Law was only to extend to Members of the Army, or to those of the opposite Army, and never was so much indulged as intended to be (executed or) exercised upon others; for others who were not listed under the Army, had no Colour of Reason to be bound by Military Constitutions, applicable only to the Army, whereof they were not Parts; but they were to be order'd and govern'd according to the Laws to which they were subject, though it were a Time of War.

Thirdly, That the Exercise of Martial Law, whereby any Person should lose his Life or Member, or Liberty, may not be permitted in Time of Peace, when the King's Courts are open for all Persons to receive Justice, according to the Laws of the Land.

. . . . .

Ninthly, The Excellency of this open Course of Evidence to the Jury in Presence of the Judge, Jury, Parties and Council, and even of the adverse Witnesses, appears in these Particulars:

1st, That it is openly; and not in private before a Commissioner or Two, and a couple of Clerks, where oftentimes Witnesses will deliver that which they will be ashamed to testify publickly.

2dly, That it is *Ore Tenus* personally, and not in Writing, wherein oftentimes, yea too often, a crafty Clerk, Commissioner, or Examiner, will make a Witness speak what he truly never meant, by his dressing of it up in his own Terms, Phrases, and Expressions; whereas on the other Hand, many times the very Manner of a Witness's delivering his Testimony will give a probable Indication whether he speaks truly or falsly; and by this Means also he has Opportunity to correct, amend, or explain his Testimony upon further Questioning with him, which he can never have after a Deposition is set down in Writing.

3dly, That by this Course of personal and open Examination, there is Opportunity for all Persons concern'd, *viz.* The Judge, or any of the Jury, or Parties, or their Council or Attornies, to propound occasional Questions, which beats and boults out the Truth much better than when the Witness only delivers a formal Series of his Knowledge without being interrogated; and on the other Side, preparatory, limited, and formal Interrogatories in Writing, preclude this Way of occasional Interrogations, and the best Method of searching and sifting out the Truth is choak'd and suppress'd.

4thly, Also by this personal Appearance and Testimony of Witnesses, there is Opportunity of confronting the adverse Witnesses, of observing the Contradiction of Witnesses sometimes of the same Side, and by this Means great Opportunities are gained for the true and clear Discovery of the Truth.

5thly, And further, The very Quality, Carriage, Age, Condition, Education, and Place of Commorance of Witnesses, is by this Means plainly and evidently set forth to the Court and the Jury, whereby the Judge and Jurors may have a full Information of them, and the Jurors, as they see Cause, may give the more or less Credit to their Testimony, for the Jurors are not only Judges of the Fact,

but many Times of the Truth of Evidence; and if there be just Cause to disbelieve what a Witness swears, they are not bound to give their Verdict according to the Evidence or Testimony of that Witness; and they may sometimes give Credit to one Witness, tho' oppos'd by more than one. And indeed, it is one of the Excellencies of this Trial above the Trial by Witnesses, that altho' the Jury ought to give a great Regard to Witnesses and their Testimony, yet they are not always bound by it, but may either upon reasonable Circumstances, inducing a Blemish upon their Credibility, tho' otherwise in themselves in Strictness of Law they are to be heard, pronounce a Verdict contrary to such Testimonies, the Truth whereof they have just Cause to suspect, and may and do often pronounce their Verdict upon one single Testimony, which Thing the Civil Law admits not of.

8

WILLIAM HAWKINS, PLEAS OF THE CROWN
2:CH. 25, §§ 99, 100; CH. 46, § 30
1721 ed.

I take it to be settled that no criminal prosecution is within the benefit of any of the statutes of Amendments; from whence it follows that no amendment can be admitted in any such prosecution, but such only as is allowed by the common law. And agreeably hereto I find it laid down as a principle in some books, that the body of an indictment removed into the King's Bench from any inferior court whatsoever, except only those of London, can in no case be amended. But it is said that the body of an indictment from London may be amended, because, by the city charter, a tenor of the record only can be removed from thence.

It seems to have been anciently the common practice, where an indictment appeared to be insufficient, either for its uncertainty or the want of proper legal words, not to put the defendant to answer it; but if it were found in the same county in which the court sat, to award process against the grand jury to come into court and amend it. And it seems to be the common practice at this day, while the grand jury who found a bill is before the court, to amend it, by their consent, in a matter of form, as the name or addition of the party.

. . . . .

As to . . . Whether a Defendant in criminal Cases have the Right to Process to bring in his Witnesses: I take it that in Prosecutions for Misdemeanors the Defendant may take out *Subpoena's* [sic] of Course, but that in Capital cases he hath no right by the Common law to any process against his witnesses without a special order of the court. But [after discussing 7 & 8 Will. 3, c. 3, § 7 (1695)] it seems that since the Statute of *1 Annae 9* . . . which ordains, That the witnesses for the prisoner shall be sworn, process may be taken out against them of course in any case whatsoever.

9

SIR MATTHEW HALE, HISTORY OF THE
PLEAS OF THE CROWN
1736 (posthumous)
Emlyn 1:34–35

If a man in his sound memory commits a capital offense, and before his arraignment he becomes absolutely mad, he ought not by law to be arraigned during such his phrenzy, but be remitted to prison until that incapacity be removed; the reason is, because he cannot advisedly plead to the indictment. . . . And if such person after his plea, and before his trial, become of *non sane memory,* he shall not be tried; or, if after his trial he become of *non sane memory,* he shall not receive judgment; or, if after judgment he become of *non sane memory,* his execution shall be spared; for were he of sound memory, he might allege somewhat in stay of judgment or execution.

10

MONTESQUIEU, SPIRIT OF LAWS, BK. 6, CH. 2
1748

*2.—Of the Simplicity of Criminal Laws in different
Governments*

We hear it generally said that justice ought to be administered with us as in Turkey. Is it possible, then, that the most ignorant of all nations should be the most clear-sighted on a point which it most behooves mankind to know?

If we examine the set forms of justice with respect to the trouble the subject undergoes in recovering his property or in obtaining satisfaction for an injury or affront, we shall find them doubtless too numerous: but if we consider them in the relation they bear to the liberty and security of every individual, we shall often find them too few; and be convinced that the trouble, expense, delays, and even the very dangers of our judiciary proceedings are the price that each subject pays for his liberty.

In Turkey, where little regard is shown to the honor, life, or estate of the subject, all causes are speedily decided. The method of determining them is a matter of indifference, provided they be determined. The pasha, after a quick hearing, orders which party he pleases to be bastinadoed, and then sends them about their business.

Here it would be dangerous to be of a litigious disposition; this supposes a strong desire of obtaining justice, a settled aversion, an active mind, and a steadiness in pursuing one's point. All this should be avoided in a government where fear ought to be the only prevailing sentiment, and in which popular disturbances are frequently attended with sudden and unforeseen revolutions. Here every man ought to know that the magistrate must not hear his name mentioned, and that his security depends entirely on his being reduced to a kind of annihilation.

But in moderate governments, where the life of the meanest subject is deemed precious, no man is stripped of his honor or property until after a long inquiry; and no man is bereft of life till his very country has attacked him—an attack that is never made without leaving him all possible means of making his defence.

Hence it is that when a person renders himself absolute, he immediately thinks of reducing the number of laws. In a government thus constituted they are more affected with particular inconveniences than with the liberty of the subject, which is very little minded.

In republics, it is plain that as many formalities at least are necessary as in monarchies. In both governments they increase in proportion to the value which is set on the honor, fortune, liberty, and life of the subject.

In republican governments, men are all equal; equal they are also in despotic governments: in the former, because they are everything; in the latter, because they are nothing.

11

BROWNSWORD V. EDWARDS
28 Eng. Rep. 157 (Ch. 1751)

Lord Chancellor. This appears a very plain case, in which defendant may protect herself from making a discovery of her marriage; and I am afraid, if the court should overrule such a plea, it would be setting up the oath *ex officio;* which then the parliament in the time of *Charles* I. would in vain have taken away, if the party might come into this court for it. The general rule is, that no one is bound to answer so as to subject himself to punishment, whether that punishment arises by the ecclesiastical law of the land. (2 Ves. sen. 389, 451; 1 Atk. 539; 2 Atk. 393; 1 Brown, 97. In case of a bankrupt smuggler, the commissioners may examine him, but he may demur to the interrogatories, and have the opinion of the court. 2 Atk. 200; 1 vol. 247; 3 Wms. 376; 1 Vern. 109.) Incest is undoubtedly punishable in ecclesiastical court; and such a crime is generally excepted out of the acts of pardon. The ecclesiastical court has conusance of incest in two respects, *diverso intuitu:* first to judge of the legality of the marriage, and to pronounce sentence of nullity; and if they do so, proceeding lawfully and rightfully, it binds all parties, being the judgment of a court having proper jurisdiction of the cause. The other is to censure and punish persons guilty by ecclesiastical censure, as for fornication, adultery, &c. Nor is it material what the nature of the punishment is. It is a punishment which must be performed or got rid of by commutation, which is like a fine. Then consider the present case. The discovery whether lawfully married takes in the whole, whether married in fact, and whether that marriage was lawful. Defendant has pleaded to it; which she may do; and in the plea it is proper to bring in facts and averments to support that plea: whereas a demurrer can be to nothing but what appears on the face of the bill, otherwise it would be a speaking demurrer. (Averments are necessary to exclude intendments which would be made against the pleader, for the court will always intend the matters charged against the pleader unless fully denied. 2 Atk. 241; Gilb. 185.) But here it was necessary to bring in such an averment, that testator was lawfully married before to her sister, and had issue; which is a fact necessary to shew; and that fact she has taken on herself to prove: the plea therefore is regular in form, and good in substance. The objection to the plea is, that one of the parties to the incestuous marriage being dead, there can be no proceeding afterward. I always took the distinction to be what is laid down in *Hicks* v. *Harris,* that by the law of the land the ecclesiastical court cannot proceed to judge of the marriage and to pronounce sentence of nullity after death of one of the married parties, especially where there is issue, because it tends to bastardise the issue; and none after death of one of the parties to that marriage is to be bastardised: but there is no rule of law standing to prevent either of the parties from punishment after death of the other. Suppose it was an offence of adultery or fornication, there is no rule of the civil or ecclesiastical law, that after death of one of the parties the survivor may not be punished for the offence: undoubtedly they may, either proceeding *ex officio,* by office of the ecclesiastical judge, or by promotion of a proper informant. Then why may not the ecclesiastical court do it in the case of incest, whether without the formality of marriage or attended with it? But it is said, *Hicks* v. *Harris* is no judicial determination in the point, and that all that was material before the court, was the joint jurisdiction; which is true: but there was a plain difference. If the court held, that the proceeding (and this is an answer to one part of the objection) even for the censure against the surviving party would have tended to affect the legitimacy of the marriage or the issue, the court of *B.R.* would have stopped there: but they went on this, that it could not be given in evidence against the issue or the plaintiff claiming under that issue: as was determined solemnly in *B.R.* on a long trial at bar, directed out of this court in *Hillyard* v. *Grantham,* in which I was of counsel. (See 3 Wooddeson, 318.) In that cause during life of the father and mother there had been a proceeding against both of them in the consistory court of *Lincoln* for living together in fornication, and sentence given against them. On the trial that sentence was offered in evidence to prove, that they were not married: the whole court were of opinion that it could not be given in evidence; because first, it was a criminal matter, and could not be given in evidence in a civil cause; next that it was *res inter alios acta,* and could not affect the issue: but they held, that if it had been a sentence on the point of the marriage on a question of the lawfulness of the marriage, it being a sentence of a court having proper jurisdiction,

might have been given in evidence. If indeed there had been collusion that might be shewn on the part of the child to take off the force of it; because collusion affects every thing: but if no collusion, it binds all the world: but in a proceeding in a criminal way that could not be given in evidence: and that was the distinction the court went on in *Hicks* v. *Harris.* But if there had not been that authority, I should not have doubted on the nature of the thing, but that the ecclesiastical court might have proceeded after death of one of the party as well for incest as fornication; in which case there is no doubt they may. Thus far as to the merits of the plea. Some collateral arguments have been used, that it is not in every case the party shall protect himself against relief in this court upon an allegation, that it will subject him to a supposed crime. It is true, it never creates a defence against relief in this court, therefore in case of usury or forgery, if a proof can be made of it, the court will let the cause go on still to a hearing, but will not force the party by his own oath to subject himself to punishment for it (if plaintiff waves the penalty, defendant shall be obliged to discover, 1 Vern. 60, or whether the penalty arises from defendant's own particular agreement, he is obliged to discover. 2 Ver. 244. Or where the discovery sought is not of a fact which can subject defendant to any penalty, but connected with some other fact which may, 2 Ves. sen. 493). In a bill to inquire into the reality of deeds on suggestion of forgery, the court has entertained jurisdiction of the cause; though it does not oblige the party to a discovery, but directs an issue to try whether forged. I remember a case where there was a deed of rent-charge suggested to be forged: it was tried twice at law, and found for the deed: a bill was afterward brought to set it aside for forgery, and to have it delivered up to be cancelled. Lord *King,* notwithstanding the two trials, which has been in *Avowry* and *Replevin,* directed an issue: wherein it was found forged, and, I remember, was cancelled and cut to pieces in court. There are several instances of that: so that the relief the party may have is no objection. As to the objection from the consequence of allowing this plea if the defendant should fail in the proof of it, that would be an objection to the allowing any plea to a discovery: though it would be no objection to a demurrer, because that must abide by the bill: but all pleas must suggest a fact (which fact must conduce to one single point, per Lord *Thurlow,* 1 Brown, 417. 1 Atk. 54): it must go to a hearing; and if the party does not prove that fact, which is necessary to support the plea, the plaintiff is not to lose the benefit of his discovery: but the court may direct an examination on interrogatories in order to supply that. The plea therefore ought to be allowed.

12

JOHN ADAMS, INSTRUCTIONS OF THE TOWN OF
BRAINTREE ON THE STAMP ACT
10 Oct. 1765
Papers 1:141–42

But the most grievous Innovation of all, is the alarming Extension of the Power of Courts of Admiralty. In these Courts, one Judge presides alone! No Juries have any Concern there!—The Law, and the Fact, are both to be decided by the same single Judge, whose Commission is only during Pleasure, and with whom, as we are told, the most mischievous of all Customs has become established, that of taking Commissions on all Condemnations; so that he is under a pecuniary Temptation always against the Subject. Now, if the Wisdom of the Mother Country has thought the Independency of the Judges, so essential to an impartial Administration of Justice, as to render them independent of every Power on Earth, independent of the King, the Lords, the Commons, the People, nay independent, in Hope and Expectation, of the Heir apparent, by continuing their Commissions after a Demise of the Crown; What Justice and Impartiality are we, at 3000 Miles distance from the Fountain to expect from such a Judge of Admiralty? We have all along thought the Acts of Trade in this Respect a Grievance: but the Stamp-Act has opened a vast Number of Sources of new Crimes, which may be committed by any Man, and cannot, but be committed by Multitudes, and prodigious Penalties are annexed, and all these are to be tried by such a Judge of such a Court!—What can be wanting, after this, but a weak or wicked Man for a Judge, to render Us the most sordid and forlorn of Slaves? We mean the Slaves of *a Slave* of the Servants of a Minister of State:—We cannot help asserting therefore, that this Part of the Act will make an essential Change in the Constitution of Juries, and is directly repugnant to the Great Charter itself. For by that Charter "No Amerciament shall be assessed, but by the Oath of honest and lawful Men of the Vicinage."—And "No Freeman shall be taken, or imprisoned, or disseized of his Freehold, or Liberties, or free Customs, nor passed upon, nor condemned, but by lawful Judgment of his Peers, or by the Law of the Land."—So that this Act will "make such a Distinction, and create such a Difference between" the Subjects in Great-Britain, and those in America as we could not have expected from the Guardians of Liberty in "Both."

13

STAMP ACT CONGRESS, DECLARATION OF RIGHTS
19 Oct. 1765
Sources 270

7th. That trial by jury is the inherent and invaluable right of every British subject in these colonies.

14

WILLIAM BLACKSTONE, COMMENTARIES, 4:298–307,
317–19, 342–50, 352–55
1769

I. A presentment, *generally* taken, is a very comprehensive term; including not only presentments properly so called, but also inquisitions of office, and indictments by a grand jury. A presentment, *properly* speaking, is the notice taken by a grand jury of any offence from their own knowledge or observation, without any bill of indictment laid before them at the suit of the king. As, the presentment of a nusance, a libel, and the like; upon which the officer of the court must afterwards frame an indictment, before the party presented as the author can be put to answer it. An inquisition of office is the act of a jury, summoned by the proper officer to enquire of matters relating to the crown, upon evidence laid before them. Some of these are in themselves convictions, and cannot afterwards be traversed or denied; and therefore the inquest, or jury, ought to hear all that can be alleged on both sides. Of this nature are all inquisitions of *felo de se;* of flight in persons accused of felony; of deodands, and the like; and presentments of petty offences in the sheriff's tourn or court-leet, whereupon the presiding officer may set a fine. Other inquisitions may be afterwards traversed and examined; as particularly the coroner's inquisition of the death of a man, when it finds any one guilty of homicide: for in such cases the offender so presented must be arraigned upon this inquisition, and may dispute the truth of it; which brings it to a kind of indictment, the most usual and effectual means of prosecution, and into which we will therefore enquire a little more minutely.

II. An *indictment* is a written accusation of one or more persons of a crime or misdemesnor, preferred to, and presented upon oath by, a grand jury. To this end the sheriff of every county is bound to return to every session of the peace, and every commission of *oyer* and *terminer*, and of general gaol delivery, twenty four good and lawful men of the county, some out of every hundred, to enquire, present, do, and execute all those things, which on the part of our lord the king shall then and there be commanded them. They ought to be freeholders, but to what amount is uncertain: which seems to be *casus omissus,* and as proper to be supplied by the legislature as the qualifications of the petit jury; which were formerly equally vague and uncertain, but are now settled by several acts of parliament. However, they are usually gentlemen of the best figure in the county. As many as appear upon this panel, are sworn upon the grand jury, to the amount of twelve at the least, and not more than twenty three; that twelve may be a majority. Which number, as well as the constitution itself, we find exactly described, so early as the laws of king Ethelred. *"Exeant seniores duodecim thani, et praefectus cum eis, et jurent super sanctuarium quod eis in manus datur, quod nolint ullum innocentem accusare, nec aliquem noxium celare."* In the time of king Richard the first (according to Hoveden) the process of electing the grand jury, ordained by that prince, was as follows: four knights were to be taken from the county at large, who chose two more out of every hundred; which two associated to themselves ten other principal freemen, and those twelve were to answer concerning all particulars relating to their own district. This number was probably found too large and inconvenient; but the traces of this institution still remain, in that some of the jury must be summoned out of every hundred. This grand jury are previously instructed in the articles of their enquiry, by a charge from the judge who presides upon the bench. They then withdraw, to sit and receive indictments, which are preferred to them in the name of the king, but at the suit of any private prosecutor; and they are only to hear evidence on behalf of the prosecution: for the finding of an indictment is only in the nature of an enquiry or accusation, which is afterwards to be tried and determined; and the grand jury are only to enquire upon their oaths, whether there be sufficient cause to call upon the party to answer it. A grand jury however ought to be thoroughly persuaded of the truth of an indictment, so far as their evidence goes; and not to rest satisfied merely with remote probabilities: a doctrine, that might be applied to very oppressive purposes.

The grand jury are sworn to enquire, only for the body of the county, *pro corpore comitatus;* and therefore they cannot regularly enquire of a fact done out of that county for which they are sworn, unless particularly enabled by act of parliament. And to so high a nicety was this matter antiently carried, that where a man was wounded in one county, and died in another, the offender was at common law indictable in neither, because no complete act of felony was done in any one of them: but by statute 2 & 3 Edw. VI. c. 24. he is now indictable in the county where the party died. And so in some other cases: as particularly, where treason is committed out of the realm, it may be enquired of in any county within the realm, as the king shall direct, in pursuance of statutes 26 Hen. VIII. c.13. 35 Hen. VIII. c. 2. and 5 & 6 Edw. VI. c.11. But, in general, all offences must be enquired into as well as tried in the county where the fact is committed.

When the grand jury have heard the evidence, if they think it a groundless accusation, they used formerly to endorse on the back of the bill, *"ignoramus;"* or, we know nothing of it; intimating, that though the facts might possibly be true, that truth did not appear to them: but now, they assert in English, more absolutely, "not a true bill;" and then the party is discharged without farther answer. But a fresh bill may afterwards be preferred to a subsequent grand jury. If they are satisfied of the truth of the accusation, they then endorse upon it, "a true bill;" antiently, *"billa vera."* The indictment is then said to be found, and the party stands indicted. But, to find a bill, there must at least twelve of the jury agree: for so tender is the law of England of the lives of the subjects, that no man can be convicted at the suit of the king of any capital offence, unless by the unanimous voice of twenty four of his equals and neighbours: that is, by twelve at least of the grand jury, in the first place, assenting to the accusation; and afterwards, by the whole petit jury, of twelve more, finding him guilty upon his trial. But, if twelve of the grand jury assent, it is a good presentment, though some of the rest disagree. And the indictment, when so found, is publicly delivered into court.

Indictments must have a precise and sufficient certainty. By statute 1 Hen. V. c. 5. all indictments must set forth the christian name, sirname, and addition of the state and degree, mystery, town, or place, and the county of the offender: and all this to identify his *person.* The *time,* and *place,* are also to be ascertained, by naming the day, and township, in which the fact was committed: though a mistake in these points is in general not held to be material, provided the *time* be laid previous to the finding of the indictment, and the *place* to be within the jurisdiction of the court. But sometimes the *time* may be very material, where there is any limitation in point of time assigned for the prosecution of offenders; as by the statute 7 Will. III. c. 3. which enacts, that no prosecution shall be had for any of the treasons or misprisions therein mentioned (except an assassination designed or attempted on the person of the king) unless the bill of indictment be found within three years after the offence committed: and, in case of murder, the time of the death must be laid within a year and a day after the mortal stroke was given. The *offence* itself must also be set forth with clearness and certainty: and in some crimes particular words of art must be used, which are so appropriated by the law to express the precise idea which it entertains of the offence, that no other words, however synonymous they may seem, are capable of doing it. Thus, in treason, the facts must be laid to be done, "treasonably, and against his allegiance;" antiently *"proditorie et contra ligeantiae suae debitum:"* else the indictment is void. In indictments for murder, it is necessary to say that the party indicted "murdered," not "killed" or "slew," the other; which till the late statute was expressed in Latin by the word *"murdravit."* In all indictments for felonies, the adverb "feloniously, *felonice,"* must be used; and for burglaries also, *"burglariter,"* or in English, "burglariously:" and all these to ascertain the intent. In rapes, the word *"rapuit,"* or "ravished," is necessary, and must not be expressed by any periphrasis; in order to render the crime certain. So in larcinies also, the words *"felonice cepit et asportavit,* feloniously took and carried away," are necessary to every indictment; for these only can express the very offence. Also in indictments for murder, the length and depth of the wound should in general be expressed, in order that it may appear to the court to have been of a mortal nature: but if it goes through the body, then it's dimensions are immaterial, for that is apparently sufficient to have been the cause of the death. Also where a limb, or the like, is absolutely cut off, there such description is impossible. Lastly, in indictments the *value* of the thing, which is the subject or instrument of the offence, must sometimes be expressed. In indictments for larcinies this is necessary, that it may appear whether it be grand or petit larciny; and whether entitled or not to the benefit of clergy: in homicide of all sorts it is necessary; as the weapon, with which it is committed, is forfeited to the king as a deodand.

The remaining methods of prosecution are without any previous finding by a jury, to fix the authoritative stamp of verisimilitude upon the accusation. One of these, by the common law, was when a thief was taken *with the mainour,* that is, with the thing stolen upon him, *in manu.* For he might, when so detected *flagrante delicto,* be brought into court, arraigned, and tried, without indictment: as by the Danish law he might be taken and hanged upon the spot, without accusation or trial. But this proceeding was taken away by several statutes in the reign of Edward the third: though in Scotland a similar process remains to this day. So that the only species of proceeding at the suit of the king, without a previous indictment or presentment by a grand jury, now seems to be that of *information.*

III. Informations are of two sorts; first, those which are partly at the suit of the king, and partly at that of a subject; and secondly, such as are only in the name of the king. The former are usually brought upon penal statutes, which inflict a penalty upon conviction of the offender, one part to the use of the king, and another to the use of the informer; and are a sort of *qui tam* actions, (the nature of which was explained in a former volume) only carried on by a criminal instead of a civil process: upon which I shall therefore only observe, that by the statute 31 Eliz. c. 5. no prosecution upon any penal statute, the suit and benefit whereof are limited in part to the king and in part to the prosecutor, can be brought by any common informer after one year is expired since the commission of the offence; nor on behalf of the crown after the lapse of two years longer; nor, where the forfeiture is originally given only to the king, can such prosecution be had after the expiration of two years from the commission of the offence.

The informations, that are exhibited in the name of the king alone, are also of two kinds: first, those which are truly and properly his own suits, and filed *ex officio* by his own immediate officer, the attorney general: secondly, those in which, though the king is the nominal prosecutor, yet it is at the relation of some private person or common informer; and they are filed by the king's coroner and attorney in the court of king's bench, usually called the master of the crown-office, who is for this purpose the standing officer of the public. The objects of the king's own prosecutions, filed *ex officio* by his own attorney general, are properly such enormous misdemesnors, as peculiarly tend to disturb or endanger his government, or to molest or affront him in the regular discharge of his royal functions. For offences so high and dangerous, in the punishment or prevention of which a moment's delay would be fatal, the law has given to the crown the power of an immediate prosecution, without waiting for any previous application to any other tribunal. A power, so necessary, not only to the ease and safety but even to the very existence of the executive magistrate, was originally reserved in the great plan of the English constitution, which has wisely provided for the due preservation of all it's parts. The objects of the other species of informations, filed by the master of the crown-office upon the complaint or relation of a private subject, are any gross and notorious misdemesnors, riots, batteries, libels, and other immoralities of an atrocious kind, not peculiarly tending to disturb the government (for those are left to the care of the attorney general) but which, on account of their magnitude or pernicious example, deserve the most public animadversion. And when an information is filed, either thus, or by the attorney general *ex officio,* it must be tried by a petit jury of the county where the offence arises: after which, if the defendant be found guilty, he must resort to the court for his punishment.

There can be no doubt but that this mode of prosecution, by information (or suggestion) filed on record by the king's attorney general, or by his coroner or master of the crown-office in the court of king's bench, is as antient as the common law itself. For as the king was bound to prosecute, or at least to lend the sanction of his name to a prosecutor, whenever a grand jury informed him upon their oaths that there was a sufficient ground for instituting a criminal suit; so, when these his immediate officers were otherwise sufficiently assured that a man had committed a gross misdemesnor, either personally against the king or his government, or against the public peace and good order, they were at liberty, without waiting for any farther intelligence, to convey that information to the court of king's bench by a suggestion on record, and to carry on the prosecution in his majesty's name. But these informations (of every kind) are confined by the constitutional law to mere misdemesnors only: for, wherever any capital offence is charged, the same law requires that the accusation be warranted by the oath of twelve men, before the party shall be put to answer it. And, as to those offences, in which informations were allowed as well as indictments, so long as they were confined to this high and respectable jurisdiction, and were carried on in a legal and regular course in his majesty's court of king's bench, the subject had no reason to complain. The same notice was given, the same process was issued, the same pleas were allowed, the same trial by jury was had, the same judgment was given by the same judges, as if the prosecution had originally been by indictment. But when the statute 3 Hen. VII. c. 1. had extended the jurisdiction of the court of star-chamber, the members of which were the sole judges of the law, the fact, and the penalty; and when the statute 11 Hen. VII. c. 3. had permitted informations to be brought by any informer upon any penal statute, not extending to life or member, at the assises or before the justices of the peace, who were to hear and determine the same according to their own discretion; then it was, that the legal and orderly jurisdiction of the court of king's bench fell into disuse and oblivion, and Empson and Dudley (the wicked instruments of king Henry VII) by hunting out obsolete penalties, and this tyrannical mode of prosecution, with other oppressive devices, continually harassed the subject and shamefully inriched the crown. The latter of these acts was soon indeed repealed by statute 1 Hen. VIII. c. 6. but the court of star-chamber continued in high vigour, and daily increasing it's authority, for more than a century longer; till finally abolished by statute 16 Car. I. c. 10.

Upon this dissolution the old common law authority of the court of king's bench, as the *custos morum* of the nation, being found necessary to reside somewhere for the peace and good government of the kingdom, was again revived in practice. And it is observable, that, in the same act of parliament which abolished the court of star-chamber, a conviction by information is expressly reckoned up, as one of the legal modes of conviction of such persons, as should offend a third time against the provisions of that statute. It is true, sir Matthew Hale, who presided in this court soon after the time of such revival, is said to have been no friend to this method of prosecution: and, if so, the reason of such his dislike was probably the ill use, which the master of the crown-office then made of his authority, by permitting the subject to be harrassed with vexatious informations, whenever applied to by any malicious or revengeful prosecutor; rather than his doubt of their legality, or propriety upon urgent occasions. For the power of filing informations, without any control, then resided in the breast of the master: and, being filed in the name of the king, they subjected the prosecutor to no costs, though on trial they proved to be groundless. This oppressive use of them, in the times preceding the revolution, occasioned a struggle, soon after the accession of king William, to procure a declaration of their illegality by the judgment of the court of king's bench. But sir John Holt, who then presided there, and all the judges, were clearly of opinion, that this proceeding was grounded on the common law, and could not be then impeached. And, in a few years afterwards, a more temperate remedy was applied in parliament, by statute 4 & 5 W. & M. c. 18. which enacts, that the clerk of the crown shall not file any information without express direction from the court of king's bench: and that every prosecutor, permitted to promote such information, shall give security by a recognizance of twenty pounds (which now seems to be too small a sum) to prosecute the same with effect; and to pay costs to the defendant, in case he be acquitted thereon, unless the judge, who tries the information, shall certify there was reasonable cause for filing it; and, at all events, to pay costs, unless the information shall be tried within a year after issue joined. But there is a proviso in this act, that it shall not extend to any other informations, than those which are exhibited by the master of the crown-office: and, consequently, informations at the king's own suit, filed by his attorney general, are no way restrained thereby.

· · · · ·

To arraign, is nothing else but to call the prisoner to the bar of the court, to answer the matter charged upon him in the indictment. The prisoner is to be called to the bar by his name; and it is laid down in our antient books, that, though under an indictment of the highest nature, he must be brought to the bar without irons, or any manner of shackles or bonds; unless there be evident danger of an escape, and then he may be secured with irons. But yet in Layer's case, *A. D.* 1722. a difference was taken between the time of arraignment, and the time of trial; and accordingly the prisoner stood at the bar in chains during the time of his arraignment.

When he is brought to the bar, he is called upon by name to hold up his hand: which, though it may seem a trifling circumstance, yet is of this importance, that by the holding up of his hand *constat de persona*, and he owns himself to be of that name by which he is called. However it is not an indispensable ceremony; for, being calculated merely for the purpose of identifying the person, any other acknowledgement will answer the purpose as well: therefore, if the prisoner obstinately and contemptuously refuses to hold up his hand, but confesses he is the person named, it is fully sufficient.

Then the indictment is to be read to him distinctly in the English tongue (which was law, even while all other proceedings were in Latin) that he may fully understand his charge. After which it is to be demanded of him, whether he be guilty of the crime, whereof he stands indicted, or not guilty. By the old common law the accessory could not be arraigned till the principal was attainted; and therefore, if the principal had never been indicted at all, had stood mute, had challenged above thirty five jurors peremptorily, had claimed the benefit of clergy, had obtained a pardon, or had died before attainder, the accessory in any of these cases could not be arraigned: for *non constitit* whether any felony was committed or no, till the principal was attainted; and it might so happen that the accessory should be convicted one day, and the principal acquitted the next, which would be absurd. However, this absurdity could only happen, where it was possible, that a trial of the principal might be had, subsequent to that of the accessory: and therefore the law still continues, that the accessory shall not be tried, so long as the principal remains liable to be tried hereafter. But by statute I Ann. c. 9. if the principal be once convicted, and before attainder, (that is, before he receives judgment of death or outlawry) he is delivered by pardon, the benefit of clergy, or otherwise; or if the principal stands mute, or challenges peremptorily above the legal number of jurors, so as never to be convicted at all; in any of these cases, in which no subsequent trial can be had of the principal, the accessory may be proceeded against, as if the principal felon had been attainted; for there is no danger of future contradiction. And upon the trial of the accessory, as well after as before the conviction of the principal, it seems to be the better opinion, and founded on the true spirit of justice, that the accessory is at liberty (if he can) to controvert the guilt of his supposed principal, and to prove him innocent of the charge, as well in point of fact as in point of law.

When a criminal is arraigned, he either *stands mute,* or *confesses* the fact; which circumstances we may call *incidents* to the arraignment: or else he *pleads* to the indictment, which is to be considered as the next stage of proceedings.

. . . . .

V. The trial by jury, or the country, *per patriam,* is also that trial by the peers of every Englishman, which, as the grand bulwark of his liberties, is secured to him by the great charter, *"nullus liber homo capiatur, vel imprisonetur, aut exulet, aut aliquo alio modo destruatur, nisi per legale judicium parium suorum, vel per legem terrae."*

The antiquity and excellence of this trial, for the settling of civil property, has before been explained at large. And it will hold much stronger in criminal cases; since, in times of difficulty and danger, more is to be apprehended from the violence and partiality of judges appointed by the crown, in suits between the king and the subject, than in disputes between one individual and another, to settle the metes and boundaries of private property. Our law has therefore wisely placed this strong and twofold barrier, of a presentment and a trial by jury, between the liberties of the people, and the prerogative of the crown. It was necessary, for preserving the admirable ballance of our constitution, to vest the executive power of the laws in the prince: and yet this power might be dangerous and destructive to that very constitution, if exerted without check or control, by justices of *oyer* and *terminer* occasionally named by the crown; who might then, as in France or Turkey, imprison, dispatch, or exile any man that was obnoxious to the government, by an instant declaration, that such is their will and pleasure. But the founders of the English laws have with excellent forecast contrived, that no man should be called to answer to the king for any capital crime, unless upon the preparatory accusation of twelve or more of his fellow subjects, the grand jury: and that the truth of every accusation, whether preferred in the shape of indictment, information, or appeal, should afterwards be confirmed by the unanimous suffrage of twelve of his equals and neighbours, indifferently chosen, and superior to all suspicion. So that the liberties of England cannot but subsist, so long as this *palladium* remains sacred and inviolate, not only from all open attacks, (which none will be so hardy as to make) but also from all secret machinations, which may sap and undermine it; by introducing new and arbitrary methods of trial, by justices of the peace, commissioners of the revenue, and courts of conscience. And however *convenient* these may appear at first, (as doubtless all arbitrary powers, well executed, are the most *convenient*) yet let it be again remembered, that delays, and little inconveniences in the forms of justice, are the price that all free nations must pay for their liberty in more substantial matters; that these inroads upon this sacred bulwark of the nation are fundamentally opposite to the spirit of our constitution; and that, though begun in trifles, the precedent may gradually increase and spread, to the utter disuse of juries in questions of the most momentous concern.

What was said of juries in general, and the trial thereby, in *civil* cases, will greatly shorten our present remarks, with regard to the trial of *criminal* suits; indictments, informa-

tions, and appeals: which trial I shall consider in the same method that I did the former; by following the order and course of the proceedings themselves, as the most clear and perspicuous way of treating it.

When therefore a prisoner on his arraignment has pleaded *not guilty,* and for his trial hath put himself upon the country, which country the jury are, the sheriff of the county must return a panel of jurors, *liberos et legales homines, de vicineto;* that is, freeholders, without just exception, and of the *visne* or neighbourhood; which is interpreted to be of the county where the fact is committed. If the proceedings are before the court of king's bench, there is time allowed, between the arraignment and the trial, for a jury to be impanelled by writ of *venire facias* to the sheriff, as in civil causes: and the trial in case of a misdemesnor is had at *nisi prius,* unless it be of such consequence as to merit a trial at bar; which is always invariably had when the prisoner is tried for any capital offence. But, before commissioners of *oyer* and *terminer* and gaol delivery, the sheriff by virtue of a general precept directed to him beforehand, returns to the court a panel of forty eight jurors, to try all felons that may be called upon their trial at that session: and therefore it is there usual to try all felons immediately, or soon, after their arraignment. But it is not customary, nor agreeable to the general course of proceedings, unless by consent of parties, to try persons indicted of smaller misdemesnors at the same court in which they have pleaded *not guilty,* or *traversed* the indictment. But they usually give security to the court, to appear at the next assises or session, and then and there to try the traverse, giving notice to the prosecutor of the same.

In cases of high treason, whereby corruption of blood may ensue, or misprision of such treason, it is enacted by statute 7 W. III. c. 3. first, that no person shall be tried for any such treason, except an attempt to assassinate the king, unless the indictment be found within three years after the offence committed: next, that the prisoner shall have a copy of the indictment, but not the names of the witnesses, five days at least before the trial; that is, upon the true construction of the act, before his arraignment; for then is his time to take any exceptions thereto, by way of plea or demurrer: thirdly, that he shall also have a copy of the panel of jurors two days before his trial: and, lastly, that he shall have the same compulsive process to bring in his witnesses *for* him, as was usual to compel their appearance *against* him. And, by statute 7 Ann. c. 21. (which did not take place till after the decease of the late pretender) all persons, indicted for high treason or misprision thereof, shall have not only a copy of the indictment, but a list of all the witnesses to be produced, and of the jurors impanelled, with their professions and places of abode, delivered to him ten days before the trial, and in the presence of two witnesses; the better to prepare him to make his challenges and defence. But this last act, so far as it affected indictments for the inferior species of high treason, respecting the coin and the royal seals, is repealed by the statute 6 Geo. III. c. 53. else it had been impossible to have tried those offences in the same circuit in which they are indicted: for ten clear days, between the finding and the trial of the indictment, will exceed the time usually allotted for any session of *oyer* and *terminer*. And no person indicted for felony is, or (as the law stands) ever can be, entitled to such copies, before the time of his trial.

When the trial is called on, the jurors are to be sworn, as they appear, to the number of twelve, unless they are challenged by the party.

Challenges may here be made, either on the part of the king, or on that of the prisoner; and either to the whole array, or to the separate polls, for the very same reasons that they may be made in civil causes. For it is here at least as necessary, as there, that the sheriff or returning officer be totally indifferent; that where an alien is indicted, the jury should be *de medietate*, or half foreigners; (which does not indeed hold in treasons, aliens being very improper judges of the breach of allegiance to the king) that on every panel there should be a competent number of hundredors; and that the particular jurors should be *omni exceptione majores;* not liable to objection either *propter honoris respectum, propter defectum, propter affectum,* or *propter delictum.*

Challenges upon any of the foregoing accounts are stiled challenges *for cause;* which may be without stint in both criminal and civil trials. But in criminal cases, or at least in capital ones, there is, *in favorem vitae,* allowed to the prisoner an arbitrary and capricious species of challenge to a certain number of jurors, without shewing any cause at all; which is called a *peremptory* challenge: a provision full of that tenderness and humanity to prisoners, for which our English laws are justly famous. This is grounded on two reasons. 1. As every one must be sensible, what sudden impressions and unaccountable prejudices we are apt to conceive upon the bare looks and gestures of another; and how necessary it is, that a prisoner (when put to defend his life) should have a good opinion of his jury, the want of which might totally disconcert him; the law wills not that he should be tried by any one man against whom he has conceived a prejudice, even without being able to assign a reason for such his dislike. 2. Because, upon challenges for cause shewn, if the reason assigned prove insufficient to set aside the juror, perhaps the bare questioning his indifference may sometimes provoke a resentment; to prevent all ill consequences from which, the prisoner is still at liberty, if he pleases, peremptorily to set him aside.

This privilege, of peremptory challenges, though granted to the prisoner, is denied to the king by the statute 33 Edw. I. st. 4. which enacts, that the king shall challenge no jurors without assigning a cause certain, to be tried and approved by the court. However it is held, that the king need not assign his cause of challenge, till all the panel is gone through, and unless there cannot be a full jury without the persons so challenged. And then, and not sooner, the king's counsel must shew the cause: otherwise the juror shall be sworn.

The peremptory challenges of the prisoner must however have some reasonable boundary; otherwise he might never be tried. This reasonable boundary is settled by the common law to be the number of thirty five; that is, one under the number of three full juries. For the law judges that five and thirty are fully sufficient to allow the most timorous man to challenge through mere caprice; and that he who peremptorily challenges a greater number, or three full juries, has no intention to be tried at all. And therefore it dealt with one, who peremptorily challenges above thirty five, and will not retract his challenge, as with one who stands mute and refuses his trial; by sentencing him to the *peine forte et dure* in felony, and by attainting him in treason. And so the law stands at this day with regard to treason, of any kind.

But by statute 22 Hen. VIII. c. 14. (which, with regard to felonies, stands unrepealed by statute 1 & 2 Ph. & Mar. c. 10.) by this statute, I say, no person, arraigned for felony, can be admitted to make any more than *twenty* peremptory challenges. But how if the prisoner will peremptorily challenge twenty one? what shall be done? The old opinion was, that judgment of *peine forte et dure* should be given, as where he challenged thirty six at the common law: but the better opinion seems to be, that such challenge shall only be disregarded and overruled. Because, first, the common law doth not inflict the judgment of penance for challenging twenty one, neither doth the statute inflict it; and so heavy a judgment shall not be imposed by implication. Secondly, the words of the statute are, "that he be not *admitted* to challenge more than twenty;" the evident construction of which is, that any farther challenge shall be disallowed or prevented: and therefore, being null from the beginning, and never in fact a challenge, it can subject the prisoner to no punishment; but the juror shall be regularly sworn.

If, by reason of challenges or the default of the jurors, a sufficient number cannot be had of the original panel, a *tales* may be awarded as in civil causes, till the number of twelve is sworn, "well and truly to try, and true deliverance make, between our sovereign lord the king, and the prisoner whom they have in charge; and a true verdict to give, according to their evidence."

When the jury is sworn, if it be a cause of any consequence, the indictment is usually opened, and the evidence marshalled, examined, and enforced by the counsel for the crown, or prosecution. But it is a settled rule at common law, that no counsel shall be allowed a prisoner upon his trial, upon the general issue, in any capital crime, unless some point of law shall arise proper to be debated. A rule, which (however it may be palliated under cover of that noble declaration of the law, when rightly understood, that the judge shall be counsel for the prisoner; that is, shall see that the proceedings against him are legal and strictly regular) seems to be not at all of a piece with the rest of the humane treatment of prisoners by the English law. For upon what face of reason can that assistance be denied to save the life of a man, which yet is allowed him in prosecutions for every petty trespass? Nor indeed is it strictly speaking a part of our antient law: for the Mirrour, having observed the necessity of counsel in civil suits, "who know how to forward and defend the cause, by the rules of law and customs of the realm," immediately afterwards subjoins; "and more necessary are they for defence upon indictments and appeals of felony, than upon other venial causes." And, to say the truth, the judges themselves are so sensible of this defect in our modern practice, that they seldom scruple to allow a prisoner counsel to stand by him at the bar, and instruct him what questions to ask, or even to ask questions for him, with respect to matters of fact: for as to matters of law, arising on the trial, they are *intitled* to the assistance of counsel. But still this is a matter of too much importance to be left to the good pleasure of any judge, and is worthy the interposition of the legislature; which has shewn it's inclination to indulge prisoners with this reasonable assistance, by enacting in statute 7 W. III. c. 3. that persons *indicted* for such high treason, as works a corruption of the blood, or misprision thereof, may make their full defence by counsel, not exceeding two, to be named by the prisoner and assigned by the court or judge: and this indulgence, by statute 20 Geo. II. c. 30. is extended to parliamentary *impeachments* for high treason, which were excepted in the former act.

. . . . .

Lastly, it was an antient and commonly received practice, (derived from the civil law, and which also to this day obtains in the kingdom of France) that, as counsel was not allowed to any prisoner accused of a capital crime, so neither should he be suffered to exculpate himself by the testimony of any witnesses. And therefore it deserves to be remembered, to the honour of Mary 1, (whose early sentiments, till her marriage with Philip of Spain, seem to have been humane and generous) that when she appointed sir Richard Morgan chief justice of the commonpleas, she injoined him, "that notwithstanding the old error, which did not admit any witness to speak, or any other matter to be heard, in favour of the adversary, her majesty being party; her highness' pleasure was, that whatsoever could be brought in favour of the subject should be admitted to be heard: and moreover, that the justices should not persuade themselves to sit in judgment otherwise for her highness than for her subject." Afterwards, in one particular instance (when embezzling the queen's military stores was made felony by statute 31 Eliz. c. 4.) it was provided that any person, impeached for such felony, "should be received and admitted to make any lawful proof that he could, by lawful witness or otherwise, for his discharge and defence:" and in general the courts grew so heartily ashamed of a doctrine so unreasonable and oppressive, that a practice was gradually introduced of examining witnesses for the prisoner, but not upon oath: the consequence of which still was, that the jury gave less credit to the prisoner's evidence, than to that produced by the crown. Sir Edward Coke protests very strongly against this tyrannical practice: declaring that he never read in any act of parliament, book-case, or record, that in criminal cases the party accused should not have witnesses sworn for him; and therefore there was not so much as *scintilla juris* against it. And the house of commons were so sensible of this absurdity, that, in the bill for abolishing hostilities between England and Scotland, when felonies committed by Englishmen in Scotland were ordered to be tried in one of the three northern counties, they insisted on a clause, and

carried it against the efforts of both the crown and the house of lords, against the practice of the courts in England, and the express law of Scotland, "that in all such trials, for the better discovery of the truth, and the better information of the consciences of the jury and justices, there shall be allowed to the party arraigned the benefit of such credible witnesses, to be examined upon oath, as can be produced for his clearing and justification." At length by the statute 7 W. III. c. 3. the same measure of justice was established throughout all the realm, in cases of treason within the act: and it was afterwards declared by statute 1 Ann. st. 2. c. 9. that in all cases of treason and felony, all witnesses *for* the prisoner should be examined upon oath, in like manner as the witnesses *against* him.

When the evidence on both sides is closed, the jury cannot be discharged till they have given in their verdict; but are to consider of it, and deliver it in, with the same forms, as upon civil causes: only they cannot, in a criminal case, give a *privy* verdict. But an open verdict may be either general, guilty, or not guilty; or special, setting forth all the circumstances of the case, and praying the judgment of the court, whether, for instance, on the facts stated, it be murder, manslaughter, or no crime at all. This is where they *doubt* the matter of law, and therefore *chuse* to leave it to the determination of the court; though they have an unquestionable right of determining upon all the circumstances, and finding a general verdict, if they think proper so to hazard a breach of their oaths: and, if their verdict be notoriously wrong, they may be punished and the verdict set aside by attaint at the suit of the king; but not at the suit of the prisoner. But the practice, heretofore in use, of fining, inprisoning, or otherwise punishing jurors, merely at the discretion of the court, for finding their verdict contrary to the direction of the judge, was arbitrary, unconstitutional and illegal: and is treated as such by sir Thomas Smith, two hundred years ago; who accounted "such doings to be very violent, tyrannical, and contrary to the liberty and custom of the realm of England." For, as sir Matthew Hale well observes, it would be a most unhappy case for the judge himself, if the prisoner's fate depended upon his directions:—unhappy also for the prisoner; for, if the judge's opinion must rule the verdict, the trial by jury would be useless. Yet in many instances, where contrary to evidence the jury have found the prisoner guilty, their verdict hath been mercifully set aside, and a new trial granted by the court of king's bench; for in such case, as hath been said, it cannot be set right by attaint. But there hath yet been no instance of granting a new trial, where the prisoner was *acquitted* upon the first.

If the jury therefore find the prisoner not guilty, he is then for ever quit and discharged of the accusation; except he be appealed of felony within the time limited by law. But if the jury find him guilty, he is then said to be *convicted* of the crime whereof he stands indicted. Which conviction may accrue two ways; either by his confessing the offence and pleading guilty; or by his being found so by the verdict of his country.

15

CONTINENTAL CONGRESS, DECLARATION AND
RESOLVES
14 Oct. 1774
Tansill 3, 4–5

Resolved, N. C. D. 5. That the respective colonies are entitled to the common law of England, and more especially to the great and inestimable privilege of being tried by their peers of the vicinage, according to the course of that law.

. . . . .

The several acts of 4 Geo. III. ch. 15, and ch. 34.—5 Geo. III. ch. 25.—6 Geo. III. ch. 52.—7 Geo. III. ch. 41. and ch. 46.—8 Geo. III. ch. 22. which impose duties for the purpose of raising a revenue in America, extend the power of the admiralty courts beyond their ancient limits, deprive the American subject of trial by jury, authorise the judges certificate to indemnify the prosecutor from damages, that he might otherwise be liable to, requiring oppressive security from a claimant of ships and goods seized, before he shall be allowed to defend his property, and are subversive of American rights.

Also 12 Geo. III. ch. 24. intituled, "An act for the better securing his majesty's dockyards, magazines, ships, ammunition, and stores," which declares a new offence in America, and deprives the American subject of a constitutional trial by jury of the vicinage, by authorising the trial of any person, charged with the committing any offence described in the said act, out of the realm, to be indicted and tried for the same in any shire or county within the realm.

16

JOHN ADAMS, NOVANGLUS, NO. 5
20 Feb. 1775
Papers 2:282–84

That the high whigs took *care* to get themselves chosen of the grand juries I don't believe. Nine tenths of the people were high whigs; and therefore it was not easy to get a grand jury without nine whigs in ten, in it. And the matter would not be much mended by the new act of parliament. The sheriff must return the same set of jurors, court after court, or else his juries would be nine tenths of them high whigs still. Indeed the tories are so envenom'd now with malice, envy, revenge and disappointed ambition, that they would be willing, for what I know, to be jurors for life, in order to give verdicts against the whigs. And many of them would readily do it, I doubt not, without any other law or evidence, than what they found in their own breasts. The suggestion of ledgerdemain, in drawing the names of petit jurors out of the box, is scandalous. Human wisdom cannot devise a method of obtaining petit jurors more fairly, and better secured against a possibility of corruption of any kind, than that established by our provincial law. They were drawn by chance out of a box, in open town meeting, to which the tories went, or might have gone, as well as the whigs, and have seen with their own eyes, that nothing unfair ever did or could take place. If the jurors consisted of whigs, it was because the freeholders were whigs, that is honest men. But now, it seems, if Massachusettensis can have his will, the sheriff who will be a person properly qualified for the purpose, is to pick out a tory jury, if he can find one in ten, or one in twenty of that character among the freeholders; and it is no doubt expected, that every news paper that presumes to deny the right of parliament to tax us, or destroy our charter, will be presented as a libel, and every member of a committee of correspondence, or a congress, &c. &c. &c. are to be indicted for rebellion. These would be pleasant times to Massachusettensis and the junto, but they will never live to see them.

"The judges pointed out seditious libels, on governors, magistrates, and the whole government to no effect." They did so. But the jurors thought some of these no libels, but solemn truths. At one time, I have heard that all the newspapers for several years, the Massachusetts Gazette, Evening Post, the Boston Chronicle, Boston-Gazette, and Massachusetts-Spy, were laid before a grand jury at once. The jurors thought there were multitudes of libels written by the tories, and they did not know who they should attack if they presented them; perhaps governor Bernard, lieut. governor Hutchinson, secretary Oliver—possibly the attorney general. They saw so many difficulties they knew not what to do.

As to the riots and insurrections, it is surprizing that this writer should say "scarce one offender was indicted, and I think not one convicted." Were not many indicted, convicted, and punished too in the county of Essex? and Middlesex, and indeed in every other county? But perhaps he will say, he means such as were connected with politicks. Yet this is not true, for a large number in Essex were punished for abusing an informer, and others were indicted and convicted in Boston, for a similar offence. None were indicted for pulling down the stamp office, because this was thought an honorable and glorious action, not a riot. And so it must be said of several other tumults. But was not this the case in royal as well as charter governments? Nor will this inconvenience be remedied by a sheriff's jury, if such an one should ever sit. For if such a jury should convict, the people will never bear the punishment. It is in vain to expect or hope to carry on government, against the universal bent and genius of the people; we may whimper and whine as much as we will, but nature made it impossible, when she made men.

17

Connecticut Constitutional
Ordinance of 1776
Poore 1:258

2. *And be it further enacted and declared,* That no Man's Life shall be taken away: No Man's Honor or good Name shall be stained: No Man's Person shall be arrested, restrained, banished, dismembered, nor any Ways punished: No Man shall be deprived of his Wife or Children: No Man's Goods or Estate shall be taken away from him, nor any Ways indamaged under the Colour of Law, or Countenance of Authority; unless clearly warranted by the Laws of this State.

18

Virginia Declaration of Rights, sec. 8
12 June 1776

8. That in all capital or criminal prosecutions a man hath a right to demand the cause and nature of his accusation, to be confronted with the accusers and witnesses, to call for evidence in his favour, and to a speedy trial by an impartial jury of his vicinage, without whose unanimous consent he cannot be found guilty, nor can he be compelled to give evidence against himself; that no man be deprived of his liberty except by the law of the land, or the judgment of his peers.

19

Delaware Declaration of Rights and
Fundamental Rules
11 Sept. 1776
Sources 339

13. That Trial by Jury of Facts where they arise is one of the greatest Securities of the Lives, Liberties and Estates of the People.

14. That in all Prosecutions for criminal Offenses, every Man hath a Right to be informed of the Accusation against him, to be allowed Counsel, to be confronted with the Accusers or Witnesses, to examine Evidence on Oath in his Favour, and to a speedy Trial by an impartial Jury, without whose unanimous Consent he ought not to be found Guilty.

15. That no Man in the Courts of common Law ought to be compelled to give Evidence against himself.

20

Georgia Constitution of 1777,
arts. 39, 58
Thorpe 2:783, 785

Art. XXXIX. All matters of breach of the peace, felony, murder, and treason against the State to be tried in the county where the same was committed. All matters of dispute, both civil and criminal, in any county where there is not a sufficient number of inhabitants to form a court, shall be tried in the next adjacent county where a court is held.

. . . . .

Art. LVIII. No person shall be allowed to plead in the courts of law in this State, except those who are authorized so to do by the house of assembly; and if any person so authorized shall be found guilty of malpractice before the house of assembly, they shall have power to suspend them. This is not intended to exclude any person from that inherent privilege of every *freeman*, the liberty to plead his own cause.

21

Vermont Constitution of 1777,
ch. 1, arts. 10, 19
Thorpe 6:3741, 3742

X. That, in all prosecutions for criminal offences, a man hath a right to be heard, by himself and his counsel—to demand the cause and nature of his accusation—to be confronted with the witnesses—to call for evidence in his favor, and a speedy public trial, by an impartial jury of the country; without the unanimous consent of which jury, he cannot be found guilty; nor can he be compelled to give evidence against himself; nor can any man be justly deprived of his liberty, except by the laws of the land or the judgment of his peers.

. . . . .

XIX. That no person shall be liable to be transported out of this State for trial, for any offence committed within this State.

22

DEBATE IN MASSACHUSETTS RATIFYING CONVENTION
30 Jan. 1788
Elliot 2:109–14

MR. HOLMES. Mr. President, I rise to make some remarks on the paragraph under consideration, which treats of the judiciary power.

It is a maxim universally admitted, that the safety of the subject consists in having a right to a trial as free and impartial as the lot of humanity will admit of. Does the Constitution make provision for such a trial? I think not; for in a criminal process, a person shall not have a right to insist on a trial in the vicinity where the fact was committed, where a jury of the peers would, from their local situation, have an opportunity to form a judgment of the *character* of the person charged with the crime, and also to judge of the *credibility* of the witnesses. There a person must be tried by a jury of strangers; a jury who *may be* interested in his conviction; and where he *may*, by reason of the distance of his residence from the place of trial, be incapable of making such a defence as he is, in justice, entitled to, and which he could avail himself of, if his trial was in the same county where the crime is said to have been committed.

These circumstances, as horrid as they are, are rendered still more dark and gloomy, as there is no provision made in the Constitution to prevent the attorney-general from filing information against any person, whether he is indicted by the grand jury or not; in consequence of which the most innocent person in the commonwealth may be taken by virtue of a warrant issued in consequence of such information, and dragged from his home, his friends, his acquaintance, and confined in prison, until the next session of the court, which has jurisdiction of the crime with which he is charged, (and how frequent those sessions are to be we are not yet informed of,) and after long, tedious, and painful imprisonment, though acquitted on trial, may have no possibility to obtain any kind of satisfaction for the loss of his liberty, the loss of his time, great expenses, and perhaps cruel sufferings.

But what makes the matter still more alarming is, that the mode of criminal process is to be pointed out by Congress, and they have no constitutional check on them, except that the trial is to be by a *jury:* but who this jury is to be, how qualified, where to live, how appointed, or by what rules to regulate their procedure, we are ignorant of as yet: whether they are to live in the county where the trial is; whether they are to be chosen by certain districts, or whether they are to be appointed by the sheriff *ex officio;* whether they are to be for one session of the court only, or for a certain term of time, or for good behavior, or during pleasure, are matters which we are entirely ignorant of as yet.

The mode of trial is altogether indetermined; whether the criminal is to be allowed the benefit of counsel; whether he is to be allowed to meet his accuser face to face; whether he is to be allowed to confront the witnesses, and have the advantage of cross-examination, we are not yet told.

These are matters of by no means small consequence; yet we have not the smallest constitutional security that we shall be allowed the exercise of these privileges, neither is it made certain, in the Constitution, that a person charged with the crime shall have the privilege of appearing before the court or jury which is to try him.

On the whole, when we fully consider this matter, and fully investigate the powers granted, explicitly given, and specially delegated, we shall find Congress possessed of powers enabling them to institute judicatories little less inauspicious than a certain tribunal in Spain, which has long been the disgrace of Christendom: I mean that diabolical institution, the *Inquisition.*

What gives an additional glare of horror to these gloomy circumstances is the consideration, that Congress have to ascertain, point out, and determine, what kind of punishments shall be inflicted on persons convicted of crimes. They are nowhere restrained from inventing the most cruel and unheard-of punishments, and annexing them to crimes; and there is no constitutional check on them, but that *racks* and *gibbets* may be amongst the most mild instruments of their discipline.

There is nothing to prevent Congress from passing laws which shall compel a man, who is accused or suspected of a crime, to furnish evidence against himself, and even from establishing laws which shall order the court to take the charge exhibited against a man for truth, unless he can furnish evidence of his innocence.

I do not pretend to say Congress *will* do this; but, sir, I undertake to say that Congress (according to the powers proposed to be given them by the Constitution) *may* do it; and if they do not, it will be owing *entirely*—I repeat it, it will be owing *entirely*—to the goodness of the men, and not in the *least degree* owing to the goodness of the Constitution.

The framers of our state constitution took particular care to prevent the General Court from authorizing the judicial authority to issue a warrant against a man for a crime, unless his being guilty of the crime was supported by oath or affirmation, prior to the warrant being granted; why it should be esteemed so much more safe to intrust Congress with the power of enacting laws, which it was deemed so unsafe to intrust our state legislature with, I am unable to conceive.

MR. GORE observed, in reply to Mr. Holmes, that it had been the uniform conduct of those in opposition to the proposed form of government, to determine, in every case where it was possible that the administrators thereof could do wrong, that they would do so, although it were demonstrable that such wrong would be against their own honor and interest, and productive of no advantage to themselves. On this principle alone have they determined that the trial by jury would be taken away in civil cases; when it had been clearly shown, that no words could be adopted, apt to the situation and customs of each state in this particular. Jurors are differently chosen in different states, and in point of qualification the laws of the several states are very diverse; not less so in the causes and disputes which are entitled to trial by jury. What is the result of this? That the laws of Congress may and will be conformable to the local laws in this particular, although the Constitution could not make a universal rule equally applying to the customs and statutes of the different states. Very few governments (certainly not this) can be interested in depriving the people of trial by jury, in questions of *meum et tuum*. In criminal cases alone are they interested to have the trial under their own control; and, in such cases, the Constitution expressly stipulates for trial by jury; but then, says the gentleman from Rochester, (Mr. Holmes,) to the safety of life it is indispensably necessary the trial of crimes should be in the vicinity; and the vicinity is construed to mean county; this is very incorrect, and gentlemen will see the impropriety, by referring themselves to the different local divisions and districts of the several states. But further, said the gentleman, the idea that the jury coming from the neighborhood, and knowing the character and circumstances of the party in trial, is promotive of justice, on reflection will appear not founded in truth. If the jury judge from any other circumstances but what are part of the cause in question, they are not impartial. The great object is to determine on the real merits of the cause, uninfluenced by any personal considerations; if, therefore, the jury could be perfectly ignorant of the person in trial, a just decision would be more probable. From such motives did the wise Athenians so constitute the famed Areopagus, that, when in judgment, this court should sit at midnight, and in total darkness, that the decision might be on the thing, and not on the person. Further, said the gentleman, it has been said, because the Constitution does not expressly provide for an indictment by grand jury in criminal cases, therefore some officer under this government will be authorized to file informations, and bring any man to jeopardy of his life, and indictment by grand jury will be disused. If gentlemen who pretend such fears will look into the constitution of Massachusetts, they will see that no provision is therein made for an indictment by grand jury, or to oppose the danger of an attorney-general filing informations; yet no difficulty or danger has arisen to the people of this commonwealth from this defect, if gentlemen please to call it so. If gentlemen would be candid, and not consider that, wherever Congress may possibly abuse power, they certainly will, there would be no difficulty in the minds of any in adopting the proposed Constitution.

23

Respublica v. Shaffer
1 Dall. 236 (Pa. 1788)

McKean, Chief Justice.—Were the proposed examination of witnesses, on the part of the defendant, to be allowed, the long-established rules of law and justice would be at an end. It is a matter well known, and well understood, that by the laws of our country, every question which affects a man's life, reputation or property, must be tried by *twelve* of his peers; and that their unanimous verdict is, alone, competent to determine the fact in issue. If, then, you undertake to inquire, not only upon what foundation the charge is made, but, likewise, upon what foundation it is denied, you will, in effect, usurp the jurisdiction of the petit jury, you will supersede the legal authority of the court, in judging of the competency and admissibility of witnesses, and having thus undertaken to try the question, that question may be determined by a bare majority, or by a much greater number of your body, than the twelve peers prescribed by the law of the land. This point has, I believe, excited some doubts upon former occasions; but those doubts have never arisen in the mind of any lawyer, and they may easily be removed by a proper consideration of the subject. For the bills or presentments, found by a grand jury, amount to nothing more than an official accusation, in order to put the party accused upon his trial; until the bill is returned, there is, therefore, no charge from which he can be required to exculpate himself; and we know that many persons, against whom bills were returned, have been afterwards acquitted by a verdict of their country. Here, then, is the just line of discrimination: it is the duty of the grand jury to inquire into the nature and probable grounds of the charge; but it is the exclusive province of the petit jury, to hear and determine, with the assistance, and under the direction of the court, upon points of law, whether the defendant is, or is not guilty, on the whole evidence, for, as well as against him. You will, therefore, readily perceive, that if you examine the witnesses on both sides, you do not confine your consideration to the probable grounds of charge, but engage completely in the trial of the cause; and your return must, consequently, be tantamount to a verdict of acquittal or condemnation. But this would involve us in another difficulty; for by the law, it is declared, that no man shall be twice put in jeopardy for the same offence: and, yet, it is certain, that the inquiry now proposed by the grand jury, would necessarily introduce the oppression of a double trial. Nor is it merely upon maxims of law, but, I think, likewise, upon principles of humanity, that this innovation should be opposed. Considering the bill as an accusation grounded entirely upon the testimony in support of the prosecution, the petit jury receive no bias from the sanction which the indorsement of the grand jury has conferred upon it. But on the other hand, would it not, in some degree, prejudice the most upright mind against the defendant, that on a full hearing of his defence, another tribunal had pronounced it insufficient?—which would then be the natural inference from every *true bill*. Upon the whole, the court is of opinion, that it would be improper and illegal to examine the witnesses, on behalf of the defendant, while the charge against him lies before the grand jury.

One of the grand inquest then observed to the court, that "there was a clause in the qualification of the jurors, upon which he, and some of his brethren, wished to hear the interpretation of the judges, to wit, what is the legal acceptation of the words *"diligently inquire?"* To this, the CHIEF JUSTICE replied, that "the expression meant, diligently to inquire into the circumstances of the charge, the credibility of the witnesses who support it, and from the whole, to judge whether the person accused ought to be put upon his trial. For (he added), though it would be improper to determine the merits of the cause, it is incumbent upon the grand jury to satisfy their minds, by a diligent inquiry, that there is a probable ground for the accusation, before they give it their authority, and call upon the defendant to make a public defence,"

24

HOUSE OF REPRESENTATIVES, AMENDMENTS TO THE CONSTITUTION
17–18 Aug. 1789
Annals 1:753, 756, 759–60

[*17 Aug.*]

The fifth clause of the fourth proposition was taken up, viz: "No person shall be subject, in case of impeachment, to more than one trial or one punishment for the same offence, nor shall be compelled to be a witness against himself, nor be deprived of life, liberty, or property, without due process of law; nor shall private property be taken for public use without just compensation."

Mr. BENSON thought the committee could not agree to the amendment in the manner it stood, because its meaning appeared rather doubtful. It says that no person shall be tried more than once for the same offence. This is contrary to the right heretofore established; he presumed it was intended to express what was secured by our former Constitution, that no man's life should be more than once put in jeopardy for the same offence; yet it was well known, that they were entitled to more than one trial. The humane intention of the clause was to prevent more than one punishment; for which reason he would move to amend it by striking out the words "one trial or."

Mr. SHERMAN approved of the motion. He said, that as the clause now stood, a person found guilty could not arrest the judgment, and obtain a second trial in his own favor. He thought that the courts of justice would never think of trying and punishing twice for the same offence. If the person was acquitted on the first trial, he ought not to be tried a second time; but if he was convicted on the first, and any thing should appear to set the judgment aside, he was entitled to a second, which was certainly favorable to him. Now the clause as it stands would deprive him of that advantage.

Mr. LIVERMORE thought the clause very essential; it was declaratory of the law as it now stood; striking out the words, would seem as if they meant to change the law by implication, and expose a man to the danger of more than one trial. Many persons may be brought to trial for crimes

they are guilty of, but for want of evidence may be acquitted; in such cases, it is the universal practice in Great Britain, and in this country, that persons shall not be brought to a second trial for the same offence; therefore the clause is proper as it stands.

Mr. SEDGWICK thought, instead of securing the liberty of the subject, it would be abridging the privileges of those who were prosecuted.

The question on Mr. BENSON's motion being put, was lost by a considerable majority.

Mr. PARTRIDGE moved to insert after "same offence," the words "by any law of the United States." This amendment was lost also.

Mr. LAWRENCE said this clause contained a general declaration, in some degree contrary to laws passed. He alluded to that part where a person shall not be compelled to give evidence against himself. He thought it ought to be confined to criminal cases, and moved an amendment for that purpose; which amendment being adopted, the clause as amended was unanimously agreed to by the committee. . . .

. . . . .

The committee then proceeded to consider the seventh proposition, in the words following:

Article 3, section 2. Strike out the whole of the third paragraph, and insert, "In all criminal prosecutions, the accused shall enjoy the right to a speedy and public trial, to be informed of the nature and cause of the accusation, to be confronted with the witnesses against him, to have compulsory process for obtaining witnesses in his favor, and to have the assistance of counsel for his defence."

Mr. BURKE moved to amend this proposition in such a manner as to leave it in the power of the accused to put off the trial to the next session, provided he made it appear to the court that the evidence of the witnesses, for whom process was granted but not served, was material to his defence.

Mr. HARTLEY said, that in securing him the right of compulsory process, the Government did all it could; the remainder must lie in the discretion of the court.

Mr. SMITH, of South Carolina, thought the regulation would come properly in, as part of the judicial system.

The question on Mr. BURKE's motion was taken and lost; ayes 9, noes 41.

Mr. LIVERMORE moved to alter the clause, so as to secure to the criminal the right of being tried in the State where the offence was committed.

Mr. STONE observed that full provision was made on the subject in the subsequent clause.

On the question, Mr. LIVERMORE's motion was adopted.

Mr. BURKE said, he was not so much discouraged by the fate of his former motions, but that he would venture upon another. He therefore proposed to add to the clause, "that no criminal prosecution should be had by way of information."

[*18 Aug.*]

The House again resolved itself into a Committee of the Whole on the subject of amendments, and took into consideration the 2d clause of the 7th proposition, in the words following, "The trial of all crimes (except in cases of impeachment, and in cases arising in the land and naval forces, or in the militia when in actual service in the time of war, or public danger,) shall be by an impartial jury of freeholders of the vicinage, with the requisite of unanimity for conviction, the right of challenge, and other accustomed requisites; and no person shall be held to answer for a capital, or otherwise infamous crime, unless on a presentment, or indictment, by a grand jury; but if a crime be committed in a place in the possession of an enemy, or in which an insurrection may prevail, the indictment and trial may by law be authorized in some other place within the same State; and if it be committed in a place not within a State, the indictment and trial may be at such place or places as the law may have directed."

Mr. BURKE moved to change the word "vicinage" into "district or county in which the offence has been committed." He said this was conformable to the practice of the State of South Carolina, and he believed to most of the States in the Union; it would have a tendency also to quiet the alarm entertained by the good citizens of many of the States for their personal security; they would no longer fear being dragged from one extremity of the State to the other for trial, at the distance of three or four hundred miles.

Mr. LEE thought the word "vicinage" was more applicable than that of "district, or county," it being a term well understood by every gentleman of legal knowledge.

The question on Mr. BURKE's motion being put was negatived.

Mr. BURKE then revived his motion for preventing prosecutions upon information, but on the question this was also lost.

The clause was now adopted without amendment.

25

HOLMES v. COMEGYS
1 Dall. 439 (Pa. 1789)

SHIPPEN, President.—It would be of very dangerous consequence, if it was established, that a commercial agent was not amenable as a witness in a court of justice, in a cause against his constituent. It is straining the matter of privilege too far. And if the law makes him a witness, we are too fond of getting at the truth, to permit him to excuse himself from declaring it, because he conceives, that, in point of delicacy, it would be a breach of confidence.

26

COMMONWEALTH v. DILLON
4 Dall. 116 (Pa. 1792)

The prisoner (a boy about 12 years old) was indicted for arson, in burning several stables, containing hay, &c. He was examined before the mayor of the city of Philadelphia, on the 20th of December 1791, and then confessed the commission of the offences, with which he was charged. But, as his own confession was the principal evidence (indeed there was no other positive evidence) against him, his counsel insisted, that it was obtained under such duress, accompanied with threats and promises, as destroyed its legal credit and validity. The evidence on that point was, substantially, as follows:

On the 18th of December, the prisoner was committed to the jail of Philadelphia, and the next day was taken before the mayor; but, at that time, he made no confession. On the 18th and 19th of December he was visited and interrogated, by several respectable citizens, who represented to him the enormity of the crime; urged a free, open, and candid, confession, which would so excite public compassion as, probably, to be the means of obtaining a pardon; while a contrary course of conduct would leave him, in case of a conviction, without hope: and they added, that they would themselves stand his friends, if he would confess. The inspectors of the prison endeavoured, likewise, to obtain from him a discovery of his offences, and of his accomplices. They carried him into the dungeon; they displayed it in all its gloom and horror; they said that he would be confined in it, dark, cold, and hungry, unless he made a full disclosure; but if he did make a disclosure, he should be well accommodated with room, fire, and victuals, and might expect pity and favour. The prisoner continued to deny his guilt for some time; and when his master visited him, he complained of the want of clothes, fire, and nourishment. At length, however, on the 19th of December, he made successive acknowledgments of the facts contained in his confession, which was formally, and, to all appearance, voluntarily, made before the mayor, on the succeeding morning; and which was repeated, with additional circumstances, at subsequent periods.

In the prisoner's defence, the following authorities were cited, principally to guard the jury against the danger of mere presumptive evidence, and an extorted confession of guilt, through force, hope, or fear, particularly in the case of an infant. 4 *Bl. Com.* 357. *Fost.* 243. 2 *Tri. per Pais.* 603. 2 *H. H. P. C.* 225. 4 *Bl. Com.* 326. *Leach C. L.* 248. 319. 3 *Com. Dig.* 511. *Staundf.* 142. 2 *H. H. P. C.* 284, 5. 3 *Bac. Abr.* 131. 3 *Inst.* 232. 2 *Hawk.* 604. 8 *Mod. Fost.* 11. 244.

For the commonwealth. The confession was delivered before the mayor, and afterwards repeated and enlarged, without the least appearance of constraint, or terror. No public officer has improperly attempted to excite fear, or hope, as the medium of extorting a discovery; and all that was said, or done, in that respect, proceeded from the avowed friends of the prisoner, and the known promoters of humanity. Besides the confession itself bears intrinsic marks of its sincerity and truth; and neither the wildness of the boy's motive, for committing the crimes, nor his youth, can afford a satisfactory answer to the charge. *Fost.* 70. And, after all, to destroy the legal effect of the confession, as evidence, it must be proved, 1st, that previous improper means were employed; and 2d, that the confession was the immediate consequence of those improper means.

By the Court: The fact of the arson is established; and it only remains to decide, whether it was committed by the prisoner? The proof against him, depends upon his own confession, slightly corroborated by the testimony of two witnesses. The confession was freely and voluntarily made, was fairly and openly received, before the mayor; and, therefore, it was regularly read in evidence. But still, it has been urged, that it was thus apparently well made before the mayor, in consequence of improper measures previously pursued with the boy. The interference of the inspectors of the prison was certainly irregular; though the public anxiety, in which they participated, upon this extraordinary occasion, may be admitted as an excuse. The manner in which he was urged, though not threatened, by the citizens who visited him, may, likewise, be objectionable. But is it reasonable to infer, that all the prisoner's confessions were falsely made under the influence of those occurrences? Consider the nature of the offence. It cannot be openly perpetrated; for, it would be instantly prevented; and if it is secretly perpetrated, how, generally speaking, can the offender be detected, but by his own declarations? If such declarations are *voluntarily* made, all the world will agree, that they furnish the strongest evidence, of imputed guilt. The hope of mercy actuates almost every criminal, who confesses his crime; and merely that he cherishes the hope, is no reason, in morality, nor in law, to disbelieve him. The true point for consideration, therefore, is, whether the prisoner has falsely declared himself guilty of a capital offence? If there is ground even to suspect, that he has done so, God forbid, that his life should be the sacrifice! While, therefore, on the one hand, it is remarked, that all the stables set on fire, were in the neighbourhood of his master's house; that he has, in part, communicated the facts to another boy; that his conduct had excited the attention and suspicion of a girl, who knew him; and that he expressed no wish to retract the statement, which he has given: the jury will, on the other hand, remember, that if they entertain a doubt upon the subject, it is their duty to pronounce an acquital. Though it is their province to administer justice, and not to bestow mercy; and though it is better not to err at all; yet, in a doubtful case, an error on the side of mercy is safer, is more venial, than error on the side of rigid justice.

Verdict, Not Guilty.*

*The humanity of the jury being gratified by an acquital of the prisoner, from the capital charge, he was indicted and convicted, on the same facts, for a misdemeanor. By the reform of our penal code, Arson is no longer a capital crime.

27

UNITED STATES v. INSURGENTS

26 Fed. Cas. 499, no. 15,443 (C.C.D.Pa. 1795)

Before PATTERSON, Circuit Justice, and PETERS, District Judge.

PETERS, District Judge. I have considered the objections made to the panels, and do not conceive these objections relevant. Although, in ordinary cases, it would be well to accommodate our practice with that of the state, yet the judiciary of the United States should not be fettered and controlled in its operations, by a strict adherence to state regulations and practice. But I see not, that in a liberal view and construction of the laws of the United States, on this subject, a rigid adherence to all the local and economical regulations of the state, is directed or necessary. It should seem, that the most pointed reference was had to the designation and qualification of jurors, and not to the exact numbers of which the panel should consist. The legislature of a state have in their consideration a variety of local arrangements, which cannot be adapted to the more expanded policy of the nation. It never could have been in the contemplation of congress, by any reference to state regulations, to defeat the operation of the national laws. Now, there are cases, which have been stated, in which some of the criminal laws of the United States may be rendered impracticable by an adherence to the rule of numberes prescribed as to jurors, in criminal cases, by the state law; and, especially, if there must be but one panel as has been contended. Yet, the most substantial requisites, to wit, the qualifications of jurors and mode of selection, may be adhered to. As to the clause in the law of the United States, directing that "the laws of the states (with great exceptions) shall be regarded as rules of decision, in trials at common law, in the courts of the United States," I do not think it applies to the case before us. All the arguments founded on the inconveniences to the defendants, if in this case particularly any such exist (of which I much doubt), weigh lightly, when set against the delays and obstructions which the objection would throw in the way of the execution of the laws of the nation.

PATTERSON, Circuit Justice. The objections that have been suggested on this occasion, are principally founded on the twenty-ninth section of the judicial act of congress, which refers the federal courts to the state laws, for certain regulations respecting juries. But the words of this reference are clearly restricted to the mode of designating the jury by lot, or otherwise; and to the qualifications which are requisite for jurors, according to the laws and practice of the respective states. Since, therefore, the act of congress does not itself fix the number of jurors, nor expressly adopt any state rule for the purpose, it is a necessary consequence, that the subject must depend on the common law; and by the common law, the court may direct any number of jurors to be summoned, on a consideration of all the circumstances under which the venire is issued. There are instances, indeed, where five juries have been summoned upon a trial for high treason, in order that after the allowance of the legal challenges, a competent number might still be insured. In the present instance, the precept requires the marshal to return at least forty-eight jurors; and he has not in my opinion been guilty of any excess in the exercise of that discretion for returning a greater number, with which he is legally invested. Neither is the mode of making his return justly exceptionable. As the act of congress directs that twelve jurors shall be summoned from the county in which the offence was committed, I cannot conceive any more proper, or more legal way of proceeding, than by issuing a venire in each case; and then there must of course be a separate panel returned, in conformity to every writ. Thus, likewise, the act of congress and the state act have been reconciled, and both put into operation; twelve jurors being returned in pursuance of the former, and sixty jurors being returned in pursuance of the latter law. With respect to the objection, that a copy of the caption of the indictment has not been furnished to the prisoners, it may be observed, that, although the practice of Pennsylvania has been different, yet the caption and the indictment seem naturally to form but one instrument; and copies of both should, therefore, be delivered under the provisions of the act of congress. There can be little inconveniency in adopting this rule; and it is calculated to avoid much difficulty and controversy. The objection, that the place of abode of the jurors and witnesses has not been sufficiently designated, in the lists furnished to the prisoners, is, likewise, in our opinion a valid one. The object of the law was to enable the party accused, to prepare for his defence, and to identify the jurors who were to try, and the witnesses who were to prove, the indictment against him. It is contrary to the spirit and intent of such a provision, that the whole range of the state, or of a county, should be allowed, as descriptive of a place of abode; and it is the duty of the judges so to mould the practice and construction of statutes, as to render them reasonable and just. With regard to the place, therefore, we think the townships in which the jurors and witnesses respectively reside, should be specified; but the act of congress does not require a specification of their occupations, and the niceties of the state act are not, in that respect, incorporated into the federal system.

In consequence of this decision, the trials were suspended, in order to give the attorney of the district the three days required by the act of congress for delivering to the prisoners amended copies of the caption and indictment, and of the lists of jurors and witnesses.

28

STATE V. GARRIGUES
1 Hayw. 241 (N.C. 1795)

PER CURIAM. The rule as laid down in 3 Co. Inst., 110, and 1 Inst., 227, is general and without exception that a jury in a capital case cannot be discharged without giving a verdict. Afterwards, however, in the reigns of the latter sovereigns of the Stuart family, a different rule prevailed, that a jury in such case might be discharged for the purpose of having better evidence against him at a future day; and this power was exercised for the benefit of the crown only; but it is a doctrine so abhorrent to every principle of safety and security that it ought not to receive the least countenance in the courts of this country. In the time of James II., and since the Revolution, this doctrine came under examination, and the rule as laid down by my Lord Coke was revived with this addition, that a jury should not be discharged in a capital case unless for the benefit of the prisoner; as if the prisoner be a woman and be taken in labor; or if the prisoner after the jury are charged with him be found to be insane, and the like; or if at the prisoner's request a jury be withdrawn to let him in to take the benefit of an exception, which otherwise he would have lost, as in the case of *Foster*. In the present case the jury were suffered by the court's officer to separate without giving a verdict. As they could not agree to convict, it is strong evidence of the party's innocence; and perhaps he could not be tried again with the same advantage to himself as then. Perhaps his witnesses are dead, or gone away, or their attendance not to be procured, or some accident may prevent their attendance. We will not again put his life in jeopardy, more especially as it is very improbable we shall be able to possess him of the same advantages.

So he was discharged.

29

ZEPHANIAH SWIFT, A SYSTEM OF LAWS OF THE STATE OF CONNECTICUT 2:398–99
1796

The attorney for the state then proceeds to lay before the jury, all the evidence against the prisoner, without any remarks or arguments. The prisoner by himself or counsel, is then allowed to produce witnesses to counteract and obviate the testimony against him; and to exculpate himself with the same freedom as in civil cases. We have never admitted that cruel and illiberal principle of the common law of England that when a man is on trial for his life, he shall be refused counsel, and denied those means of defence, which are allowed, when the most trifling pittance of property is in question. The flimsy pretence, that the court are to be counsel for the prisoner will only highten our indignation at the practice: for it is apparent to the least consideration, that a court can never furnish a person accused of a crime with the advice, and assistance necessary to make his defence. This doctrine might with propriety have been advanced, at the time when by the common law of England, no witnesses could be adduced on the part of the prisoner, to manifest his innocence, for he could then make no preparation for his defense. One cannot read without horror and astonishment, the abominable maxims of law, which deprived persons accused, and on trial for crimes, of the assistance of counsel, except as to points of law, and the advantage of witnesses to exculpate themselves from the charge. It seems by the ancient practice, that whenever a person was accused of a crime, every expedient was adopted to convict him and every privilege denied him, to prove his innocence. In England, however, as the law now stands, prisoners are allowed the full advantage of witnesses, but excepting in a few cases, the common law is enforced, in denying them counsel, except as to points of law.

Our ancestors, when they first enacted their laws respecting crimes, influenced by the illiberal principles which they had imbibed in their native country, denied counsel to prisoners to plead for them to anything but points of law. It is manifest that there is as much necessity for counsel to investigate matters of fact, as points of law, if truth is to be discovered.

The legislature has become so thoroughly convinced of the impropriety and injustice of shackling and restricting a prisoner with respect to his defence, that they have abolished all those odious laws, and every person when he is accused of a crime, is entitled to every possible privilege in making his defence, and manifesting his innocence, by the instrumentality of counsel, and the testimony of witnesses.

30

STATE V. SQUIRES
1 Tyler 147 (Vt. 1801)

WOODBRIDGE, Chief Judge. The attorney in this case must be considered as the keeper of these notes for his client. If so, in contemplation of law they are in the possession of *Thomas Mallery*. I doubt the propriety of ordering papers thus situated out of his possession for the purpose of making use of them against him. It is true there are search warrants for the discovery of stolen goods; and magistrates who may seize base coin, are authorised to examine persons through whose hands it may have passed, under oath. But these are *statute* provisions, which do not controvert the bill of rights. There are no instances of warrants to search for papers correctly issuable at common law.

If *Mallery* makes use of these notes to support an action, the Court before whom such action is tried may and ought

to direct them to be stopped. The case in *Burrows* I conceive to be in point.

HALL, Judge. I consider the only power the Court have over such papers, while in possession of the party or his attorney, whom I consider to be one in contemplation of law, must be when they are attempted to be exhibited in evidence in this Court. I do not think we have any more power over these notes than we have over any other private papers which Mr. Attorney may suggest are in the custody of *Mallery*, and which he may esteem requisite to maintain a prosecution against him. I am for discharging the rule.

SMITH, Judge. I am of the same opinion.

Rule discharged.

31

RESPUBLICA V. GIBBS
3 Yeates 429 (Pa. 1802)

Besides, it has been objected, that the questions propounded to the electors, contravene an established principle of law. The maxim is, *neme tenetur seipsum accusare, (seu prodere.)* It is founded on the best policy, and runs throughout our whole system of jurisprudence. It is the uniform practice of courts of justice as to witnesses and jurors. It is considered cruel and unjust to propose questions which may tend to criminate the party. And so jealous have the legislature of this commonwealth been, of this mode of discovery of facts, that they refused their assent to a bill brought in, to compel persons to disclose on oath, papers as well as facts, relating to questions of mere property. And may we not justly suppose, that they would not be less jealous of securing our citizens against this mode of self accusation. The words *accusare* or *prodere* are general terms, and their sense is not confined to cases, where the answers to the questions proposed would induce to the punishment of the party; if they would involve him in shame or reproach, he is under no obligation to answer them. The avowed object of putting them, is to shew, that the party is under a legal disability to elect or be elected; and they might create an incapacity to take either by purchase or descent, to be a witness or juror, &c. We are all clear on this point, that the inspectors were not justified in proposing the questions objected to, though it is probable they did not wrong intentionally. Nevertheless, if by exacting an illegal oath, the election was obstructed or interrupted, it seems most reasonable to attribute it to them.

32

PEOPLE v. BARRETT

1 Johns. R. 66 (N.Y. 1806)

TOMPKINS, J. In discussing the points in this cause, I shall take for granted, what was not controverted upon the argument, that the proceedings of the first trial of the defendants, amounted to a general verdict of acquittal.

The principal grounds upon which the first point is attempted to be supported, are, that in the first indictment, it is stated, that the defendants conspired to defraud one *Darren* of his *money,* goods and chattels, whereas, in the second, they are charged with conspiring, to defraud him of his goods and chattels only; that the date of an endorsement of the note, mentioned in both indictments, is mentioned in the former to have been on a particular day, and in the latter, on a different day. These variances between the record of acquittal and the indictment to which it is pleaded, are wholly immaterial. The same evidence would have supported either indictment. Testimony of defrauding *Darren* of his money, would have been sufficient to support the charge for defrauding him of his goods and chattels. And the endorsement of the note, for aught that appears, being in blank, according to the customary mode of negotiating promissory notes, it was discretionary with the prosecutor, to allege the endorsement to have been made at any day after the date of the note, of which the defendants could not take any advantage. If the nature of the crime be substantially the same, a variance between the indictments, in other respects, may be helped by averments in the plea. The cases in which variances have been thus helped, as mentioned in *Hawkins,* (c. 25. § 3.) and in *Pulton, de pace regis,* (title *Indictment,* § 39 and 40.) are much stronger than the present. It is there laid down, that the party indicted may plead the former acquittal, and notwithstanding a variance may, by averments, show the truth of the case, and be discharged. In this case, the conspirators, the facts of conspiracy, the security in relation to which the fraud is charged, and the person intended to be defrauded, are the same, and in every substantial matter, the two indictments coincide. The first point, therefore, is untenable.

The second point is one of great importance. The general principle established in the history and reports of the pleas of the crown, is, that no one shall be twice put in jeopardy for the same offence.

The doctrine here contended for originated with *Vaux's* case, (4 *Co.* 44.) in which it was decided, that unless the party has been lawfully acquitted, upon a sufficient indictment for the same offence, he cannot have the benefit of the plea of *autrefois acquit.* By a lawful acquittal, must be understood an acquittal by a general verdict. If, therefore, the accused escape a trial by the entry of a *nolle prosequi,* by quashing the indictment, upon an issue of *demurrer,* or in *abatement,* he is not *lawfully* acquitted, and cannot in those, and the like cases, evade a trial by the country, for the same offence. The same observation applies to the cases of withdrawing a juror, *ex necessitate.*

It may perhaps be questioned, whether by an insufficient indictment, in the authorities relating to this subject, is not meant, one which states facts and circumstances that do not amount to an offence, or which wants the legal and technical words to denote the crime. Thus in *Pulton* (*tit. Indictment,* § 42.) it is laid down, that the plea of *autrefois acquit,* is not a good plea to an indictment for felony, unless the record vouched does contain *sufficient matter of felony.*

In 2 *Hale* (247.) it is also said, that *autrefois acquit* was not a good plea in the case there mentioned, because the first indictment was *insufficient,* for it contained *no matter of felony.* But, on examination, the cases cited do not appear to me to apply to the present case, because the defendants availed themselves of the defects in the indictment, or finding. In *Vaux's* case there was not a general verdict of not guilty, on the first trial; but his counsel took advantage of an insufficient finding in the special verdict. In *Cogan's* case, where there was a verdict of not guilty upon the first indictment, the plea in bar to the second did not prevail, because the offences were not the same, which is the reason assigned by the court for their decision.

The defendants in this cause did not avail themselves of any defects in the first indictment, but were acquitted, because the public prosecutor had not sufficient proof at the time to establish the charge against them. To allow him, now, by pointing out defects in his own pleading, to place the defendants in jeopardy a second time, would contravene a salutary maxim, that no one shall take advantage of his own wrong. The defects, if any, in the former indictment, are to be attributed to the district attorney; and if he can take advantage of them, when will the peril of the defendants cease? A second, third, or fourth acquittal will not secure them, if the ingenuity of the prosecutor discover defects in the antecedent indictments. I am inclined to think the presumption, that the court will not render judgment upon a conviction, if the indictment be defective, ought not to have much weight at the present day. As offenders appear by counsel, or have counsel assigned them by the court in almost all cases, unless advantage is taken by them or their counsel, the court will seldom, of its own motion, seek for defects in an indictment where there is a conviction, if an offence be substantially stated. Since, therefore, the matter in the first indictment is substantially the same for which they are arraigned the second time; since the defendants took no advantage of any defect in the indictment on their first trial, and have been acquitted by the proceedings which this court considered as equivalent to a general verdict of not guilty, I think their plea constitutes a good bar to the second indictment, and that they ought, therefore, to be discharged.

SPENCER, J. It is contended that owing to the imperfections in the first indictment, the present plea is not a bar. The case of *William Vaux* (4 *Term Rep.* 44.) is a leading case. *Vaux* had been indicted for poisoning *Nicholas Ridley;* a special verdict was found, and judgment of acquittal was given. He was indicted again for the same murder, and pleaded the former acquittal. On this plea, it was resolved, that when the offender is discharged on an insufficient indictment, there, the law not having had its end, nor the life of the party ever in danger, he may be again indicted, and tried; under this opinion, *Vaux* was tried a second time, convicted and executed. This case is sanctioned by *Hale* and *Hawkins*, (2 *Hale*, 248. 4 *Hawk.* 317.) the latter of whom says, "he takes it to be settled, that wherever the indictment is so erroneous, for want of substance in setting out the crime, that no good judgment could be given on it, against the defendant, an acquittal is no bar to a subsequent indictment, because, in judgment of law, the defendant never was in danger."

The defendants' counsel has obviated all the exceptions taken to the first indictment but one. There appears to be no *venue* either expressly, or by implication, as to the fraudulent representations made by *Barrett* to *Darren*, that *Gun*, the maker of the note imposed on *Darren*, was in solvent circumstances. This representation is the very *gist* of the indictment; and had the defendants been convicted on it, I should have held the judgment liable to be arrested; for it is a fundamental principle in criminal law, that every material fact must be clearly and fully set out, so that nothing can be taken by intendment. It does not then appear that the essence of the offence was committed in the county of *Washington*, or even within the state; for this reason I conceive the first indictment radically defective, and, consequently, that the defendants are bound to plead over to the second.

THOMPSON, J. From the case presented to the court, we are to consider the defendants as acquitted, at a former trial, upon an indictment for the same offence for which they now stand charged; and the two questions presented for decision are, 1. Whether the former indictment was materially defective; if so, then, 2. Whether an acquittal thereon is a bar to the present prosecution.

I think the first indictment defective for want of a *venue* in that part which charges *Barrett* with making a fraudulent pretence, pursuant to the conspiracy previously entered into between him and *Ward*. It is well settled that an indictment ought to contain a proper *venue*, for the purpose of showing where the offence was committed. (2 *Hawk.* c. 25. s. 83. 5 *Term Rep.* 162.) Every act material to constitute the offence charged, must be alleged to have been done at some place. The fraudulent pretence practised by *Barrett* was a material allegation, and required a *venue* as much as any part of the indictment.

Will an acquittal then, on such a defective indictment, discharge the party accused from any further prosecution for the same offence? I think not. It appears to me, that the law on this subject has been long since settled, and were I disposed to question the propriety of the principle, I should not feel myself at liberty to overturn what I have considered an established doctrine. The rule as laid down by Serjeant *Hawkins*, in his valuable *Treatise on Criminal Law*, (book 2. c. 25. s. 8.) and which is supported by the authorities there cited, is plain and explicit. He says, "I take it to be settled at this day, that wherever the indictment or appeal whereon a man is acquitted is so far erro-

neous, either for want of substance in setting out the crime, or of authority in the judge before whom it was taken, that no good judgment could have been given thereon against the defendant, the acquittal can be no bar of a subsequent indictment or appeal." The reason assigned for it is, "because in judgment of law, the defendant was never in danger of his life from the first. For the law will presume, *prima facie*, that the judges would not have given a judgment which would have been liable to have been reversed." Without further examination, therefore, I am satisfied that the plea of *autrefois acquit* is no bar to the present prosecution.

LIVINGSTON, J. The plea of *autrefois acquit* is thought not to apply here; because, the first indictment is erroneous, and the second not for the same offence.

If an opinion had been pronounced, at the instance of the party, on the insufficiency of the first bill, either on a special verdict, or after a general finding, on a motion in arrest of judgment, this case would bear some resemblance to, and might be governed by, that of *Vaux*, (4 *Co.* 44.) which has given rise to all the *dicta* on this subject. *Vaux* was indicted a second time for murder. He pleaded a former acquittal, but it appearing that on the first trial there had been a special verdict only, upon which judgment was rendered in his favour, for an insufficiency in the indictment, it was held that the plea was bad, and *Vaux* was again tried, convicted, and hanged. The court, in giving its opinion, is made very gravely to say, that the prisoner's life, although tried for murder, had *never* been in jeopardy, because the first indictment was imperfect; and yet not one counsel in a hundred would have had discernment enough to point out the defect, which, for that time, had saved him from the gallows.

Without denying the law, though not at all satisfied with the reason on which it is founded, it is totally inapplicable to the question before us. In *Vaux's* case, an acquittal had been pronounced by the court, at the prisoner's instance, *before* a second bill was presented, and had thus become matter of record, and formed a part of his plea. Even thus far, a court should very reluctantly go; for to tell a man who had been within an ace of being executed, that his life had been in no danger at all, savours a little of refinement, and was sporting, to say the least, with the feelings of the prisoner.

But, without disputing a decision which, notwithstanding the sayings of several learned and great men to which it has given rise, does not appear ever to have been practised on in *England*, it will be sufficient to show a very great and essential difference between the case of these defendants, and that of *Vaux*. The jury had *not acquitted*, nor given *any opinion* on his guilt, but had referred the whole matter to the court. *Barrett* and *Ward*, on the contrary, are found not guilty by the jury themselves; for the discharge, on the motion in arrest of judgment, is considered by this case, as a general verdict of acquittal. *Vaux* laid hold of a defect in the indictment. These defendants have availed themselves of no such imperfection, if any there were, nor has any judgment to that effect been pronounced. This case, in short, presents the novel and unheard of spectacle, of a public officer, whose business it was to frame a correct bill, openly alleging his own inaccuracy, or neglect, as a reason for a second trial, when it is not pretended that the merits were not fairly in issue on the first. That a party shall be deprived of the benefit of an acquittal by a jury, on a suggestion of this kind, coming too from the officer who drew the indictment, seems not to comport with that universal and humane principle of criminal law, "that no man shall be brought into danger more than once for the same offence." It is very like permitting a party to take advantage of his own wrong. If this practice be tolerated, when are trials of the accused to end? If a conviction take place, whether an indictment be good, or otherwise, it is ten to one that judgment passes; for if he read the bill, it is not probable he will have penetration enough to discern its defects. His counsel, if any be assigned to him, will be content with hearing the substance of the charge, without looking farther, and the court will hardly, of its own accord, think it a duty to examine the indictment to detect errors in it. Many hundreds, perhaps, are now in the state-prison on erroneous indictments, who, however, have been fairly tried on the merits. But reverse the case, and suppose an acquittal to take place, the prosecutor, if he be dissatisfied and bent on conviction, has nothing to do but to tell the court that his own indictment was good for nothing; that it has no *venue*, or is deficient in other particulars, and that, therefore, he has a right to a second chance of convicting the prisoner, and so on, *toties quoties*.

Of the alleged imperfection in this indictment we should never have heard, if the verdict had been the other way. I am glad there is not one precedent which compels me to listen to this application; a power to try *ad infinitum,* as often as some latent defect be discovered in an indictment, may not only be abused in the hands of an attorney general, but is unsafe in those of a court. If judges have the power of putting a party on his defence a second, and a third time, because of imperfections of this kind, there is no man who may not, if the court please, be finally convicted, or cruelly harassed by such a course of proceeding. It is a sufficient argument against the assumption of such power, that it is subversive of the trial by jury, and that it is liable, in seasons of political conflicts, to great abuse. Judges are but men, and not more secure than others against improper influence.

The objection, that the second indictment is not for the same offence, is not founded on fact. Both prosecutions are for the same conspiracy. This was conceded on the argument, and the indictments correspond in every essential point. It would, therefore, be little better than a mockery to permit trials to proceed, as often as by a slight change of phraseology, or ingenuity in a district attorney, the last indictment may be made to vary from the preceding. In my opinion, the defendants are entitled to their discharge.

KENT, Ch. J. The first question that arises upon this case, is, whether the indictment of 1803 was erroneous, so that a good judgment could not have been given against the defendants, if they had been convicted? The indictment does not contain a *venue* in that part of it, which avers that the defendant, *Barrett,* made a *fraudulent pretence,* in pursuance of the conspiracy, previously, and at another day, formed. This is a material allegation, and it required a *venue,* as much at least, as any part of the indictment; for the act done in pursuance of the conspiracy, was the *gist* of the charge. This omission, as it appears to me, was an error, for which the judgment to have been given thereon, might have been arrested or reversed. (2 *Hawk. c.* 25. § 83. and *The King* v. *Matthews,* 5 *Term Rep.* 162.)

It is very questionable, also, whether the indictment be not bad, in another respect. The *specific* pretences by which the fraud was to be effected, are not laid as having been agreed upon, at the time of the conspiracy. The conspiracy is laid generally, that they conspired to cheat, by the transfer of a note; but the false tokens by which that was effected, appear to have been the *separate* and voluntary acts of each defendant by himself, and may not have been previously known to each other. The defendants are only answerable upon such a charge, for acts to the doing of which they had *jointly* conspired. Unless the acts were done in pursuance of a joint agreement, they became the *distinct acts* of each individual, though they may have conduced to effect a *joint object.* It is not necessary, however, to give any strong, or decided opinion upon this point, since the want of a *venue* appears to be an objection more clearly fatal.

The next question is, whether the defendants can lawfully plead an *acquittal* upon an erroneous indictment, in bar of a new prosecution for the same offence?

The general rule of law, as laid down by Serjeant *Hawkins,* (vol. 2. c. 35. s. 8.) and which he takes to be settled at this day, is this, "that wherever the indictment, whereon a man is acquitted, is so far erroneous, (either for want of substance in setting out the crime, or of authority in the judge, before whom it was taken,) that no good judgment could have been given upon it against the defendant, the acquittal can be no bar of a subsequent indictment, because, in judgment of law, the defendant was never in danger of his life from the first; for the law will presume, *prima facie,* that the judges would not have given a judgment which would have been liable to have been reversed." *Vaux's* case (4 *Co.* 44.) is generally referred to as the leading authority in support of this position. He was indicted for murder, for poisoning one *Ridley,* and pleaded not guilty; he was tried, and the jury gave a *special verdict,* and the court gave judgment thereon, that the facts, as set forth in the verdict, did not support the indictment, and the defendant was discharged. He was afterwards indicted again, for the same crime. The indictment being removed into the K. B. he pleaded the former acquittal in bar, and it was resolved by the court that the first indictment was insufficient, and the plea of *autrefois acquit* was no bar; for that plea meant only a *lawful acquittal,* or conviction; that if the conviction or acquittal was not lawful, his life was never in jeopardy; and because the indictment was insufficient, he was not *legitimo modo acquietatus.* A case in the *Year Books* of 19 *Edw.* IV. (1 *Bulst.* 142.) was referred to, in support of the decision, and *Vaux* was accordingly tried again, convicted, and executed. This case fully supports the doctrine in *Hawkins;* and if good law, (of which no doubt has ever been entertained in the books,) it goes completely to overrule the plea in the present case. An acquittal by special verdict, and judgment thereon, is equal to an acquittal by a general verdict of not guilty, and certainly as operative as the acquittal before us. This case of *Vaux* is cited and recognised as good law, in Sir *Mathew Hale's Pleas of the Crown,* (vol. 2. p. 248.) and a distinction is there taken between an erroneous judgment, arising from error in the court, upon a verdict which is held to be conclusive upon the *king,* till reversed, and a judgment of acquittal, in a case where the indictment itself, which is the foundation of the action, is bad; that in the latter case it shall be presumed, that the judgment of acquittal was given upon the defect in the *indictment,* and not upon the *verdict,* for the judgment is the same in both cases, and the judges are bound to look into the indictment. *Brooke,* in his *Abridgment,* (*Corone,* 35.) cites 9 *Hen.* V. 2. and says, it was agreed, that if a man be arraigned of felony and acquitted without original, he shall be again arraigned at the suit of the *king;* but where he is arraigned upon good original, as good appeal, or indictment, and acquitted, and the *mesne* process or return be ill, there he shall not be again arraigned.

I am satisfied, therefore, that the law is not now to be questioned, that if the indictment be defective, so that no good judgment could have been given upon it, an acquittal upon such indictment is no bar.

The present plea must be overruled, and the defendants plead *de novo.*

33

UNITED STATES v. BURR

25 Fed. Cas. 25, no. 14,692b (C.C.D.Va. 1807)

MARSHALL, Chief Justice, delivered the following opinion:

In considering the question which was argued yesterday, it appears to be necessary to decide: 1st. Whether the court, sitting as a court, possesses the power to commit any person charged with an offence against the United States. 2d. If this power be possessed, whether circumstances exist in this case which ought to restrain its exercise.

The first point was not made in the argument, and would, if decided against the attorney for the United States, only change the mode of proceeding. If a doubt can exist respecting it, that doubt arises from the omission in the laws of the United States to invest their courts, sitting as courts, with the power in question. It is expressly given to every justice and judge, but not to a court. This objection was not made on the part of Colonel Burr, and is now mentioned, not because it is believed to present any intrinsic difficulty, but to show that it has been considered. This power is necessarily exercised by courts in discharge of their functions, and seems not to have been expressly given, because it is implied in the duties which a court must perform, and the judicial act contemplates it in this light. They have cognizance of all crimes against the United States; they are composed of the persons who can commit for those crimes; and it is obviously understood, by the legislature, that the judges may exercise collectively the power which they possess individually, so far as is necessary to enable them to retain a person charged with an offence in order to receive the judgment which may finally be rendered in his case. The court say, this is obviously understood by the legislature, because there is no clause expressly giving to the court the power to bail or to commit a person who appears in discharge of his recognizance, and against whom the attorney of the United States does not choose to proceed; and yet the thirty-third section of the judicial act evinces a clear understanding in the legislature that the power to take bail is in possession of the court. If a person shall appear in conformity with his recognizance, and the court passes away without taking any order respecting him, he is discharged. A new recognizance, therefore, or a commitment on the failure to enter into one, is in the nature of an original commitment, and this power has been uniformly exercised.

It is believed to be a correct position, that the power to commit for offences of which it has cognizance is exercised by every court of criminal jurisdiction, and that courts as well as individual magistrates are conservators of the peace. Were it otherwise, the consequence would only be that it would become the duty of the judge to descend from the bench, and, in his character as an individual magistrate, to do that which the court is asked to do. If the court possesses the power, it is certainly its duty to hear the motion which has been made on the part of the United States; for, in cases of the character of that under consideration, its duty and its power are co-extensive with each other. It was observed when the motion was made, and the observation may now be repeated, that the arguments urged on the part of the accused rather prove the motion on the part of the United States unnecessary, or that inconveniencies may arise from it, than the want of a legal right to make it. The first is, that the grand jury being now in session ready to receive an indictment, the attorney for the United States ought to proceed by bill instead of applying to the court, since the only purpose of a commitment is to bring the accused before a grand jury. This statement contains an intrinsic error which destroys its operation. The commitment is not made for the sole purpose of bringing the accused before a grand jury; it is made for the purpose of subjecting him personally to the judgment of the law, and the grand jury is only the first step towards that judgment. If, as has been argued, the commitment was simply to detain the person until a grand jury could be obtained, then its operation would cease on the assembling of a grand jury; but such is not the fact. The order of commitment retains its force while the jury is in session, and if the prosecutor does not proceed, the court is accustomed to retain a prisoner in confinement, or to renew his recognizance to a subsequent term.

The arguments drawn from the general policy of our laws; from the attention which should be bestowed on prosecutions, instituted by special order of the executive;

from the peculiar inconveniencies and hardships of this particular case; from the improper effects which inevitably result from this examination, are some of them subjects for the consideration of those who make the motion, rather than of the court; and others go to the circumspection with which the testimony in support of the motion ought to be weighed, rather than to the duty of hearing it.

It has been said that Colonel Burr already stands charged with treason, and that, therefore, a motion to commit him for the same offence is improper. But the fact is not so understood by the court. The application to charge him with treason was rejected by the judge to whom it was made, because the testimony offered in support of the charge did not furnish probable cause for the opinion that the crime had been committed. After this rejection, Colonel Burr stood, so far as respected his legal liability to have the charge repeated, in precisely the same situation as if it had never been made. He appears in court now as if the crime of treason had never before been alleged against him. That it has been alleged, that the government had had time to collect testimony for the establishment of the fact, that an immense crowd of witnesses are attending for the purpose, that the prosecutor in his own judgment has testimony to support the indictment, are circumstances which may have their influence on the motion for a commitment, or on a continuance, but which cannot deprive the attorney for the United States of the right to make his motion. If he was about to send up a bill to the grand jury, he might move that the person he designed to accuse should be ordered into custody, and it would be in the discretion of the court to grant or to reject the motion.

The court perceives and regrets that the result of this motion may be publications unfavorable to the justice and to the right decision of the case; but if this consequence is to be prevented, it must be by other means than by refusing to hear the motion. No man, feeling a correct sense of the importance which ought to be attached by all to a fair and impartial administration of justice, especially in criminal prosecutions, can view, without extreme solicitude, any attempt which may be made to prejudice the public judgment, and to try any person, not by the laws of his country and the testimony exhibited against him, but by public feelings, which may be and often are artificially excited against the innocent as well as the guilty. But the remedy, for a practice not less dangerous than it is criminal, is not to be obtained by suppressing motions which either party may have a legal right to make.

If it is the choice of the prosecutor on the part of the United States to proceed with this motion, it is the opinion of the court that he may open his testimony.

34

United States v. Burr
25 Fed. Cas. 38, no. 14,692e (C.C.D.Va. 1807)

Marshall, Chief Justice. In point of law, the question now before the court relates to the witness himself. The attorney for the United States offers a paper in cipher, which he supposes to have proceeded from a person against whom he has preferred an indictment for high treason, and another for a misdemeanor, both of which are now before the grand jury, and produces a person said to be the secretary or clerk of the accused, who is supposed either to have copied this paper by his direction, or to be able to prove, in some other manner, that it has proceeded from his authority. To a question demanding whether he understands this paper the witness has declined giving an answer, saying that the answer might criminate himself; and it is referred to the court to decide whether the excuse he has offered be sufficient to prevent his answering the question which has been propounded to him.

It is a settled maxim of law that no man is bound to criminate himself. This maxim forms one exception to the general rule, which declares that every person is compellable to bear testimony in a court of justice. For the witness who considers himself as being within this exception it is alleged that he is, and from the nature of things must be, the sole judge of the effect of his answer; that he is consequently at liberty to refuse to answer any question if he will say upon his oath that his answer to that question might criminate himself.

When this opinion was first suggested, the court conceived the principle laid down at the bar to be too broad, and therefore required that authorities in support of it might be adduced. Authorities have been adduced, and have been considered. In all of them the court could perceive that an answer to the question propounded might criminate the witness, and he was informed that he was at liberty to refuse an answer. These cases do not appear to the court to support the principle laid down by the counsel for the witness in the full latitude in which they have stated it. There is no distinction which takes from the court the right to consider and decide whether any direct answer to the particular question propounded could be reasonably supposed to affect the witness. There may be questions no direct answer to which could, in any degree, affect him; and there is no case which goes so far as to say that he is not bound to answer such questions. The case of Goosely, in this court, is, perhaps, the strongest that has been adduced. But the general doctrine of the judge in that case must have referred to the circumstances, which showed that the answer might criminate him.

When two principles come in conflict with each other, the court must give them both a reasonable construction, so as to preserve them both to a reasonable extent. The principle which entitles the United States to the testimony of every citizen, and the principle by which every witness is privileged not to accuse himself, can neither of them be entirely disregarded. They are believed both to be preserved to a reasonable extent, and according to the true intention of the rule and of the exception to that rule, by observing that course which it is conceived courts have generally observed. It is this:

When a question is propounded, it belongs to the court to consider and to decide whether any direct answer to it can implicate the witness. If this be decided in the negative, then he may answer it without violating the privilege which is secured to him by law. If a direct answer to it may criminate himself, then he must be the sole judge what his answer would be. The court cannot participate with him in this judgment, because they cannot decide on the effect of his answer without knowing what it would be; and a disclosure of that fact to the judges would strip him of the privilege which the law allows, and which he claims. It follows necessarily then, from this statement of things, that if the question be of such a description that an answer to it may or may not criminate the witness, according to the purport of that answer, it must rest with himself, who alone can tell what it would be, to answer the question or not. If, in such a case, he say upon his oath that his answer would criminate himself, the court can demand no other testimony of the fact. If the declaration be untrue, it is in conscience and in law as much a perjury as if he had declared any other untruth upon his oath; as it is one of those cases in which the rule of law must be abandoned, or the oath of the witness be received.

The counsel for the United States have also laid down this rule according to their understanding of it; but they appear to the court to have made it as much too narrow as the counsel for the witness have made it too broad. According to their statement a witness can never refuse to answer any question unless that answer, unconnected with other testimony, would be sufficient to convict him of a crime. This would be rendering the rule almost perfectly worthless. Many links frequently compose that chain of testimony which is necessary to convict any individual of a crime. It appears to the court to be the true sense of the rule that no witness is compellable to furnish any one of them against himself. It is certainly not only a possible but a probable case that a witness, by disclosing a single fact, may complete the testimony against himself, and to every effectual purpose accuse himself as entirely as he would by stating every circumstance which would be required for his conviction. That fact of itself might be unavailing, but all other facts without it would be insufficient. While that remains concealed within his own bosom he is safe; but draw it from thence, and he is exposed to a prosecution. The rule which declares that no man is compellable to accuse himself would most obviously be infringed by compelling a witness to disclose a fact of this description.

What testimony may be possessed, or is attainable, against any individual the court can never know. It would seem, then, that the court ought never to compel a witness to give an answer which discloses a fact that would form a necessary and essential part of a crime which is punishable by the laws.

To apply this reasoning to the particular case under consideration: To know and conceal the treason of another is misprision of treason, and is punishable by law. No witness, therefore, is compellable by law to disclose a fact which would form a necessary and essential part of this crime. If the letter in question contain evidence of treason, which is a fact not dependent on the testimony of the witness before the court, and, therefore, may be proved without the aid of his testimony; and if the witness were acquainted with that treason when the letter was written, he may probably be guilty of misprision of treason, and, therefore, the court ought not to compel him to answer any question, the answer to which might disclose his former knowledge of the contents of that letter.

But if the letter should relate to misdemeanor and not to the treason, the court is not apprized that a knowledge and concealment of the misdemeanor would expose the witness to any prosecution whatever. On this account the court was, at first, disposed to inquire whether the letter could be deciphered, in order to determine from its contents how far the witness could be examined respecting it. The court was inclined to this course from considering the question as one which might require a disclosure of the knowledge which the witness might have had of the contents of this letter when it was put in cipher, or when it was copied by himself; if, indeed, such were the fact. But, on hearing the question more particularly and precisely stated, and finding that it refers only to the present knowledge of the cipher, it appears to the court that the question may be answered without implicating the witness, because his present knowledge would not, it is believed, in a criminal prosecution, justify the inference that his knowledge was acquired previous to this trial, or afford the means of proving that fact.

The court is, therefore, of opinion that the witness may answer the question now propounded.

The gentlemen of the bar will understand the rule laid down by the court to be this: It is the province of the court to judge whether any direct answer to the question which may be proposed will furnish evidence against the witness. If such answer may disclose a fact which forms a necessary and essential link in the chain of testimony, which would be sufficient to convict him of any crime, he is not bound to answer it so as to furnish matter for that conviction. In such a case the witness must himself judge what his answer will be; and if he say on oath that he cannot answer without accusing himself, he cannot be compelled to answer.

35

UNITED STATES V. BURR
25 Fed. Cas. 49, no. 14,692g (C.C.D.Va. 1807)

MARSHALL, Chief Justice. The great value of the trial by jury certainly consists in its fairness and impartiality. Those who most prize the institution, prize it because it furnishes a tribunal which may be expected to be uninfluenced by an undue bias of the mind. I have always conceived, and still conceive, an impartial jury as required by the common law, and as secured by the constitution, must be composed of men who will fairly hear the testimony which may be offered to them, and bring in their verdict according to that testimony, and according to the law arising on it. This is not to be expected, certainly the law does not expect it, where the jurors, before they hear the testimony, have deliberately formed and delivered an opinion that the person whom they are to try is guilty or innocent of the charge alleged against him. The jury should enter upon the trial with minds open to those impressions which the testimony and the law of the case ought to make, not with those preconceived opinions which will resist those impressions. All the provisions of the law are calculated to obtain this end. Why is it that the most distant relative of a party cannot serve upon his jury? Certainly the single circumstance of relationship, taken in itself, unconnected with its consequences, would furnish no objection. The real reason of the rule is, that the law suspects the relative of partiality; suspects his mind to be under a bias, which will prevent his fairly hearing and fairly deciding on the testimony which may be offered to him. The end to be obtained is an impartial jury; to secure this end, a man is prohibited from serving on it whose connexion with a party is such as to induce a suspicion of partiality. The relationship may be remote; the person may never have seen the party; he may declare that he feels no prejudice in the case; and yet the law cautiously incapacitates him from serving on the jury because it suspects prejudice, because in general persons in a similar situation would feel prejudice.

It would be strange if the law was chargeable with the inconsistency of thus carefully protecting the end from being defeated by particular means, and leaving it to be defeated by other means. It would be strange if the law would be so solicitous to secure a fair trial as to exclude a distant, unknown relative from the jury, and yet be totally regardless of those in whose minds feelings existed much more unfavorable to an impartial decision of the case. It is admitted that where there are strong personal prejudices, the person entertaining them is incapacitated as a juror; but it is denied that fixed opinions respecting his guilt constitute a similar incapacity. Why do personal prejudices constitute a just cause of challenge? Solely because the individual who is under their influence is presumed to have a bias on his mind which will prevent an impartial decision of the case, according to the testimony. He may declare that notwithstanding these prejudices he is determined to listen to the evidence, and be governed by it; but the law will not trust him. Is there less reason to suspect him who has prejudged the case, and has deliberately formed and delivered an opinion upon it? Such a person may believe that he will be regulated by testimony, but the law suspects him, and certainly not without reason. He will listen with more favor to that testimony which confirms, than to that which would change his opinion; it is not to be expected that he will weigh evidence or argument as fairly as a man whose judgment is not made up in the case. It is for this

reason that a juror who has once rendered a verdict in a case, or who has been sworn on a jury which has been divided, cannot again be sworn in the same case. He is not suspected of personal prejudices, but he has formed and delivered an opinion, and is therefore deemed unfit to be a juror in the cause.

Were it possible to obtain a jury without any prepossessions whatever respecting the guilt or innocence of the accused, it would be extremely desirable to obtain such a jury; but this is perhaps impossible, and therefore will not be required. The opinion which has been avowed by the court is, that light impressions which may fairly be supposed to yield to the testimony that may be offered, which may leave the mind open to a fair consideration of that testimony, constitute no sufficient objection to a juror; but that those strong and deep impressions which will close the mind against the testimony that may be offered in opposition to them, which will combat that testimony, and resist its force, do constitute a sufficient objection to him. Those who try the impartiality of a juror ought to test him by this rule. They ought to hear the statement made by himself or given by others, and conscientiously determine, according to their best judgment, whether in general men under such circumstances ought to be considered as capable of hearing fairly, and of deciding impartially, on the testimony which may be offered to them, or as possessing minds in a situation to struggle against the conviction which that testimony might be calculated to produce. The court has considered those who have deliberately formed and delivered an opinion on the guilt of the prisoner as not being in a state of mind fairly to weigh the testimony, and therefore as being disqualified to serve as jurors in the case.

This much has been said relative to the opinion delivered yesterday, because the argument of to-day appears to arraign that opinion, and because it seems closely connected with the point which is now to be decided. The question now to be decided is whether an opinion formed and delivered, not upon the full case, but upon an essential part of it, not that the prisoner is absolutely guilty of the whole crime charged in the indictment, but that he is guilty in some of those great points which constitute it, does also disqualify a man in the sense of the law and of the constitution from being an impartial juror. This question was adjourned yesterday for argument and for further consideration. It would seem to the court that to say that any man who had formed an opinion on any fact conducive to the final decision of the case would therefore be considered as disqualified from serving on the jury, would exclude intelligent and observing men, whose minds were really in a situation to decide upon the whole case according to the testimony, and would perhaps be applying the letter of the rule requiring an impartial jury with a strictness which is not necessary for the preservation of the rule itself. But if the opinion formed be on a point so essential as to go far towards a decision of the whole case, and to have a real influence on the verdict to be rendered, the distinction between a person who has formed such an opinion and one who has in his mind decided the whole case appears too slight to furnish the court with solid ground for distinguishing between them. The question must always depend on the strength and nature of the opinion which has been formed. In the case now under consideration, the court would perhaps not consider it as a sufficient objection to a juror that he did believe, and had said, that the prisoner at a time considerably anterior to the fact charged in the indictment entertained treasonable designs against the United States. He may have formed this opinion, and be undecided on the question whether those designs were abandoned or prosecuted up to the time when the indictment charges the overt act to have been committed. On this point his mind may be open to the testimony. Although it would be desirable that no juror should have formed and delivered such an opinion, yet the court is inclined to think it would not constitute sufficient cause of challenge. But if the juror have made up and declared the opinion that to the time when the fact laid in the indictment is said to have been committed the prisoner was prosecuting the treasonable design with which he is charged, the court considers the opinion as furnishing just cause of challenge, and cannot view the juror who has formed and delivered it as impartial, in the legal and constitutional sense of that term.

The cases put by way of illustration appear to the court to be strongly applicable to that under consideration. They are those of burglary, of homicide, and of passing counterfeit money, knowing it to be counterfeit, cases in which the intention and the fact combine to constitute the crime. If, in case of homicide, where the fact of killing was admitted or was doubtful, a juror should have made up and delivered the opinion that, though uninformed relative to the fact of killing, he was confident as to the malice, he was confident that the prisoner had deliberately formed the intention of murdering the deceased, and was prosecuting that intention up to the time of his death, or if on the charge of passing counterfeit bank notes, knowing them to be counterfeit, the juror had declared that, though uncertain as to the fact of passing the notes, he was confident that the prisoner knew them to be counterfeit, few would think such a person sufficiently impartial to try the cause according to testimony. The court considers these cases as strikingly analogous.

It has been insisted that in Callender's Case an opinion was given different from that which is now delivered. I acknowledge that I had not recollected that case accurately. I had thought that Mr. Basset had stated himself to have read the book charged as a libel, and to have formed the opinion that the publication was a libel. I find by a reference to the case itself that I was mistaken; that Mr. Basset had not read the book, and had only said that if it were such a book as it had been represented to him he had no doubt of its being a libel. This was going no further than Mr. Morris has gone, the challenge against whom has been overruled. Mr. Morris had frequently declared that if the allegations against the prisoner were true he was guilty, and Mr. Morris was determined to be an impartial juror.

With respect to the general question put in Callender's Case, the court considers it as the same with the general question put in this case. It was, "Have you made up and delivered the opinion that the prisoner is guilty or innocent of the charge laid in the indictment?" That is in substance, "Have you made up and delivered the opinion that the prisoner has been guilty of publishing a false, wicked, and malicious libel, which subjects him to punishment, under the act of congress on which he is indicted?" The same question is now substantially put. Explanatory questions are now put when they are necessary, and certain explanatory questions might have been put in Callender's Case, had they been necessary. Had the case of Mr. Basset even been such as I thought it, had he read "The Prospect Before Us," and thought it a libel, without deciding who was its author, he would have gone no further than to have formed an opinion that certain allegations were libellous, which is not dissimilar to the opinion that certain acts amount to treason. If, for example, a juror had said that levying an army for the purpose of subverting the government of the United States by force, and arraying that army in a warlike manner, amounted to treason, no person could suppose him on that account unfit to serve on the jury. The opinion would be one in which all must concur, and so was the opinion that "The Prospect Before Us" was a libel. Without determining whether the case put by Hawk. bk. 2, c. 43, § 28, be law or not, it is sufficient to observe that this case is totally different. The opinion which is there declared to constitute no cause of challenge is one formed by the juror on his own knowledge; in this case the opinion is formed on report and newspaper publications.

The argument drawn from the situation of England during the rebellions of 1715 and 1745, with respect to certain prominent characters whose situations made it a matter of universal notoriety that they were the objects of the law, is founded entirely on the absolute necessity of the case, and the total and obvious impossibility of obtaining a jury whose minds were not already made up. Where this necessity exists the rule perhaps must bend to it, but the rule will bend no further than is required by actual necessity. The court cannot believe that at present the necessity does exist. The cases bear no resemblance to each other. There has not been such open, notorious war as to force conviction on every bosom respecting the fact and the intention. It is believed that a jury may be obtained composed of men who, whatever their general impressions may be, have not deliberately formed and delivered an opinion respecting the guilt or innocence of the accused.

In reflecting on this subject, which I have done very seriously since the adjournment of yesterday, my mind has been forcibly impressed by contemplating the question precisely in its reverse. If, instead of a panel composed of gentlemen who had almost unanimously formed and publicly delivered an opinion that the prisoner was guilty, the marshal had returned one composed of persons who had openly and publicly maintained his innocence; who had insisted that, notwithstanding all the testimony in possession of the public, they had no doubt that his designs were perfectly innocent; who had been engaged in repeated, open and animated altercation to prove him innocent, and that his objects were entirely opposite to those with which he was charged—would such men be proper and impartial jurors? I cannot believe they would be thought so. I am confident I should not think them so. I cannot declare a juror to be impartial who has advanced opinions against the prisoner which would be cause of challenge if advanced in his favor.

The opinion of the court is that to have made up and delivered the opinion that the prisoner entertained the treasonable designs with which he is charged, and that he retained those designs and was prosecuting them when the act charged in the indictment is alleged to have been committed, is good cause of challenge.

36

United States v. Charles
25 Fed. Cas. 409, no. 14,786 (C.C.D.C. 1813)

Indictment for arson. Mr. Lufborough, the magistrate before whom the prisoner was brought, told him there was evidence enough to commit him at all events, and therefore he had better confess the whole truth, and that probably he would fare the better for it.

THE COURT (nem. con.) refused to suffer the confession to be given in evidence against the prisoner. Peake, Ev. 13; McNal. Ev. 42.

Mr. Jones, for United States, then called some of the grand jurors to testify as to what he swore when examined by the grand jury as a witness against negro Jacob Bruce.

Mr. Key and Mr. Morsell objected, that what he swore cannot be given in evidence against him. McNal. Ev. 47.

But THE COURT overruled the objection.

Mr. Rapine, one of the grand jurors, testified that the prisoner was not told that he need not answer any questions tending to criminate himself.

Mr. Key objected to the evidence for want of such caution to the prisoner.

But THE COURT said that the prisoner was presumed to know the law in his favor, without such caution.

Doctor Ott testified, that on the day after the examination of the prisoner by Mr. Lufborough, he was examined by Doctor Ott and Mr. Lufborough as a witness against Jacob Bruce; and after being told that if what he had before stated was not true, he might retract, made the same declaration.

Mr. Key objected, that the prisoner might have been influenced by the hope and fear excited by Mr. Lufborough on the former day. McNal. Ev. 43.

But THE COURT overruled the objection.

The jury found the prisoner guilty, but recommended him to mercy on account of his youth and apparent candor.

On the next day the counsel for the prisoner moved for a new trial, because the confessions of the prisoner, made upon oath, in his examination before the grand jury as a witness against negro Jacob Bruce, were permitted to be given in evidence against him by the testimony of grand jurors.

Mr. Key, for prisoner. There is no case in the books in which a grand juror has been permitted to give such testimony. 12 Vin. Abr. tit. "Evidence," H, pls. 20, 38. Judge Foster refused to suffer a grand juror to disclose the evidence, because sworn to keep secret, &c. So the clerk of the grand jury shall not be allowed to reveal that which was given in evidence before the inquest. McNal. Ev. 253.

Mr. Jones, contra. The rule of law that a witness is not bound to answer any question tending to criminate himself, would be useless if his declarations upon oath could not be given in evidence against him. The same rule applies to an examination before a grand jury. McNal. Ev. 246, 250, 253, 254. General Wilkinson, in Burr's trial, was protected by the rule from testifying anything which might criminate himself; and grand jurors were sworn to testify what General Wilkinson testified before them, to discredit his oath in court. U. S. v. Burr [Case No. 14,692a]. The grand juror's oath only prevents a disclosure of confidential communications by the public functionaries, or by a grand juror to his fellow jurors; it does not prevent him from disclosing when called upon in a judicial manner. The grand jury may hear evidence at the bar (2 Hale, P. C. 159, 160): and it is the practice of the general court in Virginia, in cases of difficulty before the grand jury, to call them to the bar, and have witnesses examined, and to instruct them upon the evidence, as in trials at bar. The grand jury are only to keep secret the king's counsel.

Mr. Key, in reply. The reason of the rule is the confidential nature of the communication. It is on the same reason that the magistrate, or counsel, shall not disclose what is committed to them. The oath of the grand juror forbids him to disclose any thing. It is all "the counsel of the United States." It is a high misdemeanor in a grand juror to inform the accused of the evidence which has been given against him before the grand jury. 4 Bl. Comm. 126, Tucker's note. The oath in Virginia is different, and that is the reason given by the chief justice, in Burr's case, for permitting Mr. Tazewell, one of the grand jurors, to be examined. The case of a popish priest, is a case of private confidence only; it is not imposed by the law of the land.

If the prisoner has been once induced to confess, by a promise or threat, it is the common practice to reject a subsequent confession of the same, or like facts. In one case it was admitted by Buller, J., but he observed that there must be very strong evidence of an explicit warning by the magistrate not to rely on any expected favor on that account; and it ought most clearly to appear that the prisoner thoroughly understood such warning before his subsequent confession can be given in evidence. 2 East, Crown Law, p. 658. c. 16. § 94.

THE COURT (THRUSTON, Circuit Judge, absent) granted a new trial because the first confession of the prisoner had been made under the impression of fear and hope excited by the observations of the magistrate, (Mr. Lufborough.) And no subsequent confession of the same facts ought to be given against him, according to the law as stated in 2 East, Crown Law. c. 16. § 94.

37

MEADE v. DEPUTY MARSHAL
1 Marshall's C.C. 324 (C.C.D.Va. 1815)

MARSHALL, C.J.: The Constitution of the United States, gives power to congress, "to provide for calling forth the militia to execute the laws of the Union," &c.

In the execution of this power, it is not doubted, that congress may provide the means of punishing those who shall fail to obey the requisitions, made in pursuance of the laws of the Union, and may prescribe the mode of proceeding against such delinquents, and the tribunal before which such proceedings should be had. Indeed, it would seem reasonable to expect, that all the proceedings against delinquents, should rest on the authority of that power, which had been offended by the delinquency.

This idea must be retained, whilst considering the acts of congress. The first section of the act of 1795, authorizes the president, "whenever the United States shall be invaded, or be in imminent danger of invasion," &c., "to call forth such number of the militia of the state, or states, most convenient to the place of danger, or scene of action, as he may judge necessary, to repel such invasion, and to issue his orders for that purpose, to such officer, or officers of the militia, as he shall think proper."

The fifth section enacts, "That every officer, non-commissioned officer, or private of the militia, who shall fail to obey the order of the President of the United States, in any of the cases before recited, shall forfeit a sum, not exceeding one year's pay, and not less than one month's pay, to be determined and adjudged by a court martial."

The sixth section enacts, "That courts martial, for the trial of militia, shall be composed of militia officers only."

Upon these sections, depends the question, whether courts martial for the assessment of fines against delinquent militia-men, should be constituted under the authority of the United States, or of the state to which the delinquent belongs. The idea orginally suggested, that the tribunal for the trial of the offence, should be constituted by, or derive its authority from, the government against which the offence had been committed, would seem to require, that the court thus referred to in general terms, should be a court sitting under the authority of the United States. It would be reasonable to expect, if the power were to be devolved on the court of a state government, that more explicit terms would be used for conveying it. And it seems, also, to be a reasonable construction, that the legislature, when in the sixth section, providing a court martial for the trial of militia, held in mind the offences described in the preceding section, and to be submitted to a court martial. If the offences described in the fifth section, are to be tried by a court, constituted according to the provisions of the sixth section, then we should be led by the language of that section, to suppose, that congress had in

contemplation a court formed of officers in actual service, since the provision that it should be composed "of militia officers only," would otherwise be nugatory.

This construction derives some aid from the act of 1814. By that act, courts martial for the trial of offences, such as that with which Mr. Meade is charged, are to be appointed according to the rules prescribed by the articles of war. The court in the present case, is not appointed according to those rules.

The only argument which occurs to me against this reasoning, grows out of the inconvenience arising from trying delinquent militia-men, who remain at home, by a court martial, composed of officers in actual service.

This inconvenience may be great, and well deserves the consideration of congress; but I doubt whether it is sufficient to justify a judge, in so construing a law, as to devolve on courts, sitting under the authority of the state, a power which, in its nature, belongs to the United States.

If, however, this should be the proper construction, then the court must be constituted according to the laws of the state.

On examining the laws of Virginia, it appears, that no court martial can be called for the assessment of fines, or for the trial of privates, not in actual service. This duty is performed by courts of inquiry, and a second court must sit to receive the excuses of those against whom a previous court may have assessed fines, before the sentence becomes final, or can be executed.

If it be supposed, that the act of congress has conferred the jurisdiction against delinquent militia privates on courts martial, constituted as those are for the trial of officers, still this court has proceeded in such a manner, that its sentence cannot be sustained.

It is a principle of natural justice, which courts are never at liberty to dispense with, unless under the mandate of positive law, that no person shall be condemned unheard, or without an opportunity of being heard. There is no law authorizing courts martial to proceed against any person, without notice. Consequently, such proceeding is entirely unlawful. In the case of the courts of inquiry, sitting under the authority of the state, the practice has, I believe, prevailed, to proceed in the first instance, without notice; but this inconvenience is, in some degree remedied, by a second court, and I am by no means prepared for such a construction of the act, as would justify rendering the sentence final, without substantial notice. But, be this as it may, this is a court martial, not a court of inquiry, and no law exists, authorizing a court martial to proceed without notice, as in this case, the court appears to have proceeded. For these reasons, I consider its sentences as entirely nugatory, and do, therefore, direct the petitioner to be discharged from the custody of the marshal.

38

People v. Casborus
13 Johns. R. 351 (N.Y. 1816)

39

State v. Edwards
2 Nott. & McC. 376 (S.C. 1819)

SPENCER, J., delivered the opinion of the Court. The defendant, on his arraignment, pleaded, that he had before been indicted, tried, and convicted, for the same felony; that, upon his motion, the judgment had been arrested, and that he had been discharged from that judgment. It is admitted, that the former and present indictment are, in every respect, similar. To this plea the district attorney demurred; the plea was overruled, and the defendant was thereupon tried and convicted, and sentenced to imprisonment in the state prison.

It was decided in the case of *The People* v. *Barret & Ward,* (1 *Johns. Rep.* 66.) that a person, after an acquittal, might be indicted and tried the second time, if the first indictment was erroneous, so that no good judgment could be given upon it; and where a Court of competent jurisdiction arrest a judgment at the instance of the defendant, it must be intended, legally, that the indictment was vicious, for the judgment cannot be reviewed on a writ of error; as an arrest of judgment is a mere refusal, on the part of the Court, to give judgment, every Court is bound to pay that respect to a Court of co-ordinate jurisdiction, as to presume its judgment to be according to law, when it is presented for consideration collaterally.

The effect of arresting a judgment is the same as quashing an indictment; the latter happens before trial, the former after; and, in this case, it appears to me, that as no writ of error could be brought upon the decision of the Court of Sessions arresting the judgment, that proceeding is not a bar to any other for the same matter. In analogy to civil cases, the arrest of judgment cannot be pleaded in bar to another prosecution for the same matter, because there is no judgment of the Court susceptible of review.

It is stated here, that the two indictments are, in every respect, similar; but this is not so pleaded, and, if it had been, the consequence would be the same; as already observed, in this collateral way, we must presume, from the judgment being arrested, that the indictment was erroneous, and if erroneous, then a conviction would not bar another good indictment. It is in vain to say, either that the former indictment was good, or that this, being like it, must be holden to be bad also, because the other was adjudged to be bad. We must take it as a settled point, that the other indictment was bad, however the fact may be; and we are not to be told, that this is a bad indictment, merely on the authority of the sessions. We must see if it be bad, and this is not even pretended.

For these reasons, I think the plea of *auterfois acquit* was properly overruled, and such is the opinion of the Court.

COLCOCK, J. I presume no rule, on the subject of evidence, is better established than that a witness shall not be bound to criminate himself. The only difficulty arises in the application of the rule. It must be admitted, that if the question has a tendency to criminate the witness, according to the rule, he is not bound to answer. But it is said, the Court should decide this point, as to some questions. It is utterly impossible, that the Court can decide without possessing a full and complete knowledge of all the facts which it may be important for the witness to conceal: therefore something must necessarily be left to the witness; and we have the same security for a knowledge of the fact, that he may be implicated by the answer, that we have for the knowledge of any other fact.

It was urged, that an ignorant man might not be able to decide. The Court will always so instruct a witness as to enable him, if he possess any understanding, to determine whether he may be jeopardized by the answer; and if the answer may form one link, in a chain of testimony, against him, he is not bound to answer. Phillips on Evid. Dunlap's Ed. 206. 2 Espinasse Dig. 405, 16 Vesey, jun'r. 242. McNally, 257. *King* v. *I. G. Cordon,* 2 Douglass, 595. *Honeywood* v. *Selwin,* 3 Atkins, 276. *Gates* v. *Hardacre,* 3 Taunton, 424. Under the Act against duelling, all who counsel one to fight, as well as the seconds who are engaged, are made liable to the penalties. If the witness stood in either of these relations, he might be implicated by answering the question. It is not necessary that the privity of the witness should at once appear by the answer; nor will it be contended, that, that would have been the case here; but it may have formed a link in a chain of testimony extracted from him, or obtained from other sources, which may have tended to criminate him. It was contended, that on a cross-examination, the witness may have refused to answer any question which had a tendency to criminate him; but that this question did not tend to criminate him. This appeared to admit the whole argument of the counsel for defendant; for both the Court and the witness thought it might when connected with other matters, produce the consequence. But supposing the answer had not such tendency, and that the State had closed there, the defendant upon his cross-examination, would naturally have asked at what time and place, and under what circumstances, was the confession made. I presume it will be admitted, that an answer to this might have implicated the witness—that he was permitted to refuse to answer—that would be the result. Could it be expected that the defendant would be convicted on the garbled testimony of a witness, and that too of so high a misdemeanor? I presume not. If, then, there be any doubt as to the tendency of the question, I think it is obvious another would have removed the doubt; and therefore, that the presiding judge decided correctly, that the witness should not be compelled to answer the question. Although we may regret, the act is defective, yet we have no power to legislate on the subject. It must be referred to the proper tribunal. I do not conceive that the doctrine is calculated (as was contended,) to protect reluctant witnesses generally. For it is clear, that if a witness swear he may be implicated in the guilt of the accused if he answer, and this afterwards appear to be false, he would be liable to an indictment for perjury. It is admitted, that it might be difficult of proof; but if that were to be an objection, much testimony, which is daily received, might be excluded. Suppose a witness called to prove the acknowledgments of a defendant, which was to operate against him, should swear, that it was made to him when alone, or to him, in the presence of a person at that time dead, and this should be false. How, I ask, could he be convicted of perjury? It was necessary that an opinion should be expressed on this point, as it may render some alteration in the act necessary.

But on the question, whether such an appeal can be sustained, I entertain no doubt. I think I may venture to say, that no case can be found where a new trial has been granted after acquittal, unless where it has been effected by the fraud or artifice of the accused. In the case of the *King* v. *Mawley,* and three others, (from 6 Term Rep. p. 620 to 640,) two were convicted, and two acquitted. The Court were clearly of opinion, and so ordered, that a new trial should be granted, as to those who had been found guilty. The difficulty was, how they should be separated, on the second trial. Two modes were suggested. One was, to alter the venue; the other, to make an entry on the record, that two had been improperly convicted, and then to award a new trial, as to them. Lord Kenyon says, (*Id.* 640,) "I do not know that the first mode is objectionable. The second mode suggested has already been adopted. It was so in *Rex* v. *Robbins,*" and of course, I conclude it was adopted by them. I confess, that, at first, it did strike me, that perhaps, a distinction might be made when the testimony, relied on by the State, had been unexpectedly excluded. But I am satisfied, that all cases, however determined, must stand on the same footing in this respect.

When a criminal case is put to a jury, it cannot be withdrawn, except by the consent of the accused, or by some unavoidable accident to one of the jury or the Court. The State, therefore, is bound to be ready when the case is put to the jury. I am against the motion on all the grounds.

GANTT and JOHNSON, JJ., concurred.

40

PEOPLE v. GOODWIN
18 Johns. R. 187 (N.Y. 1820)

SPENCER, Ch. J., delivered the opinion of the court. A motion has been made to discharge the defendant, on the ground that it appears, by the return to the *certiorari,* that he has been once tried, and, therefore, cannot legally be tried again. He was indicted in the Sessions in *New-York* for manslaughter; the trial continued for five days, and the jury, after having received the charge of the court, retired to consider of their verdict; were kept together 17 hours, and, declaring there was no probability of their agreeing on their verdict, were discharged after 11 o'clock at night, on the last day in which the court could sit. It appears that the jury had, in the mean time, between their receiving the charge of the court, and their discharge, come into court, and, on being asked if they had agreed on their verdict, answered, through their foreman, that they had agreed, and that they found the prisoner guilty, but recommended him to mercy; but, on being polled, the third juror called upon, declared his disagreement to the verdict. These are all the facts material to be noticed in considering the present motion.

The defendant's counsel rely, principally, on the 5th article of the amendments to the constitution of the *United States,* which contains this provision: *"Nor shall any person be subject for the same offence, to be twice put in jeopardy of life or limb."* It has been urged by the prisoner's counsel, that this constitutional provision operates upon state courts *proprio vigore.* This has been denied on the other side. I do not consider it material whether this provision be considered as extending to the state tribunals or not; the principle is a sound and fundamental one of the common law, that no man shall be twice put in jeopardy of life or limb for the same offence. I am, however, inclined to the opinion, that the article in question does extend to all judicial tribunals in the *United States,* whether constituted by the Congress of the *United States,* or the states individually. The provision is general in its nature, and unrestricted in its terms; and the sixth article of the constitution declares, that that constitution shall be the supreme law of the land; and the judges in every state shall be bound thereby, any thing in the constitution or laws of any state to the contrary notwithstanding. These general and comprehensive expressions extend the provisions of the constitution of the *United States* to every article which is not confined, by the subject matter, to the national government, and is equally applicable to the states. Be this as it may, the principle is undeniable, that no person can be twice put in jeopardy of life or limb, for the same offence.

The expression, *jeopardy of limb,* was used in reference to the nature of the offence, and not to designate the punishment for an offence; for no such punishment as loss of limb was inflicted by the laws of any of the states, at the adoption of the constitution. Punishment by deprivation of the limbs of the offender would be abhorrent to the feelings and opinions of the enlightened age in which the constitution was adopted, and it had grown into disuse in *England,* for a long period antecedently. We must understand the term, "jeopardy of limb," as referring to offences which, in former ages, were punishable by dismemberment, and as intending to comprise the crimes denominated in the law, felonies. The crime of manslaughter is, undoubtedly, a felony; and therefore, the prisoner is entitled to the protection afforded by the article of the constitution, whether we regard it as binding upon us by its own force, or as an acknowledged axiom of the common law.

The question then recurs, What is the meaning of the rule that no person shall be subject, for the same offence, to be twice put in jeopardy of life or limb? Upon the fullest consideration which I have been able to bestow on the subject, I am satisfied that it means no more than this: *that no man shall be twice tried for the same offence.* Should it be said, that we can scarcely conceive, that a maxim so universally acknowledged, and so interwoven with our institutions, should need an explicit and solemn recognition in the fundamental principles of the government of the *United States,* we have only to recur to the history of that period, and to some other of the amendments, in proof of the assertion, that there existed such a jealousy or extreme caution, on the part of the state governments, as to require an explicit avowal in that instrument, of some of the plainest and best established principles in relation to the rights of the citizens, and the rules of the common law. The first article of the amendments prohibits Congress from making any law respecting an establishment of religion, or prohibiting the free exercise thereof, or abridging the freedom of speech, or of the press, or of the right of the people peaceably to assemble and petition government for a redress of grievances; the second secures the right of the people to bear arms; and, indeed, without going into them minutely, nearly all the amendments to that instrument indicate either great precaution in defining the powers of the national government, and the rights of the people and the states, or they evince a jealousy and apprehension that those fundamental rights might be impugned, so as to leave no doubt that, in the article under consideration, no new principle was intended to be introduced. The test by which to decide whether a person has been once tried, is perfectly familiar to every lawyer—it can only be by a plea of *auterfois acquit,* or a plea of *auterfois convict.* The plea of a former acquittal, Judge *Blackstone* says, (4 *Com.* 335.) is grounded on this universal maxim of the common law of *England,* that no man is to be brought into jeopardy of his life more than once for the same offence; and hence (he says) it is allowed as a consequence, that where a man is once fairly found not guilty upon an indictment, or other prosecution, before any court having competent jurisdiction of the offence, he may plead such acquittal in bar of any subsequent accusation for the same crime. The plea of a former conviction depends on the same principle, that no man ought twice to be brought in danger for the same crime. To render the plea of a former acquittal, a bar, it must be a legal acquittal, by judgment, upon a trial for substantially the same offence, and the verdict of a petit jury. (1 *Chitty's Crim. Law,* 372.) In the present case, it is not pretended that the prisoner has been acquitted, unless the discharge of the jury, without having agreed upon their verdict, and without the prisoner's consent, shall amount, in judgment of law, to an acquittal. This brings us to the question, whether the Court of Sessions could discharge the jury, under the circumstances of this case. If they could not, then I should be of the opinion, that, although there could be no technical plea of *auterfois acquit,*

the same matter might be moved in arrest of judgment; and, if so, I can see no objection to the discussion of the question in its present shape, on a motion to discharge the prisoner.

In the case of the *People v. Olcott,* (2 *Johns. Cases,* 301.) all the authorities then extant upon the power of the court to discharge a jury in criminal cases, and the consequences of such discharge, were very ably and elaborately examined by Mr. Justice *Kent;* and it would be an unpardonable waste of time to enter upon a re-examination of them. In that case, the jury, after having remained out from 8 o'clock on *Saturday* evening, until near two o'clock the next day, and having, in the mean while, come into court two or three times for advice, declared there was no prospect of their agreeing in any verdict, and were discharged without the consent of the prisoner: One of the questions was, whether the discharge of the jury entitled the defendant to be discharged, or whether he could be re-tried. After examining and commenting on all the authorities, the position of the learned judge was this: "If the court are satisfied that the jury have made long and unavailing efforts to agree, that they are so far exhausted as to be incapable of further discussion and deliberation, this becomes a case of necessity, and requires an interference." He observed, "all the authorities admit that, when any juror becomes mentally disabled, by sickness or intoxication, it is proper to discharge the jury; and whether the mental inability be produced by sickness, fatigue or incurable prejudice, the application of the principle must be the same." Again, he observed, "every question of this kind must rest with the court, under all the particular or peculiar circumstances of the case. There is no alternative—either the court must determine when it is requisite to discharge, or the rule must be inflexible, that, after the jury are once sworn, no other jury can, in any court, be sworn and charged in the same cause. The moment cases of necessity are admitted to form exceptions, that moment a door is opened to the discretion of the court to judge of that necessity, and to determine what combination of circumstances will create one." The learned judge inveighs, with force and eloquence, against the monstrous doctrine of compelling a jury to unanimity, by the pains of hunger and fatigue, so that the verdict is not founded on temperate discussion, but on strength of body. Although the case of the *People v. Olcott* was a case of misdemeanor, the reasoning is, in my judgment, entirely applicable to cases of felony; and, although the opinion was confined to the case under consideration, a perusal of it will show that it embraces every possible case of a trial for crimes. The opinion was delivered in 1801, and since that time this question has come under consideration in several cases. In the case of the *King v. Edwards,* (4 *Taunt. Rep.* 309.) the indictment was for a felony; and while the prosecutor was giving his evidence, one of the jurors fell down in a fit, and he was pronounced by a physician, on oath, incapable of proceeding in his duty as a juryman on that day; whereupon the jury was discharged, and a new jury sworn, and the defendant was convicted. The point whether the prisoner could be tried, after the discharge of the jury, without consent, was argued before all the judges in *England,* except *Mans-*

field, Chief Justice, and *Lawrence*, Justice; all the cases were cited, and the judges, without hearing the counsel for the crown, said, that it had been decided in so many cases, it was now the settled law of the country, and gave judgment against the prisoner. The same course was adopted, upon nearly the same state of facts, in *Ann Scalbert's* case; (*Leach's C. C.* 706.) and in the case of the *King* v. *Stevenson*, (*Leach's C. C.* 618.) the prisoner fell down in a fit during the trial, and the jury was discharged, and, upon his recovery, he was tried and convicted by another jury. In the case of the *United States* v. *Coolidge*, (2 *Gallis. Rep.* 364.) a witness refusing to be sworn, the trial was suspended during the imprisonment of the witness for the contempt, and Mr. Justice *Story* held, that the discretion to discharge a jury existed in all cases; but that it was to be exercised only in very extraordinary and striking circumstances. In the case of the *Commonwealth* v. *Bowden*, (9 *Mass. Rep.* 494.) upon an indictment for highway robbery, the jury, after a full hearing of the cause, being confined together during part of a day, and a whole night, returned into court, and informed the judge that they had not agreed on a verdict, and it was not probable they ever could agree; whereupon, one of the jurors was withdrawn from the panel, without the defendant's consent, and the jury were discharged, and during the same term, another jury was impanneled for his trial, and he was found guilty. On a motion in arrest of judgment, the court refused the motion, saying that the ancient strictness of the law upon this subject had very much abated in the *English* courts; that it would neither be consistent with the genius of our government or laws, to use compulsory means to effect an agreement among jurors; that the practice of withdrawing a juror, where there existed no prospect of a verdict, had frequently been adopted in criminal trials in that court.

Upon full consideration, I am of opinion that, although the power of discharging a jury is a delicate and highly important trust, yet, that it does exist in cases of extreme and absolute necessity; and that it may be exercised without operating as an acquittal of the defendant; that it extends as well to felonies as misdemeanors; and that it exists, and may discreetly be exercised in cases where the jury, from the length of time they have been considering a cause, and their inability to agree, may be fairly presumed as never likely to agree, unless compelled so to do from the pressing calls of famine or bodily exhaustion. And, in the present case, considering the great length of time the jury had been out, that the period for which the court could legally sit, was nearly terminated, and that it was morally certain the jury could not agree before the court must adjourn, I think the exercise of the power was discreet and legal. Much stress has been placed on the fact, that the defendant was in jeopardy during the time the jury were deliberating. It is true, that his situation was critical, and there was, as regards him, danger, that the jury might agree on a verdict of guilty; but, in a legal sense, he was not in jeopardy, so that it would exonerate him from another trial. He has not been tried for the offence imputed to him; to render the trial complete and perfect, there should have been a verdict, either for or against him. A literal observance of the constitutional provision would extend to and embrace those cases where, by the visitation of God, one of the jurors should either die, or become utterly unable to proceed in the trial. It would extend, also, to a case where the defendant himself should be seized with a fit, and become incapable of attending to his defence; and it would extend to a case where the jury were necessarily discharged in consequence of the termination of the powers of the court. In a legal sense, therefore, a defendant is not once put in jeopardy, until the verdict of the jury is rendered for or against him; and if for or against him, he can never be drawn in question again for the same offence. I entirely concur in reprobating the proceeding of withdrawing a juror, and attempting to subject a person to a second trial, because the public prosecutor was not prepared with his proofs. In the case of the *People* v. *Barrett & Ward*, (2 *Caines's Rep.* 304.) this court considered it equivalent to an acquittal.

41

UNITED STATES V. MILLER
26 Fed. Cas. 1254, no. 15,772 (C.C.D.C. 1821)

Indictment [against Samuel Miller] for fighting a duel with one R. Smith. Doctor John A. Kearney, a witness for the United States, was asked whether he saw the defendant shoot at Smith. The witness objected to answer, and said that he could not answer the question without disclosing a fact which might be material and important evidence to criminate himself as participator in the same offence for which the prisoner then stood indicted.

Mr. Jones, for defendant, in behalf of the witness, contended that he was not bound to answer the question, because it might compel him to disclose a fact which would be a necessary link in the chain of evidence to support a prosecution against himself, if such a one should be instituted, for being concerned in the same misdemeanor, and cited the opinion of Chief Justice Marshall, in Burr's Case [Case No. 14,693], in which he says: "The gentlemen of the bar will understand the rule laid down by the court to be this: It is the province of the court to judge whether any direct answer to the question which may be proposed will furnish evidence against the witness. If such answer may disclose a fact which forms a necessary and essential link in the chain of testimony which would be sufficient to convict him of any crime, he is not bound to answer it so as to furnish matter for that conviction. In such a case the witness must himself judge what his answer will be; and if he says on oath that he cannot answer without accusing himself, he cannot be compelled to answer." Mr. Jones also cited St. 46 Geo. III. c. 37; Peake, Ev. 128, 134, 138, 139, 160, 161, 167, 184; Phil. Ev. 206; Rex v. Edwards, 4 Term R. 440; Rex v. Inhabitants of Castell Careinion, 8 East. 77; Cooke's Case, 1 Salk. 153, 4 State Tr. 748; Lord Geo. Gordon's Case, Doug. 593; Title v. Grevett, Ld. Raym. 1008; Cates v. Hardacre, 3 Taunt. 424; People v. Herrick, 13

Johns. 82; U. S. v. Burr [Case No. 14,693]; 4 Bl. Comm. 329; 1 Hale, P. C. 301; McNal. Ev. 256. The fact that the witness was present at the duel was a fact which it would be necessary to prove upon a prosecution against him for being concerned in the misdemeanor. He could not answer the question affirmatively, therefore, without furnishing matter for his conviction.

THE COURT, however (CRANCH, Chief Judge, contra), was of opinion that no direct answer to the question could furnish evidence against the witness, and that he was bound to answer it. This the witness still refused to do; and THE COURT committed him for the contempt. He petitioned the supreme court of the United States for a writ of habeas corpus, at February term, 1822, but it was refused upon the ground that that court had no appellate jurisdiction in criminal causes. [Ex parte Kearney] 7 Wheat. [20 U. S.] 38.

42

COMMONWEALTH v. COOK
6 Serg. & Rawle 577 (Pa. 1822)

TILGHMAN, C. J.—A bill of indictment having been found against the three prisoners during the present session of this Court, for the murder of *Samuel Alwine*, they put in a plea, supposed by them to be of the same import as a plea of *autrefois acquit*, to which the attorney for the Commonwealth demurred, and the prisoners joined in demurrer. The prisoners have likewise entered on the record a motion to be discharged from this indictment for the same reasons as are set forth in their plea. The plea is, in substance, as follows: That at a former Court of Oyer and Terminer, held before the Judges of the Court of Common Pleas for the county of *Philadelphia*, in the months of *April* and *May* last, they were indicted for the same murder, whereupon they pleaded *not guilty*, and issue having been joined, a jury was sworn, evidence given for the Commonwealth and for themselves, pleadings of counsel heard on both sides, and a charge delivered by the Court to the jury. At half an hour past nine in the evening of the 1st *May*, the jury retired to consider of their verdict. They returned to the Court several times, without having agreed, and being sent back by the Court, they came in for the last time about half past twelve in the afternoon of the 2d *May*, having been out in the whole about fifteen hours. Being then asked whether they had agreed on their verdict, they answered, that they had agreed as to two of the prisoners, and had not agreed as to the third, nor was there the least probability of their agreeing. Thereupon, the Court refused to permit the jury to pronounce the verdict which they had agreed upon, *and without, and against the consent of the prisoners*, the jury were discharged by the Court from saying any thing of their verdict in and upon the premises.

Before I enter on the question, I think proper to declare, that I have no doubt of the integrity of the learned Court by which this jury was discharged. And however my opinion may differ from theirs, it must be confessed, that as to the general discretionary power of discharging juries, they are not without countenance from Judges of high character in other States.

In considering this matter, I shall confine my opinion to the case before the Court, which is a case of *murder*, a crime of which one species, viz: of the *first degree*, is punishable by our laws with death.

Concerning the power of the Court to discharge a jury in a *capital* case, Judges have not always agreed. It is one of those questions which remained long unsettled, nor even yet has any general rule been established which embraces all cases. Indeed, from the nature of the thing, such a rule is not to be expected. The judges have, therefore, thought it safest to decide, from time to time, the cases which have been brought before them, taking care not to commit themselves on general principles. There is, indeed, one principle which cannot be contradicted, and that is, that the jury may be discharged in cases of *absolute necessity;* but what constitutes that necessity has been ascertained only in the particular cases that have arisen. There was an ancient tradition among the *English* lawyers, that a jury charged in a *capital* case, could not be discharged without giving a verdict, *even with the consent of the attorney general and the prisoner.* This is laid down for law by Sir EDWARD COKE, in his 1 *Inst.* 227b. and 3 *Inst.* 110. It is a doctrine altogether unreasonable; for why should not the jury be discharged, when it is desired by all parties interested in the verdict? Accordingly, we find that it could not stand, though supported by so great a name. Lord COKE cited a case in the *Year Books,* 21 *Edw. III.*, which being thoroughly examined, was found not to support his opinion. The matter was fully discussed in the case of the *Kinlocks, Foster,* 22, and the law, *in cases of consent,* settled on a foundation too firm to be be shaken. The *Kinlocks* having been indicted for treason, pleaded *not guilty,* and were put upon their trial; and after the jury were sworn, they asked permission to withdraw their plea, in order to plead another matter of which they were advised they could not have the advantage on the general issue. Leave was given, with the consent of the attorney general, and a juror withdrawn, after which their second plea being overruled, they were tried by another jury and convicted of high treason. They then moved in arrest of judgment, because the first jury had been discharged; but it was decided by nine Judges against WRIGHT, (the only dissentient,) that the discharge of the jury was legal, and judgment was pronounced against the prisoners. We may conclude, then, that in cases of consent, *fairly given, where the prisoner is assisted by counsel, and the discharge of the jury is intended for his benefit,* they may be discharged without giving a verdict. But that is not the present case, for the prisoners *expressly dissented.* If the proceedings of the Court can be supported, then it must be on the principle of *necessity.* And it is contended, that upon this ground it may be supported, because, when the jury are so exhausted as not to be able to continue their deliberations, they must either be discharged or perish. If that were the alternative, no doubt

281

they ought to be discharged; but I cannot perceive any such necessity on this record, although the Court appears to have recorded very fairly all the circumstances of the case. Indeed, as to two of the prisoners, there was evidently no necessity, because, as to them, the jury were prepared, and offered to give their verdict. I presume the Court was of opinion that the verdict could not be taken unless it embraced all the prisoners, and, therefore, the necessity extended to all. If the law were so, it would certainly be a reflection on the administration of justice; for it is flagrantly unjust that one who had put himself for life or death on a jury of the country, and had satisfied that jury of his innocence, after a full hearing of the evidence, the pleadings of course on both sides, and the charge of the Court, should be deprived of the benefit of a verdict, because the jury could not agree on the guilt or innocence of *another person* who happened to be tried with him. If the prisoners had been tried by different juries, as they might have been, though charged in the same indictment, no question of this kind could have arisen. And yet, where is the difference, or why should their case be the worse because all were tried together? Their offences were distinct; and it is not denied that the jury might have convicted some and acquitted others. They had a right to sever in their challenges, which shows that the law protects their several rights. It is true, that a verdict may be called an entire thing, though it includes the case of several persons. Yet it is a *whole,* consisting of parts essentially distinct; so that, in *substance,* there are as many verdicts as there are defendants. When the jury are about to give their verdict, they are asked as to each of the prisoners, severally, Is *A.* guilty or not? Is *B.* guilty or not? Is *C.* guilty or not? Extraordinary indeed, then, must it be, if the case of the prisoners is to be considered as *several,* in all these minor points, and yet *joint* as to the verdict on which their lives depend. Nothing less than the most imperious authority should induce the Court to yield to such a doctrine. But I am happy to find that the authorities place us quite at ease. It is unnecessary to give an opinion on the law in *civil* cases. There are two cases in 21 *Viner,* 481, (Trial *S.* g. pl. 1 and 2,) one of which is reported in 12 *Mod.* 275, the other in 3 *Salk.* 362, from which it may be collected, that as the law was then held in actions against several for a joint *trespass,* if some were acquitted and others unjustly convicted, the Court would not grant a new trial, because it could not be done without putting those who were acquitted to a second trial. And yet, in joint *trespass* against several defendants, where no evidence is given against one, it has been the practice to take a verdict for him, and then suffer him to be a witness for the others. 1 *Phill. Ev.* 61. *Bull. N. P. Gilb. Ev.* 117, 6 *Binn.* 316. *3 Esp. N. P. Cases,* 25. Now, in such a case, if the other defendants should be convicted, *against evidence,* I should suppose the Court would ponder well before it suffered justice to be defeated by a technical difficulty. The difficulty is, that the new *venire facias* must include *all* the defendants. The ingenuity of the Court, which it would be their duty to exert in such a cause, might, I should think, find means to evade or conquer this objection. In *civil* cases, however, I will only say, that I do not consider it as settled, that a new trial cannot

be granted for some of the defendants only. As to criminal cases, it was decided, in *Fern's Case, Hil. Term,* 27 and 28, *Car.* 2, mentioned in *Buller's Nisi Prius,* 326, that in an information exhibited against *three,* and verdict against *all,* a new trial might be granted as to *one only.* Upon this case *Buller* makes the following remarks: "Yet the authority of this case may be well doubted; for where there were several defendants, and the verdict, as to *some,* was against evidence, yet the Court would not grant a new trial, for they said the verdict must stand or fall *in toto.*" And for this, he cites *Collier* v. *Morris, Mich.* 1755, and *Captain Crabb's Case, Mich.* 23, *Geo. II.* The authority of *Buller* is of weight. His opinion was, however, bottomed altogether on the cases he cited. No good reason is given in support of it; and it has been since overruled as unreasonable, and tending to obstruct justice. These are *English* authorities: Let us now turn to our own country. In *Pennsylvania,* I know of no authority in point. In *The People* v. *Olcott,* 2 *Johns. Cases,* 301, as I understand the report of the case, two were indicted for conspiracy, and tried by the same jury. As to *one,* there was a verdict of acquittal, but as to the other, the jury, not being able to agree, were discharged by the Court. This was before the Supreme Court of *New York.* It is not quite certain, however, that both the defendants were tried by the *same* jury. The report is not so clear as could be wished on that point. But in the case of the *Commonwealth* v. *Wood,* in the Supreme Court of *Massachusetts,* 12 *Mass. Rep.* 313, there is no doubt. Two were indicted for larceny, the jury acquitted one, and were discharged as to the other, *because they could not agree.* That is precisely the case before us, and I embrace the principle of the Court of *Massachusetts* in receiving the verdict with all my heart, because it advances justice and prevents injustice. I conclude, then, that the verdict ought to have been received as to two of the prisoners. But what was that verdict, and to which of the prisoners did it relate? On both these points the record is silent. In such a case, I think myself bound to presume in favour of the prisoners, that it was a verdict of acquittal. But I can make no presumption as to the *persons* intended to be acquitted. What, then, is to be done? Parol evidence cannot be received. It must, therefore, remain unknown which of the three prisoners occasioned the doubt in the minds of the jury, and who were the two they had agreed to acquit. Under these circumstances, it would be impossible to order either of them to a second trial without the hazard of exposing one of those whom the jury had agreed to acquit. There is no certainty, therefore, of avoiding injustice but by saying that neither of them shall be brought to a second trial. This is my opinion, considering the case simply on the refusal of the Court to receive the verdict. But another and much more important view remains to be taken. In considering the refusal to receive the verdict, I have supposed that the record exhibited a case of necessity, which would have authorized the Court to discharge the jury from that part of their verdict in which they had not come to an agreement. But this is denied by the counsel for the prisoners; and it is a question which demands our most serious deliberation. In the state of purity and independence in which I verily believe the judiciary of the several States, as well as of the *United States,* at present stands, there might be no danger of oppression from its enjoyment of a very large discretionary power as to the discharge of juries. But other times may come, in which other Judges might abuse their discretion, and it is fortunate, perhaps, that the point has occurred now, when the subject may be considered without prejudice or passion. In this Commonwealth, we allow the authority of the *English* decisions down to the 4th *July,* 1776. I will, therefore, first consider the *English* law as it then stood. I am not aware of any established principle of *English* law, at that day, by which the Court could discharge a jury merely because they could not agree, even in a *civil* case; but in a *criminal* and *capital* case, I take it to be quite clear, that the Courts did not consider themselves as invested with any such authority. It was not until the case of the *Kinlocks,* (in 1746,) that this subject seems to have been well considered. Many bad precedents are to be found in the latter part of *Charles II.* and the whole of *James II.'s* reigns; but these were disregarded after the revolution in 1688. The rebellion of 1745, in which the *Kinlocks* took part, excited warm passions; but the opinion of Sir MICHAEL FOSTER, delivered in that case, is so replete with candour, learning, and good sense, that we cannot but admire it. That was a case in which the jury was discharged at the request of the prisoners, assisted by able counsel, and with the intent of imparting to them a privilege which they could not otherwise have enjoyed. But there is not to be found in FOSTER's opinion, any vestige of an argument in favour of the power to discharge a jury, merely because they could not agree. Indeed, I think it is manifest that his opinion was to the contrary; for, in his remarks on *Mansell's* case, (reported in 1 *And.* 103,) he thus expresses himself: "The truth of the case was no more than this: the jury were not agreed on any verdict at all, *and, therefore, nothing remained to be done by the Court but to send them back, and keep them together, until they should agree to such a verdict as the Court could have received and recorded."* And, now that I have mentioned this case of *Mansell,* it is proper to remark, that there, the Court seemed to be aware that it had no power to discharge the jury without the prisoner's consent, (who was on his trial for murder,) for it took the precaution of obtaining his consent, and placing it on the record; for which proceeding FOSTER censures the Court—"For," says he, "the prisoner ought not to have been drawn into any consent at all, for, in *capital* cases, I think the Court is so far of counsel with the prisoner, that it should not suffer him to consent to any thing manifestly wrong, and to his own prejudice." *Serjeant Hawkins* lays it down, (*book* 2, *ch.* 47, *sect.* 1,) "that a jury sworn and charged in a capital case, cannot be discharged *without the prisoner's consent,* till they have given a verdict, and notwithstanding some authorities to the contrary in the reign of king *Charles II.,* this hath been holden for *clear law,* both in the reign of king *James II.,* and since the revolution." Although this rule is laid down generally, yet it is to be understood that cases of *necessity* are excepted. It is to be considered, then, what those cases are. There is a class of cases which depend on what may be called the *necessity of doing justice;* such as where the prisoner has tampered with some of the jury, or has contrived to keep back the witnesses for the prosecution. It was once thought necessary in *England* to discharge a jury, (2 *Hob.* 295,) where it was found that the evidence for the King was defective, and the attorney general suggested that sufficient evidence might be had another time. So where the indictment had been badly drawn by the negligence of the Crown officer. Such reasons, (I mean, want of evidence, or negligence in drawing the indictment,) would not be listened to in this country. This class of cases does not comprehend that before the Court, and I only mention it to show, that there may be a kind of necessity arising from the duty of the Court to guard the administration of justice against fraudulent practices. But the necessity which applies to the present question is *absolute;* and I will mention some of the cases from which its nature may be understood. It is said by Lord HALE, (1 *Hale,* 34, 35,) that if the prisoner, after his plea, and before trial, becomes *insane,* he shall not be tried; and if after his trial he becomes *insane,* he shall not receive judgment; and if after judgment, he becomes *insane,* his execution shall be spared; because, if he was of sound mind, he might allege something in stay of judgment or execution. He has omitted the case of insanity happening *during the trial;* but, upon the principle of the other cases, no doubt in such case the jury should be discharged from giving a verdict. In the case of *Elizabeth Meadow,* (*Foster,* 76, A. D. 1750,) the prisoner *was taken in labour* during the trial, and the jury were discharged. So the jury has been discharged where one of the jurymen fell down in a fit, and was unable to proceed in his duty. And Sir M. HALE mentions a case, (2 *Hale,* 295,) where, after the jury were sworn and departed from the bar, one of them *went out of town;* the other eleven were discharged, and the one who went out of town was fined for his misbehaviour, and the prisoner tried by another jury. A jury has likewise been discharged on account of the *intoxication of one of the jurors,* which rendered him incapable of performing his duty. These are the *English* cases, and not one of them touches the principle on which the jury were discharged in the present case, that is to say, *because they could not agree upon a verdict.* When we look to the State of *Pennsylvania,* we must, first of all, advert to her Constitution, art. 9. sect. 10, by which it is declared, "that no man shall, for the same offence, be twice put in jeopardy of life or limb." Where one is tried and acquitted on a bad indictment, he may be tried again, because his life was not in jeopardy. The Court could not have given judgment against him, if he had been convicted. But where the indictment is good, and the jury are charged with the prisoner, his life is undoubtedly in jeopardy during their deliberation. If they are divided in opinion, and especially if there should be a great majority in favour of the prisoner, he has gained an advantage of which he is deprived if the Court discharge the jury. I grant that in case of necessity they may be discharged; but if there be any thing short of absolute necessity, how can the Court, without violating the Constitution, take from the prisoner his right to have the jury kept together until they have agreed, so that he may not be put in jeopardy a second time? We should look at both sides of the question, and not forget that, in our anxiety to relieve the jury, we may be sacrificing the life of the prisoner. In the next place, it is to be observed, that in this State there is neither adjudged case nor tradition to warrant the discharge of this jury. I think myself safe in asserting, that there is no evidence of any instance since *William Penn* obtained his charter from *Charles II.*, in which a jury was discharged without the consent of the prisoner in a *capital* case. The general understanding has been against it, and of this, powerful evidence is to be found in the act of 21st *March*, 1806, in which the ancient oath of a juryman is altered; but the alteration is confined to *civil* cases. In those cases the oath prescribed by the act is to "give a true verdict according to the evidence, *unless dismissed by the Court, or the cause be withdrawn by the parties.*" Two inferences arise from this act: 1st. That it was not not supposed that the Court had power to discharge the jury, at their discretion, even in *civil* cases. 2d. That it was not thought expedient to give them that power in *criminal* cases. And, indeed, the expediency of investing the Courts with such power in capital cases, may be well questioned, notwithstanding the opinion of Judges of high standing in some of our sister States. There is strong proof of its not being necessary, from the fact of its never before having been exercised in *Pennsylvania.* Indeed, in general, the task of a jury is not hard in capital cases, because, when the evidence leaves reasonable ground for doubt, it is their duty to acquit. But a case may arise in which a jury may find great difficulty in agreeing, and some of them may be so exhausted as to put their health in danger. No one can think for a moment that they are to be starved to death. God forbid that so absurd and inhuman a principle should be contended for. Very far from it. The moment it is made to appear to the Court, by satisfactory evidence, that the health of a single juryman is so affected as to incapacitate him to do his duty, a case of necessity has arisen which authorizes the Court to discharge the jury. But it is said to be in vain to keep people together for the purpose of agreeing, when it is certain they never will agree. But by what evidence is the Court to arrive at this certainty? There is nothing for it but the declaration of the jurors, that they never can agree. Now nothing is more delusive than that kind of evidence. I have repeatedly known a jury to declare, that they never could agree, and yet when assured by the Court that they could not in conscience permit their discharge, they have agreed, and that, too, in no great length of time. But once establish the principle, that the Court has a right to discharge them, in capital cases, merely because they cannot agree, and we shall probably have few verdicts in cases of murder. In such cases there is already considerable difficulty in procuring a jury. Some persons think it criminal to be instrumental in taking the life of a man, even under the sanction of law. This Court has recently been reduced to the painful necessity of inflicting penalties on two respectable members of a respectable Society, because they absolutely refused to serve on the jury, and the prisoners would not consent to their discharge. Now all persons of that description, rather than submit to fine and imprisonment, might safely serve as jurors, under a certainty of being discharged without giving a verdict, after a few hours fasting. These are some of the reasons which induce

me to doubt whether any good would arise from a change in the law, if the Court had power to change it, which it certainly has not. That is a power which belongs to the Legislature.

I will now take notice of the decisions in the Courts of other States, and it will be found that not one of them was in a *capital* case. The counsel for the Commonwealth has contended for the broad principle, that the Court has a discretionary power to discharge the *jury in all cases.* But this is expressly contradicted by the Supreme Court of *New York*, on whose decisions, as to the power of discharging juries, the counsel for the Commonwealth relies, for that Court decided, in the case of *The People* v. *Barrett & Ward*, 2 *Caines' Cases*, 100. 304, that where the jury were discharged against the consent of the defendants, (in a case of misdemeanor only,) because the district attorney was not prepared with evidence to support the prosecution, such discharge was *equivalent to an acquittal*, and the defendants could never be brought to trial again for the same offence. The case of *The People* v. *Olcott*, 2 *Johns. Cases*, 301, was a *misdemeanor.* The opinion of the Court was deliverd by KENT, J. who considered the subject thoroughly, and went through all the cases at that time reported. He was clear in opinion, that the Court had a right to discharge the jury when satisfied that they never could agree. But he confined his opinion to the case before him, and I remark the following expressions: "If the question in *capital* cases be *doubtful*, there is nothing to render it so in cases of misdemeanor." The case of *The People* v. *Denton*, 2 *Johns. Cases*, 275, was also a *misdemeanor.* The Court said, "That the power of discharging a jury in cases of *misdemeanor*, as in *civil* cases, rests in sound discretion, and is to be exercised with great caution. Where every reasonable endeavour has been used to obtain a verdict, and it is found that the jury cannot, or will not, agree, they must, of necessity, be discharged." The case in 2 *Day.* 504, *(Connecticut,)* was a *misdemeanor. The People* v. *Goodwin*, 18 *Johns.* 187, was a case of *felony*, (manslaughter,) but it did not touch the life of the prisoner. SPENCER, C. J. delivered the opinion of the Court, and cited, with approbation, the case of *The People* v. *Olcott.* His *argument*, it must be confessed, reached to all cases of felony, but still he confined his *opinion* to the case before the Court, in which there was an ingredient of some weight, not found in any other case; and that was, that the legal termination of the Sessions was to be in half an hour, and there was a moral certainty that the jury would not agree in so short a time. The *United States* v. *Coolidge*, was before STORY, J. It was a case of *misdemeanor;* and after the jury was sworn, an essential witness for the *United States*, from scruples of conscience, refused to take the oath prescribed by law. The Court suspended the trial, in hopes that the witness, who was committed for contempt, would get over his scruples before the end of the Term; and he did get over them, but the cause was not tried. The indictment was quashed, because it had been found in part on the evidence of the same witness who had been before the grand jury, and given his evidence without being legally sworn. The case of *The Commonwealth* v. *Bowden*, was decided by the Supreme Court of *Massachusetts*, 9 *Mass.* 494. It was an indictment for a highway robbery, which, I understand, was not, at that time, a capital felony. The jury was discharged, because they said they never could agree. The authority of this Court is great; but, from the report of the case, the subject does not seem to have undergone much discussion or consideration. The Court said, "That the ancient strictness of the law, in that respect, had very much abated in the *English* Courts, nor would it be consistent with the genius of our Government to use compulsory means to effect an agreement among jurors." I presume it could not have been intended to apply these expressions to *capital felonies;* for, as to them, there can be no ground for saying, that the *English* Courts of the present day have assumed the right of discharging the jury because they could not agree. In other respects, their strictness has been relaxed, particularly in the adjournment of a jury in cases of high treason, without the consent of the prisoner. These are all the *American* authorities which have been cited, and none of them come up to the case before us.

Upon the whole, then, this is a case which affects the *lives* of the prisoners; and the jury were discharged *without, and against* the consent of the prisoners, merely because they had not agreed, and said they never could agree as to the case of one of the prisoners, though, as to two of them, they had agreed, and were ready to give their verdict, if the Court would receive it. In such a case, I may be permitted to doubt whether the Judges who have discharged juries in other States, (for whose characters I entertain the most unfeigned respect,) would not have *paused* before they discharged the jury, and thus took away from the prisoners that chance for life which they were unwilling to relinquish. For my own part, thinking that their blood would be upon us if they were convicted of murder in the *first degree* on a second trial in this Court, I am of opinion, that they should be discharged from this indictment.

43

UNITED STATES v. PEREZ
9 Wheat. 579 (1824)

March 17th, 1824. STORY, Justice, delivered the opinion of the court.—This cause comes up from the Circuit Court for the Southern District of New York, upon a certificate of division in the opinions of the judges of that court.

The prisoner, Joseph Perez, was put upon trial for a capital offence, and the jury, being unable to agree, were discharged by the court from giving any verdict upon the indictment, without the consent of the prisoner, or of the attorney for the United States. The prisoner's counsel, thereupon, claimed his discharge as of right, under these circumstances; and this forms the point upon which the judges were divided. The question, therefore, arises, whether the discharge of the jury, by the court, from giving any verdict upon the indictment, with which they

were charged, without the consent of the prisoner, is a bar to any future trial for the same offence. If it be, then he is entitled to be discharged from custody; if not, then he ought to be held in imprisonment until such trial can be had.

We are of opinion, that the facts constitute no legal bar to a future trial. The prisoner has not been convicted or acquitted, and may again be put upon his defence. We think, that in all cases of this nature, the law has invested courts of justice with the authority to discharge a jury from giving any verdict, whenever, in their opinion, taking all the circumstances into consideration, there is a manifest necessity for the act, or the ends of public justice would otherwise be defeated. They are to exercise a sound discretion on the subject; and it is impossible to define all the circumstances, which would render it proper to interfere. To be sure, the power ought to be used with the greatest caution, under urgent circumstances, and for very plain and obvious causes; and in capital cases especially, courts should be extremely careful how they interfere with any of the chances of life, in favor of the prisoner. But, after all, they have the right to order the discharge; and the security which the public have for the faithful, sound and conscientious exercise of this discretion, rests, in this, as in other cases, upon the responsibility of the judges, under their oaths of office. We are aware, that there is some diversity of opinion and practice on this subject, in the American courts; but, after weighing the question with due deliberation, we are of opinion, that such a discharge constitutes no bar to further proceedings, and gives no right of exemption to the prisoner from being again put upon trial. A certificate is to be directed to the circuit court, in conformity to this opinion.

44

CRENSHAW v. TENNESSEE
1 Mart. & Y. 134 (Tenn. 1827)

CATRON, J. delivered the opinion of the Court. The single question in this cause is, can a defendant plead in bar a conviction, judgment, and execution upon one indictment, for a felony not capital, to all other indictments for felonies not capital, committed before such conviction, judgment, and execution? It is frankly avowed by the Attorney for the government that the object of this cause having been brought here was to test this point, which is deemed a doubtful one by the Circuit Courts, as we are informed.

The first inquiry is, what was the common law upon the subject, as regulated by the Statutes of 8 Eliz. ch. 4, and 18 Eliz. ch. 7? By the common law, all felons convicted of crimes, not affecting the king, were entitled to the benefit of clergy for the first offence. All laymen who could read were burnt in the hand, and those who were of the clergy and peers were not branded; after which, the offender was delivered to the ordinary, to be dealt with according to the ecclesiastical canons. Then the defendant went through another trial, the object of which was to acquit and restore him to all his civil rights, in point of fact; but should the jury agree in the justice of the common law conviction, the culprit was degraded, and compelled to do penance. 2 Hawk. P. C. § 5, ch. 33; 1 Chitty's Cr. Law, 667.

That this latter trial was a mere mockery, and intended to support the ascendency of the Church over the State, will be admitted; yet many of the consequences of this mode of proceeding still remain a part of the English law. The 18 Eliz. ch. 7, provides that upon a defendant being admitted to his clergy, he should not be delivered to the ordinary, but should be branded and discharged. 2 Hawk. P. C. ch. 33, § 124.

The branding followed the prayer of the benefit of clergy by the Act of 4 H. 7, ch. 13—M for murder, and T for any other felony, was inflicted in open court, not as a punishment, but as an evidence that clergy had been allowed to the defendant; by force of which statute, branding is to this day inflicted in open court in cases of manslaughter; and by analogy, in other cases, where the branding is a part of the punishment by statute; although no good reason can be seen for this practice, in cases where it is inflicted as a part of the punishment for the offence.

Up to the 8th of Queen Elizabeth, it seems to be pretty well settled that a conviction, judgment, branding, and then delivering the culprit over to the ordinary, to be dealt with by the Church according to its canons, was a bar to an arraignment for any other felony, excepting perhaps such as affected the king. This will be pretty clearly seen by the cause of the Queen v. Stone, reported by Dyer, Vol. II. 214 b.

Stone, in the 4th year of Queen Elizabeth, was indicted for a clergyable felony, convicted, prayed his benefit of clergy, and the Court took time to advise, without ordering the defendant to be delivered to the ordinary. At a subsequent session the defendant was indicted for a felony, from which the benefit of clergy had been taken away by statute, to wit, by robbing the High Treasurer of England, and his servant Devyck. Defendant pleaded not guilty, was tried and convicted. It was then moved that he be discharged, by reason of his former conviction; and it was contended that, forasmuch as the culprit had not been delivered over to the ordinary, there was a conviction without execution, which was no bar to an indictment for the second offence; but the Court decided that the execution was well enough, and he entitled to the same benefit thereof as if delivered over to the ordinary, in which case he could not have been arraigned on the second indictment. 114 Pl. Com. 374. On the 28th of May, in the 8th Elizabeth, Stone was a third time indicted, for the murder of Agner, the son of Devyck, who was principally privy to the robbery, which murder was done the next day after the robbery was committed, was convicted and had judgment to be hanged; the execution was respited from time to time by command of the Chief Justice, but finally Stone was executed.

In the latter part of the year of the 8th of Elizabeth the statute (8 Eliz. ch. 4, § 4) was passed, declaring that a con-

viction, judgment, and delivery to the ordinary should not bar an indictment for a felony not clergyable, which was committed before such conviction and judgment; but that the felon in such case should be arraigned, tried, and, if found guilty, executed, notwithstanding his former conviction and delivery over to the ordinary. This statute is good evidence that before the passage of the Act the law was otherwise, to wit, that such conviction and delivery over was a bar to an arraignment for any felony committed previous to the former conviction. Armstrong v. Lille, Kelyng's Rep. 103, 104. A similar provision is found in the 18 Eliz. ch. 7, § 5; which provision is a recognition of the 8 Eliz. ch. 4, See 2 Hawk. ch. 33, § 127. By the 2d and 3d section of the 18 Eliz. defendants praying their clergy shall be allowed the same, branded and discharged, without being delivered over to the ordinary; provided that the justices may cause them to be imprisoned at their discretion, not exceeding one year. By this statute the defendant is entitled to the same privileges as if delivered to the ordinary. By the common law this was a bar to all felonies committed; the exceptions in the 8th and 18th of Elizabeth are only partial; that felonies not clergyable, and committed before the conviction and judgment, shall not be barred by such conviction and judgment. But all felonies not capital stood as they did at common law, and a conviction and punishment for one felony is a discharge of all precedent felonies not capital; nor ought the defendant to be arraigned for such subsequent felony if he plead the former conviction and punishment in bar. 2 Hawk. ch. 33, §§ 127, 128, ch. 36, S. N.; 2 Hale, 253; 4 Bl. Com. 374.

The next inquiry is, have our statutes against horse-stealing and forgery altered the common law upon this subject? The Act of 1807, ch. 74, § 4, declares horse-stealing to be felony; and the Act of 1811, ch. 1, § 2, declares the forgery laid in the indictment felony; but neither of the crimes are capital for the first offence.

It struck us with some force in the first instance, when considering these statutes, that the defendant, if found guilty, is ordered to pay for the horse stolen and the costs of the prosecution. But it will readily occur that the plea in bar is an admission of the facts alleged in the indictment, there having been no plea of not guilty over; therefore the costs and value of the horse stolen could be awarded by the Court in the same manner as if the defendant had pleaded guilty; yet by law his plea was a good one in bar of any further prosecution on the first and second indictments. The demurrer must be overruled, the defendant taxed with the costs of the prosecutions up to the time of filing said pleas; the State with the residue of the costs and the costs of the Court.

45

UNITED STATES v. GOODING
12 Wheat. 460 (1827)

Mr. Justice STORY. . . . The first instruction prayed puts the point, whether the burden of proof of the offences charged in the indictment did not rest upon the United States. Without question, it does, in all cases where a party stands charged with an offence, unless a different provision is made by some statute; for the general rule of our jurisprudence is, that the party accused need not establish his innocence; but it is for the government itself to prove his guilt, before it is entitled to a verdict or conviction. This question has been abandoned at the argument here, and is too plain for controversy, since there is no statutable provision altering the general principle in this particular.

. . . . .

It remains only to consider the point, whether these objections to the sufficiency of the indictment could be properly taken at this stage of the proceedings. Undoubtedly, according to the regular course of practice, objections to the form and sufficiency of an indictment ought to be discussed, upon a motion to quash the indictment, which may be granted or refused in the discretion of the court, or upon demurrer to the indictment, or upon a motion in arrest of judgment, which are matters of right. The defendant has no right to insist that such objections should be discussed or decided, during the trial of the facts by the jury. It would be very inconvenient and embarrassing, to allow a discussion of such topics, during the progress of the cause before the jury, and introduce much confusion into the administration of public justice. But, we think, it is not wholly incompetent for the court to entertain such questions, during the trial, in the exercise of a sound discretion. It should, however, be rarely done, and only under circumstances of an extraordinary nature. The circuit court, in the present case, did allow the introduction and discussion of these questions, during the trial, and were divided upon the propriety of the practice. We can only certify, that the court possessed the authority, but that it ought not to be exercised except on very urgent occasions. A certificate will be sent to the circuit court of the district of Maryland, according to this opinion.

46

UNITED STATES v. MARCHANT
12 Wheat. 480 (1827)

March 12th, 1827. The opinion of the court in this case was delivered by STORY, Justice.—The question, which comes before us upon a certificate of a division of opinion of the judges of the circuit court of Massachusetts, is this, whether two or more persons, jointly charged, in the same indictment, with a capital offence, have a right, by the laws of the country, to be tried severally, separately and apart, the counsel for the United States objecting thereto, or whether it is a matter to be allowed in the discretion of the court. We have considered the question, and are of opinion, that it is a matter of discretion in the court, and not of right in the parties. And it has become my duty briefly to expound some of the reasons which urge us to that conclusion.

The subject is not provided for by any act of congress; and therefore, if the right can be maintained at all, it must be as a right derived from the common law, which the courts of the United States are bound to recognise and enforce. The crimes act of 1790, ch. 9, provides, in the 29th section, for the right of peremptory challenge in capital cases; and this right, to the extent of the statute, must, in all cases, be allowed the prisoners, whether they are tried jointly or separately. Upon a joint trial, each prisoner may challenge his full number, and every juror challenged as to one, is withdrawn from the panel as to all the prisoners on the trial, and thus, in effect, the prisoners in such a case possess the power of peremptory challenge to the aggregate of the numbers, to which they are respectively entitled. This is the rule clearly laid by Lord Coke, Lord Hale and Sergeant Hawkins, and, indeed, by all the elementary writers. Hawk. P. C. b. 2, ch. 41, § 9; 2 Hale H. P. C. 268; Co. Litt. 156; *Beauchamp's Case,* 9 Edw. IV. folio 27, pl. 40; Plowd. 100; Kelyng 9.

One consequence of this, in ancient times, was, that embarrassments often arose at trials at the assizes, on account of a defect of sufficient jurors. The statute of Westminster II., c. 38, ordained, "that in one assize, no more shall be returned than twenty-four." The common practice under this statute used to be, for the sheriff to return forty-eight jurors, although the precept named but twenty-four. It was, indeed, held, at an early period, that the statute of Westminster did not apply to criminal cases; but, notwithstanding this, the usual practice prevailed, unless the court directed a larger number to be returned. And it was not until the reign of George II., that a larger number was required by law to be returned at the assizes. The history of this branch of the subject is very clearly stated in 3 Bac. Abr. tit. Juries, B., 6, and in Kelyng 16. It is obvious, that on joint panels, returned for joint trials, at the assizes, a defect of jurors might, from this limitation, often take place. And it became a question, in very early times, whether, under such circumstances, the court had power, against the will of the prisoners, to sever the panel, and to try them severally, if they insisted upon their right of several challenge. It was decided, upon full consideration, that the court had this power. To this effect are the cases in Plowd. 100, in Dyer 152 *b*, and in Kelyng 9; and the doctrine has received the sanction of Lord HALE, and other writers of the highest authority. Whether, then, prisoners, who are jointly indicted, can, against their wishes, be tried separately, does not admit of a doubt. It remains to consider, whether they can insist upon a several trial.

The sole ground upon which this claim can rest must

be, if maintainable at all, that they have a right to select their jury out of the whole panel, and that as, upon a joint trial, one may desire to retain a juror who is challenged by another, and, if challenged by one, he must be withdrawn as to all, this right of selection is virtually impaired. But it does not appear to us, that this reasoning can, upon the principles of the common law, be supported. The right of peremptory challenge is not, of itself, a right to select, but a right to reject jurors. It excludes from the panel those whom the prisoner objects to, until he has exhausted his challenges, and leaves the residue to be drawn for his trial, according to the established order or usage of the court. The elementary writers nowhere assert a right of this nature in the prisoner, but uniformly put the allowance of peremptory challenges upon distinct grounds. Mr. Justice Blackstone, in his Commentaries (4 Bl. Com. 353), puts it upon the ground, that the party may not be tried by persons against whom he has conceived a prejudice, or who, if he has unsuccessfully challenged them for cause, may, on that account, conceive a prejudice against the prisoner. The right, therefore, of challenge, does not necessarily draw after it the right of selection, but merely of exclusion. It enables the prisoner to say who shall not try him; but not to say who shall be the particular jurors to try him. The law presumes, that every juror sworn in the case is indifferent and above legal exception; for otherwise he may be challenged for cause. What jurors, in particular, shall try the cause, depends upon the order in which they are called; and the result is a mere incident following the challenges, and not the absolute selection of the prisoner, resulting from his power of challenge.

This view of the general principle of the common law is very much confirmed by other considerations. It is laid down by Hawkins (Pl. C. b. 2, ch. 41, § 8), that where several persons are arraigned on the same indictment, and severally plead not guilty, it is in the election of the prosecutor either to take out joint *venires* against them all, or several against each of them. This plainly supposes that it is in the election of the prosecutor, whether there should be a joint or separate trial. If there had been any known right in the prisoner to control this election, it seems incredible, that so accurate and learned an author should not have stated it, when the occasion indispensably required him to take notice of a qualification so important to his text. His silence is, under such circumstances, very significant.

But a still more direct conclusion against the right may be drawn from the admitted right of the crown to challenge in criminal cases, and the practice under that right. We do not say, that the same right belongs to any of the states in the Union; for there may be a diversity in this respect as to the local jurisprudence or practice; the inquiry here is, not as to what is the state prerogative, but, simply, what is the common-law doctrine as to the point under consideration. Until the statute of 33 Edw. I., the crown might challenge peremptorily any juror, without assigning any cause; but that statute took away that right, and narrowed the challenges of the crown to those for cause shown. But the practice, since this statute, has uniformly been, and it is clearly settled, not to compel the

crown to show cause, at the time of objection taken, but to put aside the juror, until the whole panel is gone through. Hawkins, on this point, says (Pl. C. b. 2, ch. 43, §§ 2, 3), "if the king challenge a juror, before the panel is perused, it is agreed, that he need not show any cause of his challenge, till the whole panel be gone through, and it appears that there will not be a full jury, without the person so challenged. And if the defendant, in order to oblige the king to show cause, presently challenge, *touts paravaile;* yet it had been adjudged, that the defendant shall be first put to show all his causes of challenge, before the king need to show any." And the learned author is fully borne out by the authorities which he cites, and the same rule has been recognised down to the present times. Hale H. P. C. ch. 36, p. 271; 3 Bac. Abr. Jury, E, 10; *Rex* v. *Conigsmarke,* 9 How. St. Tr. 1; *Rex* v. *Stapleton,* 3 Ibid. 502; *Rex* v. *Borosky,* 9 Ibid. 1; *Rex* v. *Gray,* Ibid. 127, s. c. T. Raym. 473; *Rex* v. *Grahme,* 12 How. St. Tr. 646; *Rex* v. *Cook,* 13 Ibid. 311; *Rex* v. *Horne Tooke,* 25 Ibid. 1, 24; 1 Chit. Cr. Law 533; *Rex* v. *Campion,* 1 How. St. Tr. 1050.

This acknowledged right of peremptory challenge existing in the crown, before the statute of 33 Edw. I., and the uniform practice which has prevailed, since that statute, to allow a qualified and conditional exercise of the same right, if other sufficient jurors remained for the trial, demonstrate, as we think, that no such power of selecting his jury belongs, or was ever supposed to belong, by the common law, to the prisoner; and that, therefore, he could not demand, as matter of right, a separate trial to enable him to exercise it. In a separate or joint trial, he could, at any time, be defeated by the crown of such choice, by its own admitted prerogative.

The circumstances already alluded to, of the right of each prisoner, on a joint trial, to exercise his full right of peremptory challenge, and the small number of jurors usually returned on the panel at the assizes, accounts in a very satisfactory manner for the language used in some of the cases, as to the necessity of directing separate trials, where the prisoners refused to join in their challenges. The plain reason was, that otherwise there could be no trial at all, for defect of jurors, at the same assizes; and therefore, the court, in furtherance of public justice, were accustomed, without the consent of the prisoners, to direct a separate trial. In this way the reason of the practice is understood by Lord Hale (2 Hale P. C. ch. 34, p. 263), and by Hawkins (Hawk. P. C. b. 2, ch. 41, § 9), and by other more recent writers on common law. In this manner, the language of Lord HOLT in *Charnock's Case* (12 Howell's State Trials 1454; s. c. 3 Salk. 81), is to be interpreted; for it is manifest, that he could not intend, that there could not be a joint trial, where the prisoners challenged separately, for no rule was better settled in his time than that they could. Indeed, in *Rex* v. *Grahme* (12 Howell's State Trials, 646, 673), the same learned judge uses similar language in a sense which admits of no other interpretation; and this was the answer given to it, when cited in a later case for the like purpose. That case is *Rex* v. *Noble and others,* in 1713, before Lord Chief Justice PARKER, and reported in the State Trials (9 Harg. St. Tr. 1; s. c. 15 Howell's St. Tr. 731). In that case, which was an indictment for murder, Noble moved the court for a separate trial, and the motion was denied. He was convicted, and when brought up for judgment, he moved in arrest of judgment this very matter, that there was a mis-trial, because (to use his own words) "we were severed in our challenges, and yet were tried together by the same jury;" and he relied upon the language of Lord HOLT in *Charnock's Case,* as in point. The court overruled the objection, and stated, that Lord HOLT's language referred solely to the public inconvenience, on account of a probable defect of jurors, and not to any matter of right in the prisoners. Sentence was accordingly passed upon the prisoner, and he was executed. There is a curious and learned commentary appended in a note to this trial, which was printed before the execution of Noble, in which an attempt was made to question the correctness of the decision. But it is therein admitted, that Noble's counsel declined to argue the point, though requested; from which we cannot but infer, that they thought the objection unfounded. The decision itself has never since been questioned or denied. We have, therefore, in the present case, not merely the absence of any authority in favor of the matter of right, but the course of practice, and the general reasoning deducible from the prerogative of the crown against it; and lastly, a direct authority, in times when the administration of criminal justice was unsuspected, on the very point.

Such is the substance of the reasons which induce us to decide against the claim as a matter of right. In our opinion, it is a matter of sound discretion, to be exercised by the court with all due regard and tenderness to prisoners, according to the known humanity of our criminal jurisprudence. A certificate is, accordingly, to be sent to the circuit court.

47

UNITED STATES v. SALINE BANK
1 Pet. 100 (1828)

Mr. Chief Justice MARSHALL delivered the opinion of the Court.—

This is a bill in equity for a discovery and relief. The defendants set up a plea in bar, alleging that the discovery would subject them to penalties under the statute of Virginia.

The Court below decided in favour of the validity of the plea, and dismissed the bill.

It is apparent that in every step of the suit, the facts required to be discovered in support of this suit would expose the parties to danger. The rule clearly is, that a party is not bound to make any discovery which would expose him to penalties, and this case falls within it.

The decree of the Court below is therefore affirmed.

48

IN THE MATTER OF SPIER
1 Dev. 491 (N.C. 1828)

HALL, J. In this case the guilt or innocence of the prisoner is as little the subject of inquiry as the merits of any case can be when it is brought before this Court on a collateral question of law. Although the prisoner, if unfortunately guilty, may escape punishment in consequence of the decision this day made in his favor, yet it should be remembered that the same decision may be a bulwark of safety to those who, more innocent, may become the subjects of persecution, and whose conviction, if not procured on one trial, might be secured on a second or third, whether they were guilty or not.

It is laid down by *Lord Coke* that the life of a man shall not be twice put in jeopardy upon the same charge for a capital offense. 3 In., 110; 1 do., 227; Foster, 16, 22, 30. In this maxim is manifested the great concern which the law has for the security of the lives of its citizens. It is intended as a barrier against oppression and persecution; and although it must have been known to the wisdom of the law that it would be a means by which the guilty may sometimes escape from merited punishment, yet it was thought better to adopt it than to leave it to the discretion of a judge to award a second trial when the jury, in whose hands the life of the prisoner had been placed on the first trial, did not return a verdict.

From the record in this case it appears that a jury was sworn and impaneled to try the prisoner on the charge contained in the indictment, but they failed to return a verdict. This was a jury of the prisoner's own choosing, and one, too, to which the State did not object. When the jury were thus charged with the prisoner, he certainly stood upon his trial—his life was jeopardized.

From this maxim there are some exceptions, but such exceptions as are under no human control—they are the offspring of necessity; as where a juror is taken suddenly sick, where a woman is taken in labor, where the prisoner becomes insane, or where the jury are discharged by consent of the prisoner or at his request.

The record states that the jury were impaneled in the case, but it assigns no reason why a verdict was not returned by the jury, and it would be worse than preposterous to say that this Court can be governed by anything else than the record. It is true, like other individuals, we are informed of the reason why the jury did not return a verdict; that the term of the court expired before they had an opportunity of doing so. Let it be supposed that this fact was spread upon the record; it is certainly an event which might have been guarded against, though it was a case not without its difficulties. The trial might have been brought on sooner in the term. The jury might have been directed to withdraw and consider of the evidence after it was given in, and this the sooner if the prisoner refused to consent to withdraw a juror. I beg to be understood as laying down no rules for the government of the courts; I am not competent to do so; if I was it would not become me. But I am proving that the reason why the jury did not return their verdict was an event which might have been guarded against; that it was not founded in uncontrollable necessity, and if it was not, it forms no exception to the maxim that a citizen shall not be twice put in danger of his life upon the same charge for a capital offense.

But this is not the first time this question has arisen in this State. It was decided in *S. v. Garrigues*, 2 N. C., 241, for murder, in the Superior Court of Halifax, in 1795. There the presiding judge retired from the bench, but did not adjourn the court, and the jury having been impaneled in the case, separated without giving any verdict. It was held by *Williams* and *Haywood, JJ.*, that the prisoner could not be put upon his trial a second time. The record there and the record in this case are alike. In both cases it appears that the jury were impaneled, but returned no verdict. It is true we learn, like other individuals, that the reason why they returned no verdict in the one case was that they could not agree; in the other, that the term expired before they considered of their verdict. But in both cases the record shows, and shows nothing else, that they were impaneled, and returned no verdict before the expiration of the term. It is certainly a difficult task to distinguish, on principle, the one case from the other. I may add that that opinion drew after it the approbation of the profession, and I believe I shall not treat with disrespect the memory of the dead or the pretensions of the living when I say that a greater criminal lawyer than *Judge Haywood* never sat upon the bench in North Carolina.

It is stated in Hale that the practice was once otherwise; that where the prisoner was put upon his trial the court might discharge the jury if it appeared that the evidence was not sufficient to convict him, and remit him to jail for further evidence. It is stated, however, in a note in the same book, that the practice is now otherwise; that a jury once charged in a capital case cannot be discharged until they have given their verdict, and *Judge Haywood* says, in *S. v. Garrigues, supra*, that "this power was exercised for the benefit of the Crown only, but is a doctrine so abhorrent to every principle of safety and security that it ought not to receive the least countenance in the courts of this country." And *Haywood* is sustained in this opinion by *Foster*, who wrote long since *Judge Hale*. I say, therefore, in the present case, it was not in the power of the court to discharge the jury, unless for the intervention of some cause that could not be foreseen nor controlled.

I admit that if the jury had been charged upon an indictment which was in itself defective, so that judgment could not be given upon it, although the prisoner was found guilty, it would be no bar to a second trial; because although such feelings of danger might have been awakened as are incident to human nature, and which such occasions are naturally calculated to excite, yet in reality the prisoner ran no risk; he was in no danger; he was tried as if upon no indictment. But in this case there is no objection to the indictment. If the prisoner had been found guilty he must have suffered the penalties of the law. He

was placed upon his trial; his life was in the hands of the jury. His breast was occupied by a commixture of hope and fear; it throbbed alternately with both, and whether the struggle terminated in a verdict of guilt or innocence, it was certainly a guarantee against any future prosecution upon the same charge, and that guarantee need not claim to be bottomed upon any extraordinary maxim marked with tenderness for the life of man. It is a plain principle of municipal jurisprudence, regulating ordinary cases of property between man and man. It does not constitute the maxim that a man's life shall not be twice put in jeopardy for the same thing, to which Lord Coke, Foster, and others, fathers of the English criminal law, have given the sanction of their names.

TAYLOR, C. J. The prisoner has been brought up on the return of a *habeas corpus*, and now moves for his discharge, or to be admitted to bail, on the ground that his life has been once put in jeopardy for the same offense for which he now stands committed for trial.

The transcript of the record accompanying the return discloses only the fact that the prisoner was put upon his trial for the murder of Williams, and that no verdict was returned by the jury. An affidavit was annexed which, though *ex parte*, states other facts which have not been controverted at the bar, and which, therefore, it may be taken for granted are correct. These are that the trial began on Friday morning; that in the course of it the witnesses on both sides were examined, the counsel on the part of the State heard, and that while the counsel for the prisoner was addressing the jury the hour of 12 of Saturday night arrived, of which the judge gave notice to the parties, and then left the bench.

The case has been ably argued on both sides, and certainly a more important principle could not be brought into discussion, whether we view on one side its connection with the interests of public justice, or, on the other, the important bearing it has on the personal security of the citizens and their immunity from undue prosecution. As it is a case in which a court has no discretion, but is bound to yield obedience to the law, without regard to consequences, it is of primary importance to ascertain, amidst the conflict of opinions, on which side the weight of principle and authority rests.

A writer of established reputation on the criminal law remarks that it seems to have been anciently an uncontroverted rule, and hath been allowed even by those of a contrary opinion to have been the general tradition of the law, that a jury sworn and charged in a capital case cannot be discharged without the prisoner's consent until they have given a verdict. It is added that notwithstanding some authorities to the contrary, in the reign of Charles II. this hath been holden for clear law, both in the reign of James II. and since the Revolution of 1688. 2 Hawkins, 619. Lord Coke, who is cited as authority for the general position, lays it down in still broader terms, and so as to render the discharge of the jury in treason, felony, or larceny illegal, even with the consent of the prisoner. 3 Inst., 110.

Much more modern authorities have introduced the exception where the discharge takes place with the prisoner's consent and for his benefit; and this being reasonable and just, may be considered as now well settled.

In the remarkable case of the *Kenlocks,* reported by Foster, that eminent judge endeavors to prove that the case quoted by Coke from the year-book of Edward III. does not show that the jury was sworn, but only that they were in court and the party arraigned. But Fitzherbert, in his abridgment, understands the case in the same way with Coke; for he alleges that the reason of the judgment was that the inquest, having been once charged, could not be discharged. A majority of the judges in that case admitted the authority of the rule as a good general one, but not as practically applicable to those cases where it would produce great hardships or manifest injustice to the prisoner. In the case quoted, the power of the court to discharge the jury with the prisoner's consent seems to have been for the first time well considered; and they rejected with just animadversion the authority of those cases which had occurred in that period of misrule and persecution preceding the revolution. In one of these the court discharged a jury in a capital case, after evidence given on the part of the Crown, merely for want of sufficient evidence to convict, and in order to bring the prisoner to a second trial, when the Crown should be better prepared! In another, where the prisoner, unassisted by counsel, consented, to his own prejudice, that the jury might be discharged.

These stains upon the administration of justice show to what extremes, in a state of civil discord, the passions of men urge them to trample upon the most salutary principles of law, and in what degree judges, holding their office at the will of the sovereign, were eager to pander to his appetite for blood and forfeitures.

Certain exceptions have been incorporated with the rule by such authority as we are not at liberty to reject, even if we were inclined to do so; but we cannot add to these exceptions without authority, unless the reason for them is equally forcible and conclusive. If the discharge take place with the prisoner's consent, and for his benefit, or where it is occasioned by an overruling necessity, beyond the reach of man's foresight and control, it cannot be the instrument of injustice or oppression to the prisoner. It is impossible to lay down a general rule which may be applicable to all cases that may occur; but to the exception sanctioned in the case of the *Kenlocks* may be fairly added that of Elizabeth Meadows, who was taken in labor during the trial. (Foster, 76.) The case where the prisoner became insane, and where a juryman fell down in a fit (*Rex v. Edwards,* 4 Taunton, 309), were decided on principles from which I do not see that any mischief could arise. Whether that class of cases where the jury have been discharged in consequence of undue practices having been used to keep back witnesses, or in consequence of a juryman's having become intoxicated, stands upon the same authoritative ground, I am not prepared to decide. There is danger to be apprehended from every exception arising from a fact which artifice and cunning may simulate. As at present advised, I think the exceptions, in addition to those I have mentioned, ought to be confined to those cases of extreme and positive necessity which are dispensed by the visitation of God, and which cannot by any contrivance of man be made the engines of obstructing that justice which the safety of all requires should be done to the State, or weakening the efficacy of and rendering illusive that maxim of civil liberty of which the prisoner claims the protection.

There is no case in the British authorities resembling the one under consideration, nor is it likely any such will ever occur. But some cases are furnished by American reporters which it is proper to notice.

In Massachusetts, Boden was indicted for a highway robbery, and the jury being impaneled, and having heard the evidence and the whole of the case, retired; and after being confined the whole night and part of the day, returned into court and informed the judge that they had not agreed on a verdict, and that it was not probable they ever could agree. A juror was withdrawn without the prisoner's consent, and he was afterwards tried and convicted by another jury, and it was holden a good conviction. 9 Mass., 494. It may be collected from this case that the offense charged was not there a capital felony; the arguments of the counsel for the State and the opinion of the court seem to show this. The maxim of the common law, therefore, under which the prisoner seeks shelter in this case, was not violated. Whether the cases of inevitable necessity, cited from the British books, apply to the case of discharging a jury, because they say they have not agreed, and are not likely to agree, appears to me questionable. Juries very often agree, after thinking and saying they could not agree. If the court possessed a discretionary power to discharge a jury in a capital case, upon their saying they could not agree, it is to be apprehended that very slight endeavors would be made among them to reason with and enlighten each other; and that a disposition would prevail to escape from a duty which every man considers painful. But the difficulties and disadvantages under which the prisoner would enter upon his second trial would probably expose him to increased danger.

It must be conceded that the case of *Goodwin,* 18 Johns., 200, if rightly decided, is an authority against the prisoner in this case; for although the offense charged was not a capital felony, yet the reasoning extends the whole length of showing that the jury may be discharged in any case, and the prisoner tried again. The distinguished judge who delivered the opinion of the court in that case thought the rule which declares that no person shall be subject for the same offense to be twice put in jeopardy of life or limb means that no person shall be twice tried for the same offense. But I cannot acquiesce in this opinion, for it would seem strange that a familiar maxim of the common law, admitted for ages without denial or controversy, should require a solemn constitutional sanction for the more effectual protection of the citizens. The pleas of "heretofore convicted" and "heretofore acquitted" are interwoven with our criminal law as essentially as the pleas of former judgment between the same parties or the pendency of another suit for the same cause are with our civil law. Could the amendment to the Constitution of the United States mean no more than this, when it provided that "no person shall be subject for the same offense to be twice put in jeopardy of life or limb"? Did the constitutions of several of the States mean no more when they adopted the same article?

As the common law of every State already protects the accused against a second trial, not only in crimes of all descriptions, but in questions of civil right, it is to be inferred that the constitutions meant much more, and that their design was to protect the accused against a trial where the first jury had been discharged without due cause.

"Twice put in jeopardy" and "twice put on trial" convey to the mind several and distinct meanings, for we can readily understand how a person has been in jeopardy upon whose case the jury have not passed. The danger and peril of a verdict do not relate to a verdict given. When the jury are impaneled upon the trial of a person charged with a capital offense, and the indictment is not defective, his life is in peril or jeopardy, and continues so throughout the trial. And this is the legal understanding of the term as explained by *Mr. Justice Foster* in the case of the *Kenlocks:* "The discharge of the jury was not to bring the prisoners' lives twice in jeopardy, which is one great inconvenience of discharging jurors in capital cases, but merely in order to give them one chance for their lives, which it was apprehended they had lost by pleading to issue." This is a full admission that one inconvenience of discharging the jury is to put the prisoner twice in jeopardy, which he could not be if trial were meant. The same meaning is ascribed to the expression, 1 Chitty Cr. Law, 63.

Besides those cases in which juries may be discharged from the casual circumstances of illness, there are some others in which the Crown, at least by the consent of the prisoner, is at liberty to withdraw a juror in order to indict him again, or put off his trial. Thus it is laid down that to let him into a ground of defense which he could not otherwise have taken before evidence given, the court may by consent discharge the jury; but it does not seem the prosecutor has the right to bring the prisoner twice into peril of his life. In the same light has the subject been viewed in the Supreme Court of Pennsylvania, in 6 Sergeant and Rawle, 6; and finally, I thought the law in this State to have been settled for thirty years, ever since the case of *S. v. Garrigues,* 2 N. C., 241, conformably to which decision other cases have occurred of a similar kind, though not reported.

Under this impression of the subject I do not feel the authority of the law to add this additional exception to the rule, since the trial of a prisoner, its conduct and duration, are under the direction and control of the court and counsel, who may in general foresee or make a reasonable conjecture as to the time it may occupy. It would be a rule subject in its very nature to operate oppressively to the prisoner, without any exterior agency or the influence of sinister design. But it would be still more capable, if such were present, of being made an engine of persecution. Not that there is reason to apprehend any such influence in the present tranquil state of the country, and under the existing purity of the administration of justice; but a rule established in such times should be calculated to protect men when strife prevails and the angry passions are let loose, for it cannot be foreseen what may ensue in future; and the law, as now established, must be the rule for posterity, unless the Legislature should think proper to interfere. Should the rule, according to this opinion, facilitate the escape of some guilty persons, the addition of their exceptions might, in other times, lead to the punishment of innocent persons; and we are admonished by the law that it is better that ten guilty persons escape than that one innocent suffer. My opinion consequently is, that the prisoner cannot be tried again on this charge.

49

SANDERSON'S CASE
21 Fed. Cas. 326, no. 12,297 (C.C.D.C. 1829)

Memorandum. August 6, 1829. The foreman of the grand jury came down, and stated that a Mr. Sanderson had refused to answer who was the author of a certain publication in "The Baltimore Republican," supposed to reflect upon the court and jury, in the trial of the cases of U. S. v. Watkins [Cases Nos. 16,649 and 16,650], although he said it was "confessedly" written in this District; and that he said he could not answer the question without implicating himself.

Before CRANCH, Chief Judge, and MORSELL, Circuit Judge.

THE COURT (THRUSTON, Circuit Judge, absent) said, that it seemed to the court that he might be implicated by answering the question, and he was the sole judge whether it would; and, if it would, he was not bound to answer the question.

MORSELL, Circuit Judge, was not clear that it could implicate him.

CRANCH, Chief Judge, thought that it might form a link in the chain of circumstances, leading to a prosecution against himself, as the publisher of the paper; for, although the paper was printed in Baltimore, it might have been published here. At least it is questionable, whether sending a paper here would not be a publication here; and, as the witness was now here, he might possibly be prosecuted here.

He was not compelled to answer.

50

BULL V. LOVELAND
10 Pick. 9 (Mass. 1830)

SHAW C. J. delivered the opinion of the Court. In this case, the general question has been argued at some length, whether a witness, without his own consent, can be called to testify to any fact pertinent to the issue between other parties, where such testimony may tend to charge him with a debt, or subject him to pecuniary loss or liability, but where it does not tend to expose him to punishment, or subject him to any penalty or forfeiture.

This question has been the subject of much discussion and difference of opinion, among eminent judges, and those of the greatest experience in nisi prius trials, both in England and in the United States.

In the case of *United States* v. *Grundy*, 3 Cranch, 344, it seemed to be taken for granted by *Marshall* C. J., that a man in a civil case is not bound to testify against his interest. But that was before the discussions in England, and the opinions of the judges in the House of Lords, growing out of questions raised in Lord Melville's trial. Besides, the question was not argued, and it arose where the witness was called to testify to a fact which would have rendered a ship forfeited under the registry acts of the United States, in which, at the time of the forfeiture, he himself claimed an interest.

In *Webster* v. *Lee*, 5 Mass. R. 334, it was stated by *Parsons* C. J., in giving the opinion of the Court, that a witness may, *if he consents*, testify against his own interest. Although this expression implied that his consent was requisite, yet the case did not call for the expression of an opinion upon the question whether he could be compulsorily required to testify, against his will.

In a later case however, *Appleton* v. *Boyd*, 7 Mass. R. 131, the same point again came before the same eminent judge at nisi prius, upon which he ruled that a witness cannot be required, without his consent, to testify against his own pecuniary interest. This point among others was reserved, but it was not argued or noticed by the counsel on either side. In giving the opinion the Court cited no authority; and in noticing this point, seemed to take the rule for granted, and considered rather, whether from the facts reported, the witness had an interest in the question, than whether by law it would excuse him from giving his testimony.

In England this subject underwent much discussion, pending the impeachment against Lord Melville, in 1806, upon which occasion the question was put to the judges by the House of Lords. The question was presented in two or three different forms, slightly varying in terms, but it was substantially the same in each. Eight judges and the chancellor were of opinion, that the witness was bound to answer a question, although his answer might render him liable to a civil action; the other four judges expressed a contrary opinion. In order to remove the doubts, which such a difference of opinion among eminent judges implied, an act was passed, 46 *Geo.* 3, *c.* 37, declaring, that a witness cannot by law refuse to answer a question relevant to the matter in issue, the answering of which has no tendency to accuse himself, or to expose him to a penalty or forfeiture of any nature whatsoever, by reason only, or on the sole ground, that the answering of such question may establish or tend to establish, that he owes a debt, or is otherwise subject to a civil suit.

This act, as a statute, of course has no authority here, but as strictly a declaratory law it is entitled to weight. Lord *Erskine*, then lord chancellor, stated, that notwithstanding some difference of opinion among high authorities, he considered the law so far precise, clear and conspicuous that it was necessary no new law should be promulgated, otherwise than in the form of a declaratory

law. In this suggestion he was countenanced by Lord *Eldon*, who was not then in judicial office. 1 Phil. Ev. (Am. ed.) 208; Peake's Ev. (3d ed.) 193; 1 Hall's Law Journal, 223; 1 Stark. Ev. 135.

This rule has recently been recognized and acted on in Maryland. *Taney* v. *Kemp*, 4 Har. & Johns. 348; *Stoddart* v. *Manning*, 2 Har. & Gill, 147. And in Pennsylvania. *Baird* v. *Cochran*, 4 Serg. & Rawle, 397.

In a recent case in this Court, it has been held, that one summoned as trustee, cannot avoid answering questions put to him, in regard to the validity of a conveyance under which he claims title to property, on the ground that it may affect his own pecuniary interest. *Devoll* v. *Brownell*, 5 Pick. 448. This is not precisely in point, but it is important as giving a construction to a constitutional provision, which might be supposed to stand in the way of the application of the rule in question in this Commonwealth. The provision is found in the 12th art. of the Declaration of Rights. "No subject shall be held to answer for any crime, &c. or be compelled to accuse, or furnish evidence against himself." In this case it was decided, that the trustee was found to answer, though he might thereby charge himself, and that the above constitutional provision does not relate to questions of property.

On the whole we think the weight of authority is in favor of the rule, that a witness may be called and examined in a matter pertinent to the issue, where his answers will not expose him to criminal prosecution, or tend to subject him to a penalty or forfeiture, although they may otherwise adversely affect his pecuniary interest, and that the witness was properly called and examined in the present case.

There seems to be no difference in principle, between compelling a witness to produce a document in his possession, under a *subpoena duces tecum*, in a case where the party calling the witness has a right to the use of such document, and compelling him to give testimony, when the facts lie in his own knowledge. It has been decided, though it was formerly doubted, that a *subpoena duces tecum* is a writ of compulsory obligation, which the court has power to issue, and which the witness is bound to obey, and which will be enforced by proper process to compel the production of the paper, when the witness has no lawful or reasonable excuse for withholding it. *Amey* v. *Long*, 9 East, 473; *Corsen* v. *Dubois*, 1 Holt's N. P. R. 239. But of such lawful or reasonable excuse the court at nisi prius, and not the witness, is to judge. And when the witness has the paper ready to produce, in obedience to the summons, but claims to retain it on the ground of legal or equitable interests of his own, it is a question to the discretion of the court, under the circumstances of the case, whether the witness ought to produce, or is entitled to withhold the paper.

Under the circumstances of the present case, we are clearly of opinion that the witness had such an equitable interest in the note, and such a right to the custody and control of it, under the agreement of the plaintiff himself, that he ought not to have been required to surrender it for the purpose proposed, that of maintaining the suit and thereby fixing a lien by attachment, upon the funds placed in the hands of the witness for the common benefit of all the creditors. Upon the faith of this agreement, all the creditors, including the plaintiffs, restrained themselves from securing their respective debts by attachment; and relying on the same agreement, the witness made considerable advances for the improvement of the trust fund, for the common benefit. When the plaintiffs and other creditors constituted Tappan & Whitney their agents to collect all the demands, including their own, and placed their notes and securities in the hands of these agents for that purpose, with power by attachment or otherwise to apply the whole of the debtor's funds for that purpose, they created not a mere naked agency, but gave an authority coupled with an interest, which could not be revoked at their mere pleasure.

If it be asked how long this agency is to continue, it may be answered, a reasonable time; and what is a reasonable time must depend upon the circumstances of the case. Here it has not been shown that the witness and his partner, intrusted with the transaction of this business, have violated their agreement, or abused their trust; no application has been made to them to accelerate the collection of the demands; and this afforded evidence of a tacit acquiescence on the part of the plaintiffs, in the course pursued by them. If it was in the power of the plaintiffs to rescind the agreement, revoke the authority given, and claim their note for the purpose of being put in suit, they ought at least to give reasonable notice of their intention so to do, in order that the other creditors might be put in the same situation, which they were in before the agreement was made.   *Plaintiffs nonsuit.*

51

UNITED STATES v. SHIVE

27 Fed. Cas. 1065, no. 16,278 (C.C.E.D.Pa. 1832)

Before BALDWIN, Circuit Justice, and HOPKINSON, District Judge.

BY THE COURT. The state law giving the defendant a right to challenge peremptorily, does not apply to proceedings in this court; forgery is not a felony at common law, and though the act of congress declares the offence laid in the indictment to be a felony, that does not carry with it a right of peremptory challenge as an incident, and it has never been allowed in this court in a case like the present.

The jury were sworn and the trial had. Among other grounds of defence taken by the counsel of the defendant, he contended that the act of congress chartering the bank which created the offence, was unconstitutional, and that therefore the jury ought to acquit the defendant.

BALDWIN, Circuit Justice, after charging the jury on the law and evidence in the case, proceeded to the objection to the constitutionality of the law.

We could have wished that these would have been the only considerations, which it was our duty to submit to you, but one of the counsel for the defendant has raised another question, on which it is necessary for us to give you our opinion, and that is, whether the act of congress on which this prosecution is founded, is valid or void.

That it has passed through all the forms and branches of legislation, that it has been sanctioned and declared to be the law of the land, by the highest branch of the judicial power; that it is clothed with every sanction and carries with it every obligation known to the constitution, has not been and cannot be denied. If there is law in the land, if there is a rule by which courts and juries are bound to administer the criminal justice of the country, it is that which, having been enacted by the legislative authority of the nation, has been solemnly pronounced by the supreme judicial power, to be within the constitutional province of the legislature. Beyond that tribunal, there is no other revision of the acts of congress, that will not end in the prostration of all law and all legitimate government, unless by an amendment to the constitution.

In courts of justice, the law of the land is the law of every case, criminal as well as civil, the safety of the public, the rights of individuals do not depend on their opinion of what the law ought to be, but on what it is. The ministers of justice are not the makers of the laws, judges and jurors are, in the words of the defendant's counsel, magistrates to enforce and execute the laws; they are as much bound by them as the criminal they condemn. We sit here by the authority of the law, our duty is prescribed and defined by law, and if we willfully violate or disregard it, if we sentence a prisoner without a previous law prescribing a punishment, or acquit in opposition to the enacted and established law of the country, we should be the greatest criminals in the nation. We are judges of law, but what is law? Not the opinions of judges and jurors merely, it is the will of the people, expressed through that department of the government, to whom they have confided the law-making power. An act of congress is the exercise of that power conferred by the nation; a judgment of the supreme court affirming its validity and decreeing its binding force, is the constitutional exercise of the judicial power of the nation, confided to that high tribunal. And when a law thus carries with it the imposing authority of the people, the states of this union, and of every department of the government created by the constitution, shall the ministers of justice, its sworn administrators, be the first to trample under their feet the supreme law of the land? Shall we, the creatures of the law, the servants of the constitution, dare to assume the power of abrogating its provisions, disobeying its injunctions, and dispensing with its penalties? The sixth article of the constitution, declares itself and all laws and treaties made pursuant thereto, to be the supreme law of the land, and that all judges shall be bound thereby, notwithstanding any thing in the law or constitution of any state to the contrary.

When the most solemn acts of a sovereign state, in opposition to an act of congress, are thus declared nullities, will a jury assume no moral responsibility by substituting their opinion for the supreme law of the land? If the defendant has violated an act of congress, though not sworn to make it his rule of action, the supreme law declares him a felon. What are you or we if we put ourselves above it? The power to judge of the law as well as the fact in a criminal case, is to ascertain the existence of a law; if you see it in the statute book, you cannot on your oaths say there is no such law, or exercise a power denied to the people of a state by the most solemn constitutional provision, declare the supreme law to be void, because it does not comport with your opinion. Should you assume and exercise this power, your opinion does not become a supreme law, no one is bound by it, other juries will decide for themselves, and you could not expect that courts would look to your verdict for the construction of the constitution, as to the powers of the legislative or judicial departments of the government; nor that you have the power of declaring what the law is, what acts are criminal, what are innocent, as a rule of action for your fellow citizens or for the court. If juries once exercise this power, we are without a constitution or laws, one jury has the same power as another, you cannot bind those who may take your places, what you declare constitutional to-day, another jury may declare unconstitutional to-morrow. We shall cease to have a government of law, when what is the law, depends on the arbitrary and fluctuating opinions of judges and jurors, instead of the standard of the constitution, expounded by the tribunal to which has been referred all cases arising under the constitution, laws and treaties of the United States.

The counsel of the defendant has referred you to the message of the president, as the true exposition of the constitution in relation to the power of congress to charter the bank. We have no jurisidiction to judge of the propriety of the course of the executive; in the exercise of his constitutional power to prevent the passage of a law, he acts on his responsibility; but the judicial power cannot be exercised on the reasons which have governed the exercise of the veto power. We therefore forbear all remarks upon it. For a similar reason we cannot look to the construction given to the constitution by the executive department as a guide to our judgment; for no appellate or supervisory power over our proceedings, has been confided to that department. We must follow the rule prescribed by the tribunal to whom has been confided the power of expounding the constitution and laws, and of directing our judgment. That tribunal has adjudged this law to be valid, we cannot, and think you will not declare it void.

The jury found the defendant guilty.

52

JOSEPH STORY, COMMENTARIES ON THE
CONSTITUTION 3:§§ 1778–83, 1785–87
1833

§ 1778. The first clause requires the interposition of a grand jury, by way of presentment or indictment, before the party accused can be required to answer to any capital and infamous crime, charged against him. And this is regularly true at the common law of all offences, above the grade of common misdemeanors. A grand jury, it is well known, are selected in the manner prescribed by law, and duly sworn to make inquiry, and present all offences committed against the authority of the state government, within the body of the county, for which they are impannelled. In the national courts, they are sworn to inquire, and present all offences committed against the authority of the national government within the state or district, for which they are impannelled, or elsewhere within the jurisdiction of the national government. The grand jury may consist of any number, not less than twelve, nor more than twenty-three; and twelve at least must concur in every accusation. They sit in secret, and examine the evidence laid before them by themselves. A presentment, properly speaking, is an accusation made *ex mero motu* by a grand jury of an offence upon their own observation and knowledge, or upon evidence before them, and without any bill of indictment laid before them at the suit of the government. An indictment is a written accusation of an offence preferred to, and presented, upon oath, as true, by a grand jury at the suit of the government. Upon a presentment the proper officer of the court must frame an indictment, before the party accused can be put to answer it. But an indictment is usually in the first instance framed by the officers of the government, and laid before the grand jury. When the grand jury have heard the evidence, if they are of opinion, that the indictment is groundless, or not supported by evidence, they used formerly to endorse on the back of the bill, "ignoramus," or we know nothing of it, whence the bill was said to be *ignored*. But now they assert in plain English, "not a true bill," or which is a better way, "not found;" and then the party is entitled to be discharged, if in custody, without farther answer. But a fresh bill may be preferred against him by another grand jury. If the grand jury are satisfied of the truth of the accusation, then they write on the back of the bill, "a true bill," (or anciently, "*billa vera.*") The bill is then said to be found, and is publicly returned into court; the party stands indicted, and may then be required to answer the matters charged against him.

§ 1779. From this summary statement it is obvious, that the grand jury perform most important public functions; and are a great security to the citizens against vindictive prosecutions, either by the government, or by political partisans, or by private enemies. Nor is this all; the indictment must charge the time, and place, and nature, and circumstances, of the offence, with clearness and certainty; so that the party may have full notice of the charge, and be able to make his defence with all reasonable knowledge and ability.

§ 1780. There is another mode of prosecution, which exists by the common law in regard to misdemeanors; though these also are ordinarily prosecuted upon indictments found by a grand jury. The mode, here spoken of, is by an information, usually at the suit of the government or its officers. An information generally differs in nothing from an indictment in its form and substance, except that it is filed at the mere discretion of the proper law officer of the government *ex officio*, without the intervention or approval of a grand jury. This process is rarely recurred to in America; and it has never yet been formally put into operation by any positive authority of congress, under the national government, in mere cases of misdemeanor; though common enough in civil prosecutions for penalties and forfeitures.

§ 1781. Another clause declares, that no person shall be subject, "for the same offence, to be twice put in jeopardy of life and limb." This, again, is another great privilege secured by the common law. The meaning of it is, that a party shall not be tried a second time for the same offence, after he has once been convicted, or acquitted of the offence charged, by the verdict of a jury, and judgment has passed thereon for or against him. But it does not mean, that he shall not be tried for the offence a second time, if the jury have been discharged without giving any verdict; or, if, having given a verdict, judgment has been arrested upon it, or a new trial has been granted in his favour; for, in such a case, his life or limb cannot judicially be said to have been put in jeopardy.

§ 1782. The next clause prohibits any person from being compelled, in any criminal case, to be a witness against himself, or being deprived of life, liberty, or property, without due process of law. This also is but an affirmance of a common law privilege. But it is of inestimable value. It is well known, that in some countries, not only are criminals compelled to give evidence against themselves, but are subjected to the rack or torture in order to procure a confession of guilt. And what is worse, it has been (as if in mockery or scorn) attempted to excuse, or justify it, upon the score of mercy and humanity to the accused. It has been contrived, (it is pretended,) that innocence should manifest itself by a stout resistance, or guilt by a plain confession; as if a man's innocence were to be tried by the hardness of his constitution, and his guilt by the sensibility of his nerves. Cicero, many ages ago, though he lived in a state, wherein it was usual to put slaves to the torture, in order to furnish evidence, has denounced the absurdity and wickedness of the measure in terms of glowing eloquence, as striking, as they are brief. They are conceived in the spirit of Tacitus, and breathe all his pregnant and indignant sarcasm. Ulpian, also, at a still later period in Roman jurisprudence, stamped the practice with severe reproof.

§ 1783. The other part of the clause is but an enlargement of the language of magna charta, *"nec super eum ibimus, nec super eum mittimus, nisi per legale judicium parium suorum, vel per legem terrae,"* neither will we pass upon him, or condemn him, but by the lawful judgment of his peers, or by the law of the land. Lord Coke says, that these latter words, *per legem terrae* (by the law of the land,) mean by due process of law, that is, without due presentment or indictment, and being brought in to answer thereto by due process of the common law. So that this clause in effect affirms the right of trial according to the process and proceedings of the common law.

. . . . .

§ 1785. The other article, in declaring, that the accused shall enjoy the right to a speedy and public trial by an impartial jury of the state or district, wherein the crime shall have been committed, (which district shall have been previously ascertained by law,) and to be informed of the nature and cause of the accusation, and to be confronted with the witnesses against him, does but follow out the established course of the common law in all trials for crimes. The trial is always public; the witnesses are sworn, and give in their testimony (at least in capital cases) in the presence of the accused; the nature and cause of the accusation is accurately laid down in the indictment; and the trial is at once speedy, impartial, and in the district of the offence. Without in any measure impugning the propriety of these provisions, it may be suggested, that there seems to have been an undue solicitude to introduce into the constitution some of the general guards and proceedings of the common law in criminal trials, (truly admirable in themselves) without sufficiently adverting to the consideration, that unless the whole system is incorporated, and especially the law of evidence, a corrupt legislature, or a debased and servile people, may render the whole little more, than a solemn pageantry. If, on the other hand, the people are enlightened, and honest, and zealous in defence of their rights and liberties, it will be impossible to surprise them into a surrender of a single valuable appendage of the trial by jury.

§ 1786. The remaining clauses are of more direct significance, and necessity. The accused is entitled to have compulsory process for obtaining witnesses in his favour, and to have the assistance of counsel. A very short review of the state of the common law, on these points, will put their propriety beyond question. In the first place, it was an anciently and commonly received practice, derived from the civil law, and which Mr. Justice Blackstone says, in his day, still obtained in France, though since the revolution it has been swept away, not to suffer the party accused in capital cases to exculpate himself by the testimony of any witnesses. Of this practice the courts grew so heartily ashamed from its unreasonable and oppressive character, that another practice was gradually introduced, of examining witnesses for the accused, but not upon oath; the consequence of which was, that the jury gave less credit to this latter evidence, than to that produced by the government. Sir Edward Coke denounced the practice as tyrannical and unjust; and denied, that, in criminal cases, the party accused was not to have witnesses sworn for him. The house of commons, soon after the accession of the house of Stuart to the throne of England, insisted, in a particular bill then pending, and, against the efforts both of the crown and the house of lords, caused a clause affirming the right, in cases tried under that act, of witnesses being sworn for, as well as against, the accused. By the statute of 7 Will. 3, ch. 3, the same measure of justice was established throughout the realm, in cases of treason; and afterwards, in the reign of Queen Anne, the like rule was extended to all cases of treason and felony. The right seems never to have been doubted, or denied, in cases of mere misdemeanors. For what causes, and upon what grounds this distinction was maintained, or even excused, it is impossible to assign any satisfactory, or even plausible reasoning. Surely, a man's life must be of infinitely more value, than any subordinate punishment; and if he might protect himself against the latter by proofs of his innocence, there would seem to be irresistible reasons for permitting him to do the same in capital offences. The common suggestion has been, that in capital cases no man could, or rather ought, to be convicted, unless upon evidence so conclusive and satisfactory, as to be above contradiction or doubt. But who can say, whether it be in any case so high, until all the proofs in favour, as well as against, the party have been heard? Witnesses for the government may swear falsely, and directly to the matter in charge; and, until opposing testimony is heard, there may not be the slightest ground to doubt its truth; and yet, when such is heard, it may be incontestible, that it is wholly unworthy of belief. The real fact seems to be, that the practice was early adopted into the criminal law in capital cases, in which the crown was supposed to take a peculiar interest, in base subserviency to the wishes of the latter. It is a reproach to the criminal jurisprudence of England, which the state trials, antecedently to the revolution of 1688, but too strongly sustain. They are crimsoned with the blood of persons, who were condemned to death, not only against law, but against the clearest rules of evidence.

§ 1787. Another anomaly in the common law is, that in capital cases the prisoner is not, upon his trial upon the general issue, entitled to have counsel, unless some matter of law shall arise, proper to be debated. That is, in other words, that he shall not have the benefit of the talents and assistance of counsel in examining the witnesses, or making his defence before the jury. Mr. Justice Blackstone, with all his habitual reverence for the institutions of English jurisprudence, as they actually exist, speaks out upon this subject with the free spirit of a patriot and a jurist. This, he says, is "a rule, which, however it may be palliated under cover of that noble declaration of the law, when rightly understood, that the judge shall be counsel for the prisoner, that is, shall see, that the proceedings against him are legal, and strictly regular, seems to be not all of a piece with the rest of the humane treatment of prisoners by the English law. For upon what face of reason can that assistance be denied to save the life of a man, which is yet allowed him in prosecutions for every petty trespass." The defect has indeed been cured in England in cases of treason; but it still remains unprovided for in all other cases, to, what one can hardly help deeming, the discredit of the free genius of the English constitution.

53

UNITED STATES v. GIBERT

25 Fed. Cas. 1287, no. 15,204 (C.C.D.Mass. 1834)

STORY, Circuit Justice. This is an indictment for a robbery on the high sea, which is declared to be a capital offence and piracy by the statute of 1790, c. 9 [1 Stat. 113]. The prisoners having been found guilty, a motion has now been made for a new trial, upon grounds stated in a written motion submitted to the court. Upon the grounds thus stated, it is unnecessary for me to say any more at present, than that so far as they purport to be founded upon what took place at the trial in the presence of the court and jury, they are not admitted by the court, to present a full, accurate, or just representation of all the facts and circumstances. This remark is made simply to prevent any misapprehension from any silence or acquiescence of the court upon this subject.

The question now to be considered is, whether this court has, by the constitution and laws of the United States, authority to grant a new trial in a case circumstanced as the present is. And, in order to free the case as much as possible from any collateral and unimportant considerations, it is proper to state, that in examining this question, we shall, for the present, assume that the court had jurisdiction of the case; that there has been no mis-trial, in a legal sense, that is, no such irregularity, or error in impannelling the jury to try the cause, or in the other proceedings, in the course of the trial, as would upon the face of the process and proceedings be fatal as matter of substance, and that the indictment is sufficient in point of law to found a just judgment against the prisoners in conformity to the verdict. In other words, for the purpose of the argument, we shall for the present assume that the jurisdiction is clear, that the indictment is good, and that the trial has been regularly had, and the verdict has been regularly rendered by a competent jury.

Under such circumstances, has this court authority, by the constitution and laws of the United States, to grant a new trial after a verdict regularly rendered of guilty against the prisoners?

. . . . .

Upon the whole, having given this subject the fullest consideration, I am, upon the most mature deliberation, of opinion that this court does not possess the power to grant a new trial, in a case of a good indictment, after a trial by a competent and regular jury, whether there be a verdict of acquittal or conviction. My judgment is, that the words in the constitution. "Nor shall any person be subject, for the same offence, to be twice put in jeopardy of life or limb," mean that no person shall be tried a second time for the same offence, where a verdict has been already given by a jury. The party tried is in a legal sense, as well as in common sense, in jeopardy of his life, when a lawful jury have once had charge of his offence as a capital offence upon a good indictment, and have delivered themselves of the charge by a verdict. In this respect I follow the doctrine of the supreme court of New York; and the doctrine of the supreme court of Pennsylvania and North Carolina goes not only to the same extent, but includes cases where the party is once put upon his trial before the jury, and they are discharged from giving a verdict without extreme necessity. This too is the clear, determinate and well settled doctrine of the common law, acting upon the same principle, as a fundamental rule of criminal jurisprudence. I deem it a privilege of inestimable value to the citizen; and that it was introduced into the constitution upon the soundest principles of prudence and justice. But if it were otherwise, it is my duty to administer the constitution as it stands and not to incorporate new provisions into it. If this clause does not prohibit a new trial, where there has already been a regular trial and verdict, then it is wholly immaterial whether the verdict is of acquittal or of conviction of the offence; and the same party may, in the discretion of the court, be put upon his trial ten, nay, twenty times, if the court should deem it fit. It was (as I think) among other things, to get rid of the terrible precedents on this subject alluded to by Lord Hale, and even acted upon by him, in the reign of Charles II., in discharging juries from giving verdicts upon frivolous or oppressive suggestions, that this great maxim of the common law was engrafted into the constitution. The constitution has also in another clause declared, that "no fact once tried by a jury shall be otherwise re-examined in any court of the United States, than according to the rules of the common law." The only modes of making this re-examination known to the common law, are by a writ of error and a new trial, and if by the common law there cannot be a new trial in a capital case, after a regular trial once had upon a good indictment, as seems to me to be conclusively established by the English authorities already cited, then this clause also carries in its bosom another virtual prohibition.

Lest I should be thought to have overlooked the case of U. S. v. Daniel, 6 Wheat. [19 U. S.] 542, where the circuit court divided upon the motion for a new trial, I beg only to say that the point whether the circuit court had jurisdiction to grant a new trial in a capital case, was not before the court. It was a mere certificate of division of opinion of the circuit court; and the supreme court held that it had no jurisdiction to entertain the point certified, so far as it regarded a new trial.

If the language used by me in the Commentaries on the Constitution (3 Story, Const. c. 38, § 1781) should be thought to inculcate a different doctrine, I can only say that I do not so understand it. I have no doubt that there are cases where there may be a new trial; as in cases of a mis-trial by an improper jury. See People v. M'Kay, 18 Johns. 212; 2 Hawk. bk. 2, c. 36, § 15; Rex v. Keite, 1 Ld. Raym. 139; 2 Hawk. P. C. c. 27, § 104; Id. c. 47, § 12; Arundel's Case, 6 Coke, 14. But in the language there used, it should be considered that the author was not summing up his own private or judicial opinions, but only gathering together the opinions of others, which had come to his knowledge, to illustrate the text. But if there be any erroneous opinions inculcated in those Commentaries, which upon more deliberate examination I should deem unfounded, I trust that I shall be the last person to insist upon them as obligatory or correct. My duty, as a judge, is to pronounce such a judgment as my conscience dictates, without reference to any preconceived opinions. But I freely admit that I see nothing in that passage of the Commentaries, so far as relates to the granting of new trials, which I deem incorrect, or which I wish to retract.

It may be thought by some, that there may be great inconvenience in the establishment of this doctrine. But if there be, it is for those who possess the power to amend the constitution to apply the proper remedy. For myself, I

entertain great doubts whether, in the actual administration of public justice, the present doctrine would not be far more safe and useful than an unlimited power to grant new trials in all capital cases, at the mere discretion of the court. It may be, that a court may sometimes err in the proper administration of the law; and it may also err in granting or refusing a new trial. But the consciousness that the trial is final, will always impress every court, mindful of its duty, with the utmost caution in all its opinions and judgments in capital cases, where the result may be unfavorable to the prisoner. It will naturally induce it to lean to the side of mercy; and it will look anxiously to the dictates of the law. But still if, after all, errors should intervene, it will be but the common infirmity of the administration of all human justice. And the prisoner, even in such a case, will not be wholly without redress. He may apply for a pardon or mitigation of the sentence, to the executive; and it cannot be doubted that the court itself, if conscious of any serious error, would cheerfully aid in his application. Hitherto this ultimate appeal to the pardoning power has been deemed satisfactory and safe in the land of our ancestors down to our own age; and it has been deemed equally satisfactory and safe in all those states whose jurisprudence does not permit a new trial in capital cases under like circumstances. But whatever might be my opinion as to the authority of this court to grant a new trial in capital cases generally, I shall, under the present circumstances go over all the grounds insisted upon by the prisoner's counsel (some of which being in arrest of judgment, are indispensable to be disposed of before judgment), because if any error in point of law has been committed by the court, injurious to the prisoners, or upon established principles of law, they ought (if the court could grant it) to have a new trial, I should feel it my duty to make a direct application in their behalf to the executive for a pardon, to redress the error. God forbid that any man in this country should suffer death against the law, from the mere infirmity of judgment of those who are appointed to preside at his trial.

. . . . .

Another cause assigned for a new trial is that the jury were furnished with newspapers in their room, and did read them during the pendency of the trial; and subsequently another ground was added in a supplementary paper, that the jury drank ardent spirits while they had the cause in charge. It is important to a right understanding of these objections, to state the real facts and circumstances attendant upon the trial. The trial lasted, I believe, about fifteen days, during which time the jury were kept together night and day in the custody of officers. Some of them were engaged in very pressing business, which required them to communicate with friends respecting that business; and one or more of them was in ill health during the trial, and was obliged to have the aid of a physician. These circumstances were stated in open court, and it was agreed between the counsel in open court, that the jury might have all reasonable refreshments during the trial, that they might communicate on business with their friends, and write and receive papers from their friends on business, the papers being previously examined, and the conversation witnessed and heard by one or more of the officers of the court. And the court requested the jury during the trial, and until the arguments were heard and the charge given, not to converse with each other on the subject of the trial, in order to keep their minds open to the last moment to all the merits of the cause. While the jury were thus kept together, they were allowed by the officers of the court attending them, to read the public newspapers, the officers first inspecting them and cutting out every thing that in any manner related to the trial. And it now appears, as well from the affidavits of the officers, as from the affidavits of the jurymen, that in point of fact they never saw any thing in any newspaper relative to the trial. The officers granted the indulgence to read the newspapers, under a mere mistake of their duty, and as soon as the charge was given by the court, the jury were not allowed to see any newspaper, until after they had delivered their verdict in open court. So far, then, as reading the newspapers went, there is not the slightest reason to believe that it could or did in fact in any manner whatsoever affect the verdict or influence the jury. The evidence, as far as it bears on the point, negatives any supposition of this sort. And, speaking for myself, I must say that considering the protracted nature of the trial, and the necessary privations of the jury, and the importance of keeping them when out of court from too constant meditation upon the subject of the trial while it was yet imperfectly before them, I do not doubt that the indulgence had a tendency to tranquillize their minds, and to keep them in a state of calmness and freedom from anxiety highly favorable and useful to the prisoners themselves. Without doubt it was a great irregularity in the officers of the court, for which they may be punishable, to have granted this indulgence without the express sanction of the counsel or of the court. I am not aware that any such sanction was given. But it is not every irregularity of officers, which would justify a court in setting aside a verdict and granting a new trial, or treating the matter as a mis-trial. The court must clearly see that it is an irregularity, which goes to the merits of the trial, or justly leads to the suspicion of improper influence, or effect, on the conduct or acts of the jurors. We must take things as they are in our days. Juries cannot now, as in former ages, be kept in capital cases upon bread and water, and shut up in a sort of gloomy imprisonment, with nothing to occupy their thoughts. It would probably be most disastrous to the administration of justice, and especially to prisoners, to attempt, in these days, the enforcement of such rigid severities, so repugnant to all the usual habits of life. And for one, I am not satisfied that the irregularity in the present case has been in the slightest manner prejudicial to the prisoners; but on the contrary, as far as the evidence leads me to any conclusion, I should deem it favorable to the prisoners. The indulgence ceased the moment when the charge was given, and the jury were then put upon their own solemn and exclusive deliberations on the case.

The other ground is, that the jury, while they had the cause in charge, drank ardent spirits. Now it is most material to state certain facts which took place at the trial, and which though wholly passed over in this motion, yet essentially affect its validity and force. After the charge was given by the court to the jury, one of the jurors in open court stated that he had been unwell for several days, and still was so, and that it was impossible for him under the circumstances to confine himself to water, without danger to his health; and he wished permission to use such spirit as might be required for his health. The counsel for the prisoners then assented in open court to this indulgence, and it was also assented to by the district attorney, who at the same time suggested that the like indulgence ought to be extended to any others of the jurors, whose state of health, from the great length of the trial, and their unusual confinement, might also require it. The counsel for the prisoners then gave their consent to this extension of the indulgence. It was accordingly stated to the jury in open court that it was so granted; but they were at the same time advised to use the indulgence as little as possible, and in as moderate a manner as practicable. Now upon this statement, where there was an express consent given by the prisoners' counsel in open court to this indulgence to the jurors, it seems to me impossible that the present objection can be sustained, unless it is shown, that the indulgence was grossly abused, and operated injuriously to the prisoners. Of this there is not the slightest proof, nor indeed was it even pretended at the argument. On the contrary, the only evidence in the case to establish the fact of drinking ardent spirits, comes from one of the jurors, who is said to have stated, after the trial was over, that he was sick and went down to the bar, and got a glass of brandy and water. The juror himself has not been examined. And this renders it wholly unnecessary to consider the authority and bearing of the cases cited at the bar on this subject: and especially the cases of People v. Douglass, 4 Cow. 26, Brant v. Fowler, 7 Cow. 562, and People v. Ransom, 7 Wend. 417, for they all turn upon very different circumstances.

. . . . .

DAVIS, District Judge. I concur with the presiding judge in the disposal of the motions before us, in this very serious case, which has so long engaged the devoted and solicitous attention of the court, counsel, and jury. With the grounds and reasons of that opinion my own views coincide, excepting in one point, and on that, from its important bearing, as a constitutional question, I consider it a duty to express my opinion. I refer to that part of the argument, which rests the denial of a power, in the courts of the United States, to grant a new trial, on the merits, in a capital case, though at the request of a person convicted, on the 5th article of amendments to the constitution, declaring, that "no person shall be subject, for the same offence, to be twice put in jeopardy of life or limb." The case of a person convicted of a capital offence, put on trial again, would certainly be embraced by the terms of the article; and yet, in my view of the question, it would not present a case within its true intent and meaning. The article, in the amendments to the constitution, corresponding to a rule of the common law, according to the prevailing spirit and character of those amendments generally, was doubtless intended for the security and benefit of the individual. As such it may be waived and relinquished.

That the request of a prisoner for a new trial, affording a chance of escape from death to which a previous conviction would assign him, should be rejected, from adherence to the letter of the rule, that his life would be again in jeopardy, would present an incongruity not readily to be admitted. It is true, that according to approved authorities, the plea of autre fois convict depends on the same principle as the plea of autre fois acquit, that no man ought to be twice brought in danger of his life, for one and the same cause. Bl. Comm. bk. 4, c. 26; 2 Hawk. P. C. 377. The doctrine establishes a right in the prisoner to resort to that defence, if it be attempted or moved, against his will, to subject him to a second trial. The case of a verdict of conviction set aside, at the request of the prisoner, is not suggested in those authorities, and would stand, in my opinion, on very different ground. The previous conviction would not, I apprehend, under such circumstances, be considered as a sufficient bar to a second trial. The concise manner in which many general maxims of the law are expressed, like general rules on other topics, admits or requires, in their application, distinctions, exceptions, and qualifications, all just, reasonable, and, in some instances, indispensable, not expressed in their terms. We have an instructive exemplification of this in an early case, in the supreme court of the United States, in which the meaning of the prohibition, in the constitution, of ex post facto laws, came in question. "I do not consider," said Mr. Justice Chase, "any law as ex post facto, that nullifies the rigor of the criminal law, but only those that create or aggravate the crime, or increase the punishment, or change the rules of evidence for the purpose of conviction." 3 Dall. 391. The benign spirit, ever pervading our law, which dictated that distinction, may, as appears to me, have a proper influence and application, in reference to the rule of law under consideration, and in other instances of analogous character. By the old common law, observes Sir W. Blackstone, the accessory could not be arraigned till the principal was attainted, "unless he choose it, for he might waive the benefit of the law." Comm. bk. 4, c. 25. And in People v. McKay, 18 Johns. 212, a case of murder, Chief Justice Spencer remarks: "We know of no case which contains the doctrine, that where a new trial is awarded, at the prayer and in favor of a person that has been found guilty, he shall not be subject to another trial." On the whole, I am not convinced that the article of the constitution under consideration, would, in just and reasonable construction, be a bar to a new trial granted at the request of a person capitally convicted. I am not aware that there is any direct decision on this point. It is an open question. If a second trial in capital cases, be inadmissible, under the article, though at the request of the prisoner, then no legislative enactment can vary the law on the subject, without an amendment of the constitution. The question may thus become highly important, though the article should be binding only in the courts of the United States; still more so if, conformably to Chief Justice Spencer's opinion, it extend to decisions in the state courts. A decision on this point, however, is not essential, as this case stands, to a determination on the motion for a new trial, in which, notwithstanding a difference in opinion in reference to the constitutional question, we come to the same result. The discretion of the court on the subject of new trials is not unlimited. They are allowable "for reasons for which new trials have usually been granted in the courts of law," and with this statute direction, we are to bear in mind the 7th article of amendments to the constitution— "No fact tried by a jury, shall be otherwise re-examined, in any court of the United States, than according to the rules of the common law." Having reference to such directories, should the motion for a new trial in this case be allowed, there would, in my opinion, be a departure from the usages of courts of law, and from the principles manifested by the great current of decisions in cases of this description.

I agree with the presiding judge, in the views which he has expressed on the motion in arrest of judgment, as well as with those on the motion for a new trial, excepting in the instance which I have specified, and in the result, that the motions be overruled.

. . . . .

STORY, Circuit Justice. This being the case of a capital conviction, when the counsel for the prisoners, a week ago, suggested an intention to offer a bill of exceptions, the court then stated, that it would be expected that he should show some authority to justify the court in allowing a bill of exceptions in a capital case. It is now admitted, that the counsel have no authority to cite, which affirms the power in this court. And it is believed by the court, that none exists. We have, however, in the interval between the suggestion and the present time, deliberately examined the point, and are fully satisfied, that no such power exists in the court; and therefore it has not been deemed necessary to examine the correctness of the exceptions stated in the bill, which has been proffered.

In the first place, no power is given by statute to this court, to allow any bill of exceptions in any criminal case whatsoever; and it seems impossible to infer it by implication from any provisions in the laws of the United States. The circuit courts have final jurisdiction of all cases of crimes; and no writ of error or appeal lies to the supreme court in any such cases. Now, the sole object of a bill of exceptions is to present the matter for the revision of some superior court; and if no revision can be had, then the authority to allow a bill of exceptions would be utterly nugatory. The only mode contemplated by the laws of the United States to revise the opinions of the judges of the cirucit courts in criminal cases is, when the judges are divided in opinion at the trial; and then the point of division may be certified to the supreme court for a final decision under the judicial act of 1802 (chapter 31, § 6). There was no such division upon the present trial. If resort be had to the common law to aid us in examining this point, it will be found, that no bill of exceptions lies, in capital cases, even since the statute of Westminster II. (13 Edw. I. St. 1) c. 31, which first gave a bill of exceptions. And the better opinion certainly now is, that that statute is confined to civil proceedings, and does not extend to any criminal proceedings whatsoever. As the authorities are not all agreed on this point in cases of mere misdemeanors, it is not necessary here to decide it in regard to the latter. But in capital cases, in cases of treason and felony, it is universally agreed in England, that no bill of exceptions lies. This was solemnly settled in the case of Rex v. Vane, which was a case of high treason. It is reported in 1 Lev. 68, and in various other Reports. See Buller, N. P. 316; 1 Chit. Cr. Law (English Ed.) 622; Willes, 535, and note (b), which cites 2 Inst. 424, and Saville, 2. The very point was made, and according to Leving's Reports, it was held by the court, "that a bill of exceptions does not lie in criminal cases, but only in actions between party and party." The application was accordingly overruled, and Sir H. Vane was executed on Tower Hill. The same doctrine is laid down in Hawkins (2 Hawk. P. C. c. 46, § 198), who says: "It hath been adjudged, that no bill of exceptions is grantable on an indictment of treason or felony, the statute of Westminster, etc., having never been thought to extend to any such case." Lord Hardwicke, in Rex v. Inhabitants of Preston, Cas. t. Hardw. 251, 2 Strange, 1040, said: "Nor was it ever pretended, that in capital cases a bill of exceptions lay. In Vane's Case, it is not said to lie in any criminal case. But that point is not settled, and therefore I will give no opinion as to that." In Bacon's Abridgment (1 Bac. Abr. "Bill of Exceptions") it is said: "It is agreed that no bill of exceptions is to be allowed in treason or felony." And the same doctrine will be found in other elementary writers (see Buller, N. P. 316; 1 Chit. Cr. Law, English Ed., 622; Willes, 535, and note b, which cites 2 Inst. 424, and Saville, 2), and no authority to the contrary can be found. In People v. Holbrook, 13 Johns. 90, S. P. 6 Cow. 565, it was held by the supreme court of New York that no bill of exceptions lies in any criminal case; and this doctrine is not only supported by Vane's Case, but by Rex v. Barkstead, 1 Kreb. 244; T. Raym. 468; 1 Sid. 85.

There is then no pretence to say, that in capital cases this court can draw in aid the doctrines of the common law, as administered in England, to confer such a power. It is not implied from any statute authority. It is not implied in any reasoning at the common law, or under the statute of Westminster. We are therefore of opinion, that this court possesses no such authority; and we dare not assume what has never been confided to the court.

If this objection were not, as we think it is, conclusive, we think, that the bill of exceptions ought not now to be allowed, upon another and a distinct ground. It was not made or tendered at the trial, nor until a long time afterwards, and after a motion made and argued for a new trial and in arrest of judgment, and the opinion of the court deliberately had thereon. Under such circumstances, where the verdict was satisfactory, and the court feel no doubt about the law, it is our opinion, that the bill of exceptions ought not to be allowed. It is not within the general principles, which regulate rights of this sort. See 1 Salk. 288; 8 Mod. 222; 2 Tidd, Prac. 788. The government has its rights, as well as the prisoners.

Bill of exceptions not allowed.

SEE ALSO:

Generally Bill of Rights
An Act to Prevent Malicious Informations in the Court of Kings Bench, 4 and 5 W. & M., c. 18 (1692)
An Act for Regulating Trials in Cases of Treason and Misprision of Treason, 7 Wm. 3, c. 3 (1695)
Sir Matthew Hale, History of the Common Law (1716), Gray 164–65
William Hawkins, Pleas of the Crown 1:ch. 1, § 3 (1716)
Sir Matthew Hale, Pleas of the Crown 1:306 (Emlyn ed. 1736)
William Blackstone, Commentaries 4:388–89 (1769)
Joseph Hawley to Elbridge Gerry, 18 Feb. 1776, Gerry, Life 1:162
Georgia Constitution of 1777, art. 45, Thorpe 2:784
James Wilson, Charge Delivered to Grand Jury, May 1791, Works 2:805–6
Kentucky Constitution of 1792, art. 12, secs. 10–14, Thorpe 3:1274–75
Zylstra v. Charleston, 1 Bay 382 (S.C. 1794)
Kentucky Constitution of 1799, art. 10, secs. 10–15, Thorpe 3:1289–90
Commonwealth v. Gibbs, 4 Dall. 253 (Pa. 1802)
Galbreath's Lessee v. Eichelberger, 3 Yeates 515 (Pa. 1803)
St. George Tucker, Blackstone's Commentaries 4:App. 64–74 (1803)
United States v. Smith, 27 Fed. Cas. 1192, no. 16,342 (C.C.D.N.Y. 1806)
Maryland Constitution of 1776, Amendment of 1807, arts. 3 and 4, Thorpe 3:1704
Commonwealth v. Hardy, 2 Mass. 303 (1807)
People v. McLean, 2 Johns. R. 381 (N.Y. 1807)
United States v. Hill, 26 Fed. Cas. 315, no. 15,364 (C.C.D.Va. 1809)
Woods v. Rowan, 5 Johns. R. 133 (N.Y. 1809)
Louisiana Constitution of 1812, art. 6, sec. 18, Thorpe 3:1389
United States v. Mann, 26 Fed. Cas. 1153, no. 15,717 (C.C.D.N.H. 1812)
House of Representatives, Punishment of Treason, 10 Jan. 1814, Annals 26:881–88
United States v. Coolidge, 25 Fed. Cas. no. 14,858 (D.Mass. 1815)
Illinois Constitution of 1818, art. 8, secs. 8–12, Thorpe 2:981–82
United States v. Wood, 28 Fed. Cas. 755, no. 16,757 (C.C.D.Pa. 1818)
William Wirt, New Trials before Courts-Martial, 14 Sept. 1818, 1 Ops. Atty. Gen. 233
M'Intyre v. Mancuis, 16 Johns. R. 592 (N.Y. 1819)
William Wirt, Courts-Martial, 29 Aug. 1819, 1 Ops. Atty. Gen. 294
United States v. Cornell, 25 Fed. Cas. 650, no. 14,868 (C.C.D.R.I. 1820)
People v. McKay, 18 Johns. R. 212 (N.Y. 1820)
Vaughan v. Commonwealth, 2 Va. Cas. 273 (1821)
United States v. Lynn, 26 Fed. Cas. 1036, no. 15,649 (C.C.D.C. 1822)
Commonwealth v. Green, 17 Mass. 515 (1822)
United States v. Haskell, 26 Fed. Cas. 207, no. 15,321 (C.C.E.D.Pa. 1823)
State v. Moor, 1 Walker 134 (Miss. 1823)
Devaughan's Case, 7 Fed. Cas. 560, no. 3,837 (C.C.D.C. 1824)
Commonwealth v. Olds, 5 Little 137 (Ky. 1824)
State v. Sexton, 3 Hawks 184 (N.C. 1824)
Southard v. Rexford, 6 Cow. 254 (N.Y. 1826)
Northrup v. Hatch, 6 Conn. 361 (1827)
James Kent, Commentaries 2:9–10 (1827)
Bank of the United States v. Washington, 2 Fed. Cas. 741, no. 940 (C.C.D.C. 1828)
Salmon v. Clagett, 3 Bland Ch. 125 (Md. 1828)
Wolf v. Wolf, 2 Har. & Gill 382 (Md. 1828)

William Rawle, A View of the Constitution of the United States, 128–30, 132–34, 205–8 (2d ed. 1829)
Ward v. State, 2 Mo. 120 (1829)
Commonwealth v. Jones, 1 Leigh 598 (Va. 1829)
People v. Mather, 4 Wend. 229 (N.Y. 1830)
State v. McKee, 1 Bailey 651 (S.C. 1830)
Fries v. Brugler, 7 Halsted 79 (N.J. 1830)
An Act Declaratory of the Law concerning Contempts of Court, 4 Stat. 487 (1831)

Skinner v. Judson, 8 Conn. 528 (1831)
Livingston v. Harris, 3 Paige Ch. 528 (N.Y. 1832)
People v. Comstock, 8 Wend. 549 (N.Y. 1832)
Bellinger v. People, 8 Wend. 595 (N.Y. 1832)
United States v. Twenty-eight Packages of Pins, 28 Fed. Cas. 244, no. 16,561 (D.E.D.Pa. 1833)
Matter of Smith, 10 Wend. 449 (N.Y. 1833)

Amendment V

(Due Process and Taking)

No person shall be held to answer for a capital, or otherwise infamous crime, unless on a presentment or indictment of a Grand Jury, except in cases arising in the land or naval forces, or in the Militia, when in actual service in time of War or public danger; nor shall any person be subject for the same offence to be twice put in jeopardy of life or limb; nor shall be compelled in any criminal case to be a witness against himself, nor be deprived of life, liberty, or property, without due process of law; nor shall private property be taken for public use, without just compensation.

1. *Dr. Bonham's Case*, 8 Co. Rep. 107a, 114a (C.P. 1610)
2. Virginia Ordinance and Constitution of 1621, art. 5
3. Controversy over Petition of Right, 3 How. St. Tr. 59, 222–34 (1628)
4. Sir Edward Coke, Second Institute (1641)
5. Sir Edward Coke, Third Institute (1641)
6. John Locke, Second Treatise §§ 138–40 (1689)
7. Montesquieu, Spirit of Laws, bk. 26, ch. 15 (1748)
8. William Blackstone, Commentaries (1765)
9. Continental Congress, Declaration and Resolves, 14 Oct. 1774
10. Virginia Declaration of Rights, sec. 1, 12 June 1776
11. Delaware Declaration of Rights and Fundamental Rules, 11 Sept. 1776
12. John Jay, A Freeholder, A Hint to the Legislature of the State of New York, Winter 1778
13. Alexander Hamilton, Remarks on an Act for Regulating Elections, New York Assembly, 6 Feb. 1787
14. *Ham v. M'Claws*, 1 Bay 93 (S.C. 1789)
15. *Bowman v. Middleton*, 1 Bay 252 (S.C. 1792)
16. *State v. ——*, 1 Hayw. 28 (N.C. 1794)
17. *Vanhorne's Lessee v. Dorrance*, 2 Dall. 304 (C.C.D.Pa. 1795)
18. *Lindsay v. Commissioners*, 2 Bay 38 (S.C. 1796)
19. *University of North Carolina v. Fox*, 1 Mur. 58 (N.C. 1805)
20. *Gardner v. Village of Newburgh*, 2 Johns. Ch. 162 (N.Y. 1816)
21. *The Thomas & Henry*, 1 Marshall's C.C. 367 (C.C.D.Va. 1818)
22. *Bradshaw v. Rogers*, 20 Johns. R. 103 (N.Y. 1822)
23. *Picquet v. Swan*, 19 Fed. Cas. 609, no. 11,134 (C.C.D.Mass. 1828)
24. *Beckman v. Saratoga & S. R.R.*, 3 Paige Ch. 45 (N.Y. 1831)
25. *Livingston v. Mayor of New York*, 8 Wend. 85 (N.Y. 1831)
26. *Barron v. Baltimore*, 7 Pet. 243 (1833)
27. *Wellington, et al., Petitioners*, 16 Pick. 87 (Mass. 1834)

1

DR. BONHAM'S CASE
8 Co. Rep. 107a, 114a (C.P. 1610)

4. The censors cannot be judges, ministers, and parties; judges to give sentence or judgment; ministers to make summons; and parties to have the moiety of the forfeiture, *quia aliquis non debet esse Judex in propria causa, imo iniquum est aliquem suae rei esse judicem;* and one cannot be judge and attorney for any of the parties, Dyer 3 E. 6. 65. 38 E. 3. 15. 8 H. 6. 19 b. 20 a. 21 E. 4. 47 a., &c. And it appears in our books, that in many cases, the common law will controul acts of parliament, and sometimes adjudge them to be utterly void: for when an act of parliament is against common right and reason, or repugnant, or impossible to be performed, the common law will controul it, and adjudge such act to be void; and, therefore, in 8 E. 3. 30 a. b. Thomas Tregor's case on the statute of W. 2. c. 38. *et artic' super chartas,* c. 9. Herle saith, some statutes are made against law and right, which those who made them perceiving, would not put them in execution: the stat. of W. 2. c. 21. gives a writ of *Cessavit haeredi petenti super haeredem tenent' et super eos quibus alienatum fuerit hujusmodi tenementum:* and yet it is adjudged in 33 E. 3. *Cessavit* 42. where the case was, two coparceners lords, and tenant by fealty and certain rent, one coparcener had issue and died, the aunt and the niece shall not join in a *Cessavit,* because the heir shall not have a *Cessavit* for the cesser in the time of his ancestor, F. N. B. 209. F. and therewith agrees Plow. Com. 110 a.; and the reason is, because in a *Cessavit* the tenant before judgment may render the arrearages and damages, &c. and retain his land, and that he cannot do when the heir brings a *Cessavit* for the cesser in the time of his ancestor, for the arrearages incurred in the life of the ancestor do not belong to the heir: and because it would be against common right and reason, the common law adjudges the said act of parliament as to that point void. The statute of Carlisle, made *anno* 35 E. 1. enacts, that the order of the Cistercians and Augustines, who have a convent and common seal, that the common seal shall be in the keeping of the prior, who is under the abbot, and four others of the most grave of the house, and that any deed sealed with the common seal, which is not so in keeping shall be void: and the opinion of the Court (*in an.* 27 H. 6. Annuity 41.) was, that this statute was void, for it is impertinent to be observed, for the seal being in their keeping, the abbot cannot seal any thing with it, and when it is in the abbot's hands, it is out of their keeping *ipso facto;* and if the statute should be observed, every common seal shall be defeated upon a simple surmise, which cannot be tried. Note, reader, the words of the said statute at Carlisle, *anno* 35 E. 1. (which is called *Statutum religiosorum*) are, *Et insuper ordinavit dominus Rex et statuit, quod Abbates Cisterc' et Praemonstraten' ordin' religiosorum, &c. de caetero habeant sigillum commune, et illud in custodia Prioris monasterii seu domus, et quatuor de dignioribus et discretioribus ejusdem loci conventus sub privato sigillo Abbatis ipsius loci custod' depo', &c. Et si forsan aliqua scripta obligationum, donationum, emptionum, venditionum, alienationum, seu aliorum quorumcunque, contractuum alio sigillo quam tali sigillo communi sicut praemittit' custodit' inveniant' a modo sigillat', pro nullo penitus habeantur omnique careant firmitate.* So the statute of 1 E. 6. c. 14. gives chauntries, &c. to the King, saving to the donor, &c. all such rents, services, &c. and the common law controuls it, and adjudges it void as to services, and the donor shall have the rent, as a rentseck, distrainable of common right, for it would be against common right and reason that the King should hold of any, or do service to any of his subjects, 14 Eliz. Dyer 313. and so it was adjudged Mich. 16 & 17 Eliz. in *Com' Banco* in Strowd's case. So if any act of parliament gives to any to hold, or to have conusans of all manner of pleas arising before him within his manor of D., yet he shall hold no plea, to which he himself is party; for, as hath been said, *iniquum est aliquem suae rei esse judicem.* 5. If he should forfeit 5*l.* for one month by the first clause, and should be punished for practising at any time by the second clause, two absurdities should follow,—1. That one should be punished not only twice but many times for one and the same offence. And the divine saith, *Quod Deus non agit bis in idipsum;* and the law saith, *Nemo debet bis puniri pro uno delicto.* 2. It would be absurd, by the first clause, to punish practising for a month, and not for a lesser time, and by the second to punish practising not only for a day, but at any time, so he shall be punished by the first branch for one month by the forfeit of 5*l.* and by the second by fine and imprisonment, without limitation for every time of the month in which he practises physic. And all these reasons were proved by two grounds, or maxims in law; 1. *Generalis clausula non porrigitur ad ea quae specialiter sunt comprehensa:* and the case between Carter and Ringstead, Hil. 34 Eliz. Rot. 120. *in Communi Banco,* was cited to this purpose, where the case in effect was, that A. seised of the manor of Staple, in Odiham, in the county of Southampton in fee, and also of other lands in Odiham aforesaid in fee, suffered a common recovery of all, and declared the use by indenture, that the recoverer should stand seised of all the lands and tenements in Odiham, to the use of A. and his wife, and to the heirs of his body begotten; and further, that the recoveror should stand seised to the use of him, and to the heirs of his body, and died, and the wife survived, and entered into the said manor by force of the said general words: but it was adjudged, that they did not extend to the said manor which was specially named: and if it be so in deed, *a fortiori,* it shall be so in an act of parliament, which (as a will) is to be expounded according to the intention of the makers. 2. *Verba posteriora propter certitudinem addita ad priora quae certitudine indigent sunt referenda.* 6 E. 3. 12 a. b. Sir Adam de Clydrow, Knight, brought a *praecipe quod reddat* against John de Clydrow; and the writ was, *quod juste, &c. reddat manerium de Wicomb et duas carucatas terrae cum pertinentiis in Clydrow,* in that case the town of Clydrow shall not relate to the manor, *quia non indiget,* for a manor may be demanded without mentioning that it lies in any town, but *cum pertinentiis,* although it comes after the town, shall relate to the manor, *quia indiget. Vide* 3 E.

4. 10. the like case. But it was objected, that where by the second clause it was granted, that the censors should have *supervisum et scrutinium, correctionem et gubernationem omnium et singulorum medicorum, &c.* they had power to fine and imprison.

To that it was answered,—1. That *this* is but part of the sentence, for by the entire sentence it appears in what manner they shall have power to punish, for the words are, *ac punitionem eorum pro delictis suis in non bene exequendo, faciendo, vel utendo illa facultate;* so that without question all their power to correct and punish the physicians by this clause is only limited to these three cases, *sc. in non bene exequendo, faciendo, vel utendo, &c.* Also this word *punitionem* is limited and restrained by these words, *ita quod punitio eorundem medicorum, &c. sic in praemissis delinquentium, &c.* which words, *sic in praemissis delinquentium,* limit the former words in the first part of this sentence, *ac punitionem eorum pro delictis suis in non bene exequendo, &c.* 2. It would be absurd, that in one and the same sentence the makers of the act should give them a general power to punish without limitation; and a special manner how they shall punish, in one and the same sentence. 3. Hil. 38 Eliz. in a *quo warranto* against the Mayor and Commonalty of London, it was held, that where a grant is made to the Mayor and Commonalty, that the Mayor for the time being should have *plenum et integrum scrutinium, gubernationem, et correctionem omnium et singulorum mysteriorum, &c.* without granting them any court, in which should be legal proceedings, that it is good for search, whereby a discovery may be made of offences and defects, which may be punished by the law in any court; but it doth not give, nor can give them any irregular or absolute power to correct or punish any of the subjects of the kingdom at their pleasure.

2

VIRGINIA ORDINANCE AND CONSTITUTION
OF 1621, ART. 5
Thorpe 7:3812

V. WHEREAS in all other Things, we require the said General Assembly, as also the said Council of State, to imitate and follow the Policy of the Form of Government, Laws, Customs, and Manner of Trial, and other Administration of Justice, used in the Realm of *England,* as near as may be, even as ourselves, by his Majesty's Letters Patent, are required.

3

CONTROVERSY OVER PETITION OF RIGHT
3 How. St. Tr. 59, 222–34 (1628)

The Petition of Right.

The PETITION exhibited to his majesty by the lords spiritual and temporal, and commons in this present parliament assembled, concerning divers Rights and Liberties of the Subjects.

To the King's most excellent majesty.

I. "Humbly shew unto our sovereign lord the king, the lords spiritual and temporal, and commons in parliament assembled, that whereas it is declared and enacted by a statute made in the time of the reign of king Edward 1, commonly called, 'statutum de tallagio non concedendo*,' that no tallage or aid shall be laid or levied, by the king or his heirs, in this realm, without the good will and assent of the archbishops, bishops, earls, barons, knights, burgesses, and other the freemen of the commonalty of this realm: and by authority of parliament holden in the 25th year of the reign of king Edward 3†, it is declared and enacted, That from thenceforth no person shall be compelled to make any Loans to the king against his will, because such Loans were against reason, and the franchise of the land; and by other‡ laws of this realm it is provided, that none should be charged by any charge or imposition, called a Benevolence, nor by such like charge; by which the statutes before-mentioned, and other the good laws and statutes of this realm, your subjects have inherited this freedom, that they should not be compelled to contribute to any tax, tallage, aid, or other like charge, not set by common consent in parliament.

II. "Yet nevertheless, of late, divers Commissions, directed to sundry commissioners in several counties, with instructions, have issued; by means whereof your people have been in divers places assembled, and required to lend certain sums of money unto your majesty, and many of them, upon their refusal so to do, have had an oath administered unto them, not warrantable by the laws or statutes of this realm, and have been constrained to become bound to make appearance, and give attendance before your privy-council, and in other places; and others of them have been therefore imprisoned, confined, and sundry other ways molested and disquieted. And divers other charges have been laid and levied upon your people in several counties, by lords lieutenants, deputy lieutenants, commissioners for musters, justices of peace, and others, by command and direction from your majesty, or your privy-council, against the laws and free customs of this realm.

* 34 Edw. 1.
† 25 Edw. 3, Rot. Parl.
‡ 1 Edw. 3, 6. 11 R. 2, 9. 1 R. 3, 2.

III. "And whereas also by the statute called*, 'The Great Charter of the Liberties of England,' it is declared and enacted, That no Freeman may be taken or imprisoned or be disseised of his freehold or liberties, or his free customs, or be outlawed or exiled, or in any manner destroyed, but by the lawful judgment of his peers, or by the law of the land.

IV. "And in the 28th year of the reign of king Edward 3†, it was declared and enacted by authority of parliament, That no man, of what estate or condition he be, should be put out of his land or tenements, nor taken, nor imprisoned, nor disherited, nor put to death, without being brought to answer by due process of law.

V. "Nevertheless, against the tenor of the said statutes‡, and other the good laws and statutes of your realm, to that end provided, divers of your subjects have of late been imprisoned, without any cause shewed; and when for their deliverance they were brought before your justices, by your majesty's Writs of Habeas Corpus, there to undergo and receive as the court should order, and their keepers commanded to certify the causes of their detainer; no cause was certified, but that they were detained by your majesty's special command, signified by the lords of your privy-council, and yet were returned back to several prisons, without being charged with any thing to which they might make answer according to the law.

VI. "And whereas of late, great companies of Soldiers and Mariners have been dispersed into divers counties of the realm, and the inhabitants, against their wills, have been compelled to receive them into their houses, and there to suffer them to sojourn against the laws and customs of this realm, and to the great grievance and vexation of the people.

VII. "And whereas, also, by authority of parliament, in the 25th year of the reign of king Edw. 3, it is declared and enacted, That no man shall be fore-judged of life or limb against the form of the Great Charter and other laws and statutes of this realm: and by the said Great Charter, and other the laws and statutes of this your realm, no man ought to be adjudged to death, but by the laws established in this your realm, either by the customs of the same realm, or by acts of parliament: and, whereas no offender of what kind soever is exempted from the proceedings to be used, and punishments to be inflicted by the laws and statutes of this your realm: nevertheless, of late, divers commissions, under your majesty's great seal, have issued forth, by which, certain persons have been assigned and appointed commissioners with power and authority to proceed, within the land, according to the justice of martial law, against such soldiers and mariners, or other dissolute persons joining with them, as should commit any murder, robbery, felony, mutiny, or other outrage or misdemeanor whatsoever; and by such summary course and orders as is agreeable to martial law, and is used in armies in time of war, to proceed to the trial and condemnation of such offenders, and them to cause to be executed and put to death, according to the martial law.

VIII. "By pretext whereof some of your majesty's subjects have been, by some of the said commissioners, put to death; when and where, if by the laws and statutes of the land they had deserved death, by the same laws and statutes also they might and by no other ought to have been adjudged and executed.

IX. "And, also, sundry grievous offenders by colour thereof, claiming an exemption, have escaped the punishment due to them by the laws and statutes of this your realm, by reason that divers of your officers and ministers of justice have unjustly refused, or forborn to proceed against such offenders, according to the same laws and statutes, upon pretence that the said offenders were punishable only by martial law, and by authority of such commissions, as aforesaid; which commissions, and all others of like nature, are wholly and directly contrary to the said laws and statutes of this your realm.

X. "They do therefore humbly pray your most excellent majesty,§ 1. That no man hereafter be compelled to make or yield any gift, loan, benevolence, tax, or such like charge, without common consent by act of parliament; 2. and that none be called to make answer, or take such oath, or to give attendance, or be confined, or otherwise molested or disquieted concerning the same, or for refusal thereof: 3. and that no freeman in any such manner as is before mentioned, be imprisoned or detained.

XI. "All which they most humbly pray of your most excellent majesty, as their rights and liberties, according to the laws and statutes of this realm: and that your majesty would also vouchsafe to declare, that the awards, doings, and proceedings, to the prejudice of your people, in any of the premises, shall not be drawn hereafter into consequence or example: and that your majesty would be also graciously pleased, for the further comfort and safety of your people, to declare your royal will and pleasure, that in the things aforesaid, all your officers and ministers shall serve you, according to the laws and statutes of this realm, as they tender the honour of your majesty, and the prosperity of this kingdom." [See Statutes at large, 3, 4 Car. 1.]

The King's ANSWER.

Which Petition being read the 2d of June, the king's Answer was thus delivered by the lord keeper:

"The king willeth that right be done according to the laws and customs of the realm; and that the statutes be put in due execution, that his subjects may have no cause to complain of any wrong or oppressions, contrary to their just Rights and Liberties: to the preservation whereof, he holds himself in conscience as well obliged, as of his prerogative."

On Tuesday, June 3, the king's Answer was read in the House of Commons, and seemed not full enough, in regard of so much expence of time and labour, as had been employed in contriving the Petition.

* 9 Hen. 3, 29.
† 28 Edw. 3, 3.
‡ 37 Edw. 3, 18. 38 Edw. 3, 9. 42 Edw. 3, 3. 17 Ric. 2, 6.

§ 25 Edw. 1, 6.

June 3. A Message was brought from the King by the Speaker,

"That his majesty having, upon the Petition exhibited by both houses, given an Answer full of justice and grace, for which we and our posterity have just cause to bless his majesty, it is now time to grow to a conclusion of the session; and therefore his majesty thinks fit to let you know, that as he doth resolve to abide by that Answer, without further change or alteration, so he will royally and really perform unto you what he hath thereby promised: and further, that he resolves to end this session upon Wednesday the 11th of this month. And therefore wisheth, that the house will seriously attend those businesses, which may best bring the session to a happy conclusion, without entertaining new matters; and so husband the time, that his majesty may with the more comfort bring us speedily together again: at which time, if there be any further grievances not contained, or expressed in the Petition, they may be more maturely considered than the time will now permit.

Another Message was brought from his Majesty
by the Speaker, Thursday 5th of June.

"His majesty wished them to remember the Message he last sent them, by which he set a day for the end of this session, and he commanded the Speaker to let them know, that he will certainly hold that day prefixed without alteration; and because that cannot be, if the house entertain more business of length, he requires them, that they enter not into, or proceed with any new business, which may spend greater time, or which may lay any scandal or aspersion upon the state-government or ministers thereof."

Sir *Robert Philips*, upon this occasion, expressed himself thus: I perceive, that towards God, and towards man, there is little hope, after our humble and careful endeavours, seeing our sins are many and so great: I consider my own infirmities, and if ever my passions were wrought upon, that now this message stirs me up especially; when I remember with what moderation we have proceeded, I cannot but wonder to see the miserable straight we are now in: what have we not done, to have merited? Former times have given wounds enough to the people's liberty, we came hither full of wounds, and we have cured what we could; and what is the return of all but misery and desolation? What did we aim at, but to have served his majesty, and to have done that which would have made him great and glorious? If this be a fault, then we are all criminous. What shall we do, since our humble purposes are thus prevented, which were not to have laid any aspersion on the government, since it tended to no other end, but to give his majesty true information of his and our danger? And to this we are enforced out of a necessity of duty to the king, our country, and to posterity; but we being stopped, and stopped in such manner, as we are enjoined, so we must now leave to be a council. I hear this with that grief, as the saddest message of the greatest loss in the world. But let us still be wise, be humble; let us make a fair declaration to the king.

Sir *John Elliot*. Our sins are so exceeding great, that unless we speedily return to God, God will remove himself

further from us: ye know with what affection and integrity we have proceeded hitherto, to have gained his majesty's heart, and out of a necessity of our duty, were brought to that course we were in: I doubt, a misrepresentation to his majesty hath drawn this mark of his displeasure upon us: I observe in the Message, amongst other sad particulars, it is conceived, that we were about to lay some aspersions on the government; give me leave to protest, that so clear were our intentions, that we desire only to vindicate those dishonours to our king and country, &c. It is said also, as if we cast some aspersions on his majesty's ministers; I am confident no minister, how dear soever, can—

Here the Speaker started up from the seat of the chair, apprehending sir John Elliot intended to fall upon the Duke, and some of the ministers of state; and said, There is a command laid upon me, that I must command you not to proceed.—Whereupon sir John Elliot sate down.

Sir *Dudley Diggs*. I am as much grieved as ever. Must we not proceed? Let us sit in silence, we are miserable, we know not what to do.

Hereupon there was a silence in the house for a while, which was broken by sir Nathaniel Rich, in these words:

Sir *Nathaniel Rich*. We must now speak or for ever hold our peace; for us to be silent when king and kingdom are in this calamity, is not fit. The question is, Whether we shall secure ourselves by silence, yea or no? I know it is more for our own security, but it is not for the security of those for whom we serve; let us think on them: some instruments desire a change, we fear his majesty's safety, and the safety of the kingdom, I do not say we now see it; and shall we now sit still and do nothing, and so be scattered? Let us go together to the lords, and shew our dangers, that we may then go to the king together.

Others said, that the Speech lately spoken by sir John Elliot had given offence (as they feared) to his majesty.

Whereupon the House declared, "That every member of the house is free from any undutiful Speech, from the beginning of the parliament to that day;" and ordered, "That the house be turned into a Committee to consider what is fit to be done for the safety of the kingdom; and that no man go out upon pain of going to the Tower." But before the Speaker left the chair, he desired leave to go forth; and the house ordered that he may go forth, if he please. And the house was hereupon turned into a Grand Committee: Mr. Whitby in the chair.

Mr. *Wandesford*. I am full of grief as others, let us recollect our English hearts, and not sit still, but do our duties: two ways are propounded, to go to the lords, or to the king; I think it is fit we go to the king, for this doth concern our Liberties, and let us not fear to make a Remonstrance of our Rights; we are his counsellors. There are some men which call evil good, and good evil, and bitter sweet; justice is now called popularity and faction.

Sir *Edward Coke*. We have dealt with that duty and moderation that never was the like, *rebus sic stantibus*, after such a violation of the Liberties of the Subject: let us take this to heart. In 30 Ed. 3, were they then in doubt in parliament to name men that misled the king? They accused John de Gaunt, the king's son, and lord Latimer, and lord

Nevil, for misadvising the king, and they went to the Tower for it; now when there is such a downfal of the state, shall we hold our tongues? How shall we answer our duties to God and men? 7 H. 4, Parl. Rot. n. 31, & 32, 11 H. 4, n. 13, there the Council are complained of, and are removed from the king; they mewed up the king, and dissuaded him from the common good; and why are we now retired from that way we were in? Why may we not name those that are the cause of all our evils? In 4 H. 3, & 27 E. 3, & 13 R. 2 the parliament moderated the king's prerogative; and nothing grows to abuse, but this house hath power to treat of it. What shall we do? Let us palliate no longer; if we do, God will not prosper us. I think the duke of Buckingham is the cause of all our miseries; and till the king be informed thereof, we shall never go out with honour, or sit with honour here: that man is the grievance of grievances: let us set down the causes of all our disasters, and all will reflect upon him. As for going to the lords, that is not *via regia;* our liberties are now impeached, we are concerned; it is not *via regia*, the lords are not participant with our liberties.

Mr. *Selden* advised, That a Declaration be drawn under four heads: 1. To express the house's dutiful carriage towards his majesty. 2. To tender their liberties that are violated. 3. To present what the purpose of the house was to have dealt in. 4. That that great person, viz. the Duke, fearing himself to be questioned, did interpose and cause this distraction. All this time, (said he) we have cast a mantle on what was done last parliament; but now being driven again to look on that man, let us proceed, with that which was then well begun, and let the charge be renewed that was last parliament against him, to which he made an answer, but the particulars were sufficient, that we might demand judgment on that answer only.

In conclusion, the house agreed upon several Heads for a Remonstrance. But the Speaker, who after he had leave to go forth, went privately to the King, brought this Message:

"That his majesty commands for the present they adjourn the house till to-morrow morning, and that all committees cease in the mean time."—And the house was accordingly adjourned.

At the same time the king sent for the Lord-Keeper to attend him presently; the house of lords was adjourned *ad libitum*. The Lord-Keeper being returned, and the house resumed, his lordship signified his majesty's desire, that the house and all committees be adjourned till to-morrow morning.

Friday, 6th of June, Mr. Speaker brought another Message from the King, and said:—In my service to this house I have had many undeserved favours from you, which I shall ever with all humbleness acknowledge, but none can be greater than that testimony of your confidence yesterday shewed unto me, whereby I hope I have done nothing, or made any representation to his majesty, but what is for the honour and service of this house; and I will have my tongue cleave to my mouth, before I will speak to the disadvantage of any member thereof: I have now a Message to deliver unto you;

"Whereas his majesty understanding, that you did conceive his last Message to restrain you in your just privileges, these are to declare his intentions, That he had no meaning of barring you from what hath been your right, but only to avoid all scandals on his council and actions past, and that his ministers might not be, nor himself, under their names, taxed for their counsel unto his majesty, and that no such particulars should be taken in hand, as would ask a longer time of consideration than what he hath already prefixed, and still resolves to hold; that so, for this time, Christendom might take notice of a sweet parting between him and his people: which if it fall out, his majesty will not be long, from another meeting, when such grievances, if there be any, at their leisure and convenience may be considered."

Mr. Speaker proceeded:

I will observe somewhat out of this Message; ye may observe a great inclination in his majesty to meet in this house. I was bold yesterday to take notice of that liberty ye gave me to go to his majesty: I know there are none here but did imagine whither I went, and but that I knew you were desirous and content that I should leave you, I would not have desired it: give me leave to say, This Message bars you not of your right in matter, nay, not in manner; but it reacheth to his counsels past, and for giving him counsel in those things which he commanded.

The House of Lords likewise received this Message by the Lord-Keeper.

"My Lords, his majesty takes notice, to your great advantage, of the proceedings of this house upon the hearing of his majesty's Message yesterday; he accounts it a fair respect, that ye would neither agree on any committee, or send any Message to his majesty, though it were in your own hearts, but yield yourselves to his majesty's Message, and defer your own resolutions till you meet again at the time appointed by his majesty. Yet his majesty takes it in extreme good part to hear what was in your heart, and especially that you were so sensible of the inconvenience that might ensue upon the breach of this parliament: which if it had happened or shall hereafter happen, his majesty assures himself, that he shall stand clear before God and men of the occasion.—But his majesty saith, Ye had just cause to be sensible of the danger of considering how the state of Christendom now stands in respect of the multitude and strength of our enemies, and weakness on our part. All which his majesty knows very exactly, and in respect thereof, called this parliament; the particulars his majesty holds it needless to recite, especially to your lordships, since they are apparent to all men: neither will it be needful to reiterate them to his majesty, whose cares are most attentive upon them, and the best remedy that can be thought on therein, is, if his subjects do their parts. Therefore his majesty gives you hearty thanks, and bid me tell you, that nothing hath been more acceptable to him all the time of this parliament, than this dutiful and discrete carriage of your lordships, which he professeth hath been a chief motive to his majesty, to suspend those intentions that were not far from a resolution."

Sir *Robert Philips* assumed the debate, upon the Message delivered by the Speaker, and said; I rise up with a disposition, somewhat in more hope of comfort than yesterday; yet, in regard of the uncertainty of counsels, I shall not change much. In the first place, I must be bold without flattering, a thing not incident to me, to tell you Mr. Speaker, you have not only at all times discharged the duty of a good Speaker, but of a good man; for which I render you many thanks.—Another respect touching his majesty's Answer to our Petition; first, if that answer fall out to be short, I free his majesty, and I believe his resolution was to give that which we all expected: but in what, as in others, we have suffered, by reason of interposed persons between his majesty and us. But this day is by intervenient accidents diverted from that, but so, as in time we go to his majesty; therefore let us remove those jealousies in his majesty of our proceedings, that by some men overgrown have been misrepresented. We have proceeded with temper, in confidence of his majesty's goodness to us, and our fidelity to him; and if any have construed, that what we have done hath been out of fear, let him know we came hither freemen, and will ever resolve to endure the worst; and they are poor men that make such interpretations of parliaments. In this way and method we proceeded, and if any thing fall out unhappily, it is not king Charles that advised himself, but king Charles misadvised by others, and misled by misordered counsel; it becomes us to consider what we were doing, and now to advise what is fit to be done. We were taking consideration of the state of the kingdom, and to present to his majesty the danger he and we are in, if since any man hath been named in particular, (though I love to speak of my betters with humility) let him thank himself and his counsels, but those necessary jealousies give us occasion to name him; I assure myself we shall proceed with temper, and give his majesty satisfaction, if we proceed in that way. His majesty's message is now explanatory in point of our liberties, that he intends not to bar us of our rights, and that he would not have any aspersion cast on the counsels past; let us present to his majesty shortly and faithfully, and declare our intentions, that we intend not to lay any aspersions upon him, but out of a necessity to prevent the imminent dangers we are surrounded with, and to present to him the affairs at home and abroad, and to desire his majesty, that no interposition or mis-information of men in fault may prevail, but to expect the issue that shall be full of duty and loyalty.

The Commons sent a Message to the Lords, that they would join in an humble request to the king, that a clear and satisfactory Answer be given by his majesty in full parliament to the Petition of Right; whereunto the lords did agree.

June 7, the King came to the Lords House, and the house of commons were sent for. And the Lord-Keeper presented the humble Petition of both houses, and said,

"May it please your most excellent majesty, the lords spiritual and temporal, and commons in parliament assembled, taking into consideration that the good intelligence between your majesty and your people doth much depend upon your majesty's Answer unto their Petition of Right formerly presented; with unanimous consent do now become most humble suitors unto your majesty, that you would be graciously pleased to give a clear and satisfactory Answer thereunto in full parliament."

Whereunto the King replied,

"The Answer I have already given you was made with so good deliberation, and approved by the judgments of so many wise men, that I could not have imagined but it should have given you full satisfaction; but to avoid all ambiguous interpretations, and to shew you that there is no doubleness in my meaning, I am willing to please you as well in words as in substance; read your Petition, and you shall have an Answer that I am sure will please you."

The Petition was read, and this Answer was returned:
Soit droit fait come il est desiré par le Petition.

C. R.

"This I am sure (said his majesty) is full, yet no more than I granted you in my first Answer; for the meaning of that was to confirm all your Liberties, knowing, according to your own protestations, that you neither mean nor can hurt my Prerogative. And I assure you, my maxim is, that the people's Liberties strengthen the king's Prerogative, and the king's Prerogative is to defend the people's Liberties. You see how ready I have shewed myself to satisfy your demands, so that I have done my part; wherefore, if this parliament have not a happy conclusion, the sin is yours, I am free from it."

Whereupon the Commons returned to their own house with unspeakable joy, and resolved so to proceed as to express their thankfulness.

The King's Message to the Lower House by
sir Humfrey May, 10th of June 1628.

His majesty is well pleased that your Petition of Right, and his Answer, be not only recorded in both houses of parliament, but also in all the courts of Westminster; and that his pleasure is, it be put in print for his honour, and the content and the satisfaction of his people, and that you proceed cheerfully to settle businesses for the good and reformation of the commonwealth.

June 26. The Speaker being sent for to the king at Whitehall, came not into the house till about nine o'clock. And after prayers, the Remonstrance concerning Tunnage and Poundage being ingrossed, was a reading in the house; and while it was a reading, the king sent for the Speaker and the whole house, and the king made a Speech as followeth:

"It may seem strange, that I came so suddenly to end this session; before I give my assent to the bills. I will tell you the cause, though I must avow, that I owe the account of my actions to God alone. It is known to every one, that a while ago the house of commons gave me a Remonstrance; how acceptable, every man may judge; and for the merit of it, I will not call that in question, for I am sure no wise men can justify it.—Now, since I am truly informed that a second Remonstrance is preparing for me to take away the profit of my Tunnage and Poundage, one of the chief maintenances of my crown, by alledging I have given away my right thereto by my Answer to your Petition:—This is so prejudicial unto me, that I am forced to end this session some few hours before I meant, being not willing to receive any more Remonstrances, to which I must give a harsh Answer. And since I see, that even the house of commons begins already to make false constructions of what I granted in your Petition, lest it be worse interpreted in the country, I will now make a Declaration concerning the true intent thereof:—The profession of both houses in the time of hammering this Petition, was no way to trench upon my Prerogative, saying, they had neither intention or power to hurt it. Therefore it must needs be conceived, that I have granted no new, but only confirmed the antient Liberties of my Subjects. Yet to shew the clearness of my intentions, that I neither repent nor mean to recede from any thing I have promised you, I do here declare myself, That those things which have been done, whereby many have had some cause to suspect the Liberties of the Subjects to be trenched upon, which indeed was the first and true ground of the Petition, shall not hereafter be drawn into example for your prejudice; and from time to time, in the word of a king, ye shall not have the like cause to complain. But as for Tunnage and Poundage, it is a thing I cannot want, and was never intended by you to ask, nor meant to me, I am sure, to grant.—To conclude, I command you all that are here to take notice of what I have spoken at this time, to be the true intent and meaning of what I grant you in your Petition; but especially you, my lords the Judges, for to you only, under me, belongs the interpretation of laws: for none of the houses of parliament, either joint or separate, (what new doctrine soever may be raised) have any power either to make or declare a law without my consent."

Then the Lord Keeper said, It is his majesty's pleasure that this session now end, and that the parliament be prorogued till the 20th of October next.

In the following sessions, viz. Wednesday, January 21st, it was ordered that Mr. Selden and others should see if the Petition of Right and his majesty's Answer thereunto were inrolled in the Parliament rolls, and the Courts at Westminster, as his majesty sent them word the last session they should be; and also in what manner they were entered; which was done accordingly, and Mr. Selden made report to the house, that his majesty's Speech made the last day of the session in the upper house is also entered by his majesty's command.—Hereupon Mr. Pym moved, that the debate hereof should be deferred till Tuesday next, by reason of the fewness of the house.

Sir *John Elliot*. This which is now mentioned, concerns the honour of the house, and the liberty of the kingdom; it is true, it deserves to be deferred till there be a full house, but it is good to prepare things. I find it is a great point; I desire a select Committee may enter into consideration thereof, and also how other Liberties of the kingdom be invaded. I find in the country the Petition of Right printed indeed, but with an Answer that never gave any satisfaction: I desire a committee may consider thereof, and present it to the house, and that the printer be sent for to give satisfaction to the house, by what warrant it was printed. Which was ordered.

Mr. *Selden*. For this Petition of Right, it is known how lately it hath been violated since our last meeting; the Liberties for life, person and freehold, how they have been invaded; and have not some been committed, contrary to that? Now we, knowing these invasions, must take notice of it. For Liberties, for State, we know of an order made in the Exchequer, that a sheriff was commanded not to execute a replevin, and men's goods are taken and must not be restored. Whereas no man ought to lose life, or limb, but by law; hath not one lately lost his ears (meaning Savage) that was censured in the Star-Chamber by an arbitrary sentence and judgment? Next, they will take away our arms, and then our lives. Let all see we are sensible of these customs creeping upon us: let us make a just presentation hereof to his majesty.

Norton the King's Printer was brought to the bar, and asked by what warrant the Additions to the Petition were printed? He answered, that there was a warrant (as he thought) from the king himself. And being asked whether there were not some copies printed without additions, he answered, there were some, but they were suppressed by warrant.

Sir *John Elliot* desired some clearer satisfaction might be made, and that he might answer directly by what warrant.—Whereupon he was called in again: who said, he did not remember the particular, but sure he was there was a warrant.

Mr. *Selden* reported from the Committee concerning the printing of the Petition of Right, that there were printed 1500 without any Addition at all, which were published in the time of the last parliament: but since the parliament, other copies have been printed, and these supprest and made waste paper; which the Printer did, as he said, by command from Mr. Attorney, which he received from his majesty. And the Printer further said, That the Attorney was with the Lord Privy-Seal at Whitehall, and there delivered unto the Printer sundry papers, with divers hands to them, and on the backside was endorsed thus, "We will and command you, that these Copies be printed."

Which put an end to this Grand Affair.

4

SIR EDWARD COKE, SECOND INSTITUTE 45, 55
1641

Magna Carta, c. 29 (1225): We will sell to no man, we will not deny or defer to any man either justice or right.

· · · · ·

And therefore, every subject of this realme, for injury done to him *in bonis, terris, vel persona,* by any other subject, be he ecclesiasticall, or temporall, free, or bond, man, or woman, old, or young, or be he outlawed, excommunicated, or any other without exception, may take his remedy by the course of the law, and have justice, and right for the injury done to him, freely without sale, fully without any deniall, and speedily without delay.

5

SIR EDWARD COKE, THIRD INSTITUTE 6
1641

It was further provided by the said Act of 33 H. 8. that if a man attainted of treason became mad, that notwithstanding he should be executed; which cruell and inhumane law lived not long, but was repealed, for in that point also it was against the common law, because by intendment of law the execution of the offender is for example, *ut poena ad paucos, metus ad omnes perveniat,* as before is said: but so it is not when a mad man is executed, but should be a miserable spectacle, both against law, and of extreame inhumanity and cruelty, and can be no example to others.

6

JOHN LOCKE, SECOND TREATISE §§ 138–40
1689

Chap. XI. Of the Extent of the Legislative Power.

. . . . .

138. *Thirdly,* The *Supream Power cannot take* from any Man any part of his *Property* without his own consent. For the preservation of Property being the end of Government, and that for which Men enter into Society, it necessarily supposes and requires, that the People should *have Property,* without which they must be suppos'd to lose that by entring into Society, which was the end for which they entered into it, too gross an absurdity for any Man to own. *Men* therefore *in Society having Property,* they have such a right to the goods, which by the Law of the Community are theirs, that no Body hath a right to take their substance, or any part of it from them, without their own consent; without this, they have no *Property* at all. For I have truly no *Property* in that, which another can by right take from me, when he pleases, against my consent. Hence it is a mistake to think, that the Supream or *Legislative Power* of any Commonwealth, can do what it will, and dispose of the Estates of the Subject *arbitrarily,* or take any part of them at pleasure. This is not much to be fear'd in Governments where the *Legislative* consists, wholly or in part, in Assemblies which are variable, whose Members upon the Dissolution of the Assembly, are Subjects under the common Laws of their Country, equally with the rest. But in Governments, where the *Legislative* is in one lasting Assembly always in being, or in one Man, as in Absolute Monarchies, there is danger still, that they will think themselves to have a distinct interest, from the rest of the Community; and so will be apt to increase their own Riches and Power, by taking, what they think fit, from the People. For a Man's *Property* is not at all secure, though there be good and equitable Laws to set the bounds of it, between him and his Fellow Subjects, if he who commands those Subjects, have Power to take from any private Man, what part he pleases of his *Property,* and use and dispose of it as he thinks good.

139. But *Government* into whatsoever hands it is put, being as I have before shew'd, intrusted with this condition, and *for this end,* that Men might have and secure *their Properties,* the Prince or Senate, however it may have power to make Laws for the regulating of *Property* between the Subjects one amongst another, yet can never have a Power to take to themselves the whole or any part of the Subjects *Property,* without their own consent. For this would be in effect to leave them no *Property* at all. And to let us see, that even *absolute Power,* where it is necessary, is *not Arbitrary* by being absolute, but is still limited by that reason, and confined to those ends, which required it in some Cases to be absolute, we need look no farther than the common practice of Martial Discipline. For the Preservation of the Army, and in it of the whole Commonwealth, requires an *absolute Obedience* to the Command of every Superiour Officer, and it is justly Death to disobey or dispute the most dangerous or unreasonable of them: but yet we see, that neither the Serjeant, that could command a Souldier to march up to the mouth of a Cannon, or stand in a Breach, where he is almost sure to perish, can command that Soldier to give him one penny of his Money; nor the *General,* that can condemn him to Death for deserting his Post, or for not obeying the most desperate Orders, can yet with all his absolute Power of Life and Death, dispose of one Farthing of that Soldiers Estate, or seize one jot of his Goods; whom yet he can command any thing, and hang for the least Disobedience. Because such a blind Obedience is necessary to that end for which the Commander has his Power, *viz.* the preservation of the rest; but the disposing of his Goods has nothing to do with it.

140. 'Tis true, Governments cannot be supported without great Charge, and 'tis fit every one who enjoys his share of the Protection, should pay out of his Estate his proportion for the maintenance of it. But still it must be with his own Consent, *i.e.* the Consent of the Majority, giving it either by themselves, or their Representatives chosen by them. For if any one shall claim a *Power to lay* and levy *Taxes* on the People, by his own Authority, and without such consent of the People, he thereby invades the *Fundamental Law of Property,* and subverts the end of Government. For what property have I in that which another may by right take, when he pleases to himself?

7

MONTESQUIEU, SPIRIT OF LAWS, BK. 26, CH. 15
1748

*15.—That we should not regulate by the Principles of
political Laws those Things which depend on the
Principles of civil Law*

As men have given up their natural independence to
live under political laws, they have given up the natural
community of goods to live under civil laws.

By the first, they acquired liberty; by the second, property. We should not decide by the laws of liberty, which,
as we have already said, is only the government of the
community, what ought to be decided by the laws concerning property. It is a paralogism to say, that the good of the
individual should give way to that of the public; this can
never take place, except when the government of the community, or, in other words, the liberty of the subject is concerned; this does not affect such cases as relate to private
property, because the public good consists in everyone's
having his property, which was given him by the civil laws,
invariably preserved.

Cicero maintains, that the Agrarian laws were unjust;
because the community was established with no other view
than that everyone might be able to preserve his property.

Let us, therefore, lay down a certain maxim, that whenever the public good happens to be the matter in question,
it is not for the advantage of the public to deprive an individual of his property, or even to retrench the least part
of it by a law, or a political regulation. In this case we
should follow the rigor of the civil law, which is the palladium of property.

Thus when the public has occasion for the estate of an
individual, it ought never to act by the rigor of political
law; it is here that the civil law ought to triumph, which,
with the eyes of a mother, regards every individual as the
whole community.

If the political magistrate would erect a public edifice, or
make a new road, he must indemnify those who are injured by it; the public is in this respect like an individual
who treats with an individual. It is fully enough that it can
oblige a citizen to sell his inheritance, and that it can strip
him of the great privilege, which he holds from the civil
law, of not being forced to alienate his possessions.

After the nations which subverted the Roman Empire
had abused their very conquests, the spirit of liberty called
them back to that of equity. They exercised the most barbarous laws with moderation: and if any one should doubt
the truth of this, they need only read Beaumanoir's admirable work on jurisprudence, written in the twelfth century.

They mended the highways in his time as we do at present. He says, that when a highway could not be repaired,
they made a new one as near the old as possible; but in-
demnified the proprietors at the expense of those who
reaped any advantage from the road. They determined at
that time by the civil law; in our days, we determine by the
law of politics.

8

WILLIAM BLACKSTONE, COMMENTARIES 1:137–38
1765

3. A third subordinate right of every Englishman is that of
applying to the courts of justice for redress of injuries.
Since the law is in England the supreme arbiter of every
man's life, liberty, and property, courts of justice must at
all times be open to the subject, and the law be duly administered therein. The emphatical words of *magna carta*,
spoken in the person of the king, who in judgment of law
(says sir Edward Coke) is ever present and repeating them
in all his courts, are these; "*nulli vendemus, nulli negabimus,
aut differemus rectum vel justitiam:* and therefore every subject," continues the same learned author, "for injury done
to him *in bonis, in terris, vel persona,* by any other subject,
be he ecclesiastical or temporal without any exception, may
take his remedy by the course of the law, and have justice
and right for the injury done to him, freely without sale,
fully without any denial, and speedily without delay." It
were endless to enumerate all the *affirmative* acts of parliament wherein justice is directed to be done according to
the law of the land: and what that law is, every subject
knows; or may know if he pleases: for it depends not upon
the arbitrary will of any judge; but is permanent, fixed,
and unchangeable, unless by authority of parliament. I
shall however just mention a few *negative* statutes, whereby
abuses, perversions, or delays of justice, especially by the
prerogative, are restrained. It is ordained by *magna carta*,
that no freeman shall be outlawed, that is, put out of the
protection and benefit of the laws, but according to the law
of the land. By 2 Edw. III. c. 8. and 11 Ric. II. c. 10. it is
enacted, that no commands or letters shall be sent under
the great seal, or the little seal, the signet, or privy seal, in
disturbance of the law; or to disturb or delay common
right: and, though such commandments should come, the
judges shall not cease to do right. And by 1 W. & M. st. 2.
c. 2. it is declared, that the pretended power of suspending, or dispensing with laws, or the execution of laws, by
regal authority without consent of parliament, is illegal.

Not only the substantial part, or judicial decisions, of the
law, but also the formal part, or method of proceeding,
cannot be altered but by parliament: for if once those outworks were demolished, there would be no inlet to all
manner of innovation in the body of the law itself. The
king, it is true, may erect new courts of justice; but then
they must proceed according to the old established forms
of the common law. For which reason it is declared in the
statute 16 Car. I. c. 10. upon the dissolution of the court
of starchamber, that neither his majesty, nor his privy

council, have any jurisdiction, power, or authority by English bill, petition, articles, libel (which were the course of proceeding in the starchamber, borrowed from the civil law) or by any other arbitrary way whatsoever, to examine, or draw into question, determine or dispose of the lands or goods of any subjects of this kingdom; but that the same ought to be tried and determined in the ordinary courts of justice, and by *course of law*.

9

CONTINENTAL CONGRESS, DECLARATION AND RESOLVES
14 Oct. 1774
Tansill 2

Resolved, N. C. D. 1. That they are entitled to life, liberty and property; and they have never ceded to any foreign power whatever, a right to dispose of either without their consent.

10

VIRGINIA DECLARATION OF RIGHTS, SEC. 1
12 June 1776

---

1. That all men are by nature equally free and independent, and have certain inherent rights, of which, when they enter into a state of society, they cannot, by any compact, deprive or divest their posterity; namely, the enjoyment of life and liberty, with the means of acquiring and possessing property, and pursuing and obtaining happiness and safety.

11

DELAWARE DECLARATION OF RIGHTS AND
FUNDAMENTAL RULES
11 Sept. 1776
Sources 339

---

10. That every Member of Society hath a Right to be protected in the Enjoyment of Life, Liberty and Property; and therefore is bound to contribute his Proportion towards the Expense of that Protection, and yield his personal Service when necessary, or an Equivalent thereto; but no Part of a Man's Property can be justly taken from him, or applied to public Uses without his own Consent or that of his legal Representatives; Nor can any Man that is conscientiously scrupulous of bearing Arms in any Case be justly compelled thereto if he will pay such Equivalent.

. . . . .

12. That every Freeman for every Injury done him in his Goods, Lands or Person, by any other Person, ought to have Remedy by the Course of the Law of the Land, and ought to have Justice and Right for the Injury done to him freely without Sale, fully without any Denial, and speedily without Delay, according to the Law of the Land.

12

JOHN JAY, A FREEHOLDER, A HINT TO THE
LEGISLATURE OF THE STATE OF NEW YORK
Winter 1778
Unpublished Papers 1:461–63

Under Governments which have just and equal Liberty for their Foundation, every Subject has a Right to give his Sentiments on all Matters of public Concern; provided it be done with Modesty and Decency. I shall therefore take the Liberty of calling the Attention of my Countrymen to a Subject, which however imporant seems to have passed without due Notice; I mean *the Practice of impressing Horses, Teems, and Carriages by the military, without the Intervention of a civil Magistrate, and without any Authority from the Law of the Land.*

It is the undoubted Right and unalienable Priviledge of a Freeman not to be divested, or interrupted in the innocent use, of Life, Liberty or Property, but by Laws to which he has assented, either personally or by his Representatives. This is the Corner Stone of every free Constitution, and to defend it from the Iron Hand of the Tyrant of Britain, all America is now in arms; every Man in America being most deeply interested in its Preservation. Violations of this inestimable Right, by the King of Great Britain, or by an American Quarter Master; are of the same Nature, equally partaking of Injustice; and differing only in the Degree and Continuance of the Injury.

That the Army either stationed in, or passing through, this State should be accommodated with Carriages etc. is not to be denied; and that it may often be necessary to impress them is equally true. The only Question is, whether the Army shall at their mere *Will and Pleasure* furnish themselves, and that *at the Point of the Bayonet;* or whether they shall be furnished under the civil Authority of the State; and that in a Manner consistant with Reason, Liberty, and the Rights of Freemen.

It is neither my Desire or Design, to dwell on the *licencious* manner, in which this unconstitutional Power has been exercised in this State, by the little Officers belonging to the Quarter masters Department. Few among us require any Information on that Head. Nor would I be thought to impute it to the Directors of that Department; several of whom deseve Credit for Humanity, Prudence, and Love of Liberty. They cannot be present on every occasion, and are often obliged to employ Persons, who are ignorant of the Circumstances of the Inhabitants, and more sollicitous to shew their Power than Discretion.

It is against the Principle, not the Manner of its Exercise, that I contend. It would equally be an Insult to our Government, which ought to be a Government of Laws, as well as a Violation of the Rights of its Subjects; for the wisest and most discreet Man in the World, with a Party of armed Men at his Heels, without any Law, but that of *the necessity of the Case,* which cloaks as many Sins in Politics, as Charity is said to do in Religion; arbitrarily and by Force, to take the Property of a free Inhabitant, for the Use of the Army.

Nor does this extraordinary Exertion of Power admit of any other Excuse, than that the Legislature of this State have passed no Laws on the Subject, but have left the Quarter Master and his Agents without any other Rule for their Conduct than what should seem right in their own Eyes. In my Opinion such Laws ought no longer to be delayed. We cannot foresee to what Lengths this dangerous Practice may extend, or where a Line can be drawn. The army may want Blankets, Shoes and many other articles besides Horses and Carriages, and there certainly is as much Propriety in deducing a Right in them to impress the one as the other, from *the necessity of the Case.* In short, it is difficult to conceive of any arbitrary Act, which that prolific Mother of Tyranny may not breed, and when in Conjunction with Power, has not bred. There is scarce a Page in the History of any Nation, which does not exhibit a black account of some of her Progeny, or which does not represent her as a common Prostitute to all the Tyrants in the World, from Great Tyrants on Thrones, down to Petty Tyrants in Village Schools.

These Impresses may I think easily be so regulated by Laws, as to relieve the Inhabitants from reasonable Cause of Complaint, and yet not, retard or embarrass the Service. It may not be improper to observe that it is no less the Interest of the Quarter Master and their agents than of the People at large that such Laws should take Place. The Time may come when Law and Justice will again pervade the State, and many who now severely feel this kind of oppression, may then bring Actions and recover Damages. This is true Doctrine, however questionable the Policy of declaring it at this Time may be. For my own Part I think it ought to be declared and sounded from one End of the State to the other. Let such oppressive Evils be examined not concealed. Let them be remedied and not permitted silently to fester in the Hearts of Freemen. In an ensuing Paper I shall communicate my Ideas of the Remedy.

13

ALEXANDER HAMILTON, REMARKS ON AN ACT FOR REGULATING ELECTIONS, NEW YORK ASSEMBLY
6 Feb. 1787
Papers 4:35

We had in a former debate, travelled largely over the ground of the constitution, as applied to legislative disqualifications; He would not repeat what he had said, but he hoped to be indulged by the house in explaining a sentence in the constitution, which seems not well understood by some gentlemen. In one article of it, it is said no man shall be disfranchised or deprived of any right he enjoys under the constitution, but by the *law of the land,* or the judgment of his peers. Some gentlemen hold that the law of the land will include an act of the legislature. But Lord Coke, that great luminary of the law, in his comment upon a similar clause, in Magna Charta, interprets the law of the land to mean presentment and indictment, and process of outlawry, as contradistinguished from trial by jury. But if there were any doubt upon the constitution, the bill of rights enacted in this very session removes it. It is there declared that, no man shall be disfranchised or deprived of any right, but by *due process of law,* or the judgment of his peers. The words *"due process"* have a precise technical import, and are only applicable to the process and proceedings of the courts of justice; they can never be referred to an act of legislature.

14

HAM v. M'CLAWS
1 Bay 93 (S.C. 1789)

The Court. It is clear, that statutes passed against the plain and obvious principles of common right, and common reason, are absolutely null and void, as *far as they are calculated to operate against those principles.* In the present instance, we have an act before us, which, were the strict letter of it applied to the case of the present claimants, would be *evidently* against *common reason.* But we would not do the legislature who passed this act, so much injustice, as to sit here and say that it was their intention to make a forfeiture of property brought in here as this was. We are, therefore, bound to give such a construction to this enacting clause of the act of 1788, as will be consistent with justice, and the dictates of natural reason, though contrary to the strict letter of the law; and this construction is, that the legislature never had it in their contemplation to make a forfeiture of the negroes in question, and subject the parties to so heavy a penalty for bringing slaves into the state, under the circumstances and for the purposes, the claimants have proved.

Present, GRIMKE, WATIES and DRAYTON, Judges.

15

BOWMAN V. MIDDLETON
1 Bay 252 (S.C. 1792)

For the defendant, an objection was taken by his counsel, that no title could be transferred by this act. That it was against common right and reason as well as against *magna charta,* therefore, *ipso facto,* void. In the first place, it went to deprive the heir at law of *Nicholls* of 146 acres of land, without being called upon to answer or defend his title; and that too without the intervention of a trial by his peers. In the next place, it went to deprive the eldest son of old *John Cattel* of his inheritance, (his father dying intestate,) by settling the estate in *William,* the second son. So that, in fact, it wrought a two-fold injury, by depriving the heir at law of *Nicholls* and the heir at law of *Cattel* of their freeholds, without a trial by jury. They admitted that there might be great and urgent occasions wherein it might be justifiable for the state to take private property from individuals, (upon a full indemnification,) for the purposes of fortifications or public works, &c. but in no case could the legislature of the country interfere with private property, by taking it from one man and giving it to another, to the prejudice of either party, or that of third persons, who might be interested in the event. That the courts of justice were always open to give redress, and determine on the right; and that these courts were the proper tribunals to apply to for redress in such cases.

This point, without further argument, was submitted to

The Court, (present, GRIMKE and BAY, Justices,) who, after a full consideration on the subject, were clearly of opinion, that the plaintiffs could claim no title under the act in question, as it was against common right, as well as against *magna charta,* to take away the freehold of one man and vest it in another, and that, too, to the prejudice of third persons, without any compensation, or even a trial by the jury of the country, to determine the right in question. That the act was, therefore, *ipso facto,* void. That no length of time could give it validity, being originally founded on erroneous principles. That the parties, however, might, if they chose, rely upon a possessory right, if they could establish it.

16

STATE V. ———
1 Hayw. 28 (N.C. 1794)

At the last session of the General Assembly it was enacted that judgments might be obtained by the Attorney-General against receivers of public money, by motion; and that their delinquencies should be sufficient notice to them that they were to be proceeded against; and upon this act the Attorney-General now moved for judgment against several, and produced the act to show how he was authorized so to do.

But WILLIAMS, J., stopped him, saying he could not permit judgments to be taken in that manner; that he conceived the act to be unconstitutional; it was to condemn a man unheard. Bill of Rights, Art. 12, says: "No freeman ought to be taken, imprisoned, or disseised of his freehold, liberties or property, etc., but by the law of the land," and these words mean, according to the course of the common law, which always required the party to be cited, and so have day in Court upon which he might appear and defend himself. Sec. 14 declares that the ancient mode of trial by jury is one of the best securities of the rights of the people, and ought to remain sacred and inviolable. The ancient mode of trial by jury was that after the defendant was cited, and had pleaded, and the other party had denied his plea, or some part of it, then the point in controversy was submitted to the decision of a jury; but here, though a jury may be sworn, what will it be upon? It will be upon a default taken against the party who does not appear and plead, because he has no knowledge that any proceedings are intended to be had against him; and so in truth it is not a trial by jury according to the ancient mode. The defendant has no opportunity of making any defensive allegations which may be submitted to the decisions of a jury; but the jury here are merely to pronounce what is the sum to be recovered, and in this they are to be governed by the report of the Comptroller, which is made evidence against the defendant by another act of the Assembly; so that in reality the jury have nothing to determine on—it is mere form for the sake of which they are to be impaneled. Such a trial is a mere farce. I think the act unconstitutional, and I cannot, as at present advised, give my assent to its being carried into effect. The judges of the land are a branch of the government, and are to administer the constitutional laws, not such as are repugnant to the Constitution. It is their duty to resist an unconstitutional act. In fact, such an act made by the General Assembly, who are deputed only to make laws in conformity to the Constitution, and within the limits it prescribes, is not any law at all. Whenever the Assembly exceeds the limits of the Constitution, they act without authority, and then their acts are no more binding than the acts of any other assembled body. Suppose, when met together, they should pass an act to continue the Assembly for two years—the Constitution says it shall continue but for one; and suppose in the second year they should pass an act—would the judges be bound to effectuate it? Surely not. No more are they bound to regard an act not made agreeable to the Constitution. I am alone on the bench. I am sorry to be obliged to prevent the execution of an act which the Legislature thought necessary to be passed, and no doubt might be of public utility. But what end is an equivalent for a precedent so dangerous as that where the Constitution is disregarded by the Legislature, and that disregard sanctioned by the judiciary? Where, then, is the safety of the people, or the freedom which the Constitution meant to secure? One precedent begets another, one breach will quickly be succeeded by another, and thus the giving way in the first instance to what seems to be a case of public convenience in fact prepares the way for the total overthrow of the Constitution—the surest palladium of our rights. I cannot consent to it; but the Attorney-General, if he pleases, may again move the subject when we have reflected a little more upon it.

Next day, at the sitting of the Court, Haywood, the Attorney-General, moved the subject again, as follows: The clauses of the Constitution that are objected to the validity of this act are declarations the people thought proper to make of their rights; not against a power they supposed their own representatives might usurp, but against oppression and usurpation in general. The second clause, for instance, could not be intended as a restraint upon the Legislature; it could not be supposed the Legislature would ever attempt to oppose the right of the people to regulate their internal government. It was intended to assert the right of the people against the power of the British King and Parliament, and against all other foreign powers who hereafter might claim a right, under any pretense whatsoever, of interfering with the affairs of this Government; and to serve as a standing and perpetual memento to posterity that the least intermeddling by any foreign power with the internal policy of this Government is an invasion of their privileges. Such, also, is the manifest meaning of section 5. Who were the convention suspicious of when they declared, "That all power of suspending laws, or the execution of laws, by any authority, without the consent of the representatives of the people, is injurious to their rights, and ought not to be exercised"? This is not a restraint upon the legislative power of the Assembly. From the experience of what had happened in older governments, they apprehended that in the vicissitudes of human affairs some ambitious men might usurp the power of dispensing with laws, or claim the right of exercising such a power. It had been frequently done in that government which they were the most intimately acquainted with, to the great oppression of the people. They also had other reasons. The event of that dangerous war in which they were then engaged was doubtful. In case of an adverse event, they were determined by this solemn declaration that the rights of the people should be proclaimed and handed down to posterity; that this solemn declaration should be a monument of them, to keep the genius of

freedom alive, and to impel posterity by this lesson left them by their ancestors, at some future day to erect again the standard of liberty. This I take to be the true meaning of the Declaration of Rights; and if we attend to the 12th clause, we shall find it was copied almost *verbatim* from the chapter 29 of *Magna Carta,* and of the occasion of which our Bill of Rights were very similar—the struggle of the people against oppression. This clause in both has nearly the same meaning. And then the spirit of this clause is in exact unison with the other clauses, not intended to restrain the Legislature from making the law of the land, but a declaration only that the people are to be governed by no other than the law of land. *Per legem terrae,* were words used in the charter granted by Henry I., King Stephen, Henry II., King John, and Henry III., whose confirmation seemed finally to give stability to this charter; and this term, in those times, had a certain appropriate meaning which in latter periods came to be a little altered. In the three former of these reigns the term *per legem terrae* was employed in contradistinction to the civil law, then called the *Italian law,* having been lately discovered and adopted in Italy, and which had been, or were then begun to be, introduced in England in exclusion of the laws of Edward the Confessor, or, in other words, in the law of England. Henry I. in his charter promised, among other things, to confirm and observe all the laws of Edward the Confessor. 1 Goldsmith's England, 133. Stephen, his immediate successor, promised a restoration of the laws of Edward the Confessor in his charter. 1 Goldsmith's England, 145. These laws of Edward the Confessor were the ancient laws, usages, and customs of the different parts of England, collected and digested into one code. 1 Bl. Com., 66; 4 Bl. Com., 405. It appears from the frequent stipulations contained in the charters of these times, promising to observe and restore these laws, that they had been neglected and some other law introduced in their place. Indeed, we are expressly informed of this in the preface to 8 Rep., page 8, where immediately after the author has been speaking of King Stephen's character, he says: "King Stephen forbade by public edict that no man should retain the laws of Italy, formerly brought into England." In these times, therefore, the term *lex terrae* meant the English law in contradistinction to the laws of Italy, or of any other foreign country. And in like manner in our Constitution, where the Convention are declaring the rights of the people, and use the words of the *Magna Carta* of England, they mean to assert, in general, that the people of North Carolina have a right to be governed by their own laws, and not to be subject to laws made by any foreign power upon earth; in like manner as in the 2d clause they declare that the people of this State ought to have the sole and exclusive right of regulating the internal government and police thereof—by all which they mean to vindicate the sovereignty of this country, and the inherent right of the people thereof to govern themselves. The term *lex terrae,* in the times of Kings John and Henry III., began to have a meaning additional to what it had in the former reigns. These princes were guilty of great abuses under the pretense of prerogative. They had confiscated the estates of many of their subjects; they had exiled and destroyed many, also, by the power of prerogative. It is remarkable that in King John's charter it is stipulated that no freeman shall be taken, or imprisoned, or disseised of his free tenements and liberties, or outlawed, or banished, unless by the legal judgment of his peers, or by the law of the land, and all who suffered otherwise in this and the two former reigns shall be restored to their rights and possessions. 1 Goldsmith's England, 233. This plainly evinces that the words *per legem terrae*, here spoken of, import an acting by a pretended prerogative against or without the authority of law. 1 Goldsmith's England, 224, 225, 219, 220. And thus the term, *law of the land,* is to be understood in our Constitution, beside the meaning already ascribed to it, to declare that the people of this State are not to be deprived of liberty, property, the benefit of the law, nor exiled from their country, by any power whatsoever acting without or contrary to the established law of the country, or by any proceeding not directed or authorized by that law. The meaning of the words *lex terrae* may, therefore, be thus shortly defined—a law for the people of North Carolina, made or adopted by themselves by the intervention of their own Legislature. This definition excludes the idea of foreign legislation, of royal or executive prerogative, and of usurped power; and leaves the power of inflicting punishments, or rather of passing laws for that purpose, in their own Legislature only. In this sense, the *lex terrae* of North Carolina at present is the whole body of law, composed partly of the common law, partly of customs, partly of the acts of the British Parliament received and enforced here, and partly of the acts passed by our own Legislature. 2 Inst., 46. If this body of laws is not the *lex terrae* designated in our Bill of Rights, but the common law only, then the common law is immutable, and the Assembly cannot alter it by any legislative act. Should the Assembly in any instance attempt to alter any rule of property, with respect to its transmission, descent, etc., so as to entitle any other person to it than is entitled by the common law, he that is entitled by the rule of the common law may say, "No man is to be deprived of his property or rights, but according to the law of the land, or the common law." If an act not punishable by the common law, or punishable only in a smaller degree, should be rendered penal, or more penal than it was by the common law, by any legislative act, the party to be affected by it might say,"I am not to be imprisoned, or exiled, or disseised of my freehold, or in any manner destroyed, but according to the law of the land, or, in other words, the common law." It is easy to see into what a labyrinth of confusion this would lead us. It would contradict the very spirit of the Constitution, which in establishing a republican form of government must have been inevitably led to foresee the great alteration that the new state of things would make necessary in the great fabric of the common law; they must have intended such changes therein by the legislative power as would more perfectly adapt it to the genius of that species of government, many of the maxims of which are so diametrically opposed to all those of the common law which have any view towards the support of the kingly power or that of the nobles. Such a construction would destroy all legisla-

tive power whatsoever, except that of making laws in addition to the common law, and for cases not provided for by that law. It would lop off the whole body of the statute law at one stroke, and leave us in the most miserable condition that can well be imagined. All capital punishments ordained by the statute law for murder, rape, arson, etc., would be done away, and every malignant passion of the human heart let loose to roam through the land, unbridled by fear, and free from all manner of restraint except those very ineffectual ones the common law imposes. This cannot, therefore, be the true meaning of the term *law of the land,* made use of in the Bill of Rights. It must be that which I have already contended for, or something very similar to it; and if that be the true meaning of the term, how do these words at all imply that the Legislature have not a right to pass such an act as that which is the subject of our present discussion? Do they not, on the other hand, prove that as this is neither the act of any foreign Legislature nor the arbitrary edict of any usurped power acting independent of the people, but the act of their representatives assembled for the purpose of legislation, and to consult together for the public welfare, is such an act as ought to be respected? Does it follow, because the Constitution hath declared the right of the people to be exempted from all foreign jurisdiction, and from all power acting independently of the laws, that their own representatives cannot make a law which is useful and necessary for the public good? There is no part of this Constitution that directs the process by which a suit shall be instituted, or carried on, and the Legislature are therefore free to direct what mode of proceeding in courts they think proper; and accordingly, in a great variety of instances, both in England after *Magna Carta* and in this country since the Constitution, judgments have been rendered against the defendants without their having had any previous actual notice, and the judges have never intimated a doubt of the constitutionality of these proceedings. I will instance in the case of statute merchant, statute staple, and recognizance in England. There, after the recognition and day of payment arrives, no process issues against the debtor to show whether he has paid or obtained a discharge, but execution issues without any further notice. I will instance in the case of outlawries: a man's whole property may be taken away, and yet he never may have had any actual notice of his appearance in court being required. Both before and since the Revolution in this country, and until 1783, bonds, called judgment bonds, were in use here, and many judgments were taken upon them, after the formation of this Constitution, without any notice at all to the defendants, and the judges did not say it was an unconstitutional proceeding; and I suppose it would have been practiced to this day had it not been for the legislative interposition in 1783. See Rev. Laws, ch. 188. The necessity for this interposition proves that it was an inconvenience the judiciary could not remedy upon the ground of its unconstitutionality. Had it been such, as it was a public evil, the judges would most certainly have opposed to it the principles of the Constitution. I would instance in the case of the attachment laws: the property of an absentee is seized, judgment is obtained against him, and his property sold, when perhaps, and very probably, too, he has not the least intimation of it. The attachment law is a law of public convenience, but yet it is liable to all the objections which have been made to this act for taking judgments. Without any previous notice actually given to the defendant, a judgment by default is taken, and the jury is sworn to ascertain the *quantum* of damages, the defendant not being present, and indeed knowing nothing of it. Yet the validity of the attachment law was never questioned by the judges, nor did they, that I ever heard, express the least reluctance to its execution. If a bill in equity is filed, and the defendant cannot be found within the State, to be served with process, it is published in the *Gazette* that such a bill is filed, and if the party should not appear by the prefixed day, though he hath no actual notice, yet a decree is passed against him. If a judgment is obtained against the principal, and two *sci fa's* against the bail are returned *nihil*, here a judgment passes against the bail, though he has no actual notice of this proceeding, and of course no opportunity to plead in his defense a matter to be submitted to a jury. All the confiscation laws lately passed in this country, what are they but proceedings to take away the property of absentees, who perhaps knew nothing of these intended proceedings? If to proceed to judgment before actual notice be given to the defendant be against this clause of the Constitution, how hath it happened that so many proceedings of this nature have been established by the uniform decisions and practice of the judiciary? It may be fairly inferred that all these are so many proofs that such a proceeding is not unconstitutional, and that the Legislature may enact such laws. But to obviate these objections in every shape, let it be granted, for the sake of argument, that the phrase *lex terrae* in our Bill of Rights really means the common law, and that the common law requires notice to be given to the defendant before the plaintiff can proceed to judgment it also allows an exception to the rule when the defendant voluntarily renounces that privilege by the nature of his contract. It is one of the maxims of this very common law that *Quilibet potest renunciare juri pro se introducto*. And maxims, being the foundations of the common law, when they are once declared by the judges, are held equal in point of authority and force to acts of Parliament. Wood's Inst., 6. The maxim that *Quilibet potest, etc.*, extends even to cases where the life of the renouncer is concerned; the accessory by renouncing his right not to be tried before the conviction of the principal may put himself upon his trial, and be hanged for it. 2 Inst., 501, 183. If the rule of renunciation extends thus far, it will hardly be contended that a man may not renounce some lesser advantage, such as the having of actual notice of the State being about to proceed to judgment against him.

17

VANHORNE'S LESSEE v. DORRANCE
2 Dall. 304 (C.C.D.Pa. 1795)

[PATERSON, J.] I. The constitutionality of the confirming act; or, in other words, whether the legislature had authority to make that act?

Legislation is the exercise of sovereign authority. High and important powers are necessarily vested in the legislative body; whose acts, under some forms of government, are irresistible and subject to no control. In England, from whence most of our legal principles and legislative notions are derived, the authority of the Parliament is transcendent and has no bounds. "The power and jurisdiction of Parliament," says Sir Edward Coke, "is so transcendent and absolute, that it cannot be confined, either for causes or persons, within any bounds. And of this high court, he adds, it may be truly said, *si antiquitatem spectes, est vetussissima; si dignitatem, est honoratissima; si jurisdictionem, est capacissima.* It has sovereign and uncontrollable authority in the making, confirming, enlarging, restraining, abrogating, repealing, reviving and expounding of laws, concerning matters of all possible denominations, ecclesiastical or temporal, civil, military, maritime or criminal: this being the place where that absolute despotic power, which must in all governments reside somewhere, is intrusted by the constitution of these kingdoms. All mischiefs and grievances, operations and remedies that transcend the ordinary course of the laws, are within the reach of this extraordinary tribunal. It can regulate or new model the succession to the crown; as was done in the reign of *Henry VIII.* and *William III.* It can alter the established religion of the land; as was done in a variety of instances, in the reigns of king *Henry VIII.* and his three children. It can change and create afresh even the constitution of the kingdom and of parliaments themselves; as was done by the act of union, and the several statutes for triennial and septennial elections. It can, in short, do everything that is not naturally impossible; and therefore, some have not scrupled to call its power, by a figure rather too bold, the omnipotence of parliament. True it is, that what the parliament doth, no authority upon earth can undo." (1 Bl. Com. 160.)

From this passage, it is evident, that, in England, the authority of the parliament runs without limits, and rises above control. It is difficult to say, what the constitution of England is; because, not being reduced to written certainty and precision, it lies entirely at the mercy of the parliament: it bends to every governmental exigency; it varies and is blown about by every breeze of legislative humor or political caprice. Some of the judges in England have had the boldness to assert, that an act of parliament, made against natural equity, is void; but this opinion contravenes the general position, that the validity of an act of parliament cannot be drawn into question by the judicial department: it cannot be disputed, and must be obeyed. The power of parliament is absolute and transcendent; it is omnipotent in the scale of political existence. Besides, in England, there is no written constitution, no fundamental law, nothing visible, nothing real, nothing certain, by which a statute can be tested. In America, the case is widely different: every state in the Union has its constitution reduced to written exactitude and precision.

What is a Constitution? It is the form of government, delineated by the mighty hand of the people, in which certain first principles of fundamental laws are established. The constitution is certain and fixed; it contains the permanent will of the people, and is the supreme law of the land; it is paramount to the power of the legislature, and can be revoked or altered only by the authority that made it. The life-giving principle and the death-doing stroke must proceed from the same hand. What are legislatures? Creatures of the constitution; they owe their existence to the constitution: they derive their powers from the constitution: it is their commission; and therefore, all their acts must be conformable to it, or else they will be void. The constitution is the work or will of the people themselves, in their original, sovereign and unlimited capacity. Law is the work or will of the legislature, in their derivative and subordinate capacity. The one is the work of the creator, and the other of the creature. The constitution fixes limits to the exercise of legislative authority, and prescribes the orbit within which it must move. In short, gentlemen, the constitution is the sun of the political system, around which all legislative, executive and judicial bodies must revolve. Whatever may be the case in other countries, yet, in this, there can be no doubt, that every act of the legislature, repugnant to the constitution, is absolutely void.

In the second article of the declaration of rights, which was made part of the late constitution of Pennsylvania, it is declared: "That all men have a natural and unalienable right to worship Almighty God, according to the dictates of their own consciences and understanding; and that no man ought, or of right can be, compelled to attend any religious worship, or erect or support any place of worship, or maintain any ministry, contrary to, or against, his own free will and consent; nor can any man, who acknowledges the being of a God, be justly deprived or abridged of any civil right as a citizen, on account of his religious sentiments, or peculiar mode of religious worship; and that no authority can, or ought to be, vested in, or assumed, by any power whatever, that shall, in any case, interfere with, or in any manner control, the right of conscience in the free exercise of religious worship." (Dec. of Rights, Art. II.)

In the thirty-second section of the same constitution, it is ordained; "that all elections, whether by the people or in general assembly, shall be by ballot, free and voluntary." (Const. Penn. § 32.)

Could the legislature have annulled these articles, respecting religion, the rights of conscience, and elections by ballot? Surely no. As to these points, there was no devolution of power; the authority was purposely withheld, and reserved by the people to themselves. If the legislature had passed an act declaring, that, in future, there should be no

trial by jury, would it have been obligatory? No: it would have been void for want of jurisdiction, or constitutional extent of power. The right of trial by jury is a fundamental law, made sacred by the constitution, and cannot be legislated away. The constitution of a state is stable and permanent, not to be worked upon by the temper of the times, nor to rise and fall with the tide of events: notwithstanding the competition of opposing interests, and the violence of contending parties, it remains firm and immovable, as a mountain amidst the strife of storms, or a rock in the ocean amidst the raging of the waves. I take it to be a clear position; that if a legislative act oppugns a constitutional principle, the former must give way, and be rejected on the score of repugnance. I hold it to be a position equally clear and sound, that, in such case, it will be the duty of the court to adhere to the constitution, and to declare the act null and void. The constitution is the basis of legislative authority; it lies at the foundation of all law, and is a rule and commission by which both legislators and judges are to proceed. It is an important principle, which, in the discussion of questions of the present kind, ought never to be lost sight of, that the judiciary in this country is not a subordinate, but co-ordinate, branch of the government.

Having made these preliminary observations, we shall proceed to contemplate the quieting and confirming act, and to bring its validity to the test of the constitution. In the course of argument, the counsel on both sides relied upon certain parts of the late bill of rights and constitution of Pennsylvania, which I shall now read, and then refer to them occasionally in the sequel of the charge. (The judge then read the 1st, 8th and 11th articles of the declaration of rights; and the 9th and 46th sections of the constitution of Pennsylvania.) (See 1 Dall. Laws, app. p. 55–6, 60.)

From these passages, it is evident, that the right of acquiring and possessing property, and having it protected, is one of the natural, inherent and inalienable rights of man. Men have a sense of property: property is necessary to their subsistence, and correspondent to their natural wants and desires; its security was one of the objects that induced them to unite in society. No man could become a member of a community, in which he could not enjoy the fruits of his honest labor and industry. The preservation of property, then, is a primary object of the social compact, and, by the late constitution of Pennsylvania, was made a fundamental law. Every person ought to contribute his proportion for public purposes and public exigencies; but no one can be called upon to surrender or sacrifice his whole property, real and personal, for the good of the community, without receiving a recompense in value. This would be laying a burden upon an individual, which ought to be sustained by the society at large. The English history does not furnish an instance of the kind; the parliament, with all their boasted omnipotence, never committed such an outrage on private property; and if they had, it would have served only to display the dangerous nature of unlimited authority; it would have been an exercise of power and not of right. Such an act would be a monster in legislation and shock all mankind. The legislature, therefore, had no authority to make an act divesting one citizen of his freehold, and vesting it in another, without a just compensation. It is inconsistent with the principles of reason, justice and moral rectitude; it is incompatible with the comfort, peace and happiness of mankind; it is contrary to the principles of social alliance, in every free government; and lastly, it is contrary both to the letter and spirit of the constitution. In short, it is what every one would think unreasonable and unjust in his own case.

The next step in the line of progression is, whether the legislature had authority to make an act, divesting one citizen of his freehold and vesting it in another, even with compensation? That the legislature, on certain emergencies, had authority to exercise this high power, has been urged from the nature of the social compact, and from the words of the constitution, which says, that the house of representatives shall have all other powers necessary for the legislature of a free state or commonwealth; but they shall have no power to add to, alter, abolish or infringe on any part of this constitution. The course of reasoning, on the part of the defendant, may be comprised in a few words. The despotic power, as it is aptly called by some writers, of taking private property, when state necessity requires, exists in every government; the existence of such power is necessary; government could not subsist without it; and if this be the case, it cannot be lodged anywhere with so much safety as with the legislature. The presumption is, that they will not call it into exercise, except in urgent cases, or cases of the first necessity. There is force in this reasoning. It is, however, difficult to form a case, in which the necessity of a state can be of such a nature, as to authorize or excuse the seizing of landed property belonging to one citizen and giving it to another citizen. It is immaterial to the state, in which of its citizens the land is vested; but it is of primary importance, that, when vested, it should be secured, and the proprietor protected in the enjoyment of it. The constitution encircles and renders it an holy thing.

We must, gentlemen, bear constantly in mind, that the present is a case of landed property; vested by law in one set of citizens, attempted to be divested, for the purpose of vesting the same property in another set of citizens. It cannot be assimilated to the case of personal property taken or used in time of war or famine, or other extreme necessity; it cannot be assimilated to the temporary possession of land itself, on a pressing public emergency, or the spur of the occasion. In the latter case, there is no change of property, no divestment of right; the title remains, and the proprietor, though out of possession for a while, is still proprietor and lord of the soil. The possession grew out of the occasion and ceases with it: then the right of necessity is satisfied and at an end; it does not affect the title, is temporary in its nature, and cannot exist for ever. The constitution expressly declares, that the right of acquiring, possessing and protecting property is natural, inherent, and inalienable. It is a right not *ex gratiâ* from the legislature, but *ex debito* from the constitution. It is sacred; for it is further declared, that the legislature shall have no power to add to, alter, abolish or infringe any part of the

constitution. The constitution is the origin and measure of legislative authority. It says to legislators, thus far ye shall go and no farther. Not a particle of it should be shaken; not a pebble of it should be removed. Innovation is dangerous; one encroachment leads to another; precedent gives birth to precedent; what has been done may be done again; thus radical principles are generally broken in upon, and the constitution eventually destroyed. Where is the security, where the inviolability of property, if the legislature, by a private act, affecting particular persons only, can take land from one citizen, who acquired it legally, and vest it in another? The rights of private property are regulated, protected and governed by general, known and established laws; and decided upon by general, known and established tribunals; laws and tribunals not made and created on an instant exigency, on an urgent emergency, to serve a present turn, or the interest of a moment. Their operation and influence are equal and universal; they press alike on all. Hence, security and safety, tranquillity and peace. One man is not afraid of another, and no man afraid of the legislature. It is infinitely wiser and safer, to risk some possible mischiefs, than to vest in the legislature so unnecessary, dangerous and enormous a power as that which has been exercised on the present occasion; a power that, according to the full extent of the argument, is boundless and omnipotent: for the legislature judged of the necessity of the case, and also of the nature and value of the equivalent.

Such a case of necessity; and judging, too, of the compensation, can never occur in any nation. Singular, indeed, and untoward must be the state of things, that would induce the legislature, supposing they had the power, to divest one individual of his landed estate, merely for the purpose of vesting it in another, even upon full indemnification; unless that indemnification be ascertained in the manner which I shall mention hereafter.

But admitting, that the legislature can take the real estate of A. and give it to B., on making compensation, the principle and reasoning upon it go no further than to show, that the legislature are the sole and exclusive judges of the necessity of the case, in which this despotic power should be called into action. It cannot, on the principles of the social alliance, or of the constitution, be extended beyond the point of judging upon every existing case of necessity. The legislature declare and enact, that such are the public exigencies, or necessities of the state, as to authorize them to take the land of A. and give it to B.; the dictates of reason and the eternal principles of justice, as well as the sacred principles of the social contract, and the constitution, direct, and they accordingly declare and ordain, that A. shall receive compensation for the land. But here the legislature must stop; they have run the full length of their authority, and can go no further: they cannot constitutionally determine upon the amount of the compensation, or value of the land. Public exigencies do not require, necessity does not demand, that the legislature should, of themselves, without the participation of the proprietor, or intervention of a jury, assess the value of the thing, or ascertain the amount of the compensation to be paid for it.

This can constitutionally be effected only in three ways. 1. By the parties—that is, by stipulation between the legislature and proprietor of the land. 2. By commissioners mutually elected by the parties. 3. By the intervention of a jury.

The compensatory part of the act lies in the ninth section. "And whereas, the late proprietaries, and divers other persons, have heretofore acquired titles to parcels of the land aforesaid, agreeably to the laws and usages of Pennsylvania, and who will be deprived thereof by the operation of this act, and as justice requires that compensation be made for the lands, of which they shall be thus divested; and as the state is possessed of other lands, in which an equivalent may be rendered to the claimants under Pennsylvania, and as it will be necessary, that their claims should be ascertained by a proper examination: Be it, therefore, enacted by the authority aforesaid, that all persons having such claims to lands, which will be affected by the operation of this act, shall be, and they are hereby required, by themselves, guardians, or other lawful agents, within twelve months from the passing of this act, to present the same to the board of property, therein clearly describing those lands, and stating the grounds of their claims, and also adducing the proper proofs, not only of their titles, but of the situations, qualities and values of the land so claimed, to enable the board to judge of the validity of their claims, and of the quantities of vacant lands proper to be granted as equivalents. And for every claim which shall be admitted by said board, as duly supported, the equivalent by them allowed, may be taken either in the old or new purchase, at the option of the claimant; and warrants and patents, and all other acts of the public offices relating thereto, shall be performed free of expense. The said board shall also allow such a quantity of vacant land, to be added to such equivalent, as shall, in their judgment, be equal to the expenses, which must necessarily be incurred in locating and surveying the same. And that the board of property may in every case, obtain satisfactory evidence of the quality and value of the land, which shall be claimed as aforesaid, under the proprietary title, they may require the commissioners aforesaid, during their sitting in the county of Luzerne, to make the necessary inquiries, by the oaths or affirmations of lawful witnesses, to ascertain those points; and it shall be the duty of the said commissioners to inquire and report accordingly." (Act of 28th March 1787, § 9. P. L. 274.)

In this section, two things are worthy of consideration. 1. The mode or manner, in which compensation for the lands is to be ascertained. 2. The nature of the compensation itself.

The Pennsylvania claimants are directed to present their claims to the board of property—and what is the board to do thereupon? Why, it is—1. To judge of the validity of their claims. 2. To ascertain, by the aid and through the medium of commissioners, appointed by the legislature, the quality and value of the land. 3. To judge of the quality of vacant land to be granted as an equivalent.

This is not the constitutional line of procedure. I have already observed, that there are but three modes, in which matters of this kind can be concluded, consistently with the principles and spirit of the constitution, and social alliance. The first of which is by the parties, that is to say, by the legislature and proprietor of the land. Of this the British history presents an illustrious example in the case of the Isle of Man.

"The distinct jurisdiction of this little subordinate royalty being found inconvenient for the purposes of public justice, and for the revenue (it affording a commodious asylum for debtors, outlaws and smugglers), authority was given to the treasury, by statute 12 *Geo. I., c.* 28, to purchase the interest of the then proprietors, for the use of the crown; which purchase was at length completed in the year 1765, and confirmed by statutes 5 *Geo. III., c.* 26 and 38, whereby the whole island and all its dependencies, so granted as aforesaid (except the landed property of the Atholl family, their manorial rights and emoluments, and the patronage of bishoprics, and other ecclesiastical benefices) are inalienably vested in the crown, and subjected to the regulations of the British excise and customs." 1 Bl. Com. 107.

Shame to American legislation! That in England, a limited monarchy, where there is no written constitution, where the parliament is omnipotent, and can mould the constitution at pleasure, a more sacred regard should have been paid to property, than in America, surrounded as we are with a blaze of political illumination; where the legislatures are limited; where we have republican governments, and written constitutions, by which the protection and enjoyment of property are rendered inviolable. The case of the Isle of Man was a fair and honorable stipulation; it partook of the spirit and essence of a contract; it was free and mutual; and was treating with the proprietors on equal terms.

But if the business cannot be effected in this way, then the value of the land, intended to be taken, should be ascertained by commissioners, or persons mutually elected by the parties, or by the intervention of the judiciary, of which a jury is a component part. In the first case, we approximate nearly to a contract; because the will of the party, whose property is to be affected, is in some degree exercised; he has a choice; his own act co-operates with that of the legislature. In the other case, there is the intervention of a court of law, or, in other words, a jury is to pass between the public and the individual, who, after hearing the proofs and allegations of the parties, will, by their verdict, fix the value of the property, or the sum to be paid for it. The compensation, if not agreed upon by the parties or their agents, must be ascertained by a jury. The interposition of a jury is, in such case, a constitutional guard upon property, and a necessary check to legislative authority. It is a barrier between the individual and the legislature, and ought never to be removed; as long as it is preserved, the rights of private property will be in no danger of violation, except in cases of absolute necessity, or great public utility. By the confirming act, the value of the land taken, and the value of the land to be paid in recompense, are to be ascertained by the board of property. And who are the persons that constitute this board? Men appointed by one of the parties, by the legislature only. The person whose property is to be divested and valued, had no volition, no choice, no co-operation in the appointment; and besides, the other constitutional guard upon property, that of a jury, is removed and done away. The board of property thus constituted, are authorised to decide upon the value of the land to be taken, and upon the value of the land to be given by way of equivalent, without the participation of the party, or the intervention of a jury.

2. The nature of the compensation. By the act, the equivalent is to be in land. No just compensation can be made, except in money. Money is a common standard, by comparison with which the value of anything may be ascertained. It is not only a sign which represents the respective values of commodities, but is an universal medium, easily portable, liable to little variation, and readily exchanged for any kind of property. Compensation is a recompense in value, a *quid pro quo,* and must be in money. True it is, that land or anything else may be a compensation, but then it must be at the election of the party; it cannot be forced upon him. His consent will legalise the act, and make it valid; nothing short of it will have the effect. It is obvious, that if a jury pass upon the subject, or value of the property, their verdict must be in money.

To close this part of the discourse: It is contended, that the legislature must judge of the necessity of interposing their despotic authority; it is a right of necessity, upon which no other power in government can decide: that no civil institution is perfect; and that cases will occur in which private property must yield to urgent calls of public utility or general danger. Be it so. But then it must be upon complete indemnification to the individual. Agreed, but who shall judge of this? Did there also exist a state necessity, that the legislature, or persons solely appointed by them, must admeasure the compensation, or value of the lands seized and taken, and the validity of the title thereto? Did a third state necessity exist, that the proprietor must take land by way of equivalent for his land? And did a fourth state necessity exist, that the value of this land-equivalent must be adjusted by the board of property, without the consent of the party, or the interference of a jury? Alas! how necessity begets necessity. They rise upon each other and become endless. The proprietor stands afar off, a solitary and unprotected member of the community, and is stripped of his property, without his consent, without a hearing, without notice, the values of that property judged upon, without his participation, or the intervention of a jury, and the equivalent therefor in lands ascertained in the same way. If this be the legislation of a republican government, in which the preservation of property is made sacred by the constitution, I ask, wherein it differs from the mandate of an Asiatic prince? Omnipotence in legislation is despotism. According to this doctrine, we have nothing that we can call our own, or are sure of, for a moment; we are all tenants at will, and hold our landed property at the mere pleasure of the legislature. Wretched situation, precarious tenure! And yet we boast of property and its security, of laws, of courts, of

constitutions, and call ourselves free! In short, gentlemen, the confirming act is void; it never had constitutional existence; it is a dead letter, and of no more virtue or avail, than if it never had been made.

18

LINDSAY V. COMMISSIONERS
2 Bay 38 (S.C. 1796)

Judges GRIMKE and BAY were of opinion, that the motion for the prohibition ought to be refused. They considered the act in question as authorized by the fundamental principles of society. That the authority of the state, as laid down by eminent civilians and jurists, to appropriate a portion of the soil of every country for public roads and highways, was one of the original rights of sovereignty, retained by the supreme power of every community at its formation, and like the power of laying on, and collecting taxes, paramount to all private rights; or in other words, that all private rights were held and enjoyed, subject to this condition.

That it was by the means of these roads and highways, that the citizens of the country had a convenient communication from one extremity of it to another; and between the intermediate towns and public places in the interior of it. It was along them also, that the citizens assembled with convenience and despatch in times of danger and alarm, for defense and protection; and along these, the productions of the country were conveyed to a market, and the produce of the soil was rendered valuable. It was therefore a matter of primary importance, that the power of making and laying off these avenues of great public convenience, and keeping them in repair, should for ever be vested in the supreme legislative body of every nation and commonwealth on earth. That the legislature of *South Carolina,* had exercised this power and authority, from the first establishment of civil government in it, to the present day. They therefore considered it, as much a part of the common law of *South Carolina,* as any other part of that great and valuable system.

That it was neither against *magna charta,* nor the state constitution, but part of the *lex terrae,* which both meant to defend and protect. The so much celebrated *magna charta* of *Great Britain,* was not a concession of rights and privileges, which had no previous existence; *but a restoration, and confirmation* of those, which had been usurped, or had fallen into disuse. It was therefore only declaratory of the well known and established laws of the kingdom.

So, in like manner, the 2d section of the 9th article of our state constitution, confirms all the before-mentioned principles. It was not declaratory of any new law, but confirmed all the ancient rights and principles, which had been in use in the state, with the additional security, that no bills of attainder, nor *ex post facto* laws, or laws impairing the obligation of contracts, should ever be passed in the state. They were therefore of opinion, that so far from interfering with, or contradicting this high and important privilege of the legislature, in laying off highways, they both confirmed and secured it; consequently that none of the cases relied on by the counsel in favour of this motion, had the least tendency to contradict or overturn these principles. They were also of opinion, that the act of the legislature was constitutional and binding, and that the city council were well warranted in appointing the commissioners to go on and finish the street in contemplation. As to the assessments on the lot owners, that point seems to have been given up in the argument, as they relied principally on the compensation for the freehold: and as to the mode of collecting them, it appears to be in conformity to the old usage and customs of levying and collecting assessments, for the building and repairing of bridges, prescribed by the ancient road acts, a century ago. Upon the whole, they were of opinion, that there were no grounds for the prohibition, and that the rule should be discharged.

BURKE, J. admitted the power of the state on great and necessary occasions, to appropriate a portion of the soil of the country, for public uses and national purposes; but was of opinion that there should be *a fair compensation made to the private individual, for the loss he might sustain by it*, to be ascertained by a jury of the country.

WATIES, concurred in opinion with BURKE, but went more fully into his reasons. He admitted the right of the state to take the property of an individual, for purposes of public *necessity*, or even for public *utility*; but in exercising this power, it was essential to its validity, *that a full compensation should be provided at the time*, for every injury that the individual might suffer. This appeared to him, he said, to be the construction given by the writers quoted on the part of defendant's counsel, to shew the lawfulness of this power. *Vattel*, b. 1. c. 20. s. 244. expressly says, that "justice demands, that the individual should be recompensed;" and *Bynkershock*, who was also quoted, explicitly declares the same thing. The common law of *England*, which has also recognised this power, does it always with the same restriction. "The legislature," says Mr. *Blackstone*, "may order a new road to be made through the private grounds of an individual, and may compel him to acquiesce in it. But how does it compel him? not by stripping him of his property, in an arbitrary manner, but by giving him a full indemnification or equivalent for it. And even this is an exertion of power which it indulges with great caution." Which is evident in the act of parliament for making a new road from *Black Fryer's Bridge*, across *St. George's Fields*. The corporation of *London* is thereby authorized and directed, to treat with the owners of lands that might be taken away by the road, for the purchase of the same; and in case of refusal to treat for the value of the lands taken, the same is to be assessed by a jury; which he said, had a strong similitude to the present case. The road in that case, most probably in some cases enhanced the value of the lands through which it passed, and therefore was productive of benefit to the owners. But parliament thought

proper, *by the sacred principle of compensation*, to provide for any possible injury. The rights of our citizens are not less valuable than those of the people of *England:* we have besides a constitution, which limits and controls the power of the legislature, the 9th article of which, declares, that no freeman shall be devested of his property, but by the judgment of his peers, *or the law of the land*. On a former occasion, (in the case of the *City Corporation* against *Zylstra*,) he said, he had gone into a long investigation of the technical import of the words *lex terrae*, and therefore should only state here, that they meant *the common law*, and *ancient statutes* down to the time of *Edward* II. which were considered as part of the common law. This was the true construction given to them by all the commentators on *magna charta*, from whence they were adopted by our constitution. If the *lex terrae* meant any law which the legislature might pass, then the legislature would be authorized by the constitution, to destroy the right, which the constitution had expressly declared, should for ever be inviolably preserved. This is too absurd a construction to be the true one. He said he understood, therefore, the constitution to mean, that no freeman shall be deprived of his property, but by such means as are authorized *by the ancient common law of the land*. According to this construction, the right of property is held under the constitution, and not at the will of the legislature. In what way, then, does the common law authorize the power of taking private property for public uses? "by providing," says Mr. *Blackstone*, "a full indemnification for it." This is the condition on which the valid exercise of this power depends. But the law under consideration does not provide any indemnification, nor does it make the public responsible in any way for any injury which might be done to the plaintiffs. It has not therefore complied with the terms of the common law, and is not conformable to the constitution. It was urged, however, that no injury could arise to any of the parties complaining, and therefore it was not necessary that the legislature should provide any indemnification. This fact may be so; but it makes no difference in the case. Was the legislature itself to be the judge of that fact? Can it prescribe what terms it pleases for the individual, and determine either the measure of compensation for property taken, or that none at all is due? This would be attributing to it a power which belongs only to despots. And yet even the greatest despots have not always felt themselves at liberty to exercise it in this way. *De Tott*, in his memoirs of the *Turkish* government, mentions a remarkable instance to the contrary, which it may not be amiss to relate on this occasion. The sultan *Mustapha* being desirous of building and endowing a new mosque, fixed upon a spot, in the city of *Constantinople*, which belonged to a number of individuals. He treated with *all* of them, for the purchase of their parts, and they all willingly complied with his wishes, except a *Jew*, who owned a small house on the place, and who refused to give it up. A considerable price was offered him, but he resisted the most tempting offers. His partiality for the spot, or his obstinacy, was stronger than his avarice. All the city was astonished at his rashness, and expected every hour to see his house demolished, and his head upon a pole. But what was the conduct of the sultan?

of one who was the absolute master of the lives of millions? He consulted his mufti, who answered that private property was sacred, that the laws of the prophet forbade his taking it absolutely, but he might compel the *Jew* to lease it to him, as long as he pleased, at a full rent. The sultan submitted to the law. He observed, that we might learn two things from this example of a despot: 1st. That the sovereign power, although absolute, is not at liberty to take away private property and decide, at its own discretion, that no compensation is due; 2d. That the principle of indemnification is deeply founded in natural justice. It was further said in this case, If any injury is done, the parties might have recourse to a court and jury for redress. But whom could they sue? not the commissioners, not the city council; for they would justify under the act. Whom then? why, no one. But suppose they could sue, what would be the nature of the action? It could not be founded on contract, for there was none. It must then be on a *tort;* it must be an action of trespass, in which the jury would give a reparation *in damages.* Is not this acknowledging that the act of the legislature is a tortious act? and can any thing prove more fully, the arbitrary character of the act, than this?

He said, it was painful to him to be obliged to question the exercise of any legislative power, but he was sworn to support the constitution, and this was the most important of all the duties which were incumbent on the judges. On the faithful performance of this high duty would depend the integrity and duration of our government. If the legislature is permitted to exercise other rules than those ordained by the constitution, and if innovations are suffered to acquire the sanction of time and practice, the rights of the people will soon become dependent on legislative will, and the constitution have no more obligation than an obsolete law. But if this court does its duty, in giving to the constitution an overruling operation over every act of the legislature which is inconsistent with it, the people will then have an independent security for their rights, which may render them perpetual. In exercising this high authority, the judges claim no judicial supremacy; they are only the administrators of the public will. If an act of the legislature is held void, it is not because the judges have any control over the legislative power, but because the act is forbidden by the constitution, and because the will of the people, which is therein declared, is paramount to that of their representatives, expressed in any law. As the act under consideration appeared to him to be repugnant to this high will, he was bound to say, that it ought not to have any operation, and that the prohibition should be granted.

As the judges were equally divided in opinion in this case, the applicants took nothing by their motion.

19

UNIVERSITY OF NORTH CAROLINA v. FOX
1 Mur. 58 (N.C. 1805)

LOCKE, J., delivered the opinion of the Court. The Legislature of North Carolina in 1789 granted to the Trustees of the University "all the property that has heretofore or shall hereafter escheat to the State." Ch. 21, sec. 2. And by another act, passed in 1794, they also granted "the confiscated property then unsold." Ch. 3, sec. 1. By an act passed in 1800 they declared, "that from and after the passing of this act, all acts and clauses of acts which have heretofore granted power to the Trustees of the University to seize and possess any escheated or confiscated property, real or personal, shall be and the same it hereby repealed and made void.

"*And be it further enacted,* That all escheated or confiscated property which the said trustees, their agents or attorneys, have not legally sold by virtue of the said laws shall from hence revert to the State, and henceforth be considered as the property of the same, as though such laws had never been passed." Chapter 5.

The Trustees of the University in pursuance of the powers vested in them by the act of 1789, have brought this suit to recover the possession of a tract of land escheated to the State before the passing of the repealing act in the year 1800. The defendants have pleaded this repealing act in bar, by which they allege the power of the trustees to support this action is entirely destroyed. It is therefore now to be considered how far the trustees have title under the act of 1789, and, in the next place, how far they are divested of that title by the repealing act of 1800.

To determine the first question, it may be necessary to take into view the objections stated to the title of the trustees, independent of the operation of repealing act, and these are two: first, that no title to escheated lands vests in the State until an inquisition or office found; and, secondly, that if the State had title, yet the trustees have derived none by the act of 1789, because the State attempted to convey the right by act of Assembly and not by grant, as required by section 36 of the Constitution. With regard to the first objection, the Court think it a sufficient answer to say that on this subject the law has been supposed to be long settled, as this objection has been made in almost every suit heretofore brought by the Trustees of the University, and always overruled. The Court approve of the decisions upon this point, and will observe the ancient and wise maxim "*stare decisis.*" 2 Black., 245; 2 Co. Rep., 52.

As to the second objection, the words of the Constitution are, "All commissions and grants shall run in the name of the State of North Carolina and bear test and be signed by the Governor," etc. It seems to be a fair and clear exposition of this part of the Constitution to say that when the State conveys land by grant, the grant shall have the requisites prescribed, to wit, run in the name of the State, bear teste and be signed by the Governor, etc., and that all grants otherwise authenticated shall be void. It became necessary that the officer whose duty it shall be to sign and authenticate grants should be pointed out, and that their form and substance should be ascertained, in order to give uniformity to such grants and to avoid that variety which would be produced by the judgment of different officers. But the Court sees nothing in this clause restricting the Legislature to this single mode of conveyance; they are left free from any control in the mode or manner of transferring their property, unless they should adopt the one pointed out in the Constitution, and then the form and ceremony are prescribed. This opinion is warranted not only by the expressions contained in the clause itself, but by the many and repeated acts of Assembly passed, since the making of the Constitution, for the purpose of transferring property. Many of these acts have been mentioned and referred to by the counsel for the lessors of the plaintiff. We are therefore of opinion that the land in question vested in the State without an inquisition or office found, and that the Legislature were competent to pass the interest in the same to the Trustees of the University by the act of 1789; and that the trustees have a good and valid title, unless the operation of the repealing act of 1800 has destroyed it.

The operation of this act is next to be considered; and it may be necessary to premise that the people of North Carolina, when assembled in convention, were desirous of having some rights secured to them beyond the control of the Legislature, and these they have expressed in the Bill of Rights and the Constitution. The preamble to the Constitution states, among other things, that "We, the representatives of the freemen of North Carolina, chosen and assembled in Congress for the express purpose of framing a constitution, under the authority of the people, most conducive to their happiness and welfare, do declare, etc." Section 13 directs the General Assembly to elect several officers of State. Section 15 directs the election of a Governor. Section 38 directs that there shall be a sheriff, coroner or coroners and constables in each county. It became necessary for the Legislature to appoint these officers or to pass such laws as would secure to the people such officers as would carry this form of government into effect. The framers of this instrument appear to have been well acquainted with the importance and necessity of education, and lest this object might escape the attention of the Legislature or be by them neglected, section 41 declares, "That a school or schools shall be established by the Legislature for the convenient instruction of youth, with such salaries to the masters paid by the public as may enable them to instruct at low prices; and all useful learning shall be encouraged and promoted in one or more universities." By this section as strong an injunction was imposed on the Legislature to establish an university as by the preceding clauses to appoint the several officers of government; these objects seem to be regarded by the framers of the Constitution with equal solicitude; they have, therefore, in the same imperative style declared that there shall be an university, and that there shall be a Governor, leaving to the Legislature to make such appropriations and create such funds for the endowment of the institution as would be sufficient to effect the purposes for which it should be established. In 1789 the Legislature obeyed this constitutional injunction and made an appropriation of escheated lands, and appointed trustees for the management of the concerns of the institution. By the act of 1800 the Legislature declared that this property should be taken from the trustees and revert to the State. Is, then, this last act authorized by the Constitution, or does it destroy a right which that instrument gave to the people, a right highly esteemed in all civilized nations, that of educating their youth at a moderate expense? a right of acquiring knowledge and good morals, which have always been deemed most conducive to the happiness and prosperity of the people?

Some light will be thrown upon this subject by examining the nature of corporations: how property can be taken from them, and how they can be dissolved. Corporations are formed for the advancement of religion, learning, commerce or other beneficial purposes. They are either aggregate or sole, and created by grant or by law. When they are once erected, they acquire many rights, powers, capacities, and some incapacities (1 Black. Com., 495), as, first, to have perpetual succession; and therefore, all aggregate corporations have necessarily the power of electing members in the room of those who die, to sue and be sued and to do all other acts as natural persons. Second, to purchase lands and to hold them for the benefit of themselves and successors. Fourth, to have a common seal. Fifth, to make by-laws for the better government of the corporation. These corporations cannot commit crimes, although their members may in their individual capacity. The duties of those bodies consist in acting up to the design for which they were instituted. Let us next inquire how their corporate property can be taken from them and how they may be dissolved. A member may be disfranchised or lose his place by his own improper conduct, or he may resign. A corporation may be dissolved by act of Parliament, which is boundless in its operation; by the natural death of all its members, in case of an aggregate corporation; by surrender of its franchises into the hands of the King, which is a kind of suicide; by forfeiture of its charter through negligence or abuse of its franchises, in which case the law judges the body politic to have broken the condition on which it was incorporated, and therefore the incorporation to be void; and the regular course is to bring an information in the nature of a *quo warranto*, to inquire by what authority the members now exercise their corporate power, having forfeited it by such and such proceedings. 1 Black. Com., 485; 3 Black. Com., 263. None of these prerequisites have been done in the present case. We are then led to inquire into the soundness of an argument greatly relied on by the defendant's counsel, that those who create can destroy. The Legislature have not pretended to dissolve the corporation, but to deprive them of a part of the funds that were deemed to be vested in them and to transfer those funds to the State. In England the King's consent to the creation of any corporation is absolutely necessary, either given expressly by charter or by act of Parliament, where his assent is a necessary ingredient or implied by prescription. 1 Black. Com., 472, 473.

The King may grant to a subject the power of erecting a corporation; and yet it is the King that erects—the subject is but the instrument. 1 Black. Com., 474. Where there is an endowment of lands, the law distinguishes and makes two species of foundation: the first, *fundatio incipiens*, or the corporation; in which sense the King is the founder of all colleges and hospitals; the other, *fundatio proficiens*, or the dotation of it, in which sense the first gift of the revenues is the foundation, and who gives them is the founder. 1 Black. Com., 431. The Constitution directed the General Assembly to establish this institution and endow it; then it would seem from the principle upon which all this doctrine is predicated, that the Constitution and not the Legislature had erected this corporation; the Legislature being only the agent or instrument, whose acts are valid and binding when they do not contravene any of the provisions of the Constitution. We view this corporation as standing on higher grounds than any other aggregate corporation; it is not only protected by the common law, but sanctioned by the Constitution. It cannot be considered that the Legislature would have complied with this constitutional requisition, by establishing a school for a month or any determinate number of years, and then abolishing the institution; because the people evidently intended this university to be as permanent as the Government itself. It would not be competent for the Legislature to declare that there should be no public school in the State, because such an act would directly oppose that important clause in the Constitution before mentioned. But if the Legislature can deprive the university of the appropriated and vested funds, they can do that which will produce the same consequences; for, deprive the institution of funds already vested and refuse to make any additional appropriations, and there never can exist in the State a public school or schools, and thus the Legislature may indirectly effect that purpose which, if expressed in the words before mentioned, they could not do. Besides, when the Legislature have established an university, appointed trustees and vested them with property which they were to hold in trust for the benefit of the institution, have they not discharged their duty as the agents of the people and transferred property, which is afterwards beyond their control? From that moment the trustees became in some measure the agents of the people, clothed with the power of disposing of and applying the property thus vested to the uses intended by the people, but over which the power of the Legislature ceased with the discharge of the constitutional injunction; unless it might be necessary in the course of time to make other or further appropriations to continue and support the institution; and this we consider to be their duty at all times, when such necessity shall exist, that the expectation of the people, as expressed in the Constitution, may not be disappointed.

But one great and important reason which influences us in deciding this question is section 10 of the Bill of Rights, which declares "that no freeman ought to be taken, imprisoned or disseized of his freehold, liberties or privileges, or outlawed or exiled, or in any manner destroyed or deprived of his life, liberty or property, but by the law of the land." It has been yielded on the part of the defendant that if the Legislature had vested an individual with the property in question, this section of the Bill of Rights would restrain them from depriving him of such right; but it is denied that this section has any operation on corporations whose members are mere naked trustees, and have no interest in the donation, and especially on a corporation erected for a public purpose. It is also insisted that the term, "law of the land," does not impose any restrictions on the Legislature, who are capable of making the law of the land, and was only intended to prevent abuses in the other branches of Government. That this clause was intended to secure to corporations as well as to individuals the rights therein enumerated, seems clear from the word *"liberties,"* which peculiarly signifies those privileges and rights which corporations have by virtue of the instruments which incorporate them, and is certainly used in this clause in contradistinction to the word *"liberty,"* which refers to the personal liberty of the citizen. We therefore infer that by this clause the Legislature are as much restrained from affecting the property of corporations as they are that of a private individual, unless the "law of the land" should receive the construction contended for on the part of the defendant. It is evident the framers of the Constitution intended the provision as a restraint upon some branch of the Government, either the executive, legislative, or judicial. To suppose it applicable to the executive would be absurd on account of the limited powers conferred on that officer; and from the subjects enumerated in that clause, no danger could be apprehended from the Executive Department, that being entrusted with the exercise of no powers by which the principles thereby intended to be secured could be affected. To apply to the judiciary would, if possible, be still more idle, if the Legislature can make the *"law of the land."* For the judiciary are only to expound and enforce the law, and have no discretionary powers enabling them to judge of the propriety or impropriety of laws. They are bound, whether agreeable to their ideas of justice or not, to carry into effect the acts of the Legislature as far as they are binding or do not contravene the Constitution. If, then, this clause is applicable to the Legislature alone, and was intended as a restraint on their acts (and to presume otherwise is to render this article a dead letter), let us next inquire what will be the operation which this clause will or ought to have on the present question. It seems to us to warrant a belief that members of a corporation as well as individuals shall not be so deprived of their liberties or properties, unless by a trial by jury in a court of justice, according to the known and established rules of decision derived from the common law and such acts of the Legislature as are consistent with the Constitution. Although the trustees are a corporation established for public purposes, yet their property is as completely beyond the control of the Legislature as the property of individuals or that of any other corporation. Indeed, it seems difficult to conceive of a corporation established for merely private purposes. In every institution of that kind the ground of the establishment is some public good or purpose intended to be promoted; but in many the members thereof have a private interest, coupled with the public object. In this case the trustees have no private interest beyond the general good; yet we conceive that circumstances will not make the property of the trustees subject to the arbitrary will of the Legislature. The property vested in the trustees must remain for the uses intended for the university, until the judiciary of the country in the usual and common form pronounce them guilty of such acts as will, in law, amount to a forfeiture of their rights or a dissolution of their body. The demurrer must therefore be allowed, and the plea in bar overruled.

HALL, J., *contra*. A question of more importance than that arising in this case cannot come before a court. It is nothing less than one branch of the Government undertaking to decide whether another branch of the same Government has or has not transcended its constitutional powers; a question which in its discussion should at all times command the best energies of the head and heart. When this shall be the case, although a difference of opinion may sometimes exist, it will be an honest one, and cannot fail to find its remedy in mutual tolerance and concession. But well convinced, indeed, ought one person to be of another's error of judgment before he passes sentence of condemnation on it, when he reflects that each has given the same pledges to support the Constitution. Before a law enacted by the Legislature should be pronounced unconstitutional, it ought to appear to the Court to be palpably so. If an honest doubt can be entertained on the subject, we owe it to ourselves, as well as to the Legislature, to carry it into effect. Far be it from me, if it were in my power, to damp that laudable and honest zeal which characterized the argument of the defendant's counsel; it cannot be too much extolled or too widely circulated; but I speak it with deference to the opinions of my brethren, that I think occasions might occur when its influence would be more happily felt and lead to more useful and correct results. In the opinion which I have formed on this question I am probably mistaken, as I have the misfortune to differ from the rest of the Court; but from the best consideration I can give to it, I am bound to say that I believe the law in question is not unconstitutional.

I feel no disposition to controvert many things urged in argument by the defendant's counsel; he has had recourse, however, to one argument which I think militates against him. It is drawn from section 41 of our Constitution, which is in the following words: "A school or schools shall be established by the Legislature for the convenient instruction of youth, with such salaries to the masters, paid by the public, as may enable them to instruct at low prices; and all useful learning shall be duly encouraged and promoted in one or more universities." He endeavors to strengthen his general proposition, namely, "That any law taking away the property of an individual or a common corporation is unconstitutional," by stating, in addition, that there was a constitutional obligation on the Assembly to set apart funds for the support of the university; and if it were constitutional and right for them to do so, it is unconstitutional and wrong to take away those funds. If the framers of the Constitution intended by that section that the Legislature should establish one or more universities and schools, and vest in them certain funds, which might be deemed sufficient at the time for the support in a con-

stitutional view; if it were intended that by doing this the Legislature had completely discharged their duty, and had nothing more to do with such schools and universities, whatever misfortunes might afterwards attend them, there might be something in the argument. I think, however, this section of the Constitution was intended for a very different purpose. It became the duty of the Legislature, created by and acting under that Constitution, to establish seminaries of learning, with salaries to the masters, etc., and afterwards to support and cherish them as long as the Constitution shall exist. If by accident the funds set apart for their support should be destroyed, it would be the duty of the Legislature to endow them with others. The Legislature is the constitutional guardian of these seminaries of learning, and should at all times keep them under their inspection and control. This is a duty which they cannot delegate or transfer to any one, and can only end with the Constitution itself. Suppose, then, that property should be given to the Trustees of the University (whom I consider in no other light than as agents of the Legislature), which property was not very productive, but sufficiently so for the support of the university; and afterwards it were to become so much so that one-third of the profits arising from it would be adequate to the wants of the institution: who would have a right to the surplus? Let us reverse the case and suppose the profits of property given to the trustees to decrease or fail altogether; would it not be the duty of the Legislature to provide other funds or give other property which would be sufficiently productive? I think it would. If so, can it be doubted but that the surplus profits would be at the disposition of the Legislature? It may be said that the trustees have no surplus funds; that the profits of their property are not equal to the wants of the institution. That may be the case; but who is to judge of it? I answer, not this Court; the Constitution gives it no such power. The Legislature must be the judge. It would be going too far to say that there was constitutional obligation on the Legislature to do a certain thing, and that this Court and not the Legislature should decide when it was properly done. If, then, the Legislature must judge how large the funds of the university ought to be, add to them when they are too small and take from them when too large, this Court are not the proper judges in such cases; and if not, how can we undertake to say that the law in question is unconstitutional? It cannot, I think, be denied that the General Assembly have a right to take from the trustees property of which the university stands in no need, and that for the best of reasons—because they are bound to furnish it with additional funds, as those which it already possesses may decrease or as its wants may increase. I have said that the General Assembly cannot delegate this constitutional power; that is, that they cannot, by giving to the trustees any quantity of property or any given sum of money, exonerate themselves from the trust and confidence which the Constitution reposed in them. It is true, they may appoint trustees as their agents to act for them, and their trustees or agents are amenable to them for their conduct: they have a naked authority without any interest. The law can have no bearing upon them as individuals; it can only affect them in their public character as trustees. And how is it to do this? They were entrusted with property for the purpose of supporting an university in conformity with the directions of the Constitution, and the General Assembly are about to take this property from them, which they contend they have no right to do. If the Assembly are bound in any event to furnish funds to support the university, they have a right to take away surplus funds. If it be said that the property in question is not of that description, I answer, who are to judge of this, but the General Assembly, on whom there is a constitutional obligation to establish and superintend an university? On the trustees no such obligation is imposed; they are the mere agents of the Legislature; and as well might it be said that any other citizens equal in number to the trustees should be placed paramount to the Legislature. I therefore can see no analogy between this case and that of a gift made to an individual or to an ordinary corporation. My opinion upon the whole case is founded upon the provisions of the Constitution, and regarding the trustees as mere agents for the management of the concerns of the university under the direction of the Legislature, I think the demurrer should be overruled and the plea in bar sustained.

20

GARDNER V. VILLAGE OF NEWBURGH
2 Johns. Ch. 162 (N.Y. 1816)

THE CHANCELLOR [James Kent]. The statute under which the trustees of the village of *Newburgh* are proceeding, (sess. 32. ch. 119.) makes adequate provision for the party injured by the laying of the conduits through his land, and also affords security to the owner of the spring or springs from whence the water is to be taken. But there is no provision for making compensation to the plaintiff, through whose land the water issuing from the spring has been accustomed to flow. The bill charges, that the trustees are preparing to divert from the plaintiff's land, the whole, or the most part of the stream, for the purpose of supplying the village. The plaintiff's right to the use of the water, is as valid in law, and as useful to him, as the rights of others who are indemnified or protected by the statute; and he ought not to be deprived of it, and we cannot suppose it was intended he should be deprived of it, without his consent, or without making him a just compensation. The act is, unintentionally, defective, in not providing for his case, and it ought not to be enforced and it was not intended to be enforced, until such provision should be made.

It is a clear principle in law, that the owner of land is entitled to the use of a stream of water which has been accustomed, from time immemorial, to flow through it, and the law gives him ample remedy for the violation of this right. To divert or obstruct a water course is a private nuisance; and the books are full of cases and decisions asserting the right and affording the remedy. (F. N. B. 184.

Moore v. *Browne, Dyer,* 319. *b. Lutterel's* case, 4 Co. 86. *Glynn* v. *Nichols, Comb.* 43. 2 *Show.* 507. *Prickman* v. *Trip Comb.* 231.)

The Court of Chancery has also a concurrent jurisdiction by injunction, equally clear and well established, in these cases of private nuisance. Without noticing nuisances arising from other causes, we have many cases of the application of equity powers on this very subject of diverting streams. In *Finch* v. *Resbridger,* (2 *Vern.* 390.) the lord keeper held, that after a long enjoyment of a water course running to a house and garden, through the ground of another, a right was to be presumed, unless disproved by the other side, and the plaintiff was quieted in his enjoyment, by injunction. So, again, in *Bush* v. *Western,* (*Prec. in Ch.* 530.) a plaintiff who had been in possession, for a long time, of a water course, was quieted by injunction, against the interruption of the defendant, who had diverted it, though the plaintiff had not established his right at law, and the Court said such bills were usual. These cases show the ancient and established jurisdiction of this Court; and the foundation of that jurisdiction is the necessity of a preventive remedy when great and immediate mischief, or material injury, would arise to the comfort and useful enjoyment of property. The interference rests on the principle of a clear and certain right to the enjoyment of the subject in question, and an injurious interruption of that right, which, upon just and equitable grounds, ought to be prevented. (*Anon.* 1 *Vern.* 120. *East India Company* v. *Sandys,* 1 *Vern.* 127. *Hills* v. *University of Oxford,* 1 *Vern.* 275. *Anon.* 1 *Vesey,* 476. *Anon.* 2 *Vesey,* 414. *Whitechurch* v. *Hide,* 2 *Atk.* 391. 2 *Vesey,* 453. *Attorney-General* v. *Nichol,* 16 *Vesey,* 338.)

In the application of the general doctrines of the Court to this case, it appears to me to be proper and necessary that the preventive remedy be applied. There is no need, from what at present appears, of sending the plaintiff to law to have his title first established. His right to the use of the stream is one which has been immemorially enjoyed, and of which he is now in the actual possession. The trustees set up no other right to the stream (assuming, for the present, the charges in the bill) than what is derived from the authority of the statute; and if they are suffered to proceed and divert the stream, or the most essential part of it, the plaintiff would receive immediate and great injury, by the suspension of all those works on his land which are set in operation by the water. In addition to this, he will lose the comfort and use of the stream for farming and domestic purposes; and, besides, it must be painful to any one to be deprived, at once, of the enjoyment of a stream which he has been accustomed always to see flowing by the door of his dwelling. A right to a stream of water is as sacred as a right to the soil over which it flows. It is a part of the freehold, of which no man can be disseised "but by lawful judgment of his peers, or by due process of law." This is an ancient and fundamental maxim of common right to be found in *Magna Charta,* and which the legislature has incorporated into an act declaratory of the rights of the citizens of this state. (*Laws,* sess. 10. ch. 1.)

I have intimated that the statute does not deprive the plaintiff of the use of the stream, until recompense be made. He would be entitled to his action at law for the interruption of his right, and all his remedies at law, and in this Court, remain equally in force. But I am not to be understood as denying a competent power in the legislature to take private property for necessary or useful *public* purposes; and, perhaps, even for the purposes specified in the act on which this case arises. But to render the exercise of the power valid, a fair compensation must, in all cases, be previously made to the individuals affected, under some equitable assessment to be provided by law. This is a necessary qualification accompanying the exercise of legislative power, in taking private property for public uses; the limitation is admitted by the soundest authorities, and is adopted by all temperate and civilized governments, from a deep and universal sense of its justice.

Grotius, (*De Jur*. B. & P. b. 8. ch. 14. s. 7.) *Puffendorf*, (*De Jur. Nat. et Gent*. b. 8. ch. 5. s. 7.) and *Bynkershoeck*, (*Quaest. Jur. Pub* b. 2. ch. 15.) when speaking of the *eminent domain* of the sovereign, admit that private property may be taken for public uses, when public necessity or utility require it; but they all lay it down as a clear principle of natural equity, that the individual, whose property is thus sacrificed, must be indemnified. The last of those jurists insists, that private property cannot be taken, on any terms, without consent of the owner, for purposes of public ornament or pleasure; and he mentions an instance in which the *Roman* senate refused to allow the praetors to carry an aqueduct through the farm of an individual, against his consent, when intended merely for ornament. The sense and practice of the *English* government are equally explicit on this point. Private property cannot be violated in any case, or by any set of men, or for any public purpose, without the interposition of the legislature. And how does the legislature interpose and compel? "Not," says *Blackstone*, (*Com.* vol. 1. p. 139.) "by absolutely stripping the subject of his property, in an arbitrary manner, but by giving him a full indemnification and equivalent for the injury thereby sustained. The public is now considered as an individual treating with an individual for an exchange. All that the legislature does is to oblige the owner to alienate his possessions for a reasonable price; and even this is an exertion of power which the legislature indulges with caution, and which nothing but the legislature can perform."

I may go further, and show that this inviolability of private property, even as it respects the acts and the wants of the state, *unless a just indemnity be afforded*, has excited so much interest, and been deemed of such importance, that it has frequently been made the subject of an express and fundamental article of right in the constitution of government. Such an article is to be seen in the bill of rights annexed to the constitutions of the states of *Pennsylvania, Delaware,* and *Ohio*; and it has been incorporated in some of the written constitutions adopted in *Europe*, (Constitutional charter of *Lewis* XVIII., and the ephemeral, but very elaborately drawn, constitution *de la Republique Française* of 1795.) But what is of higher authority, and is absolutely decisive of the sense of the people of this country, it is made a part of the constitution of the *United States*, "that private property shall not be taken for public use, without just compensation." I feel myself, therefore, not only authorized, but bound to conclude, that a provision for compensation is an indispensable attendant on the due and constitutional exercise of the power of depriving an individual of his property; and I am persuaded that the legislature never intended, by the act in question, to violate or interfere with this great and sacred principle of private right. This is evident from the care which this act bestows on the rights of the owners of the spring, and of the lands through which the conduits are to pass. These are the only cases in which the legislature contemplated or intended that the act could or should interfere with private right, and in these cases due provision is made for its protection, or for compensation. There is no reason why the rights of the plaintiff should not have the same protection as the rights of his neighbors; and the necessity of a provision for his case could not have occurred, or it, doubtless, would have been inserted. Until, then, some provision be made for affording him compensation, it would be unjust, and contrary to the first principles of government, and equally contrary to the intention of this statute, to take from the plaintiff his undoubted and prescriptive right to the use and enjoyment of the stream of water.

In the case of *Agar* v. *The Regents' Canal Company,* (*Cooper's Eq. Rep.* 77.) an injunction was granted, on filing a bill supported by affidavit, restraining defendants acting under a private act of parliament, from cutting a canal through the land of the plaintiff, in a line and mode not supposed to be within the authority of the statute.

I shall, accordingly, upon the facts charged in the bill, and supportd by affidavits, as a measure immediately necessary to prevent impending injury, allow the injunction, and wait for the answer, to see whether the merits of the case will be varied.

Injunction granted.

21

THE THOMAS & HENRY
1 Marshall's C.C. 367 (C.C.D.Va. 1818)

[MARSHALL, C.J.] The act under which this seizure was made, declares that "in actions, suits, or informations to be brought, where any seizure shall be made pursuant to this act, if the property be claimed by any person, in every such case the *onus probandi* shall be upon such claimant." [See Story's Laws of U.S., vol. 1, ch. 128, § 71, p. 633.]

In this case, then, the United States are not required to establish guilt, but the claimants must prove innocence.

It is not the duty of the judge to justify the legislature, but surely, if, in any case, such a legislative provision be proper, it is in this. The fact is generally premeditated, and is perpetrated under all the precautions and in all the secrecy which ingenuity can suggest, and the means of proving innocence, at least, to a reasonable extent, which is all that can be required, are in possession of the accused. In such a case, he may, without a violation of principle, be required to prove his innocence.

In such a case, the absence of testimony, clearly in the power of the claimants, if not supplied by other equivalent testimony, must be fatal. It is impossible to smuggle so large a part of a cargo, as is charged to have been smuggled in this case, without the knowledge of the master and crew. Consequently, their testimony against the fact, if believed, would be nearly conclusive. Why is it not produced? The master, being himself liable to a fine under one of the charges in this libel, was perhaps not admissible as a witness; but to the crew, no objection existed. Why were they not examined? If they were unattainable, this fact ought to have been shown, and might have excused their non-production. The deposition of one of them only was offered, and his was taken so irregularly, as to be rejected. No attempt appears to have been made to take it again, or to take the depositions of other mariners.

22

BRADSHAW V. ROGERS
20 Johns. R. 103 (N.Y. 1822)

SPENCER, Ch. J., delivered the opinion of the Court.

The same objections which were urged against the defence set up in the Court below, have been made here, as grounds for the reversal of the judgment. The third section of the act of the 40th session, ch. 262, does not apply to this case, because, the plaintiff's land has not been entered upon for the prosecution of the canal improvements intended by that section. For such objects it does not admit of a doubt, that the canal commissioners, and their agents, have a right to enter upon and occupy lands necessary to effectuate the objects of their appointment, without having first paid the loss and damage which the proprietor of the lands may sustain. It is true, that the fee simple of the land is not vested in the people of the state, until the damages are appraised and paid; but the authority to enter is absolute, and does not depend on the appraisal and payment; and that act provides fully for the payment of the loss and damage sustained by any person, whose lands are taken for the purposes of the canal. This case turns upon the construction of the 21st section of the act of the 13th of *April*, 1820, (sess. 43. ch. 202.) which provides, that in all cases in which it shall be deemed necessary by the principal engineer, in laying out the line of the *Erie* or *Champlain* canals, to discontinue, or alter *any part of a public road, or highway*, on account of its interfering with a proper location or construction of either of the canals, such engineer shall be authorized to make such discontinuance, or alteration; and upon his drawing up, in writing and figures, a true description of all such parts of any public road, or highway, as he may discontinue and new lay, on the account aforesaid, and filing the same in the clerk's office of the town in which such discontinuance and alteration may be situated, the same shall be lawful. The proviso requires the commissioners to open and work the newly laid road before the former is discontinued. With

every disposition to uphold and justify the commissioners, and their agents, in the great and valuable work in which they are engaged, consistent with law, I must say, and I say it with regret, I think the proceedings in this case indefensible. It has been already observed, that the plaintiff's land was not entered upon for any purpose immediately connected with the canal; but was taken as a substitute for part of a turnpike road, which was broken up and taken for the canal; and without some legislative authority, independently of the act of the 40th session, ch. 262. the trespass now complained of, could not be justified. This must have been the sense of the legislature, and, probably, of the canal commissioners, in the enactment of the act of the 43rd session, ch. 202. sec. 21. The first objection is, that the act last referred to, applies only to a public road, or highway, and that the turnpike road is not a public road, or highway, but the property of the turnpike corporation. It is, undoubtedly, true, that there is a material and manifest distinction between a public road and highway, and a turnpike road. The former is open and public for the passage of every person, without any toll, or other imposition; whereas, the latter is private property, subject to be travelled over, on first paying an equivalent for its use, prescribed by the legislature. It is impossible to extend the provision relative to a public road and highway, to embrace a turnpike road, without doing violence to the expressed and declared intention of the legislature. The act, in requiring the principal engineer to draw up and file a description of the parts of the road discontinued and laid anew, in the clerk's office of the town in which such discontinuance and alteration may be situated, evidently shows that the legislature meant, as the act purports, to authorize such discontinuance and alteration as to public roads and highways only; for they have adopted the provisions of the existing laws, as to laying out and altering public roads and highways, by the commissioners of roads, of the several towns, and which provisions are wholly inapplicable to turnpike roads. The present, then, is a *casus omissus*.

If we could surmount this difficulty, a more serious one presents itself. The act under consideration contains no provision to compensate, at any time, those whose lands may be taken as a substitute for a public road, or highway, altered, or discontinued by the principal engineer, for the damages they sustain. This is directly opposed to the fifth article of the amendments of the constitution of the *United States*, which forbids the taking of private property for public use, without just compensation. The same inhibition to the power of the legislature, is contained in the late amendments to the constitution of this state. I do not rely on either, as having a binding constitutional force upon the act under consideration. The former related to the powers of the national government, and was intended as a restraint on that government; and the latter is not yet operative. But they are both declaratory of a great and fundamental principle of government; and any law violating that principle must be deemed a nullity, as it is against natural right and justice. This all important and essential principle was somewhat illustrated in the case of *The People v. Platt*, (17 *Johns. Rep.* 215.)

We are bound, on both points, to declare that the judgment below is erroneous.

23

PICQUET V. SWAN

19 Fed. Cas. 609, no. 11,134
(C.C.D.Mass. 1828)

STORY, Circuit Justice. This suit was commenced by a writ, which is known in this state as the "trustee process," but is better known elsewhere as the "process of foreign attachment," and was returnable to May term, 1827, of this court. By the state laws it is a process equally applicable to cases, where the suit is against an inhabitant, and where it is against a non-resident, whether he has ever been an inhabitant or not. In the writ the parties are described as follows: The plaintiff as "of the city of Paris in the kingdom of France, an alien, and subject of his most Christian majesty the king of France, in his capacity as administrator," &c., and the defendant, as "now commorant of the city of Paris in the kingdom of France, of the city of Boston, in the commonwealth of Massachusetts, one of the United States of America, and a citizen of the said United States." The return of the marshal on the writ is as follows: "Boston, April 18, 1827. Pursuant hereunto I have attached all the real estate of the said James Swan lying and being in the district of Massachusetts, especially a lot of land in Boston in said district, bounded, &c., called the Washington Garden, &c., and summoned William Sullivan, Esq., agent for the said Swan, and on the same day I summoned the within named Sullivan, Otis, and Howard (the supposed trustees) to appear and show cause as within commanded, by leaving a true and attested copy of this writ at their last and usual places of abode. The said Swan has not been an inhabitant or resident within this district for three years last past."

At the last term the trustees summoned in the suit were duly discharged. [Case No. 11,133.] The defendant has never appeared as a party to the suit; and it is now contended, that the plaintiff is entitled to consider him in default, and to have a judgment by default entered against him. That is the point, which has been argued, and is now to be decided by the court. I will briefly advert, in the first instance, to the local laws regulating this process, as they may be important to illustrate the conclusion, to which the court has arrived, and also more fully to explain the grounds of the argument at the bar. The trustee process, under which the present suit is brought before the court, owes its origin to the act of 28th of February, 1795 (Act 1794, c. 65), which was a substitute for the provincial act of 32 Geo. II. c. 2, to enable creditors to receive their just debts out of the effects of their absent or absconding debtors. It provides, that "the officer to whom the writ is directed shall serve the same by attaching the goods and estate of the principal in his hands and possession of the value required, if so much may be found in his precinct, by reading the said writ to him, or by leaving an attested copy thereof at his last and usual place of abode, if he had been an inhabitant or resident within this commonwealth at any time within three years next before the suing out such writ, and by reading the same to each of the trustees, or by leaving an attested copy thereof at such trustees' usual place of abode; and in case the principal has not been an inhabitant or resident as aforesaid, a service made on the supposed trustee or trustees in manner as aforesaid, shall be deemed a sufficient service," &c. It further provides, that in case all the trustees are discharged, "the plaintiff may, notwithstanding, proceed against the principal to trial, judgment, and execution." A subsequent statute (Act 1798, c. 5) has however provided, that "in all such cases, the plaintiff shall not proceed in his suit against the principal, unless there shall have been such service of the original writ upon the principal as would have authorized the court to proceed to render a judgment against him, in an action brought and commenced in the common and ordinary mode of process." But the principal might voluntarily come into court and take upon himself the defence of the suit. In the very case before the court all the trustees have been discharged; so that it is necessary to ascertain what service would be sufficient to entitle the plaintiff to judgment in an action by the common and ordinary mode of process, which is, by our local laws, by a writ known by the name of a writ of "capias" or "attachment," and authorizing either an arrest of the person of the defendant, or an attachment of his goods or estate. The act of 17th of February, 1798 (Act 1797, c. 50), provides for the mode of service of this process. Of course it can be used as a capias, only when the party is found within the state. When used as an attachment, the officer attaches the goods or estate of the defendant and a summons in due form is to be delivered to him, or left at "his dwelling-house, or place of last and usual abode," fourteen days before the return day; and "in case the defendant was at no time an inhabitant or resident within this commonwealth," then such summons is to be left with his or her tenant, agent, or attorney, &c.; otherwise the writ shall abate. There is also provision made in this act, that if the defendant is not an inhabitant or present in the state at the time of the service, and does not return before the time of trial, the court may continue the same to the next term upon a suggestion of the fact on the record. If at such term the defendant does not appear, and be so remote, that notice of the suit could not probably be conveyed to him during the vacancy, the court may continue the same to the next term, and no longer. After these two continuances, if he does not appear, judgment by default may be entered up against him. It is not material to follow up the proceedings consequent upon such judgment. But it may not be useless to add, that the trustee act of 1794 (chapter 65) adopts regulations of a similar nature, in substance, to them. Of their own force these processes and modes of service could have no validity in the courts of the United States. But by the act of congress of 29th of September, 1789, c. 21 [1 Stat. 93], the then existing forms of writs and modes of process (by which was meant modes of proceeding) in the supreme courts of the states, respectively, were adopted into the judicial proceedings of the courts of the United States; and by a subsequent act (Act 1792, c. 36 [1 Stat. 275]) the same forms were perpetuated, subject to the authority in the courts to alter and add to the same, in their discretion, so as to conform to the state jurisprudence. After the very elaborate expositions of this subject by the supreme court in Wayman v. Southard, 10 Wheat. [23 U. S.] 1, and United States Bank v. Halstead, Id. 51, it is unnecessary farther to discuss the nature and extent to which the state process applies in the courts of the United States. The state acts of 1795, c. 65; of 1797, c. 50; and of 1798, c. 5,—have never been adopted by any formal rule of the circuit court in this district; but they have constantly been used in it, both as to process and service, ever since their first enactment; and must now be admitted to be of as high authority, by usage, as if any promulgation by rule, however formal, had taken place. They can have no effect, where they contravene the positive legislation of congress; nor can they give a jurisdiction to this court, which it might not independently of them maintain. Where jurisdiction is given by any act of congress, this court may use the appropriate state process to enforce it. But the state laws can confer no authority on this court to extend its jurisdiction over persons or property, whom it could not otherwise reach.

Let us, then, first examine the existing legislation of congress on this subject. The constitution of the United States has, among other things, extended the judicial power to controversies between citizens of different states, and between citizens of a state and foreign citizens or subjects. The actual legislation of congress has not as yet been coextensive with this constitutional boundary of jurisdiction. The judiciary act of 1789 (chapter 20) provides, "that the circuit courts shall have original cognizance, concurrent with the courts of the several states, of all suits of a civil nature where the matter in dispute, exclusive of costs, exceeds 500 dollars, and the United States are plaintiffs, or petitioners; or an alien is a party; or the suit is between a citizen of the state, where the suit is brought, and a citizen of another state." As to citizens, therefore, there exists no jurisdiction, unless either the plaintiff, or the defendant is a citizen of the state, where the suit is brought. As to aliens, by which must be understood, in the language of the constitution, "a foreign citizen or subject," the jurisdiction is in all cases given, where an alien is a party. In a subsequent part of the same section is the clause, which has been so much commented on at the bar. "But no person shall be arrested in one district for trial in another in any civil action before any circuit or district court. And no civil action shall be brought before either of said courts against an inhabitant of the United States by any original process in any other district than that, whereof he is an inhabitant, or in which he shall be found at the time of serving the writ." It is observable, that the language is confined to original process, and does not apply to final process, or process of execution. If this clause had not been inserted, what would have been the legal operation of the other clauses of the act? A prior section had divided the United States into certain judicial districts, whose limits generally were coextensive with the territorial limits of a single state. Within these districts a circuit court is required to be held at certain times and places prescribed by the act. The circuit court of each district sits within and for the same, and is bounded by its local limits. In the exercise of jurisdiction within those limits, the general principles of law must be presumed to apply to them all. Whatever might be the extent of their jurisdiction over the subject matter of suits, in respect to persons and property, that jurisdiction is available only within the limits of the district. The courts of a state, however general may be their jurisdiction, are necessarily confined to the territorial limits of the state. Their process cannot be executed beyond those limits; and any attempt to act upon persons or things beyond them, would be deemed an usurpation of foreign sovereignty, not justified or acknowledged by the law of nations. Even the court of king's bench in England, though a court of general jurisdiction, never imagined, that it could serve process in Scotland, Ireland, or the colonies, to compel an appearance, or justify a judgment against persons residing therein at the time of the commencement of the suit. This results from the general principle, that a court created within and for a particular territory is bounded in the exercise of its power by the limits of such territory. It matters not, whether it be a kingdom, a state, a county, or a city, or other local district. If it be the former, it is necessarily bounded and limited by the sovereignty of the government itself, which cannot be extra-territorial; if the latter, then the judicial interpretation is, that the sovereign has chosen to assign this special limit, short of his general authority. It was doubtless competent for congress to have authorized original as well as final process, to have issued from the circuit courts and run into every state in the Union. But it has conferred no such general authority. In a single case only has it authorized—by the statute of 3d of March, 1797, c. 74 [Folwell's Ed., vol. 3, p. 423], § 6 [1 Stat. 515, c. 20]—writs of execution to run throughout the United States; and that is, upon judgments obtained for the use of the United States in any of the courts of the United States. By the act of 2d of March, 1793, c. 66 (22), § 6 [1 Story's Laws, 312; 1 Stat. 335], it has also authorized subpoenas for witnesses to attend the courts of the United States to be served in other districts within certain limited distances. And until a very recent statute—Act May 20, 1826, c. 123 [3 Story's Laws, 2034; 4 Stat. 184, c. 124]—no authority existed to serve writs of execution, in favour of private persons, in any other district, than that where the judgment was rendered, although both districts were within the territorial limits of the same state. This very course of legislation, during a period of almost forty years, demonstrates the understanding of congress, as well as of the profession, that the process of the circuit court could not be served in ordinary cases out of the limits of the judicial district for which it was established. My Brother Washington, in his able judgment in the case Ex parte Graham [Case No. 5,657], has gone largely into the consideration of this doctrine; and I follow with undoubting confidence the whole course of his reasoning. I owe it, perhaps, as a matter of justice to myself to add, that the process in that case, from the circuit court of Rhode Island, was issued at the peril of the party, without any deliberate examination of the law on the part of the court, the party being anxious to take it, valere quantum valere possit. If, therefore, the restraining clause already mentioned were not in the eleventh section of the act of 1789 (chapter 20) I should be of opinion, for the reasons so forcibly given by my Brother Washington, that the exercise of the jurisdiction of the circuit courts by compulsive process, was essentially confined, by their very organization, within the limits of their respective districts. It would otherwise follow, that final process might in all cases run into every district of the Union, since the terms of the clause apply to original process only. Yet the professional opinion and practice, as well as the positive legislation of congress in the cases above mentioned, demonstrate, that the contrary is the true construction of the act.

The jurisdiction of the circuit court in this case, so far as it depends upon the citizenship and alienage of the parties, may for the present be assumed de bene esse to be complete. But this alone is not sufficient to give the court complete authority to proceed to judgment. There must exist other facts and circumstances as a just foundation of jurisdiction. Cases are familiar of actions, which cannot be maintained, although the parties are within the reach of process, from the nature and locality of the cause of action. Suits, which concern the realty, such as writs of entry, dower, ejectment, and trespass, quare clausum fregit, cannot be maintained in the circuit court unless the land lie within the district, although the party may reside there, and, in a personal view, the jurisdiction is unexceptionable. The reason is, that the title to real estate can by the general principles of law be litigated only in the state, where the land lies, and where the process may go to bind and reach the land, and enforce the title of the party. If, therefore, the land be sought, or in other respects the suit be purely local, it must be brought, where the law of the place acts on it directly. See Massie v. Watts, 6 Cranch [10 U. S.] 148. Collateral suits for other purposes, binding the conscience, or controlling the acts of the party personally, may be brought and decided elsewhere. Id. This principle is recognized at the common law; but it has, to a certain extent at least, a foundation also in universal jurisprudence. I have already intimated, that no sovereignty can extend its process beyond its territorial limits, to subject either persons or property to its judicial decisions. Every exertion of authority beyond this limit is a mere nullity, and incapable of binding such persons or property in any other tribunals. If a state were to pass an act declaring, that upon personal notice of a suit brought against a foreigner, resident in a foreign country, proceedings might be had against him, and a judgment obtained in invitum, for aught I know, the local tribunals might give a binding efficacy to such judgments. But elsewhere they would be utterly void, as an usurpation of general sovereignty over independent nations and their subjects. Lord Ellenborough, in Buchanan v. Rucker, 9 East, 102, has put the case with great clearness and force. "Supposing," said he, "however, that the act had said in terms, that though a person sued in the island (of Tobago) had never been present within its jurisdiction, yet, that it should bind him,

upon proof of nailing up the summons at the court door; how could that be obligatory upon the subjects of other countries? Can the island of Tobago pass a law to bind the rights of the whole world? Would the world submit to such a jurisdiction?" Nor would it in such a case vary the legal result, that the party had actual notice of the suit; for he is not bound to appear to it. No sovereign has a just right to issue such a notice, and thereby to acquire a jurisdiction to draw the party from his own proper forum ad alium examen. Where a party is within a territory, he may justly be subjected to its process, and bound personally by the judgment pronounced, on such process, against him. Where he is not within such territory, and is not personally subject to its laws, if on account of his supposed or actual property being within the territory, process by the local laws may by attachment go to compel his appearance, and for his default to appear, judgment may be pronounced against him, such a judgment must, upon general principles, be deemed only to bind him to the extent of such property, and cannot have the effect of a conclusive judgment in personam, for the plain reason, that except so far as the property is concerned, it is a judgment coram non judice. If the party chooses to appear and take upon himself the defence of the suit, that might vary the case, for he may submit to the local jurisdiction, and waive his personal immunity. Such appear to me to be the principles established by the better opinions in the cases cited at the bar, and particularly in Phelps v. Holker, 1 Dall. [1 U. S.] 261; Killburn v. Woodworth, 5 Johns. 37; Smith v. Brush, 8 Johns. 84; Fenton v. Garlick, Id. 151; Pawling v. Bird's Ex'rs, 13 Johns. 192; Borden v. Fitch, 15 Johns. 121; and Bissell v. Briggs, 9 Mass. 462. In the two last cases, the learned chief justices of New York and Massachusetts reasoned out the doctrine with great acuteness and ability. The principles of the common law (which are never to be lost sight of in the construction of our own statutes) proceed yet farther. In general, it may be said, that they authorize no judgment against a party, until after his appearance in court. He may be taken on a capias and brought into court, or distrained by attachment and other process against his property to compel his appearance; and for nonappearance be outlawed. But still, even though a subject, and within the kingdom, the judgment against him can take place only after such appearance. So anxious was the common law to guard the rights of private persons from judgments obtained without notice, and regular personal appearance in court.

The conclusion, to be deduced from the foregoing considerations, which must necessarily have been in the contemplation of the framers of the judiciary act of 1789, is, that the whole structure of that act proceeded upon the supposition, that, independent of some positive provision to the contrary, no judgment could be rendered in the circuit court against any person, upon whom process could not be personally served within the district. This was the natural result of the principles of the common law in relation to jurisdiction and process. In this view of the matter, the clause in the eleventh section already cited was introduced, as my Brother Washington supposes it to have been, from abundant caution, to guard against every possibility of latent doubt. And it should be remembered in this connexion, that the process act of 1789 [1 Stat. 93,] which alone gave life to the state process in the United States courts, formed no necessary part of the system, and was brought forward by an independent and temporary statute.

Let us, then, consider, what is the true interpretation to be put upon this clause. It first provides, that "no person shall be arrested in one district for trial in another, in any civil action before a circuit or district court." So that it is clear, that the process of capias is limited to the local boundaries of the court by which it is issued. It next provides, that "no civil suit shall be brought before either of said courts against an inhabitant of the United States by any original process in any other district than that, whereof he is an inhabitant, or in which he shall be found at the time of serving the writ." Now the argument is, that this last provision applies only to persons, who, at the time of the suit are inhabitants of the United States. It is a restriction of the general authority of the courts to bring before them by original process any person, who, as a citizen or alien, was amenable by the general grant of jurisdiction to these courts. Swan was either an inhabitant of Massachusetts at the time, when the present suit was brought, or he was not. If he was an inhabitant, then the suit is brought in the proper district; if not an inhabitant, then the restriction is inapplicable to him. Such is the dilemma, into which the argument supposes the adverse party to be driven, and on which it seeks to suspend him. It appears to me, that such is not the true interpretation of the words of the clause. They admit of an interpretation, in my view, much more natural, and consonant with the principles of justice. The argument supposes, that as a general jurisdiction is given in cases, where an alien is party, if he is not an inhabitant of the United States, and has not any property within it, (for to this extent it must reach,) still he is amenable to the jurisdiction of any circuit court, sitting in any state in this Union. So that a subject of England, or France, or Russia, having a controversy with one of our own citizens, may be summoned from the other end of the globe to obey our process, and submit to the judgment of our courts. Such an intention, so repugnant to the general rights and sovereignty of other nations, ought not to be presumed, unless it is established by irresistible proof. My opinion is, that congress never had any such intention; that it presupposed, that no suit would lie against any person, who was not locally present, either as an inhabitant, or in transitu in the United States; and that it designedly enlarged the power to proceed in cases of inhabitancy, where the party happened at the time to be absent without any intentional change of domicil, as well as allowed it in any district, where the party might, at the time, be found. The words of the clause are, "against an inhabitant of the United States." But I lay no particular stress upon the word "inhabitant," and deem it a mere equivalent description of "citizen" and "alien" in the general clause conferring jurisdiction over parties. A person might be an inhabitant, without being a citizen; and a citizen might not be an inhabitant, though he retained his citizenship. Alienage or citizenship is one thing; and inhabitancy, by which I understand local residence, animo manendi, quite another. I read, then, the clause thus: "No civil suit shall be brought before either of said courts against an alien or a citizen, by any original process, in any other district than that, whereof he is an inhabitant, or in which he shall be found, at the time of serving the writ." It cannot be presumed, that congress meant to say, that if an alien or citizen were not an inhabitant of, or commorant in the United States, a suit might be maintained against him in any district, and process served abroad upon him, or a judgment given against him without any notice or process served upon him. If it be said, that process may be served upon his property within the district, what is to be done, when there is no such property to be found, or it is merely nominal? If in the latter cases an exception is to be implied upon general principles, why not in the former? The judiciary act of 1789 (chapter 20) has not provided for either case in terms; and the right to serve process upon the property of the party, and thereby to bring him into court, when an absentee, so as to bind that property, or him personally, by the judgment, is not a right growing out of the common law, but everywhere, at least in countries governed by the common law, depends upon statute regulations. Looking, therefore, to the plain tenor of this act, and construing it by the real objects, which it avows, my judgment is, that it contemplates no effective exercise of jurisdiction by the circuit court, except in cases where the party defendant is an inhabitant of, or found within, such district, at the time of serving the writ. If no forms of process or modes of proceeding had been prescribed by any other law, I do not see how the courts could have exercised their jurisdiction at all, except by reference to writs, process, and service according to the common law, a construction, which seems naturally to flow from the provisions of the fourteenth section of the act.

The process acts of 1789 (chapter 21) and of 1792 (chapter 36), have prescribed the forms of process, and modes of service, to be according to the state jurisprudence. But they do not appear to me to be intended to enlarge the sphere of jurisdiction of the circuit courts. Whenever the person is an inhabitant of, or found within, the district, the proper writ may issue, and the process may be served against him, whether it be a capias, summons, attachment, or otherwise, as the local jurisprudence authorizes. I cannot judicially say, that the general phraseology of these process acts ought to receive a more extensive intepretation, so as to break down or interfere with the policy of the judiciary act of 1789 (chapter 20), founded, as it seems to me to be, in principles of public law, public convenience, and immutable justice. If the state jurisprudence authorizes its own courts to take cognizance of suits against non-residents, by summoning their tenants, attornies, or agents, or attaching their property, whether it be a farm or a debt, or a glove, or a chip, it is not for us to say, that such legislation may not be rightful, and bind the state courts. But when the circuit courts are called upon to adopt the same rule, it ought to be seen, that congress have, in an unambiguous manner, made it imperative upon them. There is no pretence to say, that the circuit court in this district has by its practice, or by rule, sanctioned such a proceeding. If such modes of service have in such cases been used, the matter has passed sub silentio, without any knowledge on the part of the court, which implied a sanction of it.

No case has been cited, in which the question has been brought directly before any court of the United States for a decision. In Hollingsworth v. Adams, 2 Dall. [2 U. S.] 396, there was a foreign attachment in the circuit court of Pennsylvania; but the principal debtor was an inhabitant of Delaware, and not found in Pennsylvania; and the court quashed the writ for want of proper jurisdiction. In Pollard v. Dwight, 4 Cranch [8 U. S.] 421, the plaintiffs were citizens of Massachusetts and Connecticut, and the defendants were citizens of Virginia, and not found in the district of Connecticut, and were sued in a foreign attachment in the state court, and the cause removed by them into the circuit court for the district of Connecticut. The question was, whether they could be so sued. The supreme court held, that "by appearing to the action, the defendants in the court below placed themselves precisely in the situation, in which they would have stood, had process been served upon them, and consequently waived all objection to non-service of process." This was a strong case; for though the suit was between citizens of different states, yet within the terms of the eleventh section of the act of 1789, it was not a suit between a citizen of the state where the suit was brought (for the plaintiffs were partly citizens of Connecticut, and partly citizens of Massachusetts) and a citizen of another state. Shute v. Davis [Case No. 12,828], and Craig v. Cummins [Id. 3,331], turned on the very words of the statute just cited. The suit in the former case was brought in Pennsylvania between citizens of New York and New Jersey; in the latter, one of the defendants was a citizen of Pennsylvania, and the other not; but the contract being joint and by the local law, capable of being pursued against one only, the severance was deemed complete by the return of non est inventus of the non-resident. Fisher v. Consequa [Id. 4,816], was a foreign attachment against a non-resident Chinese merchant; but there seems to have been a general appearance for him, and at all events no exception was taken on this particular point. In Bissell v. Horton [Id. 1,448], in the circuit court in Connecticut, the plaintiffs were described as partly citizens of Vermont, and partly citizens of Connecticut. The defendant was described as a citizen of New York, now dwelling in Hebron in Connecticut. The court held, that they had no jurisdiction, and on motion dismissed the suit. Mr. Justice Livingston said, "the plaintiffs are partly in Vermont and partly in Connecticut. They are not, therefore, citizens of Vermont within the constitution and laws of the United States. With regard to the defendant, it is admitted, that he now resides in Connecticut, and has resided here during the time, in which he has been in possession of the demanded premises, which clearly evinces a determination in him to remain here permanently." This case may, from the shape given to the opinion of the learned judge in the report, be open to some critical observation. Upon the motion to dismiss, the citizenship of the defendant in New York, as alleged in the writ, must have been taken to be true. The process was duly served upon him in Connecti-

cut. And upon the authority of Pollard v. Dwight, 4 Cranch [8 U. S.] 421, the jurisdiction was maintainable; for the citizenship of one of the plaintiffs in Connecticut was there thought sufficient to bring the case within the act of congress. I have not met with any other cases, in which the question has been judicially discussed, except Ex parte Graham [supra], already referred to, where the reasoning, so far as it bears at all on this subject, presents itself unfavourably to the maintenance of the present suit. If, therefore, I were called upon to decide this case exclusively upon principle, my judgment would lead me to adopt these conclusions: That by the general provisons of the laws of the United States, the circuit courts could issue no process beyond the limits of their districts. That independent of positive legislation, the process can only be served upon persons within the same districts. That the acts of congress, adopting the state process, adopt the forms and modes of service only so far as the persons are rightfully within the reach of such process, and did not intend to enlarge the sphere of the jurisdiction of the circuit courts. That the right to attach property to compel the appearance of persons can properly be used only in cases in which such persons are amenable to the process of the court in personam,—that is, where they are inhabitants, or found within the United States,—and not where they are aliens or citizens resident abroad at the commencement of the suit, and have no inhabitancy here.

There are two reasons, which have great weight with me in support of these positions. One is, that otherwise the judgments in the courts of the United States would not, in cases of non-residents, be binding, as general judgments in personam; but if at all, only as proceedings in rem to the extent of the property attached, whether it be a chip, or a bale of goods, upon the principles of the cases of Bissell v. Briggs, 9 Mass. 462; Buchanan v. Rucker, 9 East, 192; and other cases before mentioned. Another is, that the forms of process in Massachusetts, (which forms are made applicable by the acts of congress to the courts of the United States,) both in the common process and the trustee process, whenever goods or estate are attached, require a summons to be served on the party. In the trustee process, the words are, "We command you to attach the goods and estate of A. B. (the defendant) to the value of——, and summons the said A. B. (the defendant), if he may be found in your precinct (district), to appear," &c. Not one word is stated in the writ itself, as to any summons, where the party is not found within the precinct or district of the officer. The mode of service in such cases, and in cases of non-residence generally, is prescribed by other distinct acts or sections of acts. So, that the exigency of the writ looks only to the fact of the party being found within the district; and unless the marshal is at liberty to make a service in a case and mode beyond the exigency of this writ, not expressly reached by the acts of congress, but dependent entirely upon state laws, made for local purposes, the service in cases of non-residence would be utterly void. The argument for the plaintiff is, that as the summons is authorized by law, it is sufficiently served by the marshal in any mode, within his district, which the local laws justify. Generally speaking, that may be true, where the party is within the district, or an inhabitant bound to obey the summons within the district, viis et modis prescribed by the law. The difficulty is, how to deal with cases, where the party is an alien, or a citizen of another state, not resident within any of the United States. Yet the state laws extend to all these cases equally with those, where the party is a non-resident citizen of the state, where the suit is brought. I know no principle, upon which the court can say, that the service as to the latter shall be good, and not as to the former; for in each case the sufficiency of the service of the summons must stand upon the same provisions of the state laws. Unless, therefore, the court can say, that an alien, who has never been within the United States, may be rightfully served with a summons or other process by any attachment of his property, however small, within the district, and be bound thereby to appear and submit to the jurisdiction of the court, or otherwise have a judgment against him in invitum, I do not perceive, how the present case can, on general principles, be maintained. If congress had prescribed such a rule, the court would certainly be bound to follow it, and proceed upon the law. The point of difficulty is, whether such a rule ought to be inferred from so general a legislation as congress has adopted, not necessarily leading to the conclusion, that such was the intent. It would seem strange, that a provision should be so solicitously made for persons inhabiting the country, that they should not be held amenable, except in the districts where they resided; and yet that no protection should be afforded to aliens or citizens, who were permanently domiciled abroad.

But supposing the preceding reasoning less well founded than, in my judgment, it seems to be; it remains to consider, whether, under the circumstances of this case, the service of the process was such, as by the local laws, would justify the judgment of default now asked of this court. We may lay out of the case all consideration of the service, so far as relates to the provisions of the trustee act of 1794 (chapter 65), because the trustees having been discharged, no judgment can, by the express provisions of the act of 1798 (chapter 5), be rendered against the principal, unless the service has been such, as would authorize the court to proceed to render judgment against him in an action commenced by the common and ordinary mode of process. The mode of service in the common process is provided for by the act of 1797 (chapter 50) already cited. In cases of attachment, a summons is required to be left at the "dwelling-house, or place of last and usual abode" of the defendant, and "in case the defendant was at no time an inhabitant or resident within this commonwealth, then such summons to be left with his or her tenant, agent, or attorney." It appears to me, that the plain intent of the statute is to apply the words of the first clause exclusively to cases, where the defendant was at the time of the suit an inhabitant or resident of the commonwealth, having a dwelling-house, or place of last and usual abode therein. Where a defendant has no such inhabitancy or residence, but has left the commonwealth, and changed his domicil, how can it be said, that he has a dwelling-house there, or a place of last and usual abode? These words "last and usual" (not "last or usual") refer to cases, where the party

has had several residences within the commonwealth. To make the service good, the last residence, if it be the usual residence of the party, is the proper place at which the summons is to be left. If the party has no place of usual abode in the commonwealth at the time, the statute has not made the service at the place of his last abode sufficient. Both must concur. And there is sound reason in this provision; for otherwise it might happen, that if the party were at one time an inhabitant, and afterwards should change his domicil, and become a citizen of another state, or have his home and usual and constant place of abode abroad for any length of time whatsoever, his property might be attached here, and without any notice to him, or to any agent or attorney, a judgment might be obtained against him, binding the property attached for ever. So monstrous and mischievous a provision could hardly be deemed a just exercise of legislative power in any civilized country. The second clause applies wholly in terms to defendants, who have been at no time inhabitants or residents within the commonwealth. Now the writ itself negatives the presumption, that Swan is in this predicament. It describes him as now commorant at Paris, but of the city of Boston; so that his inhabitancy or residence at some time, in the commonwealth, is distinctly averred. The return of the marshal states, that such inhabitancy has not been within three years. So that the case before the court is of a defendant, who has once been an inhabitant, and for three years last past has ceased to be an inhabitant. No mode of service is provided for in such a case by the statute of 1797 (chapter 50); and the trustees having been discharged, it is not provided for by the act of 1794 (chapter 65). It is a casus omissus. In respect to the service of process in such a new and extraordinary manner, varying so much from the principles and practice of the common law, and in many instances so little consonant to the principles of public law, or general justice, there can be no ground to extend the statute provision by implication or equity. The state court itself has not so construed them; and in the cases of Tingley v. Bateman, 10 Mass. 344, Lawrence v. Smith, 5 Mass. 362, and Gardner v. Baker, 12 Mass. 36, has been disposed rather to narrow down than widen the means, by which non-residents are to be brought within the sphere of our process. It appears to me, therefore, that as the service of the summons on an agent is not authorized, except where the defendant has at no time been an inhabitant or resident, such service is void; and as no summons was in fact left at any place of abode of the defendant, either last or usual, in the commonwealth, there has been no compliance with the other branch of the statute. Either way, therefore, the service is, according to the local laws, defective and nugatory.

There is another defect in the description of the writ, which would be fatal, if every other were surmounted. Swan is not described to be a citizen of Massachusetts, or of any particular state, but only as "a citizen of the United States." Now, such a specific description is, according to the known course of decisions, indispensable to give the circuit courts jurisdiction. Although the judiciary act of 1789 has given to the circuit courts jurisdiction of causes, where "an alien is a party," yet this must be construed and controlled by the provisions of the constitution itself. The latter does not extend the judicial power of the United States to such an extent, but limits it to controversies between citizens of a state, and foreign citizens or subjects. Hence the uniform interpretation of the act of 1789 has been, that if an alien is one party, a citizen of some particular state must be the other party. The constitution does not recognize such a description of persons as "citizens of the United States," as the objects of its judicial power. The circuit courts have no jurisdiction of suits between aliens, or between persons having no other description than "citizens of the United States." A citizen of one of our territories is a citizen of the United States; but he is not by law entitled to sue or be sued in the circuit courts of the United States. This doctrine was settled at an early period in the circuit courts, as appears from the case of Irving v. Frazier [Case No. 7,075], Story, Pl. 9, and other cases cited in the note to Rea v. Hayden, 3 Mass. 24, 25, and has been affirmed in the supreme court in Hepburn v. Ellzey, 2 Cranch [6 U. S.] 445, and Montalet v. Murray, 4 Cranch [8 U. S.] 46.

Upon the whole, in every view, which I have been able to take of the present case, it is the duty of the court to stay further proceedings, upon the ground, that there has been no sufficient service of the process to compel the appearance of Swan, or authorize a judgment of default against him.

24

BECKMAN V. SARATOGA & S. R.R.
3 Paige Ch. 45 (N.Y. 1831)

WADSWORTH, Ch. . . . The constitution of the United States does not come in question in this cause. It is admitted that the complainant held the land in fee; and probably under a title derived from the crown, to the rights of which the people have now succeeded. A law declaring the grant from the crown void, and divesting his title on that ground, would impair the obligation of the contract. But it was no part of the contract between the crown and its grantees or their assigns, that the property should not be taken for public use, upon paying a fair compensation therefor, whenever the public interest or necessities required that it should be so taken. All separate interests of individuals in property are held of the government under this tacit agreement or implied reservation. Notwithstanding the grant to individuals, the *eminent domain*, the highest and most exact idea of property, remains in the government, or in the aggregate body of the people in their sovereign capacity; and they have a right to resume the possession of the property, in the manner directed by the constitution and laws of the state, whenever the public interest requires it. This right of resumption may be exercised not only where the safety, but also where the interest or even the expediency of the state is concerned; as where the land of the individual is wanted for a road, canal or

other public improvement. The only restriction upon this power, in cases where the public or the inhabitants of any particular section of the state have an interest in the contemplated improvement as citizens merely, is that the property shall not be taken for the public use without just compensation to the owner, and in the mode prescribed by law. The right of *eminent domain* does not however imply a right in the sovereign power to take the property of one citizen and transfer it to another, even for a full compensation, where the public interest will be in no way promoted by such transfer. And if the legislature should attempt thus to transfer the property of one individual to another, where there could be no pretence of benefit to the public by such exchange, it would probably be a violation of the contract by which the land was granted by the government to the individual, or to those under whom he claimed title, and repugnant to the constitution of the United States. But if the public interest can be in any way promoted by the taking of private property, it must rest in the wisdom of the legislature to determine whether the benefit to the public will be of sufficient importance to render it expedient for them to exercise the right of *eminent domain*, and to authorize an interference with the private rights of individuals for that purpose. (2 *Kent's Com.* 340.) It is upon this principle that the legislatures of several of the states have authorized the condemnation of the lands of individuals for mill sites, where from the nature of the country such mill sites could not be obtained for the accommodation of the inhabitants without overflowing the lands thus condemned. Upon the same principle of public benefit, not only the agents of the government, but also individuals and corporate bodies, have been authorized to take private property for the purpose of making public highways, turnpike roads, and canals; of erecting and constructing wharves and basins; of establishing ferries; of draining swamps and marshes; and of bringing water to cities and villages. In all such cases the object of the legislative grant of power, is the public benefit derived from the contemplated improvement, whether such improvement is to be effected directly by the agents of the government, or through the medium of corporate bodies, or of individual enterprize. And according to the opinion of Chief Justice Marshall, in the case of *Wilson* v. *The Black Bird Creek Marsh Company*, (2 *Peters' Rep.* 251,) measures calculated to produce such benefits to the public, though effected through the medium of a private incorporation, are undoubtedly within the powers reserved to the states, provided they do not come in collision with those of the general government. It is objected, however, that a rail road differs from other public improvements, and particularly from turnpikes and canals, because travellers cannot use it with their own carriages, and farmers cannot transport their produce in their own vehicles; that the company in this case are under no obligation to accommodate the public with transportation; and that they are unlimited in the amount of tolls which they are authorized to take. If the making of a rail road will enable the traveller to go from one place to another without the expense of a carriage and horses, he derives a greater benefit from the improvement than if he was compelled to travel with his own conveyance over a turnpike road at the same expense. And if a mode of conveyance has been discovered by which the farmer can procure his produce to be transported to market at half the expense which it would cost him to carry it there with his own waggon and horses, there is no reason why the public should not enjoy the benefit of the discovery. And if any individual is so unreasonable as to refuse to have the rail road made through his lands, for a fair compensation, the legislature may lawfully appropriate a portion of his property for this public benefit, or may authorize an individual or a corporation thus to appropriate it, upon paying a just compensation to the owner of the land for the damage sustained. The objection that the corporation is under no legal obligation to transport produce or passengers upon this road, and at a reasonable expense, is unfounded in fact. The privilege of making a road and taking tolls thereon is a franchise, as much as the establishment of a ferry or a public wharf and taking tolls for the use of the same. The public have an interest in the use of the rail road, and the owners may be prosecuted for the damage sustained, if they should refuse to transport an individual, or his property, without any reasonable excuse, upon being paid the usual rate of fare. The legislature may also from time to time regulate the use of the franchise and limit the amount of toll which it shall be lawful to take, in the same manner as they may regulate the amount of tolls to be taken at a ferry, or for grinding at a mill, unless they have deprived themselves of that power by a legislative contract with the owners of the road.

The mode of ascertaining damages by commission has been adopted by the legislature in a great variety of cases; and I can see nothing in the provisions of the constitution which render such a course exceptionable. It was well known to the framers of the new constitution that such had been the practice in relation to the assessment of damages for private property taken for the Erie and Champlain canal, and for a great number of turnpike roads, as well as for other public uses. When, therefore, the constitution provided that private property should not be taken for public uses without just compensation, and without prescribing any mode in which the amount of compensation should be ascertained, it is fairly to be presumed the framers of that instrument intended to leave that subject to be regulated by law, as it had been before that time; or in such other manner as the legislature in their discretion might deem best calculated to carry into effect the constitutional provision, according to its spirit and intent.

The provision of the constitution which declares that the right of trial by jury in all cases in which it has heretofore been used shall remain inviolate forever, relates to the trial of issues of fact in civil and criminal causes in courts of justice, as is evident from what follows this provision in the same section; and it has no relation to cases of the kind now under consideration. Although the writ ad quod damnum had sometimes been used for the purpose of assessing damages where individual property was taken for public use, yet that was never considered a jury trial within the meaning of the constitution. There is no doubt that it is a very proper mode of estimating damages in such cases;

and probably where a single assessment was to be provided for, it would be much the most judicious and satisfactory mode of fixing the amount.

I have no doubt of the constitutionality of the statute under which the property of the complainant has been taken; and as all the requisites of the statute have been complied with, this property has been taken by due course of law, and after making just compensation therefor. From the moment that compensation was paid or deposited as the law had directed, the right to this property was absolutely vested in the defendants for the use of the rail road, and they have a perfect right to enter upon it and appropriate it to that use.

25

LIVINGSTON v. MAYOR OF NEW YORK
8 Wend. 85 (N.Y. 1831)

By the CHANCELLOR [Reuben H. Walworth]. . . . But it is said that the law which authorizes the taking of private property in the city of New York for a public street is unconstitutional, on the ground that the legislature can not authorize private property to be taken for public use without the intervention of a jury. If the plaintiff is right on this point, then no damages could be awarded to him, and his right to the street remains as it was before the commencement of these proceedings; and all the streets which have been laid out in the city of New York for the last twenty years are wholly unauthorized and invalid, except in those cases where the owners of the land have voluntarily given up their property for the use of streets. I apprehend, however, this court will not arrive at such a conclusion. The assessment of damages by *commissioners*, instead of a *jury*, is supposed to be in violation of those amendments of the constitution of the United States which provide that no person shall be deprived of his property without due process of law; that private property shall not be taken for public use without just compensation; and that in suits at common law, where the value in controversy shall exceed twenty dollars, the right of trial by jury shall be preserved. I have formerly had occasion to examine the question how far these amendments of the constitution of the United States were restrictive upon the power of the individual states; and the conclusion at which I arrived was, that all the amendments adopted by congress at its first session, and afterwards sanctioned by the requisite number of states, were intended to be restrictive upon the government of the United States and upon its officers exclusively (see *Jackson* v. *Wood*, 2 *Cowen*, 818, n. b). The preamble which was prefixed to these amendments, as adopted by congress, is important to show in what light that body considered them. This preamble has not usually been published in connection with these amendments; it will be found in the journal of the federal convention, as published in conformity to a resolution of congress, and is as follows: "The conventions of a number of the states having at the time of their adopting the constitution expressed a desire, in order to prevent misconstruction and abuse of its powers, that further declaratory and restrictive clauses should be added; and as extending the grounds of public confidence in the government will best ensure the beneficent ends of its institution: resolved," &c., that the following articles be proposed, &c. When we take into consideration the fact that this preamble was added by the senate, after they had amended the resolution of the house by expunging therefrom the only article proposed as restrictive upon the powers of the states; and when it is known that these amendments were introduced into congress by Mr. Madison, in consequence of the objections which had been made in the state conventions to the unlimited powers given by the constitution to the general government, I think it is very evident that the amendments were intended to apply to the general government only, for the purpose of restricting and limiting its powers, but without any intention of limiting or controlling state legislation. But as the same provisions substantially are now contained in the constitution of this state, it becomes necessary to inquire whether there is any thing in the manner in which the property of individuals is taken for public streets in the city of New York, or in the mode of ascertaining compensation therefor, which conflicts with the provisions of that instrument.

It is not denied that the legislature have the power to authorize the taking of private property for the purpose of public streets, upon making just compensation to the owners; but it is insisted by the plaintiff's counsel that the increased value of adjacent property belonging to the same individual can not be set off against the loss or damage sustained by him in taking his property for a street, and be considered as a just compensation for the property so taken: and that in all cases the damage must be ascertained by the verdict of a jury. I have recently had occasion to examine these questions also, in the case of *Beekman* v. *The Saratoga and Schenectady Rail Road Company* (which is not yet reported), and came to the conclusion that both of these objections were untenable. The owner of the property taken is entitled to a full compensation for the damage he sustains thereby, but if the taking of his property for the public improvement is a benefit rather than an injury to him, he certainly has no equitable claim to damages. Besides, it is a well settled principle, that where any particular county, district or neighborhood is exclusively benefited by a public improvement, the inhabitants of that district may be taxed for the whole expenses of the improvement, and in proportion to the supposed benefit received by each. In this case, if the whole value of the property taken for a street in the city of New York is allowed to the individual owner, the proprietors of the adjacent lots must be assessed for the purpose of paying that amount, and if the individual whose property is taken is the owner of a lot adjacent, that lot must be assessed rateably with the others. It therefore makes no difference whether he is allowed the whole value of the property taken in the first instance, and is assessed for his portion of the damage, or whether the one sum is offset against the other in the first place, and the balance only is allowed.

The mode of ascertaining damages by *commissioners*, had been extensively practiced in this state previous to the adoption of the new constitution. As this was well known to the members of the convention who framed that instrument, and to the people who adopted it, when they directed that private property should not be taken for public use without just compensation, but said nothing as to the manner in which such compensation should be ascertained, it is to be presumed they intended to leave that subject to the discretion of the legislature, to be regulated in such manner as might be prescribed by law.

The provision of the constitution relative to the trial by jury relates to the trial of issues of fact, in civil and criminal proceedings in courts of justice, and has no relation to cases of this kind. Although damages have frequently been ascertained by the oaths of twelve freeholders, both before and since the adoption of the constitution, yet these are not jury trials within the spirit or meaning of that provision.

I am therefore of opinion that the plaintiff in error has received full compensation for the land taken for the street, by the enhanced value which he must have obtained on the sale of the lots adjacent to the same, and that the amount of nominal damages, to which he was probably entitled, has been legally ascertained and allowed to him in the report of the commissioners of estimate and assessment. The judgment of the supreme court should therefore be affirmed.

SHERMAN, Senator. . . . As to the constitutional question, I admit that taking a man's property without his consent, is one of the highest powers that is exercised under the constitution, and ought to be used with great caution. Yet such are the terms of that instrument or compact, made by the sovereign people of this state, of whom Mr. Livingston is one, that private property may be taken for public purposes, on making a just compensation therefor. This compact has been reconfirmed by the people since the passage of the act in question. The next inquiry is, has this property been taken by due process of law, and has a just compensation been made therefor? On this last point I have given my views. On the other, I am of opinion that if the mode of taking rests with the legislature, and they have prescribed one which operates alike on all whom it affects, and is not individual or partial, that it is valid, and embraced within the constitutional limits.

Without entering further into this inquiry, I must say that the arguments advanced are not sufficient to convince my mind that the law under which the commissioners acted is invalid. The law has been so long recognized by the state courts, and by various acts of the legislature, and the principle introduced into so many other laws, that I should require other and stronger reasons than those urged in argument, to convince my mind of its unconstitutionality; the effect of which would probably be to throw open to litigation all acts done under the same, for the twenty years it has been in operation. I am of opinion that justice has been done in this case, and am therefore in favor of affirming the judgment.

The court being unanimously of the opinion that the

judgment of the supreme court ought to be affirmed, it was *affirmed* accordingly.

26

BARRON V. BALTIMORE
7 Pet. 243 (1833)

Mr. Chief Justice MARSHALL delivered the opinion of the court.

The judgment brought up by this writ of error having been rendered by the court of a state, this tribunal can exercise no jurisdiction over it, unless it be shown to come within the provisions of the twenty-fifth section of the judicial act.

The plaintiff in error contends that it comes within that clause in the fifth amendment to the constitution, which inhibits the taking of private property for public use, without just compensation. He insists that this amendment, being in favour of the liberty of the citizen, ought to be so construed as to restrain the legislative power of a state, as well as that of the United States. If this proposition be untrue, the court can take no jurisdiction of the cause.

The question thus presented is, we think, of great importance, but not of much difficulty.

The constitution was ordained and established by the people of the United States for themselves, for their own government, and not for the government of the individual states. Each state established a constitution for itself, and, in that constitution, provided such limitations and restrictions on the powers of its particular government as its judgment dictated. The people of the United States framed such a government for the United States as they supposed best adapted to their situation and best calculated to promote their interests. The powers they conferred on this government were to be exercised by itself; and the limitations on power, if expressed in general terms, are naturally, and, we think, necessarily applicable to the government created by the instrument. They are limitations of power granted in the instrument itself; not of distinct governments, framed by different persons and for different purposes.

If these propositions be correct, the fifth amendment must be understood as restraining the power of the general government, not as applicable to the states. In their several constitutions they have imposed such restrictions on their respective governments as their own wisdom suggested; such as they deemed most proper for themselves. It is a subject on which they judge exclusively, and with which others interfere no farther than they are supposed to have a common interest.

The counsel for the plaintiff in error insists that the constitution was intended to secure the people of the several states against the undue exercise of power by their respective state governments; as well as against that which might be attempted by their general government. In support of this argument he relies on the inhibitions contained in the tenth section of the first article.

We think that section affords a strong if not a conclusive argument in support of the opinion already indicated by the court.

The preceding section contains restrictions which are obviously intended for the exclusive purpose of restraining the exercise of power by the departments of the general government. Some of them use language applicable only to congress: others are expressed in general terms. The third clause, for example, declares that "no bill of attainder or ex post facto law shall be passed." No language can be more general; yet the demonstration is complete that it applies solely to the government of the United States. In addition to the general arguments furnished by the instrument itself, some of which have been already suggested, the succeeding section, the avowed purpose of which is to restrain state legislation, contains in terms the very prohibition. It declares that "no state shall pass any bill of attainder or ex post facto law." This provision, then, of the ninth section, however comprehensive its language, contains no restriction on state legislation.

The ninth section having enumerated, in the nature of a bill of rights, the limitations intended to be imposed on the powers of the general government, the tenth proceeds to enumerate those which were to operate on the state legislatures. These restrictions are brought together in the same section, and are by express words applied to the states. "No state shall enter into any treaty," &c. Perceiving that in a constitution framed by the people of the United States for the government of all, no limitation of the action of government on the people would apply to the state government, unless expressed in terms; the restrictions contained in the tenth section are in direct words so applied to the states.

It is worthy of remark, too, that these inhibitions generally restrain state legislation on subjects entrusted to the general government, or in which the people of all the states feel an interest.

A state is forbidden to enter into any treaty, alliance or confederation. If these compacts are with foreign nations, they interfere with the treaty making power which is conferred entirely on the general government; if with each other, for political purposes, they can scarcely fail to interfere with the general purpose and intent of the constitution. To grant letters of marque and reprisal, would lead directly to war; the power of declaring which is expressly given to congress. To coin money is also the exercise of a power conferred on congress. It would be tedious to recapitulate the several limitations on the powers of the states which are contained in this section. They will be found, generally, to restrain state legislation on subjects entrusted to the government of the union, in which the citizens of all the states are interested. In these alone were the whole people concerned. The question of their application to states is not left to construction. It is averred in positive words.

If the original constitution, in the ninth and tenth sections of the first article, draws this plain and marked line of discrimination between the limitations it imposes on the powers of the general government, and on those of the state; if in every inhibition intended to act on state power, words are employed which directly express that intent; some strong reason must be assigned for departing from this safe and judicious course in framing the amendments, before that departure can be assumed.

We search in vain for that reason.

Had the people of the several states, or any of them, required changes in their constitutions; had they required additional safeguards to liberty from the apprehended encroachments of their particular governments: the remedy was in their own hands, and would have been applied by themselves. A convention would have been assembled by the discontented state, and the required improvements would have been made by itself. The unwieldy and cumbrous machinery of procuring a recommendation from two-thirds of congress, and the assent of three-fourths of their sister states, could never have occurred to any human being as a mode of doing that which might be effected by the state itself. Had the framers of these amendments intended them to be limitations on the powers of the state governments, they would have imitated the framers of the original constitution, and have expressed that intention. Had congress engaged in the extraordinary occupation of improving the constitutions of the several states by affording the people additional protection from the exercise of power by their own governments in matters which concerned themselves alone, they would have declared this purpose in plain and intelligible language.

But it is universally understood, it is a part of the history of the day, that the great revolution which established the constitution of the United States, was not effected without immense opposition. Serious fears were extensively entertained that those powers which the patriot statesmen, who then watched over the interests of our country, deemed essential to union, and to the attainment of those invaluable objects for which union was sought, might be exercised in a manner dangerous to liberty. In almost every convention by which the constitution was adopted, amendments to guard against the abuse of power were recommended. These amendments demanded security against the apprehended encroachments of the general government—not against those of the local governments.

In compliance with a sentiment thus generally expressed, to quiet fears thus extensively entertained, amendments were proposed by the required majority in congress, and adopted by the states. These amendments contain no expression indicating an intention to apply them to the state governments. This court cannot so apply them.

We are of opinion that the provision in the fifth amendment to the constitution, declaring that private property shall not be taken for public use without just compensation, is intended solely as a limitation on the exercise of power by the government of the United States, and is not applicable to the legislation of the states. We are therefore of opinion that there is no repugnancy between the several acts of the general assembly of Maryland, given in evidence by the defendants at the trial of this cause, in the court of that state, and the constitution of the United

States. This court, therefore, has no jurisdiction of the cause; and it is dismissed.

27

WELLINGTON, ET AL., PETITIONERS
16 Pick. 87 (Mass. 1834)

SHAW C. J. delivered the opinion of the Court. In considering the question, whether the act passed June 5, 1830, providing for the enclosure and appropriation of Cambridge common is a constitutional act, having the force and effect of law, the delicacy and importance of the subject may render it not improper to repeat what has been so often suggested by courts of justice, that when called upon to pronounce the invalidity of an act of legislation passed with all the forms and solemnities requisite to give it the force of law, courts will approach the question with great caution, examine it in every possible aspect, and ponder upon it as long as deliberation and patient attention can throw any new light on the subject, and never declare a statute void, unless the nullity and invalidity of the act are placed, in their judgment, beyond reasonable doubt. Still however it cannot be doubted, and I believe it is nowhere denied, that in a limited government like ours, acting under a written constitution with numerous and detailed provisions, a constitution which is in itself perpetual and irrepealable except by the people themselves, and which imposes many restraints upon the power of the legislature by express provisions and many others by necessary implication, and where the same constitution has provided for the establishment of a judiciary as a coördinate department of the government, with power in all cases to expound the laws, to declare what has and what has not the force of law, and to apply them to the investigation and adjustment of the rights, duties, and obligations of citizens, in the actual administration of justice, it is clearly within the power, and sometimes the imperative duty of courts, to declare that a particular enactment is not warranted by the power vested in the legislature, and therefore to the extent, to which it thus exceeds the power of the legislature, it is without efficacy, inoperative, and void. Perhaps, however, it may be well doubted, whether a formal act of legislation can ever with strict legal propriety be said to be void; it seems more consistent with the nature of the subject, and the principles applicable to analogous cases, to treat it as voidable. But whether or not a case can be imagined, in which an act of the legislature can be deemed absolutely void, we think it quite clear, that when such act is alleged to be void, on the ground that it exceeds the just limits of legislative power, and thus injuriously affects the rights of others, it is to be deemed void only in respect to those particulars, and as against those persons, whose rights are thus affected. *Primâ facie*, and upon the face of the act itself, nothing will generally appear to show that the act is not valid; and it is only when some person attempts to resist its operation and calls in the aid of the judicial power, to pronounce it void, as to him, his property, or his rights, that the objection of unconstitutionality can be presented and sustained. Respect for the legislature, therefore, concurs with well established principles of law, in the conclusion, that such act is not void, but voidable only; and it follows as a necessary legal inference from this position, that this ground of avoidance can be taken advantage of, by those only who have a right to question the validity of the act, and not by strangers. To this extent only is it necessary to go, in order to secure and protect the rights of all persons, against the unwarranted exercise of legislative power, and to this extent only, therefore, are courts of justice called on to interpose.

Besides, and this is another argument leading to the same result, if a legislative act may or may not be valid according to circumstances, courts are bound by the plainest principles of exposition, as well as by a just deference to the legislature, to presume the existence of those circumstances which will support it and give it validity. For instance, if an act of the legislature appears on the face of it to be an encroachment on the rights of any persons, but would nevertheless be valid if passed with the consent of those persons, the court is bound to presume that such consent was given. And this presumption must prevail in favor of the validity of the act, until the contrary is shown, and shown too by a person having an interest in the maintenance of the rights supposed to be thus injuriously affected, and having a right to call for the interposition of the court for their support and protection, and a stranger can have no right to appear and contest the validity of the act upon such a ground.

Several objections have been taken to the constitutionality of this act, which deserve consideration.

1. The first is, that the commonwealth did not own the soil, and that the legislature had no authority to appropriate the land to public use, without the express consent of the owners; and if such consent is not given, the act is of itself illegal and void. This objection, we think, cannot be sustained; the consent of the owners in such case may be subsequent as well as previous, presumed and tacit, as well as express and proved by some positive act. But whether so or not, the objection cannot be taken by a stranger who has and claims no title or interest in the soil. It may often happen in a newly settled township or other place, that a qualified appropriation of a portion of the property to certain specified public uses, with a provision for its embellishment and improvement, will enhance the value of the property and confer a great benefit on the owner, a benefit so obvious, that the legislature may think it quite superfluous to wait for the owner's consent. Shall not his assent be presumed? Can a stranger treat the act as a nullity and destroy the improvement? It is said, that if this act can be sustained, the legislature might appropriate all the property in the town of Cambridge to public use. Suppose it were so. If the legislature were to provide for laying out walks over all the farms in Cambridge, for levelling, improving, and embellishing such walks, and all the owners of those farms should acquiesce, I know no principle which should authorize a stranger to interfere and treat the law providing for the making and for the protection of these improvements as a nullity.

But it is contended, that if this act is to depend for its validity upon the consent of the town of Cambridge, then such consent must be deemed equivalent to a positive act of the town, appropriating the land to the same uses declared by the act of the legislature, that this would be a breach of the condition of the grant under which the town holds it, and the proprietors of common and undivided lands might enter for condition broken, revest the title in themselves, and thus having become owners, would be in a condition to contest the validity of the act and resist its operation. Although it is obvious to remark, that this looks to many contingencies and that it is time enough to discuss this question when it is raised by the proprietors, it may tend to a more satisfactory elucidation of the general question, to give it a passing consideration. The vote of the proprietors in 1769 designates the land as the town commons, and it is probable from the buildings around it, that it had remained open for public use, from the first settlement of the town. By the terms of the grant, this land is to be used as a training field, to lie undivided, and to remain for that use for ever. To take these clauses separately. It is insisted, that the act of the legislature and the proceedings of the special commissioners under it are contrary to this condition, because the common is thereby *divided* into several distinct enclosures. We think this implies a misapplication of the term. When this term *undivided* is used and applied to lands by proprietors of common and undivided lands, it implies land set apart from their general domain, and not subject to partition, and not to be divided, set off and allotted to individual proprietors, to hold in severalty. The substance of the provision is, that it is to remain common and public.

As to the other branch of this condition, that it is to be used as a training field, and declaring a forfeiture, if the town should dispose of, grant or appropriate the same to any other use, it is to be considered what the effect of this condition is, and whether, had the town done the same acts, and made the same improvements, contemplated by the act of the legislature, it would have been a breach of this condition.

By the grant the town became owners of the soil with full power, as such owners, to make any use of the property, which owners of land can make, subject only to the restraint and limitation expressed in the condition. All such limitations and restrictions, especially those which go to create a forfeiture, are to be construed strictly, and not to be extended beyond the plain terms of the clauses in which they are expressed, and the obvious purposes for which they are introduced. Any other construction would impose a useless embarrassment upon the rights of property in the grantee, without benefit to the grantor. It appears to us, construing this grant according to these rules, that the intent of the restriction and condition in this deed was, that the land should remain common and open, in contradistinction to being divided to be held in severalty, and appropriated to private use, and that no disposition or appropriation should be made of it, inconsistent with its use as a training field. To what various uses, not incompatible with these purposes, the town as owners might appropriate it, it is not necessary here to inquire; it is sufficient for all the purposes of this view of the subject, if the use contemplated by the act of the legislature, is not inconsistent with those expressed in the condition of the grant from the proprietors to the town. And we think upon the best consideration we have been able to give the subject, that the use contemplated, is not inconsistent with those in the condition, and perhaps it is not saying too much to add, that they are in furtherance and promotion of the same object. It is declared by the act to be forever appropriated to public use only, as a public park, promenade, and place for military parade, with a strong negative clause, for greater caution, that no part thereof shall on any pretence be appropriated to any purpose of private use or emolument. Nor are any of the powers conferred on the persons named in the act, nor the acts which they are authorized to do, such as will render the place unfit for the purposes of military parade. They are authorized to enclose the grounds with a fence, to level the surface, to plant trees, to lay out and make walks, all being done with the approbation of the selectmen of the town, leaving suitable and convenient avenues for persons passing on foot. All these improvements would rather increase than diminish the fitness and convenience of the place, as a military parade; and if required to be opened for the evolutions of artillery or cavalry, the provision in the act appropriating it generally to public use as a place of military parade, would be a sufficient authority for so using it.

As to the general principle above stated, that the terms of the condition do not restrain the town from such a use of the property, as will be perfectly consistent with the use contemplated by the condition of the grant, and even promotive of its general object, it may serve as an illustration to inquire, whether a highway or town road over the land would be a breach of the condition and cause of forfeiture. Roads are not only not incompatible with the purposes of military parade, but are necessary to military operations. Suppose the town had laid out a town way, or petitioned the proper authorities to lay out a highway over this common, could it be contended that this was appropriating it to a purpose other than that of keeping it undivided and appropriating it for a place of military parade? If this were so, the laying out of the Cambridge and Concord Turnpike, the subsequent laying out of a highway by the commissioners, the loss of which these petitioners so much lament, supposing it done, as it probably was, with the consent of the town, was a breach of condition and forfeiture of the land; nay, the very act which the petitioners are now urging the commissioners to do, if done with the consent of the town, which must be presumed, where the considerations of common convenience and necessity are so obvious and urgent as the petitioners represent them, would subject the town to a forfeiture.

On the whole, on this part of the case, we are of opinion, that the condition in this grant of the proprietors to the town, does not restrain them or expose them to any forfeiture, by consenting to the improvements and appropriations contemplated by the act of June 1830, because they are in no degree inconsistent with the purposes and appropriations, declared in the grant, but rather tend to promote, confirm, and perpetuate the use and appropriation therein contemplated.

2. It is objected, that there was no adjudication that the laying out of Cambridge common, and the enclosure thereof, were of common convenience and necessity. But the legislature are bound to no particular form. Representing the sovereign authority of the Commonwealth, if the act done is within the scope of their authority, the mode of doing it is optional, and it is sufficient if done in any mode that is intelligible. The act itself is sufficient evidence of the opinion and judgment of the legislature, that the public use contemplated would be of public convenience.

3. It is objected, that no provision is made in the act for compensation to parties aggrieved for damage done to private property. If there were any force in this objection, in a case where such an act could affect private property, it can have no effect here, because it contemplated no property not already appropriated to public use, it was exclusively the property of the town of Cambridge, and was calculated to enhance the benefit, instead of injuriously affecting the property.

4. Another objection was, that nobody is charged with the duty of keeping this common or the roads around it in repair. This objection, we think, is not sustained in point of fact as to the roads. The special commissioners were authorized to make alterations in the roads by which the common was then traversed; that is, they were empowered to discontinue some roads and lay out others, regard being had to the common convenience and necessity. When they had executed this authority and made their return as they did, the roads by them laid out as a substitute for those which crossed the enclosure, became lawful public highways, and the town became liable to the duty of supporting them as such. As to the other branch of the objection, that no provision is made for the preservation and support of the improvements when made, this may be a defect in the act, but cannot affect its validity or constitutionality.

5. Another objection taken and somewhat relied on, was, that the legislature had no power to declare that any portion of territory should be *forever* appropriated to any one public use, because it had a tendency to encroach upon the acknowledged sovereign power of the State, in case of emergency, to take any property, public or private, which the exigencies of the country might require. We think there is no weight in this objection. Nothing in this act supersedes, or has a tendency to supersede, that sovereign power over all property, inherent in all governments, sometimes called the right of *eminent domain*, the power of taking property for public use, as the exigencies of the country may require. All acts of legislation not in terms limited in their operation to a particular term of time, are in legal contemplation perpetual or declared to be in force *forever*; which means, until duly altered or changed by competent authority.

Upon a consideration of all the objections, we are of opinion, that the act of June 1830, did not exceed the just limits of legislative power, and is not unconstitutional. We have considered this question, because it was freely discussed in the very able argument in this cause; and yet it cannot escape observation, that if this act was unconstitutional, and as contended, absolutely null and void, then all acts done under it are void, the highways over this common have not been legally discontinued, there is already a highway on the precise place where the petitioners now pray to have one laid out, and therefore any act of the commissioners laying out a highway as prayed for, would be wholly nugatory and inoperative.

. . . . .

It is manifest, that in cases of rare occurrence, as that of a railroad, or other similar work, if property could not be appropriated to public use by the legislature, it could not be done at all, because there is no provision by law for its being done in any other way. The right of the sovereign power of the State is incontestable. No other provision being made for its exercise, it is therefore necessarily vested in the legislature. Such is the present case, that of a public park, promenade, and place for military parade. Cases may be supposed, in which the exercise of the power would be important, not only to the convenience and comfort, but to the security and military defence of the inhabitants; but this power must be exercised by the legislature, either in each particular instance, or by general law, or must lie dormant.

. . . . .

It appears to us that this decision does not involve the sovereign right of eminent domain, or affect the power of the legislature to appropriate this property to other public uses, as public exigencies may arise. The sole question is, whether it supersedes the ordinary power and action of the county commissioners, and we are of opinion, for the reason already stated, that it does, and that the decision of the commissioners, refusing to inquire into the question whether a highway in the place proposed, was of common convenience and necessity, and dismissing the petition, was correct.

SEE ALSO:

Generally Bill of Rights
New York Constitution of 1777, art. 13, Thorpe 5:2632
Vermont Constitution of 1777, ch. 1, arts. 1, 2, 9, Thorpe 6:3739–40, 3740–41
Vermont Constitution of 1786, ch. 1, art. 10, Thorpe 6:3753
Holden v. *James*, 11 Mass. 395 (1814)
Commonwealth v. *Lewis*, 6 Binn. 266 (Pa. 1814)
Alabama Constitution of 1819, art. 1, sec. 14, Thorpe 1:97
Dawson v. *Shaver*, 1 Blackf. 204 (Ind. 1822)
Stuyvesant v. *Mayor of New York*, 7 Cow. 588 (N.Y. 1827)
Lansing v. *Smith*, 8 Cow. 146 (N.Y. 1828)
Crenshaw v. *Slate River Co.*, 6 Rand. 245 (Va. 1828)
Baker v. *Boston*, 12 Pick. 184 (Mass. 1831)
Wally's Heirs v. *Kennedy*, 2 Yerg. 554 (Tenn. 1831)
State Bank v. *Cooper*, 2 Yerg. 599 (Tenn. 1831)
Joseph Story, Commentaries on the Constitution 3:§ 1784 (1833)
In the Matter of Albany Street, 11 Wend. 149 (N.Y. 1834)
Bloodgood v. *M. & H. R.R. Co.*, 14 Wend. 51 (N.Y. 1835)

Amendment VII

In Suits at common law, where the value in controversy shall exceed twenty dollars, the right of trial by jury shall be preserved, and no fact tried by a jury, shall be otherwise re-examined in any Court of the United States, than according to the rules of the common law.

1

GILES DUNCOMBE, TRYALS PER PAIS
1665

And first as to their [the Jury's] number twelve: and this number is no less esteemed by our law than by Holy Writ. If the twelve apostles on their twelve thrones must try us in our eternal state, good reason hath the law to appoint the number of twelve to try our temporal. The tribes of Israel were twelve, the patriarchs were twelve, and Solomon's officers were twelve. I Kings, IV, 7. . . . Therefore not only matters of fact were tried by twelve, but of ancient times twelve judges were to try matters in law, in the Exchequer Chamber, and there were twelve counsellors of state for matters of state; and he that wageth his law must have eleven others with him who believe he says true. And the law is so precise in this number of twelve, that if the trial be by more or less, it is a mistrial.

2

WILLIAM BLACKSTONE, COMMENTARIES,
3:349–67, 370–81, 383–85
1768

The subject of our next enquiries will be the nature and method of the trial *by jury*; called also the trial *per pais*, or *by the country*. A trial that hath been used time out of mind in this nation, and seems to have been co-eval with the first civil government thereof. Some authors have endeavoured to trace the original of juries up as high as the Britons themselves, the first inhabitants of our island; but certain it is, that they were in use among the earliest Saxon colonies, their institution being ascribed by bishop Nicolson to Woden himself, their great legislator and captain. Hence it is, that we may find traces of juries in the laws of all those nations which adopted the feodal system, as in Germany, France, and Italy; who had all of them a tribunal composed of twelve good men and true, *"boni homines,"* usually the vasals or tenants of the lord, being the equals or peers of the parties litigant: and, as the lord's vasals judged each other in the lord's courts, so the king's vasals, or the lords themselves, judged each other in the king's court. In England we find actual mention of them so early as the laws of king Ethelred, and that not as a new invention. Stiernhook ascribes the invention of the jury, which in the Teutonic languages is denominated *nembda*, to Regner, king of Sweden and Denmark, who was co-temporary with our king Egbert. Just as we are apt to impute the invention of this, and some other pieces of juridical polity, to the superior genius of Alfred the great; to whom, on account of his having done much, it is usual to attribute

every thing: and as the tradition of antient Greece placed to the account of their one Hercules whatever atchievement was performed superior to the ordinary prowess of mankind. Whereas the truth seems to be, that this tribunal was universally established among all the northern nations, and so interwoven in their very constitution, that the earliest accounts of the one give us also some traces of the other. It's establishment however and use, in this island, of what date soever it be, though for a time greatly impaired and shaken by the introduction of the Norman trial by battel, was always so highly esteemed and valued by the people, that no conquest, no change of government, could ever prevail to abolish it. In *magna carta* it is more than once insisted on as the principal bulwark of our liberties; but especially by chap. 29. that no freeman shall be hurt in either his person or property, *"nisi per legale judicium parium suorum vel per legem terrae."* A privilege which is couched in almost the same words with that of the emperor Conrad, two hundred years before: *"nemo beneficium suum perdat, nisi secundum consuetudinem antecessorum nostrorum et per judicium parium suorum."* And it was ever esteemed, in all countries, a privilege of the highest and most beneficial nature.

But I will not mispend the reader's time in fruitless encomiums on this method of trial: but shall proceed to the dissection and examination of it in all it's parts, from whence indeed it's highest encomium will arise; since, the more it is searched into and understood, the more it is sure to be valued. And this is a species of knowlege most absolutely necessary for every gentleman in the kingdom: as well because he may be frequently called upon to determine in this capacity the rights of others, his fellow-subjects; as because his own property, his liberty, and his life, depend upon maintaining, in it's legal force, the constitutional trial by jury.

Trials by jury in civil causes are of two kinds; *extraordinary*, and *ordinary*. The extraordinary I shall only briefly hint at, and confine the main of my observations to that which is more usual and ordinary.

The first species of extraordinary trial by jury is that of the *grand assise*, which was instituted by king Henry the second in parliament, as was mentioned in the preceding chapter, by way of alternative offered to the choice of the tenant or defendant in a writ of right, instead of the barbarous and unchristian custom of duelling. For this purpose a writ *de magna assisa eligenda* is directed to the sheriff, to return four knights, who are to elect and chuse twelve others to be joined with them, in the manner mentioned by Glanvil; who, having probably advised the measure itself, is more than usually copious in describing it: and these, all together, form the grand assise, or great jury, which is to try the matter of right, and must consist of sixteen jurors.

Another species of extraordinary juries, is the jury to try an *attaint;* which is a process commenced against a former jury, for bringing in a false verdict; of which we shall speak more largely in a subsequent chapter. At present I shall only observe, that this jury is to consist of twenty four of the best men in the county, who are called the *grand* jury in the attaint, to distinguish them from the first or *petit* jury; and these are to hear and try the goodness of the former verdict.

With regard to the *ordinary* trial by jury in civil cases, I shall pursue the same method in considering it, that I set out with in explaining the nature of prosecuting actions in general, *viz.* by following the order and course of the proceedings themselves, as the most clear and perspicuous way of treating it.

When therefore an issue is joined, by these words, "and this the said A prays may be enquired of by the country," or, "and of this he puts himself upon the country, and the said B does the like," the court awards a writ of *venire facias* upon the roll or record, commanding the sheriff "that he cause to come *here* on such a day, twelve free and lawful men, *liberos et legales homines*, of the body of his county, by whom the truth of the matter may be better known, and who are neither of kin to the aforesaid A, nor the aforesaid B, to recognize the truth of the issue between the said parties." And such writ is accordingly issued to the sheriff.

Thus the cause stands ready for a trial *at the bar* of the court itself: for all trials were there antiently had, in actions which were there first commenced; which never happened but in matters of weight and consequence, all trifling suits being ended in the court-baron, hundred, or county courts: and all causes of great importance or difficulty are still usually retained upon motion, to be tried at the bar in the superior courts. But when the usage began, to bring actions of any trifling value in the courts of Westminster-hall, it was found to be an intolerable burthen to compel the parties, witnesses, and jurors, to come from Westmorland perhaps or Cornwall, to try an action of assault at Westminster. Therefore the legislature took into consideration, that the king's justices came usually twice in the year into the several counties, *ad capiendas assisas*, to take or try writs of assise, of *mort d' ancestor, novel disseisin, nusance*, and the like. The form of which writs we may remember was stated to be, that they commanded the sheriff to summon an assise or jury, and go to view the land in question; and then to have the said jury ready at the next coming of the justices of assise (together with the parties) to recognize and determine the disseisin, or other injury complained of. As therefore these judges were ready in the country to administer justice in real actions of assise, the legislature thought proper to refer other matters in issue to be also determined before them, whether of a mixed or personal kind. And therefore it was enacted by statute Westm. 2. 13 Edw. I. c. 30. that a clause of *nisi prius* should be inserted in all the aforesaid writs of *venire facias*; that is, "that the sheriff should cause the jurors to come to Westminster (or wherever the king's courts should be held) on such a day in easter and michaelmas terms; *nisi prius*, unless before that day the justices assigned to take assises shall come into his said county." By virtue of which the sheriff returned his jurors to the court of the justices of assise, which was sure to be held in the vacation before easter and michaelmas terms; and there the trial was had.

An inconvenience attended this remedy: principally because, as the sheriff made no return of the jury to the court at Westminster, the parties were ignorant who they were till they came upon the trial, and therefore were not ready with their challenges or exceptions. For this reason by the statute 42 Edw. III. c. 11. the method of trials by *nisi prius* was altered; and it was enacted that no inquests (except of assise and gaol-delivery) should be taken by writ of *nisi prius*, till after the sheriff had returned the names of the jurors to the court above. So that now the clause of *nisi prius* is left out of the writ of *venire facias*, which is the sheriff's warrant to warn the jury; and is inserted in another part of the proceedings, as we shall see presently.

For now the course is, to make the sheriff's *venire* returnable on the last return of the same term wherein issue is joined, *viz.* hilary or trinity terms, which from the making up of the issues therein are usually called *issuable* terms. And he returns the names of the jurors in a *panel* (a little pane, or oblong piece of parchment) annexed to the writ. This jury is not summoned, and therefore, not appearing at the day, must unavoidably make default. For which reason a compulsive process is now awarded against the jurors, called in the common pleas a writ of *habeas corpora juratorum*, and in the king's bench a *distringas*, commanding the sheriff to have their bodies, or to distrein them by their lands and goods, that they may appear upon the day appointed. The entry therefore on the roll or record is, "that the jury is respited, through defect of the jurors, till the first day of the next term, then to appear at Westminster; unless before that time, *viz.* on wednesday the fourth of March, the justices of our lord the king, appointed to take assises in that county, shall have come to Oxford, that is, to the place assigned for holding the assises. Therefore the sheriff is commanded to have their bodies at Westminster on the said first day of next term, or before the said justices of assise, if before that time they come to Oxford; *viz.* on the fourth of March aforesaid." And, as the judges are sure to come and open the circuit commissions on the day mentioned in the writ, the sheriff returns and summons this jury to appear at the assises, and there the trial is had before the justices of *assise* and *nisi prius*: among whom (as hath been said) are usually two of the judges of the courts at Westminster, the whole kingdom being divided into six circuits for this purpose. And thus we may observe that the trial of common issues, at *nisi prius*, was in it's original only a collateral incident to the original business of the justices of assise; though now, by the various revolutions of practice, it is become their principal employment: hardly any thing remaining in use of the real *assises*, but the name.

If the sheriff be not an indifferent person; as if he be a party in the suit, or be related by either blood or affinity to either of the parties, he is not then trusted to return the jury; but the *venire* shall be directed to the coroners, who in this, as in many other instances, are the substitutes of the sheriff, to execute process when he is deemed an improper person. If any exception lies to the coroners, the *venire* shall be directed to two clerks of the court, or two persons of the county named by the court, and sworn. And these two, who are called *elisors*, or electors, shall indifferently name the jury, and their return is final.

Let us now pause awhile, and observe (with sir Matthew Hale) in these first preparatory stages of the trial, how admirably this constitution is adapted and framed for the investigation of truth, beyond any other method of trial in the world. For, first the *person returning* the jurors is a man of some fortune and consequence; that so he may be not only the less tempted to commit wilful errors, but likewise be responsible for the faults of either himself or his officers: and he is also bound by the obligation of an oath faithfully to execute his duty. Next, as to the *time of their return*: the panel is returned to the court upon the original *venire*, and the jurors are to be summoned and brought in many weeks afterwards to the trial, whereby the parties may have notice of the jurors, and of their sufficiency or insufficiency, characters, connections, and relations, that so they may be challenged upon just cause; while at the same time by means of the compulsory process (of *distringas* or *habeas corpora*) the cause is not like to be retarded through defect of jurors. Thirdly, as to the *place* of their appearance: which in causes of weight and consequence is at the bar of the court; but in ordinary cases at the assises, held in the county where the cause of action arises, and the witnesses and jurors live: a provision most excellently calculated for the saving of expense to the parties. For, though the preparation of the causes in point of pleading is transacted at Westminster, whereby the order and uniformity of proceeding is preserved throughout the kingdom, and multiplicity of forms is prevented; yet this is no great charge or trouble, one attorney being able to transact the business of forty clients. But the troublesome and most expensive attendance is that of jurors and witnesses at the trial; which therefore is brought home to them, in the country where most of them inhabit. Fourthly, the *persons before whom* they are to appear, and before whom the trial is to be held, are the judges of the superior court, if it be a trial at bar; or the judges of assise, delegated from the courts at Westminster by the king, if the trial be held in the country: persons, whose learning and dignity secure their jurisdiction from contempt, and the novelty and very parade of whose appearance have no small influence upon the multitude. The very point of their being strangers in the county is of infinite service, in preventing those factions and parties, which would intrude in every cause of moment, were it tried only before persons resident on the spot, as justices of the peace, and the like. And, the better to remove all suspicion of partiality, it was wisely provided by the statutes 4 Edw. III. c. 2. 8 Ric. II. c. 2. and 33 Hen. VIII. c. 24. that no judge of assise should hold pleas in any county wherein he was born or inhabits. And, as this constitution prevents party and faction from intermingling in the trial of right, so it keeps both the rule and the administration of the laws uniform. These justices, though thus varied and shifted at every assises, are all sworn to the same laws, have had the same education, have pursued the same studies, converse and consult together, communicate their decisions and resolutions, and preside in those courts which are mutually connected and their judgments blended together, as they are interchangeably courts of appeal or advice to each other. And hence their administration of justice, and conduct of trials, are consonant and uniform; whereby that confusion and contrariety are avoided, which would naturally arise from a variety of un-communicating judges, or from any provincial establishment. But let us now return to the assises.

When the general day of trials is fixed, the plaintiff or his attorney must bring down the record to the assises, and enter it with the proper officer, in order to it's being called on in course. If it be not so entered, it cannot be tried; therefore it is in the plaintiff's breast to delay any trial by not carrying down the record: unless the defendant, being fearful of such neglect in the plaintiff, and willing to discharge himself from the action, will himself undertake to bring on the trial, giving proper notice to the plaintiff. Which proceeding is called the trial by *proviso*; by reason of the clause then inserted in the sheriff's *venire*, viz. "*proviso*, provided that if two writs come to your hands, (that is one from the plaintiff and another from the defendant) you shall execute only one of them." But this practice begins to be disused, since the statute 14 Geo. II. c. 17. which enacts, that if, after issue joined, the cause is not carried down to be tried according to the course of the court, the plaintiff shall be esteemed to be nonsuited, and judgment shall be given for the defendant as in case of a nonsuit. In case the plaintiff intends to try the cause, he is bound to give the defendant (if he lives within forty miles of London) eight days notice of trial; and, if he lives at a greater distance, then fourteen days notice, in order to prevent surprize: and if the plaintiff then changes his mind, and does not countermand the notice six days before the trial, he shall be liable to pay costs to the defendant for not proceeding to trial, by the same last mentioned statute. The defendant however, or plaintiff, may, upon good cause shewn to the court above, as upon absence or sickness of a material witness, obtain leave upon motion to defer the trial of the cause till the next assises.

But we will now suppose all previous steps to be regularly settled, and the cause to be called on in court. The record is then handed to the judge, to peruse and observe the pleadings, and what issues the parties are to maintain and prove, while the jury is called and sworn. To this end the sheriff returns his compulsive process, the writ of *habeas corpora*, or *distringas*, with the panel of jurors annexed, to the judge's officer in court. The jurors contained in the panel are either *special* or *common* jurors. *Special* juries were originally introduced in trials at bar, when the causes were of too great nicety for the discussion of ordinary freeholders; or where the sheriff was suspected of partiality, though not upon such apparent cause, as to warrant an exception to him. He is in such cases, upon motion in court and a rule granted thereupon, to attend the prothonotary or other proper officer with his freeholder's book; and the officer is to take indifferently forty eight of the principal freeholders in the presence of the attornies on both sides; who are each of them to strike off twelve, and the remaining twenty four are returned upon the panel. By the statute 3 Geo. II. c. 25. either party is intitled upon motion to have a special jury struck upon the trial of any issue, as well as the assises as at bar; he paying the extraordinary expense, unless the judge will certify (in pursuance of the statute 24 Geo. II. c. 18.) that the cause required such special jury.

A common jury is one returned by the sheriff according

to the directions of the statute 3 Geo. II. c. 25. which appoints, that the sheriff shall not return a separate panel for every separate cause, as formerly; but one and the same panel for every cause to be tried at the same assises, containing not less than forty eight, nor more than seventy two, jurors: and that their names, being written on tickets, shall be put into a box of glass; and when each cause is called, twelve of these persons, whose names shall be first drawn out of the box, shall be sworn upon the jury, unless absent, challenged, or excused; and unless a previous view of the lands, or tenements, or other matters in question, shall have been thought necessary by the court: in which case six or more of the jurors returned, to be agreed on by the parties, or named by a judge or other proper officer of the court, shall be appointed to take such view; and then such of the jury as have appeared upon the view (if any) shall be sworn on the inquest previous to any other jurors. These acts are well calculated to restrain any suspicion of partiality in the sheriff, or any tampering with the jurors when returned.

As the jurors appear, when called, they shall be sworn, unless *challenged* by either party. Challenges are of two sorts; challenges to the *array*, and challenges to the *polls*.

Challenges to the array are at once an exception to the whole panel, in which the jury are arrayed or set in order by the sheriff in his return; and they may be made upon account of partiality or some default in the sheriff, or his under-officer who arrayed the panel. And, generally speaking, the same reasons that before the awarding the *venire* were sufficient to have directed it to the coroners or elisors, will be also sufficient to quash the array, when made by a person or officer of whose partiality there is any tolerable ground of suspicion. Also, though there be no personal objection against the sheriff, yet if he arrays the panel at the nomination, or under the direction of either party, this is good cause of challenge to the array. Formerly, if a lord of parliament had a cause to be tried, and no knight was returned upon the jury, it was a cause of challenge to the array: but an unexpected use having been made of this dormant privilege by a spiritual lord, (though *his* title to such privilege was very doubtful) it was abolished by statute 24 Geo. II. c. 18. Also, by the policy of the antient law, the jury was to come *de vicineto*, from the neighbourhood of the vill or place where the cause of action was laid in the declaration; and therefore some of the jury were obliged to be returned from the hundred in which such vill lay; and, if none were returned, the array might be challenged for defect of hundredors. Thus the Gothic jury, or *nembda*, was also collected out of every quarter of the country; "*binos, trinos, vel etiam senos, ex singulis territorii quadrantibus.*" For, living in the neighbourhood, they were properly the very country, or *pais*, to which both parties had appealed; and were supposed to know before-hand the characters of the parties and witnesses, and therefore the better knew what credit to give to the facts alleged in evidence. But this convenience was overballanced by another very natural and almost unavoidable inconvenience; that jurors, coming out of the immediate neighbourhood, would be apt to intermix their prejudices and partialities in the trial of right. And this

our law was so sensible of, that it for a long time has been gradually relinquishing this practice; the number of necessary hundredors in the whole panel, which in the reign of Edward III were constantly *six*, being in the time of Fortescue reduced to *four*. Afterwards indeed the statute 35 Hen. VIII. c. 6. restored the antient number of *six*, but that clause was soon virtually repealed by statute 27 Eliz. c. 6. which required only *two*. And sir Edward Coke also gives us such a variety of circumstances, whereby the courts permitted this necessary number to be evaded, that it appears they were heartily tired of it. At length, by statute 4 & 5 Ann. c. 16. it was entirely abolished upon all civil actions, except upon penal statutes; and upon those also by the 24 Geo. II. c. 18. the jury being now only to come *de corpore comitatus*, from the body of the county at large, and not *de vicineto*, or from the particular neighbourhood. The array by the antient law may also be challenged, if an alien be party to the suit, and, upon a rule obtained by his motion to the court for a jury *de medietate linguae*, such a one be not returned by the sheriff, pursuant to the statute 28 Edw. III. c. 18. which enacts, that where either party is an alien born, the jury shall be one half aliens and the other denizens, if required, for the more impartial trial. A privilege indulged to strangers in no other country in the world; but which is as antient with us as the time of king Ethelred, in whose statute *de monticolis Walliae* (then aliens to the crown of England) *cap.* 3. it is ordained, that "*duodeni legales homines, quorum sex Walli et sex Angli erunt, Anglis et Wallis jus dicunto.*" But where both parties are aliens, no partiality is to be presumed to one more than another; and therefore by the statute 21 Hen. VI. c. 4. the whole jury are then directed to be denizens. And it may be questioned, whether the statute 3 Geo. II. c. 25. (before referred to) hath not in civil causes undesignedly abridged this privilege of foreigners, by the positive directions therein given concerning the manner of impanelling jurors, and the persons to be returned in such panel. So that the court might probably hesitate, especially in the case of *special* juries, how far it has now a power to direct a panel to be returned *de medietate linguae*, and to alter the method prescribed for striking a special jury, or balloting for common jurymen.

Challenges to the polls, *in capita*, are exceptions to particular jurors; and seem to answer the *recusatio judicis* in the civil and canon laws: by the constitutions of which a judge might be refused upon any suspicion of partiality. By the laws of England also, in the times of Bracton and Fleta, a judge might be refused for good cause; but now the law is otherwise, and it is held that judges or justices cannot be challenged. For the law will not suppose a possibility of biass or favour in a judge, who is already sworn to administer impartial justice, and whose authority greatly depends upon that presumption and idea. And should the fact at any time prove flagrantly such, as the delicacy of the law will not presume beforehand, there is no doubt but that such misbehaviour would draw down a heavy censure from those, to whom the judge is accountable for his conduct.

But challenges to the polls of the jury (who are judges of fact) are reduced to four heads by sir Edward Coke:

propter honoris respectum; propter defectum; propter affectum; and *propter delictum.*

1. *Propter honoris respectum;* as if a lord of parliament be impanelled on a jury, he may be challenged by either party, or he may challenge himself.

2. *Propter defectum;* as if a juryman be an alien born, this is defect of birth; if he be a slave or bondman, this is defect of liberty, and he cannot be *liber et legalis homo.* Under the word *homo* also, though a name common to both sexes, the female is however excluded, *propter defectum sexus:* except when a widow feigns herself with child, in order to exclude the next heir, and a suppositious birth is suspected to be intended; then upon the writ *de ventre inspiciendo,* a jury of women is to be impanelled to try the question, whether with child, or not. But the principal deficiency is defect of estate, sufficient to qualify him to be a juror. This depends upon a variety of statutes. And, first, by the statute Westm. 2. 13 Edw. I. c. 38. none shall pass on juries in assises within the county, but such as may dispend 20s. by the year at the least; which is encreased to 40s. by the statute 21 Edw. I. st. 1. and 2 Hen. V. st. 2. c. 3. This was doubled by the statute 27 Eliz. c. 6. which requires in every such case the jurors to have estate of freehold to the yearly value of 4l. at the least. But, the value of money at that time decreasing very considerably, this qualification was raised by the statute 16 & 17 Car. II. c. 3. to 20l. *per annum,* which being only a temporary act, for three years, was suffered to expire without renewal, to the great debasement of juries. However by the statute 4 & 5 W. & M. c. 24. it was again raised to 10l. *per annum* in England and 6l. in Wales, of freehold lands *or copyhold;* which is the first time that copyholders (as such) were admitted to serve upon juries in any of the king's courts, though they had before been admitted to serve in some of the sheriff's courts, by statutes 1 Ric. III. c. 4. and 9 Hen. VII. c. 13. And, lastly, by statute 3 Geo II. c. 25. any leaseholder for the term of five hundred years absolute, or for any term determinable upon life or lives, of the clear yearly value of 20l. *per annum* over and above the rent reserved, is qualified to serve upon juries. When the jury is *de medietate linguae,* that is, one moiety of the English tongue or nation, and the other of any foreign one, no want of lands shall be cause of challenge to the alien; for, as he is incapable to hold any, this would totally defeat the privilege.

3. Jurors may be challenged *propter affectum,* for suspicion of biass or partiality. This may be either a *principal* challenge, or *to the favour.* A *principal* challenge is such, where the cause assigned carries with it *prima facie* evident marks of suspicion, either of malice or favour: as, that a juror is of kin to either party within the ninth degree; that he has been arbitrator on either side; that he has an interest in the cause; that there is an action depending between him and the party; that he has taken money for his verdict; that he has formerly been a juror in the same cause; that he is the party's master, servant, counsellor, steward or attorney, or of the same society or corporation with him: all these are principal causes of challenge; which, if true, cannot be overruled, for jurors must be *omni exceptione majores.* Challenges *to the favour,* are where the party

hath no principal challenge; but objects only some probable circumstances of suspicion, as acquaintance, and the like; the validity of which must be left to the determination of *triors,* whose office it is to decide whether the juror be favourable or unfavourable. The triors, in case the first man called be challenged, are two indifferent persons named by the court; and, if they try one man and find him indifferent, he shall be sworn; and then he and the two triors shall try the next; and when another is found indifferent and sworn, the two triors shall be superseded, and the two first sworn on the jury shall try the rest.

4. Challenges *propter delictum* are for some crime or misdemesnor, that affects the juror's credit and renders him infamous. As for a conviction of treason, felony, perjury, or conspiracy; or if he hath received judgment of the pillory, tumbrel, or the like; or to be branded, whipt, or stigmatized; or if he be outlawed or excommunicated, or hath been attainted of false verdict, *praemunire,* or forgery; or lastly, if he hath proved recreant when champion in the trial by battel, and thereby hath lost his *liberam legem.* A juror may himself be examined on oath of *voir dire, veritatem dicere,* with regard to the three former of these causes of challenge, which are not to his dishonour; but not with regard to this head of challenge, *propter delictum,* which would be to make him either forswear or accuse himself, if guilty.

Besides these challenges, which are exceptions against the fitness of jurors, and whereby they may be *excluded* from serving; there are also other causes to be made use of by the jurors themselves, which are matter of exemption; whereby their service is *excused,* and not *excluded.* As by statute Westm. 2. 13 Edw. I. c. 38. sick and decrepit persons, persons not commorant in the county, and men above seventy years old; and by the statute of 7 & 8 W. III. c. 32. infants under twenty one. This exemption is also extended by divers statutes, customs, and charters, to physicians and other medical persons, counsel, attorneys, officers of the courts, and the like; all of whom, if impanelled, must shew their special exemption. Clergymen are also usually excused, out of favour and respect to their function: but, if they are seised of lands and tenements, they are in strictness liable to be impanelled in respect of their lay fees, unless they be in the service of the king or of some bishop; *"in obsequio domini regis, vel alicujus episcopi."*

If by means of challenges, or other cause, a sufficient number of unexceptionable jurors doth not appear at the trial, either party may pray a *tales.* A *tales* is a supply of *such* men, as are summoned upon the first panel, in order to make up the deficiency. For this purpose a writ of *decem tales, octo tales,* and the like, was used to be issued to the sheriff at common law, and must be still so done at a trial at bar, if the jurors make default. But at the assises or *nisi prius,* by virtue of the statute 35 Hen. VIII. c. 6. and other subsequent statutes, the judge is impowered at the prayer of either party to award a *tales de circumstantibus,* of persons present in court, to be joined to the other jurors to try the cause; who are liable however to the same challenges as the principal jurors. This is usually done, till the legal number of twelve be completed; in which patriarchal and apostolical number sir Edward Coke hath discovered abundance of mystery.

When a sufficient number of persons impanelled, or *tales*-men, appear, they are then separately sworn, well and truly to try the issue between the parties, and a true verdict to give according to the evidence; and hence they are denominated the jury, *jurata*, and jurors, *sc. juratores.*

We may here again observe, and observing we cannot but admire, how scrupulously delicate and how impartially just the law of England approves itself, in the constitution and frame of a tribunal, thus excellently contrived for the test and investigation of truth; which appears most remarkably, 1. In the avoiding of frauds and secret management, by electing the twelve jurors out of the whole panel by lot. 2. In it's caution against all partiality and biass, by quashing the whole panel or array, if the officer returning is suspected to be other than indifferent; and repelling particular jurors, if probable cause be shewn of malice or favour to either party. The prodigious multitude of exceptions or challenges allowed to jurors, who are the judges of fact, amounts nearly to the same thing as was practised in the Roman republic, before she lost her liberty: that the select judges should be appointed by the praetor with the mutual consent of the parties. Or, as Tully expresses it: *"neminem voluerunt majores nostri, non modo de existimatione cujusquam, sed ne pecuniaria quidem de re minima, esse judicem; nisi qui inter adversarios convenisset."*

. . . . .

The jury are now ready to hear the merits; and, to fix their attention the closer to the facts which they are impanelled and sworn to try, the pleadings are opened to them by counsel on that side which holds the affirmative of the question in issue. For the issue is said to lie, and proof is always first required, upon that side which affirms the matter in question: in which our law agrees with the civil; *"ei incumbit probatio, qui dicit, non qui negat: cum per rerum naturam factum-negantis probatio nulla sit."* The opening counsel briefly informs them what has been transacted in the court above; the parties, the nature of the action, the declaration, the plea, replication, and other proceedings, and lastly upon what point the issue is joined, which is there sent down to be determined. Instead of which formerly the whole record and process of the pleadings was read to them in English by the court, and the matter in issue clearly explained to their capacities. The nature of the case, and the evidence intended to be produced, are next laid before them by counsel also on the same side; and, when their evidence is gone through, the advocate on the other side opens the adverse case, and supports it by evidence; and then the party which began is heard by way of reply.

. . . . .

All witnesses, that have the use of their reason, are to be received and examined, except such as are *infamous*, or such as are *interested* in the event of the cause. All others are *competent* witnesses; though the jury from other circumstances will judge of their *credibility*. Infamous persons are such as may be challenged as jurors, *propter delictum;*

and therefore never shall be admitted to give evidence to inform that jury, with whom they were too scandalous to associate. Interested witnesses may be examined upon a *voir dire*, if suspected to be secretly concerned in the event; or their interest may be proved in court. Which last is the only method of supporting an objection to the former class; for no man is to be examined to prove his own infamy. And no counsel, attorney, or other person, intrusted with the secrets of the cause by the party himself, shall be compelled, or perhaps allowed, to give evidence of such conversation or matters of privacy, as came to his knowlege by virtue of such trust and confidence: but he may be examined as to mere matters of fact, as the execution of a deed or the like, which might have come to his knowlege without being intrusted in the cause.

. . . . .

Positive proof is always required, where from the nature of the case it appears it might possibly have been had. But, next to *positive* proof, *circumstantial* evidence or the doctrine of *presumptions* must take place: for when the fact itself cannot be demonstratively evinced, that which comes nearest to the proof of the fact is the proof of such circumstances which either *necessarily*, or *usually*, attend such facts; and these are called presumptions, which are only to be relied upon till the contrary be actually proved. *Stabitur praesumptioni donec probetur in contrarium. Violent* presumption is many times equal to full proof; for there those circumstances appear, which *necessarily* attend the fact. As if a landlord sues for rent due at michaelmas 1754, and the tenant cannot prove the payment, but produces an acquittance for rent due at a subsequent time, in full of all demands, this is a violent presumption of his having paid the former rent, and is equivalent to full proof; for though the actual payment is not proved, yet the acquittance in full of all demands is proved, which could not be without such payment: and it therefore induces so forcible a presumption, that no proof shall be admitted to the contrary. *Probable* presumption, arising from such circumstances as *usually* attend the fact, hath also it's due weight: as if, in a suit for rent due 1754, the tenant proves the payment of the rent due in 1755; this will prevail to exonerate the tenant, unless it be clearly shewn that the rent of 1754 was retained for some special reason, or that there was some fraud or mistake; for otherwise it will be presumed to have been paid before that in 1755, as it is most usual to receive first the rents of longest standing. *Light*, or rash, presumptions have no weight or validity at all.

The oath administred to the witness is not only that what he deposes shall be true, but that he shall also depose the *whole* truth: so that he is not to conceal any part of what he knows, whether interrogated particularly to that point or not. And all this evidence is to be given in open court, in the presence of the parties, their attorneys, the counsel, and all by-standers; and before the judge and jury: each party having liberty to except to it's competency, which exceptions are publicly stated, and by the judge are openly and publicly allowed or disallowed, in the face of the country; which must curb any secret biass or partiality, that might arise in his own breast. And if, either in his directions or decisions, he mis-states the law by ignorance, inadvertence, or design, the counsel on either side may require him publicly to seal a *bill of exceptions;* stating the point wherein he is supposed to err: and this he is obliged to seal by statute Westm. 2. 13 Edw. I. c. 31. or, if he refuses so to do, the party may have a compulsory writ against him, commanding him to seal it, if the fact alleged be truly stated: and if he returns, that the fact is untruly stated, when the case is otherwise, an action will lie against him for making a false return. This bill of exceptions is in the nature of an appeal; examinable, not in the court out of which the record issues for the trial at *nisi prius,* but in the next immediate superior court, upon a writ of error, after judgment given in the court below. But a *demurrer* to evidence shall be determined by the court, out of which the record is sent. This happens, where a record or other matter is produced in evidence, concerning the legal consequences of which there arises a doubt in law: in which case the adverse party may if he pleases demur to the whole evidence; which admits the truth of every fact that has been alleged, but denies the sufficiency of them all in point of law to maintain or overthrow the issue: which draws the question of law from the cognizance of the jury, to be decided (as it ought) by the court. But neither these demurrers to evidence, nor the bills of exceptions, are at present so much in use as formerly; since the more frequent extension of the discretionary powers of the court in granting a new trial, which is now very commonly had for the misdirection of the judge at *nisi prius.*

This open examination of witnesses *viva voce,* in the presence of all mankind, is much more conducive to the clearing up of truth, than the private and secret examination taken down in writing before an officer, or his clerk, in the ecclesiastical courts, and all others that have borrowed their practice from the civil law: where a witness may frequently depose that in private, which he will be ashamed to testify in a public and solemn tribunal. There an artful or careless scribe may make a witness speak what he never meant, by dressing up his depositions in his own forms and language; but he is here at liberty to correct and explain his meaning, if misunderstood, which he can never do after a written deposition is once taken. Besides the occasional questions of the judge, the jury, and the counsel, propounded to the witnesses on a sudden, will sift out the truth much better than a formal set of interrogatories previously penned and settled: and the confronting of adverse witnesses is also another opportunity of obtaining a clear discovery, which can never be had upon any other method of trial. Nor is the presence of the judge, during the examination, a matter of small importance; for besides the respect and awe, with which his presence will naturally inspire the witness, he is able by use and experience to keep the evidence from wandering from the point in issue. In short by this method of examination, and this only, the persons who are to decide upon the evidence have an opportunity of observing the quality, age, education, understanding, behaviour, and inclinations of the witness; in which points all persons must appear alike, when their depositions are reduced to writing, and read to the judge, in the absence of those who made them: and

yet as much may be frequently collected from the manner in which the evidence is delivered, as from the matter of it. These are a few of the advantages attending this, the English, way of giving testimony, *ore tenus.* Which was also indeed familiar among the *antient* Romans, as may be collected from Quinctilian; who lays down very good instructions for examining and cross-examining witnesses *viva voce.* And this, or somewhat like it, was continued as low as the time of Hadrian: but the civil law, as it is now modelled, rejects all public examination of witnesses.

As to such evidence as the jury may have in their own consciences, by their private knowlege of facts, it was an antient doctrine, that this had as much right to sway their judgment as the written or parol evidence which is delivered in court. And therefore it hath been often held, that though no proofs be produced on either side, yet the jury might bring in a verdict. For the oath of the jurors, to find according to their evidence, was construed to be, to do it according to the best of their own knowlege. Which construction was probably made out of tenderness to juries; that they might escape the heavy penalties of an *attaint,* in case they could shew by any additional proof, that their verdict was agreeable to the truth, though not according to the evidence produced: with which additional proof the law presumed they were privately acquainted, though it did not appear in court. But this doctrine was gradually exploded, when *attaints* began to be disused, and *new trials* introduced in their stead. For it is quite incompatible with the grounds, upon which such new trials are every day awarded, *viz.* that the verdict was given *without,* or *contrary to,* evidence. And therefore, together with new trials, the practice seems to have been first introduced, which now universally obtains, that if a juror knows any thing of the matter in issue, he may be sworn as a witness, and give his evidence publicly in court.

When the evidence is gone through on both sides, the judge in the presence of the parties, the counsel, and all others, sums up the whole to the jury; omitting all superfluous circumstances, observing wherein the main question and principal issue lies, stating what evidence has been given to support it; with such remarks as he thinks necessary for their direction, and giving them his opinion in matters of law arising upon that evidence.

The jury, after the proofs are summed up, unless the case be very clear, withdraw from the bar to consider of their verdict: and, in order to avoid intemperance and causeless delay, are to be kept without meat, drink, fire, or candle, unless by permission of the judge, till they are all unanimously agreed. A method of accelerating unanimity not wholly unknown in other constitutions of Europe, and in matters of greater concern. For by the golden bulle of the empire, if, after the congress is opened, the electors delay the election of a king of the Romans for thirty days, they shall be fed only with bread and water, till the same is accomplished. But if our juries eat or drink at all, or have any eatables about them, without consent of the court, and before verdict, it is fineable; and if they do so at his charge for whom they afterwards find, it will set aside the verdict. Also if they speak with either of the parties or their agents, after they are gone from the bar; or if they receive any fresh evidence in private; or if to prevent disputes they cast lots for whom they shall find; any of these circumstances will entirely vitiate the verdict. And it has been held, that if the jurors do not agree in their verdict before the judges are about to leave the town, though they are not to be threatened or imprisoned, the judges are not bound to wait for them, but may carry them round the circuit from town to town in a cart. This necessity of a total unanimity seems to be peculiar to our own constitution; or, at least, in the *nembda* or jury of the antient Goths, there was required (even in criminal cases) only the consent of the major part; and in case of an equality, the defendant was held to be acquitted.

When they are all unanimously agreed, the jury return back to the bar; and, before they deliver their verdict, the plaintiff is bound to appear in court, by himself, attorney, or counsel, in order to answer the amercement to which by the old law he is liable, as has been formerly mentioned, in case he fails in his suit, as a punishment for his false claim. To be *amerced*, or *a mercie*, is to be at the king's mercy with regard to the fine to be imposed; *in misericordia domini regis pro falso clamore suo*. The amercement is disused, but the form still continues; and if the plaintiff does not appear, no verdict can be given, but the plaintiff is said to be *nonsuit, non sequitur clamorem suum*. Therefore it is usual for a plaintiff, when he or his counsel perceives that he has not given evidence sufficient to maintain his issue, to be voluntarily nonsuited, or withdraw himself: whereupon the crier is ordered to *call the plaintiff;* and if neither he, nor any body for him, appears, he is nonsuited, the jurors are discharged, the action is at an end, and the defendant shall recover his costs. The reason of this practice is, that a nonsuit is more eligible for the plaintiff, than a verdict against him: for after a nonsuit, which is only a default, he may commence the same suit again for the same cause of action; but after a verdict had, and judgment consequent thereupon, he is for ever barred from attacking the defendant upon the same ground of complaint. But, in case the plaintiff appears, the jury by their foreman deliver in their verdict.

A verdict, *vere dictum*, is either *privy*, or *public*. A *privy* verdict is when the judge hath left or adjourned the court; and the jury, being agreed, in order to be delivered from their confinement, obtain leave to give their verdict privily to the judge out of court: which privy verdict is of no force, unless afterwards affirmed by a public verdict given openly in court; wherein the jury may, if they please, vary from their privy verdict. So that the privy verdict is indeed a mere nullity; and yet it is a dangerous practice, allowing time for the parties to tamper with the jury, and therefore very seldom indulged. But the only effectual and legal verdict is the *public* verdict; in which they openly declare to have found the issue for the plaintiff, or for the defendant; and if for the plaintiff, they assess the damages also sustained by the plaintiff, in consequence of the injury upon which the action is brought.

Sometimes, if there arises in the case any difficult matter of law, the jury for the sake of better information, and to avoid the danger of having their verdict attainted, will find a *special* verdict; which is grounded on the statute Westm.

2. 13 Edw. I. c. 30. §. 2. And herein they state the naked facts, as they find them to be proved, and pray the advice of the court thereon; concluding conditionally, that if upon the whole matter the court shall be of opinion that the plaintiff had cause of action, they then find for the plaintiff; if otherwise, then for the defendant. This is entered at length on the record, and afterwards argued and determined in the court at Westminster, from whence the issue came to be tried.

Another method of finding a species of special verdict, is when the jury find a verdict generally for the plaintiff, but subject nevertheless to the opinion of the judge or the court above, on a *special case* stated by the counsel on both sides with regard to a matter of law: which has this advantage over a special verdict, that it is attended with much less expense, and obtains a much speedier decision; the *postea* (of which in the next chapter) being stayed in the hands of the officer of *nisi prius*, till the question is determined, and the verdict is then entered for the plaintiff or defendant as the case may happen. But, as nothing appears upon the record but the general verdict, the parties are precluded hereby from the benefit of a writ of error, if dissatisfied with the judgment of the court or judge upon the point of law. Which makes it a thing to be wished, that a method could be devised of either lessening the expense of special verdicts, or else of entering the case at length upon the *postea*. But in both these instances the jury may, if they think proper, take upon themselves to determine at their own hazard, the complicated question of fact and law; and, without either special verdict or special case, may find a verdict absolutely either for the plaintiff or defendant.

When the jury have delivered in their verdict, and it is recorded in court, they are then discharged. And so ends the trial by jury: a trial, which besides the other vast advantages which we have occasionally observed in it's progress, is also as expeditious and cheap, as it is convenient, equitable, and certain; for a commission out of chancery, or the civil law courts, for examining witnesses in one cause will frequently last as long, and of course be full as expensive, as the trial of a hundred issues at *nisi prius:* and yet the fact cannot be determined by such commissioners at all; no, not till the depositions are published and read at the hearing of the cause in court.

Upon these accounts the trial by jury ever has been, and I trust ever will be, looked upon as the glory of the English law. And, if it has so great an advantage over others in regulating civil property, how much must that advantage be heightened, when it is applied to criminal cases! But this we must refer to the ensuing book of these commentaries: only observing for the present, that it is the most transcendent privilege which any subject can enjoy, or wish for, that he cannot be affected either in his property, his liberty, or his person, but by the unanimous consent of twelve of his neighbours and equals. A constitution, that I may venture to affirm has, under providence, secured the just liberties of this nation for a long succession of ages. And therefore a celebrated French writer, who concludes, that because Rome, Sparta, and Carthage have lost their liberties, therefore those of England in time must perish, should have recollected that Rome, Sparta, and Carthage, were strangers to the trial by jury.

Great as this eulogium may seem, it is no more than this admirable constitution, when traced to it's principles, will be found in sober reason to deserve. The impartial administration of justice, which secures both our persons and our properties, is the great end of civil society. But if that be entirely entrusted to the magistracy, a select body of men, and those generally selected by the prince or such as enjoy the highest offices in the state, their decisions, in spight of their own natural integrity, will have frequently an involuntary biass towards those of their own rank and dignity: it is not to be expected from human nature, that *the few* should be always attentive to the interests and good of *the many*. On the other hand, if the power of judicature were placed at random in the hands of the multitude, their decisions would be wild and capricious, and a new rule of action would be every day established in our courts. It is wisely therefore ordered, that the principles and axioms of law, which are general propositions, flowing from abstracted reason, and not accommodated to times or to men, should be deposited in the breasts of the judges, to be occasionally applied to such facts as come properly ascertained before them. For here partiality can have little scope: the law is well known, and is the same for all ranks and degrees; it follows as a regular conclusion from the premises of fact pre-established. But in settling and adjusting a question of fact, when intrusted to any single magistrate, partiality and injustice have an ample field to range in; either by boldly asserting that to be proved which is not so, or more artfully by suppressing some circumstances, stretching and warping others, and distinguishing away the remainder. Here therefore a competent number of sensible and upright jurymen, chosen by lot from among those of the middle rank, will be found the best investigators of truth, and the surest guardians of public justice. For the most powerful individual in the state will be cautious of committing any flagrant invasion of another's right, when he knows that the fact of his oppression must be examined and decided by twelve indifferent men, not appointed till the hour of trial; and that, when once the fact is ascertained, the law must of course redress it. This therefore preserves in the hands of the people that share which they ought to have in the administration of public justice, and prevents the encroachments of the more powerful and wealthy citizens. Every new tribunal, erected for the decision of facts, without the intervention of a jury, (whether composed of justices of the peace, commissioners of the revenue, judges of a court of conscience, or any other standing magistrates) is a step towards establishing aristocracy, the most oppressive of absolute governments. The feodal system, which, for the sake of military subordination, pursued an aristocratical plan in all it's arrangements of property, had been intolerable in times of peace, had it not been wisely counterpoised by that privilege, so universally diffused through every part of it, the trial by the feodal peers. And in every country on the continent, as the trial by the peers has been gradually disused, so the nobles have increased in power, till the state has been torn to pieces by rival factions, and oligarchy in effect has been established, though under the shadow of regal government; unless where the miserable commons have taken shelter under absolute monarchy, as the lighter evil of the two. And, particularly, it is a circumstance well worthy an Englishman's observation, that in Sweden the trial by jury, that bulwark of northern liberty, which continued in it's full vigour so lately as the middle of last century, is now fallen into disuse: and that there, though the regal power is in no country so closely limited, yet the liberties of the commons are extinguished, and the government is degenerated into a mere aristocracy. It is therefore, upon the whole, a duty which every man owes to his country, his friends, his posterity, and himself, to maintain to the utmost of his power this valuable constitution in all it's rights; to restore it to it's antient dignity, if at all impaired by the different value of property, or otherwise deviated from it's first institution; to amend it, wherever it is defective; and, above all, to guard with the most jealous circumspection against the introduction of new and arbitrary methods of trial, which, under a variety of plausible pretences, may in time imperceptibly undermine this best preservative of English liberty.

. . . . .

4. The administration of justice should not only be chaste, but (like Caesar's wife) should not even be suspected. A jury coming from the neighbourhood is in some respects a great advantage; but is often liable to strong objections: especially in small jurisdictions, as in cities which are counties of themselves, and such where assises are but seldom holden; or where the question in dispute has an extensive local tendency; where a cry has been raised and the passions of the multitude been inflamed; or where one of the parties is popular, and the other a stranger or obnoxious. It is true that if a whole county is interested in the question to be tried, the trial by the rule of law must be in some adjoining county: but, as there may be a strict interest so minute as not to occasion any biass, so there may be the strongest biass, where the whole county cannot be said to have any pecuniary interest. In all these cases, to summon a jury, labouring under local prejudices, is laying a snare for their consciences: and, though they should have virtue and vigour of mind sufficient to keep them upright, the parties will grow suspicious, and resort under various pretences to another mode of trial. The courts of law will therefore in *transitory* actions very often change the *venue*, or county wherein the cause is to be tried: but in *local* actions, though they sometimes do it indirectly and by mutual consent, yet to effect it directly and absolutely, the parties are driven to the delay and expense of a court of equity; where, upon making out a proper case, it is done upon the ground of being necessary to a fair, impartial, and satisfactory trial.

The locality of trial required by the common law seems a consequence of the antient locality of jurisdiction. All over the world, actions transitory follow the person of the defendant, territorial suits must be discussed in the territorial tribunal. I may sue a Frenchman here for a debt contracted abroad; but lands lying in France must be sued for there, and English lands must be sued for in the kingdom of England. Formerly they were usually demanded only in the court-baron of the manor, where the steward could summon no jurors but such as were the tenants of the lord. When the cause was removed to the hundred court, (as seems to have been the course in the Saxon times) the lord of the hundred had a farther power to convoke the inhabitants of different vills to form a jury; observing probably always to intermix among them a stated number of tenants of that manor wherein the dispute arose. When afterwards it came to the county court, the great tribunal of Saxon justice, the sheriff had wider authority, and could impanel a jury from the men of his county at large: but was obliged (as a mark of the original locality of the cause) to return a competent number of hundredors; omitting the inferior distinction, if indeed it ever existed. And when at length, after the conquest, the king's justiciars drew the cognizance of the cause from the county court, though they could have summoned a jury from any part of the kingdom, yet they chose to take the cause as they found it, with all it's local appendages; triable by a stated number of hundredors, mixed with other freeholders of the county. The restriction as to hundredors hath gradually worn away, and at length intirely vanished; that of counties still remains, for many beneficial purposes: but, as the king's courts have a jurisdiction co-extensive with the kingdom, there surely can be no impropriety in departing from the general rule, when the great ends of justice warrant and require an exception.

3

VIRGINIA DECLARATION OF RIGHTS, SEC. 11
12 June 1776

11. That in controversies respecting property, and in suits between man and man, the ancient trial by jury is preferable to any other, and ought to be held sacred.

4

PENNSYLVANIA CONSTITUTION OF 1776, SEC. 25
Thorpe 5:3088

SECT. 25. Trials shall be by jury as heretofore: And it is recommended to the legislature of this state, to provide by law against every corruption or partiality in the choice, return, or appointment of juries.

5

NEW JERSEY CONSTITUTION OF 1776, ART. 22
Thorpe 5:2598

XXII. That the common law of England, as well as so much of the statute law, as have been heretofore practised in this Colony, shall still remain in force, until they shall be altered by a future law of the Legislature; such parts only excepted, as are repugnant to the rights and privileges contained in this Charter; and that the inestimable right of trial by jury shall remain confirmed as a part of the law of this Colony, without repeal, forever.

6

GEORGIA CONSTITUTION OF 1777, ARTS. 40–43
Thorpe 2:783

ART. XL. All causes, of what nature soever, shall be tried in the supreme court, except as hereafter mentioned; which court shall consist of the chief-justice, and three or more of the justices residing in the county. In case of the absence of the chief-justice, the senior justice on the bench shall act as chief-justice, with the clerk of the county, attorney for the State, sheriff, coroner, constable, and the jurors; and in case of the absence of any of the aforementioned officers, the justices to appoint others in their room *pro tempore*. And if any plaintiff or defendant in civil causes shall be dissatisfied with the determination of the jury, then, and in that case, they shall be at liberty, within three days, to enter an appeal from that verdict, and demand a new trial by a special jury, to be nominated as follows, viz: each party, plaintiff and defendant, shall choose six, six more names shall be taken indifferently out of a box provided for that purpose, the whole eighteen to be summoned, and their names to be put together into the box, and the first twelve that are drawn out, being present, shall be the special jury to try the cause, and from which there shall be no appeal.

ART. XLI. The jury shall be judges of law, as well as of fact, and shall not be allowed to bring in a special verdict; but if all or any of the jury have any doubts concerning points of law, they shall apply to the bench, who shall each of them in rotation give their opinion.

ART. XLII. The jury shall be sworn to bring in a verdict according to law, and the opinion they entertain of the evidence; provided it be not repugnant to the rules and regulations contained in this constitution.

ART. XLIII. The special jury shall be sworn to bring in a verdict according to law, and the opinion they entertain of the evidence; provided it be not repugnant to justice, equity, and conscience, and the rules and regulations contained in this constitution, of which they shall judge.

7

FEDERAL FARMER, NO. 4
12 Oct. 1787
Storing 2.8.53–55

The trials by jury in civil causes, it is said, varies so much in the several states, that no words could be found for the uniform establishment of it. If so, the federal legislation will not be able to establish it by any general laws. I confess I am of opinion it may be established, but not in that beneficial manner in which we may enjoy it, for the reasons beforementioned. When I speak of the jury trial of the vicinage, or the trial of the fact in the neighbourhood,—I do not lay so much stress upon the circumstance of our being tried by our neighbours: in this enlightened country men may be probably impartially tried by those who do not live very near them: but the trial of facts in the neighbourhood is of great importance in other respects. Nothing can be more essential than the cross examining witnesses, and generally before the triers of the facts in question. The common people can establish facts with much more ease with oral than written evidence; when trials of facts are removed to a distance from the homes of the parties and witnesses, oral evidence becomes intolerably expensive, and the parties must depend on written evidence, which to the common people is expensive and almost useless; it must be frequently taken ex parte, and but very seldom leads to the proper discovery of truth.

The trial by jury is very important in another point of view. It is essential in every free country, that common people should have a part and share of influence, in the judicial as well as in the legislative department. To hold open to them the offices of senators, judges, and offices to fill which an expensive education is required, cannot answer any valuable purposes for them; they are not in a situation to be brought forward and to fill those offices; these, and most other offices of any considerable importance, will be occupied by the few. The few, the well born, etc. as Mr. Adams calls them, in judicial decisions as well as in legislation, are generally disposed, and very naturally too, to favour those of their own description.

The trial by jury in the judicial department, and the collection of the people by their representatives in the legislature, are those fortunate inventions which have procured for them, in this country, their true proportion of influence, and the wisest and most fit means of protecting themselves in the community. Their situation, as jurors and representatives, enables them to acquire information and knowledge in the affairs and government of the society; and to come forward, in turn, as the centinels and guardians of each other. I am very sorry that even a few of our countrymen should consider jurors and representatives in a different point of view, as ignorant troublesome bodies, which ought not to have any share in the concerns of government.

8

A DEMOCRATIC FEDERALIST
17 Oct. 1787
Storing 3.5.5–9

The second and most important objection to the federal plan, which Mr. Wilson pretends to be made *in a disingenuous form*, is the entire *abolition of the trial by jury in civil cases.* It seems to me that Mr. Wilson's pretended answer, is much more *disingenuous* than the objection itself, which I maintain to be strictly founded in fact. He says "that the cases open to trial by jury differing in the different States, it was therefore impracticable to have made a general rule." This answer is extremely futile, because a reference might easily have been made to the *common law of England,* which obtains through every State, and cases in the maritime and civil law courts would of course have been excepted. I must also directly contradict Mr. Wilson when he asserts that there is no trial by jury in the courts of chancery—It cannot be unknown to a man of his high professional learning, that whenever a difference arises about a matter of fact in the courts of equity in America or England, the fact is sent down to the courts of common law to be tried by a jury, and it is what the lawyers call a *feigned issue.* This method will be impracticable under the proposed form of judicial jurisdiction for the United States.

But setting aside the equivocal answers of Mr. Wilson, I have it in my power to prove that under the proposed Federal Constitution, *the trial of facts in civil cases by a jury of the Vicinage* is entirely and effectually abolished, and will be absolutely impracticable. I wish the learned gentleman had explained to us what is meant by the *appellate* jurisdiction as to law and *fact* which is vested in the superior court of the United States? As he has not thought proper to do it, I shall endeavour to explain it to my fellow citizens, regretting at the same time that it has not been done by a man whose abilities are so much superior to mine. The word *appeal,* if I understand it right, in its proper legal signification includes the *fact* as well as the *law,* and precludes every idea of a trial by jury—It is a word of *foreign growth,* and is only known in England and America in those courts which are governed by the civil or ecclesiastical law of the *Romans.* Those courts have always been considered in England as a grievance, and have all been established by the usurpations of the *ecclesiastical* over the *civil* power. It is well known that the courts of chancery in England were formerly entirely in the hands of *ecclesiastics,* who took advantage of the strict forms of the common law, to introduce a foreign mode of jurisprudence under the specious name of *Equity.* Pennsylvania, the freest of the American States has wisely rejected this establishment, and knows not even the name of a court of chancery—And in fact, there can not be any thing more absurd than a distinction between LAW and EQUITY. It might perhaps have suited those barbarous times when the law of England, like almost every other science, was perplexed with quibbles and *Aristotelian* distinctions, but it would be shameful to keep it up in these more enlightened days. At any rate, it seems to me that there is much more *equity* in a trial by jury, than in an appellate jurisdiction from the fact.

An *appeal* therefore is a thing unknown to the common law. Instead of an appeal from facts, it admits of a second, or even third trial by different juries, and mistakes in points of *law,* are rectified by superior courts in the form of a *writ of error*—and to a mere common lawyer, unskilled in the forms of the *civil law* courts, the words *appeal from law and fact,* are mere nonsense, and unintelligible absurdity.

But even supposing that the superior court of the United States had the authority to try facts by *juries of the vicinage,* it would be impossible for them to carry it into execution. It is well known that the supreme courts of the different states, at stated times in every year, go round the different counties of their respective states to try issues of fact, which is called *riding the circuits.* Now, how is it possible that the supreme continental court, which we will suppose to consist at most of five or six judges, can travel at least twice in every year, through the different counties of America, from New Hampshire to Kentuckey and from Kentuckey to Georgia, to try facts by juries of the vicinage. Common sense will not admit of such a supposition. I am therefore right in my assertion, that *trial by jury in civil cases, is, by the proposed constitution entirely done away, and effectually abolished.*

Let us now attend to the consequences of this enormous innovation, and daring encroachment, on the liberties of the citizens. Setting aside the oppression, injustice, and partiality that may take place in the trial of questions of property between man and man, we will attend to one single case, which is well worth our consideration. Let us remember that all cases arising under the new constitution, and all matters between *citizens of different states,* are to be submitted to the new jurisdiction. Suppose therefore, that the military officers of congress, by a wanton abuse of power, imprison the free citizens of America, suppose the excise or revenue officers (as we find in Clayton's Reports, page 44 Ward's case)—that a constable, having a warrant to search for stolen goods, pulled down the clothes of a bed in which there was a woman, and searched under her shift,—suppose, I say, that they commit similar, or greater indignities, in such cases a trial by jury would be our safest resource, heavy damages would at once punish the offender, and deter others from committing the same: but what satisfaction can we expect from a lordly court of justice, always ready to protect the officers of government against the weak and helpless citizen, and who will perhaps sit at the distance of many hundred miles from the place where the outrage was committed?—What refuge shall we then have to shelter us from the iron hand of arbitrary power?—O! my fellow citizens, think of this while it is yet time, and never consent to part with the glorious privilege of trial by jury, but with your lives.

9

DEBATE IN PENNSYLVANIA RATIFYING CONVENTION
7, 11 Dec. 1787
Elliot 2:488–89, 515–19

[*7 Dec.*]

[JAMES WILSON]. It is very true that trial by jury is not mentioned in civil cases; but I take it that it is very improper to infer from hence that it was not meant to exist under this government. Where the people are represented, where the interest of government cannot be separate from that of the people, (and this is the case in trial between citizen and citizen,) the power of making regulations with respect to the mode of trial may certainly be placed in the legislature; for I apprehend that the legislature will not do wrong in an instance from which they can derive no advantage. These were not all the reasons that influenced the Convention to leave it to the future Congress to make regulations on this head.

By the Constitution of the different states, it will be found that no particular mode of trial by jury could be discovered that would suit them all. The manner of summoning jurors, their qualifications, of whom they should consist, and the course of their proceedings, are all different in the different states; and I presume it will be allowed a good general principle, that, in carrying into effect the laws of the general government by the judicial department, it will be proper to make the regulations as agreeable to the habits and wishes of the particular states as possible; and it is easily discovered that it would have been impracticable, by any general regulation, to give satisfaction to all. We must have thwarted the custom of eleven or twelve to have accommodated any one. Why do this when there was no danger to be apprehended from the omission? We could not go into a particular detail of the manner that would have suited each state.

Time, reflection, and experience, will be necessary to suggest and mature the proper regulations on this subject; time and experience were not possessed by the Convention; they left it therefore to be particularly organized by the legislature—the representatives of the United States—from time to time, as should be most eligible and proper. Could they have done better?

I know, in every part where opposition has arisen, what a handle has been made to this objection; but I trust, upon examination, it will be seen that more could not have been done with propriety. Gentlemen talk of bills of rights. What is the meaning of this continual clamor, after what has been urged? Though it may be proper, in a single state, whose legislature calls itself the sovereign and supreme power, yet it would be absurd in the body of the people, when they are delegating from among themselves persons to transact certain business, to add an enumeration of those things which they are not to do. "But trial by jury is secured in the bill of rights of Pennsylvania; the parties have a right to trials by jury, which *ought* to be held sacred." And what is the consequence? There have been more violations of this right in Pennsylvania, since the revolution, than are to be found in England in the course of a century.

[*11 Dec.*]

[Mr. WILSON.] We have been told, sir, by the honorable member from Fayette, (Mr. Smilie,) "that the trial by jury was intended to be given up, and the civil law was intended to be introduced into its place, in civil cases."

Before a sentiment of this kind was hazarded, I think, sir, the gentleman ought to be prepared with better proof in its support than any he has yet attempted to produce. It is a charge, sir, not only unwarrantable, but cruel: the idea of such a thing, I believe, never entered into the mind of a single member of that Convention; and I believe further, that they never suspected there would be found, within the United States, a single person that was capable of making such a charge. If it should be well founded, sir, they must abide by the consequences; but if (as I trust it will fully appear) it is ill founded, then he or they who make it ought to abide by the consequences.

Trial by jury forms a large field for investigation, and numerous volumes are written on the subject; those who are well acquainted with it may employ much time in its discussion; but in a country where its excellences are so well understood, it may not be necessary to be very prolix in pointing them out. For my part, I shall confine myself to a few observations in reply to the objections that have been suggested.

The member from Fayette (Mr. Smilie) has labored to infer that, under the Articles of Confederation, the Congress possessed no appellate jurisdiction; but this being decided against him by the words of that instrument, by which is granted to Congress the power of "establishing courts for receiving, and determining finally, appeals in all cases of capture, he next attempts a distinction, and allows the power of appealing from the decisions of the judges, but not from the verdict of a jury; but this is determined against him also by the practice of the states; for, in every instance which has occurred, this power has been claimed by Congress, and exercised by the Courts of Appeals. But what would be the consequence of allowing the doctrine for which he contends? Would it not be in the power of a jury, by their verdict, to involve the whole Union in a war? They may condemn the property of a neutral, or otherwise infringe the law of nations; in this case, ought their verdict to be without revisal? Nothing can be inferred from this to prove that trials by jury were intended to be given up. In Massachusetts, and all the Eastern States, their causes are tried by juries, though they acknowledge the appellate jurisdiction of Congress.

I think I am not now to learn the advantages of a trial by jury. It has excellences that entitle it to a superiority over any other mode, in cases to which it is applicable.

Where jurors can be acquainted with the characters of the parties and the witnesses,—where the whole cause can be brought within their knowledge and their view,—I know no mode of investigation equal to that by a jury: they hear every thing that is alleged; they not only hear the words, but they see and mark the features of the countenance; they can judge of weight due to such testimony; and moreover, it is a cheap and expeditious manner of distributing justice. There is another advantage annexed to the trial by jury; the jurors may indeed return a mistaken or ill-founded verdict, but their errors cannot be systematical.

Let us apply these observations to the objects of the judicial department, under this Constitution. I think it has been shown, already, that they all extend beyond the bounds of any particular state; but further, a great number of the civil causes there enumerated depend either upon the law of nations, or the marine law, that is, the general law of mercantile countries. Now, sir, in such cases, I presume it will not be pretended that this mode of decision ought to be adopted; for the law with regard to them is the same here as in every other country, and ought to be administered in the same manner. There are instances in which I think it highly probable that the trial by jury will be found proper; and if it is highly probable that it will be found proper, is it not equally probable that it will be adopted? There may be causes depending between citizens of different states; and as trial by jury is known and regarded in all the states, they will certainly prefer that mode of trial before any other. The Congress will have the power of making proper regulations on this subject, but it was impossible for the Convention to have gone minutely into it; but if they could, it must have been very improper, because alterations, as I observed before, might have been necessary; and whatever the Convention might have done would have continued unaltered, unless by an alteration of the Constitution. Besides, there was another difficulty with regard to this subject. In some of the states they have courts of chancery, and other appellate jurisdictions, and those states are as attached to that mode of distributing justice as those that have none are to theirs.

I have desired, repeatedly, that honorable gentlemen, who find fault, would be good enough to point out what they deem to be an improvement. The member from Westmoreland (Mr. Findley) tells us that the trial between citizens of different states ought to be by a jury of that state in which the cause of action rose. Now, it is easy to see that, in many instances, this would be very improper and very partial; for, besides the different manner of collecting and forming juries in the several states, the plaintiff comes from another state; he comes a stranger, unknown as to his character or mode of life, while the other party is in the midst of his friends, or perhaps his dependants. Would a trial by jury, in such a case, insure justice to the stranger? But again: I would ask that gentleman whether, if a great part of his fortune was in the hands of some person in Rhode Island, he would wish that his action to recover it should be determined by a jury of that country, under its present circumstances.

The gentleman from Fayette (Mr. Smilie) says that, if the Convention found themselves embarrassed, at least they might have done thus much—they should have declared that the substance should be secured by Congress. This would be saying nothing unless the cases were particularized.

Mr. SMILIE. I said the Convention ought to have declared that the legislature should establish the trial by jury by proper regulations.

Mr. WILSON. The legislature shall establish it by proper regulations! So, after all, the gentleman has landed us at the very point from which we set out. He wishes them to do the very thing they have done—to leave it to the discretion of Congress. The fact, sir, is, nothing more could be done.

It is well known that there are some cases that should not come before juries; there are others, that, in some of the states, never come before juries, and in those states where they do come before them, appeals are found necessary, the facts reëxamined, and the verdict of the jury sometimes is set aside; but I think, in all cases where the cause has come originally before a jury, that the last examination ought to be before a jury likewise.

The power of having appellate jurisdiction, as to facts, has been insisted upon as a proof, "that the Convention *intended* to give up the trial by jury in civil cases, and to introduce the civil law." I have already declared my own opinion on this point, and have shown not merely that it is founded on reason and authority;—the express declaration of Congress (*Journals of Congress*, March 6, 1779) is to the same purpose. They insist upon this power, as requisite to preserve the peace of the Union; certainly, therefore, it ought always to be possessed by the head of the confederacy. We are told, as an additional proof, that the trial by jury was intended to be given up; "that appeals are unknown to the common law; that the term is a civil-law term, and with it the civil law is intended to be introduced." I confess I was a good deal surprised at this observation being made; for Blackstone, in the very volume which the honorable member (Mr. Smilie) had in his hand, and read us several extracts from, has a chapter entitled "Of Proceeding in the Nature of Appeals,"—and in that chapter says, that the principal method of redress for erroneous judgments, in the king's courts of record, is by writ of error to some superior "*court of appeal.*" (3 *Blackstone,* 406.) Now, it is well known that his book is a commentary upon the common law. Here, then, is a strong refutation of the assertion, "that appeals are unknown to the common law."

I think these were all the circumstances adduced to show the truth of the assertion, that, in this Constitution, the trial by jury was *intended* to be given up by the late Convention in framing it. Has the assertion been proved? I say not; and the allegations offered, if they apply at all, apply in a contrary direction. I am glad that this objection has been stated, because it is a subject upon which the enemies of this Constitution have much insisted. We have now had an opportunity of investigating it fully; and the result is, that there is no foundation for the charge, but it must proceed from ignorance, or something worse.

10

JAMES IREDELL, MARCUS, ANSWERS TO MR. MASON'S OBJECTIONS TO THE NEW CONSTITUTION 1788

Pamphlets 361–62

In respect to the trial by jury in civil cases, it must be observed it is a mistake to suppose that such a trial takes place in all civil cases now. Even in the common law courts, such a trial is only had where facts are disputed between the parties, and there are even some facts triable by other methods. In the Chancery and Admiralty Courts, in many of the States, I am told they have no juries at all. The States in these particulars differ very much in their practice from each other. A general declaration therefore to preserve the trial by jury in all civil cases would only have produced confusion, so that the courts afterwards in a thousand instances would not have known how to have proceeded.—If they had added, "as heretofore accustomed," that would not have answered the purpose, because there has been no uniform custom about it.—If therefore the Convention had interfered, it must have been by entering into a detail highly unsuitable to a fundamental constitution of government; if they had pleased some States they must have displeased others by innovating upon the modes of administering justice perhaps endeared to them by habit, and agreeable to their settled conviction of propriety. As this was the case it appears to me it was infinitely better, rather than endanger everything by attempting too much, to leave this complicated business of detail to the regulation of the future Legislature, where it can be adjusted coolly and at ease, and upon full and exact information. There is no danger of the trial by jury being rejected, when so justly a favorite of the whole people. The representatives of the people surely can have no interest in making themselves odious, for the mere pleasure of being hated, and when a member of the House of Representatives is only sure of being so for two years, but must continue a citizen all his life, his interest as a citizen, if he is a man of common sense, to say nothing of his being a man of common honesty, must ever be uppermost in his mind. We know the great influence of the monarchy in the British government, and upon what a different tenure the Commons there have their seats in Parliament from that prescribed to our representatives. We know also they have a large standing army. It is in the power of the Parliament, if they dare to exercise it, to abolish the trial by jury altogether. But woe be to the man who should dare to attempt it. It would undoubtedly produce an insurrection, that would hurl every tyrant to the ground who attempted to destroy that great and just favorite of the English nation. We certainly shall be always sure of this guard at least upon any such act of folly or insanity in our representatives. They soon would be taught the consequence of sporting with the feelings of a free people. But when it is evident that such an attempt cannot be rationally apprehended, we have no reason to anticipate unpleasant emotions of that nature. There is indeed little probability that any degree of tyranny which can be figured to the most discolored imagination as likely to arise out of our government, could find an interest in attacking the trial by jury in civil cases;—and in criminal ones, where no such difficulties intervene as in the other, and where there might be supposed temptations to violate the personal security of a citizen, it is sacredly preserved.

11

FEDERAL FARMER, NO. 16
20 Jan. 1788
Storing 2.8.199

The trial by jury in criminal as well as in civil causes, has long been considered as one of our fundamental rights, and has been repeatedly recognized and confirmed by most of the state conventions. But the constitution expressly establishes this trial in criminal, and wholly omits it in civil causes. The jury trial in criminal causes, and the benefit of the writ of habeas corpus, are already as effectually established as any of the fundamental or essential rights of the people in the United States. This being the case, why in adopting a federal constitution do we now establish these, and omit all others, or all others, at least with a few exceptions, such as again agreeing there shall be no ex post facto laws, no titles of nobility, &c. We must consider this constitution, when adopted, as the supreme act of the people, and in construing it hereafter, we and our posterity must strictly adhere to the letter and spirit of it, and in no instance depart from them: in construing the federal constitution, it will be not only impracticable, but improper to refer to the state constitutions. They are entirely distinct instruments and inferior acts: besides, by the people's now establishing certain fundamental rights, it is strongly implied, that they are of opinion, that they would not otherwise be secured as a part of the federal system, or be regarded in the federal administration as fundamental. Further, these same rights, being established by the state constitutions, and secured to the people, our recognizing them now, implies, that the people thought them insecure by the state establishments, and extinguished or put afloat by the new arrangement of the social system, unless re-established.—Further, the people, thus establishing some few rights, and remaining totally silent about others similarly circumstanced, the implication indubitably is, that they mean to relinquish the latter, or at least feel indifferent about them. Rights, therefore, inferred from general principles of reason, being precarious and hardly ascertainable in the common affairs of society, and the people, in forming a federal constitution, explicitly shewing they conceive these rights to be thus circumstanced,

and accordingly proceed to enumerate and establish some of them, the conclusion will be, that they have established all which they esteem valuable and sacred. On every principle, then, the people especially having began, ought to go through enumerating, and establish particularly all the rights of individuals, which can by any possibility come in question in making and executing federal laws. I have already observed upon the excellency and importance of the jury trial in civil as well as in criminal causes, instead of establishing it in criminal causes only: we ought to establish it generally:—instead of the clause of forty or fifty words relative to this subject, why not use the language that has always been used in this country, and say, "the people of the United States shall always be entitled to the trial by jury." This would shew the people still hold the right sacred, and enjoin it upon congress substantially to preserve the jury trial in all cases, according to the usage and custom of the country. I have observed before, that it is *the jury trial* we want; the little different appendages and modifications tacked to it in the different states, are no more than a drop in the ocean: the jury trial is a solid uniform feature in a free government; it is the substance we would save, not the little articles of form.

12

ALEXANDER HAMILTON, FEDERALIST, NO. 83,
558–74
28 May 1788

The objection to the plan of the convention, which has met with most success in this state, and perhaps in several of the other states, is *that* relative to *the want of a constitutional provision* for the trial by jury in civil cases. The disingenuous form in which this objection is usually stated, has been repeatedly adverted to and exposed; but continues to be pursued in all the conversations and writings of the opponents of the plan. The mere silence of the constitution in regard to *civil causes*, is represented as an abolition of the trial by jury; and the declamations to which it has afforded a pretext, are artfully calculated to induce a persuasion that this pretended abolition is complete and universal; extending not only to every species of civil, but even to *criminal causes*. To argue with respect to the latter, would, however, be as vain and fruitless, as to attempt the serious proof of the *existence* of *matter,* or to demonstrate any of those propositions which by their own internal evidence force conviction, when expressed in language adapted to convey their meaning.

With regard to civil causes, subtleties almost too contemptible for refutation, have been adopted to countenance the surmise that a thing, which is only *not provided for,* is entirely *abolished.* Every man of discernment must at once perceive the wide difference between *silence* and *abolition.* But as the inventors of this fallacy have attempted to support it by certain *legal maxims* of interpretation, which they have perverted from their true meaning, it may not be wholly useless to explore the ground they have taken.

The maxims on which they rely are of this nature, "a specification of particulars is an exclusion of generals"; or, "the expression of one thing is the exclusion of another." Hence, say they, as the constitution has established the trial by jury in criminal cases, and is silent in respect to civil, this silence is an implied prohibition of trial by jury in regard to the latter.

The rules of legal interpretation are rules of *common sense,* adopted by the courts in the construction of the laws. The true test therefore, of a just application of them, is its conformity to the source from which they are derived. This being the case, let me ask if it is consistent with reason or common sense to suppose, that a provision obliging the legislative power to commit the trial of criminal causes to juries, is a privation of its right to authorise or permit that mode of trial in other cases? Is it natural to suppose, that a command to do one thing, is a prohibition to the doing of another, which there was a previous power to do, and which is not incompatible with the thing commanded to be done? If such a supposition would be unnatural and unreasonable, it cannot be rational to maintain that an injunction of the trial by jury in certain cases is an interdiction of it in others.

A power to constitute courts, is a power to prescribe the mode of trial; and consequently, if nothing was said in the constitution on the subject of juries, the legislature would be at liberty either to adopt that institution, or to let it alone. This discretion in regard to criminal causes is abridged by the express injunction of trial by jury in all such cases; but it is of course left at large in relation to civil causes, there being a total silence on this head. The specification of an obligation to try all criminal causes in a particular mode, excludes indeed the obligation or necessity of employing the same mode in civil causes, but does not abridge *the power* of the legislature to exercise that mode if it should be thought proper. The pretence therefore, that the national legislature would not be at full liberty to submit all the civil causes of federal cognizance to the determination of juries, is a pretence destitute of all just foundation.

From these observations, this conclusion results, that the trial by jury in civil cases would not be abolished, and that the use attempted to be made of the maxims which have been quoted, is contrary to reason and common sense, and therefore not admissible. Even if these maxims had a precise technical sense, corresponding with the ideas of those who employ them upon the present occasion, which, however, is not the case, they would still be inapplicable to a constitution of government. In relation to such a subject, the natural and obvious sense of its provisions, apart from any technical rules, is the true criterion of construction.

Having now seen that the maxims relied upon will not bear the use made of them, let us endeavour to ascertain their proper use and true meaning. This will be best done by examples. The plan of the convention declares that the power of congress or in other words of the *national legislature,* shall extend to certain enumerated cases. This specification of particulars evidently excludes all pretension to a general legislative authority; because an affirmative grant of special powers would be absurd as well as useless, if a general authority was intended.

In like manner, the judicial authority of the federal judicatures, is declared by the constitution to comprehend certain cases particularly specified. The expression of those cases marks the precise limits beyond which the federal courts cannot extend their jurisdiction; because the objects of their cognizance being enumerated, the specification would be nugatory if it did not exclude all ideas of more extensive authority.

These examples might be sufficient to elucidate the maxims which have been mentioned, and designate the manner in which they should be used. But that there may be no possibility of misapprehension upon this subject I shall add one case more, to demonstrate the proper use of these maxims, and the abuse which has been made of them.

Let us suppose that by the laws of this state, a married woman was incapable of conveying her estate, and that the legislature, considering this as an evil, should enact that she might dispose of her property by deed executed in the presence of a magistrate. In such a case there can be no doubt but the specification would amount to an exclusion of any other mode of conveyance; because the woman having no previous power to alienate her property, the specification determines the particular mode which she is, for that purpose, to avail herself of. But let us further suppose that in a subsequent part of the same act it should be declared that no woman should dispose of any estate of a determinate value without the consent of three of her nearest relations, signified by their signing the deed; could it be inferred from this regulation that a married woman might not procure the approbation of her relations to a deed for conveying property of inferior value? The position is too absurd to merit a refutation, and yet this is precisely the position which those must establish who contend that the trial by juries, in civil cases, is abolished, because it is expressly provided for in cases of a criminal nature.

From these observations it must appear unquestionably true that trial by jury is in no case abolished by the proposed constitution, and it is equally true that in those controversies between individuals in which the great body of the people are likely to be interested, that institution will remain precisely in the same situation in which it is placed by the state constitution, and will be in no degree altered or influenced by the adoption of the plan under consideration. The foundation of this assertion is that the national judiciary will have no cognizance of them, and of course they will remain determinable as heretofore by the state courts only, and in the manner which the state constitutions and laws prescribe. All land causes, except where claims under the grants of different states come into question, and all other controversies between the citizens of the same state, unless where they depend upon positive violations of the articles of union by acts of the state legislatures, will belong exclusively to the jurisdiction of the state tribunals. Add to this that admiralty causes, and almost all those which are of equity jurisdiction are determinable under our own government without the intervention of a jury, and the inference from the whole will be that this institution, as it exists with us at present, cannot possibly be affected to any great extent by the proposed alteration in our system of government.

The friends and adversaries of the plan of the convention, if they agree in nothing else, concur at least in the value they set upon the trial by jury: Or if there is any difference between them, it consists in this; the former regard it as a valuable safeguard to liberty, the latter represent it as the very palladium of free government. For my own part, the more the operation of the institution has fallen under my observation, the more reason I have discovered for holding it in high estimation; and it would be altogether superfluous to examine to what extent it deserves to be esteemed useful or essential in a representative republic, or how much more merit it may be entitled to as a defence against the oppressions of an hereditary monarch, than as a barrier to the tyranny of popular magistrates in a popular government. Discussions of this kind would be more curious than beneficial, as all are satisfied of the utility of the institution, and of its friendly aspect to liberty. But I must acknowledge that I cannot readily discern the inseparable connection between the existence of liberty and the trial by jury in civil cases. Arbitrary impeachments, arbitrary methods of prosecuting pretended offences, and arbitrary punishments upon arbitrary convictions have ever appeared to me to be the great engines of judicial despotism; and these have all relation to criminal proceedings. The trial by jury in criminal cases, aided by the *habeas corpus* act, seems therefore to be alone concerned in the question. And both of these are provided for in the most ample manner in the plan of the convention.

It has been observed, that trial by jury is a safeguard against an oppressive exercise of the power of taxation. This observation deserves to be canvassed.

It is evident that it can have no influence upon the legislature, in regard to the *amount* of the taxes to be laid, to the *objects* upon which they are to be imposed, or to the *rule* by which they are to be apportioned. If it can have any influence therefore, it must be upon the mode of collection, and the conduct of the officers entrusted with the execution of the revenue laws.

As to the mode of collection in this state, under our own constitution, the trial by jury is in most cases out of use. The taxes are usually levied by the more summary proceedings of distress and sale, as in cases of rent. And it is acknowledged on all hands, that this is essential to the efficacy of the revenue laws. The dilatory course of a trial at law to recover the taxes imposed on individuals, would neither suit the exigencies of the public, nor promote the convenience of the citizens. It would often occasion an accumulation of costs, more burthensome than the original sum of the tax to be levied.

And as to the conduct of the officers of the revenue, the provision in favor of trial by jury in criminal cases, will afford the security aimed at. Wilful abuses of a public authority, to the oppression of the subject, and every species of official extortion, are offences against the government; for which, the persons who commit them, may be indicted and punished according to the circumstances of the case.

The excellence of the trial by jury in civil cases, appears to depend on circumstances foreign to the preservation of liberty. The strongest argument in its favour is, that it is a security against corruption. As there is always more time and better opportunity to tamper with a standing body of magistrates than with a jury summoned for the occasion, there is room to suppose, that a corrupt influence would more easily find its way to the former than to the latter. The force of this consideration, is however, diminished by others. The sheriff who is the summoner of ordinary juries, and the clerks of courts who have the nomination of special juries, are themselves standing officers, and acting individually, may be supposed more accessible to the touch of corruption than the judges, who are a collective body. It is not difficult to see that it would be in the power of those officers to select jurors who would serve the purpose of the party as well as a corrupted bench. In the next place, it may fairly be supposed that there would be less difficulty in gaining some of the jurors promiscuously taken from the public mass, than in gaining men who had been chosen by the government for their probity and good character. But making every deduction for these considerations the trial by jury must still be a valuable check upon corruption. It greatly multiplies the impediments to its success. As matters now stand, it would be necessary to corrupt both court and jury; for where the jury have gone evidently wrong, the court will generally grant a new trial, and it would be in most cases of little use to practice upon the jury, unless the court could be likewise gained. Here then is a double security; and it will readily be perceived that this complicated agency tends to preserve the purity of both institutions. By increasing the obstacles to success it discourages attempts to seduce the integrity of either. The temptations to prostitution, which the judges might have to surmount, must certainly be much fewer while the co-operation of a jury is necessary, than they might be if they had themselves the exclusive determination of all causes.

Notwithstanding therefore the doubts I have expressed as to the essentiality of trial by jury, in civil cases, to liberty, I admit that it is in most cases, under proper regulations, an excellent method of determining questions of property; and that on this account alone it would be entitled to a constitutional provision in its favour, if it were possible to fix the limits within which it ought to be comprehended. There is however, in all cases, great difficulty in this; and men not blinded by enthusiasm, must be sensible that in a federal government which is a composition of societies whose ideas and institutions in relation to the matter materially vary from each other, that difficulty must be not a little augmented. For my own part, at every new view I take of the subject, I become more convinced of the reality of the obstacles, which we are authoritatively informed, prevented the insertion of a provision on this head in the plan of the convention.

The great difference between the limits of the jury trial in different states is not generally understood. And as it must have considerable influence on the sentence we ought to pass upon the omission complained of, in regard to this point, an explanation of it is necessary. In this state our judicial establishments resemble more nearly, than in any other, those of Great-Britain. We have courts of common law, courts of probates (analogous in certain matters to the spiritual courts in England) a court of admiralty, and a court of chancery. In the courts of common law only the trial by jury prevails, and this with some exceptions. In all the others a single judge presides and proceeds in general either according to the course of the cannon or civil law, without the aid of a jury.* In New-Jersey there is a court of chancery which proceeds like ours, but neither courts of admiralty, nor of probates, in the sense in which these last are established with us. In that state the courts of common law have the cognizance of those causes, which with us are determinable in the courts of admiralty and of probates, and of course the jury trial is more extensive in New-Jersey than in New-York. In Pennsylvania this is perhaps still more the case, for there is no court of chancery in that state, and its common law courts have equity jurisdiction. It has a court of admiralty, but none of probates, at least on the plan of ours. Delaware has in these respects imitated Pennsylvania. Maryland approaches more nearly to New-York, as does also Virginia, except that the latter has a plurality of chancellors. North-Carolina bears most affinity to Pennsylvania; South-Carolina to Virginia. I believe however that in some of those states which have distinct courts of admiralty, the causes depending in them are triable by juries. In Georgia there are none but common law courts, and an appeal of course lies from the verdict of one jury to another, which is called a special jury, and for which a particular mode of appointment is marked out. In Connecticut they have no distinct courts, either of chancery or of admiralty, and their courts of probates have no jurisdiction of causes. Their common law courts have admiralty, and to a certain extent, equity jurisdiction. In cases of importance their general assembly is the only court of chancery. In Connecticut therefore the trial by jury extends in *practice* further than in any other state yet mentioned. Rhode Island is I believe in this particular pretty much in the situation of Connecticut. Massachusetts and New-Hampshire, in regard to the blending of law, equity and admiralty, jurisdictions are in a similar predicament. In the four eastern states the trial by jury not only stands upon a broader foundation than in the other states, but it is attended with a peculiarity unknown in its full extent to any of them. There is an appeal *of course* from one jury to another till there have been two verdicts out of three on one side.

From this sketch it appears, that there is a material diversity as well in the modification as in the extent of the institution of trial by jury in civil cases in the several states; and from this fact, these obvious reflections flow. First, that no general rule could have been fixed upon by the convention which would have corresponded with the circumstances of all the states; and secondly, that more, or at least as much might have been hazarded, by taking the system of any state for a standard, as by omitting a provision altogether, and leaving the matter as it has been left, to legislative regulations.

The propositions which have been made for supplying the omission, have rather served to illustrate than to obviate the difficulty of the thing. The minority of Pennsylvania have proposed this mode of expression for the purpose—"trial by jury shall be as heretofore"—and this I maintain would be absolutely senseless and nugatory. The United States, in their united or collective capacity, are the OBJECT to which all general provisions in the constitution must necessarily be construed to refer. Now it is evident, that though trial by jury with various limitations is known in each state individually, yet in the United States *as such,* it is at this time altogether unknown, because the present federal government has no judiciary power whatever; and consequently there is no proper antecedent or previous establishment to which the term *heretofore* could relate. It would therefore be destitute of a precise meaning, and inoperative from its uncertainty.

As on the one hand, the form of the provision would not fulfil the intent of its proposers, so on the other, if I apprehend that intent rightly, it would be in itself inexpedient. I presume it to be, that causes in the federal courts should be tried by jury, if in the state where the courts sat, that mode of trial would obtain in a similar case in the state courts—that is to say admiralty causes should be tried in Connecticut by a jury, and in New-York without one. The capricious operation of so dissimilar a method of trial in the same cases, under the same government, is of itself sufficient to indispose every well regulated judgment towards it. Whether the cause should be tried with or without a jury, would depend in a great number of cases, on the accidental situation of the court and parties.

But this is not in my estimation the greatest objection. I feel a deep and deliberate conviction, that there are many cases in which the trial by jury is an ineligible one. I think it so particularly in cases which concern the public peace with foreign nations; that is in most cases where the question turns wholly on the laws of nations. Of this nature among others are all prize causes. Juries cannot be supposed competent to investigations, that require a thorough knowledge of the laws and usages of nations, and they will sometimes be under the influence of impressions which will not suffer them to pay sufficient regard to those considerations of public policy which ought to guide their enquiries. There would of course be always danger that the rights of other nations might be infringed by their decisions, so as to afford occasions of reprisal and war. Though the proper province of juries be to determine matters of fact, yet in most cases legal consequences are complicated with fact in such a manner as to render a separation impracticable.

It will add great weight to this remark in relation to prize causes to mention that the method of determining them has been thought worthy of particular regulation in various treaties between different powers of Europe, and that pursuant to such treaties they are determinable in Great-Britain in the last resort before the king himself in

*It has been erroneously insinuated, with regard to the court of chancery, that this court generally tries disputed facts by a jury. The truth is, that references to a jury in that court rarely happen, and are in no case necessary, but where the validity of a devise of land comes into question.

his privy council, where the fact as well as the law undergoes a re-examination. This alone demonstrates the impolicy of inserting a fundamental provision in the constitution which would make the state systems a standard for the national government in the article under consideration, and the danger of incumbering the government with any constitutional provisions, the propriety of which is not indisputable.

My convictions are equally strong that great advantages result from the separation of the equity from the law jurisdiction; and that the causes which belong to the former would be improperly committed to juries. The great and primary use of a court of equity is to give relief *in extraordinary cases,* which are *exceptions** to general rules. To unite the jurisdiction of such cases with the ordinary jurisdiction must have a tendency to unsettle the general rules and to subject every case that arises to a *special* determination. While the separation of the one from the other has the contrary effect of rendering one a sentinel over the other, and of keeping each within the expedient limits. Besides this the circumstances that constitute cases proper for courts of equity, are in many instances so nice and intricate, that they are incompatible with the genius of trials by jury. They require often such long, deliberate and critical investigation as would be impracticable to men called from their occupations and obliged to decide before they were permitted to return to them. The simplicity and expedition which form the distinguishing characters of this mode of trial require that the matter to be decided should be reduced to some single and obvious point; while the litigations usual in chancery frequently comprehend a long train of minute and independent particulars.

It is true that the separation of the equity from the legal jurisdiction is peculiar to the English system of jurisprudence; which is the model that has been followed in several of the states. But it is equally true, that the trial by jury has been unknown in every case in which they have been united. And the separation is essential to the preservation of that institution in its pristine purity. The nature of a court of equity will readily permit the extension of its jurisdiction to matters of law, but it is not a little to be suspected, that the attempt to extend the jurisdiction of the courts of law to matters of equity will not only be unproductive of the advantages which may be derived from courts of chancery, on the plan upon which they are established in this state, but will tend gradually to change the nature of the courts of law, and to undermine the trial by jury, by introducing questions too complicated for a decision in that mode.

These appear to be conclusive reasons against incorporating the systems of all the states in the formation of the national judiciary; according to what may be conjectured to have been the intent of the Pennsylvania minority. Let us now examine how far the proposition of Massachusetts is calculated to remedy the supposed defect.

It is in this form—"In civil actions between citizens of different states, every issue of fact, arising in *actions at common law,* may be tried by a jury, if the parties, or either of them, request it."

This at best is a proposition confined to one description of causes; and the inference is fair either that the Massachusetts convention considered that as the only class of federal causes, in which the trial by jury would be proper; or that if desirous of a more extensive provision, they found it impracticable to devise one which would properly answer the end. If the first, the omission of a regulation respecting so partial an object, can never be considered as a material imperfection in the system. If the last, it affords a strong corroboration of the extreme difficulty of the thing.

But this is not all: If we advert to the observations already made respecting the courts that subsist in the several states of the union, and the different powers exercised by them, it will appear, that there are no expressions more vague and indeterminate than those which have been employed to characterise *that* species of causes which it is intended shall be entitled to a trial by jury. In this state the boundaries between actions at common law and actions of equitable jurisdiction are ascertained in conformity to the rules which prevail in England upon that subject. In many of the other states, the boundaries are less precise. In some of them, every cause is to be tried in a court of common law, and upon that foundation every action may be considered as an action at common law, to be determined by a jury, if the parties or either of them chuse it. Hence the same irregularity and confusion would be introduced by a compliance with this proposition, that I have already noticed as resulting from the regulation proposed by the Pennsylvania minority. In one state a cause would receive its determination from a jury, if the parties or either of them requested it; but in another state a cause exactly similar to the other must be decided without the intervention of a jury, because the state judicatories varied as to common law jurisdiction.

It is obvious therefore that the Massachusetts proposition, upon this subject, cannot operate as a general regulation until some uniform plan, with respect to the limits of common law and equitable jurisdictions shall be adopted by the different states. To devise a plan of that kind is a task arduous in itself, and which it would require much time and reflection to mature. It would be extremely difficult, if not impossible, to suggest any general regulation that would be acceptable to all the states in the union, or that would perfectly quadrate with the several state institutions.

It may be asked, why could not a reference have been made to the constitution of this state, taking that, which is allowed by me to be a good one, as a standard for the United States? I answer that it is not very probable the other states should entertain the same opinion of our institutions which we do ourselves. It is natural to suppose that they are hitherto more attached to their own, and that each would struggle for the preference. If the plan of taking one state as a model for the whole had been thought of in the convention, it is to be presumed that the adoption

---

*It is true that the principles by which that relief is governed are now reduced to a regular system, but it is not the less true that they are in the main, applicable to SPECIAL circumstances which form exceptions to general rules.

of it in that body, would have been rendered difficult by the predilection of each representation in favour of its own government; and it must be uncertain which of the states would have been taken as the model. It has been shewn that many of them would be improper ones. And I leave it to conjecture whether, under all circumstances, it is most likely that New-York or some other state would have been preferred. But admit that a judicious selection could have been effected in the convention, still there would have been great danger of jealousy and disgust in the other states, at the partiality which had been shewn to the institutions of one. The enemies of the plan would have been furnished with a fine pretext for raising a host of local prejudices against it, which perhaps might have hazarded in no inconsiderable degree, its final establishment.

To avoid the embarrassments of a definition of the cases which the trial by jury ought to embrace, it is some times suggested by men of enthusiastic tempers, that a provision might have been inserted for establishing it in all cases whatsoever. For this I believe no precedent is to be found in any member of the union; and the considerations which have been stated in discussing the proposition of the minority of Pennsylvania, must satisfy every sober mind that the establishment of the trial by jury in *all* cases, would have been an unpardonable error in the plan.

In short, the more it is considered, the more arduous will appear the task of fashioning a provision in such a form, as not to express too little to answer the purpose, or too much to be advisable; or which might not have opened other sources of opposition to the great and essential object of introducing a firm national government.

I cannot but persuade myself on the other hand, that the different lights in which the subject has been placed in the course of these observations, will go far towards removing in candid minds, the apprehensions they may have entertained on the point. They have tended to shew that the security of liberty is materially concerned only in the trial by jury in criminal cases, which is provided for in the most ample manner in the plan of the convention; that even in far the greatest proportion of civil cases, and those in which the great body of the community is interested, that mode of trial will remain in its full force, as established in the state constitutions, untouched and unaffected by the plan of the convention: That it is in no case abolished* by that plan; and that there are great if not insurmountable difficulties in the way of making any precise and proper provision for it in a constitution for the United States.

The best judges of the matter will be the least anxious for a constitutional establishment of the trial by jury in civil cases, and will be the most ready to admit that the changes which are continually happening in the affairs of society, may render a different mode of determining questions of property, preferable in many cases, in which that

mode of trial now prevails. For my own part, I acknowledge myself to be convinced that even in this state, it might be advantageously extended to some cases to which it does not at present apply, and might as advantageously be abridged in others. It is conceded by all reasonable men, that it ought not to obtain in all cases. The examples of innovations which contract its ancient limits, as well in these states as in Great-Britain, afford a strong presumption that its former extent has been found inconvenient; and give room to suppose that future experience may discover the propriety and utility of other exceptions. I suspect it to be impossible in the nature of the thing, to fix the salutary point at which the operation of the institution ought to stop; and this is with me a strong argument for leaving the matter to the discretion of the legislature.

This is now clearly understood to be the case in Great-Britain, and it is equally so in the state of Connecticut; and yet it may be safely affirmed, that more numerous encroachments have been made upon the trial by jury in this state since the revolution, though provided for by a positive article of our constitution, than has happened in the same time either in Connecticut or Great-Britain. It may be added that these encroachments have generally originated with the men who endeavour to persuade the people they are the warmest defenders of popular liberty, but who have rarely suffered constitutional obstacles to arrest them in a favourite career. The truth is that the general GENIUS of a government is all that can be substantially relied upon for permanent effects. Particular provisions, though not altogether useless, have far less virtue and efficacy than are commonly ascribed to them; and the want of them will never be with men of sound discernment a decisive objection to any plan which exhibits the leading characters of a good government.

It certainly sounds not a little harsh and extraordinary to affirm that there is no security for liberty in a constitution which expressly establishes the trial by jury in criminal cases, because it does not do it in civil also; while it is a notorious fact that Connecticut, which has been always regarded as the most popular state in the union, can boast of no constitutional provision for either.

13

THOMAS JEFFERSON TO THE ABBÉ ARNOUX
19 July 1789
Papers 15:282–83

Books on the subject of Juries.

Complete juryman, or a compendium of the laws relating to jurors.
12mo. 3/
Guide to English juries. 12mo. 1/. 1682.
Hawles's Englishman's right. 8vo. and 12mo. 1/
Jurors judges both of law and fact by Jones. 3/

---

*Vide No. LXXXI, in which the supposition of its being abolished by the appellate jurisdiction in matters of fact being vested in the supreme court is examined and refuted.

Security of Englishmen's lives, or the duty of grand juries. 12mo. 1/

Walwin's juries justified. 4to. 1/

Dear Sir   Paris July 19. 1789.

The above is a catalogue of all the books I recollect on the subject of juries. With respect to the value of this institution I must make a general observation. We think in America that it is necessary to introduce the people into every department of government as far as they are capable of exercising it; and that this is the only way to ensure a long-continued and honest administration of it's powers. 1. They are not qualified to exercise themselves the EXECUTIVE department: but they are qualified to name the person who shall exercise it. With us therefore they chuse this officer every 4. years. 2. They are not qualified to LEGISLATE. With us therefore they only chuse the legislators. 3. They are not qualified to JUDGE questions of *law*; but they are very capable of judging questions of *fact*. In the form of JURIES therefore they determine all matters of fact, leaving to the permanent judges to decide the law resulting from those facts. But we all know that permanent judges acquire an Esprit de corps, that being known they are liable to be tempted by bribery, that they are misled by favor, by relationship, by a spirit of party, by a devotion to the Executive or Legislative; that it is better to leave a cause to the decision of cross and pile, than to that of a judge biassed to one side; and that the opinion of 12 honest jurymen gives still a better hope of right, than cross and pile does. It is left therefore to the juries, if they think the permanent judges are under any biass whatever in any cause, to take upon themselves to judge the law as well as the fact. They never exercise this power but when they suspect partiality in the judges, and by the exercise of this power they have been the firmest bulwarks of English liberty. Were I called upon to decide whether the people had best be omitted in the Legislative or Judiciary department, I would say it is better to leave them out of the Legislative. The execution of the laws is more important than the making them. However it is best to have the people in all the three departments where that is possible.

14

GEORGIA V. BRAILSFORD
3 Dall. 1 (1794)

[JAY, Chief Justice, charging jury:] It may not be amiss, here, gentlemen, to remind you of the good old rule that on questions of fact, it is the province of the jury, on questions of law it is the province of the court, to decide. But it must be observed, that by the same law, which recognises this reasonable distribution of jurisdiction you have, nevertheless, a right to take upon yourselves to judge of both, and to determine the law as well as the fact in controversy. On this, and on every other occasion, however, we have no

doubt, you will pay that respect which is due to the opinion of the court: for as, on the one hand, it is presumed, that juries are the best judges of facts; it is, on the other hand, presumable, that the court are the best judges of law. But still, both objects are lawfully within your power of decision.

15

REASON V. BRIDGES
20 Fed. Cas. 370, no. 11,617 (C.C.D.C. 1807)

[This was an action by Reuben Reason, a negro, against John Bridges.]

The defendant having challenged twelve of the jurors peremptorily, challenged Mr. Smith, one of the tales, for favor. Eight jurors having been sworn, were sworn as triors.

THE COURT refused to suffer Mr. Smith to be examined on oath as to his religious opinions, whether he was a Methodist, and whether the Methodists had religious scruples as to the legality of slavery. A witness was sworn, who testified that it was not an essential tenet of their religion that slavery was contrary to the divine law; but some of them were of that opinion.

THE COURT refused to permit the witness to be asked whether it was the prevailing opinion among the people called Methodists, and decided that it was incumbent on the party challenging to show, either that it was an essential tenet of their religion, or was the individual opinion of the juror.

16

MIMA QUEEN V. HEPBURN
7 Cranch 290 (1813)

MARSHALL, C. J.: . . . The fourth exception also applies to an opinion given by the circuit court, respecting the service of one of the persons summoned as a juror. James Reed, when called, was questioned, and appeared to have formed and expressed no opinion on the particular case; but on being further questioned, he avowed his detestation of slavery to be such that, in a doubtful case, he would find a verdict for the plaintiffs; and that he had so expressed himself with regard to this very cause. He added, that if the testimony were equal, he should certainly find a verdict for the plaintiffs. The court then instructed the tryers that he did not stand indifferent between the parties. To this instruction an exception was taken.

It is certainly much to be desired that jurors should enter upon their duties with minds entirely free from every prejudice. Perhaps on general and public questions it is scarcely possible to avoid receiving some prepossessions, and where a private right depends on such a question, the difficulty of obtaining jurors whose minds are entirely uninfluenced by opinions previously formed is undoubtedly considerable. Yet they ought to be superior to every exception, they ought to stand perfectly indifferent between the parties; and although the bias which was acknowledged in this case might not perhaps have been so strong as to render it positively improper to allow the juror to be sworn on the jury, yet it was desirable to submit the case to those who felt no bias either way; and therefore the court exercised a sound discretion in not permitting him to be sworn.

17

Bank of Columbia v. Okely
4 Wheat. 235 (1819)

Johnson, J., delivered the opinion of the court: In this case the defendant contended, that his right to a trial by jury, as secured to him by the constitution of the United States, and of the state of Maryland, has been violated. The question is one of the deepest interest; and if the complaint be well founded, the claims of the citizen on the protection of this court are peculiarly strong.

The 7th amendment to the constitution of the United States is in these words:

"In suits at common law, where the value in controversy shall exceed $20, the right of the trial by jury shall be preserved, and no fact tried by a jury shall be otherwise re-examined in any court of the United States than according to the rules of the common law."

The 21st article of the Declaration of Rights of the state of Maryland, is in the words of *Magna Charta:*

"No freeman ought to be taken or imprisoned, &c., or deprived of his life, liberty, or property, but by the judgment of his peers, or by the law of the land."

The act by which this bank is incorporated, gives a summary remedy for the recovery of notes indorsed to it, provided those notes be made expressly negotiable at the bank in their creation. This is a note of that description; but it is contended that the act authorizing the issuing of an execution, either against the body or effects of the debtor, without the judgment of a court, upon the oath and demand of the president of the bank, is so far a violation of the rights intended to be secured to the individual, under the constitution of the United States, and of the state of Maryland. And as the clause in the act of incorporation, under which this execution issued, is express as to the courts in which it is to be executed, it is further contended, that there is no provision in the law of Congress for executing it in this district.

We readily admit that the provisions of this law are in derogation of the ordinary principles of private rights,

and, as such, must be subjected to a strict construction, and under the influence of this admission, will proceed to consider the several questions which the case presents.

The laws of the state of Maryland derive their force, in this district, under the first section of the act of Congress of the 27th of February, 1801. But we cannot admit that the section which gives effect to those laws amounts to a re-enactment of them, so as to sustain them, under the powers of exclusive legislation, given to Congress over this district. The words of the act are, "The laws of the state of Maryland, as they now exist, shall be and continue in force in that part of the said district, which was ceded by that state to the United States." These words could only give to those laws that force which they previously had in this tract of territory under the laws of Maryland; and if this law was unconstitutional in that state, it was void there, and must be so here. It becomes, then, unnecessary to examine the question, whether the powers of Congress be despotic in this district, or whether there are any, and what, restrictions imposed upon it, by natural reason, the principles of the social compact, or constitutional provisions.

Was this act void, as a law of Maryland? If it was, it must have become so under the restrictions of the constitution of the state, or of the United States. What was the object of those restrictions? It could not have been to protect the citizen from his own acts, for it would then have operated as a restraint upon his rights. It must have been against the acts of others. But, to constitute particular tribunals for the adjustment of controversies among them, to submit themselves to the exercise of summary remedies, or to temporary privation of rights of the deepest interest, are among the common incidents of life. Such are submissions to arbitration; such are stipulation bonds, forthcoming bonds, and contracts of service. And it was with a view to the voluntary acquiescence of the individual, nay, the solicited submission to the law of the contract, that this remedy was given. By making the note negotiable at the bank of Columbia, the debtor chose his own jurisdiction; in consideration of the credit given him, he voluntarily relinquished his claims to the ordinary administration of justice, and placed himself only in the situation of an hypothecator of goods, with power to sell on default, or a stipulater in the admiralty, whose voluntary submission to the jurisdiction of that court subjects him to personal coercion. It is true, cases may be supposed, in which the policy of a country may set bounds to the relinquishment of private rights. And this court would ponder long before it would sustain this action, if we could be persuaded that the act in question produced a total prostration of the trial by jury, or even involved the defendant in circumstances which rendered that right unavailing for his protection. But a power is reserved to the judges to make such rules and orders "as that justice may be done;" and as the possession of judicial power imposes an obligation to exercise it, we flatter ourselves that in practice the evils so eloquently dilated on by the counsel do not exist. And if the defendant does not avail himself of the right given him, of having an issue made up, and the trial by jury, which is tendered to him by the act, it is presumable that he cannot dispute the justice of the claim. That this view of the subject is giving full effect to the seventh amendment of the constitution, is not only deducible from the general intent, but from the express wording of the article referred to. Had the terms been, that "the trial by jury shall be preserved," it might have been contended that they were imperative, and could not be dispensed with. But the words are, that the right of trial by jury shall be preserved, which places it on the foot of a *lex pro se introducta*, and the benefit of it may therefore be relinquished. As to the words from *Magna Charta*, incorporated into the constitution of Maryland, after volumes spoken and written with a view to their exposition, the good sense of mankind has at length settled down to this: that they were intended to secure the individual from the arbitrary exercise of the powers of government, unrestrained by the established principles of private rights and distributive justice. With this explanation, there is nothing left to this individual to complain of. What he has lost, he has voluntarily relinquished, and the trial by jury is open to him, either to arrest the progress of the law in the first instance or to obtain redress for oppression, if the power of the bank has been abused. The same answer is equally applicable to the argument founded on the third article of the Maryland constitution.

18

UNITED STATES V. ROSE
2 Cranch C.C. 567 (C.C.D.C. 1825)

NOTE. After the jury was sworn, and the cause had been opened, the COURT (*nem. con.*) made the following order:—

"In this case, the Court being of opinion that this is an action in which it is necessary to examine and determine on accounts between the parties, it is ordered that the jury sworn in this cause be discharged, and that the accounts and dealings between the parties be audited and stated by Joseph Forrest, the auditor of this Court, agreeably to the 12th section of the Act of November, 1785, c. 80, and that he report to this Court."

19

UNITED STATES V. RATHBONE
27 Fed. Cas. 711, no. 16,121 (C.C.S.D.N.Y. 1828)

THOMPSON, Circuit Justice. The general question presented by the record sent up from the district court is, whether that court had authority to order the cause to be referred to referees. It has been urged, however, on the part of the defendants in error, that this general question

does not necessarily arise in this case, for that by the record it appears that the reference was by consent of parties, and not the act of the court. If such be the fair construction of this record, the judgment ought not certainly to be reversed. For, admitting the court had no authority to order the cause referred, yet there can be no doubt this could be done by the consent of parties. It is not a question of jurisdiction, but simply whether the parties will waive the right of trial by jury, and resort to that of trial by referees. The right of trial by jury, secured by the constitution of the United States, is for the benefit of the parties litigating in courts of justice, and is a privilege they may dispense with if they choose. This is a proposition too clear to require any argument or authority in support of it; but if any was wanted, it is found in the case of Bank of Columbia v. Okely, 4 Wheat. [17 U.S.] 235.

The first inquiry then is, whether it is fairly to be inferred from the record, that the reference was by consent of parties. If we look at the rule of court by which the reference was ordered, and which comes up as a part of the record in the court below, it will be seen that the cause was referred on the application of the defendants, and upon notice given to the opposite party of the intended motion; which clearly shows a hostile proceeding, and is at war with any presumed consent. But if this rule is not to be taken as a part of the record, technically considered, still it appears to me that the record proper does not show such consent on the part of the plaintiffs below as to preclude them from taking the exception here. Whenever a party is concluded by his own act, and held to have waived any right or privilege, such act should not be left doubtful, but should plainly and explicitly appear. Every reasonable presumption should be made against the waiver, especially when it relates to a right or privilege deemed so valuable as to be secured by the constitution. The record, so far as it relates to the reference, states that, "it now appearing probable to the court here that the trial of the matters aforesaid, between the parties aforesaid, will require the examination of a long account, it is therefore ordered by the same court, now here, that the matters aforesaid, in controversy between the parties aforesaid, be and the same are referred, according to the statute in such case made and provided, to J.G.S., &c., referees agreed upon and named by the parties aforesaid, to hear and examine the matters aforesaid, and report," &c. The statute here referred to in the record must be the statute of the state, for there is no act of congress on the subject; and it is reasonable to conclude, from this form of record, that the state practice under that statute has been pursued throughout; and the record shows no more than that the parties agreed upon the referees. The appointment of referees was necessarily, in order of time, an act posterior to the order to refer, and does not imply an assent to such order. The record states that order to have been the act of the court, founded upon the fact that it appeared probable that the trial of the matters in controversy would require the examination of long accounts, and not upon the agreement or consent of parties.

The examination of long accounts is the ground upon which a reference is authorized, under the state law; and it was evidently this law and the state practice under it by which the district court was governed. That law could not, however, control the rights of parties in the courts of the United States, and take away privileges secured by the constitution and laws of the United States. I think, therefore, that the plaintiffs in error are not precluded by any consent they have given to the order of reference, from raising that objection here; and the question is open for consideration, whether the district court had authority to order the reference against the consent of either party. The convenience and utility of adopting this mode of trial by referees, where the controversy involves the examination of long accounts, have led me to look at the question with a wish to find the practice sanctioned by the constitution and laws of the United States, but have not been able to find any ground upon which such authority can be sustained. The constitution (Amend. art. 7) declares that, in suits at common law, where the value in controversy shall exceed twenty dollars, the right of trial by jury shall be preserved; and no fact tried by a jury shall be otherwise re-examined in any court of the United States, than according to the rules of the common law. And the judiciary act of 1789 (2 Bior. & D. Laws, 60 [1 Stat. 73]) provides for the trial of issues of fact in all the courts of the United States, in conformity with this provision. The ninth section declares that the trial of issues of fact in the district courts, in all causes except civil causes of admiralty and maritime jurisdiction, shall be by jury. The twelfth section contains the like provision for trials in the circuit courts: "The trial of issues in fact in the circuit courts, shall, in all suits, except those of equity and of admiralty and maritime jurisdiction, be by jury." And the thirteenth section declares that the trial of issues in fact in the supreme court, in all actions at law against citizens of the United States, shall be by jury.

These provisions are too plain to be mistaken, and too positive to be disregarded. If the power to order a cause referred to referees in any case whatever, is possessed by the courts of the United States, where is the limitation of that power to be found? There is no act of congress on the subject, even admitting the constitution not to stand in the way of such a law. There is no law restricting this power to cases involving the examination of long accounts; and if the power exists at all, it may be exercised in every case, and the trial by jury abolished by the courts. The thirty-fourth section of the judiciary act, which declares, "that the laws of the several states, except where the constitution, treaties, or statutes of the United States shall otherwise require or provide, shall be regarded as rules of decision in trials at common law in the courts of the United States, in cases where they apply," has no application whatever to this case, so as to require the adoption of the state law on the subject. [Wayman v. Southard] 10 Wheat. [23 U.S.] 24; Serg. Const. Law, 149, 150, and cases there cited. And that law, at all events, falls within the excepted cases; the constitution and laws of the United States having provided for trial of issues in fact by jury, instead of by referees. How far this view of the case may affect the validity of the state law is a point not drawn in question, or intended to be considered. Although the constitution of the state of New York secures the trial by jury (article 41), it is a modified provision not at variance with the reference act; it declares, "that trial by jury, in all cases in which it hath heretofore been used in the colony of New York, shall be established, and remain inviolate forever." And references were authorized under the colonial laws as early as the year 1768. See 2 R. L. 516, note, and Id. (U. S. Ed.) 517.

In whatever light this case is considered, I can find no ground upon which the order of the district court, referring the cause to referees for trial, can be sustained. The judgment must, accordingly, be reversed, and a venire de novo issued returnable in this court.

SEE ALSO:

Generally 3.3.3; Bill of Rights
New York Constitution of 1777, art. 41, Thorpe 5:2637
Vermont Constitution of 1777, ch. 1, sec. 13, ch. 2, sec. 22, Thorpe 6:3741, 3746
Vermont Constitution of 1786, ch. 1, art. 14, ch. 2, art. 28, Thorpe 6:3753, 3759
Federal Farmer, no. 15, 18 Jan. 1788, Storing 2.8.190–93
Edmund Randolph, Virginia Ratifying Convention, 6 June 1788, Elliot 3:68
George Nicholas, Virginia Ratifying Convention, 10 June 1788, Elliot 3:247
House of Representatives, Amendments to the Constitution, 18 Aug. 1789, Annals 1:760
Cochran v. Street, Wythe 133 (Va. 1791)
Kentucky Constitution of 1799, art. 10, sec. 6, Thorpe 3:1286
Smith v. Carrington, 4 Cranch 62 (1807)
Consequa v. Willings, 6 Fed. Cas. 336, no. 3,128 (C.C.D.Pa. 1816)
Illinois Constitution of 1818, art. 8, sec. 6, Thorpe 2:981
Harrison v. Rowan, 11 Fed. Cas. 663, no. 6,142 (C.C.D.N.J. 1820)
William Wirt, Rights of Defendants in Patent Suits, 20 June 1820, 1 Ops. Atty. Gen. 376
Matilda v. Mason, 16 Fed. Cas. 1106, no. 9,280 (C.C.D.C. 1822), rev'd 12 Wheat. 590
Doe dem. Elmore v. Grymes, 1 Pet. 469 (1828)
M'Lanahan v. Universal Ins. Co., 1 Pet. 170 (1828)
William Rawle, A View of the Constitution of the United States 135 (2d ed. 1829)
Parsons v. Bedford, 3 Pet. 433 (1830)
Crane v. Morris, 6 Pet. 598 (1832)

Amendment VIII

Excessive bail shall not be required, nor excessive fines imposed, nor cruel and unusual punishments inflicted.

1

CASE OF TITUS OATES
10 How. St. Tr. 1079, 1316 (K.B. 1685)

"First, The Court does order for a fine, that you pay 1000 marks upon each Indictment.

"Secondly, That you be stript of all your Canonical Habits.

"Thirdly, the Court does award, That you do stand upon the Pillory, and in the Pillory, here before Westminster-hall gate, upon Monday next, for an hour's time, between the hours of 10 and 12; with a paper over your head (which you must first walk with round about to all the Courts in Westminister-hall) declaring your crime. And that is upon the first Indictment.

"Fourthly, (on the Second Indictment), upon Tuesday, you shall stand upon, and in the Pillory, at the Royal Exchange in London, for the space of an hour, between the hours of twelve and two; with the same inscription.

"You shall upon the next Wednesday be whipped from Aldgate to Newgate.

"Upon Friday, you shall be whipped from Newgate to Tyburn, by the hands of the common hangman.

"But, Mr. Oates, we cannot but remember, there were several particular times you swore false about; and therefore, as annual commemorations, that it may be known to all people as long as you live, we have taken special care of you for an annual punishment.

"Upon the 24th of April every year, as long as you live, you are to stand upon the Pillory and in the Pillory, at Tyburn, just opposite to the gallows, for the space of an hour, between the hours of ten and twelve.

"You are to stand upon, and in the Pillory, here at Westminster-hall gate, every 9th of August, in every year, so long as you live. And that it may be known what we mean by it, 'tis to remember, what he swore about Mr. Ireland's being in town between the 8th and 12th of August.

"You are to stand upon, and in the Pillory, at Charing-cross, on the 10th of August, every year, during your life, for an hour, between ten and twelve.

"The like over-against the Temple gate, upon the 11th.

"And upon the 2d of September, (which is another notorious time, which you cannot but be remember'd of) you are to stand upon, and in the Pillory, for the space of one hour, between twelve and two, at the Royal Exchange; and all this you are to do every year, during your life; and to be committed close prisoner, as long as you live."

Dissenting statement of a minority of the House of Lords:

"1. For that the king's bench, being a temporal court, made it part of the judgment, that Titus Oates, being a clerk, should for his said perjuries, be divested of his canonical and priestly habit, and to continue divested all his life; which is a matter wholly out of their power, belonging to the ecclesiastical courts only.

"2. For that the said judgments are barbarous, inhuman, and unchristian; and there is no precedents to warrant the punishments of whipping and committing to prison for life, for the crime of perjury; which yet were but part of the punishments inflicted upon him.

"3. For that the particular matters upon which the indictments were found, were the points objected against Mr. Titus Oates' testimony in several of the trials, in which he was allowed to be a good and credible witness, though testified against him by most of the same persons, who witnessed against him upon those indictments.

"4. For that this will be an encouragement and allowance for giving the like cruel, barbarous, and illegal judgments hereafter, unless this judgment be reversed.

"5. Because sir John Holt, sir Henry Pollexfen, the two chief justices, and sir Robert Atkins chief baron, with six judges more (being all that where then present), for these and many other reasons, did, before us, solemnly deliver their opinions, and unanimously declare, That the said judgments were contrary to law and ancient practice, and therefore erroneous, and ought to be reversed.

"6. Because it is contrary to the declaration on the twelfth of February last, which was ordered by the Lords Spiritual and Temporal and Commons then assembled, and by their declaration engrossed in parchment, and enrolled among the records of parliament, and recorded in chancery; whereby it doth appear, that excessive bail ought not to be required, nor excessive fines imposed, nor cruel nor unusual punishments inflicted."

2

BILL OF RIGHTS, SEC. 10
1 W. & M., 2d sess., c. 2, 16 Dec. 1689

---

10. That excessive bail ought not to be required, nor excessive fines imposed; nor cruel and unusual punishments inflicted.

3

MONTESQUIEU, SPIRIT OF LAWS,
BK. 6, CHS. 12, 16
1748

12.—Of the Power of Punishments

Experience shows that in countries remarkable for the lenity of their laws the spirit of the inhabitants is as much affected by slight penalties as in other countries by severer punishments.

If an inconvenience or abuse arises in the state, a violent government endeavors suddenly to redress it; and instead of putting the old laws in execution, it establishes some cruel punishment, which instantly puts a stop to the evil. But the spring of government hereby loses its elasticity; the imagination grows accustomed to the severe as well as the milder punishment; and as the fear of the latter diminishes, they are soon obliged in every case to have recourse to the former. Robberies on the highway became common in some countries; in order to remedy this evil, they invented the punishment of breaking upon the wheel, the terror of which put a stop for a while to this mischievous practice. But soon after robberies on the highways became as common as ever.

Desertion in our days has grown to a very great height; in consequence of which it was judged proper to punish those delinquents with death; and yet their number did not diminish. The reason is very natural: a soldier accustomed to venture his life, despises, or affects to despise, the danger of losing it. He is habituated to the fear of shame; it would have been therefore much better to have continued a punishment which branded him with infamy for life; the penalty was pretended to be increased, while it really diminished.

Mankind must not be governed with too much severity; we ought to make a prudent use of the means which nature has given us to conduct them. If we inquire into the cause of all human corruptions, we shall find that they proceed from the impunity of criminals, and not from the moderation of punishments.

Let us follow nature, who has given shame to man for his scourge; and let the heaviest part of the punishment be the infamy attending it.

But if there be some countries where shame is not a consequence of punishment, this must be owing to tyranny, which has inflicted the same penalties on villains and honest men.

And if there are others where men are deterred only by cruel punishments, we may be sure that this must, in a great measure, arise from the violence of the government which has used such penalties for slight transgressions.

It often happens that a legislator, desirous of remedying an abuse, thinks of nothing else; his eyes are open only to this object, and shut to its inconveniences. When the abuse is redressed, you see only the severity of the legislator; yet there remains an evil in the state that has sprung from this severity; the minds of the people are corrupted, and become habituated to despotism.

Lysander having obtained a victory over the Athenians, the prisoners were ordered to be tried, in consequence of an accusation brought against that nation of having thrown all the captives of two galleys down a precipice, and of having resolved in full assembly to cut off the hands of those whom they should chance to make prisoners. The Athenians were therefore all massacred, except Adymantes, who had opposed this decree. Lysander reproached Phylocles, before he was put to death, with having depraved the people's minds, and given lessons of cruelty to all Greece.

"The Argives," says Plutarch, "having put fifteen hundred of their citizens to death, the Athenians ordered sacrifices of expiation, that it might please the gods to turn the hearts of the Athenians from so cruel a thought."

There are two sorts of corruptions—one when the people do not observe the laws; the other when they are corrupted by the laws: an incurable evil, because it is in the very remedy itself.

. . . . .

16.—Of the just Proportion between Punishments and Crimes

It is an essential point, that there should be a certain proportion in punishments, because it is essential that a great crime should be avoided rather than a smaller, and that which is more pernicious to society rather than that which is less.

"An impostor, who called himself Constantine Ducas, raised a great insurrection at Constantinople. He was taken and condemned to be whipped; but upon informing against several persons of distinction, he was sentenced to be burned as a calumniator." It is very extraordinary that they should thus proportion the punishments between the crime of high treason and that of calumny.

This puts me in mind of a saying of Charles II, King of Great Britain. He saw a man one day standing in the pillory; upon which he asked what crime the man had committed. He was answered, "Please your majesty, he has written a libel against your ministers." "The fool!" said the King, "why did he not write against me? They would have done nothing to him."

"Seventy persons having conspired against the Emperor Basil, he ordered them to be whipped, and the hair of their heads and beards to be burned. A stag, one day, having taken hold of him by the girdle with his horn, one of his retinue drew his sword, cut the girdle, and saved him; upon which he ordered that person's head to be cut off, 'for having,' said he, 'drawn his sword against his sovereign.'" Who could imagine that the same prince could ever have passed two such different judgments?

It is a great abuse amongst us to condemn to the same punishment a person that only robs on the highway and another who robs and murders. Surely, for the public security, some difference should be made in the punishment.

In China, those who add murder to robbery are cut in pieces: but not so the others; to this difference it is owing that though they rob in that country they never murder.

In Russia, where the punishment of robbery and murder is the same, they always murder. The dead, say they, tell no tales.

Where there is no difference in the penalty, there should be some in the expectation of pardon. In England they never murder on the highway, because robbers have some hopes of transportation, which is not the case in respect to those that commit murder.

Letters of grace are of excellent use in moderate governments. This power which the prince has of pardoning, exercised with prudence, is capable of producing admirable effects. The principle of despotic government, which neither grants nor receives any pardon, deprives it of these advantages.

4

WILLIAM BLACKSTONE, *COMMENTARIES*
4:293–97, 369–74
1769

The justice, before whom such prisoner is brought, is bound immediately to examine the circumstances of the crime alleged: and to this end by statute 2 & 3 Ph. & M. c. 10. he is to take in writing the examination of such prisoner, and the information of those who bring him: which, Mr. Lambard observes, was the first warrant given for the examination of a felon in the English law. For, at the common law, *nemo tenebatur prodere seipsum;* and his fault was not be wrung out of himself, but rather to be discovered by other means, and other men. If upon this enquiry it manifestly appears, either that no such crime was committed, or that the suspicion entertained of the prisoner was wholly groundless, in such cases only it is lawful totally to discharge him. Otherwise he must either be committed to prison, or give bail; that is, put in securities for his appearance, to answer the charge against him. This commitment therefore being only for safe custody, wherever bail will answer the same intention, it ought to be taken; as in most of the inferior crimes: but in felonies, and other offences of a capital nature, no bail can be a security equivalent to the actual custody of the person. For what is there that a man may not be induced to forfeit, to save his own life? and what satisfaction or indemnity is it to the public, to seize the effects of them who have bailed a murderer, if the murderer himself be suffered to escape with impunity? Upon a principle similar to which, the Athenian magistrates, when they took a solemn oath, never to keep a citizen in bonds that could give three sureties of the same quality with himself, did it with an exception to such as had embezzled the public money, or been guilty of treasonable practices. What the nature of bail is, hath been shown in the preceding book; *viz.* a delivery, or bailment, of a person to his sureties, upon their giving (together with himself) sufficient security for his appearance: he being supposed to continue in their friendly custody, instead of going to gaol. In civil cases we have seen that every defendant is bailable; but in criminal matters it is otherwise. Let us therefore enquire, in what cases the party accused ought, or ought not, to be admitted to bail.

And, first, to refuse or delay to bail any person bailable, is an offence against the liberty of the subject, in any magistrate, by the common law; as well as by the statute Westm. 1. 3 Edw. I. c. 15. and the *habeas corpus* act, 31 Car. II. c. 2. And lest the intention of the law should be frustrated by the justices requiring bail to a greater amount than the nature of the case demands, it is expressly declared by statute 1 W. & M. st. 2. c. 1. that excessive bail ought not to be required: though what bail shall be called excessive, must be left to the courts, on considering the circumstances of the case, to determine. And on the other hand, if the magistrate takes insufficient bail, he is liable to be fined, if the criminal doth not appear. Bail may be taken either in court, or in some particular cases by the sheriff, coroner, or other magistrate; but most usually by the justices of the peace. Regularly, in all offences either against the common law or act of parliament, that are below felony, the offender ought to be admitted to bail, unless it be prohibited by some special act of parliament. In order therefore more precisely to ascertain what offences *are* bailable.

Let us next see, who may *not* be admitted to bail, or, what offences are *not* bailable. And here I shall not consider any one of those cases in which bail is ousted by statute, from prisoners *convicted* of particular offences; for then such imprisonment without bail is part of their sentence and punishment. But, where the imprisonment is only for safe custody *before* the conviction, and not for punishment *afterwards,* in such cases bail is ousted or taken away, wherever the offence is of a very enormous nature: for then the public is entitled to demand nothing less than the highest security that can be given; *viz.* the body of the accused, in order to ensure that justice shall be done upon him, if guilty. Such persons therefore, as the author of the mirror observes, have no other sureties but the four walls of the prison. By the antient common law, before and since the conquest, all felonies were bailable, till murder was excepted by statute: so that persons might be admitted to bail before conviction almost in every case. But the statute Westm. 1. 3 Edw. I. c. 15. takes away the power of bailing in treason, and in divers instances of felony. The statute 1 & 2 Ph. & Mar. c. 13. gives farther regulations in this matter: and upon the whole we may collect, that no justices of the peace can bail, 1. Upon an accusation of treason: nor, 2. Of murder: nor, 3. In case of manslaughter, if the prisoner be clearly the slayer, and not barely suspected to be so; or if any indictment be found against him: nor, 4. Such as, being committed for felony, have broken prison; because it not only carries a presumption of guilt, but is also superadding one felony to another: 5. Persons outlawed: 6. Such as have abjured the realm: 7. Approvers, of whom we shall speak in a subsequent chapter, and persons by them accused: 8. Persons taken with the mainour, or in the fact of felony: 9. Persons charged with arson: 10. Excommunicated persons, taken by writ *de excommunicato capiendo:* all which are clearly not admissible to bail. Others are of a dubious nature, as, 11. Thieves openly defamed and known: 12. Persons charged with other felonies, or manifest and enormous offences, not being of good fame: and 13. Accessories to felony, that labour under the same want of reputation. These seem to be in the discretion of the justices, whether bailable or not. The last class are such as *must* be bailed upon offering sufficient surety; as, 14. Persons of good fame, charged with a bare suspicion of manslaughter, or other inferior homicide: 15. Such persons being charged with petit larciny or any felony, not

before specified: or, 16. With being accessory to any felony. Lastly it is agreed that the court of king's bench (or any judge thereof in time of vacation) may bail for any crime whatsoever, be it treason, murder, or any other offence, according to the circumstances of the case. And herein the wisdom of the law is very manifest. To allow bail to be taken commonly for such enormous crimes, would greatly tend to elude the public justice: and yet there are cases, though they rarely happen, in which it would be hard and unjust to confine a man in prison, though accused even of the greatest offence. The law has therefore provided one court, and only one, which has a discretionary power of bailing in any case: except only, even to this high jurisdiction, and of course to all inferior ones, such persons as are committed by either house of parliament, so long as the session lasts; or such as are committed for contempts by any of the king's superior courts of justice.

Upon the whole, if the offence be not bailable, or the party cannot find bail, he is to be committed to the county gaol by the *mittimus* of the justice, or warrant under his hand and seal, containing the cause of his commitment; there to abide till delivered by due course of law. But this imprisonment, as has been said, is only for safe custody, and not for punishment: therefore, in this dubious interval between the commitment and trial, a prisoner ought to be used with the utmost humanity; and neither be loaded with needless fetters, or subjected to other hardships than such as are absolutely requisite for the purpose of confinement only: though what are so requisite, must too often be left to the discretion of the gaolers; who are frequently a merciless race of men, and, by being conversant in scenes of misery, steeled against any tender sensation. Yet the law will not justify them in fettering a prisoner, unless where he is unruly, or has attempted an escape: this being the humane language of our antient lawgivers, *"custodes poenam sibi commissorum non augeant, nec eos torqueant; sed omni saevitia remota, pietateque adhibita, judicia debite exequantur."*

. . . . .

If all these resources fail, the court must pronounce that judgment, which the law hath annexed to the crime, and which hath been constantly mentioned, together with the crime itself, in some or other of the former chapters. Of these some are capital, which extend to the life of the offender, and consist generally in being hanged by the neck till dead; though in very atrocious crimes other circumstances of terror, pain, or disgrace are superadded: as, in treasons of all kinds, being drawn or dragged to the place of execution; in high treason affecting the king's person or government, embowelling alive, beheading, and quartering; and in murder, a public dissection. And, in case of any treason committed by a female, the judgment is to be burned alive. But the humanity of the English nation has authorized, by a tacit consent, an almost general mitigation of such part of these judgments as savour of torture or cruelty: a sledge or hurdle being usually allowed to such traitors as are condemned to be drawn; and there being very few instances (and those accidental or by negligence) of any person's being embowelled or burned, till previously deprived of sensation by strangling. Some punishments consist in exile or banishment, by abjuration of the realm, or transportation to the American colonies: others in loss of liberty, by perpetual or temporary imprisonment. Some extend to confiscation, by forfeiture of lands, or moveables, or both, or of the profits of lands for life: others induce a disability, of holding offices or employments, being heirs, executors, and the like. Some, though rarely, occasion a mutilation or dismembering, by cutting off the hand or ears: others fix a lasting stigma on the offender, by slitting the nostrils, or branding in the hand or face. Some are merely pecuniary, by stated or discretionary fines: and lastly there are others, that consist principally in their ignominy, though most of them are mixed with some degree of corporal pain; and these are inflicted chiefly for crimes, which arise from indigence, or which render even opulence disgraceful. Such as whipping, hard labour in the house of correction, the pillory, the stocks, and the ducking-stool.

Disgusting as this catalogue may seem, it will afford pleasure to an English reader, and do honour to the English law, to compare it with that shocking apparatus of death and torment, to be met with in the criminal codes of almost every other nation in Europe. And it is moreover one of the glories of our English law, that the nature, though not always the quantity or degree, of punishment is *ascertained* for every offence; and that it is not left in the breast of any judge, nor even of a jury, to alter that judgment, which the law has beforehand ordained, for every subject alike, without respect of persons. For, if judgments were to be the private opinions of the judge, men would then be slaves to their magistrates; and would live in society, without knowing exactly the conditions and obligations which it lays them under. And besides, as this prevents oppression on the one hand, so on the other it stifles all hopes of impunity or mitigation; with which an offender might flatter himself, if his punishment depended on the humour or discretion of the court. Whereas, where an established penalty is annexed to crimes, the criminal may read their certain consequence in that law, which ought to be the unvaried rule, as it is the inflexible judge, of his actions.

The discretionary fines and discretionary length of imprisonment, which our courts are enabled to impose, may seem an exception to this rule. But the general nature of the punishment, *viz.* by fine or imprisonment, is in these cases fixed and determinate: though the duration and quantity of each must frequently vary, from the aggravations or otherwise of the offence, the quality and condition of the parties, and from innumerable other circumstances. The *quantum*, in particular, of pecuniary fines neither can, nor ought to be, ascertained by any invariable law. The value of money itself changes from a thousand causes; and, at all events, what is ruin to one man's fortune, may be matter of indifference to another's. Thus the law of the twelve tables at Rome fined every person, that struck another, five and twenty *denarii:* this, in the more opulent days of the empire, grew to be a punishment of so little consideration, that Aulus Gellius tells a story of one Lucius

Neratius, who made it his diversion to give a blow to whomever he pleased, and then tender them the legal forfeiture. Our statute law has not therefore often ascertained the quantity of fines, nor the common law ever; it directing such an offence to be punished by fine, in general, without specifying the certain sum: which is fully sufficient, when we consider, that however unlimited the power of the court may seem, it is far from being wholly arbitrary; but it's discretion is regulated by law. For the bill of rights has particularly declared, that excessive fines ought not to be imposed, nor cruel and unusual punishments inflicted: (which had a retrospect to some unprecedented proceedings in the court of king's bench, in the reign of king James the second) and the same statute farther declares, that all grants and promises of fines and forfeitures of particular persons, before conviction, are illegal and void. Now the bill of rights was only declaratory, throughout, of the old constitutional law of the land: and accordingly we find it expressly holden, long before, that all such previous grants are void; since thereby many times undue means, and more violent prosecution, would be used for private lucre, than the quiet and just proceeding of law would permit.

The reasonableness of fines in criminal cases has also been usually regulated by the determination of *magna carta*, concerning amercements for misbehaviour in matters of civil right. "*Liber homo non amercietur pro parvo delicto, nisi secundum modum ipsius delicti; et pro magno delicto, secundum magnitudinem delicti; salvo contenemento suo: et mercator eodem modo, salva mercandisa sua; et villanus eodem modo amercietur, salvo wainagio suo.*" A rule, that obtained even in Henry the second's time, and means only, that no man shall have a larger amercement inposed upon him, than his circumstances or personal estate will bear: saving to the landholder his contenement, or land; to the trader his merchandize; and to the countryman his wainage, or team and instruments of husbandry. In order to ascertain which, the great charter also directs, that the amercement, which is always inflicted in general terms ("*Sit in misericordia*") shall be set, *ponatur*, or reduced to a certainty, by the oath of a jury. This method, of liquidating the amercement to a precise sum, is usually done in the court-leet and court-baron by *affeerors*, or jurors sworn to *affeere*, that is, tax and moderate, the *general* amercement according to the *particular* circumstances of the offence and the offender. In imitation of which, in courts superior to these, the antient practice was to enquire by a jury, when a fine was imposed upon any man, "*quantum inde regi dare valeat per annum, salva sustentatione sua, et uxoris, et liberorum suorum.*" And, since the disuse of such inquest, it is never usual to assess a larger fine than a man is able to pay, without touching the implements of his livelyhood; but to inflict corporal punishment, or a stated imprisonment, which is better than an excessive fine, for that amounts to imprisonment for life. And this is the reason why fines in the king's court are frequently denominated ransoms, because the penalty must otherwise fall upon a man's person, unless it be redeemed or ransomed by a pecuniary fine: according to an antient maxim, *qui non habet in crumena luat in corpore.* Yet, where any statute speaks both of fine and ransom, it is holden, that the ransom shall be treble to the fine at least.

When sentence of death, the most terrible and highest judgment in the laws of England, is pronounced, the immediate inseparable consequence by the common law is *attainder.* For when it is now clear beyond all dispute, that the criminal is no longer fit to live upon the earth, but is to be exterminated as a monster and a bane to human society, the law sets a note of infamy upon him, puts him out of it's protection, and takes no farther care of him than barely to see him executed. He is then called attaint, *attinctus,* stained, or blackened. He is no longer of any credit or reputation; he cannot be a witness in any court; neither is he capable of performing the functions of another man: for, by an anticipation of his punishment, he is already dead in law. This is after *judgment:* for there is great difference between a man *convicted,* and *attainted;* though they are frequently through inaccuracy confounded together. After conviction only, a man is liable to none of these disabilities: for there is still in contemplation of law a possibility of his innocence. Something may be offered in arrest of judgment: the indictment may be erroneous, which will render his guilt uncertain, and thereupon the present conviction may be quashed: he may obtain a pardon, or be allowed the benefit of clergy; both which suppose some latent sparks of merit, which plead in extenuation of his fault. But when judgment is once pronounced, both law and fact conspire to prove him completely guilty; and there is not the remotest possibility left of any thing to be said in his favour. Upon judgment therefore of death, and not before, the attainder of a criminal commences: or upon such circumstances as are equivalent to judgment of death; as judgment of outlawry on a capital crime, pronounced for absconding or fleeing from justice, which tacitly confesses the guilt. And therefore either upon judgment of outlawry, or of death, for treason or felony, a man shall be said to be attainted.

5

VIRGINIA DECLARATION OF RIGHTS, SEC. 9
12 June 1776

9. That excessive bail ought not to be required, nor excessive fines imposed, nor cruel and unusual punishments inflicted.

6

CONNECTICUT CONSTITUTIONAL ORDINANCE OF 1776
Poore 1:258

4. And that no Man's Person shall be restrained, or imprisoned, by any authority whatsoever, before the Law hath sentenced him thereunto, if he can and will give sufficient Security, Bail, or Mainprize for his Appearance and good Behaviour in the mean Time, unless it be for Capital Crimes, Contempt in open Court, or in such Cases wherein some express Law doth allow of, or order the same.

7

DELAWARE DECLARATION OF RIGHTS AND FUNDAMENTAL RULES
11 Sept. 1776
Sources 339

16. That excessive Bail ought not to be required, nor excessive Fines imposed, nor cruel or unusual Punishments inflicted.

8

PENNSYLVANIA CONSTITUTION OF 1776, SECS. 29, 38, 39
Thorpe 5:3089, 3090

Sec. 29. Excessive bail shall not be exacted for bailable offences: And all fines shall be moderate.

. . . . .

Sect. 38. The penal laws as heretofore used shall be reformed by the legislature of this state, as soon as may be, and punishments made in some cases less sanguinary, and in general more proportionate to the crimes.

Sect. 39. To deter more effectually from the commission of crimes, by continued visible punishments of long duration, and to make sanguinary punishments less necessary; houses ought to be provided for punishing by hard labour, those who shall be convicted of crimes not capital; wherein the criminals shall be imployed for the benefit of the public, or for reparation of injuries done to private persons: And all persons at proper times shall be admitted to see the prisoners at their labour.

9

THOMAS JEFFERSON TO EDMUND PENDLETON
26 Aug. 1776
Papers 1:505

The fantastical idea of virtue and the public good being a sufficient security to the state against the commission of crimes, which you say you have heard insisted on by some, I assure you was never mine. It is only the sanguinary hue of our penal laws which I meant to object to. Punishments I know are necessary, and I would provide them, strict and inflexible, but proportioned to the crime. Death might be inflicted for murther and perhaps for treason if you would take out of the description of treason all crimes which are not such in their nature. Rape, buggery &c. punish by castration. All other crimes by working on high roads, rivers, gallies &c. a certain time proportioned to the offence. But as this would be no punishment or change of condition to slaves (me miserum!) let them be sent to other countries. By these means we should be freed from the wickedness of the latter, and the former would be living monuments of public vengeance. Laws thus proportionate and mild should never be dispensed with. Let mercy be the character of the law-giver, but let the judge be a mere machine. The mercies of the law will be dispensed equally and impartially to every description of men; those of the judge, or of the executive power, will be the eccentric impulses of whimsical, capricious designing man.

10

THOMAS JEFFERSON, A BILL FOR PROPORTIONING
CRIMES AND PUNISHMENTS
1778
Papers 2:492–504

Whereas it frequently happens that wicked and dissolute men resigning themselves to the dominion of inordinate passions, commit violations on the lives, liberties and property of others, and, the secure enjoyment of these having principally induced men to enter into society, government would be defective in it's principal purpose were it not to restrain such criminal acts, by inflicting due punishments on those who perpetrate them; but it appears at the same time equally deducible from the purposes of society that a member thereof, committing an inferior injury, does not wholly forfeit the protection of his fellow citizens, but, after suffering a punishment in proportion to his offence is entitled to their protection from all greater pain, so that it becomes a duty in the legislature to arrange in a proper scale the crimes which it may be necessary for them to re-press, and to adjust thereto a corresponding gradation of punishments.

And whereas the reformation of offenders, tho' an object worthy the attention of the laws, is not effected at all by capital punishments, which exterminate instead of reforming, and should be the last melancholy resource against those whose existence is become inconsistent with the safety of their fellow citizens, which also weaken the state by cutting off so many who, if reformed, might be restored sound members to society, who, even under a course of correction, might be rendered useful in various labors for the public, and would be living and long continued spectacles to deter others from committing the like offences.

And forasmuch the experience of all ages and countries hath shewn that cruel and sanguinary laws defeat their own purpose by engaging the benevolence of mankind to withold prosecutions, to smother testimony, or to listen to it with bias, when, if the punishment were only proportioned to the injury, men would feel it their inclination as well as their duty to see the laws observed.

For rendering crimes and punishments therefore more proportionate to each other: Be it enacted by the General assembly that no crime shall be henceforth punished by deprivation of life or limb except those hereinafter ordained to be so punished.

If a man do levy war against the Commonwealth or be adherent to the enemies of the commonwealth giving to them aid or comfort in the commonwealth, or elsewhere, and thereof be convicted of open deed, by the evidence of two sufficient witnesses, or his own voluntary confession, the said cases, and no others, shall be adjudged treasons which extend to the commonwealth, and the person so convicted shall suffer death by hanging, and shall forfiet his lands and goods to the Commonwealth.

If any person commit Petty treason, or a husband murder his wife, a parent his child, or a child his parent, he shall suffer death by hanging, and his body be delivered to Anatomists to be dissected.

Whosoever committeth murder by poisoning shall suffer death by poison.

Whosoever committeth murder by way of duel, shall suffer death by hanging; and if he were the challenger, his body, after death, shall be gibbeted. He who removeth it from the gibbet shall be guilty of a misdemeanor; and the officer shall see that it be replaced.

Whosoever shall commit murder in any other way shall suffer death by hanging.

And in all cases of Petty treason and murder one half of the lands and goods of the offender shall be forfieted to the next of kin to the person killed, and the other half descend and go to his own representatives. Save only where one shall slay the Challenger in at duel, in which case no part of his lands or goods shall be forfieted to the kindred of the party slain, but instead thereof a moiety shall go to the Commonwealth.

The same evidence shall suffice, and order and course of trial be observed in cases of Petty treason as in those of other murders.

Whosoever shall be guilty of Manslaughter, shall for the first offence, be condemned to hard labor for seven years, in the public works, shall forfiet one half of his lands and goods to the next of kin to the person slain; the other half to be sequestered during such term, in the hands and to the use of the Commonwealth, allowing a reasonable part of the profits for the support of his family. The second offence shall be deemed Murder.

And where persons, meaning to commit a trespass only, or larceny, or other unlawful deed, and doing an act from which involuntary homicide hath ensued, have heretofore been adjudged guilty of manslaughter, or of murder, by transferring such their unlawful intention to an act much more penal than they could have in probable contemplation; no such case shall hereafter be deemed manslaughter, unless manslaughter was intended, nor murder, unless murder was intended.

In other cases of homicide the law will not add to the miseries of the party by punishments or forfietures.

Whenever sentence of death shall have been pronounced against any person for treason or murder, execution shall be done on the next day but one after such sentence, unless it be Sunday, and then on the Monday following.

Whosoever shall be guilty of Rape, Polygamy, or Sodomy with man or woman shall be punished, if a man, by castration, if a woman, by cutting thro' the cartilage of her nose a hole of one half inch diameter at the least.

But no one shall be punished for Polygamy who shall have married after probable information of the death of his or her husband or wife, or after his or her husband or wife hath absented him or herself, so that no notice of his or her being alive hath reached such person for 7. years together, or hath suffered the punishments before prescribed for rape, polygamy or sodomy.

Whosoever on purpose and of malice forethought shall maim another, or shall disfigure him, by cutting out or disabling the tongue, slitting or cutting off a nose, lip or ear, branding, or otherwise, shall be maimed or disfigured in like sort: or if that cannot be for want of the same part, then as nearly as may be in some other part of at least equal value and estimation in the opinion of a jury and moreover shall forfiet one half of his lands and goods to the sufferer.

Whosoever shall counterfiet any coin current by law within this Commonwealth, or any paper bills issued in the nature of money, or of certificates of loan on the credit of this Commonwealth, or of all or any of the United States of America, or any Inspectors notes for tobacco, or shall pass any such counterfieted coin, paper bills, or notes, knowing them to be counterfiet; or, for the sake of lucre, shall diminish, case, or wash any such coin, shall be condemned to hard labor six years in the public works, and shall forfiet all his lands and goods to the Commonwealth.

Whosoever committeth Arson shall be condemned to hard labor five years in the public works, and shall make good the loss of the sufferers threefold.

If any person shall within this Commonwealth, or being a citizen thereof shall without the same, wilfully destroy, or run away with any sea-vessel or goods laden on board thereof, or plunder or pilfer any wreck, he shall be condemned to hard labor five years in the public works, and shall make good the loss of the sufferers three-fold.

Whosoever committeth Robbery shall be condemned to hard labor four years in the public works, and shall make double reparation to the persons injured.

Whatsoever act, if committed on any Mansion house, would be deemed Burglary, shall be Burglary if committed on any other house; and he who is guilty of Burglary, shall be condemned to hard labor four years in the public works, and shall make double reparation to the persons injured.

Whatsoever act, if committed in the night time, shall constitute the crime of Burglary, shall, if committed in the day be deemed Housebreaking; and whosoever is guilty thereof shall be condemned to hard labor three years in the public works, and shall make reparation to the persons injured.

Whosoever shall be guilty of Horsestealing shall be condemned to hard labor three years in the public works, and shall make reparation to the person injured.

Grand Larceny shall be where the goods stolen are of the value of five dollars, and whosoever shall be guilty thereof shall be forthwith put in the pillory for one half hour, shall be condemned to hard labor two years in the public works, and shall make reparation to the person injured.

Petty Larceny shall be where the goods stolen are of less value than five dollars; whosoever shall be guilty thereof shall be forthwith put in the pillory for a quarter of an hour, shall be condemned to hard labor one year in the public works, and shall make reparation to the person injured.

Robbery or Larceny of Bonds, bills obligatory, bills of exchange, or promisory notes for the paiment of money or tobacco, lottery tickets, paper bills issued in the nature of money, or of certificates of loan on the credit of this commonwealth, or of all or any of the United States of America, or Inspectors notes for tobacco, shall be punished in the same manner as robbery or larceny of the money or tobacco due on, or represented by such papers.

Buyers and Receivers of goods taken by way of robbery or larceny, knowing them to have been so taken, shall be deemed Accessaries to such robbery or larceny after the fact.

Prison breakers also shall be deemed Accessories after the fact to traitors or felons whom they enlarge from prison.

All attempts to delude the people, or to abuse their understanding by exercise of the pretended arts of witchcraft, conjuration, inchantment, or sorcery or by pretended prophecies, shall be punished by ducking and whipping at the discretion of a jury, not exceeding 15. stripes.

If the principal offender be fled, or secreted from justice, in any case not touching life or member, the Accessories may notwithstanding be prosecuted as if their principal were convicted.

If any offender stand mute of obstinancy, or challenge peremptorily more of the jurors than by law he may, being first warned of the consequence thereof, the court shall proceed as if he had confessed the charge.

Pardon and Privilege of clergy shall henceforth be abolished, that none may be induced to injure through hope of impunity. But if the verdict be against the defendant, and the court before whom the offence is heard and determined, shall doubt that it may be untrue for defect of testimony, or other cause, they may direct a new trial to be had.

No attainder shall work corruption of blood in any case.

In all cases of forfeiture, the widow's dower shall be saved to her, during her title thereto; after which it shall be disposed of as if no such saving had been.

The aid of Counsel, and examination of their witnesses on oath shall be allowed to defendants in criminal prosecutions.

Slaves guilty of any offence punishable in others by labor in the public works, shall be transported to such parts in the West Indies, S. America or Africa, as the Governor shall direct, there to be continued in slavery.

11

JAMES IREDELL, MARCUS, ANSWERS TO MR. MASON'S
OBJECTIONS TO THE NEW CONSTITUTION
1788

Pamphlets 359–60

As to the constituting of new crimes, and inflicting unusual and severe punishment, certainly the cases enumerated wherein the Congress are empowered either to define offences, or prescribe punishments, are such as are proper for the exercise of such authority in the general Legislature of the Union. They only relate to "counterfeiting the securities and current coin of the United States," to "piracies and felonies committed on the high seas, and offences against the law of nations," and to "treason against the United States." These are offences immediately affecting the security, the honor or the interest of the United States at large, and of course must come within the sphere of the Legislative authority which is intrusted with their protection. Beyond these authorities, Congress can exercise no other power of this kind, except in the enacting of penalties to enforce their acts of legislation in the cases where express authority is delegated to them, and if they could not enforce such acts by the enacting of penalties those powers would be altogether useless, since a legislative regulation without some sanction would be an absurd thing indeed. The Congress having, for these reasons, a just right to authority in the above particulars, the question is, whether it is practicable and proper to prescribe limits to its exercise, for fear that they should inflict punishments unusual and severe. It may be observed, in the first place, that a declaration against "cruel and unusual punish-ments" formed part of an article in the Bill of Rights at the revolution in England in 1688. The prerogative of the Crown having been grossly abused in some preceding reigns, it was thought proper to notice every grievance they had endured, and those declarations went to an abuse of power in the Crown only, but were never intended to limit the authority of Parliament. Many of these articles of the Bill of Rights in England, without a due attention to the difference of the cases, were eagerly adopted when our constitutions were formed, the minds of men then being so warmed with their exertions in the cause of liberty as to lean too much perhaps towards a jealousy of power to repose a proper confidence in their own government. From these articles in the State constitutions many things were attempted to be transplanted into our new Constitution, which would either have been nugatory or improper. This is one of them. The expressions "unusual and severe" or "cruel and unusual" surely would have been too vague to have been of any consequence, since they admit of no clear and precise signification. If to guard against punishments being too severe, the Convention had enumerated a vast variety of cruel punishments, and prohibited the use of any of them, let the number have been ever so great, an inexhaustible fund must have been unmentioned, and if our government had been disposed to be cruel their invention would only have been put to a little more trouble. If to avoid this difficulty, they had determined, not negatively what punishments should not be exercised, but positively what punishments should, this must have led them into a labyrinth of detail which in the original constitution of a government would have appeared perfectly ridiculous, and not left a room for such changes, according to circumstances, as must be in the power of every Legislature that is rationally formed. Thus when we enter into particulars, we must be convinced that the proposition of such a restriction would have led to nothing useful, or to something dangerous, and therefore that its omission is not chargeable as a fault in the new Constitution. Let us also remember, that as those who are to make those laws must themselves be subject to them, their own interest and feelings will dictate to them not to make them unnecessarily severe; and that in the case of treason, which usually in every country exposes men most to the avarice and rapacity of government, care is taken that the innocent family of the offender shall not suffer for the treason of their relation. This is the crime with respect to which a jealousy is of the most importance, and accordingly it is defined with great plainness and accuracy, and the temptations to abusive prosecutions guarded against as much as possible. I now proceed to the three great cases: The liberty of the press, the trial by jury in civil cases, and a standing army in time of peace.

12

ABRAHAM HOLMES, MASSACHUSETTS RATIFYING
CONVENTION
30 Jan. 1788
Elliot 2:111

What gives an additional glare of horror to these gloomy circumstances is the consideration, that Congress have to ascertain, point out, and determine, what kind of punishments shall be inflicted on persons convicted of crimes. They are nowhere restrained from inventing the most cruel and unheard-of punishments, and annexing them to crimes; and there is no constitutional check on them, but that *racks* and *gibbets* may be amongst the most mild instruments of their discipline.

13

DEBATE IN VIRGINIA RATIFYING CONVENTION
16 June 1788
Elliot 3:447–48, 451–52

PATRICK HENRY: . . . Congress, from their general powers, may fully go into business of human legislation. They may legislate, in criminal cases, from treason to the lowest offence—petty larceny. They may define crimes and prescribe punishments. In the definition of crimes, I trust they will be directed by what wise representatives ought to be governed by. But when we come to punishments, no latitude ought to be left, nor dependence put on the virtue of representatives. What says our [Virginia] bill of rights?—"that excessive bail ought not to be required, nor excessive fines imposed, nor cruel and unusual punishments inflicted." Are you not, therefore, now calling on those gentlemen who are to compose Congress, to . . . define punishments without this control? Will they find sentiments there similar to this bill of rights? You let them loose; you do more—you depart from the genius of your country. . . .

In this business of legislation, your members of Congress will loose the restriction of not imposing excessive fines, demanding excessive bail, and inflicting cruel and unusual punishments. These are prohibited by your declaration of rights. What has distinguished our ancestors?— That they would not admit of tortures, or cruel and barbarous punishment.

But Congress may introduce the practice of the civil law, in preference to that of the common law. They may introduce the practice of France, Spain, and Germany—of torturing, to extort a confession of the crime. They will say that they might as well draw examples from those countries as from Great Britain, and they will tell you that there

is such a necessity of strengthening the arm of government, that they must have a criminal equity, and extort confession by torture, in order to punish with still more relentless severity. We are then lost and undone.

. . . . .

Mr. NICHOLAS: . . . But the gentleman says that, by this Constitution, they have power to make laws to define crimes and prescribe punishments; and that, consequently, we are not free from torture. . . . If we had no security against torture but our declaration of rights, we might be tortured to-morrow; for it has been repeatedly infringed and disregarded.

Mr. GEORGE MASON replied that the worthy gentleman was mistaken in his assertion that the bill of rights did not prohibit torture; for that one clause expressly provided that no man can give evidence against himself; and that the worthy gentleman must know that, in those countries where torture is used, evidence was extorted from the criminal himself. Another clause of the bill of rights provided that no cruel and unusual punishments shall be inflicted; therefore, torture was included in the prohibition.

Mr. NICHOLAS acknowledged the bill of rights to contain that prohibition, and that the gentleman was right with respect to the practice of extorting confession from the criminal in those countries where torture is used; but still he saw no security arising from the bill of rights as separate from the Constitution, for that it had been frequently violated with impunity.

14

HOUSE OF REPRESENTATIVES, AMENDMENTS
TO THE CONSTITUTION
17 Aug. 1789
Annals 1:754

Mr. SMITH, of South Carolina, objected to the words "nor cruel and unusual punishments;" the import of them being too indefinite.

Mr. LIVERMORE.—The clause seems to express a great deal of humanity, on which account I have no objection to it; but as it seems to have no meaning in it, I do not think it necessary. What is meant by the terms excessive bail? Who are to be the judges? What is understood by excessive fines? It lies with the court to determine. No cruel and unusual punishment is to be inflicted; it is sometimes necessary to hang a man, villains often deserve whipping, and perhaps having their ears cut off; but are we in future to be prevented from inflicting these punishments because they are cruel? If a more lenient mode of correcting vice and deterring others from the commisssion of it could be invented, it would be very prudent in the Legislature to adopt it; but until we have some security that this will be done, we ought not to be restrained from making necessary laws by any declaration of this kind.

The question was put on the clause, and it was agreed to by a considerable majority.

15

James Wilson, A Charge Delivered to the Grand Jury
May 1791
Works 2:803–4

Gentlemen of the grand jury, to prevent crimes is the noblest end and aim of criminal jurisprudence. To punish them is one of the means necessary for the accomplishment of this noble end and aim. The impunity of an offender encourages him to repeat his offences. The witnesses of his impunity are tempted to become his disciples in his guilt. These considerations form the strongest—some view them as the sole argument for the infliction of punishments by human laws.

There are, in punishments, three qualities, which render them the fit preventives of crimes. The first is their moderation. The second is their speediness. The third is their certainty.

We are told by some writers, that the number of crimes is unquestionably diminished by the severity of punishments. If we inspect the greatest part of the criminal codes; their unwieldy bulk and their ensanguined hue will force us to acknowledge, that this opinion may plead, in its favour, a very high antiquity, and a very extensive reception. On accurate and unbiassed examination, however, it will appear to be an opinion unfounded and pernicious, inconsistent with the principles of our nature, and, by a necessary consequence, with those of wise and good government.

So far as any sentiment of generous sympathy is suffered, by a merciless code, to remain among the citizens, their abhorrence of crimes is, by the barbarous exhibitions of human agony, sunk in their commiseration of criminals. These barbarous exhibitions are productive of another bad effect—a latent and gradual, but a powerful, because a natural, aversion to the laws. Can laws, which are a natural and a just object of aversion, receive a cheerful obedience, or secure a regular and uniform execution? The expectation is forbidden by some of the strongest principles in the human frame. Such laws, while they excite the compassion of society for those who suffer, rouse its indignation against those who are active in the steps preparatory to their sufferings.

We may easily conjecture the result of those combined emotions, operating vigorously in concert. The criminal will, probably, be dismissed without prosecution by those whom he has injured. If prosecuted and tried, the jury will probably find, or think they find, some decent ground, on which they may be justified, or at least excused, in giving a verdict of acquittal. If convicted, the judges will, with avidity, receive and support every, the nicest exception to the proceedings against him; and, if all other things should fail, will have recourse to the last expedient within their reach for exempting him from rigorous punishment—that of recommending him to the mercy of the pardoning power. In this manner, the acerbity of punishment deadens the execution of the law.

The criminal, pardoned, repeats the crime, under the expectation that the impunity also will be repeated. The habits of vice and depravity are gradually formed within him. Those habits acquire, by exercise, continued accessions of strength and inveteracy. In the progress of his career, he is led to engage in some desperate attempt. From one desperate attempt he boldly proceeds to another, till, at last, he necessarily becomes the victim of that preposterous rigour, which repeated impunity had taught him to despise, because it had persuaded him that he might always escape.

When, on the other hand, punishments are moderate and mild, every one will, from a sense of interest and of duty, take his proper part in detecting, in exposing, in trying, and in passing sentence on crimes. The consequence will be, that criminals will seldom elude the vigilance, or baffle the energy, of publick justice.

True it is, that, on some emergencies, excesses of a temporary nature may receive a sudden check from rigorous penalties: but their continuance and their frequency introduce and diffuse a hardened insensibility among the citizens; and this insensibility, in its turn, gives occasion or pretence to the farther extension and multiplication of those penalties. Thus one degree of severity opens and smooths the way for another, till, at length, under the specious appearance of necessary justice, a system of cruelty is established by law.

Such a system is calculated to eradicate all the manly sentiments of the soul, and to substitute, in their place, dispositions of the most depraved and degrading kind. It is the parent of *pusillanimity*. A nation broke to cruel punishments becomes dastardly and contemptible. For, in nations, as well as individuals, cruelty is always attended by cowardice. It is the parent of *slavery*. In every government, we find the genius of freedom depressed in proportion to the sanguinary spirit of the laws. It is hostile to the prosperity of nations, as well as to the dignity and virtue of men.

16

Benjamin Rush, On Punishing Murder by Death
1792
Selected Writings 35–37, 52–53

In an essay upon the effects of public punishments upon criminals and upon society, published in the second volume of the *American Museum*, I hinted, in a short paragraph, at the injustice of punishing murder by death. I shall attempt in the following essay, to support that opinion, and to answer all the objections that have been urged against it.

I. Every man possesses an absolute power over his own liberty and property, but not over his own life. When he becomes a member of political society, he commits the disposal of his liberty and property to his fellow citizens; but as he has no right to dispose of his life, he cannot commit the power over it to any body of men. To take away life, therefore, for any crime, is a violation of the first political compact.

II. The punishment of murder by death, is contrary to reason, and to the order and happiness of society.

1. It lessens the horror of taking away human life, and thereby tends to multiply murders.

2. It produces murder, by its influence upon people who are tired of life, and who, from a supposition, that murder is a less crime than suicide, destroy a life (and often that of a near connexion) and afterwards deliver themselves up to justice, that they may escape from their misery by means of a halter.

3. The punishment of murder by death, multiplies murders, from the difficulty it creates of convicting persons who are guilty of it. Humanity, revolting at the idea of the severity and certainty of a capital punishment, often steps in, and collects such evidence in favour of a murderer, as screens him from justice altogether, or palliates his crime into manslaughter. If the punishment of murder consisted in long confinement, and hard labor, it would be proportioned by the measure of our feelings of justice, and every member of society would be a watchman or a magistrate, to apprehend a destroyer of human life, and to bring him to punishment.

4. The punishment of murder by death, checks the operations of universal justice, by preventing the punishment of every species of murder. Quack doctors frauds of various kinds—and a licentious press, often destroy life, and sometimes with malice of the most propense nature. If murder were punished by confinement and hard labour, the authors of the numerous murders that have been mentioned, would be dragged forth, and punished according to their deserts. How much order and happiness would arise to society from such a change in human affairs! But who will attempt to define these species of murder, or to prosecute offenders of this stamp, if death is to be the punishment of the crime after it is admitted, and proved to be wilful murder?—only alter the punishment of murder, and these crimes will soon assume their proper names, and probably soon become as rare as murder from common acts of violence.

5. The punishment of murder by death, has been proved to be contrary to the order and happiness of society by the experiments of some of the wisest legislators in Europe. The Empress of Russia, the King of Sweden, and the Duke of Tuscany, have nearly extirpated murder from their dominions, by converting its punishment into the means of benefiting society, and reforming the criminals who perpetrate it.

III. The punishment of murder by death, is contrary to divine revelation. A religion which commands us to forgive and even to do good to our enemies, can never authorise the punishment of murder by death. "Vengeance is mine," said the Lord; "I will repay." It is to no purpose to say here, that this vengeance is taken out of the hands of an individual, and directed against the criminal by the hand of government. It is equally an usurpation of the prerogative of heaven, whether it be inflicted by a single person, or by a whole community.

. . . . .

I cannot take leave of this subject without remarking that capital punishments are the natural offspring of monarchical governments. Kings believe that they possess their crowns by a *divine* right: no wonder, therefore, they assume the divine power of taking away human life. Kings consider their subjects as their property: no wonder, therefore, they shed their blood with as little emotion as men shed the blood of their sheep or cattle. But the principles of republican governments speak a very different language. They teach us the absurdity of the divine origin of kingly power. They approximate the extreme ranks of men to each other. They restore man to his God—to society—and to himself. They revive and establish the relations of fellow-citizen, friend, and brother. They appreciate human life, and increase public and private obligations to preserve it. They consider human sacrifices as no less offensive to the sovereignty of the people, than they are to the majesty of heaven. They view the attributes of government, like the attributes of the Deity, as infinitely more honoured by destroying evil by means of *merciful* than by exterminating punishments. The United States have adopted these peaceful and benevolent forms of government. It becomes them therefore to adopt their mild and benevolent principles. An execution in a republic is like a human sacrifice in religion. It is an offering to monarchy, and to that malignant being, who has been styled a murderer from the beginning, and who delights equally in murder, whether it be perpetrated by the cold, but vindictive arm of the law, or by the angry hand of private revenge.

17

STATE V. HOWELL
R. M. Charlton 120 (Ga. 1821)

The prisoner being brought up by the writ of *habeas corpus*, *D'Lyon* moved for his discharge, upon the ground:

1st. That the offence charged was committed, if committed at all, in the State of South Carolina—and that therefore, the prisoner could not be detained, but upon the requisition of the Governor of that State for the prisoner, as a fugitive from justice—and if this objection was overruled, then that the prisoner was entitled to be bailed—to answer to any offence charged to have been committed in the State of Georgia.

On the first ground, I am of the opinion, that a person charged with a felony in another state, and fleeing to this, may upon a principle of comity, which obtains in such cases between sovereign States, be detained for a reasonable period, for the purpose of affording time for an application to the Governor of the State, where the felony is charged to have been committed, to make the demand as stated in the Constitution. Not only the morality and reasonableness of the thing, as involved in the general principle of comity, but the cases referred to by the States' counsel, support the opinion.

2d. As to the application for bail: the prisoner is charged with having in his *possession* a counterfeit Bank Bill, with an intention to pass the same in this State. By the 53d Sect. of the 6th Division of the penal code of this State, that offence is punished by imprisonment at hard labor, for any period of time not exceeding fifteen years. In this high grade of felony, whether the prisoner shall be bailed or not, *rests* in the sound discretion of the Court. The positiveness of the affidavit in this case, and there being no extrinsic circumstances in favor of the prisoner, will not permit me to accede to this branch of the motion, particularly as the proximity of the session of the Superior Court, excludes the idea of any hardship or rigour, in continuing the imprisonment.

It is *ordered*, that the prisoner be remanded and detained in custody, to answer to such bill of indictment as may be preferred against him, at the next Superior Court.

18

BARKER V. PEOPLE
20 Johns. R. 457 (N.Y. 1823)

SPENCER, Ch. J., delivered the opinion of the court.

The plaintiff in error contends that the judgment of the Sessions is erroneous; and that the act on which it is founded, declaring that such disability shall ensue, on a conviction for sending a challenge to fight a duel, is unconstitutional: 1st. As regards the original constitution of this state. 2. As regards the constitution of the *United States;* and, 3d. As regards the amended constitution of this state. The 1st, 9th, 13th and 33d articles of the original constitution of this state, are said to bear upon this question, and the statute is supposed to be in repugnance to the provisions of those articles. The first article forbids the exercise of any authority over the people, but such as shall be derived from or granted by them. The powers of the state legislature are not conferred by any express grant, but result from the institution of a supreme legislature; and it is an axiom, that the legislature possess all power not expressly forbidden either by the constitution of the state, or the *United States,* which relates to the prevention of crime, or the well ordering of society. The ninth article constitutes the assembly judges of their own members. I presume, it is intended, by the plaintiff, by referring to that article, to infer, that no other power, not even the legislative, can divest the assembly of this right. If this be so, and it is not necessary to deny it, the only consequence would be, that should the assembly consider the judgment as no disqualification, its operation would be so far defeated, but not, necessarily, any further. The

thirteenth article forbids the disfranchisement of any member of this state, unless by the law of the land, or the judgment of his peers. If the duelling act is not otherwise unconstitutional, then the injunctions of this article have been complied with; for the act is the law of the land, and the verdict is the judgment of the plaintiff's peers. The thirty-third article relates to judgments on impeachments, and restrains their operation to removal from office, and disqualification to hold any place of honor, trust or profit, under this state. The application of this article to the question before us, is not perceived. I am, therefore, of opinion, that there is nothing in the original constitution which the act violates. When it was before the council of revision, the objections which some of the council, and I was one of them, had to the act, related to other parts of it, and not to the one now objected to. The supposed repugnancy of the act to the constitution of the *United States,* as it is urged, is to the eighth amendment, which declares, that cruel and unusual punishments shall not be inflicted. The disfranchisement of a citizen is not an unusual punishment; it was the consequence of treason, and of infamous crimes, and it was altogether discretionary in the legislature to extend that punishment to other offences.

The judgment rendered in the court below, is supposed to be erroneous, as repugnant to, and contravening the third section of the first article, the second section of the second article, the second section of the fifth article, the first and thirteenth sections of the seventh article, and the first section of the ninth article of the amended constitution. The third section of the first article, giving to the senate and assembly the right to judge of the qualifications of their members, has been commented on, as well as the second section of the fifth article, which relates to judgments on impeachments; and also the first section of the seventh article. The second section of the second article ordains, *that laws may be passed, excluding from the right of suffrage, persons who have been, or may be, convicted of infamous crimes.* The thirteenth section of the seventh article, among other things, ordains, that such acts of the legislature as were then in force, should be, and continue the law of this state, subject to such alterations as the legislature shall make concerning the same; but all such parts of the common law, and *such of the said acts, or parts thereof, as are repugnant to this constitution, are hereby abrogated.* The first section of the ninth article ordains, among other things, that those parts of the amended constitution which relate to the right of suffrage; the number of members of assembly thereby directed to be elected; the apportionment of members of assembly; the elections thereby directed to commence on the first *Monday* of *November,* 1822, should be in force, and take effect from the last day of *February* then next. The sixth article has also been relied on, which ordains, *that no other oath, declaration or test shall be required, as a qualification for any office or public trust* than the one prescribed, which is to support the constitutions of the *United States* and of this state, and faithfully to discharge the duties of the office, according to the best ability of the officer.

It may admit of much doubt, whether the legislature are not restrained from excluding from the right of suffrage, any other persons than such as have been, or may be, convicted of infamous crimes. The enumeration of offences, on the conviction for which power is given to the legislature, to exclude the persons convicted, by necessary implication, denies the power in any other cases. The offence of which the plaintiff has been convicted, is not an infamous one. The law has settled what crimes are infamous; they are treason, felony, and every species of the *crimen falsi,* such as perjury, conspiracy and barratry. (*Peake's Evid.* 126, 127.) If this be so, then the inquiry is, whether the right of suffrage, necessarily implies the right of being voted for. The amended constitution does not prescribe the qualifications of members of assembly; and, with respect to senators, it requires only that they shall be freeholders. There are particular qualifications for a governor, but for all other offices the constitution is silent as to qualification. I cannot think, that the right of voting and being voted for are convertible terms; indeed, we see they are not, for a great class of voters are not required to be freeholders, and yet it is necessary to the qualification of a senator or a governor, that he should be a freeholder; and, with respect to the governor, he must be a native citizen of the *United States,* thirty years of age, and a resident within the state for five years. The right of suffrage is, therefore, distinct from the right of being eligible to an office.

As to the oath of office, prescribed by the 6th article, and the provision, that no other oath, declaration or test shall be required; it is contended, that the word *test* has a most extensive meaning, and prohibits the establishing any other rule by which the capacity of a person to hold an office shall be determined, than that defined, the oath of the person appointed or elected. I cannot accede to this. In my judgment, the exclusion of any other oath, declaration or test, as a qualification for an office or public trust, means only, that no other oath of office shall be required. It was intended to abolish the oath of allegiance and abjuration, or any political or religious test, as a qualification. The provision, that no other oath is to be required as a test, imports nothing with respect to the other qualifications. In the case of a person elected a senator, or a governor, the oath has no reference to the qualifications required, and they may be inquired into by some other tribunals. If an alien should be elected, he can well take the oath; but surely, the question whether he could hold the office would be open to inquiry.

Upon the whole, it appears to us, that there exists no constitutional objection to the conviction; and the judgment must be affirmed.

19

James v. Commonwealth
12 Serg. & Rawle 220 (Pa. 1824)

Duncan, J. The judgment was, "that the defendant be placed in a ducking or cucking stool, and be plunged three times in the water." This sentence, we are informed, has created much ferment and excitement in the public mind. It is considered as a cruel, unusual, unnatural, and ludicrous judgment. But whatever prejudices may exist against it, still, if it be the law of the land, the court must pronounce judgment for it. But, as it is revolting to humanity, and is of that description that only could have been invented in an age of barbarism, we ought to be well persuaded, either that it is the appropriate judgment of the common law, or is inflicted by some positive law; and that that common law or statutory provision has been adopted here, and is now in force. I have employed some time not very pleasantly, certainly not very profitably, in tracing the punishment *ad ludibrium* to its source, and have followed this stream until it has sunk in oblivion in the general improvement of society, and the reformation of criminal punishment, and been dried up by Time, that great innovator.

It must strike all, as a peculiar feature of this offence, that it is of the feminine gender, that it degrades woman to a mere *thing,* to a *nuisance,* and does not consider her as a person. But this is not to be wondered at, when we reflect on the generally degraded state of woman, when this punishment was introduced. She was in some respects the servant or slave of the husband; so that he might correct her with a stick as thick as his own thumb. There is a tradition, that at the publication of *Bracton's* learned work, in which the dimension of this instrument of correction was first stated, the women of the town in which he lived, seized him and ducked him in a horse pond. At the common law, women were denied the benefit of clergy, merely because their sex precluded them from holy orders, however learned they might be, while their more ignorant husbands, who could with difficulty read even the neck verse, were burnt in the hand with a cold iron, for the offence for which they were doomed to die on the gallows. And female virtue, by the temporal law, stood and now stands in *England,* exposed to the slanders and malignity of falsehood; for any one in conversation, may proclaim the purest maid or chastest matron, as the most meretricious or incontinent of women, with impunity from the animadversion of the civil courts; and thus female honour, which is dearer to the sex than their lives, is left by the common law to be the sport of every malignant and abandoned calumniator.

The learned Judge Blackstone seems to consider the female sex a great favourite of the law of *England,* yet his more just editor, *Christian,* in his notes, expresses a fear that there is little cause to pay a compliment to our laws, for their favour and respect to the female sex. The right of the husband is to beat his wife, *"ex causa regiminis et castigationis."* It is true, he was only allowed— *modicam castigationem adhibere,* and this was never doubted until the polite reign of *Charles* II. Yet the lower rank of people, as *Blackstone* observes, who were always fond of, and adhere to the common law, still claim and exert their ancient privileges; and the civil law allowed the husband a larger authority over his wife, permitting him for some misdemeanors, *"flagellies et fustibus acriter verberare uxorem"*—and if we add the present instance of partiality, that a scolding woman is to be ducked, while the most scandalously abusive and railing man goes unpunished, the iniquity and injustice will be very striking. The ludicrous local customs of some of the manor courts, give us some idea of the low grade in which women were placed. The widow, to redeem her free bench, rode into the steward's court, sitting upon a ram with the tail in her hand, repeating some ribald verses:—

"Here I am, riding on a black ram, &c."

The punishment of the ducking, or cucking stool, is from the cuckoo, *"qui odiose jurgat et rixatur,"* as Lord COKE has it, in 3d *Inst.* 219; or, as *Jacobs* has it, in his dictionary, the gogen stool, and by some thought to be corrupted from the choke stool; and the instrument is called in *Stat.* 51, *Hen.* 3, a trebucket, a pitfall, and in law, as Lord COKE says, signifies, a stool that falls into a pit of water; whereas the last instrument that was seen in *England,* as *Morgan,* an editor of *Jacob's Dictionary* mentions, consisted of a beam or rafter, moving on a fulcrum, and extending to the centre of a large pond, on which end the stool used to be placed; while on the other hand, *Daines Barrington,* a learned antiquarian, in his observations on the *Statutes,* 40, says, it is a machine anciently used in the siege of towns, and the etymology is from the *Celtic* tre, that is, ville, and our own bucket, and signifies a town bucket.

Thus in our very outset, we are involved in doubt, and who shall decide, where there is such a difference among the learned? The officer would not know what to do, whether to fix *Nancy James* on a stool or in a bucket, whether she is to be run into the river on wheels, or to be soused into a pond, from a beam or rafter. From the country from which it is suggested we have borrowed it, we could obtain no information, nor expect a model, for not a vestige of it is there to be found; unless perhaps, along side of the Rack, (the Duke of *Exeter's* daughter,) which is still shown as a curiosity by a yeoman of the King's guard, as an instrument of punishment, which, like the trebucket, was once used in *England,* (*Barrington,* 366,) for no poor woman in that country has suffered under the edge of a law so barbarous, for the last century—like unscoured armour, it is hung up by the wall—like the law of witchcraft, it has remained unused; for no one has suffered under that law, either at the stake or on the gibbet, since the reign of *Charles* II.; although the law stood unrepealed on the Statute Book, until 9th *Geo.* 2., as our own law against the same offence, until several years after the revolution; or, like the act against the gypsies, which punished those with death, without the benefit of clergy, who remained one month within the realm; and Lord HALE, in his *Pleas of the Crown,* 671, says, "I have not known these statutes much put in execution, only about twenty years since, at the Assizes at *Bury,* about thirteen were condemned and executed for this offence." On this judgment, *Blackstone,* 4th vol. 166, remarks, "but to the honour of our national humanity, there are no instances more modern."

Thus we see two bloody statutes repealed by the voice of humanity, and not by positive law; so that it seems most probable that hanging of women as witches and gypsies, and ducking them as scolds, ceased about the same time, viz. the time of the restoration, and before the charter to *William Penn.* Yet it is to be remarked, that the statute of 6 *Jac.* 1, against witchcraft was adopted in *Pennsylvania,* and ordered to be duly put in force and execution; and in the first address of the elder Mr. *Rawle* to the associated members of the *Philadelphia* bar, (which is only the proeme of a work of general interest on the civil institutions of this state from its earliest day; and from the great learning and deep research of that eminent lawyer, we may justly look for a work of vast utility to all employed in the practice or in the administration of the law,) we have the record of a trial for witchcraft before the governor and council, in which there was a verdict either of a great simplicity or a deep policy, to get rid of a most insane prosecution for an impossible crime, without acting in open hostility to the deep rooted prejudices of the day. The jury find "that *Mary Mattser* is guilty of having the common fame of being a witch." Indeed, it appears that at the same period, the race of witches and scolds became extinct, when the law ceased to hang the witches and duck the scolds.

The instances are numerous of statutes being repealed in fact—a kind of silent legislation. As to the abrogation of statutes by *"non user,"* there may rest some doubt; for myself, I own my opinion is, that *"non user"* may be such as to render them obsolete, when their objects vanish or their reason ceases. The common law (and this is but a customary punishment) what is it, but common usage? The long disuetude of any law amounts to its repeal. Mr. *Woodeson,* in his second lecture, (vol. 1st, 63,) of civil, positive and instituted laws, observes "that the last consideration is the period of their existence." They may be repealed either expressly or by implication founded on disuse. He cites this passage from the *Digest,*—*"rectissime illud receptum est— ut magis non solus suffragio legislatorum; sed etiam tacito consensu omnium per desuetudinem abrogatur."* It certainly requires very strong grounds to presume a law obsolete, yet as the whole community includes as well the legislative power as its subjects, total disuse of any civil institution for ages past, may afford just and rational objections against disrespected and superannuated ordinances. Judge WILSON, (2d *Wilson's Works,* 38, 39,) observes, "that it is the characteristic of a system of common law, that it may be accommodated to the circumstances, the exigencies, and the conveniences of the people by whom it is appointed. Now, as these circumstances, exigencies, and conveniences silently change, a proportionate change in time and in degree must take place in the accomodated system. Time silently and gradually introduces; it silently and gradually withdraws its customary laws."

What was the criminal punishment in conspiracy, the villainous judgment, viz. to lose the *"liberam legem,"* whereby they are discredited as jurors or witnesses, to forfeit their goods and chattels and lands for life, to have their fields wasted, houses razed, their trees rooted up, their own bodies committed to prison. But this villainous judgment, by long disuse, has become obsolete, it not having been pronounced for ages; but instead thereof, the delinquents are usually condemned to fine and imprisonment, or the pillory, (4 *Blackstone*, 136). The barbarous writ of attaint, which has as strong a foundation as any principle in common law, has been long banished. That such crimes and punishments existed at the common law, every treatise to the present day states—but this does not prove that they now exist. They are nothing more than the memorials of times that are past, as the usages of our uncivilized ancestors; and in nothing is the gradual change of the common law more apparent, and in nothing does it accommodate itself more to the change of manners and effect of education, than in the silent and gradual disuse of barbarous criminal punishments.

Lambert, who first published his *Treatise on the Office of the Justice of the Peace,* in 1610, *lib.* i. *c.* 12, states that corporal punishments are either *capital,* or not *capital;* that capital are inflicted "sundrie ways; as by hanging, burning, boiling, pressing: not capital are of divers sorts, as cutting off the hand or ear, burning or branding the hand, face, shoulders, whipping, inprisoning, stocking, sitting in the pillory, or on the cucking stool." Of this kind of punishment, our old laws had more sorts than we now have; as pulling out the tongue for false rumours, cutting off the nose, and, for adultery, taking away the privy parts. So they had more sorts of punishments, when *Lambert* wrote, than we now have. Blessed be GOD! I feel a conviction, (and I have examined every book upon which I could lay my hands,) that there is no judicial record, certainly no report, of this punishment being inflicted for more than one hundred years. The case in 2 *Strange,* 849, *The King* v. *Taylor,* was quashed generally; it was not against her as *communis vexatrix,* but as *calumniatrix, et communis pertur batrix;* and, in *The King* v. *Margaret Cooper, Id.* 1246, the judgment was not rendered as for a common scold; and the last of them was as long ago as 19th *Geo.* 2, nearly eighty years ago.

In *The Queen* v. *Foxby,* 6 *Mod.* 11, in the second of *Anne,* the judgment was likewise arrested for mistake in the indictment. The note of the reporter is, the punishment of a scold is ducking, but the counsel for the prisoner said, "he knew no law for ducking of scolds." Lord HOLT did not give any opinion as to the judgment; he only mentioned that it was indictable in the *Leets, "and that it was better ducking in a Trinity,* than a *Michaelmas* term"—better in warm than in cold weather. But it was too much even for the gravity of the grave and learned Chief Justice of the King's Bench, to treat the subject with any solemnity. In page 178, she was brought up again, (for the sheriff had let her go at large,) and the court let her run again until the next term. *Holt* could not conceal his contempt for this farce of ducking; he sneered at the trebucket, declaring that ducking would only harden the criminal; and, if she were once ducked, she would scold all the days of her life. I think that the trebucket then made its final exit, or afterwards was only heard of in the courts of justice, as *John Doe* and *Richard Roe,* pledges of prosecution; a mere nominal thing.

Judge WILSON, certainly a learned and eminent person, to whom the state committed the revision of her laws, in his third volume, page 311, treats the trebucket with the same contempt with which Lord HOLT had done before

him. After giving the judgment against a common scold, in a public lecture, he sneeringly says—"So she shall be plunged into the water by way of punishment and prevention;" and thus scornfully winds up the trebucket—"Our modern men of gallantry would not surely decline the honour of her company; I therefore humbly propose, that in future, the cucking stool shall be made to hold double." And those only who knew that great man, can form an idea what that look of scorn was.

This cucking stool was a species of the *tumbrellum;*— Lord COKE laments that there was no good *Latin* word for the dung cart, and says, that the pillory and the trebucket were of the dung cart family. By the statute 51 *Hen.* 1., the pillory is the appropriate punishment for the bakers who broke the assize of bread, and the punishment of brocatrix, or a she brewer, is the trebucket. *Barrington St.* 40. Now, I ask, with as much gravity as I can command, if Mrs. *Thrale,* the widow of the great brewer *Thrale,* the rich, learned, accomplished, and fashionable Mrs. *Thrale,* had not put sufficient malt in her liquor, if she should be exposed to the punishment of the cucking stool, and be ducked in stinking water; or if the celebrated Dr. *Johnson,* the leviathan of learning, the executor of Mr. *Thrale's* will, had broken the assize, if the pillory would have been his punishment? for I think we are informed by Mr. *Boswell,* that he saw him in the brewery, attending to its concerns, and bustling about, with his ink-horn tied to the button of his coat: or would he be ducked in *stercore,* for *Jacobs,* in his Dictionary, informs us, the trebucket was a punishment for brewers and bakers, who were ducked in *stercore,* or in stinking water; and we must never forget, that the law professes *equality* of punishment; that the common law, which stamps freedom and equality upon all who are subject to it, which protects and punishes with an equal hand the high and the low, the proud and the humble, I say professes, for in the trebucket punishment we shall presently see, that it was never intended for the rich, and never was inflicted on beauty and youth.

These scolds were indictable in the sheriff's tourn—in terms *de la ley,* this is the definition: "a cucking stool is an engine, invented for the punishment of scolding and unquiet women, and by the judgment in *Eyre,* in the time of *Edward* III., a pillory and a tumbrel were appendant to a leet, *without which right* cannot be administered within the view." Very possibly, as both men and women were in those days rude and disorderly, the women were put in the trebucket and the men in the pillory, for disturbing or making a noise in this great court; and Lord COKE, *Inst.* 219, says, *"furea, pillore et tumbrel appendant al view de frank pledge,* and every one who hath a leet or market, ought to have a pillory and trebucket to punish offenders; for want whereof, the lord may be fined, or his liberty seized." And this is something like the heritable jurisdiction in *Scotland,* only that was more extensive; for it added to the pillory and the tumbrel, the gallows.

There is no ground, whatever may be the antiquated theory of the law, that it now exists in fact and in practice, as a legal punishment. *Barrington* says, it was a punishment formerly used in this country for female offenders, and not confined to the offence of *scolding;* and *Jacobs* says the punishment is disused. Mr. *Morgan,* one of his editors, informs us, that he saw the *remains* of one on a private estate in *Warwickshire;* and Mr. *Tomlins,* in his last edition of this work, mentions there had been one, which had lately been removed, at *Banbury,* in *Oxfordshire,* but that was not a machine for legal punishment, but was used to make sport for the mob, in ducking common women; for this usage, this propensity to ducking women, was pretty inveterate. Old women were generally ducked by the common people, by way of primary or experimental trial, before they were delivered over to the civil magistrate to be hanged as witches. Many of the accused died under the experiment. This does not depend on a work of fiction, (many of which, in the present day, present the real manners and habits of the times in which they lay the scenes,) but on authentic history.

I do not know that all the members of the court agree with me in the conclusion, as to the abrogation of this punishment in *England* by disuse; but in the inquiry most important, there is no difference of opinion. We all agree in this, that this customary ancient punishment for ducking scolds was never adopted, and therefore is not the common law of *Pennsylvania.*

It has been already stated, that the ducking stool, cucking stool, or choaking stool, *(quocunque nomine gaudet,)* and the pillory, the *collisstrigium,* or neck stretch, are punishments, *ejusdem generis,* of the same family, of *the dung cart race*—and were intended, *magis ad ludibrium, quam in poenam.* Barrington 41, 63. In *The King* v. *Beardmore,* Mr. Justice DENNISON says, "that standing with the head in the pillory is by way of disgrace, *ad ludibrium,* which is the intent of this kind of punishment;" and it is very certain, that the legislature never considered the ducking stool a legal punishment, which could be inflicted by the sentence of the law, or when they abolished the pillory and whipping post, &c. they would have included it. The object of the framers of the act of 1790, was the abolition of all infamous, disgraceful public punishments—all cruel and unnatural punishments—for all the classes of minor offences and misdemeanor, to which they had been before applied. This was the object of the author of our humane penal code. I need not mention the name of Mr. *Bradford,* to whom the civilized world is so much indebted; and the wisdom, humanity, and policy of our *Pennsylvania* plan, has crossed the *Atlantic*—*England,* attached as she is to her own system, has adopted ours; and very lately, by stat. 56 *Geo.* 3., has abolished pillory, in all cases but perjury and subornation of perjury. Long before to the honour of her humanity, in the case of punishments inflicted for clergiable offences, she had extended the benefit of clergy to women, provided that the whipping should be in private, and in the presence of the female sex alone, 19 *Geo.* 2. *c.* 26; and I believe the punishment of whipping, as to females, has been altogether abolished.

The late Judge INGERSOLL, a name respected and honoured, when attorney general, in his report to the legislature in 1813, stated, that by several acts of assembly, "cruel and unnatural punishments, which tended only to harden and confirm the criminal, had been abolished for all inferior offences." It is apparent that those two distinguished

men were of opinion, that all infamous corporal punishments, and disgraceful public spectacles, *ad ludibrium,* were abolished; and that the legislature so considered it when they passed the several acts, reforming the penal laws, I think we have the most conclusive evidence.

The sanguinary code of *England* could be no favourite with *William Penn* and his followers, who fled from persecution. Cruel punishments were not likely to be introduced by a society who denied the right to touch the life of man, even for the most atrocious crime. For had they brought with them the whole body of the *British* criminal law, then we should have had the appeal of death, and the impious spectacle of a trial by battle in a Quaker colony; and it is worthy of remembrance, that the charter of *William Penn* empowered him, with the advice and assent of the freemen, to make laws for their own government, and until this was done, the laws of *England,* in respect to real and personal property, and as to *felonies,* were to continue the same. Thus, as to misdemeanors, the common law punishments were not brought over by the first settlers.

The first body of laws, (called the great body of laws,) contains an act passed in 1682, against scolding, imposing the penalty five shillings, or three days' confinement at hard labour. (Chap. 34.) The second act, in 1683, (chap. 12,) inflicts the same penalty, or standing one hour in the most public place, with a gag in the mouth; and, eleven years after this, in 1693, in the petition of right to Governor *Fletcher,* they state the laws contained in that list had not been repealed by the King in council, and that it had pleased the King and Queen so tenderly to regard their happy government, as to confirm their own laws and constitutions, so fitly accommodated to their circumstances, and conclude by earnestly desiring him to govern them according to these laws, including the laws against scolding; and the governor commanded them to be enforced. These acts certainly continued in force until 1700, when another act against scolding passed, inflicting the same penalty, of imprisonment five days at hard labour, or to be gagged and stand at some convenient place, at the discretion of the magistrate. These acts are not in the printed laws, but were procured by me from the secretary's office.

The act of 1700 was repealed by the Queen in council, but I have not been able to find the repeal of the acts of 1682 and 1683. It seems to have been the opinion of the late Judge BRADFORD, that all in the great body of laws was repealed, and I would not venture totally to dissent from so high an authority, though I must confess I think this very doubtful. Nor do I see how, consistently with the charter, this could otherwise be repealed, than by act of assembly. If they were not directly repealed, they were not virtually repealed by the repeal of the act of 1700. Certain of these laws were enforced by indictment in 1685, as appears in *Hall's Journal of Jurisprudence,* (1st vol. No. III. p. 324.) One *Rambo* was tried and convicted of fornication, and enjoined to marry the woman he had seduced, or pay a fine of ten pounds. The law of 1700 differed in some respects; its repeal left the others in full force. Because the people did not obtain a sanction from the crown to the act of 1700, it by no means followed that they were deprived of the former laws, and the common law forced on them. Mr. *Smith,* in his edition of the laws, gives us the heads of the several laws contained in the great body of laws, including these two, and adds this note:—"Most of these laws mentioned in the foregoing list, were subsequently supplied; the remainder became obsolete." Whatever be the fact, the conclusion is the same,—that the common law punishment of ducking was not received nor embodied by usage, so as to become a part of the common law of *Pennsylvania.* It was rejected, as not accommodated to the circumstances of the country, and against all the notions of punishment entertained by this primitive and humane community; and, though they adopted the common law doctrines as to inferior offences, yet they did not follow their punishments. One remarkable instance I will notice. A gross libel in *England* was sometimes punished by the pillory: I believe Mr. *Prynne* lost both his ears. Though the offence is the same here, yet the sentence is very different.

It is not true, that our ancestors brought with them all the common law offences; for instance, that of champarty and maintenance, this court decided in *Stoever* v. *Whitman's Lessee,* 6 *Binn.* 416, did not exist here. I do not find the rule on this subject more satisfactorily laid down any where, than by the Chief Justice, in *The Guardians of the Poor of Philadelphia* v. *Green,* 5 *Binn.* 558. Every country, he observed, had its common law—ours is composed partly of the common law of *England,* and partly of our own usages. Our ancestors, when they emigrated, took with them such of the *English* principles as were convenient for the situation in which they were about to place themselves. By degrees, as circumstances demanded, we adopted the *English* usages, or substituted others better suited to our wants; until before the revolution, we had formed a system of our own, founded in general on the *English* constitution, but not without considerable variation; and in nothing was the variation greater, than in the trial and punishment of crimes. Judge CHASE, in *The United States* v. *Worrall,* 2 *Dall,* 384, on the same subject, thus expresses himself: "When the *American* colonies were first settled by our ancestors, it was held, as well among the settlers as by the judges and lawyers of *England,* that they brought hither as their birthright and inheritance, so much of the common law as was applicable to their local situation and change of circumstances; but each colony judged for itself what part of the common law was applicable to its new condition, and by various modes, by legislative acts, by judicial decisions, or *by constant usage,* adopted some parts and rejected others."

Here all our legislation has been opposed to this punishment—judicial decisions there are none. I cannot give to the two precedents from the Quarter Sessions of *Philadelphia,* the weight of decisions. In *Winn's Dialogues, (Eunomus,)* there is a scale given, by which the weight of legal precedents may be measured. Precedents *sub silentio* would obtain the lowest place. Next above these, (though in comparison the first are almost as the freezing point in the thermometer to the spring temperature,) I consider an opinion of a judge at *nisi prius;* the determination of any court in *Westminster* Hall much higher than this; that very determination confirmed by another court on writ of error; and the highest of all, the determination of the same in a court of last resort. The two instances in the Quarter Sessions, which are principally relied upon to sustain the judgment, are too slight a foundation on which to rest a sentence, so hostile to all the policy and humanity of our penal code, and so much opposed to the sense of the community. Common law rights are to be found in the opinions of lawyers delivered by axioms; or in judicial decisions, well considered and established; or to be collected from the universal usage through the country.

What is the evidence here? In 1769, eighty years after the settlement of the colony, in *The King* v. *Mary Conway,* the indictment was against her as a common scold: she pleaded guilty. The sentence was, that she should be publicly ducked at the end of Market street wharf, in the *Delaware.* All this passed without debate, and, we may presume, without the assistance of counsel for the woman. In 1779, ten years after there was a trial and conviction—*The State* v. *Ann Maize*—and the same sentence. In 1781, there was an indictment for the same offence, against *Mary Swann*—verdict, guilty; continued for advisement; continued from *March,* 1781, to *June,* 1782, when there is this most extraordinary entry:—"Defendant having demeaned herself peaceably, kept under further advisement; and, in the next term, on motion of Mr. *Bankson,* the defendant was recognised, that she will, within one month, leave the neighbourhood and pay the costs." The highly respectable court whose decision we are now revising, were probably governed by these precedents, considering them exclusive evidence of the adoption of this punishment, and making it the law of the land. And I am satisfied that it will afford to every member of it great satisfaction to have the error corrected, in a judgment which they most *conscientiously,* and, as we are informed, most reluctantly gave, having first called upon the defendant's counsel to suggest any reason why it should not be given; and, when it was given, recommending a writ of error, and humanely suspending the execution of the sentence, until the opinion of this court should be taken:—the entry in the last case overturning every thing like proving a settled usage. Why this long delay? Why enter into a compromise with the woman? Why dispense with the judgment of the law? Because they were doubtful of the sentence to be given; therefore they were glad, as well as the neighbourhood, to get rid of her. Mr. *Bradford* was then Attorney General—most probably, all was transacted under his advice—we can thus readily account for this unusual judgment. The Court of Quarter Sessions was, when this judgment was given, composed entirely of men who, (however high their standing in society, and however intelligent,) were unversed in law. Since 1782, until the last case in the Mayor's Court, forty years ran round, and there has been no instance of this punishment. There has been one of an acquittal. That case, therefore proves nothing.

This is a very different question from the common law rules of real and personal property,—the modes of acquisition and alienation of estates. For although the reasons of many of those rules have ceased, yet it might be dangerous, on that account, to abolish them; as it would lessen the security of property, of titles to land, which should always be firm and stable; and, by the charter, they were to remain the same as in *England*, except when altered by the representatives of the people. But I am far from professing the same reverence for all the degrading and ludicrous punishments of the early days of the common law—I am far from thinking that this is an unbroken pillar of the common law, or that to remove this rubbish, would impair a structure, which no man can admire more than I do. But I must confess, I am not so idolatrous a worshipper as to tie myself to the tail of this dung-cart of the common law.

In coming to the conclusion, that the ducking stool is not the punishment of scolds, I do not take into consideration the humane provisions of the constitutions of the *United States* and of this state, as to cruel and unusual punishments, further than they show the sense of the whole community. If the reformation of the culprit, and prevention of the crime, be the just foundation and objects of all punishments, nothing could be further removed from these salutary ends, than the infliction in question. It destroys all personal respect—the women thus punished, would scold on for life, and the exhibition would be far from being beneficial to the spectators. What a spectacle would it exhibit! What a congregation of the idle and disorderly, of black and white spirits! and the day would produce more *scolding*, in this polite city, than would otherwise take place in a year. The city is rescued from this ignominious and odious show, and the state from the opprobrium of the continuance of so barbarous an institution; which would pluck from the brow of our legislators, that diadem of humanity, which the civilized world has awarded. The courts of our sister states of *New York* and *Massachusetts*, governed by the same common law as we are, have declared that this strange and ludicrous punishment no longer exists with them.

Although I admire the impartiality of the first laws against scolding, confirmed by Governor *Fletcher*, in the punishment of men and women equally, as the offence (if it be an indictable one, or within the control of human laws,) would be common to both sexes—yet I cannot applaud their justice or equality, in a country where all are born equally free and independent, and where there is no distinction of ranks; for it is only the poor who are to be gagged—a woman was not gagged for scolding, but because she was so very poor as not to be able to raise five shillings. But this was treading in the steps of ancient legislatures, which punished the peccant member, and commuted the offence for money; and it was following the principle of the tumbril law, which was a punishment and a disgrace, fixed on the poor only; for Lord COKE, in his chapter on the trebucket, says, (3 *Inst.* 220,) "*Nobiles magis plectuntur pecunia, plebii vero in corpore.*"

In considering this question, I own, I have some hesitation in deciding whether the offence of *communis vexatrix* exists as indictable, but I have acceded to the opinion of the Chief Justice and my brother GIBSON; it now is to be considered as indictable and punishable as a common nuisance, by fine, or by fine and imprisonment, at the discretion of the court, the acts of assembly being obsolete, and the common law punishment of ducking, not being received here; and I join in the hope of a learned antiquar-

ian and jurist of our own country, "that we shall hereafter hear nothing of the ducking stool, or other remains of the customs of barbarous ages." *Duponceau on Jurisdiction*, 96. It is therefore the opinion of the court, that the judgment of the Court of Quarter Sessions be reversed.

20

COMMONWEALTH V. WYATT
6 Rand. 694 (Va. 1828)

The first proposition involves a question of the greatest magnitude, which should never be lightly and unnecessarily introduced into the deliberations of this court. Whether this court has authority to declare an act of the general assembly to be unconstitutional, and therefore void, is a question which admits of a great variety of opinion. Judicially to assert or to deny such authority, unless upon an occasion which palpably required such an opinion by the court, would expose it to the censure of all, without calling to its support the talents and influence of those who might concur in the principle asserted, if such principle were palpably applicable to the case decided. This court therefore declines the discussion, not because it would not firmly meet it if a palpable case were to require it, but because the case now under consideration does not require it, further than the notice now to be taken of it.

It is urged that the act of 1823, already referred to, while it properly limits the authority of the court to a reasonable extent of punishment to be inflicted on the party convicted, by imprisonment not less than one nor more than six months, yet authorises the court to inflict the lightest punishment by stripes imaginable, or the most cruel, even extending necessarily to death itself, for an offence of the same character and grade. For that, as the court may impose an imprisonment for six months, and may also direct the party imprisoned to receive any number of stripes, at different times, not exceeding thirty-nine at any one time, during his confinement, at the *discretion* of the court, it is perfectly evident that the court, by virtue of this law, might exercise its discretion to subserve vindictive passions, and so as to direct the party convicted to be subjected to thirty-nine stripes every day of the six months, which would inevitably terminate in death; a death produced by the most *cruel torture*. That by the bill of rights, properly regarded as part of the constitution of Virginia, the general assembly is restrained from authorising by law, "cruel and unusual punishments (to be) inflicted," and that therefore the authority delegated to the courts, as above described by the act aforesaid, being prohibited to the legislature, by the Constitution, cannot by it be delegated to the courts, and that the act aforesaid is therefore void, and ought so to be regarded by this court.

It may be allowed, that the act in question might be regarded as less objectionable, if the aggregate number of stripes, which might be inflicted for any one offence, had been limited as the term of imprisonment is; but this imperfection, if one, does not involve the consequences contended for, nor is it allowed that the discretion of the court mentioned in the act, can rightfully be regarded as unlimited. The responsibility of the court might have been lighter, if the act had been more cautiously dictated; but in all cases, where by law, whether statute or common law, a subject is referred to the discretion of the court, that must be regarded as a *sound discretion,* to be exercised according to the circumstances of each particular case. If the judge should not so limit the authority of his discretion, but extend it further to subserve motives of oppression, or his own vindictive passions, he might and would be impeached. The punishment of offences by stripes is certainly odious, but cannot be said to be *unusual.* This court, regarding the discretion delegated by the act in question, as being of the same character with the discretion always exercised by Common Law Courts to inflict fine and imprisonment, and subject to be restrained by the same considerations, does not feel itself at liberty in this case to refuse to obey the legislative will, nor to execute that will by its judgments.

21

WILLIAM RAWLE, A VIEW OF THE CONSTITUTION
OF THE UNITED STATES 130–32
1829 (2d ed.)

During the arbitrary reigns of the Stuarts in Britain, particularly of the two last, one frequent mode of oppressing those who were obnoxious to the court, was to cause criminal proceedings to be instituted against them, to demand bail in extravagant sums, and on their failing to procure it, to commit them to prison.

When the revolution took place, among other provisions demanded by the people, and readily assented to by William III. was the clause which has been transcribed into this amendment. If excessive bail is demanded by one magistrate, another may moderate it on a *habeas corpus,* issued to the keeper of the prison in whose custody the party is. This power is not, however, to be abused, by reducing the bail below a reasonable sum. In such a case, the latter magistrate would himself be liable to a fine, if the criminal should not *appear* at the appointed time.

Excessive fines constitute one mode of inflicting cruel punishments.

This restriction applies equally to the legislative and to the judicial authority. In respect to the former, however, it is rather to be considered in the light of a recommendation than as a condition on which the constitutionality of the law depends. The judicial authority would not undertake to pronounce a law void, because the fine it imposed appeared to them excessive; and, therefore, if the legislature should commit, and persist in, gross errrors in this respect, the ultimate remedy must be sought among the checks on the legislative power, which will hereafter be brought into view.

The prohibition of unusual punishments applies alike, under the qualifications already noticed, to the legislative and to the judicial power.

The laws of a free country seldom leave the sort of punishment to be inflicted to the discretion of the judge, although the measure or extent of it, as for instance the *quantum* of a limited fine, or the duration of a term of imprisonment, which, by the law is not to be exceeded, is often submitted to him. The peculiar circumstances of each case, the contrition or general good character of the offender, may suggest and justify a moderation of the full extent of the punishment. But a law which subjects an offender to any sort of punishment, is unknown to our civil code. If the law is silent in respect to the mode of punishment, which is sometimes the case when an act is prohibited in general terms, without saying more, the court is understood to be confined to the usual moderate punishment of fine and imprisonment, or one of them. If a fine alone is imposed, imprisonment may be an adjunct, to enforce the payment of it.

The obligation on the legislature not to pass laws inflicting unusual punishments must be considered as subject to some qualification. The established forms of punishment may have proved ineffectual to prevent the commission of some kinds of offences. We may instance the practice of duelling, an offence against God and society, which no law has yet been found sufficient to prevent. It would be no violation of the Constitution if congress, within the sphere of their separate legislation, could by the invention of some new punishment, striking at the false honour which leads folly to the field, put an end to a custom so inhuman and absurd.

SEE ALSO:

Generally Bill of Rights
Georgia Constitution of 1777, art. 59, Thorpe 2:785
Vermont Constitution of 1777, ch. 2, secs. 26, 35, Thorpe 6:3746, 3747
Act of 30 Apr. 1790, secs. 16–18, 1 Stat. 116
Kentucky Constitution of 1792, art. 12, cls. 15–17, Thorpe 3:1275
United States v. *Hamilton,* 3 Dall. 17 (1795)
House of Representatives, Intercourse with the Indians, 9 Apr. 1796, Annals 5:899–904
Palmer v. *Allen,* 7 Cranch 550 (1813)
William Wirt, Powers of the President concerning Bail, 23 June 1818, 1 Ops. Atty. Gen. 213
Illinois Constitution of 1818, art. 8, secs. 13–15, 17, Thorpe 2:982
Barker v. *People,* 3 Cowen 686 (N.Y. 1824), aff'd 20 Johns. 457
William Wirt, Fees of Imprisoned Witnesses, 21 Mar. 1830, 1 Ops. Atty. Gen. 424–46
Joseph Story, Commentaries on the Constitution 3:§§ 1896–97 (1833)

Amendment IX

The enumeration in the Constitution, of certain rights, shall not be construed to deny or disparage others retained by the people.

1

WILLIAM BLACKSTONE, COMMENTARIES 1:120–41
1765

For the principal aim of society is to protect individuals in the enjoyment of those absolute rights, which were vested in them by the immutable laws of nature; but which could not be preserved in peace without that mutual assistance and intercourse, which is gained by the institution of friendly and social communities. Hence it follows, that the first and primary end of human laws is to maintain and regulate these *absolute* rights of individuals. Such rights as are social and *relative* result from, and are posterior to, the formation of states and societies: so that to maintain and regulate these, is clearly a subsequent consideration. And therefore the principal view of human laws is, or ought always to be, to explain, protect, and enforce such rights as are absolute, which in themselves are few and simple; and, then, such rights as are relative, which arising from a variety of connexions, will be far more numerous and more complicated. These will take up a greater space in any code of laws, and hence may appear to be more attended to, though in reality they are not, than the rights of the former kind. Let us therefore proceed to examine how far all laws ought, and how far the laws of England actually do, take notice of these absolute rights, and provide for their lasting security.

The absolute rights of man, considered as a free agent, endowed with discernment to know good from evil, and with power of choosing those measures which appear to him to be most desirable, are usually summed up in one general appellation, and denominated the natural liberty of mankind. This natural liberty consists properly in a power of acting as one thinks fit, without any restraint or control, unless by the law of nature: being a right inherent in us by birth, and one of the gifts of God to man at his creation, when he endued him with the faculty of free-will. But every man, when he enters into society, gives up a part of his natural liberty, as the price of so valuable a purchase; and, in consideration of receiving the advantages of mutual commerce, obliges himself to conform to those laws, which the community has thought proper to establish. And this species of legal obedience and conformity is infinitely more desirable, than that wild and savage liberty which is sacrificed to obtain it. For no man, that considers a moment, would wish to retain the absolute and uncontroled power of doing whatever he pleases; the consequence of which is, that every other man would also have the same power; and then there would be no security to individuals in any of the enjoyments of life. Political therefore, or civil, liberty, which is that of a member of society, is no other than natural liberty so far restrained by human laws (and no farther) as is necessary and expedient for the general advantage of the publick. Hence we may collect that the law, which restrains a man from doing mischief to his fellow citizens, though it diminishes the natural, increases the civil liberty of mankind: but every wanton and causeless restraint of the will of the subject, whether practiced by a monarch, a nobility, or a popular assembly, is a degree of tyranny. Nay, that even laws themselves, whether made with or without our consent, if they regulate and constrain our conduct in matters of mere indifference, without any good end in view, are laws destructive of liberty: whereas if any public advantage can arise from observing such precepts, the control of our private inclinations, in one or two particular points, will conduce to preserve our general freedom in others of more importance; by supporting that state, of society, which alone can secure our independence. Thus the statute of king Edward IV, which forbad the fine gentlemen of those times (under the degree of a lord) to wear pikes upon their shoes or boots of more than two inches in length, was a law that savoured of oppression; because, however ridiculous the fashion then in use might appear, the restraining it by pecuniary penalties could serve no purpose of common utility. But the statute of king Charles II, which prescribes a thing seemingly as indifferent; viz. a dress for the dead, who are all ordered to be buried in woollen; is a law consistent with public liberty, for it encourages the staple trade, on which in great measure depends the universal good of the nation. So that laws, when prudently framed, are by no means subversive but rather introductive of liberty; for (as Mr Locke has well observed) where there is no law, there is no freedom. But then, on the other hand, that constitution or frame of government, that system of laws, is alone calculated to maintain civil liberty, which leaves the subject entire master of his own conduct, except in those points wherein the public good requires some direction or restraint.

The idea and practice of this political or civil liberty flourish in their highest vigour in these kingdoms, where it falls little short of perfection, and can only be lost or destroyed by the folly or demerits of it's owner: the legislature, and of course the laws of England, being peculiarly adapted to the preservation of this inestimable blessing even in the meanest subject. Very different from the modern constitutions of other states, on the continent of Europe, and from the genius of the imperial law; which in general are calculated to vest an arbitrary and despotic power of controlling the actions of the subject in the prince, or in a few grandees. And this spirit of liberty is so deeply implanted in our constitution, and rooted even in our very soil, that a slave or a negro, the moment he lands in England, falls under the protection of the laws, and with regard to all natural rights becomes *eo instanti* a freeman.

The absolute rights of every Englishman (which, taken in a political and extensive sense, are usually called their liberties) as they are founded on nature and reason, so they are coeval with our form of government; though subject at times to fluctuate and change: their establishment (excellent as it is) being still human. At some times we have seen them depressed by overbearing and tyrannical princes; at others so luxuriant as even to tend to anarchy, a worse state than tyranny itself, as any government is better than none at all. But the vigour of our free constitution has always delivered the nation from these embarassments, and, as soon as the convulsions consequent on the struggle have been over, the ballance of our rights and liberties has settled to it's proper level; and their fundamental articles have been from time to time asserted in parliament, as often as they were thought to be in danger.

First, by the great charter of liberties, which was obtained, sword in hand, from king John; and afterwards, with some alterations, confirmed in parliament by king Henry the third, his son. Which charter contained very few new grants; but, as sir Edward Coke observes, was for the most part declaratory of the principal grounds of the fundamental laws of England. Afterwards by the statute called *confirmatio cartarum*, whereby the great charter is directed to be allowed as the common law; all judgments contrary to it are declared void; copies of it are ordered to be sent to all cathedral churches, and read twice a year to the people; and sentence of excommunication is directed to be as constantly denounced against all those that by word, deed, or counsel act contrary thereto, or in any degree infringe it. Next by a multitude of subsequent corroborating statutes, (sir Edward Coke, I think, reckons thirty two,) from the first Edward to Henry the fourth. Then, after a long interval, by *the petition of right;* which was a parliamentary declaration of the liberties of the people, assented to by king Charles the first in the beginning of his reign. Which was closely followed by the still more ample concessions made by that unhappy prince to his parliament, before the fatal rupture between them; and by the many salutary laws, particularly the *habeas corpus* act, passed under Charles the second. To these succeeded *the bill of rights,* or declaration delivered by the lords and commons to the prince and princess of Orange 13 February 1688; and afterwards enacted in parliament, when they became king and queen: which declaration concludes in these remarkable words; "and they do claim, demand, and insist upon all and singular the premises, as their undoubted rights and liberties." And the act of parliament itself recognizes "all and singular the rights and liberties asserted and claimed in the said declaration to be the true, antient, and indubitable rights of the people of this kingdom." Lastly, these liberties were again asserted at the commencement of the present century, in the *act of settlement,* whereby the crown is limited to his present majesty's illustrious house, and some new provisions were added at the same fortunate aera for better securing our religion, laws, and liberties; which the statute declares to be "the birthright of the people of England;" according to the antient doctrine of the common law.

Thus much for the *declaration* of our rights and liberties. The rights themselves thus defined by these several statutes, consist in a number of private immunities; which will appear, from what has been premised, to be indeed no other, than either that *residuum* of natural liberty, which is not required by the laws of society to be sacrificed to public convenience; or else those civil privileges, which society hath engaged to provide, in lieu of the natural liberties so given up by individuals. These therefore were formerly, either by inheritance or purchase, the rights of all mankind; but, in most other countries of the world being now more or less debased and destroyed, they at present may be said to remain, in a peculiar and emphatical manner, the rights of the people of England. And these may be reduced to three principal or primary articles; the right of personal security, the right of personal liberty; and the right of private property: because as there is no other known method of compulsion, or of abridging man's natural free will, but by an infringement or diminution of one or other of these important rights, the preservation of these, inviolate, may justly be said to include the preservation of our civil immunities in their largest and most extensive sense.

I. The right of personal security consists in a person's legal and uninterrupted enjoyment of his life, his limbs, his body, his health, and his reputation.

1. Life is the immediate gift of God, a right inherent by nature in every individual; and it begins in contemplation of law as soon as an infant is able to stir in the mother's womb. For if a woman is quick with child, and by a potion, or otherwise, killeth it in her womb; or if any one beat her, whereby the child dieth in her body, and she is delivered of a dead child; this, though not murder, was by the antient law homicide or manslaughter. But at present it is not looked upon in quite so atrocious a light, though it remains a very heinous misdemesnor.

An infant *in ventre sa mere,* or in the mother's womb, is supposed in law to be born for many purposes. It is capable of having a legacy, or a surrender of a copyhold estate made to it. It may have a guardian assigned to it; and it is enabled to have an estate limited to it's use, and to take afterwards by such limitation, as if it were then actually born. And in this point the civil law agrees with ours.

2. A man's limbs, (by which for the present we only understand those members which may be useful to him in fight, and the loss of which only amounts to mayhem by the common law) are also the gift of the wise creator; to enable man to protect himself from external injuries in a state of nature. To these therefore he has a natural inherent right; and they cannot be wantonly destroyed or disabled without a manifest breach of civil liberty.

Both the life and limbs of a man are of such high value, in the estimation of the law of England, that it pardons even homicide if committed *se defendendo,* or in order to preserve them. For whatever is done by a man, to save either life or member, is looked upon as done upon the highest necessity and compulsion. Therefore if a man through fear of death or mayhem is prevailed upon to execute a deed, or do any other legal act; these, though accompanied with all other the requisite solemnities, are totally void in law, if forced upon him by a well-grounded apprehension of losing his life, or even his limbs, in case of his non-compliance. And the same is also a sufficient excuse for the commission of many misdemesnors, as will appear in the fourth book. The constraint a man is under in these circumstances is called in law *duress,* from the Latin *durities,* of which there are two sorts; duress of imprisonment, where a man actually loses his liberty, of which we shall presently speak; and duress *per minas,* where the hardship is only threatened and impending, which is that we are now discoursing of. Duress *per minas* is either for fear of loss of life, or else for fear of mayhem, or loss of limb. And this fear must be upon sufficient reason; *"non,"* as Bracton expresses it, *"suspicio cujuslibet vani et meticulosi hominis, sed talis qui possit cadere in virum constantem; talis enim debet esse metus, qui in se contineat vitae periculum, aut corporis cruciatum."* A fear of battery, or being beaten, though never so well grounded, is no duress; neither is the fear of having one's house burnt, or one's goods taken away and destroyed; because in these cases, should the threat be performed, a man may have satisfaction by recovering equivalent damages: but no suitable atonement can be made for the loss of life, or limb. And the indul-

gence shewn to a man under this, the principal, sort of duress, the fear of losing his life or limbs, agrees also with that maxim of the civil law; *ignoscitur ei qui sanguinem suum qualiter qualiter redemptum voluit.*

The law not only regards life and member, and protects every man in the enjoyment of them, but also furnishes him with every thing necessary for their support. For there is no man so indigent or wretched, but he may demand a supply sufficient for all the necessities of life, from the more opulent part of the community, by means of the several statutes enacted for the relief of the poor, of which in their proper places. A humane provision; yet, though dictated by the principles of society, discountenanced by the Roman laws. For the edicts of the emperor Constantine, commanding the public to maintain the children of those who were unable to provide for them, in order to prevent the murder and exposure of infants, an institution founded on the same principle as our foundling hospitals, though comprized in the Theodosian code, were rejected in Justinian's collection.

These rights, of life and member, can only be determined by the death of the person; which is either a civil or natural death. The civil death commences if any man be banished the realm by the process of the common law, or enters into religion; that is, goes into a monastery, and becomes there a monk professed: in which cases he is absolutely dead in law, and his next heir shall have his estate. For, such banished man is entirely cut off from society; and such a monk, upon his profession, renounces solemnly all secular concerns: and besides, as the popish clergy claimed an exemption from the duties of civil life, and the commands of the temporal magistrate, the genius of the English law would not suffer those persons to enjoy the benefits of society, who secluded themselves from it, and refused to submit to it's regulations. A monk is therefore accounted *civiliter mortuus,* and when he enters into religion may, like other dying men, make his testament and executors; or, if he makes none, the ordinary may grant administration to his next of kin, as if he were actually dead intestate. And such executors and administrators shall have the same power, and may bring the same actions for debts due *to* the religious, and are liable to the same actions for those due *from* him, as if he were naturally deceased. Nay, so far has this principle been carried, that when one was bound in a bond to an abbot and his successors, and afterwards made his executors and professed himself a monk of the same abbey, and in process of time was himself made abbot thereof; here the law gave him, in the capacity of abbot, an action of debt against his own executors to recover the money due. In short, a monk or religious is so effectually dead in law, that a lease made even to a third person, during the life (generally) of one who afterwards becomes a monk, determines by such his entry into religion: for which reason leases, and other conveyances, for life, are usually made to have and to hold for the term of one's *natural* life.

This natural life being, as was before observed, the immediate donation of the great creator, cannot legally be disposed of or destroyed by any individual, neither by the person himself nor by any other of his fellow creatures, merely upon their own authority. Yet nevertheless it may, by the divine permission, be frequently forfeited for the breach of those laws of society, which are enforced by the sanction of capital punishments; of the nature, restrictions, expedience, and legality of which, we may hereafter more conveniently enquire in the concluding book of these commentaries. At present, I shall only observe, that whenever the *constitution* of a state vests in any man, or body of men, a power of destroying at pleasure, without the direction of laws, the lives or members of the subject, such constitution is in the highest degree tyrannical: and that whenever any *laws* direct such destruction for light and trivial causes, such laws are likewise tyrannical, though in an inferior degree; because here the subject is aware of the danger he is exposed to, and may by prudent caution provide against it. The statute law of England does therefore very seldom, and the common law does never, inflict any punishment extending to life or limb, unless upon the highest necessity: and the constitution is an utter stranger to any arbitrary power of killing or maiming the subject without the express warrant of law. *"Nullus liber homo,* says the great charter, *aliquo modo destruatur, nisi per legale judicium parium suorum aut per legem terrae."* Which words, *"aliquo modo destruatur,"* according to sir Edward Coke, include a prohibition not only of *killing,* and *maiming,* but also of *torturing* (to which our laws are strangers) and of every oppression by colour of an illegal authority. And it is enacted by the statute 5 Edw. III. c. 9. that no man shall be forejudged of life or limb, contrary to the great charter and the law of the land: and again, by statute 28 Ed. III. c. 3. that no man shall be put to death, without being brought to answer by due process of law.

3. Besides those limbs and members that may be necessary to man, in order to defend himself or annoy his enemy, the rest of his person or body is also entitled by the same natural right to security from the corporal insults of menaces, assaults, beating, and wounding; though such insults amount not to destruction of life or member.

4. The preservation of a man's health from such practices as may prejudice or annoy it, and

5. The security of his reputation or good name from the arts of detraction and slander, are rights to which every man is intitled, by reason and natural justice; since without these it is impossible to have the perfect enjoyment of any other advantage or right. But these three last articles (being of much less importance than those which have gone before, and those which are yet to come) it will suffice to have barely mentioned among the rights of persons; referring the more minute discussion of their several branches, to those parts of our commentaries which treat of the infringement of these rights, under the head of personal wrongs.

II. Next to personal security, the law of England regards, asserts, and preserves the personal liberty of individuals. This personal liberty consists in the power of locomotion, of changing situation, or removing one's person to whatsoever place one's own inclination may direct; without imprisonment or restraint, unless by due course of law. Concerning which we may make the same observations as upon the preceding article; that it is a right strictly natural; that the laws of England have never abridged it without sufficient cause; and, that in this kingdom it cannot ever be abridged at the mere discretion of the magistrate, without the explicit permission of the laws. Here again the language of the great charter is, that no freeman shall be taken or imprisoned, but by the lawful judgment of his equals, or by the law of the land. And many subsequent old statutes expressly direct, that no man shall be taken or imprisoned by suggestion or petition to the king, or his council, unless it be by legal indictment, or the process of the common law. By the petition of right, 3 Car. I, it is enacted, that no freeman shall be imprisoned or detained without cause shewn, to which he may make answer according to law. By 16 Car. I. c. 10. if any person be restrained of his liberty by order or decree of any illegal court, or by command of the king's majesty in person, or by warrant of the council board, or of any of the privy council; he shall, upon demand of his counsel, have a writ of *habeas corpus,* to bring his body before the court of king's bench or common pleas; who shall determine whether the cause of his commitment be just, and thereupon do as to justice shall appertain. And by 31 Car. II. c. 2. commonly called *the habeas corpus act,* the methods of obtaining this writ are so plainly pointed out and enforced, that, so long as this statute remains unimpeached, no subject of England can be long detained in prison, except in those cases in which the law requires and justifies such detainer. And, lest this act should be evaded by demanding unreasonable bail, or sureties for the prisoner's appearance, it is declared by 1 W. & M. st. 2. c. 2. that excessive bail ought not to be required.

Of great importance to the public is the preservation of this personal liberty: for if once it were left in the power of any, the highest, magistrate to imprison arbitrarily whomever he or his officers thought proper, (as in France it is daily practiced by the crown) there would soon be an end of all other rights and immunities. Some have thought, that unjust attacks, even upon life, or property, at the arbitrary will of the magistrate, are less dangerous to the commonwealth, than such as are made upon the personal liberty of the subject. To bereave a man of life, or by violence to confiscate his estate, without accusation or trial, would be so gross and notorious an act of despotism, as must at once convey the alarm of tyranny throughout the whole kingdom. But confinement of the person, by secretly hurrying him to gaol, where his sufferings are unknown or forgotten; is a less public, a less striking, and therefore a more dangerous engine of arbitrary government. And yet sometimes, when the state is in real danger, even this may be a necessary measure. But the happiness of our constitution is, that it is not left to the executive power to determine when the danger of the state is so great, as to render this measure expedient. For the parliament only, or legislative power, whenever it sees proper, can authorize the crown, by suspending the *habeas corpus* act for a short and limited time, to imprison suspected persons without giving any reason for so doing. As the senate of Rome was wont to have recourse to a dictator, a magistrate of absolute authority, when they judged the republic in any imminent danger. The decree of the senate, which usually preceded the nomination of this magistrate, *"dent operam consules, nequid respublica detrimenti capiat,"* was called the *senatus consultum ultimae necessitatis.* In like manner this experiment ought only to be tried in cases of extreme emergency; and in these the nation parts with it's liberty for a while, in order to preserve it for ever.

The confinement of the person, in any wise, is an imprisonment. So that the keeping a man against his will in a private house, putting him in the stocks, arresting or forcibly detaining him in the street, is an imprisonment. And the law so much discourages unlawful confinement, that if a man is under *duress of imprisonment,* which we before explained to mean a compulsion by an illegal restraint of liberty, until he seals a bond or the like; he may alledge this duress, and avoid the extorted bond. But if a man be lawfully imprisoned, and either to procure his discharge, or on any other fair account, seals a bond or a deed, this is not by duress of imprisonment, and he is not at liberty to avoid it. To make imprisonment lawful, it must either be, by process from the courts of judicature, or by warrant from some legal officer, having authority to commit to prison; which warrant must be in writing, under the hand and seal of the magistrate, and express the causes of the commitment, in order to be examined into (if necessary) upon a *habeas corpus.* If there be no cause expressed, the gaoler is not bound to detain the prisoner. For the law judges in this respect, saith sir Edward Coke, like Festus the Roman governor; that it is unreasonable to send a prisoner, and not to signify withal the crimes alleged against him.

A natural and regular consequence of this personal liberty, is, that every Englishman may claim a right to abide in his own country so long as he pleases; and not to be driven from it unless by the sentence of the law. The king indeed, by his royal prerogative, may issue out his writ *ne exeat regnum,* and prohibit any of his subjects from going into foreign parts without licence. This may be necessary for the public service, and safeguard of the commonwealth. But no power on earth, except the authority of parliament, can send any subject of England *out of* the land against his will; no not even a criminal. For exile, or transportation, is a punishment unknown to the common law; and, wherever it is now inflicted, it is either by the choice of the criminal himself, to escape a capital punishment, or else by the express direction of some modern act of parliament. To this purpose the great charter declares that no freeman shall be banished, unless by the judgment of his peers, or by the law of the land. And by the *habeas corpus* act, 31 Car. II, c. 2. (that second *magna carta,* and stable bulwark of our liberties) it is enacted, that no subject of this realm, who is an inhabitant of England, Wales, or Berwick, shall be sent prisoner into Scotland, Ireland, Jersey, Guernsey, or places beyond the seas; (where they cannot have the benefit and protection of the common law) but that all such imprisonments shall be illegal; that the person, who shall dare to commit another contrary to this law, shall be disabled from bearing any office, shall incur the penalty of a praemunire, and be incapable of receiving the king's pardon: and the party suffering shall also have his private action against the person committing, and all his

aiders, advisers and abettors, and shall recover treble costs; besides his damages, which no jury shall assess at less than five hundred pounds.

The law is in this respect so benignly and liberally construed for the benefit of the subject, that, though *within* the realm the king may command the attendance and service of all his liegemen, yet he cannot send any man *out of* the realm, even upon the public service; he cannot even constitute a man lord deputy or lieutenant of Ireland against his will, nor make him a foreign embassador. For this might in reality be no more than an honorable exile.

III. The third absolute right, inherent in every Englishman, is that of property: which consists of the free use, enjoyment, and disposal of all his acquisitions, without any control or diminution, save only by the laws of the land. The original of private property is probably founded in nature, as will be more fully explained in the second book of the ensuing commentaries: but certainly the modifications under which we at present find it, the method of conserving it in the present owner, and of translating it from man to man, are entirely derived from society; and are some of those civil advantages, in exchange for which every individual has resigned a part of his natural liberty. The laws of England are therefore, in point of honor and justice, extremely watchful in ascertaining and protecting this right. Upon this principle the great charter has declared that no freeman shall be disseised, or divested, of his freehold, or of his liberties, or free customs, but by the judgment of his peers, or by the law of the land. And by a variety of antient statutes it is enacted, that no man's lands or goods shall be seised into the king's hands, against the great charter, and the law of the land; and that no man shall be disinherited, nor put out of his franchises or freehold, unless he be duly brought to answer, and be forejudged by course of law; and if any thing be done to the contrary, it shall be redressed, and holden for none.

So great moreover is the regard of the law for private property, that it will not authorize the least violation of it; no, not even for the general good of the whole community. If a new road, for instance, were to be made through the grounds of a private person, it might perhaps be extensively beneficial to the public; but the law permits no man, or set of men, to do this without consent of the owner of the land. In vain may it be urged, that the good of the individual ought to yield to that of the community; for it would be dangerous to allow any private man, or even any public tribunal, to be the judge of this common good, and to decide whether it be expedient or no. Besides, the public good is in nothing more essentially interested, than in the protection of every individual's private rights, as modelled by the municipal law. In this, and similar cases the legislature alone can, and indeed frequently does, interpose, and compel the individual to acquiesce. But how does it interpose and compel? Not by absolutely stripping the subject of his property in an arbitrary manner; but by giving him a full indemnification and equivalent for the injury thereby sustained. The public is now considered as an individual, treating with an individual for an exchange. All that the legislature does is to oblige the owner to alienate his possessions for a reasonable price;

and even this is an exertion of power, which the legislature indulges with caution, and which nothing but the legislature can perform.

Nor is this the only instance in which the law of the land has postponed even public necessity to the sacred and inviolable rights of private property. For no subject of England can be constrained to pay any aids or taxes, even for the defence of the realm or the support of government, but such as are imposed by his own consent, or that of his representatives in parliament. By the statute 25 Edw. I. c. 5 and 6. it is provided, that the king shall not take any aids or tasks, but by the common assent of the realm. And what that common assent is, is more fully explained by 34 Edw. I. st. 4. cap. 1. which enacts, that no talliage or aid shall be taken without assent of the arch-bishops, bishops, earls, barons, knights, burgesses, and other freemen of the land: and again by 14 Edw. III. st. 2. c. 1. the prelates, earls, barons, and commons, citizens, burgesses, and merchants shall not be charged to make any aid, if it be not by the common assent of the great men and commons in parliament. And as this fundamental law had been shamefully evaded under many succeeding princes, by compulsive loans, and benevolences extorted without a real and voluntary consent, it was made an article in the petition of right 3 Car. I, that no man shall be compelled to yield any gift, loan, or benevolence, tax, or such like charge, without common consent by act of parliament. And, lastly, by the statute 1 W.&M. st. 2. c. 2. it is declared, that levying money for or to the use of the crown, by pretence of prerogative, without grant of parliament; or for longer time, or in other manner, than the same is or shall be granted, is illegal.

In the three preceding articles we have taken a short view of the principal absolute rights which appertain to every Englishman. But in vain would these rights be declared, ascertained, and protected by the dead letter of the laws, if the constitution had provided no other method to secure their actual enjoyment. It has therefore established certain other auxiliary subordinate rights of the subject, which serve principally as barriers to protect and maintain inviolate the three great and primary rights, of personal security, personal liberty, and private property. These are,

1. The constitution, powers, and privileges of parliament, of which I shall treat at large in the ensuing chapter.

2. The limitation of the king's prerogative, by bounds so certain and notorious, that it is impossible he should exceed them without the consent of the people. Of this also I shall treat in it's proper place. The former of these keeps the legislative power in due health and vigour, so as to make it improbable that laws should be enacted destructive of general liberty: the latter is a guard upon the executive power, by restraining it from acting either beyond or in contradiction to the laws, that are framed and established by the other.

3. A third subordinate right of every Englishman is that of applying to the courts of justice for redress of injuries. Since the law is in England the supreme arbiter of every man's life, liberty, and property, courts of justice must at all times be open to the subject, and the law be duly administred therein. The emphatical words of *magna carta*,

spoken in the person of the king, who in judgment of law (says sir Edward Coke) is ever present and repeating them in all his courts, are these; "*nulli vendemus, nulli negabimus, aut differemus rectum vel justitiam:* and therefore every subject," continues the same learned author, "for injury done to him *in bonis, in terris, vel persona,* by any other subject, be he ecclesiastical or temporal without any exception, may take his remedy by the course of the law, and have justice and right for the injury done to him, freely without sale, fully without any denial, and speedily without delay." It were endless to enumerate all the *affirmative* acts of parliament wherein justice is directed to be done according to the law of the land: and what that law is, every subject knows; or may know if he pleases: for it depends not upon the arbitrary will of any judge; but is permanent, fixed, and unchangeable, unless by authority of parliament. I shall however just mention a few *negative* statutes, whereby abuses, perversions, or delays of justice, especially by the prerogative, are restrained. It is ordained by *magna carta,* that no freeman shall be outlawed, that is, put out of the protection and benefit of the laws, but according to the law of the land. By 2 Edw. III. c. 8. and 11 Ric. II. c. 10. it is enacted, that no commands or letters shall be sent under the great seal, or the little seal, the signet, or privy seal, in disturbance of the law; or to disturb or delay common right: and, though such commandments should come, the judges shall not cease to do right. And by 1 W.&M. st. 2. c. 2. it is declared, that the pretended power of suspending, or dispensing with laws, or the execution of laws, by regal authority without consent of parliament, is illegal.

Not only the substantial part, or judicial decisions, of the law, but also the formal part, or method of proceeding, cannot be altered but by parliament: for if once those outworks were demolished, there would be no inlet to all manner of innovation in the body of the law itself. The king, it is true, may erect new courts of justice; but then they must proceed according to the old established forms of the common law. For which reason it is declared in the statute 16 Car. I. c. 10. upon the dissolution of the court of starchamber, that neither his majesty, nor his privy council, have any jurisdiction, power, or authority by English bill, petition, articles, libel (which were the course of proceeding in the starchamber, borrowed from the civil law) or by any other arbitrary way whatsoever, to examine, or draw into question, determine or dispose of the lands or goods of any subjects of this kingdom; but that the same ought to be tried and determined in the ordinary courts of justice, and by *course of law.*

4. If there should happen any uncommon injury, or infringement of the rights beforementioned, which the ordinary course of law is too defective to reach, there still remains a fourth subordinate right appertaining to every individual, namely, the right of petitioning the king, or either house of parliament, for the redress of grievances. In Russia we are told that the czar Peter established a law, that no subject might petition the throne, till he had first petitioned two different ministers of state. In case he obtained justice from neither, he might then present a third petition to the prince; but upon pain of death, if found to be in the wrong. The consequence of which was, that no

one dared to offer such third petition; and grievances seldom falling under the notice of the sovereign, he had little opportunity to redress them. The restrictions, for some there are, which are laid upon petitioning in England, are of a nature extremely different; and while they promote the spirit of peace, they are no check upon that of liberty. Care only must be taken, lest, under the pretence of petitioning, the subject be guilty of any riot or tumult; as happened in the opening of the memorable parliament in 1640: and, to prevent this, it is provided by the statute 13 Car. II. st. 1. c. 5. that no petition to the king, or either house of parliament, for any alterations in church or state, shall be signed by above twenty persons, unless the matter thereof be approved by three justices of the peace or the major part of the grand jury, in the country; and in London by the lord mayor, aldermen, and common council; nor shall any petition be presented by more than two persons at a time. But under these regulations, it is declared by the statute 1 W. & M. st. 2. c. 2. that the subject hath a right to petition; and that all commitments and prosecutions for such petitioning are illegal.

5. The fifth and last auxiliary right of the subject, that I shall at present mention, is that of having arms for their defence, suitable to their condition and degree, and such as are allowed by law. Which is also declared by the same statute 1 W. & M. st. 2. c. 2. and is indeed a public allowance, under due restrictions, of the natural right of resistance and self-preservation, when the sanctions of society and laws are found insufficient to restrain the violence of oppression.

In these several articles consist the rights, or, as they are frequently termed, the liberties of Englishmen: liberties more generally talked of, than thoroughly understood; and yet highly necessary to be perfectly known and considered by every man of rank or property, lest his ignorance of the points whereon it is founded should hurry him into faction and licentiousness on the one hand, or a pusillanimous indifference and criminal submission on the other. And we have seen that these rights consist, primarily, in the free enjoyment of personal security, of personal liberty, and of private property. So long as these remain inviolate, the subject is perfectly free; for every species of compulsive tyranny and oppression must act in opposition to one or other of these rights, having no other object upon which it can possibly be employed. To preserve these from violation, it is necessary that the constitution of parliaments be supported in it's full vigor; and limits certainly known, be set to the royal prerogative. And, lastly, to vindicate these rights, when actually violated or attacked, the subjects of England are entitled, in the first place, to the regular administration and free course of justice in the courts of law; next to the right of petitioning the king and parliament for redress of grievances; and lastly to the right of having and using arms for self-preservation and defence. And all these rights and liberties it is our birthright to enjoy entire; unless where the laws of our country have laid them under necessary restraints. Restraints in themselves so gentle and moderate, as will appear upon farther enquiry, that no man of sense or probity would wish to see them slackened. For all of us have it in our choice to do every thing that a good man would desire to do; and are restrained from nothing, but what would be pernicious either to ourselves or our fellow citizens. So that this review of our situation may fully justify the observation of a learned French author, who indeed generally both thought and wrote in the spirit of genuine freedom; and who hath not scrupled to profess, even in the very bosom of his native country, that the English is the only nation in the world, where political or civil liberty is the direct end of it's constitution. Recommending therefore to the student in our laws a farther and more accurate search into this extensive and important title, I shall close my remarks upon it with the expiring wish of the famous father Paul to his country, "ESTO PERPETUA!"

2

MASSACHUSETTS HOUSE OF REPRESENTATIVES, CIRCULAR LETTER TO THE COLONIAL LEGISLATURES
11 Feb. 1768
S. Adams Writings 1:185

The House have humbly represented to the ministry, their own Sentiments that His Majestys high Court of Parliament is the supreme legislative Power over the whole Empire: That in all free States the Constitution is fixd; & as the supreme Legislative derives its Power & Authority from the Constitution, it cannot overleap the Bounds of it without destroying its own foundation: That the Constitution ascertains & limits both Sovereignty & allegiance, & therefore, his Majestys American Subjects who acknowledge themselves bound by the Ties of Allegiance, have an equitable Claim to the full enjoymt of the fundamental Rules of the British Constitution. That it is an essential unalterable Right in nature, ingrafted into the British Constitution, as a fundamental Law & ever held sacred & irrevocable by the Subjects within the Realm, that what a man has honestly acquird is absolutely his own, which he may freely give, but cannot be taken from him without his consent: That the American Subjects may therefore exclusive of any Consideration of Charter Rights, with a decent firmness adapted to the Character of free men & Subjects assert this natural and constitutional Right.

3

SAMUEL ADAMS, THE RIGHTS OF THE COLONISTS
20 Nov. 1772
Writings 2:350–59

The Committee appointed by the Town the second Instant "to State the Rights of the Colonists and of this Province in particular, as Men, as Christians, and as Subjects; to communicate and publish the same to the several Towns in this Province and to the World as the sense of this Town with the Infringements and Violations thereof that have been, or from Time to Time may be made. Also requesting of each Town a free Communication of their Sentiments Reported—

First, a State of the *Rights* of the Colonists and of this Province in particular—

Secondly, A List of the *Infringements,* and Violations of those Rights.—

Thirdly, A Letter of Correspondence with the other Towns.—

1st. Natural Rights of the Colonists as Men.—

Among the Natural Rights of the Colonists are these First. a Right to *Life;* Secondly to *Liberty;* thirdly to *Property;* together with the Right to support and defend them in the best manner they can—Those are evident Branches of, rather than deductions from the Duty of Self Preservation, commonly called the first Law of Nature—

All Men have a Right to remain in a State of Nature as long as they please: And in case of intollerable Oppression, Civil or Religious, to leave the Society they belong to, and enter into another.—

When Men enter into Society, it is by voluntary consent; and they have a right to demand and insist upon the performance of such conditions, And previous limitations as form an equitable *original compact.*—

Every natural Right not expressly given up or from the nature of a Social Compact necessarily ceded remains.—

All positive and civil laws, should conform as far as possible, to the Law of natural reason and equity.—

As neither reason requires, nor religeon permits the contrary, every Man living in or out of a state of civil society, has a right peaceably and quietly to worship God according to the dictates of his conscience.—

"Just and true liberty, equal and impartial liberty" in matters spiritual and temporal, is a thing that all Men are clearly entitled to, by the eternal and immutable laws Of God and nature, as well as by the law of Nations, & all well grounded municipal laws, which must have their foundation in the former.—

In regard to Religeon, mutual tolleration in the different professions thereof, is what all good and candid minds in all ages have ever practiced; and both by precept and example inculcated on mankind: And it is now generally agreed among christians that this spirit of toleration in the fullest extent consistent with the being of civil society "is the chief characteristical mark of the true church"* & In so much that Mr. Lock has asserted, and proved beyond the possibility of contradiction on any solid ground, that such toleration ought to be extended to all whose doctrines are not subversive of society. The only Sects which he thinks ought to be, and which by all wise laws are excluded from such toleration, are those who teach Doctrines subversive of the Civil Government under which they live. The Roman Catholicks or Papists are excluded by reason of such Doctrines as these "that Princes excommunicated

may be deposed, and those they call *Hereticks* may be destroyed without mercy; besides their recognizing the Pope in so absolute a manner, in subversion of Government, by introducing as far as possible into the states, under whose protection they enjoy life, liberty and property, that solecism in politicks, Imperium in imperio† leading directly to the worst anarchy and confusion, civil discord, war and blood shed—

The natural liberty of Men by entring into society is abridg'd or restrained so far only as is necessary for the Great end of Society the best good of the whole—

In the state of nature, every man is under God, Judge and sole Judge, of his own rights and the injuries done him: By entering into society, he agrees to an Arbiter or indifferent Judge between him and his neighbours; but he no more renounces his original right, than by taking a cause out of the ordinary course of law, and leaving the decision to Referees or indifferent Arbitrations. In the last case he must pay the Referees for time and trouble; he should be also willing to pay his Just quota for the support of government, the law and constitution; the end of which is to furnish indifferent and impartial Judges in all cases that may happen, whether civil ecclesiastical, marine or military.—

"The natural liberty of man is to be free from any superior power on earth, and not to be under the will or legislative authority of man; but only to have the law of nature for his rule."—

In the state of nature men may as the *Patriarchs* did, employ hired servants for the defence of their lives, liberty and property: and they should pay them reasonable wages. Government was instituted for the purposes of common defence; and those who hold the reins of government have an equitable natural right to an honourable support from the same principle "that the labourer is worthy of his hire" but then the same community which they serve, ought to be assessors of their pay: Governors have no right to seek what they please; by this, instead of being content with the station assigned them, that of honourable servants of the society, they would soon become Absolute masters, Despots, and Tyrants. Hence as a private man has a right to say, what wages he will give in his private affairs, so has a Community to determine what they will give and grant of their Substance, for the Administration of publick affairs. And in both cases more are ready generally to offer their Service at the proposed and stipulated price, than are able and willing to perform their duty.—

In short it is the greatest absurdity to suppose it in the power of one or any number of men at the entering into society, to renounce their essential natural rights, or the means of preserving those rights when the great end of civil government from the very nature of its institution is for the support, protection and defence of those very rights: the principal of which as is before observed, are life liberty and property. If men through fear, fraud or mistake, should *in terms* renounce and give up any essential natural right, the eternal law of reason and the great end of society, would absolutely vacate such renunciation; the

---

*See Locks Letters on Toleration.

†A Government within a Government—

right to freedom being *the gift* of God Almighty, it is not in the power of Man to alienate this gift, and voluntarily become a slave—

2d. *The Rights of the Colonists as Christians*—

These may be best understood by reading—and carefully studying the institutes of the great Lawgiver and head of the Christian Church: which are to be found clearly written and promulgated in the *New Testament*—

By the Act of the British Parliament commonly called the Toleration Act, every subject in England Except Papists &c was restored to, and re-established in, his natural right to worship God according to the dictates of his own conscience. And by the Charter of this Province it is granted ordained and established (that it is declared as an original right) that there shall be liberty of conscience allowed in the worship of God, to all christians except Papists, inhabiting or which shall inhabit or be resident within said Province or Territory.* Magna Charta itself is in substance but a constrained Declaration, or proclamation, and promulgation in the name of King, Lord, and Commons of the sense the latter had of their original inherent, indefeazible natural Rights,† as also those of free Citizens equally perdurable with the other. That great author that great jurist, and even that Court writer Mr. Justice Blackstone holds that this recognition was justly obtained of King John sword in hand: and peradventure it must be one day sword in hand again rescued and preserved from total destruction and oblivion.—

3d. *The Rights of the Colonists as Subjects*

A Common Wealth or state is a body politick or civil society of men, united together to promote their mutual safety and prosperity, by means of their union.‡

The *absolute Rights* of Englishmen, and all freemen in or out of Civil society, are principally, *personal security personal liberty* and *private property.*

All Persons born in the British American Colonies are by the laws of God and nature, and by the Common law of England, *exclusive of all charters from the Crown,* well Entitled, and by the Acts of the British Parliament are declared to be entitled to all the natural essential, inherent & inseperable Rights Liberties and Privileges of Subjects born in Great Britain, or within the Realm. Among those Rights are the following; which no men or body of men, consistently with their own rights as men and citizens or members of society, can for themselves give up, or take away from others

First, "The first fundamental positive law of all Commonwealths or States, is the establishing the legislative power; as the first fundamental *natural* law also, which is to govern even the legislative power itself, is the preservation of the Society."§

Secondly, The Legislative has no right to absolute arbitrary power over the lives and fortunes of the people: Nor can mortals assume a prerogative, not only too high for men, but for Angels; and therefore reserved for the exercise of the *Deity* alone.—

"The Legislative cannot Justly *assume* to itself a power to rule by extempore arbitrary decrees; but it is bound to see that Justice is dispensed, and that the rights of the subjects be decided, by promulgated, standing and known laws, and authorized *independent Judges;*" that is independent as far as possible of Prince or People. *"There shall be one rule of Justice for rich and poor; for the favorite in Court, and the Countryman at the Plough."*‖

Thirdly, The supreme power cannot Justly take from any man, any part of his property without his consent, in person or by his Representative.—

These are some of the first principles of natural law & Justice, and the great Barriers of all free states, and of the British Constitution in particular. It is utterly irreconcileable to these principles, and to many other fundamental maxims of the common law, common sense and reason, that a British house of commons, should have a right, at pleasure, to give and grant the property of the Colonists. That these Colonists are well entitled to all the essential rights, liberties and privileges of men and freemen, born in Britain, is manifest, not only from the Colony charter, in general, but acts of the British Parliament. The statute of the 13th of George 2. c. 7. naturalizes even foreigners after seven years residence. The words of the Massachusetts Charter are these, "And further our will and pleasure is, and we do hereby for us, our heirs and successors, grant establish and ordain, that all and every of the subjects of us, our heirs and successors, which shall go to and inhabit within our said province or territory and every of their children which shall happen to be born there, or on the seas in going thither, or returning from thence shall have and enjoy, all liberties and immunities of free and natural subjects within any of the dominions of us, our heirs and successors, to all intents constructions & purposes whatsoever as if they and every of them were born within this our Realm of England." Now what liberty can there be, where property is taken away without consent? Can it be said with any colour of truth and Justice, that this Continent of three thousand miles in length, and a breadth as yet unexplored, in which however, its supposed, there are five millions of people, has the least voice, vote or influence in the decisions of the British Parliament? Have they, all together, any more right or power to return a single member to that house of commons, who have not inadvertently, but deliberately assumed a power to dispose of their lives,# Liberties and properties, than to choose an Emperor of China! Had the Colonists a right to return members to the british parliament, it would only be hurtfull; as from their local situation and circumstances it is impossible they should be ever truly and properly represented there. The inhabitants of this country in all probability in a few years will be more numerous, than those of Great Britain and Ireland together; yet it is absurdly ex-

---

*See 1. Wm. and Mary. St. 2. C. 18—and Massachusetts Charter.

†Lord Cokes Inst. Blackstone, Commentaries—Vol. 1st. Page 122.

‡See Lock and Vatel—

§Locke on Government. Salus Populi Suprema Lex esto—

‖Locke—

#See the Act of the last Session, relating to the Kings Dock Yards—

pected by the promoters of the present measures, that these, with their posterity to all generations, should be easy while their property, shall be disposed of by a house of commons at three thousand miles distant from them; and who cannot be supposed to have the least care or concern for their real interest: Who have not only no natural care for their interest, but must be *in effect* bribed against it; as every burden they lay on the colonists is so much saved or gained to themselves. Hitherto many of the Colonists have been free from Quit Rents; but if the breath of a british house of commons can originate an act for taking away all our money, our lands will go next or be subject to rack rents from haughty and relentless landlords who will ride at ease, while we are trodden in the dirt. The Colonists have been branded with the odious names of traitors and rebels, only for complaining of their grievances; How long such treatment will, or ought to be born is submitted.

4

CONTINENTAL CONGRESS, DECLARATION AND
RESOLVES
14 Oct. 1774
Tansill 1–5

Whereas, since the close of the last war, the British parliament, claiming a power, of right, to bind the people of America by statutes in all cases whatsoever, hath, in some acts, expressly imposed taxes on them, and in others, under various pretences, but in fact for the purpose of raising a revenue, hath imposed rates and duties payable in these colonies, established a board of commissioners, with unconstitutional powers, and extended the jurisdiction of courts of admiralty, not only for collecting the said duties, but for the trial of causes merely arising within the body of a county.

And whereas, in consequence of other statutes, judges, who before held only estates at will in their offices, have been made dependant on the crown alone for their salaries, and standing armies kept in times of peace: And whereas it has lately been resolved in parliament, that by force of a statute, made in the thirty-fifth year of the reign of King Henry the Eighth, colonists may be transported to England, and tried there upon accusations for treasons and misprisions, or concealments of treasons committed in the colonies, and by a late statute, such trials have been directed in cases therein mentioned:

And whereas, in the last session of parliament, three statutes were made; one entitled, "An act to discontinue, in such manner and for such time as are therein mentioned, the landing and discharging, lading, or shipping of goods, wares and merchandise, at the town, and within the harbour of Boston, in the province of Massachusetts-Bay in North-America;" another entitled, "An act for the better regulating the government of the province of Massachusetts-Bay in New England;" and another entitled, "An act for the impartial administration of justice, in the cases of persons questioned for any act done by them in the execution of the law, or for the suppression of riots and tumults, in the province of the Massachusetts-Bay in New England;" and another statute was then made, "for making more effectual provision for the government of the province of Quebec, etc." All which statutes are impolitic, unjust, and cruel, as well as unconstitutional, and most dangerous and destructive of American rights:

And whereas, assemblies have been frequently dissolved, contrary to the rights of the people, when they attempted to deliberate on grievances; and their dutiful, humble, loyal, and reasonable petitions to the crown for redress, have been repeatedly treated with contempt, by his Majesty's ministers of state:

The good people of the several colonies of New-Hampshire, Massachusetts-Bay, Rhode-Island and Providence Plantations, Connecticut, New-York, New-Jersey, Pennsylvania, Newcastle, Kent, and Sussex on Delaware, Maryland, Virginia, North-Carolina, and South-Carolina, justly alarmed at these arbitrary proceedings of parliament and administration, have severally elected, constituted, and appointed deputies to meet, and sit in general Congress, in the city of Philadelphia, in order to obtain such establishment, as that their religion, laws, and liberties, may not be subverted: Whereupon the deputies so appointed being now assembled, in a full and free representation of these colonies, taking into their most serious consideration, the best means of attaining the ends aforesaid, do, in the first place, as Englishmen, their ancestors in like cases have usually done, for asserting and vindicating their rights and liberties, DECLARE,

That the inhabitants of the English colonies in North-America, by the immutable laws of nature, the principles of the English constitution, and the several charters or compacts, have the following RIGHTS:

Resolved, N. C. D. 1. That they are entitled to life, liberty and property: and they have never ceded to any foreign power whatever, a right to dispose of either without their consent.

Resolved, N. C. D. 2. That our ancestors, who first settled these colonies, were at the time of their emigration from the mother country, entitled to all the rights, liberties, and immunities of free and natural-born subjects, within the realm of England.

Resolved, N. C. D. 3. That by such emigration they by no means forfeited, surrendered, or lost any of those rights, but that they were, and their descendants now are, entitled to the exercise and enjoyment of all such of them, as their local and other circumstances enable them to exercise and enjoy.

Resolved, 4. That the foundation of English liberty, and of all free government, is a right in the people to participate in their legislative council: and as the English colonists are not represented, and from their local and other circumstances, cannot properly be represented in the British parliament, they are entitled to a free and exclusive power of legislation in their several provincial legislatures, where their right of representation can alone be preserved, in all cases of taxation and internal polity, subject only to the negative of their sovereign, in such manner as has been heretofore used and accustomed: But, from the necessity of the case, and a regard to the mutual interest of both countries, we cheerfully consent to the operation of such acts of the British parliament, as are bona fide, restrained to the regulation of our external commerce, for the purpose of securing the commercial advantages of the whole empire to the mother country, and the commercial benefits of its respective members; excluding every idea of taxation internal or external, for raising a revenue on the subjects, in America, without their consent.

Resolved, N. C. D. 5. That the respective colonies are entitled to the common law of England, and more especially to the great and inestimable privilege of being tried by their peers of the vicinage, according to the course of that law.

Resolved, 6. That they are entitled to the benefit of such of the English statutes, as existed at the time of their colonization; and which they have, by experience, respectively found to be applicable to their several local and other circumstances.

Resolved, N. C. D. 7. That these, his majesty's colonies, are likewise entitled to all the immunities and privileges granted and confirmed to them by royal charters, or secured by their several codes of provincial laws.

Resolved, N. C. D. 8. That they have a right peaceably to assemble, consider of their grievances, and petition the king; and that all prosecutions, prohibitory proclamations, and commitments for the same, are illegal.

Resolved, N. C. D. 9. That the keeping a standing army in these colonies, in times of peace, without the consent of the legislature of that colony, in which such army is kept, is against law.

Resolved, N. C. D. 10. It is indispensably necessary to good government, and rendered essential by the English constitution, that the constituent branches of the legislature be independent of each other; that, therefore, the exercise of legislative power in several colonies, by a council appointed, during pleasure, by the crown, is unconstitutional, dangerous and destructive to the freedom of American legislation.

All and each of which the aforesaid deputies, in behalf of themselves, and their constituents, do claim, demand, and insist on, as their indubitable rights and liberties; which cannot be legally taken from them, altered or abridged by any power whatever, without their own consent, by their representatives in their several provincial legislatures.

In the course of our inquiry, we find many infringements and violations of the foregoing rights, which, from an ardent desire, that harmony and mutual intercourse of affection and interest may be restored, we pass over for the present, and proceed to state such acts and measures as have been adopted since the last war, which demonstrate a system formed to enslave America.

Resolved, N. C. D. That the following acts of parliament are infringements and violations of the rights of the colonists; and that the repeal of them is essentially necessary, in order to restore harmony between Great-Britain and the American colonies, viz.

The several acts of 4 Geo. III. ch. 15, and ch. 34.—5 Geo. III. ch. 25.—6 Geo. III. ch. 52.—7 Geo. III. ch. 41. and ch. 46.—8 Geo. III. ch. 22. which impose duties for the purpose of raising a revenue in America, extend the power of the admiralty courts beyond their ancient limits, deprive the American subject of trial by jury, authorise the judges certificate to indemnify the prosecutor from damages, that he might otherwise be liable to, requiring oppressive security from a claimant of ships and goods seized, before he shall be allowed to defend his property, and are subversive of American rights.

Also 12 Geo. III. ch. 24. intituled, "An act for the better securing his majesty's dockyards, magazines, ships, ammunition, and stores," which declares a new offence in America, and deprives the American subject of a constitutional trial by jury of the vicinage, by authorising the trial of any person, charged with the committing any offence described in the said act, out of the realm, to be indicted and tried for the same in any shire or county within the realm.

Also the three acts passed in the last session of parliament, for stopping the port and blocking up the harbour of Boston, for altering the charter and government of Massachusetts-Bay, and that which is entitled, "An act for the better administration of justice, etc."

Also the act passed in the same session for establishing the Roman Catholic religion, in the province of Quebec, abolishing the equitable system of English laws, and erecting a tyranny there, to the great danger (from so total a dissimilarity of religion, law and government) of the neighbouring British colonies, by the assistance of whose blood and treasure the said country was conquered from France.

Also the act passed in the same session, for the better providing suitable quarters for officers and soldiers in his majesty's service, in North-America.

Also, that the keeping a standing army in several of these colonies, in time of peace, without the consent of the legislature of that colony, in which such army is kept, is against law.

To these grievous acts and measures, Americans cannot submit, but in hopes their fellow subjects in Great-Britain will, on a revision of them, restore us to that state, in which both countries found happiness and prosperity, we have for the present, only resolved to pursue the following peaceable measures: 1. To enter into a non-importation, non-consumption, and non-exportation agreement or association. 2. To prepare an address to the people of Great-Britain, and a memorial to the inhabitants of British America: and 3. To prepare a loyal address to his majesty, agreeable to resolutions already entered into.

5

"John DeWitt," no. 2
Oct. 1787

Storing 4.3.8

The Compact itself is a recital upon paper of that proportion of the subject's natural rights, intended to be parted with, for the benefit of adverting to it in case of dispute. Miserable indeed would be the situation of those individual States who have not prefixed to their Constitutions a Bill of Rights, if, as a very respectable, learned Gentleman at the Southward observes, "the People, when they established the powers of legislation under their separate Governments, invested their Representatives with every right and authority which they did not, in explicit terms, reserve; and therefore upon every question, respecting the jurisdiction of the House of Assembly, if the Frame of Government is silent, the jurisdiction is efficient and complete." In other words, those powers which the people by their Constitutions expressly give them, they enjoy by positive grant, and those remaining ones, which they never meant to give them, and which the Constitutions say nothing about, they enjoy by tacit implication, so that by one means and by the other, they became possessed of the whole.—This doctrine is but poorly calculated for the meridian of America, where the nature of compact, the mode of construing them, and the principles upon which society is founded, are so accurately known and universally diffused. That insatiable thirst for unconditional controul over our fellow-creatures, and the facility of sounds to convey essentially different ideas, produced the first Bill of Rights ever prefixed to a Frame of Government. The people, altho' fully sensible that they reserved every tittle of power they did not expressly grant away, yet afraid that the words made use of, to express those rights so granted might convey more than they originally intended, they chose at the same moment to express in different language those rights which the agreement did not include, and which they never designed to part with, endeavoring thereby to prevent any cause for future altercation and the intrusion into society of that doctrine of tacit implication which has been the favorite theme of every tyrant from the origin of all governments to the present day.

6

Federal Farmer, no. 16
20 Jan. 1788

Storing 2.8.199

We must consider this constitution, when adopted, as the supreme act of the people, and in construing it hereafter,

we and our posterity must strictly adhere to the letter and spirit of it, and in no instance depart from them: in construing the federal constitution, it will be not only impracticable, but improper to refer to the state constitutions. They are entirely distinct instruments and inferior acts: besides, by the people's now establishing certain fundamental rights, it is strongly implied, that they are of opinion, that they would not otherwise be secured as a part of the federal system, or be regarded in the federal administration as fundamental. Further, these same rights, being established by the state constitutions, and secured to the people, our recognizing them now, implies, that the people thought them insecure by the state establishments, and extinguished or put afloat by the new arrangement of the social system, unless re-established.—Further, the people, thus establishing some few rights, and remaining totally silent about others similarly circumstanced, the implication indubitably is, that they mean to relinquish the latter, or at least feel indifferent about them. Rights, therefore, inferred from general principles of reason, being precarious and hardly ascertainable in the common affairs of society, and the people, in forming a federal constitution, explicitly shewing they conceive these rights to be thus circumstanced, and accordingly proceed to enumerate and establish some of them, the conclusion will be, that they have established all which they esteem valuable and sacred. On every principle, then, the people especially having began, ought to go through enumerating, and establish particularly all the rights of individuals, which can by any possibility come in question in making and executing federal laws.

7

James Madison, House of Representatives
8 June 1789

Annals 1:439

It has been objected also against a bill of rights, that, by enumerating particular exceptions to the grant of power, it would disparage those rights which were not placed in that enumeration; and it might follow by implication, that those rights which were not singled out, were intended to be assigned into the hands of the General Government, and were consequently insecure. This is one of the most plausible arguments I have ever heard urged against the admission of a bill of rights into this system; but, I conceive, that it may be guarded against. I have attempted it, as gentlemen may see by turning to the last clause of the fourth resolution [the Ninth Amendment].

8

HOUSE OF REPRESENTATIVES, AMENDMENTS TO THE CONSTITUTION
17 Aug. 1789
Annals 1:754–55

The eighth clause of the fourth proposition was taken up, which was, "The enumeration in this constitution of certain rights shall not be construed to deny or disparage others retained by the people."

Mr. GERRY said, it ought to be "deny or impair," for the word "disparage" was not of plain import; he therefore moved to make that alteration, but not being seconded, the question was taken on the clause, and it passed in the affirmative,

9

JOSEPH STORY, COMMENTARIES ON THE CONSTITUTION 3:§ 1898
1833

§ 1898. The next amendment is: "The enumeration in the constitution of certain rights shall not be construed to deny, or disparage others retained by the people." This clause was manifestly introduced to prevent any perverse, or ingenious misapplication of the well known maxim, that an affirmation in particular cases implies a negation in all others; and *é converso*, that a negation in particular cases implies an affirmation in all others. The maxim, rightly understood, is perfectly sound and safe; but it has often been strangely forced from its natural meaning into the support of the most dangerous political heresies. The amendment was undoubtedly suggested by the reasoning of the Federalist on the subject of a general bill of rights.

Amendment X

The powers not delegated to the United States by the Constitution, nor prohibited by it to the States, are reserved to the States respectively, or to the people.

1. Articles of Confederation, art. 2, 1 Mar. 1781
2. James Wilson, Pennsylvania Ratifying Convention, 4 Dec. 1787
3. Federal Farmer, no. 16, 20 Jan. 1788
4. James Madison, Federalist, no. 45, 26 January 1788
5. James Iredell, Proposed Amendment, North Carolina Ratifying Convention, 1 Aug. 1788
6. House of Representatives, Amendments to the Constitution, 18, 21 Aug. 1789
7. St. George Tucker, Blackstone's Commentaries (1803)
8. James Monroe, Views of the President of the United States on the Subject of Internal Improvements, 4 May 1822
9. Joseph Story, Commentaries on the Constitution (1833)

1

ARTICLES OF CONFEDERATION, ART. 2
1 Mar. 1781

ARTICLE II. Each state retains its sovereignty, freedom, and independence, and every Power, Jurisdiction and right, which is not by this confederation expressly delegated to the United States, in Congress assembled.

2

JAMES WILSON, PENNSYLVANIA RATIFYING CONVENTION
4 Dec. 1787
Elliot 2:418–82

Sir, I think there is another subject with regard to which this Constitution deserves approbation. I mean the accuracy with which the *line is drawn* between the powers of the *general government* and those of the *particular state governments*. We have heard some general observations, on this subject, from the gentlemen who conduct the opposition. They have asserted that these powers are unlimited and undefined. These words are as easily pronounced as *limited* and *defined*. They have already been answered by my honorable colleague, (Mr. M'Kean;) therefore I shall not enter into an explanation. But it is not pretended that the line is drawn with mathematical precision; the inaccuracy of language must, to a certain degree, prevent the accomplishment of such a desire. Whoever views the matter in a true light, will see that the powers are as minutely enumerated and defined as was possible, and will also discover that the general clause, against which so much exception is taken, is nothing more than what was necessary to render effectual the particular powers that are granted.

But let us suppose—and the supposition is very easy in the minds of the gentlemen on the other side—that there is some difficulty in ascertaining where the true line lies. Are we therefore thrown into despair? Are *disputes* between the *general* government and the *state* governments to be necessarily the consequence of inaccuracy? I hope, sir, they will not be the enemies of each other, or resemble comets in conflicting orbits, mutually operating destruction; but that their motion will be better represented by that of the planetary system, where each part moves harmoniously within its proper sphere, and no injury arises by interference or opposition. Every part, I trust, will be considered as a part of the United States. Can any cause of distrust arise here? Is there any increase of risk? Or, rather, are not the enumerated powers as well defined here, as in the present Articles of Confederation?

3

FEDERAL FARMER, NO. 16
20 Jan. 1788
Storing 2.8.196–98

Having gone through with the organization of the government, I shall now proceed to examine more particularly those clauses which respect its powers. I shall begin with those articles and stipulations which are necessary for accurately ascertaining the extent of powers, and what is given, and for guarding, limiting, and restraining them in their exercise. We often find, these articles and stipulations placed in bills of rights; but they may as well be incorporated in the body of the constitution, as selected and placed by themselves. The constitution, or whole social compact, is but one instrument, no more or less, than a certain number of articles or stipulations agreed to by the people, whether it consists of articles, sections, chapters, bills of rights, or parts of any other denomination, cannot be material. Many needless observations, and idle distinctions, in my opinion, have been made respecting a bill of

rights. On the one hand, it seems to be considered as a necessary distinct limb of the constitution, and as containing a certain number of very valuable articles, which are applicable to all societies: and, on the other, as useless, especially in a federal government, possessing only enumerated power—nay, dangerous, as individual rights are numerous, and not easy to be enumerated in a bill or rights, and from articles, or stipulations, securing some of them, it may be inferred, that others not mentioned are surrendered. [These appear] to me to be general indefinite propositions without much meaning—and the man [James Wilson] who first advanced those of the latter description, in the present case, signed the federal constitution, which directly contradicts him. The supreme power is undoubtedly in the people, and it is a principle well established in my mind, that they reserve all powers not expressly delegated by them to those who govern; this is as true in forming a state as in forming a federal government. There is no possible distinction but this founded merely in the different modes of proceeding which take place in some cases. In forming a state constitution, under which to manage not only the great but the little concerns of a community: the powers to be possessed by the government are often too numerous to be enumerated; the people to adopt the shortest way often give general powers, indeed all powers, to the government, in some general words, and then, by a particular enumeration, take back, or rather say they however reserve certain rights as sacred, and which no laws shall be made to violate: hence the idea that all powers are given which are not reserved: but in forming a federal constitution, which *ex vi termine*, supposes state governments existing, and which is only to manage a few great national concerns, we often find it easier to enumerate particularly the powers to be delegated to the federal head, than to enumerate particularly the individual rights to be reserved; and the principle will operate in its full force, when we carefully adhere to it. When we particularly enumerate the powers given, we ought either carefully to enumerate the rights reserved, or be totally silent about them; we must either particularly enumerate both, or else suppose the particular enumeration of the powers given adequately draws the line between them and the rights reserved, particularly to enumerate the former and not the latter, I think most advisable: however, as men appear generally to have their doubts about these silent reservations, we might advantageously enumerate the powers given, and then in general words, according to the mode adopted in the 2d art. of the confederation, declare all powers, rights and privileges, are reserved, which are not explicitly and expressly given up. People, and very wisely too, like to be express and explicit about their essential rights, and not to be forced to claim them on the precarious and unascertained tenure of inferences and general principles, knowing that in any controversy between them and their rulers, concerning those rights, disputes may be endless, and nothing certain:—But admitting, on the general principle, that all rights are reserved of course, which are not expressly surrendered, the people could with sufficient certainty assert their rights on all occasions, and establish them with ease, still there are infinite advantages in particularly enumerating many of the most essential rights reserved in all cases: and as to the less important ones, we may declare in general terms, that all not expressly surrendered are reserved. We do not by declarations change the nature of things, or create new truths, but we give existence, or at least establish in the minds of the people truths and principles which they might never otherwise have thought of, or soon forgot. If a nation means its systems, religious or political, shall have duration, it ought to recognize the leading principles of them in the front page of every family book. What is the usefulness of a truth in theory, unless it exists constantly in the minds of the people, and has their assent:—we discern certain rights, as the freedom of the press, and the trial by jury, &c. which the people of England and of America of course believe to be sacred, and essential to their political happiness, and this belief in them is the result of ideas at first suggested to them by a few able men, and of subsequent experience; while the people of some other countries hear these rights mentioned with the utmost indifference; they think the privilege of existing at the will of a despot much preferable to them. Why this difference amongst beings every way formed alike. The reason of the difference is obvious—it is the effect of education, a series of notions impressed upon the minds of the people by examples, precepts and declarations. When the people of England got together, at the time they formed Magna Charta, they did not consider it sufficient, that they were indisputably entitled to certain natural and unalienable rights[;] not depending on silent titles, they, by a declaratory act, expressly recognized them, and explicitly declared to all the world, that they were entitled to enjoy those rights; they made an instrument in writing, and enumerated those they then thought essential, or in danger, and this wise men saw was not sufficient: and therefore, that the people might not forget these rights, and gradually become prepared for arbitrary government, their discerning and honest leaders caused this instrument to be confirmed near forty times, and to be read twice a year in public places, not that it would lose its validity without such confirmations, but to fix the contents of it in the minds of the people, as they successively come upon the stage.—Men, in some countries do not remain free, merely because they are entitled to natural and unalienable rights; men in all countries are entitled to them, not because their ancestors once got together and enumerated them on paper, but because, by repeated negociations and declarations, all parties are brought to realize them, and of course to believe them to be sacred. Were it necessary, I might shew the wisdom of our past conduct, as a people in not merely comforting ourselves that we were entitled to freedom, but in constantly keeping in view, in addresses, bills of rights, in news-papers, &c. the particular principles on which our freedom must always depend.

It is not merely in this point of view, that I urge the engrafting in the constitution additional declaratory articles. The distinction, in itself just, that all powers not given are reserved, is in effect destroyed by this very constitution, as I shall particularly demonstrate—and even independent of this, the people, by adopting the constitution, give many general undefined powers to congress, in the constitutional exercise of which, the rights in question may be effected. Gentlemen who oppose a federal bill of rights, or further declaratory articles, seem to view the subject in a very narrow imperfect manner. These have for their objects, not only the enumeration of the rights reserved, but principally to explain the general powers delegated in certain material points, and to restrain those who exercise them by fixed known boundaries. Many explanations and restrictions necessary and useful, would be much less so, were the people at large all well and fully acquainted with the principles and affairs of government. There appears to be in the constitution, a studied brevity, and it may also be probable, that several explanatory articles were omitted from a circumstance very common. What we have long and early understood ourselves in the common concerns of the community, we are apt to suppose is understood by others, and need not be expressed; and it is not unnatural or uncommon for the ablest men most frequently to make this mistake. To make declaratory articles unnecessary in an instrument of government, two circumstances must exist; the rights reserved must be indisputably so, and in their nature defined; the powers delegated to the government, must be precisely defined by the words that convey them, and clearly be of such extent and nature as that, by no reasonable construction, they can be made to invade the rights and prerogatives intended to be left in the people.

The first point urged, is, that all power is reserved not expressly given, that particular enumerated powers only are given, that all others are not given, but reserved, and that it is needless to attempt to-restrain congress in the exercise of powers they possess not. This reasoning is logical, but of very little importance in the common affairs of men; but the constitution does not appear to respect it even in any view. To prove this, I might cite several clauses in it. I shall only remark on two or three. By article 1, section 9, "No title of nobility shall be granted by congress" Was this clause omitted, what power would congress have to make titles of nobility? in what part of the constitution would they find it? The answer must be, that congress would have no such power—that the people, by adopting the constitution, will not part with it. Why then by a negative clause, restrain congress from doing what it would have no power to do? This clause, then, must have no meaning, or imply, that were it omitted, congress would have the power in question, either upon the principle that some general words in the constitution may be so construed as to give it, or on the principle that congress possess the powers not expressly reserved. But this clause was in the confederation, and is said to be introduced into the constitution from very great caution. Even a cautionary provision implies a doubt, at least, that it is necessary; and if so in this case, clearly it is also alike necessary in all similar ones. The fact appears to be, that the people in forming the confederation, and the convention, in this instance, acted, naturally, they did not leave the point to be settled by general principles and logical inferences; but they settle the point in a few words, and all who read them at once understand them.

4

JAMES MADISON, FEDERALIST, NO. 45, 313–14
26 Jan. 1788

The powers delegated by the proposed Constitution to the Federal Government, are few and defined. Those which are to remain in the State Governments are numerous and indefinite. The former will be exercised principally on external objects, as war, peace, negociation, and foreign commerce; with which last the power of taxation will for the most part be connected. The powers reserved to the several States will extend to all the objects, which, in the ordinary course of affairs, concern the lives, liberties and properties of the people; and the internal order, improvement, and prosperity of the State.

The operations of the Federal Government will be most extensive and important in times of war and danger; those of the State Governments, in times of peace and security. As the former periods will probably bear a small proportion to the latter, the State Governments will here enjoy another advantage over the Federal Government. The more adequate indeed the federal powers may be rendered to the national defence, the less frequent will be those scenes of danger which might favour their ascendency over the governments of the particular States.

If the new Constitution be examined with accuracy and candour, it will be found that the change which it proposes, consists much less in the addition of NEW POWERS to the Union, than in the invigoration of its ORIGINAL POWERS. The regulation of commerce, it is true, is a new power; but that seems to be an addition which few oppose, and from which no apprehensions are entertained. The powers relating to war and peace, armies and fleets, treaties and finance, with the other more considerable powers, are all vested in the existing Congress by the articles of Confederation. The proposed change does not enlarge these powers; it only substitutes a more effectual mode of administering them. The change relating to taxation, may be regarded as the most important: And yet the present Congress have as compleat authority to REQUIRE of the States indefinite supplies of money for the common defence and general welfare, as the future Congress will have to require them of individual citizens; and the latter will be no more bound than the States themselves have been, to pay the quotas respectively taxed on them. Had the States complied punctually with the articles of confederation, or could their compliance have been enforced by as peaceable means as may be used with success towards single persons, our past experience is very far from countenancing an opinion that the State Governments would have lost their constitutional powers, and have gradually undergone an entire consolidation. To maintain that such an event would have ensued, would be to say at once, that the existence of the State Governments is incompatible with any system whatever that accomplishes the essential purposes of the Union.

5

JAMES IREDELL, PROPOSED AMENDMENT, NORTH
CAROLINA RATIFYING CONVENTION
1 Aug. 1788
Elliot 4:249

1. Each state in the Union shall respectively retain every power, jurisdiction, and right, which is not by this Constitution delegated to the Congress of the United States, or to the departments of the general government; nor shall the said Congress, nor any department of the said government, exercise any act of authority over any individual in any of the said states, but such as can be justified under some power particularly given in this Constitution; but the said Constitution shall be considered at all times a solemn instrument, defining the extent of their authority, and the limits of which they cannot rightfully in any instance exceed.

6

HOUSE OF REPRESENTATIVES, AMENDMENTS
TO THE CONSTITUTION
18, 21 Aug. 1789
Annals 1:761, 767–68

[*18 Aug.*]

The 9th proposition, in the words following, was considered, "The powers not delegated by the constitution, nor prohibited by it to the States, are reserved to the States respectively."

Mr. TUCKER proposed to amend the proposition, by prefixing to it "all powers being derived from the people." He thought this a better place to make this assertion than the introductory clause of the Constitution, where a similar sentiment was proposed by the committee. He extended his motion also, to add the word "expressly," so as to read "the powers not expressly delegated by this Constitution."

Mr. MADISON objected to this amendment, because it was impossible to confine a Government to the exercise of express powers; there must necessarily be admitted powers by implication, unless the Constitution descended to recount every minutia. He remembered the word "expressly" had been moved in the convention of Virginia, by the opponents to the ratification, and, after full and fair discussion, was given up by them, and the system allowed to retain its present form.

Mr. SHERMAN coincided with Mr. MADISON in opinion, observing that corporate bodies are supposed to possess all powers incident to a corporate capacity, without being absolutely expressed.

Mr. Tucker did not view the word "expressly" in the same light with the gentleman who opposed him; he thought every power to be expressly given that could be clearly comprehended within any accurate definition of the general power.

Mr. Tucker's motion being negatived,

Mr. Carroll proposed to add to the end of the proposition, "or to the people;" this was agreed to.

[21 Aug.]

The ninth proposition Mr. Gerry proposed to amend by inserting the word "expressly," so as to read "the powers not expressly delegated by the Constitution, nor prohibited to the States, are reserved to the States respectively, or to the people." As he thought this an amendment of great importance, he requested the yeas and nays might be taken. He was supported in this by one-fifth of the members present; whereupon they were taken, and were as follows:

YEAS.—Messrs. Burke, Coles, Floyd, Gerry, Grout, Hathorn, Jackson, Livermore, Page, Parker, Partridge, Van Rensselaer, Smith, (of South Carolina,) Stone, Sumter, Thatcher, and Tucker.—17.

NAYS.—Messrs. Ames, Benson, Boudinot, Brown, Cadwalader, Carroll, Clymer, Fitzsimons, Foster, Gale, Gilman, Goodhue, Hartley, Heister, Lawrence, Lee, Madison, Moore, Muhlenburg, Schureman, Scott, Sedgwick, Seney, Sherman, Sylvester, Sinnickson, Smith, (of Maryland,) Sturges, Trumbull, Vining, Wadsworth, and Wynkoop.—32.

Mr. Sherman moved to alter the last clause, so as to make it read, "the powers not delegated to the United States by the Constitution, nor prohibited by it to the States, are reserved to the States respectively, or to the people."

This motion was adopted without debate.

7

St. George Tucker,
Blackstone's Commentaries
1:App. 185–87
1803

The twelfth article of the amendments to the constitution of the United States, declares, that the powers not delegated to the United States by the constitution, nor prohibited by it to the states, are reserved to the states respectively, or to the people.

The powers absolutely prohibited to the states by the constitution, are, shortly, contained in article 1. section 10. viz.

1. No state shall enter into any treaty, alliance or confederation.

2. Nor grant letters of marque and reprisal.

3. Nor coin money.

4. Nor emit bills of credit.

5. Nor make any thing but gold and silver coin a tender in payment of debts.

6. Nor pass any bill of attainder.

7. Nor any expost facto law.

8. Nor any law impairing the obligation of contracts.

9. Nor grant any title of nobility. . . . Concerning all which, we shall make some few observations hereafter.

All other powers of government whatsoever, except these, and such as fall properly under the first or third heads above-mentioned, consistent with the fundamental laws, nature, and principle of a democratic state, are therefore reserved to the state governments.

From this view of the powers delegated to the federal government, it will clearly appear, that those exclusively granted to it have no relation to the domestic economy of the state. The right of property, with all it's train of incidents, except in the case of authors, and inventors, seems to have been left exclusively to the state regulations; and the rights of persons appear to be no further subject to the control of the federal government, than may be necessary to support the dignity and faith of the nation in it's federal or foreign engagements, and obligations; or it's existence and unity as the depository and administrator of the political councils and measures of the united republics. . . . Crimes and misdemeanors, if they affect not the existence of the federal government; or those objects to which it's jurisdiction expressly extends, however heinous in a moral light, are not cognizable by the federal courts; unless committed within certain fixed and determinate territorial limits, to which the exclusive legislative power granted to congress, expressly extends. Their punishment, in all other cases, exclusively, belongs to the state jurisprudence.

The federal government then, appears to be the organ through which the united republics communicate with foreign nations, and with each other. Their submission to it's operation is voluntary: it's councils, it's engagements, it's authority are theirs, modified, and united. It's sovereignty is an emanation from theirs, not a flame by which they have been consumed, nor a vortex in which they are swallowed up. Each is still a perfect state, still sovereign, still independent, and still capable, should the occasion require, to resume the exercise of it's functions, as such, in the most unlimited extent.

But until the time shall arrive when the occasion requires a resumption of the rights of sovereignty by the several states (and far be that period removed when it shall happen) the exercise of the rights of sovereignty by the states individually, is wholly suspended, or discontinued, in the cases before mentioned: nor can that suspension ever be removed, so long as the present constitution remains unchanged, but by the dissolution of the bonds of union. An event which no good citizen can wish, and which no good, or wise administration will ever hazard.

8

JAMES MONROE, VIEWS OF THE PRESIDENT OF
THE UNITED STATES ON THE SUBJECT OF
INTERNAL IMPROVEMENTS
4 May 1822
Richardson 2:152–55

Having presented above a full view of all the powers granted to the United States, it will be proper to look to those remaining to the States. It is by fixing the great powers which are admitted to belong to each government that we may hope to come to a right conclusion respecting those in controversy between them. In regard to the National Government, this task was easy because its powers were to be found in specific grants in the Constitution; but it is more difficult to give a detail of the powers of the State governments, as their constitutions, containing all powers granted by the people not specifically taken from them by grants to the United States, can not well be enumerated. Fortunately, a precise detail of all the powers remaining to the State governments is not necessary in the present instance. A knowledge of their great powers only will answer every purpose contemplated, and respecting these there can be no diversity in opinion. They are sufficiently recognized and established by the Constitution of the United States itself. In designating the important powers of the State governments it is proper to observe, first, that the territory contemplated by the Constitution belongs to each State in its separate character and not to the United States in their aggregate character. Each State holds territory according to its original charter, except in cases where cessions have been made to the United States by individual States. The United States had none when the Constitution was adopted which had not been thus ceded to them and which they held on the conditions on which such cession had been made. Within the individual States it is believed that they held not a single acre; but if they did it was as citizens held it, merely as private property. The territory acquired by cession lying without the individual States rests on a different principle, and is provided for by a separate and distinct part of the Constitution. It is the territory within the individual States to which the Constitution in its great principles applies, and it applies to such territory as the territory of a State and not as that of the United States. The next circumstance to be attended to is that the people composing this Union are the people of the several States, and not of the United States in the full sense of a consolidated government. The militia are the militia of the several States; lands are held under the laws of the States; descents, contracts, and all the concerns of private property, the administration of justice, and the whole criminal code, except in the cases of breaches of the laws of the United States made under and in conformity with the powers vested in Congress and of the laws of nations, are regulated by State laws. This enumeration shows the great extent of the powers of the State governments.

The territory and the people form the basis on which all governments are founded. The militia constitutes their effective force. The regulation and protection of property and of personal liberty are also among the highest attributes of sovereignty. This, without other evidence, is sufficient to show that the great office of the Constitution of the United States is to unite the States together under a Government endowed with powers adequate to the purposes of its institution, relating, directly or indirectly, to foreign concerns, to the discharge of which a National Government thus formed alone could be competent.

This view of the exclusive jurisdiction of the several States over the territory within their respective limits, except in cases otherwise specially provided for, is supported by the obvious intent of the several powers granted to Congress, to which a more particular attention is now due. Of these the right to declare war is perhaps the most important, as well by the consequences attending war as by the other powers granted in aid of it. The right to lay taxes, duties, imposts, and excises, though necessary for the support of the civil government, is equally necessary to sustain the charges of war; the right to raise and support armies and a navy and to call forth and govern the militia when in the service of the United States are altogether of the latter kind. They are granted in aid of the power to make war and intended to give effect to it. These several powers are of great force and extent, and operate more directly within the limits and upon the resources of the States than any of the other powers. But still they are means only for given ends. War is declared and must be maintained, an army and a navy must be raised, fortifications must be erected for the common defense, debts must be paid. For these purposes duties, imposts, and excises are levied, taxes are laid, the lands, merchandise, and other property of the citizens are liable for them; if the money is not paid, seizures are made and the lands are sold. The transaction is terminated; the lands pass into other hands, who hold them, as the former proprietors did, under the laws of the individual States. They were means only to certain ends; the United States have nothing further to do with them. The same view is applicable to the power of the General Government over persons. The militia is called into the service of the United States; the service is performed; the corps returns to the State to which it belongs; it is the militia of such State, and not of the United States. Soldiers are required for the Army, who may be obtained by voluntary enlistment or by some other process founded in the principles of equality. In either case the citizen after the tour of duty is performed is restored to his former station in society, with his equal share in the common sovereignty of the nation. In all these cases, which are the strongest which can be given, we see that the right of the General Government is nothing more than what it is called in the Constitution, a power to perform certain acts, and that the subject on which it operates is a means only to that end; that it was both before and after that act under the protection and subject to the laws of the individual State within which it was.

To the other powers of the General Government the same remarks are applicable and with greater force. The right to regulate commerce with foreign powers was necessary as well to enable Congress to lay and collect duties and imposts as to support the rights of the nation in the intercourse with foreign powers. It is executed at the ports of the several States and operates almost altogether externally. The right to borrow and coin money and to fix its value and that of foreign coin are important to the establishment of a National Government, and particularly necessary in support of the right to declare war, as, indeed, may be considered the right to punish piracy and felonies on the high seas and offenses against the laws of nations. The right to establish an uniform rule of naturalization and uniform laws respecting bankruptcies seems to be essentially connected with the right to regulate commerce. The first branch of it relates to foreigners entering the country; the second to merchants who have failed. The right to promote the progress of useful arts and sciences may be executed without touching any of the individual States. It is accomplished by granting patents to inventors and preserving models, which may be done exclusively within the Federal district. The right to constitute courts inferior to the Supreme Court was a necessary consequence of the judiciary existing as a separate branch of the General Government. Without such inferior court in every State it would be difficult and might even be impossible to carry into effect the laws of the General Government. The right to establish post-offices and post-roads is essentially of the same character. For political, commercial, and social purposes it was important that it should be vested in the General Government. As a mere matter of regulation, and nothing more, I presume, was intended by it, it is a power easily executed and involving little authority within the States individually. The right to exercise exclusive legislation in all cases whatsoever over the Federal district and over forts, magazines, arsenals, dockyards, and other needful buildings with the consent of the State within which the same may be is a power of a peculiar character, and is sufficient in itself to confirm what has been said of all the other powers of the General Government. Of this particular grant further notice will hereafter be taken.

I shall conclude my remarks on this part of the subject by observing that the view which has been presented of the powers and character of the two Governments is supported by the marked difference which is observable in the manner of their endowment. The State governments are divided into three branches—a legislative, executive, and judiciary—and the appropriate duties of each assigned to it without any limitation of power except such as is necessary to guard against abuse, in the form of bills of right. But in instituting the National Government an entirely different principle was adopted and pursued. The Government itself is organized, like the State governments, into three branches, but its powers are enumerated and defined in the most precise form. The subject has already been too fully explained to require illustration by a general view of the whole Constitution, every part of which affords proof of what is here advanced. It will be sufficient to advert to the eighth section of the first article, being that more particularly which defines the powers and fixes the character of the Government of the United States. By this

section it is declared that Congress shall have power, first, to lay and collect taxes, duties, imposts, and excises, etc.

Having shown the origin of the State governments and their endowments when first formed; having also shown the origin of the National Government and the powers vested in it, and having shown, lastly, the powers which are admitted to have remained to the State governments after those which were taken from them by the National Government, I will now proceed to examine whether the power to adopt and execute a system of internal improvement by roads and canals has been vested in the United States.

9

JOSEPH STORY, COMMENTARIES ON THE CONSTITUTION 3:§§ 1900–1901
1833

§ 1900. This amendment is a mere affirmation of what, upon any just reasoning, is a necessary rule of interpreting the constitution. Being an instrument of limited and enumerated powers, it follows irresistibly, that what is not conferred, is withheld, and belongs to the state authorities, if invested by their constitutions of government respectively in them; and if not so invested, it is retained BY THE PEOPLE, as a part of their residuary sovereignty. When this amendment was before congress, a proposition was moved, to insert the word "expressly" before "delegated," so as to read "the powers not *expressly* delegated to the United States by the constitution," &c. On that occasion it was remarked, that it is impossible to confine a government to the exercise of express powers. There must necessarily be admitted powers by implication, unless the constitution descended to the most minute details. It is a general principle, that all corporate bodies possess all powers incident to a corporate capacity, without being absolutely expressed. The motion was accordingly negatived. Indeed, one of the great defects of the confederation was, (as we have already seen,) that it contained a clause, prohibiting the exercise of any power, jurisdiction, or right, not *expressly delegated*. The consequence was, that congress were crippled at every step of their progress; and were often compelled by the very necessities of the times to usurp powers, which they did not constitutionally possess; and thus, in effect, to break down all the great barriers against tyranny and oppression.

§ 1901. It is plain, therefore, that it could not have been the intention of the framers of this amendment to give it effect, as an abridgment of any of the powers granted under the constitution, whether they are express or implied, direct or incidental. Its sole design is to exclude any interpretation, by which other powers should be assumed beyond those, which are granted. All that are granted in the original instrument, whether express or implied, whether direct or incidental, are left in their original state. All powers not delegated, (not all powers not *expressly* delegated,) and not prohibited, are reserved. The attempts, then, which have been made from time to time, to force upon this language an abridging, or restrictive influence, are utterly unfounded in any just rules of interpreting the words, or the sense of the instrument. Stripped of the ingenious disguises, in which they are clothed, they are neither more nor less, than attempts to foist into the text the word "expressly;" to qualify, what is general, and obscure, what is clear, and defined. They make the sense of the passage bend to the wishes and prejudices of the interpreter; and employ criticism to support a theory, and not to guide it. One should suppose, if the history of the human mind did not furnish abundant proof to the contrary, that no reasonable man would contend for an interpretation founded neither in the letter, nor in the spirit of an instrument. Where is controversy to end, if we desert both the letter and the spirit? What is to become of constitutions of government, if they are to rest, not upon the plain import of their words, but upon conjectural enlargements

and restrictions, to suit the temporary passions and interests of the day? Let us never forget, that our constitutions of government are solemn instruments, addressed to the common sense of the people and designed to fix, and perpetuate their rights and their liberties. They are not to be frittered away to please the demagogues of the day. They are not to be violated to gratify the ambition of political leaders. They are to speak in the same voice now, and for ever. They are of no man's private interpretation. They are ordained by the will of the people; and can be changed only by the sovereign command of the people.

SEE ALSO:

Generally vol. 1, ch. 8; 1.8.18
House of Representatives, Cod Fisheries, 7–8 Feb. 1792, Annals 3:393–96, 397–400
State v. Antonio, 2 Treadway 776 (S.C. 1816)
James Kent, Commentaries 1:363–79 (1826)
State v. Tutt, 2 Bailey 44 (S.C. 1830)

Amendment XI

The Judicial power of the United States shall not be construed to extend to any suit in law or equity, commenced or prosecuted against one of the United States by Citizens of another State, or by Citizens or Subjects of any Foreign State.

The Eleventh Amendment was proposed by Congress on 4 Mar. 1794, when it passed the House, having previously passed the Senate on 14 Jan. (Annals 4:30–31, 477–78). It appears officially in 1 Stat. 402. Ratification was completed on 7 Feb. 1795, when the twelfth State (North Carolina) approved the amendment, there being then fifteen States in the Union. Official announcement of ratification was not made until 8 Jan. 1798, when President John Adams in a message to Congress stated that the 11th Amendment had been adopted by three-fourths of the States and that it "may now be deemed to be a part of the Constitution"

(Richardson 1:260). In the interim South Carolina had ratified, and Tennessee had been admitted into the Union as the sixteenth State.

The several State legislatures ratified the Eleventh Amendment on the following dates: New York, 27 Mar. 1794; Rhode Island, 31 Mar. 1794; Connecticut, 8 May 1794; New Hampshire, 16 June 1794; Massachusetts, 26 June 1794; Vermont, between 9 Oct. and 9 Nov. 1794; Virginia, 18 Nov. 1794; Georgia, 29 Nov. 1794; Kentucky, 7 Dec. 1794; Maryland, 26 Dec. 1794; Delaware, 23 Jan. 1795; North Carolina, 7 Feb. 1795; South Carolina, 4 Dec. 1797.

---

1. *Chisholm v. Georgia*, 2 Dall. 419 (1793)
2. *Hollingsworth v. Virginia*, 3 Dall. 378 (1798)
3. *Cohens v. Virginia*, 6 Wheat. 264 (1821)
4. *Osborn v. Bank of the United States*, 9 Wheat. 738 (1824)
5. *Bank of the United States* v. *Planters' Bank of Georgia*, 9 Wheat. 904 (1824)

1

CHISHOLM V. GEORGIA
2 Dall. 419 (1793)

IREDELL, Justice.—This great cause comes before the court, on a motion made by the attorney-general, that an order be made by the court to the following effect: "That unless the state of Georgia shall, after reasonable notice of this motion, cause an appearance to be entered on behalf of the said state, on the fourth day of next term, or show cause to the contrary, judgment shall be entered for the plaintiff, and a writ of inquiry shall be awarded." Before such an order be made, it is proper that this court should be satisfied it hath cognisance of the suit; for, to be sure, we ought not to enter a conditional judgment (which this would be), in a case where we were not fully persuaded we had authority to do so.

This is the first instance wherein the important question involved in this cause has come regularly before the court. In the Maryland case, it did not, because the attorney-general of the state voluntarily appeared. We could not, therefore, without the greatest impropriety, have taken up the question suddenly. That case has since been compromised; but had it proceeded to trial, and a verdict been given for the plaintiff, it would have been our duty, previous to our giving judgment, to have well considered whether we were warranted in giving it. I had then great doubts upon my mind, and should, on such a case, have proposed a discussion of the subject. Those doubts have increased since, and after the fullest consideration I have been able to bestow on the subject, and the most respectful attention to the able argument of the attorney-general, I am now decidedly of opinion, that no such action as this before the court can legally be maintained.

The action is an action of *assumpsit*. The particular question then before the court, is, will an action of *assumpsit* lie against a state? This particular question (abstracted from the general one, viz., whether, a state can in any instance be sued?) I took the liberty to propose to the consideration of the attorney-general, last term. I did so, because I have often found a great deal of confusion to arise from taking too large a view at once, and I had found myself embarrassed on this very subject, until I considered the abstract question itself. The attorney-general has spoken to it, in deference to my request, as he has been pleased to intimate, but he spoke to this particular question slightly, conceiving it to be involved in the general one; and after establishing, as he thought, that point, he seemed to consider the other followed of course. He expressed, indeed, some doubt how to prove what appeared so plain. It seemed to him (if I recollect right), to depend principally on the solution of this simple question; can a state assume? But the attorney-general must know, that in England, certain judicial proceedings, not inconsistent with the sovereignty, may take place against the crown, but that an ac-

tion of *assumpsit* will not lie. Yet, surely, the King can assume as well as a state. So can the United States themselves, as well as any state in the Union: yet, the attorney-general himself has taken some pains to show, that no action whatever is maintainable against the United States. I shall, therefore, confine myself, as much as possible, to the particular question before the court, though every thing I have to say upon it will effect every kind of suit, the object of which is to compel the payment of money by a state.

The question, as I before observed, is—will an action of *assumpsit* lie against a state? If it will, it must be in virtue of the constitution of the United States, and of some law of congress conformable thereto. The part of the constitution concerning the judicial power, is as follows, viz: Art. III., § 2. The judicial power shall extend, (1) To all cases, in law and equity, arising under the constitution, the laws of the United States, and treaties made, or which shall be made, under their authority: (2) To all cases affecting ambassadors, or other public ministers and consuls: (3) To all cases of admiralty and maritime jurisdiction: (4) To all controversies to which the United States shall be a party: (5) To controversies between two or more states; between a state and citizens of another state; between citizens of different states; between citizens of the same state, claiming lands under grants of different states; and between a state or the citizens thereof, and foreign states, citizens or subjects. The constitution, therefore, provides for the jurisdiction wherein a state is a party, in the following instances: 1st. Controversies between two or more states: 2d. Controversies between a state and citizens of another state: 3d. Controversies between a state, and foreign states, citizens or subjects. And it also provides, that in all cases in which a state shall be a party, the supreme court shall have original jurisdiction.

The words of the general judicial act, conveying the authority of the supreme court, under the constitution, so far as they concern this question, are as follows: § 13. "That the supreme court shall have exclusive jurisdiction of all controversies of a civil nature, where a state is a party, except between a state and its citizens; and except also, between a state and citizens of other states or aliens, in which latter case, it shall have original, but not exclusive jurisdiction. And shall have, exclusively, all jurisdiction of suits or proceedings against ambassadors or other public ministers, or their domestics or domestic servants, as a court of law can have or exercise consistently with the law of nations; and original, but not exclusive jurisdiction, of all suits brought by ambassadors or other public ministers, or in which a consul or vice-consul shall be a party."

The supreme court hath, therefore, *first*, exclusive jurisdiction in every controversy of a civil nature: 1st. Between two or more states: 2d. Between a state and a foreign state: 3d. Where a suit or proceeding is depending against ambassadors, other public ministers, or their domestics or domestic servants. *Second*, original, but not exclusive jurisdiction, 1st. Between a state and citizens of other states: 2d. Between a state and foreign citizens or subjects: 3d. Where a suit is brought by ambassadors or other public ministers: 4th. Where a consul or vice-consul is a party. The suit now before the court (if maintainable at all) comes within the latter description, it being a suit against a state by a citizen of another state.

The constitution is particular in expressing the parties who may be the objects of the jurisdiction in any of these cases, but in respect to the subject matter upon which such jurisdiction is to be exercised, used the word "controversies" only. The act of congress more particularly mentions civil controversies, a qualification of the general word in the constitution, which I do not doubt every reasonable man will think well warranted, for it cannot be presumed, that the general word "controversies" was intended to include any proceedings that relate to criminal cases, which in all instances that respect the same governor only, are uniformly considered of a local nature, and to be decided by its particular laws. The word "controversy" indeed, would not naturally justify any such construction, but nevertheless it was perhaps a proper instance of caution in congress to guard against the possibility of it.

A general question of great importance here occurs. What controversy of a civil nature can be maintained against a state by an individual? The framers of the constitution, I presume, must have meant one of two things— Either, 1. In the conveyance of that part of the judicial power which did not relate to the execution of the other authorities of the general government (which it must be admitted are full and discretionary, within the restrictions of the constitution itself), to refer to antecedent laws for the construction of the general words they use: or, 2. To enable congress in all such cases to pass all such laws as they might deem necessary and proper to carry the purposes of this constitution into full effect, either absolutely at their discretion, or, at least, in cases where prior laws were deficient for such purposes, if any such deficiency existed.

The attorney-general has indeed suggested another construction, a construction, I confess, that I never heard of before, nor can I now consider it grounded on any solid foundation, though it appeared to me to be the basis of the attorney-general's argument. His construction I take to be this: "That the moment a supreme court is formed, it is to exercise all the judicial power vested in it by the constitution, by its own authority, whether the legislature has prescribed methods of doing so, or not." My conception of the constitution is entirely different. I conceive, that all the courts of the United States must receive, not merely their *organization* as to the number of judges of which they are to consist; but all their authority, as to the manner of their proceeding, from the legislature only. This appears to me to be one of those cases, with many others, in which an article of the constitution cannot be effectuated, without the intervention of the legislative authority. There being many such, at the end of the special enumeration of the powers of congress in the constitution, is this general one: "To make all laws which shall be necessary and proper for carrying into execution the foregoing powers, and all other powers vested by this constitution in the government of the United States, or in any department or officer thereof." None will deny, that an act of legislation is nec-

essary to say, at least, of what number the judges are to consist; the President, with the consent of the senate, could not nominate a number at their discretion. The constitution intended this article so far, at least, to be the subject of a legislative act. Having a right thus to establish the court, and it being capable of being established in no other manner, I conceive it necessarily follows, that they are also to direct the manner of its proceedings. Upon this authority, there is, that I know, but one limit; that is, "that they shall not exceed their authority." If they do, I have no hesitation to say, that any act to that effect would be utterly void, because it would be inconsistent with the constitution, which is a fundamental law, paramount to all others, which we are not only bound to consult, but sworn to observe; and therefore, where there is an interference, being superior in obligation to the other, we must unquestionably obey that in preference. Subject to this restriction, the whole business of organizing the courts, and directing the methods of their proceeding, where necessary, I conceive to be in the discretion of congress. If it shall be found, on this occasion, or on any other, that the remedies now in being are defective, for any purpose, it is their duty to provide for, they no doubt will provide others. It is their duty to *legislate*, so far as is necessary to carry the constitution into effect. It is *ours* only to *judge*. We have no reason, nor any more right to distrust their doing their duty, than they have to distrust that we all do ours. There is no part of the constitution that I know of, that authorizes this court to take up any business where they left it, and in order that the powers given in the constitution may be in full activity, supply their omission by making *new laws* for *new cases;* or, which I take to be the same thing, applying *old principles* to *new cases* materially different from those to which they were applied before.

With regard to the attorney-general's doctrine of incidents, that was founded entirely on the supposition of the other I have been considering. The authority contended for is certainly not one of those necessarily incident to all courts merely as such.

If therefore, this court is to be (as I consider it) the organ of the constitution and the law, not of the *constitution* only, in respect to the manner of its proceeding, we must receive our directions from the legislature in this particular, and have no right to constitute ourselves an *officina brevium*, or take any other short method of doing what the constitution has chosen (and, in my opinion, with the most perfect propriety) should be done, in another manner.

But the act of congress has not been altogether silent upon this subject. The 14th section of the judicial act, provides in the following words: "All the before-mentioned courts of the United States shall have power to issue writs of *scire facias, habeas corpus,* and all other writs not specially provided for by statute, which may be necessary for the exercise of their respective jurisdictions, and agreeable to the principles and usages of law." These words refer as well to the supreme court as to the other courts of the United States. Whatever writs we issue, that are necessary for the exercise of our jurisdiction, must be agreeable to the principles and usages of law. This is a direction, I apprehend, we cannot supersede, because it may appear to us not sufficiently extensive. If it be not, we must wait until other remedies are provided by the same authority. From this it is plain, that the legislature did not choose to leave to our own discretion the path to justice, but has prescribed one of its own. In doing so, it has, I think, wisely, referred us to principles and usages of law, already well known, and by their precision calculated to guard against that innovating spirit of courts of justice, which the attorney-general, in another case, reprobated with so much warmth, and with whose sentiments in that particular, I most cordially join.The principles of law to which reference is to be had, either upon the general ground I first alluded to, or upon the special words I have above cited, from the judicial act, I apprehend, can be, either, 1st. Those of the particular laws of the state, against which the suit is brought. Or 2d. Principles of law, common to all the states. I omit any consideration arising from the word "usages," though a still stronger expression. In regard to the principles of the particular laws of the state of Georgia, if they in any manner differed, so as to affect this question, from the principles of law, common to all the states, it might be material to inquire, whether, there would be any propriety or congruity in laying down a rule of decision which would induce this consequence, that an action would lie in the supreme court against some states, whose laws admitted of a compulsory remedy against their own governments, but not against others, wherein no such remedy was admitted, or which would require, perhaps, if the principle was received, fifteen different methods of proceeding against states, all standing in the same political relation to the general government, and none having any pretence to a distinction in its favor, or justly liable to any distinction to its prejudice. If any such difference existed in the laws of the different states, there would seem to be a propriety, in order to induce uniformity (if a constitutional power for that purpose exists), that congress should prescribe a rule, fitted to this new case, to which no equal, uniform and impartial mode of proceeding could otherwise be applied.

But this point, I conceive, it is unnecessary to determine, because I believe there is no doubt, that neither in the state now in question, nor in any other in the Union, any particular legislative mode, authorizing a compulsory suit for the recovery of money against a state, was in being, either when the constitution was adopted, or at the time the judicial act was passed. Since that time, an act of assembly for such a purpose has been passed in Georgia. But that surely could have no influence in the construction of an act of the legislature of the United States, passed before.

The only principles of law, then, that can be regarded, are those common to all the states. I know of none such, which can affect this case, but those that are derived from what is properly termed "the common law," a law which I presume is the ground-work of the laws in every state in the Union, and which I consider, so far as it is applicable to the peculiar circumstances of the country, and where no special act of legislation controls it, to be in force in each state, as it existed in England (unaltered by any stat-

ute), at the time of the first settlement of the country. The statutes of England that are in force in America differ perhaps in all the states; and therefore, it is probable, the common law in each is in some respects different. But it is certain, that in regard to any common-law principle which can influence the question before us, no alteration has been made by any statute, which could occasion the least material difference, or have any partial effect. No other part of the common law of England, it appears to me, can have any reference to this subject, but that part of it which prescribes remedies against the crown. Every state in the Union, in every instance where its sovereignty has not been delegated to the United States, I consider to be as completely sovereign, as the United States are in respect to the powers surrendered. The United States are sovereign as to all the powers of government actually surrendered: each state in the Union is sovereign, as to all the powers reserved. It must necessarily be so, because the United States have no claim to any authority but such as the states have surrendered to them: of course, the part not surrendered must remain as it did before. The powers of the general government, either of a legislative or executive nature, or which particularly concerns treaties with foreign powers, do for the most part (if not wholly) affect individuals, and not states: they require no aid from any state authority. This is the great leading distinction between the old articles of confederation, and the present constitution. The judicial power is of a peculiar kind. It is indeed commensurate with the ordinary legislative and executive powers of the general government, and the power which concerns treaties. But it also goes further. Where certain parties are concerned, although the subject in controversy does not relate to any of the special objects of authority of the general government, wherein the separate sovereignties of the states are blended in one common mass of supremacy, yet the general government has a judicial authority in regard to such subjects of controversy, and the legislature of the United States may pass all laws necessary to give such judicial authority its proper effect. So far as states, under the constitution, can be made legally liable to this authority, so far, to be sure, they are subordinate to the authority of the United States, and their individual sovereignty is in this respect limited. But it is limited no further than the necessary execution of such authority requires. The authority extends only to the decision of controversies in which a state is a party, and providing laws necessary for that purpose. That surely can refer only to such controversies in which a state *can* be a party; in respect to which, if any question arises, it can be determined, according to the principles I have supported, in no other manner than by a reference either to pre-existent laws, or laws passed under the constitution and in conformity to it.

Whatever be the true construction of the constitution in this particular; whether it is to be construed as intending merely a transfer of jurisdiction from one tribunal to another, or as authorizing the legislature to provide laws for the decision of all possible controversies in which a state may be involved with an individual, without regard to any prior exemption; yet it is certain, that the legislature has in fact proceeded upon the former supposition, and not upon the latter. For, besides what I noticed before, as to an express reference to principles and usages of law, as the guide of our proceeding, it is observable, that in instances like this before the court, this court hath a *concurrent jurisdiction* only; the present being one of those cases where, by the judicial act, this court hath *original* but not *exclusive* jurisdiction. This court, therefore, under that act, can exercise no authority, in such instances, but such authority as, from the subject-matter of it, may be exercised in some other court. There are no courts with which such a concurrence can be suggested but the circuit courts, or courts of the different states. With the former, it cannot be, for admitting that the constitution is not to have a restrictive operation, so as to confine all cases in which a state is a party, exclusively to the supreme court (an opinion to which I am strongly inclined), yet, there are no words in the definition of the powers of the circuit court, which give a color to an opinion, that where a suit is brought against a state, by a citizen of another state, the circuit court could exercise any jurisdiction at all. If they could, however, such a jurisdiction, by the very terms of their authority, could be only concurrent with the courts of the several states. It follows, therefore, unquestionably, I think, that looking at the act of congress, which I consider is on this occasion the limit of our authority (whatever further might be constitutionally enacted), we can exercise no authority, in the present instance, consistently with the clear intention of the act, but such as a proper state court would have been, at least, competent to exercise, at the time the act was passed.

If, therefore, no new remedy be provided (as plainly is the case), and consequently, we have no other rule to govern us, but the principles of the pre-existent laws, which must remain in force until superseded by others, then it is incumbent upon us to inquire, whether, previous to the adoption of the constitution (which period, or the period of passing the law, in respect to the object of this inquiry, is perfectly equal), an action of the nature like this before the court could have been maintained against one of the states in the Union, upon the principles of the common law, which I have shown to be alone applicable. If it could, I think, it is now maintainable here: if it could not, I think, as the law stands at present, it is not maintainable; whatever opinion may be entertained, upon the construction of the constitution as to the power of congress to authorize such a one. Now, I presume, it will not be denied, that in every state in the Union, previous to the adoption of the constitution, the only common-law principles in regard to suits that were in any manner admissible in respect to claims against the state, were those which, in England, apply to claims against the crown; there being certainly no other principles of the common law which, previous to the adoption of this constitution, could, in any manner, or upon any color, apply to the case of a claim against a state, in its own courts, where it was solely and completely sovereign, in respect to such cases, at least. Whether that remedy was strictly applicable or not, still, I apprehend, there was no other. The only remedy, in a case like that before the court, by which, by any possibility, a suit can be maintained against the crown, in England, or, at any period from which the common law, as in force in America, could be derived, I believe, is that which is called a *Petition of right*. It is stated, indeed, in Com. Dig. 105, that "until the time of Edward I., the King might have been sued in all actions, as a common person." And some authorities are cited for that position, though it is even there stated as a doubt. But the same authority adds—"but now, none can have an action against the King, but one shall be put to sue to him by petition." This appears to be a quotation or abstract from Theloall's Digest, which is also one of the authorities quoted in the former case. And this book appears (from the law catalogue) to have been printed so long ago as the year 1579. The same doctrine appears (according to a quotation in Blackstone's Commentaries, 1 vol. 243) to be stated in Finch's Law 253, the first edition of which, it seems, was published in 1579. This also more fully appears in the case of *The Bankers,* and particularly from the celebrated argument of SOMERS, in the time of Wm. III., for, though that case was ultimately decided against Lord SOMERS's opinion, yet, the ground on which the decision was given, no way invalidates the reasoning of that argument, so far as it respects the simple case of a sum of money demandable from the King, and not by him secured on any particular revenues. The case is reported in Freeman, vol. 1, p. 331; 5 Mod. 29; Skin. 601; and lately very elaborately in a small pamphlet published by Mr. Hargrave, which contains all the reports at length, except Skinner's, together with the argument at large of Lord Somers; besides some additional matter.

The substance of the case was as follows: King Charles II. having received large sums of money from bankers, on the credit of the growing produce of the revenue, for the payment of which, tallies and orders of the exchequer were given (afterwards made transferable by statute), and the payment of these having been afterwards postponed, the King at length, in order to relieve the bankers, in 1677, granted annuities to them out of the hereditary excise, equal to six per cent. interest on their several debts, but redeemable on payment of the principal. This interest was paid until 1683, but it then became in arrear, and continued so at the revolution; and the suits which were commenced to enforce the payment of these arrears, were the subject of this case. The bankers presented a petition to the barons of the exchequer, for the payment of the arrears of the annuities granted; to which petition the attorney-general demurred. Two points were made: First, whether the grant out of the excise was good; second, whether a petition to the barons of the exchequer was a proper remedy. On the first point, the whole court agreed, that, in general, the King could alienate the revenues of the crown; but Mr. Baron Lechmere differed from the other barons, by thinking that this particular revenue of the excise, was an exception to the general rule. But all agreed, that the petition was a proper remedy. Judgment was, therefore, given for the petition, by directing payment to the complainants, at the receipt of the exchequer. A writ of error was brought on this judgment, by the attorney-general, in the exchequer-chamber. There, all the judges who argued held the grant out of the excise good.

A majority of them, including Lord Chief Justice Holt, also approved of the remedy by petition to the barons. But Lord Chief Justice Treby was of opinion, that the barons of the exchequer were not authorized to make order for payments on the receipt of the exchequer, and therefore, that the remedy by petition to the barons was inapplicable. In this opinion, Lord Somers concurred. A doubt then arose, whether the Lord Chancellor and Lord High Treasurer were at liberty to give judgment, according to their own opinion, in opposition to that of a majority of the attendant judges; in other words, whether the judges called by the Lord Chancellor and Lord High Treasurer were to be considered as mere assistants to them, without voices. The opinion of the judges being taken on this point, seven against three, held, that the Lord Chancellor and Lord Treasurer were not concluded by the opinions of the judges, and therefore, that the Lord Keeper, in the case in question, there being then no Lord Treasurer, might give judgment according to his own opinion. Lord Somers concurring in this idea, reversed the judgment of the court of exchequer. But the case was afterwards carried by error into parliament, and there the Lords reversed the judgment of the exchequer-chamber, and affirmed that of the exchequer. However, notwithstanding this final decision in favor of the bankers and their creditors, it appears by a subsequent statute, that they were to receive only one-half of their debts; the 12 & 14 *Wm. III.*, after appropriating certain sums out of the hereditary excise for public uses, providing that in lieu of the annuities granted to the bankers and all arrears, the hereditary excise should, after the 26th of December 1601, be charged with annual sums equal to an interest of three per cent., until redeemed by payment of one moiety of the principal sums. *Hargrave's Case of the Bankers*, 1, 2, 3.

Upon perusing the whole of this case, these inferences naturally follow: 1st. That admitting the authority of that decision, in its fullest extent, yet, it is an authority only in respect to such cases, where letters-patent from the crown have been granted for the payment of certain sums out of a particular revenue. 2d. That such relief was grantable in the exchequer, upon no other principle than that that court had a right to direct the issues of the exchequer as well after the money was deposited there, as while (in the exchequer language) it was *in transitu*. 3d. That such an authority could not have been exercised by any other court in Westminster Hall, nor by any court, that, from its particular constitution, had no control over the revenues of the kingdom. Lord C. J. Holt, and Lord Somers (though they differed in the main point) both agreed in that case, that the court of King's bench could not send a writ to the treasury. Hargrave's case, 45, 89. Consequently, no such remedy could, under any circumstances, I apprehend, be allowed in any of the American states, in none of which it is presumed any court of justice hath any express authority over the revenues of the state such as has been attributed to the court of exchequer in England.

The observations of Lord Somers, concerning the general remedy by petition to the King, have been extracted and referred to by some of the ablest law characters since; particularly, by Lord C. Baron Comyns, in his digest. I

shall, therefore, extract some of them, as he appears to have taken uncommon pains to collect all the material learning on the subject; and indeed is said to have expended several hundred pounds in the procuring of records relative to that case. Hargrave's Preface to the Case of the Bankers.

After citing many authorities, Lord Somers proceeds thus: "By all these authorities, and by many others, which I could cite, both ancient and modern, it is plain, that if the subject was to recover a rent or annuity, or other charge from the crown; whether it was a rent or annuity, originally granted by the King, or issuing out of lands, which by subsequent title came to be in the King's hands; in all cases, the remedy to come at it was, by petition to the person of the King; and no other method can be shown to have been practised at common law. Indeed, I take it to be generally true, that in all cases where the subject is in the nature of a plaintiff, to recover anything from the King, his only remedy, at common law, is to sue by petition to the person of the King. I say, where the subject comes as a plaintiff. For, as I said before, when, upon a title found for the King by office, the subject comes in to traverse the King's title, or to show his own right, he comes in the nature of a defendant; and is admitted to interplead in the case, with the King, in defence of his title, which otherwise would be defeated by finding the office. And to show that this was so, I would take notice of several instances. That, in cases of debts owing by the crown, the subject's remedy was by petition, appears by *Aynesham's Case*, Ryley, 251, which is a petition for 19*l*. due for work done at Carnarvon castle. So, Ryley 251, the executors of John Estrateling petition for 132*l*. due to the testator, for wages. The answer is remarkable; for there is a latitude taken, which will very well agree with the notion that is taken up in this case; *habeant bre. de liberate in canc. thes. et camerar, de 32l. in partem solutionis*. So, the case of *Yerward de Galeys*, for 56*l*. Ryley 414. In like manner, in the same book, 253 (33 *Edw. I.*), several parties sue by *petition* for money and goods taken for the King's use; and also for wages due to them; and for debts owing to them by the king. The answer is, *rex ordinavit per concilium thesaurarii et baronum de scaccario, quod satisfiet iis quam citius fieri poterit; ita quod contertos se tenebunt.* And this is an answer given to a petition presented to the king in parliament; and therefore, we have reason to conclude it to be warranted by law. They must be content, and they shall be paid, *quam citius fieri poterit.* The parties, in these cases, first go to the King by petition: it is by him they are sent to the exchequer; and it is by writ under the great seal, that the exchequer is impowered to act. Nor can any such writ be found (unless in a very few instances, where it is mere matter of account), in which the treasurer is not joined with the barons. So far was it from being taken to be law at that time, that the barons had any original power of paying the King's debts; or of commanding annuities, granted by the King or his progenitors, to be paid, when the person applied to them for such payment. But, perhaps, it may be objected, that it is not to be inferred, because petitions were brought in these cases, that, therefore, it was of necessity, that the subject should pursue that course, and could take no other way. It might be reasonable to require from those who object thus, that they should produce some precedents, at least, of another remedy taken. But I think, there is a good answer to be given to this objection. All these petitions which I have mentioned, are after the Stat. 8 *Edw. I.* (Ryley 442), where notice is taken that the business of parliament is interrupted by a multitude of petitions, which might be redressed by the chancellor and justices. Wherefore, it is thereby enacted, that petitions which touch the seal shall come first to the chancellor; those which touch the exchequer, to the exchequer; and those which touch the justices, or the law of the land, should come to the justices; and if the business be so great, or *fi de grace*, that the chancellor, or others, cannot do them without the King, then the petitions shall be brought before the King, to know his pleasure; so that no petitions come before the King and his council, but by the hands of the chancellor, and other chief ministers; that the King and his council may attend the great affairs of the King's realm, and his sovereign dominions. This law being made; there is reason to conclude, that all petitions brought before the King or parliament, after this time, and answered there, were brought according to the method of this law; and were of the nature of such petitions as ought to be brought before the person of the King. And that petitions did lie for a chattel, as well as for a freehold, does appear, 37 Ass. pl. ii.; Bro. Pet. 17. If tenant by the statute-merchant be ousted, he may have petition, and shall be restored. *Vide* 9 *Hen. IV.*, 4; Bro. Pet. 9; 9 *Hen. VI.*, 21; Bro. Pet. 2. If the subject be ousted of his term, he shall have his petition. 7 *Hen. VII.*, 2. Of a chattel real, a man shall have his petition of right, as of his freehold. 34 *Hen. VI.*, 51; Bro. Pet. 3. A man shall have a petition of right, for goods and chattels, and the King indorses it in the usual form. It is said, indeed, 1 *Hen. VII.*, 3; Bro. Pet. 19, that a petition will not lie on a chattel. And admitting there was any doubt as to that point, in the present suit, we are in the case of a freehold." Lord Somers's argument in Hargrave's Case of the Bankers, 103–105.

The solitary case, noticed at the conclusion of Lord Somers's argument, "that a petition will not lie of a chattel," certainly is deserving of no consideration, opposed to so many other instances mentioned, and unrecognised (as I believe it is) by any other authority, either ancient or modern, whereas, the contrary, it appears to me, has long been received and established law. In Comyn's Dig. 4 vol. 458, it is said, expressly, "suit shall be to the king by petition, for goods as well as for land." He cites Staundf. Praer. 75 *b*, 72 *b*, for this authority, and takes no notice of any authority to the contrary. The same doctrine is also laid down, with equal explicitness, and without noticing any distinction whatever, in Blackstone's Commentaries, 3 vol. 256, where he points out the petition of right as one of the common-law methods of obtaining possession or restitution from the crown, either of real or personal property; and says expressly, the petition of right "is of use, where the King is in full possession of any hereditaments or chattels, and the petitioner suggests such a right as controverts the title of the crown, grounded on facts disclosed in the petition itself."

I leave out of the argument, from which I have made so long a quotation, everything concerning the restriction on the exchequer, so far as it concerned the case then before the court, as Lord Somers (although more perhaps by weight of authority than reasoning) was overruled in that particular. As to all others, I consider the authorities on which he relied, and his deduction from them, to be unimpeached.

Blackstone, in the first volume of his Commentaries (p. 203), speaking of demands in point of property upon the King, state the general remedy thus: "If any person has, in point of property, a just demand upon the King, he must petition him in his court of chancery, where his chancellor will administer right, as a matter of grace, though not upon compulsion." (For which he cites Finch L. 255.) "And this is exactly consonant to what is laid down by the writers on natural law. A subject, says Puffendorf, so long as he continues a subject, hath no way to oblige his prince to give him his due when he refuses it; though no wise prince will ever refuse to stand to a lawful contract. And if the prince gives the subject leave to enter an action against him upon such contract, in his own courts, the action itself proceeds rather upon natural equity than upon the municipal laws. For the end of such action is not to compel the prince to observe the contract, but to persuade him."

It appears, that when a petition to the person of the King is properly presented, the usual way is, for the King to indorse or to underwrite *soit droit fait al partie* (let right be done to the party); upon which, unless attorney-general confesses the suggestion, a commission is issued to inquire into the truth of it; after the return of which, the King's attorney is at liberty to plead in bar, and the merits shall be determined upon issue or demurrer, as in suits between subject and subject. If the attorney-general confesses the suggestion, there is no occasion for a commission, his admission of the truth of the facts being equally conclusive, as if they had been found by a jury. See 3 Blackstone's Commentaries, 256; and 4 Com. Dig. 458, and the authorities there cited. Though the above-mentioned endorsement be the usual one Lord Somers, in the course of his voluminous search, discovered a variety of other answers to what he considered were unquestionable petitions of right, in respect to which he observes: "The truth is, the manner of answering petitions to the person of the King was very various; which variety did sometimes arise from the conclusion of the party's petition; sometimes, from the nature of the thing; and sometimes, from favor to the person; and according as the indorsement was, the party was sent into chancery or the other courts. If the indorsement was general, *soit droit fait al partie*, it must be delivered to the chancellor of England, and then a commission was to go, to find the right of the party, and that being found, so that there was a record for him, thus warranted, he is let in to interplead with the King; but if the indorsement was special, then the proceeding was to be according to the indorsement in any other court. This is fully explained by Staundfort in his treatise of the Prerogative, c. 22. The case Mich. 10 *Hen. IV.*, No. 4, 8, is full as to this matter. The King recovers in a *quare impedit*, by default, against one who was never summoned; the party cannot have a writ of deceit, without a petition. If, then, says the book, he concludes his petition generally *'que le Roy lui face droit'* (that the King will cause right to be done), and the answer be general, it must go into the chancery, that the right may be inquired of by commission; and upon the inquest found, an original writ must be directed to the justices, to examine the deceit, otherwise, the justices before whom the suit was, cannot meddle. But if he concludes his petition especially, that it may please his highness to command his justices to proceed to the examination, and the indorsement be accordingly, *that* had given the justices a jurisdiction. They might, in such case, have proceeded upon the petition, without any commission or any writ to be sued out, the petition and answer indorsed giving a sufficient jurisdiction to the court to which it was directed. And as the book I have mentioned proves this, so many other authorities may be cited." He, accordingly, mentions many other instances, immaterial to be recited here, particularly remarking a very extraordinary difference in the case belonging to the revenue, in regard to which he said, he thought there was not an instance, to be found, where petitions were answered, *soit droit fait aux parties* (let right be done to the parties). The usual reference appears to have been to the treasurer and barons, commanding them to do justice. Sometimes, a writ under the great seal was directed to be issued to them for that purpose: sometimes, a writ from the chancery directing payment of money immediately, without taking notice of the barons. And other varieties appear to have taken place. See Hargrave's Case of the Bankers, p. 73, *et seq.* But in all cases of petition of right, of whatever nature is the demand, I think it is clear, beyond all doubt, that there must be some indorsement or order of the King himself, to warrant any further proceedings. The remedy, in the language of Blackstone, being a matter of grace and not on compulsion.

In a very late case in England, this point was incidentally discussed. The case I refer to, is that of *Macbeath* v. *Haldimand*, reported 1 T. R. 172. The action was against the defendant, for goods furnished by the defendant's order, in Canada, when the defendant was governor of Quebec. The defence was, that the plaintiff was employed by the defendant, in his official capacity, and not upon his personal credit, and that the goods being, therefore, furnished for the use of government, and the defendant not having undertaken personally to pay, he was not liable. The defence was set up at the trial, on the plea of the general issue, and the jury, by Judge BULLER's direction, found a verdict for the defendant. Upon a motion for a new trial, he reported particularly all the facts given in evidence, and said, his opinion had been at the trial, that the plaintiff should be nonsuited; "but the plaintiff's counsel appearing for their client, when he was called, he left the question to the jury, telling them that they were bound to find for the defendant in point of law. And upon their asking him whether, in the event of the defendant not being liable, any other person was, he told them, that was no part of their consideration, but being willing to give them any information, he added, that he was of opinion, that if the plaintiff's demands were just, his proper rem-

edy was by a petition of right to the crown. On which, they found a verdict for the defendant. The rule for granting a new trial was moved for, on the misdirection of two points. 1st. That the defendant had, by his own conduct, made himself liable, which question should have been left to the jury. 2d. That the plaintiff had no remedy against the crown, by a petition of right, on the supposition of which the jury had been induced to give their verdict." "Lord MANSFIELD, Chief Justice, now declared, that the court did not feel it necessary for them to give any opinion on the second ground. His lordship said, that great difference had arisen, since the revolution, with respect to the expenditure of the public money. Before that period, all the public supplies were given to the King, who, in his individual capacity, contracted for all expenses. He alone had the disposition of the public money. But since that time, the supplies had been appropriated by parliament to particular purposes, and now, whoever advances money for the public service, trusts to the faith of parliament. That according to the tenor of Lord Somer's argument in the *Banker's case*, though a petition of right would lie, yet it would probably produce no effect. No benefit was ever derived from it in the *Banker's case;* and parliament was afterwards obliged to provide a particular fund for the payment of those debts. Whether, however, this alteration in the mode of distributing the supplies had made any difference in the law upon this subject, it was necessary to determine; at any rate, if there were a recovery against the crown, application must be made to parliament, and it would come under the head of supplies for the year." The motion was afterwards argued on the other ground (with which I have at present nothing to do), and rejected.

In the old authorities, there does not appear any distinction between debts that might be contracted personally by the King, for his own private use, and such as he contracted in his political capacity, for the service of the kingdom. As he had, however, then, fixed and independent revenues, upon which depended the ordinary support of government, as well as the expenditure for his own private occasions, probably, no material distinction, at that time, existed, or could easily be made. A very important distinction may, however, perhaps, now subsist between the two cases, for the reasons intimated by Lord MANSFIELD; since the whole support of government depends now on parliamentary provisions, and except in the case of the civil list, those for the most part annual.

Thus, it appears, that in England, even in the case of a private debt contracted by the King, in his own person, there is no remedy but by petition, which must receive his express sanction, otherwise there can be no proceeding upon it. If the debts contracted be avowedly for the public uses of government, it is at least doubtful, whether that remedy will lie, and if it will, it remains afterwards in the power of parliament to provide for it, or not, among the current supplies of the year.

Now, let us consider the case of a debt due from a state. None can, I apprehend, be directly claimed but in the following instances. 1st. In case of a contract with the legislature itself. 2d. In case of a contract with the executive, or any other person, in consequence of an express authority from the legislature. 3d. In case of a contract with the executive, without any special authority. In the first and second cases, the contract is evidently made on the public faith alone. Every man must know that no suit can lie against a legislative body. His only dependence, therefore, can be, that the legislature, on principles of public duty, will make a provision for the execution of their own contracts, and if that fails, whatever reproach the legislature may incur, the case is certainly without remedy in any of the courts of the state. It never was pretended, even in the case of the crown in England, that if any contract was made with parliament or with the crown, by virtue of an authority from parliament, that a petition to the crown would in such case lie. In the third case, a contract with the governor of a state, without any special authority. This case is entirely different from such a contract made with the crown in England. The crown there has very high prerogatives; in many instances, is a kind of trustee for the public interest; in all cases, represents the sovereignty of the kingdom, and is the only authority which can sue or be sued in any manner, on behalf of the kingdom, in any court of justice. A governor of a state is a mere executive officer; his general authority very narrowly limited by the constitution of the state; with no undefined or disputable prerogatives; without power to effect one shilling of the public money, but as he is authorized under the constitution, or by a particular law; having no color to represent the sovereignty of the state, so as to bind it in any manner, to its prejudice, unless specially authorized thereto. And therefore, all who contract with him, do it at their own peril, and are bound to see (or take the consequence of their own indiscretion) that he has strict authority for any contract he makes. Of course, such contract, when so authorized, will come within the description I mentioned, of cases where public faith alone is the ground of relief, and the legislative body, the only one that can afford a remedy, which, from the very nature of it, must be the effect of its discretion, and not of any compulsory process. If, however, any such cases were similar to those which would entitle a party to relief, by petition to the King, in England, that petition being only presentable to him, as he is the sovereign of the kingdom, so far as analogy is to take place, such petition in a state could only be presented to the sovereign power, which surely the governor is not. The only constituted authority to which such an application could, with any propriety, be made, must undoubtedly be the legislature, whose express consent, upon the principle of analogy, would be necessary to any further proceeding. So that this brings us (though by a different route) to the same goal—the discretion and good faith of the legislative body.

There is no other part of the common law, besides that which I have considered, which can, by any person, be pretended, in any manner, to apply to this case, but that which concerns corporations. The applicability of this, the attorney-general, with great candor, has expressly waived. But as it may be urged on other occasions, and as I wish to give the fullest satisfaction, I will say a few words to that doctrine. Suppose, therefore, it should be objected, that the reasoning I have now used, is not conclusive, because,

inasmuch as a state is made subject to the judicial power of congress, its sovereignty must not stand in the way of the proper exercise of that power, and therefore, in all such cases (though in no other), a state can only be considered as a subordinate corporation merely. I answer: 1st. That this construction can only be allowed, at the utmost, upon the supposition that the judicial authority of the United States, as it respects states, cannot be effectuated, without proceeding against them in that light: a position, I by no means admit. 2d. That according to the principles I have supported in this argument, admitting that states ought to be so considered for that purpose, an act of the legislature is necessary to give effect to such a construction, unless the old doctrine concerning corporations will naturally apply to this particular case. 3d. That as it is evident, the act of congress has not made any special provision in this case, grounded on any such construction, so it is to my mind perfectly clear, that we have no authority, upon any supposed analogy between the two cases, to apply the common doctrine concerning corporations, to the important case now before the court. I take it for granted, that when any part of an ancient law is to be applied to a new case, the circumstances of the new case must agree in all essential points with the circumstances of the old cases to which that ancient law was formerly appropriated. Now, there are, in my opinion, the most essential differences between the old cases of corporations, to which the law intimated has reference, and the great and extraordinary case of states separately possessing, as to everything simply relating to themselves, the fullest powers of sovereignty, and yet, in some other defined particulars, subject to a superior power, composed out of themselves, for the common welfare of the whole. The only law concerning corporations, to which I conceive the least reference is to be had, is the common law of England on that subject. I need not repeat the observations I made in respect to the operation of that law in this country. The word "corporations," in its largest sense, has a more extensive meaning than people generally are aware of. Any body politic (sole or aggregate), whether its power be restricted or transcendent, is in this sense, "a corporation." The king, accordingly, in England, is called a corporation. 10 Co. 29 b. So also, by a very respectable author (Sheppard, in his Abridgement, 1 vol. 431), is the parliament itself. In this extensive sense, not only each state singly, but even the United States may, without impropriety, be termed "corporations." I have, therefore, in contradistinction to this large and indefinite term, used the term "subordinate corporations," meaning to refer to such only (as alone capable of the slightest application, for the purpose of the objection) whose creation and whose powers are limited by law.

The differences between such corporations, and the several states in the Union, as relative to the general government, are very obvious, in the following particulars. 1st. A corporation is a mere creature of the king, or of parliament; very rarely, of the latter; most usually, of the former only. It owes its existence, its name, and its laws (except such laws as are necessarily incident to all corporations merely as such), to the authority which create it. A state does not owe its origin to the government of the United

States, in the highest or in any of its branches. It was in existence before it. It derives its authority from the same pure and sacred source as itself: the voluntary and deliberate choice of the people. 2d. A corporation can do no act but what is subject to the revision either of a court of justice, or of some other authority within the government. A state is altogether exempt from the jurisdiction of the courts of the United States, or from any other exterior authority, unless in the special instances where the general government has power derived from the constitution itself. 3d. A corporation is altogether dependent on that government to which it owes its existence. Its charter may be forfeited by abuse: its authority may be annihilated, without abuse, by an act of the legislative body. A state, though subject, in certain specified particulars, to the authority of the government of the United States, is, in every other respect, totally independent upon it. The people of the state created, the people of the state can only change, its constitution. Upon this power, there is no other limitation but that imposed by the constitution of the United States; that it must be of the republican form. I omit minuter distinctions. These are so palpable, that I never can admit that a system of law, calculated for one of these cases, is to be applied, as a matter of course, to the other, without admitting (as I conceive) that the distinct boundaries of law and legislation may be confounded, in a manner that would make courts arbitrary, and, in effect, makers of a new law, instead of being (as certainly they alone ought to be) expositors of an existing one. If still it should be insisted, that though a state cannot be considered upon the same footing as the municipal corporations I have been considering, yet, as relative to the powers of the general government, it must be deemed in some measure dependent; admitting that to be the case (which to be sure is, so far as the necessary execution of the powers of the general government extends), yet, in whatever character this may place a state, this can only afford a reason for a new law, calculated to effectuate the powers of the general government in this new case: but it affords no reason whatever for the court admitting a new action to fit a case, to which no old ones apply, when the *application* of law, not the *making* of it, is the sole province of the court.

I have now, I think, established the following particulars. 1st. That the constitution, so far as it respects the judicial authority, can only be carried into effect, by acts of the legislature, appointing courts, and prescribing their methods of proceeding. 2d. That congress has provided no new law in regard to this case, but expressly referred us to the old. 3d. That there are no principles of the old law, to which we must have recourse, that in any manner authorize the present suit, either by precedent or by analogy. The consequence of which, in my opinion, clearly is, that the suit in question cannot be maintained, nor, of course, the motion made upon it be complied with.

From the manner in which I have viewed this subject, so different from that in which it has been contemplated by the attorney-general, it is evident, that I have not had occasion to notice many arguments offered by the attorney-general, which certainly were very proper, as to his extended view of the case, but do not affect mine. No part

of the law of nations can apply to this case, as I apprehend, but that part which is termed, "The conventional Law of Nations;" nor can this any otherwise apply, than as furnishing rules of interpretation, since, unquestionably, the people of the United States had a right to form what kind of union, and upon what terms they pleased, without reference to any former examples. If, upon a fair construction of the constitution of the United States, the power contended for really exists, it undoubtedly may be exercised, though it be a power of the first impression. If it does not exist upon that authority, ten thousand examples of similar powers would not warrant its assumption. So far as this great question affects the constitution itself, if the present afforded, consistently with the particular grounds of my opinion, a proper occasion for a decision upon it, I would not shrink from its discussion. But it is of extreme moment, that no judge should rashly commit himself upon important questions, which it is unnecessary for him to decide. My opinion being, that even if the constitution would admit of the exercise of such a power, a new law is necessary for the purpose, since no part of the existing law applies, this alone is sufficient to justify my determination in the present case. So much, however, has been said on the constitution, that it may not be improper to intimate, that my present opinion is strongly against any construction of it, which will admit, under any circumstances, a compulsive suit against a state for the recovery of money. I think, every word in the constitution may have its full effect, without involving this consequence, and that nothing but express words, or an insurmountable implication (neither of which I consider, can be found in this case), would authorize the deduction of so high a power. This opinion, I hold, however, with all the reserve proper for one, which, according to my sentiments in this case, may be deemed in some measure extra-judicial. With regard to the policy of maintaining such suits, that is not for this court to consider, unless the point in all other respects was very doubtful. Policy might then be argued from, with a view to preponderate the judgment. Upon the question before us, I have no doubt. I have, therefore, nothing to do with the policy. But I confess, if I was at liberty to speak on that subject, my opinion on the policy of the case would also differ from that of the attorney-general. It is, however, a delicate topic. I pray to God, that if the attorney-general's doctrine, as to the law, be established by the judgment of this court, all the good he predicts from it may take place, and none of the evils with which, I have the concern to say, it appears to me to be pregnant.

BLAIR, Justice.—In considering this important case, I have thought it best to pass over all the strictures which have been made on the various European confederations; because, as, on the one hand, their likeness to our own is not sufficiently close to justify any analogical application; so, on the other, they are utterly destitute of any binding authority here. The constitution of the United States is the only fountain from which I shall draw; the only authority to which I shall appeal. Whatever be the true language of that, it is obligatory upon every member of the Union; for no state could have become a member, but by an adoption of it by the people of that state. What then do we find there, requiring the submission of individual states to the judicial authority of the United States? This is expressly extended, among other things, to controversies between a state and citizens of another state. Is, then, the case before us one of that description? Undoubtedly, it is, unless it may be a sufficient denial to say, that it is a controversy between a citizen of one state and another state. Can this change of order be an essential change in the thing intended? And is this alone a sufficient ground from which to conclude, that the jurisdiction of this court reaches the case where a state is plaintiff, but not where it is defendant? In this latter case, should any man be asked, whether it was not a controversy between a state and citizen of another state, must not the answer be in the affirmative? A dispute between A. and B. is surely a dispute between B. and A. Both cases, I have no doubt, were intended; and probably, the state was first named, in respect to the dignity of a state. But that very dignity seems to have been thought a sufficient reason for confining the sense to the case where a state is plaintiff. It is, however, a sufficient answer to say, that our constitution most certainly contemplates, in another branch of the cases enumerated, the maintaining a jurisdiction against a state, as defendant; this is unequivocally asserted, when the judicial power of the United States is extended to controversies between two or more states; for there, a state must, of necessity, be a defendant. It is extended also to controversies between a state and foreign states; and if the argument taken from the order of designation were good, it would be meant here, that this court might have cognisance of a suit, where a state is plaintiff, and some foreign state a defendant, but not where a foreign state brings a suit against a state. This, however, not to mention that the instances may rarely occur, when a state may have an opportunity of suing, in the American courts, a foreign state, seems to lose sight of the policy which, no doubt, suggested this provision, viz., that no state in the Union should, by withholding justice, have it in its power to embroil the whole confederacy in disputes of another nature. But if a foreign state, though last named, may, nevertheless, be a plaintiff against an individual state, how can it be said, that a controversy between a state and a citizen of another state means, from the mere force of the order of the words, only such cases where a state is plaintiff? After describing, generally, the judicial powers of the United States, the constitution goes on to speak of it distributively, and gives to the supreme court original jurisdiction, among other instances, in the case where a state shall be a *party;* but is not a state a party as well in the condition of a defendant, as in that of a plaintiff? And is the whole force of that expression satisfied, by confining its meaning to the case of a plaintiff-state? It seems to me, that if this court should refuse to hold jurisdiction of a case where a state is defendant, it would renounce part of the authority conferred, and consequently, part of the duty imposed on it by the constitution; because, it would be a refusal to take cognisance of a case, where a state is a party.

Nor does the jurisdiction of this court, in relation to a state, seem to me to be questionable, on the ground, that congress has not provided any form of execution, or pointed out any mode of making the judgment against a state effectual; the argument *ab inutile* may weigh much, in cases depending upon the construction of doubtful legislative acts, but can have no force, I think, against the clear and positive directions of an act of congress and of the constitution. Let us go on so far as we can; and if, at the end of the business, notwithstanding the powers given us in the 14th section of the judicial law, we meet difficulties insurmountable to us, we must leave it to those departments of government which have higher powers; to which, however, there may be no necessity to have recourse. Is it altogether a vain expectation, that a state may have other motives than such as arise from the apprehension of coercion, to carry into execution a judgment of the supreme court of the United States, though not conformable to their own ideas of justice? Besides, this argument takes it for granted, that the judgment of the court will be against the state; it possibly may be in favor of the state: and the difficulty vanishes. Should judgment be given against the plaintiff, could it be said to be void, because extra-judicial? If the plaintiff, grounding himself upon that notion, should renew his suit against the state, in any mode in which she may permit herself to be sued in her own courts, would the attorney-general for the state be obliged to go again into the merits of the case, because the matter, when here, was *coram non judice?* Might he not rely upon the judgment given by this court, in bar of the new suit? To me, it seems clear, that he might. And if a state may be brought before this court, as a defendant, I see no reason for confining the plaintiff to proceed by way of petition; indeed, there would even seem to be an impropriety in proceeding in that mode. When sovereigns are sued in their own courts, such a method may have been established, as the most respectful form of demand; but we are not now in a state court; and if sovereignty be an exemption from suit, in any other than the sovereign's own courts, it follows, that when a state, by adopting the constitution, has agreed to be amenable to the judicial power of the United States, she has, in that respect, given up her right of sovereignty.

With respect to the service of the summons to appear, the manner in which it has been served, seems to be as proper as any which could be devised for the purpose of giving notice of the suit, which is the end proposed by it, the governor being the head of the executive department, and the attorney-general the law officer, who generally represents the state in legal proceedings: and this mode is the less liable to exception, when it is considered, that in the suit brought in this court, by the state of *Georgia* against *Brailsford* and others, it is conceived in the name of the governor in behalf of the state. If the opinion which I have delivered, respecting the liability of a state to be sued in this court, should be the opinion of the court, it will come, in course, to consider, what is the proper step to be taken for inducing appearance, none having been yet entered in behalf of the defendant. A judgment by default, in the present state of the business, and writ of inquiry for damages, would be too precipitate in any case, and too incompatible with the dignity of a state in this. Further opportunity of appearing to defend the suit ought to be given. The conditional order moved for the last term, the consideration of which was deferred to this, seems to me to be a very proper mode; it will warn the state of the meditated consequence of a refusal to appear, and give an opportunity for more deliberate consideration. The order, I think, should be thus: "Ordered, that unless the state of Georgia should, after due notice of this order, by a service thereof upon the governor and attorney-general of the said state, cause an appearance to be entered in behalf of the state, on the 5th day of the next term, or then show cause to the contrary, judgment be then entered up against the state, and a writ of inquiry of damages be awarded."

WILSON, Justice—This is a case of uncommon magnitude. One of the parties to it is a State, certainly respectable, claiming to be sovereign. The question to be determined is, whether this state, so respectable, and whose claim soars so high, is amenable to the jurisdiction of the supreme court of the United States? This question, important in itself, will depend on others, more important still; and may, perhaps, be ultimately resolved into one, no less *radical* than this—"do the People of the United States form a Nation?"

A cause so conspicuous and interesting, should be carefully and accurately viewed, from every possible point of sight. I shall examine it, 1st. By the principles of general jurisprudence. 2d. By the laws and practice of particular states and kingdoms. From the law of nations, little or no illustration of this subject can be expected. By that law, the several states and governments spread over our globe, are considered as forming a society, not a nation. It has only been by a very few comprehensive minds, such as those of Elizabeth and the Fourth Henry, that this last great idea has been even contemplated. 3d. And chiefly, I shall examine the important question before us, by the constitution of the United States, and the legitimate result of that valuable instrument.

I. I am first to examine this question by the principles of general jurisprudence. What I shall say upon this head, I introduce, by the observation of an original and profound writer, who, on the philosophy of mind, and all the sciences attendant on this prime one, has formed an era not less remarkable, and far more illustrious, than that formed by the justly celebrated Bacon, in another science, not prosecuted with less ability, but less dignified as to its object; I mean the philosophy of nature. Dr. Reid, in his excellent inquiry into the human mind, on the principles of common sense, speaking of the sceptical and illiberal philosophy, which, under bold, but false, pretensions to liberality, prevailed in many parts of Europe before he wrote, makes the following judicious remark: "The language of philosophers, with regard to the original faculties of the mind, is so adapted to the prevailing system, that it cannot fit any other; like the coat that fits the man for whom it was made, and shows him to advantage, which yet will fit very awkward upon one of a different make, although as handsome and well proportioned. It is hardly possible to make any innovation in our philosophy concerning the mind and its operations, without using new words and phrases, or giving a different meaning to those that are received." With equal propriety, may this solid remark be applied to the great subject, on the principles of which the decision of this court is to be founded. The perverted use of *genus* and *species* in logic, and of *impressions* and *ideas* in metaphysics, have never done mischief so extensive or so practically pernicious, as has been done by *states* and *sovereigns*, in politics and jurisprudence; in the politics and jurisprudence even of those who wished and meant to be free. In the place of those expressions, I intend not to substitute new ones; but the expressions themselves I shall certainly use for purposes different from those, for which hitherto they have been frequently used; and one of them I shall apply to an object still more different from that, to which it has been hitherto, most frequently, I may say, almost universally, applied. In these purposes, and in this application, I shall be justified by example the most splendid, and by authority the most binding; the example of the most refined as well as the most free nation known to antiquity; and the authority of one of the best constitutions known to modern times. With regard to one of the terms, "state," this authority is declared: with regard to the other, "sovereign," the authority is implied only; but it is equally strong: for, in an instrument well drawn, as in a poem well composed, silence is sometimes most expressive.

To the constitution of the United States the term *sovereign* is totally unknown. There is but one place where it could have been used with propriety. But even in that place, it would not, perhaps, have comported with the delicacy of those who ordained and established that constitution. They might have announced themselves *sovereign* people of the United States: but serenely conscious of the past, they avoided the ostentatious declaration.

Having thus avowed my disapprobation of the purposes for which the terms *state* and *sovereign*, are frequently used, and of the object to which the application of the last of them is almost universally made; it is now proper, that I should disclose the meaning which I assign to both, and the application which I make of the latter. In doing this, I shall have occasion incidentally to evince, how true it is, that states and governments were made for man; and at the same time, how true it is, that his creatures and servants have first deceived, next vilified, and at last, oppressed their master and maker.

Man, fearfully and wonderfully made, is the workmanship of his all-perfect Creator: a state, useful and valuable as the contrivance is, is the inferior contrivance of man; and from his native dignity, derives all its acquired importance. When I speak of a state, as an inferior contrivance, I mean that it is a contrivance inferior only to that which is divine: Of all human contrivances, it is certainly most transcendently excellent. It is concerning this contrivance, that Cicero says so sublimely, "Nothing which is exhibited upon our globe, is more acceptable to that divinity which governs the whole universe, than those communities and assemblages of men, which, lawfully associated, are denominated states."

Let a state be considered as subordinate to the People:

but let everything else be subordinate to the state. The latter part of this position is equally necessary with the former. For in the practice, and even, at length, in the science of politics, there has very frequently been a strong current against the natural order of things, and an inconsiderate or an interested disposition to sacrifice the end to the means. As the state has claimed precedence of the people; so, in the same inverted course of things, the government has often claimed precedence of the state; and to this perversion in the second degree, many of the volumes of confusion concerning sovereignty owe their existence. The ministers, dignified very properly by the appellation of the magistrates, have wished, and have succeeded in their wish, to be considered as the sovereigns of the state. This second degree of perversion is confined to the old world, and begins to diminish even there: but the first degree is still too prevalent, even in the several states of which our Union is composed. By a state, I mean, a complete body of free persons united together for their common benefit, to enjoy peaceably what is their own, and to do justice to others. It is an artificial person. It has its affairs and its interests: it has its rules: it has its rights: and it has its obligations. It may acquire property, distinct from that of its members: it may incur debts, to be discharged, out of the public stock, not out of the private fortunes of individuals. It may be bound by contracts; and for damages arising from the breach of those contracts. In all our contemplations, however, concerning this feigned and artificial person, we should never forget, that, in truth and nature, those who think and speak and act, are men.

Is the foregoing description of a state, a true description? It will not be questioned, but it is. Is there any part of this description, which intimates, in the remotest manner, that a state, any more than the men who compose it, ought not to do justice and fulfil engagements? It will not be pretended, that there is. If justice is not done; if engagements are not fulfilled; is it, upon general principles of right, less proper, in the case of a great number, than in the case of an individual, to secure, by compulsion, that which will not be voluntarily performed? Less proper, it surely cannot be. The only reason, I believe, why a free man is bound by human laws, is, that he binds himself. Upon the same principles, upon which he becomes bound by the laws, he becomes amenable to the courts of justice, which are formed and authorised by those laws. If one free man, an original sovereign, may do all this, why may not an aggregate of free men, a collection of original sovereigns, do this likewise? If the dignity of each, singly, is undiminished; the dignity of all, jointly, must be unimpaired. A state, like a merchant, makes a contract. A dishonest state, like a dishonest merchant, wilfully refuses to discharge it: the latter is amenable to a court of justice: upon general principles of right, shall the former, when summoned to answer the fair demands of its creditor, be permitted, Proteus-like, to assume a new appearance, and to insult him and justice, by declaring I am a *sovereign* state? Surely not. Before a claim, so contrary, in its first appearance, to the general principles of right and equality, be sustained by a just and impartial tribunal, the person, natural or artificial, entitled to make such claim, should

certainly be well known and authenticated. Who, or what, is a sovereignty? What is his or its sovereignty? On this subject, the errors and the mazes are endless and inexplicable. To enumerate all, therefore, will not be expected: to take notice of some, will be necessary to the full illustration of the present important cause. In one sense, the term *sovereign* has for its correlative, *subject*. In this sense, the term can receive no application; for it has no object in the constitution of the United States. Under that constitution, there are *citizens*, but no *subjects*. "Citizens of the *United States*." "Citizens of another state." "Citizens of different states." "A state or citizen thereof." The term *subject* occurs, indeed, once in the instrument; but to mark the contrast strongly, the epithet "foreign" is prefixed. In this sense, I presume the state of Georgia has no claim upon her own citizens: in this sense, I am certain, she can have no claim upon the citizens of another state.

In another sense, according to some writers, every state, which governs itself, without any dependence on another power, is a sovereign state. Whether, with regard to her own citizens, this is the case of the state of Georgia; whether those citizens have done, as the individuals of England are said, by their late instructors, to have done, surrendered the supreme power to the state or government, and reserved nothing to themselves; or whether, like the people of other states, and of the United States, the citizens of Georgia have reserved the supreme power in their own hands; and on that supreme power, have made the state dependent, instead of being sovereign; these are questions, to which, as a judge in this cause, I can neither know nor suggest the proper answers; though, as a citizen of the Union, I know, and am interested to know, that the most satisfactory answers can be given. As a citizen, I know, the government of that state to be republican; and my short definition of such a government is—one constructed on this principle, that the supreme power resides in the body of the people. As a judge of this court, I know, and can decide, upon the knowledge, that the citizens of Georgia, when they acted upon the large scale of the Union, as a part of the "People of the United States," did *not* surrender the supreme or sovereign power to that state; but, *as to the purposes of the Union*, retained it to themselves. *As to the purposes of the Union*, therefore, Georgia *is not a sovereign state*. If the judicial decision of this case forms one of those purposes; the allegation that Georgia is a sovereign state, is unsupported by the fact. Whether the judicial decision of this cause is, or is not, one of those purposes, is a question which will be examined particularly, in a subsequent part of my argument.

There is third sense, in which the term sovereign is frequently used, and which it is very material to trace and explain, as it furnishes a basis for what, I presume, to be one of the principal objections against the jurisdiction of this court over the State of Georgia. In this sense, sovereignty is derived from a feudal source; and like many other parts of that system, so degrading to man, still retains its influence over our sentiments and conduct, though the cause, by which that influence was produced, never extended to the American states. The accurate and well informed President Henault, in his excellent chronological abridgment of the History of France, tells us, that, about the end of the second race of Kings, a new kind of possession was acquired, under the name of fief. The governors of cities and provinces usurped equally the property of land, and the administration of justice; and established themselves as proprietary seigniors over those places in which they had been only civil magistrates or military officers. By this means, there was introduced into the state a new kind of authority, to which was assigned the appellation of sovereignty. In process of time, the feudal system was extended over France, and almost all the other nations of Europe; and every kingdom became, in fact, a large fief. Into England, this system was introduced by the conqueror; and to this era we may, probably, refer the English maxim, that the King or sovereign is the fountain of justice. But in the case of the King, the sovereignty had a double operation. While it vested him with jurisdiction over others, it excluded all others from jurisdiction over him. With regard to him, there was no superior power; and consequently, on feudal principles, no right of jurisdiction. "The law," says Sir William Blackstone, "ascribes to the King, the attribute of sovereignty: he is sovereign and independent, within his own dominions; and owes no kind of subjection to any other potentate upon earth. Hence it is, that no suit or action can be brought against the King, even in civil matters; because no court can have jurisdiction over him: for all jurisdiction implies superiority of power." This last position is only a branch of a much more extensive principle, on which a plan of systematic despotism has been lately formed in England, and prosecuted with unwearied assiduity and care. Of this plan, the author of the Commentaries was, if not the introducer, at least, the great supporter. He has been followed in it, by writers later and less known; and his doctrines have, both on the other and this side of the Atlantic, been implicitly and generally received by those, who neither examined their principles nor their consequences. The principle is, that all human law must be prescribed by a superior: this principle I mean not now to examine: suffice it, at present, to say, that another principle, very different in its nature and operations, forms, in my judgment, the basis of sound and genuine jurisprudence; laws derived from the pure source of equality and justice must be founded on the *consent* of those whose obedience they require. The sovereign, when traced to his source, must be found in the man.

I have now fixed, in the scale of things, the grade of a state; and have described its composure: I have considered the nature of sovereignty; and pointed its application to the proper object. I have examined the question before us, by the principles of general jurisprudence. In those principles, I find nothing, which tends to evince an exemption of the State of Georgia, from the jurisdiction of the court. I find everything to have a contrary tendency.

II. I am, in the second place, to examine this question by the laws and practice of different states and kingdoms. In ancient Greece, as we learn from Isocrates, whole nations defended their rights before crowded tribunals. Such occasions as these excited, we are told, all the powers of persuasion; and the vehemence and enthusiasm of the sentiment was gradually infused into the Grecian language, equally susceptible of strength and harmony. In those days, law, liberty and refining science made their benign progress in strict and graceful union; the rude and degrading league between the bar and feudal barbarism was not yet formed.

When the laws and practice of particular states have any application to the question before us, that application will furnish what is called an argument *à fortiori;* because all the instances produced will be instances of subjects instituting and supporting suits against those who were deemed their own sovereigns. These instances are stronger than the present one, because between the present plaintiff and defendant, no such unequal relation is alleged to exist.

Columbus achieved the discovery of that country which, perhaps, ought to bear his name. A contract made by Columbus furnished the first precedent for supporting, in his discovered country, the cause of injured merit against the claims and pretensions of haughty and ungrateful power. His son Don Diego wasted two years in incessant, but fruitless, solicitation at the Court of Spain, for the rights which descended to him, in consequence of his father's original capitulation. He endeavored, at length, to obtain, by a legal sentence, what he could not procure from the favor of an interested monarch. He commenced a suit against Ferdinand, before the Council which managed Indian affairs, and that court, with integrity which reflects honor on its proceedings, decided against the King, and sustained Don Diego's claim.

Other states have instituted officers to judge the proceedings of their Kings. Of this kind, were the Ephori of Sparta; of this kind also, was the mayor of the palace, and afterwards, the constable of France.

But of all the laws and institutions relating to the present question, none is so striking as that described by the famous Hottoman, in his book entitled Franco Gallia. When the Spaniards of Arragon elect a King, they represent a kind of play, and introduce a personage whom they dignify by the name of Law, *la Justiza,* of Arragon. This person they declare, by a public decree, to be greater and more powerful than their king, and then address him in the following remarkable expressions: "We, who are of as great worth as you, and can do more than you can do, elect you to be our King, upon the conditions stipulated. But between you and us, there is one of greater authority than you."

In England, according to Sir William Blackstone, no suit can be brought against the King, even in civil matters. So, in that kingdom, is the law at this time received. But it was not always so. Under the Saxon government, a very different doctrine was held to be orthodox. Under that government, as we are informed by the Mirror of Justice, a book said by Sir Edward Coke, to have been written, in part, at least, before the conquest; under that government, it was ordained, that the King's court should be open to all plaintiffs, by which, without delay, they should have remedial writs, as well against the King or against the Queen, as against any other of the people. The law continued to be the same, for some centuries after the conquest. Until the time of Edward I., the King might have been sued as a common person. The form of the process was even imperative. *"Praecipe Henrico Regi Angliae,"* &c. "Command Henry, King of England," &c. Bracton, who wrote in the time of Henry III., uses these very remarkable expressions concerning the King: *"In justitia recipienda, minimo de regno suo comparetur"*—in receiving justice, he should be placed on a level with the meanest person in the kingdom. True it is, that now, in England, the King must be sued in his courts, by petition; but even now, the difference is only in the form, not in the thing. The judgments or decrees of those courts will substantially be the same upon a precatory as upon a mandatory process. In the courts of justice, says the very able author of the considerations on the laws of forfeiture, the King enjoys many privileges; yet not to deter the subject from contending with him freely. The judge of the high court of admiralty, in England, made, in a very late cause, the following manly and independent declaration: "In any case, where the crown is a party, it is to be observed, that the crown can no more withhold evidence of documents in its possession than a private person. If the court thinks proper to order the production of any public instrument, that order must be obeyed. It wants no *insignia* of an authority derived from the crown."

"Judges ought to know, that the poorest peasant is a man, as well as the king himself: all men ought to obtain justice, since, in the estimation of justice, all men are equal, whether the prince complain of a peasant, or a peasant complain of the prince." These are the words of a king, of the late Frederic of Prussia. In his courts of justice, that great man stood upon his native greatness, and disdained to mount upon the artificial stilts of sovereignty.

Thus much concerning the laws and practice of other states and kingdoms. We see nothing against, but much in favor of, the jurisdiction of this court over the state of Georgia, a party to this cause.

III. I am, thirdly, and chiefly, to examine the important question now before us, by the constitution of the United States, and the legitimate result of that valuable instrument. Under this view, the question is naturally subdivided into two others. 1. Could the constitution of the United States vest a jurisdiction over the state of Georgia? 2. Has that constitution vested such jurisdiction in this court? I have already remarked, that in the practice, and even in the science of politics, there has been frequently a strong current against the natural order of things; and an inconsiderate or an interested disposition to sacrifice the end to the means. This remark deserves a more particular illustration. Even in almost every nation which has been denominated free, the state has assumed a supercilious preeminence above the people who have formed it: hence, the haughty notions of state independence, state sovereignty, and state supremacy. In despotic governments, the government has usurped, in a similar manner, both upon the state and the people: hence, all arbitrary doctrines and pretensions concerning the supreme, absolute, and uncontrollable power of government. In each, man is degraded from the prime rank, which he ought to hold in human affairs: in the latter, the state as well as the man is degraded. Of both degradations, striking instances occur in history, in politics, and in common life. One of them is drawn from an anecdote, which is recorded concerning Louis XIV., who has been styled the Grand Monarch of France. This prince, who diffused around him so much dazzling splendor, and so little vivifying heat, was vitiated by that inverted manner of teaching and of thinking, which forms kings to be tyrants, without knowing or even suspecting that they are so. The oppression under which he held his subjects, during the whole course of his long reign, proceeded chiefly from the principles and habits of his erroneous education. By these, he had been accustomed to consider his kingdom as his patrimony, and his power over his subjects as his rightful and undelegated inheritance. These sentiments were so deeply and strongly imprinted on his mind, that when one of his ministers represented to him the miserable condition, to which those subjects were reduced, and in the course of his representation, frequently used the word *L'Etat*, the state, the King, though he felt the truth and approved the substance of all that was said, yet was shocked at the frequent repetition of the expression *L'Etat;* and complained of it as an indecency offered to his person and character. And, indeed, that kings should imagine themselves the final causes, for which men were made, and societies were formed, and governments were instituted, will cease to be a matter of wonder or surprise, when we find, that lawyers and statesmen and philosophers have taught or favored principles which necessarily lead to the same conclusion. Another instance, equally strong, but still more astonishing, is drawn from the British government, as described by Sir William Blackstone and his followers. As described by him and them, the British is a despotic government. It is a government without a people. In that government, as so described, the sovereignty is possessed by the parliament: in the parliament, therefore, the supreme and absolute authority is vested: in the parliament resides that uncontrollable and despotic power, which, in all governments, must reside somewhere. The constituent parts of the parliament are the King's Majesty, the Lords spiritual, the Lords temporal, and the Commons. The King and these three estates together form the great corporation or body politic of the kingdom. All these sentiments are found; the last expressions are found *verbatim*, in the Commentaries upon the Laws of England. The parliament form the great body politic of England! What, then, or where, are the people? Nothing! Nowhere! They are not so much as even the "baseless fabric of a vision!" From legal contemplation, they totally disappear! Am I not warranted in saying that, if this is a just description, a government, so and justly so described, is a despotic government? Whether this description is or is not a just one, is a question of very different import.

In the United States, and in the several states which compose the Union, we go not so far: but still, we go one step farther than we ought to go, in this unnatural and inverted order of things. The states, rather than the *people*, for whose sakes the states exist, are frequently the objects which attract and arrest our principal attention. This, I believe, has produced much of the confusion and perplexity, which have appeared in several proceedings and several publications on state-politics, and on the politics, too, of the United States. Sentiments and expressions of this inaccurate kind prevail in our common, even in our convivial, language. Is a toast asked? "The United States," instead of the "People of the United States," is the toast given. This is not politically correct. The toast is meant to present to view the first great object in the Union: it presents only the second: it presents only the artificial person, instead of the natural persons, who spoke it into existence. A *state*, I cheerfully admit, is the noblest work of man: but man himself, free and honest, is, I speak as to this world, the noblest work of GOD!

Concerning the prerogative of Kings, and concerning the sovereignty of states, much has been said and written; but little has been said and written, concerning a subject much more dignified and important, the majesty of the people. The mode of expression, which I would substitute in the place of that generally used, is not only politically, but also (for between true liberty and true taste there is a close alliance) classically, more correct. On the mention of Athens, a thousand refined and endearing associations rush at once into the memory of the scholar, the philosopher, and the patriot. When Homer, one of the most correct, as well as the oldest of human authorities, enumerates the other nations of Greece, whose forces acted at the siege of Troy, he arranges them under the names of their different Kings or Princes: but when he comes to the Athenians, he distinguishes them by the peculiar appellation of the People of Athens. The well-known address used by Demosthenes, when he harangued and animated his assembled countrymen, was "O! men of Athens." With the strictest propriety, therefore, classical and political, our national scene opens with the most magnificent object, which the nation could present: "The People of the United States" are the first personages introduced. Who were those people? They were the citizens of thirteen states, each of which had a separate constitution and government, and all of which were connected together by articles of confederation. To the purposes of public strength and felicity, that confederacy was totally inadequate. A requisition on the several states terminated its legislative authority: executive or judicial authority it had none. In order, therefore, to form a more perfect union, to establish justice, to insure domestic tranquility, to provide for common defence, and to secure the blessings of liberty, those people, among whom were the people of Georgia, ordained and established the present constitution. By that constitution, legislative power is vested, executive power is vested, judicial power is vested.

The question now opens fairly to our view, could the people of those states, among whom were those of Georgia, bind those states, and Georgia, among the others, by the legislative, executive, and judicial power so vested? If the principles on which I have founded myself, are just and true; this question must unavoidably receive an affirmative answer. If those states were the work of those people; those people, and, that I may apply the case closely, the people of Georgia, in particular, could alter, as they pleased, their former work: to any given degree, they could *diminish* as well as enlarge it: any or all of the former

state-powers, they could extinguish or transfer. The inference, which necessarily results, is, that the constitution ordained and established by those people; and, still closely to apply the case, in particular, by the people of Georgia, could vest jurisdiction or judicial power over those states, and over the state of Georgia in particular.

The next question under this head is—has the constitution done so? Did those people mean to exercise this, their undoubted power? These questions may be resolved, either by fair and conclusive deductions, or by direct and explicit declarations. In order, ultimately, to discover, whether the people of the United States intended to bind those states by the judicial power vested by the national constitution, a previous inquiry will naturally be: Did those people intend to bind those states by the legislative power vested by that constitution? The articles of confederation, it is well known, did not operate upon individual citizens, but operated only upon states. This defect was remedied by the national constitution, which, as all allow, has an operation on individual citizens. But if an opinion, which some seem to entertain, be just; the defect remedied, on one side, was balanced by a defect introduced on the other: for they seem to think, that the present constitution operates only on individual citizens, and not on states. This opinion, however, appears to be altogether unfounded. When certain laws of the states are declared to be "subject to the revision and control of the congress;" it cannot, surely, be contended, that the legislative power of the national government was meant to have no operation on the several states. The fact, uncontrovertibly established in one instance, proves the principle in all other instances, to which the facts will be found to apply. We may then infer, that the people of the United States intended to bind the several states, by the legislative power of the national government.

In order to make the discovery, at which we ultimately aim, a second previous inquiry will naturally be—Did the people of the United States intend to bind the several states, by the executive power of the national government? The affirmative answer to the former question directs, unavoidably, an affirmative answer to this. Ever since the time of Bracton, his maxim, I believe, has been deemed a good one—"*Supervacuum esset, leges condere, nisi esset qui leges tueretur.*" (It would be superfluous to make laws, unless those laws, when made, were to be enforced.) When the laws are plain, and the application of them is uncontroverted, they are enforced immediately by the executive authority of government. When the application of them is doubtful or intricate, the interposition of the judicial authority becomes necessary. The same principle, therefore, which directed us from the first to the second step, will direct us from the second to the third and last step of our deduction. Fair and conclusive deduction, then, evinces that the people of the United States did vest this court with jurisdiction over the state of Georgia. The same truth may be deduced from the declared objects, and the general texture of the constitution of the United States. One of its declared objects is, to form an union more perfect than, before that time, had been formed. Before that time, the Union possessed legislative, but unenforced legislative power over the states. Nothing could be more natural than to intend that this legislative power should be enforced by powers executive and judicial. Another declared object is, "to establish justice." This points, in a particular manner, to the judicial authority. And when we view this object, in conjunction with the declaration, "that no state shall pass a law impairing the obligation of contracts;" we shall probably think, that this object points, in a particular manner, to the jurisdiction of the court over the several states. What good purpose could this constitutional provision secure, if a state might pass a law, impairing the obligation of its own contracts; and be amenable, for such a violation of right, to no controlling judiciary power? We have seen, that on the principles of general jurisprudence, a state, for the breach of a contract, may be liable for damages. A third declared object is—"to insure domestic tranquillity." This tranquillity is most likely to be disturbed by controversies between states. These consequences will be most peaceably and effectually decided, by the establishment and by the exercise of a superintending judicial authority. By such exercise and establishment, the law of nations—the rule between contending states—will be enforced among the several states, in the same manner as municipal law.

Whoever considers, in a combined and comprehensive view, the general texture of the constitution, will be satisfied, that the people of the United States intended to form themselves into a nation, for national purposes. They instituted, for such purposes, a national government, complete in all its parts, with powers legislative, executive and judiciary; and in all those powers, extending over the whole nation. Is it congruous, that, with regard to such purposes, any man or body of men, any person, natural or artificial, should be permitted to claim successfully, an entire exemption from the jurisdiction of the national government? Would not such claims, crowned with success, be repugnant to our very existence as a nation? When so many trains of deduction, coming from different quarters, converge and unite at last, in the same point, we may safely conclude, as the legitimate result of this constitution, that the state of Georgia is amenable to the jurisdiction of this court.

But in my opinion, this doctrine rests not upon the legitimate result of fair and conclusive deduction from the constitution: it is confirmed, beyond all doubt, by the direct and explicit declaration of the constitution itself. "The judicial power of the United States shall extend, to controversies between *two* states." Two states are supposed to have a controversy between them: this controversy is supposed to be brought before those vested with the judicial power of the United States: Can the most consummate degree of professional ingenuity devise a mode by which this "controversy between two states" can be brought before a court of law; and yet neither of those states be a defendant? "The judicial power of the United States shall extend to controversies, between a state and citizens of another state." Could the strictest legal language; could even that language, which is peculiarly appropriated to an art, deemed, by a great master, to be one of the most honorable, laudable and profitable things in our law; could this

strict and appropriated language, describe, with more precise accuracy, the cause now depending before the tribunal? Causes, and not parties to causes, are weighed by justice, in her equal scales: on the former solely, her attention is fixed: to the latter, she is, as she is painted, blind.

I have now tried this question by all the touchstones, to which I proposed to apply it. I have examined it by the principles of general jurisprudence; by the laws and practice of states and kingdoms; and by the constitution of the United States. From all, the combined inference is, that the action lies.

CUSHING, Justice.—The grand and principal question in this case is, whether a state can, by the federal constitution, be sued by an individual citizen of another state?

The point turns not upon the law or practice of England, although, perhaps, it may be in some measure elucidated thereby, nor upon the law of any other country whatever; but upon the constitution established by the people of the United States; and particularly, upon the extent of powers given to the federal judiciary in the 2d section of the 3d article of the constitution. It is declared, that "the judicial power shall extend to all cases in law and equity arising under the constitution, the laws of the United States, or treaties made or which shall be made under their authority; to all cases affecting ambassadors or other public ministers and consuls; to all cases of admiralty and maritime jurisdiction; to controversies, to which the United States shall be a party; to controversies between two or more states and citizens of another state; between citizens of different states; between citizens of the same state, claiming lands under grants of different states; and between a state and citizens thereof and foreign states, citizens or subjects." The judicial power, then, is expressly extended to "controversies between a state and citizens of another state." When a citizen makes a demand against a state, of which he is not a citizen, it is as really a controversy between a state and a citizen of another state, as if such state made a demand against such citizen. The case, then, seems clearly to fall within the letter of the constitution. It may be suggested, that it could not be intended to subject a state to be a defendant, because it would affect the sovereignty of states. If that be the case, what shall we do with the immediate preceding clause—"controversies between two or more states," where a state must of necessity be defendant? If it was not the intent, in the very next clause also, that a state might be made defendant, why was it so expressed, as naturally to lead to and comprehend that idea? Why was not an exception made, if one was intended?

Again, what are we to do with the last clause of the section of judicial powers, viz., "controversies between a state, or the citizens thereof, and foreign states or citizens." Here again, states must be suable or liable to be made defendants by this clause, which has a similar mode of language with the two other clauses I have remarked upon. For if the judicial power extends to a controversy between one of the United States and a foreign state, as the clause expresses, one of them must be defendant. And then, what becomes of the sovereignty of states so far as suing affects it? But although the words appear reciprocally to affect the state here and a foreign state, and put them on the same footing so far as may be, yet ingenuity may say that the state here may sue, but cannot be sued; but that the foreign state may be sued, but cannot sue. We may touch foreign sovereignties, but not our own. But I conceive, the reason of the thing, as well as the words of the constitution, tend to show that the federal judicial power extends to a suit brought by a foreign state against any one of the United States. One design of the general government was, for managing the great affairs of peace and war and the general defence, which were impossible to be conducted, with safety, by the states separately. Incident to these powers, and for preventing controversies between foreign powers or citizens from rising to extremities and to an appeal to the sword, a national tribunal was necessary, amicably to decide them, and thus ward off such fatal, public calamity. Thus, states at home and their citizens, and foreign states and their citizens, are put together without distinction, upon the same footing, so far as may be, as to controversies between them. So also, with respect to controversies between a state and citizens of another state (at home), comparing all the clauses together, the remedy is reciprocal; the claim to justice equal. As controversies between state and state, and between a state and citizens of another state, might tend gradually to involve states in war and bloodshed, a disinterested civil tribunal was intended to be instituted to decide such controversies, and preserve peace and friendship. Further, if a state is entitled to justice in the federal court, against a citizen of another state, why not such citizen against the state, when the same language equally comprehends both? The rights of individuals and the justice due to them, are as dear and precious as those of states. Indeed, the latter are founded upon the former; and the great end and object of them must be, to secure and support the rights of individuals, or else, vain is government.

But still it may be insisted, that this will reduce states to mere corporations, and take away all sovereignty. As to corporations, all states whatever are corporations or bodies politic. The only question is, what are their powers? As to individual states and the United States, the constitution marks the boundary of powers. Whatever power is deposited with the Union by the people, for their own necessary security, is so far a curtailing of the power and prerogatives of states. This is, as it were, a self-evident proposition; at least, it cannot be contested. Thus, the power of declaring war, making peace, raising and supporting armies for public defence, levying duties, excises and taxes, if necessary, with many other powers, are lodged in congress; and are a most essential abridgement of state sovereignty. Again, the restrictions upon states: "No state shall enter into any treaty, alliance or confederation, coin money, emit bills of credit, make anything but gold and silver a tender in payment of debts, pass any law impairing the obligations of contracts;" these, with a number of others, are important restrictions of the power of states, and were thought necessary to maintain the Union; and to establish some fundamental uniform principles of public justice, throughout the whole Union. So that, I think, no argument of force can be taken from the sovereignty of states. Where it has been abridged, it was thought necessary for the greater indispensable good of the whole. If the constitution is found inconvenient in practice, in this or any other particular, it is well that a regular mode is pointed out for amendment. But while it remains, all officers, legislative, executive and judicial, both of the states and of the Union, are bound by oath to support it.

One other objection has been suggested, that if a state may be sued by a citizen of another state, then the United States may be sued by a citizen of any of the states, or, in other words, by any of their citizens. If this be a necessary consequence, it must be so. I doubt the consequence, from the different wording of the different clauses, connected with other reasons. When speaking of the United States, the constitution says, "controversies to which the United States shall be a party," not controversies between the United States and any of their citizens. When speaking of states, it says, "controversies between two or more states; between a state and citizens of another state." As to reasons for citizens suing a different state, which do not hold equally good for suing the United States; one may be, that as controversies between a state and citizens of another state, might have a tendency to involve both states in contest, and perhaps in war, a common umpire to decide such controversies may have a tendency to prevent the mischief. That an object of this kind was had in view, by the framers of the constitution, I have no doubt, when I consider the clashing interfering laws which were made in the neighboring states, before the adoption of the constitution, and some affecting the property of citizens of another state, in a very different manner from that of their own citizens. But I do not think it necessary to enter fully into the question, whether the United States are liable to be sued by an individual citizen? in order to decide the point before us. Upon the whole, I am of opinion, that the constitution warrants a suit against a state, by an individual citizen of another state.

A second question made in the case was, whether the particular action of *assumpsit* could lie against a state? I think *assumpsit* will lie, if any suit; provided a state is capable of contracting.

The third question respects the competency of service, which I apprehend is good and proper; the service being by summons and notifying the suit to the governor and the attorney-general; the governor, who is the supreme executive magistrate and representative of the state, who is bound by oath to defend the state, and by the constitution to give information to the legislature of all important matters which concern the interest of the state; the attorney-general, who is bound to defend the interests of the state in courts of law.

JAY, Chief Justice.—The question we are now to decide has been accurately stated, viz.: Is a state suable by individual citizens of another state?

It is said, that Georgia refuses to appear and answer to the plaintiff in this action, because she is a sovereign state, and therefore, not liable to such actions. In order to ascertain the merits of this objection, let us inquire, 1st. In what sense, Georgia is a sovereign state. 2d. Whether suability is compatible with such sovereignty. 3d. Whether the constitution (to which Georgia is a party) authorizes such an action against her.

Suability and suable are words not in common use, but they concisely and correctly convey the idea annexed to them.

1st. In determining the sense in which Georgia is a sovereign state, it may be useful to turn our attention to the political situation we were in, prior to the revolution, and to the political rights which emerged from the revolution. All the country, now possessed by the United States, was then a part of the dominions appertaining to the crown of Great Britain. Every acre of land in this country was then held, mediately or immediately, by grants from that crown. All the people of this country were then subjects of the King of Great Britain, and owed allegiance to him; and all the civil authority then existing, or exercised here, flowed from the head of the British Empire. They were, in strict sense, fellow-subjects, and in a variety of respects, one people. When the revolution commenced, the patriots did not assert that only the same affinity and social connection subsisted between the people of the colonies, which subsisted between the people of Gaul, Britain and Spain, while Roman provinces, viz., only that affinity and social connection which result from the mere circumstance of being governed by the same prince; different ideas prevailed, and gave occasion to the Congress of 1774 and 1775.

The revolution, or rather the Declaration of Independence, found the people already united for general purposes, and at the same time, providing for their more domestic concerns, by state conventions, and other temporary arrangements. From the crown of Great Britain, the sovereignty of their country passed to the people of it; and it was then not an uncommon opinion, that the unappropriated lands, which belonged to the crown, passed, not to the people of the colony or states within whose limits they were situated, but to the whole people; on whatever principles this opinion rested, it did not give way to the other, and thirteen sovereignties were considered as emerged from the principles of the revolution, combined with local convenience and considerations; the people, nevertheless, continued to consider themselves, in a national point of view, as one people; and they continued, without interruption, to manage their national concerns accordingly; afterwards, in the hurry of the war, and in the warmth of mutual confidence, they made a confederation of the states, the basis of a general government. Experience disappointed the expectations they had formed from it; and then the people, in their collective and national capacity, established the present constitution. It is remarkable, that in establishing it, the people exercised their own rights, and their own proper sovereignty, and conscious of the plenitude of it, they declared with becoming dignity, "We, the people of the United States, do ordain and establish this constitution." Here we see the people acting as sovereigns of the whole country; and in the language of sovereignty, establishing a constitution by which it was their will, that the state governments, should be bound, and to which the state constitutions should be made to conform. Every state constitution is a compact made by and between the citizens of a state, to govern themselves in a certain manner; and the constitution of the United States is likewise a compact made by the people of the United States, to govern themselves, as to general objects, in a certain manner. By this great compact, however, many prerogatives were transferred to the national government, such as those of making war and peace, contracting alliances, coining money, &c.

If, then, it be true, that the sovereignty of the nation is in the people of the nation, and the residuary sovereignty of each state in the people of each state, it may be useful to compare these sovereignties with those in Europe, that we may thence be enabled to judge, whether all the prerogatives which are allowed to the latter, are so essential to the former. There is reason to suspect, that some of the difficulties which embarrass the present questions, arise from inattention to differences which subsist between them.

It will be sufficient to observe briefly, that the sovereignties in Europe, and particularly in England, exist on feudal principles. That system considers the prince as the sovereign, and the people as his subjects; it regards his person as the object of allegiance, and excludes the idea of his being on an equal footing with a subject, either in a court of justice or elsewhere. That system contemplates him as being the fountain of honor and authority; and from his grace and grant, derives all franchises, immunities and privileges; it is easy to perceive, that such a sovereign could not be amenable to a court of justice, or subjected to judicial control and actual constraint. It was of necessity, therefore, that suability became incompatible with such sovereignty. Besides, the prince having all the executive powers, the judgment of the courts would, in fact, be only monitory, not mandatory to him, and a capacity to be advised, is a distinct thing from a capacity to be sued. The same feudal ideas run through all their jurisprudence, and constantly remind us of the distinction between the prince and the subject. No such ideas obtain here; at the revolution, the sovereignty devolved on the people; and they are truly the sovereigns of the country, but they are sovereigns without subjects (unless the African slaves among us may be so called) and have none to govern but themselves; the citizens of America are equal as fellow-citizens, and as joint-tenants in the sovereignty.

From the differences existing between feudal sovereignties and governments founded on compacts, it necessarily follows, that their respective prerogatives must differ. Sovereignty is the right to govern; a nation or state-sovereign is the person or persons in whom that resides. In Europe, the sovereignty is generally ascribed to the prince; here it rests with the people; there, the sovereign actually administers the government; here, never in a single instance; our governors are the agents of the people, and at most stand in the same relation to their sovereign, in which regents in Europe stand to their sovereigns. Their princes have personal powers, dignities and pre-eminences, our rulers have none but official; nor do they partake in the sovereignty otherwise, or in any other capacity, than as private citizens.

2d. The second object of inquiry now presents itself, viz., whether suability is compatible with state sovereignty.

Suability by whom? Not a subject, for in this country there are none; not an inferior, for all the citizens being, as to civil rights, perfectly equal, there is not, in that respect, one citizen inferior to another. It is agreed, that one free citizen may sue another; the obvious dictates of justice, and the purposes of society demanding it. It is agreed, that one free citizen may sue any number on whom process can be conveniently executed; nay, in certain cases, one citizen may sue forty thousand; for where a corporation is sued, all the members of it are actually sued, though not personally sued. In this city, there are forty odd thousand free citizens, all of whom may be collectively sued by any individual citizen. In the state of Delaware, there are fifty odd thousand free citizens, and what reason can be assigned why a free citizen who has demands against them, should not prosecute them? Can the difference between forty odd thousand, and fifty odd thousand make any distinction as to right? Is it not as easy, and as convenient to the public and parties, to serve a summons on the governor and attorney-general of Delaware, as on the mayor or other officers of the corporation of Philadelphia? Will it be said, that the fifty odd thousand citizens in Delaware, being associated under a state government, stand in a rank so superior to the forty odd thousand of Philadelphia, associated under their charter, that although it may become the latter to meet an individual on an equal footing in a court of justice, yet that such a procedure would not comport with the dignity of the former? In this land of equal liberty, shall forty odd thousand, in one place, be compellable to do justice, and yet fifty odd thousand, in another place, be privileged to do justice only as they may think proper? Such objections would not correspond with the equal rights we claim; with the equality we profess to admire and maintain; and with that popular sovereignty in which every citizen partakes. Grant that the governor of Delaware holds an office of superior rank to the mayor of Philadelphia, they are both nevertheless the officers of the people; and however more exalted the one may be than the other, yet, in the opinion of those who dislike aristocracy, that circumstance cannot be a good reason for impeding the course of justice.

If there be any such incompatibility as is pretended, whence does it arise? In what does it consist? There is at least one strong undeniable fact against this incompatibility, and that is this, any one state in the Union may sue another state, in this court, that is, all the people of one state may sue all the people of another state. It is plain, then, that a state may be sued, and hence it plainly follows, that suability and state sovereignty are not incompatible. As one state may sue another state in this court, it is plain, that no degradation to a state is thought to accompany her appearance in this court. It is not, therefore, to an appearance in this court, that the objection points. To what does it point? It points to an appearance at the suit of one or more citizens. But why it should be more incompatible, that all the people of a state should be sued by one citizen, than by one hundred thousand, I cannot perceive, the process in both cases being alike; and the consequences of a judgement alike. Nor can I observe any greater inconveniencies in the one case than in the other, except what may arise from the feelings of those who may regard a lesser number in an inferior light. But if any reliance be made on this inferiority as an objection, at least one-half of its force is done away, by this fact, viz., that it is conceded that a state may appear in this court, as plaintiff, against a single citizen, as defendant; and the truth is, that the state of Georgia is at this moment prosecuting an action in this court against two citizens of South Carolina.

The only remnant of objection, therefore, that remains is, that the state is not bound to appear and answer as a defendant, at the suit of an individual; but why it is unreasonable that she should be so bound, is hard to conjecture; that rule is said to be a bad one, which does not work both ways; the citizens of Georgia are content with a right of suing citizens of other states; but are not content that citizens of other states should have a right to sue them.

Let us now proceed to inquire, whether Georgia has not, by being a party to the national compact, consented to be suable by individual citizens of another state. This inquiry naturally leads our attention, 1st. To the design of the constitution. 2d. To the letter and express declaration in it.

Prior to the date of the constitution, the people had not any national tribunal to which they could resort for justice; the distribution of justice was then confined to state judicatories, in whose institution and organization the people of the other states had no participation, and over whom they had not the least control. There was then no general court of appellate jurisdiction, by whom the errors of state courts, affecting either the nation at large, or the citizens of any other state, could be revised and corrected. Each state was obliged to acquiesce in the measure of justice which another state might yield to her, or to her citizens; and that, even in cases where state considerations were not always favorable to the most exact measure. There was danger that from this source animosities would in time result; and as the transition from animosities to hostilities was frequent in the history of independent states, a common tribunal for the termination of controversies became desirable, from motives both of justice and of policy.

Prior also to that period, the United States had, by taking a place among the nations of the earth, become amenable to the law of nations; and it was their interest, as well as their duty, to provide, that those laws should be respected and obeyed; in their national character and capacity, the United States were responsible to foreign nations for the conduct of each state, relative to the laws of nations, and the performance of treaties; and there the inexpediency of referring all such questions to state courts, and particularly to the courts of delinquent states, became apparent. While all the states were bound to protect each, and the citizens of each, it was highly proper and reasonable, that they should be in a capacity, not only to cause justice to be done to each, and the citizens of each; but also to cause justice to be done by each, and the citizens of each; and that, not by violence and force, but in a stable, sedate and regular course of judicial procedure.

These were among the evils which it was proper for the

nation, that is, the people of all the United States, to provide by a national judiciary, to be instituted by the whole nation, and to be responsible to the whole nation.

Let us now turn to the constitution. The people therein declare, that their design in establishing it, comprehended six objects. 1st. To form a more perfect union. 2d. To establish justice. 3d. To ensure domestic tranquility. 4th. To provide for the common defence. 5th. To promote the general welfare. 6th. To secure the blessings of liberty to themselves and their posterity. It would be pleasing and useful, to consider and trace the relations which each of these objects bears to the others; and to show that they collectively comprise everything requisite, with the blessing of Divine Providence, to render a people prosperous and happy: on the present occasion, such disquisitions would be unseasonable, because foreign to the subject immediately under consideration.

It may be asked, what is the precise sense and latitude in which the words "to establish justice," as here used, are to be understood? The answer to this question will result from the provisions made in the constitution on this head. They are specified in the 2d section of the 3d article, where it is ordained, that the judicial power of the United States shall extend to ten descriptions of cases, viz.: 1st. To all cases arising under this constitution; because the meaning, construction and operation of a compact ought always to be ascertained by all the parties, or by authority derived only from one of them. 2d. To all cases arising under the laws of the United States; because as such laws, constitutionally made, are obligatory on each state, the measure of obligation and obedience ought not to be decided and fixed by the party from whom they are due, but by a tribunal deriving authority from both the parties. 3d. To all cases arising under treaties made by their authority; because, as treaties are compacts made by, and obligatory on, the whole nation, their operation ought not to be affected or regulated by the local laws or courts of a part of the nation. 4th. To all cases affecting ambassadors, or other public ministers and consuls; because, as these are officers of foreign nations, whom this nation are bound to protect and treat according to the laws of nations, cases affecting them ought only to be cognisable by national authority. 5th. To all cases of admiralty and maritime jurisdiction; because, as the seas are the joint property of nations, whose right and privileges relative thereto, are regulated by the law of nations and treaties, such cases necessarily belong to national jurisdiction. 6th. To controversies to which the United States shall be a party; because in cases in which the whole people are interested, it would not be equal or wise to let any one state decide and measure out the justice due to others. 7th. To controversies between two or more states; because domestic tranquillity requires, that the contentions of states should be peaceably terminated by a common judiciary; and because, in a free country, justice ought not to depend on the will of either of the litigants. 8th. To controversies between a state and citizens of another state; because, in case a state (that is, all the citizens of it) has demands against some citizens of another state, it is better that she should prosecute their demands in a national court, than in a court of the state to which those citizens belong; the danger of irritation and criminations arising from apprehensions and suspicions of partiality, being thereby obviated. Because, in cases where some citizens of one state have demands against all the citizens of another state, the cause of liberty and the rights of men forbid, that the latter should be the sole judges of the justice due to the latter; and true republican government requires, that free and equal citizens should have free, fair and equal justice. 9th. To controversies between citizens of the same state, claiming lands under grants of different states: because, as the rights of the two states to grant the land, are drawn into question, neither of the two states ought to decide the controversy. 10th. To controversies between a state, or the citizens thereof, and foreign states, citizens or subjects; because, as every nation is responsible for the conduct of its citizens towards other nations, all questions touching the justice due to foreign nations or people, ought to be ascertained by, and depend on national authority. Even this cursory view of the judicial powers of the United States, leaves the mind strongly impressed with the importance of them to the preservation of the tranquillity, the equal sovereignty and the equal right of the people.

The question now before us renders it necessary to pay particular attention to that part of the 2d section, which extends the judicial power "to controversies between a state and citizens of another state." It is contended, that this ought to be construed to reach none of these controversies, excepting those in which a state may be plaintiff. The ordinary rules for construction will early decide, whether those words are to be understood in that limited sense.

This extension of power is remedial, because it is to settle controversies. It is, therefore, to be construed liberally. It is politic, wise and good, that, not only the controversies in which a state is plaintiff, but also those in which a state is defendant, should be settled; both cases, therefore, are within the reason of the remedy; and ought to be so adjudged, unless the obvious, plain and literal sense of the words forbid it. If we attend to the words, we find them to be express, positive, free from ambiguity, and without room for such implied expressions: "The judicial power of the United States shall extend to controversies between a state and citizens of another state." If the constitution really meant to extend these powers only to those controversies in which a state might be plaintiff, to the exclusion of those in which citizens had demands against a state, it is inconceivable, that it should have attempted to convey that meaning in words, not only so incompetent, but also repugnant to it; if it meant to exclude a certain class of these controversies, why were they not expressly excepted; on the contrary, not even an intimation of such intention appears in any part of the constitution. It cannot be pretended, that where citizens urge and insist upon demands against a state, which the state refuses to admit and comply with, that there is no controversy between them. If it is a controversy between them, then it clearly falls not only within the spirit, but the very words of the constitution. What is it to the cause of justice, and how can it affect the definition of the word *controversy,* whether the demands which cause the dispute, are made by a state against citizens of another state, or by the latter against the former? When power is thus extended to a *controversy,* it necessarily, as to all judicial purposes, is also extended to those between whom it subsists.

The exception contended for, would contradict and do violence to the great and leading principles of a free and equal national government, one of the great objects of which is, to ensure justice to all: to the few against the many, as well as to the many against the few. It would be strange, indeed, that the joint and equal sovereigns of this country, should, in the very constitution by which they professed to establish justice, so far deviate from the plain path of equality and impartiality, as to give to the collective citizens of one state, a right of suing individual citizens of another state, and yet deny to those citizens a right of suing them. We find the same general and comprehensive manner of expressing the same ideas, in a subsequent clause; in which the constitution ordains, that "in all cases affecting ambassadors, other public ministers and consuls, and those in which a state shall be a party, the supreme court shall have original jurisdiction." Did it mean here party-plaintiff? If that only was meant, it would have been easy to have found words to express it. Words are to be understood in their ordinary and common acceptation, and the word party being, in common usage, applicable both to plaintiff and defendant, we cannot limit it to one of them, in the present case. We find the legislature of the United States expressing themselves in the like general and comprehensive manner; they speak in the 13th section of the judicial act, of controversies where a state is a party, and as they do not, impliedly or expressly, apply that term to either of the litigants, in particular, we are to understand them as speaking of both. In the same section, they distinguish the cases where ambassadors are plaintiffs, from those in which ambassadors are defendants, and make different provisions respecting those cases; and it is not unnatural to suppose, that they would, in like manner, have distinguished between cases where a state was plaintiff, and where a state was defendant, if they had intended to make any difference between them; or if they had apprehended that the constitution had made any difference between them.

I perceive, and therefore candor urges me to mention, a circumstance, which seems to favor the opposite side of the question. It is this: the same section of the constitution which extends the judicial power to controversies "between a state and the citizens of another state," does also extend that power to controversies to which the United States are a party. Now, it may be said, if the word party comprehends both plaintiff and defendant, it follows, that the United States may be sued by any citizen, between whom and them there may be a controversy. This appears to me to be fair reasoning; but the same principles of candor which urge me to mention this objection, also urge me to suggest an important difference between the two cases. It is this, in all cases of actions against states or individual citizens, the national courts are supported in all their legal and constitutional proceedings and judgments, by the arm of the executive power of the United States; but in cases of actions against the United States, there is no power which the courts can call to their aid. From this distinction, important conclusions are deducible, and they place the case of a state, and the case of the United States, in very different points of view.

I wish the state of society was so far improved, and the science of government advanced to such a degree of perfection, as that the whole nation could, in the peaceable course of law, be compelled to do justice, and be sued by individual citizens. Whether that is, or is not, now the case, ought not to be thus collaterally and incidentally decided: I leave it a question.

As this opinion, though deliberately formed, has been hastily reduced to writing, between the intervals of the daily adjournments, and while my mind was occupied and wearied by the business of the day, I fear, it is less concise and connected than it might otherwise have been. I have made no references to cases, because I know of none that are not distinguishable from this case: nor does it appear to me necessary to show that the sentiments of the best writers on government and the rights of men, harmonise with the principles which direct my judgment on the present question. The acts of the former congresses, and the act of many of the state conventions, are replete with similar ideas; and to the honor of the United States, it may be observed, that in no other country are subjects of this kind better, if so well, understood. The attention and attachment of the constitution to the equal rights of the people are discernible in almost every sentence of it; and it is to be regretted that the provision in it which we have been considering, has not, in every instance, received the approbation and acquiescence which it merits. Georgia has, in strong language, advocated the cause of republican equality: and there is reason to hope, that the people of that state will yet perceive that it would not have been consistent with that equality, to have exempted the body of her citizens from that suability, which they are at this moment exercising against citizens of another state.

For my own part, I am convinced, that the sense in which I understand and have explained the words "controversies between states and citizens of another state," is the true sense. The extension of the judiciary power of the United States to such controversies appears to me to be wise, because it is honest, and because it is useful. It is honest, because it provides for doing justice, without respect of persons, and by securing individual citizens, as well as states, in their respective rights, performs the promise which every free government makes to every free citizen, of equal justice and protection. It is useful, because it is honest, because it leaves not even the most obscure and friendless citizen without means of obtaining justice from a neighboring state; because it obviates occasions of quarrels between states on account of the claims of their respective citizens; because it recognises and strongly rests on this great moral truth, that justice is the same whether due from one man or a million, or from a million to one man; because it teaches and greatly appreciates the value of our free republican national government, which places all our citizens on an equal footing, and enables each and every of them to obtain justice, without any danger of being overborne by the weight and number of their opponents; and because it brings into action and enforces this great and glorious principle, that the people are the sovereign of this country, and consequently, that fellow-citizens and joint-sovereigns cannot be degraded, by appearing with each other, in their own courts, to have their controversies determined. The people have reason to prize and rejoice in such valuable privileges; and they ought not to forget, that nothing but the free course of constitutional law and government can ensure the continuance and enjoyment of them.

For the reasons before given, I am clearly of opinion, that a state is suable by citizens of another state; but lest I should be understood in a latitude beyond my meaning, I think it necessary to subjoin this caution, viz.: That such suability may nevertheless not extend to all the demands, and to every kind of action; there may be exceptions. For instance, I am far from being prepared to say, that an individual may sue a state on bills of credit issued before the constitution was established, and which were issued and received on the faith of the state, and at a time when no ideas or expectations of judicial interposition were entertained or contemplated.

2

Hollingsworth v. Virginia
3 Dall. 378 (1798)

The Court, on the day succeeding the argument, delivered a unanimous opinion, that the [11th] amendment being constitutionally adopted, there could not be exercised any jurisdiction, in any case, past or future, in which a state was sued by the citizens of another state, or by citizens or subjects of any foreign state.

3

Cohens v. Virginia
6 Wheat. 264 (1821)

Mr. Chief Justice MARSHALL delivered the opinion of the Court.

This is a writ of error to a judgment rendered in the Court of Hustings for the borough of Norfolk, as an information for selling lottery tickets, contrary to an act of the Legislature of Virginia. In the State Court, the defendant claimed the protection of an act of Congress. A case was agreed between the parties, which states the act of Assembly on which the prosecution was founded, and the act of Congress on which the defendant relied, and concludes in these words: "If upon this case the Court shall be of

opinion that the acts of Congress before mentioned were valid, and, on the true construction of those acts, the lottery tickets sold by the defendants as aforesaid, might lawfully be sold within the State of Virginia, notwithstanding the act or statute of the general assembly of Virginia prohibiting such sale, then judgment to be entered for the defendants; And if the Court should be of opinion that the statute or act of the General Assembly of the State of Virginia, prohibiting such sale, is valid, notwithstanding the said acts of Congress, then judgment to be entered that the defendants are guilty, and that the Commonwealth recover against them one hundred dollars and costs."

Judgment was rendered against the defendants; and the Court in which it was rendered being the highest Court of the State in which the cause was cognizable, the record has been brought into this Court by writ of error.[a]

The defendant in error moves to dismiss this writ, for want of jurisdiction.

In support of this motion, three points have been made, and argued with the ability which the importance of the question merits. These points are—

1st. That a State is a defendant.

2d. That no writ of error lies from this Court to a State Court.

3d. The third point has been presented in different forms by the gentlemen who have argued it. The counsel who opened the cause said, that the want of jurisdiction was shown by the subject matter of the case. The counsel who followed him said, that jurisdiction was not given by the judiciary act. The Court has bestowed all its attention on the arguments of both gentlemen, and supposes that their tendency is to show that this Court has no jurisdiction of the case, or, in other words, has no right to review the judgment of the State Court, because neither the constitution nor any law of the United States has been violated by that judgment.

The questions presented to the Court by the two first points made at the bar are of great magnitude, and may be truly said vitally to affect the Union. They exclude the inquiry whether the constitution and laws of the United States have been violated by the judgment which the plaintiffs in error seek to review; and maintain that, admitting such violation, it is not in the power of the government to apply a corrective. They maintain that the nation does not possess a department capable of restraining peaceably, and by authority of law, any attempts which may be made, by a part, against the legitimate powers of the whole; and that the government is reduced to the alternative of submitting to such attempts, or of resisting them by force. They maintain that the constitution of the United States has provided no tribunal for the final construction of itself, or of the laws or treaties of the nation; but that this power may be exercised in the last resort by the Courts of every State in the Union. That the constitution, laws, and treaties, may

[a]The plaintiff in error prayed an appeal from the judgment of the Court of Hustings, but it was refused, on the ground that there was no higher State tribunal which could take cognizance of the case.

receive as many constructions as there are States; and that this is not a mischief, or, if a mischief, is irremediable. These abstract propositions are to be determined; for he who demands decision without permitting inquiry, affirms that the decision he asks does not depend on inquiry.

If such be the constitution, it is the duty of the Court to bow with respectful submission to its provisions. If such be not the constitution, it is equally the duty of this Court to say so; and to perform that task which the American people have assigned to the judicial department.

1st. The first question to be considered is, whether the jurisdiction of this Court is excluded by the character of the parties, one of them being a State, and the other a citizen of that State?

The second section of the third article of the constitution defines the extent of the judicial power of the United States. Jurisdiction is given to the Courts of the Union in two classes of cases. In the first, their jurisdiction depends on the character of the cause, whoever may be the parties. This class comprehends "all cases in law and equity arising under this constitution, the laws of the United States, and treaties made, or which shall be made, under their authority." This clause extends the jurisdiction of the Court to all the cases described, without making in its terms any exception whatever, and without any regard to the condition of the party. If there be any exception, it is to be implied against the express words of the article.

In the second class, the jurisdiction depends entirely on the character of the parties. In this are comprehended "controversies between two or more States, between a State and citizens of another State," "and between a State and foreign States, citizens or subjects." If these be the parties, it is entirely unimportant what may be the subject of controversy. Be it what it may, these parties have a constitutional right to come into the Courts of the Union.

The counsel for the defendant in error have stated that the cases which arise under the constitution must grow out of those provisions which are capable of self-execution; examples of which are to be found in the 2d section of the 4th article, and in the 10th section of the 1st article.

A case which arises under a law of the United States must, we are likewise told, be a right given by some act which becomes necessary to execute the powers given in the constitution, of which the law of naturalization is mentioned as an example.

The use intended to be made of this exposition of the first part of the section, defining the extent of the judicial power, is not clearly understood. If the intention be merely to distinguish cases arising under the constitution, from those arising under a law, for the sake of precision in the application of this argument, these propositions will not be controverted. If it be to maintain that a case arising under the constitution, or a law, must be one in which a party comes into Court to demand something conferred on him by the constitution or a law, we think the construction too narrow. A case in law or equity consists of the right of the one party, as well as of the other, and may truly be said to arise under the constitution or a law of the United States, whenever its correct decision depends on the construction of either. Congress seems to have in-

tended to give its own construction of this part of the constitution in the 25th section of the judiciary act; and we perceive no reason to depart from that construction.

The jurisdiction of the Court, then, being extended by the letter of the constitution to all cases arising under it, or under the laws of the United States, it follows that those who would withdraw any case of this description from that jurisdiction, must sustain the exemption they claim on the spirit and true meaning of the constitution, which spirit and true meaning must be so apparent as to overrule the words which its framers have employed.

The counsel for the defendant in error have undertaken to do this; and have laid down the general proposition, that a sovereign independent State is not suable, except by its own consent.

This general proposition will not be controverted. But its consent is not requisite in each particular case. It may be given in a general law. And if a State has surrendered any portion of its sovereignty, the question whether a liability to suit be a part of this portion, depends on the instrument by which the surrender is made. If, upon a just construction of that instrument, it shall appear that the State has submitted to be sued, then it has parted with this sovereign right of judging in every case on the justice of its own pretensions, and has entrusted that power to a tribunal in whose impartiality it confides.

The American States, as well as the American people, have believed a close and firm Union to be essential to their liberty and to their happiness. They have been taught by experience, that this Union cannot exist without a government for the whole; and they have been taught by the same experience that this government would be a mere shadow, that must disappoint all their hopes, unless invested with large portions of that sovereignty which belongs to independent States. Under the influence of this opinion, and thus instructed by experience, the American people, in the conventions of their respective States, adopted the present constitution.

If it could be doubted, whether from its nature, it were not supreme in all cases where it is empowered to act, that doubt would be removed by the declaration, that "this constitution, and the laws of the United States, which shall be made in pursuance thereof, and all treaties made, or which shall be made, under the authority of the United States, shall be the supreme law of the land; and the judges in every State shall be bound thereby; any thing in the constitution or laws of any State to the contrary notwithstanding."

This is the authoritative language of the American people; and, if gentlemen please, of the American States. It marks, with lines too strong to be mistaken, the characteristic distinction between the government of the Union, and those of the States. The general government, though limited as to its objects, is supreme with respect to those objects. This principle is a part of the constitution; and if there be any who deny its necessity, none can deny its authority.

To this supreme government ample powers are confided; and if it were possible to doubt the great purposes for which they were so confided, the people of the United

States have declared, that they are given "in order to form a more perfect union, establish justice, ensure domestic tranquillity, provide for the common defence, promote the general welfare, and secure the blessings of liberty to themselves and their posterity."

With the ample powers confided to this supreme government, for these interesting purposes, are connected many express and important limitations on the sovereignty of the States, which are made for the same purposes. The powers of the Union, on the great subjects of war, peace, and commerce, and on many others, are in themselves limitations of the sovereignty of the States; but in addition to these, the sovereignty of the States is surrendered in many instances where the surrender can only operate to the benefit of the people, and where, perhaps, no other power is conferred on Congress than a conservative power to maintain the principles established in the constitution. The maintenance of these principles in their purity, is certainly among the great duties of the government. One of the instruments by which this duty may be peaceably performed, is the judicial department. It is authorized to decide all cases of every description, arising under the constitution or laws of the United States. From this general grant of jurisdiction, no exception is made of those cases in which a State may be a party. When we consider the situation of the government of the Union and of a State, in relation to each other; the nature of our constitution; the subordination of the State governments to that constitution; the great purpose for which jurisdiction over all cases arising under the constitution and laws of the United States, is confided to the judicial department; are we at liberty to insert in this general grant, an exception of those cases in which a State may be a party? Will the spirit of the constitution justify this attempt to control its words? We think it will not. We think a case arising under the constitution or laws of the United States, is cognizable in the Courts of the Union, whoever may be the parties to that case.

Had any doubt existed with respect to the just construction of this part of the section, that doubt would have been removed by the enumeration of those cases to which the jurisdiction of the federal Courts is extended, in consequence of the character of the parties. In that enumeration, we find "controversies between two or more States, between a State and citizens of another State," "and between a State and foreign States, citizens, or subjects."

One of the express objects, then, for which the judicial department was established, is the decision of controversies between States, and between a State and individuals. The mere circumstance, that a State is a party, gives jurisdiction to the Court. How, then, can it be contended, that the very same instrument, in the very same section, should be so construed, as that this same circumstance should withdraw a case from the jurisdiction of the Court, where the constitution or laws of the United States are supposed to have been violated? The constitution gave to every person having a claim upon a State, a right to submit his case to the Court of the nation. However unimportant his claim might be, however little the community might be interested in its decision, the framers of our constitution thought it necessary for the purposes of justice, to provide a tribunal as superior to influence as possible, in which that claim might be decided. Can it be imagined, that the same persons considered a case involving the constitution of our country and the majesty of the laws, questions in which every American citizen must be deeply interested, as withdrawn from this tribunal, because a State is a party?

While weighing arguments drawn from the nature of government, and from the general spirit of an instrument, and urged for the purpose of narrowing the construction which the words of that instrument seem to require, it is proper to place in the opposite scale those principles, drawn from the same sources, which go to sustain the words in their full operation and natural import. One of these, which has been pressed with great force by the counsel for the plaintiffs in error, is, that the judicial power of every well constituted government must be co-extensive with the legislative, and must be capable of deciding every judicial question which grows out of the constitution and laws.

If any proposition may be considered as a political axiom, this, we think, may be so considered. In reasoning upon it as an abstract question, there would, probably, exist no contrariety of opinion respecting it. Every argument, proving the necessity of the department, proves also the propriety of giving this extent to it. We do not mean to say, that the jurisdiction of the Courts of the Union should be construed to be co-extensive with the legislative, merely because it is fit that it should be so; but we mean to say, that this fitness furnishes an argument in construing the constitution which ought never to be overlooked, and which is most especially entitled to consideration, when we are inquiring, whether the words of the instrument which purport to establish this principle, shall be contracted for the purpose of destroying it.

The mischievous consequences of the construction contended for on the part of Virginia, are also entitled to great consideration. It would prostrate, it has been said, the government and its laws at the feet of every State in the Union. And would not this be its effect? What power of the government could be executed by its own means, in any State disposed to resist its execution by a course of legislation? The laws must be executed by individuals acting within the several States. If these individuals may be exposed to penalties, and if the Courts of the Union cannot correct the judgments by which these penalties may be enforced, the course of the government may be, at any time, arrested by the will of one of its members. Each member will possess a *veto* on the will of the whole.

The answer which has been given to this argument, does not deny its truth, but insists that confidence is reposed, and may be safely reposed, in the State institutions; and that, if they shall ever become so insane or so wicked as to seek the destruction of the government, they may accomplish their object by refusing to perform the functions assigned to them.

We readily concur with the counsel for the defendant, in the declaration, that the cases which have been put of direct legislative resistance for the purpose of opposing the acknowledged powers of the government, are extreme cases, and in the hope, that they will never occur; but we cannot help believing, that a general conviction of the total incapacity of the government to protect itself and its laws in such cases, would contribute in no inconsiderable degree to their occurrence.

Let it be admitted, that the cases which have been put are extreme and improbable, yet there are gradations of opposition to the laws, far short of those cases, which might have a baneful influence on the affairs of the nation. Different States may entertain different opinions on the true construction of the constitutional powers of Congress. We know, that at one time, the assumption of the debts contracted by the several States, during the war of our revolution, was deemed unconstitutional by some of them. We know, too, that at other times, certain taxes, imposed by Congress, have been pronounced unconstitutional. Other laws have been questioned partially, while they were supported by the great majority of the American people. We have no assurance that we shall be less divided than we have been. States may legislate in conformity to their opinions, and may enforce those opinions by penalties. It would be hazarding too much to assert, that the judicatures of the States will be exempt from the prejudices by which the legislatures and people are influenced, and will constitute perfectly impartial tribunals. In many States the judges are dependent for office and for salary on the will of the legislature. The constitution of the United States furnishes no security against the universal adoption of this principle. When we observe the importance which that constitution attaches to the independence of judges, we are the less inclined to suppose that it can have intended to leave these constitutional questions to tribunals where this independence may not exist, in all cases where a State shall prosecute an individual who claims the protection of an act of Congress. These prosecutions may take place even without a legislative act. A person making a seizure under an act of Congress, may be indicted as a trespasser, if force has been employed, and of this a jury may judge. How extensive may be the mischief if the first decisions in such cases should be final!

These collisions may take place in times of no extraordinary commotion. But a constitution is framed for ages to come, and is designed to approach immortality as nearly as human institutions can approach it. Its course cannot always be tranquil. It is exposed to storms and tempests, and its framers must be unwise statesmen indeed, if they have not provided it, as far as its nature will permit, with the means of self-preservation from the perils it may be destined to encounter. No government ought to be so defective in its organization, as not to contain within itself the means of securing the execution of its own laws against other dangers than those which occur every day. Courts of justice are the means most usually employed; and it is reasonable to expect that a government should repose on its own Courts, rather than on others. There is certainly nothing in the circumstances under which our constitution was formed; nothing in the history of the times, which would justify the opinion that the confidence reposed in the States was so implicit as to leave in them and their tribunals the power of resisting or defeating, in the form

of law, the legitimate measures of the Union. The requisitions of Congress, under the confederation, were as constitutionally obligatory as the laws enacted by the present Congress. That they were habitually disregarded, is a fact of universal notoriety. With the knowledge of this fact, and under its full pressure, a convention was assembled to change the system. Is it so improbable that they should confer on the judicial department the power of construing the constitution and laws of the Union in every case, in the last resort, and of preserving them from all violation from every quarter, so far as judicial decisions can preserve them, that this improbability should essentially affect the construction of the new system? We are told, and we are truly told, that the great change which is to give efficacy to the present system, is its ability to act on individuals directly, instead of acting through the instrumentality of State governments. But, ought not this ability, in reason and sound policy, to be applied directly to the protection of individuals employed in the execution of the laws, as well as to their coercion. Your laws reach the individual without the aid of any other power; why may they not protect him from punishment for performing his duty in executing them?

The counsel for Virginia endeavour to obviate the force of these arguments by saying, that the dangers they suggest, if not imaginary, are inevitable; that the constitution can make no provision against them; and that, therefore, in construing that instrument, they ought to be excluded from our consideration. This state of things, they say, cannot arise until there shall be a disposition so hostile to the present political system as to produce a determination to destroy it; and, when that determination shall be produced, its effects will not be restrained by parchment stipulations. The fate of the constitution will not then depend on judicial decisions. But, should no appeal be made to force, the States can put an end to the government by refusing to act. They have only not to elect Senators, and it expires without a struggle.

It is very true that, whenever hostility to the existing system shall become universal, it will be also irresistible. The people made the constitution, and the people can unmake it. It is the creature of their will, and lives only by their will. But this supreme and irresistible power to make or to unmake, resides only in the whole body of the people; not in any sub-division of them. The attempt of any of the parts to exercise it is usurpation, and ought to be repelled by those to whom the people have delegated their power of repelling it.

The acknowledged inability of the government, then, to sustain itself against the public will, and, by force or otherwise, to control the whole nation, is no sound argument in support of its constitutional inability to preserve itself against a section of the nation acting in opposition to the general will.

It is true, that if all the States, or a majority of them, refuse to elect Senators, the legislative powers of the Union will be suspended. But if any one State shall refuse to elect them, the Senate will not, on that account, be the less capable of performing all its functions. The argument founded on this fact would seem rather to prove the subordination of the parts to the whole, than the complete independence of any one of them. The framers of the constitution were, indeed, unable to make any provisions which should protect that instrument against a general combination of the States, or of the people, for its destruction; and, conscious of this inability, they have not made the attempt. But they were able to provide against the operation of measures adopted in any one State, whose tendency might be to arrest the execution of the laws, and this it was the part of true wisdom to attempt. We think they have attempted it.

It has been also urged, as an additional objection to the jurisdiction of the Court, that cases between a State and one of its own citizens, do not come within the general scope of the constitution; and were obviously never intended to be made cognizable in the federal Courts. The State tribunals might be suspected of partiality in cases between itself or its citizens and aliens, or the citizens of another State, but not in proceedings by a State against its own citizens. That jealousy which might exist in the first case, could not exist in the last, and therefore the judicial power is not extended to the last.

This is very true, so far as jurisdiction depends on the character of the parties; and the argument would have great force if urged to prove that this Court could not establish the demand of a citizen upon his State, but is not entitled to the same force when urged to prove that this Court cannot inquire whether the constitution or laws of the United States protect a citizen from a prosecution instituted against him by a State. If jurisdiction depended entirely on the character of the parties, and was not given where the parties have not an original right to come into Court, that part of the 2d section of the 3d article, which extends the judicial power to all cases arising under the constitution and laws of the United States, would be mere surplusage. It is to give jurisdiction where the character of the parties would not give it, that this very important part of the clause was inserted. It may be true, that the partiality of the State tribunals, in ordinary controversies between a State and its citizens, was not apprehended, and therefore the judicial power of the Union was not extended to such cases; but this was not the sole nor the greatest object for which this department was created. A more important, a much more interesting object, was the preservation of the constitution and laws of the United States, so far as they can be preserved by judicial authority; and therefore the jurisdiction of the Courts of the Union was expressly extended to all cases arising under that constitution and those laws. If the constitution or laws may be violated by proceedings instituted by a State against its own citizens, and if that violation may be such as essentially to affect the constitution and the laws, such as to arrest the progress of government in its constitutional course, why should these cases be excepted from that provision which expressly extends the judicial power of the Union to *all* cases arising under the constitution and laws?

After bestowing on this subject the most attentive consideration, the Court can perceive no reason founded on the character of the parties for introducing an exception which the constitution has not made; and we think that the judicial power, as originally given, extends to all cases arising under the constitution or a law of the United States, whoever may be the parties.

It has been also contended, that this jurisdiction, if given, is original, and cannot be exercised in the appellate form.

The words of the constitution are, "in all cases affecting ambassadors, other public ministers, and consuls, and those in which a State shall be a party, the Supreme Court shall have original jurisdiction. In all the other cases before mentioned, the Supreme Court shall have appellate jurisdiction."

This distinction between original and appellate jurisdiction, excludes, we are told, in all cases, the exercise of the one where the other is given.

The constitution gives the Supreme Court original jurisdiction in certain enumerated cases, and gives it appellate jurisdiction in all others. Among those in which jurisdiction must be exercised in the appellate form, are cases arising under the constitution and laws of the United States. These provisions of the constitution are equally obligatory, and are to be equally respected. If a State be a party, the jurisdiction of this Court is original; if the case arise under a constitution or a law, the jurisdiction is appellate. But a case to which a State is a party may arise under the constitution or a law of the United States. What rule is applicable to such a case? What, then, becomes the duty of the Court? Certainly, we think, so to construe the constitution as to give effect to both provisions, as far as it is possible to reconcile them, and not to permit their seeming repugnancy to destroy each other. We must endeavour so to construe them as to preserve the true intent and meaning of the instrument.

In one description of cases, the jurisdiction of the Court is founded entirely on the character of the parties; and the nature of the controversy is not contemplated by the constitution. The character of the parties is every thing, the nature of the case nothing. In the other description of cases, the jurisdiction is founded entirely on the character of the case, and the parties are not contemplated by the constitution. In these, the nature of the case is every thing, the character of the parties nothing. When, then, the constitution declares the jurisdiction, in cases where a State shall be a party, to be original, and in all cases arising under the constitution or a law, to be appellate—the conclusion seems irresistible, that its framers designed to include in the first class those cases in which jurisdiction is given, because a State is a party; and to include in the second, those in which jurisdiction is given, because the case arises under the constitution or a law.

This reasonable construction is rendered necessary by other considerations.

That the constitution or a law of the United States, is involved in a case, and makes a part of it, may appear in the progress of a cause, in which the Courts of the Union, but for that circumstance, would have no jurisdiction, and which of consequence could not originate in the Supreme Court. In such a case, the jurisdiction can be exercised only in its appellate form. To deny its exercise in this form is to deny its existence, and would be to construe a clause, dividing the power of the Supreme Court, in such manner, as in a considerable degree to defeat the power itself. All must perceive, that this construction can be justified only where it is absolutely necessary. We do not think the article under consideration presents that necessity.

It is observable, that in this distributive clause, no negative words are introduced. This observation is not made for the purpose of contending, that the legislature may "apportion the judicial power between the Supreme and inferior Courts according to its will." That would be, as was said by this Court in the case of *Marbury* v. *Madison*, to render the distributive clause "mere surplusage," to make it "form without substance." This cannot, therefore, be the true construction of the article.

But although the absence of negative words will not authorize the legislature to disregard the distribution of the power previously granted, their absence will justify a sound construction of the whole article, so as to give every part its intended effect. It is admitted, that "affirmative words are often, in their operation, negative of other objects than those affirmed;" and that where "a negative or exclusive sense must be given to them, or they have no operation at all," they must receive that negative or exclusive sense. But where they have full operation without it; where it would destroy some of the most important objects for which the power was created; then, we think, affirmative words ought not to be construed negatively.

The constitution declares, that in cases where a State is a party, the Supreme Court shall have original jurisdiction; but does not say that its appellate jurisdiction shall not be exercised in cases where, from their nature, appellate jurisdiction is given, whether a State be or be not a party. It may be conceded, that where the case is of such a nature as to admit of its originating in the Supreme Court, it ought to originate there; but where, from its nature, it cannot originate in that Court, these words ought not to be so construed as to require it. There are many cases in which it would be found extremely difficult, and subversive of the spirit of the constitution, to maintain the construction, that appellate jurisdiction cannot be exercised where one of the parties might sue or be sued in this Court.

The constitution defines the jurisdiction of the Supreme Court, but does not define that of the inferior Courts. Can it be affirmed, that a State might not sue the citizen of another State in a Circuit Court? Should the Circuit Court decide for or against its jurisdiction, should it dismiss the suit, or give judgment against the State, might not its decision be revised in the Supreme Court? The argument is, that it could not; and the very clause which is urged to prove, that the Circuit Court could give no judgment in the case, is also urged to prove, that its judgment is irreversible. A supervising Court, whose peculiar province it is to correct the errors of an inferior Court, has no power to correct a judgment given without jurisdiction, because, in the same case, that supervising Court has original jurisdiction. Had negative words been employed, it would be difficult to give them this construction if they would admit of any other. But, without negative words, this irrational construction can never be maintained.

So, too, in the same clause, the jurisdiction of the Court is declared to be original, "in cases affecting ambassadors, other public ministers, and consuls." There is, perhaps, no part of the article under consideration so much required by national policy as this; unless it be that part which extends the judicial power "to all cases arising under the constitution, laws, and treaties of the United States." It has been generally held, that the State Courts have a concurrent jurisdiction with the federal Courts, in cases to which the judicial power is extended, unless the jurisdiction of the federal Courts be rendered exclusive by the words of the third article. If the words, "to all cases," give exclusive jurisdiction in cases affecting foreign ministers, they may also give exclusive jurisdiction, if such be the will of Congress, in cases arising under the constitution, laws, and treaties of the United States. Now, suppose an individual were to sue a foreign minister in a State Court, and that Court were to maintain its jurisdiction, and render judgment against the minister, could it be contended, that this Court would be incapable of revising such judgment, because the constitution had given it original jurisdiction in the case? If this could be maintained, then a clause inserted for the purpose of excluding the jurisdiction of all other Courts than this, in a particular case, would have the effect of excluding the jurisdiction of this Court in that very case, if the suit were to be brought in another Court, and that Court were to assert jurisdiction. This tribunal, according to the argument which has been urged, could neither revise the judgment of such other Court, nor suspend its proceedings: for a writ of prohibition, or any other similar writ, is in the nature of appellate process.

Foreign consuls frequently assert, in our Prize Courts, the claims of their fellow subjects. These suits are maintained by them as consuls. The appellate power of this Court has been frequently exercised in such cases, and has never been questioned. It would be extremely mischievous to withhold its exercise. Yet the consul is a party on the record. The truth is, that where the words confer only appellate jurisdiction, original jurisdiction is most clearly not given; but where the words admit of appellate jurisdiction, the power to take cognizance of the suit originally, does not necessarily negative the power to decide upon it on an appeal, if it may originate in a different Court.

It is, we think, apparent, that to give this distributive clause the interpretation contended for, to give to its affirmative words a negative operation, in every possible case, would, in some instances, defeat the obvious intention of the article. Such an interpretation would not consist with those rules which, from time immemorial, have guided Courts, in their construction of instruments brought under their consideration. It must, therefore, be discarded. Every part of the article must be taken into view, and that construction adopted which will consist with its words, and promote its general intention. The Court may imply a negative from affirmative words, where the implication promotes, not where it defeats the intention.

If we apply this principle, the correctness of which we believe will not be controverted, to the distributive clause under consideration, the result, we think, would be this: the original jurisdiction of the Supreme Court, in cases where a State is a party, refers to those cases in which, according to the grant of power made in the preceding clause, jurisdiction might be exercised in consequence of the character of the party, and an original suit might be instituted in any of the federal Courts; not to those cases in which an original suit might not be instituted in a federal Court. Of the last description, is every case between a State and its citizens, and, perhaps, every case in which a State is enforcing its penal laws. In such cases, therefore, the Supreme Court cannot take original jurisdiction. In every other case, that is, in every case to which the judicial power extends, and in which original jurisdiction is not expressly given, that judicial power shall be exercised in the appellate, and only in the appellate form. The original jurisdiction of this Court cannot be enlarged, but its appellate jurisdiction may be exercised in every case cognizable under the third article of the constitution, in the federal Courts, in which original jurisdiction cannot be exercised; and the extent of this judicial power is to be measured, not by giving the affirmative words of the distributive clause a negative operation in every possible case, but by giving their true meaning to the words which define its extent.

The counsel for the defendant in error urge, in opposition to this rule of construction, some *dicta* of the Court, in the case of *Marbury* v. *Madison.*

It is a maxim not to be disregarded, that general expressions, in every opinion, are to be taken in connection with the case in which those expressions are used. If they go beyond the case, they may be respected, but ought not to control the judgment in a subsequent suit when the very point is presented for decision. The reason of this maxim is obvious. The question actually before the Court is investigated with care, and considered in its full extent. Other principles which may serve to illustrate it, are considered in their relation to the case decided, but their possible bearing on all other cases is seldom completely investigated.

In the case of *Marbury* v. *Madison*, the single question before the Court, so far as that case can be applied to this, was, whether the legislature could give this Court original jurisdiction in a case in which the constitution had clearly not given it, and in which no doubt respecting the construction of the article could possibly be raised. The Court decided, and we think very properly, that the legislature could not give original jurisdiction in such a case. But, in the reasoning of the Court in support of this decision, some expressions are used which go far beyond it. The counsel for Marbury had insisted on the unlimited discretion of the legislature in the apportionment of the judicial power; and it is against this argument that the reasoning of the Court is directed. They say that, if such had been the intention of the article, "it would certainly have been useless to proceed farther than to define the judicial power, and the tribunals in which it should be vested." The Court says, that such a construction would render the clause, dividing the jurisdiction of the Court into original and appellate, totally useless; that "affirmative words are often, in their operation, negative of other objects than those which are affirmed; and, in this case, (in the case of

Marbury v. *Madison,*) a negative or exclusive sense must be given to them, or they have no operation at all." "It cannot be presumed," adds the Court, "that any clause in the constitution is intended to be without effect; and, therefore, such a construction is inadmissible, unless the words require it."

The whole reasoning of the Court proceeds upon the idea that the affirmative words of the clause giving one sort of jurisdiction, must imply a negative of any other sort of jurisdiction, because otherwise the words would be totally inoperative, and this reasoning is advanced in a case to which it was strictly applicable. If in that case original jurisdiction could have been exercised, the clause under consideration would have been entirely useless. Having such cases only in its view, the Court lays down a principle which is generally correct, in terms much broader than the decision, and not only much broader than the reasoning with which that decision is supported, but in some instances contradictory to its principle. The reasoning sustains the negative operation of the words in that case, because otherwise the clause would have no meaning whatever, and because such operation was necessary to give effect to the intention of the article. The effort now made is, to apply the conclusion to which the Court was conducted by that reasoning in the particular case, to one in which the words have their full operation when understood affirmatively, and in which the negative, or exclusive sense, is to be so used as to defeat some of the great objects of the article.

To this construction the Court cannot give its assent. The general expressions in the case of *Marbury* v. *Madison* must be understood with the limitations which are given to them in this opinion; limitations which in no degree affect the decision in that case, or the tenor of its reasoning.

The counsel who closed the argument, put several cases for the purpose of illustration, which he supposed to arise under the constitution, and yet to be, apparently, without the jurisdiction of the Court.

Were a State to lay a duty on exports, to collect the money and place it in her treasury, could the citizen who paid it, he asks, maintain a suit in this Court against such State, to recover back the money?

Perhaps not. Without, however, deciding such supposed case, we may say, that it is entirely unlike that under consideration.

The citizen who has paid his money to his State, under a law that is void, is in the same situation with every other person who has paid money by mistake. The law raises an assumpsit to return the money, and it is upon that assumpsit that the action is to be maintained. To refuse to comply with this assumpsit may be no more a violation of the constitution, than to refuse to comply with any other; and as the federal Courts never had jurisdiction over contracts between a State and its citizens, they may have none over this. But let us so vary the supposed case, as to give it a real resemblance to that under consideration. Suppose a citizen to refuse to pay this export duty, and a suit to be instituted for the purpose of compelling him to pay it. He pleads the constitution of the United States in bar of the action, notwithstanding which the Court gives judgment against him. This would be a case arising under the constitution, and would be the very case now before the Court.

We are also asked, if a State should confiscate property secured by a treaty, whether the individual could maintain an action for that property?

If the property confiscated be debts, our own experience informs us that the remedy of the creditor against his debtor remains. If it be land, which is secured by a treaty, and afterwards confiscated by a State, the argument does not assume that this title, thus secured, could be extinguished by an act of confiscation. The injured party, therefore, has his remedy against the occupant of the land for that which the treaty secures to him, not against the State for money which is not secured to him.

The case of a State which pays off its own debts with paper money, no more resembles this than do those to which we have already adverted. The Courts have no jurisdiction over the contract. They cannot enforce it, nor judge of its violation. Let it be that the act discharging the debt is a mere nullity, and that it is still due. Yet the federal Courts have no cognizance of the case. But suppose a State to institute proceedings against an individual, which depended on the validity of an act emitting bills of credit: suppose a State to prosecute one of its citizens for refusing paper money, who should plead the constitution in bar of such prosecution. If his plea should be overruled, and judgment rendered against him, his case would resemble this; and, unless the jurisdiction of this Court might be exercised over it, the constitution would be violated, and the injured party be unable to bring his case before that tribunal to which the people of the United States have assigned all such cases.

It is most true that this Court will not take jurisdiction if it should not: but it is equally true, that it must take jurisdiction if it should. The judiciary cannot, as the legislature may, avoid a measure because it approaches the confines of the constitution. We cannot pass it by because it is doubtful. With whatever doubts, with whatever difficulties, a case may be attended, we must decide it, if it be brought before us. We have no more right to decline the exercise of jurisdiction which is given, than to usurp that which is not given. The one or the other would be treason to the constitution. Questions may occur which we would gladly avoid; but we cannot avoid them. All we can do is, to exercise our best judgment, and conscientiously to perform our duty. In doing this, on the present occasion, we find this tribunal invested with appellate jurisdiction in *all* cases arising under the constitution and laws of the United States. We find no exception to this grant, and we cannot insert one.

To escape the operation of these comprehensive words, the counsel for the defendant has mentioned instances in which the constitution might be violated without giving jurisdiction to this Court. These words, therefore, however universal in their expression, must, he contends, be limited and controlled in their construction by circumstances. One of these instances is, the grant by a State of a patent of nobility. The Court, he says, cannot annul this grant.

This may be very true; but by no means justifies the inference drawn from it. The article does not extend the judicial power to every violation of the constitution which may possibly take place, but to "a case in law or equity," in which a right, under such law, is asserted in a Court of justice. If the question cannot be brought into a Court, then there is no case in law or equity, and no jurisdiction is given by the words of the article. But if, in any controversy depending in a Court, the cause should depend on the validity of such a law, that would be a case arising under the constitution, to which the judicial power of the United States would extend. The same observation applies to the other instances with which the counsel who opened the cause has illustrated this argument. Although they show that there may be violations of the constitution, of which the Courts can take no cognizance, they do not show that an interpretation more restrictive than the words themselves import ought to be given to this article. They do not show that there can be "a *case* in law or equity," arising under the constitution, to which the judicial power does not extend.

We think, then, that, as the constitution originally stood, the appellate jurisdiction of this Court, in all cases arising under the constitution, laws, or treaties of the United States, was not arrested by the circumstance that a State was a party.

This leads to a consideration of the 11th amendment.

It is in these words: "The judicial power of the United States shall not be construed to extend to any suit in law or equity commenced or prosecuted against one of the United States, by citizens of another State, or by citizens or subjects of any foreign State."

It is a part of our history, that, at the adoption of the constitution, all the States were greatly indebted; and the apprehension that these debts might be prosecuted in the federal Courts, formed a very serious objection to that instrument. Suits were instituted; and the Court maintained its jurisdiction. The alarm was general; and, to quiet the apprehensions that were so extensively entertained, this amendment was proposed in Congress, and adopted by the State legislatures. That its motive was not to maintain the sovereignty of a State from the degradation supposed to attend a compulsory appearance before the tribunal of the nation, may be inferred from the terms of the amendment. It does not comprehend controversies between two or more States, or between a State and a foreign State. The jurisdiction of the Court still extends to these cases: and in these a State may still be sued. We must ascribe the amendment, then, to some other cause than the dignity of a State. There is no difficulty in finding this cause. Those who were inhibited from commencing a suit against a State, or from prosecuting one which might be commenced before the adoption of the amendment, were persons who might probably be its creditors. There was not much reason to fear that foreign or sister States would be creditors to any considerable amount, and there was reason to retain the jurisdiction of the Court in those cases, because it might be essential to the preservation of peace. The amendment, therefore, extended to suits commenced or prosecuted by individuals, but not to those brought by States.

The first impression made on the mind by this amendment is, that it was intended for those cases, and for those only, in which some demand against a State is made by an individual in the Courts of the Union. If we consider the causes to which it is to be traced, we are conducted to the same conclusion. A general interest might well be felt in leaving to a State the full power of consulting its convenience in the adjustment of its debts, or of other claims upon it; but no interest could be felt in so changing the relations between the whole and its parts, as to strip the government of the means of protecting, by the instrumentality of its Courts, the constitution and laws from active violation.

The words of the amendment appear to the Court to justify and require this construction. The judicial power is not "to extend to any suit in law or equity commenced or prosecuted against one of the United States by citizens of another State, &c."

What is a suit? We understand it to be the prosecution, or pursuit, of some claim, demand, or request. In law language, it is the prosecution of some demand in a Court of justice. The remedy for every species of wrong is, says Judge Blackstone, "the being put in possession of that right whereof the party injured is deprived." "The instruments whereby this remedy is obtained, are a diversity of suits and actions, which are defined by the Mirror to be 'the lawful demand of one's right.' Or, as Bracton and Fleta express it, in the words of Justinian, 'jus prosequendi in judicio quod alicui debetur.'" Blackstone then proceeds to describe every species of remedy by suit; and they are all cases where the party suing claims to obtain something to which he has a right.

To commence a suit, is to demand something by the institution of process in a Court of justice; and to prosecute the suit, is, according to the common acceptation of language, to continue that demand. By a suit commenced by an individual against a State, we should understand process sued out by that individual against the State, for the purpose of establishing some claim against it by the judgment of a Court; and the prosecution of that suit is its continuance. Whatever may be the stages of its progress, the actor is still the same. Suits had been commenced in the Supreme Court against some of the States before this amendment was introduced into Congress, and others might be commenced before it should be adopted by the State legislatures, and might be depending at the time of its adoption. The object of the amendment was not only to prevent the commencement of future suits, but to arrest the prosecution of those which might be commenced when this article should form a part of the constitution. It therefore embraces both objects; and its meaning is, that the judicial power shall not be construed to extend to any suit which may be commenced, or which, if already commenced, may be prosecuted against a State by the citizen of another State. If a suit, brought in one Court, and carried by legal process to a supervising Court, be a continuation of the same suit, then this suit is not commenced nor prosecuted against a State. It is clearly in its commencement the suit of a State against an individual, which suit is transferred to this Court, not for the purpose of asserting any claim against the State, but for the purpose of asserting a constitutional defence against a claim made by a State.

A writ of error is defined to be, a commission by which the judges of one Court are authorized to examine a record upon which a judgment was given in another Court, and, on such examination, to affirm or reverse the same according to law. If, says my Lord Coke, by the writ of error, the plaintiff may recover, or be restored to any thing, it may be released by the name of an action. In *Bacon's Abridgment, tit. Error,* L. it is laid down, that "where by a writ of error, the plaintiff shall recover, or be restored to any personal thing, as debt, damage, or the like, a release of all actions personal is a good plea; and when land is to be recovered or restored in a writ of error, a release of actions real is a good bar; but where by a writ of error the plaintiff shall not be restored to any personal or real thing, a release of all actions, real or personal, is no bar." And for this we have the authority of Lord Coke, both in his Commentary on *Littleton* and in his *Reports.* A writ of error, then, is in the nature of a suit or action when it is to restore the party who obtains it to the possession of any thing which is withheld from him, not when its operation is entirely defensive.

This rule will apply to writs of error from the Courts of the United States, as well as to those writs in England.

Under the judiciary act, the effect of a writ of error is simply to bring the record into Court, and submit the judgment of the inferior tribunal to re-examination. It does not in any manner act upon the parties; it acts only on the record. It removes the record into the supervising tribunal. Where, then, a State obtains a judgment against an individual, and the Court, rendering such judgment, overrules a defence set up under the constitution or laws of the United States, the transfer of this record into the Supreme Court, for the sole purpose of inquiring whether the judgment violates the constitution or laws of the United States, can, with no propriety, we think, be denominated a suit commenced or prosecuted against the State whose judgment is so far re-examined. Nothing is demanded from the State. No claim against it of any description is asserted or prosecuted. The party is not to be restored to the possession of any thing. Essentially, it is an appeal on a single point; and the defendant who appeals from a judgment rendered against him, is never said to commence or prosecute a suit against the plaintiff who has obtained the judgment. The writ of error is given rather than an appeal, because it is the more usual mode of removing suits at common law; and because, perhaps, it is more technically proper where a single point of law, and not the whole case, is to be re-examined. But an appeal might be given, and might be so regulated as to effect every purpose of a writ of error. The mode of removal is form, and not substance. Whether it be by writ of error or appeal, no claim is asserted, no demand is made by the original defendant; he only asserts the constitutional right to have his defence examined by that tribunal whose province it is to construe the constitution and laws of the Union.

The only part of the proceeding which is in any manner

personal, is the citation. And what is the citation? It is simply notice to the opposite party that the record is transferred into another Court, where he may appear, or decline to appear, as his judgment or inclination may determine. As the party who has obtained a judgment is out of Court, and may, therefore, not know that his cause is removed, common justice requires that notice of the fact should be given him. But this notice is not a suit, nor has it the effect of process. If the party does not choose to appear, he cannot be brought into Court, nor is his failure to appear considered as a default. Judgment cannot be given against him for his nonappearance, but the judgment is to be re-examined, and reversed or affirmed, in like manner as if the party had appeared and argued his cause.

The point of view in which this writ of error, with its citation, has been considered uniformly in the Courts of the Union, has been well illustrated by a reference to the course of this Court in suits instituted by the United States. The universally received opinion is, that no suit can be commenced or prosecuted against the United States; that the judiciary act does not authorize such suits. Yet writs of error, accompanied with citations, have uniformly issued for the removal of judgments in favour of the United States into a superior Court, where they have, like those in favour of an individual, been re-examined, and affirmed or reversed. It has never been suggested, that such writ of error was a suit against the United States, and, therefore, not within the jurisdiction of the appellate Court.

It is, then, the opinion of the Court, that the defendant who removes a judgment rendered against him by a State Court into this Court, for the purpose of re-examining the question, whether that judgment be in violation of the constitution or laws of the United States, does not commence or prosecute a suit against the State, whatever may be its opinion where the effect of the writ may be to restore the party to the possession of a thing which he demands.

But should we in this be mistaken, the error does not affect the case now before the Court. If this writ of error be a suit in the sense of the 11th amendment, it is not a suit commenced or prosecuted "by a citizen of another State, or by a citizen or subject of any foreign State." It is not then within the amendment, but is governed entirely by the constitution as originally framed, and we have already seen, that in its origin, the judicial power was extended to all cases arising under the constitution or laws of the United States, without respect to parties.

2d. The second objection to the jurisdiction of the Court is, that its appellate power cannot be exercised, in any case, over the judgment of a State Court.

This objection is sustained chiefly by arguments drawn from the supposed total separation of the judiciary of a State from that of the Union, and their entire independence of each other. The argument considers the federal judiciary as completely foreign to that of a State; and as being no more connected with it in any respect whatever, than the Court of a foreign State. If this hypothesis be just, the argument founded on it is equally so; but if the hypothesis be not supported by the constitution, the argument fails with it.

This hypothesis is not founded on any words in the constitution, which might seem to countenance it, but on the unreasonableness of giving a contrary construction to words which seem to require it; and on the incompatibility of the application of the appellate jurisdiction to the judgments of State Courts, with that constitutional relation which subsists between the government of the Union and the governments of those States which compose it.

Let this unreasonableness, this total incompatibility, be examined.

That the United States form, for many, and for most important purposes, a single nation, has not yet been denied. In war, we are one people. In making peace, we are one people. In all commercial regulations, we are one and the same people. In many other respects, the American people are one; and the government which is alone capable of controling and managing their interests in all these respects, is the government of the Union. It is their government, and in that character they have no other. America has chosen to be, in many respects, and to many purposes, a nation; and for all these purposes, her government is complete; to all these objects, it is competent. The people have declared, that in the exercise of all powers given for these objects, it is supreme. It can, then, in effecting these objects, legitimately control all individuals or governments within the American territory. The constitution and laws of a State, so far as they are repugnant to the constitution and laws of the United States, are absolutely void. These States are constituent parts of the United States. They are members of one great empire—for some purposes sovereign, for some purposes subordinate.

In a government so constituted, is it unreasonable that the judicial power should be competent to give efficacy to the constitutional laws of the legislature? That department can decide on the validity of the constitution or law of a State, if it be repugnant to the constitution or to a law of the United States. Is it unreasonable that it should also be empowered to decide on the judgment of a State tribunal enforcing such unconstitutional law? Is it so very unreasonable as to furnish a justification for controling the words of the constitution?

We think it is not. We think that in a government acknowledgedly supreme, with respect to objects of vital interest to the nation, there is nothing inconsistent with sound reason, nothing incompatible with the nature of government, in making all its departments supreme, so far as respects those objects, and so far as is necessary to their attainment. The exercise of the appellate power over those judgments of the State tribunals which may contravene the constitution or laws of the United States, is, we believe, essential to the attainment of those objects.

The propriety of entrusting the construction of the constitution, and laws made in pursuance thereof, to the judiciary of the Union, has not, we believe, as yet, been drawn into question. It seems to be a corollary from this political axiom, that the federal Courts should either possess exclusive jurisdiction in such cases, or a power to revise the judgment rendered in them, by the State tribunals. If the federal and State Courts have concurrent jurisdiction in all cases arising under the constitution, laws, and treaties of the United States; and if a case of this description brought in a State Court cannot be removed before judgment, nor revised after judgment, then the construction of the constitution, laws, and treaties of the United States, is not confided particularly to their judicial department, but is confided equally to that department and to the State Courts, however they may be constituted. "Thirteen independent Courts," says a very celebrated statesman, (and we have now more than twenty such Courts,) "of final jurisdiction over the same causes, arising upon the same laws, is a hydra in government, from which nothing but contradiction and confusion can proceed."

Dismissing the unpleasant suggestion, that any motives which may not be fairly avowed, or which ought not to exist, can ever influence a State or its Courts, the necessity of uniformity, as well as correctness in expounding the constitution and laws of the United States, would itself suggest the propriety of vesting in some single tribunal the power of deciding, in the last resort, all cases in which they are involved.

We are not restrained, then, by the political relations between the general and State governments, from construing the words of the constitution, defining the judicial power, in their true sense. We are not bound to construe them more restrictively than they naturally import.

They give to the Supreme Court appellate jurisdiction in all cases arising under the constitution, laws, and treaties of the United States. The words are broad enough to comprehend all cases of this description, in whatever Court they may be decided. In expounding them, we may be permitted to take into view those considerations to which Courts have always allowed great weight in the exposition of laws.

The framers of the constitution would naturally examine the state of things existing at the time; and their work sufficiently attests that they did so. All acknowledge that they were convened for the purpose of strengthening the confederation by enlarging the powers of the government, and by giving efficacy to those which it before possessed, but could not exercise. They inform us themselves, in the instrument they presented to the American public, that one of its objects was to form a more perfect union. Under such circumstances, we certainly should not expect to find, in that instrument, a diminution of the powers of the actual government.

Previous to the adoption of the confederation, Congress established Courts which received appeals in prize causes decided in the Courts of the respective States. This power of the government, to establish tribunals for these appeals, was thought consistent with, and was founded on, its political relations with the States. These Courts did exercise appellate jurisdiction over those cases decided in the State Courts, to which the judicial power of the federal government extended.

The confederation gave to Congress the power "of establishing Courts for receiving and determining finally appeals in all cases of captures."

This power was uniformly construed to authorize those Courts to receive appeals from the sentences of State Courts, and to affirm or reverse them. State tribunals are not mentioned; but this clause in the confederation necessarily comprises them. Yet the relation between the general and State governments was much weaker, much more lax, under the confederation than under the present constitution; and the States being much more completely sovereign, their institutions were much more independent.

The Convention which framed the constitution, on turning their attention to the judicial power, found it limited to a few objects, but exercised, with respect to some of those objects, in its appellate form, over the judgments of the State Courts. They extend it, among other objects, to all cases arising under the constitution, laws, and treaties of the United States; and in a subsequent clause declare, that in such cases, the Supreme Court shall exercise appellate jurisdiction. Nothing seems to be given which would justify the withdrawal of a judgment rendered in a State Court, on the constitution, laws, or treaties of the United States, from this appellate jurisdiction.

Great weight has always been attached, and very rightly attached, to contemporaneous exposition. No question, it is believed, has arisen to which this principle applies more unequivocally than to that now under consideration.

The opinion of the *Federalist* has always been considered as of great authority. It is a complete commentary on our constitution; and is appealed to by all parties in the questions to which that instrument has given birth. Its intrinsic merit entitles it to this high rank; and the part two of its authors performed in framing the constitution, put it very much in their power to explain the views with which it was framed. These essays having been published while the constitution was before the nation for adoption or rejection, and having been written in answer to objections founded entirely on the extent of its powers, and on its diminution of State sovereignty, are entitled to the more consideration where they frankly avow that the power objected to is given, and defend it.

In discussing the extent of the judicial power, the *Federalist* says, "Here another question occurs: what relation would subsist between the national and State Courts in these instances of concurrent jurisdiction? I answer, that an appeal would certainly lie from the latter, to the Supreme Court of the United States. The constitution in direct terms gives an appellate jurisdiction to the Supreme Court in all the enumerated cases of federal cognizance in which it is not to have an original one, without a single expression to confine its operation to the inferior federal Courts. The objects of appeal, not the tribunals from which it is to be made, are alone contemplated. From this circumstance, and from the reason of the thing, it ought to be construed to extend to the State tribunals. Either this must be the case, or the local Courts must be excluded from a concurrent jurisdiction in matters of national concern, else the judicial authority of the Union may be eluded at the pleasure of every plaintiff or prosecutor.

Neither of these consequences ought, without evident necessity, to be involved; the latter would be entirely inadmissible, as it would defeat some of the most important and avowed purposes of the proposed government, and would essentially embarrass its measures. Nor do I perceive any foundation for such a supposition. Agreeably to the remark already made, the national and State systems are to be regarded as ONE WHOLE. The Courts of the latter will of course be natural auxiliaries to the execution of the laws of the Union, and an appeal from them will as naturally lie to that tribunal which is destined to unite and assimilate the principles of natural justice, and the rules of national decision. The evident aim of the plan of the national convention is, that all the causes of the specified classes shall, for weighty public reasons, receive their original or final determination in the Courts of the Union. To confine, therefore, the general expressions which give appellate jurisdiction to the Supreme Court, to appeals from the subordinate federal Courts, instead of allowing their extension to the State Courts, would be to abridge the latitude of the terms, in subversion of the intent, contrary to every sound rule of interpretation."

A contemporaneous exposition of the constitution, certainly of not less authority than that which has been just cited, is the judiciary act itself. We know that in the Congress which passed that act were many eminent members of the Convention which formed the constitution. Not a single individual, so far as is known, supposed that part of the act which gives the Supreme Court appellate jurisdiction over the judgments of the State Courts in the cases therein specified, to be unauthorized by the constitution.

While on this part of the argument, it may be also material to observe that the uniform decisions of this Court on the point now under consideration, have been assented to, with a single exception, by the Courts of every State in the Union whose judgments have been revised. It has been the unwelcome duty of this tribunal to reverse the judgments of many State Courts in cases in which the strongest State feelings were engaged. Judges, whose talents and character would grace any bench, to whom a disposition to submit to jurisdiction that is usurped, or to surrender their legitimate powers, will certainly not be imputed, have yielded without hesitation to the authority by which their judgments were reversed, while they, perhaps, disapproved the judgment of reversal.

This concurrence of statesmen, of legislators, and of judges, in the same construction of the constitution, may justly inspire some confidence in that construction.

In opposition to it, the counsel who made this point has presented in a great variety of forms, the idea already noticed, that the federal and State Courts must, of necessity, and from the nature of the constitution, be in all things totally distinct and independent of each other. If this Court can correct the errors of the Courts of Virginia, he says it makes them Courts of the United States, or becomes itself a part of the judiciary of Virginia.

But, it has been already shown that neither of these consequences necessarily follows: The American people may certainly give to a national tribunal a supervising power over those judgments of the State Courts, which may conflict with the constitution, laws, or treaties, of the United States, without converting them into federal Courts, or converting the national into a State tribunal. The one Court still derives its authority from the State, the other still derives its authority from the nation.

If it shall be established, he says, that this Court has appellate jurisdiction over the State Courts in all cases enumerated in the 3d article of the constitution, a complete consolidation of the States, so far as respects judicial power is produced.

But, certainly, the mind of the gentleman who urged this argument is too accurate not to perceive that he has carried it too far; that the premises by no means justify the conclusion. "A complete consolidation of the States, so far as respects the judicial power," would authorize the legislature to confer on the federal Courts appellate jurisdiction from the State Courts in all cases whatsoever. The distinction between such a power, and that of giving appellate jurisdiction in a few specified cases in the decision of which the nation takes an interest, is too obvious not to be perceived by all.

This opinion has been already drawn out to too great a length to admit of entering into a particular consideration of the various forms in which the counsel who made this point has, with much ingenuity, presented his argument to the Court. The argument in all its forms is essentially the same. It is founded, not on the words of the constitution, but on its spirit, a spirit extracted, not from the words of the instrument, but from his view of the nature of our Union, and of the great fundamental principles on which the fabric stands.

To this argument, in all its forms, the same answer may be given. Let the nature and objects of our Union be considered; let the great fundamental principles, on which the fabric stands, be examined; and we think the result must be, that there is nothing so extravagantly absurd in giving to the Court of the nation the power of revising the decisions of local tribunals on questions which affect the nation, as to require that words which import this power should be restricted by a forced construction. The question then must depend on the words themselves; and on their construction we shall be the more readily excused for not adding to the observations already made, because the subject was fully discussed and exhausted in the case of *Martin* v. *Hunter*.

3d. We come now to the third objection, which, though differently stated by the counsel, is substantially the same.

. . . . .

If the 25th section of the judiciary act be inspected, it will at once be perceived that it comprehends expressly the case under consideration.

But it is not upon the letter of the act that the gentleman who stated this point in this form, founds his argument. Both gentlemen concur substantially in their views of this part of the case. They deny that the act of Congress, on which the plaintiff in error relies, is a law of the United States; or, if a law of the United States, is within the second clause of the sixth article.

In the enumeration of the powers of Congress, which is made in the 8th section of the first article, we find that of exercising exclusive legislation over such District as shall become the seat of government. This power, like all others which are specified, is conferred on Congress as the legislature of the Union: for, strip them of that character, and they would not possess it. In no other character can it be exercised. In legislating for the District, they necessarily preserve the character of the legislature of the Union; for, it is in that character alone that the constitution confers on them this power of exclusive legislation. This proposition need not be enforced.

The 2d clause of the 6th article declares, that "This constitution, and the laws of the United States, which shall be made in pursuance thereof, shall be the supreme law of the land."

The clause which gives exclusive jurisdiction is, unquestionably, a part of the constitution, and, as such, binds all the United States. Those who contend that acts of Congress, made in pursuance of this power, do not, like acts made in pursuance of other powers, bind the nation, ought to show some safe and clear rule which shall support this construction, and prove that an act of Congress, clothed in all the forms which attend other legislative acts, and passed in virtue of a power conferred on, and exercised by Congress, as the legislature of the Union, is not a law of the United States, and does not bind them.

One of the gentlemen sought to illustrate his proposition that Congress, when legislating for the District, assumed a distinct character, and was reduced to a mere local legislature, whose laws could possess no obligation out of the ten miles square, by a reference to the complex character of this Court. It is, they say, a Court of common law and a Court of equity. Its character, when sitting as a Court of common law, is as distinct from its character when sitting as a Court of equity, as if the powers belonging to those departments were vested in different tribunals. Though united in the same tribunal, they are never confounded with each other.

Without inquiring how far the union of different characters in one Court, may be applicable, in principle, to the union in Congress of the power of exclusive legislation in some places, and of limited legislation in others, it may be observed, that the forms of proceedings in a Court of law are so totally unlike the forms of proceedings in a Court of equity, that a mere inspection of the record gives decisive information of the character in which the Court sits, and consequently of the extent of its powers. But if the forms of proceedings were precisely the same, and the Court the same, the distinction would disappear.

Since Congress legislates in the same forms, and in the same character, in virtue of powers of equal obligation, conferred in the same instrument, when exercising its exclusive powers of legislation, as well as when exercising those which are limited, we must inquire whether there be any thing in the nature of this exclusive legislation, which necessarily confines the operation of the laws made in virtue of this power to the place with a view to which they are made.

Connected with the power to legislate within this District, is a similar power in forts, arsenals, dock yards, &c. Congress has a right to punish murder in a fort, or other place within its exclusive jurisdiction; but no general right to punish murder committed within any of the States. In the act for the punishment of crimes against the United States, murder committed within a fort, or any other place or district of country, under the sole and exclusive jurisdiction of the United States, is punished with death. Thus Congress legislates in the same act, under its exclusive and its limited powers.

The act proceeds to direct, that the body of the criminal, after execution, may be delivered to a surgeon for dissection, and punishes any person who shall rescue such body during its conveyance from the place of execution to the surgeon to whom it is to be delivered.

Let these actual provisions of the law, or any other provisions which can be made on the subject, be considered with a view to the character in which Congress acts when exercising its powers of exclusive legislation.

If Congress is to be considered merely as a local legislature, invested, as to this object, with powers limited to the fort, or other place, in which the murder may be committed, if its general powers cannot come in aid of these local powers, how can the offence be tried in any other Court than that of the place in which it has been committed? How can the offender be conveyed to, or tried in, any other place? How can he be executed elsewhere? How can his body be conveyed through a country under the jurisdiction of another sovereign, and the individual punished, who, within that jurisdiction, shall rescue the body.

Were any one State of the Union to pass a law for trying a criminal in a Court not created by itself, in a place not within its jurisdiction, and direct the sentence to be executed without its territory, we should all perceive and acknowledge its incompetency to such a course of legislation. If Congress be not equally incompetent, it is because that body unites the powers of local legislation with those which are to operate through the Union, and may use the last in aid of the first; or because the power of exercising exclusive legislation draws after it, as an incident, the power of making that legislation effectual, and the incidental power may be exercised throughout the Union, because the principal power is given to that body as the legislature of the Union.

So, in the same act, a person who, having knowledge of the commission of murder, or other felony, on the high seas, or within any fort, arsenal, dock yard, magazine, or other place, or district of country within the sole and exclusive jurisdiction of the United States, shall conceal the same, &c. he shall be adjudged guilty of misprision of felony, and shall be adjudged to be imprisoned, &c.

It is clear, that Congress cannot punish felonies generally; and, of consequence, cannot punish misprision of felony. It is equally clear, that a State legislature, the State of Maryland for example, cannot punish those who, in another State, conceal a felony committed in Maryland. How, then, is it that Congress, legislating exclusively for a fort, punishes those who, out of that fort, conceal a felony committed within it?

The solution, and the only solution of the difficulty, is, that the power vested in Congress, as the legislature of the United States, to legislate exclusively within any place ceded by a State, carries with it, as an incident, the right to make that power effectual. If a felon escape out of the State in which the act has been committed, the government cannot pursue him into another State, and apprehend him there, but must demand him from the executive power of that other State. If Congress were to be considered merely as the local legislature for the fort or other place in which the offence might be committed, then this principle would apply to them as to other local legislatures, and the felon who should escape out of the fort, or other place, in which the felony may have been committed, could not be apprehended by the marshal, but must be demanded from the executive of the State. But we know that the principle does not apply; and the reason is, that Congress is not a local legislature, but exercises this particular power, like all its other powers, in its high character, as the legislature of the Union. The American people thought it a necessary power, and they conferred it for their own benefit. Being so conferred, it carries with it all those incidental powers which are necessary to its complete and effectual execution.

Whether any particular law be designed to operate without the District or not, depends on the words of that law. If it be designed so to operate, then the question, whether the power so exercised be incidental to the power of exclusive legislation, and be warranted by the constitution, requires a consideration of that instrument. In such cases the constitution and the law must be compared and construed. This is the exercise of jurisdiction. It is the only exercise of it which is allowed in such a case. For the act of Congress directs, that "no other error shall be assigned or regarded as a ground of reversal, in any such case as aforesaid, than such as appears on the face of the record, and immediately respects the before mentioned questions of validity or construction of the said constitution, treaties," &c.

The whole merits of this case, then, consist in the construction of the constitution and the act of Congress. The jurisdiction of the Court, if acknowledged, goes no farther. This we are required to do without the exercise of jurisdiction.

The counsel for the State of Virginia have, in support of this motion, urged many arguments of great weight against the application of the act of Congress to such a case as this; but those arguments go to the construction of the constitution, or of the law, or of both; and seem, therefore, rather calculated to sustain their cause upon its merits, than to prove a failure of jurisdiction in the Court.

After having bestowed upon this question the most deliberate consideration of which we are capable, the Court is unanimously of opinion, that the objections to its jurisdiction are not sustained, and that the motion ought to be overruled.

Motion denied.

4

OSBORN V. BANK OF THE UNITED STATES
9 Wheat. 738 (1824)

Chief Justice MARSHALL. . . . 6. We proceed now to the 6th point made by the appellants, which is, that if any case is made in the bill, proper for the interference of a Court of Chancery, it is against the State of Ohio, in which case the Circuit Court could not exercise jurisdiction.

The bill is brought, it is said, for the purpose of protecting the Bank in the exercise of a franchise granted by a law of the United States, which franchise the State of Ohio asserts a right to invade, and is about to invade. It prays the aid of the Court to restrain the officers of the State from executing the law. It is, then, a controversy between the Bank and the State of Ohio. The interest of the State is direct and immediate, not consequential. The process of the Court, though not directed against the State by name, acts directly upon it, by restraining its officers. The process, therefore, is substantially, though not in form, against the State, and the Court ought not to proceed without making the State a party. If this cannot be done, the Court cannot take jurisdiction of the cause.

The full pressure of this argument is felt, and the difficulties it presents are acknowledged. The direct interest of the State in the suit, as brought, is admitted; and, had it been in the power of the Bank to make it a party, perhaps no decree ought to have been pronounced in the cause, until the State was before the Court. But this was not in the power of the Bank. The eleventh amendment of the constitution has exempted a State from the suits of citizens of other States, or aliens; and the very difficult question is to be decided, whether, in such a case, the Court may act upon the agents employed by the State, and on the property in their hands.

Before we try this question by the constitution, it may not be time misapplied, if we pause for a moment, and reflect on the relative situation of the Union with its members, should the objection prevail.

A denial of jurisdiction forbids all inquiry into the nature of the case. It applies to cases perfectly clear in themselves; to cases where the government is in the exercise of its best established and most essential powers, as well as to those which may be deemed questionable. It asserts, that the agents of a State, alleging the authority of a law void in itself, because repugnant to the constitution, may arrest the execution of any law in the United States. It maintains, that if a State shall impose a fine or penalty on any person employed in the execution of any law of the United States, it may levy that fine or penalty by a ministerial officer, without the sanction even of its own Courts; and that the individual, though he perceives the approaching danger, can obtain no protection from the judicial department of the government. The carrier of the mail, the collector of the revenue, the marshal of a district, the recruiting officer, may all be inhibited, under ruinous penalties, from the performance of their respective duties; the warrant of a ministerial officer may authorize the collection of these penalties, and the person thus obstructed in the performance of his duty, may indeed resort to his action for damages, after the infliction of the injury, but cannot avail himself of the preventive justice of the nation to protect him in the performance of his duties. Each member of the Union is capable, at its will, of attacking the nation, of arresting its progress at every step, of acting vigorously and effectually in the execution of its designs, while the nation stands naked, stripped of its defensive armour, and incapable of shielding its agent or executing its laws otherwise than by proceedings which are to take place after the mischief is perpetrated, and which must often be ineffectual, from the inability of the agents to make compensation.

These are said to be extreme cases; but the case at bar, had it been put by way of illustration in argument, might have been termed an extreme case; and, if a penalty on a revenue officer, for performing his duty, be more obviously wrong than a penalty on the Bank, it is a difference in degree, not in principle. Public sentiment would be more shocked by the infliction of a penalty on a public officer for the performance of his duty, than by the infliction of this penalty on a Bank which, while carrying on the fiscal operations of the government, is also transacting its own business; but, in both cases, the officer levying the penalty acts under a void authority, and the power to restrain him is denied as positively in the one as in the other.

The distinction between any extreme case, and that which has actually occurred, if, indeed, any difference of principle can be supposed to exist between them, disappears, when considering the question of jurisdiction; for, if the Courts of the United States cannot rightfully protect the agents who execute every law authorized by the constitution, from the direct action of State agents in the collection of penalties, they cannot rightfully protect those who execute any law.

The question, then, is, whether the constitution of the United States has provided a tribunal which can peacefully and rightfully protect those who are employed in carrying into execution the laws of the Union, from the attempts of a particular State to resist the execution of those laws.

The State of Ohio denies the existence of this power, and contends, that no preventive proceedings whatever, or proceedings against the very property which may have been seized by the agent; of a State, can be sustained against such agent, because they would be substantially against the State itself, in violation of the 11th amendment of the constitution.

That the Courts of the Union cannot entertain a suit brought against a State by an alien, or the citizen of another State, is not to be controverted. Is a suit, brought against an individual, for any cause whatever, a suit against a State, in the sense of the constitution?

The 11th amendment is the limitation of a power supposed to be granted in the original instrument; and to understand accurately the extent of the limitation, it seems proper to define the power that is limited.

The words of the constitution, so far as they respect this question, are, "The judicial power shall extend to controversies between two or more States, between a State and citizens of another State, and between a State and foreign states, citizens, or subjects."

A subsequent clause distributes the power previously granted, and assigns to the Supreme Court original jurisdiction in those cases in which "a State shall be a party."

The words of the 11th amendment are, "The judicial power of the United States shall not be construed to extend to any suit in law or equity, commenced or prosecuted against one of the United States, by citizens of another State, or by citizens or subjects of a foreign state."

The Bank of the United States contends, that in all cases in which jurisdiction depends on the character of the party, reference is made to the party on the record, not to one who may be interested, but is not shown by the record to be a party.

The appellants admit, that the jurisdiction of the Court is not ousted by any incidental or consequential interest, which a State may have in the decision to be made, but is to be considered as a party where the decision acts directly and immediately upon the State, through its officers.

If this question were to be determined on the authority of English decisions, it is believed that no case can be adduced, where any person has been considered as a party, who is not made so in the record. But the Court will not review those decisions, because it is thought a question growing out of the constitution of the United States, requires rather an attentive consideration of the words of that instrument, than of the decisions of analogous questions by the Courts of any other country.

Do the provisions, then, of the American constitution, respecting controversies to which a State may be a party, extend, on a fair construction of that instrument, to cases in which the State is not a party on the record?

The first in the enumeration, is a controversy between two or more States.

There are not many questions in which a State would be supposed to take a deeper or more immediate interest, than in those which decide on the extent of her territory. Yet the constitution, not considering the State as a party to such controversies, if not plaintiff or defendant on the record, has expressly given jurisdiction in those between citizens claiming lands under grants of different States. If each State, in consequence of the influence of a decision on her boundary, had been considered, by the framers of the constitution, as a party to that controversy, the express grant of jurisdiction would have been useless. The grant of it certainly proves, that the constitution does not consider the State as a party in such a case.

Jurisdiction is expressly granted, in those cases only where citizens of the same State claim lands under grants of different States. If the claimants be citizens of different States, the Court takes jurisdiction for that reason. Still, the right of the State to grant, is the essential point in dispute; and in that point the State is deeply interested. If that interest converts the State into a party, there is an end of the cause; and the constitution will be construed to forbid the Circuit Courts to take cognizance of questions to which it was thought necessary expressly to extend their jurisdiction, even when the controversy arose between citizens of the same State.

We are aware, that the application of these causes may be denied, because the title of the State comes on incidentally, and the appellants admit the jurisdiction of the Court, where its judgment does not act directly upon the property or interests of the State; but we deemed it of some importance to show, that the framers of the constitution contemplated the distinction between cases in which a State was interested, and those in which it was a party, and made no provision for a case of interest, without being a party on the record.

In cases where a State is a party on the record, the question of jurisdiction is decided by inspection. If jurisdiction depend, not on this plain fact, but on the interest of the State, what rule has the constitution given, by which this interest is to be measured? If no rule be given, is it to be settled by the Court? If so, the curious anomaly is presented, of a Court examining the whole testimony of a cause, inquiring into, and deciding on, the extent of a State's interest, without having a right to exercise any jurisdiction in the case. Can this inquiry be made without the exercise of jurisdiction?

The next in the enumeration, is a controversy between a State and the citizens of another State.

Can this case arise, if the State be not a party on the record? If it can, the question recurs, what degree of interest shall be sufficient to change the parties, and arrest the proceedings against the individual? Controversies respecting boundary have lately existed between Virginia and Tennessee, between Kentucky and Tennessee, and now exist between New-York and New-Jersey. Suppose, while such a controversy is pending, the collecting officer of one State should seize property for taxes belonging to a man who supposes himself to reside in the other State, and who seeks redress in the federal Court of that State in which the officer resides. The interest of the State is obvious. Yet it is admitted, that in such a case the action would lie, because the officer might be treated as a trespasser, and the verdict and judgment against him would not act directly on the property of the State. That it would not so act, may, perhaps, depend on circumstances. The officer may retain the amount of the taxes in his hands, and, on the proceedings of the State against him, may plead in bar the judgment of a Court of competent jurisdiction. If this plea ought to be sustained, and it is far from being certain that it ought not, the judgment so pleaded would have acted directly on the revenue of the State, in the hands of its officer. And yet the argument admits, that the action, in such a case, would be sustained. But, suppose, in such a case, the party conceiving himself to be injured, instead of bringing an action sounding in damages, should sue for the specific thing, while yet in possession of the seizing officer. It being admitted, in argument, that the action sounding in damages would lie, we are unable to perceive the line of distinction between that and the action of detinue. Yet the latter action would claim the specific article seized for the tax, and would obtain it, should the seizure be deemed unlawful.

It would be tedious to pursue this part of the inquiry

farther, and it would be useless, because every person will perceive that the same reasoning is applicable to all the other enumerated controversies to which a State may be a party. The principle may be illustrated by a reference to those other controversies where jurisdiction depends on the party. But, before we review them, we will notice one where the nature of the controversy is, in some degree, blended with the character of the party.

If a suit be brought against a foreign minister, the Supreme Court alone has original jurisdiction, and this is shown on the record. But, suppose a suit to be brought which affects the interest of a foreign minister, or by which the person of his secretary, or of his servant, is arrested. The minister does not, by the mere arrest of his secretary, or his servant, become a party to this suit, but the actual defendant pleads to the jurisdiction of the Court, and asserts his privilege. If the suit affects a foreign minister, it must be dismissed, not because he is a party to it, but because if affects him. The language of the constitution in the two cases is different. This Court can take cognizance of all cases "affecting" foreign ministers; and, therefore, jurisdiction does not depend on the party named in the record. But this language changes, when the enumeration proceeds to States. Why this change? The answer is obvious. In the case of foreign ministers, it was intended, for reasons which all comprehend, to give the national Courts jurisdiction over all cases by which they were in any manner affected. In the case of States, whose immediate or remote interests were mixed up with a multitude of cases, and who might be affected in an almost infinite variety of ways, it was intended to give jurisdiction in those cases only to which they were actual parties.

In proceeding with the cases in which jurisdiction depends on the character of the party, the first in the enumeration is, "controversies to which the United States shall be a party."

Does this provision extend to the cases where the United States are not named in the record, but claim, and are actually entitled to, the whole subject in controversy?

Let us examine this question.

Suits brought by the Postmaster-General are for money due to the United States. The nominal plaintiff has no interest in the controversy, and the United States are the only real party. Yet, these suits could not be instituted in the Courts of the Union, under that clause which gives jurisdiction in all cases to which the United States are a party; and it was found necessary to give the Court jurisdiction over them, as being cases arising under a law of the United States.

The judicial power of the Union is also extended to controversies between citizens of different States; and it has been decided, that the character of the parties must be shown on the record. Does this provision depend on the character of those whose interest is litigated, or of those who are parties on the record? In a suit, for example, brought by or against an executor, the creditors or legatees of his testator are the persons really concerned in interest; but it has never been suspected that, if the executor be a resident of another State, the jurisdiction of the federal Courts could be ousted by the fact, that the creditors or legatees were citizens of the same State with the opposite party. The universally received construction in this case is, that jurisdiction is neither given nor ousted by the relative situation of the parties concerned in interest, but by the relative situation of the parties named on the record. Why is this construction universal? No case can be imagined, in which the existence of an interest out of the party on the record is more unequivocal than in that which has been just stated. Why, then, is it universally admitted, that this interest in no manner affects the jurisdiction of the Court? The plain and obvious answer is, because the jurisdiction of the Court depends, not upon this interest, but upon the actual party on the record.

Were a State to be the sole legatee, it will not, we presume, be alleged, that the jurisdiction of the Court, in a suit against the executor, would be more affected by this fact, than by the fact that any other person, not suable in the Courts of the Union, was the sole legatee. Yet, in such a case, the Court would decide directly and immediately on the interest of the State.

This principle might be further illustrated by showing that jurisdiction, where it depends on the character of the party, is never conferred in consequence of the existence of an interest in a party not named; and by showing that, under the distributive clause of the 2d section of the 3d article, the Supreme Court could never take original jurisdiction, in consequence of an interest in a party not named in the record.

But the principle seems too well established to require that more time should be devoted to it. It may, we think, be laid down as a rule which admits of no exception, that, in all cases where jurisdiction depends on the party, it is the party named in the record. Consequently, the 11th amendment, which restrains the jurisdiction granted by the constitution over suits against States, is, of necessity, limited to those suits in which a State is a party on the record. The amendment has its full effect, if the constitution be construed as it would have been construed, had the jurisdiction of the Court never been extended to suits brought against a State, by the citizens of another State, or by aliens.

The State not being a party on the record, and the Court having jurisdiction over those who are parties on the record, the true question is, not one of jurisdiction, but whether, in the exercise of its jurisdiction, the Court ought to make a decree against the defendants; whether they are to be considered as having a real interest, or as being only nominal parties.

In pursuing the arrangement which the appellants have made for the argument of the cause, this question has already been considered. The responsibility of the officers of the State for the money taken out of the Bank, was admitted, and it was acknowledged that this responsibility might be enforced by the proper action. The objection is, to its being enforced against the specific article taken, and by the decree of this Court. But, it has been shown, we think, that an action of detinue might be maintained for that article, if the Bank had possessed the means of describing it, and that the interest of the State would not have been an obstacle to the suit of the Bank against the individual in possession of it. The judgement in such a suit might have been enforced, had the article been found in possession of the individual defendant. It has been shown, that the danger of its being parted with, of its being lost to the plaintiff, and the necessity of a discovery, justified the application to a Court of equity. It was in a Court of equity alone that the relief would be real, substantial, and effective. The parties must certainly have a real interest in the case, since their personal responsibility is acknowledged, and, if denied, could be demonstrated.

It was proper, then, to make a decree against the defendants in the Circuit Court, if the law of the State of Ohio be repugnant to the constitution, or to a law of the United States made in pursuance thereof, so as to furnish no authority to those who took, or to those who received, the money for which this suit was instituted.

5

BANK OF THE UNITED STATES V. PLANTERS' BANK OF GEORGIA

9 Wheat. 904 (1824)

Mr. Chief Justice MARSHALL delivered the opinion of the Court.

In this case, the petition of the plaintiffs, which, according to the practice of the State of Georgia, is substituted for a declaration, is founded on promissory notes, payable to a person named in the note, *"or bearer,"* and states, that the notes were "duly transferred, assigned and delivered" to the plaintiffs, "who thereby became the lawful bearer thereof, and entitled to payment of the sums therein specified; and that the defendants, in consideration of their liability, assumed," &c.

The Planters' Bank pleads to the jurisdiction of the Court, and alleges, that it is a corporation, of which the State of Georgia, and certain individuals, who are citizens of the same State with some of the plaintiffs, are members. The plea also alleges, that the persons to whom the notes mentioned in the petition were made payable, were citizens of the State of Georgia, and, therefore, incapable of suing the said Bank in a Circuit Court of the United States; and being so incapable, could not, by transferring the notes to the plaintiffs, enable them to sue in that Court.

To this plea the plaintiffs demurred, and the defendants joined in demurrer.

. . . . .

1. Is the State of Georgia a party defendant in this case? If it is, then the suit, had the 11th amendment never been adopted, must have been brought in the Supreme Court of the United States. Could this Court have entertained jurisdiction in the case?

We think it could not. To have given the Supreme Court original jurisdiction, the State must be plaintiff or defendant as a State, and must, as a State, be a party on the record. A suit against the Planters' Bank of Georgia, is no more a suit against the State of Georgia, than against any other individual corporator. The State is not a party, that is, an entire party, in the cause.

If this suit could not have been brought originally in the Supreme Court, it would be difficult to show, that it is within the 11th amendment. That amendment does not purport to do more than to restrain the construction which might otherwise be given to the constitution; and if this case be not one of which the Supreme Court could have taken original jurisdiction, it is not within the amendment. This is not, we think, a case in which the character of the defendant gives jurisdiction to the Court. If it did, the suit could be instituted only in the Supreme Court. This suit is not to be sustained because the Planters' Bank is suable in the federal Courts, but because the plaintiff has a right to sue any defendant in that Court, who is not withdrawn from its jurisdiction by the constitution, or by law. The suit is against a corporation, and the judgment is to be satisfied by the property of the corporation, not by that of the individual corporators. The State does not, by becoming a corporator, identify itself with the corporation. The Planters' Bank of Georgia is not the State of Georgia, although the State holds an interest in it.

It is, we think, a sound principle, that when a government becomes a partner in any trading company, it devests itself, so far as concerns the transactions of that company, of its sovereign character, and takes that of a private citizen. Instead of communicating to the company its privileges and its prerogatives, it descends to a level with those with whom it associates itself, and takes the character which belongs to it associates, and to the business which is to be transacted. Thus, many States of this Union who have an interest in Banks, are not suable even in their own Courts; yet they never exempt the corporation from being sued. The State of Georgia, by giving to the Bank the capacity to sue and be sued, voluntarily strips itself of its sovereign character, so far as respects the transactions of the Bank, and waives all the privileges of that character. As a member of a corporation, a government never exercises its sovereignty. It acts merely as a corporator, and exercises no other power in the management of the affairs of the corporation, than are expressly given by the incorporating act.

The government of the Union held shares in the old Bank of the United States; but the privileges of the government were not imparted by that circumstance to the Bank. The United States was not a party to suits brought by or against the Bank in the sense of the constitution. So with respect to the present Bank. Suits brought by or against it are not understood to be brought by or against the United States. The government, by becoming a corporator, lays down its sovereignty, so far as respects the transactions of the corporation, and exercises no power or privilege which is not derived from the charter.

We think, then, that the Planters' Bank of Georgia is not exempted from being sued in the federal Courts, by the circumstance that the State is a corporator.

. . . . .

Mr. Justice JOHNSON. . . . So, also, with regard to the State of Georgia. An original suit against that State for the recovery of a debt, could not be maintained. Yet, if an original suit against a corporation, be an original suit against each corporator, I see not wherein the case differs from that of a direct suit against the State. Suppose the case of a joint bond, given by a State and individuals, to an individual contractor, citizen of another State, what would except a suit on such a bond from the operation of the 11th amendment of the constitution? If it be said that the amendment alluded to has regard only to suits instituted against States in their sovereign capacity, I would ask, in what other capacity can a State appear, or even exist? In every possible form and shape, it is a sovereign State, or it is nothing. And this very stock, held in this Bank, is the property of the people of Georgia, held by them in the name and capacity of the State of Georgia. If any dispute were to arise on the title to the stock, in what capacity could they sue or be sued for the interest held by them in the stock, unless in their sovereign capacity? It is not because it imparts its own immunities to the other stockholders, that this action cannot be maintained, but because that the judicial power must reach each and every defendant, in order to bring a case within the prescribed limits of the constitution. Each defendant occupies his own peculiar rank, claims his own peculiar immunities; but they are not suable in the Courts of the United States, as long as any one of them is exempted from suit in those Courts.

I am here expressing a technical opinion, founded on the authority of the case of *The Bank v. Deveaux.* That decision brings it strictly within the letter of the 11th amendment; although I am ready to admit, that, unaffected by that decision, it is not within its purview. Although not responsible for that decision, I acknowledge its obligation, until overruled.

SEE ALSO:

Generally 3.2.1; Bill of Rights
Records of the Federal Convention, Farrand 2:39, 146–47
Federal Farmer, no. 3, 10 Oct. 1787, Storing 2.8.43
Alexander Hamilton, Federalist, nos. 17, 32, 81, Dec. 1787–May 1788
James Madison, Federalist, nos. 39, 45, 46, Jan. 1788
Brutus, no. 13, 21 Feb. 1788, Storing 2.9.163–67
Debate in Virginia Ratifying Convention, 19–21 June 1788, Elliot 3:526–27, 529, 533, 542–43, 549, 555–56, 573–75
Amendments Proposed and Ratified, 1789, Elliot 1:340–41
Vanstophorst v. Maryland, 2 Dall. 401 (1791)
Senate, Amendment to the Constitution, 20 Feb. 1793, Annals 3:651–52
Senate, Amendment to the Constitution, 2, 14 Jan. 1794, Annals 4:25, 30
House of Representatives, Amendment to the Constitution, 4 Mar. 1794, Annals 4:476–78
Hollingsworth v. Virginia, 3 Dall. 378 (1798)
United States v. Peters, 5 Cranch 115 (1808)
United States v. Bright, 24 Fed. Cas. 1232, no. 14,647 (C.C.D.Pa. 1809)
Gale v. Babcock, 9 Fed. Cas. 1077, no. 5,188 (C.C.D.N.J. 1822)
Governor of Georgia v. Madrazo, 1 Pet. 110 (1828)
Joseph Story, Commentaries on the Constitution 3:§§ 1677–83 (1833)

Amendment XII

The Electors shall meet in their respective states and vote by ballot for President and Vice-President, one of whom, at least, shall not be an inhabitant of the same state with themselves; they shall name in their ballots the person voted for as President, and in distinct ballots the person voted for as Vice-President, and they shall make distinct lists of all persons voted for as President, and of all persons voted for as Vice-President, and of the number of votes for each, which lists they shall sign and certify, and transmit sealed to the seat of the government of the United States, directed to the President of the Senate;—The President of the Senate shall, in the presence of the Senate and House of Representatives, open all the certificates and the votes shall then be counted;—The person having the greatest number of votes for President, shall be the President, if such number be a majority of the whole number of Electors appointed; and if no person have such majority, then from the persons having the highest numbers not exceeding three on the list of those voted for as President, the House of Representatives shall choose immediately, by ballot, the President. But in choosing the President, the votes shall be taken by states, the representation from each state having one vote; a quorum for this purpose shall consist of a member or members from two-thirds of the states, and a majority of all the states shall be necessary to a choice. And if the House of Representatives shall not choose a President whenever the right of choice shall devolve upon them, before the fourth day of March next following, then the Vice-President shall act as President, as in the case of the death or other constitutional disability of the President—The person having the greatest number of votes as Vice-President, shall be the Vice-President, if such number be a majority of the whole number of Electors appointed, and if no person have a majority, then from the two highest numbers on the list, the Senate shall choose the Vice-President; a quorum for the purpose shall consist of two-thirds of the whole number of Senators, and a majority of the whole number shall be necessary to a choice. But no person constitutionally ineligible to the office of President shall be eligible to that of Vice-President of the United States.

The Twelfth Amendment was proposed by Congress on 9 Dec. 1803, when it passed the House, having previously passed the Senate on 2 Dec. (Annals 13:209, 775–76). It was not signed by the presiding officers of the House and Senate until 12 Dec. It appears officially in 2 Stat. 306. Ratification was probably completed on 15 June 1804, when the legislature of the thirteenth State (New Hampshire) approved the amendment, there being then seventeen States in the Union. The Governor of New Hampshire, however, vetoed this act of the legislature on 20 June, and the act failed to pass again by two-thirds vote then required by the State constitution. Inasmuch as Article 5 of the Federal Constitution specifies that amendments shall become effective "when ratified by the legislatures of three-fourths of the several States or by conventions in three-fourths thereof," it has been generally believed that an approval or veto by a governor is without significance. If the ratification by New Hampshire be deemed ineffective, then the amendment became operative by Tennessee's ratification on 27 July 1804. On 25 Sept. 1804, in a circular letter to the Governors of the several States, Secretary of State Madison declared the amendment ratified by three-fourths of the States.

The several State legislatures ratified the Twelfth Amendment on the following dates: North Carolina, 22 Dec. 1803; Maryland, 24 Dec. 1803; Kentucky, 27 Dec. 1803; Ohio, between 5 Dec. and 30 Dec. 1803; Virginia, between 20 Dec. 1803 and 3 Feb. 1804; Pennsylvania, 5 Jan. 1804; Vermont, 30 Jan. 1804; New York, 10 Feb. 1804; New Jersey, 22 Feb. 1804; Rhode Island, between

27 Feb. and 12 Mar. 1804; South Carolina, 15 May 1804; Georgia, 19 May 1804; New Hampshire, 15 June 1804; and Tennessee, 27 July 1804. The amendment was re-

jected by Delaware on 18 Jan. 1804, and by Connecticut at its session begun 10 May 1804. Massachusetts ratified this amendment in 1961.

1

HOUSE OF REPRESENTATIVES, AMENDMENTS TO THE CONSTITUTION
22 Jan. 1801
Annals 10:941–46

Mr. NICHOLAS, from the committee to whom was referred on the twenty-first of November last, a motion for amending the Constitution of the United States, made a report; which was read, and ordered to be committed to a Committee of the whole House on Monday next. The report is as follows:

Resolved by the Senate and House of Representatives of the United States, (two-thirds of both Houses concurring,) That the following articles be proposed to the Legislatures of the several States, as amendments to the Constitution of the United States:

"1. That, after the third day of March, in the year one thousand eight hundred and one, the choice of electors of President and Vice President shall be made by dividing each State into a number of districts, equal to the number of electors to be chosen in such State, and by the persons in each of those districts, who shall have the qualifications requisite for electors of the most numerous branch of the Legislature of such State, choosing one elector in the manner which the Legislature thereof shall prescribe.

"2. That the election of Representative to Congress, who are to serve after the third day of March, in the year one thousand eight hundred and three, shall be by dividing each State into a number of districts, equal to the number of Representatives to which such State shall be entitled, and by the people within each of those districts who shall have the qualifications requisite for electors of the most numerous branch of the Legislature of such State choosing one Representative in the manner which the Legislature thereof shall prescribe."

The committee, to whom were referred the foregoing resolutions, have had the same under their consideration,

and, as the result of that consideration, beg leave to make the following report:

It is conceived that it may be assumed as one of the most indisputable maxims of American policy, that no change in the Constitution of the United States be admitted without a well-grounded assurance of the attainment of some greater good under the proposed change than under the existing provisions of the Constitution.

In relation to the object of the first of the aforesaid resolutions, the existing provisions of the Constitution of the United States are expressed in the following terms:

"Each State shall appoint, in such manner as the Legislature thereof may direct, a number of electors equal to the whole number of Senators and Representatives to which the State may be entitled in Congress; but no Senator or Representative, or person holding an office of trust or profit under the United States, shall be appointed an elector.

"The electors shall meet in their respective States, and vote, by ballot, for two persons, of whom one at least shall not be an inhabitant of the same State with themselves; and they shall make a list of all the persons voted for, and of the number of votes for each; which list they shall sign and certify, and transmit, sealed, to the seat of Government of the United States, directed to the President of the Senate. The President of the Senate shall, in the presence of the Senate and House of Representatives, open all the certificates, and the votes shall then be counted. The person having the greatest number of votes shall be the President, if such number be a majority of the whole number of electors appointed; and if there be more than one who have such a majority, and have an equal number of votes, then the House of Representatives shall immediately choose, by ballot, one of them for President; and if no person have a majority, then, from the five highest on the list, the said House shall, in like manner, choose the President. But in choosing the President, the votes shall be taken by States, the representation from each State having one vote; a quorum for this purpose shall consist of a member or members from two-thirds of the States, and a majority of all the States shall be necessary to a choice. In every case, after the choice of the President, the person having the greatest number of votes of the electors shall be the Vice President. But if there should remain two or more who have equal votes, the Senate shall choose from them, by ballot, the Vice President.

"The Congress may determine the time of choosing the electors, and the day on which they shall give their votes; which day shall be the same throughout the United States."

Under the latitude of expression used in the foregoing provisions, considerable variety of practice has been found to prevail, not only in the different States, but at different periods in the same States. The modes adopted may be considered as capable of designation under two general descriptions: the one an appointment of electors by popular vote; the other, an appointment of electors by legislative choice.

In each mode considerable varieties have prevailed. Under the first general mode, the States have been sometimes divided into districts, in proportion to the number of electors to be appointed in each State respectively; and the inhabitants of each district, having the right of suffrage, have appointed, by vote, the elector for such district, respectively, nearly in the manner proposed by the first resolution referred to your committee. In other instances, the whole people of a State, having the right of suffrage, have appointed, by general vote, such number of electors as the State was respectively entitled to. The electors appointed under the latter modification have been sometimes taken from the body of the people at large, in other instances, they have been selected from certain districts or divisions of the State, in conformity with certain previous legislative requisitions. In cases of death, absence, or other disability of electors appointed by popular vote, provisions have been made by law, in the same States, to supply the vacancies which might be occasioned by such accidents, by means of a legislative choice.

Under the other general mode of appointment, the electors in some States have been appointed by a joint ballot of both Houses of the Legislature. In some instances, the electors appointed by legislative choice have been taken from the body of the people at large without previous limitation; in other instances, from a restricted list, nominated in certain proportions by each House of the Legislature, respectively.

In the same States one general mode of appointment has prevailed at one time, and another general mode at another time; the changes having been made as well from one general mode as from the other.

Such are the existing provisions of the Constitution of the United States, and such has been the practice under these provisions. The modes thus used are presumed to have been within the legitimate construction of the Constitution, since the votes of electors appointed under almost every variety of these modes have been admitted in former elections of President and Vice President of the United States. The latitude of expression used in those provisions, and the variety of modes practically adopted under them, seem to have been considered in the first of the resolutions referred to your committee as inconveniences which ought to be remedied.

Your committee are persuaded that the provisions of the Constitution of the United States can, in no instance, be reasonably considered as mere pleonasms or inadvertencies; and, therefore, that the particular phraseology used on the above subject, was not adopted without due consideration. Your committee are equally persuaded that the varieties which have practically taken place under the terms used, are not beyond the contemplation of those who framed the Constitution. These varieties, it is reasonable to suppose, were foreseen, and, being foreseen, were viewed not without favor, as the best means of enabling the people of the United States to combine the advantages of experience with the speculations of theory in relation to this acknowledgedly the most difficult part of their Government in the adjustment, so that they may ultimately settle down into one uniform mode within Constitutional limits, not from Constitutional restriction, but from the convictions of reason founded on experience.

The mode proposed to be exclusively established being clearly within the expressions of the Constitution, if upon experience and comparison with other modes, equally within those expressions, it shall be found to possess superior advantages, or, possessing equal advantages, to be liable to fewer or less considerable inconveniences, your committee will not distrust the good sense of the people of the United States, in ultimately selecting this mode without Constitutional restraint, as their uniform mode of electing the President and Vice President of the United States.

Your committee hold it foreign to their duty to enter into a comparative view of the merits and demerits of the various modes which have been or may be adopted under the existing provisions of the Constitution of the United States; they hold it sufficient to authorize the rejection of any proposition for the exclusive establishment of any particular mode, if such mode shall, upon candid examination, be found liable to serious abuses of most dangerous consequence to the public peace; against which abuses, under such mode, no practicable means have been, or probably can be found, for prevention or remedy.

The liability of the mode proposed to such abuses cannot be made more manifest than by a brief review of the essential details of that mode.

To carry into effect the mode proposed to be exclusively established, every State must necessarily be divided into a number of districts in proportion to the number of electors to be appointed in each State, respectively. These districts must, of necessity, be again sub-divided, for the convenient reception of the votes of the people. Authority must be delegated to one or more officers in every subdivision of every electoral district thoughout the United States for the purpose of receiving those votes.

Amidst so great a variety of officers thus to be intrusted, it would be against the calculations of all experience to suppose there would not be found some who might be reasonably suspected of a liability to the deviations of error, if not to those of a worse nature. No government upon earth has, or can have, competent knowledge of so great a variety of individuals, as to insure, through the cautiousness of appointment, against such deviations in all instances. Absolute prevention, then, is not to be expected.

The votes of some, possessing the right of suffrage, may

be rejected; the votes of others, not possessing the right of suffrage, may be admitted; whether such rejection or admission proceed from error of judgment, or from design, it will equally lay the foundation of a contested or disputed election between the candidates for the electorship.

When the votes of the several sub-divisions of an electoral district have been taken, the polls, or lists of those votes, must be brought together for an addition and comparison; and a return must be made of the person appointed an elector. Whether that return be made by the officers (authorized originally to receive the votes) in a collective body, or whether it be made by some other authority, to which those officers may be directed to transmit the polls or lists of the votes taken by them, there may (amidst the conflict of passions, too likely to prevail on such occasions) too probably be found means of suppressing the polls, or lists of votes of some of the sub-divisions of a district, or of preventing or delaying the transmission thereof; so that one man might be returned in apparent conformity with law, the elector of a district, when, in reality, another may have been appointed by the people of that district.

The common experience of elective governments evinces that cases, such as those above suggested, are by no means out of the course of probable occurrence. Instances of disputed elections, contested upon similar grounds, frequently occur in ordinary legislative bodies, notwithstanding the knowledge that a remedy exists within the scope of the power of those bodies. The protracted periods of their sessions give time for investigating and deciding upon the merits of such contested elections. The knowledge of the practicability of such remedy probably tends to discourage the greater frequency of such occurrences.

But the bodies of electors in each State, respectively, from the necessarily restricted periods of their sessions, are incapacitated to collect the necessary evidence, and to pursue such other steps as are essential to the investigation of and decision upon the merits of a contested election of one of their members, were they otherwise competent thereto. Those, therefore, who may be returned electors, whether duly and really appointed or not, will, in practice, exercise the important functions of electors of the President and Vice President of the United States. No practicable remedy against such abuses appears to exist in the present stage of the proposed system; a knowledge of the defect of such remedy, moreover, it is to be feared, might act as an additional temptation to the frequency of abuse.

The votes of the electors in the several States are next to be rendered by ballot, and, when so rendered, they are to be transmitted in the form of certificates, giving the result of the ballot to certain officers of the Government of the United States. When the period arrives for opening those certificates, and counting the votes in the presence of the Senate and House of Representatives of the United States, if error or abuse shall have taken place, no means exist (in case the ballot be in favor of more than two persons as President and Vice President) for discriminating between the votes of those who shall have been duly appointed and returned, and those who shall have been de-

fectively appointed and unduly returned as electors. To set aside votes given by persons not duly appointed, and consequently wanting the competent authority of electors, no course presents itself in such case, save that of vacating the whole ballot, of which the defective vote or votes may be a component part. Thus, to deprive a State of all participation in the election of the President and Vice President of the United States, on account of the defective appointment of one or a few of its electors, would be a serious and painful duty. To vacate such ballot, and thereby to deprive those candidates for whom the sound votes of such ballot may have been given, of the aid of that ballot, in order at the same time to destroy the effect of the unsound votes, might result in giving to others a priority, to which, if effect could be given to the really sound votes, those others might not be entitled. This also presents an embarrassing consideration.

The vacation of a ballot, composed of sound and defective votes, ought to be the result of uniform principle; it ought to take place on all occasions where a discrimination cannot be made, or on none. Not to vacate such ballot, but to permit the election of a Chief Magistrate to be carried, on any occasion, by the aid of one or more defective votes, would be to hazard, in a most eminent degree, the peace of the Union. It is of the last importance to the happiness of the people of the United States, that a complete conviction should prevail at all times that the person who may be elected Chief Magistrate of the Union has been really elected by electors duly and really appointed by those having competent authority for that purpose. It were painful to anticipate the consequences which would too probably attend a disputed election to the Presidency; those consequences might be more calamitous than can be foreseen.

A mode of electing the President and Vice President of the United States, which might at once combine the expression of the public sentiments of the people of the respective States, with a perfect assurance of the due appointment of the electors for that important purpose, is a discovery greatly to be desired; that such mode may be found, under the present provisions of the Constitution of the United States, and will be discovered by the good sense of the American people, when aided by further experience, is confidently hoped. Under such circumstances, to adopt exclusively the mode proposed by the first resolution referred to your committee, might not only preclude the advantages of further experience, and the adoption of a more eligible mode, but might tend to perpetuate, as well as to render more frequent the occurrence of those exceptionable incidents which have been before suggested, and for which it is difficult, if not impracticable, to find adequate and convenient means of prevention or remedy.

These considerations induce your committee to prefer the existing provisions of the Constitution of the United States to the change proposed by the first of the resolutions referred to them.

In relation to the second resolution referred to your committee, they report, that the objects directly contemplated therein are already within the limits of the Legislative authority of the Government of the United States. To convert a Constitutional provision for the exercise of Legislative authority, to which recurrence may be had at all times, and under which such modifications may be introduced, from time to time, as the public good or convenience may require, in the ordinary forms of legislation, into a specific Constitutional prescription, seems to be both superfluous and inconvenient.

The adoption of the change proposed in the second resolution would also, in the opinion of your committee, indirectly tend to withdraw from the Government of the United States its existing control over the appointment of one of its most essential branches, and to vest that authority exclusively in the State Governments. Such arrangement might produce consequences not contemplated, and too unpleasant to be anticipated. Your committee, therefore, conceive it to be inexpedient to adopt the proposed change on this subject, and submit the following resolutions to the consideration of the House:

Resolved, That it is inexpedient to change the Constitution of the United States, in the manner proposed by the first of the aforesaid resolutions, in relation to the election of the President and Vice President of the United States.

Resolved, That it is inexpedient to change the Constitution of the United States, in the manner proposed by the second of the aforesaid resolutions, in relation to the election of members of the House of Representatives of the United States.

2

JAMES A. BAYARD TO ALEXANDER HAMILTON
8 Mar. 1801
Hamilton Papers 25:344–45

In one case I was willing to take Burr, but I never considered it as a case likely to happen. If by his conduct he had completely forfeited the confidence and friendship of his Party and left himself no resort but the support of the federalists, there are many considerations which would have induced me to prefer him to Jefferson. But I was enabled soon to discover that he was determined not to shackle himself with federal principles and it became evident that if he got in without being absolutely committed in relation to his own Party, that he would be disposed & obliged to play the game of McKean upon an improved plan and enlarged scale.

In the origin of the business I had contrived to lay hold of all the doubtful votes in the House which enabled me according to views which presented themselves to protract or terminate the controversy.

This arrangement was easily made, from the opinion readily adopted from the consideration, that representing a small state without resources which could supply the means of self protection I should not dare to proceed to any length which would jeopardize the constitution or the safety of any state. When the experiment was fully made, I acknowledged upon all hands to have completely ascer-

tained, that Burr was resolved not to commit himself, and that nothing remained but to appoint a President by law, or have the government without one. I came out with the most explicit & determined declaration of voting for Jefferson. You cannot well imagine the clamour & vehement invective to which I was subjected for some days. We had several caucuses. All acknowledged that nothing but desperate measures remained, which several were disposed to adopt, & but few were willing openly to disapprove. We broke up each time in confusion and discord, and the manner of the last ballot was arranged but a few minutes before the ballot was given. Our former harmony however has since been restored.

The public declarations of my intention to vote for Jefferson to which I have alluded were made without a general consultation, knowing that it would be an easier task to close the breach which I foresaw, when it was the result of an act done without concurrence than if it had proceeded from one against a decision of the Party. Had it not been for a single gentleman from Connecticut, the eastern states would finally have voted in blank in the same manner as done by S. Carolina & Delaware. But because he refused, the rest of the Delegation refused and because connecticut insisted upon continuing the ballot for Burr New Hampshire Massachusetts & Rhode Island refused to depart from their former vote.

The means existed of electing Burr, but they required his cooperation. By deceiving one Man (a great blockhead) and tempting two (not incorruptible) he might have secured a majority of the States. He will never have another chance of being president of the U.states and the little use he has made of the one which has occurred gives me but a humble opinion of the talents of an unprincipled man.

3

ALEXANDER HAMILTON, DRAFT OF A RESOLUTION
FOR THE LEGISLATURE OF NEW YORK FOR THE
AMENDMENT OF THE CONSTITUTION
OF THE UNITED STATES
29 Jan. 1802
Papers 25:512–13

Resolved, as the sense of the Legislature, that the following amendments ought to be incorporated into the Constitution of the United States as a necessary safeguard in the choice of a President and Vice President against pernicious dissensions as the most eligible mode of obtaining a full and fair expression of the public will in such election.

1st. That Congress shall from time to time divide each State into Districts equal to the whole number of Senators and Representatives from such state in the Congress of the United States, and shall direct the mode of choosing an Elector of President and Vice President in each of the said Districts, who shall be chosen by Citizens who have the qualifications requisite for Electors of the most numerous branch of the State Legislature, and that the districts shall be formed, as nearly as may be, with an equal proportion of population in each, and of Counties and, if necessary, parts of Counties contiguous to each other, except when there may be any detached portion of territory not sufficient of itself to form a District which then shall be annexed to some other part nearest thereto.

2nd. That in all future elections of President and Vice President the persons voted for shall be particularly designated by declaring which is voted for as President and which as Vice President.

Resolved that the President of the Senate and Speaker of the Assembly transmit a copy of the preceding Resolutions to the Senators and Representatives in Congress from this State with an earnest request that they would use their best exertions for obtaining the adoption of the above amendments or other amendments in substance equivalent so as that the President and Vice President may be separately designated in voting for them and that the electors for both may be chosen in distinct Districts.

4

ALEXANDER HAMILTON TO GOUVERNEUR MORRIS 4 Mar. 1802

Papers 25:558–59

You have seen certain resolutions unanimously pass our legislature for amending the Constitution 1 by designating separately the candidates for President and Vice President 2 by having the Electors chosen by the people in districts under the direction of the National Legislature.

After mature reflection I was thoroughly confirmed in my first impression, that it is true Federal policy to promote the adoption of these amendments.

Of the first, not only because it is in itself right that the people should know whom they are choosing & because the present mode gives all possible scope to intrigue and is dangerous as we have seen to the public tranquillity—but because in every thing which gives opportunity for juggling arts our adversaries will Nine times out of Ten excell us.

Of the second, because it removes thus far the intervention of the state Governments and strengthens the connection between the Foederal head and the people, and because it diminishes the means of party combination, in which also the burning zeal of our opponents will be generally an overmatch for our temperate flame.

I shall be very happy that our friends may think with me & that no temporary motive may induce them to let slip the precious occasion, in which personal motives induce the other party to forget their true policy.

We are told here that at the close of your birth day feast a strange *apparition* which was taken for the *V P* appeared among you and toasted "the union of all honest men." I

often hear at the corner of the streets important foederal secrets of which I am ignorant. This may be one.

If the story be true, tis a good thing if we use it well. As an *instrument* the person will be an auxiliary of *some* value, as a chief he will disgrace and destroy the party. I suspect however the folly of the mass will make him the latter, and from the moment it shall appear that this is the plan it may be depended upon much more will be lost than gained. I know of no important character who has a less *founded* interest than the man in question. His talents may do well enough for a particular plot but they are illsuited to a great and wise *Drama*. But what has wisdom to do with weak man? Adieu

5

SENATE, AMENDMENT TO THE CONSTITUTION 1–2 Dec. 1803

Annals 13:129–53, 155–56, 159–75, 180–81

[*1 Dec.*]

Mr. HILLHOUSE.— . . . The complex mode provided by the Constitution was conceived in great wisdom. It was necessary, when the country was agitated, to operate as a check upon party and irregular passions. Parties will always have their champions, and they will be always well known; to attack another champion is to restrain the passions by some degree of uncertainty during the contest. But, by the new amendment, it would be every man to his own book, and every demagogue would be a leader and a champion, and, in the contest, parties would be divided between the two principal champions, and a third would come in and win the race.

If every man were to act correctly, no party passions would prevail on an occasion so important; but carry the champions of two opposite parties to the House of Representatives, and instead of voting thirty-seven times before they decide, as on the last occasion, they will vote thirty hundred times. You are told that, at the last election, one was intended by the people for President, and the other for Vice President; but the Constitution knows no vote for Vice President. Alter it as you now propose, and let two candidates be equal, and then you will be told that they were both intended for President. What will be the consequences? On the third day of March neither party will give out, and it will end in the choice of a third man, who will not be the choice of the people, but one who will, by artful contrivances, bring himself to that place with the sole intention of getting in between them. Choice by lot would certainly be better than this. Would not any man prefer a choice by lot rather than such a course, as it would break up the Constitution, and leave the people without a President in whom they would confide?

The principle of the Constitution, of electing by electors,

is certainly preferable to all others. One of the greatest evils that can happen is the throwing of the election into the House of Representatives. There, Pennsylvania, Virginia, Massachusetts, and New York, may combine; they may say to the other States, we will not vote for your man; for either of those States giving their whole votes to a third character may bring him in. We see the practice daily in Congressional elections, when both parties obstinately adhere to their candidate; a third is set up and carried in to the rejection of both. By the new mode proposed every man will have an interest to intrigue for himself to obtain the eminent station. Gentlemen may suppose that such is the predominancy of their party, they may carry in any President. But no party can long hold an ascendancy in power; they will ill treat each other—or some of them will disagree, and from the fragments new parties will arise, who will gain power and forget themselves, and again disagree, to make way for new parties. The Constitution was predicated upon the existence of parties; they will always exist, and names will not be wanting to rally under, and difference of interests will not be wanting for pretexts: the agricultural will be arrayed against the mercantile; the South against the East; the seaboard against the inland. As to what he had heard about cutting off heads, he supposed that could not have been meant as a threat; in his part of the country such a crime could not take place. The gentleman, however, must be supposed to know his neighbors better than he did, but he could not suspect such danger from a valiant people.

Mr. PICKERING said the amendment he had offered was suggested to him by the alarming picture of danger drawn by the gentleman from Maryland. He thought the dangers indeed exaggerated, though possibly they might not be; but he thought it proper to provide how elections should be conducted, and to determine between tumult or civil war and law.

Mr. SMITH did say that, at the last Presidential election, the party opposed to the present Chief Magistrate did contemplate laying aside the popular choice and electing a President by a law to be passed for the occasion, at the time: he had also said, that had the measure been carried into effect, the person, whoever he might have been, would have met the fate of an usurper, and his head would not have remained on his shoulders twenty-four hours.

Mr. WRIGHT.—It had been said, that we meant to precipitate this amendment of the Constitution—to make the minority swallow it; he hoped the gentlemen, in their eagerness to render it insipid, would not make it totally unpalatable to us: as they had proceeded, the modes they had proposed struck him at least by their novelty. Since what was offered was not satisfactory, and they were willing to commit it to chance, why did they not take up the ancient mode of *grande battaile?* we should have no objection to have it decided by the champions of both parties armed with tomahawks! Gentlemen talk of the danger and of the rights of the small States, do they expect that any man can think their professions serious, when they are, at the same time, willing to commit their rights to the chance

of a lottery? The rights of freemen are not to be gambled away, or committed to chance, or sorcery, or witchcraft; we look to reason and experience for our guides; we seek for the means most conducive to the general happiness; to this, reason conducts us. By experience, we correct what may have escaped our sagacity at first, or may have been defective or erroneous in practice. It is upon these principles our Constitution is founded; it is for these words that the provision is made in the Constitution itself for its own amendment; and it is not compatible with reason, or with the principles of the Constitution, to commit anything to capricious fortune, in which reason and human rights are concerned. Gentlemen charge us now with a wish to press this amendment forward with precipitation; what do gentlemen mean by this? A few days only have passed, when the same gentlemen were eager for an immediate decision; they declared their readiness to decide immediately; that the subject was as well understood then as ever it would be; and that we delayed the decision to the exhaustion of their patience. The subject has, nevertheless, undergone a long discussion, and the time has only served to prove that the gentlemen were at first mistaken, or that the numerous amendments which they have brought forward have their origin in other considerations.

Mr. ADAMS had declared that he was ready to give his vote upon the amendment in the first stage; but it did not therefore follow, that when his opinion on the whole was not likely to prevail, that he should endeavor to render it as palatable as possible. He was totally adverse to any decision by lot, and agreed perfectly with the gentleman from Maryland, that it was not a mode suited to the principles of our Government. But gentlemen say there is a defect, and wish to provide a remedy. He had drawn up an amendment which he should offer to the House, if that of his colleague should not be approved. He confessed he did approve of the designating principle, and for one among other reasons, that the present mode is too much like choice by lot. For instance, A may be intended by a large majority of the people for President, and B as Vice President; yet the votes might be so disposed, or chance might operate so contrary to intention, that the votes for B should exceed by a vote those for A. This was a defect in the Constitution; and there was a further reason why he was in favor of the designating principle, and that was, that it appeared to be called for from all parts of the United States. It was very true, as had been observed, that some time ago the opposers of the amendment did press for a decision; but he had seen those dispositions prevail alternately; but the minority had not so much pressed for a decision as for the discussion of the question.

Mr. PICKERING suggested his wish to substitute forty-eight hours for twenty-four, in his amendment; and if the election should not then take place, a choice to be made in such manner as the House should direct.

The question, on Mr. PICKERING's motion, was then put and negatived, without a division.

Mr. ADAMS then moved the following amendment: In the 37th line, after the word "choice," insert—

"And in case the House of Representatives shall not, within —— days, effect the choice in manner aforesaid, and there be a Vice President duly elected, the said Vice President shall discharge the powers and duties of the President of the United States. But if the office of Vice President be also vacant, then the said powers and duties of President of the United States shall be discharged by such person as Congress may by law direct, until a new election shall be had, in manner already prescribed by law."

Mr. HILLHOUSE thought that there should be provision made for the choice so made, to remain only until such period as the Electors could be called again.

Mr. DAYTON hoped the gentleman did not mean to lay a larger patch upon the Constitution than the hole they make in it required. Had gentlemen considered, that when there is a Vice President, that in case of death or inability, he alone can exercise the powers of the Executive, and that you cannot place any person over his head?

Mr. ADAMS.—The gentleman is certainly right; he had offered his proposition hastily. The observations which arise in this discussion evidently prove that we have not as full a consideration of the subject as it is susceptible of.

Mr. WRIGHT.—Gentlemen did not perceive that the House of Representatives are Constitutionally bound and impelled to choose when it devolves upon them: they are sworn to do their duty. The amendments offered are wholly founded on the presumed corruption of the House of Representatives. You may as well make provisions against the corruption of a jury.

Mr. HILLHOUSE.—There is another point which gentlemen appear not to have taken into view: how the objections of their oaths are to operate or be enforced, when the functions themselves expire on the third of March. There is another view of the subject, which ought not to be passed over: The members are sworn, to be sure, but one half of the House may sincerely believe that A is the popular choice; while the other half may as sincerely believe that the wishes of the majority are with B; and how are we to compel them by moral obligations, when the obligation rests wholly on the consciences of the individuals? The true principle, then, would be to make provision for the appointment of a person who should carry on the functions of Government till the Electors may again meet and choose a President. A provision vesting in the Senate the right of choice, even for one year, may be a motive for the other House to perform their duty promptly. It was not pleasant to discuss some topics, but we must discuss them, if we mean to avoid evil. We must suppose the existence of faction, of party, and even corruption, for we know that evil passions do and will exist, and that, by discussing, we guard against them. A House of Representatives elected two years before your Presidential election, may hold sentiments very different from him; the public mind may change in the time; and a party losing power may be led away by passion to conspire and throw every difficulty in the way.

Mr. BRADLEY thought the sentiments of the gentleman last up perfectly correct. He was satisfied that, if the House made no choice, the Vice President would administer the Government.

Mr. WRIGHT said that although the functions of the House of Representatives would expire with the third of March, yet there was, assuredly, time enough between the second Wednesday in February, and the third of March, to make a proper choice; nothing but obstinacy, or worse, would prevent an election; he would shut them up, like a jury, until they had made a choice: he could not conceive a case wherein any number of men in Congress would dare to set themselves up against the country, and put its happiness and their own lives at hazard, in such a way as the gentleman supposed.

Mr. S. SMITH.—The gentleman from Massachusetts (Mr. ADAMS) appears not to be perfectly satisfied with his own amendment; and certainly the gentleman from Connecticut had shown that the amendment was defective; the candor of that gentleman he must acknowledge, he had taken the strongest hold possible of the subject; he had laid the fruits of experience before you, and pointed out the weakness which you had to protect. He would recommend it to the gentleman from Massachusetts to alter his amendment, so as to make it, that, in case the House should fail to choose, then, in four days after, the Vice President shall be President.

Mr. ADAMS saw a new difficulty there also, for there may not be a majority for both, and provision will be necessary for the vacancy of the Vice Presidency.

Mr. HILLHOUSE thought there would be no danger of the Senate omitting to elect their President, who is, on a vacancy, the Vice President in fact. As to shutting the House up like a jury in a dark room, depriving them of fire, light, and food, he thought the measure too strong; he did not wish to see them at the mercy of the sheriff, who upon their laches might call in the *posse comitatus*, and trundle them out of the District, or send them to Coventry. If the House of Representatives should not make a choice, he saw no reason why the Government should not go on until an election should take place.

Mr. COCKE was astonished to see gentlemen going over so much unnecessary ground. Could they suppose the people so indifferent to their own rights as not to make an election? Or, do gentlemen mean all these cavillings as amusement—to display their ingenuity at finding fault? If there should be any failure of choice, why could not the Secretary of State arrange and carry on the Executive business until an election should again take place?

Mr. TRACY rose.

Mr. COCKE called for the question—the question!

Mr. TRACY.—Does the gentleman mean to call for the question while I am on the floor? I will not sit down upon such a call. What is the question, sir?

Mr. DAYTON hoped the gentleman from Massachusetts (Mr. ADAMS) would withdraw his amendment.

Mr. ADAMS thought the deliberation of one or two hours could not be thrown away.

Mr. WRIGHT hoped the decision on the amendment would not be pressed upon the House. What! is it proposed to take the choice of President out of the hands of the Electors and place it wholly in the House of Representatives, and tell them, hold out only four days, and you will then have the whole power in your hands; you may set aside all consideration for the wishes of your constituents—set popular opinion at defiance, and please yourselves by choosing a President of whom the people never thought? Gentlemen should avoid this dangerous path which they wish to prepare; the people will not bear to be frowned upon by those whom their breath has made, and can unmake.

Sir, it is our wish to prevent all these dangerous or fatal courses and consequences; and we should keep in mind, that whatever we may conclude upon here, is completely guarded, not alone by the necessary consent of the other House, but that of three-fourths of the States. The Constitution, sir, would be preferable as it is, without the odious and anti-republican forms which gentlemen propose to engross upon it. What, sir, determine a most important principle of effective government by a non-effective act—determine an election by holding out a temptation to non-election! He should prefer having the choice open to the Representatives bound by oath, by duty, and by the Constitution, to such an alternative.

. . . . .

An observation of the gentleman from Massachusetts (Mr. ADAMS) produced a sensation which at once showed that something besides the care of the people's rights had an influence here. He proposes that the proper officer, the Vice President, should succeed to the Presidential chair upon a failure of election or vacancy after a few short months. Whence arose the agitation and interest excited by this proposition? Is it because we wish not to see a man seated in the Executive chair whom the people never contemplated to place there, and who never had a vote?

Mr. DAYTON.—You are about to designate who shall be President and who Vice President; and some gentlemen have gone so far as to favor the choice of one who had not a vote for either office. The gentleman from Massachusetts, (Mr. ADAMS,) indeed, professes to have in view the succession of the Vice President to the Executive Chair when vacant. But gentlemen should perceive, that if you designate, the principle will be totally changed. He could not assent to the conclusion of some gentlemen on another point. If anything could be understood from the Constitution more clearly than another, it was that the votes are given to two persons for President, and that, as has been observed before, the Constitution never notices a vote for the office of Vice President. How, then, can it be said which was the person intended? The gentleman from Maryland (Mr. WRIGHT) had said that one of the candidates at the late election had not a single vote for President, while the official returns show that each and every vote was the same for both candidates as President.

Mr. TAYLOR.—That matter appears susceptible of a very simple explanation. There can be no question that in form, the votes for each candidate were equal; but that is not the question; the *quo animo* must be taken into view. Would any gentleman say no preference was intended? It is very true that such was the form, but looking to the well known intention, have you not in the very fact stated an evidence that the principle of designation is essential, were

it only to prevent the consummation of an act never contemplated or expected?

[*2 Dec.*]

Mr. TAYLOR, of Virginia, desired to withdraw his motion of the preceding day in order to accommodate the terms of his proposition to the wishes of gentlemen. His only object was to obtain the principle, and provided that was obtained in such a manner as to promise an accomplishment of the good intended thereby, he should consider the words in which the provision was to be couched of inferior moment. In lieu of the addition which he offered before, he now proposed to insert after the word *choice*, in the 37th line, the following words:

> "And if the House of Representatives shall not choose a President whenever the right of choice shall devolve upon them, before the 4th day of March next following, then the Vice President shall act as President, as in case of the death or other Constitutional disability of the President."

Mr. ADAMS had no sort of objection to this addition to the paragraph; it reached his ideas as far as it went; but he conceived that though this made a very necessary provision for the case of the President, it did not go far enough, inasmuch as no provision was made in case there should be no Vice President. He would submit this case to gentlemen, that if there was no Vice President existing nor any more than a President chosen, in the event of a high state of party spirit, would it be difficult to foresee that there would be much room left for contention and evil? Unless provision should be made against the contingency, therefore, the amendment would be imperfect, in his mind. Like the gentleman from Virginia, he was not tied to words, but he thought it worth while to employ two lines to provide against the danger.

Mr. PICKERING objected to the length of time allowed for the House of Representatives to decide. We have been told that the small States, from the smaller number of votes, are exposed to corruption; he wished no time to be left for corruption to operate, and he therefore desired that the period for the House of Representatives to decide should be limited to forty-eight hours or three days. . . .

The amendment was agreed to—. . . .

Mr. ADAMS offered another amendment, of the following effect, to be added to the provisions concerning the election of Vice President:

"And if there shall be no Vice President duly elected within ten days after the fourth of March, then the power and duties of the President of the United States shall be discharged by such person as shall be by law invested with that power, until such time as a new election by Electors shall take place." . . .

Mr. HILLHOUSE was not disposed to concur with the proposed amendment; he did not think a period of agitation a proper one to make choice of an officer of so much power; he would prefer making provision by law before the happening of the event; for, in a high state of party he could see no likelihood of an agreement, and out of disagreement confusion might arise. His wish was to have some person designated who should discharge the Executive duties until an election should take place, and that this officer should be previously fixed upon, so that party spirit should have no room for agitation.

Mr. JACKSON could not discern the necessity of the proposition now offered; the case proposed to be provided against, he thought so extreme as likely never to happen. Besides, the mover appeared not to have taken it into consideration that one-third of the Senate go out at the close of the second session of every Congress by rotation, and would he have only two-thirds to make the law which was to provide for this choice? Upon the principle of the general amendment, he had not at first made up his convictions, but the amendment adopted had removed his doubts, and he thought this addition to this amendment unnecessary. He hoped the Senate would abide by that they had already agreed to, and preserve the right of choice to the people.

Mr. WRIGHT.—There was another difficulty which the gentleman from Massachusetts appears not to have foreseen. To make a law it is not enough that the Senate are present even if complete; the House of Representatives is necessary to an act of legislation, and that body can have no existence after the fourth day of March, nor within the ten days suggested, for they could not, if all elected, be called even by proclamation within that time; and further, if there should be no election of President, there would be no power to convene Congress; so that the proposed addition is improper altogether.

Mr. ADAMS did not feel extremely solicitous for the proposition; when the Constitution is proposed to be amended, however, he was disposed to offer every suggestion which might appear to him calculated to render it more perfect. The objections offered by the gentleman from Georgia, highly as he respected his opinion, did not appear to him conclusive; for his calculations of time and circumstances do not entirely correspond with experience past. The President has at all times heretofore been inaugurated after the House of Representatives had closed its session by limitation, and the Senate had been uniformly assembled for the purpose of the inauguration. Here then is a body in session, and if there shall not be a Vice President chosen, they can and must proceed to choose one, and that choice would of course fall, as proposed, upon one of the candidates. The gentleman from Connecticut (Mr. HILLHOUSE) had mistaken his view, concerning the choice of a person by law; his intention certainly was to provide for the future contingency by a previous law.

Mr. JACKSON still conceived the gentleman's proposition founded in mistake; for it would be impracticable for the Senate to act, since, according to the rules of the Senate, two-thirds of the whole are necessary to form a quorum; one third must Constitutionally go out of that body at the time, and the absence of a single member would disable the Senate from business.

Mr. ADAMS.—There would remain still two-thirds of the Senate, and it would be the duty of the Executive to call them together, as had been done in some cases; and as to the deduction of the third by rotation, there are several of the small States that elected their Senators several months before the period. To argue that they would neglect it, would be to argue that the States are indifferent to their representation on this floor.

Mr. JACKSON—We know that vacancies do occur from other causes than indifference or neglect of States; we know that at this moment New York has but one Representative on this floor, and that New Jersey had but very lately been so much embarrassed by a faction as to leave her for sometime without more than one Senator.

. . . . .

Mr. WHITE, of Delaware, rose and addressed the Chair as follows:

Mr. President, it may be expected that we, who oppose the present measure, and especially those of us who belong to the smaller States, and who think the interests of those States will be most injuriously affected by its adoption, shall assign some reasons for our opinion, and for the resistance we give it: I will for myself endeavor to do so. I know well the prejudices of many in favor of this proposed amendment to the Constitution; I know too, and acknowledge with pleasure, the weight of abilities on the other side of the House by which those prejudices, if I may so be permitted to call them, will be sustained; this might perhaps be sufficient to create embarrassment or even silence on my part, but for the consciousness I feel in the rectitude of my views, and my full reliance on the talents of those with whom I have the honor generally to think and act. Upon a subject of the nature and importance of the one before us a great diversity of sentiment must be expected, and is perhaps necessary to the due and proper investigation of it. Without detaining the Senate with further preliminary remarks, presuming upon that patience and polite indulgence that are at all times extended by this honorable body to gentlemen who claim their attention, I will proceed immediately to the subject of the resolution; barely premising that notwithstanding the opinions of the gentleman from Virginia (Mr. TAYLOR) and the gentleman from Georgia, (Mr. JACKSON,) whose opinions I highly respect, I must yet think with my honorable friend from New Jersey (Mr. DAYTON) that the Constitution of the United States bears upon the face of it the strongest marks of its having been made under the influence of State classifications. It was a work of compromise, though not formed, as stated by the gentleman from Virginia, by the large States yielding most, but by the smaller States yielding much more to the general good.

It will be recollected that, previous to the adoption of the Constitution, on all Legislative subjects, in fact, on every measure of the Constitution each State had an equal voice; but very different is the case now, when, in the popular branch of your Government, you see one State represented by twenty-two members, and another by but one voting according to numbers. So that, notwithstanding the ideas of those gentlemen, and the declaration of an honorable member from Maryland, on my right, (Mr. SMITH,) that, during his ten years' service in Congress, he had never seen anything like State jealousies, State divisions, or State classification, I must be permitted to predicate part of my argument upon this business. Should any gentleman be able to show that the foundation is unsound, the super-structure of course will be easily demolished. Admitting, then, sir, for the sake of argument, that there were no very great objections to this proposed alteration in the mode of electing a President and Vice President, and that it were now part of the Constitution, it might be unwise to strike it out; unless much stronger arguments had been urged against than I have heard in favor of it, yet I would not now vote for its adoption. What appears specious in theory, may prove very inconvenient and embarrassing in practice, and my objections go to any alteration of the Constitution at this time; we have not given it a fair experiment, and it augurs not well to the peace and happiness of the United States to see so much increasing discontent upon this subject, so many projected alterations to the great charter of our Union and our liberties; not less than four are now upon our tables, and which, if adopted, will materially change the most valuable features of the Constitution. The first alters the mode of electing the President and Vice President; the second changes the ground upon which the Vice President is to be appointed by the Senate, in case one is not elected by the Electors, according to the Constitution; the third extends the powers of the Senate in the choice of this latter officer beyond what was ever contemplated by the people of this country; and the fourth, which is not now immediately before us, goes to incapacitate any citizen from being eligible to the office of President more than a certain number of years. All these important changes we are about to introduce into the Constitution at once; and, indeed, were attempted to be forced into a final vote upon them, in little more than the space of one day from the moment they were submitted to us. Are we aware of what we are about? Is this the way in which the Constitution was formed? Was it put together with as much facility and as little reflection as we are tearing it to pieces? No, Mr. President, it was constructed after much thought, after long and mature deliberation, by the collected wisdom and patriotism of America, by such a set of men as I fear this country will never again see assembled; and we should be cautious how we touch it. The fewer changes we make in it, the longer it remains; the older it grows the higher veneration will every American entertain for it; the man born to its blessings, will respect it more than him who saw its birth; he will regard it not only as the great bulwark of his liberties, but as the price of the blood of his ancestors—as a sacred legacy from his father, deposited with him for the benefit of himself, and in trust for his posterity. But if, in this way, every succeeding Congress, every party enjoying the short-lived triumph of a day, shall be mutilating it with alterations, from whatever motives, either to thwart their political opponents, or to answer particular purposes, ere long no trace of the original instrument will remain; it will be kept in a state of tottering infancy, until some Gallic Caesar, turning to his advantage an unhappy moment of popular phrenzy, may make the last change, by trampling upon its ruins, and substituting the strong arm of power in its place.

What, sir, let me ask, are the objects of these proposed amendments? The first, we are told, will so mark, so designate the man to be President, as to close forever the doors upon that subject! Could this be the effect, the adoption of it would indeed be wise and provident; but I fear a directly contrary tendency, that will open a new and immense field for intrigue.

The United States are now divided, and will probably continue so, into two great political parties; whenever, under this amendment, a Presidential election shall come round, and the four rival candidates be proposed, two of them only will be voted for as President—one of these two must be the man; the chances in favor of each will be equal. Will not this increased probability of success afford more than double the inducement to those candidates, and their friends, to tamper with the Electors, to exercise intrigue, bribery, and corruption, as in an election upon the present plan, where the whole four would be voted for alike, where the chances against each are as three to one, and it is totally uncertain which of the gentlemen may succeed to the high office? And there must, indeed, be a great scarcity of character in the United States, when, in so extensive and populous a country, four citizens cannot be found, either of them worthy even of the Chief Magistracy of the nation. But, Mr. President, I have never yet seen the great inconvenience that has been so much clamored about, and that will be provided against in future by substituting this amendment. There was, indeed, a time when it became necessary for the House of Representatives to elect, by ballot, a President of the United States from the two highest in vote, and they were engaged here some days, as I have been told, in a very good-humored way, in the exercise of that Constitutional right; they at length decided; and what was the consequence? The people were satisfied, and here the thing ended. What does this prove? that the Constitution is defective? No, sir, but rather the wisdom and efficiency of the very provision intended to be stricken out, and that the people are acquainted with the nature of their Government; and give me leave to say, if fortune had smiled upon another man, and that election had eventuated in another way, the consequence would have been precisely the same; the great mass of the people would have been content and quiet; and those factious, restless disorganizers, that are the eternal disturbers of all well administered Governments, and who then talked of resistance, would have had too much prudence to hazard their necks in so dangerous an enterprise. I will not undertake to say that there was no danger apprehended on that occasion. I know many of the friends of the Constitution had their fears; the experiment however, proved them groundless; but what was the danger apprehended pending the election in the House of Representatives? Was it that they might choose Colonel Burr or Mr. Jefferson President? Not at all; they had, notwithstanding what had been said on this subject by the gentleman from Maryland, (Mr. WRIGHT,) a clear Constitutional right to choose either of them, as much so as the Electors in the several States had to vote for them in the first instance; the particular man was a consideration of but secondary importance to the country; the only ground of alarm was, lest the House should separate without making any choice, and the Government be without a head, the consequences of which no man could well calculate. The present attempt, to say the least of it, as has been well observed by my honorable friend from Jersey, (Mr. DAYTON,) is taking advantage of a casualty to alter the Constitution that astonished every one when it happened, and that no man can imagine, in the ordinary course of events, will ever arise again. Sir, every hour that is added to the age of our Government, every day's increasing population of our country, every State admitted into the Union, renders still more remote even this improbable contingency. Gentlemen have urged, with exulting confidence, and particularly the honorable gentleman from Maryland, (Mr. SMITH,) that the people have long thought on this subject, and prepared for the amendment, and expect its adoption. I respect the sentiments of the people as highly as any man when they are well digested and clearly expressed; but in my mind this is a dangerous ground to advance far upon, without examining it well for ourselves; it is an argument that will apply alike to almost every question of importance, and goes to preclude debate upon them; for it is well known that there are few such submitted to us that have not been previously the subject of thought and speculative conversation out of doors. Ours is a country of politicians, and from the nature of our Government must continue so; every member of society feels such a portion of interest in the affairs of the nation as to excite inquiry; be his lot humble or exalted, be his sentiments right or wrong, he expresses them, as he is entitled to do, with freedom; but is it abroad in the country that the most important measures of the Government are to be matured and decided upon? Is it in private circles, in caucuses, in clubs, in coffee-houses, streets, and bar-rooms, that great Constitutional questions are to be settled? And are we convened here but to register the crude decrees of such assemblages, or only for the humble purpose of answering to the call of our Secretary with a yea or nay? If the argument proves anything, it amounts to this. Would the gentleman from Maryland, or any other honorable member, be content to hold his seat upon such terms? If so, he may indulge himself in one consolation, that no private citizen would envy him the place; but for myself I claim the exercise of higher and more responsible privileges of thinking and acting for myself, holding it my duty, so far as I am capable, to assign to my constituents the reasons that govern my public conduct.

It has of late, Mr. President, become fashionable to attach very little importance to the office of Vice President, to consider it a matter but of small consequence who the man may be; to view his post merely as an idle post of honor, and the incumbent as a cypher in the Government; or according to the idea expressed by an honorable member from Georgia, (Mr. JACKSON,) quoting, I believe, the language of some Eastern politician, as a fifth wheel to a coach; but in my humble opinion this doctrine is both incorrect and dangerous. The Vice President is not only the second officer of Government in point of rank, but of importance, and should be a man possessing, and worthy of the confidence of the nation. I grant, sir, should this designating mode of election succeed, it will go very far to destroy, not the certain or contingent duties of the office, for the latter by this resolution are considerably extended, but what may be much more dangerous, the personal consequence and worth of the officer; by rendering the Electors more indifferent about the reputation and qualification of the candidate, seeing they vote for him but as a secondary character; and which may occasion this high and important trust to be deposited in very unsafe hands. By a provision in the first section of the second article of the Constitution, "in case of the removal of the President from office, or of his death, resignation or inability to discharge the powers and duties of the said office, the same shall devolve on the Vice President"—and he is Constitutionally the President, not until another can be made only, but of the residue of the term, which may be nearly four years; and this is not to be supposed a remote or improbable case. In the State to which I have the honor to belong, within a few years past, two instances have happened of the place of Governor becoming vacant, and the duties of the office, according to the constitution of that State, devolving upon the Speaker of the Senate. We know well too, generally speaking, that before any man can acquire a sufficient share of the public confidence to be elected President, the people must have long been acquainted with his character and his merit; he must have proved himself a good and faithful servant, and will of course be far advanced in years, when the chances of life will be much against him. It may indeed, owing to popular infatuation, or some other extraordinary causes, be the ill fate of our country, that an unworthy designing man, grown old and gray, in the ways of vice and hypocrisy, shall for a time dishonor the Presidential chair, or it may be the fortune of some young man to be elected, but those will rarely happen. The Convention in constructing this part of the Constitution, in settling the first and second offices of the Government, and pointing out the mode of filling, aware of the probability of the Vice President succeeding to the office of President, endeavored to attach as much importance and respectability to his office as possible by making it uncertain at the time of voting, which of the persons voted for should be President, and which Vice President; so as to secure the election of the best men in the country, or at least those in whom the people reposed the highest confidence, to the two offices—thus filling the office of Vice President, with one of our most distinguished citizens, who would give respectability to the Government, and in case of the Presidency becoming vacant, having at his post a man Constitutionally entitled to succeed, who had been honored with the second largest number of the suffrages of the people for the same office, and who of consequence would be probably worthy of the place, and competent to its duties. Let us now, Mr. President, examine for a moment the certain effect of the change about to be made, or what must be the operation of this designating principle, if you introduce it into the Constitution; now the Elector cannot designate, but must vote for two persons as President, leaving it to circumstances not within his power to control which shall be the man: of course he will select two characters, each suitable for that office, and the second highest in vote must be the Vice President; but upon this designating plan the public attention will be entirely engrossed in the election of the President, in making one great man. The eyes of each contending party will be fixed exclusively upon their candidate for this first and highest office, no surrounding object can be viewed at the same time, they will be lost in his disc. The office of President, is in point of honor, profit, trust, and influential patronage so infinitely superior to any other place attainable in this Government, that, in the pursuit and disposal of it, all minor considerations will be forgotten, everything will be made to bend, in order to subserve the ambitious views of the candidates and their friends. In this angry conflict of parties, against the heat and anxiety of this political warfare, the Vice Presidency will either be left to chance, or what will be much worse, prostituted to the basest purposes; character, talents, virtue, and merit, will not be sought after, in the candidate. The question will not be asked, is he capable? is he honest? But can he by his name, by his connexions, by his wealth, by his local situation, by his influence, or his intrigues, best promote the election of a President? He will be made the mere stepping stone of ambition. Thus, by the death or other Constitutional inability of the President to do the duties of the office, you may find at the head of your Government as First Magistrate of the nation, a man who has either smuggled or bought himself into office. Who, not having the confidence of the people, or feeling the Constitutional responsibility of his place, but attributing his elevation merely to accident, and conscious of the superior claims of others, will be without restraint upon his conduct, without that strong inducement to consult the wishes of the people, and to pursue the true interests of the nation, that the hope of popular applause, and the prospect of re-election, would offer. Such a state of things might be productive of incalculable evils; for it is, as I fear time will show, in the power of a President of the United States to bring this Government into contempt, and this country to disgrace, if not to ruin. Again, sir, if this amendment succeeds, if you designate the person voted for as President, and the person voted for as Vice President, you hold out an irresistible temptation to contracts and compromises among the larger States for these offices; it will be placing the choice of the two highest officers in the Government so completely in their power, that the five largest States, viz: Massachusetts, New York, Pennsylvania, Virginia, and North Carolina, may not only act in every previous arrangement relative to the appointment of these officers without the necessity of consulting the other twelve, but may totally exclude them from any participation in the election. The whole number of Electors, according to the present representation in Congress, will be one hundred and seventy-seven; these five States will have ninety-six of them, a clear majority of eight, and should they agree among themselves they can say absolutely who shall be the President. The other twelve States will not have even the humble privilege of choosing between their candidates; for their whole number of votes being but eighty-one given to the candidate for the Vice Presidency as President, would be but thrown away, since the other would still have his designated majority of eight for that place. Should it be said that such a coalition is improbable, I answer that my opinion is different, and it is enough for me that it is possible. Again, sir, counting only the States of Massachusetts, New

York, Pennsylvania, and Virginia, these four will be found to be entitled to eighty-two Electors, wanting seven of a majority of the whole number; so that, leaving North Carolina among the smaller States, if they unite, and can by any species of influence, by promises of offices, bribery, or corruption, gain over to their interest but seven of the Electors belonging to the other States, they can in like manner appoint who they please. I might go on to show that lopping even Massachusetts from the list, the other four, viz: New York, Pennsylvania, Virginia, and North Carolina, could with very little difficulty effect the same object, since they are entitled to seventy-seven Electors. And now let me ask gentlemen representing the twelve smaller States, if they are prepared to yield up not only the high and honorable ground upon which the Constitution has placed them in the House of Representatives in case of an election for a President to be had there, but to vest in the five larger States, or even in a smaller number of them, whenever they shall be pleased to exercise it, the exclusive power of appointing the President and Vice President of the United States?

Again, Mr. President, admitting these coalitions of the larger States, of which I have been speaking, for the purpose of appointing a President and Vice President by themselves, may none of them ever take place under this amendment, if adopted, notwithstanding its strong and natural tendency to such an effect, (and this is certainly admitting much more than gentlemen on the other side of the House could in argument have any right to demand of me,) yet there is one other which I am sure, in candor, they must grant me, is not only possible, but very probable, indeed, upon a subject of this kind—I mean the States of Virginia, North and South Carolina, Georgia, Kentucky, and Tennessee, together with the Territories upon the waters of the Mississippi, that are every day growing into States. And such is the rapidly increasing population of that country, that, after the next census, it will be forever in their power, upon this designating plan of election, to appoint the President and Vice President of the United States. The other ten Middle and Eastern States will have only to acquiesce in the choice, without, as I before observed, the power even of electing between the candidates, and much less the right of being consulted, in the first instance, as to the suitable and proper characters. Gentlemen will, I hope, do me the justice to believe that I mention these coalitions as likely to be entered into, only in relation to this particular object. I have no doubt but that these States are as well disposed, and as much attached to the Union, as any that belong to it; but who does not know the indissoluble bonds that will bind together the citizens of that Southern and Western country, in the pursuit of an object of this kind? Their similarity of manners, of habits, of laws, of civil institutions, of local interests, added to their native prejudices and ties of consanguinity, unite them inseparably, and make their views the same. Yet gentlemen, to my utter astonishment, tell us that this amendment is intended to preclude intrigue. Sir, no other measure could be adopted that would so effectually produce it. It will create ill blood between the smaller and the larger States—between one part of the Union and another. It will give rise to local prejudices, to envious territorial distinctions, to State schisms; and I should not wonder if, in the end, it were to be the means of plunging this country into a civil war, and of producing a separation.

As to the second and third alterations proposed in this resolution, that of enlarging the ground upon which the Vice President may be appointed by the Senate, by giving them authority to elect from the two highest, whenever no person has a majority of the whole number of votes, whereas now they can choose but in the case of two persons being upon a vote, and thus extending the powers of the Senate in the election of this officer, they would, at first view, seem to be mere matters of speculation, introduced for the sake of change only, or for the want of something else to employ ourselves about. No inconvenience is even pretended to have been experienced under those provisions of the Constitution, as they now stand; yet we, in the plenitude of our wisdom, are about to recommend to the several State Legislatures an alteration of them; and so every successive Congress, which will no doubt in the same ratio as the present be more wise, more learned, more enlightened, and more patriotic, than their predecessors, will improve upon our example, until the Constitution shall be entirely regenerated. But the gentleman from Vermont (Mr. BRADLEY) now tells us—and I believe correctly—that these amendments, though not before contemplated, result necessarily from the introduction of the designating principle into the Constitution. Does not this show us, most clearly, the danger of meddling with the Constitution at all? Out of the single amendment proposed by the gentleman from New York, (Mr. CLINTON,) that of designating the person voted for as President, and the person voted for as Vice President, these two other very important changes have already grown—have forced themselves upon our consideration; and another of still greater importance immediately presents itself, which gentlemen on all sides seem to think must shortly follow—that of abolishing entirely the office of Vice President. Several honorable members have told us that their minds have long been made up on this subject; that they had long since seen the necessity of introducing this change in the mode of electing a President and Vice President; but never before saw its operation upon other parts of the Constitution, or that any other alterations must be the necessary consequence of its adoption. The honorable mover of this subject, from New York, who, according to his own account, had been two years maturing it in his mind, and who pressed the immediate adoption of it, with even more than his usual eloquence, had never before seen the bearing of his own resolution upon the Constitution, and was himself one of the first to vote for striking out part, and to second a motion of a gentleman from Vermont, (Mr. BRADLEY,) who I do not now see in his place, for a very important amendment to another part, of it. Indeed, sir, after all the deep deliberation bestowed upon it by the learned mover, the resolution, as at first introduced, provided very carefully for an impossible case, that in the nature of things could never happen—that of two candidates, upon the designating plan of election, having each a majority of the whole number of votes for President. Added to all this, sir, recollect the awkward and embarrassed situation of the Senate for a week past on this subject. Every step we have taken has involved us in new difficulties. We have several times been so completely lost in the mazes of our own amendments as to be under the necessity of adjourning, in order to have them printed, that we might see what we had done; and no sooner were they laid before us, than they directed our eyes to some other part of the Constitution where an unexpected injury had been sustained; and all this has arisen from the attempt to introduce the designating principle into the Constitution. The favorers of the amendments have been alternately at variance with themselves and with each other, and sometimes so scattered that no two of them could agree; at other times, all were entirely lost. These are the most irresistible arguments, the strongest circumstances, to show how dangerous it is to attempt any alteration in the Constitution; and that, as has been urged on a former occasion, every comma has its meaning. You cannot strike out a word from one section without inflicting a wound upon some other. So nicely has it been woven together, that no thread can be spared. Every principle it contains is a keystone, and no one of them can be removed without endangering the edifice. No man can tell how these amendments may operate—how they enfeeble and shackle other parts of the Constitution—or what other alterations they may render necessary. Look at this paper now, and recollect what it has been. At different times it has assumed different shapes—at one time proposing but one alteration; at another, four or five. Thus one alteration will beget the necessity for another and so we shall have to go on in this work *ad infinitum,* as the regular series of cause and effect. It may be said that this second amendment, so far as it goes to extend the powers of the Senate in the election of the Vice President, if adopted, may prove advantageous to the smaller States. I grant the possibility, but such advantage is too casual, too remote and unimportant, to induce me, as a Representative from one of the smaller States, to vote for any alteration in the Constitution. It is the true interest of the smaller States, especially, to preserve sacred and untouched the Constitution and not be weakening it by alterations—expecting temporary advantages that may or may never arise; and which, if attained, would be little—would be less than insignificant—compared with the infinite importance of this instrument to those States, as it stands at present. Their independence, nay, their very existence, as States, hangs upon their preservation of it. They could never get such another, and they should be the last to tamper with it: when they do so, they risk their only stake. And now let me entreat gentlemen representing the twelve smaller States in the Senate (for it is here, and here only, they are felt in the Government) to weigh well their amendments before, by their affirmative votes, they do an act that may encroach upon the Constitutional rights of those States. I know well that, with some of the States, it is the highest source of mortification that the Constitution has placed the larger and smaller ones so nearly upon an equality in certain respects. The pride of some of the larger States will, for instance, never submit that, by any possible contingency, the State of Delaware, of Rhode Island, of Vermont, or New Hampshire, should have an equal voice with them in the choice of a President, as in case of an election by the House of Representatives. This is an evil that must be cured; and if alterations shall prove insufficient, a more effectual remedy, I fear, will be prescribed, the moment that the national pulse can be prepared for the application.

So far, Mr. President, as human wisdom, or rather human frailty, might be permitted to judge of the future from the past and the present, I should think it no act of rashness to foretell that the next alteration attempted, will be to destroy the influence of the smaller States in this branch of the Legislature, not directly by expunging that provisions of the Constitution which gives to each State an equal representation upon this floor, for that cannot be done with the consent of every State, but indirectly in conformity with the idea of the gentleman from Kentucky, (Mr. BRECKENRIDGE,) expressed the other day, by shortening the period for which Senators shall be elected, and which, in effect, will amount to the same thing. I know too well the weight and influence of the gentleman from Kentucky in this Government at present, to treat lightly what he says upon a subject of such magnitude, and must consider the charge of aristocracy, which he has been pleased to bring against the Senate as the denunciation of this body. Indeed, sir, I shall not be surprised to hear at the next session, that the people are prepared for the change, or even that some of the smaller States have recommended it, for such is at present the infatuated confidence of many of them in those who, I fear, are encompassing their ruin, that they seem to be constantly acting under instructions, and to have resigned both themselves and the Constitution to the guardianship of others. The gentleman from Virginia, (Mr. TAYLOR,) in order to lull our fears and divert our attention from the threat uttered by him to the smaller States, has very artfully called the alarm sounded on that subject by my honorable friend from New Jersey, (Mr. DAYTON,) at one time a stratagem, and at another an ambuscade; and asked, how he, as a general, could lay an ambuscade so unconcealed, so exposed to the enemy? Sir, we resort to no stratagems or ambuscades, our opposition is public, and our movements undisguised; and it was on the part of my friend only a prompt attack upon an ambuscade laid by the gentleman from Virginia himself, who has been entrusted with the chief command in this campaign, and which by him had been incautiously too soon uncovered; whilst gentler means succeed so well, threats are unnecessary, and might be dangerous. I was not a little surprised, Mr. President, to hear an honorable member from Maryland, (Mr. SMITH,) after reminding us that he belonged to a small State, come out on this occasion the mighty champion of the large ones, and whilst exhibiting himself to the greatest possible advantage in this new and enviable character, calling upon my friend from Massachusetts before me, (Mr. ADAMS,) to know why he, representing a large State, had been pleased to give himself any concern about the interests of the small States, intimating that such conduct concealed views not intended to be discovered, or, in the courtly language of the day, that it was

stratagem; I wonder it had not been an ambuscade too. The honorable member from Virginia (Mr. TAYLOR) has prudently attempted to conceal again the ambuscade that had been so much annoyed by the fire of my friend from New Jersey, endeavoring to soften down and explain away an expression used by him, and which, by a very natural construction, was considered a threat to the smaller States; the gentleman has indeed told us since that he intended no threat, and we are bound to accept his explanation. I mean not to scrutinize his meaning, especially after what the honorable member has said; but let us see how far the gentleman from Maryland was correct, when he declared that his friend from Virginia had used no language that could amount to a threat to the smaller States. If, sir, the language, I will say the menacing language of the gentleman from Virginia used on this subject, taken according to its common import, was not sufficient to rally and unite the smaller States, then the rancor of party has stifled more noble sentiments, we are a house divided against itself, and our day has passed.

After reproaching us with our weakness, the gentleman proclaimed in the language of triumph, (for I will give his very words as noted down by myself and others at the time,) "Let the smaller States beware how they rouse the resentment of the larger ones. What," asked he, "must become of them in such a collison?" And is this no threat? Sir, I answer, we might sink; but it is to avoid this very collision that I resist, with my feeble efforts, the present measure. We are now safely entrenched behind the barriers of the Constitution, and shall we ourselves demolish this great bulwark of our defence? Shall we not rather make our stand here, whilst the means of protection and resistance are within our power? Ambition is insatiable; the more we give up the more will be demanded of us, and every inch of ground we yield, the less tenable does the rest become. The honorable member from Virginia has told us, that the present mode of electing the President and Vice President was the road to Monarchy. I have often, sir, heard it intimated, that the Government of the United States had a tendency to Monarchy, a doctrine I could never accede to, (I mean as the Government is at present organized.) I speak and judge from things as they now present themselves; what effect these many speculative changes that are at present taking place in the Constitution may have, I know not, I presume not to foretell. but one thing was, years since, foretold and denied, and I now call it up to the recollection of gentlemen on the other side of the House, not to upbraid or offend them—but short-sighted man feels a kind of pleasure, (it is indeed though, Mr. President, on this occasion a melancholy one,) in having foretold truly the events of futurity. It was foretold that the Constitution would not suit those who were coming into power; that it was obnoxious to them, or to their leaders, which is in effect the same, and that the moment they should lay their hands upon it, if they could not get rid of it entirely under the pretence of amending and altering, they would fritter it away, until the shadow, the empty shadow, should remain. How far the proceedings of this session, which is the first that the present majority ever consisted of two-thirds of both branches of the Legislature, will go to justify this prediction, I will leave the world and the consciences of those honorable gentlemen on the other side of the House to judge. But such was the anxiety on this subject, that scarcely had we convened before the long wished for, hallowed work, was commenced, and the order of almost every day since has been a resolution to alter the Constitution. If, sir, the Constitution was suffered to remain as it is, I have no idea, from my acquaintance with the people of this country, and from the nature of our civil institutions, that any set of men, entrusted with the management of our public affairs, could ever, by a system of measures tending to such an end, succeed in the subversion of our rights and liberties. The people watch their servants with a jealous eye. If they err at all, it is on this side, and this is the safe side. No, Mr. President, what we have most to fear to our Government, and our liberties, must come from another and a very different source, from the licentiousness of democracy. This is what Republican Governments have forever to guard against; this is the vortex in which they are most likely to be swallowed up. God grant it may never be the case with ours, and I fear nothing else. By the licentiousness of democracy, I mean no imputation or offence to any portion of this community; I refer not to the political sentiments of any honorable gentlemen, or to the sentiments of their constituents—but to that wild infuriated spirit that we have seen in France, under the prostituted name of liberty, anarchizing the world, and rioting in the destruction of everything dear and valuable to society; and after having sported itself in all the wantonness of excess with the terrors, the crimes, the miseries and the murders of mankind, has seated a Corsican adventurer upon the high and dignified throne of the Bourbons—has riveted the manacles of tyranny upon a great, a brave, but a deluded people, and is now reclining in the shade of a military despotism.

. . . . .

Mr. COCKE.—The gentleman from Delaware thinks the minority should govern—that is his argument, however he may disguise it. I think the majority should govern; I like to speak out—I do not wish to have a man put upon us contrary to our wishes. What! shall the majority abandon the right of choosing a man whose opinions are conformable to theirs, and suffer a man of principles hostile to theirs to be put upon them? I am, sir, for a government of the people, whether well born or born by accident; I am for a government not of checks and balances, but one that will not suffer a bad check upon good principles.

But we are once more told of a Gallic Caesar, and our fears are to be provoked this way too—but this more than the rest of alarms will not do; we fear no Caesar, foreign or domestic. We have indeed seen the day when we were near getting a President not of our choice; but because we have escaped from the danger and the intrigue of that day, are we to take no precaution against such measures again. It is to guard against such danger we wish to amend this Constitution. But gentlemen tell us we have not given it a fair trial. I think we have, and found it defective. Here we have been a week and upwards, laboring and bewildered in every kind of discussion, and what have we come

to? exactly where we set out. Not one of us has altered our opinions—we have argued and listened and done nothing. Why? Because gentlemen have been attempting impossibilities; there is no such thing as moving either side from their principles. One side thinks the minority should give the law; we think with the Constitution the right is in the majority, and we will submit to no other law. I am for the amendment, and for a discrimination.

. . . . .

It has been said, the people require this amendment; but of this fact we have no evidence.

This amendment affects the relative interest and importance of the smaller States. The Constitution requires the Electors of each State to vote for two men, one of whom to be President of the United States. This affords a degree of security to the small States against the views and ambition of the large States. It gives them weight and influence in the choice. By destroying this complex mode of choice, and introducing the simple principle of designation, the large States can with more ease elect their candidate. This amendment will enable the Electors from four States and a half to choose a President, against the will of the remaining twelve States and a half. Can such a change tend to conciliate and strengthen the Union?

This amendment has a tendency to render the Vice President less respectable. He will be voted for not as President of the United States, but as President of the Senate, elected to preside over forms in this House. In electing a subordinate officer the Electors will not require those qualifications requisite for supreme command. The office of Vice President will be a sinecure. It will be brought to market and exposed to sale to procure votes for the President. Will the ambitious, aspiring candidate for the Presidency, will his friends and favorites promote the election of a man of talents, probity, and popularity for Vice President, and who may prove his rival? No! They will seek a man of moderate talents, whose ambition is bounded by that office, and whose influence will aid them in electing the President. This mode of election is calculated to increase corruption, promote intrigue, and aid inordinate ambition. The Vice President will be selected from some of the large States; he will have a casting vote in this House; and feeble indeed must his talents be, if his influence will not be equal to that of a member. This will, in fact, be giving to that State a third Senator.

In the Southern States the blacks are considered as property, and the States in which they live are thereby entitled to eighteen additional Electors and Representatives. A number equal to all the Electors and Representatives that four States and a half are entitled to elect. Will you, by this amendment, lessen the weight and influence of the Eastern States in the election of your first officers, and still retain this unequal article in your Constitution? Shall property in one part of the Union give an increase of Electors, and be wholly excluded in other States? Can this be right? Will it strengthen the Union?

This amendment is designed to prevent the evils that occurred at the last Presidential election. That was an extraordinary event; it was a casualty that can seldom happen. Two men had a majority of all the electoral votes, but neither of them was chosen. But what was the consequence? Why, the House of Representatives in a peaceable manner completed the choice, and that, fourteen days before the President could enter upon the duties of his office. It may be desirable to prevent the choice being carried into the House of Representatives, but this amendment will not do it. It expressly provides for such an event. And if two or more candidates of different parties are carried there, (and if the state's parties should be nearly equal it will happen,) the House must then decide between candidates of different parties.

Mr. P. said that the amendment appeared calculated to give power to the strong; enfeeble and weaken the small States; to lessen the respectability of the Vice President, and not to prevent the evil it was designed to remedy; and therefore that he should vote against it.

. . . . .

Mr. TRACY. . . . The merits have never, until now, been before us, for, although considerable time has been consumed in debate, it has chiefly been directed to the subordinate amendments, and not to the main resolution. But, since the Senate have refused to adjourn, I will now offer some observations on the merits; in doing which, I will study brevity, as much as the importance of the subject will permit.

. . . . .

Propriety, therefore, requires that we attentively examine the Constitution itself, not only to obtain correct ideas upon these observations, so repeatedly urged, but to place in the proper light the operations and effects of the resolution in debate. If we attend to the Constitution, we shall immediately find evident marks of concession and compromise, and that the parties to these concessions were the great and small States. And the members of the Convention who formed the instrument have, in private information and public communications, united in the declaration, that the Constitution was the result of concession and compromise between the great and small States. In this examination of the Constitution it will be impossible to keep out of view our political relations under the first Confederation. We primarily united upon the footing of complete State equality—each State had one, and no State had more than one vote in the Federal Council or Congress. With such a Confederation we successfully waged war, and became an independent nation. When we were relieved from the pressure of war, that Confederation, both in structure and power, was found inadequate to the purposes for which it was established. Under these circumstances, the States, by their Convention, entered into a new agreement, upon principles better adapted to promote their mutual security and happiness. But this last agreement, or Constitution, under which we are now united, was manifestly carved out of the first Confederation. The small States adhered tenaciously to the principles of State equality; and gave up only a part of that federative principle, complete State equality, and that, with evident caution and reluctance. To this federative principle they were attached by habit; and their attachment was sanctioned and corroborated by the example of most if not all the ancient and the modern Confederacies. And when the great States claimed a weight in the Councils of the nation proportionate to their numbers and wealth, the novelty of the claim, as well as its obvious tendency to reduce the sovereignty of the small States, must have produced serious obstacles to its admission. Hence it is, that we find in the Constitution but one entire departure from the Federal principle. The House of Representatives is established upon the popular principle, and given to numbers and wealth, or to the great States, which, in this view of the subject, are synonymous. It was thought, by the Convention, that a consolidation of the States into one simple Republic, would be improper. And the local feelings and jealousies of all, but more especially of the small States, rendered a consolidation impracticable.

The Senate, who have the power of a legislative check upon the House of Representatives, and many other extensive and important powers, is preserved as an entire federative feature of Government as it was enjoyed by the small States, under the first Confederacy.

In the article which obliges the Electors of President to vote for one person not an inhabitant of the same State with themselves, is discovered State jealousy. In the majorities required for many purposes by the Constitution, although there were other motives for the regulations, yet the jealousy of the small States is clearly discernible. Indeed, sir, if we peruse the Constitution with attention, we shall find the small States are perpetually guarding the federative principle, that is, State equality. And this, in every part of it, except in the choice of the House of Representatives, and in their ordinary legislative proceedings. They go so far as to prohibit any amendment which may affect the equality of States in the Senate.

This is guarding against almost an impossibility, because the Senators of small States must be criminally remiss in their attendance, and the Legislatures extremely off their guard, if they permit such alterations, which aim at their own existence. But, lest some accident, some unaccountable blindness or perfidy should put in jeopardy the federative principle in the Senate, they totally and forever prohibit all attempts at such a measure. In the choice of President, the mutual caution and concession of the great and small States, is, if possible, more conspicuous than in any other part of the Constitution.

He is to be chosen by Electors appointed as the State Legislatures shall direct, not according to numbers entirely, but adding two Electors in each State as representatives of State sovereignty. Thus Delaware obtains three votes for President, whereas she could have but one in right of numbers. Yet, mixed as this mode of choice is, with both popular and federative principles, we see the small States watching its motions and circumscribing it to one attempt only, and, on failure of an Electoral choice, they instantly seize upon the right of a Federal election, and select from the candidates a President by States and not by numbers. In confirmation of my assertion, that this part of the Constitution was peculiarly the effect of compromise between the great and small States, permit me to quote an authority which will certainly have great weight, not only in the Senate, but through the Union, I mean that of the present Secretary of State, (Mr. Madison,) who was a leading member of the Federal Convention who formed, and of the Virginia Convention who adopted the Constitution.

In the Debates of the Virginia Convention, volume 3, page 77, Mr. Madison says, speaking of the mode of electing the President:

> "As to the eventual voting by States it has my approbation. The lesser States and some larger States will be generally pleased by that mode. The Deputies from the small States argued, and there is some force in their reasoning, that, when the people voted, the large States evidently had the advantage over the rest, and, without varying the mode, the interests of the little States might be neglected or sacrificed. Here is a compromise. For in the eventual election, the small States will have the advantage."

After this view of the Constitution, let us inquire, what is the direct object of the proposed alteration in the choice of President?

To render more practicable and certain the choice by Electors—and for this reason: that the people at large, or in other words, that the great States, ought to have more weight and influence in the choice. That it should be brought nearer to the popular and carried further from the federative principle. This claim we find was made at the formation of the Constitution. The great States naturally wished for a popular choice of First Magistrate. This mode was sanctioned by the example of many of the States in the choice of Governor. The small States claimed a choice on the federative principle, by the Legislatures, and to vote by States; analogies and examples were not wanting to sanction this mode of election. A consideration of the weight and influence of a President of this Union, must have multiplied the difficulties of agreeing upon the mode of choice. But as I have before said, by mutual concession, they agreed upon the present mode, combining both principles and dividing between the two parties, thus mutually jealous, as they could, this important privilege of electing a Chief Magistrate.

This mode then became established, and the right of the small States to elect upon the federative principle, or by States, in case of contingency of electoral failure of choice, cannot with reason and fairness be taken from them, without their consent, and on a full understanding of its operation; since it was meant to be secured to them by the Constitution, and was one of the terms upon which they became members of the present Confederacy; and for which privilege they gave an equivalent to the great States, in sacrificing so much of the federative principle, or State equality.

The Constitution is nicely balanced, with the federative and popular principles; the Senate are the guardians of the former, and the House of Representatives of the latter; and any attempts to destroy this balance, under whatever specious names or pretences they may be presented, should be watched with a jealous eye. Perhaps a fair definition of the Constitutional powers of amending is, that

you may upon experiment so modify the Constitution in its practice and operation, as to give it, upon its own principles, a more complete effect. But this is an attack upon a fundamental principle established after a long deliberation, and by mutual concession, a principle of essential importance to the instrument itself, and an attempt to wrest from the small States a vested right, and, by it, to increase the power and influence of the large States. I shall not pretend, sir, that the parties to this Constitutional compact cannot alter its original essential principles, and that such alterations may not be effected under the name of amendment; but, let a proposal of that kind come forward in its own proper and undisguised shape; let it be fairly stated to Congress, to the State Legislatures, to the people at large, that the intention is to change an important federative feature in the Constitution, which change in itself and all its consequences, will tend to a consolidation of this Union into a simple Republic; let it be fairly stated, that the small States have too much agency in the important article of electing a Chief Magistrate, and that the great States claim the choice; and we shall then have a fair decision. If the Senators of the small States, and if their State Legislatures, will then quietly part with the right they have, no person can reasonably complain.

Nothing can be more obvious, than the intention of the plan adopted by our Constitution for choosing a President. The Electors are to nominate two persons, of whom they cannot know which will be President; this circumstance not only induces them to select both from the best men; but gives a direct advantage into the hands of the small States even in the electoral choice. For they can always select from the two candidates set up by the Electors of large States, by throwing their votes upon their favorite, and of course giving him a majority; or, if the Electors of the large States should, to prevent this effect, scatter their votes for one candidate, then the Electors of the small States would have it in their power to elect a Vice President. So that, in any event, the small States will have a considerable agency in the election. But if the discriminating or designating principal is carried, as contained in this resolution, the whole or nearly the whole right and agency of the small States, in the electoral choice of Chief Magistrate is destroyed, and their chance of obtaining a federative choice by States if not destroyed, is very much diminished.

For this identical purpose is the principle of electoral discrimination and designation introduced into the resolution before you; for the same purpose is the number of candidates reduced from five to three, from whom the House of Representatives may elect, in case of electoral failure of choice; that is, to destroy or diminish the agency of the small States in the choice of President.

For what purpose else are we perpetually told and from all parts of the Senate, that the public will is opposed by the present mode, and public will cannot be gratified, without the introduction of the discriminating principle?

By the public will thus mentioned, the gentlemen mean the will of a popular majority, or, the will of the great States, which in this case, I repeat it, are the same. How is it possible for the gentlemen to increase the chances of gratifying this description of the public will, without decreasing the agency of the small States?

The whole power of election is now vested in the two parties; numbers and States, or, great and small States; and it is demonstration itself if you increase the power of the one, in just such proportion you diminish that of the other. Do the gentlemen suppose that the public will, when Constitutionally expressed by a majority of States in pursuance of the federative principle of our Government, is of less validity, or less binding upon the community at large, than the public will expressed by a popular majority? The framers of your Constitution, the people who adopted it, meant, that the public will, in the choice of President, should be expressed by Electors, if they could agree, and if not, the public will should be expressed by a majority of the States, acting in their federative capacity, and that in both cases the expression of the public will should be equally binding.

It is pretended that the public will can never, properly or Constitutionally, be expressed but by a majority of numbers of the people, or of the House of Representatives. This may be a pleasing doctrine enough to great States; but it is certainly incorrect. Our Constitution has given the expression of the public will, in a variety of instances, other than that of the choice of President, into very different hands from either House of Representatives or the people at large. The President and Senate, and in many cases the President alone, can express the public will, in apointments of high trust and responsibility, and it cannot be forgotten that the President sometimes expresses the public will by removals. Treaties, highly important expressions of the public will, are made by the President and Senate; and they are the supreme law of the land. In the several States, many great offices are filled, and even the Chief Magistracy, by various modes of election. The public will is sometimes expressed by pluralities instead of majorities, sometimes by both branches of the Legislatures, and sometimes by one, and in certain contingencies, elections are settled by lot. The people have adopted constitutions containing such regulations, and experience has proved that they are well calculated to preserve their liberties and promote their happiness. From what good or even pardonable motive, then, can it be urged that the present mode of electing our President has a tendency to counteract the public will? Do gentlemen intend to destroy every federal feature in this Constitution? And is this resolution a precursor to a complete consolidation of the Union, and to the establishment of a simple Republic?— Or will it suffice to break down every federative feature which secures to one portion of the Union, to the small States, their rights?

. . . . .

The Constitution is of recent date; it was formed by the mutual concessions of conflicting parties, and balanced with a view to the securing of all. Experience alone can test its utility, and time and practice discover its faults. It is a sound position that you should never attempt an alteration in an instrument so complicated, and calculated to serve so many various and opposite interests, without being able, by the test of experiment, to discern clearly the necessity of alteration, and without a moral certainty that the change shall not only remove an existing evil, but that it shall not produce any itself. The article in the Constitution establishing the mode of electing a Chief Magistrate, and which is now proposed to be altered, was undoubtedly one of the most difficult parts of the whole at its formation. I am convinced, sir, that the public mind is not sufficiently impressed with the difficulty of adopting, not only an unexceptionable but even a tolerable and practicable mode of electing a Chief Magistrate, possessing such important and extensive powers as are Constitutionally vested in the President of the United States. An attempt to detail the number and magnitude of his powers, to this Senate, would be impertinent. But it must and will be acknowledged by all, that the President is vested with powers vastly extensive and important, and that he will bring with him into the Government more or less of State politics and State prejudices, and these facts, to which may be added the probability that he will be taken from a large State, must have increased the difficulties of the Convention in fixing on a mode of choice.

How often have contests, wars, and bloodshed, the destruction of confederacies, of liberty and of vast portions of the human race, arisen from the election of Chief Magistrates? When we consider that the powers vested in the President of this Union are sufficiently important to excite the avarice and ambition of the human heart, its two most active principles, to gain possession of the office; when we consider the difference of sentiment, habit, and interest, in this country; State pride and State jealousy, which could never be laid asleep; the difficulties of fixing upon a proper mode of election must be also infinitely multiplied. And yet this article is now selected for alteration. All the amendments which have been hitherto adopted, went to some general explanation upon very general principles, not changing but rather expounding the Constitution.

This, as I have before said, is taking up the most difficult and most important article in the Constitution, both in relation to rights and principles. But it is said that experience has shown us the necessity of an alteration in this article; that an evil has been found in practice to grow out of the Constitutional provision, which calls imperiously for remedy.

At the last election of President two persons had an equal number of votes, and that number was a majority of the votes of all the Electors appointed, which circumstance gave the House of Representatives a Constitutional right to select one of them for President. In exercising this Constitutional right, they voted by States, and there was at first a division, no choice being made until the sixth day; when an election was effected, of the very man whom the great States, and the advocates of this resolution, wished.

It ought to be noted here, that although they voted by States, yet it happened, in this division, that a majority, in point of numbers, voted for the person as President who eventually became Vice President. As to intrigue, by either of the candidates, or by their friends, I know of none; the sentiments and conduct of the Vice President, as published, were perfectly fair and honorable, containing a declaration of his wishes not to stand in the way of the other candidate.

After the view of the Constitution which we have taken, and comparing this fact, or set of facts, with the provisions for electing a President, we shall really be at a loss to find out the mighty evil, which the experience of this election has discovered, and which is said to call so imperiously for a remedy. But the advocates of this resolution have had the goodness to put their finger on the spot. They say, that in the certificates of the Electors, Mr. Jefferson's name stood first; this is called a sort of record testimony, and, in addition, some, if not all the Electors said they meant to elect Mr. Jefferson President, and Mr. Burr Vice President; and this is declared to be the public will, expressed by the Constitutional organ, the Electors. Notwithstanding this expression of the public will, say the gentlemen, a large portion of the House of Representatives withstood and opposed the public will for the space of six days, and wilfully voted for the man to be President, who, they knew by the evidence just mentioned, was meant to be Vice President. One gentleman (Mr. WRIGHT) has said, that if he had been a member of that House, possessing such sentiments upon the subject as he now does, such voting would in him have amounted to the crime of perjury, or words to the same effect. I mean to quote his ideas, as expressed, and believe I have given nearly his very words. And, it is added, that thus there was imminent danger of a person being imposed upon the United States as Chief Magistrate, who was not originally intended for that high office, and that civil war must have been the consequence; and, as is common in such cases, the picture is filled—in the back ground, with brother raising his murderous hand against brother, father against son, and with an afflicting group of *et ceteras;* and to avoid a repetition of this tremendous crisis, as it is called, the present resolution, it is said, must pass.

Let this statement of facts be kept in view while we examine the duties assigned by the Constitution to the several agents concerned. The duty of the Electors is precisely defined. They are each to bring forward two candidates fully qualified for President, because they cannot know at the time of giving their ballots upon which the choice will fall. The circumstance of two having a majority, and both being equal in number of votes, is an expression of the public will, through the only Constitutional organ, by which, in this case, the public will can be expressed, that both had the requisite qualifications. The public will, then, was in this instance clearly and unequivocally expressed, by a Constitutional and numerous majority, that both candidates were worthy of the office; but here the expression of the public will ceased, and which of these two should be President was now to be decided by another Constitutional organ, that is, by the House of Representatives, voting by States.

The framers of the Constitution so intended, and the people who adopted it have so ordained, that their will in this case should be expressed by a majority of the States, acting by their representation in the House of Represen-

tatives. The right of selection is a right complete in itself, to be exercised by these second Electors, uninfluenced by any extraneous consideration, and governed only by their own sense of propriety and rectitude. The opinion of the people had been expressed by the Electors, but it only reached a certain point, and then was totally silent as to which of the two should be President, and their sense upon this point could only be collected through their Constitutional organ, the House of Representatives, voting by States. Any interference of the first Electors, or of an individual or individuals, must be informal and improper. The advice of sensible and candid men, as in every other case, might be useful; but could have no binding force whatever. The first Electors had no right to choose a Vice President. To claim it was overstepping their duty, and arrogating to themselves a power not given to them by the Constitution.

If there is anything in this whole transaction which has the most distant appearance of a breach of duty, it was in the Electors, by attempting to designate, and by exercising the important office of an Elector under the influence of improper motives; that is, by officiously attempting to decide the question, which of the two persons was proper for Vice President, which they were constitutionally incompetent to decide. By this conduct they attempted to break down an important guard provided by the Constitution, and improperly to release themselves from its obligations, which made it their duty to select two men qualified to be President. But if there can be a shadow of reason in this claim of the Electors to designate under the present Constitutional regulations, of which, to doubt, seems to be so heinous, what necessity can there be for this amendment? The object of the amendment, or certainly its chief object, is to establish the designating principle; but why this, if it can already be effected by the simple mode of placing one name first on the ballot, which is so easy to be done that it can scarcely be avoided? And if done, by the doctrine of gentlemen, it is so far binding on the House of Representatives, that if they even doubt, they are damned?

The fact certainly was, that at the last election, the great States brought forward the two candidates. They were both of the same political sentiments. This they had a Constitutional right to do. But it now seems that their language to the small States was: "because you will not give up your Constitutional rights to us, and let us go on and designate, we will stir up a civil war, and lay the blame to you; and of this improper conduct of ours we will take the advantage, and obtain an alteration of the Constitution, which will hereafter gratify us in every respect." A gentleman from Maryland (Mr. SMITH) had said, that he heard, though he could not prove it, that the Federal majority, at the time of the last election, contemplated making a law authorizing or appointing some person as President, in case no choice had been made by the House of Representatives. I was then, sir, a member of the Government, and knew nothing of such a project; it might have been so; but supposing it was, what then? Why, says the gentleman, the person thus appointed could not have kept his head on his shoulders twenty-four hours; and this would have made a civil war. If the majority now should contemplate a measure which the Constitution does not authorize—as it clearly did not authorize the measure suspected by the gentleman, though he cannot prove it—the best thing in the world for them to do would be to give up, without any attempt to effect it, as it seems the Federal majority did. But what argument all this can afford in favor of the amendment, or why it was mentioned in this debate, is beyond my comprehension. In the result of the last election, the great States and the ruling political party were certainly gratified, and there does not appear the least reasonable ground of complaint against the small States, in the use of their Constitutional rights on the occasion. All support, therefore, to the amendment, drawn from that transaction, must fail.

I have said that the article fixing the mode of electing a Chief Magistrate was, from its nature, attended with many difficulties. A more strict inquiry into the Constitutional mode, and a comparison of it in some other and more particular points with the proposed alteration, will be useful in forming an opinion of their relative merits.

As the Constitution stands each Elector is to write the names of two persons on a piece of paper called a ballot. Either of the two persons thus voted for may be President, and the Elector cannot know which. This affords the most powerful inducement to vote for two, both of whom are qualified for the very important office. For it is not only uncertain upon whom the choice will fall at first, but the one remaining will certainly be President upon any contingency which shall remove or incapacitate the first. The Convention seem to have selected a mode of proceeding the most simple, the least liable to accident, and the best calculated to insure the main object, that is, that both should be really worthy of the trust. If one candidate wishes to make interest with the Electors, as each must vote for two, it will be impossible for bribery or intrigue to succeed; for, without corrupting the whole, or certainly many more than half, he may be defeated by the other candidate on the ballot. This is, perhaps, the most effectual bar to intrigue that was ever contrived; for, unless all, or a great proportion of the Electors are corrupted, an extreme case of depravity not probable in any country, intrigue can have no assurance of success. The danger and difficulty which must always attend such an important election as that of Chief Magistrate of the United States, was meant to be avoided by diminishing the chances of its frequent recurrence. So, two persons are placed in condition to act as President in succession, to prevent both the evils of vacancy and a recurrence of choice more frequently than once in four years: and it seems merely incidental to this second person to be called Vice President, and neither the first nor second description of Electors can have any right to vote for him as such. Indeed, he can have no existence till the first character is designated, and then seems to be discovered, not elected. The Senate, in case of an equal number of votes for two or more remaining persons, after the President is elected, are vested with authority to choose a Vice President, for as such he is to preside over this body, and this body therefore seems to be the only Constitutional organ to designate him. Both the other descriptions of Electors have nothing to do with

such a character or office, but are confined to act with a single reference to the character and office of President, and are trusted with no power to give any opinion of the character or qualifications of a Vice President; and it is remarkable that there are no appropriate qualifications made necessary by the Constitution for a Vice President; but every qualification has reference to President. There is another important feature in this part of the Constitution. It was known by the Convention that in this country, in common with all others where there is freedom of opinion and of speech, there would be parties. They likewise knew, that the intolerance of the major or ruling sect and political party, was frequently exercised upon the minor party, and that the rights of the minority ought to be protected to them.

As well then to secure the rights of the minority, as to check the intolerance of the majority, they placed the majority in jeopardy, if they should attempt at grasping all the benefits of a President and Vice President within themselves, to the total exclusion of the minority. This very case which happened at the last session was contemplated, in which the majority attempted totally to exclude the minority from any participation. The language of the Constitution to such majorities is, "take care that you aim not at too much, for if you do, it is put into the power of the minority to check you, and, by a judicious disposition of their few votes, determine the choice of President." To avoid this event the majority will probably be cautious in the exercise of power; and thus the rights, the proper weight and influence of a minority, are secured against the conduct of the majority, which is certainly liable to be intolerant and oppressive. In this respect the spirit of the Constitution is, political moderation. And it is clear to my mind, that the experience of the last election has taught a lesson to all majorities, which will in future completely secure them from again incurring a similar risk. I recollect well that it was thought probable, when the electoral votes were given, that Mr. Burr would have a vote or two in some of the Eastern States. If he had received but one, he would have been by an electoral choice the Constitutional President. If the majority in future have powers of recollection, they will undoubtedly avoid the evil, if it is one, which happened at the last election, with such unfailing certainty, that there will be no need of the remedy proposed by the amendment. But the majority say, if their votes are so scattered for one candidate as to avoid this danger, that another will be incurred; and that is, the minority will elect a Vice President. The language of the Constitution to them is, again, "that this was meant as a security for the minority against the majority." But the majority exclaim against both these provisions as very unreasonable indeed. "What!" say they, "are minorities to govern majorities?" The answer of the Constitution is, "no, but their due weight and influence shall be secured to them, and the danger of your intolerance guarded against." For the security of small States and minorities, there is in the Constitution a mixture of the federative with the popular principles. And as it is well known that when popular majorities alone prevail, and exercise power uncontrolled by Constitutional checks, the minorities, who generally possess their proportion of integrity and virtue, are overwhelmed, and liberty itself, by the same means, destroyed; so it is in kindness to both parties, to the country and to humanity, that these wholesome checks are Constitutionally provided. Had the majority or the great States been willing fairly to have submitted to the Constitutional checks in the last election, no evil could have happened. And it is remarkable that the Constitution completely protects them, as long as they obey its precepts, in the creation of which they had an agency, and to which they have solemnly agreed. To prove that I am correct in these ideas, I not only refer to the Constitution but to the Secretary of State, (Mr. Madison.) In the Virginia Debates, volume 1, page 96, he says:

"But on a candid examination of history, we shall find that turbulence, violence, and abuse of power, by the majority trampling on the rights of the minority, have produced factions and commotions which, in Republics, have more frequently than any other cause produced despotism. If we go over the whole history of ancient and modern Republics, we shall find their destructions to have generally resulted from those causes. If we consider the peculiar situation of the United States, and what are the resources of that diversity of sentiments which pervades its inhabitants, we shall find great danger that the same causes may terminate here in the same fatal effects which they produced in those Republics. This danger ought to be wisely guarded against. Perhaps, in the progress of this discussion, it will appear that the only possible remedy for those evils, and means of preserving and protecting the principles of republicanism, will be found in that very system which is now exclaimed against as the parent of oppression."

Mr. President, it has been often said by the discerning and judicious of this and other countries, that our Constitution, for its brevity, its comprehensiveness, its perspicuity, and the political skill contained in it, was the best State paper extant. I believe all this and even more is a tribute justly due to its merits; and I am persuaded that the article which fixes a mode for the choice of a Chief Magistrate stands most prominent among its excellencies.

Let us now, sir, examine and compare the merits of the amendment with a special reference to this last view we have taken of the Constitutional provision.

The amendment authorizes the Electors to vote for a President and Vice President by a specific designation. Is ambition in your country? Here is a direct and inviting object for its operation.—Is the integrity of your Electors assailable? You place it here in the most encouraging attitude for an assault. A fear of detection, and a sense of shame, upon the exposure of an improper action, has been, perhaps, a better security against political errors or crimes, than all the moral virtues united, when the temptation has been attended with an impossibility of detection. An intrigue with an Elector can be carried on without much danger of detection; but when your election is car-

ried into the House of Representatives, besides the ordinary weight of character in favor of the members of that House, a detection of an intrigue with a candidate is almost certain. It will be recollected that at the last election two or three members held the choice perfectly in their own hands. If I mistake not, three gentlemen, that is, a member from New Jersey, a member from Vermont, and one from either Maryland, Delaware, or Tennessee, could have given a President to the United States. The particular gentlemen mentioned were above suspicion of bribery; but, in addition to this circumstance, if they had in the contest gone over from improper motives, or under the influence of bribery, a detection was certain.

This will remain forever the criterion, as it respects the relative danger of intrigue and bribery, in the two modes of choice. And the amendment is avowedly intended to secure a choice by Electors, and to prevent a resort to the House; because, says the gentleman from Virginia, (Mr. TAYLOR.) "if you permit the election to go into the House, there are small States, and minorities, and all the evils of a diet election;" meaning that corruption must be the consequence. But, he says, "let there be a divided election by the Electors, meeting by States separately, and you lessen the tendency to corruption." This may look plausible in theory, but I think practice will show its fallacy.

It may be better for the Electors to meet by States than for all to be together, but this can never prove that they are less liable to corruption than the House of Representatives; which is the only point in question.

The manner of electing the Vice President, as proposed by the amendment, not only invites ambition to an unchecked operation, but exposes us to the selection of a less important and more unfit person than the Constitutional provision. In addition to his importance in the Government, arising from his incidental succession to the Chief Magistracy, the Vice President is *ex officio* President of the Senate, and gives a direct influence to the State from which he is chosen, of a third vote in this body, in all cases of equal division, which are usually the cases of most importance. Besides, his influence as presiding officer is, perhaps, more than equal to the right of a vote. It becomes therefore peculiarly important to the small States, and to minorities, whose security rests in this body, not only that their influence in the election of Vice President should not be diminished, but that no measure be adopted which may tend to bestow the office upon an unworthy character. By the proposed amendment, this character must necessarily become a sort of make-weight and stepping-stone for the Presidency. As in recruiting for an army, a man, active, and of a particular cast of character, but not very proper for a Commander-in-Chief, is employed to obtain recruits, and, upon condition that he obtains a given number, is to be rewarded with a sergeant's warrant; so, in this case, the man who can procure a given number of votes for President will be encouraged to hope for the Vice Presidency; and where will such characters be sought after? In Delaware or Rhode Island? No, sir, but in the great States; there the recruiting talents will be put in operation, because the number of recruits, or votes, will be sufficient to test his active and recruiting merits. And thus the office of Vice President will be sent to market with hardly a possible chance to meet an honest purchaser.

I have already remarked upon the alteration made by the Senate in the resolution passed by the House of Representatives, changing the number five to three. But, one addition, made this morning, deserves attention. I mean that which authorizes the Vice President to administer the Government in case neither the first nor the second Constitutional Electors effect a choice of President. This is a new principle, and its operation is more uncertain than that of any other part of the proposed amendment. Viewing it in one point of light, it may be thought to confer a new power upon the Senate, that of giving a President to the Union. And, it is said, that this part will recompense the small States, who have the ascendency in the Senate, for the injury inflicted by the other parts of the amendment. If it be true that the last part restores all which the former parts have taken away from us, it is inconceivable why any man can wish to pass a resolution the parts of which thus mutually destroy each other. It is possible that, by the force of intrigue and faction, the Electors may be induced to scatter their votes for both President and Vice President, in such manner as to present several candidates to the House for President, and two or more to the Senate for Vice President; in which case the senate might immediately choose or select a Vice President. In this state of things, there is an opportunity afforded for intrigue of a very extensive and alarming nature. The Senate, I mean a majority of them, might wish that the man whom they had elected Vice President should administer the Government, and if the House could be prevented from agreeing, their wishes would be gratified. The facility of preventing over that of producing a choice is very obvious.

A bold address may be made to any member of the House, without wounding his pride or offending his morality, to adhere to his candidate, and not change his vote so as to effect a choice. He can be told that there is no danger of leaving the United States without a President, as there is one already chosen to his hand by the Senate; and this person may be more the object of his wishes than any of the other candidates, his favorite excepted. In this process the Senate may give a President to the United States. But if the probability of such a process and such an event is increased by the amendment of this morning, it cannot certainly greatly recommend it. For myself I wish for no alteration in the Constitution, not even if its operations were directly in favor of the small States, more especially if such a favor is to be derived through a sort of double conspiracy of intrigue; in the first place, to operate on the Electors, and then on the House of Representatives. It seems to me, that the small States had better be contented to enjoy the rights now secured to them by the Constitution, which they can honestly do, rather than submit to a deprivation of their rights for the sake of dishonestly obtaining a restoration of them. We may charitably and safely conclude that the majority do not intend, by this part of the amendment, to expose the country to such a scene of iniquity. And the uncertainty of its operations

alone, is, in my mind, a sufficient ground for rejection. However the operation of this part of the amendment may appear in theory, as to other points, it seems to me that, in one point, all must agree: and that is, when the House of Representatives know that the United States will be left without an Executive Magistrate, in case they do not agree. This awful responsibility will speak in a voice too loud for the hardihood of party entirely to disregard. And may I not suggest, without giving offence, that the operation of this very responsibility has been proved, at least in some degree, in the proceedings of the last Presidential election?

If this last-mentioned security be worth preserving, it follows, of course, that the part of the amendment alluded to ought not to pass.

There is another view of the Constitution which has a reference to the general subject before us; and that is, the caution exhibited with respect to the introduction of amendments. In an instrument so important, and containing many features new, if not to the world, at least to ourselves, although we might approve of its principles, yet experience might discover errors as to the mode devised for carrying those principles into effect. Hence it was the part of wisdom and caution to provide for such alterations in practice as would give the fairest operation to principles, without incurring the confusion and agitation incidental to a general Convention. But, lest the daring and restive spirit of innovation should injure or destroy, under the specious name of amendment, that same wisdom and caution hath provided salutary checks.

"Two-thirds of both Houses of the Congress shall deem it necessary" to propose amendments; and three-fourths of the State Legislatures shall ratify such amendments, before they acquire validity. I speak now, sir, of the mode which has always been, and probably will be, put in practice to obtain amendments. The other Constitutional mode is equally guarded as to numbers, but, as it has no relation to the subject now in debate, may be laid aside. "Two-thirds of both Houses," must, I think, on every fair principle of construction, mean two-thirds of all the members. The number of Senators is thirty-four, two-thirds being twenty-three. And as there is no representation from New Jersey, the number of Representatives is one hundred thirty-six, two-thirds being ninety-one.

My impressions are, sir, that this amendment cannot constitutionally be proposed to the State Legislatures unless it is agreed to in the two Houses by those numbers twenty-three and ninety-one, respectively. This is a Constitutional point, which, I am told, has never been agitated, but is certainly worthy of attention. If the construction should prevail that two-thirds of the members present, at any time, might propose amendments, the consequence is that twelve Senators, being two-thirds of a quorum, and forty-eight Representatives, being a similar two-thirds, might propose any and the most important amendments. I am aware sir, that it may be said such propositions are not final, they may yet be ratified or rejected by the State Legislatures. But the spirit of the Constitution seems to require two-thirds of the nation, acting by its proper organs, to propose amendments; and that, in so interesting a subject as a Constitutional alteration a less number should have no authority.

. . . . .

Mr. TAYLOR.—The opposition to this discriminating amendment to the Constitution is condensed into a single stratagem, namely: an effort to excite the passion of jealousy in various forms. Endeavors have been made to excite geographical jealousies—a jealousy of the smaller against the larger States—a jealousy in the people against the idea of amending the Constitution; and even a jealousy against individual members of this House. Sir, is this passion a good medium through which to discern truth, or is it a mirror calculated to reflect error? Will it enlighten or deceive? Is it planted in good or in evil—in moral or in vicious principles? Wherefore, then, do gentlemen endeavor to blow it up? Is it because they distrust the strength of their arguments, that they resort to this furious and erring passion? Is it because they know that

> ———"Trifles light as air,
> Are, to the jealous, confirmation strong
> As proofs of holy writ?"

So far as these efforts have been directed towards a geographical demarcation of the interests of the Union into North and South, in order to excite a jealousy of one division against another; and, so far as they have been used to create suspicions of individuals, they have been either so feeble, inapplicable, or frivolous, as to bear but lightly upon the question, and to merit but little attention. But the attempts to array States against States because they differ in size, and to prejudice the people against the idea of amending their Constitution, bear a more formidable aspect, and ought to be repelled, because they are founded on principles the most mischievous and inimical to the Constitution, and could they be successful, are replete with great mischiefs.

Towards exciting this jealousy of smaller States against larger States, the gentleman from Connecticut (Mr. TRACY) had labored to prove that the federal principle of the Constitution of the United States was founded in the idea of minority invested with operative power. That, in pursuance of this principle, it was contemplated and intended that the election of a President should frequently come into the House of Representatives, and to divert it from thence by this amendment would trench upon the federal principle of our Constitution, and diminish the rights of the smaller States, bestowed by this principle upon them. This was the scope of his argument to excite their jealousy, and is the amount also of several other arguments delivered by gentlemen on the same side of the question. He did not question the words, but the ideas of gentlemen. Words, selected from their comrades, are easily asserted to misrepresent opinions, as he had himself experienced during the discussion on the subject.

This idea of federalism ought to be well discussed by the smaller States, before they will suffer it to produce the intended effect—that of exciting their jealousy against the larger. To him it appeared to be evidently incorrect. Two principles sustain our Constitution: one a majority of the people, the other a majority of the States; the first was necessary to preserve the liberty or sovereignty of the people; the last, to preserve the liberty or sovereignty of the States. But both are founded in the principle of majority; and the effort of the Constitution is to preserve this principle in relation both to the people and the States, so that neither species of sovereignty or independence should be able to destroy the other. Many illustrations might be adduced. That of amending the Constitution will suffice. Three-fourths of the States must concur in this object, because a less number or a majority of States might not contain a majority of people; therefore, the Constitution is not amendable by a majority of States, lest a species of State sovereignty might, under color of amending the Constitution, infringe the right of the people. On the other hand, a majority of the people residing in the large States cannot amend the Constitution, lest they should diminish or destroy the sovereignty of the small States, the federal Union, or federalism itself. Hence a concurrence of the States to amend the Constitution became necessary, not because federalism was founded in the idea of minority, but for a reason the very reverse of that idea—that is, to cover the will both of a majority of the people and a majority of States, so as to preserve the great element of self-government, as it regarded State sovereignty, and also as it regarded the sovereignty of the people.

For this great purpose certain political functions are assigned to be performed, under the auspices of the State or federal principle, and certain others under the popular principle. It was the intention of the Constitution that these functions should be performed in conformity to its principle. If that principle is in fact a government of a minority, then these functions ought to be performed by a minority. When the federal principle is performing a function, according to this idea, a majority of the States ought to decide. And, by the same mode of reasoning, when the popular principle is performing a function, then a minority of the people ought to decide. This brings us precisely to the question of the amendment. It is the intention of the Constitution that the popular principle shall operate in the election of a President and Vice President. It is also the intention of the Constitution that the popular principle, in discharging the functions committed to it by the Constitution, should operate by a majority and not by a minority. That the majority of the people should be driven, by an unforeseen state of parties, to the necessity of relinquishing their will in the election of one or the other of these officers, or that the principle of majority, in a function confided to the popular will, should be deprived of half its rights, and be laid under a necessity of violating its duty to preserve the other half, is not the intention of the Constitution.

But the gentleman from Connecticut has leaped over all this ground, and gotten into the House of Representatives, without considering the principles of the Constitution, as applicable to the election of President and Vice President by Electors, and distinguishing them from an election by the House of Representatives. And by mingling and interweaving the two modes of electing together, a considerable degree of complexity has been produced. If, however, it is admitted that in an election of a President and Vice President by Electors, that the will of the electing majority ought fairly to operate, and that an election by the will of a minority would be an abuse or corruption of the principles of the Constitution, then it follows that an amendment, to avoid this abuse, accords with, and is necessary to save these principles. In like manner, had an abuse crept into the same election, whenever it was to be made under the federal principle by the House of Representatives, enabling a minority of States to carry the election, it would not have violated the intention of the Constitution to have corrected this abuse, also, by an amendment. For, sir, I must suppose it to have been the intention of the Constitution that both the federal principle and the popular principle should operate in those functions respectively assigned to them, perfectly and not imperfectly—that is, the former by a majority of States, and the latter by a majority of the people.

Under this view of the subject, the amendment ought to be considered. Then the question will be, whether it is calculated or not to cause the popular principle, applied by the Constitution in the first instance, to operate perfectly, and to prevent the abuse of an election by a minority? If it is, it corresponds with the intention, diminishes nothing of the rights of the smaller States, and, of course, affords them no cause of jealousy.

Sir, it could never have been the intention of the Constitution to produce a state of things by which a majority of the popular principle should be under the necessity of voting against its judgment to secure a President, and by which a minor faction should acquire a power capable of defeating the majority in the election of President, or of electing a Vice President contrary to the will of the electing principle. To permit this abuse would be a fraudulent mode of defeating the operation of the popular principle in this election, in order to transfer it to the federal principle—to disinherit the people for the sake of endowing the House of Representatives; whereas it was an accidental and not an artificial disappointment in the election of a President, against which the Constitution intended to provide. A fair and not an unfair attempt to elect was previously to be made by the popular principle, before the election was to go into the House of Representatives. And if the people of all the States, both large and small, should by an abuse of the real design of the Constitution, be bubbled out of the election of Executive power, by leaving to them the nominal right of an abortive effort, and transferring to the House of Representatives the substantial right of a real election, nothing will remain but to corrupt the election in that House by some of those abuses of which elections by diets are susceptible, to bestow upon Executive power an aspect both formidable and inconsistent with the principles by which the Constitution intended to mould it.

The great check imposed upon Executive power was a popular mode of election; and the true object of jealousy, which ought to attract the attention of the people of every State, is any circumstance tending to diminish or destroy that check. It was also a primary intention of the Constitution to keep Executive power independent of Legislative; and although a provision was made for its election by the House of Representatives in a possible case, that possible case never was intended to be converted into the active rule, so as to destroy in a degree the line of separation and independency between the Executive and Legislative power. The controversy is not therefore between larger and smaller States, but between the people of every State and the House of Representatives. Is it better that the people—a fair majority of the popular principle—should elect Executive power; or, that a minor faction should be enabled to embarrass and defeat the judgment and will of this majority, and throw the election into the House of Representatives? This is the question. If this amendment should enable the popular principle to elect Executive power, and thus keep it separate and distinct from legislation, the intention of the Constitution, the interest of the people, and the principles of our policy, will be preserved; and if so, it is as I have often endeavored to prove in this debate, the interest of the smaller States themselves, that the amendment should prevail. For, sir, is an exposure of their Representatives to bribery and corruption (a thing which may possibly happen at some future day, when men lose that public virtue which now governs them) an acquisition more desirable than all those great objects best (if not exclusively) attainable by the election of Executive power by the popular principle of the Federal Government, as the Constitution itself meditates and prefers?

So far, then, the amendment strictly coincides with the Constitution and with the interests of the people of every State in the Union. But suppose by some rare accident the election should still be sent into the House of Representatives, does not the amendment then afford cause of jealousy to the smaller States? Sir, each State has but one vote, whether it is large or small; and the President and Vice President are still to be chosen out of five persons. Such is the Constitution in both respects now. To have enlarged the number of nominees, would have increased the occurrence of an election by the House of Representatives; and if, as I have endeavored to prove, it is for the interest of every State, that the election should be made by the popular principle of Government and not by that House, then it follows, that whatever would have a tendency to draw the election to that House, is against the interest of every State in the Union; and that every State in the Union is interested to avoid an enlargement of the nominees, if it would have such a tendency.

Sir, the endeavor to excite a national jealousy against the idea of amending the Constitution, is in my view infinitely more dangerous and alarming than even the attempt to marshal States against States. The gentleman from Connecticut (Mr. TRACY) has twice pronounced with great emphasis, "man is man," and attempted to make inferences against all attempts to amend our Constitution from the evil moral qualities with which human nature is afflicted! Sir, he has forgotten that Governments as well as nations are constituted of men, and that if the vices of governed man ought to alarm us for the safety of liberty, the vices of governing man are not calculated to assuage our apprehensions. Sir, it is this latter species of depravity which has suggested to the people of America a new idea, enforced by constitutions. Permit me to illustrate this new idea by the terms political law and municipal law. The former is that law, called Constitutional, contrived and enacted in the United States, to control those evil moral qualities to which this creature "man" is liable when invested with power. The latter is that law enacted to control the vices of man in his private capacity. If the former species of law should be suffered to remain unchanged, the effects would be the same as if the latter should remain unchanged. Both, unaltered, would be evaded by the ingenuity, avarice, and ambition of public man, as well as private man. And, therefore, it is as necessary for the preservation of liberty, that constitutions or political law should be amended from time to time, in order to preserve liberty against the avarice and ambition of men in power, by meeting and controlling their artifices, as it is occasionally to amend municipal law, for the preservation of property against the vicious practices of men not in power.

6

James Madison to Thomas Jefferson
14 Jan. 1824
Writings 9:174–76

You have probably noticed that the manner in which the Constitution as it stands may operate in the approaching election of President, is multiplying projects for amending it. If electoral districts, and an eventual decision by joint ballot of the two Houses of Congress could be established, it would, I think, be a real improvement, and as the smaller States would approve the one, and the larger the other, a spirit of compromise might adopt both.

An appeal from an abortive ballot in the first meeting of the Electors, to a reassemblage of them, a part of the several plans, has something plausible, and in comparison with the existing arrangement, might not be inadmissible. But it is not free from material objections. It relinquishes, particularly, the policy of the Constitution in allowing as little time as possible for the Electors to be known & tampered with. And beside the opportunities for intrigue furnished by the interval between the first and second meeting, the danger of having one electoral Body played off against another, by artful misrepresentations rapidly transmitted, a danger not to be avoided, would be at least doubled. It is a fact within my own knowledge, that the equality of votes which threatened such mischief in 1801 was the result of false assurances despatched at the critical moment to the Electors of one State, that the votes of another would be different from what they proved to be.

Having received letters from certain quarters on the subject of the proposed amendments, which I could not decline answering, I have suggested for consideration, "that each Elector should give two votes, one naming his first choice, the other naming his next choice. If there be a majority for the first, he to be elected; if not, and a ma-jority for the next, he to be elected: If there be not a majority for either, then the names having the two highest number of votes on the two lists taken together, to be referred to a joint ballot of the Legislature." It is not probable that this modification will be relished by either of those to whom it has been suggested; both of them having in hand projects of their own. Nor am I sure that there may not be objections to it which have been overlooked. It was recommended to my reflections by its avoiding the inconveniĕes of a second meeting of Electors, and at the same time doubling the chance of avoiding a final resort to Congress. I have intimated to my correspondents my disinclination to be brought in any way into the public discussion of the subject; the rather as every thing having a future relation only to a Presidential Election may be misconstrued into some bearing on that now depending.

7

James Madison to Henry Lee
14 Jan. 1825
Writings 9:216–17

The nature & extent of the obligation on a representative to be guided by the known will of his Constituents, though an old question, seems yet to be in a controvertible state. In general it may be said to be often a verbal controversy. That the obligation is not in strictness constitutional or legal, is manifest; since the vote of the Representative is equally valid & operative whether obeying or violating the instruction of his constituents. It can only be a moral obligation to be weighed by the conscience of the Representative, or a prudential one to be enforced by the penal displeasure of his Constituents.

In what degree a plurality of votes is evidence of the will of the Majority of voters, must depend on circumstances more easily estimated in a given case than susceptible of general definition. The greater the number of candidates among whom the votes are divided, the more uncertain, must, of course, be the inference from the plurality with respect to the majority.

In our complex system of polity, the public will, as a source of authority, may be the Will of the People as composing one nation; or the will of the States in their distinct & independent capacities; or the federal will as viewed, for example, thro' the Presidential Electors, representing in a certain proportion both the Nation & the States. If in the eventual choice of a President the same proportional rule had been preferred, a joint ballot by the two Houses of Congress would have been substituted for the mode which gives an equal vote to every State however unequal in size. As the Constitution stands, and is regarded as the result of a compromise between the larger & smaller States, giving to the latter the advantage in selecting a president from the Candidates, in consideration of the advantage possessed by the former in selecting the Candidates from the people, it cannot be denied whatever may be thought of the Constitutional provision, that there is, in making the eventual choice, no other controul on the votes to be given, whether by the representatives of the smaller or larger States, but their attention to the views of their respective Constituents and their regard for the public good.

8

WILLIAM RAWLE, A VIEW OF THE CONSTITUTION OF THE UNITED STATES 57–59
1829 (2d ed.)

It must however be acknowledged that in no respect have the enlarged and profound views of those who framed the constitution, nor the expectations of the public when they adopted it, been so completely frustrated as in the practical operation of the system so far as relates to the independence of the electors.

It was supposed that the election of these two high officers would be committed to men not likely to be swayed by party or personal bias, who would act under no combination with others, and be subject neither to intimidation or corruption. It was asserted that the choice of several persons to form an intermediate body of electors, would be much less apt to convulse the community with extraordinary movements, than the choice of one who was himself to be the final object of their wishes.

Whether ferments and commotions would accompany a general election by the whole body of the people, and whether such a mode of election could be conveniently practised in reference to the ratio of representatives prescribed in the constitution, is yet to be ascertained; but experience has fully convinced us, that the electors do not assemble in their several states for a free exercise of their own judgments, but for the purpose of electing the particular candidate who happens to be preferred by the predominant political party which has chosen those electors. In some instances the principles on which they are chosen are so far forgotten, that the electors publicly pledge themselves to vote for a particular individual, and thus the whole foundation of this elaborate system is destroyed.

Another innovation has also been introduced. Members of congress, entrusted only with the power of ordinary legislation, have frequently formed themselves into a regular body at the seat of government, and undertaken to point out to the people certain persons as proper objects of their choice. Although the mild and plausible garb of recommendation is alone assumed, yet its effect is known and felt to have been often great and sometimes irresistible.

If the Constitution, as originally proposed, had contained a direct provision that the president and vice president should be chosen by a majority of the two houses of congress, it is not probable that this part of it would have been adopted.

That the chief executive magistrate should be the creature of the legislature; that he should view in them the source from which he sprung, and by which he was to be continued, would at once destroy the dignity and independence of his station, and render him no longer what the Constitution intended,—an impartial and inflexible administrator of the public interests. To the people alone he would no longer consider himself responsible, but he would be led to respect, and would be fearful to offend, a power higher than the people.

Such principles cannot be found in the Constitution; and it is wholly inconsistent with its spirit and its essence, to effectuate indirectly, that which directly is not avowed or intended. These instances fully prove that the safety of the people greatly depends on a close adherence to the letter and spirit of their excellent Constitution; but it is probable that a late failure will prevent a renewal of the last mentioned attempt. And in reference to the election of 1828, it has not been renewed, but, with a strict adherence to the forms prescribed, the voice of a great majority of the people has decided the choice.

Before we close the subject, it is proper to add that, in one respect, the caution of the Constitution cannot be violated—no senator or representative or person holding an office of trust or profit under the United States can be an elector, and therefore the vote of every such person would be void.

SEE ALSO:

Constitution of the United States and the First Twelve Amendments

We the People of the United States, in Order to form a more perfect Union, establish Justice, insure domestic Tranquility, provide for the common defence, promote the general Welfare, and secure the Blessings of Liberty to ourselves and our Posterity, do ordain and establish this Constitution for the United States of America.

Article. I.

SECTION 1. All legislative Powers herein granted shall be vested in a Congress of the United States, which shall consist of a Senate and House of Representatives.

SECTION 2. The House of Representatives shall be composed of Members chosen every second Year by the People of the several States, and the Electors in each State shall have the Qualifications requisite for Electors of the most numerous Branch of the State Legislature.

No person shall be a Representative who shall not have attained to the Age of twenty five Years, and been seven Years a Citizen of the United States, and who shall not, when elected, be an Inhabitant of that State in which he shall be chosen.

Representatives and direct Taxes shall be apportioned among the several States which may be included within this Union, according to their respective Numbers, which shall be determined by adding to the whole Number of free Persons, including those bound to Service for a Term of Years, and excluding Indians not taxed, three fifths of all other Persons. The actual Enumeration shall be made within three Years after the first Meeting of the Congress of the United States, and within every subsequent Term of ten Years, in such Manner as they shall by Law direct. The Number of Representatives shall not exceed one for every thirty Thousand, but each State shall have at Least one Representative; and until such enumeration shall be made, the State of New Hampshire shall be entitled to chuse three, Massachusetts eight, Rhode-Island and Providence Plantations one, Connecticut five, New-York six, New Jersey four, Pennsylvania eight, Delaware one, Maryland six, Virginia ten, North Carolina five, South Carolina five, and Georgia three.

When vacancies happen in the Representation from any State, the Executive Authority thereof shall issue Writs of Election to fill such Vacancies.

The House of Representatives shall chuse their Speaker and other Officers; and shall have the sole Power of Impeachment.

SECTION 3. The Senate of the United States shall be composed of two Senators from each State, chosen by the Legislature thereof, for six Years; and each Senator shall have one Vote.

Immediately after they shall be assembled in Consequence of the first Election, they shall be divided as equally as may be into three Classes. The Seats of the Senators of the first Class shall be vacated at the Expiration of the second Year, of the second Class at the Expiration of the fourth Year, and of the third Class at the Expiration of the sixth Year, so that one third may be chosen every second Year; and if Vacancies happen by Resignation, or otherwise, during the Recess of the Legislature of any State, the Executive thereof may make temporary Appointments until the next Meeting of the Legislature, which shall then fill such Vacancies.

No Person shall be a Senator who shall not have attained to the Age of thirty Years, and been nine Years a Citizen of the United States, and who shall not, when elected, be an Inhabitant of that State for which he shall be chosen.

The Vice President of the United States shall be President of the Senate, but shall have no Vote, unless they be equally divided.

The Senate shall chuse their other Officers, and also a President pro tempore, in the Absence of the Vice President, or when he shall exercise the Office of President of the United States.

The Senate shall have the sole Power to try all Impeachments. When sitting for that Purpose, they shall be on Oath or Affirmation. When the President of the United States is tried, the Chief Justice shall preside: And no Person shall be convicted without the Concurrence of two thirds of the Members present.

Judgment in Cases of Impeachment shall not extend further than to removal from Office, and disqualification to hold and enjoy any Office of honor, Trust or Profit under the United States: but the Party convicted shall nevertheless be liable and subject to Indictment, Trial, Judgment and Punishment, according to Law.

SECTION 4. The Times, Places and Manner of holding Elections for Senators and Representatives, shall be prescribed in each State by the Legislature thereof; but the Congress may at any time by Law make or alter such Regulations, except as to the Places of chusing Senators.

The Congress shall assemble at least once in every Year, and such Meeting shall be on the first Monday in December, unless they shall by Law appoint a different Day.

SECTION 5. Each House shall be the Judge of the Elections, Returns and Qualifications of its own Members, and a Majority of each shall constitute a Quorum to do Business; but a smaller Number may adjourn from day to day, and may be authorized to compel the Attendance of absent Members, in such Manner, and under such Penalties as each House may provide.

Each House may determine the Rules of its Proceedings, punish its Members for disorderly Behaviour, and, with the Concurrence of two thirds, expel a Member.

Each House shall keep a Journal of its Proceedings, and from time to time publish the same, excepting such Parts as may in their Judgment require Secrecy; and the Yeas and Nays of the Members of either House on any question shall, at the Desire of one fifth of those Present, be entered on the Journal.

Neither House, during the Session of Congress, shall, without the Consent of the other, adjourn for more than three days, nor to any other Place than that in which the two Houses shall be sitting.

SECTION 6. The Senators and Representatives shall receive a Compensation for their Services, to be ascertained by Law, and paid out of the Treasury of the United States. They shall in all Cases, except Treason, Felony and Breach of the Peace, be privileged from Arrest during their Attendance at the Session of their respective Houses, and in going to and returning from the same; and for any Speech or Debate in either House, they shall not be questioned in any other Place.

No Senator or Representative shall, during the Time for which he was elected, be appointed to any civil Office under the Authority of the United States, which shall have been created, or the Emoluments whereof shall have been encreased during such time; and no Person holding any Office under the United States, shall be a Member of either House during his Continuance in Office.

SECTION 7. All Bills for raising Revenue shall originate in the House of Representatives; but the Senate may propose or concur with Amendments as on other Bills.

Every Bill which shall have passed the House of Representatives and the Senate, shall, before it become a Law, be presented to the President of the United States; If he approve he shall sign it, but if not he shall return it, with his Objections to that House in which it shall have originated, who shall enter the Objections at large on their Journal, and proceed to reconsider it. If after such Reconsideration two thirds of that House shall agree to pass the Bill, it shall be sent, together with the Objections, to the other House, by which it shall likewise be reconsidered, and if approved by two thirds of that House, it shall become a Law. But in all such Cases the Votes of both Houses shall be determined by yeas and Nays, and the Names of the Persons voting for and against the Bill shall be entered on the Journal of each House respectively. If any Bill shall not be returned by the President within ten days (Sundays excepted) after it shall have been presented to him, the Same shall be a Law, in like Manner as if he had signed it, unless the Congress by their Adjournment prevent its Return in which Case it shall not be a Law.

Every Order, Resolution, or Vote to which the Concurrence of the Senate and House of Representatives may be necessary (except on a question of Adjournment) shall be presented to the President of the United States; and before the Same shall take Effect, shall be approved by him, or being disapproved by him, shall be repassed by two thirds of the Senate and House of Representatives, according to the Rules and Limitations prescribed in the Case of a Bill.

SECTION 8. The Congress shall have Power To lay and collect Taxes, Duties, Imposts and Excises, to pay the Debts and provide for the common Defence and general Welfare of the United States; but all Duties, Imposts and Excises shall be uniform throughout the United States;

To borrow Money on the credit of the United States;

To regulate Commerce with foreign Nations, and among the several States, and with the Indian Tribes;

To establish an uniform Rule of Naturalization, and uniform Laws on the subject of Bankruptcies throughout the United States;

To coin Money, regulate the Value thereof, and of foreign Coin, and fix the Standard of Weights and Measures;

To provide for the Punishment of counterfeiting the Securities and current Coin of the United States;

To establish Post Offices and post Roads;

To promote the progress of Science and useful Arts, by securing for limited Times to Authors and Inventors the exclusive Right to their respective Writings and Discoveries;

To constitute Tribunals inferior to the supreme Court;

To define and punish Piracies and Felonies committed on the high Seas, and Offences against the Law of Nations;

To declare War, grant Letters of Marque and Reprisal, and make Rules concerning Captures on Land and Water;

To raise and support Armies, but no Appropriation of Money to that Use shall be for a longer Term than two Years;

To provide and maintain a Navy;

To make Rules for the Government and Regulation of the land and naval Forces;

To provide for calling forth the Militia to execute the Laws of the Union, suppress Insurrections and repel Invasions;

To provide for organizing, arming, and disciplining, the Militia, and for governing such Part of them as may be employed in the Service of the United States, reserving to the States respectively, the Appointment of the Officers, and the Authority of training the Militia according to the discipline prescribed by Congress;

To exercise exclusive Legislation in all Cases whatsoever, over such District (not exceeding ten Miles square) as may, by Cession of particular States, and the Acceptance of Congress, become the Seat of the Government of the United States, and to exercise like Authority over all Places purchased by the Consent of the Legislature of the State in which the Same shall be, for the Erection of Forts, Magazines, Arsenals, dock-Yards, and other needful Buildings;—And

To make all Laws which shall be necessary and proper for carrying into Execution the foregoing Powers, and all other Powers vested by this Constitution in the Government of the United States, or in any Department or Officer thereof.

SECTION 9. The Migration or Importation of such Persons as any of the States now existing shall think proper to admit, shall not be prohibited by the Congress prior to the Year one thousand eight hundred and eight, but a Tax or duty may be imposed on such Importation, not exceeding ten dollars for each Person.

The Privilege of the Writ of Habeas Corpus shall not be suspended, unless when in Cases of Rebellion or Invasion the public Safety may require it.

No Bill of Attainder or ex post facto Law shall be passed.

No Capitation, or other direct, Tax shall be laid, unless in Proportion to the Census or Enumeration herein before directed to be taken.

No Tax or Duty shall be laid on Articles exported from any State.

No Preference shall be given by any Regulation of Commerce or Revenue to the Ports of one State over those of another: nor shall Vessels bound to, or from, one State, be obliged to enter, clear, or pay Duties in another.

No Money shall be drawn from the Treasury, but in Consequence of Appropriations made by Law; and a regular Statement and Account of the Receipts and Expenditures of all public Money shall be published from time to time.

No Title of Nobility shall be granted by the United States: And no Person holding any Office of Profit or Trust under them, shall, without the Consent of the Congress, accept of any present, Emolument, Office, or Title, of any kind whatever, from any King, Prince, or foreign State.

SECTION 10. No State shall enter into any Treaty, Alliance, or Confederation; grant Letters of Marque and Reprisal; coin Money; emit Bills of Credit; make any Thing but gold and silver Coin a Tender in Payment of Debts; pass any Bill of Attainder, ex post facto Law, or Law impairing the Obligation of Contracts, or grant any Title of Nobility.

No State shall, without the Consent of the Congress, lay any Imposts or Duties on Imports or Exports, except what may be absolutely necessary for executing it's inspection Laws: and the net Produce of all Duties and Imposts, laid by any State on Imports or Exports, shall be for the Use of the Treasury of the United States; and all such Laws shall be subject to the Revision and Controul of the Congress.

No State shall, without the Consent of Congress, lay any Duty of Tonnage, keep Troops, or Ships of War in time of Peace, enter into any Agreement or Compact with another State, or with a foreign Power, or engage in War, unless actually invaded, or in such imminent Danger as will not admit of delay.

Article. II.

SECTION 1. The executive Power shall be vested in a President of the United States of America. He shall hold his Office during the Term of four Years, and, together with the Vice President, chosen for the same Term, be elected as follows

Each State shall appoint, in such Manner as the Legislature thereof may direct, a Number of Electors, equal to the whole Number of Senators and Representatives to which the State may be entitled in the Congress: but no Senator or Representative, or Person holding an Office of Trust or Profit under the United States, shall be appointed an Elector.

The Electors shall meet in their respective States, and vote by Ballot for two Persons, of whom one at least shall not be an Inhabitant of the same State with themselves. And they shall make a List of all the Persons voted for, and of the Number of Votes for each; which List they shall sign and certify, and transmit sealed to the Seat of the Government of the United States, directed to the President of the Senate. The President of the Senate shall, in the Presence of the Senate and House of Representatives, open all the Certificates, and the Votes shall then be counted. The Person having the greatest Number of Votes shall be the President, if such Number be a Majority of the whole Number of Electors appointed; and if there be more than one who have such Majority, and have an equal Number of Votes, then the House of Representatives shall immediately chuse by Ballot one of them for President; and if no Person have a Majority, then from the five highest on the List the said House shall in like Manner chuse the President. But in chusing the President, the Votes shall be taken by States, the Representation from each State having one Vote; A quorum for this Purpose shall consist of a Member or Members from two thirds of the States, and a Majority of all the States shall be necessary to a Choice. In every Case, after the Choice of the President, the Person having the greatest Number of Votes of the Electors shall be the Vice President. But if there should remain two or more who have equal Votes, the Senate shall chuse from them by Ballot the Vice President.

The Congress may determine the Time of chusing the Electors, and the Day on which they shall give their Votes; which Day shall be the same throughout the United States.

No Person except a natural born Citizen, or a Citizen of the United States, at the time of the Adoption of this Constitution, shall be eligible to the Office of President; neither shall any Person be eligible to that Office who shall not have attained to the Age of thirty five Years, and been fourteen Years a Resident within the United States.

In Case of the Removal of the President from Office, or of his Death, Resignation, or Inability to discharge the Powers and Duties of the said Office, the Same shall devolve on the Vice President, and the Congress may by Law provide for the Case of Removal, Death, Resignation or Inability, both of the President and Vice President, declaring what Officer shall then act as President, and such Officer shall act accordingly, until the Disability be removed, or a President shall be elected.

The President shall, at stated Times, receive for his Services, a Compensation, which shall neither be encreased nor diminished during the Period for which he shall have been elected, and he shall not receive within that Period any other Emolument from the United States, or any of them.

Before he enter on the Execution of his Office, he shall take the following Oath or Affirmation:—"I do solemnly swear (or affirm) that I will faithfully execute the Office of President of the United States, and will to the best of my Ability, preserve, protect and defend the Constitution of the United States."

SECTION 2. The President shall be Commander in Chief of the Army and Navy of the United States, and of the Militia of the several States, when called into the actual Service of the United States; he may require the Opinion, in writing, of the principal Officer in each of the executive Departments, upon any Subject relating to the Duties of their respective Offices, and he shall have Power to grant Reprieves and Pardons for Offences against the United States, except in Cases of Impeachment.

He shall have Power, by and with the Advice and Consent of the Senate, to make Treaties, provided two thirds of the Senators present concur; and he shall nominate, and by and with the Advice and Consent of the Senate, shall appoint Ambassadors, other public Ministers and Consuls, Judges of the supreme Court, and all other Officers of the United States, whose Appointments are not herein otherwise provided for, and which shall be established by Law: but the Congress may by Law vest the Appointment of such inferior Officers, as they think proper, in the President alone, in the Courts of Law, or in the Heads of Departments.

The President shall have Power to fill up all Vacancies that may happen during the Recess of the Senate, by granting Commissions which shall expire at the End of their next Session.

SECTION 3. He shall from time to time give to the Congress Information of the State of the Union, and recommend to their Consideration such Measures as he shall judge necessary and expedient; he may, on extraordinary Occasions, convene both Houses, or either of them, and in Case of Disagreement between them, with Respect to the Time of Adjournment, he may adjourn them to such Time as he shall think proper; he shall receive Ambassadors and other public Ministers; he shall take Care that the Laws be faithfully executed, and shall Commission all the Officers of the United States.

SECTION 4. The President, Vice President and all civil Officers of the United States, shall be removed from Office on Impeachment for, and Conviction of, Treason, Bribery, or other high Crimes and Misdemeanors.

Article. III.

SECTION 1. The judicial Power of the United States, shall be vested in one supreme Court, and in such inferior Courts as the Congress may from time to time ordain and establish. The Judges, both of the supreme and inferior Courts, shall hold their Offices during good Behaviour, and shall, at stated Times, receive for their Services, a Compensation, which shall not be diminished during their Continuance in Office.

SECTION 2. The judicial Power shall extend to all Cases, in Law and Equity, arising under this Constitution, the Laws of the United States, and Treaties made, or which shall be made, under their Authority;—to all Cases affecting Ambassadors, other public Ministers and Consuls;—to all Cases of admiralty and maritime Jurisdiction;—to Controversies to which the United States shall be a Party;—to Controversies between two or more States;—between a State and Citizens of another State;—between Citizens of different States,—between Citizens of the same State claiming Lands under Grants of different States, and between a State, or the Citizens thereof, and foreign States, Citizens or Subjects.

In all Cases affecting Ambassadors, other public Ministers and Consuls, and those in which a State shall be Party, the supreme Court shall have original Jurisdiction. In all the other Cases before mentioned, the supreme Court shall have appellate Jurisdiction, both as to Law and Fact, with such Exceptions, and under such Regulations as the Congress shall make.

The Trial of all Crimes, except in Cases of Impeachment, shall be by Jury; and such Trial shall be held in the State where the said Crimes shall have been committed; but when not committed within any State, the Trial shall be at such Place or Places as the Congress may by Law have directed.

SECTION 3. Treason against the United States, shall consist only in levying War against them, or in adhering to their Enemies, giving them Aid and Comfort. No Person shall be convicted of Treason unless on the Testimony of two Witnesses to the same overt Act, or on Confession in open Court.

The Congress shall have Power to declare the Punishment of Treason, but no Attainder of Treason shall work Corruption of Blood, or Forfeiture except during the Life of the Person attainted.

Article. IV.

SECTION 1. Full Faith and Credit shall be given in each State to the public Acts, Records, and judicial Proceedings of every other State. And the Congress may by general Laws prescribe the Manner in which such Acts, Records and Proceedings shall be proved, and the Effect thereof.

SECTION 2. The Citizens of each State shall be entitled to all Privileges and Immunities of Citizens in the several States.

A Person charged in any State with Treason, Felony, or other Crime, who shall flee from Justice, and be found in another State, shall on Demand of the executive Authority of the State from which he fled, be delivered up, to be removed to the State having Jurisdiction of the Crime.

No Person held to Service or Labour in one State, under the Laws thereof, escaping into another, shall, in Consequence of any Law or Regulation therein, be discharged from such Service or Labour, but shall be delivered up on

Claim of the Party to whom such Service or Labour may be due.

SECTION 3. New States may be admitted by the Congress into this Union; but no new State shall be formed or erected within the Jurisdiction of any other State; nor any State be formed by the Junction of two or more States, or Parts of States, without the Consent of the Legislatures of the States concerned as well as of the Congress.

The Congress shall have Power to dispose of and make all needful Rules and Regulations respecting the Territory or other Property belonging to the United States; and nothing in this Constitution shall be so construed as to Prejudice any Claims of the United States, or of any particular State.

SECTION 4. The United States shall guarantee to every State in this Union a Republican Form of Government, and shall protect each of them against Invasion; and on Application of the Legislature, or of the Executive (when the Legislature cannot be convened) against domestic Violence.

Article. V.

The Congress, whenever two thirds of both Houses shall deem it necessary, shall propose Amendments to this Constitution, or, on the Application of the Legislatures of two thirds of the several States, shall call a Convention for proposing Amendments, which, in either Case, shall be valid to all Intents and Purposes, as Part of this Constitution, when ratified by the Legislatures of three fourths of the several States, or by Conventions in three fourths thereof, as the one or the other Mode of Ratification may be proposed by the Congress; Provided that no Amendment which may be made prior to the Year One thousand eight hundred and eight shall in any Manner affect the first and fourth Clauses in the Ninth Section of the first Article; and that no State, without its Consent, shall be deprived of it's equal Suffrage in the Senate.

Article. VI.

All Debts contracted and Engagements entered into, before the Adoption of this Constitution, shall be as valid against the United States under this Constitution, as under the Confederation.

This Constitution, and the Laws of the United States which shall be made in Pursuance thereof; and all Treaties made, or which shall be made, under the Authority of the United States, shall be the supreme Law of the Land; and the Judges in every State shall be bound thereby, any Thing in the Constitution or Laws of any State to the Contrary notwithstanding.

The Senators and Representatives before mentioned, and the Members of the several State Legislatures, and all executive and judicial Officers, both of the United States and of the several States, shall be bound by Oath or Affirmation, to support this Constitution; but no religious Test shall ever be required as a Qualification to any Office or public Trust under the United States.

Article. VII.

The Ratification of the Conventions of nine States, shall be sufficient for the Establishment of this Constitution between the States so ratifying the Same.

The Word, "the," being interlined between the seventh and eighth Lines of the first Page, The Word "Thirty" being partly written on an Erazure in the fifteenth Line of the first Page, The Words "is tried" being interlined between the thirty second and thirty third Lines of the first Page and the Word "the" being interlined between the forty third and forty fourth Lines of the second Page. Attest WILLIAM JACKSON Secretary

done in Convention by the Unanimous Consent of the States present the Seventeenth Day of September in the Year of our Lord one thousand seven hundred and Eighty seven and of the Independance of the United States of America the Twelfth In witness whereof We have hereunto subscribed our Names,

Go: WASHINGTON—Presidt. and deputy from Virginia

New Hampshire	{ John Langdon Nicholas Gilman }
Massachusetts	{ Nathaniel Gorham Rufus King
Connecticut	{ Wm. Saml. Johnson Roger Sherman
New York	Alexander Hamilton
New Jersey	{ Wil: Livingston David Brearley. Wm. Paterson. Jona: Dayton
Pensylvania	{ B Franklin Thomas Mifflin Robt Morris Geo. Clymer Thos. FitzSimons Jared Ingersoll James Wilson Gouv Morris
Delaware	{ Geo: Read Gunning Bedford jun John Dickinson Richard Bassett Jaco: Broom
Maryland	{ James McHenry Dan of St Thos. Jenifer Danl Carroll
Virginia	{ John Blair— James Madison Jr.
North Carolina	{ Wm. Blount Richd. Dobbs Spaight. Hu Williamson
South Carolina	{ J. Rutledge Charles Cotesworth Pinckney Charles Pinckney Pierce Butler.
Georgia	{ William Few Abr Baldwin

Amendments to the Constitution

Article I

Congress shall make no law respecting an establishment of religion, or prohibiting the free exercise thereof; or abridging the freedom of speech, or of the press; or the right of the people peaceably to assemble, and to petition the Government for a redress of grievances.

Article II

A well regulated Militia, being necessary to the security of a free State, the right of the people to keep and bear Arms, shall not be infringed.

Article III

No Soldier shall, in time of peace be quartered in any house, without the consent of the Owner, nor in time of war, but in a manner to be prescribed by law.

Article IV

The right of the people to be secure in their persons, houses, papers, and effects, against unreasonable searches and seizures, shall not be violated, and no Warrants shall issue, but upon probable cause, supported by Oath or affirmation, and particularly describing the place to be searched, and the persons or things to be seized.

Article V

No person shall be held to answer for a capital, or otherwise infamous crime, unless on a presentment or indictment of a Grand Jury, except in cases arising in the land or naval forces, or in the Militia, when in actual service in time of War or public danger; nor shall any person be subject for the same offence to be twice put in jeopardy of life or limb; nor shall be compelled in any criminal case to be a witness against himself, nor be deprived of life, liberty, or property, without due process of law; nor shall private property be taken for public use, without just compensation.

Article VI

In all criminal prosecutions, the accused shall enjoy the right to a speedy and public trial, by an impartial jury of the State and district wherein the crime shall have been committed, which district shall have been previously ascertained by law, and to be informed of the nature and cause of the accusation; to be confronted with the witnesses against him; to have compulsory process for obtaining witnesses in his favor, and to have the Assistance of Counsel for his defence.

Article VII

In Suits at common law, where the value in controversy shall exceed twenty dollars, the right of trial by jury shall be preserved, and no fact tried by a jury, shall be otherwise re-examined in any Court of the United States, than according to the rules of the common law.

Article VIII

Excessive bail shall not be required, nor excessive fines imposed, nor cruel and unusual punishments inflicted.

Article IX

The enumeration in the Constitution, of certain rights, shall not be construed to deny or disparage others retained by the people.

Article X

The powers not delegated to the United States by the Constitution, nor prohibited by it to the States, are reserved to the States respectively, or to the people.

Article XI

The Judicial power of the United States shall not be construed to extend to any suit in law or equity, commenced or prosecuted against one of the United States by Citizens of another State, or by Citizens or Subjects of any Foreign State.

Article XII

The Electors shall meet in their respective states, and vote by ballot for President and Vice-President, one of whom, at least, shall not be an inhabitant of the same state with themselves; they shall name in their ballots the person voted for as President, and in distinct ballots the person voted for as Vice-President, and they shall make distinct lists of all persons voted for as President, and of all persons voted for as Vice-President, and of the number of votes for each, which lists they shall sign and certify, and transmit sealed to the seat of the government of the United States, directed to the President of the Senate;— The President of the Senate shall, in the presence of the Senate and House of Representatives, open all the certificates and the votes shall then be counted;—The person having the greatest number of votes for President, shall be the President, if such number be a majority of the whole number of Electors appointed; and if no person have such majority, then from the persons having the highest numbers not exceeding three on the list of those voted for as President, the House of Representatives shall choose immediately, by ballot, the President. But in choosing the President, the votes shall be taken by states, the representation from each state having one vote; a quorum for this purpose shall consist of a member or members from two-thirds of the states, and a majority of all the states shall be necessary to a choice. And if the House of Representatives shall not choose a President whenever the right of choice shall devolve upon them, before the fourth day of March next following, then the Vice-President shall act as President, as in the case of the death or other constitutional disability of the President. The person having the greatest number of votes as Vice-President, shall be the Vice-President, if such number be a majority of the whole number of Electors appointed, and if no person have a majority, then from the two highest numbers on the list, the Senate shall choose the Vice-President; a quorum for the purpose shall consist of two-thirds of the whole number of Senators, and a majority of the whole number shall be necessary to a choice. But no person constitutionally ineligible to the office of President shall be eligible to that of Vice-President of the United States.

Short Titles Used

Documentary citations given in short-title forms as "Life," "Papers," "Works," etc., are to be understood as referring to editions of the author of that particular document. Exceptions are clearly noted.

John Adams, Diary *Diary and Autobiography of John Adams.* Edited by L. H. Butterfield et al. 4 vols. Cambridge: Belknap Press of Harvard University Press, 1961.

John Adams, Papers *Papers of John Adams.* Edited by Robert J. Taylor et al. Cambridge: Belknap Press of Harvard University Press, 1977–.

John Adams, Works *The Works of John Adams.* Edited by Charles Francis Adams. 10 vols. Boston: Little, Brown & Co., 1850–56.

See also: Butterfield; Cappon; Warren-Adams Letters

J. Q. Adams, Writings *Writings of John Quincy Adams.* Edited by Worthington Chauncey Ford. 7 vols. New York: Macmillan Co., 1913–17.

Samuel Adams, Writings *The Writings of Samuel Adams.* Edited by Harry Alonzo Cushing. 4 vols. New York: G. P. Putnam's Sons, 1904–8.

American Archives *American Archives.* Edited by M. St. Clair Clarke and Peter Force. 4th ser., 6 vols. Washington, D.C., 1837–46. 5th ser., 3 vols. Washington, D.C., 1848–53.

American Colonial Documents Jensen, Merrill, ed. *American Colonial Documents to 1776.* English Historical Documents, edited by David C. Douglas, vol. 9. New York: Oxford University Press, 1969.

Annals *Annals of Congress. The Debates and Proceedings in the Congress of the United States.* "History of Congress." 42 vols. Washington, D.C.: Gales & Seaton, 1834–56.

Bailyn Bailyn, Bernard, ed. *Pamphlets of the American Revolution, 1750–1776.* Vol. 1, *1750–1765.* Cambridge: Belknap Press of Harvard University Press, 1965.

Blackstone, Commentaries Blackstone, William. *Commentaries on the Laws of England: A Facsimile of the First Edition of 1765–1769.* Chicago: University of Chicago Press, 1979.

Boyd Boyd, Julian P., ed. *Fundamental Laws and Constitutions of New Jersey, 1664–1964.* New Jersey Historical Series, vol. 17. Princeton: D. Van Nostrand Co., Inc., 1964.

Bradford, Of Plymouth Plantation Bradford, William. *Of Plymouth Plantation, 1620–1647.* Edited by Samuel Eliot Morison. New York: Modern Library, 1967.

Burgh [Burgh, James.] *Political Disquisitions: or, An Enquiry into Public Errors, Defects, and Abuses. . . .* 3 vols. London, 1774–75.

Burke, Works *The Works of the Right Honourable Edmund Burke.* 6 vols. London: Henry G. Bohn, 1854–56.

Burnett Burnett, Edmund C., ed. *Letters of Members of the Continental Congress.* 8 vols. Washington: Carnegie Institution of Washington, 1921–36.

Butterfield Adams, Abigail Smith. *The Book of Abigail and John: Selected Letters of the Adams Family, 1762–1784.* Edited by L. H. Butterfield et al. Cambridge: Harvard University Press, 1975.

Cannon *The Letters of Junius.* Edited by John Cannon. Oxford: At the Clarendon Press, 1978.

Cappon *The Adams-Jefferson Letters: The Complete Correspondence between Thomas Jefferson and Abigail and John Adams.* Edited by Lester J. Cappon. 2 vols. Chapel Hill: University of North Carolina Press for the Institute of Early American History and Culture, Williamsburg, Virginia, 1959.

Chase Chase, Frederick. *A History of Dartmouth College and the Town of Hanover New Hampshire.* Edited by John K. Lord. 2 vols. Cambridge: John Wilson & Son, 1891.

Colonial Records *The Colonial Records of North Carolina.* Edited by William L. Saunders. 10 vols. Raleigh: Josephus Daniels, 1886–90.

Crèvecoeur Crèvecoeur, J. Hector St. John. *Letters from an American Farmer.* New York: Albert & Charles Boni, 1925.

Documentary History *Documentary History of the Constitution of the United States of America, 1786–1870.* 5 vols. Washington, D.C.: Department of State, 1901–5.

Dumbauld Dumbauld, Edward. *The Bill of Rights and What It Means Today.* Norman: University of Oklahoma Press, 1957.

Early History *Early History of the University of Virginia, as Contained in the Letters of Thomas Jefferson and Joseph C. Cabell, Hitherto Unpublished. . . .* Richmond: J. W. Randolph, 1856.

Elliot Elliot, Jonathan, ed. *The Debates in the Several State Conventions on the Adoption of the Federal Constitution as Recommended by the General Convention at Philadelphia in 1787. . . .* 5 vols. 2d ed. 1888. Reprint. New York: Burt Franklin, n.d.

Emlyn Hale, Sir Matthew. *Historia Placitorum Coronae. The History of the Pleas of the Crown.* Edited by Sollom Emlyn. 2 vols. London, 1736. Reprint. Classical English Law Texts. London: Professional Books, Ltd., 1971.

Essays Ford, Paul Leicester, ed. *Essays on the Constitution of the United States, Published during Its Discussion by the People, 1787–1788.* Brooklyn: Historical Printing Club, 1892.

Farrand Farrand, Max, ed. *The Records of the Federal Convention of 1787.* Rev. ed. 4 vols. New Haven and London: Yale University Press, 1937.

Federalist Hamilton, Alexander; Madison, James; and Jay, John. *The Federalist.* Edited by Jacob E. Cooke. Middletown, Conn.: Wesleyan University Press, 1961.

Foster Foster, Sir Michael. *A Report of Some Proceedings on the Commission . . . for the Trial of the Rebels in the Year 1746 . . . , and of Other Crown Cases.* London, 1762. Reprint. Classical English Law Texts. Abingdon, England: Professional Books, Ltd., 1982.

Four Letters on Interesting Subjects *Four Letters on Interesting Subjects.* Philadelphia: 1776. Evans 14759.

Franklin, Papers *The Papers of Benjamin Franklin.* Edited by Leonard W. Labaree et al. New Haven: Yale University Press, 1959–.

Franklin, Writings *The Writings of Benjamin Franklin.* Edited by Albert Henry Smyth. 10 vols. New York: Macmillan Co., 1905–7.

Gerry, Life Austin, James T. *The Life of Elbridge Gerry. With Contemporary Letters.* 2 vols. Boston, 1828–29.

Gray Hale, Sir Matthew. *The History of the Common Law of England.* Edited by Charles M. Gray. Classics of British Historical Literature. Chicago: University of Chicago Press, 1971.

Gwyn Gwyn, W. B. *The Meaning of the Separation of Powers: An Analysis of the Doctrine from Its Origin to the Adoption of the United States Constitution.* Tulane Studies in Political Science, vol. 9. New Orleans: Tulane University, 1965.

Hamilton, Papers *The Papers of Alexander Hamilton.* Edited by Harold C. Syrett et al. 26 vols. New York and London: Columbia University Press, 1961–79.

See also: Federalist

Handlin Handlin, Oscar, and Handlin, Mary, eds. *The Popular Sources of Political Authority: Documents on the Massachusetts Constitution of 1780.* Cambridge: Belknap Press of Harvard University Press, 1966.

Harrington *The Political Writings of James Harrington: Representative Selections.* Edited by Charles Blitzer. New York: Liberal Arts Press, 1955.

History of Congress *History of Congress; Exhibiting a Classification of the Proceedings of the Senate, and the House of Representatives, from March 4, 1789, to March 3, 1793. . . .* Philadelphia: Lea & Blanchard, 1843.

Hume Hume, David. *Essays Moral, Political and Literary.* 1742, 1752.

Hurst Hurst, James Willard. *The Law of Treason in the United States: Collected Essays.* Westport, Conn.: Greenwood Publishing Corp., 1971.

Iredell, Life *Life and Correspondence of James Iredell.* Edited by Griffith J. McRee. 2 vols. New York: D. Appleton & Co., 1857.

Iredell, Papers *The Papers of James Iredell.* Edited by Don Higginbotham. Raleigh: North Carolina Division of Archives and History, 1976–.

Jacobson Trenchard, John, and Gordon, Thomas. *Cato's Letters.* In *The English Libertarian Heritage*, edited by David L. Jacobson. American Heritage Series. Indianapolis: Bobbs-Merrill, 1965.

Jamestown, The Three Charters of the Virginia Company of London *The Three Charters of the Virginia Company of London.* Jamestown 350th Anniversary Historical Booklet, no. 4. 1957

Jay, Correspondence *The Correspondence and Public Papers of John Jay.* Edited by Henry P. Johnston. 4 vols. New York and London: G. P. Putnam's Sons, 1890–93.

Jay, Unpublished Papers *John Jay: Unpublished Papers.* Edited by Richard B. Morris et al. New York: Harper & Row, 1975–.

See also: Federalist

Jefferson, Notes on the State of Virginia Jefferson, Thomas. *Notes on the State of Virginia.* Edited by William Peden. Chapel Hill: University of North Carolina Press for the Institute of Early American History and Culture, Williamsburg, Virginia, 1954.

Jefferson, Papers *The Papers of Thomas Jefferson.* Edited by Julian P. Boyd et al. Princeton: Princeton University Press, 1950–.

Jefferson, Works *The Works of Thomas Jefferson.* Collected and edited by Paul Leicester Ford. Federal Edition. 12 vols. New York and London: G. P. Putnam's Sons, 1904–5.

Jefferson, Writings *The Writings of Thomas Jefferson.* Edited by Andrew A. Lipscomb and Albert Ellery Bergh. 20 vols. Washington: Thomas Jefferson Memorial Association, 1905.

Jensen *The Documentary History of the Ratification of the Constitution.* Edited by Merrill Jensen et al. Madison: State Historical Society of Wisconsin, 1976–.

Journals *Journals of the Continental Congress, 1774–1789.* Edited by Worthington C. Ford et al. 34 vols. Washington, D.C.: Government Printing Office, 1904–37.

Kent Kent, James. *Commentaries on American Law.* 4 vols. New York, 1826–30.

King, Life *The Life and Correspondence of Rufus King.* Edited by Charles R. King. 6 vols. New York: G. P. Putnam's Sons, 1894–1900.

Land Eddis, William. *Letters from America.* Edited by Aubrey C. Land. Cambridge: Belknap Press of Harvard University Press, 1969.

Leake Leake, Isaac Q. *Memoir of the Life and Times of General John Lamb.* Albany, N.Y., 1857.

Lee, Letters *The Letters of Richard Henry Lee.* Edited by James Curtis Ballagh. 2 vols. New York: Macmillan Co., 1911–14.

Lincoln, Collected Works *The Collected Works of Abraham Lincoln.* Edited by Roy P. Basler et al. 8 vols. New Brunswick, N.J.: Rutgers University Press, 1953.

Locke, Second Treatise Locke, John. *Two Treatises of Government.* Edited by Peter Laslett. New York: Mentor Books, New American Library, 1965.

See also: Montuori

Machiavelli Machiavelli, Niccolò. *Discourses on the First Ten Books of Titus Livius.* Translated by Christian E. Detmold. New York: Modern Library, 1940.

McMaster McMaster, John Bach, and Stone, Frederick D., eds. *Pennsylvania and the Federal Constitution, 1787–1788.* Lancaster: Published for the Subscribers by the Historical Society of Pennsylvania, 1888.

Madison, Letters *Letters and Other Writings of James Madison.* Published by order of Congress. 4 vols. Philadelphia: J. B. Lippincott & Co., 1865.

Madison, Papers *The Papers of James Madison.* Edited by William T. Hutchinson et al. Chicago and London: University of Chicago Press, 1962–77 (vols. 1–10); Charlottesville: University Press of Virginia, 1977– (vols. 11–).

Madison, W. & M. Q. Fleet, Elizabeth. "Madison's 'Detached Memoranda.'" *William and Mary Quarterly*, 3d ser., 3 (1946): 534–68.

Madison, Writings *The Writings of James Madison.* Edited by Gaillard Hunt. 9 vols. New York: G. P. Putnam's Sons, 1900–1910.

See also: Federalist

Marshall, Life Beveridge, Albert J. *The Life of John Marshall.* 4 vols. Boston: Houghton Mifflin Co., 1916–19.

Marshall, Papers *The Papers of John Marshall.* Edited by Herbert A. Johnson et al. Chapel Hill: University of North Carolina Press, in association with the Institute of Early American History and Culture, Williamsburg, Virginia, 1974–.

Maryland Archives *Archives of Maryland: Proceedings and Acts of the General Assembly of Maryland.* Edited by William Hand Browne. Vol. 1. Baltimore: Maryland Historical Society, 1883.

Mason, Papers *The Papers of George Mason, 1725–1792.* Edited by Robert A. Rutland. 3 vols. Chapel Hill: University of North Carolina Press, 1970.

Meade Meade, Robert Douthat. *Patrick Henry: Patriot in the Making.* Philadelphia: J. B. Lippincott Co., 1957.

MHS Collections *Collections of the Massachusetts Historical Society.*

Monroe, Writings *The Writings of James Monroe.* Edited by Stanislaus Murray Hamilton. 7 vols. New York and London: G. P. Putnam's Sons, 1898–1903.

Montesquieu *The Spirit of Laws.* 1748. Translated by Thomas Nugent, 1750.

Montuori Locke, John. *A Letter concerning Toleration.* Latin and English texts revised and edited by Mario Montuori. The Hague: Martinus Nijhoff, 1963.

Gouverneur Morris, Amerikastudien Adams, Willi Paul. "'The Spirit of Commerce Requires that Property be Sacred': Gouverneur Morris and the American Revolution." *Amerikastudien* 21 (1976): 309–31.

Gouverneur Morris, Life *The Life of Gouverneur Morris, with Selections from His Correspondence and Miscellaneous Papers.* Edited by Jared Sparks. 3 vols. Boston, 1832.

Robert Morris, Papers *The Papers of Robert Morris, 1781–1784.* Edited by E. James Ferguson et al. Pittsburgh: University of Pittsburgh Press, 1973–.

New England Federalism Adams, Henry, ed. *Documents Relating to New-England Federalism.* Boston: Little, Brown & Co., 1877.

Niles Niles, Hezekiah, *Principles and Acts of the Revolution in America.* Centennial Offering. New York: A. S. Barnes & Co., 1876.

Old Family Letters Biddle, Alexander. *Old Family Letters.* Ser. A. Philadelphia: J. B. Lippincott Co., 1892.

Otis, Political Writings "Some Political Writings of James Otis." Collected by Charles F. Mullett. *University of Missouri Studies* 4 (1929): 257–432.

Paine, Life *The Life and Works of Thomas Paine.* Edited by William M. Van der Weyde. Patriots' Edition. 10 vols. New Rochelle, N.Y.: Thomas Paine National Historical Association, 1925.

Pamphlets Ford, Paul Leicester, ed. *Pamphlets on the Constitution of the United States, Published during Its Discussion by the People, 1787–1788.* Brooklyn, 1888. Reprint. New York: De Capo Press, 1968.

Penn, Select Works *The Select Works of William Penn.* 5 vols. 3d ed. London, 1782.

Pickering, Life Upham, Charles W. *The Life of Timothy Pickering.* 2 vols. Boston: Little, Brown & Co., 1873.

Pinkney Wheaton, Henry. *Some Account of the Life, Writings, and Speeches of William Pinkney.* Baltimore: E. J. Coale, 1826.

Randolph, History of Virginia Randolph, Edmund. *History of Virginia.* Edited by Arthur H. Shaffer. Charlottesville: University Press of Virginia for the Virginia Historical Society, 1970.

Rawle Rawle, William. *A View of the Constitution of the United States of America.* 2d ed. Philadelphia, 1829. Reprint. New York: Da Capo Press, 1970.

Read, Life Read, William Thompson. *Life and Correspondence of George Read.* Philadelphia: J. B. Lippincott & Co., 1870.

Records of the Federal Convention. *See* Farrand

Remonstrance and Petition, W. & M. Q. Schmidt, F. T., and Wilhelm, B. R. "Early Proslavery Petitions in Virginia." *William and Mary Quarterly*, 3d ser., 30 (1973): 133–46.

Richardson Richardson, James D., comp. *A Compilation of the Messages and Papers of the Presidents, 1789–1897.* 10 vols. Washington, D.C.: Government Printing Office, 1896–99.

Robertson Robertson, C. Grant, ed. *Select Statutes, Cases and Documents to Illustrate English Constitutional History, 1660–1832.* 4th ed., rev. London: Methuen & Co., Ltd., 1923.

Rush, Letters *Letters of Benjamin Rush.* Edited by L. H. Butterfield. 2 vols. Memoirs of the American Philosophical Society, vol. 30, parts 1 and 2. Princeton: Princeton University Press, for the American Philosophical Society, 1951.

Rush, Selected Writings *The Selected Writings of Benjamin Rush.* Edited by Dagobert D. Runes. New York: Philosophical Library, 1947.

Scribner *Revolutionary Virginia: The Road to Independence.* Vol 6, *The Time for Decision, 1776: A Documentary Record*, edited by Robert L. Scribner and Brent Tarter. Charlottesville: University Press of Virginia for the Virginia Independence Bicentennial Commission, 1981.

Sidney, Works *The Works of Algernon Sydney. A New Edition.* London, 1772.

Sources *Sources of Our Liberties.* Edited by Richard L. Perry under the general supervision of John C. Cooper. [Chicago:] American Bar Foundation, 1952.

State Trials *State Trials of the United States during the Administrations of Washington and Adams.* Edited by Francis Wharton. Philadelphia: Carey & Hart, 1849.

Stokes Stokes, Anton Phelps, ed. *Church and State in the United States.* 3 vols. New York: Harper & Bros., 1950.

Storing Storing, Herbert J., ed. *The Complete Anti-Federalist.* 7 vols. Chicago: University of Chicago Press, 1981.

Story Story, Joseph. *Commentaries on the Constitution of the United States.* 3 vols. Boston, 1833.

Tansill *Documents Illustrative of the Formation of the Union of the American States.* Edited by Charles C. Tansill. 69th Cong., 1st sess. House Doc. No. 398. Washington, D.C.: Government Printing Office, 1927.

Taylor Taylor, Robert J., ed. *Massachusetts, Colony to Commonwealth: Documents on the Formation of Its Constitution, 1775–1780.* Chapel Hill: University of North Carolina Press for the Institute of Early American History and Culture, Williamsburg, Virginia, 1961.

Thorpe Thorpe, Francis Newton, ed. *The Federal and State Constitutions, Colonial Charters, and Other Organic Laws of the States, Territories, and Colonies Now or Heretofore Forming the United States of America.* 7 vols. Washington, D.C.: Government Printing Office, 1909.

Tucker, Blackstone's Commentaries Tucker, St. George. *Blackstone's Commentaries: With Notes of Reference to the Constitution and Laws of the Federal Government of the United States and of the Commonwealth of Virginia.* 5 vols. Philadelphia, 1803. Reprint. South Hackensack, N.J.: Rothman Reprints, 1969.

Walker, U. Pa. L. Rev. Radin, Max. "The Doctrine of the Separation of Powers in Seventeenth Century Controversies." *University of Pennsylvania Law Review* 86 (1938): 842–66.

Warren, Life Frothingham, Richard. *Life and Times of Joseph Warren.* Boston: Little, Brown & Co., 1865.

Warren-Adams Letters *Warren-Adams Letters, Being Chiefly a Correspondence among John Adams, Samuel Adams, and James Warren.* Vol. 2, 1778–1814. Collections of the Massachusetts Historical Society, vol. 73. [Boston:] Massachusetts Historical Society, 1925.

Washington, Writings *The Writings of George Washington from the Original Manuscript Sources, 1745–1799.* Edited by John C. Fitzpatrick. 39 vols. Washington, D.C.: Government Printing Office, 1931–44.

Webster, Collection Webster, Noah. *A Collection of Essays and Fugitiv Writings on Moral, Historical, Political and Literary Subjects.* Boston, 1790. Reprint. Delmar, N.Y.: Scholars' Facsimiles & Reprints, 1977.

Webster, Political Papers Webster, Noah. *A Collection of Papers on Political, Literary and Moral Subjects.* New York, 1843. Reprint. New York: Burt Franklin, 1968.

Wharton Wharton, Francis, ed. *The Revolutionary Diplomatic Correspondence of the United States.* 6 vols. Washington, D.C.: Government Printing Office, 1889.

Wilson, Works *The Works of James Wilson.* Edited by Robert Green McCloskey. 2 vols. Cambridge: Belknap Press of Harvard University Press, 1967.

Winthrop Winthrop, John. *The History of New England from 1630 to 1649.* Edited by James Savage. 2 vols. Boston: Little, Brown & Co., 1853.

Woodhouse Woodhouse, A. S. P., ed. *Puritanism and Liberty, Being the Army Debates (1647–9) from the Clarke Manuscripts with Supplementary Documents.* 2d ed. London: J. M. Dent & Sons Ltd., 1951.

Index of Constitutional Provisions

Table of Cases

Grumon v. *Raymond*, 1 Conn. 40 (1814), Amend. IV, no. 18

Hall v. *Williams*, 6 Pick. 232 (Mass. 1828), 4.1, no. 13
Ham v. *M'Claws*, 1 Bay 93 (S.C. 1789), Amend. V (due process), no. 14
Harrison v. *Sterry*, 5 Cranch 289 (1809), 1.8.4 (bankruptcy), no. 5
Hawkins v. *Barney's Lessee*, 5 Pet. 457 (1831), 1.10.3, no. 4
Hayburn's Case, 2 Dall. 409 (1792), 3.2.1, no. 31
Hepburn v. *Ellzey*, 2 Cranch 445 (1804), 1.8.17, no. 12
Hitchcock v. *Aicken*, 1 Caines 460 (N.Y. 1803), 4.1, no. 8
Hodgson & Thompson v. *Bowerbank*, 5 Cranch 303 (1809), 3.2.1, no. 52
Holiday v. *Pitt*, 93 Eng. Rep. 984 (K.B. 1734), 1.6.1, no. 2
Hollingsworth v. *Virginia*, 3 Dall. 378 (1798), Amend. XI, no. 2
Holmes v. *Comegys*, 1 Dall. 439 (Pa. 1789), Amends. V–VI, no. 25
Houston v. *Moore*, 5 Wheat. 1 (1820), 1.8.15, no. 20
Huckle v. *Money*, 95 Eng. Rep. 768 (C.P. 1763), Amend. IV, no. 3
Hunter v. *Fulcher*, 1 Leigh 172 (Va. 1829), 1.9.1, no. 27
Hurst's Case, 4 Dall. 387 (C.C.D.Pa. 1804), 1.6.1, no. 23
Hylton v. *United States*, 3 Dall. 171 (1796), 1.9.4, no. 13

Isaac Williams, Case of, 27 Feb. 1797, in St. George Tucker, *Blackstone's Commentaries*, 1:App. 436–38 (1803), 1.8.4 (citizenship), no. 13

Jack v. *Martin*, 14 Wend. 507 (N.Y. 1835), 4.2.3, no. 15
Jackson v. *Rose*, 2 Va. Cas. 34 (1814), 3.2.1, no. 59
James v. *Allen*, 1 Dall. 188 (Pa. 1786), 4.1, no. 2
James v. *Commonwealth*, 12 Serg. & Rawle 220 (Pa. 1824), Amend. VIII, no. 19
Jansen v. *Vrow Christina Magdalena*, 13 Fed. Cas. 356, no. 7,216 (D.S.C. 1794), 3.2.1, no. 39
Johnson v. *Duncan*, 3 Mart. 530 (La. 1815), 4.4, no. 12
Johnson & Graham v. *M'Intosh*, 8 Wheat. 543 (1823), 1.8.3 (Indians), no. 9
Jose Ferreira dos Santos, Case of, 2 Marshall's C.C. 493 (C.C.D.Va. 1835), 4.2.2, no. 9

Kibbe v. *Kibbe*, Kirby 119 (Conn. 1786), 4.1, no. 3
King v. *Dedham Bank*, 15 Mass. 447 (1819), 1.10.1, no. 18
The King v. *Dr. Purnell*, 96 Eng. Rep. 20 (K.B. 1748), Amend. IV, no. 1
Knight's Case, 87 Eng. Rep. 75 (K.B. 1686), Amend. II, no. 2

Lindsay v. *Commissioners*, 2 Bay 38 (S.C. 1796), Amend. V (due process), no. 18
Little v. *Bareme*, 2 Cranch 170 (1804), 1.8.11, no. 13
Livingston v. *Mayor of New York*, 8 Wend. 85 (N.Y. 1831), Amend. V (due process), no. 25
Livingston v. *Moore*, 7 Pet. 469 (1833), 3.1, no. 37
Livingston v. *Van Ingen*, 15 Fed. Cas. 697, no. 8,420 (C.C.S.D.N.Y. 1811), 3.2.1, no. 55
Livingston v. *Van Ingen*, 9 Johns. R. 507 (N.Y. 1812), 1.8.3 (commerce), no. 13
Lord Sackville's Case, 28 Eng. Rep. 940 (Ch. 1760), 3.2.1, no. 2
Loughborough v. *Blake*, 5 Wheat. 317 (1820), 1.9.4, no. 16

M'Clung v. *Silliman*, 6 Wheat. 598 (1821), 3.2.1, no. 75
McCormick v. *Sullivant*, 10 Wheat. 192 (1825), 4.1, no. 12
McCulloch v. *Maryland*, 4 Wheat. 316 (1819), Preamble, no. 19; 1.8.18, no. 14; 6.2, no. 34
McIntire v. *Wood*, 7 Cranch 504 (1813), 3.2.1, no. 57
McKim v. *Voorhies*, 7 Cranch 279 (1812), 6.2, no. 31
McPherson v. *Blacker*, 146 U.S. 1 (1892), 2.1.2–3, no. 6
Marbury v. *Madison*, 1 Cranch 137 (1803), 3.2.1, no. 47
Martin v. *Hunter's Lessee*, 1 Wheat. 304 (1816), 3.2.1, no. 65
Martin v. *Mott*, 12 Wheat. 19 (1827), 1.8.15, no. 22
Mason v. *Haile*, 12 Wheat. 370 (1827), 1.10.1, no. 20
Meade v. *Deputy Marshal*, 1 Marshall's C.C. 324 (C.C.D.Va. 1815), 1.8.15, no. 19; Amends. V–VI, no. 37
Mills v. *Duryee*, 7 Cranch 480 (1813), 4.1, no. 10

Mima Queen v. *Hepburn*, 7 Cranch 290 (1813), Amend. VII, no. 16
Money v. *Leach*, 97 Eng. Rep. 1075 (K.B. 1765), Amend. IV, no. 7
Morgan's Heirs v. *Morgan*, 2 Wheat. 290 (1817), 3.2.1, no. 68
Morton v. *Naylor*, 1 Hill 439 (S.C. 1833), 4.1, no. 14
Mossman v. *Higginson*, 4 Dall. 12 (1800), 3.2.1, no. 44
Murray v. *McCarty*, 2 Munf. 393 (Va. 1811), 4.2.3, no. 7

New Orleans v. *Winter*, 1 Wheat. 91 (1816), 3.2.1, no. 64

Ogden v. *Saunders*, 12 Wheat. 213 (1827), 1.10.1, no. 19
Osborn v. *Bank of the United States*, 9 Wheat. 738 (1824), 3.2.1, no. 79; Amend. XI, no. 4
Owings v. *Norwood's Lessee*, 5 Cranch 344 (1809), 3.2.1, no. 53
Owings v. *Speed*, 5 Wheat. 419 (1820), 7, no. 16

Pawlet v. *Clark*, 9 Cranch 292 (1815), 3.2.1, no. 62
Pennsylvania v. *Morrison*, 1 Addison 274 (Pa. 1795), Amend. I (petition), no. 18
People v. *Barrett*, 1 Johns. R. 66 (N.Y. 1806), Amends. V–VI, no. 32
——— v. *Casborus*, 13 Johns. R. 351 (N.Y. 1816), Amends. V–VI, no. 38
——— v. *Croswell*, 3 Johns. Cas. 337 (N.Y. 1804), Amend. I (speech), no. 28
——— v. *Godfrey*, 17 Johns. R. 225 (1819), 1.8.17, no. 17
——— v. *Goodwin*, 18 Johns. R. 187 (N.Y. 1820), Amends. V–VI, no. 40
——— v. *Lynch*, 11 Johns. R. 549 (N.Y. 1814), 3.3.1–2, no. 24
——— v. *Ruggles*, 8 Johns. R. 290 (N.Y. 1811), Amend. I (religion), no. 62
Phipps, Case of, reported in *Cummington* v. *Springfield*, 2 Pick. 394 (Mass. 1824), 1.8.4 (citizenship), no. 20
Picquet v. *Swan*, 19 Fed. Cas. 609, no. 11,134 (C.C.D.Mass. 1828), Amend. V (due process), no. 23
Pirate v. *Dalby*, 1 Dall. 167 (Pa. 1786), 1.9.1, no. 2
Poulson, Ex parte, 19 Fed. Cas. 1205, no. 11,350 (C.C.E.D.Pa. 1835), 3.1, no. 39

Reason v. *Bridges*, 20 Fed. Cas. 370, no. 11,617 (C.C.D.C. 1807), Amend. VII, no. 15
Respublica v. *Carlisle*, 1 Dall. 35 (Pa. 1778), 3.3.1–2, no. 12
——— v. *Chapman*, 1 Dall. 53 (Pa. 1781), 3.3.1–2, no. 13
——— v. *De Longchamps*, 1 Dall. 111 (Pa. 1784), 1.8.10, no. 2
——— v. *Gibbs*, 3 Yeates 429 (Pa. 1802), Amends. V–VI, no. 31
——— v. *Oswald*, 1 Dall. 319 (Pa. 1788), Amend. I (speech), no. 13
——— v. *Passmore*, 3 Yeates 441 (Pa. 1802), 3.1, no. 19
——— v. *Shaffer*, 1 Dall. 236 (Pa. 1788), Amends. V–VI, no. 23
——— v. *Weidle*, 2 Dall. 88 (Pa. 1781), 3.3.1–2, no. 14
Rex v. *Wilkes*, 95 Eng. Rep. 737 (C.P. 1763), Amend. IV, no. 5

Sanderson's Case, 21 Fed. Cas. 326, no. 12,297 (C.C.D.C. 1829), Amends. V–VI, no. 49
The Santissima Trinidad, 7 Wheat. 283 (1822), 1.8.4 (citizenship), no. 19
The Sarah, 8 Wheat. 391 (1823), 3.2.1, no. 76
The Schooner Exchange v. *McFaddon*, 7 Cranch 116 (1812), 1.8.10, no. 7
Sere v. *Pitot*, 2 Cranch 332 (1810), 4.3.2, no. 4
Seven Bishops, Trial of, for Publishing a Libel, 12 How. St. Tr. 183, 415 (1688), Amend. I (petition), no. 6
Shaftesbury's Trial, 8 How. St. Tr. 759 (1681), Amends. V–VI, no. 3
Shanks v. *DuPont*, 3 Pet. 242 (1830), 1.8.4 (citizenship), no. 24
Shedden v. *Curtis*, 21 Fed. Cas. 1218, no. 12,736 (C.C.D.Va. 1793), 3.2.1, no. 35
Sommersett's Case, 20 How. St. Tr. 1, 80–82 (K.B. 1771), 4.2.3, no. 2
Spier, In the Matter of, 1 Dev. 491 (N.C. 1828), Amends. V–VI, no. 48

Index of Authors and Documents

References are to chapter or to constitutional section, and to document number. References to volume 1 are by chapter and document number (e.g., ch. 15, no. 23); references to constitutional provisions in volumes 2–4 are by article, section, clause, and document number (e.g., 1.8.8, no. 12); and references to volume 5 are by Amendment and document number (e.g., Amend. I [religion], no. 66). In the case of documents whose several clauses are ranged under a large number of headings (e.g., the Bill of Rights of 1689, the Massachusetts Constitution of 1780, and the like), reference is made only to appearances of the complete text.